THE SPURS ALPHABET

THE SPURS ALPHABET

A COMPLETE WHO'S WHO OF
TOTTENHAM HOTSPUR FC

BOB GOODWIN

ROBWIN PUBLISHING HOUSE

First published in Great Britain by
Robwin Publishing House
20 Roundcroft, West Cheshunt, Herts EN7 6DL
2017

© Bob Goodwin

All rights reserved. No part of this publication may be reproduced, stored in a retrieval system, or transmitted in any form, or by any means, electronic, mechanical, photocopying, recording or otherwise without the prior permission in writing of the Copyright holder, nor be otherwise circulated in any form or binding or cover other than in which it is puiblished and without a similar condition being imposed on the subsequent publisher.

ISBN 0-9540434-2-1

CONTENTS

A-Acimovic-Ayres 1

B-Baardsen-Button 20

C-Cable-Curtis 72

D-Daines-Dyson 112

E-Eadon-Evans 137

F-Fairclough-Furr 147

G-Gain-Guthrie 163

H-Haddow-Hyde 188

I-Ifil-Iversen 222

J-Jack-Jull 225

K-Kaboul-Kyle 239

L-Lacy-Lyons 254

Mc-McAllister-McVey 272

M-Mabbutt-Murray 285

N-Nash-Nuttall 316

O-Oakes-Owen 326

P-Page-Purdie 333

Q-Quinn 355

R-Raby-Ryden 355

S-Sage-Sykes 376

T-Taarabt-Tyrell 413

U-Upex-Upton 428

V-Van den Hauwe-Vorm 429

W-Waddle-Wright 435

Y-Yates-Young 463

Z-Zamora-Zokora 466

In memory of Andy Porter.

Introduction

Tottenham Hotspur Football Club was formed in 1882 by a group of local schoolboys and was originally known simply as the Hotspur Football Club. For the first ten years of its existence, Spurs played only friendly matches and in local cup competitions such as the London Association Cup, London Senior Cup and Middlesex Senior Cup. It was not until the 1892-93 season that a League competition was entered and that only lasted for the one season as several clubs failed to fulfil all their fixtures in the Southern Alliance.

In 1894 Spurs entered the FA Cup for the first time. When I first produced the Spurs Alphabet back in 1992, the criteria for inclusion was that a player had to have played in a competitive game since that event. I am pleased to have been able to dispense with that restriction, allowing this book to feature every player known to have played in a first team game from the club's founding until the end of the 2016-17 season. As a schoolboy outfit, there was little interest in Spurs in the early days, and even less interest in recording its history. This means that there are several players included about whom little, if anything, is known

For each player, I have tried to provide the following information: -full name, recognised position, period as a Spurs player, height and weight, date and place of birth/death, career details, Spurs debut, biography and details of appearances made and goals scored.

I hope that most of the information is self-explanatory, but a few notes may be helpful.

The period as a Spurs player covers the date from when a player made his first team debut (whether in a competitive match or not) to the date of his last first team appearance and covers the seasons concerned, i.e. 1954-59 means seasons 1954-55 to 1958-59.

Heights and weights should only be regarded as approximate figures as they varied throughout the player's career. The same caution must apply to transfer fees. Third party ownership, sell-on clauses and commissions make any calculation difficult and it is rare for any club to confirm exactly how much it paid or received for a player's registration.

The debut given is the player's first appearance in a competitive game if he played in one, with any preceding non-competitive appearance detailed in brackets.

In the details of appearances and goals the following abbreviations have been used: -

League	=	Football/Premier League
Southern	=	Southern League
FA Cup	=	FA Cup
FL Cup	=	Football League Cup in all its guises, Milk Cup, Worthington Cup and so on

Euro	=	European Competition-European Champions Cup, Champions League, European Cup-Winners' Cup, UEFA Cup and Europa League
Others:	=	Any other matches, such as those in war-time competition, the several minor leagues Spurs competed in prior to joining the Football League in 1908, testimonials, tour matches and friendlies.

In the debuts, I have dispensed with "Others" and given rather more detail with the following:

AmC	=	Amateur Cup
EL	=	Europa League
FAC	=	FA Cup
FLC	=	Football League Cup in all its guise
FLS	=	Football League South
FLSC	=	Football League South Cup
Fr	=	Friendly
JTF	=	Jubilee Trust Fund
LAC	=	London Association Cup
LCC	=	London Charity Cup
LFACC	=	London Challenge Cup
LFC	=	London Football Combination
LL	=	London League
LPFCF	=	London Professional Football Charity Fund
LSC	=	London Senior Cup
LutCC	=	Luton Charity Cup
LWC	=	London War Cup
LWL	=	London War League
NWF	=	National War Fund
MSC	=	Middlesex Senior Cup
PL	=	Premier League
SA	=	Southern Alliance
SDC	=	Southern District Combination
SL	=	Southern League
TML	=	Thames & Medway League
UEFA	=	UEFA Cup
UL	=	United League
WChC	=	Wellingborough Charity Cup
WL	=	Western League

To provide a full record, appearances and goals in matches that were later expunged, like those at the start of the 1939-40 season and those against clubs who later withdraw from the Southern League, are included. Abandoned matches that were later replayed are also included with a specific note to that effect.

In compiling a book such as this it would be foolish to think that errors cannot creep in. If any are found, then first; apologies. Secondly, please let me know so they can be corrected in any future edition.

Some of the pictures are not as good as I would have liked. I took the view, especially with the more obscure players, that it was better to have a poor picture than none at all.

If any reader can shed further light on players' details/careers, or provide photographs of any players not portrayed here, then please contact me. In particular, if anyone knows who "Slender" was …!

Bob Goodwin

Cheshunt, Hertfordshire

July 2017

Acknowledgements

No amount of research could have enabled me to compile this and the previous version of the Spurs Alphabet without the help of others, and their assistance must be acknowledged. There are far too many to try and list them individually and, sadly, some of them are no longer with us. I must mention, in no particular order, Mike Davage, Doug Lamming, Les Yates, Barry Hugman, Ray Spiller, James Creasy, John Harris, Carolyn Tingay, "Ossie", John Fennelly, Julian Baskcomb, Julia Byrne, Ian Scott, Fred Dowry, Andy Scott, John Davies, Peter Lee, the staff of the Football League, Bruce Castle Museum and the British Newspaper Library and the authors of the numerous football Who's Who that have been produced over the years.

The photographs that appear in this book have come from my private collection plus a vast number of people, ranging from players and their families through to supporters, photographers and collectors. If I could remember them all, I would need a couple of pages to list their names. They should all know how grateful I am for their help. A very special word of thanks must go to Steve Martin, Wayne Baker and, especially, Les Gold.

I have not been able to trace the source of the pictures, but any photographer involved is cordially invited to contact me in writing with proof of copyright.

Finally, a very special thank you to the late Andy Porter, a great friend who will never be forgotten.

A

AČIMOVIČ, MILENKO

Role: Midfielder 2002-04
6ft.1ins. 12st.8lbs.
Born: Ljubljana, Yugoslavia, 15th February 1977

CAREER: Železničar NK Ljubljana (Yugoslavia) Jul 1994/NK Olimpija Ljubljana (Yugoslavia) Jul 1996/Red Star Belgrade (Yugoslavia) Jan 1998/**SPURS** May 2002/Lille (France) loan Jan 2004, perm Apr 2004/Al-Ittihad (Saudi Arabia) Aug 2006/FK Austria (Austria) Jan 2007/retired Sep 2010/NK Olimpija Ljubljana (Slovenia) Director of Football Jan 2011-Sep 2012/SK Austria Klagenfurt (Austria) training Sep 2013/NK Olimpija Ljubljana (Slovenia) Director of Football Jul 2014-May 2015.

Debut v Everton (sub) (PL) (a) 17.8.2002
(Stevenage Borough (Fr) 21.7.2002)

A tall, elegant midfielder, much was expected of Milenko Ačimovič when he signed for Spurs in May 2002, but things did not work out for him at White Hart Lane and barely 18 months later he was on his way out. Ačimovič first made his name as a 17-year old with Železničar Ljubljana and quickly moved on to Olimpija Ljubljana before joining Yugoslavia's top club, Red Star Belgrade, the club his father, Jovan "Kule" Ačimovič, had played for in the 1970s. Helping them win the League title in 2000 and 2001 and Yugoslav Cup in 1999, 2000 and 2002, several of Europe's top clubs were watching Ačimovič's progress when Spurs stepped in to sign him. He began his time at Spurs in the first team squad but was rarely able to make the starting eleven and spent most of his time on the bench or in the reserves. Although it was evident he was possessed of talent, he seemed unable, perhaps unwilling, to make the effort to adjust to the more physical side of the game. Never more than on the fringes of the team, Ačimovič was loaned to Lille in January 2004, with the move being made permanent three months later. He spent two years in France without ever really establishing himself as a regular performer and had a few months in Saudi Arabia, before joining FK Austria of Vienna. He, at last, held down a regular starting role until a persistent knee injury led to retirement in September 2010. Although of Croat descent, Ačimovič played for Slovenia after the break-up of Yugoslavia, winning his first cap against the Czech Republic in April 1998. He went on to score 13 goals in 74 appearances for his country before announcing his retirement from international football in August 2007. He almost collected the most unwanted record of being the player sent off quickest in international football. Against the Italians in August 2002 he went on as a substitute, committed a foul after only two minutes and was promptly shown a yellow card. The referee thought he had already booked Ačimovič and produced the red card, but the error was drawn to his attention and Ačimovič was called back before he had even left the pitch.

Appearances:
League: 4 (13) apps.
FL Cup: 1 app.
Others: 13 (2) apps. 1 gl.
Total: 18 (15) apps. 1 gl.

ACQUROFF, John

Role: Centre-forward 1945-46
5ft.10ins. 10st.12lbs.
Born: Chelsea, London, 9th September 1911
Died: Launceston, Tasmania, Australia, 14th November 1987

CAREER: Willesden Polytechnic/**SPURS** am. Jun 1931, pro. Aug 1931/Northfleet United Aug 1931/**SPURS** Nov 1932/Folkestone Jun 1934/Hull City Nov 1934/Bury Oct 1936/Norwich City Feb 1939/(guest for Birmingham, Fulham, Millwall, **SPURS**, Walsall, West Bromwich Albion and Wolverhampton Wanderers during World War Two)/Metro (Australia) 1950/Wanderers (Australia)/Caledonians Down Under (Australia)/retired Aug 1957/Telecom (Australia).

Debut v West Bromwich Albion (FLS) (h) 29.9.1945 (scored twice)

Although Jack Acquroff first joined Spurs as a junior in June 1931, it was over 14 years before he made his first team debut and when he did it was as a guest player. Sent to the nursery club at Northfleet, Acquroff was the Kent League's top scorer in his two seasons there, but although he moved up to White Hart Lane in late 1932, Spurs decided not to keep him on and he joined Folkestone. Too talented for Southern League football, he quickly moved into the Football League giving good service to Hull City, Bury and Norwich City before the Second World War began. A typical pre-war centre-forward, his hopes of making a name for himself at Spurs had been limited by the presence of George Hunt, but he showed the type of finishing that had first interested Spurs by scoring twice on his first guest appearance. Possibly the only pre-war Football League player of Russian extraction; his parents had been naturalised, his only other game was two weeks later against Birmingham. Acquroff retired at the end of the transitional 1945-46 season and in December 1949 emigrated to Hobart, Tasmania. He played there for Metro and Caledonians Down Under and represented Tasmania before finally retiring from the game at the age of 49. He still played the odd game, scoring a hat-trick for Telecom against Postal Institute in Launceston in 1983, aged 72!

Appearances:
Others: 2 apps. 2 gls.
Total: 2 apps. 2 gls.

ADAMS, Christopher James

Role: Forward 1950-53
5ft.7ins. 10st.0lbs.
Born: *Hornchurch, Essex, 6th September 1927*
Died: *Brentwood, Essex, 24th June 2012*

CAREER: Essex Schoolboys/Suttons/Leytonstone/Romford/Army/**SPURS** am. Jun 1947, pro. Nov 1948/Norwich City Dec 1952/Watford Mar 1954/Dartford Nov 1956-1964.

Debut v Derby County (FL) (h) 1.3.1952 (scored once)
(Tennis-Borussia (Fr) (a) 18.5.1950)

Although Chris Adams made his first team debut in Berlin during Spurs' 1950 European tour and was with the club for four years he made only six League appearances. In the first of those he stood in for the injured Les Medley and scored in a 5-0 defeat of Derby County. Four more outings followed before Medley returned and Adams was to play only one more League game for Spurs, in October 1952 when Medley was on international duty. A couple of months later he joined Norwich City as part of the deal that saw Roy Hollis move to White Hart Lane, but by the end of the following season he had moved on to Watford. Refusing part-time terms at the end of the 1955-56 season, it took an appeal to the Football League for Adams to secure a free transfer and a move into non-League football. He turned out for Dartford for eight seasons before retiring to save further damage to a troublesome knee injury.

Appearances:
League: 6 apps. 1 gl.
Others: 5 (1) apps. 5 gls.
Total: 11 (1) apps. 6 gls.

ADAMS, Dexter William

Role: Centre-half 1954-55

Born: *Handsworth, Birmingham, 4th April 1925*
Died: *Stamford, Lincolnshire, 31st January 2015*

CAREER: Hendon 1947-1958, coach/**SPURS** (guest)/Barnet manager 1962-1970.

Debut v Queens Park Rangers (Fr) (a) 11.10.1954

A well-regarded centre-half with Hendon, Dexter Adams made two guest appearances for Spurs in friendly games during the 1954-55 season, when matches under floodlights, although limited to friendlies, were just becoming established. His first outing was at Queens Park Rangers, with the second three weeks later when the German club, Essen-Rot-Weiss, visited White Hart Lane. An England regular at amateur level, Adams had been on Spurs' radar for some time and his two appearances showed he had what was needed to make the step up to the professional game. Spurs offered him the chance, but he preferred to play the game for fun, rebuffed their advances and went on to give Hendon many years of dedicated service while winning 20 amateur caps. He was later manager of Hendon's great rivals, Barnet, leading them from 1962 until 1970. In charge when they turned semi-professional in 1965, he helped lay the foundations for the modern-day club.

Appearances:
Others: 2 apps. 0 gls.
Total: 2 apps. 0 gls.

ADAMS, William Henry

Role: Full-back 1943-46
5ft.7ins. 10st.10lbs.
Born: *Arlecdon, Cumberland, 8th January 1919*
Died: *Cockermouth, Cumbria, 1st March 1989*

CAREER: Whitehaven School/Northumberland Schools/Hartlepools United am./Tottenham Juniors 1935/**SPURS** am. Jan 1937/Northfleet United am. Sep 1938, pro. Jan 1939/**SPURS** pro. May 1939/(guest for Bradford City, Brighton and Hove Albion, Carlisle United, Hartlepools United, Linfield, Middlesbrough, Millwall and Reading during World War Two)/Carlisle United Jun 1946/Cheltenham Town Jun 1947/Workington Jun 1951.

Debut v Brentford (FAC) (a) 10.1.1946
(Brentford (FLS) (h) 8.1.1944)

Another of the numerous players sent to learn their trade at the Northfleet nursery club, although Bill Adams was recognised as a full-back, he made only two appearances for Spurs during the Second World War in that position. He played most of his games at outside-left, a not unfamiliar role, having operated as a winger in his schoolboy days. Adams' first appearance was at left-back in a Football League South fixture but the rest of his games in 1943-44, including the League South Cup semi-final with Charlton Athletic at Stamford Bridge, were in the number eleven shirt. Due to his service postings, he was rarely available to Spurs and most of his war-time football was as a guest for Hartlepools United and Bradford City. In June 1946, he was transferred to Carlisle United where he played under another of Spurs' war-time players, Ivor Broadis. Adams spent only one season in Cumbria before moving into non-League football although he did turn out in the League again, making three appearances for Workington in their first Football League campaign.

Appearances:
FA Cup: 1 app.
Others: 11 apps.
Total: 12 apps. 0 gls.

ADEBAYOR, Sheyi Emmanuel

Role: Striker 2011-15

6ft.3ins. 11st.11lbs.

Born: Lome, Togo, 26 February 1984

CAREER: Sporting Club de Lomé (Togo) 1997/OC Agaza (Togo) 1998/ FC Metz (France) 1999/AS Monaco (France) Jul 2003/Arsenal Jan 2006/ Manchester City Jul 2009/(Real Madrid (Spain) loan Jan 2011)/**SPURS** loan Aug 2011, perm. Aug 2012-Sep 2015/Crystal Palace Jan 2016/ released Jun 2016/İstanbul Başakşehir (Turkey) Jan 2017.

Debut v Wolverhampton Wanderers (PL) (a) 10.9.2011 (scored one)

Another of the many talented young Africans identified by French clubs in the country's former colonies, Adebayor was only 15 when spotted playing in a tournament in Sweden. Taken into the youth set-up at Metz, within two years he was playing regularly in the French League and two years later made the first big transfer of his career when he joined AS Monaco after helping Metz secure promotion to Ligue 1. In his first season at the Stade Louis II, Adebayor had to content himself with the role of back-up to loanee Fernando Morientes as Monaco marched through to the Champions League final, but when the Spaniard returned to Real Madrid, Adebayor was left to shoulder the main goal-scoring burden. He did it so well that Arsène Wenger was soon making another of his renowned swoops on the French League to take Adebayor to Arsenal in a £7million deal. The signing proved another shrewd piece of business by Wenger as Adebayor's talent flourished and he quickly succeeded Thierry Henry as Arsenal's most potent goal scorer. As mega money began to flow into Manchester City's coffers from Abu Dhabi, it was no surprise when Adebayor was identified as the man to lead City's all-star attack. £25million was paid to secure his transfer. For a year he did the job City wanted, but as more, and more expensive, signings made their way to the City of Manchester Stadium, Adebayor fell down the pecking order. Having already acquired a reputation for being difficult when things were not going his way, it was not a situation he was prepared to accept. When Real Madrid offered him the chance of escape, even if only for a few months on loan, it was an opportunity he could not reject. Five goals in 14 games for Real, the only two of real importance coming against Spurs in the first leg of the Champions League quarter-final in April 2011, were not enough to make his move to Spain permanent. With no-one prepared to match his City wages, Adebayor was expected to play no more than a bit part for them in the 2011-12 season, but when heavy defeats in the opening two Premier League fixtures exposed Spurs' weaknesses up front, Adebayor was one of the few proven goal scorers available. As City were desperate to get him off the wage bill, Spurs were able to negotiate a deal that did not wreck the club's wage structure. With his ability to hold up play and operate as a lone front man or alongside a second striker, Adebayor's signing proved a smart move on the part of Harry Redknapp. He scored regularly as Spurs only missed out on another Champions League spot when Chelsea surprisingly won the trophy. Tall and gangly, adept at rolling his marker and with great strength, Adebayor was an awkward player for any defender to deal with. Although his attitude was often questioned, he made enough of an impact on loan for Spurs to seek a permanent transfer, but it was only as the transfer window drew to a close that a deal was done. Spurs reportedly paid a bargain £5million transfer fee, though they took on his hefty wages. Sadly, having got a permanent transfer, Adebayor seemed to think he need do no more. Following a poor 2012-13 season, he was so out of favour that he was not even training with the senior squad. There seemed only one way for Adebayor to go, but when Tim Sherwood replaced Andrea Villas-Boas, he managed to re-kindle Adebayor's interest. The decision not to appoint Sherwood as permanent head coach, saw Adebayor's career go further back and it did not take Mauricio Pochettino long to decide Adebayor was not the type of character he wanted. With no buyer prepared to meet Adebayor's wage demands, his registration was released by Spurs once the August 2015 transfer window had closed. However, his contract continued, so Spurs were left to pick up his wages. Even when Crystal Palace signed Adebayor on a short-term deal, the wages they paid him only went to reduce Spurs' outlay. When his Spurs' contract came to an end Adebayor was unable to secure a new club for six months, only signing a deal with Turkey's Başakşehir after impressing for Togo in the Africa Cup of Nations. As Adebayor's parents were Nigerian he qualified to play for both Nigeria and Togo. He chose Togo and, when not in dispute with the manager or national FA, proved a regular scorer on the international stage. As a Spurs' player, he made 17 international appearances. The decision to play for Togo was one that almost cost Adebayor his life. In January 2010, he was on the bus carrying the Togo team to the African Cup of Nations in Angola when it was attacked by a terrorist group in the Cabanda province. Eight members of the party were injured, with three killed.

Appearances:
League: 79 (13) apps. 35 gls.
FA Cup: 5 (2) apps. 1 gl.
FL Cup: 2 apps. 1 gl.
Euro: 11 (1) apps. 5 gls.
Others: 4 (2) apps. 3 gls.
Total: 101 (18) apps. 45 gls.

ADLINGTON, Edward Hewitt

Role: Goalkeeper 1885-89
Born: Tottenham, London, 1867

Debut v Rutland (Fr) (a) 14.11.1885

Little is known about Edward Adlington other than that he was one of the pioneers of Spurs' early days and spent most of his time as captain of the reserve side. A local lad, like most of the early members he was still at school when first associated with the club. Like many youngsters of his age he was happy to turn out in any position, but appears to have principally played in goal for the Second XI. He is only known to have made three appearances in the first team, all in friendly matches. In 1889 Adlington emigrated to South Africa. He helped found a football club in Johannesburg before moving on to Australia where he did the same thing in Perth.

Appearances:
Others: 3 apps. 0 gls.
Total: 3 apps. 0 gls.

AITCHISON, Barrie George

Role: Winger 1954-64
5ft.6ins. 9st.8lbs.
Born: Colchester, Essex, 15th November 1937

CAREER: Colchester Casuals/**SPURS** am. Feb 1954, pro. Jan 1955/ Colchester United Aug 1964/Cambridge City Jun 1966/Bury Town cs. 1967.

Debut v Army XI (Fr) (h) 24.10.1960 (scored once)

Barry Aitchison was associated with Spurs as a youth for some time before signing professional, but while he proved a consistent performer at reserve level, he was unable to make the step up to the League team. His only first team outing was in a side depleted by international calls for a friendly match against an Army XI in October 1960. Aitchison remained in the reserves until the end of the 1963-64 season when he was released and joined his home town team, Colchester United. He spent two years at Layer Road, the last of which was decimated by a leg injury that forced him to retire from League football in the summer of 1966. He then joined Cambridge City, linking up with his former Spurs' colleague Tony Marchi, the Cambridge manager and later played for Bury Town. Aitchison's brother, Peter, also played for Colchester.

Appearances:
Others: 1 app. 1 gl.
Total: **1 app. 1 gl.**

AITKEN, W

Role: Outside-left 1893-94

Debut v City Ramblers (Fr) (h) 3.2.1894

Nothing is known about Aitken whose only recorded first team appearance was in a friendly match against City Ramblers in February 1894.

Appearances:
Others: 1 app.
Total: **1 app. 0 gls.**

ALDERWEIRELD, Tobias Albertine Maurits

Role: Defender 2015-
6ft.2ins. 13st. 13lbs.
Born: Antwerp, Belgium, 2nd March 1989

CAREER: Germinal Beerschot (Belgium) 1999/Ajax (Holland) Academy Aug 2004, pro. Feb 2007/Atlético Madrid (Spain) Sep 2013/(Southampton loan Sep 2014)/**SPURS** Jul 2015.

Debut v Manchester United (PL) (a) 7.8.2015
(MLS All-Stars (Fr) (a) 29.7.2015)

Toby Alderweireld is one of many graduates of the successful Ajax youth scouting structure to reach the peak of European football. Plucked from his native Antwerp as a 15-year old, Alderweireld followed Jan Vertonghen through the Ajax Academy into the Dutch masters' first team and the Belgian national line-up. He made his debut for Belgium against Chile in May 2009 and soon established himself as a first choice in defence, though not in his favoured central role. The presence of two master defenders in Vertonghen and Vincent Kompany meant Alderweireld had to settle for a place at full-back. It was a role he filled more than competently, showing power, pace and attacking desire. With Ajax, Alderweireld won the Dutch Eredivisie title in 2011, 2012 and 2013. He was not to make it four-in-a-row as he

was tempted away to Atlético Madrid. While unable to displace either Diego Godin or Miranda, the established central defensive pairing, Alderweireld did enough to help Atletico win the La Liga title in his one season in Spain. Still developing, he was surprisingly allowed to move to Southampton on loan in September 2014. He proved one of the Saint's outstanding performers and it was no surprise when they sought to exercise an option to sign him on a permanent basis. Whether they had an enforceable option was a matter of debate, and there was talk of Southampton taking legal action when it was announced that Alderweireld had decided to join Spurs. Whatever the merits of a claim, Southampton quickly realised there was nothing to be gained from trying to force through a transfer and Alderweireld joined his compatriots, Vertonghen, Mousa Dembélé and Nacer Chadli at White Hart Lane. Alongside Vertonghen, he has formed a formidable barrier in front of Hugo Lloris and the pair have played a major part in Spurs' upward progress.

Appearances:
League: 68 apps. 5 gls.
FA Cup: 5 apps.
Euro: 14 (1) apps. 1 gl.
Others: 4 apps.
Total: **91 (1) apps. 6 gls.**

ALEKSIC, Milija Antony

Role: Goalkeeper 1978-82
6ft.1ins. 13st.11lbs.
Born: *Newcastle-Under-Lyme, Staffordshire, 14th April 1951*
Died: *Johannesburg, South Africa, 17th October 2012*

CAREER: Staffordshire Schools/Port Vale am./Eastwood/Stafford Rangers/Plymouth Argyle Feb 1973/(Oxford United loan Jul 1976)/(Ipswich Town loan Nov 1976)/Luton Town loan Dec 1976, perm. Jan 1977/**SPURS** Dec 1978/(Sheffield United loan Mar 1979)/(Luton Town loan Nov 1981)/Wits University (South Africa) player-coach 1982-86.

Debut v Altrincham (FAC) (Maine Road) 16.1.1979
(El Nasr (Fr) (a) 18.12.1978)

Born of a Yugoslavian father and nicknamed "Elastic", Milija Aleksic was released by his local League side, Port Vale, when manager, Sir Stanley Matthews, decided he would not make the grade. He joined the local amateur side Eastwood, then moved up the non-league ladder with Stafford Rangers. His performance for Rangers in the 1972 FA Trophy Final led several higher League clubs to look closely at him, but it was with Plymouth Argyle that he turned professional. Some impressive displays led to loan spells with Oxford United and Ipswich Town, before Luton Town decided to turn a loan into a permanent move. Aleksic soon established himself as first choice 'keeper and, with Spurs looking for Pat Jennings' long term Burkinshaw to part with £100,000 to secure his transfer. In four seasons with Spurs, Aleksic was to play only 32 senior games as a series of unfortunate injuries prevented him playing more often. A brave 'keeper with replacement, his consistent performances persuaded manager Keith Burkinshaw to part with £100,000 to secure

his transfer. In four seasons with Spurs, Aleksic was to play only 32 senior games as a series of unfortunate injuries prevented him playing more often. A brave 'keeper with good reflexes, ironically it was an injury to Barry Daines that gave Aleksic the opportunity to win his one major honour. Called into the team at the semi-final stage, he went on to play his part in the thrilling 1981 FA Cup Final defeat of Manchester City. In August 1981 Ray Clemence was signed and with further opportunities limited Aleksic was released in the summer of 1982. He joined the "rebel" tour of South Africa, where he later took up coaching.

Appearances:
League: 25 apps.
FA Cup: 7 apps
Others: 23 (3) apps.
Total: 55 (3) apps. 0 gls.

ALEXANDER, Stanley

Role: Forward 1936-38
5ft.7ins. 10st.7lbs.
Born: Percy Main, Northumberland, 17th September 1905
Died: Anlaby, Hull, East Yorkshire, 5th June 1961

CAREER: England Schools/Percy Main Amateurs/Hull City Jun 1926/Bradford City Nov 1931/Millwall Oct 1933/**SPURS** Jun 1936/Accrington Stanley Jul 1938/Royal Navy 1940/Hull City juniors coach in the 1950s.

Debut v West Ham United (FL) (a) 29.8.1936

An experienced inside-forward or winger, at 31 Stan Alexander's best years were probably in the past by the time he joined Spurs. A member of the FA touring party to Canada in 1930, he made his Spurs' debut in the opening match of the 1936-37 season but was unable to hold down a permanent first team place and made only nine sporadic League appearances. He spent the following season in the reserves before being given a free transfer in May 1938 and joining Accrington Stanley. Alexander stayed with the former League club until retiring during the Second World War, after which he returned to Hull City and coached their juniors. Alexander's brother, John, played for Hull City, Ashington, Workington and Bury.

Appearances:
League: 9 apps. 1 gl.
Total: 9 apps. 1 gl.

ALLEN, Clive Darren

Role: Striker 1984-88
5ft.10ins. 12st.3lbs.
Born: Stepney, London, 20th May 1961

CAREER: Gaynes School/County Park Rangers/Havering Schools/Essex Schools/London Schools/England Schools/Queens Park Rangers app. Jun 1977, pro. Sep 1978/Arsenal Jun 1980/Crystal Palace Aug 1980/Queens Park Rangers Jun 1981/**SPURS** Aug 1984/Bordeaux (France) Mar 1988/Manchester City Jul 1989/Chelsea Dec 1991/West Ham United Mar 1992/Millwall Mar 1994/Bristol City trial Jul 1995/Dagenham and Redbridge trial Jul 1995/Carlisle United trial Sep 1995/Luton Town trial Oct 1995/Cambridge United trial Nov 1995/Colchester United trial 1995-96/England Youth team coach Jul 1999/**SPURS** caretaker reserve team manager Oct 2003-May 2004, Development Coach Jun 2004, caretaker manager Oct 2007, first team assistant coach 2010-Jun 2012.

Debut v Everton (FL) (a) 25.8.1984 (scored twice)
(Brentford (sub) (Fr) (a) 11.8.1984 (scored twice))

Clive Allen's arrival at White Hart Lane made him the second member of the Allen footballing family to wear the white shirt of Spurs. Although not to win as many trophies as his father, Les, netting no less than 42 goals in the 1986-87 season gave him the distinction of scoring more competitive goals for Spurs in one season than anyone else. Allen's prowess as a marksman was evident from an early age and all London's major clubs were keen to sign him, but, after training at Spurs as a schoolboy, it was Queens Park Rangers, his father's last club, that he chose to join. He was soon scoring goals and winning England youth and Under-21 caps. After only one full season of League football Allen was transferred to Arsenal for £1.25 million. His stay at Highbury was remarkably short as, within two months and after only three friendly games for the Gunners, he moved again, this time to Terry Venables' Crystal Palace in an exchange deal for Kenny Sansom valued at £1.25 million. Venables left Selhurst Park for Queens Park Rangers just two months later and, not surprisingly after all the turmoil the teenager had been through, Allen had a difficult ten months with Palace, although he did manage to add two more Under-21 caps to the one he had collected with Rangers. In June 1981, he renewed acquaintance with Venables by returning to Loftus Road and lost no time getting back to the old routine of scoring goals. In his first season back, he played for Rangers in the 1982 FA Cup Final against Spurs, but departed with an injury after only ten minutes and was forced to miss the replay. The amazing regularity of his goal-scoring for Rangers led to selection for the England tour of South America in 1984 and a first full cap as substitute against Brazil. A £700,000 move to White Hart Lane followed and Allen's Spurs' career began in the best possible way with two goals on his League debut. Unfortunately, life did not continue in the same happy vein as a string of injuries limited his appearances in his first two seasons. It was only in 1986-87 that Allen shook off his injury problems and then, playing as a lone striker in David Pleat's new look Spurs team, really showed the full depth of his clinical finishing abilities with those 49 goals, including the first against Coventry City after only two minutes of the FA Cup Final. Sadly, however, he was again destined to collect a loser's medal after Coventry's extra-time victory, although some consolation came from being voted Player of the Year by both the Football Writers' and Professional Footballer's' Associations. After such a wonderful season, it was perhaps to be expected he would have difficulty maintaining such incredible standards in 1987-88 and, although he started off the season representing the Football League in the League's Centenary celebration match against the Rest of the World, events off the pitch at Spurs did not help and it was only after the appointment of Venables as manager that Allen started to find flashes of his old form. However, Venables decided Allen did not figure in his future plans and in March 1988, a month after winning his fifth England cap, he made the third £1,000,000 move of his career and signed for the French club Bordeaux, although he remained with Spurs until the end of the season. He only spent a year in France without enjoying much success before a further £1,000,000 move took him to newly-promoted Manchester City. Although Allen maintained an excellent strike rate at Maine Road, it was apparent early in the 1991-92 season that he did not figure in City's long-term thinking. In December 1991 he joined Chelsea, another of his father's old clubs, for a modest £250,000. Regarded as one of the bargain buys of the season, he was surprisingly transferred to West Ham United on transfer deadline day in March 1992 for a similar fee. Unable to save the Hammers from relegation, he did help them return at the first attempt before joining his seventh London club, Millwall, but, badly affected by injuries, he was released at the end of 1994-95. He had trials with several clubs without being taken on before accepting a role in the television industry with Sky TV. In February 1997 Allen signed on as kicker for the London Monarchs in the World League of American Football but spent only one season in the gridiron game before combining his media work with coaching the England Under-16 team. He was to make one further appearance for Spurs, playing as a substitute in the October 2002 Tottenham Trust Fund match against DC United. In October 2003 Allen returned to the White Hart Lane staff as caretaker reserve team manager before taking on the new role of development coach. With the departure of Martin Jol in October 2007 Allen, along with youth coach Alex Inglethorpe, was put in temporary charge of the first team. Harry Redknapp's appointment saw Allen back as Development Coach but his abilities soon shone through and he proved a valuable member of Redknapp's first team coaching staff. When Redknapp was sacked in June 2012, Allen also lost his position and returned to work in the media.

Appearances:
League: 97 (8) apps. 60 gls.
FA Cup: 11 (1) apps. 9 gls.
FL Cup: 13 (1) apps. 13 gls.
Euro: 3 (1) apps. 2 gls.
Others: 32 (7) apps. 29 gls.
Total: 156 (18) apps. 113 gls.

ALLEN, Jimmy

Role: Utility 1896-97
5ft.7ins. 11st.3lbs.

CAREER: Clapton/SPURS Mar 1897/Mansfield.

Debut v Swindon Town (SL) (a) 9.1.1897
(Northfleet (Fr) (h) 29.12.1896)

Jimmy Allen appeared in a variety of positions for Spurs during the 1896-97 season, their first in the Southern League. Initially a guest from Clapton, he ceased to be a member of the famous amateur club in March 1897 and turned out regularly for Spurs for the rest of the season, usually at centre-half or right-back. A London representative player, he was not retained at the end of the season and later played for Mansfield, although not the current former League outfit.

Appearances:
Southern: 4 apps.
Others: 19* apps. 3 gls.
Total: 23 apps. 3 gls.
* Includes 1 abandoned match.

ALLEN, Joseph

Role: Inside-forward 1932-33
5ft.8ins. 11st.4lbs.
Born: Bilsthorpe, Nottinghamshire, 30th December 1909
Died: Rainworth, Mansfield, Nottinghamshire, 29th November 1978

CAREER: Bilsthorpe Colliery/Mansfield Town am. Aug 1928, pro. Aug 1929/Bilsthorpe Colliery cs. 1930/SPURS Aug 1932/Northfleet United Aug 1932/Queens Park Rangers Jun 1933/Mansfield Town Jun 1935/Racing Club De Roubaix (France) Nov 1935/Clapton Orient trial May 1937/Racing Club De Roubaix (France) 1937/Nancy (France) 1938 /(guest for Mansfield Town and Northampton Town during World War Two).

Debut v Bradford City (FL) (h) 8.4.1933 (scored once)

Although Joe Allen had played regularly in the Midland League since 1929, when he joined Spurs from Mansfield Town he was immediately sent to the nursery club at Northfleet to further his football education. He did so well in the early part of the 1932-33 season that by December 1932 he was called up to join the White Hart Lane staff. Allen spent most of his time in the reserves, making his only senior appearance in April 1933 as stand-in for Willie Hall, when he scored Spurs' goal in a 1-1 draw with Bradford City. Two months later he was released and spent two years with Queens Park Rangers until returning to Mansfield. His second spell there only no more than six months before a transfer to the French club, Racing Club De Roubaix where he played for a few months before moving on to Nancy. Returning to Nottinghamshire from France because of the Second World War, Allen worked in the local mines but still turned out for Mansfield and Northampton Town as a guest in war-time competition.

Appearances:
League: 1 app. 1 gl.
Total: 1 app. 1 gl.

ALLEN, Leslie William

Role: Centre or inside-forward 1959-65
5ft.10ins 10st.3lbs.
Born: Dagenham, Essex, 4th September 1937

CAREER: Briggs Sports/West Ham United trial Sep 1952/SPURS am. 1953/Chelsea Sep 1954/SPURS Dec 1959/Queens Park Rangers Jul 1965, player-manager Dec 1968-Jan 1971/Aris Thessalonika (Greece) manager Feb-May 1971/Woodford Town player-manager Aug 1971-72/Swindon Town chief scout, manager Nov 1972-Feb 1974.

Debut v Newcastle United (FL) (h) 19.12.1959

Bill Nicholson's signing of Les Allen was a considerable surprise, for he let popular former England international Johnny Brooks move to Stamford Bridge as part of the £20,000 part-exchange deal, but it did not take long for Allen to prove what a shrewd bargain Nicholson had secured. A sixteen-year-old in Briggs Sports' 1954 Amateur Cup semi-final team, Allen had scored 11 goals in 44 League games for Chelsea,

but was struggling to escape their reserves as a certain Jimmy Greaves was banging in the goals for their senior team. Allen did not score on his debut, but netted twice in his second match and was soon scoring regularly, including five in a 13-2 FA Cup replay defeat of Crewe Alexandra in February 1960. His arrival took some of the weight off Bobby Smith up front and his value as an instinctive scorer and unselfish, hard-working member of the team who enjoyed a near-perfect understanding with his team-mates, was shown by his ever-present tag in the "Double" winning team of 1961, when he netted 27 League and Cup goals. Rewarded with selection for the England Under-23 side against Wales in February 1961, the arrival of Jimmy Greaves in November of that year was expected to mark the end of Allen's days at White Hart Lane. In fact, Allen competed with Smith to partner Greaves, even winning a place in the Football League side that played the Italian League in November 1962. It was only after Alan Gilzean's arrival that Allen left Spurs for Queens Park Rangers in a £21,000 deal. At Loftus Road, his experience was invaluable in helping a young Rangers side climb from the Third to First Division, winning the first Football League Cup Final at Wembley in 1967 on its way. On Tommy Docherty's departure in December 1968, Allen was appointed Rangers' manager, but he only held the post until January 1971. After a brief spell in Greece and a year or so as player-manager at Woodford Town, he returned to League management with Swindon Town. When his football career ended Allen worked in the car industry back in his native Essex.

Appearances:
League: 119 apps. 47gls.
FA Cup: 15 apps. 13 gls.
Euro: 3 apps. 1 gl.
Others: 10 apps. 14 gls.
Total: 147 apps. 75 gls.

ALLEN, Paul Kevin

Role: Midfielder 1985-94
5ft.7ins. 11st.0lbs.
Born: Aveley, Essex, 26th August 1962

CAREER: Thurrock Schools/Essex Schools/West Ham United app. Jul 1978, pro. Aug 1979/**SPURS** Jun 1985/Southampton Sep 1993/(Luton Town loan Dec 1994)/(Stoke City loan Jan 1995)/Southend United training Jul 1995/Swindon Town Oct 1995/Bristol City Jan 1997/Purfleet Jul 1997/Millwall trial Jul 1997/**SPURS** coach/Ashford Town 1998.

Debut v Watford (FL) (h) 17.8.1985 (scored once)
(Wycombe Wanderers (Fr) (Bisham Abbey) 18.7.1985)

When Paul Allen joined Spurs, he became the third member of the remarkable Allen footballing family to play for the club, following his uncle Les and cousin Clive. As a schoolboy, Allen trained with Queens Park Rangers and Crystal Palace and had a trial with Arsenal, but it was for West Ham that he signed apprentice forms. England youth caps and a professional contract were quickly followed by his League debut in September 1979. At the end of his first season, and only 17 years and 256 days old, he made history as the youngest player to appear in an FA Cup Final as a member of the "Hammers" team that beat favourites Arsenal 1-0. Paul also made headlines that day as the victim of a notorious "professional foul" by "Gunners" defender Willie Young when clean through on goal. By the time of his £400,000 move to Spurs Allen had already won two England Under-21 caps and collected another against Rumania in September 1985. Not helped by some personal problems off the field, he had difficulty reproducing his best form at White Hart Lane and it took two years for him to really establish himself as a valuable member of Spurs' senior squad. A wide midfielder, able to play at full-back if the need arose, he returned to Wembley for the 1987 FA Cup Final with Coventry City, although this time he had to be content with a loser's medal. A busy, non-stop player with his own unique scampering run, Allen's contribution to the team's performances was often overlooked, but his consistency was rewarded at the end of the 1988-89 season with selection for the England "B" team tour. Unfortunately, injury forced him to withdraw from the squad, but he continued to be one of the most dependable players at White Hart Lane and deservedly won another FA Cup winner's medal against Nottingham Forest in 1991. Out of favour under Ossie Ardiles, Allen moved to Southampton in September 1993 for £550,000. His popularity was recognised by Spurs' travelling support as they stood as one on their next visit to the Dell to salute him. Given a free transfer by Southampton, Allen went on to serve Bristol City and Millwall before dropping into the non-League game. He later joined Spurs' academy coaching staff, whilst also working in the PFA's London offices. Apart from Clive, Les and Paul, the Allen family has seen Les' brother Dennis play

for Charlton Athletic, Reading and AFC Bournemouth, his son Martin play for Queens Park Rangers, West Ham United and Portsmouth and Clive's brother Bradley play for Queens Park Rangers, Charlton and Grimsby Town.

Appearances:
League: 276 (16) apps. 23 gls.
FA Cup: 26 (1) apps. 1 gl.
FL Cup: 42 (2) apps. 4 gls.
Euro: 6 (1) apps.
Others: 94 (7) apps. 3 gls.
Total: 444 (27) apps. 31 gls.

ALLEN, Rory William

Role: Striker 1996-99
5ft.11ins. 11st.7lbs.
Born: Beckenham, Kent, 17th October 1977

CAREER: Langley Park Boys School/Beckenham Schools/Kent Schools/**SPURS** assoc. schl. Jul 1992, trainee Jul 1994, pro. March 1996/(Luton Town loan Mar 1998)/Portsmouth Jul 1999.

Debut v Wimbledon (FL) (sub) (h) 4.9.1996
(Ham Kam (Fr) (a) 23.7.1996)

A tall young striker who developed through Spurs' junior ranks, Rory Allen moved quickly through to the fringes of the first team, but with competition from the likes of Chris Armstrong, Steffen Iversen, and Teddy Sheringham he was always going to face an uphill task to make the breakthrough to a regular first team place. That task was made all the harder with the arrival of Les Ferdinand, but Allen was not helped by long spells of injury just when he needed to be learning his trade from such experienced players. With opportunities looking few, he was allowed to move to Portsmouth for a £1 million fee, but injuries continued to haunt him and eventually simply became too much. In November 2002 Allen called time on his career, walking out on Portsmouth to join the "Barmy Army" watching the Ashes matches in Australia. Allen's grandfather, Des Quinn played for Millwall and Blackburn Rovers.

Appearances:
League: 10 (11) apps. 2 gls.
FA Cup: 1 app.
FL Cup: 3 (3) apps. 2 gls.
Others: 9 (5) apps. 3 gls.
Total: 23 (19) apps. 7 gls.

ALLI, Bamidele Jermaine

Role: Midfielder 2015-
6ft.2ins. 12st.6lbs.
Born: Milton Keynes, Buckinghamshire, 11th April 1996

CAREER: City Colts/Milton Keynes Dons 2007/**SPURS** Feb 2015/
(Milton Keynes Dons loan Feb 2015).

Debut v Manchester United (sub) (PL) (a) 7.8.2015
(MLS All-Stars (sub) (Fr) (a) 29.7.2015)

Few players have made such an immediate impact on English football as Dele Alli. Taken under the wing of his local club MK Dons as an 11-year old, Alli made his senior debut at 16 and within a year was holding down a regular midfield spot. Scouts from the bigger clubs were soon making tracks for the Buckinghamshire town and it was just a question of when he would move on. While others pondered, Spurs moved to secure his transfer. An initial £5 million fee was handed over in February 2015, with Alli remaining at MK Dons on loan for the rest of the season. The step-up from League One to the Premier League is a big one and little more was expected of Alli than that he would establish a place in the senior squad. However, from the very first minute it was obvious Alli had all that was needed to become a first team regular. Strong, hard-running and possessed of an attacking instinct that immediately put opponents on the back foot, Alli had a freshness and a total lack of fear. He was prepared to try anything, and even if it went wrong, he just tried again until he got it right. With just seven Premier League games to his credit Alli was called up to the full England squad in October 2015 and made his debut as a substitute against Estonia. A month later he started against France and netted his first goal, past his Spurs team-mate, Hugo Lloris. Capable of playing as a deep-lying midfielder, or either side of a midfield three, Alli appears best suited to what is being termed a "no 10" role. Operating between the midfield and a lone striker, Alli's pace, willingness to get forward, eye for an opening and coolness in front of goal, have made him the perfect foil for Harry Kane.

Appearances:
League: 63 (7) apps. 27 gls.
FA Cup: 4 (4) apps. 3 gls.
FL Cup: (1) app.
Euro: 15 (2) apps. 1 gl.
Others: 2 (3) apps. 1 gl.
Total: 94 (17) apps. 32 gls.

ALMOND, William

Role: Half-back 1895-97
Born: Blackburn, Lancashire, 5th April 1863

CAREER: Witton/Blackburn Rovers May 1888/Accrington Oct 1892/Northwich Victoria/Middlesbrough cs. 1893/Millwall Athletic cs. 1894/**SPURS** Aug 1895/Millwall Athletic cs. 1897/Clapton/Wandsworth.

Debut v Wolverton (SL) (a) 12.9.1896
(Old Westminsters (LCC) (h) 9.11.1895)

Willie Almond started his football career with his local club, Witton, rather than the better-known Blackburn Rovers, Blackburn Olympic or Blackburn Park Lane. A determined, attacking half-back he came to prominence when he joined Blackburn Rovers in May 1888, one of several signings they made in preparation for the first season of League football. He became a valued and regular member of their team of the late 1880s/early 1890s and, although he missed the FA Cup Finals of 1890 and 1891, gave

Blackburn over four years sterling service before joining Accrington. He made only a handful of appearances for Accrington before moving on to Middlesbrough and had a year with Millwall Athletic before reverting to amateur status. He joined Spurs for the start of the 1895-96 campaign, making his first appearance in a London Charity Cup tie in November 1895. A month later Spurs decided to adopt professionalism, but Almond continued to play as an amateur. This allowed him to turn out for other clubs such as Clapton and Millwall during his two years at Tottenham. After helping Spurs in their first season of Southern League football of 1896-97 Almond, together with practically all the other players on the Spurs' staff, was released. He returned to Millwall for one season before winding down his career with London's senior amateur clubs such as Clapton and Wandsworth. Almond had the opportunity to collect an England cap, but turned down the chance to play against Ireland in March 1889 so that he could turn out for Blackburn in an important FA Cup tie against Aston Villa. In May 1888, shortly after joining Blackburn Rovers, Almond joined his team-mates on a rowing boat at

Derwentwater in the Lake District. A non-swimmer, he slipped into the water without realising its depth and was soon in trouble. In an effort to assist, goalkeeper Billy Townley threw an oar towards Almond, but it just struck Almond, sending him under again. Fortunately, Herbie Arthur and Alf Woolfall proved rather more adept at life-saving and pulled Almond to safety.

Appearances:
Southern: 16 apps. 2 gls.
FA Cup: 7 apps.
Others: 37 apps. 8 gls.
Total: 60 apps. 10 gls

ALNWICK, Benjamin Robert

Role: Goalkeeper 2006-11
6ft.2ins. 15st.0lbs.
Born: Prudhoe, Northumberland, 1st January 1987

CAREER: Sunderland Scholar Jul 2003, pro Mar 2004/**SPURS** Jan 2007/(Luton Town loan Sep 2007)/(Leicester City loan Jan 2008)/(Carlisle United loan Oct 2008)/(Norwich City loan Jul 2009)/(Leeds United loan Oct 2010)/(Doncaster Rovers loan Mar 2011)/Middlesbrough trial Jul 2011/(Leyton Orient loan Sep 2011)/Barnsley Jul 2012/Charlton Athletic Sep 2013/Leyton Orient Jan-Mar 2014/Huddersfield Town training Apr 2014/Blackpool trial Jul 2014/Peterborough United Jul 2014/Bolton Wanderers Aug 2016.

Debut v Burnley (FLC) (a) 21.1.2009

Having represented England at all levels up to Under-21, Ben Alnwick was viewed as one of the country's most promising young 'keepers even before he had fully established himself with Sunderland. With little more than twenty senior games to his credit, Spurs paid out £900,000 to secure his transfer in January 2007, a figure that would rise to £1.3 million if Alnwick proved as talented as expected. Despite Paul Robinson having a tough time, Alnwick failed to challenge Radek Černý's position as Robinson's number two and when overlooked with the signings of Heurelho Gomes and Carlo Cudicini, he was allowed out on loan, a situation that prevailed for most of his Spurs'

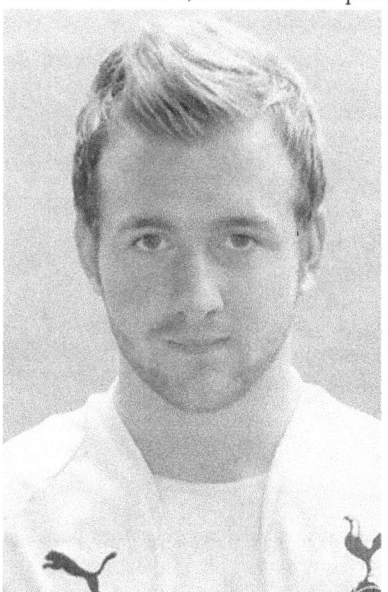

career. In January 2009, he was recalled from Carlisle United to make his Spurs' senior debut in the Carling Cup semi-final at Burnley. He retained his place for the following FA Cup game, but it was not until May 2010 that he made his sole Premier League appearance for Spurs. Even his loan travels did little to enhance his career, most of his time being spent on the substitutes' bench. By June 2012 it was clear Alnwick was not going to make the grade at White Hart Lane. His contract was cancelled and he signed for Barnsley, quickly moving on to Charlton Athletic and Leyton Orient. His contract at Brisbane Road was cancelled after only one game when illness prevented him training or playing. By the summer he was fit to resume playing and had offers from both Blackpool and Peterborough United. He chose Peterborough, at last establishing himself as a regular starter before having his contract cancelled and joining Bolton Wanderers. Alnwick's brother, Jak, was also a goalkeeper, playing for Newcastle United and Port Vale.

Appearances:
League: 1 app.
FA Cup: 1 app.
FL Cup: 1 app.
Others: (1) app.
Total: 3 (1) apps.

ALSFORD, Walter John

Role: Half-back 1930-37
5ft.11ins. 11st.11lbs.
Born: Edmonton, London, 6th November 1911
Died: Bedford, Bedfordshire, 3rd June 1968

CAREER: Lancastrian School/Edmonton Schools/London Schools/**SPURS** am. May 1929/Cheshunt/Northfleet United 1929/**SPURS** pro. Aug 1930/Nottingham Forest Jan 1937/(guest for Aldershot, Arsenal, Doncaster Rovers, Grantham Town and Nottingham Forest during World War Two).

Debut v Reading (FL) (a) 27.12.1930
(Chelsea (LFACC) (a) 27.10.1930)

A local product, Wally Alsford was under Spurs' wing from his early days and, after signing as an amateur, was "farmed out" to the club's junior nursery at Cheshunt before moving to the senior outfit at Northfleet. In August 1930, he moved on to the White Hart Lane staff and made his first team debut the following October in a London FA Charity Cup tie with Chelsea. By then, the competition was of little more than reserve team status and his senior debut came two months later. A wing-half who could also play centre-half or inside-forward, he was with Spurs for over six years but, despite the 1930's being a time of ups and downs for the club with both promotion and relegation experienced, Alsford was unable to establish himself as a first team regular. His best season was the relegation year of 1934-35 when he not only appeared in half the League games, but also won an England cap against Scotland in April 1935 after impressing in the previous month's international trial. After more than seven years with Spurs, Alsford was allowed to move to Nottingham Forest, but within twelve months of the transfer was found to be suffering from osteomyelitis, a bone marrow inflammation. Told he would not be able to play again he retired in May 1938, but did turn out for Nottingham Forest and guest for several other clubs during the early years of the Second World War. After the war, he was a licensee in Nottingham, Brighton and Bedford.

Appearances:
League: 81 apps.
FA Cup: 9 apps.
Others: 10 apps. 2 gls.
Total: 100 apps. 2 gls.

AMBLER, Charles James

Role: Goalkeeper 1894-1900
5ft.10ins. 10st.11lbs.
Born: Alverstone, Isle of Wight, 13th August 1868
Died: September qtr. 1952

CAREER: Bostal Rovers/Royal Arsenal am. 1891, pro./Clapton am. 1892/Dartford cs. 1893/Luton Town Sep 1894/**SPURS** Oct 1894/Woolwich Arsenal Nov 1895/Gravesend United 1900/New Brompton Sep 1900/West Ham United Sep 1901/Millwall Athletic cs. 1902.

Debut v Wolverton (FAC) (h) 3.11.1894

Born under the surname Toby, Charlie Ambler played for one season with Royal Arsenal as a professional but was re-instated as an amateur in the summer of 1892 so he could turn out for Clapton-although he continued to be associated with Arsenal. After a year with Dartford and just one month at Luton Town he joined Spurs in October 1894, making his first appearance in an FA Cup 2nd Qualifying Round tie and quickly establishing himself as first choice 'keeper. As Spurs were not, at the time, competing in any organised League competition, Ambler was free to play for other clubs. In October 1895, he signed Southern League forms for Luton Town and the following month Football League forms for Woolwich Arsenal. He did not turn out for Luton, but he did play for Woolwich Arsenal, deputising for the suspended Harry Storer in one Football League game. One of London's very best 'keepers, Ambler won several representative honours as a Spurs' player, notably playing for London in inter-county competition. Although he missed only one game in Spurs first Southern League season of 1896-97, the summer of 1897 saw wholesale changes in the playing staff and, with the arrival of Joe Cullen, Ambler found himself in the reserves. He remained with Spurs until the summer of 1900-making only rare appearances in the first team when Cullen was unavailable-when he was released and moved to Gravesend United. After a very short spell there, he spent one season at New Brompton, following that with similar spells at West Ham United and Millwall Athletic.

Appearances:
Southern: 22 apps.
FA Cup: 12 apps.
Others: 98* (1) apps.
Total: 132 (1) apps. 0 gls.
* Includes 1 abandoned match.

AMOS, Luke Ayodele

Role: Midfielder 2016-
5ft.10ins. 11st.1lb.
Born: *Welwyn Garden City, Hertfordshire, 23rd February 1997*

CAREER: John Warner School, Hoddesdon/Ware Youth/**SPURS** Academy Scholar Jul 2013, pro. Jun 2015/(Southend United loan Jan 2017).

Debut v Juventus (sub) (Fr) (Melbourne) 26.7.2016

Associated with Spurs since nine-years old, Luke Amos is a strong, central defensive midfielder, with strength and stamina who has represented England at Under-16 and Under-18 level. He made his debut during Spurs trip to Australia for the International Champions Cup in July 2016, impressing with his hard work and composure. A regular in the senior youth sides, Amos followed the well-trodden route of going out to loan when he joined Southend United in January 2017 for the rest of the season. Amos struggled to make much of an impression, but did make three senior appearances for the Shrimpers before returning to Spurs.

Appearances:
Others: (3) apps.
Total: (3) apps. 0 gls.

AMOS, Robert Henry

Role: Forward 1884-86
Born: 1862

Debut v Woodgrange (Fr) (h) 18.10.1884

Another of the young men from Spurs' pioneering days of whom little is known, Robert Amos played as a forward in some of the club's earliest recorded matches. His first known appearance was on 18th October 1884 and it is likely he only joined Spurs that season after playing for one of the many other local clubs. Probably only with the club for two seasons he played in Spurs' first ever cup-tie against St Albans, a London clearing house, on 17th October 1885 in the London Association Cup.

Appearances:
Others: 6 apps. 5 gls.
Total: 6 apps. 5 gls.

ANDERSON, Alexander

Role: Goalkeeper 1944-45
5ft.9ins. 11st.0lbs.
Born: Gorbals, Glasgow, 8th January 1922
Died: Ainsdale, Southport, Lancashire, 10th October 1984

CAREER: Provanside Hibs/Petershill Juniors/Heart of Midlothian Aug 1941/(guest for Chelsea, Raith Rovers and **SPURS** during World War Two)/Stirling Albion 1947/Third Lanark 1947/Rochdale Feb 1948/Dundalk cs. 1948/Southport trial and perm. Nov 1949/Bangor City cs. 1951/Runcorn cs. 1953/Lancaster City Oct 1954-1957.

Debut v Charlton Athletic (FLS) (a) 13.1.1945

Hearts' goalkeeper Alex Anderson was a regular guest for Chelsea at the time of his one appearance for Spurs, only playing because the usual guest 'keeper, Archie Hughes, was engaged in a Services representative match. After the War Anderson moved rapidly from Hearts to Stirling Albion and Third Lanark before joining Rochdale, but played only four League games before moving on to Dundalk. He had a more successful spell in Ireland, winning an FA of Ireland Cup Winner's medal in 1949 and even representing the League of Ireland against the Scottish League back in his native Glasgow in September 1948. He later played for Southport and finished his career in non-League circles. After football Anderson settled in Southport working as a painter and decorator. He always insisted on wearing a yellow jersey; even though the colour was reserved for international matches only.

Appearances:
Others: 1 app.
Total: 1 app. 0 gls.

ANDERSON, John Connell

Role: Goalkeeper 1885-92
Born: *Edmonton, London, Sep qtr. 1868*

Debut v Park (Fr) (h) 10.4.1886

A pupil at St Johns Middle Class School and one of the original founders of Spurs, little more is known about Anderson apart from the fact his association with the club lasted for at least the first ten years of its existence. His first known appearance was on 10th April 1886 but it is almost certain he had played in many matches before that date.

Appearances:
Others: 11 apps.
Total: 11 apps. 0 gls.

ANDERTON, Darren Robert

Role: Forward 1992-2004
6ft.1ins. 12st.7lbs.
Born: *Southampton, Hampshire, 3rd March 1972*

CAREER: Itchen Saints/AFC Totton/Portsmouth trainee cs. 1988, pro. Feb 1990/**SPURS** Jun 1992/Birmingham City Aug 2004/ Wolverhampton Wanderers Aug 2005/AFC Bournemouth Sep 2006-Dec 2008.

Debut v Southampton (PL) (a) 15.8.1992
(Heart of Midlothian (Fr) (a) 24.7.1992

To many people Terry Venables' £2 million signing of Darren Anderton was a gamble. The youngster had played barely 18 months of First Division football and while he clearly possessed ability, it was still a lot of money to lay out on a 20-year old some viewed as a bit of an old-fashioned winger. Anderton had made his name as the outstanding performer for Portsmouth as they made their way to the 1992 FA Cup semi-finals, and proved the star of the battles with Liverpool they were unfortunate to lose on penalties. Venables was always regarded as a good judge of young players and not afraid to back his judgment with big money, so while others dithered, he moved quickly to secure Anderton's services in June 1992. With Portsmouth, Anderton played out wide, tracking back when needed but very much an attacking player, a real handful for any full-back with his pace and trickery. Since the departure of Chris Waddle, Spurs had been lacking pace and guile on the flanks. Anderton was expected to fill the void. Initially he struggled, not helped by a niggling injury that took some time to diagnose and the inevitable comparisons with Waddle, but as he overcame his injury problems and found his feet in the top flight, there were signs he would more than justify Venables' confidence. Principally operating on the right, Anderton had a coltish style of running and the ability to beat his marker before swinging in dangerous crosses, just the type of service demanded by Teddy Sheringham. When he got into his stride there were few full-backs who could keep up with him, but once clear he did not just hammer the ball into the middle. He was an intelligent player and would hold the ball up until making a calculated pass or rolling the ball into the path of a colleague. Anderton was not just a winger in the old sense of the word. There was far more to his game. His incredible stamina allowed him to work back and defend and he also had a penchant for moving into midfield where his passing could come to the fore or he could show the range of his shooting. Shortly after joining Spurs, Anderton made his England Under-21 debut. In March 1994, he collected the first of thirty full caps, playing against Denmark in Venables' first game as England coach. He gave a performance that marked him out as a natural for football at the highest level. In 1994-95 Anderton, along with Nick Barmby, Jürgen Klinsmann, Ilie Dumitrescu and Sheringham, was lauded as one of Ossie Ardiles "Famous Five", the attacking gems in a team that only knew how to go forward. When results turned against Ardiles and he was sacked, Anderton found himself having to show his controlled and defensive qualities in the more rigid midfield Ardiles' replacement Gerry Francis preferred. Now established as an England regular, even a £5 million approach from Manchester United would not tempt Spurs to part with Anderton. That approach came at what proved to be the peak of Anderton's career. Injured early in the 1995-96 season, he only recovered just in time for Euro '96. He proved himself one of the stars of the competition, but from then on, he suffered one injury after another and for two years made only sporadic appearances. The press cruelly labelled him "Sicknote", a tag that was to remain with him for the rest of his career. The injuries took their toll. Anderton no longer had the pace to beat his marker, and perhaps no longer had the desire to take on his opponent for fear of suffering further injuries. The work ethic remained as strong as ever though, particularly useful as Anderton adapted to a more central role, providing the ammunition for his strikers with passes played through the defence rather than crosses from out wide. He played a full part in helping Spurs lift the Worthington Cup in 1999. When fit, Anderton remained as near an automatic choice as one could be, but he was unavailable too often and despite being on a "pay-as-you-play" deal, when his contract expired in the summer of 2004 he was released. He moved to Birmingham City and played there for one season before a similar spell with his former Spurs' and England manager, Glenn Hoddle, at Wolves. Anderton then returned to the South Coast with AFC Bournemouth until retiring in December 2008. Anderton's brother, Ben, was given a try-out with Spurs juniors, but injured in his only game in February 1994.

Appearances:
League: 273 (26) apps. 34 gls.
FA Cup: 26 (2) apps. 6 gls.
FL Cup: 30 (1) apps. 8 gls.
Others: 60 (9) apps. 18 gls.
Total: 389 (38) apps. 66 gls.

ANDREWS, Daniel Mark

Role: Goalkeeper 1983-84
Born: *Stratford, London, 28th September 1967*

CAREER: Waltham Forest Schools/London Schools/**SPURS** YTS cs. 1984/released cs. 1985/Southend United YTS Aug 1985/Cheshunt 1989 –95/Collier Row 1995-96/Saffron Walden Town 1995-96.

Debut v Wimbledon (sub) (Fr) (a) 26.3.1984

Young Danny Andrews made his only first team appearance for Spurs

when he played as a substitute in a testimonial match for Dave Bassett at Plough Lane. At that time, he had only been associated with the club for a few months, playing mostly for the junior team. During the following summer, he signed on under the Youth Training Scheme and spent the 1984-85 season turning out with the Junior and Youth teams with one appearance in the reserves. He was not retained at the end of that season and joined Southend United before dropping into the non-League game.

Appearances:
Others: (1) app.
Total: (1) app. 0 gls.

ANSON, William Charles

Role: Full-back 1900-01
Born: Islington, London, September qtr. 1882

CAREER: SPURS pro. Sep 1900

Debut v Bristol City (WL) (a) 27.3.1901
(Clapton (Fr) (h) 5.1.1901)

Apart from the fact he was a local lad who had helped the reserves for some time and signed professional in September 1900, little is known about Bill Anson. A regular in the reserves, his senior competitive debut was in a Western League fixture and all his first team appearances were in matches when Spurs effectively fielded reserve elevens to keep the first team fresh for forthcoming FA Cup ties, including the Final itself. He was still with the club in January 1902 but did not make the first team again.

Appearances:
Southern: 4 apps.
Others: 2 apps.
Total: 6 apps. 0 gls.

ARBER, Mark Andrew

Role: Central defender 1997-99
6ft.1ins. 12st.11lbs.
Born: Johannesburg, South Africa, 9th October 1977

CAREER: Canon Palmer School/Redbridge Schools/Essex Schools/**SPURS** assoc. schl. Oct 1991, trainee Jul 1994, pro. March 1996/Barnet loan Sep 1998, perm. Nov 1998/Peterborough United Dec 2002/Oldham Athletic Jun 2004/Peterborough United loan Dec 2004, perm Jan 2005/(Dagenham & Redbridge loan Mar 2007)/Stevenage Borough Aug 2007/Dagenham & Redbridge loan Feb 2008, perm. Jul 2008/Dartford Jul 2012/Arsenal academy coach/Corby Town player-coach Jun 2013 (and Arsenal Academy coach till Dec 2013)/(Huntingdon Town loan Jan 2014, asst. manager Nov 2013–Aug 2014)/West Bromwich Albion scout Aug 2014.

Debut v Faaberg (Fr) 17.07.1997

Mark Arber was born in Johannesburg, South Africa when his father, Bobby, best known for his time with Orient, was playing for the Rangers club. Arber worked his way through the junior ranks at Spurs, but while he played in three matches during the pre-season tour to Norway in 1997, he was not to get another chance. Allowed to join Barnet on loan in September 1998, the move was made permanent a couple of months later as Arber settled to show himself a central defender with class and confidence. He seemed set to become a permanent fixture in the Bee's defence, but a dispute over Barnet's failure to make a loyalty payment Arber was entitled to, led to him departing. He moved to Peterborough and for almost four years, apart from a brief spell at Oldham Athletic, was the rock around which Posh's defence was built. In total, he played over 300 League games before dropping into non-League football with Dagenham, but returned to take his League appearances total over the 500 mark with Stevenage. Dropping down to non-League level, Arber began coaching at Arsenal's Academy where his father held a senior position. Unfortunately, Arber proudly announced on social media that, with his inside knowledge of Arsenal's transfer activity, he had placed a bet on Arsenal signing Mesut Ozil. Arber was fortunate that the FA decided not to take disciplinary action, but Arsenal viewed his conduct as a serious breach of trust and terminated its relationship with him. In April 2004 Arber was selected for a South African training camp in preparation for the World Cup qualifiers, but after an investigation into his background, FIFA decided his birth certificate was not sufficient evidence of his eligibility to play for Bafana Bafana.

Appearances:
Others: 3 apps.
Total: 3 apps. 0 gls.

ARCHER, Arthur

Role: Full-back 1903-04
5ft.9ins. 12st.7lbs.
Born: Ashby-de-la-Zouch, Leicestershire, October qtr. 1877
Died: Islington, London, 4th October 1927

CAREER: Burton St Edmunds 1892/Tutbury Hampton 1894/Swadlincote Town Jan 1895/Burton Wanderers Sep 1895/Small Heath Jul 1897/New Brompton May 1902/Wingfield House Apr 1903/Queens Park Rangers Aug 1903/(**SPURS** guest 1903-05)/Norwich City Aug 1905/Brighton and Hove Albion May 1907/Millwall Aug 1908/retired cs. 1909/coach in Germany 1910-12/coach in Ghent (Belgium) 1914, 1920/coach in Italy 1921/coach in Ghent (Belgium) 1922/Watford coach May 1924.

Debut v Brentford (LL) (a) 16.11.1903

A left-back who had spent the 1902-03 season as a regular with Spurs' Southern League rivals, New Brompton, Arthur Archer was a tough, no-nonsense player with plenty of top level experience. He had spent the best years of his career at Small Heath, helping them to promotion to the First Division in 1900-01 and appearing regularly until his move to New Brompton. When he joined Queens Park Rangers in August 1903 he only signed Southern League forms for them so was able to make five first team appearances for Spurs in the London League, the minor first team competition in which the club competed. He appeared regularly for Rangers throughout that and the following season, when he also played for Spurs reserves. He later played for Norwich City, Brighton and Hove Albion and Millwall. Archer worked as a coach and trainer in Germany from 1910-12 and returned briefly to England before coaching in Ghent until the outbreak of war. He joined the army in 1915, survived the conflict and by 1920 was again back coaching in Ghent. A year in Italy was followed by two more in Belgium before he became Watford's trainer in May 1924.

Appearances:
Others: 5 apps.
Total: 5 apps. 0 gls.

ARCHER, Jordan Gideon

Role: Goalkeeper 2013-14
6ft.2ins. 13st.12lbs.
Born: Walthamstow, London, 12th April 1993

CAREER: SPURS Academy Scholar Jul 2009, pro. Jul 2011/(Bishops Stortford loan Sep 2011)/(Wycombe Wanderers loan Sep 2012)/(Northampton Town loan Aug 2014)/Millwall loan Feb 2015, perm Jun 2015.

Debut v Ledley King XI (Fr) (h) (sub) 11.5.2014

Jordan Archer had been associated with Charlton Athletic prior to joining Spurs Academy ranks in July 2009. A tall, confident lad, he easily made the move up to professional status and then embarked on a series of loan moves. While he gained plenty of experience in the lower leagues and was on the substitutes bench for Spurs, notably in Europa League games, his only first team appearance was as a substitute in Ledley King's Testimonial match. When his contract ran down Archer was allowed to leave and was quickly snapped up by Millwall. Archer was a regular for Scotland at Under-21 level, winning his first cap against Belgium in August 2012 and picking up a total of 14 in his days as a Spurs player.

Appearances:
Others: (1) app.
Total: (1) app. 0 gls.

ARCHIBALD, James Mitchell

Role: Half-back 1919-22
5ft.8ins. 11st.2lbs.
Born: Falkirk, 18th September 1892
Died: Walthamstow, London, 25th January 1975

CAREER: Cambuslang Rangers/Bellshill Athletic/Motherwell Oct 1914/**SPURS** Aug 1919/Aberdare Athletic Jun 1922/Clapton Orient Jun 1923/Southend United Sep 1926/Margate Town Dec 1927/Tunbridge Wells Rangers Jul 1929/Ashford Sep 1930.

Debut v Bristol City (FL) (h) 28.2.1920
(Arsenal (LPFCF) (a) 29.9.1919)

In September 1918, Motherwell gave Jimmy Archibald four weeks' notice of termination of his contract after accusing him of not trying in their match with Hibernians. It is not clear what happened to him then, but by March 1919 Spurs were prepared to pay £100 to secure his services. Signed to provide half-back cover as Spurs rebuilt for the Second Division promotion campaign after being voted out of the First Division following the increase to 22 clubs, Archibald made his first team debut in September 1919 when he played out of position at centre-forward in the London Professional Football Charity Fund match with Arsenal. Tall and constructive, he found his first team opportunities restricted by the fine form of Spurs' England international wing-halves Bert Smith and Arthur Grimsdell and it was only due to injury to centre-half Charlie Rance (with Smith switching to the central position) that Archibald was able to secure a place at right-half in the team running away with the Second Division title. He retained his place until the end of the season, but the return to fitness of Rance and the emergence of Charlie Walters the following season left Archibald out in the cold. Further appearances were limited to those occasions when Smith was unavailable and it was no surprise when Archibald was allowed to move to Third Division Aberdare Athletic. After one season with the Welsh club, four years with Orient and a brief spell with Southend, Archibald finished his career with Margate, Tunbridge Wells Rangers and Ashford.

Appearances:
League: 24 apps. 1 gl.
FA Cup: 1 app.
Others: 8 apps. 0 gls.
Total: 33 apps. 1 gl.

ARCHIBALD, Steven

Role: Striker 1980-88
5ft.10ins. 11st.2lbs.
Born: Glasgow, 27th September 1956

CAREER: Crofoot United/Fernhill Athletic/East Stirling trial Mar 1974/Clyde 1974/Aberdeen Jan 1978/**SPURS** May 1980/Barcelona (Spain) Jul 1984/(Blackburn Rovers loan Dec 1987)/Hibernian Aug 1988/Espanyol (Spain) Jan 1990/St Mirren Nov 1990/Reading trial Jan 1992/Ayr United trial Feb 1992/Clyde Mar 1992/Fulham (non-contract) Sep 1992/East Fife player-manager Aug 1994-Sep 1996/Home Farm Everton Nov 1996/Benfica (Portugal) non-executive director Aug 1998/Airdrieonians manager/owner designate Aug 2000-Mar 2001.

Debut v Nottingham Forest (FL) (h) 16.8.1980
(Southend United (Fr) (a) 28.7.1980 (scored once))

Immediately on joining Spurs, Steve Archibald struck up a marvellous rapport with Garth Crooks, who was signed from Stoke City to partner him up front. At £800,000, Archibald was Spurs' record buy at the time and also the most expensive cross-border transfer, but he proved to be worth every penny of the fee. Having started with junior clubs Crofoot United and Fernhill Athletic, he joined Clyde as a part-timer although he had previously played one match on trial for East Stirling. A member of Clyde's 1978 Scottish Second Division winning team, Archibald continued his training as a Rolls-Royce mechanic and it was only when he joined Aberdeen for £25,000 that he became a full-time professional. A slim but instinctive goal-scorer, he helped Aberdeen to the Scottish League Cup Finals of 1979 and 1980 and the Scottish League title in 1980 and, by the time of his move to White Hart Lane, had already won four Scottish Under-21 caps and made a goal-scoring debut for the full Scotland side as a substitute against Portugal in March 1980. His skill, strong-running, razor sharpness in the box and seemingly unquenchable thirst for goals made him a great favourite of Spurs' fans and, with Crooks the perfect foil, he led the attack in both the 1981 and 1982 FA Cup Final successes and scored Spurs' goal in the 1982 League (Milk) Cup Final against Liverpool. He added one Under-21 and 22 full caps to his tally while with Spurs, but unfortunately fell out with manager Keith Burkinshaw. This hastened his departure from White Hart Lane and, having helped Spurs lift the UEFA Cup in 1984, he signed for Terry Venables' Barcelona for £1,250,000. In his first season in Spain he added the Spanish title to a growing list of honours and led Barcelona's attack in the 1986 European Champions Cup Final against Steaua Bucharest which they lost on penalties. Four more Scottish caps were won, but with the signing of Mark Hughes and Gary Lineker for the 1987-88 season, Barcelona made it clear Archibald's services would only be needed in an emergency. Midway through the campaign he was allowed to join Blackburn Rovers on loan in their Second Division promotion battle where, for a time, he was re-united with former Spurs team-mate Ossie Ardiles. During that season, he also returned to White Hart Lane on two occasions to guest in the Tony Galvin Testimonial and Danny Thomas Benefit matches and showed he had lost few of his talents by scoring in both games. In August 1988, his contract with Barcelona was paid up and he returned to Scottish football with Hibernian, where he continued to score regularly in his first season. Unable to get in the team the following year, he bought up his own contract. He went back to Barcelona where he signed for the Second Division side Espanyol, but returned to Scotland ten months later to join St Mirren. Released in May 1991, he was unable to find another club until February 1992 when he signed for Ayr United having had a week's trial with Reading the previous month. He left Ayr for Clyde and played briefly for Fulham on a non-contract basis. In August 1994, he took on the player-manager's role at East Fife and at the end of his second season in charge led them to promotion from the Second Division. Only six matches into the new season though, and with the Fifers bottom of the table, he was sacked.

Initially combining his business interests in Spain with television punditry, Archibald always had in mind to move up the football hierarchy and after gaining some experience as a director of Benfica he tried to buy control of Airdrieonians. Given preferred bidder status, he installed himself as manager and used his connections to bring in some useful players, but, despite a long fight was unable to complete a purchase and eventually had to pull out of the venture.

Appearances:
League: 128 (3) apps. 58 gls.
FA Cup: 17 (1) apps. 5 gls.
FL Cup: 18 apps. 7 gls.
Euro: 22 apps. 7 gls.
Others: 25 (2) apps. 18 gls.
Total: 210 (6) apps. 95 gls.

ARDILES, Osvaldo Cesar

Role: Midfielder 1978-91
5ft.6ins. 9st.10lbs.
Born: Cordoba, Argentina, 3rd August 1952

CAREER: Red Star Córdoba (Argentina)/Instituto Atlético Central Córdoba (Argentina) am., pro. 1969/Atlético Belgrano (Argentina) 1974/Atlético Huracán (Argentina) 1975/**SPURS** Jul 1978/(Paris St Germain (France) loan Jul 1982)/(St George Saints (Australia) guest Jun 1985)/(Blackburn Rovers loan Mar 1988)/Queens Park Rangers Aug 1988/Fort Lauderdale Strikers (USA) Jun 1989/Swindon Town manager Jul 1989/Newcastle United manager Mar 1991-Feb 1992/West Bromwich Albion manager May 1992/**SPURS** manager Jun 1993-Oct 1994/Chivas de Guadalajara (Mexico) coach Jun-Oct 1995/Shimizu S-Pulse (Japan) coach Jan 1996/Croatia Zagreb (Croatia) coach Jun-Oct 1999/Yokohama F Marinos (Japan) manager Dec 1999-Jun 2001/Al Ittihad (Saudi Arabia) manager Sep-Nov 2001/Racing Club of Buenos Aires (Argentina) Technical Director Jul 2002-May 2003/Tokyo Verdy (Japan) coach May 2003-Jul 2005/Beitar Jerusalem (Israel) coach May-Oct 2006/Atlético Huracán (Argentina) head coach Sep-Dec 2007/Cerro Porteño (Paraguay) coach Apr-Aug 2008/Machida Zelvia (Japan) coach Jan-Nov 2012.

Debut v Nottingham Forest (FL) (a) 19.8.1978
(Royal Antwerp (Fr) (a) 8.8.1978)

Ossie Ardiles sprang to such prominence with his performances for the host nation, Argentina, when they won the World Cup in 1978 that England manager Ron Greenwood described him as "the best right-sided midfield player in the World Cup". When Spurs' manager Keith Burkinshaw sensationally signed him for £325,000 with his compatriot Ricardo Villa in July of that year, a new chapter in the history of British football was opened. Spurs had only just won back their First Division status and the signing of two South Americans who could not speak English and were unfamiliar with the rigours of the Football League was something of a gamble. The cynics were forced to eat humble pie as the rewards proved greater than anybody could have expected. Ardiles had begun his football career in his home town with the junior club Red Star before joining the youth set-up of Instituto Córdoba. In 1975, he moved to Huracán of Buenos Aires and continued to add minor representative honours to those he had won with Instituto. In August 1975, he won his first full cap and soon established himself as an international regular. From his first team debut for Spurs in a pre-season friendly against Royal Antwerp, football fans were flocking to admire the silky Latin skills and precision passing which were quickly harnessed to the more robust attributes of the English game. Although frail-looking at only 5ft.6ins tall and around 10 stone in weight, Ardiles had a remarkable ability to ride challenges and a unique style of holding off his opponent while running with the ball, but perhaps his greatest quality was the mental toughness that allowed him to accept and conquer the many obstacles that came his way. Continuing to pick up international honours, Ardiles was adored by the fans as one of the central virtuosos of Spurs 1981 FA Cup-winning side and also played in the team that lost the 1982 League (Milk) Cup Final to Liverpool. His last game for Spurs in

1982 was in the FA Cup semi-final against Leicester City for he then returned home to help Argentina's preparations for their defence of the World Cup. It was still expected he would appear in the FA Cup Final, but the Falklands conflict put an end to his chances of being released and he was forced to watch the two matches against Queens Park Rangers from the other side of the Atlantic. The conflict was to have a deeper effect on Ardiles' Spurs' career however. He felt it would be unwise to return after the World Cup in Spain, so joined Paris St Germain on loan for the 1982-83 season. Things did not work out in France and in December 1982 he was back at White Hart Lane. Further misfortune immediately befell this intelligent, disarmingly charming man when he broke a shin at Maine Road in only his fourth game back. It was more than ten long months before he was able to play again in the League, but a succession of injuries restricted further appearances, although he did collect a UEFA Cup Winners medal in

1984 playing as a substitute in the second leg of the final against Anderlecht. Typically, he did not keep the medal for long, handing it to Spurs' stalwart captain Steve Perryman who was forced to miss the match through suspension. Still hounded by injury, Ardiles was honoured with a Benefit match against Inter Milan in May 1986 and many felt it an appropriate time for him to retire, but he thought otherwise, and the following season he was back to his best and another appearance at Wembley in the 1987 FA Cup Final against Coventry City. In August 1987, he added another accolade to an illustrious career when he played as a substitute for the Football League in the Centenary Celebration match against the Rest of the World, and the following month captained the League side against the Irish League in Belfast. It was only the arrival of Terry Venables with his plans to rebuild Spurs that saw the end of Ardiles' great career at White Hart Lane. In March 1988, he was loaned to Blackburn Rovers in an effort to provide the final impetus in their vain push for promotion and, at the end of the season, given a free transfer. Chased by many clubs, Ardiles choose to join Queens Park Rangers where one of his ex-bosses at Spurs, Peter Shreeve, was assistant manager, but after only a few games suffered a broken leg. In his early days with Spurs Ardiles had completed the legal studies he had started at home in Argentina and qualified as a lawyer, but he had no thoughts of giving up football. He recovered from the injury and joined the American club Fort Lauderdale Strikers. After only one month, Ardiles returned to England to take over as manager of Swindon Town where he built an exciting team combining the best of British and South American football styles. He guided Swindon to promotion from the Second Division via the play-offs in 1990, but then saw his efforts dashed as the "Robins" were immediately relegated for financial irregularities. Economic problems for the Wiltshire club forced Ardiles to sell several of his best players and although Swindon failed to make the same impact in 1990-91, Ardiles had already established his managerial reputation. In March 1991, he took over as manager of struggling giants Newcastle United. Sadly, he met different financial constraints at St James Park and was cruelly dismissed less than twelve months later. However, the little man was soon back in football, charged with reviving the flagging fortunes of West Bromwich Albion and quickly appointed his old mentor Keith Burkinshaw as his assistant. Following the departure of Terry Venables after his infamous falling out with Chairman Alan Sugar, Ardiles returned to White Hart Lane as manager. Determined to give Spurs' supporters the exciting football they demand, he invested heavily in top flight entertainers and gave the team the freedom to play attacking football. While entertainment was guaranteed, results were not, but Ardiles refused to compromise his beliefs and paid the ultimate price with dismissal in October 1994. After a brief but unsuccessful spell in Mexico, Ardiles took over as manager of Shimizu S-Pulse in Japan leading them to Yamasaki Nabisco Cup success in 1996. He spent three years in Japan before deciding to return to England but with no British club willing to take him on, he surprisingly accepted the coach's position with Croatia Zagreb. Harshly dismissed after just four months when Zagreb failed to progress past the first league stage of the Champions League, he returned to Japan with Yokohama F Marinos. Unable to repeat his earlier success in Japan, Ardiles was dismissed. He quickly found a new post in Saudi Arabia with the Al Ittihad club, but again suffered cruel dismissal with his team top of the table. In July 2002, he returned to Argentina taking up the technical director's post with Racing Club of Buenos Aires. A year later it was back to Japan for a two-year spell in charge of Tokyo Verdy. Ardiles wound down his managerial career with short spells in charge of Beitar Jerusalem, Cerro Porteño of Paraguay and Japan's Machida Zelvia. When his playing days with Spurs had ended, Ardiles returned to play for his beloved "Tottingham" in testimonial matches for several former team-mates. In 1981 Spurs' FA Cup hit record "Ossie's Dream" captured the popular imagination of the general public as well as Spurs supporters.

Appearances:
League: 222 (16) apps. 16 gls.
FA Cup: 32 apps. 4 gls.
FL Cup: 31 (1) apps. 3 gls.
Euro: 8 (1) apps. 2 gls.
Others: 92 (15) apps. 12 gls.
Total: 385 (33) apps. 37 gls.

ARMSTRONG, Christopher Peter

Role: Striker 1995-2001
6ft.0ins. 12st.12lbs.
Born: Newcastle, Tyne & Wear, 19th June 1971

CAREER: Clwyd Schools/North Wales Schools/Llay Welfare/Wrexham non-contract Oct 1988, pro. March 1989/Millwall Aug 1991/Crystal Palace Sep 1992/**SPURS** Jun 1995-May 2002/Bolton Wanderers Aug 2002/Wrexham Jul 2003-Jun 2005.

Debut v Manchester City (PL) (a) 19.8.1995
(Silkeborg (Fr) (Bjerringbro) 22.7.1995)

North-east born Chris Armstrong moved to London when three years old. Five years later he made the further move to Wrexham to live with foster parents. Although he played at local schoolboy level it was only while playing for Llay Welfare that he was spotted by his local club. That was probably because Armstrong played in goal while at school whereas with the Welsh National League side he played up front. Armstrong gave up his job as a packer in a local factory to sign for Wrexham, initially as a non-contract player but soon elevated to full professional status. Within a couple of years, he was on his way back to London, Millwall investing £125,000 in a player they hoped could replace Nottingham Forest bound Teddy Sheringham. A year later he was on the move again, joining Crystal Palace for £1 million. At Selhurst Park Armstrong made rapid progress and even though Palace were going through one of those up-and-down spells Armstrong was soon attracting attention from the big clubs. Having helped Palace win the Football League in 1993-94, Armstrong collected an England "B" cap in May 1994. As Palace struggled in the Premiership the following season, Armstrong was one of the few bright spots, but his career almost came to an abrupt end when he became the first top-level player to fail a drugs test in March 1995, testing positive for cannabis. Having undergone a rehabilitation programme, Gerry Francis signed Armstrong for Spurs in June 1995, the £4.5 million fee reflecting the widely acknowledged potential he possessed. It was a difficult move for Armstrong, particularly as he had the unenviable task of replacing Jürgen Klinsmann after the charismatic German had decided to return home. Athletically built and with terrific pace, Armstrong initially found the job difficult but with the experienced Sheringham alongside him slowly began to settle and find the target. Armstrong could not have been more different to Klinsmann. His control and appreciation of others often let him down while his pace and a willingness to run non-stop were his greatest assets. Those attributes were perfect for the long ball style Francis favoured with Armstrong frequently haring into the corners to chase the ball, but it was not the style Spurs supporters expected. Francis seemed content to make the most of Armstrong's abilities rather than improve his all-round game. It did little to endear Armstrong to the Spurs' crowd but, after a first season that could not be criticised, Armstrong was not helped by constant injuries. Continually out of action and unable to get a consistent run he became a peripheral figure before being released in May 2002. Bolton Wanderers took a chance on him but he made only one appearance in a year at the Reebok before finishing his career with two years back at Wrexham.

Appearances:
League: 117 (24) apps. 48 gls.
FA Cup: 10* (5) apps. 4 gls.
FL Cup: 15 apps. 10 gls.
Euro: 3 apps.
Others: 21 (8) apps. 13 gls.
Total: 166 (37) apps. 75 gls.
* Includes 1 abandoned match.

ARMSTRONG, Gerard Joseph

Role: Striker 1975-81
6ft.0ins. 13st.0lbs.
Born: Belfast, Northern Ireland, 23rd May 1954

CAREER: St Paul's Swifts/Cromac United/Bangor Aug 1972/**SPURS** Nov 1975/Watford Nov 1980/Real Mallorca (Spain) Aug 1983/West Bromwich Albion Aug 1985/Chesterfield loan Jan 1986, perm. Mar 1986/Brighton and Hove Albion Jul 1986/(Millwall loan Jan 1987)/Carlisle United trial Jul 1987/Brighton and Hove Albion player-coach cs. 1988/Gillingham trial Feb 1989/Crawley Town player-coach Feb 1989-Mar 1990/Glenavon Mar 1990/Waterford/Bromley Apr 1990/Southwick/Worthing United player-manager Nov 1991-1993/Watford scout/Northern Ireland coach 1993, asst. manager 1994-Oct 1997/Southwick/Sussex FA Youth coach/development officer Mar 1996, manager/Whitehawk player-coach/Lewes coach/Northern Ireland asst. manager Jan 2004-Aug 2006/Irish FA elite player mentor Aug 2011-Sep 2012.

Debut v Ipswich Town (FL) (a) 21.8.1976
(Brighton and Hove Albion (sub) (Fr) (a) 23.3.1976 (scored once))

Gerry Armstrong gave up his job as a senior clerical officer with the Northern Ireland Housing Executive in order to seek fame and fortune on the football field. As a boy, he played Gaelic football and hurling, not taking up football until he was 17 and suspended from the Gaelic game after getting involved in one of the fights the Gaelic game was all too well known for. He played with the local junior clubs St. Paul's Swifts and Cromac United before joining Bangor as a part-timer, then making the move to Spurs. Armstrong spent the 1975-76 season quite successfully in the reserves, scoring 10 goals in 24 Football Combination matches, and made his first team debut in March 1976 in a testimonial match for Joe Kinnear, when he scored after

going on as a substitute. Continuing to net goals in friendly and tour matches, the barrel-chested Armstrong was given his chance in the senior eleven in August 1976 and, although he did not retain his place, by the end of the season was the regular centre-forward. Sadly, however, the season was a disaster for Spurs-the club being relegated for the first time since promotion in 1950. For the next three seasons, he vied for one of the central striking positions with Colin Lee, John Duncan, Ian Moores and Chris Jones without ever really establishing himself as first choice and even played as an emergency centre-half. With the arrival of Steve Archibald and Garth Crooks in the summer of 1980, it was no surprise Spurs were prepared to release Armstrong when Watford made a £250,000 approach. His style, based on never-ending hard work and direct running, was perhaps more suited to the Watford way, but he still found it hard to establish himself and it was somewhat surprising the upturn in his career should come on the international scene. Having made his debut for Northern Ireland in April 1977 and won 27 full caps as a Spurs player, he was already an established member of the province's team when they travelled to Spain for the 1982 World Cup. His whole-hearted commitment and non-stop battling qualities were one of the principal reasons for the unexpected success of the Irish and Armstrong left such an impression with the host nation's clubs that a year later he was transferred to Real Mallorca. He spent two years in Spain before returning to the Football League with West Bromwich Albion, but only stayed at the Hawthorns a short time before joining Chesterfield, initially on loan. His contract was cancelled at the end of the 1985-86 season and he joined Brighton and Hove Albion. The 1986-87 season saw Brighton relegated to the Third Division, but Armstrong remained with the South Coast club as youth officer although still registered as a player. His League career came to a sad end in February 1989 when he left the Goldstone Ground after being convicted of assaulting a fan. He then joined Beazer Homes League Crawley Town. In March 1990, he resigned from Crawley after a dispute with the manager, but in November 1991 was appointed player-manager of Worthing. He left Worthing in 1995 and took up a coaching post with the Sussex FA combining that job with the assistant manager's job for Northern Ireland and commentating on Spanish football for Sky TV, a role he has made his own. Apart from his Irish caps won as a Spurs' player Armstrong won a further 21 whilst with Watford, nine with Real Mallorca, four with West Bromwich Albion and two with Chesterfield. Such was Gerry's impact in the 1982 World Cup that he was voted Ireland's "Personality of the Year" in 1983.

Appearances:
League: 65 (19) apps. 10 gls.
FA Cup: 6 (4) apps. 3 gls.
FL Cup: 3 (1) apps. 3 gls.
Others: 22 (13) apps. 16 gls.
Total: 96 (37) apps. 32gls.

ARMSTRONG, James William

Role: Centre or inside-forward 1927-30
5ft.8ins 10st.6lbs.
Born: Swalwell-On-Tyne, 6th September 1901
Died: Gateshead, Tyneside, 12th August 1977

CAREER: Spen Black & White/Chelsea Oct 1922/**SPURS** May 1927/Luton Town Jul 1930/Bristol Rovers Mar 1931/Walker Celtic cs. 1931.

Debut v Birmingham (FL) (a) 31.12.1927

Spotted by Chelsea playing for a junior club in his home town, Jimmy Armstrong's League debut was at White Hart Lane on 23rd December 1922 when he scored Chelsea's goal in a 1-3 defeat. Failing to establish himself at Stamford Bridge, he moved to Tottenham in May 1927, but had to wait until the last day of December 1927 before making his Spurs' debut as stand-in for Jack Elkes. Happy at either centre or inside-forward, Armstrong was unable to command a place in the team despite the fact Spurs were struggling, being relegated at the end of his first season and unable to escape from the Second Division. In April 1930, he was released and joined Luton Town, from where he moved to Bristol Rovers and quickly drifted out of the League game.

Appearances:
League: 28 apps. 5 gls.
FA Cup: 5 apps.
Others: 12 apps. 9 gls.
Total: 45 apps. 14 gls.

ARNOLD, W

Role: Winger 1940-41

CAREER: Leicester City/(guest for **SPURS** during World War Two).

Debut v Leicester City (FLS) (a) 17.5.1941

Arnold is one of the war-time guest players who so helped Spurs to field a full eleven in all their fixtures and a perfect example of the way clubs co-operated in those difficult times. Spurs arrived for a fixture at Leicester with only ten men and the home club allowed Arnold, one of the junior members of their staff, to turn out for Spurs. It was his only game for the club.

Appearances:
Others: 1 app.
Total: 1 app. 0 gls.

ASSOU-EKOTTO, Benoît Pierre David

Role: Full-back 2006-15
5ft.10ins. 11st.13lbs.
Born: Arras, France, 24th March 1984

CAREER: Racing Club Lens 1995/**SPURS** Jun 2006/(Queens Park Rangers loan Sep 2013), released Feb 2015/Saint-Étienne (France) Jul 2015/Metz (France) Aug 2016.

Debut v Bolton Wanderers (PL) (a) 19.8.2006
(Girondins de Bordeaux (Fr) (Albertville) 13.7.2006)

The signing of Benoît Assou-Ekotto, one of the most promising full-backs in France, was another example of Martin Jol's determination to invest in young players of quality from around the world, who would develop to give Spurs a team that would go from strength to strength. Assou-Ekotto was first associated with RC Lens as a 10-year old, following his brother, Mathieu, and developed through the youth ranks to make his senior debut days after turning twenty. Capable of playing at full-back, in the centre of defence or left midfield, his father was from Cameroon and Assou-Ekotto turned down the chance to play for France at youth level, hoping for the call from his father's country. His consistent displays for the French club soon attracted attention and Spurs had to fight off interest from Arsenal to sign Assou-Ekotto for £3.5 million. He started his first season as the regular left-back and while initially lacking the attacking instincts of Lee Young-Pyo, proved a competent performer, solid, unspectacular and concentrating on his defensive responsibilities. Injury struck early in 2007 causing Assou-Ekotto to miss almost eighteen months of action, but on his return, he seemed stronger, more relaxed and determined to enjoy his football. Free from injury and playing regularly, Assou-Ekotto blossomed, pushing forward and showing a whole new dimension to his game as he linked with Gareth Bale. Sometimes taking risks when caution would have been the safest course of action and with a down-to-earth attitude that endeared him to the fans, his popularity increased with one outstanding performance after another.

His reward at last came on the international stage when he was selected to play for Cameroon in February 2009 and he soon established himself as a regular international performer in the often-chaotic arena of African football. Having made the left-back position at Spurs his own, injury early in 2012-13 set his progress back just when he needed to impress new coach Andre Villas-Boas. Given few opportunities when fit again, Assou-Ekotto was quick to accept an offer from former manager Harry Redknapp to join Queens Park Rangers on a season long loan. Assou-Ekotto's admission that for him football was just another job, did not endear him to those who took the game more seriously. Side-lined by Mauricio Pochettino, Assou-Ekotto was content to see out his contract until released in February 2015. He did not immediately find a new club, waiting until the following pre-season before accepting an offer from St Etienne, then quickly moving to Metz. Mathieu Assou-Ekotto did not make the grade with Lens, but went on to play for Royal Excelsior Mouscron, Créteil-Lusitanosl, Valenciennes, Grenoble, Louviéroise, Standard Liège and Willem II.

Appearances:
League: 151 (4) apps. 4 gls.
FA Cup: 12* apps.
FL Cup: 10 apps.
Euro: 25 (3) apps.
Others: 25 (7) apps.
Total: 223 (14) apps. 4 gls.
* Includes 1 abandoned match

THE SPURS ALPHABET

ASTWOOD, Marischal

Role: Forward 1979

CAREER: PHC Zebras (Bermuda).

Debut v Bermuda Select XI (sub) (Fr) (a) 6.6.1979

Mop Astwood was one of four local players who guested for Spurs in a friendly match in Hamilton, Bermuda at the end of Spurs 1979 summer tour. Due to injuries and players having returned home early, Spurs were forced to field a scratch side containing physioerapist Mike Varney, assistant Secretary Peter Day and goalkeeper Milija Aleksic as an outfield player. Astwood, a Bermudian international, was a second-half substitute for Varney.

Appearances:
Others: (1) app.
Total: (1) app. 0 gls.

ATHERTON, Thomas Henry

Role: Inside-forward 1898-99
5ft.5ins. 10st.0lbs.
Born: West Derby, Liverpool, 1879
Died: 1955

CAREER: Benburb/**SPURS** May 1898/Dunfermline Juniors/St Bernards May 1899/Partick Thistle Aug 1900/Dundee May 1901/Grimsby Town May 1902/Brentford Jul 1903/Motherwell Jul 1904.

Debut v New Brompton (SL) (h) 18.3.1899
(Surrey Wanderers (Fr) (a) 21.12.1898)

As was quite common in the later days of the last century, Tom Atherton was signed by Spurs purely as a reserve. It was not until December 1898 that he made his first team debut and even then, only in a friendly. When he made his competitive debut, it was at centre-half in a Thames and Medway League match. He only stayed with Spurs the one season, at the end of which he returned to Scotland where he was more successful, representing the Scottish League against the Irish League in February 1901, whilst with Partick Thistle. He then played for one season with Dundee, Grimsby Town and Brentford before finishing his career with Motherwell. He was reported to have passed away in the 1950s, but the exact date is as yet unknown.

Appearances:
Southern: 2 apps.
Others: 11 apps. 4 gls.
Total: 13 apps. 4 gls.

ATOUBA, Thimothée Essama

Role: Full-back 2004-05
6ft.3ins. 12st.8lbs.
Born: Douala, Cameroon, 17th February 1982

CAREER: Mineduc (Cameroon)/Union Sportive Douala (Cameroon) 1996/Neuchâtel Xamax (Switzerland) Jun 2000/Basel (Switzerland) Jan 2002/**SPURS** Aug 2004/Hamburg SV (Germany) Jul 2005/Ajax (Holland) Jul 2009-May 2011/Montreal Impact (Canada) trial May 2012/UD Las Palmas (Spain) Nov 2012-Jun 2014.

Debut v Liverpool (sub) (PL) (h) 14.8.2004

One of the flood of players who arrived at White Hart Lane following the appointment of Frank Arnesen and Jacques Santini, Thimothée Atouba was a powerful Cameroonian international who could play either on the left of midfield or at full-back. Taken to Switzerland as an 18-year old by Neuchâtel Xamax, he quickly moved on to Basel helping them clinch the Swiss League title in his first season, but it was on the international stage that he really sprang to prominence. One of the stars of the 2004 African Cup of Nations, his strength and forward thrusts marked him out as a player who looked ideally suited to the English game.

He made a wonderful start to his Spurs' career with a superb goal to secure three points at Newcastle in August 2004, but from then onwards it was all downhill for Atouba. He looked out of his depth, lacking in finesse and guile and too often caught out of position. He lasted only one season with Spurs before moving to SV Hamburg. He settled to a regular place with the German outfit, though that not without its problems. In December 2006, he was given a two-match ban and hefty fine for making an obscene gesture to his own fans as they booed him off having been substituted in a Champions' League game against CSKA Moscow. When Martin Jol moved to Ajax, he took Atouba with him, but Atouba had a miserable two years in Amsterdam, disciplinary and injury problems seeing him play only two games. Without a club for a year, he had a trial with Montreal Impact before securing a short-term deal with Las Palmas.

Appearances:
League: 15 (3) apps. 1 gl.
FA Cup: 5 apps.
FL Cup: 1 app.
Total: 21 (3) apps. 1 gl.

AUSTIN, Dean Barry

Role: Full-back 1992-98
6ft.0ins. 12st.4lbs.
Born: Hemel Hempstead, Hertfordshire, 26th April 1970

CAREER: Astley Cooper Secondary School/Forest United/Comets, Hemel Hempstead/Hendon trainee cs. 1986/Watford trainee cs. 1987/St Albans City cs. 1988/Southend United Mar 1990/**SPURS** Jun 1992/Crystal Palace Jul 1998/Watford training Nov 2002/Woking Nov 2002-Jun 2003/retired Jul 2003/Southend United caretaker reserve team manager Apr 2004/Farnborough Town Director of Football Jun 2004, caretaker manager Jun 2004, manager Jul 2004, player-manager Aug 2004-Feb 2005/Reading scout/Southend United coach May 2007, chief scout, chief scout/reserve team manager Jun 2007/Watford asst. manager Nov 2008-Jun 2009/Reading asst. manager Jun-Dec 2009/Crystal Palace coach Jun 2010-May 2011/Bolton Wanderers scout Feb-Dec 2012/Notts County asst. manager Feb-May 2013/Birmingham City scout/Watford coach Jan 2015-Jun 2016.

Debut v Crystal Palace (sub) (PL) (h) 22.8.1992
(Heart of Midlothian (sub) (Fr) (a) 24.7.1992)

Dean Austin may not be remembered as one of the best full-backs to have played for Spurs, but for five years he held down a regular place in the team, much of that time partnering Justin Edinburgh who had made the same move from Southend United to Spurs two years earlier. Austin was highly rated at the time of his transfer, so much so that the transfer tribunal set not only a basic fee of £375,000, but also ordered Spurs to pay Southend an additional £50,000 when he had made 25 appearances, another £50,000 when he made 50 appearances and a final £50,000 when he collected an international cap. Much like Edinburgh, it was expected Austin would spend some time in the reserves before making the move up, but injury to Terry Fenwick allowed Austin an early opportunity and he grasped it well. He settled in quickly, showing a willingness to push forward, link well with his attackers and send in some dangerous crosses. The defensive side of his game sometimes left something to be desired, but that was often due to his desire to attack and it was expected that experience would bring about a vast improvement. The future looked good for Austin but a broken leg early in September 1993 set him back. Ossie Ardiles signed the experienced David Kerslake as cover and Austin never really recovered his place. With the emergence of Steve Carr, Austin found himself on the fringes and in May 1998 he was given a free transfer. He joined Crystal Palace, linking up with Terry Venables who had signed him for Spurs, and gave Palace four years' good service. After a brief spell in the non-League game, Austin moved into managing and coaching.

Appearances:
League: 117 (7) apps.
FA Cup: 17* (1) apps.
FL Cup: 7 (2) apps.
Others: 24 (7) apps.
Total: 165 (17) apps. 0 gls.
* Includes 1 abandoned match

AUSTIN, Percy Charles

Role: Centre-forward 1926-28
5ft.9ins. 10st.12lbs.
Born: Watford, Hertfordshire, 1st July 1903
Died: St Albans, Hertfordshire, 15th August 1961

CAREER: Farnham United Breweries/**SPURS** Jan 1926, released May 1928, scout.

Debut v Birmingham (FL) (a) 31.12.1927
(Clapton Orient (LPFCF) (h) 7.11.1927)

Percy Austin only played two matches in Spurs' first team, the first against Clapton Orient for the benefit of the London Professional Football Charity Fund in November 1927. For the second, his only Football League appearance, Spurs were so badly hit by injuries that Austin was called into the team to replace injured half-back Arthur Grimsdell. He was not retained at the end of the season.

Appearances:
League: 1 app.
Others: 1 app.
Total: 2 apps. 0 gls.

AYRES J

Role: Half-back 1889-90

Debut v Royal Arsenal (Fr) (a) 21.9.1889

Nothing is known about this player who made only one recorded first team appearance in a friendly against Royal Arsenal. As it was the first match of the season it is likely he was playing as a trialist in a match Spurs lost 1-10.

Appearances:
Others: 1 app.
Total: 1 app. 0 gls.

AYRES

Role: Winger 1917-18

Debut v Queens Park Rangers (LFC) (h) 30.3.1918

As often happened during the First World War, Spurs were struggling to get eleven players together for a match against Queens Park Rangers at Clapton Orient's Homerton ground. Without a recognised outside-left available, they called upon the services of Ayres, "an amateur with a good class Essex amateur team". He retained a place for the next game which he played at left-half, but they were his only appearances for the club.

Appearances:
Others: 2 apps.
Total: 2 apps. 0 gls.

B

BAARDSEN, Per Espen

Role: Goalkeeper 1996-2000
6ft.5ins. 13st.7lbs.
Born: San Rafael, California, 7th December 1977

CAREER: Lamorinda Soccer Club (USA)/Tri-Valley (USA)/California State (USA)/San Francisco All Blacks/**SPURS** Jul 1996/Watford Aug 2000/Everton Dec 2002/retired Jul 2003.

Debut v Liverpool (sub) (PL) (a) 3.5.1997
(Ham Kam (Fr) (a) 23.7.1996)

If ever there was an example of Spurs letting a highly-talented youngster leave for peanuts, Espen Baardsen is the man. Born in California to Norwegian parents, Baardsen was always regarded as one of the best young 'keepers around. At just 16-years old he was called up for the American Under-18 squad. He was already on Spurs' radar, first training with the club in 1992 and frequently coming over to England for further coaching as Spurs kept a close eye on his progress. Baardsen only made one appearance for the American Under-18s, ironically against Norway, before deciding to switch allegiance to his parent's homeland. After playing at Under-18 and Under-20 level he won his first Norwegian Under-21 cap in February 1996 against the USA. Offered a contract by Spurs in July 1995, Baardsen finished his schooling a year later before moving to White Hart Lane. With competition from the likes of Erik Thorstvedt and Ian Walker it was never going to be easy for Baardsen to establish himself, but he made steady progress, establishing himself as Norway's regular Under-21 'keeper. Early in the 1998-99 season Baardsen replaced Walker as the season began in poor fashion and won the first of his four full caps as a Spurs' player against Latvia in September 1998. He looked to have established himself, but the arrival of George Graham changed all that. Not only did Graham clearly prefer Walker, but he also had little regard for Baardsen. A player who thrived on confidence, Graham shattered Baardsen's. His form suffered dramatically and without being given another chance, he was released and moved to Watford. At last Baardsen had a regular platform on which to display his talents, but when he was dropped by the Hornets his confidence was shattered again and he began to question his desire to play the game. With Watford in financial troubles, Baardsen's contract was paid up in December 2002 and he signed for Everton on a short-term contract. Everton were facing a goalkeeping crisis, but as that eased Baardsen was surplus to requirements. He decided he had had enough of football and retired. After spending a year travelling the world, he carved out a new career for himself as an investment analyst in the City.

Appearances:
League: 22 (1) apps.
FA Cup: 2 (1) apps.
FL Cup: 3 apps.
Others: 6 (7) apps.
Total: 33 (9) apps. 0 gls.

BADENOCH, George Huntly

Role: Outside-right 1906-07
5ft.8ins. 11st.4lbs.
Born: Kelton, Castle Douglas, Castlehouse, Kirkcudbrightshire, 9th April 1882
Died: Givenchy, France, 15th June 1915 (killed in action)

CAREER: Douglas Wanderers/Heart of Midlothian Apr 1901/Glossop Oct 1901/Watford Aug 1903/**SPURS** May 1906/Northampton Town May 1907/retired 1909.

Debut v Watford (SL) (a) 5.9.1906

Another of the many players signed purely as reserve cover for the first team regulars, George Badenoch made a total of only three senior appearances in his one year at Spurs. Not helped by a bout of appendicitis, he was unable to challenge Joe Walton for the regular outside-right position. Released in April 1907, he spent two years with Northampton, helping them win the Southern League title in 1909, before a knee injury forced him to retire. He then emigrated to Canada, where he played cricket for the Indian Head club of Saskatchewan, but returned to Britain during the First World War. Serving with the Western Ontario Regiment of the Canadian Infantry he lost his life on active service in France.

Appearances:
Southern: 1 app.
Others: 2 apps.
Total: 3 apps. 0 gls.

BADGER, Herbert Osborne

Role: Centre-forward 1903-04
Born: Islington, London, 4th October 1882
Died: Colchester, Essex, 16th March 1965

CAREER: Clacton Town/Colchester Town/Ilford/**SPURS** am. Oct 1903/Woolwich Arsenal pro. Sep 1904/Watford Aug 1906/Brentford Jul 1908/Nottingham Forest Sep 1909/Brentford Dec 1910/released 1911.

Debut v Millwall (LL) (h) 23.11.1904 (scored once)

Bert Badger was an amateur with the Ilford club when he made several guest appearances for Spurs. Although he played two games at centre-half he was principally a centre-forward at the time and made his debut in that position scoring once. Only associated with Spurs for one

season, he later reverted to the centre-half position and turned professional with Woolwich Arsenal, but failed to make their first eleven in his two years there. He appeared regularly for Watford and Brentford in the Southern League before a brief spell with Nottingham Forest, making only two Football League appearances for the Midlanders before returning to Brentford.

Appearances:
Others: 10 apps. 5 gls.
Total: 10 apps. 5 gls.

BAILLIE

Role: Forward 1883-84

Debut v Sekford Rovers (Fr) (a) 24.11.1883

Baillie, who "was acquainted with first class football", joined Spurs for their second season of existence, 1883-84, as a coach as well as player. Apart from the fact he is known to have played three friendly matches, nothing is known about him.

Appearances:
Others: 3 apps.
Total: 3 apps. 0 gls.

BAILY, Edward Francis

Role: Inside-forward 1945-56
5ft.7ins. 10st.0lbs.
Born: Clapton, London, 6th August 1925
Died: Welwyn Garden City, Hertfordshire, 13th October 2010

CAREER: Hackney Schools/Middlesex Schools/ Tottenham Juniors/ Finchley/**SPURS** am./Chelsea am/**SPURS** am. Feb 1946, pro. Oct 1946/Port Vale Jan 1956/Nottingham Forest Oct 1956/Leyton Orient Dec 1958, coach 1960/ **SPURS** asst. manager Oct 1963/West Ham United scout Sep 1974/Chesham United coach/West Ham United chief scout Aug 1976-Oct 1977/ Birmingham City asst. manager Oct 1977/Ipswich Town scout.

Debut v West Bromwich Albion (FL) (h) 4.1.1947
(Aston Villa (FLS) (h) 20.2.1946)

One of the most important names in Spurs post-war history, both as a player and coach, but were it not for the good grace of Chelsea, Eddie Baily may never have appeared in a Spurs shirt at all! First coming to the club's attention as a schoolboy, he was taken under Spurs' wing and played for Tottenham Juniors, before being placed with Finchley where several Spurs stars of the future learnt the basics of their trade. He signed as an amateur on leaving school during the war, but then had to serve with the Royal Scots Fusiliers. Spurs heard he had been reported missing in action and allowed his registration to lapse. Unaware of this, but having heard nothing from Spurs, when he returned to the UK Baily was persuaded to sign amateur forms for Chelsea, and it was only when he popped into White Hart Lane that the Army's error became known. The situation was explained to Chelsea and they agreed to cancel his registration so Baily could re-sign for Spurs. In the forces, he had gained plenty of football experience, representing the British Army on the Rhine against the Polish, Swiss, Czech and French armies. When home on leave he made his debut for Spurs in a Football League South match. His League debut came on 4th January 1947 against West Bromwich Albion, but it was not until October of the same year that he signed a professional contract. An archetypal chirpy Cockney character, Baily immediately established himself in the first team and was soon recognised as one of the game's finest inside-forwards, a player with superb one-touch skills, the vision to create opportunities for others and the ability to score goals himself. Affectionately known as "The Cheeky Chappie", he was superbly suited to, and one of the key cogs in, the flowing "Push and Run" team that won the Second Division in 1949-50 and the League Championship the following season. His outstanding performances were soon rewarded with international honours; three caps for England "B" followed by a full England debut in June 1950 against Spain in Rio De Janeiro during the World Cup Finals. In total, he won nine England caps, appeared for the Rest of the UK against Wales, played for the Football League five times and was still considered good enough to play for an England team against Young England in May 1957. Having made almost 300 League appearances for Spurs in ten years, he was allowed to leave in January 1956 for Port Vale, but only stayed for nine months before joining Nottingham Forest, helping them win promotion to the First Division. Baily finished his playing career with Leyton Orient, joined the coaching staff there and helped the club gain promotion in 1962. In October 1963, he returned to White Hart Lane as assistant manager to his old Spurs team-mate Bill Nicholson. He held the post for eleven years, earning a reputation as a strict but fair disciplinarian, before leaving again following Nicholson's resignation in 1974. A man with an encyclopaedic football knowledge, he was not allowed to remain out of football for long, joining West Ham United as Chief scout. He discovered Alan Devonshire who cost the "Hammers" just £5,000 from non-League Southall. For a short time, the assistant manager to his former Spurs and England colleague, Alf Ramsey, at Birmingham City, Baily also worked in the England set-up until his retirement from a full-time role in 1992. In May 1993 Spurs met Enfield in a Testimonial match for him.

Appearances:
League: 297* apps. 64 gls.
FA Cup: 29 apps. 5 gls.
Others: 56 apps. 21 gls.
Total: 382 apps. 90 gls.
*Includes 1 abandoned match.

BAILY, W

Role: Inside-forward 1894-95

Debut v London Welsh (LSC) (h) 26.1.1895

Baily's three appearances for Spurs were all in the 1894-95 London Senior Cup competition when he played at inside-forward. His first performance was described as not creating "a good impression", but he went on to play in the two second round matches against Old Westminsters, scoring his only goal for the club in the replay that Spurs lost 4-5. Baily was from Woolwich.

Appearances:
Others: 3 apps. 1 gl.
Total: 3 apps. 1 gl.

BAKARI, Dagui Orphie

Role: Striker 2004-05
6ft.4ins. 14st.2lbs.
Born: Paris, France, 6th September 1974

CAREER: Romainville (France)/Olympique Noisy-Le-Sec (France) 1994/Amiens (France) 1995/Le Mans (France) 1996/Lille Olympique (France) 1999/RC Lens (France) Jun 2002/(Valladolid (Spain) loan Mar 2004)/**SPURS** trial Jul 2004/Wigan Athletic trial Aug 2005/Nancy Lorraine (France) Aug 2005/retired Oct 2005.

Debut v Nottingham Forest (sub) (Fr) (a) 31.7.2004

A 29-year old on the books of RC Lens given a trial in the early days of the Frank Arnesen/Jacques Santini regime, Daqui Bakari was a journeyman striker who had spent his whole career in his native France, only really tasting any success with Lille. He had left France once, in March 2004 when he was unveiled as Valladolid's three-month loan signing, but within days a dispute broke out over the terms of his move and he quickly returned to Lens. Two months later he played his first game for the Ivory Coast. Bakari was born in Paris of Ivorian parents and had many opportunities to play for his parent's country but turned them down hoping to get the call from the country of his birth. When he realised that call was not going to come, he accepted the chance to play for the "Elephants" and went on to score four goals in six appearances. A big, strong, willing worker, he played in four pre-season games during his trial spell with Spurs, but was no better than the strikers already on the books and not taken on. He continued with Lens for another season, had an unsuccessful trial at Wigan Athletic and signed for Nancy Lorraine. After only one game for his new club, Bakari was found to suffer from heart hypertrophy, a cardiac problem that meant his heart would balloon to twice its normal size. There was no choice but for him to retire from football. Bakari's brother, Oumar, played for French Second Division outfit Wasquehal.

Appearances:
Others: 1 (3) apps.
Total: 1 (3) apps. 0 gls.

BAKER

Role: Centre-forward 1893-94

Debut v Enfield (Fr) (a) 16.9.1893

Nothing is known about a player whose one and only appearance for Spurs was as a trialist. Playing at centre-forward he "made a regular hash of it" and was described by a local scribe as a "lamentable failure who would have been better off at home".

Appearances:
Others: 1 app.
Total: 1 app. 0 gls.

BAKER, Peter Russell Barker

Role: Full-back 1952-65
5ft.10ins. 10st.8lbs.
Born: Hampstead, London, 10th December 1931
Died: Enfield, Middlesex, 27th January 2016

CAREER: Southgate County Grammar School/Edmonton Boys/Middlesex Boys/Enfield/**SPURS** am. Jun 1949, pro. Sep 1952/Durban United (South Africa) May 1965, coach/Addington (South Africa)/Durban Spurs 1969/Durban United (South Africa) asst. coach 1970, manager 1971-72.

Debut v Sunderland (FL) (a) 18.4.1953

While Peter Baker and his full-back partner Ron Henry were the most under-rated members of Spurs' 1960-61 "Double" winning team, they probably formed the best full-back pairing of the time. Their contribution to Spurs' successes was immeasurable. First spotted by Spurs while playing for Enfield, Baker had already won Middlesex and England youth honours when he signed for Spurs as an amateur. He continued to play for Enfield until signing as a professional, making his League debut in April 1953 when Alf Ramsey was on international duty. He understudied Ramsey for the next two seasons, only making the occasional appearance when the England man was unavailable, but his chances of becoming the long-term replacement for the future England manager appeared to fade when Spurs signed Maurice Norman from Norwich City in November 1955. However, injury to Norman early in 1956-57 allowed Baker the chance to really stake a claim to the right-back position, and so impressive was he that when Norman was fit to resume he had to move to centre-half to find a regular  place. When it seemed, he had made the right-back position his own, Baker then had to fight off the challenge of John Hills, but by the time of Bill Nicholson's appointment as manager in October 1958 Baker was firmly established in the team. Fast and fearless, strong-sometimes even tough-in the tackle, good with his head, positionally solid and cool under pressure in an era when virtually every team had a useful winger, Baker's neat short passing was also an integral part of turning defence into attack. He was almost immovable during the Glory Days of the early sixties, part of the team that won the FA Cup in 1962 and the European Cup-Winners Cup the following season to add to the "Double". He deserved international recognition but was unfortunate in being unable to displace Jimmy Armfield from the England team. Baker was eventually replaced at Spurs by Cyril Knowles as Nicholson sought to rebuild, and in May 1965 his contract was cancelled by mutual consent so he could join Durban United in South Africa. He settled in the Republic managing Durban United and coaching Abbinton of Durban before opening an office furniture and stationery business. He later returned to the UK, living back in Enfield until his death.

Appearances:
League: 299 apps. 3 gls.
FA Cup: 27 apps.
Euro: 16 apps.
Others: 58* (2) apps.
Total: 400 (2) apps. 3 gls.
* Includes 1 abandoned match

BAKER, Sean

Role: Striker 1984-85
Born: 7th March 1962

CAREER: Boreham Wood/(**SPURS** trial Nov 1984)/Maidstone United/Finchley/Barnet/Finchley/Harrow Borough/Leyton Wingate/Hendon Jul

1989-1991/Boreham Wood/Spalding Town.

Debut v Sutton United (sub) (Fr) (a) 13.11.1984

A young trialist striker with Boreham Wood, Sean Baker was only associated with Spurs for about a month in late 1984 during which time he played a couple of games in the reserves. His one first team appearance was in a testimonial match for long-serving England amateur international Larry Pritchard when he appeared on as a substitute. Spurs decided the Hertfordshire Youth player did not have what it takes to make the grade at the highest level, but Baker went on to enjoy a successful career in the non-League game.

Appearances:
Others: (1) app.
Total: (1) app. 0 gls.

BALDOCK, George Rowlett

Role: Half-back 1887-93
Born: London

Debut v Hendon (LSC) (a) 8.10.1887

Yet another of the players from Spurs' early days, George Baldock is one of only two known members of the Spurs' team that played Arsenal for the first time in November 1887. In his first season, he played all his known matches at half-back, but like many players in those days he was just happy to get a game when he could. Although principally a half-back, he also played in goal, particularly for the reserve side. Associated with Spurs for several years both as a player and on the administrative side, it was only after the decision in December 1895 to turn professional that Baldock ceased to have an involvement with the club.

Appearances:
Others: 11 apps. 1 gl.
Total: 11 apps. 1 gl.

BALDWIN, A

Role: Goalkeeper 1917-18

Debut v West Ham United (LFC) (h) 16.3.1918

Apart from the fact Baldwin was an inexperienced young player from Ponders End in north London, nothing is known about a player whose only appearance was as a last-minute replacement in a London Football Combination match at Highbury in March 1918. This was a home game for Spurs played on one of the two grounds they used at the time (Clapton Orient's Homerton being the other) due to the requisitioning of White Hart Lane for the manufacture of gasmasks.

Appearances:
Others: 1 app.
Total: 1 app. 0 gls.

BALE, Gareth Frank

Role: Full-back/Midfield 2007-13
6ft.0ins. 12st.7lbs.
Born: Cardiff, Wales, 16th July 1989

CAREER: Cardiff Civil Service/Whitchurch High School/Southampton Academy Scholar Jul 2005, pro. Jul 2006/**SPURS** May 2007/Real Madrid (Spain) Sep 2013.

Debut v Manchester United (PL) (a) 26.8.2007
(St Patricks Athletic (Fr) (a) 12.7.2007)

Signed as a 17-year-old of enormous potential, Gareth Bale was one of the most sought-after youngsters in the British game as evidenced by the £5 million, rising to £10 million, Spurs agreed to pay for his transfer. As it was, they only had to lay out £7 million, cutting a deal with Southampton to pay a lesser sum early because of the Saints' serious financial problems. Even at the original price, Bale would have been a bargain. Starting out as an attacking left-back with tremendous pace, in his one season of senior football he had already built a reputation as something of a free-kick expert, four of his five senior goals for the Saints coming from dead-ball situations. Given an early chance with Spurs, Bale looked set to justify all expectations, but with one injury after another and the ever-improving form of Benoit Assou-Ekotto, Bale struggled to hold down a regular place until given a more advanced role. Playing wide on the left of midfield, where his sustained power and pace was best utilised, Bale's performances improved as his confidence grew. Never afraid to take a man on, a change of pace would take him past his opponent, while his ability to sustain speed over distance left his markers trailing in his wake. Pace was not his only asset though. He

could cross a ball with whip and accuracy and a superb heading ability combined with a tremendous spring made him a serious threat in the air. If that was not enough, Bale's shooting prowess was not just from free-kicks. Cutting in from the wing and unleashing a vicious shot, he was always a threat. His performances against Inter Milan in the 2010-11 Champions League, a hat-trick in the first game in the San Siro followed by another goal in the return as he completely dominated Maicon, saw Bale on every club's wish-list and as he continued to improve, so the biggest clubs in the world coveted his services. With the arrival of Andre Villas-Boas as coach, Bale's career took a further leap forward. Released from the shackles of playing on the wing and allowed to roam where he felt he could do most damage, Bale gave one masterful performance after another. His return of 21 goals in the Premier League alone inspired Spurs to another ultimately unsuccessful bid to qualify for the Champions League. Improving with every game, Bale continued to come up with the unexpected, but even when opponents knew what was coming, there was no way they could stop him. Favourably compared with Cristiano Ronaldo and Lionel Messi, Bale had yet to produce their sustained level of performance, but it was not difficult to see that he possessed every attribute needed to take him to their level. Real Madrid certainly recognised that and forked out a world record £86million to add him to their galaxy of stars. Bale became Wales' youngest player when he made his debut against Trinidad and Tobago in May 2006, a month after making his League debut for Southampton, and its youngest scorer when he netted against Slovakia five months later.

Appearances:
League: 136 (10) apps. 42 gls.
FA Cup: 17* apps. 3 gls.
FL Cup: 8 (2) apps. 2 gls.
Euro: 27 (4) apps. 8 gls.
Others: 16 (8) apps. 5 gls.
Total: 204 (24) apps. 60 gls.
* Includes 1 abandoned match

BALL, Dominic

Role: Defender 2016-17
6ft.1in. 12st.5lbs.
Born: Welwyn Garden City, Hertfordshire, 2nd August 1995

CAREER: Welwyn Pegasus/Watford/**SPURS** Academy Scholar Jul 2011, pro. Sep 2013/(Cambridge United loan Jan 2015)/(Rangers loan Aug 2015)/Rotherham United Aug 2016/(Peterborough United loan Jan 2017).

Debut v Juventus (Fr) (Melbourne) 26.7.2016

With his father, Tom, a former Stevenage Borough player, business manager of the Watford Academy, it is no surprise that Dominic Ball should have trained with the Hornets as a boy. He joined Spurs as a 16-year old, quickly adding representative honours for Northern Ireland at Under-17 and Under-19 level to those he had collected as an Under-15 and Under-16. Principally regarded as a central defender, his outstanding potential saw him make two appearances at Under-21 level, before accepting an offer to represent England. Quickly establishing himself in the youth teams at Spurs, Ball gained Football League experience in five months on loan at Cambridge United. For the 2015-16 season, he moved up to Scotland with Rangers and played regularly as the former giants of Scottish football continued their return to the top, winning the Scottish Championship and Scottish Challenge Cup. Ball impressed a great deal, playing both in the centre of defence and as a holding midfielder. While Rangers were keen to secure Ball on another season long loan, Mauricio Pochettino decided to have a good close look at Ball and took him to Australia for the pre-season International Champions Cup. Ball played in both games against Juventus and Atlético Madrid, but with the likes of Toby Alderweireld and Eric Dier ahead of him, the coach decided Ball's career would benefit from a permanent move. With several clubs interested in acquiring his services, Ball moved to Rotherham United. Expected to benefit from the experience of manager Alan Stubbs, a former top-class centre-half, Ball found the going tough as the struggling Miller's chopped and changed managers. Ball's brother, Matt, failed to make the grade at Norwich, but has since played for several clubs including Stevenage, Wealdstone and St Albans.

Appearances:
Others: 1 (1) apps.
Total: 1 (1) apps. 0 gls.

BANKS, James Andrew

Role: Forward 1913-24
5ft.8ins. 11st.12lbs.
Born: Ashington, County Durham, 28th April 1893
Died: Chelsea, London, 25th August 1942

CAREER: Starcliffe Celtic/St Gregorys/Spennymoor United/All Saints FC/Willington Athletic/**SPURS** Dec 1913/Norwich City Sep 1923/Luton Town Aug 1927/London Public Omnibus Company player-coach till Aug 1929/Worthing coach Aug 1938.

Debut v Manchester United (FL) (h) 7.2.1914

Signed as an inside-forward, Jimmy Banks' best days at Spurs came when he played at outside-right. He did not make his debut until late in the 1913-14 season and, although he finished the season with a run in the first team due to the indisposition of Billy Minter, was not able to establish a regular place until the outbreak of the First World War. When war arrived he joined the Services, but unlike many of his contemporaries was not posted abroad and therefore available to play regularly. During this time, he played mainly at centre-forward and proved very successful, top-scoring in 1916-17 and 1917-18.

Whether he would have fared so well in League football must be a matter of conjecture, but the resumption of normal football saw Banks revert to an inside-forward role and he was only able to establish a place in the team midway through the promotion season of 1919-20. However, Jimmy Seed arrived in February 1920 and by the start of the following campaign Banks found himself back in the reserves. In January 1921, outside-right Fanny Walden was injured and Spurs' manager Peter McWilliam decided to give Banks the opportunity to replace the magical little winger. Banks took the chance well, his direct, resolute style playing an important role in helping Spurs lift the FA Cup for the second time. Although he started the next term in the first team, he was unable to retain a place and early the following season moved to Norwich City where he played for four years. Finishing his career with Luton Town, he became a bus driver with the London Public Omnibus Company playing on permit for their works team in the Northern Suburban Intermediate League. He was also coach to the team until succeeded by his former Spurs colleague Bill Sage, but continued to be involved in the game in a coaching capacity.

Appearances:
League: 68 apps. 6 gls.
FA Cup: 9 apps. 4 gls.
Others: 133* apps. 81# gls.
Total: 210 apps. 91 gls.
* Includes 1 abandoned match.
# Includes 1 in abandoned match.

BANKS, Kingsley Peter

Role: Goalkeeper 1985-87
Born: Enfield, Middlesex, 6th December 1968

CAREER: Essex Schools/North East Essex Schools/London Schools/**SPURS** app. Jul 1985, pro. cs. 1986/Gillingham/Dartford May 1987/Basildon United/Enfield/Barking/Witham Town 1994-95/Heybridge Swifts Jul 1995/retired Jul 2003.

Debut v West Ham United (Fr) (a) 12.5.1986

Kingsley Banks had trained with West Ham United and Fulham before joining Spurs as an apprentice. A regular with the youth team in 1985-86 his one first team appearance was as a substitute in a Benefit match at West Ham for Gerhard Ampofo in May 1986. Upgraded to professional status shortly afterwards, Banks was unable to displace the senior keepers Ray Clemence and Tony Parks and with a steady stream of talented young keepers coming through the ranks he was released in May 1987. After a short spell at Gillingham without making the first team he went into non-League football, spent several years as the rock around which Heybridge Swifts built their team and was widely regarded as possibly the best goalkeeper outside the League.

Appearances:
Others: (1) app.
Total: (1) app. 0 gls.

BANN, William Edward

Role: Full-back 1923-30
5ft.10ins. 11st.6lbs.
Born: Broxburn, West Lothian, 15th August 1902
Died: Haringey, London, 16th March 1973

CAREER: Winchburgh Thistle/Broxburn United Jun 1922/SPURS Feb 1923/Brentford May 1930/Bristol Rovers Jun 1932/Aldershot Sep 1933.

Debut v Newcastle United (FL) (h) 25.3.1926
(Chelsea (Fr) (a) 2.2.1924)

Bill Bann joined Spurs from Scottish Second Division Broxburn United in February 1923, but did not make his first team debut until twelve months later and that was only in a friendly. It was to be another two years before his competitive debut. That was in March 1926 when he turned out as replacement for Tommy Clay. Although he retained a place for the rest of the season, he did not play a further League game until September 1928 and made his final appearances for the club that season. Initially released in May 1929, he was then re-signed, but released again in May 1930. He joined Brentford before moving, after two years, to Bristol Rovers. He finished his career with one season at Aldershot.

Appearances:
League: 12 apps.
Others: 5 apps.
Total: 17 apps. 0 gls.

BANNERMAN, Alec C

Role: Forward 1893-94

CAREER: London Hospital/(SPURS guest Dec 1893).

Debut v Friars (Fr) (h) 19.12.1893

A member of the London Hospital's football team, Alec Bannerman played for Spurs as a guest in four friendly matches during the 1893-94 season. In the first, Spurs entertained "The Friars", a team made up of members of the London Press Club. Bannerman's three other games all came in March 1894.

Appearances:
Others: 4 apps. 1 gl.
Total: 4 apps. 1 gl.

BARBER

Role: Forward 1891-92

CAREER: Tottenham/(SPURS guest Feb 1892).

Debut v Grenadier Guards (Fr) ((h) 27.2.1892

A forward who played most of his football for the Tottenham club, Barber made his only appearance for Spurs in a friendly match against the Grenadier Guards when he scored once in a 9-0 victory.

Appearances:
Others: 1 app. 1 gl.
Total: 1 app. 1 gl.

BARCHAM, Andrew

Role: Forward 2006-08
5ft.8ins. 12st.3lbs.
Born: Basildon, Essex, 16th December 1986

CAREER: SPURS Academy Scholar Jul 2003, pro. Jul 2005/(Leyton Orient loan Nov 2007)/Gillingham loan Sep 2008, perm. Jan 2009/Scunthorpe United Jun 2011/Portsmouth May 2013/AFC Wimbledon Jul 2015.

Debut v Port Vale (FLC) (h) 8.11.2006

A hard-running little winger, Andy Barcham joined Spurs' professional staff after completing his scholarship and performed reasonably well at youth and reserve level. He was not the most talented or naturally gifted player, but was prepared to give everything in an effort to get a result. His only senior appearance for Spurs came in November 2006 when he was given the task of playing up front in a weak team against Port Vale in the Carling Cup. He was not to get near the first team again, spending most of the following season on loan at Leyton Orient before joining Gillingham, initially on loan. Playing as an out-and-out striker, Barcham did particularly well in two years with Gillingham before moving on to Scunthorpe United. When the "Iron" were relegated, Barcham was released and joined Portsmouth. The continuing financial problems Pompey faced saw his contract cancelled after two of the three years it was due to run so that he could switch to AFC Wimbledon.

Appearances:
FL Cup: 1 app.
Others: (1) app.
Total: 1 (1) app. 0 gls.

BARKER, George

Role: Full-back 1894-95
Born: Blakenhall, Wolverhampton, Staffordshire, 12th February 1875
Died: 1940

CAREER: 3rd Battalion Grenadier Guards/Royal Ordnance Factories/(SPURS guest Mar 1895)/Royal Ordnance/Wolverhampton Wanderers am./Everton May 1896/Bristol City cs. 1898/Bedminster Nov 1899/Wolverhampton Wanderers Jan 1901/retired Sep 1901.

Debut v Old Carthusians (LCC) (a) 21.3.1895 (scored once)

An army corporal serving with the Grenadier Guards and captain of their 3rd Battalion football team, Barker also made a few appearances for Royal Ordnance Factories in the early days of the Southern League and represented Middlesex. He made his first appearance for Spurs in a London Charity Cup second round match with Old Carthusians and appeared in a friendly three weeks later. In May 1896 Everton bought Barker out of the army and for two years he played on Merseyside, usually for the reserve side of which he was captain. At the end of the 1897-98 season Everton transfer-listed Barker, looking for a fee of £100. As it was only Football League clubs that were required to pay a fee for his transfer, Everton could do nothing to prevent Barker signing for Southern League Bristol City. He played at the St John's Lane ground for 18 months before moving on to Bedminster. Without a club for 1900-01, Barker sought a free transfer from Everton in December 1900. They refused to grant him one, but when Wolverhampton Wanderers offered £30 for his services a month later, it was accepted. Unfortunately, injury ended his career nine months later.

Appearances:
Others: 2 apps.
Total: 2 apps. 0 gls.

BARLOW, John

Role: Inside-forward 1901-1903
5ft.7ins. 12st.0lbs.
Born: Prescot, Lancashire, 19th May 1875
Died: Seaforth, Crosby, Lancashire, 21st October 1951

CAREER: Prescot/Everton Feb 1898/Reading May 1899/**SPURS** May 1901/Reading Feb 1903/Leicester Fosse May 1903-May 1904.

Debut v Bristol Rovers (WL) (h) 21.10.1901
(Rest of the Southern League (Fr) (h) 16.10.1901)

John Barlow only played four League games in his two seasons with Everton, but then spent two reasonably successful seasons with Reading before joining Spurs. He made his first team debut in a friendly against the Rest of the Southern League five days before his competitive debut in a Western League fixture, but was only ever a reserve at White Hart Lane. He played just seven matches in the Southern League in his two years with the club, and it was no surprise when he was allowed to return to Reading in February 1903. However, his second spell with the Berkshire club was very short for in May of the same year he was released and joined Leicester Fosse where he played for one season.

Appearances:
Southern: 7 apps.
Others: 19 apps. 9 gls.
Total: 26 apps. 9 gls.

BARMBY, Nicholas Jonathan

Role: Forward 1991-1996
5ft.6ins. 11st.4lbs.
Born: Hull, Humberside, 11th February 1974

CAREER: Springhead Boys/Kingston-Upon-Hull Schools/England Schools/FA-GM School of Excellence/**SPURS** trainee Jul 1990, pro. Mar 1991/Middlesbrough Aug 1995/Everton Oct 1996/Liverpool Jul 2000/Leeds United Aug 2002/(Nottingham Forest loan Feb 2004)/Hull City Jul 2004, player-coach Jun 2010, player-caretaker manager Nov 2011, manager Jan-May 2012/Westella and Willerby Juniors manager/Wyke College football academy coach Sep 2015.

Debut v Sheffield Wednesday (PL) (a) 27.9.1992
(Hull City XI (Fr) (a) 8.5.1992)

One of the most sought-after schoolboy stars, Nicky Barmby graduated from the FA-GM School of Excellence to sign for Spurs in the face of competition from all the top clubs. Within a couple of years, he was starring for Spurs alongside the likes of Teddy Sheringham, Jürgen Klinsmann and Darren Anderton. A pocket dynamo who could operate up front, in midfield or, where he was probably most effective, between the two, Barmby was all action, whether running with the ball at pace, seeking out space to receive the ball or playing a perceptive pass through a defence. Given a chance early in the 1992-93 season, he was immediately at home in the rarefied atmosphere of top level football, displaying a level of maturity far beyond his years. Towards the end of his first full season, shin splints, part of the growing up process, caused Barmby problems and it was some time before he had fully recovered. He was soon back, playing and scoring regularly and quickly worked his way through the Under-21s and "B" team to make his full England debut against Uruguay in March 1995. Barmby looked destined for a long and distinguished career in a Tottenham shirt but towards the end of the 1994-95 campaign stories began that he was homesick and desperate for a return north. Although denied, when Middlesbrough made a £5 million plus offer for his transfer, he made it clear it was a move he wanted and Spurs had little choice but to accept the offer. Barmby spent only a year on Teesside, before moving on to Everton, Liverpool and Leeds United. While he continued to perform at the highest level and collect international honours, his career never reached the heights his early years with Spurs had promised. Reaching his thirties, Barmby joined his home town club, Hull City, where he continued to play into the veteran stage. He coached for a while and took over the managerial reins on a permanent basis in January 2012 when he quit playing. His time in management was short, being sacked after three months when he publicly expressed concerns about the availability of funds to strengthen the team. Barmby's son, Jack, was on the books of Manchester United and Leicester City.

Appearances:
League: 81 (6) apps. 20 gls.
FA Cup: 12 (1) apps. 5 gls.
FL Cup: 7 (1) apps. 2 gls.
Others: 25 (9) 8 gls.
Total: 125 (17) apps. 35 gls.

BARNARD, J

Role: Forward 1916-19

Debut v Queens Park Rangers (LFC) (a) 13.10.1917 (scored twice)
(West Ham United (Fr) (a) 5.5.1917 (scored once))

A forward who only played for Spurs during the First World War, it has proved impossible to ascertain any information about this player apart from the fact that he was a local man. He made his first appearance in Spurs' colours in a friendly match at West Ham United on 5th May 1917. He scored one of Spurs' goals in a 3-3 draw and went one better than that on his competitive debut five months later.

Appearances:
Others: 9 apps. 5 gls.
Total: **9 apps. 5 gls.**

BARNARD, Lee James

Role: Forward 2001-08
5ft.10ins. 10st.10lbs.
Born: Romford, Essex, 18th July 1984

CAREER: Perry Street School/Mayflower School/Basildon and Brentwood District Schools/**SPURS** Scholar Jul 2000, pro. Jul 2002/(Exeter City loan Nov 2002)/(Stevenage Borough loan Mar 2004)/(Leyton Orient loan Nov 2004)/(Northampton Town loan Mar 2005)/(Crewe Alexandra loan Aug 2007)/Southend United Jan 2008/Southampton Jan 2010/(AFC Bournemouth loan Aug 2012)/(Oldham Athletic loan Jan 2013)/Southend United loan Jan 2014, perm. May 2014-Jun 2015/(Stevenage loan Oct 2014)/Crawley Town trial and perm. Jul 2015/Braintree Town Jun 2016.

Debut v Manchester United (sub) (PL) (h) 17.4.2006
(Stevenage Borough (sub) (Fr) (a) 13.7.2001)

Lee Barnard was another in a long list of talented young strikers who never quite made the grade with Spurs, but went on to carve out a good career lower down the football ladder. Associated with Spurs as a boy, he proved a prolific scorer at youth and reserve level, but never had a real chance to make the breakthrough into the first team, spending much of his time out on loan to lower league clubs in an effort to give him experience. A neat, deceptively strong central striker he relied on guile and finesse far more than sheer strength. Easy on the eye, he had a few outings in friendly games but only three appearances as a substitute in League games. Competing with the likes of Les Ferdinand, Teddy Sheringham, Robbie Keane and Jermaine Defoe, Barnard seemed to lack the physical presence they all possessed and when Dimitar Berbatov arrived it was time for Barnard to move on. He joined Southend United, scoring at the rate of almost a goal every other game in his two years there, before moving to Southampton. Instrumental in helping them return to the second tier of English football, injuries limited his appearances in the Championship and when promotion to the Premier League was secured Barnard found himself surplus to requirements. After loans to Bournemouth and Oldham Athletic, he returned to Southend for a year, then moved on to Crawley Town and Braintree Town.

Appearances:
League: (3) apps.
Others: 5 (9) apps. 3 gls,
Total: **5 (12) apps. 3 gls.**

BARNES, F W

Role: Forward 1891-92

CAREER: Tottenham College/**SPURS** guest Feb 1892/Edmonton/Old Tottonians.

Debut v Grenadier Guards (Fr) (h) 27.2.1892 (scored once)

A player with the Tottenham College football team, Barnes, like Barber, made his only appearance for Spurs in their 9-0 victory over the Grenadier Guards in February 1892. Again, like Barber, he scored one of Spurs' goals. He was later noted playing for Old Tottonians, the College Old Boys team.

Appearances:
Others: 1 app. 1 gl.
Total: **1 app. 1 gl.**

BARNES, John Charles Bryan

Role: Forward 1987-88
5ft.11ins. 12st. 0lbs.
Born: Kingston, Jamaica, West Indies, 7th November 1963

CAREER: Sudbury Court/Watford Jul 1981/Liverpool Jun 1987/(**SPURS** guest Mar 1988)/Newcastle United Aug 1997/Charlton Athletic Feb-May 1999/Celtic coach Jun 1999-Feb 2000/Jamaica coach Sep 2008/Tranmere Rovers manager Jun-Oct 2009.

Debut v Manchester United (Fr) (h) 28.3.1988

England international John Barnes guested for Spurs in a Benefit match for Danny Thomas in March 1988. At the time he was with Liverpool, having established himself as one of the most exciting players in the game. As a winger, he was capable of dominating the opposing full-back, making goals for his team-mates and scoring stunning goals such as the one he netted for England against Brazil in the Maracanã Stadium in June 1984. A member of Watford's losing FA Cup Final team of 1983-84, he won two England Under-21 and 31 full caps before moving to Liverpool. He soon slotted into the Anfield machine bringing, with Peter Beardsley, a flair that had not always been welcome at a club more concerned with team than individual performances. Playing in midfield, his first season on Merseyside was quite incredible with Liverpool winning the Football League and reaching the FA Cup Final and Barnes picking up individual accolades as Player of the Year from both the Football Writers' and Professional Footballers' Associations. A member of the Liverpool side that won the FA Cup in 1989 and was only seconds away from adding the Football League title, he helped Liverpool regain the title in 1990. Forced to compete with former Spurs' star Chris Waddle for the winger's role in the England team, it was only towards the end of Bobby Robson's reign as England manager that a place in the team was found for both of them. After ten years' service to Liverpool, Barnes joined his old team-mate and manager Kenny

Dalglish at Newcastle, but the arrival of Ruud Gullit as manager saw Barnes move on to struggling Charlton Athletic. His stay at the Valley was very short for, unable to keep the south Londoner's in the Premiership, he soon linked up with Dalglish again, taking on the coach's role at Celtic. Unable to challenge the dominance of great rivals Rangers, Barnes was dismissed in February 2000. He later had a spell as manager of his native Jamaica, followed by another unsuccessful spell in charge of Tranmere Rovers before concentrating on a career as a TV pundit.

Appearances:
Others: 1 app.
Total: 1 app. 0 gls.

BARNETT, Frederick William

Role: Outside-right 1922-29
5ft.6ins. 10st.9lbs.
Born: *Dartford, Kent, 4th April 1898*
Died: *Gravesend, Kent, June 1982*

CAREER: Hawley/Bolton Wanderers trial Feb 1920/SPURS/Northfleet United cs. 1921/SPURS Feb 1923/Southend United Apr 1929/Watford Jun 1934/Dartford Jul 1935.

Debut v Bolton Wanderers (FL) (a) 11.4.1923

Fred Barnett had a trial with Bolton Wanderers after the First World War, but despite scoring three goals in eight games was not offered a position and returned to his junior club, Hawley. He had better luck with Spurs and was placed with the Northfleet nursery, before graduating to the senior ranks at White Hart Lane. His debut came in April 1923 when he played against Bolton Wanderers as Spurs' manager Peter McWilliam shuffled his forward line to compensate for the absence of the injured Jimmy Seed. However, Barnett was never able to displace players of the quality of Fanny Walden, Andy Thompson, Tich Handley and Frank Osborne and in April 1929 was released. He joined Southend United, later moving on to Watford and Dartford.

Appearances:
League: 16 apps. 1 gl.
Others: 1 apps.
Total: 17 apps. 1 gl.

BARRON, George Patrick

Role: Goalkeeper 1942-43
5ft.10ins. 11st.4lbs.
Born: *Marylebone, London, 23rd November 1914*

CAREER: Cray Wanderers 1933/SPURS am. Aug 1936/Northfleet United 1937/Erith and Belvedere 1937/Bromley Oct 1942/Canterbury City 1948-1950.

Debut v Reading (LWL) (a) 17.10.1942

First associated with Spurs in August 1936 when he signed amateur forms, George Barron was sent down to Northfleet where he played until the arrival of Ted Ditchburn saw Barron loaned to Erith and Belvedere. Although still on Spurs' books, he was only called upon to play the once, against Reading in October 1942. Most of his football was seen with Erith and Belvedere until shortly after his one outing for Spurs, when he joined Bromley. When the War was over Barron was not offered terms by Spurs, but continued to play regularly with Bromley, until concluding his career with a couple of years at Canterbury City. Barron's son, Paul, was also a goalkeeper. He enjoyed a lengthy career in both League and non-League circles, his best days coming with Arsenal, Crystal Palace, West Bromwich Albion and Queens Park Rangers.

Appearances:
Others: 1 app.
Total: 1 app. 0 gls.

BARTON, Kenneth Rees

Role: Full-back 1954-1965
5ft.9ins. 10st.6lbs.
Born: *Caernarvon, 20th September 1937*
Died: *Chester, 6th September 1982*

CAREER: Caernarvon Schools/Caernarvon Boys Club/Welsh Boys Club/Wales Schools/SPURS am. May 1953, trial Jan 1954, pro. Oct 1954/Millwall Sep 1964/Luton Town Dec 1964/Dunstable Town.

Debut v Manchester United (FL) (a) 16.1.1961
(Plymouth Argyle (Fr) (a) 24.10.1955)

Ken Barton made only four Football League appearances during a ten-year career with Spurs that started with a trial in January 1954, although he had been on the amateur books for some time before then. He made his first team debut in a friendly with Plymouth Argyle in October 1955 and signed professional forms twelve months later, but it was more than four years before his League debut. The outstanding consistency of Peter Baker never gave Barton much of a look-in and even when Baker was absent the experienced Mel Hopkins was usually preferred. Barton made only three more League appearances for Spurs before being transferred to Millwall. He stayed there for just three months without a single League outing and then moved to Luton Town. One season at Kenilworth Road saw him add just a further eleven appearances to his Football League total. When his playing career was over Ken worked as a representative for a pharmaceutical company.

Appearances:
League: 4 apps.
Others: 2 apps.
Total: 6 apps. 0 gls.

BARTON, Percival A

Role: Half-back 1915-19
5ft.8ins. 11st.0lbs.
Born: *Edmonton, London, 20th January 1893*
Died: *Birmingham, October 1961*

CAREER: Montague Road School/Edmonton Amateurs/Corinthians/Tottenham Thursday/Sultan FC/Birmingham Jul 1913/(SPURS during World War One)/Stourbridge Aug 1929/retired Jun 1933.

Debut v Arsenal (LFC) (a) 4.9.1915

A former Corinthians player born on Spurs doorstep, Percy Barton really was a player Spurs let slip. He joined Birmingham from Tottenham Thursday, not just one of Spurs' local junior clubs, but a club who played their matches on Spurs' own White Hart Lane pitch on Thursdays. After playing briefly for Sultan FC, he made his League debut in January 1914 and immediately established himself as Birmingham's regular left-half. As he was posted to London on service duties he was able to play for Spurs throughout the war years. Capable of playing at full-back or inside-forward when the shortage of players demanded, he was particularly valuable during the first two seasons of the London Football Combination, being almost ever-present and compensating for the absence of Arthur Grimsdell. Back with Birmingham after the war, he really came to the fore, helping them win the Second Division title in 1921 and, after playing in two England trials, won his first cap against Belgium in May 1921. He collected seven England caps over the next four years, competing with Grimsdell for the left-half position. Moving to full-back towards the end of his career, Barton left Birmingham after thirteen years and played for four years at Stourbridge until retiring from the game.

Appearances:
Others: 91* apps. 6 gls.
Total: 91 apps. 6 gls.
*Includes 1 abandoned match.

BASSETT, Edward John

Role: Forward 1915-18
5ft.7ins. 10st.4lbs.
Born: Deptford, London, 1st January 1889
Died: Watford, Hertfordshire, 25th November 1970

CAREER: Woolwich Arsenal/Deptford Invicta/Dartford Jan 1909/Croydon Common trial Sep 1909/Metrogas Oct 1909/Charlton Albion 1910/**SPURS**/Millwall Nov 1911/Newark Stanley Works 1912/Dartford cs. 1912/Notts County Sep 1913/(guest for Fulham and **SPURS** during World War One)/Watford Jun 1919/Luton Town Jun 1921/Dartford Aug 1922/Fordsons, Cork (Ireland)/Finchley Nov 1930.

Debut v Arsenal (LFC) (a) 4.9.1915

Having worked his way up the ranks of junior clubs, Ted Bassett had been on Spurs' books for a while, but was released without making the first team. He joined Millwall where he was only marginally more successful, making one Southern League appearance in 1911-12. He then moved to Notts County and helped them win the Second Division in 1914. He was still on their books when he played regularly for Spurs during the early years of the First World War, making his debut against Arsenal in the first match of the newly-formed London Football Combination. Playing at inside-right he proved a very valuable performer for Spurs during those times, finding the net with consistency and linking well with Bert Bliss and Jimmy Banks. After only six games of the 1917-18 season Bassett was unavailable due to service demands. W and when he was able to re-join Spurs the inside-right position had been taken by Bliss. Bassett therefore assisted Fulham for the rest of the War, returned to Meadow Lane at the end of hostilities and was then transferred to Watford. He wound down his playing career with Luton Town, Dartford and the Irish club, Fordsons, but was still playing in the early 1930s for Finchley.

Appearances:
Others: 74* apps. 37 gls.
Total: 74 apps. 37 gls.
* Includes 1 abandoned match.

BASSETT, G

Role: Full-back or half-back 1889-92

Debut v Vulcan (Fr) (h) 8.2.1890 (scored once)

A local player who turned out regularly for three years, Bassett was one of the first players connected with Spurs to win a representative honour when he played for East Middlesex against West Middlesex at Southall on 25 November 1891.

Appearances:
Others: 12 apps. 3 gls.
Total: 12 apps. 3 gls.

BASSONG, Sébastien Aymar (Nguena)

Role: Central Defender 2009-13
6ft.2ins. 11st. 7lbs.
Born: Paris, France, 9th July 1986

CAREER: INF Clairefontaine (France) 1999/FC Metz (France) 2002/Newcastle United trial and perm. Jul 2008/**SPURS** Aug 2009/(Wolverhampton Wanderers loan Jan 2012)/Norwich City Aug 2012/(Watford loan Oct 2014).

Debut v Liverpool (PL) (h) 16.8.2009 (scored once)
(Olympiacos (Fr) (h) 9.8.2009)

Another product of France's famous Clairefontaine Academy, Sébastien Bassong joined Metz as a 16-year old defensive midfielder of strength and power. He made two appearances for France at Under-21 level in that position, but his lack of pace and mobility meant he was never going to reach the top in that role. Moved back into central defence, he soon excelled and after just a year Newcastle United were impressed enough to lay out £1.5 million to sign him. He spent a year on Tyneside, the outstanding player in a Newcastle side that was relegated on the last day of the season. Bassong was not prepared to accept playing outside the top flight and with injury problems raising concerns over the availability of both Ledley King and Jonathan Woodgate, Harry Redknapp was happy to invest £8 million to secure a more than competent Premiership performer. It appeared money well spent, especially when Bassong scored on his competitive debut against

Liverpool. That was just a few days after he had won his first full cap for Cameroon against Austria having decided he was not going to get a call up to the full French team. Bassong settled well at Spurs, whether paired alongside King or Michael Dawson, but all too often he would let his concentration lapse. The consequences could be costly. With the return of Younes Kaboul and the signing of William Gallas, Bassong all too often found himself on the bench. He began to agitate for regular action and in January 2012 was loaned to Wolverhampton Wanderers for the rest of the season. With their relegation ending any hopes of a permanent move to the Midlands, Bassong was grateful when Norwich City offered him the chance of regular first team football. At the end of his second year in Norfolk, City became the third team Bassong had played for to be relegated from the Premier League. Unlike previously, he initially remained with the club, but then spent three months on loan at Watford. He returned to help Norwich successfully return to the top flight at the first time of asking, finishing just behind Watford. A year later, the Canaries were relegated again.

Appearances:
League: 33 (12) apps. 2 gls.
FA Cup: 9 apps.
FL Cup: 5 apps.
Euro: 10 (1) apps. 1 gl.
Others: 6 (4) apps.
Total: 63 (17) apps. 3 gls.

BAUCHOP, James Rae

Role: Inside-forward 1913-14
5ft.10ins. 11st.12lbs.
Born: Sauchie, Scotland, 22nd May 1886
Died: Bradford, Yorkshire, 13th June 1968

CAREER: Sauchie May 1902/Alloa Athletic May 1904/Celtic Jan 1906/Norwich City May 1907/Crystal Palace Mar 1908/Derby County May 1909/SPURS May 1913/Bradford Park Avenue Dec 1913/(Guest for Bradford City, Celtic and Rangers during World War One)/Doncaster Rovers Jun 1922/Lincoln City Sep 1923/Bradford Park Avenue trainer 1924.

Debut v Sheffield United (FL) (a) 1.9.1913 (scored twice)

A typical Scottish inside-forward of his time with a love of dribbling and an almost selfish desire to go for goal, Jimmy Bauchop was a success with Alloa Athletic and Celtic before moving into English football with Southern League Norwich City. He spent less than one season in Norfolk, and was Norwich's top scorer when he moved to Crystal Palace. He achieved the same feat with Palace the next season before moving to Derby County. Scoring at a goal every other game, it was his performances for Derby that attracted Spurs' attention and led to his move to White Hart Lane. Although he scored twice on his debut, he was unable to retain a place and after being dropped in November 1913 demanded a transfer. The request was granted and he moved to Bradford Park Avenue the following month. His first season saw Park Avenue promoted to the First Division and when Spurs visited Yorkshire in March 1915 Bauchop must have derived enormous pleasure from scoring a hat-trick-his third of the season. He played for Bradford for nine years before leaving for Doncaster Rovers.

He finished his playing career with one season at Lincoln City and then returned to Bradford as a coach. Bauchop's brother, Willie, was a winger with Alloa Athletic, Plymouth Argyle, Heart of Midlothian, Carlisle United, Stockport County, Leicester City and Norwich City before the First World War.

Appearances:
League: 10 apps. 6 gls.
Others: 3 apps. 4 gls.
Total: 13 apps. 10 gls.

BAXTER, J M

Role: Inside-forward 1890-94

CAREER: SPURS/Old St Marks.

Debut v Luton Town (Fr) (a) 18.10.1890 (scored once)

A goal-scoring forward in the days when Spurs were beginning to establish themselves as one of the clubs in London that had a big future, Baxter played for the club for four years. It is not known what became of him thereafter, though in October 1893 he did turn out for Old St Marks against Spurs.

Appearances:
Others: 12 apps. 7 gls.
Total: 12 apps. 7 gls.

BAY

Role: Centre-forward 1918-19

Debut v Fulham (NWF) (h) 10.5.1919

Nothing is known about Bay who made his only appearance for Spurs at centre-forward in a National War Fund match towards the end of the First World War.

Appearances:
Others: 1 app.
Total: 1 app. 0 gls.

BEADLE, Peter Clifford William James

Role: Striker 1992-94
6ft.1ins. 10st.12lbs.
Born: Lambeth, London, 13 May 1972

CAREER: Lordswood Boys Club/Gillingham YTS Jul 1988, pro. May 1990/(Margate loan Mar 1990)/SPURS Jun 1992/(AFC Bournemouth loan Mar 1993)/(Southend United loan Mar 1994)/Watford Sep 1994/Bristol Rovers Nov 1995/Port Vale Aug 1998/Notts County Feb 1999/Bristol City Oct 1999-May 2003/Cheltenham Town trial Jul 2003/Brentford trial and perm. Jul 2003/Barnet Sep-Dec 2003/Team Bath player-coach Dec 2003/Clevedon Town player-asst. manager/commercial manager Jun 2004/Taunton Town manager May 2005/AFC Newport County manager Oct 2005-Apr 2008/West Bromwich Albion academy coach/Clevedon Town manager Mar-May 2010/Cheltenham Town coach Dec 2010/Hereford United Director of Youth Football Apr 2013, caretaker manager Mar 2014/Sutton United head coach May 2014/Hereford manager May 2015.

Debut v Brighton & Hove Albion (sub) (Fr) (a) 29.7.1992

A strapping 6 foot plus striker, Peter Beadle had been under scrutiny by Spurs even before making the breakthrough into the Gillingham first team and it was just a question of time before they made their move. That

came in June 1992 with £300,000 laid out for a player reckoned to have great potential. Beadle made his first appearance as a substitute in a pre-season friendly, but that turned out to be his only first team outing. The potential may have been there, but it did not develop. After loan spells at Bournemouth and Southend United, he was allowed to move to Watford, but it was only when he joined Bristol Rovers that he began to show some of the form that had earned his move to White Hart Lane. Beadle was a big lad who could prove troublesome to any defence, if he was in the mood. Never really of top flight quality, he proved quite successful at lower level playing over 300 League games before embarking on an extensive managerial and coaching career.

Appearances:
Others: (1) app.
Total: (1) app. 0 gls.

BEAL, Phillip

Role: Defender 1960-75
5ft.10ins. 11st.11lbs.
Born: Godstone, Surrey, 8th January 1945

CAREER: Surrey Schools/**SPURS** am. May 1960, pro. Jan 1962/Brighton and Hove Albion Jul 1975/Los Angeles Aztecs (USA) Apr 1977/Memphis Rogues (USA) Apr 1978/Chelmsford City Sep 1978/Crewe Alexandra non-contract Aug 1979/Oxford City Nov 1979/Woking.

Debut v Aston Villa (FL) (a) 16.9.1963

In 13 seasons as a first team player Phil Beal, surely one of the most loyal players ever on Spurs' books, scored only one goal, but it was a strike nobody present will ever forget. It came against Queens Park Rangers in January 1969 when Beal broke up a Ranger's attack on the edge of his own penalty box, raced out of defence, exchanged passes with Jimmy Greaves and cracked the ball home off the crossbar from the edge of the Rangers' penalty area. One goal in over 400 appearances is hardly an impressive scoring record, but England Youth international Beal was first and foremost a defender, a role in which he was more than impressive. As a home-grown player Beal had difficulty establishing himself as a regular member of the first team in the 1960s when Spurs were renowned as a club that bought the big names. His consistently

reliable performances, cool head under pressure and willingness to occupy any of the defensive positions were attributes that could not be ignored and by 1966-67 he was firmly entrenched as first choice right-back. Robbed of a place in the 1967 FA Cup winning side by a broken arm, he found stiff opposition from Joe Kinnear for that position when fit to return. However, his versatility soon allowed him to re-establish himself, this time in a tight-marking central defensive role. It was in that position he played in the League Cup winning teams of 1971 and 1973, the UEFA Cup winning team of 1972 and the losing team in the same competition in 1974. He was awarded a testimonial match, but it was reported that he lost money on the game against Bayern Munich in December 1973, due to the large fee agreed with the Germans. After Spurs, and a free transfer for one season at Brighton, Beal joined the flood of players nearing the end of their careers in the USA. He spent one year in Los Angeles and a spell in Memphis before returning to the UK in July 1979. He retired after a few games for Crewe, Oxford City and Woking during the 1979-80 season, during which he also returned to guest in Terry Naylor's testimonial match. Although Phil netted only one goal in nearly 500 games for Spurs, he scored in his first match for Los Angeles Aztecs!

Appearances:
League: 330 (3) apps. 1 gl.
FA Cup: 30 apps.
FL Cup: 27 apps.
Euro: 30 apps.
Others: 62 (1) apps.
Total: **479 (4) apps. 1 gl.**

BEAN, Ralph

Born: Hamilton, Bermuda, 1953

CAREER: Philadelphia Atoms (USA) 1975/North Village Community Club (Bermuda) by 1978/Vasco da Gama Volcanoes (Bermuda) 1981-82.

Debut v Bermuda Select XI (sub) (Fr) (a) 6.6.1979 (scored once)

Ralph "Gumbo" Bean is one of the Bermudan players who made a guest appearance for Spurs as a substitute at the end of Spurs' 1979 summer tour. Going on as a replacement for Milija Aleksic, who was playing in an outfield position due to the absence of so many players, Bean scored one of Spurs' goals in a 3-1 victory. He was one of Bermuda's most experienced players having played for Philadelphia Atoms in the North American Soccer League in 1975. His son, also Ralph, also played for North Village, Bermuda Hogges and the Bermuda national team and coached North Village.

Appearances:
Others: (1) app. 1 gl.
Total: **(1) app. 1 gl.**

BEARMAN, John Garland

Role: Inside-forward 1916-17

Debut v Watford (LFC) (h) 30.12.1916

A nephew of Spurs' director Fred Bearman, John Bearman was studying at Charterhouse when he made his one appearance for Spurs in a 3-0

London Football Combination victory over Watford at Highbury in December 1916. He later went to Exeter College, Oxford and played for Spurs reserves in 1922.

Appearances:
Others: 1 app.
Total: **1 app. 0 gls.**

BEASLEY, Albert Edward

Role: Forward or half-back 1942-46
5ft.7ins. 10st.8lbs.
Born: Stourbridge, Worcestershire, 27th July 1912
Died: Taunton, Somerset, 3rd March 1986

CAREER: Ambercote School/Brierley Hill Schools/Cookesley/Stourbridge Feb 1931/Arsenal May 1931/Huddersfield Town Oct 1936/(guest for Arsenal, Brentford, Charlton Athletic, Derby County, Fulham, Reading, **SPURS** and York City during World War Two)/Fulham Dec 1945/Bristol City Jul 1950, player-manager May 1952/Birmingham City joint manager Feb 1958, manager Sep 1958/retired May 1960/Fulham scout 1960-61/Dover manager May 1961-Apr 1964.

Debut v Charlton Athletic (FLS) (h) 12.9.1942 (scored once)

A war-time guest from Huddersfield Town, Pat Beasley was one of the most regular players to guest for Spurs during the Second World War. He was familiar with the North London area having spent six years with Arsenal, joining them despite keen interest from Aston Villa. A winger who played on either flank or could occupy an inside-forward position, he never truly established himself at Highbury, but with competition from the likes of Cliff Bastin, Joe Hulme and Alf Kirchen that was no disgrace. Although a member of the 1934 League Championship team, he was otherwise most unfortunate in his Highbury career. Selected for the 1932 FA Cup Final, but replaced at the last minute when Joe Hulme made a miraculous recovery from injury, he missed out on a League Championship medal in 1935 when he made only 20 appearances (one less than needed for a medal) and lost his place for the 1936 FA Cup Final when manager George Allison decided Arsenal could not do without Ted Drake, even though he had played only one game following a cartilage operation. Beasley finally played at Wembley in 1938, a member of the Huddersfield team that lost to Preston North End in the FA Cup Final. In April 1939, he made his one appearance for England, scoring against Scotland, and may well have added to his international honours but for the War. As it was, his only other honours came on the 1939 FA Tour of South Africa. During the War Beasley moved to half-back, a position he continued to occupy after his December 1945 transfer from Huddersfield to Fulham. He led Fulham to the Second Division title in 1948-49 before finishing his playing career as player-manager of Bristol City. Beasley then turned to management full-time taking City to the Third Division (South) title in 1955, but in January 1958 resigned. The following month he was appointed joint manager of Birmingham City, taking sole control when Arthur Turner left eight months later. He remained with Birmingham until his retirement in May 1960, served Fulham as a scout and then gave up retirement to have three years as manager of Dover.

Appearances:
Others: 98 apps. 31 gls.
Total: **98 apps. 31 gls.**

BEATON, Simon

Role: Half-back 1917-19
5ft.8ins. 10st.10lbs.
Born: Inverness, 1888
Died: Middlesbrough, 1959

CAREER: Aston Villa 1907/Newcastle United 1908/Middlesbrough Feb 1910/Newcastle United/Huddersfield Town May 1910/(guest for Crystal Palace and **SPURS** during World War One)/retired Jan 1919.

Debut v Queens Park Rangers (LFC) (a) 2.2.1918

Having failed to make the senior side at Villa Park or St James' Park, Sam Beaton joined Middlesbrough, but by the end of the 1909-10 season had made only two appearances in their League side. It was an expensive adventure for Middlesbrough. Beaton was still registered with Newcastle and 'Boro were fined 10 guineas for fielding him. Beaton returned to Newcastle to be immediately released. He signed for Huddersfield Town in time for their Football League debut season of 1910-11 and went on to make over 100 League appearances for them before the outbreak of the First World War. Beaton played for Spurs as a guest whilst in London. He retired at the end of hostilities.

Appearances:
Others: 9 apps.
Total: **9 apps. 0 gls.**

BEAVON, Michael Stuart

Role: Midfielder 1975-80
5ft.7ins. 10st.4lbs.
Born: Wolverhampton, Staffordshire, 30th November 1958

CAREER: Oxford Schools/**SPURS** app. Mar 1975, pro. Jul 1976/(Notts County loan Dec 1979)/Reading Jul 1980/Northampton Town Aug 1990, player-asst. manager Apr 1992/Newbury Town player-coach cs. 1993, player-asst. manager/Chesham United Feb 1995/Kintbury Rangers/Oxford City Feb 1996/Reading Town Jan 1998/Reading Borough/Pewsey during 1999-2000/Ardley United Oct 2001/Abbey Rangers coach by May 2005.

Debut v Manchester City (FL) (h) 3.2.1979 (Aldershot (sub) (Fr) (a) 19.9.1978)

Like many home-produced players, Stuart Beavon was unable to make the grade at White Hart Lane, but proved capable of doing a first-class job for a club lower down the Football League ladder. He made his first team debut in a friendly with Aldershot in September 1978, but his chances at Spurs were always going to be limited by the presence of players like Glenn Hoddle, Ossie Ardiles and the emerging Micky Hazard. After a spell on loan to Notts County, he was transferred to Reading. At Elm Park, he became an almost permanent fixture as midfield playmaker and his service to the Berkshire club was rewarded when he scored one of their goals in the surprise Simod Cup victory over Luton Town at Wembley in 1988. After ten years' service to Reading, Beavon was released on a free transfer and in the summer of 1990 joined Northampton Town. Three years later, another free transfer saw him leave League football to join Newbury Town as player-coach, and he continued to appear in non-League circles for some time. Even after giving up the game to concentrate on a painting and decorating business, he played for Ardley United alongside his striker son, Stuart junior, who went on to play for Wallingford, Didcot, Weymouth, Wycombe Wanderers and Preston North End. Stuart's father, Cyril, was a full-back with Wolverhampton Wanderers and Oxford United which accounts for the fact that although born in Wolverhampton Stuart played for Oxford as a schoolboy.

Appearances:
League: 3 (1) apps.
FL Cup: (1) app.
Others: 3 (12) apps. 3 gls
Total: **6 (14) apps. 3 gls.**

BEE

Role: Centre-forward 1918-19

CAREER: Sutton Town/(guest for **SPURS** during World War One).

Debut v Queens Park Rangers (LFC) (a) 25.12.1918

Bee made his only appearance for Spurs as a guest from Sutton Town on Christmas Day 1918.

Appearances:
Others: (1) app.
Total: **(1) app. 0 gls.**

BELL A C

Role: Centre-forward 1892-93

CAREER: Old St Marks/(**SPURS** guest Jan 1893).

Debut v Slough (SA) (a) 21.1.1893 (scored twice)

Initially playing under the name of "Sharpshot", "AC Bell" was another pseudonym of a prominent member of the Old St Marks club who helped Spurs out in January and February 1893. He certainly lived up to the original pseudonym, scoring five goals in his four appearances for Spurs in the Southern Alliance competition of 1892-93. That competition only lasted for one season, but may be regarded as a forerunner of the Southern League.

Appearances:
Others: 4 apps. 5 gls.
Total: **4 apps. 5 gls.**

BELL, Samuel

Role: Inside-forward 1934-37
5ft.8ins. 10st.3lbs.
Born: Burnhope, County Durham, 6th February 1909
Died: Southend, Essex, 6th January 1982

CAREER: Burnhope Institute/Norwich City Apr 1930/Luton Town Apr 1934/**SPURS** Mar 1935/Southend United May 1937/(guest for Millwall during World War Two)/Chelmsford City Jul 1948/Tonbridge Jul 1949.

Debut v Portsmouth (FL) (a) 9.3.1935

Although hailing from the North-East, it was with Norwich City that

Sam Bell started his senior football career in April 1930, before joining Luton Town four years later. Whilst principally an inside-forward, it was the 20 goals he scored for Luton in his one season with the Bedfordshire club that persuaded Percy Smith to secure his transfer. He finished his initial season in the first team, but the arrival of Jack Tresadern as manager saw Bell out of favour, and he spent the next term as little more than a reserve. Released in April 1937, he moved to Southend United and remained with the seaside club until 1948, later playing for Chelmsford City and Tonbridge. He continued to live in Southend where he worked as manager of the local greyhound stadium.

Appearances:
League: 15 apps. 6 gls.
FA Cup: 1 app.
Others: 1 app. 1 gl.
Total: **17 apps. 7 gls.**

BELLAMY, Walter Richard

Role: Winger 1926-35
5ft.8ins. 11st.2lbs.
Born: Tottenham, north London, 6th November 1904
Died: Hadley, Hertfordshire, 19th October 1978

CAREER: Leysian Mission/Tufnell Park/Dulwich Hamlet/**SPURS** pro. Feb 1927/Brighton and Hove Albion Sep 1935/(New Camp (Gibraltar) during World War Two).

Debut v Liverpool (FL) (a) 30.4.1927
(Millwall (LFACC) (a) 27.9.1926)

Playing for Dulwich Hamlet, Walter Bellamy had been associated with Spurs as an amateur for some time before signing professional. With the south London club, he had won many honours, played for the Isthmian League, the FA and Middlesex XIs, the Amateurs against the Professionals in the FA Charity Shield matches of 1925 and 1926 and won England amateur caps against Ireland in 1926 and 1927. A typical winger of his day, he got his head down and went for the goal-line before sending over accurate crosses for the centre-forward to feed off. His first team debut came in September 1926 when he played in a London FA Cup-tie, but there was no League debut until the end of the season. For most of his Spurs' career Bellamy had to compete first with England international Jimmy

Dimmock and then with Welsh international Willie Evans and rarely managed to get a lengthy run in the first team. He served Spurs for eight years before being released in May 1935 to join Brighton and Hove Albion where he spent just one season, not being retained in May 1936. Whilst serving in Gibraltar in 1942 and 1943 he played in the Gibraltar League for the New Camp club. After retiring from football Bellamy established a successful heating oil business in north London and was a regular visitor to White Hart Lane until his death on a golf course in 1978.

Appearances:
League: 70 apps. 9 gls.
FA Cup: 3 apps.
Others: 11 apps. 2 gls.
Total: 84 apps. 11 gls.

BENNETT, F J

Role: Goalkeeper 1941-42

CAREER: St James' Old Boys/Tottenham Argyle/Enfield/(SPURS during World War Two).

Debut v Fulham (LWL) (a) 1.11.1941

An amateur who trained at White Hart Lane, Bennett originally played for the St James' Old Boys club of Enfield Highway, but when they folded joined Tottenham Argyle, where he represented the Northern Suburban Intermediate League against the London League. He made three appearances for Spurs in the London War League in 1941-42

Appearances:
Others: 3 apps.
Total: 3 apps. 0 gls.

BENNETT, J Kenneth

Role: Outside-right 1918-19
Born: Sheffield, Yorkshire

CAREER: Nelson/Cardiff City/Southend United cs. 1914/(guest for Croydon Common, Luton Town and SPURS during World War One).

Debut v Arsenal (LFC) (a) 1.2.1919 (scored once)

Yet another of those players whose only games for Spurs were during a period of war, Ken Bennett had played for Nelson, Cardiff City and Southend United. With normal football disrupted, he joined Croydon Common during the early part of the First World War, but when they ceased playing turned out for Luton Town. He made four appearances for Spurs in the London Football Combination scoring his only goal on his debut against Arsenal at Highbury.

Appearances:
Others: 4 apps. 1 gl.
Total: 4 apps. 1 gl.

BENNETT, Kenneth Edgar

Role: Inside-forward 1940-41
Born: Wood Green, North London, 2nd October 1921
Died: Rochford, Essex, December 1994

CAREER: Wood Green Town/SPURS am. Aug 1939/(guest for Millwall and Southend United during World War Two)/Southend United Jun 1946/Bournemouth and Boscombe Athletic Jun 1948/Guildford City Jul 1949/Brighton and Hove Albion May 1950/Crystal Palace Jul 1953/Tonbridge Jul 1954/Headington United Dec 1954/Plessey FC/Clacton Town.

Debut v Chelsea (FLS) (a) 21.9.1940

Like his elder brother, Les, Ken Bennett started his football career with his local club Wood Green Town, where their father was trainer. He signed for Spurs during the Second World War, but it was only in the 1940-41 season that he made any appearances in the first team. Also like his brother, Ken was recognised as an inside-forward, although he also played on the wing and at half-back in his matches for Spurs. Released in 1946 he spent two years at Southend and a year each with Bournemouth and Guildford before enjoying the best spell of his career with Brighton and Hove Albion, for whom he made 101 Football League appearances netting 37 goals. Three years with Brighton were followed by one at Crystal Palace before the move into non-League circles. He finished his career with Clacton Town where brother Les was manager.

Appearances:
Others: 6 apps. 1 gl.
Total: 6 apps. 1 gl.

BENNETT, Leslie Donald

Role: Inside-forward 1939-55
5ft.11ins. 11st.0lbs.
Born: Wood Green, north London, 10th January 1918
Died: Hackney, London 29th April 1999

CAREER: Alexandra School/Wood Green Schools/London Schools/Middlesex Schools/Alexandra Old Boys/Tottenham Juniors 1935/Northfleet United 1938/SPURS am. Aug 1935, pro. May 1939/(guest for Distillery, Millwall and Torquay United during World War Two)/West Ham United Dec 1954/Clacton Town player-manager Jul 1956/Romford Aug 1959-May 1960.

Debut v Birmingham City (FL) (h) 31.8.1946
(Watford (FLS) (h) 11.11.1939 (scored three))

Tall, elegant and long-striding, Les Bennett was one of the stalwarts of the Spurs side for almost ten years after the Second World War and a crucial member of Arthur Rowe's remarkable "Push and Run" team that won the Second Division in 1950 and the League Championship the following season. A local discovery, he was placed with the Tottenham Juniors whilst at school before being sent along to the Northfleet nursery. Brought up to White Hart Lane in May 1939, his career was immediately put on hold by the outbreak of war, though the problems caused by the hostilities meant Bennett did have an early taste of senior football. He scored a hat-trick on his debut in November 1939 and went on to make eleven appearances in that season of turmoil, also guesting for Torquay United in what was to be their only season of war-time football. Military service in Egypt, India and Burma meant Bennett was rarely able to turn out for Spurs, but he guested for Distillery while on duty in the province and even represented the Northern Ireland Regional League against the League of Ireland in April 1943. On being demobbed he immediately

secured a place as first choice inside-right at White Hart Lane and, despite having lost some peak years before his football League debut at the age of 28, rarely relinquished the position until time began to take its toll. Bennett had everything an inside-forward needed; balance, speed, control, mobility, good positional sense, brilliant dribbling ability, a tremendous hunger for work, shrewdness and a flair for the unpredictable and unconventional that created goals both for colleagues and for himself. He was most unlucky never to represent England, but did make twelfth man for one match during the 1951-52 season. By 1954 Bennett was 36 years old and when Spurs signed Johnny Brooks, Les decided his future at White Hart Lane was limited. He was allowed to join West Ham United and spent just over one season at Upton Park, including a spell as captain. He then joined Clacton Town as manager, finishing his involvement with football with a brief spell at Romford. He later worked on the security staff at the University of Essex. Les' brother, Ken, was on Spurs' books during the Second World War. An inside-forward, he played during the 1940-41 season, but was released when the war was over and went on to make a good career in the game with Southend, Bournemouth, Brighton and Crystal Palace. In 1947 Les Bennett appeared in the film "The Odd Man".

Appearances:
League: 273 apps. 103 gls.
FA Cup: 22 apps. 14 gls.
Others: 84* apps. 52# gls.
Total: 379 apps. 169 gls.
* Includes 1 abandoned match.
# Includes 1 in an abandoned match.

BENT, Darren Ashley

Role: Striker 2007-10
5ft.11ins. 13st.4lbs.
Born: Tooting, London, 6th February 1984

CAREER: Godmanchester Rovers/Ipswich Town Scholar Jul 2000, pro. Jul 2001/Charlton Athletic Jun 2005/**SPURS** Jul 2007/Sunderland Aug 2009/Aston Villa Jan 2011/(Fulham loan Aug 2013)/(Brighton and Hove Albion loan Nov 2014)/Derby County loan Jan 2015, perm. Jun 2015.

Debut v Sunderland (sub) (PL) (a) 11.8.2007
(Stevenage Borough (Fr) (a) 7.7.2007)

With his goal-scoring record, the signing of Darren Bent for a record £16.5 million was considered a good investment on a player who could only get better. Sadly, for club and player, it did not turn out that way as Bent's career stalled at White Hart Lane. It was only after he had left that he got it back on track. A natural goal-scorer from his earliest days, Bent represented England at all levels as he worked his way through the youth ranks at Ipswich Town, making his Premier League debut as a 17-year-old during the Suffolk's clubs unsuccessful relegation battle of 2001-02. Bent honed his talents in the First Division, leading Ipswich's scoring charts, but lacking the support needed to take them back to the Premier League. While Ipswich missed out in the play-offs in 2005, Bent got a move into the top flight, signing for Charlton Athletic for £2.5 million. He proved at home in the Premier League, scoring almost a goal a game for Charlton and winning two full caps for England. Again, though, he lacked the necessary back-up and after two years Charlton were relegated. Strong-running, ready and willing to chase the ball down, hustle defenders and never afraid to have a crack at goal, Bent had quality players around him at Spurs and should have flourished, but he never lived up to expectations. With Dimitar Berbatov and Robbie Keane the first-choice strikers, Bent was rarely able to find a place in the team and when he did get a chance, his lack of the

finer subtleties required of all top strikers was all too evident. Bent was used to chasing balls played through or over a defence, the main man whose principle job was to score goals. With Spurs, he was expected to hold the ball up and bring others into the game. It was a job he struggled with. He did make two international appearances as a Spurs' player, but that was more a reflection on England's lack of quality strikers, than Bent's ability. Even with the departures of Berbatov and Keane and the arrival of a mis-firing Roman Pavlyuchenko, Bent still struggled, his confidence visually evaporating. He was not helped by Harry Redknapp's thoughtless comment after Bent had failed to convert an easy opening that Mrs Redknapp could have scored! It was a comment that marked the end of Bent's Tottenham career. When Sunderland made an offer that gave Spurs the chance to recover most of what they had laid out to sign Bent, they were quick to accept. At the Stadium of Light, Bent re-discovered his scoring touch so effectively that within 18 months Aston Villa had tabled a bid that could have reached £24 million for his services. The offer was one Sunderland could not refuse, particularly when Bent handed in a transfer request. A promising start to Bent's Villa career was halted by injury. When fit (and amid rumours further appearances would involve Villa having to pay more money to Sunderland), Bent found new manager Paul Lambert preferring the younger Christian Benteke as his main striker. With little prospect of displacing the young Belgian, Bent accepted a season long loan to Fulham, linking up again with Martin Jol. He struggled in a struggling team that was relegated to the Championship. Early in 2014-15 Villa manager Paul Lambert made it clear Bent did not figure in his plans, no matter how badly Villa were doing. Bent was sent out on loan, initially to Brighton and Hove Albion, then to Derby County. At Pride Park, he began to rebuild his reputation, helping Derby challenge for promotion until results fell away towards the end of the season. He did not do enough for Villa to offer him a new contract, but he had impressed Derby enough for them to offer him acceptable terms.

Appearances:
League: 32 (28) apps. 18 gls.
FA Cup: 1 app.
FL Cup: 1 (3) apps. 1 gl.
Euro: 9 (5) apps. 6 gls.
Others: 14 (3) apps. 18 gls.
Total: 57 (39) apps. 43 gls.

BENTALEB, Nabil

Role: Midfielder 2013-
5ft.10ins. 13st.4lbs.
Born: Lille (France) 24th November 1994

THE SPURS ALPHABET

CAREER: JS Lille Wazemmes (France) Sep 2001/Lille Olympique (France) Jul 2004/Royal Excelsior Mouscron (Belgium) Jul 2009/US Littoral Dunkerque (France) Jul 2010/Birmingham City trial Aug 2011// SPURS trial Sep 2011, Academy Scholar Jan 2012, pro. Sep 2012/(Schalke 04 (Germany) loan Aug 2016).

Debut v Southampton (sub) (PL) (a) 22.12.2013
(Swindon Town (Fr) (a) 16.7.2013)

When Tim Sherwood took on the first team coaching duties after the dismissal of Andre Villas-Boas, one of his first acts was to promote Nabil Bentaleb from the Under-21 squad Sherwood had previously been responsible for. It was a surprise decision, but while Spurs had plenty of attacking midfielders, they were in need of someone who could provide a defensive shield in front of a back line that was all too often exposed. Sherwood decided that Bentaleb was the man, a strong combative player not afraid to put his foot in; in many ways, a player from the same mould as Sherwood. Bentaleb had been with his local junior club, Wazemmes, from the age of six until 10, when he joined Lille's Academy. Released at 15, he did not give up dreams of making a career in football and after playing for RE Mouscron and Dunkerque found himself on trial at Birmingham City. It was there that Spurs spotted his talent, offered him a trial, followed by a Scholarship and finally professional terms. Sherwood's promotion of Bentaleb to the first team proved a sound decision. Bentaleb did the job required of him exceptionally well. In March 2014, he made his international debut for Algeria, opting to play for the country of his parents despite having collected one cap for France at Under-19 level and in the summer of 2014 he represented his country at the World Cup Finals. The departure of Sherwood and the signings of Benjamin Stambouli and Étienne Capoue saw Bentaleb's position in jeopardy. He rose to the challenge so well that after just one season it was the experienced French internationals who departed White Hart Lane. With Mauricio Pochettino giving Eric Dier an opportunity to impress in midfield, injury early in the 2015-16 season did Bentaleb no favours. The arrival of Victor Wanyama increased the competition for places and Bentaleb went on loan to Schalke 04 in an effort to get his career back on track. He quickly impressed the Germans enough for a deal to be done to make the move permanent at the end of the loan period.

Appearances:
League: 38 (8) apps.
FA Cup: 4 (1) apps.
FL Cup: 3 apps. 1 gl.
Euro: 7 (5) apps.
Others: 5 (5) apps.
Total: 57 (19) apps. 1 gl.

BENTLEY, David Michael

Role: Midfielder 2008-13
5ft.10ins. 12st.0lbs.
Born: Peterborough, Cambridgeshire, 27th August 1984

CAREER: Wormley/Arsenal Scholar Jul 2000, pro. Sep 2001/(Norwich City loan Aug 2004)/Blackburn Rovers loan Aug 2005, perm. Jan 2006/ SPURS Jul 2008/(Birmingham City loan Jan 2011)/(West Ham United loan Aug 2011)/(Rostov (Russia) loan Sept 2012)/(Blackburn Rovers loan Feb 2013)/released May 2013/retired Jun 2014.

Debut v Middlesbrough (PL) (a) 16.8.2008
(Celtic (sub) (Fr) (Rotterdam) 1.8.2008)

From his early days as an Arsenal scholar, David Bentley was marked down as a skilful midfield player destined for great things. With the same initials, shirt number, role, dead ball skills and happiness in the public glare, Bentley was seen as the natural successor to David Beckham, but while Beckham became a world superstar, Bentley's star hardly shone further than Blackburn. Progressing through the England youth teams as he climbed the ranks at Arsenal, Bentley made his senior debut for Arsenal in January 2003, but barely figured again as Arsenal seemed to prefer foreign talent to home grown youngsters. In 15 months Bentley struggled to take his number of first team appearances to nine, growing increasingly frustrated at the lack of opportunities. In an effort to advance his career he agitated for a loan move and was allowed to join Norwich City on a season long deal in August 2004. At last given the stage on which to perform, he began to look the part, proving increasingly influential from a position wide right of midfield even as Norwich were relegated. A further season long loan was then arranged with Blackburn Rovers, but so well did Bentley perform that Blackburn pushed through a permanent deal in January 2006. For three seasons Bentley pulled Rovers' attacking strings from his wide right role in a fashion very similar to that of Beckham. Neither were blessed with great pace or dribbling ability but both were adept at finding the space to put over accurate centres and were free-kick specialists, not only creating chances but also scoring from range. Despite incurring public wrath when he cited "fatigue" for his refusal to join the England Under-21 squad for the 2007 European championships, Bentley's talent was too good to be ignored and in the following season he played six games for the full England team. His career looked set to really take off when he joined Spurs for a reported £15 million fee, an early, perhaps the only, highlight coming in October 2008 when he scored with an incredible 45-yard volley against Arsenal at the Emirates. Sadly, it was all downhill from there. Unable to find his form, Bentley became a peripheral figure, drifting aimlessly and failing to have any impact on games. More often than not on the bench, he was rarely called upon and a move seemed the only hope of Bentley resurrecting his career. His hefty wages proved a problem though and Bentley had to content himself with loan moves to West Ham, Blackburn and the Russian side, Rostov. It was no surprise when Spurs announced in May 2013 that Bentley was being released. More of a surprise was that, despite many clubs reportedly being interested in him, he was unable to find a new stage on which to display his talents. He retired before he was 30, a talent wasted.

Appearances:
League: 32 (10) apps. 3 gls.
FA Cup: 6 (1) apps. 1 gl.
FL Cup: 7 (1) apps. 1 gl.
Euro: 5 apps. 1 gl.
Others: 10 (4) apps. 3 gls.
Total: 60 (16) apps. 9 gls.

BENTLEY, Frank William

Role: Half-back 1908-12
5ft.9ins. 11st.0lbs.
Born: Butt Lane, Staffordshire, 9th October 1886
Died: Hartshill, Stoke-On-Trent, Staffordshire, 19th November 1958

CAREER: Butt Lane Swifts/Stoke/**SPURS** Jul 1908/Brentford Aug 1912/Butt Lane White Star 1914/Butt Lane by 1920.

Debut v Notts County (FL) (h) 30.10.1909
(Queens Park Rangers (LFACC) (h) 5.10.1908)

Signed from Stoke just after Spurs had been voted into the Football League in place of his former club, Frank Bentley made his first team debut in a London FA Charity Cup tie in October 1908, but did not make a League appearance for Spurs in their first League season. Indeed, it was not until October 1909 that he was selected for the League side, being brought in to strengthen the defence after Spurs had picked up only five points from their first eight games in the First Division. When Bentley did make his debut, it was to last only 50 minutes, as the game, at Preston North End, was abandoned due to rain, and so his official League debut came seven days later. In a difficult season when Spurs only managed to finish 15th out of the 20 clubs in the First Division, Bentley could not establish himself and the story was identical the next season. He was clearly not good enough for First Division football and on his release in July 1912 joined Southern League Brentford where he played for two years.

Appearances:
League: 38* apps.
FA Cup: 5 apps.
Others: 10 apps.
Total: 53 apps. 0 gls.
* Includes 1 abandoned match.

BERBATOV, Dimitar Ivanov

Role: Striker 2006-2009
6ft.2ins. 13st.0lbs.
Born: Blagoevgrad, Bulgaria, 30th January 1981

CAREER: Pirin Blagoevgrad (Bulgaria)/CSKA Sofia (Bulgaria) 1997/Bayer 04 Leverkusen (Germany) Jan 2001/**SPURS** Jul 2006/Manchester United Aug 2008/Fulham Aug 2012/Monaco (France) Jan 2014/PAOK (Greece) Sep 2015.

Debut v Bolton Wanderers (PL) (a) 19.8.2006
(v Girondins de Bordeaux (Fr) (Albertville) 13.7.2006)

It was obvious within weeks of his signing that while Spurs had laid out a near club record £10.9 million to secure the services of Dimitar Berbatov, Martin Jol had got a real bargain. The Bulgarian striker, known as "The devil with an angel's face", began his career with his local club Pirin, where his father Ivan had played, but was soon spirited away to one of his country's biggest clubs, CSKA Sofia, another of his father's former clubs. Breaking into the team as an 18-year old he quickly showed the cool finishing skills Spurs fans came to admire and by November 1999 had taken his talents onto the international stage, collecting his first cap against Greece. Bayer Leverkusen wasted no time in swooping for his signature but it took "Berba" time to settle in Germany. While he was establishing himself as his country's first choice striker, he found it more difficult to make his mark in the tougher Bundesliga, but as he got to know those around him so the goals began to flow and envious glances were cast in the direction of the Bay Arena. Many of Europe's top clubs were interested in signing him, but Martin Jol showed great determination to bring Berbatov to White Hart Lane. From the start, it was obvious Berbatov would bring something different to Spurs. His silky skills and subtlety did not catch the eye immediately, but they caused as much damage as the power and pace that was becoming a pre-requisite for many strikers. While tall and rangy, Berbatov did not appear muscular but even the toughest of defenders found he would not shy away from the physical side of the game and had a knack of using their strength to his advantage as he would draw them in before twisting away. His all-round game made him the ideal front man. He climbed well, whether to get a header on goal or lay the ball off to a fast-breaking colleague, but could hold the ball up to allow teammates to make runs into space and had an eye for the pass any midfield creator would envy. Blistering pace was not one of his attributes, but he was deceptively fast at covering the ground and no slouch at running with the ball, perfect balance and control keeping it just out of his opponent's reach. At times Berbatov seemed to almost float across the surface, as graceful and elegant as a ballet dancer. When an opening presented itself Berbatov was quick to seize the chance with instant power and precision, whether from inside the six-yard box or thirty yards from goal, but he was far more than a goal-scorer. With an appreciation of space and the ability to create time for himself he had a wonderful talent for bringing others into the game. At Leverkusen Berbatov formed a deadly partnership with Andriy Voronin, at White Hart Lane, his strike partner, whether Robbie Keane or Jermain Defoe, found Berbatov the ideal foil, opening defences for them, but also on hand to finish off the chances they created. Having helped Spurs win the Carling Cup in 2008, the stage seemed set for Berbatov to spearhead Spurs' attempts to re-join the upper echelons of English football, but in the summer of 2009, Manchester United announced that they wanted to sign him. It was not an approach appreciated by Spurs or its supporters but the idea of playing for the biggest club in England, and in the Champions League, was enough to turn Berbatov's head. Having made it clear he wanted to move, it was left to Spurs' chairman, Daniel Levy, to play hardball with United to secure the best deal for the club. He took it to the edge, a deal of over £31 million being agreed on the last day of the transfer window. While it was described as a dream move for Berbatov, it was not to turn out that way. He finished his first

season at Old Trafford with a Premier League winner's medal but, his contribution was not without some criticism. While his languid style was accepted at Spurs, at United it was seen as a sign of laziness, as if he was not working hard enough. It was unfair criticism for Berbatov was not one to hare around the pitch. He preferred to reserve his hard work for when it really mattered. It was a style that while more effective, drew unfavourable comparisons with the likes of Carlos Tevez and Wayne Rooney and meant that no matter how many goals he scored or created, he could never be truly sure of his position.

Berbatov collected a Carling Cup winners' medal in 2010 and another Premier League title the following season, but with the signing of Robin Van Persie, his days in Manchester were numbered. When Martin Jol called, Berbatov accepted a move to Fulham. The focal point of the team, Berbatov quickly showed he had lost none of the class that will forever be his trademark. With Fulham struggling, Berbatov moved on to Monaco and PAOK. He played a total of 77 full internationals for Bulgaria, scoring 48 goals and captaining his country for four years before retiring from the international game in May 2010.

Appearances:
League: 63 (7) apps. 27 gls.
FA Cup: 6 (1) apps. 5 gls.
FL Cup: 7 (2) apps. 2 gls.
Euro: 15 (1) apps. 11 gls.
Others: 13 (2) apps. 7 gls.
Total: 104 (13) apps. 52 gls.

BERGSSON, Guðni

Role: Defender 1988-1993
6ft.1ins. 12st.3lbs.
Born: Reykjavik, Iceland, 21st July 1965

CAREER: Valur/Aston Villa trial 1985/(TSV 1860 Munich loan Mar 1988)/SPURS trial Nov 1988, pro. Feb 1989/released Sep 1993/Valur Jan 1994/Crystal Palace trial Dec 1994/SPURS trial Jan 1995/Bolton Wanderers Mar 1995/retired May 2003/Bolton Wanderers scout/Icelandic FA chairman Feb 2017.

Debut v Luton Town (FL) (h) 26.12.1988

When Icelandic Player of the Year Guðni Bergsson joined Spurs on trial in November 1988 he was a law student at Reykjavik University, playing as an amateur for his local club, Valur. One of Iceland's most outstanding prospects he had helped Valur win the Icelandic League title in 1987 and Icelandic Cup in 1988. With 24 caps to his credit, having also represented his country at junior, youth and Under-21 level, he had made his Icelandic League debut in 1983, won his first cap against the Faroe Islands in August 1984 and in 1985 had an unsuccessful trial with Aston Villa. Bergsson was to do much better at White Hart Lane, making his League debut in December 1988 when, although primarily regarded as a sweeper, he performed so well at left-back he was immediately offered professional terms. At the time, he only had a temporary work permit, but full clearance was soon forthcoming and in February 1989 he joined the paid ranks, a bargain signing as no transfer fee was involved. Although unable to maintain a regular place in the side, he proved a valuable member of the first team squad, able to play with some style in any of the defensive positions. A quiet, unassuming player, he continued to add to his international honours winning his first cap as a Spurs' player in May 1989 when he played against the England "B" side on their short end of season tour. Captain of his country, but unable to get in the Spurs team early in the 1993-94 season, he was given a free transfer and returned to Iceland to continue his law studies and play for Valur. With his studies completed, he returned to England, had a trial with Crystal Palace and returned to White Hart Lane to try and impress Ossie Ardiles. When an offer came in from Bolton he was keen to accept and, with Spurs having retained his registration, a fee of £65,000 was agreed. A regular at the heart of their defence he was unable to prevent their relegation from the Premier League after just one season. That was the start of a yo-yo period that saw Bolton promoted and relegated before firmly establishing themselves in the Premier League. Bergsson became a modern-day legend, making well over 250 appearances for the Trotters in eight years. For much of that time he captained his country but in September 1997 he fell out with manager Guðjón Thordarson over whether he should return direct to England from Bucharest or, as the manager wanted, via Reykjavik. The dispute led to Bergsson making himself unavailable for future internationals after winning 77 caps, although he did return to the international team late 2002-03. Having carved a niche for himself in Bolton's history, Bergsson retired in May 2003 and returned to Iceland to practise law. He continued to scout for Bolton while acting as President of the club's ex-players' association, and then moved into the administrative side of the game when elected Chairman of the Icelandic FA.

Appearances:
League: 51 (20) apps. 2 gls.
FA Cup: 2 (2) apps.
FL Cup: 4 (2) apps.
Euro: 5 (1) apps.
Others: 26 (9) apps. 1 gl.
Total: 88 (34) apps. 3 gls.

BERRY, Frank

Role: Winger 1900-01

CAREER: Edmonton White Star/SPURS trial Oct 1900, pro. Oct 1900/Clapton Orient cs. 1901.

Debut v Gravesend United (SL) (a) 3.4.1901
(Luton Town (Fr) (h) 22.10.1900)

An Edmonton lad playing for one of the local junior clubs, Frank Berry made his Spurs' debut as a trialist in a friendly match in October 1900 when he played at outside-right in the absence of Tom Smith. He had only played his first reserve match two days earlier and, although described as being a "bit nervous", obviously did enough, as Spurs then signed him as a professional. He spent the rest of the season in the reserves, making only two more senior appearances, both in April 1901 when the first team was rested prior to important FA Cup ties and the reserve team fulfilled their fixtures. At the end of the season he was released and returned to his junior club although he also turned out for Clapton Orient's reserves.

Appearances:
Southern: 1 app.
Others: 2 apps.
Total: 3 apps. 0 gls.

BERRY, William Alexander

Role: Centre-forward 1903-07
5ft.7ins. 10st.12lbs.
Born: Sunderland, September qtr. 1884
Died: 1st March 1943

CAREER: Oakhill/Sunderland Royal Rovers/Sunderland Sep 1902/SPURS Jan 1904/Manchester United Nov 1906/Stockport County Feb 1909/Sunderland Royal Rovers cs. 1910.

Debut v Plymouth Argyle (WL) (h) 29.2.1904 (scored once)

"Burglar" Berry, as he was nicknamed, joined Spurs having failed to make the grade with his home town club Sunderland, but was never more than a reserve at White Hart Lane. He had few opportunities to impress, for at the time the great Vivian J Woodward was Spurs' regular centre-forward and he was undoubtedly the best in the country in that position. However, Berry stayed with Spurs as Woodward's understudy for almost three years before moving to Manchester United where he was required to fill the gap created by the suspension of Billy Meredith following the illegal payments scandal. Meredith had signed for United from Manchester City in May 1906, but his subsequent suspension meant he would not be available until January 1907. Berry stayed with United for almost 18 months, but with few opportunities moved on to Stockport County where he played for two seasons before returning to the North East.

Appearances:
Southern: 19 apps. 1 gl.
FA Cup: 1 app.
Others: 20 apps. 12 gls.
Total: 40 apps. 13 gls.

BERTI, Nicola

Role: Midfielder 1997-99
6ft.1ins. 12st.3lbs.
Born: Salsomaggiore Terme, Italy 14th April 1967

CAREER: Parma (Italy) 1982/Fiorentina (Italy) cs. 1985/Internazionale (Italy) cs. 1988/SPURS Jan 1998/Deportivo Alavés (Spain) Dec 1998-May 1999/Charlton Athletic trial Oct 1999/Northern Spirit (Australia) Dec 1999.

Debut v Manchester United (PL) (a) 10.1.1998

One of Italy's most renowned midfielders, Nicola Berti was well into the veteran stage when he joined Spurs in January 1998 as Christian Gross's side struggled against the spectre of relegation. A tough-tackling, no-nonsense battler, Berti had a very English style about his play, relishing a hard midfield battle. In addition, he still possessed the polish and style expected of the Italians. Berti had spent almost ten years with Inter, the engine room of the team that won the Scudetto in 1988-89 and the UEFA Cup in 1991, 1994 and 1998. He had also collected 39 full caps for his country, a member of the team that only lost the 1994 World Cup final to Brazil on penalties. Spurs did not see the best of Berti. Injury had seen him on the side-lines at Milan for a year before his arrival at White Hart Lane, but his experience and willingness to battle was a definite factor in helping Gross's side climb away from the foot of the table. With the departure of Gross and the arrival of George Graham, Berti found himself out of favour. Rarely given a chance, he was allowed to move to Alavés in December 1998 where he played for the rest of the season. After that he had a brief flirtation with Australian football, but age had taken its toll and on poor quality pitches, and often with even poorer quality players around him, he was not a success. He soon returned to Italy to take up a career in television.

Appearances:
League: 21 apps. 3 gls.
FA Cup: 2 apps.
Others: 7 (2) apps. 1 gl.
Total: 30 (2) apps. 4 gls.

BEVERIDGE, T

Role: Right-back 1895-96

CAREER: Royal Scots/SPURS guest Feb 1896/Northfleet.

Debut v Luton Town (Fr) (a) 10.2.1896

A member of the Royal Scots, Beveridge made his only appearance for Spurs in a friendly match at Luton Town two days after playing for the soldiers against Spurs. He played in a weak Spurs' team that included his fellow soldier Buchan as Spurs lost 0-9. Later in the season he turned out for Spurs' Southern League rivals Northfleet.

Appearances:
Others: 1 app.
Total: 1 app. 0 gls.

BING, Thomas Edward

Role: Winger 1954-58
5ft.10ins. 10st.3lbs.
Born: Broadstairs, Kent, 24th November 1931
Died: Margate, Kent, 18th May 2015

CAREER: St Johns Secondary School/Margate Schools/Margate 1947, part-time pro 1949, (guest for professional side in Germany during 1952-53) full pro. Nov 1953/SPURS Sep 1954/Margate Jul 1959-Jan 1962, 1963-Nov 1963, scout, coach.

Debut v Bolton Wanderers (FL) (a) 19.10.1957
(Essex County All Stars (sub) (Fr) (a) 22.5.1957)

Tommy Bing had been a part-timer with Margate when signed by Spurs in the face of competition from Wolverhampton Wanderers and West Ham United. He had been with Margate since he was 16-years old although he had only progressed to their first team shortly before joining Spurs, replacing his brother, Doug, who had signed for West Ham United. Bing had been under scrutiny for some time, but Spurs decided to move for him following a reserve team friendly when Bing had been pitched against Bill Nicholson. Bing was, reportedly, suddenly withdrawn during a match by his manager and former Spurs' forward, Almer Hall, in order to sign for Spurs. Recognised as a wing-half or inside-forward when he made the move to White Hart Lane, Bing was soon moved to the outside-right berth. He made his first team debut as a substitute in a friendly against the Essex County All Stars during Spurs' 1957 North American tour, but his only League game was in October 1957 when he stood in for Terry Medwin who was playing for Wales against England. Bing never got another look-in at Spurs before returning to Margate. Unfortunately, his career back in Kent was soon disrupted by injury and a cartilage problem forced him to retire in January 1962. He attempted a comeback the following season, but without success. Doug Bing spent four and a half years with West Ham United before also returning to Margate.

Appearances:
League: 1 app.
Others: 2 (2) apps.
Total: 3 (2) apps. 0 gls.

BIRD

Role: Outside-left 1917-18

Debut v Brentford (LFC) (a) 5.1.1918

When Spurs arrived for a match at Brentford in January 1918 they were a player short. Brentford allowed Bird, one of the younger members of their staff, to turn out for Spurs.

Appearances:
Others: 1 app.
Total: 1 app. 0 gls.

BIRD, J

Role: Outside-left 1887-88

Debut v Hendon (LSC) (a) 8.10.1887

Bird is known to have made only one first team appearances for Spurs, in a 0-6 defeat at the hands of Hendon in a London Senior Cup-tie.

Appearances:
Others: 1 app.
Total: 1 app. 0 gls.

BIRNIE, Edward Lawson

Role: Half-back 1910-11
5ft.10ins. 12st.9lbs.
Born: Sunderland, 25th August 1878
Died: Rochford, Essex, 22nd December 1935

CAREER: Sunderland Seaburn 1896/Northumberland/Newcastle United Jun 1898/Crystal Palace May 1905/Chelsea Aug 1906/**SPURS** Jul 1910/Mulheim (Germany) player-coach-secretary Aug 1911/Rochdale Jul 1912/Newcastle City player-manager/Leyton player-manager Jul 1914/Sunderland asst. trainer Aug 1919/Rochdale trainer Jun 1921/Southend United manager Jan 1922-Apr 1934/manager and coach in Germany 1934.

Debut v Middlesbrough (FL) (a) 4.10.1910
(Clapton Orient (LFACC) (h) 19.9.1910)

Ted Birnie was unable to claim a regular first team place with Newcastle in the early years of the 20th century and joined the newly-formed Crystal Palace, their first captain. Originally a winger, he moved to half-back and, after only one season in south London, joined Chelsea. He became a regular in their League side until early in the 1909-10 season when he lost his place after breaking a leg. Not retained at the end of the season, he joined Spurs, but only stayed for one season making just five senior appearances. Released in the summer of 1911 he took up a playing plus coaching/secretarial position with Mulheim in Germany and spent one year there before returning to end his senior playing career with Rochdale. After ending his playing days and gaining managerial experience at non-League level, he was appointed assistant trainer with his native Sunderland and Rochdale. He then moved onto the management side of the game, reaching his peak with Southend United. He remained with the Essex club until 1934 when he went back to coach in Germany, but returned after a year to settle in Southend where he passed away.

Appearances:
League: 4 apps. 1 gl.
Others: 1 app.
Total: 5 apps. 1 gl.

BLACK, David George

Role: Outside-left 1897-98
5ft.5ins. 10st.0lbs.
Born: Irvine, Ayrshire, 29th March 1868
Died: 1940

CAREER: Rovers FC/Hurlford/Grimsby Town May 1889/Middlesbrough May 1891/Wolverhampton Wanderers Jul 1893/Burnley Dec 1896/**SPURS** May 1897/Woolwich Arsenal May 1898/Clyde Sep 1898/retired 1900.

Debut v Sheppey United (SL) (a) 4.9.1897
(Glossop North End (Fr) (h) 2.9.1897 (scored once))

David Black was signed from Burnley in May 1897 to replace Richard McElhaney when, as was the way in those days, almost the entire forward line moved on. At 29 he was nearing the end of a career that had started with Rovers FC and Hurlford, with whom he had played for Scotland against Ireland in March 1889. He then played for Grimsby Town in their first two seasons in the Football Alliance, followed that with two years at Middlesbrough and then moved to Wolverhampton Wanderers. He scored their goal in the 1896 FA Cup Final defeat by Sheffield Wednesday before transferring to Burnley. A diminutive but speedy, direct winger who knew where the goal was and went for it, he was a great success at Northumberland Park, missing only three competitive matches throughout the whole season, a testament to his strength and resilience in days when opposing full-backs would mete out

uncompromisingly rough treatment to dangerous opponents. Black was only absent from the team in January 1898 and that was due to injury. At the end of the season he moved to Woolwich Arsenal, but had no opportunity to establish himself before joining Clyde. He retired after two years at Clyde.

Appearances:
Southern: 20 apps. 8 gls.
FA Cup: 2 apps. 2 gls.
Others: 35 apps. 15 gls.
Total: 57 apps. 25 gls.

BLAIR, James

Role: Centre-forward 1945-46
Born: Glasgow

CAREER: Wood Green Town Aug 1945/SPURS am. Feb 1946.

Debut v Arsenal (FLS) (a) 9.2.1946 (scored once)

Twenty-five-year-old Jimmy Blair made two guest appearances for Spurs in the transitional 1945-46 season. His football experience had been limited to junior clubs in his native Glasgow until joining Wood Green, but he made an immediate impact scoring 56 goals by the time he Spurs signed him to amateur forms. Within days of signing he made his debut, scoring Spurs' goal in a 1-1 draw with Arsenal. His only other appearance came a week later when the clubs played the return fixture. Both matches were played at White Hart Lane for, although no longer required for war-work, Highbury had suffered quite severe bomb damage and in the view of the authorities, there were more important buildings to be repaired than football grounds.

Appearances:
Others: 2 apps. 1 gl.
Total: 2 apps. 1 gl.

BLAIR, John Guthrie

Role: Inside-forward 1925-28
5ft.11ins. 12st.6lbs.

Born: Neilston, Renfrewshire, 23rd August 1905
Died: Kilmarnock, Ayrshire, 1st January 1972

CAREER: Thornliebank/Neilston/Aston Villa/Neilston Victoria/Glasgow Pollock/Third Lanark May 1923/SPURS Apr 1926/Sheffield United Nov 1927/Fordsons, Cork (Ireland) Nov 1929-1932.

Debut v Everton (FL) (h) 28.8.1926 (scored once) (West Ham United (Fr) (a) 3.5.1926 (scored once))

John Blair had an outstanding season with Third Lanark in 1925-26 and, whilst he had only eighteen months experience of senior football, Spurs decided to invest in his talent. Signed after the 1926 transfer deadline, he made a goal-scoring first team debut in a friendly at West Ham United, but had to wait until the start of the following season before making his League debut. Blair scored nine goals in his first eleven League games for Spurs before being side-lined by injury, but, whilst regaining his first team place, he could not recapture his goal-scoring form. The emergence of Taffy O'Callaghan saw Blair out of favour come the end of the campaign. He managed to get back in the team early the following season, but could not secure his place and when Sheffield United made an offer, Spurs allowed him to leave.

Appearances:
League: 29 apps. 15 gls.
FA Cup: 1 app.
Others: 2 apps. 1 gl.
Total: 32 apps. 16 gls.

BLAKE, Frederick James Carter

Role: Centre-forward 1918-19
Born: Walthamstow, London, 1892

CAREER: Avenue Old Boys/Bronze Athletic/Clapton Orient/Ilford 1911/ (guest for Clapton Orient and Queens Park Rangers during World War One)/SPURS trial Oct 1918/Walthamstow Grange 1923/Clapton 1924/ Argonauts committee Feb 1929/Catford Wanderers 1929, secretary.

Debut v Arsenal (LFC) (a) 12.10.1918

Captain Blake, to give him his full title at the time, was an army officer who made one appearance for Spurs as a trialist in October 1918 in a London Football Combination match with Arsenal. The centre-forward position was one Spurs were having a great deal of difficulty trying to fill at the time, but Blake was not a success and his association with the club finished after that one game. Blake had started his football career with Avenue Old Boys, the club that went on to become Walthamstow Avenue and Bronze Athletic, a club in Deptford. An amateur on Clapton Orient's books, in 1911 he joined Ilford and, playing at full-back, went on to give them incredible service over the next twelve years, He then had a brief spell with Walthamstow Grange before switching to Clapton, helping them win the FA Amateur Cup in 1924 and 1925.

Appearances:
Others: 1 app.
Total: 1 app. 0 gls.

BLAKE, Herbert Charles Edwin

Role: Goalkeeper 1921-24
5ft.10ins. 11st.9lbs.
Born: Bristol, 26th August 1894
Died: Bristol, 21st January 1958

CAREER: Eastville School/Fishponds Amateurs/Ovendale/St Philips Adult School/Fishponds City/Glenmore/Gloucestershire/Bristol City trial and perm. Oct 1914/Mid-Rhondda cs. 1915/Preston North End trial Oct 1919/Mid-Rhondda 1919/**SPURS** Feb 1922/Kettering Jun 1925/retired 1929.

Debut v Sunderland (FL) (a) 5.4.1922

Throughout the 1920s Spurs had concerns over the goalkeeping position and Bert Blake was one of several players obtained to try and solve the problem. After the war, the position had been held by Bill Jacques, apart from a brief spell when Alex Hunter had taken over, but in 1921-22 Jacques contracted the illness which eventually led to his premature death. Spurs felt Hunter was not consistent enough for First Division football and so Blake was acquired from Mid-Rhondda when that club was on the verge of breaking up. He was 27-years old and had played most of his career with the Welsh club, having made just one appearance for Bristol City in the 1914-15 season. He made his League debut for Spurs in April 1922, kept his place for the rest of the season and remained first choice 'keeper for most of the one that followed. However, the defence still let in too many goals and towards the end of 1922-23 Blake's place was taken by Geordie Maddison. Blake was to play few more League games and the arrival of Fred Hinton spelt the end of his career at White Hart Lane. He stayed with the club until April 1925 when he was given a free transfer, and moved to Kettering.

Appearances:
League: 51 apps.
FA Cup: 5 apps.
Others: 5 apps.
Total: 61 apps. 0 gls.

BLAKE, John Joseph

Role: Outside-left 1905-06
5ft.10ins. 11st.4lbs.
Born: Belchamp Walter, Essex, October qtr. 1882
Died: Sholing, Southampton, Hampshire, 23rd February 1931

CAREER: Woodbridge Grammar School/Colchester Crown/Church of England Young Men's Society/Ilford/**SPURS** guest Oct 1905/Cowes/Southampton am. Dec 1907, pro. May 1908/(Thorneycrofts guest during World War One)/Thorneycrofts Mar 1920.

Debut v Fulham (WL) (h) 16.10.1905

An amateur with Ilford, Joe Blake made three appearances for Spurs in the Western League, the minor first team League in which Spurs competed at the time, in 1905-06. The target of several professional sides, he is one of many players of the period who played in such matches by way of a trial, but were not subsequently taken on. In Blake's case Spurs undoubtedly made a mistake for, after playing for Cowes, he joined Southampton and as a skilful dribbler with an accurate centre rendered great service to the South Coast club until the outbreak of the First World War. At that time, he worked in Thorneycrofts shipyards and turned out for both Thorneycrofts and Southampton during the conflict. When peace returned he went back to Southampton on a permanent basis, but made only a handful of further appearances before leaving in March 1920 to re-join Thorneycrofts.

Appearances:
Others: 3 apps. 1 gl.
Total: 3 apps. 1 gl.

BLANCHFLOWER, Robert Dennis

Role: Half-back 1954-64
5ft.10ins. 10st.7lbs.
Born: Belfast, 10th February 1926
Died: Cobham, Surrey, 9th December 1993

CAREER: Belfast Technical College/Connsbrook 1940/Bloomfield United 1941/Glentoran am. Dec 1945, pro. Jan 1946/(guest for Swindon Town during World War Two)/Barnsley Apr 1949/Aston Villa Mar 1951/**SPURS** Dec 1954/Toronto City (Canada) guest Jun 1961/(Boksburg (South Africa) guest May 1962)/(Durban City (South Africa) guest Jun 1963)/retired Jun 1964/Durban City (South Africa) guest coach 1965/Northern Ireland manager Jun 1976-Nov 1978/Chelsea manager Dec 1978-Sep 1979.

Debut v Manchester City (FL) (a) 11.12.1954

Danny Blanchflower is quite simply one of the most famous players in Spurs history, not merely because he captained the club to its greatest ever triumph of the League and FA Cup "Double" in 1961, but also because he was one of the finest players ever to wear a Spurs shirt. He had every attribute an attacking wing-half needed. He was cool, skilful, artful and graceful, a perfect passer of the ball, a superb reader of the game, in short, poetry in motion. Never flustered and always in total command, he was an absolute delight to watch. More than that though, he was a truly inspirational captain who earned the genuine respect of the players around him. A great theorist and tactician himself, Danny could take the manager's ideas and plans from the dressing room onto the pitch and put them into action; if necessary, honing, refining and developing them with his own unique style and panache as situations demanded. His illustrious career started with Glentoran, who were managed by former Spurs player Frank Grice. He played once for Swindon Town during the war and by the time of his £6,500 transfer to Barnsley had represented the Irish League five times and the Northern Ireland Regional League once, although he had not played for his country. That was put to rights within six months of his becoming a full-time professional at Barnsley with his international debut against Scotland in October 1949. For the next 13 years he was almost ever-present in the Northern Ireland team, captaining it for most of that time and setting a record of 56 appearances. Having cost Aston Villa £15,000 in 1951, Arthur Rowe secured Blanchflower's transfer for £30,000 in December 1954 as replacement for the ageing Bill Nicholson. From his Spurs' debut until his retirement he was rarely absent from the team unless injured or on international duty. Footballer of the Year for 1957-58, he led Northern Ireland in their surprisingly successful World Cup campaign of 1958, a campaign that may have been even better had Danny's brother, Manchester United's Jackie, not been injured in the Munich Air Disaster. The "Double" was followed by the Footballer of the Year award for the second time and a summer spent playing in Canada. He then captained Spurs to the FA Cup Final victory of 1962 and Britain's first European trophy, the European Cup-Winners Cup in 1963. Having won four caps with Barnsley and nine with Aston Villa he added a further 43 as a Spurs' player and also played for Great Britain against Europe in August 1955 and the Football League against the Irish League in October 1960. Troubled by a knee injury for some time, Blanchflower retired from football on 30th June 1964. He then made a career for himself in journalism, displaying in his writing the same innovative, forceful and at times controversial attributes that had marked his playing career. Such was his high standing in the football world that, despite an absence of several years from the game, he had spells as manager both of Chelsea and Northern Ireland. In May 1990 Blanchflower received an honour never open to him in his playing days, when Spurs met a Northern Ireland XI in a Benefit match for one of the true all-time greats in the club's history.

Appearances:
League: 337 apps. 15 gls.
FA Cup: 33 apps. 4 gls.
Euro: 12 apps. 2 gls.
Others: 54 (1) apps. 6 gls.
Total: 436 (1) apps. 27 gls.

BLISS, Herbert

Role: Inside-forward 1911-23
5ft.6ins. 10st.1lbs.
Born: Willenhall, Staffordshire, 29th March 1890
Died: Wood Green, London, 14th June 1968

CAREER: New Invention/Bilston United/Willenhall Swifts/Willenhall Pickwick/**SPURS** Apr 1912/Clapton Orient Dec 1922/Bournemouth and Boscombe Athletic Jul 1925-May 1926/Wellington Town/Hednesford Town cs. 1932.

Debut v Manchester City (FL) (h) 8.4.1912

Bert Bliss was spotted by Spurs playing for Birmingham and District Juniors against Scotland Juniors in March 1912. So impressed were they by the little inside-left with a "blistering" shot, that within a month his transfer had been secured and he had made his Football League debut. A confident, shoot-on-sight player, somewhat reminiscent of the legendary Steve Bloomer, he quickly fitted into the team, finishing top scorer with 21 goals in the miserable 1914-15 season that saw Spurs finish bottom of Division One. In the first two seasons of war-time football it was Bliss's goals that helped Spurs do so well in the London Football Combination and when service demands prevented him playing, Spurs' performance suffered. It will always be a matter of conjecture what honours his ferocious shooting powers might have won had the best years of his career not been lost to the war, but when normal football resumed it had not affected his goal-scoring prowess. Prompted by the skilful lines of supply provided by Jimmy Dimmock and Arthur Grimsdell, he top-scored with 31 goals in the team that ran away with the Second Division title in 1919-20. Although he did not score in the 1921 FA Cup Final, it was his two goals in the semi-final that saw off Preston North End. His consistent strike-rate was finally recognised when, after playing in two England trial matches, he won a place in the team that played Scotland in April 1921. He must have felt at home on what was to be his only international appearance, for not only was Spurs team-mate Dimmock his wing partner but behind him was the Spurs half-back pairing of Bert Smith and Grimsdell. By the end of the 1921-22 season Bliss's power was beginning to wane and in December 1922 he transferred to Clapton Orient, finishing his League career with one season at Bournemouth and Boscombe Athletic. He could have remained with Bournemouth, but they were not happy he wanted to continue living in Edmonton, so he moved into the non-League game.

Appearances:
League: 195* apps. 91 gls.
FA Cup: 21 apps. 13 gls.
Others: 99 apps. 64 gls.
Total: 315 apps. 168 gls.
* Includes 1 abandoned match.

BLONDEL, Jonathan

Role: Midfielder 2002-04
5ft.7ins. 10st.12lbs.
Born: Ypres, Belgium, 3rd April 1984

CAREER: Union Ploegsteert (Belgium) 1990/Royal Excelsior Mouscron (Belgium) 1996/Manchester United trial Jul 2002/**SPURS** Jul 2002/Brugge (Belgium) Jan 2004/retired Jan 2015.

Debut v Southampton (sub) (PL) (h) 31.8.2002
(Crystal Palace (sub) (Fr) (a) 31.7.2002)

Belgium's brightest young star, Jonathan Blondel was very much "one for the future" when signed from Royal Excelsior Mouscron in the summer of 2002 for a fee in the region of £1 million. Unfortunately, the tough-tackling midfielder who had scored for Mouscron in the 2002 Belgian Cup final and rejected the chance of trials at Manchester United and Schalke 04, soon displayed a distinct lack of patience. Although he was given a few outings in pre-season friendlies and quickly found himself winning his first full cap, it was clear Blondel would need time to develop and learn how to survive in the Premiership. An attacking player always prepared to make forward runs and never afraid to put himself about in the midfield engine-room, Blondel was soon complaining at his lack of first team opportunities. On Glenn Hoddle's departure, David Pleat gave Blondel a chance, but he failed to impress, returned to the reserves and agitated for a return home. His wish was granted in January 2004 when he moved to Club Brugge. Helping them to win the Belgian title in 2005 he proved himself a competent, if not outstanding, performer in the Belgian League. He made over 200 appearances for Brugge before injury caused him to retire.

Appearances:
League: (2) apps.
FL Cup: 1 (1) apps.
Others: 3 (3) apps.
Total: 4 (6) apps. 0 gls.

BLYTH, James Banes

Role: Centre-half 1936-37
5ft.8ins. 10st.12lbs.
Born: Stobhill, Edinburgh, 9th August 1911
Died: Gorebridge, Midlothian, 10th December 1979

CAREER: Newtongrange Star/Arniston Rovers/**SPURS** Feb 1936/Hull City May 1937/Heart of Midlothian May 1939/(Falkirk loan Jan 1942)/St Johnstone Dec 1945/retired 1950.

Debut v Newcastle United (FL) (a) 12.9.1936

Jim Blyth was signed from the Scottish Junior club Arniston Rovers with a view to replacing Arthur Rowe who was nearing the end of his playing career. He had to wait until September 1936 before making his League debut, brought into the team after Spurs had failed to register a win in their first three games of the season. On the whole, the 1930's were not a very successful period for the club and 1936-37 was to be one of the poorer seasons. Blyth played just eleven League games, mainly as stand-in for Rowe, was released in April 1937 and moved to Hull City. Two years later he joined Heart of Midlothian and finished his career with St Johnstone.

Appearances:
League: 11 apps.
Total: 11 apps. 0 gls.

BO, Qu

Role: Striker 2002-03
5ft.11ins. 10st.10lbs.
Born: Tianjin, China, 15th July 1981

CAREER: Tianjin Locomotive 1996/Qingdao Hainiu (renamed Qingdao Jonoon) (China) 2000/**SPURS** trial Jul 2002/Feyenoord (Holland) trial Jan 2003/Blackburn Rovers trial Oct 2003/Shaanxi Zhongxin (China) Feb 2010/Qingdao Hainiu (China) Jun 2014/ Tianjin Teda (China) Jan 2016.

Debut v Crystal Palace (sub) (Fr) (a) 31.7.2002

China's young player of the year, 21-year old Qu Bo had come to the fore as a member of the Chinese team in the 2002 World Cup. Offered a trial at White Hart Lane, he played in two first team games at the start of the 2002-03 season and looked a player of tremendous potential. A forward with blistering pace and a good goal-scoring record despite having been converted from a central striker to more of a winger, Glenn Hoddle was sufficiently impressed to agree a £2 million deal with Bo's Chinese club, but the deal never went through. Bo had made his debut for China against Portugal in May 2002 and had played in practically all their games since, but he had not played in 75% of their internationals in the preceding two years, most of his appearances being in the junior international teams. A work permit was refused, even on appeal. Bo returned to his Chinese team Qingdao and flirted with further efforts to make it in the European game, having trials with Feyenoord and Blackburn Rovers. Neither came to anything, but Bo remained a regular with Qingdao until moving on to Shaanxi Zhongxin who changed their name to Guiazho Renhe when the club relocated to Guizhao.

Appearances:
Others: 1 (1) apps.
Total: 1 (1) apps. 0 gls.

BOATENG, Kevin-Prince

Role: Midfielder 2007-10
6ft.0ins. 13st.4lbs.
Born: Berlin, Germany, 6th March 1987

CAREER: Füchse Berlin Reinickendorf (Germany) 1994/Hertha Berlin (Germany) Jul 1994/**SPURS** Jul 2007/(Borussia Dortmund (Germany) loan Jan 2009)/Portsmouth Sep 2009/Genoa (Italy) Aug 2010/AC Milan (Italy) loan Aug 2010, perm May 2011/Schalke 04 (Germany) Aug 2013-Dec 2015/AC Milan (Italy) Jan 2016/Las Palmas (Spain) Aug 2016.

Debut v Anorthosis (UEFA) (a) 4.10.2007

Associated with Hertha Berlin from the age of seven, Kevin-Prince Boateng (he added the Prince to his registered name in honour of his father) worked his way through their junior ranks to make his Bundesliga debut in August 2005. A confident, flamboyant midfielder, who could be brilliant at times, his progress was monitored for some while before Spurs moved to secure his transfer in July 2007, reportedly paying about £7 million for his signature. Barely 20-years old and with less than fifty top level games to his credit, Boateng was impatient for first team action, but he needed time to settle to a different country, let alone a different style of football. He clearly thought otherwise and was not afraid to voice his opinion, not an attitude that endeared itself to Martin Jol. Barely given a chance by the big Dutchman, the arrival of Juande Ramos saw Boateng given more opportunities, but it was not hard to see that Jol was right, Boateng was not ready for a regular place. At times neat and controlled, too often Boateng had to show off, try something outrageous when a simple pass would have been more effective. He clearly had ability, but wanted to be the star, rather than harness his talent for the team's benefit. Rarely even considered for first team action, Boateng continued to make his feelings public and pressed for a move. In January 2009, his wish was granted with a return to Germany on loan to Borussia Dortmund, but it was three months before he played his first game for them. When Boateng returned to Spurs it was clear he had little future at White Hart Lane. While it meant a substantial loss on the investment, Portsmouth's surprise £4 million bid for his services was quickly accepted by Spurs, the only question being whether Boateng was prepared to forsake the bright lights of London to try his luck on the south coast. He was, and as he settled to produce some polished performances, it looked to be a good decision. Given responsibility in the centre of Portsmouth's midfield, even though Portsmouth were struggling, Boateng began to blossom. He gave one of his best performances in the 2010 FA Cup semi-final against Spurs, netting Portsmouth's second goal. Despite his best efforts, Portsmouth were at the start of a desperate decline that saw them placed into Administration and, come the end of the season, relegated from the Premier League. Boateng was one of their most saleable assets and quickly signed for Genoa, though within hours of the signing he was loaned to AC Milan. It was a transaction described as "complicated", but Boateng was always destined for a permanent move to Milan. In Italy, Boateng at last began to harness his talents to those of the team, though never afraid to embellish performances when the chance arose. He helped Milan win the Scudetto in 2012 and established himself as a consistent performer. In the summer of 2013 he was transferred to Schalke 04, having surprised Milan with an unexpected transfer request. In May 2015 Boateng and two team-mates were suspended by Schalke for bad behaviour that was said to have contributed to some poor results.

It led to his contract being cancelled in December 2015 and an immediate return to Milan. On the international stage, Boateng represented Germany at all levels up to Under-21, but in May 2010 announced he would play at full level for his father's homeland, Ghana. He played in the 2010 World Cup, announced in November 2011, with nine full caps to his name, that he had given up international football, but reversed that decision in June 2013. Boateng's uncle, Robert, was a Ghanaian international who played for Rosenborg and his brother, Jérôme, a German international who played for Hertha Berlin, Hamburger, Manchester City and Bayern Munich. The brothers appeared on opposing sides in a World Cup match in June 2010. In January 2013 Boateng led his team-mates from the field in protest at racist abuse being hurled at him and others during a friendly match with Pro Patria. It earned Boateng worldwide praise and the March 2013 appointment as a UN anti-racism ambassador.

Appearances:
League: 7 (7) apps.
FA Cup: 1 (1) apps.
FL Cup: 1 (4) apps.
Euro: 1 (2) apps.
Others: 1 (3) apps.
Total: 11 (17) apps. 0 gls.

BOLAN, Leonard Arthur

Role: Outside-right 1933-36
5ft.8ins. 10st.7lbs.
Born: Lowestoft, Suffolk, 16th March 1909
Died: Lowestoft, Suffolk, 17th May 1973

CAREER: Lowestoft Town 1929/Norwich City am. Feb 1931/Suffolk/West Ham United am. Oct 1931/**SPURS** am. Feb 1933, pro. Jun 1933/Southend United Jul 1935/(guest for Coventry City and Northampton Town during World War Two)/retired Aug 1940.

Debut v Huddersfield Town (FL) (a) 26.12.1933

Although Len Bolan joined Spurs as an amateur in early 1933 he had to wait until December that year before making his League debut and then until the following season for his next appearance. At the time Jimmy McCormick was Spurs' regular outside-right and Bolan was always going to have a difficult time trying to oust him from the team. Indeed, it was only when McCormick was injured that Bolan managed to get a game. He scored three goals in nine appearances in the 1934-35 season, but it soon became clear Bolan did not have what it took to make the grade at the highest level and he was allowed to move to Southend United. He was not, though, to be easily forgotten at White Hart Lane, scoring the lowly Third Division (South) club's first goal as they surprisingly held Spurs to a 4-4 draw at Southend in the third round of the FA Cup in January 1936. He then netted their goal in a replay that Spurs were a shade fortunate to win 2-1. Bolan continued to play for Southend until the end of the war. As part of Bolan's signing, in February 1934 Spurs sent an "A" team to play a friendly at Lowestoft, for whom Bolan had first played in 1929-30.

Appearances:
League: 10 apps. 3 gls.
Others: 3 apps.
Total: 13 apps. 3 gls.

BOND, Dennis Joseph Thomas

Role: Midfielder 1966-71
5ft.7ins. 10st.10lbs.
Born: Walthamstow, London, 17th March 1947

CAREER: Walthamstow Schools/London Schools/England Schools/Watford app. May 1962, pro. Mar 1964/**SPURS** Mar 1967/Charlton Athletic Oct 1970/Watford loan Feb 1973, perm Jul 1973/Dagenham Aug 1978/Highfield Sports player-manager by Oct 1981/Boreham Wood 1982-83/Waltham Abbey player-manager/St Margaretsbury/Potters Bar Town asst. manager 1986-87/Mount Grace Old Boys manager by Nov 1988.

Debut v Liverpool (sub) (FL) (h) 1.4.1967

Although born almost on Spurs' doorstep, it was with Watford that England Youth international Dennis Bond first caught the eye of the bigger clubs. He made his debut for the Hornets when only 17 and under the care of ex-Spurs star Ron Burgess, then the Watford manager, had made over 100 senior appearances by the time of his £20,000 transfer to Spurs. A creative midfield player, his debut was as a substitute against Liverpool, but unfortunately, he never fulfilled his true potential. He was perhaps typical of the many home-produced or cheaply acquired players who suffered due to Spurs' reputation as a club who would buy bigger names, and although he stayed with

Tottenham for over three years he never really had the opportunity to make a place in the team his own and scored just one goal in the League- a penalty against Everton. Once transferred to Charlton Athletic for £25,000, he soon became a regular with the south London club and then returned to Watford to make another 200 senior appearances before moving into non-League football.

Appearances:
League: 20 (3) apps. 1 gl.
FL Cup: 2 (1) apps.
Euro: 1 app.
Others: 8 (1) apps. 2 gls.
Total: 31 (5) apps. 3 gls.

BOOTH, Andrew David

Role: Striker 2000-01
6ft.0ins. 12st.9lbs.
Born: Huddersfield, Yorkshire, 6th December 1973

CAREER: Lindley Junior School/Lindley/Elland Athletic/Huddersfield Town trainee Jul 1990. pro. Jul 1992/Sheffield Wednesday Jul 1996/ (**SPURS** loan Jan 2001)/Huddersfield Town Mar 2001/retired May 2009.

Debut v West Ham United (PL) (a) 31.1.2001

When Spurs were left struggling for power up front in January 2001 due to injuries to Les Ferdinand, Steffen Iversen and Chris Armstrong, Director of Football, David Pleat, suggested to manager George Graham that Andy Booth could be the man to fill the breach for a short while. Booth had made his name as a strong, powerful central striker with Huddersfield Town, Huddersfield Town, collecting three England Under-21 caps, and Pleat had signed him for Sheffield Wednesday for £2.7 million when manager at Hillsborough. While not an elegant player, Booth was as honest as they come. A true battler, he put everything he had into every game and while he played just four games during his month's loan at White Hart Lane, he never let the side down. When his loan was over he returned to Hillsborough but within a couple of months had gone back to his first love, Huddersfield. He continued to give his best to his home-town club for another eight years, taking his goals tally to 150 before retiring and becoming a club ambassador.

Appearances:
League: 3 (1) apps.
Total: 3 (1) apps. 0 gls.

BORBÁS, Dr Gáspár

Role: Forward 1912
5ft.11ins. 12st.1lb.
Born: Budapest, Hungary, 26th July 1884
Died: Budapest, Hungary, 20th September 1976

CAREER: Ferencvárosi Torna (Hungary) 1901/Magyar Atlétikai Club (Hungary) 1904/Ferencvárosi Torna (Hungary) 1910/**SPURS** guest Jun 1912/retired 1916.

Debut v Austrian Olympic Players (Fr) (Vienna) 2.6.1912.

Towards the end of their 1912 European tour Spurs played three matches in Budapest, the first against Ferencvárosi, the others against Hungary's squad for the forthcoming Stockholm Olympics. Gáspár Borbás was one of their opponents and made such a considerable impression that when the Spurs directors realised injuries were going to prevent them putting out a full team for the final game of the tour, Borbás was asked to fill-in. He accompanied the team to Vienna and played at outside-left against the Austrian's Olympic squad. It was no surprise Borbás stood out, for he was rated the finest player Hungary had produced by then. A flying winger with speed and dribbling ability, he was a member of Hungary's first international team, played in the 1912 Olympics and represented his country 41 times, scoring eleven goals in a career that spanned 16 years. A doctor of law, he only gave up playing when appointed the prosecutor in Budapest. A small stadium in Kerekegyháza, southern Hungary is named after Borbás.

Appearances:
Others: 1 app.
Total: 1 app. 0 gls.

BOREHAM, Frederick

Role: Goalkeeper 1908-10
5ft.11ins. 13st.0lbs.
Born: Rye, Sussex, 8th July 1885
Died: Hastings, Sussex, August 1951

CAREER: Rother Invicta/Rye by 1900/Tunbridge Wells Rangers/Leyton/ **SPURS** May 1908/Leyton May 1910.

Debut v Gainsborough Trinity (FL) (h) 27.3.1909
(Millwall (LFACC) (Upton Park) 22.3.1909)

Fred Boreham spent the first two seasons of Spurs' Football League career at White Hart Lane, but played a total of only 20 League games. Having started in his native Sussex with Rother Invicta, he was a schoolboy star in Rye's Sussex Junior Cup winning team of 1901 before moving on to Tunbridge Wells Rangers. There, he again proved the star of the show as they won the Tunbridge Wells Charity Cup in 1904. He progressed from there to make his name with Leyton. Signed by Spurs in May 1908, he had to wait almost a year for his first team debut. That came in March 1909 in the semi-final of the London FA Charity Cup, with his League debut five days later. Boreham retained his place until the end of a season that saw Spurs promoted to the First Division but, while he started the following term in the side, the club found the top Division much tougher and the defence particularly so. After only twelve games Boreham had to give way to the more experienced Jim Joyce who was signed from Millwall to strengthen the defence. Boreham remained with Spurs, but with the signing of Tom Lunn in April 1910 was clearly surplus to requirements and returned to Leyton.

Appearances:
League: 20 apps.
Others: 13 apps.
Total: 33 apps. 0 gls.

BORTOLOZZO, Diego

Role: Midfielder 2002-03
5ft.11ins. 11st 11lbs
Born: Brazil, 29th September 1982

CAREER: Castello Branco Athletic Assoc. (Brazil)/Treviso (Italy) 2000-01/Barnet trial/Estrela Do Norte (Brazil)/**SPURS** trial Jul 2002, perm Aug 2002-Dec 2002/Dynamo Kyiv (Ukraine) trial Feb 2003/América MG (Brazil) trial Mar 2003/AO Kavalas (Greece) 2004/Palmeirense (Brazil) May-Aug 2004/Royal Francs Borains (Belgium) Feb 2005/Royale Union Saint-Gilloise (Belgium) Jul 2005/Pétange (Luxembourg) Jul 2006/Atlético Colatinense (Brazil) by Jan 2007/SC Wiedenbrück (Germany) Jul 2007/SV Meppen (Germany) Jul 2008/BSV Kickers Emden (Germany) trial Jul 2009/FC Solothurn (Switzerland) Nov 2009/SV Lippstadt (Germany) Jul 2010/SC Roland Beckum (Germany) Jul 2011/Warendorfer SU (Germany) Jul 2013/SC Wiedenbrück II Jun 2015.

Debut v Stevenage Borough (sub) (Fr) (a) 21.7.2002

A young Brazilian midfielder with an Italian passport, Diego Bortolozzo did enough in a month's trial in July 2002 to be offered a three-month contract. Talented and with the basic football skills expected of all Brazilians, he played regularly for the reserves but never quite looked as though he had what it takes to make it to the top level in England. Released at the end of his three months, Bortolozzo has since moved rapidly around lower level, semi-professional clubs back in Brazil and throughout Europe.

Appearances:
Others: 2 (3) apps.
Total: 2 (3) apps. 0 gls.

BOSTOCK, John Joseph

Role: Midfielder 2008-12
5ft.11ins. 13st.1lbs.
Born: Lambeth, London, 15th January 1992

CAREER: Ajax 95/Crystal Palace 2007/**SPURS** scholar May 2008/(Brentford loan Nov 2009)/(Hull City loan Aug-Dec 2010)/(Sheffield Wednesday loan Jan-Mar 2012)/(Swindon Town loans Mar 2012 and Aug 2012)/(LA Galaxy (USA) trial Feb 2013)/(Toronto (Canada) loan Mar 2013)/released Jun 2013/Royal Antwerp (Belgium) Jul 2013/Oud-Heverlee Leuven (Belgium) Aug 2014/RC Lens (France) Jul 2016.

Debut v Dinamo Zagreb (sub) (UEFA) (h) 6.11.2008
(Hercules (sub) (Fr) (a) 24.7.2008)

One of the most hyped young talents of modern times, John Bostock was reputedly a world beater by the time he was 15 if claims that clubs like Manchester United, Barcelona and Chelsea were desperate to secure his transfer from boyhood club Crystal Palace are to be believed. He was certainly a player full of potential, well-built, confident and with obvious ability. A midfielder with strength and passing skills beyond his years, he was still a schoolboy when he became Palace's youngest ever player, making his debut at 15 years and 287 days in October 2007. At the end of the season and with only four senior games to his credit, Spurs announced his signing with the fee to be determined by a tribunal if a deal could not be reached with Palace. That proved impossible with Palace reportedly demanding anything up to £4.5 million and in July 2008 the tribunal made its decision. Spurs were to pay £700,000 with add-ons depending on appearances potentially taking the figure up to £1.25 million. Another £200,000 was payable if Bostock played for England at full international level. Bostock

made his senior competitive debut for Spurs in November 2008 as a substitute in a UEFA Cup tie against Dinamo Zagreb. At 16 years, 295 days he beat Ally Dick's record of being Spurs youngest player by just six days. Although he made three more substitute appearances in senior games, that first outing was probably the highlight of his Spurs' career. Bostock never looked like progressing from schoolboy wonder to anything more than a competent performer outside the top level. Sent out on loan to gain experience, he returned early from spells with Hull City and Sheffield Wednesday amid stories of a poor attitude. Only at Swindon Town did he buckle down and turn in any sort of notable performances. In an effort to resurrect a career that appeared to be going nowhere, Bostock went to the USA, having a trial at LA Galaxy before signing on loan for Toronto, but even that arrangement was terminated early. On his return to White Hart Lane, Bostock was released and signed for Royal Antwerp. In three years in Belgium he rebuilt his career before trying his luck in France with RC Lens.

Appearances:
FA Cup: (1) app.
Euro: (3) apps.
Others: 2 (4) apps.
Total: 2 (8) apps. 0 gls.

BOULTON, Frank Preece

Role: Goalkeeper 1944-45
Born: Chipping Sodbury, Wiltshire, 12th August 1917
Died: Swindon, Wiltshire, 12th June 1987

CAREER: Bristol City Nov 1934/Bath City Jul 1936/Arsenal Oct 1936/Derby County Aug 1938/(guest for Aldershot, Arsenal, Chelsea, Crystal Palace, Fulham, Swansea Town, **SPURS** and Watford during World War Two)/Swindon Town Jul 1946/Crystal Palace Oct 1950/Bedford Town Feb 1951.

Debut v Chelsea (FLS) (h) 14.10.1944

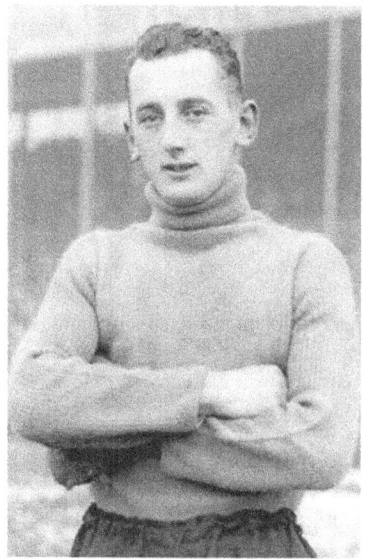

Another of the war-time guest players who played only one match for Spurs, Frank Boulton started his career with Bristol City and Bath

City before being transferred to Arsenal, where he became one of several keepers used by them during their great days of the 1930s. He stayed at Highbury until moving on to Derby County and it was as a Derby player that he guested for Spurs and several other clubs during the War. Injury forced him to miss the 1946 FA Cup Final and with Derby having signed Vic Woodley, Boulton was allowed to move to Swindon Town. He made over 100 appearances for Swindon, but failed to make the first eleven in his four months at Crystal Palace before joining Bedford Town.

Appearances:
Others: 1 app.
Total: **1 app. 0 gls.**

BOWEN, Rosslyn Mark

Role: Full-back or midfield 1983-87
5ft.8ins. 11st.13lbs.
Born: Neath, Glamorgan, 7th December 1963

CAREER: Afan Nedd Schools/Wales Schools/**SPURS** app. Jun 1980, pro. Dec 1981/Norwich City Jul 1987/West Ham United Jul 1996/Shimuzu S Pulse (Japan) Mar 1997/Charlton Athletic Sep 1997-May 1999/Bristol City trial Jul 1999/Oxford United trial Jul 1999/Wigan Athletic non-contract Aug 1999/Wales Under-21 coach Aug 1999/Reading non-contract Dec 1999/FA of Wales technical director Aug 1999/Wales asst. manager/ Crystal Palace reserve team manager Jun 2001/Birmingham City first team coach Dec 2001-Jun 2004/Blackburn Rovers asst. manager Oct 2004/ Manchester City asst. manager Jun 2008-Dec 2009/Fulham asst. manager Aug 2010, academy coach Jul 2011/Queens Park Rangers asst. manager Jan 2012, caretaker manager Nov 2012/Stoke City asst. manager Jun 2013.

Debut v Coventry City (FL) 29.8.1983
(Enfield (Fr) (a) 4.8.1983)

Principally regarded as a full-back but quite capable of playing in midfield, Mark Bowen, who played rugby at District Schoolboy level, had played for Wales at both Youth and Under-21 level by the time of his first team debut in a friendly at Enfield in August 1983. A quiet but confident defender who enjoyed getting forward, he won his first full cap during Wales' summer tour of Canada in 1986, twice appearing as substitute in games with the home nation. Unfortunately, he was unable to win a regular place at Spurs due to competition from the likes of Chris Hughton, Mitchell Thomas, Danny Thomas and Gary Stevens and was allowed to move to Norwich City for a modest £90,000 fee. Linking-up with former Spurs reserve team-mates Ian Crook and Ian Culverhouse, Bowen developed into a top class full-back with considerable attacking flair and played a big part in Norwich's challenge for the League title in 1988-89. A regular for his country, he gave Norwich nine years' great service before returning to London and the best part of a year with West Ham, winning another four caps to add to the 35 he had collected with Norwich. In March 1997 Bowen was persuaded to join Shimuzu S Pulse in Japan, linking up with Ossie Ardiles and Steve Perryman, but was unable to settle in the country. He returned to London the following September to help Charlton reach the Premiership via the play-offs. With injury all but decimating his 1998-99 season, he could do little to prevent Charlton returning to the First Division and at the end of the season was released. He joined Wigan, but quickly moved on to Reading, playing only one game for the "Royals" before taking up a coaching position with the Welsh FA, where he first worked with Mark Hughes. When Steve Bruce took over as manager at Crystal Palace, he persuaded Bowen to become his assistant and six months later the pair of them moved to Birmingham City. Bowen fell out with Bruce when the manager refused to allow Bowen to carry out his assistant manager duties with Wales. Bowen then linked up with Mark Hughes at Blackburn, following him to Manchester City, Fulham, Queens Park Rangers and Stoke City.

Appearances:
League: 14 (3) apps. 2 gls.
FA Cup: 3 apps.
Others: 7 (14) apps.
Total: **24 (17) apps. 2 gls.**

BOWERING, Ernest George

Role: Half-back 1911-12
5ft.10ins. 11st.9lbs.
Born: Wandsworth, London, 30th March 1891
Died: Speldhurst, Kent, 23rd November 1961

CAREER: London Schools/Tottenham Thursday/**SPURS** am. Feb 1910, pro. Feb 1911/Fulham Oct 1912/Merthyr Town cs. 1913/Chelsea Aug 1915 /Rice & Son Nov 1933.

Debut v Blackburn Rovers (FL) (a) 27.1.1912

Ernest Bowering signed professional immediately on joining Spurs from the local junior club Tottenham Thursday, but went on to make only nine senior appearances in the 1911-12 season. A half-back, he was a reserve for Dan Steel and Jabez Darnell, but with the signings of Arthur Grimsdell and Finlay Weir during the 1912 close season it was clear Bowering would have to be patient if he was ever to have an extended run in the first team. When Spurs received an offer from Fulham Bowering was allowed to make the move to west London. He fared little better at Craven Cottage, making only one League appearance before moving on to Merthyr Town. He signed for Chelsea during the First World War but never played for them. Late in November 1933 he was reported playing for the works team of Rice & Son.

Appearances:
League: 7 apps.
Others: 3 apps.
Total: **10 apps. 0 gls.**

BOWGETT, Paul

Role: Central defender 1977-79
Born: Stevenage, Hertfordshire, 17th June 1955

CAREER: North Herts Schools/Stevenage Youth/Hertfordshire Youth/ Letchworth Garden City/**SPURS** trial Jan 1978, pro. Feb 1978/ Wimbledon Mar 1979/Wealdstone Sep 1980/Baldock Town player-joint manager 1988 Hitchin Town/Stevenage Borough 1992-93/Baldock Town 1993-94.

Debut v Wolverhampton Wanderers (sub) (Fr) (a) 16.10.1978

Although Paul Bowgett performed well at schoolboy and youth level he must have thought a career in top class football had passed him by when he joined Letchworth Garden City. However, Spurs saw his potential and after a trial period he was signed as a professional, giving up his job as a toolmaker to accept the opportunity. As it was he made only one first team appearance, as a substitute in a testimonial match at Wolverhampton Wanderers, before joining Fourth Division Wimbledon in March 1979. After just a year with Wimbledon, Bowgett returned to non-League football with Wealdstone, captaining them to the Southern League and Southern League Cup "Double" in 1981-82 and the Gola League and FA Trophy "Double" in 1984-85. He went on to play for Baldock Town, Hitchin Town and Stevenage Borough.

Appearances:
Others: (1) app.
Total: (1) app. 0 gls.

BOWLER, George Henry

Role: Half-back 1913-1919
5ft.10ins. 12st.0lbs.
Born: *Newhall, Derbyshire, 23rd January 1890*
Died: *Bethnal Green, London, October qtr. 1948*

CAREER: Tottenham Thursday by Oct 1909/Newhall Swifts/Gresley Rovers/Derby County May 1911/SPURS May 1913/Luton Town Jul 1919.

Debut v Blackburn Rovers (FL) (a) 28.2.1914
(Crystal Palace (LPFCF) (h) 27.10.1913)

George Bowler spent two years at the Baseball Ground as a reserve, playing only one League game for Derby County in 1912-13. He did little better with Spurs. After making his first team debut in the London Professional Football Charity Fund match with Crystal Palace in October 1913, he went on to make only three League appearances that season. He remained a permanent reserve-making just one appearance during the war-until his release in the 1919 close season. He then joined Luton Town but, even then, rarely progressed past the Hatters' reserve side.

Appearances:
League: 3 apps.
Others: 3 apps.
Total: 6 apps. 0 gls.

BOWYER

Role: Centre-forward 1893-94

Debut v Old St Marks (LSC) (h) 28.10.1893

Bowyer made his one appearance for Spurs in a London Senior Cup match with Old St Marks. The match was a replay, Spurs having drawn the first game at home 0-0. Although the game was staged at Northumberland Park by mutual consent it did Spurs little good as they were beaten 1-6. Bowyer played at centre-forward and was described as "no good", an "absolute failure" and "the worst" of four or five centre-forwards Spurs had tried.

Appearances:
Others: 1 app.
Total: 1 app. 0 gls.

BRACE, Robert Leon

Role: Forward 1983-84
5ft.8ins. 10st. 9lbs.
Born: *Waltham Abbey, Hertfordshire, 19th December 1964*

CAREER: Cheshunt Youth Club/Abbey Youth Club/SPURS app. Apr 1981, pro. Dec 1982/Waterschei (Belgium) May 1984/FC De Graafschap (Holland) 1984-85/1. FC Saarbrücken (Germany) cs. 1985-87/FK Pirmasens (Germany) 1987-90/Eintracht Trier 05 (Germany) 1990-91/TUS Koblenz Verbands (Germany) 1991-95/Eintracht Glas-Chemie Wirges + Eisbachtal (Germany) 1995-2000/Eintracht Glas-Chemie Wirges (Germany) coach 2000-2002/SC 07 Moselweiss (Germany) trainer Jan-Sep 2005/TUS Immendorf (Germany) trainer Sep 2005/SG Mülheim-Kärlich (Germany) coach Mar-May 2012/SV Niederwerth (Germany) May 2013-May 2015.

Debut v Southampton (sub) (FL) (a) 7.5.1984

Robby Brace worked his way through Spurs' junior ranks to professional status, but made only one Football League appearance. That was in May 1984 as a substitute in a League match at Southampton played only two days before Spurs were due to meet Anderlecht in the first leg of the UEFA Cup Final. Spurs fielded almost a complete reserve side, lost 0-5 and received a hefty fine from the League for not naming their strongest team. Less than a month later Brace was given a free transfer and moved to Waterschei of Belgium. He later played for De Grafscaap in Holland and several lower level German clubs before turning to coaching.

Appearances:
League: (1) app.
Total: (1) app. 0 gls.

BRADSHAW, Thomas Henry

Role: Outside-left 1898-99
5ft.6ins. 10st.7lbs.
Born: *Liverpool, Merseyside, 24th August 1873*
Died: *Tottenham, London, 25th December 1899*

CAREER: Lansdown/Liverpool Nomads 1889-91/Everton 1891-92/Northwich Victoria/Liverpool Oct 1893/**SPURS** May 1898/Thames Ironworks cs. 1899.

Debut v Thames Ironworks (TML) (h) 3.9.1898 (scored once)
(Gainsborough Trinity (Fr) (h) 1.9.1898)

Originally a centre-forward who worked his way through local junior football, Tom Bradshaw was a regular member of Liverpool's Second Division winning team of 1894 but, while an ever-present and top-scorer, he was unable to stop them being relegated after just one season in the top flight. They came straight back up in 1896, by which time Bradshaw had moved to outside-left, the position in which he played twice for the Football League and won an England cap against Ireland in February 1897, the first Liverpool player to win international honours. A founder member of the Association Footballers' Union, he joined Spurs in May 1898, a fast, direct winger who instinctively made for the touchline before firing over crosses for the in-rushing forwards to run on to. Almost ever-present, he was, however, only with Spurs for one season, but in that time represented the United League against the Thames and Medway League, played for the South against the North in the annual international trial match and turned out for an England XI against a Scotland XI in a match to raise funds for the Players' Union. In the summer of 1899 he moved to Thames Ironworks, but did not complete a full season for them. While with Liverpool, Bradshaw had been kicked in the head during a match. In October 1899, he sustained another such kick that caused him some problems for a few weeks. On Christmas Day 1899 he watched Spurs beat Portsmouth 3-0 at White Hart Lane. When he returned to his home nearby he was seriously ill with pains in the head and chest. Before a doctor could attend on him, Bradshaw had a fit and died. Officially, his premature death-he was only 26-was attributed to tuberculosis, even though a post-mortem showed a ruptured blood vessel in his brain. On 2nd April 1900 Spurs met Thames Ironworks in a match to raise funds for his dependants.

Appearances:
Southern: 24 apps. 5 gls.
FA Cup: 9 apps. 5 gls.
Others: 36 apps. 9 gls.
Total: **69 apps. 19 gls.**

BRADY, Garry

Role: Midfielder 1994-98
5ft.10ins. 10st.6lbs.
Born: Glasgow, 7th September 1976

CAREER: St Margaret Mary's School/Glasgow Schools/Glasgow County Schools/Scotland Schools/Scotland Youth/Celtic Boys Club 1990/**SPURS** trainee Jul 1992, pro. Sep 1993/Newcastle United Jul 1998-Jan 2001/(Norwich City loan Mar 2000 and Sep 2000)/Portsmouth trial Feb 2001, perm Mar 2001-May 2002/(Kilmarnock trial Jan 2002)/Walsall trial Jul 2002/Dundee trial Aug 2002, perm. Sep 2002/St Mirren Jul 2006/Brechin City Jun 2011-May 2013.

Debut v Fulham (FA Cup) (h) 5.1.1998
(Reading (sub) (Fr) (a) 11.11.1994)

Young Scottish midfielder Garry Brady began to make a breakthrough into the Spurs' team towards the end of the 1997-98 season. An industrious midfielder who seemed destined to challenge for what was proving a difficult spot wide on the left, he was one of a new breed of talented youngsters from whom much was expected. Unfortunately, Brady was impatient for regular first team action, not prepared to wait and establish himself. With his contract up at the end of the season, he refused to sign the new one Spurs offered and instead took himself off to Newcastle. As he was under 24, Spurs were allowed to recover their costs of developing him and in November 1998 Newcastle were ordered by a tribunal to pay £650,000. It was a fair reflection of the investment Spurs had made and an indication of his potential, but for Newcastle it proved a stiff fee. Brady made barely a dozen senior appearances for the Magpies before being shipped off to Norwich City on loan for the first of two such spells. Released by Newcastle, he secured a move to Portsmouth, but he was little more than a year at Fratton Park before again being released. Brady joined Dundee, where he played for four years and made over 100 appearances before a contractual dispute saw him depart for St Mirren. After five years there and well into the vintage stage, he moved on to Brechin City. His brother, Darren, played for Airdrie, Dundee, Livingston, Raith, Partick Thistle, Ross County, Forfar and Pollock.

Appearances:
League: (9) apps.
FA Cup: 1 (1) apps.
Others: 1 (5) apps.
Total: **2 (15) apps. 0 gls.**

BRADY, William Liam

Role: Midfielder 1983-84
5ft.8ins. 12st.7lbs.
Born: Dublin, 13th February 1956

CAREER: St Kevin's Boys club/Eire Schools/Arsenal app. Jun 1971, pro. Aug 1973/Juventus (Italy) Jul 1980/Sampdoria (Italy) cs. 1982/Internazionale (Italy) Jun 1984/Ascoli (Italy) cs. 1986/West Ham United Mar 1987/retired cs. 1990/Celtic manager Jun 1991-Oct 1993/Brighton and Hove Albion manager Dec 1993-Nov 1995/Arsenal Youth Team manager Aug 1996, Head of Youth Development to May 2014.

Debut v England XI (Fr) (h) 29.5.1984 (scored once)

Liam Brady, who made his only appearance in a Spurs' shirt as a guest in Keith Burkinshaw's Testimonial whilst with Sampdoria, will always be associated with Arsenal where he made his name before enjoying a lengthy career in Italian football. Within two months of signing professional for Arsenal he had made his full League debut, against Spurs at White Hart Lane, and within two years his first appearance for the Republic of Ireland, playing against the USSR on 30th October 1974. A youth international, he won 25 caps for his country and made more than 300 appearances for Arsenal before moving to Italian giants Juventus. The Professional Footballers' Association Player of the Year in 1979, during his time with Arsenal Brady won an FA Cup winners medal in 1979, loser's medals in the same competition in 1978 and 1980, a loser's medal in the European Cup-Winners' Cup in 1980 and established himself not only as a regular for his country, but one of the finest creative midfield players of the time. In Italy Brady considerably enhanced his reputation, helping Juventus win the Italian League title in both his

seasons with them and collecting another 10 caps. Restrictions on foreign players meant Brady had to leave Juventus following their signing of Michel Platini and Zbigniew Boniek. He moved to Sampdoria, won nine more caps, and after two years with them joined Internazionale. After two years and another twelve caps he finished his Italian career with Ascoli where he won four more caps. Brady then returned to London with West Ham United, and whilst in the veteran class proved to be one of their most influential players. With West Ham, he took his number of caps for the Republic to a record 72 before retiring at the end of the 1989-90 season. Initially working as a player's agent, he was surprisingly appointed manager of Celtic in June 1991, but was unable to take the magic he showed on the pitch into the manager's job at either Celtic or Brighton. In July 1996, he returned to Highbury charged with the important job of developing Arsenal's young players. It was a job he loved, helping set many talented youngsters on the way to stardom. Brady's uncle Frank played for Ireland in 1920s, while his brothers Ray and Pat both played for Millwall and Queens Park Rangers, with Ray going on to play for Ireland.

Appearances:
Others: 1 app. 1 gl.
Total: 1 app. 1 gl.

BRAIN, James

Role: Centre or inside-forward 1931-35
5ft.9ins. 13st.3lbs.
Born: Bristol, 11th September 1900
Died: Barnet, Hertfordshire, October qtr. 1971

CAREER: Cardiff City trial/Ton Pentre/Arsenal May 1923/SPURS Sep 1931, player-coach Aug 1933/Kings Lynn manager May 1935/Cheltenham Town manager 1937-48, player-manager Sep 1938-May 1940/Arsenal scout.

Debut v Manchester United (FL) (a) 12.9.1931

Jimmy Brain scored 137 goals in 232 senior appearances during seven great years with Arsenal, but when Spurs moved to sign him in September 1931 he was languishing in their reserves. Working as a miner, he played for Cardiff City in the Welsh League before turning professional with Ton Pentre. He joined Arsenal in preference to Spurs. A mobile player who used skill and guile to unlock opposing defences, Brain was equally at home at inside or centre-forward, although he did not have the brawn and muscle attributes of most centre-forwards of the era. However, he was still highly successful and played for Arsenal in the 1927 FA Cup Final which they lost to Cardiff City. With his Welsh football background, it was assumed he could play for Wales and it was only when selected for the principality that he admitted to actually being born in Bristol. That "confession" led to him playing in the 1926 England international trial, but it was the closest Jimmy got to appearing for his country. A regular in his first season with Spurs, Percy Smith then preferred George Greenfield and Taffy O'Callaghan as his inside-forwards and Brain became little more than a reserve, making only spasmodic first team appearances. In May 1933, he was made available for transfer, but Spurs subsequently decided to retain him to help coach the younger players and he remained with Spurs as a player/coach until taking the manager's job at Kings Lynn. He later had spells managing Cheltenham Town and scouting for Arsenal. Brain made his debut for Arsenal against Spurs on 25th October 1924 and scored the only goal of the game, although it was not one he knew a great deal about. He was struck by a fierce shot from Jock Rutherford which deflected into the Spurs' net and left Brain unconscious!

Appearances:
League: 45 apps. 10 gls.
FA Cup: 2 apps.
Others: 2 apps.
Total: 49 apps. 10 gls.

BRANDHAM, James

Role: Goalkeeper 1918-19
Born: St. Albans, Hertfordshire

CAREER: St. Albans City 1911/(guest for Brentford, Fulham, Luton Town and SPURS during World War One)/Luton Town.

Debut v Haydn Price's XI (Fr) (St Albans) 31.8.1918

A half-back for his local club, Brandham made his one appearance for Spurs in a Charity match at St. Albans against a team selected by Corporal Haydn Price, a Welsh international who also guested for Spurs that season. Only minutes before kick-off Spurs chosen keeper was injured and Brandham was an emergency stand-in. After the war, he played for Luton.

Appearances:
Others: 1 app.
Total: 1 app. 0 gls.

BRAWN, William Frederick

Role: Outside-left 1918-19
6ft.1ins. 13st.5lbs.
Born: Wellingborough, Northamptonshire, 1st August 1878
Died: Brentford, London, 18th August 1932

CAREER: Rock Street School/Wellingborough Schools/Wellingborough St Marks/Wellingborough Town Aug 1893/Northampton Town Jul 1898/Sheffield United Jan 1900/Aston Villa Dec 1901/Middlesbrough Mar 1906/Chelsea Nov 1907/Brentford May 1911/retired Apr 1913/(guest for SPURS during World War One)/Brentford advisory manager Jul 1919-Jun 1921, director.

Debut v Brentford (LFC) (a) 9.11.1918

When Billy Brawn made his one appearance for Spurs he was over 40 and had not played first class football for several years. Spurs arrived for a London Football Combination fixture at Brentford with only nine men and the former England international was pressed into service as emergency outside-right. An amateur with Wellingborough St Marks, Wellingborough Town and Northampton Town, it was only when Brawn joined Sheffield United that he first became a professional. Just under two years with Sheffield saw him improve steadily, but it was with Aston Villa that he had the most successful years of his career. He won

two England caps, against Wales in February 1904 and Ireland the following month, and was a member of Villa's FA Cup winning team of 1905. Less than twelve months later he left Villa and after playing for Middlesbrough and Chelsea made the final move of his career to Brentford. He played there until his retirement in April 1913 to run a local public house. "Advisory" manager of Brentford for two years, he later served the club as a director.

Appearances:
Others: 1 app.
Total: 1 app. 0 gls.

BRAZIL, Alan Bernard

Role: Striker 1982-84
6ft.0ins. 12st.4lbs.
Born: Simshill, Glasgow, 15th June 1959

CAREER: Glasgow Schools/Celtic Boys Club/Ipswich Town app. Aug 1975, pro. May 1977/(Detroit Express loan May 1978)/**SPURS** Mar 1983/Manchester United Jun 1984/Coventry City Jan 1986/Queens Park Rangers Jun 1986/retired Jan 1987/Witham Town cs. 1987/Woolongong City (Australia) 1988/Chelmsford City Jul 1988/FC Baden (Switzerland) Sep 1988/Chelmsford City 1989/Southend Manor 1989/Bury Town 1989-90/Stambridge 1990/Chelmsford City Nov 1990/Wivenhoe Town 1991/Saffron Walden Town 1991/Slough Town Director of Football Aug 1998.

Debut v Watford (FL) (a) 19.3.1983

While the famous Celtic Boys Club was not officially linked with the Glasgow giants, Celtic were usually very quick to spot the available talent, but they overlooked Alan Brazil, who joined the apprentice ranks at Ipswich before turning professional. A Scottish Youth international, he made his League debut in January 1978 and was a member of the entertaining and highly successful side built by Bobby Robson that challenged for major honours and won the UEFA Cup in 1981. Having played for the Scotland Under-21 team, Brazil made his full international debut against Poland in May 1980 and, by the time of his £450,000 move to Spurs, had won eight Under-21 and eleven full caps. A consistent goalscorer, exceptionally good at turning his marker, he won two more full caps as a Tottenham player but, unfortunately, found his style of play did not really fit in with that of Spurs. He was allowed to move to Manchester United, who had been keen to sign him when he left Ipswich, for £750,000. Again, Brazil was unable to recapture his outstanding Portman Road form or adapt his play to the pattern of his club and, after an unhappy time at Old Trafford, he moved to Coventry City with former Spurs man Terry Gibson moving in the opposite direction. At Highfield Road, he began to rediscover his old touch. After only five months he returned to London, this time signing for Queens Park Rangers. However, he played only four League games for Rangers before suffering a serious back injury. It forced him to retire from League football, although he was able to continue playing in non-League circles. Brazil finally gave up the game completely to become a publican in Ipswich and TV pundit for Sky TV. When his pub business failed, Brazil set out on a new career as a radio presenter.

Appearances:
League: 29 (2) apps. 9 gls.
FA Cup: 1 app.
FL Cup: (1) app.
Euro: 3 (2) apps. 4 gls.
Others: 14 (2) apps. 7 gls.
Total: 47 (7) apps. 20 gls.

BREARLEY, John

Role: Centre-forward or half-back 1903-07
5ft.9ins. 11st.0lbs.
Born: West Derby, Liverpool, 11th November 1875
Died: Southend, Essex, October 1944

CAREER: Liverpool South End Aug 1896/Notts County Feb 1897/Kettering Dec 1897 Chatham Jun 1898/Millwall Athletic May 1899/Notts County May 1900/Middlesbrough Apr 1901/Everton May 1902/**SPURS** May 1903/Crystal Palace May 1907/Millwall player-coach Sep 1909-May 1911/Viktoria 89 Berlin (Germany) coach to 1915.

Debut v Woolwich Arsenal (LL) (h) 1.9.1903

When John Cameron went back to his former club, Everton, to sign John Brearley it was with a view to Brearley replacing him in the Spurs' side so Cameron could concentrate on his managerial duties. The centre-forward had built quite a reputation in a career that had started with Kettering and then encompassed one game with Notts County and one season each with Chatham, Millwall, Notts County and Middlesbrough before his year at Everton, but it was to be as a half-back that Brearley was to give his best service to Spurs. He made his debut in the first match of the 1903-04 season and maintained the centre-forward position until the great Vivian J Woodward was ready to resume the role of focal point of the Spurs' attack, on the conclusion of the cricket season. With Woodward available Brearley was unable to get in the team, but towards the end of the campaign he deputised at half-back when Tom Morris or Ted Hughes were unable to play. He settled well in the middle line and continued to fill one of the half-back positions for the next two seasons, playing for the Professionals of the South against the Amateurs of the South in an international trial match at White Hart Lane in January 1905. He could also fill in at inside-forward when necessary, and such was his all-round ability that he finished his Spurs' career playing at outside-left. At the end of the 1906-07 season he was released and joined the emerging Crystal Palace club where he played for two years. He then joined the coaching staff at Millwall but still turned out for a few games in the 1909-10 season. Brearley ran the Grove Tavern at Snells Road, Edmonton in 1910 but by the outbreak of the First World War he was coaching in Germany. He was interned at Ruhleben prison camp along with several other well-known footballers and sportsmen-including his former manager, Cameron!

Appearances:
Southern: 71 apps. 7 gls.
FA Cup: 8 apps.
Others: 55* apps. 17 gls.
Total: 134 apps. 24 gls.
* Includes 1 abandoned match.

BRENNAN, A

Role: Inside-forward 1894-95

CAREER: Woolwich Clarence/**SPURS** trial Mar 1895.

Debut v City Ramblers (Fr) (h) 30.3.1895

Brennan made his only appearance for Spurs as a trialist inside-right from the Woolwich Clarence club in a friendly with City Ramblers in March 1895.

Appearances:
Others: 1 app.
Total: 1 app. 0 gls.

BREWSTER

Role: Outside-right 1907-08

CAREER: SPURS trial Oct 1907, pro. Oct 1907.

Debut v Plymouth Argyle (SL) (h) 20.1.1907

A local lad who had learnt his football while serving in the Army, Brewster was given a trial by Spurs' manager Fred Kirkham in October 1907 and, although one local reporter described him as being "out of his class", was immediately signed as a professional. He spent the whole of the campaign in the reserve team, save for his one first team game against Plymouth Argyle in January 1908. At the end of that season, Spurs' final one in the Southern League, he was not retained by the club.

Appearances:
Southern: 1 app.
Total: 1 app. 0 gls.

BRIGDEN, J

Role: Inside-forward 1891-94

CAREER: Edmonton Albion by Oct 1886/(**SPURS** guest Jan 1892)/**SPURS** cs. 1892/Edmonton All Saints cs. 1893/(**SPURS** guest)/Edmonton Albion.

Debut v Westminster Criterion (Fr) (h) 23.1.1892

Another of the players from the early 1890s who helped establish Spurs as one of London's most attractive and popular teams, "Motor" Brigden was with the Edmonton Albion club when he made his first recorded appearance for Spurs. He joined the club for the 1892-93 season and appeared frequently as Spurs competed for the first time in a league competition; the Southern Alliance, but made only three more appearances the following season. By then he was playing for Edmonton All Saints. He remained active in local football playing for Edmonton All Saints and later back with Edmonton Albion. "Motor's" brother, W, played for Novocastrians.

Appearances:
Others: 22 apps. 3 gls.
Total: 22 apps. 3 gls.

BRIGGS, Charles Edward

Role: Goalkeeper 1942-44
6ft.0ins. 11st.2lbs.
Born: Newtown, South Wales, 4th April 1910

CAREER: SPURS am. Apr 1930/Haywards Sports/Guildford/Fulham/Crystal Palace/Bradford Park Avenue/Halifax Town/(guest for Aldershot, Brentford, Fulham and **SPURS** during World War Two)/Clyde Jun 1946/Rochdale May 1947/Chesterfield Dec 1947.

Debut v Aldershot (FLS) (h) 3.10.1942

First associated with the club as an amateur, Spurs arranged for Charlie Briggs to play with Hayward Sports, but decided not to sign him as a professional. He joined Guildford before graduating to the Football League with Crystal Palace, Bradford Park Avenue and Halifax Town. It was as a war-time guest from Halifax that he made his appearances for Spurs. The first was when he arrived for a Football League South game at White Hart Lane as Aldershot's reserve keeper only to be was asked to stand-in for Spurs at the last moment as their selected keeper was unavailable. It was only after the game when he was approached by Spurs' acting manager Arthur Turner to see if he could assist the club again, that it was realised he had previously been connected with Spurs. After two appearances, his services were not required again until twelve months later when, with Ted Ditchburn on service in Scotland and Percy Hooper injured, Briggs was called up to play against Aldershot. After the war, he joined Clyde but only remained there for one year before returning to England to assist Rochdale. After seven months with Rochdale he moved to Chesterfield although he did not play a League match for them.

Appearances:
Others: 3 apps.
Total: 3 apps. 0 gls.

BRIGGS, Stanley S

Role: Half-back 1891-98
6ft.3ins. 13st.10lbs.
Born: Stamford Hill, London, 7th February 1872
Died: Canada, September 1935

CAREER: Grove House School/Folkestone/Hermitage 1890/Tottenham FC/**SPURS** Jan 1892/(guest for Clapton, Corinthians, Evesham Wanderers, Friars, London Caledonians, Millwall Athletic, Richmond Association, Upton Park, Woolwich Arsenal am. Oct 1893)/Clapton cs. 1895/Richmond Association 1901/Shepherds Bush Oct 1902, committee 1905-1907.

Debut v West Herts (FAC) (h) 13.10.1894
(Westminster Criterion (Fr) (h) 23.1.1892)

Stanley Briggs was one of the most famous names in London amateur football at the end of the 19th century and played an important role in helping Spurs establish themselves as one of the premier amateur clubs in the South. Although born locally, his footballing talent first developed whilst studying at Grove House School in Folkestone and by the age of only 14 he was a regular with the Folkestone club. Returning to London four years later, he joined Hermitage FC which developed into the Tottenham club. Within two years he switched allegiance to Spurs and his first known appearance was in January 1892. From then on, his football career took off, and as his reputation spread so did that of Spurs. Professional clubs were soon offering Briggs the opportunity to join the paid ranks, but he rejected all advances, preferring to remain true to his amateur principles. In those days, a player in his early twenties was still regarded as barely out of his youth, but Briggs exhibited a maturity far beyond his years and found himself in demand with numerous other clubs. A tall, commanding, half-back, he was a tireless worker, equally adept at breaking-up opposition attacks, going forward and unleashing a powerful long range shot or moving into the penalty area where his height was always a threat. As an amateur, he was free to turn out for any club he wished and in October 1893 he signed Football League forms for Woolwich Arsenal. He was to play only two League games for them the following season, preferring Spurs or the famous amateur club Clapton. Spurs' captain and a regular for London and Middlesex, he assisted many other clubs in his time with Spurs. He would doubtless have played for Spurs for many years were it not for the club's momentous decision in December 1895 to adopt professionalism. Briggs was totally against this, even refusing to attend the meeting at which the proposal was put and passed. Although he continued to play for Spurs for the rest of the season his involvement with the club rapidly diminished and he concentrated on playing for Clapton. Had he embraced the paid game, he would surely have played for England. As it was, the nearest he got to winning international honours was selection to play for the South against the North in an international trial match in February 1899, although he did play for and captain the FA XI that toured Germany and Bohemia in November 1899 and was regarded in some quarters as an unofficial England team. By the early years of the twentieth century he found that business demanded most of his attention and he slowly wound down his playing career with Shepherds Bush. His versatility was shown with west London's senior amateur outfit for he frequently played for them in goal. When his football career was over he emigrated to Canada. Briggs passed away while playing tennis.

Appearances:
Southern: 7 apps. 1 gl.
FA Cup: 10 apps.
Others: 95 apps. 10 gls.
Total: 112 apps. 11 gls.

BRITTAN, Colin

Role: Wing-half 1950-58
5ft.11ins. 11st.10lbs.
Born: Bristol, 2nd June 1927
Died: Bristol, Avon, 4th April 2013

CAREER: Bristol North Old Boys/SPURS am. Jan 1948, pro. Oct 1949/Bedford Town Nov 1958/Tunbridge Wells United cs. 1960.

Debut v Burnley (FL) (h) 7.10.1950

Although with Spurs for almost ten years, Colin Brittan was rarely more than a reserve. Competing with the likes of Ron Burgess, Bill Nicholson and Danny Blanchflower, he proved a valuable member of the club's staff and never let the team down when called upon. He made his League debut in October 1950 when Burgess was out injured and for the next three seasons played only when Burgess or Nicholson were unavailable. With the departure of Burgess in April 1954 Brittan found himself first choice left-half at the start of the following season, but the emergence of young Tony Marchi and the arrival of Blanchflower soon returned Brittan to the reserve team. He remained with Spurs, filling in whenever needed, but proving more valuable to the club as an elder statesman in the reserve side, until moving to Bedford Town late in 1958.

Appearances:
League: 41 apps. 1 gl.
FA Cup: 4 apps.
Others: 10 apps.
Total: 55 apps. 1 gl.

BRITTAN, Richard Charles

Role: Full-back 1911-14
5ft.11ins. 12st.8lbs.
Born: Isle of Wight, 7th August 1887
Died: Leigh, Kent, 31st July 1949

CAREER: Portsmouth 1904/ Northampton Town cs. 1906/ SPURS Oct 1911/Cardiff City Nov 1913/retired 1924.

Debut v Notts County (FL) (h) 21.10.1911

Charlie Brittan had established himself as possibly the best right-back in the Southern League when Spurs signed him from Northampton Town. Having begun as a sixteen-year-old at Portsmouth, he moved to Northampton and in five years with the "Cobblers" made five appearances for the Southern League in Inter-League matches. He improved steadily under the guidance of Northampton manager Herbert Chapman who was able to extract a stiff fee plus reserve forward "Darkie" Tull from Spurs for his transfer. However, he was not quite able to live up to his reputation in the higher grade of football and could never be sure of a place in the team. At the start of the 1913-14 season he was unable to displace Tom Collins or Fred Webster and when, in November 1913, manager Peter McWilliam preferred to replace the injured Collins with Bill Cartwright, Brittan demanded a transfer. His request was granted and he moved back to the Southern League, joining Cardiff City where he made a further appearance for the Southern League, two appearances for the Welsh League and helped Cardiff win the Welsh Cup in 1920 and 1922. He retired in 1924 to follow a business career and later went into politics as a member of Cardiff City Council.

Appearances:
League: 42* apps.
FA Cup: 2 apps.
Others: 11 apps.
Total: 55 apps. 0 gls.
* Includes 2 abandoned matches.

BRITTON, John

Role: Goalkeeper 1925-28
6ft.0ins. 12st.8lbs.
Born: Campsie, Lennoxtown, 18th March 1900
Died: Campsie, Lennoxtown, 8th October 1953

CAREER: Duntocher Hibernians/Albion Rovers Oct 1920/Dundee Aug 1924/**SPURS** Mar 1926/released May 1928/Celtic/Kirkintilloch Rob Roy Dec 1931.

Debut v West Ham United (FL) (a) 20.3.1926

The 1920s were a difficult time for Spurs as far as the goalkeeping position was concerned, and particularly so in the middle part of the decade. The club seemed unable to find anybody who could provide either the strength or reliability needed to help turn Spurs from a middle of the table team to one capable of challenging for the title. When Jock Britton was signed in March 1926 he became the fourth 'keeper Spurs had tried that season, following Fred Hinton, Bill Kaine and Jimmy Smith. He completed the campaign as number one choice, but when injured in pre-season training found Smith back in favour. Britton battled back to again finish the season in the team, saw Joe Nicholls replace him at the start of 1927-28, but once more recovered his place. However, Spurs were struggling from the start of the following season and in December 1928 manager Billy Minter invested in the experienced Cyril Spiers. With the club still getting relegated, Minter began to plan for the future and in May 1928 Britton was released. He subsequently joined Celtic although never making their first eleven.

Appearances:
League: 40 apps.
Others: 3 apps.
Total: **43 apps. 0 gls.**

BROADIS, Ivan Arthur

Role: Inside-forward 1940-46
5ft.9ins. 11st.5lbs.
Born: Isle of Dogs, London, 18th December 1922

CAREER: Glengall Road School/Coopers Company School/Middlesex Schools/Tottenham Juniors/Golders Green/Finchley/**SPURS** am. Aug 1939/Northfleet United/(guest for Bradford Park Avenue, Carlisle United, Distillery, Manchester United and Millwall during World War Two)/Carlisle United player-manager Aug 1946/Sunderland Feb 1949/Manchester City Oct 1951/Newcastle United Oct 1953/Carlisle United player-coach Jul 1955/Queen of the South Jul 1959, coach Jul 1960-1962.

Debut v Clapton Orient (LWC) (h) 4.1.1941

Ivor Broadis was one of the most skilful inside-forwards of his generation, a man with excellent ball control, the ability to make space for himself and to create chances for his colleagues, and an eye for goal that bought him more than his fair share of goals. However, while he started his career at White Hart Lane, it was with Manchester City and Newcastle United that he enjoyed his best days. He was an amateur throughout his time with Spurs, signing as such during the Second World War. Too young to join the forces, he was able to turn out regularly for Spurs in the 1940-41 season and the whole of the next, winning his first representative honour in April 1942 when he played for a Football Association XI against the Metropolitan Police. Many players lost the best years of their career to the war, but for Broadis it was a benefit as he was playing against first class opponents at an age when, were it not for the war, he would still have been in the junior side. After joining the forces,

Broadis was not so readily available to Spurs, but was in demand as a guest and spent the bulk of the 1945-46 season assisting Carlisle United. In August 1946 Carlisle offered him professional terms, not just as a player but as player/manager and Spurs allowed him to leave. It was, perhaps, a poor decision by the Spurs management for Broadis was highly successful with the Third Division (North) club and in February 1949 transferred himself to Sunderland. A member of England's 1950 World Cup squad, he moved on to Manchester City and made his England debut against Austria in November 1951. He played for the Football League three times and won seven more caps before making the move to Newcastle United where he won another six caps. In July 1955, he went back to Carlisle as player/coach and played for them for another three years, still good enough to play for the Third Division (North) against the Third Division (South) each season, until finishing his playing career with one year at Queen of the South. He later worked as a coach while building the career as a respected sports journalist that eventually took up all his time. In July 2006 one of the stands at Carlisle's Brunton Park ground was named after Broadis.

Appearances:
Others: 85 apps. 38 gls.
Total: **85 apps. 38 gls.**

BROOKE, Garry James

Role: Midfielder 1980-85
5ft.6ins. 10st.5lbs.
Born: Bethnal Green, London, 24th November 1960

CAREER: Winns School/Sidney Chaplin Junior High School/Waltham Forest District Schools/McEntree Seniors/Essex County/**SPURS** app. Jun 1977, pro. Oct 1978/(GAIS (Sweden) loan Apr-Oct 1980)/Norwich City May 1985/Groningen (Holland) Dec 1986/Wimbledon Mar 1988/(Stoke City loan Mar 1990)/Brentford Aug 1990/Baldock Town Jan 1991/(Colchester United loan Jan 1991)/Reading non-contract Feb 1991/Wivenhoe Town Apr 1991/St Albans City Sep 1991/Romford Oct 1992/Worthing Nov 1992/Cornard United Aug 1993/Braintree Town Oct 1994/Worthing Sep 1996.

Debut v West Bromwich Albion (sub) (FL) (h) 29.11.1980
(Weymouth (Fr) (a) 17.11.1980)

A stocky, strongly-built midfield player with a cracking long-range shot, Garry Brooke worked his way through the junior ranks at White Hart Lane to make his League debut in November 1980. At the end of that season he won an FA Cup winner's medal playing as substitute in the first match against Manchester City and remaining on the bench in the replay. He repeated the feat in 1981 82, playing as substitute in both matches against Queens Park Rangers, and was beginning to establish himself as replacement for the exiled Ossie Ardiles when he suffered serious injuries in a car crash in February 1983. Happily, he recovered, but he was never quite the same player again and was allowed to join Norwich City for £50,000. Unable to find a place in the Canaries team he moved to Groningen of Holland, impressing particularly in the small Dutch club's UEFA Cup challenge. However, Brooke's wife was unable to settle in Holland and he returned to London with Wimbledon.

Unhappy with their direct style of play, he was rarely able to break into the League side and at the end of the season was given a free transfer. He signed for Brentford and linked up with former Spurs reserve Phil Holder who had taken on the role of caretaker manager following the surprise resignation of Steve Perryman. Still unable to establish himself back in the Football League, Brooke joined Colchester United on what was intended to be a long-term loan with a view to a permanent transfer. Within a month he was on trial with Reading, before signing for Wivenhoe Town where he joined former Spurs team-mates John Lacy and Paul Price. In the summer of 1991 he moved, along with Price, to St Albans City and then moved around the non-League scene until taking on the role of a statistics recorder for the PFA and Press Association.

Appearances:
League: 49 (24) apps. 15 gls.
FA Cup: 4 (8) apps. 1 gl.
FL Cup: 4 (1) apps. 1 gl.
Euro: 6 (5) apps. 1 gl.
Others: 21 (7) apps. 7 gls.
Total: 84 (45) apps. 25 gls.

BROOKS, John

Role: Inside-forward 1952-60
5ft.10ins. 12st.0lbs.
Born: Reading, Berkshire, 23rd December 1931
Died: Bournemouth, Dorset, 7th June 2016

CAREER: Reading Schools/Berkshire Schools/Coley Old Boys/Mount Pleasant Youth Club/Castle Street Institute/Reading am. Feb 1949, pro. Apr 1949/**SPURS** Feb 1953/Chelsea Dec 1959/Brentford Sep 1961/Crystal Palace Jan 1964/Toronto City (Canada) May 1964/Stevenage Town Oct 1964/Toronto City (Canada) May 1965/Cambridge City cs. 1968/Cleveland Stokers (USA) May 1968/Knebworth player-manager 1973-/Letchworth/Knebworth/Moordown Youth coach/Bournemouth FC President.

Debut v Stoke City (FL) (a) 6.4.1953

Johnny Brooks, who had signed professional for Reading after only six weeks on their ground-staff, joined Spurs in preference to Newcastle United for a £3,000 fee, with Dennis Uphill and Harry Robshaw making the reverse journey in part-exchange. The mid 1950's were a transitional time for Spurs, the "Push and Run" team breaking up before the "Double" side took shape, and at first Brooks found it hard to made the step up to the First Division. However, by the end of the 1954-55 season he had established a place and with the departure of Eddie Baily in January 1956, assumed the main creative role. A thoughtful but naturally gifted player, Brooks had great dribbling ability and an amazing body-swerve that enabled him to cut a swathe through defences. His fine distribution, shrewd positional sense and shooting ability soon caught the eye of the England selectors. He won his first cap against Wales in November 1956 and although he scored in each of his first two games the third, against Denmark, was to be his last. Unfortunately, he did not work well with Johnny Haynes, England's senior schemer. Brooks then found himself under threat in the Spurs team from Alfie Stokes and, unable to retain a regular place, was even tried as a winger. If Brooks had one fault it was that he was perhaps not consistent enough; his concentration tending to wander. With Bill Nicholson looking to build a new team, Brooks moved to Chelsea in a £20,000 part-exchange deal for Les Allen, linking-up with his former Reading manager Ted Drake. Less than two years later he joined Brentford and was a member of their 1963 Fourth Division Championship team. He finished his League career with Crystal Palace and then moved into non-League circles although he also spent two summers in Toronto. When his football career was over, Brooks worked for several years as a broker's messenger in the City of London. His son, Shaun, was a midfielder who played for Crystal Palace, Orient, AFC Bournemouth and Barnet. In November 1945 Brooks scored 19 goals as his Castle Street Institute side beat Suttons 44-1 in a Reading Minor Cup-tie.

Appearances:
League: 166 apps. 46 gls.
FA Cup: 13 apps. 5 gls.
Others: 43* apps. 21 gls.
Total: 222 apps. 72 gls.
* Includes 1 abandoned match

BROOKS, Samuel Ernest

Role: Outside-left 1922-24
5ft.3ins. 9st.8lbs.
Born: Brierley Hill, Staffordshire, 27th March 1890
Died: Wolverhampton, Staffordshire, 13th January 1960

CAREER: Bent Street School/Brierley Hill Corinthians/Brierley Hill Alliance/Bilston United Sep 1906/Cradley Heath & St Luke's/Wolverhampton Wanderers am.1908, pro. Aug 1910/(guest for Birmingham and Grimsby Town during World War One)/**SPURS** Jul 1922/Kidderminster Harriers cs. 1924/Southend United Jan 1925/Kidderminster Harriers Jun 1925/Cradley Heath Alliance/Stourbridge/Kidderminster Harriers Sep 1926/retired 1927.

Debut v Arsenal (FL) (a) 30.9.1922
(Corinthians (Fr) (a) 11.9.1922 (scored once))

As a boy, Sammy Brooks played local junior football until as a 16-year old, joining Bilston United, where he was spotted by Wolverhampton Wanderers. Initially associated with Wolves as an amateur, within two years of signing professional forms he was the established first choice left-winger. He represented the Football League against the Irish League in October 1914, played for England against Wales in a 1919-20 Victory

international, and appeared in the 1921 FA Cup Final. Indeed, Brooks had a great chance to score an equaliser in that game and had it not been for a desperate tackle by Charlie Walters it might have been Brooks, and not Jimmy Dimmock, who was the hero of the day. Only 5ft.3ins tall, he was very similar in style to Fanny Walden and with his signing for Spurs great things were expected with the two little men on opposite wings. However, it was not to be. Brooks proved a major disappointment and in May 1924, after only three goals in 16 appearances, was placed on the transfer list. At first no club came in for him and he played for Birmingham League Kidderminster, with Spurs retaining his Football League registration, until a transfer to Southend United. He later played for Cradley Heath and Stourbridge. Brooks' brother, Ernie, played for Blackburn Rovers, Wolverhampton Wanderers and Brierley Hill Alliance.

Appearances:
League: 10 apps. 1 gl.
Others: 6 apps. 2 gls.
Total: **16 apps. 3 gls.**

BROOKS

Role: Outside-right 1918-19

Debut v Haydn Price's XI (Fr) (St Albans) 31.8.1918

Brooks only game for Spurs was when he played in a "scratch" Spurs team that met Corporal Haydn Price's XI in a charity friendly match at St Albans. He appeared as a trialist but did not perform well enough to have any further association with the club.

Appearances:
Others: 1 app.
Total: **1 app. 0 gls.**

BROTHERSTON, Noel

Role: Winger 1975-76
5ft.8ins. 10st.8lbs.
Born: Dundonald nr. Belfast, 18th November 1956
Died: Blackburn, Lancashire, 6th May 1995

CAREER: Dundonald Boys High School/North Down Schools/Northern Ireland Schools/**SPURS** app. Sep 1972, pro. Apr 1974/Blackburn Rovers Jul 1977/Bury Jun 1987/(Scarborough loan Oct 1988)/(Motola (Sweden) loan Feb 1989)/Chorley cs. 1990.

Debut v Aston Villa (FL) (h) 13.3.1976
(Millwall (sub) (Fr) (a) 27.10.1975)

Regarded by Spurs as a pure and simple winger, Noel Brotherston was not really given a chance at White Hart Lane, making only one League appearance before being released on a free transfer. He joined Blackburn Rovers where, operating in the then more fashionable withdrawn winger/midfield role, he proved a great, and successful, servant playing over 300 League games, representing Northern Ireland in their first Under-21 international and collecting 27 caps for the full international team before signing for Bury. He had one good season with Bury, played on loan to League newcomers Scarborough and the Swedish club, Motola, before being joining Chorley on a free transfer at the end of the 1989-90 season. Having finished with regular football, Brotherston worked as a roofer and was still playing for Blackburn Veterans when he died of a heart attack in May 1995.

Appearances:
League: 1 app.
Others: 1 (1) apps.
Total: **2 (1) apps. 0 gls.**

BROUGH, Joseph

Role: Half-back 1908-09
5ft.7ins. 10st.10lbs.
Born: Burslem, Staffordshire, 9th November 1886
Died: Stockton Brook, 5th October 1968

CAREER: Burslem Park Boys/Smallthorne FC/Burslem Port Vale am. 1906, pro. Feb 1907/Stoke Sep 1907/**SPURS** Jul 1908/Burslem Port Vale Sep 1909/Liverpool Aug 1910/Bristol City Jan 1912/Burslem Port Vale Apr 1913/retired cs. 1922.

Debut v Wolverhampton Wanderers (FL) (a) 28.12.1908
(West Ham United (LFACC) (a) 30.11.1908)

Joe Brough was signed from Stoke in July 1908, after Spurs had taken their place in the Football League, and perhaps as part of the deal done between the clubs whereby Stoke initially agreed to support Spurs as their replacements. A centre-forward with Burslem Port Vale, Brough was hampered by ill-health in his time at White Hart Lane and made only three senior appearances before returning to the Staffordshire club. He then had brief spells with Liverpool and Bristol City before re-joining Burslem for a third spell. He remained with the Potteries club until 1922, during which time they replaced Leeds City in the Football League.

Appearances:
League: 1 app.
FA Cup: 1 app.
Others: 1 app.
Total: **3 apps. 0 gls.**

BROWN, Alexander

Role: Centre-forward 1900-02
5ft.10ins. 11st.6lbs.
Born: Glenbuck, Ayrshire, 7th April 1879
Died: Glranity, New Zealand, ?? March 1944

CAREER: Glenbuck Athletic/Kilsyth Wanderers/Edinburgh St Bernards pro. Jul 1895/Preston North End cs. 1896/Portsmouth cs. 1899/**SPURS** May 1900/Portsmouth May 1902/Middlesbrough May 1903/Luton Town cs. 1905/Kettering cs. 1907.

Debut v Millwall Athletic (SL) (h) 1.9.1900

A truly prodigious goal-scorer in his short time with Spurs, "Sandy" Brown had quickly moved up through the ranks of Scottish football

before moving down to England with Preston North End. Given few chances in his three years in Lancashire, he moved on to Portsmouth for their inaugural season. His talents were quickly spotted by Spurs, and after just the one season on the south coast his transfer was secured. Brown's impact was immediate, for it was his goals that were responsible for the club winning the FA Cup for the first time at the end of his initial season. He scored both the goals in the 1901 Final and then added the deciding strike in the Final Replay to give him a goal in every round of the competition and a total of 15-a record that stands to this day and will probably never be bettered. Although he looked idle when not in possession, Brown was a true opportunist and as soon as the ball arrived there was only one place he would go-straight for goal. With his two compatriots John Cameron and David Copeland at inside-forward, he was given plenty of opportunities to do just that. His scoring continued unabated the following season and, having played for the Anglo-Scots against the Home-Scots in an international trial in March 1902, he was selected for the full Scotland team against England on 5th April 1902, an ill-fated match subsequently declared void due to the Ibrox Disaster. Brown did not get a further chance to be one of Spurs' Scottish internationalists for at the end of the season he was allowed to return to Portsmouth. He spent one season with Pompey, before enjoying two years at Middlesbrough. During that time, he at last won a Scottish cap playing against England in April 1904. Twelve months later he joined Luton Town and continued to find the back of the net regularly before finishing his career in 1907-08 with Kettering. He later emigrated to New Zealand with his wife, a daughter of WF Gilboy, landlord of the White Hart. His last match for Spurs was in April 1907 when he returned to White Hart Lane to play for the 1901 FA Cup-winning side against a "Team of the South" in a benefit match for former Spurs' trainer Sam Mountford. Brown's brother, Tom, played a few games for Portsmouth in 1903-04. After the FA Cup success of 1901 Brown reputedly took the trophy to his home village of Glenbuck in Ayrshire and put it on display in the window of the local Co-op.

Appearances:
Southern: 46 apps. 30 gls.
FA Cup: 11 apps. 15 gls.
Others: 56 apps. 51 gls.
Total: 113 apps. 96 gls.

BROWN, Charles

Role: Half-back 1902-04
5ft.8ins. 11st.9lbs.
Born: Greenock

CAREER: New Brighton Tower/Stalybridge Rovers cs. 1899/Everton May 1901/**SPURS** May 1902/released cs. 1904/Hull City trial Sep 1904/Reading Sep 1904/Luton Town cs. 1905.

Debut v Brentford (LL) (a) 6.10.1902

Having started his career with New Brighton Tower and spent two years with Stalybridge, helping them win the Lancashire League title, Charles Brown joined Everton for the 1901-02 season and, although restricted to the reserves, was developing well with the club keen to retain his services. However, when Spurs invited him to sign in the summer of 1902 he was glad to accept the offer. Although only 5ft.7ins tall, Brown was powerfully built and expected to provide stiff opposition at half-back to the likes of John and Ollie Burton, Jimmy McNaught, Ted Hughes, Jack Jones and Tom Morris. Unfortunately, he proved a disappointment and made few first team appearances in the main competition of the time, the Southern League. He made his debut in a London League match in October 1902 and whilst almost a regular until about February, by the next season he had to be content with a place in the reserves. Come the summer of 1904 he was released. Unable to find a new club immediately, he had a month's trial with Hull City before signing for Reading. A year later he moved on to Luton Town.

Appearances:
Southern: 14 apps.
Others: 24* apps. 1 gl.
Total: 38 apps. 1 gl.
* Includes 1 abandoned match

BROWN, David Crichton

Role: Centre-forward 1909-11
5ft.8ins. 10st.12lbs.
Born: Broughty Ferry, Angus, 26th July 1889

CAREER: Forthill Athletic/**SPURS** May 1909/Reading trial Aug 1911 /Birmingham trial Sep 1911/Merthyr Town trial Oct 1911/Morton Oct 1911.

Debut v Liverpool (FL) (a) 26.3.1910

David Brown joined Spurs in May 1909 from Forthill Athletic, a north of Scotland club, but was to make only one first team appearance in his two seasons with the club. That came in March 1910 when he played at Liverpool, standing-in for the injured Percy Humphries. At the end of the season he was released, but Spurs changed their mind and re-signed him for the following campaign which he again spent in the reserve side. Released once more at the end of the 1910-11 season, he had trials with Reading, Birmingham and Merthyr Town before signing for Morton.

Appearances:
League: 1 app.
Others: 1 app. 1 gl.
Total: 2 apps. 1 gl.

BROWN, Harold Thomas

Role: Goalkeeper 1944-45
6ft.0ins. 11st. 4lbs.
Born: Kingsbury, London, 9th April 1924
Died: Abingdon, Oxfordshire, ?? June 1982.

CAREER: Queens Park Rangers Jun 1940/(guest for Arsenal, Brentford, Crystal Palace and **SPURS** during World War Two)/Chelsea trial/Notts County Apr 1946/Derby County Oct 1949/Queens Park Rangers Aug 1951/Plymouth Argyle Aug 1956/Exeter City Sep 1958.

Debut v Aldershot (FLS) (h) 4.11.1944

A young keeper with Queens Park Rangers, Harry Brown played three matches for Spurs as a guest in November 1944. During the war, he also guested for Crystal Palace and Brentford and played as a substitute for Arsenal in their famous match against Moscow Dynamo at White Hart Lane in November 1945. At the end of the War he moved from Rangers to Notts County and then spent two years with Derby County before returning to Loftus Road. Five years later he signed for Plymouth Argyle and after two years made his final move to Exeter City, although he did not make their League side.

Appearances:
Others: 3 apps.
Total: 3 apps. 0 gls.

BROWN, Ivor Erwin Ronald John

Role: Centre-forward 1909-11
5ft.8ins. 11st.0lbs.
Born: Shardlow, Derbyshire, 1st April 1888
Died: Swansea, 1966

CAREER: Ripley Town/**SPURS** trial Oct 1909, pro. Nov 1909/Coventry City Jul 1911/Reading May 1913/Swansea Town Feb 1914/Porth Athletic cs. 1920.

Debut v Notts County (FL) (h) 30.10.1909
(Croydon Common (LFACC) (h) 11.10.1909 (scored once))

Born under the name Ivor Erwin and signed on trial from the Derbyshire League club Ripley Town, Ivor Brown was a 5ft.8ins centre-forward of whom much was expected. With a reputation as a great opportunist at Ripley, he went straight into Spurs' first team making his debut in a London FA Charity Cup match with Croydon Common. His first League appearance was against Preston North End on 23rd October 1909 but the match was abandoned after fifty minutes due to rain and so his "official" League bow came the following week. Signed professional after a month's trial, he showed great promise to start with, scoring in the Charity Cup matches, but was unable to find the net in any of the eight League matches he played that first season. The same applied the following season at the end of which he was released and joined Southern League Coventry City. He spent two years with Coventry, one with Reading and then joined Swansea Town with whom he appeared after the First World War.

Appearances:
League: 13* apps.
Others: 5 apps. 4 gls.
Total: 18 apps. 4 gls.
* Includes 1 abandoned match

BROWN, John James

Role: Inside-forward 1936-37
6ft.1ins. 12st.8lbs.
Born: Kilmarnock, 31st December 1908
Died: Berkeley Heights, New Jersey, USA, 9th November 1994

CAREER: Loans Athletic Juniors/Plainfield/Bayonne Rovers (USA) 1927/Newark Skeeters (USA) 1928-29/New York Nationals (USA)/New York Giants (USA) 1929-30/New York Soccer Club (USA)/Brooklyn Wanderers (USA) 1930-31/Newark Americans (USA)/Manchester United Aug 1932/Brentford May 1934/**SPURS** Sep 1936/Guildford Jul 1937/Clydebank 1940/Greenwich High School (USA) coach 1950-51/Greensport United player-president 1951-52/Brunswick School (USA) senior coach 1952-75/Polish Falcons manager 1957-58.

Debut v Bradford Park Avenue (FL) (h) 19.9.1936

Attending a school where only rugby was played, Jimmy Brown's early football experience was limited to juvenile level at home in Scotland. In September 1927, he moved to America to join his father, where he played for Bayonne Rovers before moving into the professional American Soccer League with Newark, New York Nationals and New York Giants. Whilst with the Giants he played at outside-right for America in all four of their 1930 World Cup Finals matches. He tried his luck in the Football League with Manchester United and looked to be a very promising player, but sadly the promise failed to develop. He spent two-and-a-half anonymous years with Brentford before his transfer to White Hart Lane, but made only four senior appearances for Spurs early in the 1936-37 season, then spent the rest of the campaign in the reserves. Not retained in April 1937, he signed for Guildford three months later where, playing alongside his brother Dick, he helped them lift the Southern League title in his first season. His career in England ended with World War Two when he returned to America. In 1950, he formed Greensport United and played for them for two years alongside his son, George, helping them win the Connecticut State Amateur League, which he also helped form, in 1951. He later moved onto coaching, serving the Brunswick School for 22 years. Two of Brown's brothers were professional goalkeepers; Tom with Ipswich Town and John with Clyde, Hibernians and Scotland, and his son, George, represented the USA against Mexico in 1957.

Appearances:
League: 4 apps.
Total: 4 apps. 0 gls.

BROWN, Laurence

Role: Centre-half or centre-forward 1963-66
6ft.0ins. 12st.10lbs.
Born: Shildon, County Durham, 22nd August 1937
Died: Aycliffe, County Durham, 30th September 1998

CAREER: Timothy Hackworth School/All Saints Sec. Modern School/Bishop Auckland Schools/Durham Schools/Shildon Workers Juniors/All Saints Rovers/Shildon Town/Woking Town/Bishop Auckland/Fulham am. Mar 1957/Darlington am. Mar 1959/Northampton Town pro. Oct 1960/Arsenal Aug 1961/**SPURS** Feb 1964/Norwich City Sep 1966/Bradford Park Avenue player-manager Dec 1968/Altrincham player-manager Nov 1969/Kings Lynn player-manager Dec 1970/Stockton manager/Tow Law Town manager.

Debut v Arsenal (FL) (h) 22.2.1964

An England amateur international centre-forward who won 14 caps at that level and represented Great Britain in the Rome Olympics of 1960, Laurie Brown made his reputation with Bishop Auckland before turning professional with Northampton Town. Associated with Fulham as an amateur, he played three League games as an amateur for Darlington in 1959-60, but it was his 21 goals in only 33 appearances for the Cobblers that attracted the attention of the big clubs and led to him joining Arsenal. Despite his goal-scoring record, Arsenal saw him as a defensive wing or centre-half and in two-and-a-half years he made over 100 senior appearances in those roles. The arrival of Ian Ure eventually forced him out of the team at Highbury and Bill Nicholson signed Brown for £40,000, rather strangely, as the likely long-term replacement for ageing centre-forward Bobby Smith. Brown made his Spurs' debut against his old club one day after his transfer, helping Spurs to a 3-1 win, but unfortunately his goal-scoring form had deserted him and by the start of the next season Brown found himself in the reserves, back in a defensive role. It was in that position that he played the majority of his games for Spurs, taking over the centre-half berth when Maurice Norman's career was ended by injury. In August 1966 Mike England was signed, and it became clear Brown's further opportunities at White Hart Lane would be limited. A £25,000 move to Norwich City followed. He finished his League career as player/manager with Bradford Park Avenue and held the same position with Altrincham and Kings Lynn before managing Stockton back in his native North East. When he left football, Laurie ran a public house and later worked as a milkman in County Durham.

Appearances:
League: 62 apps. 3 gls.
FA Cup: 3 apps.
Others: 21 (1) apps.
Total: **86 (1) apps. 3 gls.**

BROWN, Michael Robert

Role: Midfielder 2003-06
5ft.8ins. 11st.8lbs.
Born: Hartlepool, County Durham, 25th January 1977

CAREER: Hartlepool St Francis/Lion Hillcarter//Manchester City trainee Jul 1993, pro. Sep 1994/(Hartlepool United loan Mar 1997)/(Portsmouth loan Nov 1997)/Sheffield United loan Dec 1999, perm Jan 2000/**SPURS** Jan 2004/Fulham Jan 2006/Wigan Athletic Jul 2007/Portsmouth Aug 2009/Leeds United Jul 2011-May 2014/Port Vale player-coach Jul 2014, asst. manager Jun 2016.

Debut v Liverpool (PL) (h) 17.1.2004

Michael Brown was the type of midfield worker who never knew when to stop running, always prepared to give of his best for every minute of every game. It was a laudable attitude, but at the very top level of football not quite enough. Brown began his career with Manchester City, hustling and bustling through midfield, bursting forward, but always doing the donkey work in defending and winning the ball. He collected four caps for England at Under-21 level, but lacked the guile and skills to make the step up to the full team. After loan spells with Hartlepool United and Portsmouth, Brown joined Sheffield United, initially on loan, but with the move quickly made permanent. With the Blades, Brown found the perfect platform for his talents in a club where the work ethic was considered an acceptable substitute for the skills demanded at many bigger clubs. Brown became a cult hero at Sheffield United, but could not resist the chance of another stab at the top flight when Spurs made a bid for him. Brown's attributes were desperately needed at the time as Spurs midfield lacked the ball-winner Brown could be. For a short while Brown did the job needed of him. but with the arrival of Frank Arnesen, Jacques Santini and Martin Jol, Brown found himself on the fringes of the first team. After two years at White Hart Lane he was allowed to move to Fulham, making the further move to Wigan Athletic eighteen months later. When he joined Portsmouth, they were comfortably placed in the Premier League but financial difficulties were just around the corner. Brown played his part in helping them reach the FA Cup final in 2010, including a semi-final victory over Spurs, but could not prevent them being relegated. Unlike many of his colleagues he remained with the relegated club, playing regularly until December 2010 when the stage was reached that one more appearance would mean an extension to his contract and an increase in wages. Pompey simply could not afford that, so Brown was left on the touchlines until his contract ran out at the end of the season, leaving him free to join Leeds United. He gave Leeds great service for three years until the financially strapped club decided it could not afford his services, allowing Port Vale to sign him.

Appearances:
League: 39 (11) apps. 2 gls.
FA Cup: 9 apps.
FL Cup: 4 (1) apps. 1 gl.
Others: 4 (2) apps. 1 gl.
Total: **56 (14) apps. 4 gls.**

BROWN, R

Role: Outside-right 1917-18

Debut v Crystal Palace (LFC) (h) 16.2.1918

Nothing is known about this player who made two appearances in the London Football Combination competition of 1917-18.

Appearances:
Others: 2 apps.
Total: **2 apps. 0 gls.**

BROWN, Robert Samuel

Role: Full-back 1919-24
5ft.9ins. 11st.7lbs.
Born: Southampton, Hampshire, 16th October 1895
Died: Isle of Wight, Hampshire, April qtr. 1980

CAREER: Cowes (Isle of Wight)/Thorneycrofts/**SPURS** cs. 1919/retired cs. 1925/Aldershot 1927/Newport (Isle of Wight) 1928.

Debut v Barnsley (FL) (h) 27.12.1919
(Crystal Palace (LFACC) (a) 6.10.1919)

Although Bob Brown made his senior debut in a London FA Charity Cup match with Crystal Palace in October 1919, he had to wait until the end of the year for a League debut. He then retained a place for the rest of the season, helping Spurs run away with the Second Division title. Thereafter, he was unable to reproduce his earlier dependable form and consigned to the reserves, although his cause was not helped by several injuries. Called upon only when one of the established full-backs was unavailable, he remained with the club until being transfer-listed in April 1925. He received several offers, but refused them all, choosing instead to retire and run a butcher's shop in his home town although he did later play for Aldershot and Newport (Isle of Wight). In later life, he was a publican for many years on the Isle of Wight.

Appearances:
League: 37 apps.
FA Cup: 8 apps.
Others: 4 apps.
Total: **49 apps. 0 gls.**

BROWN, Roy Ernest Eric

Role: Goalkeeper 1962-68
6ft.1ins. 12st.10lbs.
Born: Hove, Sussex, 5th October 1945

CAREER: Sussex Schools/**SPURS** app. Sep 1961, pro. Oct 1962/Reading Jul 1968/(Dartford loan Mar 1970)/Notts County Jul 1970/Mansfield Town non-contract Nov 1975.

Debut v Blackpool (FL) (h) 15.10.1966

Roy Brown's only appearance for Spurs came four years to the day after he had signed professional forms when, with Bill Brown transferred to Northampton Town only two days earlier, Pat Jennings was injured. Having gained local schoolboy honours, he first came to Spurs' attention playing for England against The Rest in a Schoolboys international trial. With two such consistent international 'keepers ahead of him as Brown and Jennings, his chances were always limited and without a further senior outing to his credit he was allowed to move to Reading. He spent two years in Berkshire and then moved on to Notts County, finishing his career at the end of 1974-75 although he was to play one further League game, turning out for Mansfield as a non-contract player in November 1975.

Appearances:
League: 1 app.
Total: **1 app. 0 gls.**

BROWN, R P

Role: Inside-forward 1896-97

CAREER: St Bartholomew's Hospital/London Welsh/London Caledonians/Clapton/**SPURS** guest.

Debut v Southampton St Marys (Fr) (h) 29.10.1896 (scored once)

A member of the Clapton club, Brown made three appearances for Spurs as a guest in the 1896-97 season. The first was in a friendly in October 1896 when he scored once, and he played in another friendly in March 1897. He would probably not have turned out for the first team again had it not been for the misdemeanours of regular inside-right James Milliken. He was suspended in April 1897 for a breach of club rules and Brown stepped up to replace him in the last friendly match of the season, although he was not available for the last game of the season, the Final of the Wellingborough Charity Cup. For that match Spurs called upon the services of Dartford's S Brown.

Appearances:
Others: 3 apps. 1 gl.
Total: **3 apps. 1 gl.**

BROWN, S

Role: Inside-forward 1895-97

CAREER: Dartford/**SPURS** Oct 1895/Dartford Feb 1896/(**SPURS** guest Apr 1897).

Debut v Old Westminsters (LCC) (a) 9.11.1895

Brown joined Spurs in October 1895 from Dartford, but was to make only one appearance before returning to his former club. His debut was in a London Charity Cup tie with Old Westminsters, and although Spurs won that match it was their last in the competition as the decision was taken the following month to turn professional and the competition was only open to amateur clubs. Brown was injured in that game and unable to play again until February 1896 when, with Spurs' agreement, he decided to return to Dartford. He did however make two further appearances for Spurs, being called upon to play one friendly and then the Final of the Wellingborough Charity Cup against Wellingborough on 29th April 1897. Spurs were in difficulty getting together a reasonable team for the last match of the season. Several players had been suspended for disciplinary reasons and with the Clapton player R P Brown, who had been helping Spurs out, unable to play, Brown was called upon to play at outside-right.

Appearances:
Others: 3 apps.
Total: **3 apps. 0 gls.**

BROWN, William

Role: Centre-forward 1895-96
13st.0lbs.
Born: Preston, Lancashire, 1875

CAREER: Thornliebank/Preston North End 1893/**SPURS** Mar 1896/Lincoln City May 1896.

Debut v 1st Battalion Scots Guards (Fr) (h) 7.3.1896

One of Spurs' first signings as a professional club, Preston had decided Willie Brown was not up to the standard they required and agreed to his release so he could join Spurs. Although he did not score on his first appearance as Spurs won 8-0, he did go on to score eight goals in a total of 18 appearances in friendly matches that season, before joining Lincoln City. He spent only one season with Lincoln, injuries limiting him to just one outing.

Appearances:
Others: 18 apps. 8 gls.
Total: 18 apps. 8 gls.

BROWN, William Dallas Fyfe

Role: Goalkeeper 1959-67
6ft.1ins. 10st.2lbs.
Born: Arbroath, Angus, 8th October 1931
Died: Simcoe, Ontario, Canada, 30 November 2004

CAREER: Arbroath High School/Arbroath Cliffburn/Carnoustie Juvenilles/Scotland Schools/Carnoustie Panmure/Dundee Sep 1949/ **SPURS** Jun 1959/Northampton Town Oct 1966/Toronto Falcons (Canada) cs. 1967.

Debut v Newcastle United (FL) (a) 22.8.1959

The sterling last line of defence in the great Spurs team of the early 1960s, Bill Brown showed such all-round ability in his school days that he had a trial for Scotland Schools at outside-left. He played for the junior clubs Arbroath Cliffburn and Carnoustie Juvenilles and, having played for Scotland Schools as a 'keeper, signed for Carnoustie Panmure from whom he joined Dundee. He helped Dundee win the Scottish League Cup in 1952, won his first senior representative honour in February 1956 playing for Scotland "B" against England "B" and played for the Scottish League eight times. However, he had to stand by as reserve on no less than 22 occasions before winning a first full cap against France in June 1958, Scotland's last match of the World Cup competition. Joining Spurs for £16,500 as part of Bill Nicholson's rebuilding plans, Brown soon established himself as a worthy successor to Ted Ditchburn. Tall and lean, with safe hands, good positional sense and an accurate kick or throw that could quickly turn defence into attack, Brown was a solid, reliable 'keeper who liked to do the simple things with the minimum of fuss. His great strength was his consistency and, despite an occasional weakness on gathering crosses, he was an unflappable character who instilled confidence and reassured those around him. His powers of concentration and calmness were among the major factors that helped Spurs land the "Double" in 1961, the FA Cup in 1962 and the European Cup-Winners' Cup in 1963, a period when he was almost ever-present. With Spurs, he won 24 Scottish caps to add to the four collected with Dundee-a Scottish record at the time. It was only injuries and the emergence of Pat Jennings that then led to his absence from the team and in October 1966 he

moved to Northampton Town for a nominal fee having played his last game for Spurs in a friendly at Dundee earlier that month. He remained with Northampton until the end of the season and then played for Toronto Falcons in the "rebel" American National Professional Soccer League. He settled in Toronto, where he went into the real estate business.

Appearances:
League: 222 apps.
FA Cup: 23 apps.
Euro: 17 apps.
Others: 30 apps.
Total: 292 apps. 0 gls.

BROWNE, John Henry

Role: Centre-forward 1940-44
5ft.4ins. 8st.9lbs.
Born: Boughton Monchelsea nr Maidstone, Kent

CAREER: SPURS am. Jun 1934/Tottenham Juniors/Northfleet United 1939/Finchley.

Debut v Luton Town (FLS) (h) 23.11.1940

Jack Browne was a young centre-forward who first joined Spurs as an amateur in June 1934. After playing for Tottenham Juniors until the outbreak of the Second World War, he was sent down to Northfleet before being "farmed out" to Finchley who had several Spurs' juniors on their books during that time. His first appearance for Spurs lasted only 60 mins as the match with Luton Town at White Hart Lane had to be abandoned because of an air raid attack. He made three further appearances in 1943-44, but failed to score in any of his matches.

Appearances:
Others: 4 apps.
Total: 4 apps. 0 gls.

BROWNE, Robert James

Role: Half-back 1942-43
Born: Londonderry, Northern Ireland, 9th February 1912
Died: 1994

CAREER:
Maleven/Cooney Rovers/ Derry City/Leeds United Sep 1935/(guest for Aldershot, Derry City, Luton Town, **SPURS**, Swansea Town and Watford during World War Two)/York City Aug 1947-Jun 1948/Thorne Colliery player-manager 1949/Halifax Town coach Aug 1954, caretaker manager Oct-Nov 1954.

Debut v Queens Park Rangers (FLS) (a) 5.9.1942

Another war-time guest player, Bobby Browne was with Leeds United when he played for Spurs. He had joined Leeds from Derry City with whom he had represented the Irish League against the Football League in September 1935. As a Leeds player, he won six full caps for Northern Ireland prior to the outbreak of war; the first against England in October 1935. Introduced by Willie Hall, his first appearance for Spurs was on 5th September 1942 and he played in the next two matches. He continued to play for Leeds in the first post-war season but finished his career after only five League matches for York. He was later player/manager of Thorne Colliery and coach and caretaker-manager of Halifax Town.

Appearances:
Others: 3 apps.
Total: 3 apps. 0 gls.

BRYANT, Bernard L

Role: Centre-forward 1943-44

CAREER: Walthamstow Avenue/Chelsea am./(guest for Arsenal, Clapton Orient, Crystal Palace and SPURS during World War Two)/Hayes 1947-48.

Debut v Aldershot (FLSC) (a) 4.3.1944 (scored once)

An amateur international with Walthamstow Avenue, Bryant was registered with the Football League as a Chelsea player and turned out for them in the 1942-43 season. However, they did not require his services the next season so he was able to help out other London clubs and scored twice in his seven matches for Spurs.

Appearances:
Others: 7 apps. 2 gls.
Total: 7 apps. 2 gls.

BUCHAN

Role: Centre-half 1895-96

Debut v Luton Town (Fr) (a) 10.2.1896

A soldier serving with the Royal Scots, Buchan's only appearance for Spurs was in February 1896 when he played against Luton Town as a weak Spurs' team went down 0-9. Two days earlier he had played for the Scots against Spurs along with his fellow soldier Beveridge who also played in the match at Luton.

Appearances:
Others: 1 app.
Total: 1 app. 0 gls.

BUCKINGHAM, Victor Frederick

Role: Defender 1935-49
5ft.10ins. 11st.3lbs.
Born: Greenwich, South London, 23rd October 1915
Died: Chichester, Sussex, 26th January 1995

CAREER: Greenwich Schools/Tottenham Juniors/England Schools/Bromley/SPURS am. Oct 1931, pro. May 1934/Northfleet United 1934-35/(guest for Crewe Alexandra, Fulham, Millwall and Portsmouth during World War Two)/Moss (Norway) coach cs. 1946/Middlesex FA coach/Stanmore coach/Oxford University coach/Pegasus coach/SPURS coach 1949/Norsemen coach/Bradford Park Avenue manager Jun 1951/West Bromwich Albion manager Feb 1953/Ajax (Holland) manager May 1959/Sheffield Wednesday manager Jun 1961-Apr 1964/Ajax (Holland) manager Jul 1964/Fulham manager Jan 1965/Ethnikos (Greece) manager May 1968/Barcelona (Spain) manager Dec 1969/Sevilla (Spain) manager Mar 1972/Ethnikos (Greece) manager by Oct 1973/Al-Salmiya (Kuwait) coach late 1970s.

Debut v Bury (FL) (h) 16.11.1935

Although Vic Buckingham played over 300 matches for Spurs, it is as a coach and manager that he is perhaps best remembered in football circles. A tall, stylish player, originally a full-back, he was spotted very early in his career by Spurs and, after playing for the Tottenham Juniors and Northfleet, made the move up to the full professional staff at White Hart Lane. A versatile player at home in any of the defensive positions, he made his League debut at centre-half. By the outbreak of hostilities, he was established at half-back, but like so many players of his generation the best years of his career were lost to the war. Serving in the RAF, he regularly appeared in service and Football Association sides and played for England in two war-time internationals; against Wales in April and June 1941. He continued to appear for Spurs when available throughout the war years and also guested for other clubs, even playing for Portsmouth against Spurs in March 1944. When hostilities ceased he resumed his first team career, but the emergence of Bill Nicholson and Ron Burgess as first choice half-backs meant Buckingham reverting to full-back. Having spent his entire career with Spurs-none of it in the First Division-he took to coaching the juniors when he retired from playing early in the 1949-50 season. Buckingham already had experience in that area for in 1946 he spent the summer coaching Moss FC of Norway and on his return had coached Stanmore. Apart from looking after Spurs juniors, he also coached Oxford University and took Pegasus, the combined Oxford and Cambridge Universities team, to Amateur Cup success in 1950-51. His coaching talents were soon noticed and in June 1951 he embarked on a lengthy managerial career, firstly with Bradford Park Avenue and then West Bromwich Albion, who won the FA Cup and finished second in Division One in his first full season. On leaving Albion he coached Ajax of Amsterdam, taking them to the Dutch League title in 1961, and in March 1961, with his contract at Ajax due to expire in June, accepted an offer to manage Plymouth Argyle. However, he never filled the manager's chair at Home Park, for in May 1961 he was offered the post at Sheffield Wednesday and Plymouth agreed to release him. In January 1965 he joined Fulham, but after a continual struggle against relegation left after three years. He later managed Ethnikos of Greece and Barcelona and Sevilla of Spain, leading Barcelona to the Spanish Cup in 1971.

Appearances:
League: 208* apps. 1 gl.
FA Cup: 26 apps.
Others: 77 apps. 1 gl.
Total: 311 apps. 2 gls.
* Includes 1 abandoned match.

BUCKINGHAM, William F

Role: Half-back 1900-01

CAREER: Novocastrians/SPURS trial Aug 1900, pro. Oct 1900/Coventry City cs. 1901/Grays United cs. 1902/Willesden Town by Sep 1904.

Debut v Bristol City (WL) (a) 27.3.1901

A young member and captain of the local Novocastrians club, Buckingham was signed as a professional after impressing with his performances in the reserves during a trial period. He only stayed with Tottenham, as a reserve, for the one season although he did make nine appearances in first team matches late in the campaign when Spurs were preoccupied with their FA Cup run. and fielded reserve teams to keep the first eleven fresh for the Cup games. Released at the end of the season, he signed for Coventry City then moved on to Grays United and Willesden Town.

Appearances:
Southern: 6 apps.
Others: 3 apps.
Total: 9 apps. 0 gls.

BUCKLE, Robert

Role: Inside-forward 1882-95
Born: Tottenham, London, 17th October 1868
Died: Mitcham, Surrey, 14th April 1959

Debut v Brownlow Rovers (Fr) (h) 6.10.83

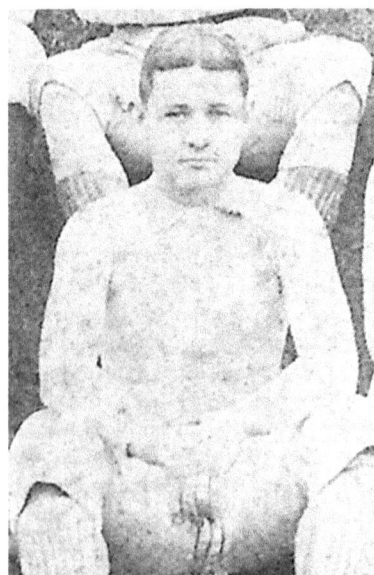

One of the pupils at Tottenham Grammar School who founded Spurs in 1882, Bobby Buckle was the club's first outside-left and turned out regularly for the first ten years of the club's existence, years when not only were the foundations laid for one of the world's best-known football clubs, but years when the style of play was developed which has ever since remained the cornerstone of the club's success. Buckle was only 14 years old when Spurs were founded, but it is evident that his left-wing partnership with Billy Harston provided a solid platform for much of the club's early success. Records of the club's early days are scant, so it is not possible to give full details of the matches he played in, but it is quite clear that in those early days a Spurs' team without Buckle was almost unthinkable. A small man, the first in a diminutive line of wingers like Fanny Walden and Terry Dyson, he was, by all accounts, a strong player who liked to be involved throughout the game. Apart from his prowess on the pitch, Buckle was a leader off it, for he was a member of the original committee, the man who put forward the resolution that the club should become professional and one of the original directors when the club became a limited company in 1898. His immediate association with Spurs ceased in June 1900 when he resigned from the board as he was leaving the Tottenham area, but he continued to follow the club's fortunes and was the man selected to propose the toast when the club won the FA Cup in 1921. Still going strong in 1951 it must have been a great thrill for Buckle to watch the club he helped create win the Football League title. In the early 1880s Buckle lived at White Cottage in White Hart Lane.

Appearances:
Others: 54 apps. 28 gls.
Total: 54 apps. 28 gls.

BUGG, James Walter

Role: Centre-half 1902-03
5ft.8ins. 10st.10lbs.
Born: Poplar, 25th May 1882

CAREER: Glengall Road School/Millwall St Johns/Millwall by 1900/West Norwood/Woolwich Arsenal/**SPURS** Sep 1902, released 1904/Norwich City Sep 1905-May 1907.

Debut v West Ham United (WL) (h) 16.2.1903

Walter Bugg was a member of the Millwall St Johns club that did so well in the 1898-99 season, winning all its 28 games with a goal record of 202 for and only 13 against, that it was adopted by Millwall as their reserve team. From Millwall Bugg moved on to West Norwood and Woolwich Arsenal, but did not progress past their reserve side and fared little better in his two years with Spurs. He made just one first team appearance. That was in February 1903 in a Western League fixture with West Ham United. Five days later Spurs were due to meet Bristol City in an FA Cup tie and almost the entire first team was rested with the fixture being fulfilled by a reserve eleven. Retained for the following season, Bugg did not make the first eleven again and was then released. In 1906-07 he played for Norwich City after turning out in some friendlies the previous season, although it was only in the last month of the campaign that he made the Canaries first team.

Appearances:
Others: 1 app.
Total: 1 app. 0 gls.

BUIST, Robert W

Role: Full-back or half-back 1895-96
Born: Kinning Park, Glasgow, 5th October 1869
Died: 1944

CAREER: Fairfield Rangers/Cowlairs/Clyde/Royal Arsenal Sep 1891/Leith Athletic Jun 1894/Royal Ordnance cs. 1895/**SPURS** trial Mar 1896/Gravesend United cs. 1896 -1899/(guest for Northfleet).

Debut v Gravesend United (Fr) (a) 4.3.1896

Bobby Buist played for Fairfield, Cowlairs and Clyde in his native Scotland before moving down to London and Royal Arsenal. He had three years there as a consistent performer and was a member of their first Football League team, before returning to Scotland and signing for Leith Athletic. Only a year later he was back in London with Royal Ordnance of the Southern League. A utility player, best at either full-back or centre-half, he played regularly for Royal Ordnance before being given a trial by Spurs late in the 1895-96 season. He played in three friendly matches, one at right-back, one at centre-half and one at outside-left. Although he did not impress Spurs sufficiently to be offered terms, he must have impressed Gravesend who provided the opposition in two of those matches, for he then joined the Kent club. He spent three years with them, during which time he also made at least one guest appearance for Northfleet. Buist's brother, George, also played for Woolwich Arsenal, joining them from Greenock Morton in September 1896.

Appearances:
Others: 3 apps.
Total: 3 apps. 0 gls.

BULL, E

Role: Half-back 1886-87

Debut v Silesia (Fr) (a) 13.11.1886

Nothing is known about this player who made his only appearance in Spurs' fourth year of existence.

Appearances:
Others: 1 app.
Total: 1 app. 0 gls.

BULL, Hedley Telfer

Role: Half-back 1882-93
Born: Keynsham, Bristol, September qtr. 1867

CAREER: SPURS cs. 1882/Robin Hood cs. 1893.

Debut v Remington (Fr) (h) 4.10.1884

Another of the club's founders, Hedley Bull made most of his known appearances in the half-back line, usually at centre-half. His first known appearance was in October 1884 in a friendly against Remington, but it has proved impossible to trace the team details for practically all Spurs' matches before then and it is certain he would have played in the majority of those early games. By all accounts a hard, rumbustious player, Bull ceased to play for Spurs at the end of the 1892-93 season when he joined the Robin Hood club, probably Spurs' most serious local rivals of the time.

Appearances:
Others: 33 apps.
Total: 33 apps. 0 gls.

BULL, Walter

Role: Half-back 1904-09
5ft.9ins. 12st.8lbs.
Born: Nottingham, 19th December 1874
Died: Nottingham, 28th July 1952

CAREER: Nuncargate/Newstead Byron/St Andrews Church/Notts County Apr 1894/**SPURS** May 1904/Heanor United Jun 1910/Gimnasia y Esgrima La Plata, Buenos Aires (Argentina) coach Apr 1911/ Northampton Town player-manager Jul 1912-Dec 1912.

Debut v Millwall (WL) (a) 3.10.1904

Walter Bull was one of the most highly rated footballers in the game when he signed for Spurs and his capture was regarded as a considerable coup for the Tottenham management, although it was not without problems. He was not able to make his debut until October 1904 due to a dispute between Spurs and Notts County over the transfer fee. Spurs offered £175, Notts County demanded £200 and when the Football Association met to decide the issue in October 1904 they ordered Spurs to pay £300! A thickset, beefy player, he could occasionally be thoughtful, but more often was far from subtle. He had the tenacity of a terrier and put it to good effect, particularly when marking an opponent. In his eight years with Notts County Bull was regarded as something of a utility player, appearing in every outfield position. Half-back was generally recognised as his best spot, indeed, he represented the Football League against the Scottish League at right-half in January 1901, but he spent his last season with County in both full-back and half-back positions. He had appeared in the first major game staged at White Hart Lane, playing a friendly against Spurs in September 1899, a match that demonstrated his remarkable versatility for when the County 'keeper Suters was injured it was Bull who replaced him between the posts. Although Bull never represented England, he did play in four trial matches (three of them as a Spurs player) and was first reserve to the England team on several occasions.

Apart from injuries he was a regular in the Spurs team until 1908-09, but even then, was called into the side for the last dozen games of the season to add experience and help ensure Spurs' promotion in their first Football League season. A member of the committee when the Players' Union was first formed in 1907, Bull left Spurs for Heanor United in June 1910. The following April he went to coach in Buenos Aires having previously visited Argentina with Spurs' touring party in 1909. He returned in July 1912, replacing Herbert Chapman as manager of Northampton Town when the former Spurs' forward moved to Leeds City. Bull was one of the founders of the Professional Footballers' Association.

Appearances:
Southern: 105 apps. 8 gls.
League: 12 apps.
FA Cup: 15 apps. 1 gl.
Others: 55* apps. 6 gls.
Total: 187 apps. 15 gls.
* Includes 1 abandoned match.

BULLING, Evelyn

Role: Full-back 1909-11
6ft.0ins. 12st.10lbs.
Born: East Retford, Nottingham, 11th December 1888
Died: Nottingham, 7th February 1963

CAREER: Nottingham Olympic/**SPURS** trial Mar 1909, pro. Apr 1909/released cs. 1911.

Debut v Liverpool (FL) (a) 29.10.1910
(Clapton Orient (LFACC) (h) 19.9.1910)

Ed Bulling was given a trial by Spurs on the recommendation of Walter Bull-who knew him from his days in Nottingham-and did enough to almost immediately be signed as a professional, quite a step up for someone who had previously played simply for fun with Nottingham Olympic. Just 20-years old when he arrived, he made only four first team appearances for Spurs, all in the 1910-11 season. The first was in a London FA Charity Cup tie with his League debut coming at Liverpool in October 1910. The following month he played his last two first team games, one each in the same competitions. At the end of the season Spurs decided not to retain his services. Bulling's brother, C, was also on Spurs' books for a short time before returning to Nottingham Olympic.

Appearances:
League: 2 apps.
Others: 2 apps.
Total: 4 apps. 0 gls.

BULLY

Role: Inside-forward 1918-19

Debut v West Ham United (LFC) (h) 16.11.1918

An air mechanic from Edmonton, Bully made his one appearance for Spurs by way of a trial in a London Football Combination fixture at Homerton, a home game for Spurs played on Clapton Orient's ground because White Hart Lane had been commandeered for war work.

Appearances:
Others: 1 app.
Total: 1 app. 0 gls.

BUMBERRY, Thomas William

Role: Goalkeeper 1882-90
Born: Islington, London, June qtr. 1867
Died: Stury, Kent, 2nd November 1924

Debut v Grange Park (Fr) (a) 17.1.1884

Goalkeeper in Spurs first ever competitive match, a London Association Cup tie with St. Albans, Tom Bumberry was a regular playing member of the club in its early days, although not one of the founders. Indeed, as he only joined the club during its first season of 1882-83 he had to pay double the membership fee the original members had paid. Detailed records of the club's earliest days are non-existent so it is impossible to give any clear idea of the number of matches he played, but he was certainly a member of the club for some years with many of his games played at reserve level. As was common in those early days, Bumberry was not a player limited to only one position. His only known appearance from 1889-90 was in the forward line.

Appearances:
Others: 5 apps. 1 gl.
Total: 5 apps. 1 gl.

BUNJEVČEVIĆ, Goran Petar

Role: Central Defender 2001-06
6ft.3ins. 12st.1lbs.
Born: Karlovac, Yugoslavia, 17th February 1973

CAREER: Hadjuk Split (Yugoslavia)/Dinamo Zagreb (Yugoslavia)/BUSK (Yugoslavia)/Grafičar Belgrade (Yugoslavia) 1992/Rad Belgrade (Yugoslavia) 1993/Red Star Belgrade (Yugoslavia) 1997/**SPURS** May 2001/ADO Den Haag (Holland) trial and permanent Aug 2006/retired May 2007/Red Star Belgrade Sporting Director Mar 2008-Aug 2008/FK Zemun (Serbia) general manager Nov 2012/Serbia FA Executive Committee vice-president, sporting director.

Debut v Aston Villa (PL) (h) 18.8.2001
(Stevenage Borough (Fr) (a) 13.7.2001)

Brought up in Split, Goran Bunjevčević was playing for the Hadjuk club and about to sign professional when his army officer father was transferred to Zagreb. The young Bunjevčević followed and looked set to build a career with Dinamo Zagreb until civil war broke out in the former Yugoslav republic. The Bunjevčević family was forced to flee to Belgrade where Bunjevčević signed for the amateur BUSK club, believing they were a nursery club to First Division outfit Čukarički. They were not, but Bunjevčević stayed with them for six months before moving on to Fourth Division Grafičar. Three years later he joined Belgrade's top club, Red Star, and quickly established himself as a crucial component of their team, helping them win the Yugoslav League title in 2000 and 2001 and the Cup in 1999 and 2000. Playing as a sweeper at the heart of the defence, Bunjevčević was not a big, powerful destroyer, but a cultured footballing defender, confident in possession, a good reader of the game and capable of making an incisive pass. Captain of Red Star, Spurs paid out £5 million to sign Bunjevčević, but almost immediately he suffered a series of injuries. Quite the opposite of his career in Yugoslavia where he had been almost injury free, he missed almost his entire first season at White Hart Lane. A stylish player, Bunjevčević was just the type of player Glenn Hoddle liked and was given ample opportunity to prove his worth both as a central defender and as a defensive midfielder operating in front of the back four. Sadly, after one good season injuries returned to haunt Bunjevčević and with Hoddle's departure he found himself out of favour, spending most of his time in the reserves. He was released in May 2006 and after a trial joined ADO Den Haag. He played regularly for most of his one season but after another injury found he was unable to continue playing and in May 2007 retired. The break-up of Yugoslavia meant Bunjevčević won full international honours as a Spurs player for two countries; Yugoslavia and Serbia-Montenegro.

Appearances:
League: 41 (10) apps.
FL Cup: 6 (1) apps. 2 gls.
Others: 32 (9) apps. 2 gls.
Total: 79 (20) apps. 4 gls.

BURCH, Robert

Role: Goalkeeper 2003-06
6ft.2ins. 12st.13lbs.
Born: Yeovil, Somerset, 8 October 1983

CAREER: Larkspur/Yeovil Town/**SPURS** Scholar Jul 2000, pro. Jul 2002/(Woking loan Feb 2003)/(Stevenage Borough loan Aug 2004)/(West Ham United loan Dec 2004)/(Stevenage Borough loan Jan 2005)/Sheffield

Wednesday training 2004-05/(Bristol City loan Aug 2005)/(Barnet loan Jan 2007)/released May 2007/Sheffield Wednesday Jul 2007/Lincoln City Jul 2008/Notts County Jun 2010-May 2012/**SPURS** coach Aug 2013.

Debut v Oxford United (Fr) (a) 20.7.2003

Rob Burch is one of many young goalkeepers who worked their way through the White Hart Lane youth ranks, only to move on before making a senior competitive appearance. Burch signed professional for Spurs in July 2002 following the completion of his scholarship, but it was only in pre-season friendly games that he made any senior appearances. Loaned out to the likes of Stevenage Borough and Woking to gain experience, the signing of more experienced 'keepers such as Márton Fülöp and Radek Černý, pushed Burch down the pecking order and it was no surprise when he was released in May 2007. He was quickly offered a position with Sheffield Wednesday and went on to play for Lincoln City and Notts County before returning to Spurs to help out on the coaching side.

Appearances:
Others: 4 (2) apps.
Total: 4 (2) apps. 0 gls.

BURCHELL, George S

Role: Full-back 1939-40

CAREER: Romford/**SPURS** am. Aug 1935/(guest for Darlington, Middlesbrough and Reading during World War Two)/Walthamstow Avenue.

Debut v Watford (FLS) (a) 30.12.1939

England amateur international George Burchell had signed amateur forms for Spurs in August 1935, but did not move into the professional ranks. Instead he continued to play as an amateur with Romford, represented Essex and the Athenian League and collected a total of 16 Amateur caps for England. Most were won prior to the war, but the last few were with Walthamstow Avenue, who he joined when hostilities were over.

Appearances:
Others: 1 app.
Total: 1 app. 0 gls.

BURDITT, Frederick Charles Kendall

Role: Inside-forward 1940-41
5ft.9ins. 11st.3lbs.
Born: Ibstock, Leicestershire, 12th November 1906
Died: Ibstock, Leicestershire, 27th October 1977

CAREER: Ibstock/Penistone Rovers/Gresley Rovers trial 1928-29/Bloxwich Strollers 1929-30/Gresley Rovers Aug 1930/Norwich City Oct 1930/Millwall Aug 1936/Notts County Jan 1938/Colchester United May 1939/(guest for Leicester City, Norwich City and **SPURS** during World War Two)/Ibstock Colliery/Pegsons/Penistone Rovers player-manager till 1959.

Debut v Leicester City (FLS) (a) 17.5.1941

When Spurs journeyed to Filbert Street for their Football League South fixture with Leicester City in May 1941 Ken Burditt arrived at the ground hoping he might get a game for the home team. However, Spurs arrived with only ten men and Leicester agreed to let Burditt make up the numbers. At the time, he was on the books of Colchester United but had returned to the Midlands because of war service. He had begun his career with Penistone Rovers and Gresley Rovers before spending six successful years with Norwich City. He then joined up with his brother, George, and helped Millwall reach the FA Cup semi-final in 1937. A short spell with Notts County was followed by his being placed on the transfer list at a fee of £1,000 after he had refused the terms offered by County. He signed for Colchester, but his career in Essex did not even get under way due to the outbreak of war. When the war was over he decided to retire from first class football, although he continued to play in non-League circles in the Midlands, still turning out for Ibstock Colliery when in his fifties. Brother George played for Millwall, Nottingham Forest and Wrexham.

Appearances:
Others: 1 app.
Total: 1 app. 0 gls.

BURGESS, William Arthur Ronald

Role: Half-back 1938-54
5ft.11ins. 11st.0lbs.
Born: Cwm, South Wales, 9th April 1917
Died: Swansea, South Wales, 14th February 2005

CAREER: Cwm Ryddach School/Ebbw Vale Schools/Cwm Villa/Cardiff City am./South Wales Juniors/**SPURS** am. May 1936/Tottenham Juniors/Northfleet United 1936, am. Apr 1937, pro. May 1938/**SPURS** pro. Aug 1938/(guest for Brighton and Hove Albion, Huddersfield Town, Millwall, Nottingham Forest, Notts County and Reading during World War Two)/Swansea Town player-coach May 1954, player-manager Jul 1955, manager cs. 1956/Watford coach Dec 1958, acting manager Feb 1959, manager Mar 1959/Hendon manager May 1963/Fulham trainer cs. 1965/Bedford Town manager till cs. 1967/Luton Town scout/Kenton coach.

Debut v Norwich City (FL) (a) 4.2.1939

One of the all-time greats, not only of Spurs, but of football in general, Ron Burgess first caught the attention of Spurs scouts playing for his local side Cwm Villa. He had signed as an amateur for Cardiff City but, with the promised trial not forthcoming, took a job as a pit boy. A forward at the time, he was taken on Spurs' junior staff, but after less than twelve months was told he would not make the grade. Before returning home, perhaps to a job in the pits, he popped into the ground to watch the "A" team play. They were a man short and Burgess was asked to fill in at right-half. It was the first time he had played in anything but a forward position, but so well did he perform that Spurs offered him a place on the ground-staff and an amateur contract at the Northfleet nursery. In his first season at Northfleet they did the "Double", winning the Kent Senior League and Kent Senior Cup, and at the end of the season signed Burgess to a professional contract. However, he played no further games for Northfleet as he reported for training to be told Spurs wanted him to sign professional at White Hart Lane. After making his debut in February

1939, he immediately secured one of the half-back positions and for the next 15 years was only absent due to injury, national service or international calls. International honours were not long in coming and he made the first of ten war-time appearances for Wales against England in November 1939. Throughout the war years he won representative honours for the RAF, FA and his country, turning out for Spurs when service demands permitted, if not, guesting for one of many clubs keen to utilise his services. An extraordinary human dynamo of a player, he was soon recognised as the best left-half in the country and one of the finest attacking wing-halves the game has known. An inspiring leader, Burgess was not only captain but also the engine-room of Arthur Rowe's "Push and Run" team that won the Second Division and the Football League Championship between 1949 and 1951. He was captain of his country, winning 32 caps between 1946 and 1954 when he missed only two internationals, was the first Welshman to play for the Football League team and played for Great Britain against the Rest of Europe. Although it was his incredible stamina and willingness to support almost every attacking foray that most caught the eye, Burgess could also defend solidly when the situation demanded. He dovetailed perfectly with half-back partner Bill Nicholson. In May 1954, shortly after making his final appearance for Wales, Burgess took up the post of player-coach with Swansea Town, soon graduating to player-manager and then taking over the manager's job full time. After four years with Swansea he moved to Watford as manager and there discovered, and transferred to Spurs, Pat Jennings. After leaving Watford he managed Hendon, had a spell as trainer under his former Spurs' team-mate Vic Buckingham at Fulham and managed Bedford Town. He finished his football career scouting for Luton Town and coaching Kenton. Burgess later worked as a stock controller for a stationery concern in Wealdstone and a warehouseman in South Harrow.

Appearances:
League: 301* apps. 16 gls.
FA Cup: 27 apps. 1 gl.
Others: 178 apps. 46 gls.
Total: 506 apps. 63 gls.
* Includes 1 abandoned match.

BURGON, Frederick Archibald

Role: Winger 1934-36
5ft.9ins. 11st.4lbs.
Born: Nottingham, 28th March 1912
Died: Metheringham, Lincolnshire, 20th September 1994

CAREER: West Bridgford Secondary School/Colwick/Burton Joyce/Grantham Town/Notts County trial/Nottingham Forest trial/Newark Town Nov 1931/Notts County pro. Jun 1932/Grantham Town Aug 1934/SPURS Jan 1935/Wrexham Oct 1935/Carlisle United Jul 1939.

Debut v Aston Villa (FL) (a) 2.2.1935

Initially a centre-forward, even though Archie Burgon scored twice in a trial match for Notts County, he was not offered terms. He joined Newark Town and performed so well, at either centre-forward or outside-left, that County decided they might have made a mistake and offered him a position on the staff. Although he scored a hat-trick on his Football League debut, he was unable to make the step up to League level and allowed to join Midland League Grantham Town from whom Spurs secured his transfer. He only stayed at White Hart Lane for nine months, playing just four League games of which two were at centre-forward and two at outside-left. Transferred to Wrexham, he joined Carlisle United in 1939 but the outbreak of war brought his career to an end.

Appearances:
League: 4 apps.
Total: 4 apps. 0 gls.

BURKE, Charles

Role: Centre-half 1944-45
Born: Isle of Arran, Scotland, 13th September 1921
Died: October 1995

CAREER: Ardeer Athletic/Bournemouth and Boscombe Athletic Jun 1939/(guest for Crystal Palace, Luton Town, Millwall, SPURS and West Ham United during World War Two)/retired 1947/Weymouth/Clyde Oct 1948-Apr 1949.

Debut v Charlton Athletic (FLS) (h) 30.9.1944

Within weeks of moving down from Scotland to join Bournemouth and Boscombe Athletic, 18-year old Charlie Burke found his career on hold due to the outbreak of the Second World War. He quickly became Bournemouth's regular centre-half, but was also able to turn out as a guest player for other clubs, including Spurs. He made 15 appearances in a Spurs' shirt during the 1944-45 season, filling in at any half-back position when needed. He was no stranger to filling in where necessary, for in February 1941 he had played for Bournemouth against Spurs in the Football League War Cup as an emergency goalkeeper. After the War Burke had one season on the south coast before retiring, though he did manage a few games for Clyde a couple of years later.

Appearances:
Others: 15 apps.
Total: 15 apps. 0 gls.

BURKE, Mark Stephen

Role: Midfielder 1994-95
5ft.10ins. 11st.12lbs.
Born: Solihull, West Midlands, 12th February 1969

CAREER: Erdington & Saltley Schools/England Schools/England Youth/Aston Villa app. Jun 1985, pro. Feb 1987/Middlesbrough Dec 1987/(Darlington loan Oct 1990)/(Ipswich Town loan Jan 1991)/Wolverhampton Wanderers Mar 1991/(Luton Town loan Mar 1994)/SPURS trial Jul 1994/Port Vale Aug 1994/Sporting Lisbon (Portugal) trial May 1995/Fortuna Sittard (Holland) trial Jan 1996, perm Feb 1996/B'Karna (Finland) trial/Tiru'su (Finland) trial/Omiya Ardila (Japan) Jul

1999/(Rapid Bucharest loan Mar 2001)/Rushden & Diamonds training/Rot-Weiss Essen (Germany) trial/TOP Oss (Holland)/IF Brommapojkarna (Sweden)/Vinkenslag (Holland) Nov 2001/Birmingham University coach.

Debut v Bristol City (Fr) (a) 29.7.1994 (sub)

Having been released by Wolverhampton Wanderers, Mark Burke was given a trial by Spurs after reportedly meeting manager Ossie Ardiles at an airport as both waited to fly out on holiday! A former England youth international who had failed to make the grade with Aston Villa, but spent four years at Middlesbrough and three at Wolves, Burke played only one game in his month at Tottenham, and that as a substitute in a pre-season friendly at Bristol City. Not offered terms by Spurs he joined Port Vale and went on to play throughout Europe and in Japan.

Appearances:
Others: (1) app.
Total: (1) app. 0 gls.

BURLEY, Benjamin

Role: Outside-left 1942-43
5ft.7ins. 11st.0lbs.
Born: *Sheffield, Yorkshire, 2nd November 1912*
Died: *Norfolk, February 2003*

CAREER: Darnall Road School/Sheffield Schools/Yorkshire Schools/Netherhope Institute/Woodhouse Mills United/Sheffield United am. Nov 1931, pro. Oct 1932/Southampton Sep 1933/Grimsby Town Jun 1934/Norwich City Jun 1935/Darlington May 1938/Chelmsford City Jun 1939/(guest for Brighton and Hove Albion, Crystal Palace, Millwall, Norwich City, Queens Park Rangers, Southend United, **SPURS** and Watford during World War Two)/Zwolle (Holland) coach cs. 1947/Chelmsford City cs. 1948, coach, secretary Jun 1951, manager Oct 1952-Oct 1954.

Debut v Arsenal (Fr) (h) 8.5.1943

As a youngster Ben Burley had been on the books of Sheffield United, but moved on without playing a senior game for them. He did slightly better with Southampton, making two appearances, and then moved around lower level clubs. In June 1939 he joined Chelmsford City, but barely played a game for them before the Second World War broke out. He played as a guest for several clubs during the War, his one appearance for Spurs being in a friendly with Arsenal. With his playing career brought to an end after one post-war season, Burley had a short spell coaching in Holland, before returning to the UK and serving Chelmsford as coach, secretary and manager.

Appearances:
Others: 1 app.
Total: 1 app. 0 gls.

BURNE, R

Role: Inside-forward 1895-96

Debut v Vampires (FAC) (a) 2.11.1895
(Royal Ordnance (Fr) (h) 28.9.1895 (scored once))

Very little is known about Burne who made three appearances for Spurs in the 1895-96 season. He made his debut as a trialist in a friendly with Royal Ordnance in September 1895, giving a reported "promising display" and scoring once from the inside-left position. Five weeks later he made his only competitive appearance at right-half in a second qualifying round FA Cup tie against Vampires. Spurs lost that match 2-4, but complained that the pitch had been incorrectly marked out. The appeal was upheld, Spurs won the replay 2-1 and went on to qualify for the competition proper for the first time where they lost 0-5 to Stoke. Burne's only other outing was in a friendly five days after the cup-tie.

Appearances:
FA Cup: 1 app.
Others: 2 apps. 1 gl.
Total: 3 apps. 1 gl.

BURNETT, Jonathan

Role: Centre-forward 1944-45

CAREER: Tooting and Mitcham/(guest for Clapton Orient, **SPURS** and West Ham United during World War Two).

Debut v Clapton Orient (FLS) (h) 21.4.1945 (scored twice)

Burnett was an amateur with Tooting and Mitcham when he made his one appearance for Spurs in a Football League South match in April 1945. A last-minute replacement for Jack Gibbons, who was stranded on a train, Burnett was recommended to Spurs by Roy White who knew him from a London Services game they had played in. He scored twice in Spurs 4-1 victory.

Appearances:
Others: 1 app. 2 gls.
Total: 1 app. 2 gls.

BURROWS, Lycurgus

Role: Full-back 1894-98
5ft.10ins. 12st.10lbs
Born: *Ashton-Under-Lyme, Lancashire, 26th June 1875*
Died: *Gosforth, Newcastle Upon Tyne, 23rd August 1952*

CAREER: Melrose/Woolwich Polytechnic/Royal Arsenal am. Jan 1892/**SPURS** Oct 1894/Sheffield United Dec 1897.

Debut v Wolverton (FAC) (h) 3.11.1894
(3rd Battalion Grenadier Guards (Fr) (h) 6.10.1894)

One of the great characters of late 19th century London football, Ly Burrows was a full-back-then one of the toughest jobs on the field. Not only did he have to contend with the trickery of a speedy winger whose sole aim was to get past him and centre the ball, but he also had to cover the opposing inside-forward whenever his half-back partner got left upfield. Consequently, most full-backs gained a reputation for being "hard men", but this also meant they were fair game for hefty challenges themselves. Although born near Manchester, Burrows' family moved around a lot and he first played football for the Melrose club of Govan near Glasgow. He played next for his school team in Sheffield and when

he moved down to London joined the Woolwich Polytechnic club. It was whilst playing for the "Poly" that he caught the attention of Royal Arsenal, as they then were. Basically, a reserve, he grew unhappy with second string football and accepted an invitation to play for Spurs, making his first appearance in October 1894. Apart from turning out for Spurs, Burrows still assisted Woolwich Arsenal and played in ten Football League games for them between 1894 and 1896. He was primarily recognised as a Spurs player, though, and when selected to play for London, it was Tottenham who were credited with being his club. He made several appearances for London and would have won many more such honours had it not been for the excellent Charlie McGahey, a City Ramblers player, who also assisted Spurs. An amateur all his career, Burrows announced in December 1897 that he was moving back to Sheffield for business reasons and joined Sheffield United, although he still managed to play a few more games for Spurs before the season ended. There is little doubt that his robust skills helped establish Spurs in the Southern League and as one of the South's most up-and-coming clubs.

Appearances:
Southern: 27 apps. 1 gl.
FA Cup: 12 apps.
Others: 79 apps. 2 gls.
Total: 118 apps. 3 gls.

BURTON, A

Role: Forward 1893-96

Debut v Old St Marks (LSC) (h) 21.10.1893

Another of those players from the dim and distant past about whom it has proved impossible to unearth any information, Burton played only two games for Spurs. The first was a London Senior Cup tie in October 1893, when he played at outside-left. He replaced H Ellis in that game, a decision for which the club was much criticised, and was described as "not fast enough". His other appearance was in October 1895 when he scored his only goal for the club from the inside-right position in a friendly.

Appearances:
Others: 2 apps. 1 gl.
Total: 2 apps. 1 gl.

BURTON, John Henry

Role: Half-back 1900-05
5ft.7ins. 12st.2lbs.
Born: Derby, Derbyshire, 13th August 1875
Died: Derby, Derbyshire, 13th May 1949

CAREER: Derby St Andrews/Derby County Oct 1896/Chatham Jun 1899/SPURS trial Mar 1901, pro. Apr 1901/Preston North End Oct 1906/West Ham United Jul 1908.

Debut v Gravesend United (SL) (a) 3.4.1901

Unable to establish himself with Derby County, John Burton moved to Chatham where he proved a competent performer. When Chatham were

forced to withdraw from the Southern League, Burton was given a trial by Spurs and did enough to be offered professional terms. A half-back at the time, he made his debut in a first team fixture in April 1901 in a Southern League match- although as Spurs were preparing for their FA Cup semi-final clash with West Bromwich Albion five days later it was, in reality, a reserve team line-up. Indeed, all Burton's outings in senior competitions that season were when Spurs put out reserve sides in order to keep the first eleven fit for pending cup-ties. Burton slowly developed, but was never secure in the first team, even in his best season of 1902-03 when he played most of his games as stand-in for the injured J L Jones. To make matters worse, he soon found his position at Spurs threatened by the arrival of his brother Oliver! John Burton left the club in the summer of 1905 and later signed for Preston North End although he did not make their first eleven. There is much confusion between Burton and another player with the same name who appeared for Grangetown, Blackburn Rovers (Aug 1906), West Ham United (Jul 1908), Birmingham (Dec 1909), (perhaps) Nelson, Cardiff City (cs. 1911) and Southend United (Sep 1914).

Appearances:
Southern: 21 apps. 3 gls.
Others: 29* apps. 2 gls.
Total: 50 apps. 5 gls.
* Includes 1 abandoned match

BURTON, Oliver

Role: Half-back or full-back 1901-10
5ft.9ins. 11st.10lbs.
Born: Derby, Derbyshire, 27th May 1879
Died: St Pancras, London, 20th January 1929

CAREER: SPURS trial Oct 1901, pro. Nov 1901.

Debut v Brentford (LL) (a) 12.1.1903

Ollie Burton was originally, like his elder brother John, a half-back but his best service to Spurs came at full-back. He was taken on after a trial in October 1901, but had to wait until January 1903 before making his debut in a London League match-very much the minor of the three league competitions Spurs competed in at the time. It was October 1903 before Burton played in the premier Southern League competition. He slowly established himself at Spurs, eventually replacing his brother as first choice reserve in the half-back positions. A strong, muscular player, Burton was basically a defender and perhaps a little out of his depth in the middle of the park where he was expected to be creative and get up and help his forwards. In December 1905 he was tried at full-back when Sandy Tait was injured and took to the

position so well that by 1907-08 he had made it his own. He was virtually ever-present for that and the following season-Spurs first in the Football League. He found the job much harder in the First Division and only managed five games before dropping out of the team.

Appearances:
Southern: 65 apps.
League: 38 apps.
FA Cup: 5 apps.
Others: 65 apps. 1 gl.
Total: 173 apps. 1 gl.
* Includes 1 abandoned match.

BUTCHER, Calum James

Role: Defender 2010-11
5ft.11ins. 12st.12lbs.
Born: Rochford, Essex, 26th February 1981

CAREER: Belfairs High School/**SPURS** scholar Jul 2007, pro. Mar 2009/(Barnet loan Dec 2009)/released Dec 2010/Ipswich Town trial Dec 2010/Sporting Kansas City (USA) trial Jan 2011/Southend United trial Apr 2011/Aldershot Town trial Jul 2011/Hjørring (Denmark) Jul 2011/Hayes & Yeading United Sep 2012/Dundee United trial Jun 2013, perm. Jul 2013/Burton Albion Jun 2015/Millwall Aug 2016.

Debut v AFC Bournemouth (Fr) (a) 10.7.2010

Calum Butcher had not even signed professional when he was on the substitute's bench as a very weak Spurs team was selected for the UEFA League match with Shakhtar Donetsk in February 2009. It was the only time Butcher got near making a competitive appearance for Spurs. Having played mainly for the academy side, he had made only a couple of appearances at reserve level when he was surprisingly called up for a first team debut in the opening friendly of the 2010-11 pre-season at AFC Bournemouth. After a substitute appearance five days later, it was back to the reserves before Butcher was released in December 2010. After several trials, he eventually joined the Danish side Hjørring, spending just over a year there before returning to the UK with non-League Hayes & Yeading United. In less than a year with the Conference South side he impressed enough for Dundee United to offer him a trial and then a contract. He moved into midfield and had two years in Scotland before signing for Burton Albion, quickly returning to London with Millwall.

Appearances:
Others: 1 (1) app.
Total: 1 (1) apps.

BUTCHER, G

Role: Full-back 1915-16

CAREER: Carrow/**SPURS** guest Apr 1916.

Debut v Norwich City (Fr) (a) 24.4.1916

A member of Norwich's Carrow club, Butcher was called upon to make his one appearance for Spurs in a friendly at Norwich City in April 1916. Spurs arrived with only nine players and Butcher was pressed into service at left-back.

Appearances:
Others: 1 app.
Total: 1 app. 0 gls.

BUTLER, E

Role: Inside-right 1895-96

Debut v Ilford (Fr) (a) 19.10.1895

Another player from the 19th century who made his only appearance for Spurs in a friendly game and about whom nothing is known, Butler played his one game at inside-right in a friendly at Ilford when he was described as "fast, but weak in front of goal".

Appearances:
Others: 1 app.
Total: 1 app. 0 gls.

BUTTERS, Guy

Role: Central defender 1988-91
6ft.3ins. 13st.7lbs.
Born: Hillingdon, Middlesex, 30th October 1969

CAREER: Hillingdon Schools/Middlesex Schools/**SPURS** trainee Jul 1986, pro. Aug 1988/(Southend United loan Jan 1990)/Portsmouth Sep 1990/(Oxford United loan Nov 1994)/Gillingham Oct 1996/Brighton & Hove Albion Aug 2002, community support officer/(Barnet loan Mar 2003)/Havant & Waterlooville May 2008/(Lewes loan Jan 2009)/Winchester City loan Aug 2009, temp. manager Aug 2010, perm. manager Sep 2010-Oct 2012/Brighton & Hove Albion Community Officer Oct 2012/Eastleigh asst. manager Oct 2012-May 2014.

Debut v Blackburn Rovers (sub) (FLC) (a) 9.11.1988
(Reading (sub) (Fr) (a) 10.8.1988)

Guy Butters trained with Chelsea whilst at school, but it was with Spurs that he accepted a position as a trainee. He made rapid progress through the youth teams at White Hart Lane and was knocking on the first team door immediately he signed professional. He made his senior debut as a substitute in a Littlewoods Cup tie in November 1988 and kept the position until the end of the season, performing so well that in March 1989 manager Terry Venables felt able to allow the experienced Chris Fairclough to move to Leeds. Adding the sort of height and muscle that had been missing for too long in the heart of defence, Butters was soon pushing for international honours and in June 1989 was included in England's Under-21 squad for the international tournament in Toulon. He played in all three of England's games and then captained the Rest of the World side that took the place of the Dutch team who returned home after several Surinam-born Dutch League players were killed in an air crash. Although Butters began the following 1989-90 season in the first team, another poor start to the campaign and the decision to move new signing Steve Sedgley from midfield to defence saw Butters out in the cold. In January 1990, he

joined Southend on loan for three months, helping them to promotion from the Fourth Division. With Sedgley and Gary Mabbutt looking more solid in the centre of defence at the start of the next campaign, Butters was simply unable to get back in the team. He was transferred to Portsmouth for £375,000 and developed to play a part in Pompey's thrilling run to the 1992 FA Cup semi-finals. He rose to be captain of Portsmouth, but soon after Terry Venables took control of the club, was transferred to Gillingham. Not the most attractive of players, his whole-hearted commitment made him a popular figure in Kent and he gave Gillingham great service for six years before moving to Brighton & Hove Albion. As he approached his thirties he moved down the football ladder until trying his hand at coaching and management.

Appearances:
League: 34 (1) apps. 1 gl.
FA Cup: 1 app.
FL Cup: 2 (1) apps.
Others: 12 (9) apps.
Total: 49 (11) apps. 1 gl.

BUTTON, David Robert Edmund

Role: Goalkeeper, 2009-11
6ft.0ins. 13st.0lbs.
Born: Stevenage, Hertfordshire, 27th February 1989

CAREER: SPURS Scholar Jul 2005, pro. Feb 2006/(Grays Athletic loan Jan 2008)/(Rochdale loan Mar 2008)/(Grays Athletic loan Sep 2008)/(AFC Bournemouth loan Jan 2009)/Luton Town loan Mar 2009)/(Dagenham & Redbridge loan Apr 2009)/(Crewe Alexandra loan Jul and Sep 2009)/(Shrewsbury Town loan Nov 2009)/(Plymouth Argyle loan Aug 2010)/(Leyton Orient loan Aug 2011)/(Doncaster Rovers loan Jan 2012)/(Barnsley loan Mar 2012)/Charlton Athletic Aug 2012/Brentford Jul 2013/Fulham Jul 2016.

Debut v Doncaster Rovers (sub) (FLC) (a) 26.8.2009

(Exeter City (sub) (Fr) (a) 15.7.2009)

In over six years as a White Hart Lane professional David Button made one competitive appearance for Spurs, and that as a substitute, whiling making over 100 appearances for lower Football League and non-League clubs. With experienced performers like Carlo Cudicini, Heurelho Gomes and Brad Friedel plus several lesser 'keepers ahead of him, it was always going to be difficult for Button to make a breakthrough and it is, perhaps, a sign of the regard in which he was held that he was on Spurs' books for so long. The one competitive outing for Button was in August 2009. He had been on loan to Crewe Alexandra at the time, but recalled when Gomes was injured. Button replaced Cudicini for the last eight minutes of the Carling Cup-tie with Doncaster Rovers. Eventually Button was allowed to move permanently, joining Charlton Athletic in August 2012. He moved on to Brentford a year later and, at last, began to establish a regular position.

Appearances:
FL Cup: (1) app.
Others: (3) apps.
Total: (4) apps. 0 gls.

CABLE, Thomas Henry

Role: Centre-half 1928-32
5ft.10ins. 11st.0lbs.
Born: Barking, London, 27th November 1900
Died: Southend, Essex, 23rd May 1986

CAREER: Sterling Athletic/Barking Town/Leyton 1924/Queens Park Rangers Nov 1925/Middlesex Wanderers/Leyton 1927/**SPURS** pro. Jul 1928/Southampton Sep 1932/Kettering Town player-manager/Leyton manager, committee Jun 1936/Grays Athletic manager cs. 1950-Sep 1951.

Debut v Hull City (FL) (h) 6.10.1928

Tommy Cable was one of the biggest names in amateur football when Spurs persuaded him to turn professional. Having played for Barking, he joined Leyton, one of the best amateur teams of the time, won an England amateur cap against Wales in March 1926 and helped Leyton carry off the Amateur Cup in 1927 and 1928. Cable scored twice in the first of those finals and once in the second. His signing by Spurs, who had just been relegated, was regarded as something of a coup, even though he was getting on for 30-years old.

Cable made his League debut in October 1928, but only played one further game that season. However, the following term he became the regular centre-half, but was still not regarded as strong enough and Spurs bought Alf Messer from Reading. Although Messer proved little better than Cable, Arthur Rowe was by now emerging and Cable was rarely in first team contention. Given a free transfer in April 1932 he joined Southampton, but soon moved on to Kettering as player/manager. An injury early in his time with Kettering ended his playing career, but he continued in management taking charge of both his former club, Leyton, and Grays Athletic.

Appearances:
League: 42 apps.
FA Cup: 2 apps.
Others: 5 apps.
Total: 49 apps. 0 gls.

CADMAN, Morton Frederick

Role: Utility 1889-92
Born: Hythe, Kent, about 1867
Died: December 1948

CAREER: Tottenham Wanderers by Nov 1886/**SPURS** Dec 1888, director Jun 1900, vice president 1913, life vice president Apr 1943.

Debut v Royal Arsenal (Fr) (a) 21.9.1889

Morton Cadman played as an amateur in Spurs' early days, though he is best remembered for the service he gave the club in an administrative capacity. Elected a member in December 1888, his first known first team appearance was in a 1-10 defeat to Royal Arsenal, but most of his games were played for the reserves and at one time he was captain of the Second XI. After he finished playing he became a member of the committee that ran the club until it was converted into a Limited Company in March 1898. Although not elected as a director on the company's incorporation, he was invited to join the board in June 1900 and in 1913 became the club's vice-president. He served as a director until April 1943 when he became the club's first life vice-president, a position he held until his death in December 1948.

Appearances:
Others: 5 apps.
Total: 5 apps. 0 gls.

CAIN, A

Role: Inside-forward 1918-19

CAREER: Dublin Bohemians/(guest for **SPURS** during World War One).

Debut v Queens Park Rangers (LFC) (a) 15.2.1919 (scored once)

Another of the guest players who turned out for the club during the First World War, Cain made his one appearance at inside-left in a London Football Combination match at Queens Park Rangers, scoring Spurs goal in a 1-7 defeat.

Appearances:
Others: 1 app. 1 gl.
Total: 1 app. 1 gl.

CAIN, Robert

Role: Full-back 1898-99
5ft.7ins. 12st.7lbs.
Born: Slammanan, Stirlingshire, 13 February 1866

CAREER: Airdrie am. 1885/Rangers am./Slammanan 1888/Everton Oct 1889/Bootle Aug 1890/Sheffield United Aug 1891/**SPURS** May 1898/Albion Rovers Jul 1899/Small Heath Oct 1899.

Debut v Thames Ironworks (TML) (h) 3.9.1898
(Gainsborough Trinity (Fr) (h) 1.9.1898)

Scottish full-back Bob Cain played for Spurs for just the one season. A strong, hard-tackling defender, he was considered quite a capture, having played for the Anglo-Scots against the Home Scots in an international trial match only two months before signing. His career began with Airdrie and he played for Everton and Bootle, but it was with Sheffield United that he made his reputation. A half-back at Everton, he reverted to full-back with Bootle and, having helped Sheffield United win the Second Division, immediately followed by the Football League title in 1897-98, was widely regarded as one of the best full-backs in the country. His invaluable service to Sheffield United was recognised with a benefit match between Scottish and English Players at Bramall Lane in January 1898, but when Spurs offered Cain £70 to sign for the club, he turned his back on Bramall Lane. As Spurs were outside the Football League, they did not have to pay a fee to Sheffield United, so could pay Cain the substantial fee. Cain's decision did not go down well in Sheffield. The championship winner's medal he was due to receive was withheld, as was his benefit bonus. When he contacted Sheffield United asking if he could re-sign for them as he could not settle in London, the approach was rejected. Almost ever-present throughout his one season in London, Cain helped Spurs battle through the qualifying rounds of the FA Cup for only the second time in their history before losing to Stoke in the Third round proper. At the end of the season, having made it plain he was not happy in London, Cain was not retained and moved to Albion Rovers. He only stayed in Scotland for a few months before being transferred to Small Heath.

Appearances:
Southern: 24 apps.
FA Cup: 10 apps.
Others: 35 apps. 1 gl.
Total: 69 apps. 1 gl.

CALDECOTT, Watson

Role: Full-back 1894-95
Born: Basingstoke, Hampshire, 1871

CAREER: Basingstoke/**SPURS** trial Oct 1894/Crouch End.

Debut v Crouch End (Fr) (a) 27.10.1894

Caldecott made his one appearance for Spurs as a trialist in a friendly fixture with Crouch End. He played at left-back but was "not impressive" and certainly not good enough to be taken on by Spurs. He did though impress Crouch End, for he immediately joined them and played with Spurs' near neighbours for at least two years. A schoolmaster, Caldecott later moved to Wolverhampton and was headmaster of Wolverhampton Grammar School between 1905 and 1923

Appearances:
Others: 1 app.
Total: 1 app. 0 gls.

CALDERWOOD, Colin

Role: Central defender 1993-99
6ft.0ins. 11st.9lbs.
Born: Stranraer, Scotland, 20th January 1965

CAREER: Lochryan Boys Club/Wigtownshire Schools/Inverness Caledonian Thistle/Scottish Juniors/Mansfield Town app. May 1981, pro. Mar 1982/Swindon Town Jul 1985/**SPURS** Jul 1993/Aston Villa Mar 1999/Nottingham Forest Mar 2000/(Notts County loan Mar 2001)/retired May 2001/**SPURS** reserve team manager cs. 2001/Northampton Town manager Oct 2003/Nottingham Forest manager May 2006-Dec 2008/Newcastle United coach Jan 2009, asst. manager Oct 2009/Hibernian manager Oct 2010-Nov 2011/Birmingham City asst. manager Nov 2011/Norwich City asst. manager Jun 2012-Apr 2014/Brighton and Hove Albion asst. manager Feb 2015/Aston Villa asst. manager Nov 2016.

Debut v Newcastle United (PL) (a) 14.8.1993
(Team Nord-Trøndelag (Fr) (Steinjker) 23.7.1993)

Colin Calderwood had been spotted by Mansfield Town playing in Scotland and taken on their apprentice staff. In March 1982, he accepted their offer of professional terms and made his debut in a 2-0 victory at Crewe Alexandra. Unfortunately, Mansfield had forgotten to notify the Football League of Calderwood's new status, resulting in a two-point deduction. Calderwood settled well to League football and after three years was persuaded to sign for Swindon Town with the transfer fee of £27,500 being set by a Football League tribunal. Already displaying leadership qualities, the 21-year old was installed as captain and led Swindon to the Fourth Division title. That was immediately followed by promotion, via the play-offs, to the Second Division and in 1990, again via the play-offs, to the First Division. Sadly, Swindon did not take their place in the top flight, an illegal payments scandal seeing them relegated to the Third Division, before an appeal allowed them to remain in the Second. Under the guidance of, first Ossie Ardiles, and then Glenn Hoddle, Swindon consolidated their Second Division status then, at last, made the step up, again via the paly-offs, into the new Premier League. Under Ardiles and Hoddle, Calderwood had developed as a footballing centre-half. Strong and well able to mix it with the toughest of strikers, the insistence of the two former Spurs' stars on football being played from the back, had allowed Calderwood to display his creative abilities, bringing the ball out of defence to initiate attacking play. With Ardiles taking charge at White Hart Lane and Calderwood's contract at Swindon coming to an end, it was no surprise when he signed for Spurs. Again, the fee was determined by a tribunal, but this time it was £1.25 million. Calderwood spent the best part of six years at White Hart Lane, proving a competent if not spectacular performer, often asked to display his footballing qualities in a midfield holding role. He made his first appearance for Scotland against Russia in March 1995 and was rarely absent from a Scotland team as he went on to collect 36 full caps. In March 1995 Calderwood left Spurs for Aston Villa, quickly moving on to Nottingham Forest and Notts County before retiring after suffering a broken leg while at Forest. He returned to White Hart Lane to work on the coaching staff, forming a useful partnership at reserve level with Chris Hughton. In October 2003 Calderwood accepted an offer to manage Northampton Town. Having led them to promotion, he was persuaded to move to Nottingham Forest, but could not repeat the success. When he was sacked, he was quickly offered a job as first coach and then assistant to Hughton at Newcastle United. Calderwood tried his hand at management again with Hibernians, but was not a success and went back to coaching as assistant manager to Hughton at Birmingham City, Norwich City and Brighton and Hove Albion, until taking on the same role at Aston Villa.

Appearances:
League: 152 (11) apps. 6 gls.
FA Cup: 16* (1) apps. 1 gl.
FL Cup: 19 (1) apps.
Others: 33 (9) apps. 3 gls.
Total: 220 (22) apps. 10 gls.
* Includes 1 abandoned match

CALDWELL, Thomas

Role: Outside-left 1916-17
Born: West Ham, London, 1886

CAREER: Ilford Alliance/West Ham St Pauls/Clapton Orient 1906/Southend United May 1908/West Ham United Aug 1909/New Brompton Jul 1912/(Clapton Orient and SPURS during World War One)/Reading.

Debut v Chelsea (LFC) (h) 2.9.1916

East Ender Tom Caldwell had started his career with Clapton Orient before moving on to Southend and West Ham United. He spent three years at Upton Park, a regular and well-respected winger, before moving to New Brompton. Although he had not played for them for over two years, he was still associated with Gillingham (as New Brompton had been renamed) when he made his one appearance for Spurs. That was in September 1916 in the first match of the season's London Football Combination competition. At Orient, Caldwell had replaced his brother, Jimmy, who also played for Queens Park Rangers and Reading.

Appearances:
Others: 1 app.
Total: 1 app. 0 gls.

CAMARA, Aboubacar Sidiki

Role: Striker 1998-99
6ft.0ins. 13st.0lbs.
Born: Conakry, Guinea 17th November 1972

CAREER: AS Kaloum Star (Guinea) Jul 1986/Saint Etienne (France) Jul 1989/Racing Lens (France) Jul 1995/Olympique Marseille (France) Jul 1997/SPURS trial Jul 1998/Liverpool May 1999/West Ham United Dec 2000/(Al-Ittihad (Saudi Arabia) loan Jan 2003)/Al Siliya (Qatar) Jul 2003/Amiens (France) Jan 2005/Guinea National Technical director May 2009 and Head coach Jun 2009 both till Sep 2009/Sports Minister of Guinea Dec 2010-Oct 2012.

Debut v Queens Park Rangers (Fr) (a) 1.8.1998

Guinea centre-forward Titi Camara, joined Spurs for a week's trial in July 1998 as Christian Gross sought to identify potential recruits for his first full season as manager. Camara made one appearance in a pre-season friendly at Queens Park Rangers before returning to Olympique Marseille. He had moved to France with St Etienne as a 16-year old and done reasonably well, establishing himself as his country's first choice striker, before moving on to Racing Lens. He moved up the ranks of French football with Olympique Marseille, but found himself unable to

establish a regular starting place, all too often finding himself a substitute, as he was in the 1999 UEFA Cup final. Having been rejected by Spurs, it was surprising that in May 1999 Liverpool should invest £2.6 million in Camara. He spent eighteen months at Anfield, a bustling striker who could sometimes thrill, but too often disappointed, before moving to

West Ham United. His most memorable moment at Anfield came in October 1999 when, only hours after learning his father had died, he fell to the turf in tears after scoring the only goal of the game against West Ham. It was all downhill for Camara after joining West Ham. He rarely played and was soon on the way out, loaned to Al-Ittihad of Saudi Arabia before his contract was terminated in July 2003. After a year in Qatar, Camara returned to France. He played for two years with SC Amiens then returned home to Guinea. He tried to stand for the Presidency of the Guinea Football Federation, but was not allowed to because of "inexperience", although he went on to become his country's Sports Minister.

Appearances:
Others: 1 app.
Total: **1 app. 0 gls.**

CAMERON, John

Role: Inside-forward 1898-1907
5ft.10ins. 11st.4lbs.
Born: Ayr, 13th April 1872
Died: Glasgow, 20th April 1935

CAREER: Ayr Grammar School/Ayr Parkhouse/Queen's Park/Everton am. Sep 1895, pro. Apr. 1896/**SPURS** May 1898, player-secretary-manager Feb 1899, manager 1906-Mar 1907/Dresdner SC (Germany) coach May 1914/Ayr United manager Aug 1918-Aug 1919.

Debut v Thames Ironworks (TML) (h) 3.9.1898 (scored once) (Gainsborough Trinity (Fr) (h) 1.9.1898)

One of the most important signings ever made by Spurs, John Cameron started his career with the local Ayr Parkhouse club before playing for Queen's Park. He then signed as an amateur for Everton, but continued to appear for Queen's Park and it was the Glasgow club who gained the credit when he won a Scottish cap against Ireland in March 1896. Moving to Liverpool, Cameron earned his living working in the offices of the Cunard shipping line, but this was not popular with his team-mates at Goodison Park, who felt an amateur could not be as committed to the game as were those whose livelihood depended on how they performed. It was this disquiet that persuaded Cameron to join the professional ranks. Originally a centre-forward, he moved to inside-forward in the 1897-98 season and it was for that position that Frank Brettell, Spurs' first manager, signed him. A typical Scottish inside-forward, he was a great dribbler but also possessed excellent passing ability and retained his centre-forward's eye for goal, top-scoring in his first season with Spurs. Not only was Cameron a good footballer, but he was also a most articulate and intelligent man. When Brettell accepted the manager's position at Portsmouth in February 1899, Cameron was the natural choice to replace him, becoming Spurs' first and only player-manager-secretary. His impact was immediate, and in his first full season in charge, Spurs won the Southern League title for the only time, following that up with the dramatic first FA Cup victory in 1901 when Cameron netted the equaliser in the 3-1 replay win over Sheffield United. He continued to play regularly the following season, but then began to take a less active role on the pitch, concentrating more on administrative and managerial duties, although in January 1906 he did successfully apply to be re-instated as an amateur player. The same year his secretarial duties were handed over to reduce the workload, but then, in March 1907 and much to everyone's surprise, he resigned as manager. The club was not doing particularly well, but there had been no pressure on the popular Cameron who, much to the chagrin of the board, cited "differences with the directorate" as the reason for his action. After a short time in sports journalism he returned to football as the first coach appointed by Dresdner SC. He was one of several British coaches working abroad who were interned by the Germans at the start of the First World War. After the hostilities Cameron had a short time as manager of Ayr United and then returned to football journalism. Cameron was one of the leading lights of efforts to establish a football players' union around the turn of the century being secretary of the Association Footballers' Union, the forerunner to the Professional Footballers' Association.

Appearances:
Southern: 117 apps. 43 gls.
FA Cup: 25 apps. 7 gls.
Others: 147* apps. 89 gls.
Total: **289 apps. 139 gls.**
* Includes 1 abandoned match.

CAMPBELL, Fraizer Lee

Role: Striker 2008-09
5ft.11ins. 11st.13lbs.
Born: Huddersfield, West Yorkshire, 13th September 1987

CAREER: Huddersfield Town Centre of Excellence/Stile Common/Manchester United Scholar Jul 2004, pro. Mar 2006/(Royal Antwerp (Belgium) loan Aug 2006)/(Hull City loan Oct 2007)/(**SPURS** loan Sep 2008)/Sunderland Jul 2009/Cardiff City Jan 2013/Crystal Palace Jul 2014.

Debut v Wisła Kraków (sub) (UEFA) (h) 18.9.2008

When Daniel Levy accepted Manchester United's £30 million plus offer for Dimitar Berbatov on the last day of the 2008 summer transfer window, he knew there was not enough time for Spurs to secure a replacement of anything like Berbatov's quality. With Darren Bent and Roman Pavlyuchenko the only recognised front line strikers on the books, Levy insisted that a season long loan of United's up and coming youngster Fraizer Campbell had to be part of the deal. Campbell had been associated with United since the age of ten, signing as a scholar and professional at the earliest opportunity. A prolific scorer at youth and reserve level, he had gained experience on loan to United's Belgian partner club, Royal Antwerp, and with Hull City, scoring regularly for both and continuing to pick up Youth and Under-21 international honours. While no-one could replace Berbatov, Campbell at least had a scoring pedigree that would lessen the loss of the Bulgarian. Sadly, injuries held Campbell back at White Hart Lane. He played most of his games in the Carling Cup and Europa League, making all but one of his Premier League appearances from the bench. Campbell had quality, of that there was little doubt, but he needed a decent run in the team to show it. The experience knocked Campbell's career back so much that when he returned to United he was disappointed to find the team he had supported since childhood had accepted an offer from Sunderland. It took Campbell some time to settle on Wearside, but just as he appeared to be finding some form, an anterior cruciate ligament injury side-lined him for months. As if that was not bad enough, he had only just resumed playing when another injury to the same ligament put him out of action for a year. The setbacks may have been too much for some players, but Campbell has a fighting spirit. Allowed to move on to Cardiff City, his goals helped the Welsh club into the Premier League for the first time. When they were unable to retain their top flight status, Campbell moved on to Crystal Palace.

Appearances:
League: 1 (9) apps. 1 gl.
FA Cup: (1) app.
FL Cup: 3 (1) apps. 2 gls.
Euro: 5 (2) apps.
Total: 9 (13) apps. 3 gls.

CAMPBELL, Sulzeer Jeremiah

Role: Central defender 1991-2001
6ft.2ins. 14st.4lbs.
Born: Newham, 18th September 1974

CAREER: Senrab/Newham Schools/England Schools/FA-GM School of Excellence/England Youth/**SPURS** trainee Jul 1991, pro. Sep 1992/Arsenal Jul 2001/Portsmouth Aug 2006-May 2009/Notts County player-coach Aug 2009-Sep 2009/Arsenal training Oct 2009, perm Jan 2010/Newcastle United Jul 2010.

Debut v Chelsea (sub) (FL) (h) 5.12.1992
(Spurs'81-82 (sub) (Fr) (h) 10.11.1991)

Throughout the 1990s Sol Campbell was the rock around whom Spurs should have built a great team. They failed to so, with the result Campbell took his immense talents to another corner of north London, in his quest for those gold and silver baubles that players pull out of the bank vault every now and then, to show what a success they have been. Campbell was an outstanding prospect as a youngster and from the minute he stepped up for his League debut as a substitute against Chelsea in December 1992 it was obvious he was destined for the very top. Big and strong, he was playing in midfield, but even then looked ideally suited for a central defensive role. As it was, he first secured a regular place at full-back where his pace and willingness to thrust forward were valuable weapons, while his speed of recovery and ability to shepherd an opponent away from the danger areas could not be faulted. Although frequently employed in the centre of defence, it was only with Gary Mabbutt's retirement that Campbell moved there permanently and he was soon seen at his majestic best. Packed with solid muscle, his mere physical presence was enormous. Standing over 6ft.2ins. and with a terrific spring in his leap, even from a standing position he would tower above a ruck of players to get his head to the ball, while his 14st plus meant players who could out-muscle him were rare indeed. He possessed pace enough to catch even the most fleet-footed of forwards and a tackle that was not only strong and solid, but timed to such perfection that he did not simply put the ball out of play, but more often than not won it cleanly. It was not the power and strength of his game that made Campbell stand out though. He had remarkable composure, confidence in his own ability, and a surprising amount of skill, often advancing from deep positions to set out on an attacking foray. First called up for England in May 1996 he was soon as dominant on the international stage as at club level, one of the stars of the 1998 World Cup. For Spurs, Campbell was the bedrock of the defence, turning in one outstanding performance after another, coveted by every club in the country and many abroad. He seemed totally committed to the Spurs' cause, frequently playing when not fully fit and throwing himself at the ball as if his life depended on it. Club captain, he led Spurs to success in the 1999 Worthington Cup final and collected forty England caps, but that was not enough. He wanted to win trophies on a regular basis, to compete against the best in the Champions League. With the continual chopping and changing of managers, there was little prospect of his ambitions being satisfied with Spurs. Campbell did not hide his feelings. There were many who could sympathise with him, who, if he had packed his bags and taken himself off to Real Madrid or Barcelona, even Liverpool or Manchester United, would have thanked him for his past services and wished him well, but Campbell did not do that. As his contract ran down in 2000-01 he appeared to toy with the club, making all the right noises of how he wanted to achieve success with Spurs, but all the time refusing to sign the best contract the club had ever offered a player. He played his last match in a Spurs' shirt in the FA Cup semi-final at Old Trafford, turning out when clearly far from fit and departing the action early. With the benefit of the Bosman ruling, Campbell allowed his contract to expire, then announced he was joining Arsenal. For many supporters it was a kick in the teeth, an act of betrayal by one they had for so long identified as the very heart and soul of Spurs. To lose their captain, their inspiration, was bad enough but to lose him to Arsenal was too much. In an instant Campbell turned from hero to less than zero. After Arsenal, Campbell spent three years at Portsmouth, a veteran, but still as good a defender as ever. After a brief spell as player-coach at Notts County, Campbell returned to Arsenal for a short time then signed for Newcastle United. By then the sparkle had gone. He played few games, was released at the end of the 2010-11 season and, unable to secure a new club, retired in May 2012. Over at Highbury, Campbell won his medals, two League titles, two FA Cups, he even scored in a Champions League Final, but at White Hart Lane he has still not been forgiven. Perhaps, in time, people will recall Campbell at his best in a lilywhite shirt, a master defender who never gave anything but total commitment while out on the pitch.

Appearances:
League: 246 (9) apps. 10 gls.
FA Cup: 29* (2) apps. 1 gl.
FL Cup: 28 apps. 4 gls.
Euro: 2 apps.
Others: 39 (12) apps. 3 gls.
Total: 344 (23) apps. 18 gls.
* Includes 1 abandoned match

CANTRELL, James

Role: Centre-forward 1912-23
5ft.9ins. 11st.8lbs.
Born: Sheepbridge, nr Chesterfield, Derbyshire, 7th May 1882
Died: Basford, Nottinghamshire, 31st July 1960

CAREER: Chesterfield & District Schools/Bulwell Red Rose/Bulwell White Star/Carey United/Hucknall Constitutional FC/Aston Villa Jul 1904/Notts County Mar 1908/**SPURS** Oct 1912/(guest for Leicester Fosse and Notts County during World War One)/Sutton Town Oct 1923/retired May 1925.

Debut v Manchester United (FL) (a) 19.10.1912

Jimmy Cantrell had scored two goals for Notts County against Spurs at White Hart Lane on 12th October 1912 when, after 80 minutes, fog descended and the match was abandoned with County 3-1 ahead. The

following Friday he signed for Spurs. In three of his four full seasons at Meadow Lane Cantrell had been top scorer and was regarded as one of the best centre-forwards around. Far removed from the typical battering ram centre-forward of his day, Cantrell was an artist, preferring to stroke goals with subtlety rather than sheer power. Unlucky never to win international honours he was selected as an England reserve on several occasions but, even when picked for the Football League side, had to miss out on the honour due to injury. The very nature of his dainty playing style made him more susceptible to injury than others, particularly when up against brawny centre-halves far more used to tangling with forwards who relied on strength not skill. However, he not only maintained a good record of appearances but goals to match. When the Great War broke out he returned to the Midlands and frequently assisted Notts County, but at the age of 37, with his best years apparently behind him, Jimmy returned to Spurs. Surprisingly, he still had enough speed of thought and skill to play regularly in the Second Division winning team of 1919-20, with only the prolific Bert Bliss scoring more goals. Although age inevitably began to take a toll, the following season he still led the line in the 1921 FA Cup Final success and played his last game for Spurs in April 1923 just weeks off his 41st birthday-the oldest player to appear for Spurs in the Football League at the time. Six months later he joined Sutton Town where he finished his football career. That was not the end of his sporting career, for he later became a golf professional.

Appearances:
League: 159 apps. 74 gls.
FA Cup: 15 apps. 10 gls.
Others: 20 apps. 11 gls.
Total: 194 apps. 95 gls.

CAPOUE, Étienne

Role: Midfielder, 2013-15
6ft.2ins. 12st.8lbs.
Born: *Niort, France, 11th July 1988*

CAREER: Chamois Niortais (France) Sep 1995/Chauray (France) Aug 2002/Angers SCO (France) Jul 2004/Toulouse (France) Jul 2005, pro. Feb 2008/**SPURS** Aug 2013/Watford Jul 2015.

Debut v Crystal Palace (sub) (PL) (a) 18.8.2013

A strong, defensive midfielder who could also play at centre-half, Étienne Capoue was a £9.3m signing from Toulouse in the summer of 2013 as the departure of Gareth Bale to Real Madrid saw Andre Villas-Boas totally rebuild his squad. On the radar of several Premier League clubs, Capoue was an established French international having elected to play for his country of birth rather than his father's homeland of Guadeloupe. After playing at junior levels, he had joined the ranks of Toulouse where he built a reputation as a midfield destroyer who was not afraid to get stuck in, as evidenced by the number of bookings he had collected. An international at all levels, he won his first full cap in August 2012 playing against Uruguay and had a total of seven appearances to his credit by the time he signed for Spurs. Sadly, things did not go well for him at White Hart Lane. An early injury saw him

side-lined, and he was rarely able to string together a run of games. After two years, and with young Nabil Bentaleb nailing down the central defensive midfield role that Capoue was best suited to, Spurs allowed Capoue to leave when newly-promoted Watford made a good offer. At Vicarage Road, Capoue re-discovered his fitness, and with it the form that had first attracted Spurs' attention. First choice in a hard-working team of limited talent where expectations were not as great as at White Hart Lane, he was one of the stars as Watford secured their place in the Premier League. Capoue's older brother, Aurélien, also a midfielder was best known as a player with Nantes and Boulogne

Appearances:
League: 19 (5) apps. 1 gl.
FA Cup: 2 apps. 1 gl.
FL Cup: 1 (1) apps.
Euro: 6 (2) apps.
Others: 4 (1) apps. 1 gl.
Total: 32 (9) apps. 3 gls.

CARR, Stephen

Role: Full back 1993-2005
5ft.9ins. 12st.11lbs.
Born: *Dublin, 29th August 1976*

CAREER: Donahies Community School/Dublin Schools/Trinity Boys/St Kevin's/Stella Maris/Republic of Ireland Schools/**SPURS** trainee Jul 1992, pro. Sep 1993/Newcastle United Aug 2004/Leicester City trial Jul 2008/retired Dec 2008/Birmingham City training/trial and perm Feb 2009/retired May 2013.

Debut v Burnley (CC Cup) (a) 22.9.1993

When 17-year old Steve Carr first broke into the Spurs team, he made two appearances in the space of five days and, having only just signed his first professional contract, might have been forgiven for thinking it was easy to make it in the big time. He was called up due to injury to Dean Austin, but Ossie Ardiles knew he could not expect the young Dubliner to cover for the more experienced Austin for long. David Kerslake was signed, and after those first two outings it was back to the youth and reserve teams for Carr. He needed time to further his football education and with Chris Hughton in charge of the

youngsters could not have had a better coach in the art of full-back play. It was to be another three years before Carr made the senior team again, but when he did, he made the number two shirt his own. Confident in his own ability and not afraid to voice his opinion to more seasoned performers, he showed a composure and maturity beyond his years in his defensive duties, sticking to his opponent before choosing the right moment to nip in and muscle the ball away or diving in with a hard challenge to put it out of play. Not the biggest of defenders, he was sometimes singled out for aerial attack, but he soon learnt there were times when he could not win the header so dropped off his man to be in position to pick up the flick on. His anticipation was excellent, frequently cutting out passes with his speed off the mark, and he appreciated the importance of shuffling across to cover for his central defenders. Defensively, Carr was more than solid, but it was going forward that he really caught the eye. With pace and strength, he was quite prepared to take on opponents in a straight race and when he had got past his man, could drop some inviting balls into the danger area. At times he could be Spurs most potent attacking weapon, always willing to launch himself forward, a continual outlet and particularly adept at playing those little one-twos before racing onto the ball played inside the full-back and cutting it back into the box. For someone who got forward as much as Carr did, he did not score too many goals, but when he did they were usually something special, a thirty-yard screamer against Manchester United in October 1999 particularly memorable. A regular for the Republic of Ireland and rated by many the equal of any full-back in the country, Carr suffered a cruciate ligament injury in July 2001 that left him side-lined for over a year. When he returned he was the same hard-working, enthusiastic player he had always been, but a little of the pace had gone out of his game. He still made those darting runs up the wing, but that vital spark was missing. Still first choice, he made it known he wanted to leave White Hart Lane and moved to Newcastle United. He gave Newcastle good service for a couple of years, but as age and injuries began to take their toll, fell down the pecking order. Released in May 2008, Carr was unable to secure a new club and in December 2008 announced his retirement. Two months later he accepted, first, an offer from Birmingham City to train with them and then the offer of a one-month contract. He went on to play over 100 games for Birmingham, a solid dependable, experienced figure who captained them to Carling Cup success over Arsenal in 2011. When a persistent knee injury struck again, Carr struggled and retired for a second time in May 2013. Carr's father played for Shelbourne.

Appearances:
League: 222 (4) apps. 7 gls.
FA Cup: 16 (1) apps.
FL Cup: 23 apps. 1 gl.
Euro: 4 apps.
Others: 57 (15) apps. 2 gls.
Total: 322 (20) apps. 10 gls.

CARRICK, Christopher

Role: Outside-left 1905-06
5ft.7ins. 11st.3lbs.
Born: Stockton, County Durham, 8th October 1882
Died: Middlesbrough, North Yorkshire, 1927

CAREER: Middlesbrough cs. 1900/West Ham United cs. 1904/**SPURS** Apr 1905/Reading cs. 1906/Bradford Park Avenue cs. 1907/Glentoran Sep 1908.

Debut v Bristol Rovers (WL) (h) 25.9.1905

After little success with Middlesbrough and West Ham United, Chris Carrick joined Spurs as they looked to replace John Kirwan who had moved on to Chelsea. A stocky little fellow, Carrick had to compete with William Murray, and it was only around the middle of the season that he began to hold down a regular place. However, in March 1906 Spurs travelled to the West Country for Western League fixtures with Bristol Rovers and Plymouth Argyle. Between the two matches Carrick and Peter Kyle were involved in some misdemeanour. On their return to London, both were suspended, officially for a breach of the club's training rules. It must have been fairly serious, as Carrick never played for Spurs again, moving on to Reading and later playing for Bradford Park Avenue and Glentoran.

Appearances:
Southern: 15 apps. 4 gls.
FA Cup: 4 apps.
Others: 5 apps. 1 gl.
Total: 24 apps. 5 gls.

CARRICK, Michael

Role: Midfielder 2004-06
6ft.1ins. 11st.11lbs.
Born: Wallsend, Tyneside, 28 July 1981

CAREER: Wallsend Boys Club/West Ham United trainee Jul 1997, pro. Aug 1998/(Swindon Town Nov 1999 loan)/(Birmingham City loan Feb 2000)/**SPURS** Aug 2004/Manchester United Jul 2006.

Debut v Portsmouth (sub) (PL) (h) 18.10.2004

Michael Carrick is another product of the Wallsend Boys Club that produced players of the quality of Alan Shearer and Peter Beardsley. Like Shearer, he moved away from the North East to make his name, only he joined West Ham United as a trainee as soon as he turned 16. Carrick quickly established himself as one of the country's most promising young midfield talents, winning his first full England cap in May 2001. Side-lined by injury for much of the 2002-03 season that saw West Ham relegated from the Premiership, Carrick helped the Irons reach the play-offs the following season, but when they lost the final decided he had to move on if his career was to progress. Spurs paid out £2.75 million to take him to White Hart Lane, but Jacques Santini seemed reluctant to play him and it was only after Santini's departure that Carrick managed to hold down a regular place in the centre of midfield. Playing in front of the back four, Carrick exhibited a range of both long and short passing, coupled with a fine positional sense that not only enabled him to break up opposing attacks with  quick interceptions, but also to initiate attacks from deep. He always seemed to have time and space, was not easily flustered and while he rarely advanced with the ball, on those odd occasions he did decide to dribble, could cut through a defence and finish with an accurate strike. Carrick had been going nowhere with West Ham, but in a Spurs' shirt his career was reignited. Called up by England again in May 2005, Carrick's impressive form as Spurs almost made the Champions' League in 2005-

06 saw him selected for the England squad in the 2006 World Cup finals where he made two appearances. Looking set to be the midfield kingpin Martin Jol could build an exciting, young and principally English team around, Carrick's performances drew envious glances from Manchester United. Alex Ferguson decided Carrick was the man around whom he would build a new United team and after several approaches, Spurs at last succumbed to an offer that was just too good to refuse, with bonuses over £18 million. Carrick immediately settled into the midfield general role at Old Trafford, quietly going about his job and collecting five Premier League titles, one Carling Cup and one European Champions' League title. There have been times when his place appeared under threat, but while new signings may have displaced him for a while, his experience and quality could not be matched and he would soon return.

Appearances:
League: 61 (3) apps. 2 gls.
FA Cup: 6 (1) apps.
FL Cup: 3 (1) apps.
Others: 6 (1) apps.
Total: 76 (6) apps. 2 gls.

CARROLL, Thomas James

Role: Midfielder 2011-17
5ft.8ins. 11st.3lbs.
Born: Watford, Hertfordshire, 28th May 1992

CAREER: Parmiter's School/Hertfordshire Schools/SPURS academy Jun 2008, pro. Jun 2010/(Leyton Orient loan Jan 2011)/(Derby County loan Jan 2012)/(Queens Park Rangers loan Sep 2013)/(Swansea City loan Aug 2014)/Swansea City Jan 2017.

Debut v Heart of Midlothian (EL) (h) 25.8.2011

A will-o-the-wisp midfielder, Tom Carroll hardly looks strong enough for Premier League football, but he is the perfect example of how deceptive appearances can be. Carroll was a striker when first associated with Spurs, but by the time he was offered academy terms he had moved back to midfield where he could be more involved in the game. Neat, tidy and comfortable on the ball, Carroll is always on hand, providing support for the man in possession and demanding the ball from colleagues. He went out on loan to Leyton Orient when barely 18-years old and did well in the hurly-burly of League One football. Back with Spurs, Carroll made his debut in a Europa League tie against Heart of Midlothian and went on to became almost a regular in the competition as Harry Redknapp used it to give some of Spurs' youngsters valuable experience. Under Andre Villa-Boas Carroll stepped up to make a few Premier League appearances, but with the arrival of Christian Eriksen, Paulinho and Etienne Capoue in the summer of 2012, opportunities for Carroll looked limited. When Redknapp asked to take him to Queens Park Rangers for a season, the chance of regular action was too good to turn down. The following season he went on loan to Swansea City, a club playing the passing style ideal for a player like Carroll. An easy player to watch, Carroll has an eye for an opening and the ability to thread a pass that creates an opening. Remarkably strong and a true 90 minute worker, he had the ability to become a regular, but Harry Winks' rapid development saw Carroll drop down the pecking order and he moved to Swansea City in search of regular action.

Appearances:
League: 4 (23) apps. 1 gl.
FA Cup: 3 (2) apps. 1 gl.
FL Cup: 5 (1) apps.
Euro: 13 (5) apps. 1 gl.
Others: 6 (16) apps. 1 gl.
Total: 31 (47) apps. 4 gls.

CARTER-VICKERS, Cameron

Role: Central Defender 2016-
6ft.1in. 14st.5lbs.
Born: Southend, Essex, 31st December 1997

CAREER: Our Lady of Lourdes RC Primary School/Eastwood Academy/Catholic United/SPURS Academy Scholar Jul 2014, pro. Dec 2014.

Debut v Gillingham (FL Cup) (h) 21.9.2016
(Juventus (Fr) (Melbourne) 26.7.2016)

An impressively powerful, well-built central defender, Cameron Carter-Vickers has long been regarded as a probable future defensive lynchpin for Spurs. An all-round sportsman, Carter-Vickers joined Spurs Academy when 11 and was soon playing for teams a year or more above his age group. It was a feature he took to the international stage. When only 16 he was called up to the US national team Under-18 squad. He qualified to play for the US through his father, Howard "Hi-C" Carter, a former basketball player who played at the highest level in America, France and Greece. Carter-Vickers did not look out of his depth and, in fact, impressed so much that before his 17th birthday he was in the Americans Under-23 team. Back at Spurs, he continued to develop rapidly and when Jan Vertonghen was injured in February 2016, Carter-Vickers looked like making a breakthrough until injury put him on the side-lines. Another injury to Vertonghen and absences after Euro 2016, saw Carter-Vickers at last make his first team debut in the International Champions Cup in Australia. His power and strength were obvious, but he also looked solid, reading the game well and quick to learn. There can be little doubt he will soon be challenging for a regular starting place. The Americans must be looking to promote Carter-Vickers to their full team soon, for he could still switch allegiance to England if the call came.

Appearances:
FA Cup: 2 apps.
FL Cup: 2.apps.
Others: 3 apps.
Total: 7 apps. 0 gls.

CARTWRIGHT, William

Role: Full-back 1913-15
5ft.10ins. 12st.9lbs.
Born: Burton-On-Trent, Staffordshire, 26th June 1884
Died: Repton, Lincolnshire, 13th July 1971

CAREER: Trent Rovers/Gainsborough Trinity Aug 1906/Chelsea May 1908/**SPURS** May 1913/Stoke Albion May 1916/Swansea Town May 1919/Gillingham Sep 1919/Southend United trainer Aug 1920, ground-staff 1946.

Debut v Newcastle United (FL) (a) 15.11.1913
(Crystal Palace (LPFCF) (h) 27.10.1913)

Bill Cartwright had spent most of his five years at Stamford Bridge in the reserve side. Although on Spurs' books for six years, four taken up by the First World War, he only managed a sustained run in the first team during his first full season. With the signing of the Armistice in late 1918 football looked to return to normality. Swansea Town had all but closed down for the duration, but began to play friendly matches and Cartwright joined them for half a season, before moving to Gillingham. He spent one season in Kent and then joined Southend United as trainer, giving the Essex club so many years of loyal service that he was granted a testimonial.

Appearances:
League: 13 apps.
FA Cup: 2 apps.
Others: 7 apps.
Total: **22 apps. 0 gls.**

CARVER

Role: Inside-left 1894-95

CAREER: Bostal Rovers/**SPURS** trial Mar 1895.

Debut v City Ramblers (Fr) (h) 30.3.1895 (scored once)

Carver's only known appearance for Spurs was as a trialist from Bostal Rovers. Although he scored in a 2-0 friendly victory over City Ramblers, he evidently did not perform well enough, for he was not taken on by Spurs.

Appearances:
Others: 1 app. 1 gl.
Total: **1 app. 1 gl.**

CASEY, Hamilton Douglas

Role: Half-back 1882-95
Born: *Hackney, London, September qtr. 1867*
Died: *March 1914*

CAREER: Radicals/**SPURS**/Old Tottonians.

Debut v Brownlow Rovers (Fr) (h) 6.10.1883

One of Spurs founding members, Ham Casey, was one of the few players known to have played for another club before Spurs, having turned out for the Radicals in 1881-82. A pupil at St John's Middle Class School and a well-known athlete with the Finchley Harriers club, like Billy Harston and Bobby Buckle, Casey retained his interest in the club for many years. His brother, Lindsay R Casey, was also a founder member although it would appear it was "Ham", also known as Sam, who served the club on the playing side. It was reportedly he and his brother who painted the club's first goalposts, supplied by their father. Casey is known to have played for Old Tottonians in 1898-99, but when too old to play he continued to be involved in football for several years as a linesman and referee in the Southern and Western Leagues. In the early years of the twentieth century Spurs' programmes carried an advertisement from Casey for picture framing.

Appearances:
Others: 48 apps.
Total: **48 apps. 0 gls.**

CASEY, Jack

Role: Outside-left 1916-17
Born: *Liverpool, Lancashire*

CAREER: Bromley/West Ham United cs. 1912/(guest for **SPURS** during World War One)/Clapton Orient cs. 1919.

Debut v West Ham United (Fr) (a) 5.5.1917

A schoolmaster, Jack Casey made his name with Bromley, helping them win the Spartan League, Isthmian League (twice) and, in 1911, the Amateur Cup. He joined West Ham United in 1912, a speedy winger and was a regular in their first team until the outbreak of war. He made many appearances for them during the time of conflict, when he also made his one appearance for Spurs. That was when Spurs arrived at Upton Park in May 1919 for a friendly match two men short and Casey was asked to help make up the numbers. He remained with West Ham for the first post-war season and then joined Clapton Orient, but never played a senior game for them.

Appearances:
Others: 1 app.
Total: **1 app. 0 gls.**

CASKEY, Darren Mark

Role: Midfielder 1991-96
5ft.8ins. 11st.9lbs.
Born: *Basildon, Essex, 21st August 1974*

CAREER: Basildon & Brentwood Schools/FA-GM School of Excellence/**SPURS** trainee Jul 1990, pro. Feb 1992/(Watford loan Oct 1995)/Reading Feb 1996/Notts County Jun 2001/Bristol City non-contract Mar-Jun 2004, trial Jul 2004/Hornchurch Aug 2004/Peterborough United non-contract Nov 2004, perm. Dec 2004/Bath City Jan 2005/Rushden & Diamonds training Jan 2005/Havant and Waterlooville Jan 2005/Virginia Beach Mariners (USA) trial and perm. Feb 2005/MK Dons trial Dec 2005/Mansfield Town trial Jan 2006/Rushden & Diamonds Jan 2006/Kettering Town player-coach Jun 2006/Halesowen Town loan player-coach Oct 2007, perm. Nov 2007/Ilkeston Town coach Jul 2009, asst. manager Jul-Sep 2010/Ilkeston FC asst. manager Dec 2010/Gateshead asst. manager Sep 2013/Wrexham asst. manager Jun 2015 - Oct 2016/York City football consultant Oct 2016.

Debut v Arsenal (sub) (PL) (h) 16.8.1993
(Hull City (sub) (Fr) (a) 8.5.1992)

England schools international Darren Caskey was not only one of the stars of the England Youth team that won the European championship in 1993, but also the team captain. Alongside Spurs youth team-mates, Sol Campbell and Ian Walker, Caskey was rated one of the players most likely to reach the pinnacle of English football and that promise soon looked like being realised. A midfielder with excellent passing skills to complement an eye for the opening, Ossie Ardiles was quick to spot Caskey's talents, and just as quick to give him his opportunity. In 1993-94, Ardiles' first season in charge, Caskey became a regular performer and while he clearly lacked pace and sometimes seemed to tire early, he was still in his teens and there was no reason to think he could not develop to become the fulcrum of the team's attacking game. The arrival of Gică Popescu early the following season saw Caskey overlooked, but it was when Gerry Francis arrived to replace Ardiles that Caskey's fortunes really took a turn for the worse. While Ardiles had been prepared to give young, attacking talent an opportunity, Francis was more concerned with experienced players he knew and trusted. Caskey was rarely given a chance under Francis, and after a loan spell at Watford, accepted that there was no future for him at White Hart Lane. He moved to Reading in a £700,000 transfer. Caskey was not playing at the highest level, but he established himself as the midfield general, notching up over 230 senior appearances in five years with the Royals, before deciding he was not willing to accept a role playing out wide on the right. He moved to Notts County where he added another hundred plus appearances to his total, before being released and signing a short term contract with Bristol City. When that had run its course, Caskey stayed on hoping to persuade the Robins to give him a longer deal, but when they decided not to make an offer he moved into non-League football with ambitious Hornchurch. The plans of the Essex club were wildly over-optimistic and as they began to disintegrate and their financial problems deepened, Caskey was one of the first they wanted to get off the wage bill. He touted his talents around looking for a new club until accepting an offer to play for Virginia Beach Mariners in the second rank of American football, the First Division of the United Soccer Leagues. In his one season in America Caskey impressed, being voted the most valuable player with the club by his team-mates and in the All-League Second team of 2005, but when the Mariners folded Caskey returned to the UK to look for a new club. Well into the veteran stage now, Caskey had to content himself with playing in the non-League game, slowly moving into coaching and managing roles. Caskey's son, Jake Forster-Caskey is on the books of Brighton & Hove Albion.

Appearances:
League: 20 (12) apps. 4 gls.
FA Cup: 6 (1) app.
FL Cup: 3 (1) apps. 1 gl.
Others: 11 (10) apps. 2 gls.
Total: 40 (24) apps. 7 gls.

CASTLE, Sidney Ernest Roland

Role: Outside-right 1919-21
5ft.8ins. 11st.2lbs.
Born: Basingstoke, Hampshire, 12th March 1892
Died: Basingstoke, Hampshire, 27th January 1978

CAREER: Basingstoke Town/Thorneycrofts/(guest for Reading & Crystal Palace during World War One)/Guildford City Aug 1919/**SPURS** Mar 1920/Charlton Athletic May 1921/Chelsea May 1923/Guildford United Jun 1926/Weymouth Sep 1926/Ajax (Holland) coach Nov 1927-Sep 1928/ZAC (Holland) coach to Jun 1930/PEC (Holland) coach Jul 1930/SC Heerenveen (Holland) coach 1932/Meppeler SC (Holland) coach 1933-1935/SC Heerenveen (Holland) coach 1936-1938.

Debut v Stoke City (FL) (a) 10.4.1920

Sid Castle's career had been rather low key before he signed for Spurs-who were pressing for promotion back to the First Division-and it did not particularly improve during his time at White Hart Lane. Two games in his first season were followed by just four more the following term, before he was released. The most successful spell of his career saw him playing regularly for Charlton Athletic in their initial seasons in the Football League and led to a move to Chelsea, where he played intermittently for three years in the League team. In the summer of 1926 he was released by Chelsea and joined Guildford United, finishing his career with Weymouth. Castle then went to coach in Holland, returning to the UK just before the outbreak of the Second World War. During the 1950's, Castle ran a works canteen in Basingstoke.

Appearances:
League: 5 apps.
Others: 1 app. 1 gl.
Total: 6 apps. 1 gl.

CATTELL, C

Role: Forward 1892-93

CAREER: Old St Marks/**SPURS** guest Mar 1893.

Debut v Windsor & Eton (SA) (h) 4.3.1893 (scored on debut)

Cattell was a forward with the Old St Marks club, one of Spurs' oldest regular opponents. He assisted Spurs as a "guest" player late in the 1892-93 season, making his first known appearance in a Southern Alliance match. The Southern Alliance was the first League competition Spurs entered, but it only survived for one season, several clubs failing to fulfil all their fixtures. While Cattell continued to play for Old St Marks for several years, he turned out for Spurs again in the FA Cup-tie with Vampires in November 1895, that was subsequently declared void by the FA due to the pitch having been incorrectly marked.

Appearances:
FA Cup: 1 app.
Others: 3 apps. 1 gl.
Total: 4 apps. 1 gl.

CAULKER, Steven Roy

Role: Central defender 2010-2014
6ft.3ins. 14st.13lbs.
Born: Feltham, Middlesex, 29th December 1991

CAREER: Lampton School/Hounslow Borough/**SPURS** Academy Scholar Jul 2008, pro. Jul 2009/(Yeovil Town loan Jul 2009)/(Bristol City loan Sep 2010)/(Swansea City loan Jul 2011)/Cardiff City Jul 2013/Queens Park Rangers Jul 2014/(Southampton loan Jul 2015)/(Liverpool loan Jan 2016).

Debut v Arsenal (FLC) (h) 21.9.2010
(AFC Bournemouth (Fr) (a) 10.7.2010)

Steven Caulker is a prime example of the benefits provided by football's loan system. An outstanding prospect as a schoolboy, Caulker played a year or two above his age level in Spurs' youth set-up, and did not look out of his depth. Having signed on as a professional, he was immediately sent out on a three-month loan to Yeovil Town, but ended up staying for the whole of the 2009-10 season; their star performer. He made his debut for Spurs in a 1-4 Carling Cup defeat to Arsenal and looked strong and confident, but up against quality forwards, his inexperience was obvious. He went out on season long loans again, first to Bristol City, then Swansea City for their first season in the Premier League. The experience he gathered over the three loans was invaluable. An England Under-21 regular, Caulker was developing so well that he was selected for the Great Britain team at the 2012 Olympic Games. He formed the bedrock of the defence, playing in all five of the nation's matches. Having proved himself a more than competent Premier League performer, Caulker began the 2012-13 season in Spurs' first team, impressing so much that he collected his first England cap against Sweden in November 2012. With competition from the likes of William Gallas, Michael Dawson and Jan Vertonghen, Caulker was not a first team regular, but in an age when few players could be regarded as certain starters, he did well enough to seem destined for a long and successful career in a Spurs' shirt. It was, therefore, a major surprise when Spurs accepted an £8 million offer for his services from Cardiff City. Caulker played every minute of all Cardiff's Premier League games in 2013-14, but could do nothing to prevent them being relegated. Far too good for Championship football, Caulker returned to London with Queens Park Rangers, but again experienced relegation in his first season at a new club. He started the 2015-16 season on loan to Southampton, expected to replace Toby Alderweireld who had moved to Spurs. What was expected to be a season long loan was surprisingly cut short in January 2016 so Caulker could join Liverpool on loan for the rest of the season.

Appearances:
League: 17 (1) apps. 2 gls.
FA Cup: 2 apps.
FL Cup: 3 apps.
Euro: 5 (1) apps.
Others: 4 (2) apps.
Total: 31 (4) apps. 2 gls.

CAWKILL

Role: Unknown 1884-85

Debut v Sekforde Rovers (Fr) (a) 1.11.1884

Another of those players from Spurs' early days that nothing is known about, Cawkill is recorded as having played in two friendly matches during the 1884-85 season. It is not even known what position he played in.

Appearances:
Others: 2 apps.
Total: 2 apps. 0 gls.

CEBALLOS, Christian Prieto

Role: Midfielder 2013-15
5ft.9ins, 11st.9lbs.
Born: Santa María de Cayón, Spain, 3rd December 1992

CAREER: Barcelona (Spain) 2004/Chelsea training Apr 2011/**SPURS** trial Apr 2011, perm Jul 2011/(Arouca (Portugal) loan Sep 2013)/Charlton Athletic Jul 2015/(Sint-Truidense (Belgium) loan Aug 2016).

Debut v Swindon Town (Fr) (a) 16.7.2013

Christian Ceballos was only 11-years old when Barcelona spotted his talent and took him into its La Masia youth set up. He developed well as he moved up through the ranks to the Catalan club's "B" team but with an abundance of attacking talent he was released after seven years. Given a trial by Spurs he did enough to impress and was quickly persuaded to move to London. A technically-gifted attacking midfielder with an eye for goal, he made the first team match day squad in his early days at White Hart Lane, but most of his playing action was limited to the Youth team. His senior debut came in a pre-season friendly in July 2013 and a couple of months later he was loaned out to Arouca, newly promoted to the Portuguese top flight. He played regularly in Portugal and returned to Spurs to again feature in pre-season games, but with Spurs blessed with a depth of midfield players, first team opportunities appeared as far away as ever and Ceballos made it known he could only see a future if he left Spurs. His wish was granted in July 2015 when he was allowed to join Charlton Athletic on a free transfer.

Appearances:
Others: 1 (3) apps.
Total: 1 (3) apps. 0 gls.

ČERNÝ, Radek

Role: Goalkeeper, 2004-08
6ft.2ins, 14st.8lbs.
Born: Prague, Czechoslovakia, 18th February 1974

CAREER: Slavia Prague (Czech Republic) 1990/(Ceske Budejovice (Czech Republic) loan 1993-95)/(Tatran Poštovná (Czech Republic) loan 1995)/(Union Cheb (Czech Republic) loan 1996)/(**SPURS** loan Jan 2005)/ Queens Park Rangers May 2008-May 2013/Slavia Prague (Czech Republic) trial Jun 2013, perm Jul 2013, goalkeeping coach Jun 2015.

Debut v Aston Villa (sub) (PL) (h) 1.5.2005

Associated with his local club, Slavia, from the age of six, Radek Černý followed his father and elder brother, Petr, onto their professional staff. Loaned out to lower division clubs, he collected eleven Under-21 caps, but it was to be six years before he made his debut for Slavia. In the next nine years he never really established himself as the first choice 'keeper, though he played nearly 200 games for them and collected three full caps. Come 2004-05, he was out of favour and with Spurs keen to have experienced cover for Paul Robinson, accepted the offer of an 18-month loan. He made his Premier League debut as a substitute for Robinson in May 2005 and played in the final game of the season, but when Robinson was fit to resume the following season, it was back to the bench for Černý. Despite knowing opportunities would be limited, he extended his stay at White Hart Lane for another two years. Only in his final season did he get a regular run in the first team, taking over from Robinson when the England 'keeper lost form. Well into the veteran stage, there was little chance of Černý making a long term career with Spurs. With Heurelho Gomes' signing in the pipeline, Černý was released and joined Queens Park Rangers. He gave Rangers four years' good service before finding Robert Green and Julio Caesar usurping his position. He was released when his contract expired in May 2013 and returned to Slavia Prague, initially as a player, then as a coach.

Appearances:
League: 15 (1) apps.
FA Cup: 4 apps.
FL Cup: 4 apps.
Euro: 4 apps.
Others: 13 (2) apps.
Total: 40 (3) apps. 0 gls.

CHADLI, Nacer

Role: Midfielder, 2013-
6ft.2ins, 13st.8lbs.
Born: Liège, Belgium, 2nd August 1989

CAREER: JS Thier-à-Liège (Belgium) 1994/Standard Liège (Belgium) 1998/MVV Maastricht (Holland) 2004/AGOVV Apeldoorn (Holland) Jul 2007/FC Twente (Holland) Jul 2010/**SPURS** Jul 2013/West Bromwich Albion Aug 2016.

Debut v Crystal Palace (PL) (a) 18.8.2013
(Monaco (Fr) (a) 3.8.2013)

In the summer of 2013 it was known that Gareth Bale would be leaving for Real Madrid. A price of up to £100 million was expected. Spurs would be flush with money, but short of true top quality players. Nacer Chadli was one of several players signed to try and fill that void. As it turned out, one of the better signings. Of Moroccan descent, Chadli was a typical example of a young boy taken under the wing of a youth team and, when potential was shown, the youth structure of a professional club. In Chadli's case, it was Standard Liege who spotted his potential, but, as so often the case with talented Belgian youngsters, it was a Dutch club, that offered the best chance of a good contract and quick progression. Chadli played youth football with MVV Maastricht and took his first professional steps with AGOVV Apeldoorn. It was when he joined the Dutch champions, Twente, that he really came to the fore. Within four months of signing he was playing international football, though not for Belgium. Morocco were quick to recognise that Chadli was qualified to play for them. He made his international debut against Northern Ireland in November 2010. A couple of months later he announced that he intended to play for Belgium, something he was able to do because his appearance for Morocco was not in a competitive match. Days later he played for Belgium against Finland. Before playing that first game for Belgium, Chadli had played for Twente against Spurs in both Champions League group games. Already Spurs were being linked with Chadli, and a goal in each game simply reinforced the stories. It was two-and-a-half years later that Spurs laid out £7 million to secure Chadli's services. In his first season at White Hart Lane Spurs were seeking to rebuild following the departure of Bale, to find a new format and style of play. With the influx of new players and the poor results it was not easy for a new signing and Chadli was not helped by injury problems. A big, strong, powerful individual, Chadli was primarily regarded as a wide player when he arrived at Spurs; not a winger with speed and trickery, but a modern wide midfielder, with pace and power, capable of dropping deep to defend, liable to pop up in a scoring position and a regular contributor to the goal-scoring charts. His physique makes him perfectly suited to a striker's role and he can play up front in an emergency, but he is at his best in midfield. In his time with Spurs Chadli has developed into an all-round midfielder, capable of playing right across the pitch or just behind the main striker. In the modern squad dominated game, few players can be regarded as certain starters. Chadli was not one of them, but he proved himself a valuable member of the squad before, surprisingly, being allowed to move to West Bromwich Albion, at £13 million, the Black Country club's record signing.

Appearances:
League: 53 (35) apps. 15 gls.
FA Cup: 4 (3) apps. 4 gls.
FL Cup: 3 (4) apps. 2 gls.
Euro: 12 (5) apps. 4 gls.
Others: 5 (4) apps. 1 gl.
Total: 77 (51) apps. 26 gls.

CHALMERS, James

Role: Outside-left 1902-04
5ft.10ins. 13st.0lbs.
Born: Old Luce, Wigtownshire, 3rd December 1877
Dies: Gallipoli, Turkey, 12th July 1915 (killed in action)

CAREER: Beith 1895/Greenock Morton Jul 1896/Sunderland May 1897/Preston North End Oct 1898/Notts County Jun 1899/Beith Sep 1900/Partick Thistle Oct-Dec 1900/Watford Jul 1901/**SPURS** May 1902/Swindon Town May 1904/Norwich City May 1906/Bristol Rovers May 1908/Beith till cs. 1913.

Debut v Northampton Town (WL) (a) 27.12.1902
(Corinthians (Fr) (h) 13.12.1902 (scored once))

Well-travelled James Chalmers was signed from Watford as understudy to John Kirwan and spent the whole of his two seasons in that role, playing only when the Irish international was unavailable. Prematurely grey-haired when scarcely out of his teens, his first senior game for Spurs was a friendly in December 1902, but he had to wait until the end of the month before making a competitive debut in a Western League fixture, and then a further month before playing for Spurs in the Southern League. Released in May 1904, he joined Swindon Town and later played for Norwich City and Beith. He is not to be confused with John "Jack" Chalmers who played for Glasgow Rangers, Stoke (Jan 1906), Clyde (Nov 1908), Woolwich Arsenal (Oct 1910) and Greenock Morton (Mar 1912). James Chalmers gave his life for his country, a victim of the Gallipoli Battle.

Appearances:
Southern: 10 apps. 1 gl.
Others: 22* apps. 5 gls.
Total: 32 apps. 6 gls.
* Includes 1 abandoned match

CHANNELL, Frederick Charles

Role: Full-back 1933-36
5ft.8ins. 10st.10lbs.
Born: Edmonton, north London, 5th May 1910
Died: Colchester, Essex, 6th August 1976

CAREER: Lancastrian Road School/Harwich and Parkeston/Haywards FC 1928/ **SPURS** ground-staff, am. Feb 1928, pro. Aug 1930/Clapton Orient trial/ Peterborough and Fletton United/Northfleet United Oct 1930/**SPURS** pro. Aug 1933.

Debut v Sunderland (FL) (h) 7.10.1933

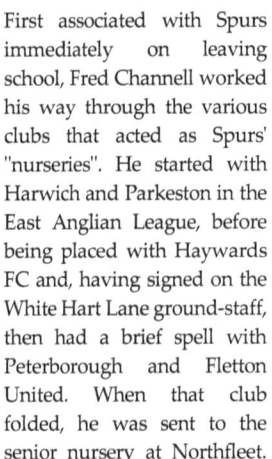

First associated with Spurs immediately on leaving school, Fred Channell worked his way through the various clubs that acted as Spurs' "nurseries". He started with Harwich and Parkeston in the East Anglian League, before being placed with Haywards FC and, having signed on the White Hart Lane ground-staff, then had a brief spell with Peterborough and Fletton United. When that club folded, he was sent to the senior nursery at Northfleet. Channell made his League debut in October 1933, standing in for the injured Bill Felton, and by the end of the season had taken to the right-back position so well that the experienced Felton was allowed to leave. A cool, stylish defender, Channell was soon regarded as international material. In March 1935 he played for The Rest in the England trial at the Hawthorns, and two months later for an English XI against an Anglo-Scots XI at Highbury. Sadly, just as his career was about to approach its peak, he was so badly injured in a match with West Ham United on 14th March 1936 that two months later, at the age of only 26, he was forced to retire. He later ran the Boundary House pub in Ponders End, Middlesex. Channell's brother, Bill, was on Spurs' books as a professional from December 1921 to May 1922 but never made the senior team before moving on to Northfleet United.

Appearances:
League: 95 apps. 1 gl.
FA Cup: 14 apps.
Others: 4 apps.
Total: 113 apps. 1 gl.

CHAPLIN, Alexander Balfour

Role: Full-back 1915-16
Born: Dundee, 6th February 1892
Died: Fulham, London, 9th March 1986

CAREER: Dundee Hibernian May 1914/Napier Munitions/**SPURS** guest Sep 1915/Fulham guest 1915, pro Jun 1919/Northfleet United player-coach Oct 1926-1929.

Debut v Arsenal (LFC) (a) 4.9.1915

Chaplin followed his elder brother John on to the staff at White Hart Lane although Alec's career with Spurs was much shorter and came during a time of upheaval. Like his brother a full-back, he moved to London during the First World War to work in a munitions factory. Recommended by his brother, he played in four of Spurs' first five matches of the London Football Combination competition, but after that was not seen in Spurs' colours again. He was spotted by Fulham playing for the factory side, Napiers, and they signed him on, the beginning of a ten-year career at Craven Cottage. Fulham's regular left-back after the war, he retired from playing at the end of the 1925-26 season and joined Spurs' Northfleet nursery as player/coach. He served there for three years. Later in life he spent 15 years as a member of Fulham council.

Appearances:
Others: 4 apps.
Total: 4 apps. 0 gls.

CHAPLIN, John Fowler

Role: Full-back 1905-08
5ft.9ins. 12st.2lbs.
Born: Dundee, 10th October 1882
Died: Doncaster, Yorkshire, 15th April 1952

CAREER: Dundee Arnot/Dundee Wanderers/Dundee May 1903/**SPURS** May 1905/Dundee May 1908/Manchester City Nov 1910/Leeds City trainer Nov 1913, asst. manager/Sheffield Wednesday trainer Oct 1919/ Bristol Rovers trainer Mar 1920/Huddersfield Town trainer Apr 1921, manager Aug 1926, trainer May 1929-1935.

Debut v Plymouth Argyle (WL) (h) 2.10.1905

A tough, hard-tackling full-back who had gained experience in his native Dundee, John Chaplin made his first team debut for Spurs in a Western League fixture in October 1905, but had to wait until the following April before making his first appearance in the senior competition, the Southern League. The following season he displaced John Watson as first choice right-back and proved very popular with Spurs fans. In May 1908 Spurs wanted to re-sign Chaplin for their anticipated entry into the Football League, but he surprisingly decided to return to Dundee instead. During two years back in his home town he played for the Scottish League against the Irish League in October 1909 and in the 1910 Scottish Cup Final, although injury meant he had to miss the replay. In November 1910, he wanted to join Manchester City, but Spurs' consent was necessary. As Spurs had offered him the maximum permitted wages to re-sign in 1908, they had first claim on his services. They did not stand in his way, even though unable to obtain any transfer fee as they had not been members of the Football League at the time of his departure. Chaplin made only 17 League appearances at Hyde Road before injury brought his career to an end and he moved onto the training side with Leeds City, Bristol Rovers and Sheffield Wednesday before joining

Huddersfield Town in the same capacity in April 1921. In August 1926, he took over as manager from Cecil Potter just as Huddersfield completed a hat-trick of Football League championships. After such successful years under Herbert Chapman and Potter, Chaplin faced an almost impossible job, but still managed to keep Huddersfield near the pinnacle and took them to the 1928 FA Cup Final. In May 1929, he stepped down and returned to the trainer's role continuing to serve Huddersfield in that position until the outbreak of World War Two. John Chaplin's two brothers were both professional full-backs. George, a Scottish international, played for Dundee, Bradford City and Coventry City and Alec, who guested for Spurs during the First World War, played for Dundee Hibernians and spent ten years with Fulham after the War. Alec later had three years as player/coach with Northfleet United.

Appearances:
Southern: 66 apps.
FA Cup: 1 app.
Others: 33 apps.
Total: 100 apps. 0 gls.

CHAPMAN, Edwin

Role: Inside-forward 1942-43
Born: East Ham, London, 3rd August 1923
Died: Ilford, Essex, 8th October 2002

CAREER: Loxford School/Ilford Schools/Essex Schools/London Schools/South of England Schools/West Ham United am. 1936, ground-staff Aug 1937/(Romford loan)/West Ham United pro. Sep 1942/(guest for Aldershot, Gillingham, Millwall and **SPURS** during World War Two)/West Ham United asst. secretary, secretary 1954, chief executive Jun 1979/retired Jun 1986/Gillingham consultant Jul 1986.

Debut v Crystal Palace (FLS) (a) 28.11.1942

Eddie Chapman was best known in football circles as an administrator, having been secretary and later chief executive of West Ham United. An England schoolboy trialist, he joined the east London club as an amateur, signed on the ground-staff and played for Romford before signing as a West Ham professional in 1942. His debut for West Ham came during the war and he played his only match for Spurs as a guest in November 1942 in a Football League South fixture. Chapman had to wait until 1948 before making his Football League debut and had played only seven League games when he

retired in 1954. Towards the end of his playing career he had been appointed assistant secretary at Upton Park and he took up the senior post on his playing retirement. Appointed chief executive in 1979, he held the post until his retirement in June 1986.

Appearances:
Others: 1 app.
Total: 1 app. 0 gls.

CHAPMAN, Herbert

Role: Inside-forward 1904-07
5ft.8ins. 12st.0lbs.
Born: Kiveton Park, Sheffield, Yorkshire, 19th January 1878
Died: Hendon, Middlesex, 6th January 1934

CAREER: Kiveton Park Schools/Kiveton Park FC May 1896/Ashton North End Aug 1896/Stalybridge Rovers Jul 1897/Rochdale Athletic pro. Oct 1897/Grimsby Town am. May 1898/Swindon Town am. Jan 1899/Sheppey United Nov 1899/Worksop Town Oct 1900/Northampton Town pro. Jul 1901/Sheffield United am. May 1902/Notts County pro. May 1903/Northampton Town May 1904/**SPURS** Mar 1905/Chesterfield Town trial Aug 1906/Northampton Town player-manager Apr 1907/Leeds City manager May 1912/Huddersfield Town secretary Sep 1920, asst. manager Feb 1921, manager Mar 1921/Arsenal manager May 1925.

Debut v Brighton and Hove Albion (SL) (h) 18.3.1905 (scored once)

Herbert Chapman's is one of the greatest names in football, but it was not for his prowess as a Spurs' player that he achieved lasting fame. He joined Spurs in March 1905, an inside-forward with plenty of experience, but only average ability, and never in the same class as his brother Harry, who played for Sheffield Wednesday. Chapman had gained experience throughout the country, starting as an amateur with Kiveton Park, Ashton North End and Stalybridge Rovers whilst studying to become a mining engineer. He played professionally for Rochdale, Grimsby Town, Swindon Town, Sheppey United, Worksop and Northampton Town, but reverted to amateur status to spend one season with Sheffield United. May 1903 saw him back in the

professional ranks with Notts County and the following season he again played for Northampton Town. Still registered with Notts County as a Football League player, when Spurs wanted to sign him, they had to pay a £70 transfer fee to County. Almost ever-present in his first season, Chapman was relegated to the reserves the following year and in April 1907 returned to Northampton, as player/manager. Northampton finished the season bottom of the Southern League, yet two years later Chapman retired from playing with the Cobblers hailed as champions. He then followed former Spurs' goalkeeper Frank Walford as manager of Leeds City as they faced re-election to the League. Whilst football standards understandably slipped during the war years, Leeds City won the League's Midland Section in both 1916-17 and 1917-18, but in 1919 were summoned before the Football League to answer charges of making illegal payments to players during the war years. Leeds refused to allow inspection of their books and as a result were thrown out of the League and their officials, Chapman included, suspended. It was, perhaps, a little harsh on Chapman, for he had been managing a munitions factory since

1916 and was probably not party to any illegalities. The suspension was lifted late in 1920 and he returned to football with Huddersfield Town, initially as secretary, but soon after as manager. Chapman's impact was little short of sensational as he led Huddersfield to FA Cup success in 1922, third place in the First Division in 1923 and the League title in 1924 and 1925. Huddersfield won their third title the next season, with Arsenal, whom Chapman had joined in May 1925, runners-up. In 1927 he took Arsenal to the FA Cup Final where they lost to Cardiff City, but he led them back to Wembley in 1930 to beat his old club Huddersfield. Arsenal now embarked on arguably the most glorious period of their history. In 1931 they won the Football League Championship, followed that with another FA Cup victory in 1932, and the League again in 1933. A truly great Arsenal side was on its way to the second of three successive titles when Chapman went down with pneumonia and died.

Appearances:
Southern: 41 apps. 15 gls.
FA Cup: 7 apps. 1 gl.
Others: 19 apps. 4 gls.
Total: 67 apps. 20 gls.

CHERRIE, T

Role: Half-back 1895-96

Debut v Gravesend (Fr) (a) 22.4.1896

Cherrie appeared in two friendly matches for Spurs in April 1896 as a trialist half-back. He could not have impressed too much for he was not subsequently signed on.

Appearances:
Others: 2 apps.
Total: 2 apps. 2 gls.

CHESTER, Arthur

Role: Winger 1918-19
5ft.7ins. 11st 2lb
Born: Hexham, Northumberland, June quarter 1886
Died: Don Valley, Yorkshire, June quarter 1943

CAREER: Wingate Albion/Preston North End 1910/Croydon Common cs. 1912/(guest for Brentford, Clapton Orient, Millwall, **SPURS** and West Ham United during World War One)/Queens Park Rangers cs. 1919/Brentford/Ramsgate cs. 1920

Debut v West Ham United (LFC) (h) 8.3.1919

Originally with Wingate Albion and Preston North End, Art Chester played regularly for Croydon Common prior to the start of the First World War, but with their demise was available to guest for any club that could do with his assistance. He made three appearances for Spurs, all late in the 1918-19 season when clubs were looking to recruit for the resumption of normal football. In the first he played at outside-right, and in the second at inside-right, but he did not impress and his only other appearance was in a friendly at Crystal Palace on 26th April 1919. With Spurs playing two friendly matches that day several trialists were given an opportunity and Chester went on a substitute for the unfortunate "Slender", who had such a bad game his true name has never been disclosed. Although not regarded as good enough for Spurs, Chester joined Queens Park Rangers for the following season. He made only one appearance for them before moving on to Brentford.

Appearances:
Others: 2 (1) apps.
Total: 2 (1) apps. 0 gls.

CHIEDOZIE, John Okay

Role: Winger 1984-88
5ft.7ins. 10st.10lbs.
Born: Owerri, Nigeria, 18th April 1960

CAREER: St Bonaventure School/Newham Schools/London Schools/Orient app. Jul 1976, pro. Apr 1977/Notts County Aug 1981/**SPURS** Aug 1984/Derby County Aug 1988/Notts County non-contract Jan 1990/Chesterfield non-contract Mar 1990/Swindon Town trial 1990/Bashley trial Oct 1991/Banks of Barking Dec 1991/Bashley cs. 1992.

Debut v Everton (FL) (a) 25.8.1984 (scored once)
(Manchester City (sub) (Fr) (a) 16.8.1984)

Coming to England when only twelve-years old, John Chiedozie immediately showed the pace and ball control that made him such an exciting winger. Having trained with West Ham United, he was pursued by a posse of London clubs, but chose to join Orient, and by the time he signed professional had already made his Football League debut. Transferred to newly-promoted Notts County he played over 100 games for the League's oldest club before they fell back into the Second Division. Several First Division outfits had been impressed with his speed and ability to cut inside for a crack at goal, but it was Spurs' manager Peter Shreeve who swooped to sign him for £375,000. If Chiedozie had a shortcoming it was that he could too often be put out of a game by an over-physical opposing full-back and this, allied to a series of injuries limited his appearances and effectiveness for Spurs. A regular Nigerian international when signed, John made three further appearances for his country whilst at White Hart Lane, but after a string of bad injuries wiped out his 1987-88 season, he was given a free transfer and returned to the Midlands with Derby County. Persistent injury worries plagued his spell at the Baseball Ground and he was again released on a free transfer. Chiedozie returned to Notts County and had a short stint at Chesterfield, before dropping into non-League circles with Banks of Barking and Bashley. Chiedozie's son, Jordan, played for Cambridge United and several non-League clubs.

Appearances:
League: 45 (8) apps. 12 gls.
FA Cup: 5 (3) apps. 2 gls.
FL Cup: 7 apps.
Euro: 7 apps.
Others: 22 (6) apps. 5 gls.
Total: 86 (17) apps. 19 gls.

CHIMBONDA, Pascal

Role: Full-back 2006-10
5ft.11ins. 12st.2lbs.
Born: Les Abymes, Guadeloupe, 21st February 1979

CAREER: Real Club (Guadeloupe)/Port-Louis (Guadeloupe)/Le Havre (France) Jul 1999/Bastia (France) Jul 2003/Wigan Athletic Jul 2005/**SPURS** Aug 2006/Sunderland Jul 2008/**SPURS** Jan 2009/Blackburn Rovers Jul 2009-Jan 2011/Queens Park Rangers Jan 2011/Doncaster Rovers Sep 2011-Jun 2012/Chicago Fire trial Feb 2013/Market Drayton Town Jul 2013/Tranmere Rovers training Aug 2013/Colwyn Bay Aug 2013/CD Fátima

(Portugal) trial Oct 2013/Carlisle United training and perm Oct 2013/ Arles-Avignon (France) Oct 2014-Feb 2015/AS Mazargues (France) coach Jul 2015.

Debut v Manchester United (PL) (a) 9.9.2006

In seven years playing top flight football in France, Pascal Chimbonda had not grabbed the attention of the bigger clubs. The fact both Le Havre and Bastia had suffered relegation with him in their ranks may have had something to do with that. When Bastia were relegated, Chimbonda decided to try his luck abroad and while clubs like Marseille were interested in signing him, he decided to join Wigan Athletic for their first season in the Premier League. While Wigan could, perhaps, not be further removed from Chimbonda's West Indies home, it proved a wise decision in football terms. Playing at right-back, he was a revelation, thrusting forward at every opportunity with strong bursts down the flank and proving a continual threat, particularly when the ball was in the air. Defensively, he was more than capable, timing his tackles well and not allowing any opponent to get the better of him. For two years he was Wigan's outstanding performer, helping them to the Carling Cup final in 2006, but he wrecked his career at the DW Stadium no more than three months later when, on the last day of the season, he demanded a transfer. As he had only agreed to extend his contract weeks earlier, it was not a demand that went down well with employer or supporters. Interest in signing Chimbonda was keen with Spurs making several offers that were turned down. Late on the last day of the transfer window, a £6 million offer found favour with Wigan and Chimbonda moved to White Hart Lane. He started his White Hart Lane career, looking solid in defence and a force going forward. He played in the 2008 Carling Cup final, but his form began to wane and he found himself sidelined. When Sunderland made a good offer for Chimbonda, it was accepted. Barely six months later, he was back at Spurs, when Harry Redknapp decided Chimbonda could do a job for a team that was struggling. It made him one of very few players to return to the club. Chimbonda's second stay was very short. Having played only five senior matches he was allowed to join Blackburn Rovers. Soon out of favour there, his contract was terminated so he could move to Queens Park Rangers on a six-months deal. After a year at Doncaster Rovers, Chimbonda found it difficult to secure a permanent deal anywhere and had to content himself with various short-term contracts until finding a role as Under-17 coach for AS Mazargues.

Appearances:
League: 65 (3) apps. 3 gls.
FA Cup: 6 apps.
FL Cup: 8 apps. 1 gl.
Euro: 21 apps.
Others: 9 (2) apps.
Total: 109 (5) apps. 4 gls.

CHIPPERFIELD, James John

Role: Forward 1919-21
5ft.9ins. 11st.4lbs.
Born: Bethnal Green, London, 4th March 1894
Died: Wandsworth, London, 6th September 1966

CAREER: Dunstable Road Council School/Luton Schoolboys/ Bedfordshire Schoolboys/Albion/Commercial Cars FC/Luton Excelsior /Luton Amateurs/Luton Clarence/Luton Town am. pro. May 1914/(guest for Arsenal during World War One)/**SPURS** Jun 1919/Notts County Dec 1921/Northfleet United Dec 1922/Charlton Athletic May 1923/Chatham Town Aug 1924.

Debut v Coventry City (FL) (a) 30.8.1919 (scored twice)

Much confusion surrounds the early career of Jimmy Chipperfield. He first came to prominence during the Great War playing for Arsenal and they were credited as his club in April 1919 when he played in an international trial match. He was in fact a Luton Town player and merely "guested" for Arsenal throughout the war. Although a Londoner by birth, Chipperfield played for Luton Clarence and it was whilst with them that he was spotted by the "Hatters". After a few games as an amateur he signed professional, but played just one Southern League match in their colours. Following the outbreak of war, he played for Arsenal, making most of his appearances at left-half or outside-left, despite being regarded as a utility player. Such was his progress during the war several clubs were keen to secure his transfer from Luton, but he chose to join Spurs who were seeking a replacement for the ageing Bert Middlemiss. Chipperfield scored twice on his League debut and played in 13 of the next 14 matches, but in December suffered an untimely cartilage injury. This gave the talented young Jimmy Dimmock a run in the team and so impressive was he, that Chipperfield was unable to win back his place. A year later he was allowed to join Notts County and later played for Northfleet and Charlton Athletic. When released by Charlton he gave up the professional game.

Appearances:
League: 15 apps. 6 gls.
Others: 2 apps.
Total: 17 apps. 6 gls.

CHIRICHES, Vlad Iulian

Role: Central defender 2013-15
6ft.2ins. 12st.1lb.
Born: Bacău, Romania, 14th November 1989

CAREER: LPS Bacău (Romania)/Ardealul Cluj (Romania) 2004/Benfica (Portugal) Jul 2007/Internaţional Curtea de Argeş (Romania) Jul 2008/ Pandurii Lignitul Târgu Jiu (Romania) Aug 2010/Steaua Bucharest (Romania) Dec 2011/**SPURS** Aug 2013/Napoli (Italy) Jul 2015.

Debut v Aston Villa (FLC) (a) 24.9.2013

The signing of Vlad Chiriches was expected to add a bit more class to Spurs defensive options. With young Steven Caulker surprisingly allowed to leave for Cardiff, Younes Kaboul and Michael Dawson were available to provide the power and strength, but only Jan Vertonghen the class. With both Kaboul and Vertonghen suspect to injury, cover was needed. Chiriches had started his career as a midfielder. It was when he joined Benfica that he began to play in defence and he might have settled with the Lisbon club were it not for two nasty injuries that caused him to return home to Romania after just a year in Portugal. He joined second division Internaţional Curtea de Argeş and helped them to promotion in

his first season. After just the one campaign in the top flight the owner of International announced he could not afford to continue losing money on the club; it was giving up its first division place. That place was taken by Pandurii Lignitul Târgu Jiu and Chiriches, along with several other International players, joined the replacement outfit. Settling to top level football and looking comfortable, Chiriches was already on the radar of Steaua Bucharest. After making his international debut against Luxembourg in September 2011, Romania's number one club moved to sign him three months later. In less than two years with Steaua Chiriches established himself as a top quality international defender, comfortable in possession, competent in his passing and not afraid to venture forward. He looked an accomplished, cultured player, similar in style to Vertonghen. If too similar to the Belgian to play alongside him, he would at least provide competition. As it was Chiriches proved a major disappointment. While he looked the part, he appeared slow, both physically and in mind. He was too often pulled out of position, bullied by more powerful opponents, easily tricked by the more subtle. His supposed forte of being comfortable on the ball was totally missing as he was too often caught in possession. When tried at full-back, a lack of pace and positional sense were apparent. While Chiriches continued to represent, and captain, his country, he was quickly marginalised at Spurs. A move was clearly the best for both sides and when Napoli offered £4.5 million, little more than half what Spurs had paid, it was an offer both were keen to accept. In Italy, Chiriches has continued to find life difficult, rarely playing and then usually as a substitute.

Appearances:
League: 24 (3) apps. 1 gl.
FA Cup: 4 apps. 1 gl.
FL Cup: 3 (1) apps.
Euro: 8 apps.
Total: **39 (4) apps. 2 gls.**

CHISHOLM, John Richardson

Role: Centre-half 1941-48
Born: Enfield, Middlesex, 9th October 1924
Died: Waltham Forest, Essex, 24th August 1977

CAREER: Tottenham Juniors/Finchley/Crossbrook Sports/**SPURS** Oct 1941/(guest for Fulham and Millwall during World War Two)/Brentford Dec 1947/Sheffield United Mar 1949/Plymouth Argyle Dec 1949/Helston manager/Finchley manager/Romford manager/Town Argyle player-manager by Jan 1958.

Debut v West Bromwich Albion (FL) (a) 23.8.1947
(Crystal Palace (Fr) (a) 25.5.1942) (scored once)

Jack Chisholm was a junior product of White Hart Lane who was thrust into first team action due to the demands of the Second World War. A strong, but constructive, centre-half he made his senior debut in a friendly in May 1942 and from then on was expected to provide the solid base for Spurs' defence. Only 17-years old he immediately established himself in the team, a star of the future amongst the stars of the day. Too young for National Service, he was ever-present in his first season and formed the backbone of the Spurs defence for two years before the club were deprived of his services by his Army call-up. His appearances were limited due to the demands of the Services for the next two years, although he was able to play for the Army and the Football Association. Available again for the 1945-46 season, a serious knee injury in the first match put Chisholm out for almost the whole season. When fit to resume, the centre-half berth was occupied by Bill Nicholson. Chisholm made only two League appearances for Spurs, at the beginning of the 1947-48 season, but both matches were lost and he found Horace Woodward installed in his place. Chisholm was allowed to move to Brentford, who were struggling at the foot of the Second Division, with Brentford's reserve centre-half Cyril Toulouse joining Spurs as part of the deal. A useful cricketer with Bedfordshire, Devon and even Middlesex, for whom he played one match in 1947, Chisholm spent less than 18 months with Brentford moving to Sheffield United and then Plymouth Argyle.

It was Plymouth who got the best out of Chisholm, and he gave them sterling service for the next five years. When his playing days were over, he had spells managing Romford and Town Argyle of the Edmonton Sunday League and ran a Mecca betting shop in Edmonton.

Appearances:
League: 2 apps.
Others: 79 apps. 1 gl.
Total: **81 apps. 1 gl.**

CHIVERS, Martin Harcourt

Role: Striker 1967-80
6ft.1ins. 13st.12lbs.
Born: Southampton, Hampshire, 27th April 1945

CAREER: Foundry Lane School/Taunton Grammar School/Hampshire Schools/CPC Sports May 1961/Southampton pro. Sep 1962/**SPURS** Jan 1968/(Durban United (South Africa) guest Apr 1975)/Servette (Switzerland) Jul 1976/Norwich City Jul 1978/Brighton and Hove Albion Mar 1979/Frankston City (Australia) Jun 1980/Dorchester Town player-manager Aug-Dec 1980/Vard (Norway) player, player-coach Mar 1981/Barnet player-manager Oct 1982/Potters Bar Rovers player-manager.

Debut v Sheffield Wednesday (FL) (a) 17.1.1968 (scored once)

Martin Chivers was signed by his local club having played for Southampton and Hampshire at Youth level and for Southampton's nursery side CPC Sports. A big, strong forward, he had a splendid tutor in the centre forward's art playing alongside the great Welsh international Ron Davies in Saints' 1967 promotion-winning team. During 175 League appearances for Southampton, he scored 97 goals and won 12 England Under 23 caps. Spurs paid out a record fee of £125,000 to sign the big man, with Frank Saul (valued at £45,000) moving to The Dell as part of the deal, and he began to repay the fee immediately by scoring on his debut and netting both goals in the next match, a 3rd round FA Cup 2-2 draw at Manchester United. Five further Under 23 caps took his total to a record 17, and Chivers was just starting to settle into Spurs' style when he suffered a serious left knee injury in September 1968 that put him out of action for the rest of the season. He struggled clumsily for form and confidence on his return, was dropped and told to study the

play of West Ham's England star Geoff Hurst. However, Bill Nicholson persevered, working hard to increase Chivers' aggression and sense of responsibility in the wake of Jimmy Greaves' departure, and was rewarded when, aided by the promptings of Martin Peters and the guile of Alan Gilzean, Chivers started to find the net again with a real vengeance in 1970-71. Having scored both Spurs' goals in the 1971 League Cup victory over Aston Villa and made his England debut against Malta, Chivers' revival was complete, and he had deservedly emerged as England's first choice centre-forward. For a big man who could brush even the top defenders aside, he at times seemed remarkably timid, and there were occasions when "Big Chiv" looked casual, even lethargic, an infuriating characteristic which at worst seemed to affect the whole team and could incur the wrath of an exasperated management. At best it was wickedly deceptive, hiding an incredible turn of speed, awesome strength in the air, a powerful and creative long throw and the ability to score the most spectacular goals. A member of the UEFA Cup winning team of 1972-he sealed the Final first leg victory over Wolves with a pair of quite brilliant strikes-and League Cup winning side of 1973, Chivers also played in both legs of the 1974 UEFA Cup Final against Feyenoord. He finally left Spurs for £80,000 to join the Swiss club Servette with 24 full England caps (13 goals) to his credit and played for Norwich City and Brighton on his return to England, but was no longer up to the demands of League football. He tried his hand at management with Vard of Norway, Dorchester Town and Barnet, before retiring from football due to injury in December 1982 to run a hotel and restaurant business in Hertfordshire. He still turned out for Spurs once more, guesting in Terry Naylor's testimonial in April 1980.

Appearances:
League: 268 (10) apps. 118 gls.
FA Cup: 22 (2) apps. 11 gls.
FL Cup: 33 apps. 23 gls.
Euro: 32 apps. 22 gls.
Others: 47 (1) apps. 28 gls.
Total: 402 (13) apps. 202 gls.

CLAESEN, Nicolas Pieter Jozef

Role: Striker 1986-88
5ft.8ins. 10st.0lbs.
Born: Leut, Belgium, 1st October 1962

CAREER: Patro Eisden Maasmechelen (Belgium)/Seraing (Belgium) pro. 1980/Vfb Stuttgart (West Germany) Jul 1984/Standard Liege (Belgium) Sep 1985/**SPURS** Oct 1986/Royal Antwerp (Belgium) Jul 1988/KFC Germinal Ekeren (Belgium) Jul 1992/Royal Antwerp (Belgium) Jul 1993/Oostende (Belgium) Jul 1994/Sint-Niklaas (Belgium) Jul 1996/Beringen (Belgium) head coach Jul 1998/KFC Turnhout (Belgium) assistant coach /Patro Eisden Maasmechelen (Belgium) coach Mar 2003/KFC Turnhout (Belgium) coach Jun 2004/Patro Eisden Maasmechelen (Belgium) coach Jun 2005/KAS Eupen (Belgium) coach May-Sep 2008 /KVV Verbroedering Maasmechelen (Belgium) coach Mar 2009/RFC Liège (Belgium) coach May-Oct 2010/Norwich City scout.

Debut v Liverpool (FL) (a) 11.10.1986

At the age of 16 Nico Claesen was playing for Patro Eisden in the Belgian Second Division. At 18 he signed for Seraing of Liege. Finishing as top scorer in the Belgian League in 1983-84 earned him a transfer to Vfb Stuttgart, but he had had an unhappy time in West Germany and soon returned to Belgium with Standard Liege. It was with Standard that he rose to prominence, playing a vital role in helping Belgium reach the semi-finals of the 1986 World Cup in Mexico. A diminutive figure, with a cracking shot from a short back-lift, he played on his own up front up in a Belgian side that operated with a five-man midfield. David Pleat paid £600,000 to sign him for Spurs, intending to link him up with Clive Allen who had scored nine of Spurs' ten League goals so far that season. Claesen soon became a firm favourite of the crowd but it was ironic Spurs' best performances came when Allen played in front of a five-man midfield. Claesen was unable to claim a regular place, having to settle for the substitute's role on many occasions, including the 1987 FA Cup Final against Coventry City. Whilst he continued to be selected for his country Claesen was not satisfied with a reserve slot at Spurs and, when he was in due course dropped from the Belgian team, made his feelings clear.

The arrival of Terry Venables did little to improve Claesen's fortunes, and he went back to Belgium with Antwerp for £500,000. The return home did not immediately restore Claesen to the international ranks, but he slowly regained the ground lost in England and was a member of Belgium's 1990 World Cup squad. He spent six years with Antwerp, broken with a single season at Germinal Ekeren, and wound down his playing career with lower level Belgian clubs before moving into coaching.

Appearances:
League: 37 (13) apps. 18 gls.
FA Cup: 1 (5) app. 2 gls.
FL Cup: 7 apps. 3 gls.
Others: 11 (3) apps. 5 gls.
Total: 56 (21) apps. 28 gls.

CLAPHAM, James Richard

Role: Full-back 1996-98
5ft.9ins. 11st.0lbs.
Born: Lincoln, Lincolnshire, 7th December 1975

CAREER: City School, Lincoln/Lincoln Schools/Lincolnshire Schools/ **SPURS** assoc. schl. Jan 1992, trainee Jul 1992, pro. Jul 1994/(Leyton Orient loan Jan 1997)/(Bristol Rovers loan Mar 1997)/Ipswich Town loan Jan 1998, perm Mar 1998/Birmingham City Jan 2003/Wolverhampton Wanders training Jul 2006, perm Aug 2006/(Leeds United loan Aug 2007)/Leicester City Jan 2008/Southend United trial Jul 2008/Notts County training and perm Sep 2008/Lincoln City Jul 2010/Kettering Town trial Jul 2011, perm Aug-Sep 2011/Middlesbrough senior professional phase development coach Jul 2012, asst. manager Sep 2013-Mar 2014/Coventry City coach Jun 2015.

Debut v Coventry City (sub) (PL) (h) 11.5.1997
(Ham-Kam (sub) (Fr) (a) 23.7.1996)

Another of the young talents developed by Spurs who did not make the grade at White Hart Lane, but went on to make a good career for

themselves in the game, Jamie Clapham was a left-back who found himself on the fringes of the first team, but never quite managed to make the breakthrough. He first appeared in League football during loan spells with Leyton Orient and Bristol Rovers, but made only one League appearance in a Spurs' shirt, in the final game of the 1996-97 season. A cool, competent performer who loved to get forward on the overlap and possessed the ability to finish with a well-placed cross, Clapham was allowed to join Ipswich Town on loan and when they made an offer for his permanent transfer it was accepted. He soon established himself as a regular performer with the Suffolk side and played for them for five years before financial cutbacks left them unable to retain Clapham. He moved on to Birmingham City and later played for Wolverhampton Wanderers and several other clubs, before moving into coaching. Clapham's father, Graham, had been an apprentice at Newcastle United, failed to make the grade there and went on to play for Chester City and Shrewsbury Town, while his maternal grandfather, Bert Wilkinson, had played for Lincoln City.

Appearances:
League: (1) app.
Others: 3 (5) apps.
Total: 3 (6) apps. 0 gls.

CLARKE, David Henry

Role: Inside-forward 1909
5ft.7ins. 10st.0lbs.
Born: Leyton, London

CAREER: Romford/Leyton/**SPURS** am. 1908/Released May 1912/ Charlton Athletic, player, director 1924, president Nov 1969.

Debut v Everton (Fr) (Palermo) 5.6.1909

An amateur with Leyton, Clarke was first associated with Spurs during the 1908-09 season when he played in the reserve side. At the end of the season, and in the absence of Bob Steel, he accompanied the club on its tour to Argentina scoring four goals in five appearances. Although he performed well in those matches, they did not provide a breakthrough to regular first team football as he was unable to displace the regular inside-forwards; Steel and Billy Minter. He continued with the reserves until the end of the 1911-12 season during which time he also turned out occasionally for Leyton. However, he never managed to make the first team at Spurs again and in the 1912 close season was released. He later played for Charlton Athletic and went on to give them many years' service as a director. Working for a building company he supervised construction work carried out at the Valley. When, in 1924, Charlton were unable to pay the outstanding bill, the builders accepted a debenture from the club and Clarke was appointed to the board in order to protect their investment. He stayed a director, even after the arrival of the Gliksten brothers had seen the builders paid and only resigned when made President of the club, a post of held for two years.

Appearances:
Others: 5 apps. 4 gls.
Total: **5 apps. 4 gls.**

CLARKE, Harold Alfred

Role: Centre-half 1948-57
6ft.3ins. 12st.7lbs.
Born: Woodford, Essex, 23rd February 1923
Died: Romford, Essex, 16th April 2000

CAREER: Woodford Schools/RAF/Lovells Athletic am., pro. Aug 1945/ **SPURS** Mar 1949, (Clarks College, Stamford Hill coach 1956-57) coach 1957/Llanelli player-manager Feb 1959/Romford manager Mar 1962-Dec 1974.

Debut v Luton Town (FL) (h) 19.3.1949

Harry Clarke was one of the best buys Arthur Rowe ever made for Spurs. His football developed in the RAF and he helped Lovells Athletic win the Welsh Cup in 1948. On joining Spurs, he was pitched straight into the first team and despite such a late entry into the League arena, maintained an ever-present place for the next two seasons, as Spurs' famous "Push and Run" side won the Second Division and Football League titles. Injury sidelined him at the start of the 1951-52 season but he was soon back as dominant as ever. At 6ft.3ins Clarke's

great strength was his ability in the air, but he was still happy enough with the ball on the ground and few centre-forwards got the better of him. He looked calm, almost casual, at times but this was misleading for Clarke usually knew exactly what he was doing and developed an excellent understanding with goalkeeper Ted Ditchburn. His consistent performances for Spurs were rewarded with an appearance for England "B" against West Germany in March 1954 and a full cap the following month against Scotland. One of Spurs' faithful regulars during the early 1950's, he retired from playing during 1956-57 but remained at White Hart Lane as a coach with the junior players, until taking the manager's job at Llanelli. He later had twelve years in the same capacity with Romford, succeeding Ted Ditchburn and leading them to the Southern League title in 1967 and Southern League Cup in 1970 before his dismissal. He then worked as an officer for a security transit company in Ilford, Essex.

Appearances:
League: 295 apps. 4 gls.
FA Cup: 27 apps.
Others: 59* apps.
Total: **381 apps. 4 gls.**
* Includes 1 abandoned match

CLARKE, Raymond Charles

Role: Centre-forward 1972-73
5ft.11ins. 11st.7lbs.
Born: Hackney, London, 25th September 1952

CAREER: Central Foundation Grammar School, Islington/Islington Schools/London Schools/Middlesex Schools/**SPURS** app. May 1968, pro. Oct 1969/England Youth/Swindon Town May 1973/Mansfield Town Aug 1974/Sparta (Holland) Jul 1976/Ajax (Holland) Jul 1978/Bruges (Belgium) Jul 1979/Brighton and Hove Albion Oct 1979/Newcastle United Jul 1980/Southampton coach-reserve team manager Jul 1996-Jul 1997/Coventry City European scout Aug 1998/Newcastle United Head scout Apr 2005/Celtic Head of International Coaching Sep 2005-Jun 2009/Portsmouth chief scout Sep 2009-Mar 2010/Middlesbrough chief scout May 2010/Blackburn Rovers chief scout Sep 2012.

Debut v Leicester City (sub) (FL) (h) 21.4.1973

Ray Clarke's only appearance for Spurs came when he substituted for Alan Gilzean in a League match against Leicester City in April 1973. He was perhaps unlucky not to have had more success at White Hart Lane, but suffered from Spurs' policy of paying big money to buy more established goal-scorers. An England Schoolboys trialist and England Youth international, whilst a prolific scorer for the reserves, he was unable to displace the established strikers like Martin Chivers and Gilzean. Allowed to move on to Swindon Town, he made only 14 appearances in 14 months before joining Mansfield Town. His good goal-scoring form began there, helping Mansfield win the Fourth Division title in 1974, and while several bigger clubs were watching Sparta Rotterdam took him to Holland. He built a good career on the continent helping Ajax Amsterdam win the Dutch League and Cup in 1979 before joining the Belgium side Bruges. On his return to England with Brighton he showed that experience abroad had clearly improved his game and was expected to do well when he signed for Newcastle United. Sadly, he never had the chance to join the long list of famous Newcastle centre-forwards, as an early injury forced a premature retirement when he should have been at his peak. He went into the hotel business in East Anglia and the Isle of Man, but returned to football as a coach at Southampton under his old Spurs' reserve team-mate Graeme Souness. Clarke left the Dell following Souness' departure. As football became more and more a global game, he took on the role of European scout for Coventry City and later scouted for Celtic, Portsmouth, Middlesbrough and Blackburn Rovers. In March 2014 Clarke was inducted into the Dutch football Hall of Fame.

Appearances:
League: (1) app.
Total: **(1) app. 0 gls.**

CLAWLEY, George

Role: Goalkeeper 1899-07
6ft.1ins. 12st.7lbs.
Born: Odd Rode, Scholar Green, Staffordshire, 10th April 1875
Died: Southampton, Hampshire, 16th July 1920

CAREER: Crewe Alexandra Aug 1893/Stoke Aug 1894/Southampton St Marys May 1896/Stoke May 1898/**SPURS** May 1899/Southampton May 1903/retired 1907.

Debut v Millwall Athletic (SL) (a) 2.9.1899

Tall and calm, George Clawley was one of the most reliable goalkeepers in an era when 'keepers received scant, if any, protection. He began his career with Crewe Alexandra and Stoke but it was with Southampton St Marys that he built himself a big reputation, helping the "Saints" win the Southern League title in 1897 and 1898. After two seasons on the South Coast, during which time he played for Hampshire and the Southern League, he returned to Stoke, but spent only one season there before John Cameron signed him for Spurs. Clawley made his debut in September 1899, but broke his leg the following month. He only managed to return in April 1900, so not playing in enough games to qualify for another Southern League championship medal. He more than compensated for that though the following season, when he played in all Spurs' matches in their victorious FA Cup run. Almost irreplaceable for the next two seasons, major representative honours eluded him although he did play in an International trial match at White Hart Lane in March 1903. At the end of that season Clawley returned to Southampton and was Saints regular 'keeper in their Southern League Championship side the next season. He remained with Southampton until his retirement in 1907 to open a public house. Brother-in-law of Spurs 1901 FA Cup hero, Sandy Brown, he was still landlord of the Wareham Arms at the time of his death.

Appearances:
Southern: 83* apps.
FA Cup: 12 apps.
Others: 90 apps.
Total: 185 apps. 0 gls.
* Includes 1 abandoned match.

CLAY, Thomas

Role: Full-back 1913-29
5ft.10ins. 11st.10lbs.
Born: Leicester, 19th November 1892
Died: Southend, Essex, 21st February 1949

CAREER: Belvoir Sunday School/Leicester Fosse Apr 1911/**SPURS** Jan 1914/(guest for Notts County during World War One)/Northfleet United player-coach May 1929/St Albans City trainer-coach Jul 1931/RV & AV Sparta Rotterdam (Holland) coach 1937/HVV Den Haag (Holland) coach 1937-1939.

Debut v Oldham Athletic (FL) (h) 17.1.1914

Tommy Clay made his debut as a 19-year old for Leicester Fosse in November 1911 and retained his place for the next two years. He so impressed Spurs' manager Peter McWilliam with his performances against Spurs in the first round of the FA Cup in 1914 that, immediately after the replay, he signed the young full-back who was to provide one of the longest and most impressive playing careers in Spurs' history. Clay was one of the finest full-backs of his day, strong in the tackle, an immaculate passer of the ball, always constructive and with an astute tactical brain; particularly in the application of the old offside law. He played throughout the First World War and when service duties meant he could not get to Spurs, he was always in demand, playing for Notts County amongst others. In April 1919 he played in an international trial

match, but did not win his first cap until March 1920 when he played against Wales at Highbury. Club captain in 1919-20 he led Spurs to the Second Division title, but then handed over the captaincy to Arthur Grimsdell and so did not have the privilege of lifting the FA Cup after a superb personal display in the 1921 Final. Cool, unflappable and ever consistent, he was almost irreplaceable for Spurs in the early 1920s, winning another four caps and representing the Football League. In May 1929, after almost fifteen years of the most accomplished service, Clay was not retained and the following month accepted an offer to become player-coach at the Spurs' nursery club of Northfleet. In October 1930, he took over a public house in St Albans, but continued with Northfleet until July 1931 when he became trainer/coach to St Albans City. Tommy Clay played a full League game for Spurs in goal. In March 1921 regular 'keepers Bill Jacques and Alex Hunter were both injured and Clay filled in between the posts at Sunderland, keeping a clean sheet as Spurs won 1-0. Clay was invited for trials by Leicestershire County Cricket Club in 1923, but football was his priority, although he later coached the summer game, both at home and in Holland.

Appearances:
League: 318 apps. 23 gls.
FA Cup: 33 apps. 1 gl.
Others: 157* apps. 13 gls.
Total: 508 apps. 37 gls.
* Includes 1 abandoned match.

CLAYTON, Edward

Role: Inside-forward 1957-68
Born: Bethnal Green, London, 7th May 1937

CAREER: Hackney Schools/Eton Manor/**SPURS** am. Mar 1955, pro. Nov 1957/Southend United Mar 1968/Ashford Town Apr 1970/Margate Jun 1970, caretaker player-manager Oct 1971/retired May 1975/Aylesbury United Aug 1975-Nov 1975/Leyton-Wingate Jan 1976/Barking & Dagenham district Schools coach/Essex Schools coach/Norwich City coach.

Debut v Everton (FL) (a) 5.4.1958 (scored twice)

Eddie Clayton is one of many fine young players developed by Spurs who never quite made the success of their careers that was expected. An intelligent, ball playing wing-half or inside-forward, with a good eye for an opening and a powerful shot, he failed to maintain the early form that saw him score twice on his debut. For most of his Spurs' career he was a reserve who could be relied upon to give a sound performance when needed. His best time at White Hart Lane was undoubtedly the transitional 1965-66 season when he was almost ever-present, but with the signing of Terry Venables it was clear Clayton did not figure in Bill Nicholson's long term plans. He was allowed to leave for Southend United. After two seasons with Southend, he moved on to Ashford and quickly to Margate, playing against Spurs in the FA Cup third round in 1973. Clayton announced he was retiring in 1975, but was then persuaded to finish his career with a short spell at Aylesbury.

Appearances:
League: 88 (4) apps. 20 gls.
FA Cup: 9 apps.
FL Cup: 1 app.
Euro: 1 app.
Others: 26 (4) apps. 6 gls.
Total: 125 (8) apps. 26 gls.

CLAYTON, S A

Role: Left-back 1916-17

CAREER: Bradford Park Avenue/(guest for **SPURS** during World War One).

Debut v Queens Park Rangers (LFC) (h) 28.10.1916

Formerly on the books of Bradford Park Avenue, Clayton made his one appearance for Spurs in a London Football Combination match with Queens Park Rangers played at Clapton Orient's Homerton ground.

Appearances:
Others: 1 app.
Total: 1 app. 0 gls.

CLAYTON, Stanley

Role: Inside-forward 1942-44
5ft.9ins. 11st. 2lbs.
Born: Castleford, Yorkshire, 21st November 1912
Died: Castleford, Yorkshire 2nd July 2002

CAREER: Castleford Town/Bradford PA am. Jan 1932/Leeds United am. Aug 1932/Castleford (Rugby League)/Upton Colliery/Notts County May 1937/(guest for **SPURS**, Aldershot, Reading and Middlesbrough during World War Two).

Debut v Crystal Palace (FLS) (h) 28.8.1943 (scored once)
(Arsenal (Fr) (h) 8.5.1943)

Stan Clayton was serving in the Army Educational Corp when he played three games for Spurs as a guest. The first was in May 1943 in a friendly with Arsenal. He followed that up with two appearances in Football League South games early the following season.

Appearances:
Others: 3 apps. 1 gl.
Total: 3 apps. 1 gl.

CLEMENCE, Raymond Neal M.B.E.

Role: Goalkeeper 1981-91
6ft.0ins. 12st.9lbs.
Born: Skegness, Lincolnshire, 5th August 1948

CAREER: Skegness Youth Club/Notts County am./Scunthorpe United pro. Aug 1965/Liverpool Jun 1967/(St George Saints (Australia) guest 1978)/**SPURS** Aug 1981, retired Mar 1988, goalkeeper coach, reserve team manager Jun 1989, asst. first team coach Jun 1992-Jul 1993/Barnet general manager Jan 1994/England goalkeeping coach Aug 1996-Oct 2013.

Debut v Middlesbrough (FL) (a) 29.8.1981
(Aston Villa (FACS) (Wembley) 22.8.1981)

When Ray Clemence joined Spurs he had won almost every honour in the game with Liverpool, but still had a thirst for more. Spotted by Scunthorpe United playing for the Skegness Youth Club, he had been associated with Notts County, playing one "A" team game for them. He played just 50 senior games for Scunthorpe, many of them behind future Spurs' manager Keith Burkinshaw, before joining Liverpool. After serving the almost mandatory spell in the reserves Clemence took over

from Tommy Lawrence as the regular 'keeper and in eleven seasons missed only six League games, amassing over 650 appearances as Liverpool dominated English football. During this time he played in Liverpool teams that won the Football League Championship (1972-73, 1975-76, 1976-77, 1978-79 and 1979-80), the European Champions Cup (1977, 1978 and 1981), the UEFA Cup (1973 and 1976), the FA Cup (1974), the League Cup (1981) and the European Super Cup (1977). He was also in the losing teams in two FA Cup Finals (1971 and 1977), one League Cup Final (1978) and one European Super Cup (1978). To this impressive list of club honours, he could add 56 full England caps, four at Under-23 level and two appearances for the Football League. Clemence was one of the best goalkeepers England has produced and would have won many more caps were it not for the fact he was forced to compete with Peter Shilton. Unflappable, consistent, confident and blessed with good reflexes and sound positional sense, he inspired confidence in his defenders with his organisational ability. Signed by Burkinshaw, Clemence made his debut at Wembley in the 1981 FA Charity Shield and soon proved that Spurs at last had a 'keeper to replace Pat Jennings. In his first season with Spurs Clemence played his part in helping them retain the FA Cup and reach the League (Milk) Cup final, where they lost to Liverpool. In his first six seasons at White Hart Lane, during which time he gained five more England caps, Clemence missed only 23 League games, most of those in 1983-84 when injury also meant he missed out on the UEFA Cup success, and again appeared in an FA Cup Final, picking up a loser's medal in 1987. Having completed 1,000 first class games in 1985, Clemence was rewarded for his services to football with the M.B.E. in the 1987 Birthday Honours List. Looking as if he could continue for ever, he sustained a serious knee injury in October 1987 and was forced to retire. However his experience was not lost to the game. He was appointed goalkeeping coach at Spurs on his retirement, took over as reserve team coach following Allen Harris' departure, and worked with Doug Livermore as first team coach following the Sugar/Venables takeover. Clemence left Spurs in the summer of 1993 following the dismissal of Venables, but was not out of football for long. He took on the general manager's role at Barnet, a position he only relinquished when invited to join Venables' England coaching set-up. He became a permanent fixture on the backroom staff, serving the FA for over 17 years, working with Venables and his successor Glenn Hoddle. He combined that with the media work he continued after Hoddle's departure. Clemence made one further appearance in a Spurs' shirt after his retirement playing against West Ham United in his testimonial in August 1990. Like his famous predecessor, Pat Jennings, Clemence also managed to score once for Spurs. That was in a friendly against a Guernsey FA XI on 8th April 1985 when he netted from a penalty.

Appearances:
League: 240 apps.
FA Cup: 25 apps.
FL Cup: 38 apps.
Euro: 27 apps.
Others: 77 apps. 1 gl.
Total: 407 apps. 1 gl.

CLEMENCE, Stephen Neal

Role: Midfielder 1997-2003

5ft.11ins. 12st.5lbs.

Born: Liverpool, Merseyside, 31st March 1978

CAREER: Lea Valley Schools/England Schools/FA National School of Excellence/England Youth/**SPURS** assoc. schl. Feb 1993, trainee Jul 1994, pro. Apr 1995/Birmingham City Jan 2003/Leicester City Jul 2007/retired Mar 2010/Sunderland coach Jul 2010, reserve/development coach Feb 2011/Hull City asst. manager Jun 2012/Aston Villa first team coach Nov 2016.

Debut v Middlesbrough (PL) (h) 10.8.1997
(Ski (sub) (Fr) (a) 15.7.1997)

Son of Spurs' 'keeper Ray, Stephen Clemence was always going to make a career in football, playing for England schools before making the move to the FA's elite National School of Excellence. Associated with Spurs from his earliest days, he was elevated to the first team squad in 1997, making his first appearance in the senior team in a pre-season friendly on Spurs' Norwegian tour. A hard-working midfielder, neat and concise in his passing, Clemence did not find it easy winning over the Spurs' fans. Too often they expect players to show outrageous flair and panache, and do not always appreciate every team need those players who are less flamboyant but just as essential. Clemence slowly established himself under Christian Gross and George Graham, but with the arrival of Glenn Hoddle found himself on the fringes. Far too good to wallow in the reserves, he moved to Birmingham City for £900,000 and for four years provided a solid base in the centre of midfield for the Blues, before moving on to Leicester City. On his retirement Clemence was recruited by his former Birmingham manager, Steve Bruce, to the coaching staff at Sunderland and has since followed Bruce to Hull City and Aston Villa.

Appearances:
League: 68 (22) apps. 2 gls.
FA Cup: 7 (1) 1 gl.
FL Cup: 7 (1) apps.
Euro: 2 (1) apps.
Others: 21 (14) apps. 4 gls.
Total: 105 (39) apps. 7 gls.

CLEMENTS, Robert William

Role: Inside-forward 1894-98
5ft.8ins. 11st.4lbs.
Born: 1875

CAREER: SPURS Mar 1895/Chatham Jun 1898/Grays United Nov 1900.

Debut v Luton Town (FAC) (a) 12.10.1895
(Old Westminsters (LSC) (h) 9.3.1895)

Bob "Topsy" Clement was one of the players who did so much to prove the wisdom of Spurs' decision to turn professional. First associated with the club in its amateur days, he was an inside-forward always likely to score and the envy of many of the country's senior clubs. Top scorer in Spurs' first Southern League season of 1896-97, he was one of only four players retained at the season's end, but then fell victim to Spurs' ambitions. To turn Spurs into the best team in London proven professional players were signed, players who would not only help the club's performances on the field but also attract the paying public. The signing of Bob Stormont in the 1897 close season meant Clement could not get in the team and, although he remained with the club throughout the season, he decided to join Chatham when it was over. He remained with Chatham, scoring regularly as they struggled in the Southern League, until they folded in November 1900. He then moved on to Grays United, where he played for several years.

Appearances:
Southern: 21 apps. 14 gls.
FA Cup: 9 apps. 4 gls.
Others: 98* apps. 53 gls.
Total: 128 apps. 71 gls.
* Includes 1 abandoned match.

CLEMENTS, J

Role: Inside-forward 1896-97

CAREER: Malvern Swifts/SPURS Oct 1895.

Debut v Vampires (Fr) (h) 26.12.1896 (scored once)

A member of the Malvern Swifts club introduced to Spurs by his elder brother "Topsy", Clements first played for Spurs reserves in October 1895, but it was only during the 1896-97 season that he played in three senior friendly games. The first was on Boxing Day 1896 against the Vampires in the first of two games Spurs played that day. His other appearances were late in the season as Spurs gave several promising youngsters the chance to impress. Unfortunately, Clements failed to grasp the opportunity and at the end of the season his association with Spurs came to an end.

Appearances:
Others: 3 apps. 1gl.
Total: 3 apps. 1 gl.

CLOSE, Shaun Charles

Role: Forward 1985-88
Born: Islington, London, 8th September 1966

CAREER: King Harold School/Harlow Schools/West Essex Schools/London Schools/SPURS YTS Sep 1983, pro. Aug 1984/(Halmstad (Sweden) loan summer 1986)/AFC Bournemouth loan Jan 1988, perm. Mar 1988/Swindon Town Sep 1989/Barnet Aug 1993/released cs. 1994/Bishops Stortford 1994-95/St Albans City 1994-95

Debut v Barnsley (FLC) (h) 8.10.1986 (scored once)
(Chelmsford City (sub) (Fr) (a) 2.4.1986)

A striker somewhat similar in style to Clive Allen in that he did his best work in the opposing penalty area, Shaun Close certainly benefited from a summer spent on loan to the Swedish club Halmstad. Following his return, he made a goal-scoring senior debut, but Clive Allen was at the absolute peak of his form. Close found first team opportunities limited and was given no chance to impress new manager Terry Venables, before being transferred to Bournemouth. Things did not work out too well for him at Dean Court and he moved on to Swindon Town, one of the first signings of his former Spurs' team mate, Ossie Ardiles. After four years he joined Barnet, but was released after just one season. He moved into the non-League game but gave that up after a year to concentrate on running a public house (The George) in Hoddesdon, Hertfordshire, he had first taken on while at Barnet.

Appearances:
League: 3 (6) apps.
FL Cup: 3 apps. 2 gls.
Others: 3 (5) apps. 8 gls.
Total: 9 (11) apps. 10 gls.

COATES, Ralph

Role: Forward 1971-81
5ft.7ins. 11st.11lbs
Born: Hetton-Le-Hole, County Durham, 26th April 1946
Died: Luton, Bedfordshire, 17th December 2010

CAREER: Lambton and District Schools/County Durham Schools/Eppleton Colliery Welfare/Burnley am. Oct 1961, pro. Jun 1963/ SPURS May 1971/(St Georges (Australia) loan April 1978)/Orient Nov 1978, coach 1982/Hertford Heath/Ware/Nazeing/Elliott Sports/Herts FA Football Development Officer.

Debut v Wolverhampton Wanderers (FL) (a) 14.8.1971

A centre-forward as a schoolboy, Ralph Coates was ignored by the professional clubs when he left school and took a job at Eppleton Colliery. It was only whilst playing for the Colliery's Welfare side that he was noticed by Burnley, and taken on by the Lancashire club famous for producing home-grown players. He made his Football League debut in December 1964 and quickly established himself as a highly promising winger/wide midfield player. In his time at Burnley Coates won eight England Under-23 caps, played for the Football League four times and won two England caps, the first against

Northern Ireland in April 1970, but like many of his team-mates was allowed to leave for economic reasons. His first appearances as a Spurs player were for England when he played against Malta and Wales at Wembley in May 1971. A tireless worker who would be back defending one minute and looking to score the next, Coates never truly fulfilled his promise and was perhaps restricted by a failure to find his best position at Spurs. He could play on the wing or in midfield, but never really settled in either position, although most people thought he would be most effective if he could combine the two roles. With a receding hairline and wisps of blonde hair, his non-stop running and endless energy portrayed him as a workmanlike Bobby Charlton. A member of the team that won the UEFA Cup in 1972 and reached the final of the same competition in 1974, his best moment at Spurs came in the 1973 League Cup Final against Norwich City when he scored the winning goal after substituting for the injured John Pratt. In the summer of 1978 Coates left White Hart Lane to play for the St George's club of Sydney. He returned in September of that year and joined Orient two months later. He later played for Hertford Heath, Ware and Nazeing, but was to be seen again in a Spurs' shirt, returning in May 1981 as a substitute in Barry Daines' Testimonial against Crystal Palace.

Appearances:
League: 173 (15) apps. 14 gls.
FA Cup: 11 (1) apps.
FL Cup: 19 (3) apps. 1 gl.
Euro: 26 apps. 9 gls.
Others: 48 (9) apps. 6 gls.
Total: **277 (28) apps. 30 gls.**

COCKRAM, Allan Charles

Role: Midfielder 1983-84
5ft.7ins. 10st.0lbs.
Born: Kensington, London, 8th October 1963

CAREER: Camden Schools/**SPURS** pro. Jan 1981/San Francisco Flyers (USA) player/coach May 1985/Bristol Rovers trial Jul 1985, perm. Aug 1985/San Jose (USA)/Farnborough Town Feb 1986-Dec 1986/Crystal Palace trial Jan 1987/St Albans City Jan 1987/Brentford non-contract Mar 1988, pro. May 1988/released Jun 1991/Brighton and Hove Albion trial Jul 1991/Charleroi (Belgium) trial Jul 1991/Reading trial Aug 1991/Woking non-contract Sep 1991/Reading non-contract Oct 1991/Farnborough Town non-contract Mar 1992/Woking May 1992/St Albans City cs. 1992, player-joint-manager Feb 1994, player-manager Jul 1995-Apr 1996/Chertsey Town player-manager 1996-Jan 1997/Leatherhead asst. manager during 1999-2000.

Debut v Watford (FL) (h) 2.1.1984

Allan Cockram played just two League games for Spurs, the first in January 1984 and the second in May of that year when Spurs fielded a reserve team at Southampton just before the UEFA Cup Final. Generally recognised as a midfield player, he was given a free transfer at the end of the 1984-85 season and joined Bristol Rovers but played only one game for Rovers before moving to America to play for San Jose in the indoor soccer league. After a fairly successful time in America, he returned to England and signed for Vauxhall-Opel League St Albans City where he linked up with former Spurs' players John Lacy and Chris Jones. It was another former Spurs' player who persuaded Cockram to return to the League game, when he signed for Steve Perryman's Brentford, initially as a non-contract player, but then as a full professional, and he was very influential in the "Bees" FA Cup run of 1988-89. However, he failed to maintain his position with Brentford and at the end of the 1990-91 season was released, eventually signing for Reading and then moving into the non-League game. Cockram moved around the non-League scene, first as a player then as a player-manager, until 2000 when he left the game to become a firefighter. but he returned to football ten years later. Along with former team-mate Gary Blissett he set up SoccerSounds, a training regime for American youngsters that combined traditional football with music.

Appearances:
League: 2 apps.
Total: **2 apps. 0 gls.**

COE

Role: Centre-half 1896-97

Debut v Chatham (Fr) (h) 28.1.1897

Another of the many soldiers who played for Spurs as a "guest", Coe made his only appearance in a friendly against Chatham in January 1897. A member of the Coldstream Guards, over six-foot tall, he was apparently very slim, for he was described as a player whose "breadth was not in proportion to his height". He did not impress too much, being described by one local reporter as "uncertain and clumsy".

Appearances:
Others: 1 app.
Total: **1 app. 0 gls.**

COLEMAN, Alf

Role: Inside-forward 1893-95

CAREER: **SPURS**/Novocastrians.

Debut v Luton Town (FAC) (a) 15.12.1894
(Uxbridge (Fr) (a) 30.12.1893)

One of Spurs' young reserves, Alf Coleman made two appearances in the middle of the 1893-94 season, but did not play for the first team again until a year later. He was then called up as a surprise replacement for Donald Goodall in an FA Cup 4th Qualifying Round replay against Luton Town in December 1894. Never able to make the grade with Spurs, he continued to play for the local junior clubs, in particular Novocastrians, for some years.

Appearances:
FA Cup: 1 app.
Others: 2 apps.
Total: **3 apps. 0 gls.**

COLLINS, James Simon

Role: Half-back 1894-97
Born: Woolwich, London, December qtr. 1874

CAREER: **SPURS** Jan 1895/Sheppey United cs. 1897/Chatham cs. 1899.

Debut v Luton Town (FAC) (a) 12.10.1895
(London Welsh (LSC) (h) 26.1.1895)

Another of the players from Spurs' early days, James Collins first appeared in the club's first team in January 1895. He slowly established himself in the team and by the start of 1895-96 was firmly established as a regular performer. That season saw the decision to turn professional and the influx of paid players that followed meant Collins was rarely able to get in the team again. However, he did not do a great deal to help

himself, being suspended for six weeks in November 1896 for "wilfully disobeying training instructions". The exact circumstances of the suspension were not publicised, but it doubtless had something to do with the fact that in December 1896 he was sentenced to two-months imprisonment for assaulting the landlord of the Sussex Arms Public House in Woolwich. Collins was not retained at the end of the season as Spurs dispensed with the services of practically all their players. He joined Sheppey United where he played for two years before moving on to Chatham.

Appearances:
Southern: 2 apps.
FA Cup: 6 apps.
Others: 60 apps. 1 gl.
Total: 68 apps. 1 gl.

COLLINS, James

Role: Inside-forward 1960-62
5ft.9ins. 12st.0lbs.
Born: Lorn, Ayrshire, 21st December 1937

CAREER: Lugar Boys Club/Lugar Boswell Thistle/**SPURS** Jun 1956/Brighton and Hove Albion Oct 1962/Wimbledon Jul 1967/Stevenage Southwick player, manager/Shoreham/Saltdean United/Corals.

Debut v West Ham United (FL) (h) 23.8.1961
(Army XI (Fr) (h) 24.10.1960)

Jimmy Collins joined Spurs after helping the Scottish junior club Lugar Boswell Thistle win the Scottish Youth Cup. He was a regular goalscorer in the reserves, but made only three first team appearances, one of those a friendly when Spurs' international stars were unavailable. His only Football League appearances were in August 1961 and April 1962, on each occasion standing in for his fellow Scot John White. With players such as White, Eddie Clayton and John Smith ahead of him, opportunities were always going to be limited for Collins and he was allowed to move to Brighton and Hove Albion. He served Brighton well for five years, playing over 200 senior games before joining the then non-League Wimbledon, where he also played for five years. He continued in the non-League game and was still making the occasional appearance for Corals when in his fifties.

Appearances:
League: 2 apps.
Others: 1 app.
Total: 3 apps. 0 gls.

COLLINS, John Lindsay

Role: Full-back 1965-66
5ft.8ins. 10st.10lbs.
Born: Rhymney, south Wales, 21st January 1949

CAREER: Tredegar Schools/Swansea Schools/Wales Schools/**SPURS** app. Apr 1964, pro. Mar 1966/Portsmouth May 1971/(Dallas Tornado (USA) summer 1973)/Halifax Town Aug 1974/Sheffield Wednesday Jul 1976/Barnsley Dec 1976/Kidderminster Harriers Aug 1980/Baltimore (USA) (6-a-side).

Debut v Sunderland (FL) (a) 26.3.1966

Making his first League appearance only eight days after signing professional and only three weeks after his first reserve outing, John Collins played one more League game, but while he won five Welsh Under-23 caps in the next two years, he suffered very much like his namesake Jimmy Collins. With regular full-backs such as Phil Beal, Joe Kinnear, Cyril Knowles and Ray Evans, he never got a real chance in the first team and did not make another senior appearance before moving to Portsmouth. He won two more Under-23 caps at Fratton Park where he played for three years till joining Halifax Town. After a short spell with Sheffield Wednesday he finished his senior career with Barnsley before moving to Kidderminster Harriers and then went to play the 6-a-side game in America.

Appearances:
League: 2 apps.
Total: 2 apps. 0 gls.

COLLINS, Peter John

Role: Central defender 1967-74
Born: Chelmsford, Essex, 29th November 1948

CAREER: Chelmsford Schools/Crompton Parkinson Youth/Chelmsford City 1965/**SPURS** Jan 1968/retired Nov 1974/Folkestone player-manager Jul-Dec 1975/Emjay late 70s/Maldon Town manager/Braintree Town joint manager/Southend United coach/Chelmsford City coach/Braintree Town manager 1990-1995/Chelmsford City asst. manager Jun 1998.

Debut v Arsenal (FL) (h) 10.8.1968
(Rangers (Fr) (h) 31.7.1968 (scored twice))

Peter Collins joined Spurs at the same time as Martin Chivers, but there was little publicity over the move. While Spurs were paying out a record fee of £125,000 for Chivers, Collins was snapped up for a bargain £5,000 from Southern League Chelmsford City. A strong, rugged and quick central defender, he was very much in the Mike England mould, unfortunate because if Collins was ever to establish himself with Spurs it was England he would have to displace. During his time at Spurs he continually challenged England and Phil Beal for one of the central defensive roles and it would be true to say that with most other First Division teams he would have held down an automatic place. His best season was 1970 71 when he stood in for the injured England and won a Football League Cup winners tankard against Aston Villa. Unfortunately, Collins then sustained a serious knee injury and after a lengthy battle to overcome it, was forced to retire from League football. He later had a spell as player-manager of Folkestone before moving into management and coaching.

Appearances:
League: 78* (6) apps. 4 gls.
FA Cup: 8 (1) apps.
FL Cup: 5 (2) apps. 1 gl.
Euro: 1 (1) apps.
Others: 14 (2) apps. 3 gls.
Total: 106 (12) apps. 8 gls.
* Includes 1 abandoned match.

COLLINS, Thomas

Role: Full-back 1910-15
5ft.10ins. 12st.9lbs.
Born: *Leven, Fife, 16th April 1882*
Died: *Edmonton, London, 13th July 1929*

CAREER: Leven Thistle/Heart of Midlothian May 1903/(Bathgate Thistle loan Mar 1905)/East Fife Jun 1905/Heart of Midlothian Jul 1906/**SPURS** Nov 1910/retired Mar 1915/East Fife Aug 1915/Dundee Hibernians Nov 1915.

Debut v Sunderland (FL) (a) 26.11.1910

Tom Collins spent several years in his native Scotland building a good career for himself before moving into the Football League with Spurs. He really came to prominence in his second spell with Hearts playing for the Scottish League against the Football League in February 1909 and for Scotland against Wales the following month. His move to Spurs followed his appearance for the Scottish League against the Southern League in October 1910 and he soon established himself as first choice right-back. A sound defender, very fast and very strong in the tackle in both 1911 and 1912 he played for the Anglo-Scots against the Home Scots in the international trial matches and was unfortunate not to win more international caps. As early optimism for a swift end to the First World War receded, Collins contract with Spurs was cancelled in March 1915 so he could return to Scotland. He joined East Fife for the following season but soon moved on to Dundee Hibernians, although he never turned out for them. His registration papers were not received by the Dundee club that was later to be renamed Dundee United, before he was called up for military service. In the trenches, he sustained serious injuries that resulted in him losing an arm and a leg.

Appearances:
League: 115* apps. 1 gl.
FA Cup: 9 apps.
Others: 10 apps.
Total: 134 apps. 1 gl.
* Includes 2 abandoned matches.

COLQUHOUN, David Wilson

Role: Half-back 1931-35
Born: *Motherwell, Lanarkshire, 23rd January 1906*
Died: *Motherwell, Lanarkshire, 3rd June 1983*

CAREER: Blantyre Victoria/St Mirren Apr 1926/**SPURS** Jul 1931/Luton Town Mar 1935/Rochdale cs. 1936/(guest for Blackpool, Bradford City, Stockport County and Walsall during World War Two).

Debut v Wolverhampton Wanderers (FL) (a) 29.8.1931

David Colquhoun had worked his way to the verge of international honours by the time of his transfer to Spurs, having played in the Scots international trial match of 1930-31. A strong, resolute wing-half, he was a regular as Spurs strove to get out of the Second Division with the target being achieved in 1932-33. He then found himself in competition for a place in the team with Tom Evans, but had to concede defeat in that battle. With Spurs on a downward cycle in 1934-35, he was transferred to Luton Town in March 1935 where he played until released in May 1936. He later joined Rochdale and guested in War-time League competition.

Appearances:
League: 81 apps. 2 gls.
FA Cup: 6 apps.
Others: 4 apps. 3 gls.
Total: 91 apps. 5 gls.

CONN, Alfred James

Role: Forward 1974-77
5ft.8ins. 11st.5lbs.
Born: *Kirkcaldy, Fife, 5th April 1952*

CAREER: Prestonpans Primary School/Tynecastle Athletic/Scotland Schools/Edina/Musselburgh Windsor/Leeds United app. (cancelled)/Rangers ground-staff Jul 1967, pro. Oct 1968/**SPURS** Jun 1974/Celtic loan Mar 1977, perm Apr 1977/Derby County trial May 1979/Hercules (Spain) trial Jul 1979/Pittsburgh Spirit (USA) Nov 1979/Hartford Hellions (USA) Mar 1980/San Jose Earthquakes (USA) Mar-May 1980/Heart of Midlothian Sep 1980/(Blackpool loan Mar 1981)/Motherwell Aug 1981/retired Jun 1984/Coatbridge manager.

Debut v Middlesbrough (sub) (FLC) (h) 2.9.1974
(Heart of Midlothian (Fr) (a) 3.8.1974)

Alfie Conn was Bill Nicholson's last signing for Spurs. As a schoolboy, he represented East of Scotland at Rugby and Scotland at soccer. He played for the junior clubs Edina and Musselburgh Windsor, before joining Rangers. Appearing in the Rangers' first team when only 16, Conn won Scottish Amateur Youth honours before signing professional. A member of Rangers' winning teams in the 1971 Scottish League Cup Final and 1973 Scottish Cup Final, he also helped them win the European Cup-Winners' Cup in 1972. He made only one appearance for Spurs under Nicholson's management before Terry Neill's arrival. In a season of continual struggle for Spurs, one League appearance as a substitute was followed by his full debut at Newcastle United on 11th January 1975.

He celebrated with a hat-trick in Spurs best victory of the season. Conn was an inside-forward out of the old Scottish school. A showman with magical dribbling skills, he was always prepared to take a man on and beat him with sheer skill. With his long, curly locks flowing he certainly gave the fans as well as the team a tremendous lift, proving very influential in the successful battle against relegation. Sadly, he was perhaps too much of an individual and it was difficult to harness his undoubted flair and talent to the benefit of the team. Not helped by injuries that were a consequence of his style of play, he had a very up-and-down career with Spurs, winning two full international caps in May 1975 followed by three Under-23 caps and then finding himself in the reserves. In March 1977 Conn joined Celtic on loan, the move being made permanent after he satisfied them as to his fitness. He played for Celtic in their 1977 Scottish Cup Final success and helped them to the Scottish League title in both 1977 and 1979. During the following season, he joined Pittsburgh Spirit of the Major Indoor Soccer League and after signing to play for Hartford Hellions in the same competition signed with the regular football outfit, San Jose Earthquakes. He had a short stay in California, playing only two games, before returning to Scotland and signing for Hearts. After a spell on loan to Blackpool in March 1981, he joined Motherwell and helped them to the Scottish First Division title in 1981-82. Early in the 1983-84 season he suffered an injury that forced him to retire at the age of only 32. He then went into management and was manager of the Coatbridge side which won the 1985-86 Scottish Amateur Cup. Alfie Conn's father, also Alfie, was an inside-forward with Heart of Midlothian and Scotland in the 1950s and also played in South Africa with Ramblers.

Appearances:
League: 35 (3) apps. 6 gls.
FA Cup: 2 apps.
FL Cup: 1 (2) apps. 1 gl.
Others: 11 (5) apps. 3 gls.
Total: **49 (10) apps. 10 gls.**

CONSORTI, Maurizio

Role: Midfielder 2001-02
Born: Rome, Italy 6th March 1982

CAREER: GS Nuova Tor Tre Teste (Italy)/Lazio Region (Italy) Youth/**SPURS** trial May 1999, trainee Jun 1999/released May 2002/Chievo (Italy) /Fidelis Andria AS (Italy) cs. 2004/ASD Castel Madama (Italy)/ASD Terranova (Italy) by Mar 2008/Ostia Mare 1945 (Italy) Jun 2009/ASD Atletico Torrenova (Italy) by Nov 2012 /Colle Di Fuori (Italy) Jan 2016.

Debut v Stevenage Borough (sub) (Fr) (a) 13.7.2001

In the late 1990s Spurs recognised that the changing nature of the game meant it was necessary to spread their scouting network throughout Europe. Maurizio Consorti was among the first of many talented foreign youngsters to be identified and offered trainee terms. A strong-running midfielder, he made his one first team appearance as a substitute in a pre-season friendly at Stevenage, but was not offered a professional contract. He returned to Italy where he has continued to play for lower level clubs.

Appearances:
Others: (1) app.
Total: **(1) app. 0 gls.**

CONU, J

Role: Half-back 1885-86

Debut v Casuals (LAC) (a) 7.11.1885

Another of the players from the club's earliest days, Conu's only known first team appearance was in a London Association Cup tie with the Casuals. Spurs lost 0-8 in a real "men versus boys" match, but the result was irrelevant. A game against the most famous amateur club in the country showed just how much Spurs had progressed in the three years since their formation.

Appearances:
Others: 1 app.
Total: **1 app. 0 gls.**

COOK, George William

Role: Inside-forward 1929-31
5ft.7ins. 10st.7lbs.
Born: Evenwood, County Durham, 27th February 1895
Died: Colwyn Bay, Colwyn, Clwyd, 31st December 1980

CAREER: Evenwood Juniors 1912-1914/Trindle Juniors 1914-1916/Royal Artillery/Bishop Auckland Aug 1919/Rotherham County May 1922/Huddersfield Town May 1923/Aston Villa Feb 1927/**SPURS** Jun 1929/Brentford Aug 1931/Colwyn Bay Aug 1932/Rhyl May 1934-Apr 1935.

Debut v Bradford Park Avenue (FL) (a) 31.8.1929

Billy Cook was an accomplished player who had won many honours in the game before joining Spurs. He first made his mark with Bishop Auckland and it was his performances helping them win the FA Amateur Cup in 1921 and 1922 that attracted the attention of League clubs. He turned professional with Rotherham County, but after only a year signed for Herbert Chapman's Huddersfield Town. He helped the Yorkshire club to three successive Football League titles between 1924 and 1927 before joining Aston Villa. Two years at Villa Park preceded his transfer to Spurs and, although over 34 when signed and approaching the twilight of his career, he gave Spurs two years sterling service before being released in April 1931. He then spent a season with Brentford before winding down his career with Colwyn Bay and Rhyl

Appearances:
League: 63 apps. 22 gls.
FA Cup: 4 apps. 2 gls.
Others: 6 apps. 6 gls.
Total: **73 apps. 30 gls.**

COOK, H J

Role: Full-back 1896-97

CAREER: Clapton/SPURS Dec 1896/Vampires.

Debut v Wolverton (WChC) (a) 16.12.1896

A well-known Clapton and London representative player, Cook signed Southern League forms for Spurs in December 1896, but did not make any appearances in that competition. His only appearance for Spurs was in a Wellingborough Charity Cup tie in December 1896. A few days later he turned out for Vampires.

Appearances:
Others: 1 app.
Total: 1 app. 0 gls.

COOK, Jason Peter

Role: Midfielder 1987-88.
Born: Edmonton, London, 29th December 1969

CAREER: South Bedfordshire Schools/Bedfordshire Schools/South of England Schools/Luton Town trial/SPURS trainee Jul 1986, pro. cs. 1988/Southend United Jun 1989/Colchester United May 1991/Braintree Town Nov 1993/Woking Feb 1994/Braintree Town 1994-95/Dagenham and Redbridge 1994-95/Romford Aug 1995/Purfleet 1995-96/Heybridge Swifts 1995-96/Chelmsford City cs. 1996/Canvey Island Nov 1996/Chertsey Town 1996-97/Halstead Town.

Debut v Brentford (sub) (Fr) (a) 5.12.1987

Apart from football, Jason Cook was also a good rugby player at school representing South Bedfordshire at that sport. He decided to make his career in football, had a trial for Luton Town, but opted to join Spurs as a trainee, being upgraded to full professional status in the summer of 1988. By then he had already made his first team debut as a substitute in a friendly at Brentford. Only making one more first team substitute appearance, Cook was given a free transfer at the end of the 1988-89 season and joined Southend United. In his first two seasons he helped them climb from the Fourth Division straight up to the Second but in May 1991 was released. He joined Colchester United, helping them to the GM Vauxhall Conference/FA Trophy "Double" in 1992. After leaving Colchester, Cook played for several years at senior non-League level for various Essex clubs.

Appearances:
Others: (2) apps.
Total: (2) apps. 0 gls.

COOK, Robert Kenneth

Role: Outside-right 1949-50
5ft.8ins. 11st.0lbs.
Born: Letchworth, Hertfordshire, 13th June 1924
Died: Ayton, Berwickshire, 6th March 1997

CAREER: Letchworth Town/Reading Mar 1948/SPURS Jul 1949/Watford Aug 1951/Canterbury City Jul 1953/Northampton Town Mar 1956/Biggleswade Town Jun 1957.

Debut v Queens Park Rangers (FL) (h) 26.11.1949

Bobby Cook had only a year's Football League experience behind him before joining Spurs, and this was perhaps evident in the three appearances he made for the club as replacement for injured Sonny Walters during the 1949-50 Second Division Championship campaign. Replaced as Walter's understudy by Jimmy Scarth, Cook was not particularly well suited to Arthur Rowe's "Push and Run" style of football and, with Walters so consistent and injury-free, was unable to mount a sustained challenge for a first team place. Without another senior outing to his name, Cook moved to Watford where he played for two years before dropping down the football ladder.

Appearances:
League: 3 apps.
Total: 3 apps. 0 gls.

COOKE, Richard Edward

Role: Winger 1982-87
5ft.6ins. 9st.0lbs.
Born: *Islington, London, 4th September 1965 place in italic font*

CAREER: Albany Comprehensive School/Enfield Schools/Middlesex Schools/London Schools/SPURS app. Jul 1982, pro. May 1983/(Birmingham City loan Sep 1986)/AFC Bournemouth Jan 1987/Luton Town Mar 1989/AFC Bournemouth Mar 1991/retired Mar 1993/Bashley Jun 1993/Kitchee (Hong Kong) Oct 1993/Dorchester Town 1993-94.

Debut v Luton Town (FL) (a) 19.11.1983 (scored once)
(Scunthorpe United (sub) (Fr) (a) 3.8.1982)

If physical appearances were all that mattered, Richard Cooke would never have been a professional footballer. A short, frail looking winger, he hardly seemed equipped for the rigours of League football, but made up for his lack of physique with pace and excellent ball skills. Pursued by several League clubs, he chose Spurs on leaving school, won England Youth and Under-19 honours and appeared as a substitute in friendlies before scoring on his competitive debut in Spurs' 4-2 victory at Luton Town in November 1983. After a promising first full season, Cooke had to be content with a place in the reserves, but still managed to win an England Under-21 cap in March 1986 as a substitute against Denmark. Unfortunately, David Pleat's new tactical plan of five men in midfield supporting a lone striker meant there was no room for an out-and-out winger and, after a loan spell with Birmingham City, Cooke was allowed to join Bournemouth for £50,000. One of the stars of the "Cherries"

attempt to win promotion to the First Division in 1988-89, he was transferred to Luton just before the March 1989 transfer deadline, making his debut as a substitute against Spurs later that month. However, things did not go too well at Kenilworth Road and he spent most of the time struggling to climb out of the reserves before returning to Bournemouth on a free transfer. A knee injury sustained in October 1992 forced a premature retirement from the higher levels of the league game, but Cooke continued to play for a short time in Hong Kong and in non-League circles. In July 1994 Spurs visited Dean Court to play a testimonial match for his benefit.

Appearances:
League: 9 (2) apps. 2 gls.
FA Cup: 1 app.
FL Cup: 1 (1) apps.
Euro: 1 (2) apps.
Others: 4 (11) apps. 2 gls.
Total: **16 (16) apps. 4 gls.**

COOMBER, George Stephen

Role: Half-back 1917-18
Born: West Hoathley, Sussex, 19th January 1890
Died: Hove, Sussex, 6th March 1960

CAREER: Tottenham Thursday/**SPURS** am. Mar 1912/Tufnell Park/Brighton and Hove Albion am. Jul 1913, pro Apr 1914/(guest for **SPURS** and Watford during World War One)/retired 1925.

Debut v Crystal Palace (LFC) (a) 1.9.1917

Although his birth name was Comber, Coomber always played under the name with an extra "o". He made his only appearances for Spurs during the First World War in the London Football Combination. Early in his career he had been on Spurs books having been signed from the local junior club Tottenham Thursday. Prior to the war he had been registered with Brighton and Hove Albion to whom he returned after the war and gave great service for many years. It was not until 1925 that he retired after a serious cartilage injury. He only assisted Spurs in the 1917-18 season making 13 appearances and scoring twice.

Appearances:
Others: 13 apps. 2 gls.
Total: **13 apps. 2 gls.**

COOPER, John Alexander

Role: Midfield 1981-82
Born: Euston, London, 9th November 1962

CAREER: Camden Schools/Inner London Schools/**SPURS** app. Apr 1979, pro. Jan 1980/Helsingborg (Sweden) cs. 1982/Enfield cs. 1984/Finchley/Gravesend and Northfleet 1990-1992.

Debut v Bahrain Select XI (Fr) (a) 24.5.1981

One of those young players who never quite made the grade at White Hart Lane, Cooper never appeared in a competitive first team match for Spurs, but made six appearances in friendlies and tour matches, all of them as a substitute. He played in all three matches on Spurs trip to Bahrain and Kuwait in May 1981 and then in three friendly matches prior to the start of the next season. Released in the summer of 1982, Cooper joined the Swedish Second Division club Helsingborg and played for them for two years before returning to England. He joined Enfield and helped Spurs non-league neighbours win the FA Trophy in 1988. He later played for Finchley and Gravesend and Northfleet.

Appearances:
Others: (6) apps.
Total: **(6) apps. 0 gls.**

COPELAND, David Campbell

Role: Inside or centre-forward 1899-1905
5ft.7ins. 11st.5lbs.
Born: Ayr, Scotland, 7th April 1875
Died: Erdington, Birmingham, 16th November 1931

CAREER: Ayr Parkhouse 1892/Walsall Oct 1893/Bedminster Jun 1898/**SPURS** May 1899/Chelsea May 1905/Glossop Sep 1907-Jun 1908/Ayr Parkhouse/Walsall Oct 1910.

Debut v Millwall Athletic (SL) (a) 2.9.1899 (scored once)

David Copeland was one of the many Scots recruited for the club by John Cameron and played a considerable part in Spurs' run of success around the turn of the century. A centre-forward or winger with Ayr Parkhouse, Walsall and Bedminster, he initially played in the centre for Spurs, but soon switched to inside-forward, swapping positions with Tom Pratt. The two of them were top scorers as Spurs clinched their only Southern League title in 1899-1900. Although injury deprived Spurs of his services for much of the following season Copeland still managed to play in all the FA Cup games, culminating in Spurs' first success in that competition. Along with Cameron-who also came from Ayr-Copeland was responsible for many of the goals scored by centre-forward "Sandy" Brown. Copeland also had a remarkable understanding with winger John Kirwan and for six years they formed one of the most effective left wing partnerships in the country. Had they been the same nationality there is little doubt Copeland would have won international honours alongside Kirwan, but as the winger was Irish, the nearest Copeland got to playing for his country was an appearance for the Anglo-Scots against the Home Scots in the 1903 international trial. He stayed with Spurs until May 1905 when he and Kirwan moved to newly-formed Chelsea. A broken leg early in the 1906-07 season effectively ended his career although he did attempt a comeback with Glossop, but was only able to play two games for them. A few seasons before the Great War he turned out for Walsall in the Birmingham League and was reported to have shown "fine judgment" but, not surprisingly, "lacked much of his former speed". Later employed at the Rose and Crown Hotel at Erdington in Birmingham, he collapsed and died of heart failure whilst chopping wood. David's interest in Spurs never waned throughout his life. Whenever the team visited the Birmingham area, he would always meet them at the station and accompany the party to the match-often assisting the trainer on the bench.

Appearances:
Southern: 144* apps. 50 gls.
FA Cup: 20* apps. 3 gls.
Others: 135 apps. 53 gls.
Total: 299 apps. 106 gls.
* Includes 1 abandoned match.

COQUET, Ernest

Role: Full-back 1907-11
6ft.0ins. 12st.7lbs.
Born: Durston-On-Tyne, County Durham, 6th January 1883
Died: Gateshead, County Durham, 26th October 1946

CAREER: Seaham White Star/Gateshead Town Aug 1904/Sunderland May 1905/Reading Aug 1907/**SPURS** Mar 1908/Burslem Port Vale May 1911/Fulham Jan 1913/retired 1919/Leadgate Park Jan 1920.

Debut v Millwall (SL) (h) 7.3.1908

In just one season with Reading Ernie Coquet built a reputation as a hard, combative player, and it was these qualities that persuaded Spurs to sign him. With Sunderland for two years before joining Reading, he was a strong, determined character who could occupy either full-back position with equal competence. He missed only one game in Spurs first season in the Football League, but by the end of the 1910-11 season found himself competing with Tom Collins, Bert Elkin and Fred Wilkes for one of the full-back positions. In May 1911 he was released and moved to Burslem Port Vale, returning to London with Fulham almost two years later. He played for Fulham until the end of the First World War when he retired, but was persuaded return for a brief spell with Leadgate Park back in his native North-east.

Appearances:
Southern: 6 apps.
League: 78* apps.
FA Cup: 8 apps. 1 gl.
Others: 17 apps.
Total: 109 apps. 1 gl.
* Includes 2 abandoned matches.

CORBETT, Patrick Avalon

Role: Defender 1980-83
6ft.0ins. 11st.0lbs.
Born: Hackney, London, 12th February 1963

CAREER: East London Schools/**SPURS** app. Jun 1979, pro. Oct 1980/GAIS (Sweden) loan summer 1981/Orient Aug 1983/Elo Kuopio (Finland) 1986/MyPa (Finland) 1991/released Sep 1991.

Debut v Southampton (sub) (FL) (a) 31.10.1981 (scored once)
(West Ham United (sub) (Fr) (h) 11.5.1981)

A strong defender, probably best at centre-half, Pat Corbett played for England at Youth level and like several Spurs youngsters of the time, spent a summer abroad playing for GAIS of Sweden. His League debut came at Southampton in October 1981 when he went on as a substitute for the last five minutes and within three minutes scored the winning goal. He made three further appearances in the League in May 1982 when Spurs were forced to complete a backlog of fixtures with several first team regulars injured, but was to make only one more substitute appearance before being transferred to Orient. He played for Orient until April 1986 when his contract was cancelled so that he could move to Finland. Latterly playing with MyPa, he helped them to promotion from the Second Division before being released in September 1991.

Appearances:
League: 3 (2) apps. 1 gl.
Others: (2) apps.
Total: 3 (4) apps. 1 gl.

CORDER, Peter Robert

Role: Goalkeeper 1983-84
Born: Loughton, Essex, 12th December 1966

CAREER: Basildon Schools/Essex Schools/Wickford Town/**SPURS** Jul 1983, pro. Oct 1984/(Peterborough United loan Oct 1985)/Nuneaton Borough Dec 1985/(Boston United loan Dec 1986)/Holbeach United/Raunds/Peterborough United asst. physio by Dec 2002/Cambridge City physio by Sep 2003/Peterborough United youth team physio, community support officer, first team physio May 2010.

Debut v West Ham United (sub) (Fr) (a) 18.5.1984

A winger turned goalkeeper, Peter Corder had a trial for England in the outfield position, but after joining Wickford Town was switched to the goalkeeper's role which resulted in him being associated with both Orient and West Ham United before joining Spurs. He made his one and only first team appearance in May 1984 when he went on as substitute in

a testimonial match at West Ham. Corder never got a look-in at First Division level, but did get some experience of League football with two games for Peterborough United whilst on a three-month loan there. He will not forget those matches for both of them were lost and in the second he conceded seven goals at Tranmere Rovers. However, Corder could hardly be blamed for the size of the defeat as three of the goals were own goals, two by experienced player-manager John Wile and the other by his assistant, the former Spurs player, Jimmy Holmes. Certainly Holmes did not blame Corder, for when he joined Nuneaton Borough as manager, he secured Corder's transfer. Corder later played for Holbeach United and Raunds and then became a qualified physiotherapist working for four years with Peterborough United and three years at Cambridge City, before returning to Peterborough.

Appearances:
Others: (1) app.
Total: (1) app. 0 gls.

ĆORLUKA, Vedran

Role: Defender, 2008-2012
6ft.3ins. 14st.1lb.
Born: Modran, Doboj, Yugoslavia, 5th February 1986

CAREER: Dinamo Zagreb (Croatia) pro. 2003/(Inter Zaprešić (Croatia) loan Jul 2004)/Manchester City Aug 2007/SPURS Sep 2008/(Bayer 04 Leverkusen (Germany) loan Jan 2012)/Lokomotiv Moscow (Russia) Jun 2012.

Debut v Aston Villa (PL) (h) 15.9.2008

Due to the Balkans conflict Vedran Ćorluka and his family were forced to leave Modran, a village in what is now Bosnia and Herzegovina, and move to the Croatian city of Zagreb. Within a short time of the move Ćorluka, only eight, began an association with Dinamo Zagreb that was to take him to the peak of Croatian football. At the first opportunity he was taken on the professional staff, a strong, hard-tackling defender, capable of playing at full-back or in the centre of defence. Along with Dinamo Zagreb team-mate, Luka Modrić, Ćorluka was sent out on loan to Inter Zaprešić to further his football education and helped the unfashionable club finish the 2004-05 season as runners-up to Hadjuk Split in the Prva HNL, while his parent club struggled in the relegation group. Returning to Dinamo, Ćorluka was immediately installed as a regular in defence and helped

Dinamo to the first two of a still unbroken run of ten successive titles. Having represented Croatia at all levels from Under-16 to Under-21, Ćorluka made his first appearance for the full international team against Italy in August 2006. Only injury has seen him absent since then. A seasoned performer, but still only 21, Manchester City laid out a reported £8 million to secure his transfer and Ćorluka immediately settled to Premier League football. With the influx of Middle East money into Manchester City and the flood of players that secured, it was still a surprise when City accepted a Spurs' offer of £5.5 million for Ćorluka, that allowed him to be re-united with Modrić. As Spurs struggled under Juande Ramos, Ćorluka had few opportunities but following the Spaniard's departure and Harry Redknapp's appointment, he was installed as first choice right-back. There was nothing fancy about Ćorluka. He was first and foremost a defender, physically strong, competent in the air and a hard tackler. When the opportunity arose he would press forward, but he always seemed most comfortable nearer his own goal. For two years Ćorluka contested the right-back spot with Alan Hutton, but the signing of Kyle Walker saw both of them lose out, the younger, more attack-minded Walker, being recognised as the better long-term prospect. Far too good to be left on the side-lines, Ćorluka went on loan to Bayer Leverkusen with a view to a permanent transfer. When that fell through due to the German club's financial difficulties, Lokomotiv Moscow were quick to make Ćorluka one of the first signings of the newly appointed, Slaven Bilić, Ćorluka's former international manager.

Appearances:
League: 76 (5) apps. 1 gl.
FA Cup: 9 apps.
FL Cup: 7 (1) apps.
Euro: 12 apps.
Others: 11 (5) apps. 2 gls.
Total: 115 (11) apps. 3 gls.

COTTRELL, Francis Skeet

Role: Inside-forward 1883-95
Born: Cambridge, 23rd March 1868

CAREER: SPURS/Park Casuals.

Debut v Brownlow Rovers (Fr) (h) 6.10.1883

Although Frank Cottrell was not one of the founder members of Spurs he was playing for the club by its second season, 1883-84, his first known appearance being against Brownlow Rovers in the initial match for which a full Spurs line-up is recorded. He was one of the longest serving players from those early days appearing regularly right up until the 1892-93 season. He then took to playing for a local junior club, Park Casuals, making only the odd appearance for Spurs.

Appearances:
Others: 51 apps. 20 gls.
Total: 51 apps. 20 gls.

COUCHMAN, H F

Role: Outside-left 1918-19
Born: London.

CAREER: Leavesden Hospital/(guest for SPURS and Watford during World War One).

Debut v Brentford (LFC) (a) 1.3.1919

A former serviceman who had played at outside-right for the British Army against the French Army towards the close of hostilities, Couchman made his one appearance for Spurs in a 1-4 defeat at Brentford. At the time he was working at Leavesden Hospital near Watford, another club he played for during the War.

Appearances:
Others: 1 app.
Total: 1 app. 0 gls.

COULIBALY, Souleymane

Role: Striker, 2012-13
5ft.8ins. 11st.13lbs.
Born: Anguededou Songon, Abidjan, Ivory Coast, 26th December 1994

CAREER: Junior Camp Arezzo Football Academy (Italy)/AS Siena (Italy)/**SPURS** Academy Scholar Jul 2011, pro Dec 2011/ (US Grosseto (Italy) loan Jan 2013)/Bari (Italy) Sep 2014/ (Pistoiese (Italy) loan Sep 2014)/ Crewe Alexandra trial Jul 2015/ Peterborough United trial and perm Jul 2015/(Newport County AFC loan Mar 2016) /Kilmarnock Jun 2016/Al Ahly (Egypt) Jan 2017.

Debut v Stevenage (Fr) (a) 18.7.2012

Civil war caused 13-year old Souleymane Coulibaly to flee the Ivory Coast and head for Italy where his father had made his home. In three years of youth football in his adopted Tuscany he impressed enough to be selected to represent the country of his birth at the Under-17 World Cup of 2011 in Mexico. The powerfully built youngster burst on to the international stage, scoring nine goals to collect the Golden Boot award and attract the attention of all Europe's leading clubs. Within weeks of the tournament ending, Coulibaly was signed to the Spurs Academy and at the first opportunity upgraded to full professional status. Signed as one for the future, he started well enough with the youth team and development squad and made a first team appearance as a substitute in a July 2012 pre-season friendly. While signed as one for the future, further progress was slow. To gain some experience of senior competitive football, Coulibaly returned to Italy for a while on loan to struggling US Grosseto. It did not produce the boost hoped for and before the 2014-15 season had really got underway he was allowed to move to Bari, although he immediately joined Pistoiese on loan. The return to Italy did not produce a change in fortunes and within a year Coulibaly was back in England looking for another club and eventually joining Peterborough. A year later he moved on to Kilmarnock.

Appearances:
Others: (1) app.
Total: (1) app. 0 gls.

COULTHIRST, Shaquile Tyshan

Role: Striker, 2013-2016
5ft.9ins. 11st.11lbs.
Born: Hackney, London, 11th November 1994

CAREER: Westward Boys/Petchey Academy/**SPURS** Academy Scholar Jul 2011, pro Apr 2012/(Leyton Orient loan Jan 2014)/(Torquay United loan Mar 2014)/(Southend United loan Aug 2014)/(York City loan Mar 2015)/(Wigan Athletic loan Aug 2015)/Peterborough United Jan 2016/(Mansfield Town loan Jan 2017).

Debut v Anzhi Makhachkala (EL) (h) (sub) 12.12.2013 (Colchester United (Fr) (a) (sub) 19.7.2013)

A pocket-sized striker with an unquenchable thirst for goals, that sometime annoyed better-placed team-mates, Shaq Coulthirst was a local lad who worked his way to the fringes of the first team before being allowed to move on. Mobile and aggressive, he looked the part as he moved up the ranks, netting regularly at all levels, whether played as a central striker or out wide. He had plenty of quality, was sharp, pacy and with the natural scorer's instinct. Having made a couple of first team substitute appearances, Coulthirst went out on loan to gain the type of senior competitive experience young players will rarely have to chance to taste at a club like Spurs. Despite the obvious lack of back-up for Harry Kane, he was surprisingly allowed to join Peterborough in January 2016.

Appearances:
Euro: (1) app.
Others: (2) apps.
Total: (3) apps. 0 gls.

COULSON, W

Role: Full-back 1891-92

Debut v Uxbridge (Fr) (h) 2.1.1892

Coulson is only known to have played in three friendly matches for Spurs during the 1891-92 season, all of them at full-back.

Appearances:
Others: 3 apps.
Total: 3 apps. 0 gls.

COUSINS, Albert Cowley

Role: Forward 1907-08
Born: Pancras, London, September qtr. 1890

CAREER: SPURS trial Nov 1907, pro. Nov 1907/Hastings & St Leonards United Aug 1908/Chelsea May 1909/ Watford Aug 1911-cs. 1912.

Debut v Millwall (WL) (h) 25.11.1907

At 17-years old, Albert Cousins was given a trial in the reserves late in 1907 and after several useful performances signed as a professional. He made his first team debut almost immediately in a Western League fixture, and followed up with two Southern League appearances the following month. However, at the end of the season the decision was taken that he was not good enough to make the grade and he was released. He joined Hastings & St Leonards, although he did make further attempts at playing at the top level with both Chelsea and Watford. His brief career at Watford came to a sad end in March 1912 when, along with another reserve team player he was suspended for 28 days for misbehaviour

Appearances:
Southern: 2 apps.
Others: 1 apps.
Total: 3 apps. 0 gls.

COX, Frederick James Arthur

Role: Winger 1938-49
5ft.7ins. 10st.2lbs.
Born: Reading, Berkshire, 1st November 1920
Died: Bournemouth, Hampshire, 7th August 1973

CAREER: Redlands Senior School/St George's Lads Club/**SPURS** am. 1936, Jun 1937/Northfleet United 1937/ **SPURS** pro. Aug 1938/(guest for Fulham, Reading, Manchester City and Swindon Town during World War Two)/Arsenal Sep 1949/Norsemen coach/ West Bromwich Albion player-coach Jul 1953, asst. manager/Bournemouth and Boscombe Athletic manager Apr 1956/Portsmouth manager Apr 1958-Feb 1961/ Gillingham manager Jun 1962-Dec 1965/Bournemouth and Boscombe Athletic manager Apr 1965-Apr 1970.

Debut v Swansea Town (FL) (a) 19.11.1938 (scored once)

In a remarkable football career that spanned over 40 years as player and manager, Freddie Cox experienced all the highs and lows which accompany such a lengthy time in the game. Spotted by Spurs playing for his local St George's Lads Club, signed as an amateur and sent to the nursery club at Northfleet, he made his Football League debut whilst still a junior. A fast, probing winger his chances of establishing a first choice place were wrecked by the war and he was only able to make the odd appearance for Spurs in the wartime competitions. Robbed of most of his best playing years by the war, during which he was awarded the Distinguished Flying Cross, he was first choice winger in the early post-war years, but with the emergence of the young Sonny Walters was allowed to move to Arsenal for £12,000. Ironically, it was with the Gunners that Freddie enjoyed his greatest successes. He certainly relished his return visits to White Hart Lane. In the 1950 FA Cup semi-final he scored against Chelsea and got another in the replay which also took place at White Hart Lane. He did even better in 1952 when Arsenal again needed two matches to overcome Chelsea. Both matches were once more staged on his old hunting ground and he scored once in the first match and twice in the replay. He played in the Final in both those years, picking up a winners' medal in 1950, but was a loser on the second occasion. Memories of that defeat were, however, largely erased the following season when he played nine games in helping Arsenal to the Football League title. In July 1953 he left Highbury to join former Spurs colleague Vic Buckingham at West Bromwich Albion, initially as player/coach but later assistant manager. He then took up the manager's chair at Bournemouth and was in command when the Third Division (South) club knocked Spurs out of the FA Cup in February 1957. Later in charge of Portsmouth and Gillingham, who he led to the Fourth Division title in 1964, he returned to Bournemouth where he remained until dismissed following their relegation to the Fourth Division in 1970. At that point he decided to retire from the game he had served so widely and so well, and concentrate on his newsagent's business in Bournemouth.

Appearances:
League: 99 apps. 15 gls.
FA Cup: 6 apps. 3 gls.
Others: 39 apps. 9 gls.
Total: 144 apps. 27 gls.

CRAIG

Role: Outside-left 1896-97

Debut v Chatham (Fr) (a) 11.1.1897

Craig's only appearance for Spurs was on 11th January 1897 when he played at outside-left in a friendly at Chatham.

Appearances:
Others: 1 app.
Total: 1 app. 0 gls.

CRAIG

Role: Left-back 1918-19

Debut v Crystal Palace (Fr) (a) 26.4.1919

A trialist, Craig made his only appearance for Spurs in a friendly match in April 1919. Spurs arranged two friendly matches that day in an effort to find new young talent for the resumption of normal football after the First World War. Presumably Craig did not impress Spurs too much, for he had no further association with the club.

Appearances:
Others: 1 app.
Total: 1 app. 0 gls.

CRESSWELL, Warneford

Role: Full-back 1917-18
5ft.10ins. 10st.10lbs.
Born: South Shields, County Durham, 5th November 1897
Died: South Shields, County Durham, 20th October 1973

CAREER: Stanhope School/ South Shields Schools/Durham Schools/England Schools/ North Shields Athletic 1914/ (guest for Heart of Midlothian, Hibernian, Morton and **SPURS** during World War One)/South Shields May 1919/Sunderland Mar 1922/Everton Feb 1927/ Port Vale manager-coach May 1936/Northampton Town manager Apr 1937-Sep 1939/ Dartford manager cs. 1946-Jan 1947.

Debut v Brentford (LFC) (a) 15.9.1917

Warney Cresswell had been associated with Manchester United prior to the First World War without making the breakthrough into their senior team. At the time of his appearances for Spurs he was serving as a gymnastics instructor at an important Army training centre. He made a total of eleven appearances for the club, spending most of his time in

Scotland where he assisted the local clubs. When the war was over he returned to South Shields, joined his local club and rapidly developed as an outstanding defender, winning his first representative honour in March 1921 when he played for the Football League against the Scottish League. Two days later he won his first England cap against Wales. After joining Sunderland Cresswell represented the Football League twice more and won five more international caps before moving to Everton. With Everton he made two more appearances for the Football League, won Football League Championship medals in 1928 and 1932, the Second Division title in 1931, an FA Cup Winner's medal in 1933 and his final cap in October 1929. After his retirement from playing, Cresswell served Port Vale as coach and manager, Northampton Town and Dartford as manager.

Appearances:
Others: 11 apps.
Total: **11 apps. 0 gls.**

CROFT, T

Role: Full-back 1916-17

Debut v Brentford (LFC) (h) 30.9.1916

A local player, Croft made three appearances for Spurs in the London Football Combination in 1916-17.

Appearances:
Others: 3 apps.
Total: **3 apps. 0 gls.**

CROFT, W

Role: Full-back 1916-17

Debut v West Ham United (LFC) (h) 28.9.1916

Brother of T Croft and another local lad, Croft also made his only appearances for Spurs in the London Football Combination competition of 1916-17 although he played one game less than his brother. His first game was in September 1916 when Tommy Clay was unavailable and his final appearance was in February 1917 when he played right-half in the absence of Jimmy Elliott.

Appearances:
Others: 2 apps.
Total: **2 apps. 0 gls.**

CROMPTON, Arthur

Role: Outside-right 1928-30
5ft.5ins. 10st.0lbs.

Born: Birmingham, 9th January 1903
Died: Congleton, Cheshire, February 1987

CAREER: St Pauls School/South Staffs Regiment/Devon County/**SPURS** Aug 1927/Southend United May 1930/Brentford Feb 1932/Crystal Palace Feb 1934/Tranmere Rovers Sep 1935/Northwich Victoria Jun 1936.

Debut v Bristol City (FL) (a) 24.11.1928 (scored once)

A gold and silversmith by trade, Arthur "Tiddler" Crompton had learned his football while serving in the Army and spent some time brushing up his skills with Spurs' reserves before making his debut. Never able to hold down a regular place, the signing of Willie Davies in February 1930 meant he was surplus to requirements and two months later he was released. He moved to Southend United and later played lower down the Football League with Brentford (helping them win the Third Division South in 1933), Crystal Palace and Tranmere Rovers.

Appearances:
League: 15 apps. 3 gls.
Others: 9 apps. 5 gls.
Total: **24 apps. 8 gls.**

CROMPTON, George Ellis

Role: Centre-forward 1910-12
5ft.8ins. 11st.7lbs.
Born: Ramsbottom, Lancashire, 17th July 1886
Died: Barnstaple, Devon, 17th May 1953

CAREER: Hupton United/Padiham/Blackburn Rovers May 1906/**SPURS** Dec 1910/Exeter City Jul 1912/Bristol Rovers May 1913/Exeter City Jul 1921/(Bristol Rovers loan Jul 1922)/Barnstaple Town player-coach Jun 1926/Llanelli player-coach 1929/Barry Town player-coach 1930.

Debut v Sheffield Wednesday (FL) (a) 31.12.1910

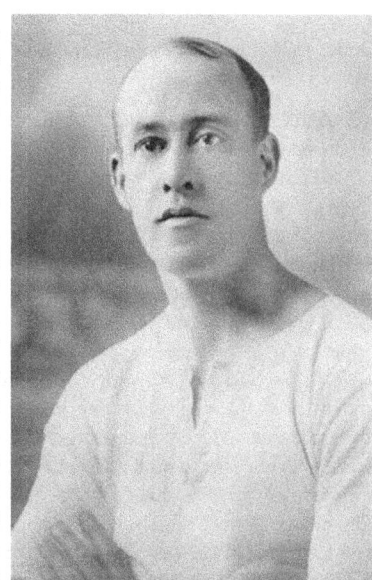

Ellis Crompton was signed to try and solve Spurs centre-forward problems caused by injury to Percy Humphreys, but was not a success. He only retained his place until Humphreys was fit to resume, and then suffered an injury himself that precluded any action for two months. Crompton did not have a bad record for Blackburn Rovers, 16 goals in 24 League outings, but that was spread over a period of six years. In the eleven games he played for Spurs, he scored only one goal and even that has been lost in the mists of time. It came in a match against Oldham Athletic that was abandoned at half-time due to fog. Released at the end of the 1911-12 season, he moved on to Exeter City and Bristol Rovers, remaining with Rovers until his return to Exeter. Having retreated into the half-back line, he served Exeter until 1926 when he joined Barnstaple Town as player/coach. He followed that with spells at Llanelli and Barry Town. He was later a publican in Barnstaple.

Appearances:
League: 9* apps. 1# gl.
FA Cup: 2 apps.
Total: **11 apps. 1 gl.**
* Includes 1 abandoned match.
# Includes 1 in an abandoned match.

CROOK, Ian Stuart

Role: Midfielder 1980-86
5ft.8ins. 11st.6lbs.
Born: Romford, Essex, 18th January 1963

CAREER: Forest Lodge Comprehensive School/Great Danes/Havering Schools/**SPURS** app. May 1979, pro. Aug 1980/Norwich City Jun 1986/Sanfrecce Hiroshima (Japan) Jun 1997/Northern Spirit (Australia) May

1998, youth team coach 1999, asst. manager Feb 2000/Newcastle United (Australia) head coach May 2001-Apr 2004/American Samoa manager May 2004-Nov 2004/Sydney FC asst. manager Nov 2004-Jan 2007/ (Australia Under-21 asst. coach)/Avispa Fukuoka (Japan) asst. manager Jan 2007-Jul 2008/Newcastle Jets (Australia) High Performance manager Oct 2008/Norwich City first team coach Jan 2009/Sydney Olympic (Australia) Director of Coaching Jun 2010/New South Wales Institute of Sport Head Coach Sep 2010/ Sydney FC (Australia) asst. coach Feb 2011/Sydney Olympic (Australia) Head of Football Development Mar 2011/Sydney FC (Australia) Youth team coach Jan 2012, manager May-Nov 2012/ Football New South Wales (Australia) coach co-ordinator Jan 2013/Western Sydney Wanderers (Australia) asst. coach Jun 2014, Elite Academy Technical Director May 2015.

Debut v Coventry City (sub) (FL) (a) 1.5.1982
(Weymouth (sub) (Fr) (a) 17.11.1980)

Ian Crook is another example of the excellent home-grown players produced by Spurs who have not quite been able to make the grade at White Hart Lane, but have proved themselves valuable contributors with a less glamorous club. An Essex County trialist, Crook, who also played cricket for Havering Schools, was spotted by Spurs playing for his local Sunday club, Great Danes. Working his way through the junior ranks, he appeared as a substitute in friendly and tour matches before making his League debut in May 1982, when Spurs were forced to give an early opportunity to several younger players as serious injury problems piled up alongside a backlog of fixtures. A cultured midfield player with vision and a lovely passing ability, he followed in the footsteps of home produced midfielders of the quality of Glenn Hoddle and Micky Hazard and it was not easy to do that, let alone displace them. The presence of such firm favourites seriously limited his openings, and when Norwich City offered Spurs a modest £80,000, and Crook the prospect of regular first team action, he was persuaded to move to Norfolk. He proved a more than competent First Division performer, appeared for the England "B" team, and was the subject of £1 million transfer speculation. Given a free transfer in the summer of 1996, he signed for Ipswich, but his contract with Norwich had not expired, and on Mike Walker being re-appointed as Norwich manager Crook re-signed for Norwich. This caused an almighty row with their East Anglian rivals. When he did leave Norwich, Crook moved a little further away than Suffolk playing in Japan before moving on to Australia where, apart from an 18-month stint back at Norwich, he has coached at various clubs and umbrella organisations.

Appearances:
League: 10 (10) apps. 1 gl.
FA Cup: (1) app.
FL Cup: 1 app.
Euro: (2) apps.
Others: 13 (22) apps. 2 gls.
Total: 24 (35) apps. 3 gls.

CROOKS, Garth Anthony O.B.E.

Role: Striker 1980-85
5ft.8ins. 11st.6lbs.
Born: Stoke-on-Trent, Staffordshire, 10th March 1958

CAREER: St Peters Comprehensive School/Stoke Schools/Staffordshire Schools/Stoke City app. Jul 1974, pro. Mar 1976/**SPURS** Jul 1980/ (Manchester United loan Nov 1983)/West Bromwich Albion Jul 1985/ Charlton Athletic Mar 1987/retired Nov 1990.

Debut v Nottingham Forest (FL) (h) 16.8.1980 (scored once)
(Southend United (Fr) (a) 28.7.1980)

When Keith Burkinshaw teamed Garth Crooks with Steve Archibald in the summer of 1980, he created for Spurs one of the most potent and exciting goal-scoring partnerships for many years; a combination which put fear into the heart of any defence. Within a month of signing professional for Stoke, Crooks made his League debut, but it was the transfer of Ian Moores to Spurs in September 1976 that really gave him the opportunity to claim a regular place in the Potters' team. He took the chance well, soon became a regular and lethal scorer, helped Stoke to promotion back to Division One in 1978-79 and won his first England Under-21 cap in November 1979 when he scored a hat-trick against Bulgaria. By the time of his £650,000 move to Spurs in July 1980, he had collected three more caps at that level. For two seasons he was almost ever-present for Spurs, helping the club to FA Cup victories in 1981 and 1982 and the League (Milk) Cup Final in 1982. Indeed, he played no less than 17 FA Cup ties for Spurs before tasting defeat. Crooks scored several important goals along the way, including the equaliser in the 1981 FA Cup Final replay. Whilst the goal was overshadowed by Ricky Villa's incredible winner, it was undoubtedly just as crucial, for it put Spurs back in the game just when it looked as if Manchester City had taken control. A natural opportunist with a crisp left foot, excellent balance, control and an ability to withstand strong challenges, Crooks was also responsible for creating many good openings for Archibald with his unselfish running and team play. Loss of form in the middle of the 1982-83 season, the arrival of Alan Brazil and the emerging talents of Mark Falco saw Crooks lose his place and he struggled to get back, even going on loan to Manchester United. In the reserves at the start of the 1984-85 season, he proved a more than capable standby when Clive Allen was injured and seemed to have recovered some of his old sparkle. However, in August 1985 he was transferred to West Bromwich Albion for £100,000, but then left the struggling West Midlanders to join Charlton Athletic in their relegation battle. Scorer and creator of many of the goals that helped keep Charlton in the First Division, persistent injury problems side-lined Crooks for most of the 1989-90 season and in his absence Charlton were relegated. Unable to overcome a back problem, he retired in November 1990. This forced him to resign as Chairman of the Professional Footballers' Association for whom he had rendered splendid service. An intelligent and articulate chairman, he had the qualities to be one of the game's leading administrators, but choose instead to work in TV and radio. In the Queen's Birthday Honours List of June 1999, Crooks was awarded the OBE for services to the Institute of Professional Sport (formerly the Sports Council).

Appearances:
League: 121 (4) apps. 48 gls.
FA Cup: 21 apps. 9 gls.
FL Cup: 19 (1) apps. 9 gls.
Euro: 15 (1) apps. 9 gls.
Others: 42 (14) apps. 31 gls.
Total: 218 (20) apps. 106 gls.

CROSSLEY, A J

Role: Full-back or half-back 1888-92

CAREER: Radicals (Tottenham)/Park/**SPURS** cs. 1888.

Debut v Old Etonians (LSC) (h) 13.10.1888

One of Spurs' greatest local rivals in the years immediately after their formation were Park FC, a club who used to play on Northumberland Park. Senior to Spurs in that their members were youths as opposed to schoolboys, although they performed quite well in local competition and were perhaps regarded as superior to the fledgling Spurs, they were not blessed with the same progressive leadership Spurs were able to call upon. When Park disbanded in the summer of 1888 several of their players opted to join Spurs, and Crossley was one of the few to appear in the first team. His first recorded appearance was in October 1888 when Spurs were thrashed 2-8 by Old Etonians in the First Round of the London Senior Cup. He is also known to have played in two friendly matches that season, but his only other recorded appearance was not until January 1892 when he played in another friendly.

Appearances:
Others: 4 apps.
Total: 4 apps. 0 gls.

CROSSLEY, Charles Arthur

Role: Centre-forward 1916-17
5ft.8ins. 12st. 2lbs.
Born: Short Heath, Hednesford, Staffordshire, 17th December 1891
Died: Wolverhampton, Staffordshire, 29th April 1965

CAREER: Hednesford United 1909/Walsall Aug 1913/Sunderland Feb 1914/ (guest for Clapton Orient, Hednesford Collieries, Huddersfield Town, **SPURS** and Walsall during World War One)/Everton Apr 1920/ West Ham United Jun 1922/ Swindon Town Jul 1923/ Ebbw Vale player-manager Sep 1925.

Debut v Portsmouth (LFC) (a) 17.2.1917

Charlie Crossley made his mark with his local clubs Hednesford United and Walsall before moving into the big time with Sunderland, for whom he made his debut, and scored, against Spurs in March 1914. His only appearance for Spurs was at Portsmouth on 17th February 1917 whilst on leave from serving as a stoker on a submarine boat destroyer. A stocky, muscular player, not afraid to mix it with bigger defenders, after the war he returned to Sunderland. He played for the North against England in an international trial before joining Everton. He later played for West Ham United and Swindon Town.

Appearances:
Others: 1 app.
Total: 1 app. 0 gls.

CROUCH, Peter James

Role: Striker 1999-2000
6ft.5ins. 11st.11lbs.
Born: Macclesfield, Cheshire, 30th January 1981

CAREER: West Middlesex Colts/Ealing District Schools/Middlesex Schools/**SPURS** assoc. schl. May 1995, trainee Jul 1997, pro. Jul 1998/ (Dulwich Hamlet loan Jan 2000)/(IFK Hässleholm (Sweden) loan Apr 2000)/Queens Park Rangers trial and perm. Jul 2000/Portsmouth Jul 2001/ Aston Villa Mar 2002/(Norwich City loan Sep 2003)/Southampton Jul 2004/Liverpool Jul 2005/Portsmouth Jul 2008/**SPURS** Jul 2009/Stoke City Aug 2011.

Debut v Liverpool (sub) (PL) (h) 17.8.2009
(Bishops Stortford (sub) (Fr) (a) 3.9.1999)

At 6ft 5ins and skinny as a beanpole, there has always been something of the footballing Bambi about Peter Crouch. Right from his earliest days as a 16-year old trainee with Spurs, it was his loping stride and gangly appearance that caught the eye, but for those who looked a little closer, there were signs even then of a centre-forward with genuine football ability. Crouch moved through the ranks with Spurs, but made only one senior appearance, as a substitute in a friendly at Bishops Stortford. Loaned out to Dulwich Hamlet and the Swedish club IFK Hässleholm, Crouch was not a bustling style of striker in the Les Ferdinand mould, or blessed with the pace of a Chris Armstrong, but a target man who could hold up the ball, feed his team-mates and bring others into the game, while still able to grab his fair share of goals. With Spurs he was not given the chance to perform at the highest level, not the type of player the manager for most of his time at White Hart Lane, George Graham, appreciated. While his height gave him an advantage in the air, he was best with the ball at his feet, deceptive control and unexpected skills surprising all but those who knew him best. With his prospects of making the grade at Spurs receding as Armstrong, Ferdinand and Steffen Iversen were preferred, he was released in May 2000 and immediately taken on by his former Spurs' manager, Gerry Francis, at Queens Park Rangers. Given a regular staring berth in the Championship side, he began to show his quality, and while Rangers were relegated at the end of his first season, his performances were enough to secure a £1.5m move to Portsmouth where Harry Redknapp was director of football. Continuing to impress, Aston Villa was Crouch's next stop, the ideal player for Graham Taylor, a manager who liked a tall man up front, but when Taylor left Villa Park, Crouch found himself out of favour, even loaned out to Norwich City. He moved on to Southampton, where Redknapp was manager. Although the Saints were relegated, Crouch impressed enough to make his full England debut against Colombia in May 2005 and a couple of months later, another big-money move, this time to Liverpool. He struggled to score his first goal for Liverpool, but once he did, kept up a regular flow until Liverpool signed Fernando Torres. With the Spaniard proving an instant hit, Crouch was rarely in the starting line-up and it was no surprise when he was on the move again, returning to Portsmouth, and Harry Redknapp, in an £11 million deal. Three months later Redknapp left Portsmouth for White Hart Lane, but he and Crouch were not apart long, the manager persuading chairman Daniel Levy to spend £10m to bring Crouch back to White Hart Lane. A regular performer, Crouch was not the most prolific of scorers at White Hart Lane, but he was instrumental in setting up many goals, particularly for Jermaine Defoe. When he did score himself, the goals were often crucial. The hat-trick against Young Boys Berne that helped take Spurs into the Champions' League group stages for the first time and the winner against AC Milan in the San Siro that set up the quarter-final clash with Real Madrid, perfect examples. It was, therefore, a bit of a surprise when Crouch was allowed to move to Stoke City in August 2011.

Appearances:
League: 42 (31) apps. 12 gls.
FA Cup: 6 (1) apps. 1 gl.
FL Cup: 2 (1) apps. 4 gls.
Euro: 9 (1) apps. 7 gls.
Others: 4 (4) apps. 1 gl.
Total: 63 (38) apps. 25 gls.

CROWL, Sydney Robert

Role: Winger 1913-18
Born: Islington, London, 18th March 1888
Died: Waterlooville, Hampshire, 9th October 1971

CAREER: Old Burghleyans/London/Middlesex/Enfield 1908-1925/**SPURS** am. Dec 1913.

Debut v Sheffield Wednesday (FL) (a) 25.4.1914

An England amateur international trialist and regular for London and Middlesex, Sid Crowl played for Enfield, but in December 1913 he was signed to amateur forms by Spurs as cover for regular outside-left Bert Middlemiss. Crowl made only one Football League appearance, in the last game of the season, and although he also played in the War Relief Fund match against Arsenal at the start of the following term, all his other appearances for Spurs came during the First World War. During a near 20-year career with Enfield, Crowl also signed amateur forms for Watford, Southend United and West ham United, though he never played for any of them at senior level,

Appearances:
League: 1 app.
Others: 15 apps. 1 gl.
Total: 16 apps. 1 gl.

CRUMP, William Harold

Role: Half-back 1895-98 and 1899-1900
5ft.8ins. 11st.8lbs.
Born: Harborne, Smethwick, Birmingham 12 February 1873
Died: Burton-on-Trent, 31st January 1918

CAREER: Smethwick Centaur/West Smethwick/Wednesfield/Wolverhampton Wanderers Sep 1894/Hereford Thistle cs. 1895/Bloxwich//**SPURS** trial and perm. Apr 1896/Luton Town May 1898/**SPURS** Sep 1899/(guest for Thames Ironworks)/Doncaster Rovers cs. 1900/Brentford cs. 1901/Watford.

Debut v Sheppey United (SL) (a) 5.9.1896 (scored once)
(Gravesend (Fr) (a) 22.4.1896)

Known as "The Baron", Harry Crump was a muscular, hard-tackling wing-half released after only one Football League appearance for Wolves, who joined Spurs for a month's trial from Hereford Thistle. He played three friendly matches and so impressed that he was immediately signed on. Possessor of a fierce long-range shot, his experience proved invaluable as Spurs took their first tentative steps into senior competitive football and was almost ever-present in their first season in the Southern League. Capable of playing in the forward line if required, he was one of

only four players retained in May 1897. He played the majority of matches the next season, but the signing of John Cameron in the 1898 close season meant Bob Stormont reverting to the half-back role Crump was released. He immediately joined Luton Town and spent a season there, but was without a club as the 1899-00 season started and Spurs decided to re-sign him. After only three appearances that season, he was again released and joined Doncaster later playing for Brentford and signing for Watford although he never made their first eleven.

Appearances:
Southern: 31 apps. 2 gls.
FA Cup: 4 apps. 3 gls.
Others: 72* apps. 8 gls.
Total: 107 apps. 13 gls.
*Includes 1 abandoned match.

CUBBERLEY, Archibald William

Role: Inside-forward 1892-95
Born: Bermondsey, London, 1st February 1875
Died: Shotgate, Wickford, Essex, 29 August 1958

CAREER: Asplin Rovers/**SPURS** Sep 1892/Park Aug 1897/Asplin Rovers/Lansdown/Manchester United during World War One.

Debut v West Herts (FAC) (h) 13.10.1894
(Polytechnic (SA) (a) 24.9.1892)

A local lad and one of the first Spurs' players to win representative honours, Archie Cubberley played for the local club Asplin Rovers before making his first recorded appearance for Spurs in their opening Southern Alliance match in September 1892. Although he continued to turn out for Asplin Rovers and is only known to have played three matches for Spurs that season, it has not been possible to trace the team details of all Spurs' matches in those days and he almost certainly played many more games.

What is more certain is that, whilst he continued with Asplin Rovers the next season, he was soon Spurs' established inside-right and a great favourite of the crowds flocking to Tottenham Marshes to watch them play. Selected for Middlesex against Kent in November 1894 when only 18, he was being favourably compared to his brother, Stanley, (who played for Cheshunt and spent several years in the Football League with Leeds City) before suffering a bad knee injury in December 1894. Although Archie tried to play again he was forced to retire without reaching the heights his talents deserved. He was, however, still able to appear in junior level football and after being re-instated as an amateur in August 1897 joined Park of the Tottenham Alliance for the following season. He then returned to Asplin Rovers, playing with them, sometimes in goal, till joining Lansdown at the end of the century. During the First War he played two games for Manchester United alongside his brother Stanley.

Appearances:
FA Cup: 5 apps. 1 gl.
Others: 44 apps. 6 gls.
Total: 49 apps. 7 gls.

CUDICINI, Carlo

Role: Goalkeeper 2008-13
6ft.1in. 12st.8lbs.
Born: Milan, Italy, 6th September 1973

CAREER: AC Milan (Italy) Sep 1991/(Como (Italy) loan Sep 1993)/Prato (Italy) Jul 1995/Lazio (Italy) Jul 1996/Castel di Sangro (Italy) Aug 1997/Chelsea loan Aug 1999, perm. Jul 2000/**SPURS** Jan 2009/LA Galaxy (USA) Dec 2012-Jan 2014/Chelsea asst. to first team coach Jul 2016..

Debut v Stoke City (PL) (h) 27.1.2009

While Carlo Cudicini was not to have as celebrated a career as his father, the legendary Fabio Cudicini who played for Udinese, Roma, Brescia and, most notably, AC Milan, Carlo still had a career that anyone would be proud of. He played only two games for AC Milan, albeit in the Champions League, before a year and six outings on loan with Como. Unable to make the breakthrough at Milan, Cudicini was transferred to Prato, where his performances in one season were enough to persuade Lazio to secure his signature. Unfortunately, a wrist injury sustained soon after the move limited his opportunities and after just a year he was allowed to move to Serie B outfit, Castel di Sangro. Injuries continued to hamper his career and it was a considerable surprise when he joined Chelsea on loan in August 1999. Initially nothing more than a reserve, he made only one senior appearance in his first season, but obviously did enough to impress the Chelsea hierarchy for a permanent transfer followed. The fee of just £160,000 was to prove an absolute bargain. Initially standing in for the injured Ed de Goey, Cudicini proved a revelation and for three years looked one of the best 'keepers in the country, international honours only eluding him due to the consistent brilliance of Gianluigi Buffon and Francesco Toldo. When injury struck Cudicini again, Chelsea invested in Petr Čech, leaving Cudicini on the side-lines. It was a position he accepted for five years, until Spurs decided Ben Alnwick was not experienced enough to act as cover for Heurelho Gomes. Signed on a free transfer, Cudicini proved a competent deputy when called upon, but rarely looked more than a reserve. With the arrival of first Brad Friedel and then Hugo Lloris, Cudicini was pushed further down the pecking order until moving to LA Galaxy.

Appearances:
League: 18 (1) apps.
FA Cup: 8* apps.
FL Cup: 2 apps.
Euro: 7 (2) apps.
Others: 13 (5) apps.
Total: 48 (8) apps. 0 gls.
*Includes 1 abandoned match.

CULLEN, Joseph

Role: Goalkeeper 1897-99
5ft.7ins. 12st.0lbs.
Born: Glasgow, 1870
Died: Glasgow, 27th October 1905

CAREER: St Francis' School/Stanley Swifts/Junior Hawthorn/Benburb/Celtic Jan 1892/**SPURS** May 1897/Lincoln City Sep 1899/Luton Town/retired Jan 1900.

Debut v Sheppey United (SL) (a) 4.9.1897
(Glossop North End (Fr) (h) 2.9.1897)

During several years with Celtic, Joe Cullen helped them win the Scottish Cup for the first time (1892) and represented the Scottish League against the Irish League (January 1894). Signed by Spurs after their first season in the Southern League, he was the regular custodian throughout his two years at Northumberland Park. He was not the tallest of players, but he was reliable, consistent and rarely absent from the team. Unlucky not to collect any major representative honours in his time with Spurs, he did play for the United League against the Thames and Medway League on his home ground in November 1898. Released in May 1899, Cullen moved to Lincoln City, but played there for less than a year. He reportedly signed for Luton, but failed to make any appearances for them before retiring. He returned to Glasgow and died suddenly from pneumonia only days after watching Celtic train.

Appearances:
Southern: 43 apps.
FA Cup: 12 apps.
Others: 70 apps.
Total: 125 apps. 0 gls.

CULVERHOUSE, David Paul

Role: Defender 1993-94
6ft.0ins. 11st.6lbs.
Born: Harlow, Essex, 9th September 1973

CAREER: SPURS trainee cs. 1990, pro Jul 1992/Dagenham and Redbridge Aug 1994/(Oldham Athletic trial during 1994-95)/Aveley Jun 1999/Billericay Town Oct 1999/Braintree Town Feb 2001/Heybridge Swifts Jul 2002/Braintree Town Feb 2003, joint caretaker manager Nov 2003, manager Dec 2003-Mar 2004.

Debut v Team Nord-Trøndelag (sub) (Fr) (Steinjker) 23.7.1993

A talented youngster who had worked his way through the junior ranks, David Culverhouse, like his brother Ian, was a competent if not spectacular defender who got to the fringes of the senior team. His only appearances came during the pre-season tour of Norway in 1993 when he appeared in two matches. Unable to challenge the likes of Dean Austin, Justin Edinburgh, David Kerslake and Sol Campbell, he was released in the summer of 1994 and moved to Dagenham & Redbridge, later playing for several of Essex's senior non-League clubs. After a short spell in management with Braintree Town, Culverhouse embarked on a career as a chiropodist.

Appearances:
Others: 1 (1) apps.
Total: 1 (1) apps. 0 gls.

CULVERHOUSE, Ian Brett

Role: Defender 1982-86
5ft.10ins. 11st.2lbs.
Born: Bishops Stortford, Hertfordshire, 22nd September 1964

CAREER: Harlow Schools/Hoddesdon United/Southampton jun./ SPURS app. May 1981, pro. Sep 1982/Norwich City Oct 1985/Swindon Town loan and perm Dec 1994/Stevenage Borough trial Jul 1998/ Kingstonians trial Jul 1998/Brighton & Hove Albion Aug 1998, reserve team coach Feb 1999/Barnet youth team coach Aug 2000, asst. manager to Jan 2002/St Albans City Jan 2001/Leyton Orient youth team coach Jan 2002, asst. manager to May 2005/Wycombe Wanderers youth team coach Jul 2005, first team coach Jul 2007/Colchester United asst. manager Oct 2008/Norwich City asst. manager Aug 2009/Aston Villa asst. manager Jul 2012-May 2014/Dagenham & Redbridge asst. manager Jan 2016.

Debut v Notts County (sub) (FL) (a) 21.2.1984
(Israeli Select XI (sub) (Fr) (a) 22.12.1982)

After a brief association as a junior with Southampton, Ian Culverhouse joined Spurs. He played for England youth and was rated highly as a potential first team centre-half, making several first team appearances in friendly matches. However, he managed just two League appearances, the first as a substitute, the second in May 1984 when Spurs fielded practically a complete reserve team at Southampton prior to the first leg of the UEFA Cup Final against Anderlecht. With opportunities at White Hart Lane severely limited, Culverhouse moved to Norwich City in October 1985 for just £50,000, but soon established himself as a more than competent performer for the Norfolk club. A stylish player with good distribution skills, he performed reliably at full-back, central defence or sweeper. He gave Norwich almost ten years' great service before moving to Swindon Town where he played for four years. Released by Swindon, Culverhouse looked set to continue his career in non-League football but struggling Brighton were desperate for an experienced defender and persuaded him to play for them for two years, while also coaching their reserve side. With his playing days over Culverhouse turned to coaching with Barnet, Leyton Orient and Wycombe Wanderers. At Colchester United he linked up as assistant manager with Paul Lambert and followed the Scot to Norwich City and Aston Villa. In April 2014, Culverhouse was suspended by Villa following claims of bullying and aggressiveness. He was sacked a month later and out of the game for almost two years, until joining Dagenham & Redbridge. As a schoolboy Culverhouse played for Harlow schools at rugby and had a trial for the Essex County team at the oval ball game.

His brother David was a Spurs trainee who failed to make the grade at White Hart Lane but played for several years in senior non-League circles.

Appearances:
League: 1 (1) apps.
Others: 5 (8) apps.
Total: 6 (9) apps.

CUNDY, Jason Victor

Role: Central defender 1991-97
6ft.1ins. 13st.10lbs.
Born: Wimbledon, London, 12th November 1969

CAREER: Chelsea trainee Apr 1986, pro. Aug 1988/SPURS loan Mar 1992, perm. Jun 1992/(Crystal Palace loan Dec 1995)/(Bristol City loan Aug 1996)/Ipswich Town loan Oct 1996, perm. Nov 1996/Portsmouth Jun 1999/retired Dec 2000/Chelsea Academy coach.

Debut v Coventry City (FL) (h) 28.3.1992

A fast, strong and steely central defender with a promising career in front of him, Jason Cundy was signed by Spurs in March 1992 on loan from Chelsea with a view to a permanent move at the end of the season. Spurs' well documented financial problems prevented them from making the signing permanent at the time, but at least the loan period gave both the club and player the chance to see if they were suited. Cundy had made his League debut for Chelsea in September 1990 and within weeks won his first England Under-21 cap against the Republic of Ireland, adding a second in March 1991. Spurs were sufficiently impressed with what they saw to sign Cundy on a permanent basis in the summer of 1992 for a £700,000 fee. With the more experienced Gary Mabbutt  or Neil Ruddock alongside him, Cundy could have gone on to prove a sound acquisition for Spurs, but continual injury problems severely restricted his appearances. In November 1996 he was allowed to move to Ipswich Town for £200,000 plus another £50,000 after 30 appearances and another £50,000 if Ipswich were promoted at the end of the season. The additional fee was not paid. but Cundy remained with Ipswich for almost three years before his release in May 1999. He moved to Portsmouth, but further injuries meant he played only nine League games before retiring in December 2000 and taking up a coaching post with Chelsea's Academy.

Appearances:
League: 23 (3) apps. 1 gl.
FL Cup: 2 apps.
Others: 17 (7) apps. 2 gls.
Total: 42 (10) apps. 3 gls.

CURRIE, Anthony William

Role: Midfield 1980-81
5ft.11ins. 12st.9lbs.
Born: Edgware, Middlesex, 1st January 1950

CAREER: Whitefield Secondary Modern School/Hendon Schools/ Chelsea assoc. schl./Queens Park Rangers assoc. schl./Watford app. Feb 1966, pro. May 1967/Sheffield United Feb 1968/Leeds United Jun 1976/

(SPURS guest May 1981)/Queens Park Rangers Aug 1979/Toronto Nationals (Canada) May 1983-Jun 1983/Chesham United Aug 1983/Southend United non-contract Sep 1983/Chesham United Nov 1983/Torquay United non-contract Mar 1984/Tranmere Rovers Oct 1984/Dunstable Town 1985/Hendon 1986/Goole Town player-coach Sep 1987/Sheffield United admin Feb 1988, Club Ambassador Feb 2008.

Debut v West Ham United (sub) (Fr) (h) 11.5.1981

England international Tony Currie made his only appearance for Spurs as a guest in Barry Daines' Testimonial match against West Ham United in May 1981, going on as a substitute in a match that was played between the FA Cup Final and Replay. A highly gifted player, he never won the honours his talent deserved in an age when work-rate seemed more important than ability. Starting out with Watford, he won England Youth honours and had nine goals in only 18 League games to his credit before being transferred to Sheffield United. His First Division debut was in February 1968 when he scored United's second goal in a 3-2 win over Spurs. He won further England Youth honours, 13 Under-23 caps, seven full caps, the first of them in May 1972 against Northern Ireland, and made three appearances for the Football League in his time at Bramall Lane. Transferred to Leeds United, he added a further ten caps to his collection before returning South to join Queens Park Rangers. Currie played for Rangers in the 1982 FA Cup Final against Spurs, giving away

the penalty converted by Glenn Hoddle which won the replay. Troubled by injury, Currie left Rangers at the end of the 1982-83 season, played for the Canadian club Toronto Nationals for two months and then joined Chesham United, although he also played for Southend United and Torquay United as a non-contract player. He then signed for Tranmere Rovers, but was clearly not up to the demands of League football. After assisting Dunstable, Hendon and Goole Town he joined the administrative staff of Sheffield United.

Appearances:
Others: (1) app.
Total: **(1) app. 0 gls.**

CURTIS, John Joseph

Role: Outside-right 1908-13
5ft.6ins. 11st.0lbs.
Born: Southbank, 13th December 1888
Died: Wimbledon, London, Jan qtr. 1955

CAREER: Eston United/Seaham White Star/Southbank St Peters/Grangetown/South Bank/Sunderland Dec 1906/South Bank Apr 1907/Shildon Athletic Dec 1907/Gainsborough Trinity May 1908/**SPURS** Apr 1909/Fulham May 1913/Brentford Jun 1914/Stockport County Jan 1915/Middlesbrough Aug 1919/Darlington 1919/Shildon Athletic Oct 1920/coach in Holland inc. Leeuwarden and Haarlem 1927-40.

Debut v Bradford Park Avenue (FL) (a) 24.4.1909 (scored once)

Jack Curtis was signed from Gainsborough Trinity to help give Spurs the final push needed to secure promotion to the First Division at the first attempt. A nippy little winger, standing only 5ft 6ins tall, he had been in senior football less than a year, having played at junior level in his native North-East and briefly been associated with Sunderland. His impact at Spurs was instant, for he scored on his debut and was soon regarded as an outstanding prospect, playing in the international trial match at Anfield in January 1910. Unfortunately, such hopeful signs were not maintained and, troubled by injuries, he was unable to compete for the right wing position against first, John McTavish and then, Walter Tattersall. In the summer of 1913 he moved across London to Fulham, but made only two League appearances before joining Brentford. A regular for Brentford in his first two seasons, the War saw Brentford offer all their players a free transfer and Curtis was the first to accept, moving to Stockport County. In 1919, he transferred to Middlesbrough for one season before being released to return to Shildon. Curtis later worked as a coach in Holland. He married the daughter of Mr WF Gilboy, landlord of the White Hart pub outside the main entrance to White Hart Lane.

Appearances:
League: 84* apps. 5 gls.
FA Cup: 7 apps.
Others: 24 apps. 7 gls.
Total: **115 apps. 12 gls.**
* Includes 2 abandoned match

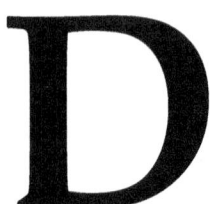

D

DAINES, Barry Raymond

Role: Goalkeeper 1971-81
6ft.0ins. 11st.8lbs.
Born: Witham, Essex, 30th September 1951

CAREER: Chelmsford Schools/Mid-Essex Schools/Essex Schools/SPURS app. Jul 1968, pro. Sep 1969/Bulova (Hong Kong) Sep 1981/Mansfield Town non-contract Oct 1983/Chelmsford City Jul 1984.

Debut v West Bromwich Albion (FL) (h) 20.11.1971

When Barry Daines-who as a schoolboy trained with West Ham United-first joined Spurs, Pat Jennings was at his peak and Daines had to show considerable patience before establishing himself as the big Irishman's successor. An England Youth cap, Daines made his debut in November 1971, but although he proved a capable deputy whenever called upon, he made only 13 senior appearances in his first five seasons, due to the consistent brilliance of Jennings. In the grim 1976-77 relegation season Jennings was injured and Daines had an extended run in the team, making such progress that at the end of the season manager Keith Burkinshaw decided Daines had more of a long-term future than Jennings. The popular Jennings was sold to Arsenal, leaving Daines as first choice. Ever-present in the promotion season that followed, Daines was a competent 'keeper, not flashy or spectacular or one who grabbed the headlines, but a player who simply got on with his job. In 1978-79 Spurs struggled back in the First Division and Daines came under increasing pressure from the home-grown Mark Kendall and the imported Milija Aleksic. Helped indirectly by injuries to the unlucky Aleksic, Daines seemed to have won the battle and was still the regular choice in 1980-81 until injured himself. That let Aleksic back in and Daines missed out on the 1981 FA Cup Final after playing in the early rounds. The arrival of Ray Clemence in August 1981 left Daines right out in the cold. He moved to Hong Kong to play for the Bulova club and on his return appeared for Mansfield Town as a non-contract player.

Appearances:
League: 146 apps.
FA Cup: 11 apps.
FL Cup: 14 apps.
Euro: 2 apps.
Others: 51 (11) apps.
Total: **224 (11) apps. 0 gls.**

DALGLISH, Kenneth Mathieson

Role: Striker 1987-88 and 1990-91
5ft.8ins. 12st.3lbs.
Born: Dalmarnock, Glasgow, 14th March 1951

CAREER: Glasgow Schools/Scotland Schools/Drumchapel Amateurs/Glasgow United/Possilpark YMCA 1962/Celtic prov. May 1967, pro. Apr 1968/(Cumbernauld United loan Jul 1967)/Liverpool Aug 1977, player-manager May 1985/retired Feb 1991/Blackburn Rovers manager Oct 1991, Director of Football Jun 1995-Aug 1996/Newcastle United manager Jan 1997-Aug 1998/Celtic Director of Football Operations Jun 1999-Jun 2000/Liverpool caretaker manager Jan 2011, manager May 2011-May 2012, non-exec director Oct 2013.

Debut v Manchester United (Fr) (h) 28.3.1988

Arguably the greatest player to have come out of Scotland, Kenny Dalglish played for Scotland at Youth level and was soon in the Celtic first team showing skills that were to be admired by football fans throughout the world. He helped Celtic win the Scottish League in 1972, 1973, 1974 and 1977, the Scottish Cup in 1972, 1974, 1975 and 1977, the Scottish League Cup in 1975 and reach the final of the Scottish Cup in 1973 and Scottish League Cup in 1972, 1973, 1974 and 1977. By August 1977 he had collected 47 full Scottish caps, the first as a substitute against Belgium in November 1971, and four at Under-23 level. He had won all the honours Scottish football could offer; all that was missing was a European title. He put that right within twelve months. Transferred to Liverpool with the formidable task of replacing Kevin Keegan, he surpassed all expectations. In his first season he helped Liverpool reach the final of the European Champions Cup and then scored the only goal of the game against FC Bruges at Wembley. In the next seven years Liverpool, with Dalglish at the forefront, dominated English and European football winning the Football League in 1979, 1980, 1982, 1983 and 1984, the European Champions Cup in 1981 and 1984 and the Football League Cup in 1981, 1982, 1983 and 1984. After the European Cup Final defeat in 1985 Joe Fagan resigned as Liverpool manager. Instead of promoting from the backroom staff as Liverpool usually did, they surprised the football world by making Dalglish player-manager. In his first season in the role he led Liverpool to the Football League and FA Cup "Double", a feat that had proved beyond the talents of even Bill Shankly, Bob Paisley and Joe Fagan-and they were managers only, they did not need to worry about playing. Voted Footballer of the Year by the Football Writers' Association in 1978-79 and 1982-83 and by the Professional Footballers' Association in 1983, Dalglish, who was awarded the MBE in 1985, effectively retired from playing at the end of the 1986-87 season. Holder of a record 100 full caps for Scotland and joint top scorer with Denis Law of 30 goals for his country, Dalglish is one of only two players to score over 100 League goals in both English and Scottish football. As manager, he kept Liverpool at the pinnacle of British football, leading them to the Football League championship in 1988 and 1990 and the FA Cup in 1989, and was voted Manager of the Year in 1986, 1988 and 1990. In February 1991 he shocked the football world when he retired, giving "pressure" as the reason for the totally unexpected announcement. In October 1991 he was persuaded to return to football taking over as manager of ambitious Blackburn Rovers and leading them from the Second Division to the pinnacle of Premier League champions in 1995. Again citing "pressure" as the problem, Dalglish moved up to become director of football, but clearly did not enjoy the job and resigned in August 1996. He was tempted back into management early in 1997 when he replaced Kevin Keegan as manager of Newcastle, but left under acrimonious circumstances early in the 1998-99 season. Having fronted a consortium bidding to take over Celtic, Dalglish returned to his old club as Director of Football Operations and was responsible for giving his former Liverpool colleague John Barnes his first chance in management. Unable to challenge Rangers' superiority in Scotland, Barnes was sacked and Dalglish followed soon after. In January 2011 he returned to Anfield as caretaker manager following the dismissal of Roy Hodgson, with the appointment being made permanent four months later. Although Liverpool added the Carling Cup to their list of honours and reached the FA Cup final, failure to qualify for the Champions League for the third season in succession was seen as too great a failure and Dalglish was dismissed again. Dalglish made two appearances for Spurs, the first in Danny Thomas' Benefit match with Manchester United on 28th March 1988 and the second in Ray Clemence's Benefit match with West Ham United on 17th August 1990.

Appearances:
Others: 2 apps.
Total: 2 apps. 0 gls.

DALMAT, Stéphane

Role: Midfield 2003-04
5ft.11ins. 12st.0lbs.
Born: Jouè-les-Tours, France, 16th February 1979

CAREER: Berrichonne de Châteauroux (France) 1996/RC Lens (France) Jul 1998/Olympique Marseille (France) Jul 1999/Paris St German (France) May 2000/Internazionale (Italy) Jan 2001/**SPURS** loan Sep 2003-Apr 2004)/(Toulouse (France) loan Jun 2004)/Racing Santander (Spain) Jul 2005/Girondins de Bordeaux (France) Aug 2006/Sochaux-Montbeliard (France) Jun 2007/Rennes (France) Jul 2010/Nîmes Olympique (France) Jul 2012/retired Jul 2012.

Debut v Chelsea (sub) (PL) (a) 13.9.2003

Stéphane Dalmat was a very talented midfielder who should have gone on to reach greater heights than he eventually achieved. Starting out with the amateur section of Châteauroux, he quickly progressed through Lens and Marseille to Paris St Germain, picking up French Under-21 caps along the way. After only six months in the French capital, and having fallen out with the coach, Dalmat was on his way to Inter Milan. He was expected to prove a gem in the Italian's midfield, but failed to establish himself, unable to take control of games and too often finding himself on the bench. With Spurs desperate for a left-sided player who could replace the injured Christian Ziege, Dalmat seemed tailor made and was signed on what was meant to be a year's loan. With pace, ball control and dribbling ability, there were times when he looked just what Spurs needed, but on other occasions he seemed uninterested and just going through the motions. He definitely had the ability and it was frustrating that he seemed unable to apply himself. In April 2004 Dalmat was involved in a training ground incident with young

Jamie O'Hara. He was told to pack his bags and return to Italy. Dalmat was now surplus to requirements at the San Siro and soon out on a season's loan with Toulouse. A full transfer to Racing Santander, where he played alongside his brother, Wilfred, followed, but Dalmat failed to impress and was soon on his travels again. In July 2012, only days after signing for Nimes Olympique, he announced he was no longer able take the strain of training and retired.

Appearances:
League: 12 (10) apps. 3 gls.
FA Cup: 2 (1) apps.
FL Cup: 1 (2) apps.
Total: 15 (13) apps. 3 gls.

DANIELS, Charlie John

Role: Defender 2007-08
5ft.10ins. 13st.4lbs.
Born: Harlow, Essex, 7th September 1986

CAREER: Highams Park School/Ridgeway Rovers/**SPURS** Academy Scholar Jul 2003, pro. Jul 2005/(Chesterfield loan Mar 2007)/(Leyton Orient loan Aug 2007)/Millwall trial Jul 2008/(Gillingham loan Aug 2008) /Leyton Orient Jan 2009/AFC Bournemouth loan Nov 2011, perm Jan 2012.

Debut v Stevenage Borough (Fr) (a) 7.7.2007

Another of the many youngsters that came through the ranks at Spurs, but never quite made it, Charlie Daniels was a busy little player equally at home on the left of midfield or at full-back. After a couple of years with Spurs and a loan to Chesterfield, he played in two of the 2007-08 pre-season games, but that was as far as he got with Spurs. Loaned to Leyton Orient and Gillingham, Daniels moved to Brisbane Road in January 2009. He proved a consistent performer over the next two years or so and when offered the chance to make a move up to Bournemouth, the fee was reported to be £200,000. He was a regular performer as the Dorset club won promotion to the top flight of English football in 2015 and one of the star performers as the Premier League newcomers fought to retain their place.

Appearances:
Others: 1 (1) apps.
Total: 1 (1) apps. 0 gls.

DARCY, Ross

Role: Defender 1998-99
6ft.0ins. 12st.2lbs.
Born: Ballybriggin, County Dublin, 21st March 1978

CAREER: Glebe North/Stella Maris/Republic of Ireland schools/**SPURS** trainee Jul 1994. pro. Jul 1995/Barnet Dec 1999/(Dover Athletic loan Nov 2000)/Dundalk (Eire) Jul 2002-Jun 2003/retired Jan 2004.

Debut v Peterborough United (Fr) (a) 15.7.1998

A cultured central defender, Ross Darcy joined Spurs as a 16-year-old having been spotted at the well-known Irish youth side, Stella Maris. Taken on the professional staff, he worked his way through the youth

THE SPURS ALPHABET

and reserve teams, collecting Irish Under-21 honours on the way, but made only two first team appearances in pre-season matches in 1998. Just as he seemed ready to make the breakthrough, a cruciate ligament injury brought this career to a shuddering halt. On his return, another injury set him back again. Struggling to recover his earlier promise, he was released and joined Barnet. Further injuries badly afflicted Darcy at Underhill and in February 2002 his contract was paid up as he had decided to retire. On his return home to Ireland he joined Dundalk, where he played for 18 months before finally succumbing to his injuries.

Appearances:
Others: 2 apps.
Total: 2 apps. 0 gls.

DARNELL, Jabez

Role: Half-back 1905-19
5ft.5ins. 10st.7lbs.
Born: *Potton, Bedfordshire, 28th March 1884*
Died: *Edmonton, London, December 1950*

CAREER: Northampton Town/**SPURS** am. Aug 1903/Potton/Biggleswade/**SPURS** pro. Oct 1904, asst. trainer cs. 1919/retired 1946.

Debut v Queens Park Rangers (WL) (a) 11.9.05

Renowned for the strength of his terrier-tackling and a never-say-die attitude which often secured victory when defeat seemed more likely, Jabez Darnell gave Spurs over 40 years' loyal service, 15 of them as a player. Although he made his debut in September 1905, Spurs had an abundance of strong wing-halves and the swarthy Darnell had to be content with a place in the reserves for his first two or three seasons. He eventually took over the left-half position from Ted Hughes and missed only one game in Spurs' first Football League season of 1908-09. For the next three years he held down a regular place, but then slipped back into the reserves where his experience proved invaluable in the development of younger players. With the calls of war taking their toll in 1914-15 and Spurs struggling against relegation, Darnell was recalled towards the end of the season, but was unable to prevent Spurs finishing bottom of the table. Well past his best, he continued to assist the club during the war years and only retired from playing when normal football resumed in 1919-20. He then took up the post of assistant trainer, a position he held until his retirement in 1946. In the late 1920s Darnell's son played a few games for Spurs' reserves.

Appearances:
Southern: 34 apps. 1 gl.
League: 153* apps. 3 gls.
FA Cup: 11 apps.
Others: 125 apps. 1 gl.
Total: 323 apps. 5 gls.
* Includes 3 abandoned matches.

DAVENPORT, Calum Raymond Paul

Role: Central Defender 2004-07
6ft.4ins. 14st 0lbs.
Born: *Bedford, Bedfordshire, 1st January 1983*

CAREER: Coventry City/**SPURS** Aug 2004/((West Ham United loan Sep 2004)/(Southampton loan Jan 2005)/(Norwich City loan Sep 2005)/West Ham United Jan 2007-Mar 2010(Watford loan Jan 2008)/(Sunderland loan Feb 2009)/Nottingham Forest training Aug 2010/Leeds United trial Aug 2010/Wootton Blue Cross Sep 2010, first team coach Nov 2010/Northampton Town trial Dec 2012/Elstow Abbey to Mar 2015.

Debut v Aston Villa (sub) (PL) (a) 22.11.2004

Rated one of the most promising young central defenders outside the Premier League, Calum Davenport was among the flood of players signed following the arrival of Frank Arnesen as Director of Football and Jacques Santini as Head Coach in the summer of 2004, but within days of his arrival he was loaned out to West Ham United. He made his Spurs' debut as a substitute at Aston Villa shortly after his return, but the New Year saw him playing the Loan Ranger again with a move to Southampton. While he was performing well enough to collect England Under-21 honours, as his second season as a Spurs player got underway he was on loan once more, Norwich City the club to benefit from his services. It was only during the 2006-07 season that Davenport got anything like a regular starting berth with Spurs, but even then it was only while Ledley King was out with injury. With Michael Dawson establishing himself as first choice at the centre of defence, Davenport was left to compete with King and Anthony Gardner for the other central defensive role. Apart from King, the others were young and inexperienced so, with Ricardo Rocha lined up as his replacement, Spurs decided to let Davenport leave when West Ham made a good offer. Davenport struggled to make his mark at Upton Park, but it was an incident off the pitch that finished his top flight career. He was stabbed in the legs in an incident that saw him lose half the blood in his body, undergo emergency surgery and then find himself charged with assaulting his sister. The injury and subsequent court case put his career on hold, and his contract with West Ham terminated. When he recovered his basic fitness, there was interest in him from League clubs. He choose to join Wootton Blue Cross of the United Counties League, ostensibly to recover full fitness before a return to the professional game, but remained in non-League football until March 2015. He was then charged with assault following an altercation with a team-mate while playing for Elstow Abbey in the Bedfordshire County Football League.

Appearances:
League: 9 (6) apps. 1 gl.
FA Cup: 1 app.
FL Cup: 2 apps.
Euro: 1 (1) apps.
Others: 8 (1) apps.
Total: 21 (8) apps. 1 gl.

DAVIDS, Edgar Steven

Role: Midfield 2005-07
5ft.6ins. 11st. 5lbs.
Born: Paramaribo, Surinam, 13th March 1973

CAREER: Schellingwoude (Holland)/Ajax (Holland) 1991/AC Milan (Italy) Jul 1996/Juventus (Italy) Dec 1997/(Barcelona (Spain) loan Jan 2004)/Internazionale (Italy) Jul 2004/**SPURS** Aug 2005/Ajax (Holland) Jan 2007-Jun 2009/Crystal Palace Aug-Nov 2010/Brixton United manager/ Ajax (Holland) Supervisory Board Jun 2011/Barnet player-joint manager Oct 2012, player-manager Dec 2012-Jan 2014.

Debut v Middlesbrough (PL) (h) 20.8.2005

One of Europe's most lauded midfielders, Edgar Davids had won just about everything that matters in a career that had seen him play for some of the most famous clubs in the game, before joining Spurs for eighteen months. Starting out with the famed Ajax academy, he helped them win the UEFA Cup in 1992, three League titles in 1994, 1995 and 1996 and the Champions League in 1995. With his biting tackles and continual hustling of opponents, he well merited the nickname of "Pitbull" given him by his manager, Louis van Gaal. It was a nickname he retained for the rest of his career. Having won all he could in Holland and established himself as a regular on the international scene, Davids took his talents to AC Milan and Italy, but his non-stop tackling and ethos of hard work was not suited to the more languid Milanese style and he struggled to make an impact. He moved on to Juventus, where he became the midfield general of "The Old Lady", helping them take the Italian title in 1998. A forthright character with immense belief in his own ability, he was never afraid to espouse his views. Sent home from Euro 96 for criticising manager, Guus Hiddink, he often fell out with his Juve coaches and was not slow to make his displeasure known, but his value was never doubted as evidenced by the way Juve stuck by him when he was found guilty in May 2001 of using the banned anabolic steroid nandrolone. Originally banned for eight months, two appeals saw the penalty reduced to three. Davids still suffered from the fall-out and at times looked to be on his way out of Juventus, but he showed the same battling qualities off the pitch as on it, and helped Juventus collect two more Italian titles in 2002 and 2003. It was another six months before Juventus decided Davids was surplus to requirements and in January 2004 he was loaned out to a struggling Barcelona, his mere presence galvanising the Catalan club and helping turn around their season. Wanted by Barcelona on a permanent basis, Davids secured his release from Juventus, but instead of moving to Spain he returned to Milan with Internazionale. The move was not a success. Davids rarely featured and, as was his way, made his unhappiness known. Spurs' manager, Martin Jol, was keen to secure an experienced and respected midfielder and Davids fitted the bill perfectly. For a year Davids performed the role Jol demanded, cajoling and bullying his younger team-mates and leading by example, but he was now into the veteran stage, and as the season wore on his performances suffered. Unable to make much of an impression in the early part of 2006-07 Spurs allowed Davids to return to Ajax in January 2007. He almost spurred his old club to another Dutch title, as they missed out by just one point. Despite a broken leg sustained in pre-season 2007, Davids gave Ajax another two years good service before, apparently, bringing his playing career to an end. It was not over though. After more than a year out of the game he suddenly returned to London signing for Crystal Palace. He stayed with Palace for three months, but remained much longer in London, settling in the capital and managing Sunday League side, Brixton United. In October 2012 Davids suddenly returned to playing when he joined Barnet as player-manager, working alongside Mark Robson. He took sole control two months later, but was unable to save Barnet from dropping out of the League. With Barnet in contention for a quick return, Davids resigned in January 2014, feeling he had become a target for referees.

Appearances:
League: 34 (6) apps. 1 gl.
FA Cup: 2 (1) apps.
FL Cup: (1) app.
Others: 5 (1) apps.
Total: 41 (9) apps. 1 gl.

DAVIDSON, James Wilkie

Role: Inside-forward 1897-98
5ft.7ins. 11st.0lbs.
Born: Edinburgh, 25th October 1873

CAREER: Leith Athletic/St Bernards/Celtic 1892/Burnley Jul 1895/ (Lincoln City loan Mar 1897)/**SPURS** May 1897/Brighton United May 1898/Burnley Apr 1900-1902.

Debut v Sheppey United (SL) (a) 4.9.1897

Signed in May 1897, "Tooty" Davidson had played regularly for Burnley in 1895-96 but, although still on their books, had spent the end of the 1896-97 season on loan to Lincoln, helping them win the Lincolnshire Cup. He made his debut for Spurs in the opening Southern League fixture of the season but, whilst he played in most of the matches that season in both the Southern and United Leagues, he was not retained when the season ended. He joined the new professional club Brighton United during the ensuing close season and played on the South Coast for two years before returning to Burnley, where he was a regular for the next two years.

Appearances:
Southern: 17 apps. 5 gls.
Others: 29 apps. 10 gls.
Total: 46 apps. 15 gls.

DAVIE, John

Role: Centre-forward 1943-44
5ft.9ins. 11st.4lbs.
Born: Dunfermline, Fife, 19th February 1913
Died: Shrewsbury, Shropshire, June 1994

CAREER: St Bernards/St Johnstone/Dunfermline Wednesday/Hibernian Apr 1934/Dundee trial/Torquay United trial/Arsenal am./Margate Nov 1935/Brighton and Hove Albion May 1936/(guest for Aldershot, Brentford, Charlton Athletic, Chesterfield, Clapton Orient, Crystal

Palace, Fulham, Leeds United, Manchester United, Mansfield Town, Millwall, Nottingham Forest, Notts County, Portsmouth, Queens Park Rangers, Reading, Southampton, Sunderland and **SPURS** during World War Two)/Stockton Aug 1946/Barnsley Dec 1946/Kiddermnister Harriers /Shrewsbury Town.

Debut v Reading (FLS) (h) 5.2.1944

A Brighton and Hove Albion player, Davie made his only appearance for Spurs as a guest in a Football League South fixture in 5th February 1944. A regular goal-scoring centre-forward, he was one of the most popular guest players of the War, turning out for numerous clubs, Davie had

started out in Scotland, before signing as an amateur for Arsenal and being placed at their Kent nursery club, Margate. After less than a season in Kent, Davie accepted Brighton's offer of professional terms and immediately transferred his goal-scoring talents to the bigger. Like so many players, just when he should have been at the peak of his powers, the War intervened and his best years were lost. As Brighton sought to rebuild after the War, Davie was released. He played for a couple of more years before retiring.

Appearances:
Others: 1 app.
Total: 1 app. 0 gls.

DAVIES, Benjamin Thomas

Role: Full-back 2014-
5ft.10ins. 12st.4lbs.
Born: Neath, West Glamorgan, 24th April 1993

CAREER: Swansea City/FF Viborg (Denmark) 2001/Swansea City Academy Scholar Jul 2009, pro Jul 2011/**SPURS** Jul 2014.

Debut v AEL Limassol (EL) (a) 21.8.2014
(Toronto (Fr) (a) 23.7.2014)

When his father's work commitments dictated the family should move

to Denmark, 8-year old Ben Davies had to leave the Swansea City Academy. He found a new football school at Viborg and for eighteen months sharpened his talents in a somewhat more relaxed atmosphere where technical skills were always to the fore. After 18 months the family returned to Wales and Davies to the Swansea Academy. Eight years later Davies was on the professional staff, pushing for a place in the starting line-up as Swansea consolidated their place in the Premier League. Davies got his chance early in the 2012-13 season and grasped it

immediately. Within no time he was first choice, displacing Neil Taylor and fitting smoothly into the sweet passing style manager Brian Laudrup insisted on. Within weeks of his Premier League debut, Davies was in the Welsh team, making his debut against Scotland in a World Cup qualifier. While Davies had quickly won the battle for the left-back slot with Taylor at club level, he found it rather more difficult to do so in the national team, but by the time of his move to Spurs he was the regular number three. Davies arrived at Spurs with Michel Vorm, former Swansea midfielder Gylfi Sigurðsson returning to the Liberty Stadium as part of the deal. At Spurs, Danny Rose had just about made the left-back position his own. The arrival of Davies put pressure on Rose to perform consistently at his best, while Davies knew he would have to do likewise if he was to become a regular. Over two years the battle between them has been quite absorbing, debate as to who deserves the starting place, never-ending. Rose is the more aggressive, his former winger tendencies seeing him looking to attack at all times. Davies is the better defender, his positional sense first class and his concentration rarely lapsing. He defends first, but when the opportunity is there to attack, he is no slouch at doing so. Pacy and strong, he looks to progress through quick, one-touch passing, beating his opponent before finishing with a sharp, accurate cross. With modern football demanding two players for every position, Spurs are lucky to have two such fine left-backs.

Appearances:
League: 41 (13) apps. 1 gl.
FA Cup: 8 apps. 1 gl.
FL Cup: 6 apps.
Euro: 22 apps.
Others: 5 (3) apps.
Total: 82 (16) apps. 2 gls.

DAVIES, R O

Debut v Iona (Fr) (h) 12.10.1899

Nothing is known about this player whose only appearances for Spurs were in friendly matches in 1889-90. The first saw Spurs won 10-0.

Appearances:
Others: 2 apps.
Total: 2 apps. 0 gls.

DAVIES, Simon

Role: Midfield 1999-2005
5ft.10ins. 12st.4lbs.
Born: Haverfordwest, Pembrokeshire, 23rd October 1979

CAREER: Pembroke Schools/Pembroke County Schools/Solva AFC/ Wrexham/Norwich City assoc. schl./Peterborough United trainee Jul 1996, pro. Jul 1997/Manchester United training Jul 1999/**SPURS** Jan 2000/ Everton May 2005/Fulham Jan 2007-May 2013/Solva AFC Aug 2013 and Sep 2014.

Debut v Liverpool (sub) (PL) (a) 9.4.2000

Simon Davies and Matthew Etherington were regarded as players for the future when signed from Peterborough United in a double deal in January 2000. They had been drawing the scouts to London Road for a while, with Manchester United even inviting the pair to Old Trafford for pre-season training. Alex Ferguson was said to be keen on signing them, but while he delayed, Spurs Director of Football, David Pleat, moved to bring them to White Hart Lane. Pleat had been charged with rebuilding a Spurs youth set-up that was failing to bring through home-produced youngsters. He spent £1.3m of his budget on signing the pair, the slightly larger part attributed to Davies who was viewed as the more developed of the two. A midfielder with guile and strength, the move to top level football soon saw him in the Wales team, his first cap coming against the Ukraine in March 2001. He found it easier to become a regular for his country than for Spurs, as it took him a couple of years to make a place

in the starting eleven his own. Davies was a perfect example of the type of wide midfielder demanded by most clubs. He had a fair amount of pace and was not afraid to take his opponent on. Often cutting in from out wide, he had an eye for the through ball, was capable of finishing off a move himself and prepared to defend when circumstances demanded. While the solid, consistent type of player you could depend upon, there were occasions when he could be quite brilliant, but too often he was predictable and could be shut out of a game. With the explosive Aaron Lennon on Spurs' radar, Davies was allowed to move to Everton in a £3.5 million deal in May 2005. Less than two years later he was back in London with Fulham. For five years he gave Fulham great service with one consistent display after another on the right flank, scoring Fulham's goal in the 2010 Europa League final against Atletico Madrid. Sadly injury then struck and after two years of trying to battle back to fitness, Davies had to concede defeat. Released by Fulham and without another club, he turned out for his old team Solva, his brother, Chris, keeping goal for the Welsh village outfit. Davies uncle is Ian Evans, the former Crystal Palace and Wales striker.

Appearances:
League: 99 (22) apps. 13 gls.
FA Cup: 10 (3) apps. 2 gls.
FL Cup: 10 (3) apps. 3 gls.
Others: 17 (12) apps. 4 gls.
Total: 136 (40) apps. 22 gls.

DAVIES, William

Role: Outside-right 1929-33
5ft.10ins. 10st.10lbs.
Born: *Troedrhiwfuwch, nr. Bargoed, Glamorgan, 16th February 1900*
Died: *Llansadwrn, Carmarthenshire, 22nd August 1953*

CAREER: Troedrhiwfuwch/Rhymney/Swansea Amateurs cs. 1920/Swansea Town pro. May 1921/Cardiff City Jun 1924/Notts County Mar 1928/**SPURS** Feb 1930/Swansea Town Sep 1933/Llanelli player-coach Apr 1936-1938.

Debut v Oldham Athletic (FL) (h) 15.2.1930

A Welsh international with 17 caps to his credit when signed by Spurs, Willie Davies played for Swansea in all the forward positions before settling down at outside-right. Signed for ten shillings and sixpence (52p), he collected the first of his three caps as a Swansea player against Scotland in February 1924. He won a further eight during four years with Cardiff, for whom he played in the 1925 FA Cup Final against Sheffield United, and six with Notts County before his transfer to Spurs. A fast raiding winger, always likely to pop up in a goal-scoring position, Davies filled what had been a problem position for Spurs, missing only four of the next 105 League and FA Cup games. With age beginning to creep up and young John McCormick coming through from the juniors, Davies played only 15 games when Spurs won promotion in 1932-33 and in May 1933 was made available for transfer. He returned to Swansea where he played for three years and then finished his career at Llanelli. In 1938 he took charge of the caretaking department of Pontarddulais schools.

Appearances:
League: 109 apps. 19 gls.
FA Cup: 6 apps.
Others: 8 apps. 5 gls.
Total: 123 apps. 24 gls.

DAVIS, Sean

Role: Midfield 2004-06
6ft.0ins. 13st.3lbs.
Born: *Clapham, London, 20th September 1979*

CAREER: Fulham trainee Jul 1996, pro. Jul 1998/**SPURS** Jul 2004/Portsmouth Jan 2006/Bolton Wanderers Jun 2009/(Bristol City loan Feb 2012)/retired Sep 2012.

Debut v Liverpool (PL) (h) 14.8.2004
(FC Copenhagen (Fr) (Gothenburg) 15.7.2004)

Sean Davis was an industrious midfield player, who made his League debut for Fulham as a 17-year-old and was soon attracting attention from the top clubs as Fulham worked their way into the top flight. A tigerish tackler, forever foraging in midfield, Davis was equally good at providing the midfield cover for his defence, as he was at bursting forward and breaking into the box. The subject of continual transfer speculation, particularly after making known his desire to join a club of ambition, Davies was another of the many players Spurs signed following the arrival of Director of Football, Frank Arnesen, and Head Coach, Jacques Santini. Initially Davies was given the holding role in midfield, but after injury saw him out of the team, he found himself struggling to get back in. He was too talented for reserve team football, so when Portsmouth approached Spurs in January 2006 for his services, he was allowed to move on, along with team-mates Pedro Mendes and Noé Pamarot. In three years on the South coast Davies played over 100 games before Portsmouth's soon to emerge serious financial problems saw him move to Bolton Wanderers on a free transfer. Sadly the transfer proved disastrous for Davis. Two serious knee injuries limited his appearances for Bolton to just three. When his knee succumbed for a third time, Davis called time on his career.

Appearances:
League: 11 (4) apps.
FL Cup: 1 (1) apps.
Others: 8 apps.
Total: 20 (5) apps. 0 gls.

DAWSON, E

Role: Full-back 1895-96

Debut v Ilford (Fr) (h) 18.1.1896

A member of the 2nd Battalion of the Coldstream Guards, Dawson made his one appearance for Spurs in January 1896 in a friendly against Ilford. He should not be confused with his fellow soldier J Dawson who played for Spurs in two matches earlier in the season.

Appearances:
Others: 1 app.
Total: **1 app. 0 gls.**

DAWSON, J

Role: Full-back 1895-96

Debut v London Welsh (Fr) (h) 30.11.1895

Dawson was a member of the 1st Battalion of the Scots Guards, who made two appearances for Spurs at right-back in friendly matches in the 1895-96 season.

Appearances:
Others: 2 apps.
Total: **2 apps. 0 gls.**

DAWSON, Michael Richard

Role: Central Defence 2004-14
6ft.4ins. 13st.6lbs.
Born: Northallerton, North Yorkshire, 18th November 1983

CAREER: Northallerton Town/Richmond Town/Nottingham Forest trainee Jul 2000, pro. Nov 2000/**SPURS** Jan 2005/Hull City Aug 2014.

Debut v Liverpool (PL) (a) 16.4.2005

When Spurs signed Michael Dawson and Andy Reid from Nottingham Forest in January 2005, Dawson was viewed as something of a makeweight, an unexpected addition to the ranks. As it transpired, he proved by far the better signing. Dawson was a big, combative central defender, raw and uncultured, but possessed of a determined, battling attitude that was to serve him, and Spurs, so well. With seasoned performers in Goran Bunjevčević and Noureddine Naybet and up-and-coming talents like Anthony Gardner and Ledley King on the books, Spurs appeared blessed with an abundance of defensive kingpins, but within months, the 21-year old Dawson had made such an impression he was first choice. At Forest, Dawson had developed alongside former England defender, Des Walker. At Spurs his partner was King. While Walker and King provided the finesse, Dawson provided the power. Particularly strong in the air, brave to a fault and never afraid to put his body on the line, Dawson won six Under-21 caps before making his full England debut in August 2010. It was the first of only four caps he was to collect, injuries taking their toll. At times Dawson could look clumsy and not quite accomplished enough for a top level performer, but what he lacked in skill, he more than made up for in attitude. There were some who felt his whole-hearted approach to the game was not enough to make up for the occasional lapse, Andre Villas-Boas amongst them. As soon as he arrived, he appeared content to let Dawson leave, but the man who captained the team in King's absence was not interested in a move.

Appointed club captain, Dawson was initially behind Jan Vertonghen, William Gallas and Steven Caulker in the pecking order, but by the end of Villas-Boas' first season in charge, he was again recognised as the rock on which Spurs' defence was built. Villas-Boas departed Spurs before Dawson did. Moving into his thirties and beginning to lose a little of the snap that was so important to Dawson, Spurs accepted a £3.5 million offer for him from Hull City. Relegated at the end of his first season, Dawson led Hull's efforts to return to the top flight at the first attempt. Dawson's elder brothers were both professional players, Andy with Scunthorpe United and Hull City, Kevin with Chesterfield.

Appearances:
League: 221 (15) apps. 7 gls.
FA Cup: 28 apps.
FL Cup: 18 (2) apps. 1 gl.
Euro: 36 (5) apps. 2 gls.
Others: 36 (8) apps. 1 gl.
Total: **339 (30) apps. 11 gls.**

DAY, Alfred

Role: Half-back 1932-36
5ft.8ins, 11st.2lbs.
Born: Ebbw Vale, Monmouthshire, 2nd October 1907

CAREER: Pontygof School/Ebbw Vale Schools/**SPURS** am. Dec 1930/Cheshunt/Barnet/Northfleet United 1928/**SPURS** pro. May 1931/Millwall May 1936/Southampton May 1937/Tranmere Rovers Aug 1938/Swindon Town Jun 1939/(guest for Bournemouth and Boscombe Athletic, Brighton and Hove Albion, Ipswich Town, Lincoln City, and Reading during World War Two).

Debut v Manchester City (FL) (h) 14.4.1934
(Jersey (Fr) (a) 16.5.1932)

Alf Day is possibly unique in modern football having made his international debut before he had played even one match in the Football League. In November 1933 the Welsh secretary-manager Ted Robbins was desperately searching for players to make up the injury-ravaged Welsh team for a fixture with Northern Ireland in Belfast. On contacting Arthur Turner, Spurs' secretary, Day was recommended as being a highly promising lad who would not let the Welsh down. Although he performed well enough, he did not win another cap and the development he showed in Spurs' reserves, as a calm, neat player who liked to keep the ball on the ground, did not fully materialise either. There was no League debut until April 1934 when he replaced Tom Evans and kept the position for the last two matches of the season. Only twelve more senior matches followed, before he was given a free transfer in May 1936 and moved to Millwall. He then had a year with Southampton and Tranmere Rovers and had just joined Swindon Town when war broke out. A telephone operator with the RAF, he was a war-time guest for several clubs, but had retired from the game by the time the conflict was over. He was later employed at Brimsdown power station in north London.

Appearances:
League: 13 apps.
FA Cup: 1 app.
Others: 3 apps.
Total: **17 apps. 0 gls.**

DAY, Christopher Nicholas

Role: Goalkeeper 1994-96
6ft.2ins. 12st.4lbs.
Born: Whipps Cross, London, 28th Jul 1975

CAREER: Ridgeway Rovers/Aveling Park School/Waltham Forest Schools/London Schools/**SPURS** trainee cs. 1991, pro. Apr 1993/Crystal Palace Aug 1996/Watford Jul 1997/(Lincoln City loan Dec 2000)/Queens Park Rangers Jul 2001/(Aylesbury United loan Oct 2002)/(Preston North End loan Feb 2005)/Coventry City trial Jul 2005/Crewe Alexandra trial Jul 2005/Oldham Athletic Sep 2005/Millwall Jun 2006/Watford training Jul 2008/Stevenage Borough Aug 2008., player-goalkeeper coach May 2016.

Debut v AFC Bournemouth (sub) (Fr) (a) 22.7.1994

A more than competent goalkeeper, Chris Day is one of the many young players developed by Spurs who found their opportunities at White Hart Lane limited so decided to move on in the hope of making the breakthrough. On completing his traineeship with Spurs, Day signed professional, but in over three years made just five appearances as a substitute, all in friendly games and four of those pre-season fixtures. With Ian Walker in excellent form and firmly established as first choice, Day declined a new contract in May 1996 and joined Crystal Palace on a conditional transfer with Palace able to pull out of the deal if they did not like the transfer fee that was to be decided by a tribunal. The fee set was one of the most convoluted of any transfer Spurs have been involved in. The initial fee of £22,500 was to be followed by payments of £25,000 after five and fifteen appearances, £50,000 after the 35th, 65th and 105th appearance, £100,000 if he played for England plus 25% of any profit Palace made on transferring him. Although Day had won three England Under-21 caps in his time with Spurs and added to his total with the Selhurst Park club, Spurs only received the first two stage payments as Day found himself in a poor Palace team that struggled. He moved on to Watford, but fared little better and it was only when he joined Queens Park Rangers that he got the regular first team football he wanted. Despite a bad leg injury, Day racked up a total of over 100 appearances for Rangers, but in May 2005 they decided to release him. He spent a year with Oldham Athletic before returning to London with Millwall. Day later joined Stevenage Borough and played over 300 games for the club, still turning out regularly when in his early forties.

Appearances:
Others: (5) apps.
Total: (5) apps. 0 gls.

DAY, Peter

Role: Full-back 1979
Born: Wolverhampton, Staffordshire, 22nd August 1946

CAREER: Wolverhampton Wanderers trial/Walsall trial/Telford United/**SPURS** asst. secretary Jun 1976, secretary 1983/Swindon Town chief executive/Birmingham City deputy managing director/Swansea City director Oct 1997-Jul 1999/Airdrieonians chairman Jul 2000.

Debut v Bermuda Select XI (Fr) (a) 6.6.1979

The only member of the club's executive staff to play in a first team match, Day turned out in a friendly at the end of Spurs' 1979 summer tour. A promising youngster, Day had trials with Wolverhampton Wanderers and Walsall, but his only experience of football at any reasonable level was with Telford United. He had joined Spurs as assistant secretary and made his one appearance in a scratch Spurs XI when several players were injured or had already returned to the UK. Day left Spurs in the summer of 1987, perhaps suffering for the debacle in the FA Cup Final against Coventry City when half the players appeared in shirts lacking the name of the club's sponsors. He later took on the role of Chief Executive at Swindon Town, where he worked with Swindon managers and former Spurs' players Ossie Ardiles and Glenn Hoddle, and took up the chairman's role at Airdrie when Steve Archibald's takeover looked likely to proceed. He lost the post when Archibald's takeover fell through.

Appearances:
Others: 1 app.
Total: 1 app. 0 gls.

DEARDEN, Kevin Charles

Role: Goalkeeper 1990-93
5ft.11ins. 12st.10lbs.
Born: Luton, Bedfordshire, 8th March 1970

CAREER: Luton Schools/Bedfordshire Schools/**SPURS** trainee Jul 1986, pro. Aug 1988/(Farnborough Town loan Sep 1988)/(Woking loan Jan 1989)/Cambridge United loan Mar 1989)/(Hartlepool United loan Aug 1989)/(Oxford United loan Dec 1989)/(Swindon Town loan Mar 1990) (Peterborough United loan Aug 1990)/(Hull City loan Jan 1991)/(Rochdale loan Aug 1991)/(Birmingham City loan Mar 1992)/(Portsmouth loan Aug 1992)/Sheffield United trial Sep 1993/Brentford Oct 1993/(Barnet loan Feb 1999)/(Huddersfield Town loan Mar 1999)/Wrexham Jun 1999/Queens Park Rangers trial Aug 2001/Stevenage Borough trial Aug 2001/Torquay United Aug 2001/Crystal Palace Academy coach/Boreham Wood Feb 2006/Brentford goalkeeping coach Jul 2006/Millwall goalkeeping coach Jul 2006-Nov 2007/Leyton Orient part-time goalkeeping coach Nov 2007, full-time goalkeeping coach/chief scout Jun 2008, temp asst. manager Jan 2009/Luton Town goalkeeping coach Dec 2014.

Debut v Hartlepool United (FLC) (a) 9.10.1990
(Millonarios (Fr) (Miami) 28.5.1987)

Kevin Dearden is clearly worthy of the title "Loan Ranger", for he spent the majority of his Spurs' career on loan to other clubs at all levels of League and senior non-League football. His initial outing in the Spurs' first team was when he was still a trainee, as a team containing several reserves and juniors was sent to Miami to play an exhibition match against the Columbian club Millonarios at the Orange Bowl. Upgraded to full professional status in the summer of 1988, he immediately began his travels, usually spending more than a month with the clubs he assisted and gaining valuable experience all the time. While on loan to Peterborough United, he was called back to make his competitive debut for Spurs in October 1990. With Erik Thorstvedt on international duty for Norway, Bobby Mimms injured and Ian Walker cup-tied having played

for Oxford United in the competition whilst on loan, Dearden turned out in the Rumbelows League Cup match with Hartlepool United. His only other senior game for Spurs was in April 1993 when he replaced Thorstvedt during a League game at Nottingham Forest. With Thorstvedt and Walker ahead of him and young Chris Day coming through the ranks, Dearden left Spurs on a free transfer in October 1993 to join Brentford, where he was first choice for the best part of five years. He spent almost as long with Torquay United, but injury caused him to retire in March 2005, when he began coaching. He played for a short while with Boreham Wood, then joined Brentford's coaching staff but within days moved on to Millwall. He later moved to Leyton Orient, where he combined coaching with the chief scouts' job and worked for a while as assistant manager, before joining the coaching staff of his hometown club.

Appearances:
League: (1) app.
FL Cup: 1 app.
Others: 4 (4) apps.
Total: 5 (5) apps. 0 gls.

DEFENDI, Rodrigo

Role: Defender 2004-07
6ft.2ins. 12st.10lbs.
Born: *Ribeirão Preto, Brazil, 16th June 1986*

CAREER: Commercial Ribeirão Preto (Brazil)/Cruzeiro (Brazil)/**SPURS** Jul 2004/(Udinese (Italy) loan Feb 2006)/(Roma (Italy) loan Aug 2006)/US Avellino (Italy) Aug 2007/Palmeiras (Brazil) Mar 2010/Paraná Clube (Brazil) Feb 2011-May 2011/Vitória Guimarães (Portugal) May 2011/ Botafogo (Brazil) Jan 2013/Vitória (Brazil) Jan 2014/Vitória Guimarães (Portugal) Jul 2014/Shijiazhuang Ever Bright (China) Feb 2015/Maribor (Slovenia) Jan 2016.

Debut v Celtic (sub) (Fr) (a) 10.8.2004

Having been with Cruzeiro from the age of six, Rodrigo Defendi was 16-years old when he became Spurs first signing following the arrival of Frank Arnesen. At £600,000 he was reckoned to be one of the finest defensive talents to come out of Brazil for years, and an example of the young talent garnered from all four corners of the globe that Arnesen had built his reputation around discovering. He made his first appearance as a substitute in a pre-season friendly with Celtic, but was not seen in the first team again. Although he played regularly in the youth and reserve sides, he did not make the progress expected. Loaned out to Udinese to gain experience, he made only two appearances for the Italians, returned to Spurs, but was again loaned out, this time to Roma. They had the option to sign Defendi on a permanent deal for £25,000, but after a season's loan decided not to exercise the option. Unlikely to make the grade with Spurs, Defendi was given a free transfer and in August 2007 joined newly-promoted US Avellino in Italy. When they went bust, he returned to Brazil for a short time. After a brief spell he tried again to make the grade in Europe with Portugal's Vitória Guimarães. He failed to establish himself and has since flitted around the world, playing intermittently in Europe, Brazil and China. His brother, Rafael, is a goalkeeper who has played for several of Brazil's lesser clubs.

Appearances:
Others: (1) app.
Total: (1) app. 0 gls.

DEFOE, Jermain Colin

Role: Striker 2003
5ft.7ins. 10st.10lbs.
Born: *Beckton, London, 7th October 1982*

CAREER: Charlton Athletic/FA National School of Excellence/West Ham United scholar Jul 1999, pro. Oct 1999/(AFC Bournemouth loan Oct 2000) /**SPURS** Feb 2004/Portsmouth loan and perm Jan 2008/**SPURS** Jan 2009/ Toronto (Canada) Jan 2014/Sunderland Jan 2015/AFC Bournemouth July 2017.

Debut v Portsmouth (PL) (h) 7.2.2004 (scored once)

With tremendous pace and the single-minded determination to find the back of the net all great goal-scorers need, Jermain Defoe was marked out as future star of the game even before making the breakthrough into senior football. While an East Ender, he was one of the most promising youngsters on the books of Charlton Athletic when West Ham United targeted him. Even though he had not played a single game for Charlton, a furious tug-of-war broke out over his services. West Ham eventually won and signed him as a scholar in 1999, but they had to pay Charlton substantial compensation. Defoe quickly justified the Hammers' outlay and within a year had scored on his senior debut. West Ham decided he needed to gain

experience lower down the League ladder and in October 2000 Defoe was loaned to AFC Bournemouth. His impact was immediate and headline grabbing. The 18-year old scored in ten successive League games and finished the season with nineteen goals. Back at Upton Park, Defoe soon showed he had what it takes to score at the top level, but as West Ham allowed their best young talent to leave, he alone was unable to keep them in the top flight. At the end of 2002-03 they were relegated. Supremely confident in his own ability, Defoe angered West Ham fans when he demanded a transfer immediately after their fate was sealed, but when it was refused, he buckled down to helping their fight for a return to the Premiership. Fifteen goals in 22 games showed that he was too good for First Division football and his frustration showed with three red cards by Christmas 2003. David Pleat rescued him from his West Ham misery in February 2004, laying out £7 million to secure his signature and allowing Bobby Zamora to move in the opposite direction. In total Defoe had scored 41 goals in 105 appearances for the "Hammers". A goal on his debut against Portsmouth, showed Spurs had secured another bright young English talent and within two months Defoe had made his full England debut to follow his 23 Under-21 caps. While he found the target regularly for Spurs, Defoe found the transition to international level more difficult. He was not helped by too often only getting brief substitute appearances, yet expected to perform the miracles others had failed to produce in ever-changing formations. Without doubt one of England's few true natural goal-scorers, Defoe was ridiculously left out of the 2006 World Cup squad as Sven-Goran Eriksson opted to take the advice of Arsene Wenger and select the untried Arsenal youngster Theo Walcott. At 5ft 7ins, Defoe does not have the build of most strikers, but what he lacks in physique he more than makes up for with his instinctive positioning, ability to find space and uncanny sense of knowing where the goal is even when he cannot see the target. A born predator, even the most imposing defenders find it impossible to shackle Defoe. To take their eye off him for a second runs the risk of Defoe bursting clear and causing havoc. Playing right up against the last defender, Defoe's speed off the mark is a continual threat as he looks to finish off a through ball, but he is not just a player who finishes off chances created by others. Comfortable with the ball at his feet, he can create chances for himself, running at defenders and committing them before getting in an effort that is usually on target. A clinical finisher, as adept at finishing with a perfectly placed pass into the net as a fiercely struck shot that beats the 'keeper for power, Defoe is at his most potent when he knows his place in the team is secure and that he does not need to score in every game to justify his selection. When Martin Jol preferred one big man and one small man as his perfect striking combination, Defoe found himself battling with Robbie Keane to partner Dimitar Berbatov at the forefront of Spurs' attack. Keane often won the battle, but Defoe remained a perennial threat, ensuring the competition for places that could make the difference between clubs near the top of the tree and those collecting the silverware. With no certainty of a regular starting berth, Defoe refused offers to sign an extended contract and when he was left out of Fabio Capello's first England squad, Spurs decided they just could not afford to lose Defoe under "freedom of contract" and accepted a £9 million offer from Portsmouth. Defoe was only on the South Coast for a year. When Harry Redknapp, who had signed Defoe for Portsmouth, was charged with rebuilding Spurs after Juande Ramos' short reign, he immediately took Defoe back to White Hart Lane. He cost almost double the amount Spurs had received for his transfer. After another five goal-laden years and supposedly approaching the veteran stage, Defoe signed for Toronto, where his former Spurs' team-mate, Ryan Nelsen, was manager, in January 2014, but remained with Spurs until the end of February that year. In just over a year in Canada, Defoe scored a dozen goals in 21 appearances. He returned to the UK to assist Sunderland's ultimately successful relegation battle, a feat that was repeated the following year. Despite being top-scorer in 2016-17 he could not keep them up for a third time, though his fantastic goal-scoring did see him recalled to the England squad. With Sunderland relegated, Defoe was available on a "free". He signed for AFC Bournemouth, almost going back to where it all began.

Appearances:
League: 182 (94) apps. 91 gls.
FA Cup: 23* (8) apps. 15 gls.
FL Cup: 20 (7) apps. 14 gls.
Euro: 29 (11) apps. 23 gls.
Others: 37 (24) apps. 32 gls.
Total: 291 (144) apps. 175 gls.
* Includes 1 abandoned match

DEMBÉLÉ, Mousa Sidi Yaya

Role: Midfielder 2012-
6ft.1ins. 13st.5lbs.

Born: *Wilrijk, Antwerp, Belgium, 16th July 1987*

CAREER: K Bercherm Sport (Belgium)/KFC Germinal Beerschott (Belgium) 2003/Willem II (Holland) Jul 2005/AZ Alkmaar (Holland) Aug 2006/Fulham Aug 2010/**SPURS** Aug 2012.

Debut v Norwich City (PL) (h) (sub) 1.9.2012

Another of the many Belgian players who had to move to Holland to find the platform and rewards for their talent, Mousa Dembélé was a youth player at home with Berchem Sport taking an early step on a professional career with Germinal Beerschott. A Belgian international at Under-16, Under-17 and Under-18 level, he was continually being watched by bigger clubs and still only 18-years old when offered the chance to play in Holland with Willem II. The Tilburg club were having a difficult time, but that did not prevent Dembélé proving their star performer, clearly destined for better things. After just one season AZ Alkmaar moved to sign him and in his first season, his dynamic midfield play had AZ challenging for the Eredivisie, a challenge that only failed due to a last day defeat. Three years later AZ did win the title, Dembélé hailed as the creative fulcrum behind their success. His outstanding performances were attracting the attention of English clubs and it was Fulham that laid out £5 million to secure his services. By the time of his arrival at Craven Cottage, Dembélé had completed his youth honours with caps at Under-19 level and established himself in the full international squad. Dembélé quickly established himself with Fulham, dominating the midfield, creating chances and chipping in with the occasional goal. He was clearly worthy of a bigger stage and a club that wanted to challenge for honours, not content just to remain in the top flight. Spurs had finished 2011-12 fourth in the Premier League. With Luka Modrić bound for Real Madrid, a midfielder capable of holding the ball up, cutting through defences and laying on chances was desperately needed. Dembélé looked the perfect solution and if he could turn Spurs from challengers to winners, worth every penny of the £15 million Fulham wanted for him. He did not take long to show his qualities but with an abundance of midfielders he was never sure of a place and all too often was expected to play out wide. Injuries did not help and he was frequently on the bench and not given the time to make a real impact on games. Only when Mauricio Pochettino paired Dembélé with Eric Dier and gave him the responsibility of pulling the strings from deep did Dembélé at last have the impact expected. Gangly and often looking unbalanced, he has an incredible ability to retain the ball in the tightest of corners, twisting and turning to escape his marker. Strong and a powerful runner from deep, he opens up space, attracts players to him and then lays the ball off to those he has freed up. If he has a weakness it is that he does not score often enough, disappointing when he does possess a good shot. An automatic choice for Belgium's squads, if not always the team, Dembélé is one of the most important components of Pochettino's favoured eleven.

Appearances:
League: 109 (34) apps. 7 gls.
FA Cup: 5 (5) apps.
FL Cup: 4 (4) apps.
Euro: 26 (10) apps. 3 gls.
Others: 7 (1) apps.
Total: 151 (54) apps. 10 gls.

THE SPURS ALPHABET

DEMPSEY, Clinton Drew

Role: Midfielder 2012-13
6ft.1ins. 13st.7lbs.
Born: *Nacogdoches, Texas, USA 9th March 1983*

CAREER: Nacgodoches High School/Dallas Texans (USA) 1998/Furman Paladins (USA) Feb 2001/New England Revolution (USA) Jan 2004/ŁKS Łomża (Poland) trial 2006/Fulham Jan 2007/**SPURS** Aug 2012/Seattle Sounders (USA) Aug 2013/(Fulham loan Dec 2013).

Debut v Reading (PL) (a) 16.9.2012

From trailer park to one of the USA's most lauded sportsmen, Clint Dempsey is an example of what can be achieved with conviction, courage and a fair amount of talent. He had it hard as a child in Texas, money always short and what little there was invested in his elder sister, a talented tennis player who sadly passed away when only 16. Dempsey was noticed by Dallas Texans when he went along to watch his brother in a trial. Reputedly spotted doing a little ball-juggling to pass the time, he was invited to join the club and quickly developed as its star player. He was forced to give up playing when the family finances were particularly stretched, but help from his team-mates and their families allowed him to resume a career that began to flourish when he attended the Furman University. A youth international, he was one of the first selected from the MLS draft in 2004 and within a year had made his first full international appearance, playing for the USA against Jamaica in November 2004 in a World Cup qualifier. In three years with New England Revolution, he proved an outstanding midfielder, capable of both creating chances and finishing them off. A move to Europe was always on the cards and in January 2007 he signed for Fulham in a deal costing £2 million, a record for an American leaving the States, and linking up with fellow internationals Carlos Bocanegra and Sean McBride. In five-and-a-half years at Craven Cottage, Dempsey proved a true star as Fulham continually won its annual relegation battle. He usually played in midfield, often operating just behind the strikers and was occasionally pushed into service up front, though that was not his best position. He was not a workhorse, but an artist, most effective shuttling between midfield and the forward line, searching out the little openings. His forte was drifting unnoticed into space in the opposition penalty box ending a move with a cool finish. In 2011-12, playing alongside Mousa Dembélé, Dempsey scored 23 goals, far and away Fulham's top scorer. When Rafael van der Vaart decided to leave Spurs for Hamburg, Dempsey looked the perfect replacement. In his one season at White Hart Lane, he did well enough, but at Fulham it had taken five years to build a team to get the best out of Dempsey. At Spurs, he was expected to slot straight into a team in which Gareth Bale was the main man and likely to be looking for the same spaces as Dempsey. He found it difficult and did not perform as well as expected. When Seattle Sounders offered Spurs the chance to recoup what they had laid out to sign Dempsey, the offer was accepted. Back in the States, Dempsey has continued to play and score regularly, taking his number of international appearances well past the 100 mark and the number of goals close to 50.

Appearances:
League: 22 (7) apps. 7 gls.
FA Cup: 2 apps. 3 gls.
FL Cup: 2 apps.
Euro: 6 (4) apps. 3 gls
Others: 2 apps. 1 gl.
Total: **34 (11) apps. 14 gls.**

DENNIS, Alan Edmund

Role: Full-back 1962-65
Born: *Ashcot, Somerset, 8th September 1944*

CAREER: Bermondsey Schools/Kent Schools/London Schools/England Schools/**SPURS** am. May 1960, pro. Sep 1961/Cambridge City cs. 1965/Dover cs. 1967/Margate cs. 1969-cs. 1970/Ramsgate trial Nov 1970/Harwich & Parkeston/Clacton Town 1973-1977/Tilbury Aug 1977/Harwich & Parkeston 1978/Clacton Town 1979/Truro City manager.

Debut v Arsenal (sub) (Fr) (h) 26.1.1963

Alan Dennis only managed to progress past reserve team level at Spurs twice. His first appearance in the senior team was in January 1963 when he substituted for Peter Baker in a friendly with Arsenal. His only other first eleven outing was in a friendly at Leytonstone in December 1964. He was released at the end of the 1964-65 season and went into the non-League game.

Appearances:
Others: 1 (1) apps.
Total: **1 (1) apps. 0 gls.**

DERVITE (-VAUSSOUE), Dorian Pierre

Role: Defender 2006-10
6ft.3ins. 14st.1lb.
Born: *Lille, France, 25th July 1988*

CAREER: La Madeleine (France) 1994/Lille OSC (France) 1999/**SPURS** Jul 2006/(Southend United loan Jan 2009)/Villarreal (Spain) Jul 2010/Huddersfield Town trial Jul 2012/Charlton Athletic trial Jul 2012, perm. Aug 2012/Bolton Wanderers Jul 2014.

Debut v Port Vale (FLC) (h) 8.12.2006

Another of the promising young talents Spurs signed in the hope they would develop in the future, Dervite was the French Under-18 captain when signed in July 2006. By November he had made his first senior appearance, against Port Vale in the Carling Cup. Rapid progress, but it was brought to a quick halt when he suffered a knee ligament injury that saw him out of the running for the rest of the season. His recovery was slow, and with competition from the likes of Michael Dawson, Ledley King, Jonathan Woodgate, Younes Kaboul and Sebastian Bassong, it was no surprise when he was released after four years on the books. He joined Villarreal, but in his two years there was unable to get past their B side. Dervite returned to London with Charlton Athletic in August 2012 He began to re-establish himself in south London, becoming a regular for the financially-strapped Addicks, before moving to Bolton Wanderers, another club with money problems. Dervite represented France at all youth levels from Under-16 to Under-21, collecting eight caps at the latter level while a Spurs' player.

Appearances:
FL Cup: 1 app.
Others: 4 (1) apps.
Total: **5 (1) apps. 0 gls.**

DEVLIN, John

Role: Half-back 1896-97
5ft.10ins.

CAREER: Mossend Celtic/Celtic Mar 1895/Airdrie Aug 1895/Chorley Sep 1895/Airdrie Nov 1895/(Hereford Thistle loan 1895)/**SPURS** May 1896/Millwall Athletic Oct 1897/Third Lanark May 1898/Albion Rovers Aug 1899/British Army Dec 1899/Albion Rovers Aug 1901/Nithsdale Wanderers May 1902/Lanemark Mar 1905/retired 1907.

Debut v Sheppey United (SL) (a) 5.9.1896

Signed from Airdrie, Johnny Devlin had spent the previous season on loan to Hereford Thistle where he played with Bill Crump who also signed for Spurs at about the same time. Devlin was a regular performer throughout almost the whole of his one season with Spurs, only absent for the last few matches of the season when, along with McElhaney, Wilson and Milliken he was suspended for "acts of insubordination". Despite this indiscretion, he was re-signed for the following season, but before it even kicked-off he was again suspended when Spurs discovered he had also signed for Millwall- Spurs' fiercest rivals of those days. The punishment suggested was to suspend Devlin for the whole season, but the situation was resolved in October 1897 when he was transferred to Millwall. In February 1898, after only ten appearances he was suspended by Millwall for the rest of the season and returned to Scotland. Devlin frequently played alongside his brother, Jimmy which has caused much confusion in their career details.

Appearances:
Southern: 21 apps. 1 gl.
FA Cup: 3 apps.
Others: 35* apps. 4 gls.
Total: **59 apps. 5 gls.**
* Includes 1 abandoned match.

DEXTER, Frederick William

Role: Full-back 1883-84
Born: Edmonton, London, September qtr. 1868

Debut v Brownlow Rovers (Fr) (h) 6.10.1883

Another of Spurs' founder members from St Johns Middle Class School, Dexter almost certainly played regularly in Spurs' first season of 1882-83. However no records exist of the games played in that first season let alone the players who turned out. The only match he is definitely known to have played in was a 9-0 victory over Brownlow Rovers, the first Spurs match to be reported in any detail in the local Tottenham and Edmonton Weekly Herald.

Appearances:
Others: 1 app.
Total: **1 app. 0 gls.**

DICK, Alistair John

Role: Winger 1981-86
5ft.9ins. 10st.7lbs.
Born: Stirling, Scotland, 25th April 1965

CAREER: Stirling Boys Club/Scotland Schools/**SPURS** app. Jul 1981, pro. May 1982/Ajax (Holland) Jul 1986/Derby County trial Feb 1988/ Newcastle United training Nov 1988/Southampton training Mar 1989/ Wimbledon Jul 1989/Brighton and Hove Albion Mar 1990/Ajax (Holland) cs. 1990/Sheffield Wednesday trial Jan 1991/Hellenic (South Africa) 1991/ Heidelberg United (Australia)/Cape Town Spurs (South Africa)/Seven Stars (South Africa) 1996/Alloa Athletic Jan 1997/Stirling Albion youth team coach Jul 2010.

Debut v Manchester City (FL) (h) 20.2.1982
(Norwich City (sub) (Fr) (a) 12.8.1981)

A schoolboy star from whom great things were expected, Spurs signed Alli Dick in the face of keen competition from several clubs, but unfortunately. he never progressed through to the highest level. He attended the same school as former Leeds United and Scotland captain Billy Bremner, but there any similarity ended, for Dick was a highly skilled out-and-out winger, not an aggressive little midfield agitator. Dick represented Scotland at all schoolboy levels and by the time he signed professional for Spurs had already made his Football League debut. Although Alli performed well for the reserves he was unable to make the step up and consequently his first team outings were sporadic. He did however have something special to show for his time at Spurs; going on as a substitute in the second leg of the 1984 UEFA Cup Final he collected a winner's medal after the tense penalty shoot-out. In the summer of 1986 Alli was given a free transfer and moved to Ajax of Amsterdam. He was unable to make headway in Holland and flitted around several English clubs before going to play in South Africa and Australia. Dick made one substitute appearance for Alloa before disappearing from the game at the higher level, eventually resurfacing on the coaching staff at Stirling Albion. When he made his League debut he became the youngest player to appear for Spurs in the Football League, aged 16 years 301 days.

Appearances:
League: 16 (1) apps. 2 gls.
FA Cup: 2 apps.
Euro: 3 (3) apps.
Others: 7 (11) apps. 4 gls.
Total: **28 (15) apps. 6 gls.**

THE SPURS ALPHABET

DICKER, Leslie Raymond

Role: Outside-left 1951-52
5ft.10ins. 10st.2lbs.
Born: *Lambeth, London, 20th December 1926*

CAREER: Hornchurch Athletic/Chelmsford City cs. 1948/**SPURS** Jun 1951/Southend United Jul 1953/Chelmsford City Jul 1955-1960.

Debut v West Bromwich Albion (FL) (h) 23.8.1951

Les Dicker was signed by Arthur Rowe from his former club, Southern League Chelmsford City, as cover for Les Medley, and it was as a replacement for the injured Medley that Dicker scored twice in ten Football League appearances in the 1952-53 season. His first match was on the opening day, but by the end of the season Spurs had signed George Robb as long term replacement for the emigrating Medley. Dicker was transfer-listed in May 1953 and moved to Southend United, where he played for two years. He then returned to Chelmsford, giving them great service over five years as he took his number of appearances over 250 and his goals tally past the 100 mark.

Appearances:
League: 10 apps. 2 gls.
Total: **10 apps. 2 gls.**

DICKIE, J S

Role: Half-back 1894-95

CAREER: SPURS 1894/Old St Stephens 1894.

Debut v Uxbridge (Fr) (a) 15.9.1894

Dickie played in the first three matches of the 1894-95 season, but then disappeared from the first team scene at Spurs. He went on to play for Old St Stephens.

Appearances:
Others: 3 apps.
Total: **3 apps. 0 gls.**

DIER, Eric Jeremy Edgar

Role: Defender/Midfielder 2014-
6ft.2ins. 14st.4lbs.
Born: *Cheltenham, Gloucestershire, 15th January 1994*

CAREER: International Preparatory School, Lisbon (Portugal)/Sporting (Portugal) pro. Apr 2010/(Everton loan Jan 2011)/**SPURS** Aug 2014.

Debut v West Ham United (PL) (a) 16.8.2014 (scored once)
(Schalke 04 (Fr) (h) 9.8.2014)

When Eric Dier was six and his family moved to Portugal, it was so his mother could take up a job preparing for Euro 2004, not so that he could learn to play football the Portuguese way. Two years later he was at Sporting's academy and when his family returned to England in 2010, he remained having joined Sporting's professional staff. He developed quickly and in 2011 joined Everton on a six months' loan that lasted for a

year more. During his stay on Merseyside Dier represented England at Under-18 and Under-19 level and continued to work his way up the international level when he returned to Lisbon. He also made the breakthrough at Sporting, playing for both their senior and B teams. Initially at centre-half, he also played at full-back with a few games as a defensive midfielder. With several English clubs watching his development, Spurs moved to secure his transfer for a bargain £4 million. He was not expected to be given a regular starting place from the outset, but with Younes Kaboul and Federico Fazio both out of form, he had plenty of opportunities and did not disappoint. Whether at centre-half or full-back he was strong and quick, dangerous in the air and confident beyond his years. Centre-half seemed his better position, but in the build-up to the 2015-16 season, Mauricio Pochettino installed Dier in the centre of midfield. It was a position he had played in Portugal, but the Premier League is different. Dier has excelled in the role, the holding player covering in front of the defence and dropping back to provide a third centre-half when the full-backs embark on forward sorties. Confident in possession, his passing ability, whether over short or long distance, has come to the fore, while his positional sense and strong tackling have proved invaluable. The switch in positions was in large part responsible for Spurs at last mounting a serious title challenge. It also boosted Dier's international career. Having been capped at Under-23 level, he was called into the full England squad for the game against Spain in November 2015 and has become an integral part of the team. At 23 there is plenty more to come from Dier.

Appearances:
League: 96 (5) apps. 7 gls.
FA Cup: 8 (1) apps.
FL Cup: 5 apps.
Euro: 19 (1) apps.
Others: 6 (2) apps.
Total: **134 (9) apps. 7 gls.**

DILLON, Michael Leslie

Role: Central defender 1972-75
5ft.11ins.
Born: *Highgate, London, 29th September 1952*

CAREER: Islington Schools/London Schools/Middlesex Schools/England Schools/**SPURS** app. May 1968, pro. Dec 1969/(Montreal Olympique (Canada) loan cs. 1972)/(Millwall loan Dec 1974)/(Swindon Town loan Mar 1975)/New York Cosmos (USA) loan cs. 1975, then perm/Cheshunt Nov 1977/Washington Diplomats (USA) Apr 1978/Georgetown Hoyas (USA) coach.

Debut v Manchester United (FL) (a) 28.10.1972

A calm, commanding central defender, Matt Dillon worked his way through Spurs junior ranks to sign professional and play for England Youth, before spending the summer of 1972 playing for Montreal Olympic in the North American Soccer League. He clearly benefited from playing with and against some of the most famous and experienced names in world football, and made his Spurs' debut within weeks of his return. At the time Spurs were blessed with an abundance of first class central defenders, Mike England, Phil Beal, Peter Collins and a young

Terry Naylor, so Dillon was rarely able to get a run in the first team. He never let the club down when he was called upon, but to get more League experience he was loaned out to Millwall and Swindon. At the end of the 1974-75 season he crossed the Atlantic again to spend the summer with New York Cosmos, and did so well in the States that he decided, with Spurs' agreement, to stay on. In October 1975 his contract was cancelled by mutual consent and he had three years playing alongside Pele with the Cosmos and another two with Washington Diplomats. In his short time with Cheshunt, Dillon played alongside his brother, Tommy, who had been a junior with Spurs in 1969-70.

Appearances:
League: 21 (3) apps. 1 gl.
FA Cup: 1 app.
FL Cup: 1 app.
Euro: 2 (1) apps.
Others: 3 (1) apps.
Total: 28 (5) apps. 1 gl.

DIMMOCK, James Henry

Role: Outside-left 1918-31
5ft.10ins. 11st.6lbs.
Born: *Edmonton, London, 5th December 1900*
Died: *Enfield, Middlesex, 23rd December 1972*

CAREER: Montague Road School/Park Avenue/Gothic Works/Edmonton Ramblers/**SPURS** am. Dec 1918, pro. May 1919/(Clapton Orient during World War One)/Thames Aug 1931/Clapton Orient Sep 1932/Ashford Town Mar 1934/Tunbridge Wells Rangers/retired cs. 1936.

Debut v Lincoln City (FL) (a) 4.10.1919
(Fulham (NWF) (h) 10.5.1919)

Jimmy Dimmock wrote his name permanently into Spurs' history when, with an angled left foot shot, he scored the winning goal against Wolverhampton Wanderers in the 1921 FA Cup Final at Stamford Bridge. However, he was just 20-years old and that was only an early chapter in the story, for Dimmock was a special talent and one of the greatest wingers ever on Spurs' books. Spotted as a schoolboy with Edmonton Ramblers, Spurs immediately signed him to amateur forms. When Dimmock was allowed to play for Clapton Orient during the First World War, he immediately showed many of the superb individual skills that made him so elusive and difficult to tie down. At the conclusion of the war both Clapton Orient and Arsenal wanted to sign him, but Dimmock chose Spurs and became a professional in May 1919. His League debut followed in October 1919, when he stood in for Jimmy Chipperfield and, when weeks later Chipperfield was injured again, the young Dimmock took his chance. From that moment on the left wing position was his, as Spurs ran away with the Second Division title in 1919-20. Touched with natural genius, much of Dimmock's football was instinctive and although some of his long, mazy dribbles along the left flank, could at times border on the self-indulgent, his clever trickery with the ball earned him enormous popularity with the adoring crowd. Stylish, elegant and splendidly balanced, Dimmock also had a tremendous shot in both feet, so it was something of a puzzle that he did not win the number of international honours his gifts deserved. After playing in two trial matches in February 1921, he won his first cap against Scotland the following April but, although he continued to shine at Spurs, his next cap did not arrive until March 1926 and only one more came after that. If anything, Dimmock got better over the next few years, scoring more regularly than in his early days, and it can perhaps only be the fact Spurs were struggling which prevented him adding to his sparse array of caps. Towards the end of his Spurs career Dimmock began to put on weight; he was still a magnificent artist, but was losing that edge of speed so important to his game. In April 1931 Spurs decided not to retain his services and he joined Thames, preferring to stay in London rather than go to Bristol Rovers. He only spent a year with Thames for, at the end of the 1931-32 season, they folded and he joined Clapton Orient. He then moved to Kent League club Ashford, but played for just two months before retiring. He later worked in the road haulage industry. Dimmock's brother was on Spurs' books shortly after the first war.

Appearances:
League: 400 apps. 100 gls.
FA Cup: 38 apps. 12 gl.
Others: 55 apps. 26 gls.
Total: 493 apps. 138 gls.

DINGWELL, W

Role: Full-back 1891-92

Debut v Coldstream Guards (LutCC) (h) 7.11.1891

Dingwell is yet another of the players from Spurs' early days about whom it has proved impossible to find any information. He is known to have played in three matches in November 1891, two Luton Charity Cup ties and a friendly, but any other appearances are not recorded.

Appearances:
Others: 3 apps.
Total: 3 apps. 0 gls.

DITCHBURN, Edwin George

Role: Goalkeeper 1939-59
6ft.1ins. 12st.9lbs.
Born: *Gillingham, Kent, 24th October 1921*
Died: *Wickham Market, 26th December 2005*

CAREER: Northfleet Schools/Kent Schools/Northfleet Paper Mills/**SPURS** ground-staff 1937, am. Jun 1938/Northfleet United Aug 1938/**SPURS** pro. May 1939/(guest for Aberdeen, Birmingham and Dartford during World War Two)/Romford Apr 1959, player-manager Jul 1960-Mar 1962/retired Apr 1965/Brentwood Town Aug 1965.

Debut v Birmingham City (FL) (h) 31.8.1946
(Chelsea (FLS) (h) 25.5.1940)

Ted Ditchburn came to Spurs via the Northfleet nursery club in 1939 and, when it is taken into account that he lost seven years of his career to the Second World War, it is quite remarkable that only Pat Jennings and Steve Perryman have played more games for Spurs. An England Schools

trialist, he played for Northfleet Paper Mills before joining the Spurs' groundstaff. On signing amateur forms, he was sent to Northfleet, but with the outbreak of war guested for Dartford. His debut was in the Football League South in May 1940, but National Service meant he was only able to turn out occasionally for Spurs-he played more games during the war as a guest for Aberdeen than for Spurs. However, the war did give Ditchburn an early taste of representative football with the Royal Air Force and Football Association XI's as well as in two England war-time internationals, the first against Scotland in February 1944. On his demob, he immediately took over the 'keeper's role at White Hart Lane and between April 1946 and March 1954 missed only two League and FA Cup games. That included a record 247 consecutive League appearances. He was ever-present in the Second Division championship team of 1949-50 and the First Division winning team the following season. Athletic, courageous, safe, a particularly good shot-stopper and possessor of a mighty kick, his one weakness-ironical for the son of a noted boxer-was his punching. Ditchburn also had a quick, accurate throw and, in conjunction with Alf Ramsey, pioneered and perfected the art of starting attacks with the sort of early distribution from the back which was so important to Spurs "Push and Run" style in the early 50s. Always consistent and maintaining excellent standards of fitness throughout his career, Ditchburn was unfortunate to play in an era when England were well served by top class 'keepers such as Frank Swift and Bert Williams, and representative honours were limited to only a handful. A member of England's World Cup squad in 1950, five appearances for the Football League were followed by his first full cap against Switzerland in December 1948. In the next eight years he won only five more caps although he also played for England "B" twice, and the Football League once more. In the mid-fifties Ditchburn lost his place for short spells to Ron Reynolds, but fought his way back, and it was only in August 1958 that he eventually relinquished the position to John Hollowbread and retired from top-flight football. From April 1959 until April 1965 he played for Romford, including a lengthy spell as player/manager until handing over to his former "Push and Run" team-mate, Harry Clarke. In August 1965 Ditchburn signed for Brentwood Town where he played a few games whilst building a successful sports outfitters business in Romford, where he also owned a toys and games shop and had an interest in a printing business.

Appearances:
League: 419* apps.
FA Cup: 34 apps.
Others: 121 apps.
Total: 574 apps. 0 gls.
* Includes 1 abandoned match

DIX, Ronald William

Role: Inside-forward 1939-48
5ft.9in. 12st.5lbs.
Born: Bristol, 5th September 1912
Died: Bristol, 2nd April 1998

CAREER: South Central School/Bristol Schools/Gloucestershire Schools/England Schools/Bristol Rovers am. Jul 1927, pro. Sep 1929/Blackburn Rovers May 1932/Aston Villa May 1933/Derby County Feb 1937/**SPURS** Jun 1939/(guest for Blackpool, Bradford Park Avenue, Bristol City, Chester, Liverpool, Wrexham and York City during World War Two)/Reading Nov 1947/retired Jun 1949.

Debut v Birmingham (FL) (h) 26.8.1939 (later expunged from record) (Arsenal (JTF) (h) 19.8.1939)

A schoolboy star in his native Bristol, Ronnie Dix made his name during five years with Bristol Rovers. He moved to Blackburn Rovers when a proposed transfer to Everton fell through, but only stayed with Blackburn for a year before transferring to Aston Villa. It was, though, with Derby County that he had his best years, playing for the Football League against the Scottish League in November 1938 and winning an England cap against Norway a week later. He scored once in a 4-0 victory. Spurs signed Dix in June 1939, but the war meant his White Hart Lane career never got off the ground. His debut came in the Jubilee Trust Fund match with Arsenal and he played in all three of the Football League matches that season which were later expunged from the records. During the war years he was rarely able to turn out for Spurs, although he guested regularly for several clubs, including Blackpool, helping them win the Football League North Cup in 1943 and reach the Final in 1944. The regular inside-left in the first full post-war season, Dix was past his best and was transferred to Reading, where he played until his retirement in June 1949. He then returned to the South West and went into business in Bristol. When he scored for Bristol Rovers against Norwich City in a Third Division (South) fixture on 3rd March 1928, Dix became the youngest player to score a goal in a Football League match. He was only 15 years and 180 days old.

Appearances:
League: 39 apps. 6 gls.
FA Cup: 4 apps.
Others: 54 apps. 14 gls.
Total: 97 apps. 20 gls.

DIXON, Arthur

Role: Full-back 1907-08
5ft.9ins. 11st.10lbs.
Born: Barrowford, Lancashire, 8th October 1879
Died: Nelson, Lancashire, Jan qtr. 1946

CAREER: Trawden Forest/Nelson/Burnley cs. 1900/**SPURS** May 1907/Bradford Park Avenue Jun 1908.

Debut v Queens Park Rangers (SL) (a) 2.9.1907

Arthur Dixon had been a regular with Burnley for six years when signed by Spurs, but was not to have much good fortune in London. Originally a half-back but converted by Burnley to full-back, he made his debut in the first Southern League match of the 1907-08 season. Playing at left-back, he made a total of only twelve more appearances before leaving in the summer of 1908 to join Bradford Park Avenue where he became re-established as a consistent League performer. He played regularly until the First World War bought his career to an end.

Appearances:
Southern: 6 apps.
Others: 7 apps.
Total: 13 apps. 0 gls.

DIXON, Kenneth George

Role: Full-back 1982-83

CAREER: Mid-Herts Schools/Hertfordshire Schools/SPURS app. Jan 1981, pro. Dec 1981/retired May 1984.

Debut v Barnet (Fr) (a) 20.9.1982

Apart from playing football at school, Kenny Dixon also excelled at rugby and represented Hertfordshire Schools at that code. Looked upon as a very promising young player his only first team appearance was when Spurs fielded a fairly weak eleven in a friendly at Barnet in September 1982. Unfortunately, Dixon sustained a serious injury early in the 1983-84 season and was forced to retire in May 1984.

Appearances:
Others: 1 app.
Total: 1 app. 0 gls.

DOCKRAY, John

Role: Outside-left 1918-19
Born: Carlisle, Cumbria, 1892
Died: Exeter, Devon, 12th September 1939

CAREER: Carlisle United/Bury 1912/Exeter City cs. 1914/(guest for SPURS during World War One)/Bideford Town player-coach cs. 1924/Friernhay Oct 1926.

Debut v Fulham (LFC) (a) 7.9.1918

An experienced player with Carlisle and Bury, John Dockray had joined Exeter City in the summer of 1914 and was still retained by them when he turned out for Spurs. His first appearance for Spurs was on 31st August 1918 when he played in a scratch Spurs XI against a team selected by Haydn Price, the former Welsh international, at St Albans in a match to raise funds for war charities. Evidently Spurs were impressed for he started the regular season in the team, but soon had to drop out due to service demands. After the war he remained with Exeter, twice representing the Southern League against the Welsh League, until the summer of 1924 when he joined Bideford Town as player-coach.

Appearances:
Others: 13 apps.
Total: 13 apps. 0 gls.

DODGE, William Charles

Role: Half-back 1958-61
5ft.7ins.
Born: Hackney, London, 10th March 1937

CAREER: Eton Manor/SPURS am. Mar 1955, pro. Oct 1957/Crystal Palace Jul 1962/Kettering Town Aug 1963/Ashford Jul 1965/Canterbury City Jun 1972/Leyton-Wingate player-coach Jan 1976/Aylesbury.

Debut v Blackburn Rovers (FL) (h) 3.1.1959
(Bela Vista (Fr) (h) 14.10.1958)

As a half-back on Spurs' staff at the same time as such greats as Danny Blanchflower and Dave Mackay, Bill Dodge had few opportunities to impress. He made his League debut in January 1959, standing in for Blanchflower, and made a total of eleven senior appearances that season, but always as understudy to Blanchflower who was rarely absent from the team. Dodge remained at White Hart Lane until July 1962, but made only one more League appearance before moving to Crystal Palace. He played just three League games for Palace in twelve months before dropping into non-League football.

Appearances:
League: 6 apps.
FA Cup: 4 apps.
Others: 3 apps.
Total: 13 apps. 0 gls.

DOHERTY, Gary Michael Thomas

Role: Striker or Central Defender 1999-2005
6ft.2ins, 13st.1lbs.
Born: Cardonough, Republic of Ireland 31st January 1980

CAREER: Luton Town trainee Jul 1996, pro. Jul 1997/SPURS Apr 2000/Norwich City Aug 2004/Charlton Athletic Jul 2010/Wycombe Wanderers loan Feb 2012, perm. Jul 2012/retired Dec 2014.

Debut v Manchester United (sub) (PL) (a) 6.5.2000

Another of the promising young talents signed by Director of Football David Pleat, Gary Doherty had spent four years with Luton Town flitting between the centre-forward and centre-half positions. At White Hart Lane he was to do much the same. At over six-foot tall, Doherty had the attributes needed for either role, physically strong, good in the air and competent with the ball at his feet. Despite playing for a Second Division club, Doherty had represented the Republic of Ireland at Under-21 level and only the day before his £1m transfer to Spurs had won his first full cap. He was just establishing himself as a defensive regular in the first team squad when his leg was broken in a Worthington Cup tie. When fit to return, he struggled to recover his form; not helped by facing competition for a central defensive berth from Ledley King, Anthony Gardner and Dean Richards. When the experienced Nourredine Naybet was signed as part of the Arnesen/Santini revolution in the summer of 2005, Doherty's prospects did not look good and Norwich City were quick to make an offer. Doherty spent six years with Norwich, the cornerstone of their

defence and one of the few bright spots in some miserable years as the financially strapped club plunged from the Premier League to League One. Having helped Norwich back to the Championship, Doherty was surprisingly released. He joined Charlton Athletic and spent 18 months there before moving on to Wycombe Wanderers.

Appearances:
League: 45 (19) apps. 4 gls.
FA Cup: 7 (1) apps. 4 gls.
FL Cup: 3 (3) apps.
Others: 22 (6) apps. 2 gls.
Total: 77 (29) apps. 10 gls.

DOMBAXE, Laste

Role: Midfielder 2013-14
5ft.7ins.
Born: Luanda, Angola, 14th May 1995

CAREER: SPURS Academy Scholar Jul 2011/(Bolton Wanderers loan Jan 2014)/(Queens Park Rangers trial Feb 2014)/released Jun 2014/Hadley Aug 2014/Carlisle United trial Jul 2015/Watford trial Sep 2015/Redbridge Aug 2016/East Grinstead Town Aug 2016/GAIS (Sweden) trial Nov 2016.

Debut v Swindon Town (sub) (Fr) (a) 16.7.2013

A muscular youngster who developed through the Academy system, Laste Dombaxe was a defensive midfielder unfortunate to be looking to progress through the youth teams at the same time as young players of the calibre of Nabil Bentaleb and Tom Carroll. Dombaxe made a couple of substitute appearances in pre-season friendlies in August 2013, but he was never seriously considered for first team action. The decision was made early in 2014 that his future did not lie with Spurs and he was allowed to try and find another club before being released at the end of the season. Unable to find a senior club, he took to playing for the Micky Hazard managed Hadley in the Spartan South Midlands League, while still harbouring thoughts of a return to the big stage.

Appearances:
Others: (2) apps.
Total: (2) apps. 0 gls.

DOMINGUEZ, Jose Manuel Martins

Role: Winger 1997-2001
5ft.3ins, 10st.0lbs.
Born: Lisbon, Portugal, 16th February 1974

CAREER: Benfica (Portugal) pro. 1990/(Sintrense (Portugal) loan 1993)/(AD Fafe (Portugal) loan Nov 1993)/Birmingham City Mar 1994/Sporting (Portugal) May 1995/**SPURS** Aug 1997/1FC Kaiserslautern (Germany) Nov 2000/Al-Ahly (Qatar) Aug 2004/Vasco da Gama (Brazil) Feb 2005/retired Aug 2005/União de Leiria (Portugal) youth team coach Mar 2010, first team coach Mar 2012/Sporting (Portugal) coach Jul 2012, reserve team manager Oct 2012/Real Cartagena (Colombia) coach Dec 2013/Real Club Recreativo de Huelva (Spain) coach Mar-Dec 2015.

Debut v Derby County (sub) (PL) (h) 23.8.1997

Jose Dominguez had not made a senior appearance for Benfica and had been loaned out to a couple of third tier clubs when signed by Birmingham City. One of the smallest players to appear in English professional football, he was unable to save the Blues from relegation, but his performances in 1994-95 not only helped them return to the Premier League at the first attempt, but led to him representing Portugal at Under-21 level and securing a £1.6 million return to Portugal with Sporting Lisbon. After a couple of years during which he won full international honours and represented his country at the 1996 Olympics, Sporting recovered their outlay when they accepted Spurs' offer. As Gerry Francis was not known to favour flair players, it was a bit of a surprise signing, particularly as David Ginola had been signed only days before Dominguez's arrival. The diminutive winger made his first appearance as a substitute against Derby County and what a debut it was. With pace, trickery and some amazing dribbling skills he totally changed the game, winning the penalty that proved the difference between the two teams. Unfortunately, that appearance was to prove the highlight of Dominguez's White Hart Lane career. With competition from Ginola and Ruel Fox, Dominguez was rarely in the starting line-up, most of his appearances coming as a substitute. Sadly, he was unable to produce the immediate impact that was expected of him after his debut. Not helped by the departure of Francis and the ill-fated rein of Christian Gross, Dominguez spent most of his time with the reserves. The appointment of George Graham spelt the end of Dominguez's Spurs' career. He moved to Kaiserslautern, where he enjoyed the most productive four years of his career before finishing with short spells in Qatar and Brazil. Out of the game for five years after his retirement, he returned as a coach, working in Portugal, Columbia and Spain.

Appearances:
League: 12 (33) apps. 4 gls.
FA Cup: 2 (1) apps.
FL Cup: 2 (6) apps. 1 gl.
Euro: (2) apps.
Others: 7 (6) apps. 4 gls.
Total: 23 (48) apps. 9 gls.

DORLING, George John

Role: Full-back 1939-40.
5ft.10ins, 10st.9lbs.
Born: Edmonton, London, 27th July 1918
Died: Enfield, Middlesex, October 1987

CAREER: Edmonton Schools/Middlesex Schools/Tottenham Juniors/**SPURS** am. May 1934/Wood Green/Northfleet United Aug 1937/**SPURS** pro. Sep 1937/(guest for Aldershot and Leeds United during World War Two)/Gillingham Apr 1947/Snowdon Colliery Welfare Oct 1951/**SPURS** ground-staff.

Debut v Southend United (FLS) (a) 21.10.1939
(Chelsea (Fr) (h) 30.9.1939)

Brought up from the nursery club at Northfleet, George Dorling did not have the opportunity to prove himself before war broke out. As with many local players he had been spotted early on by Spurs and was sent to Northfleet after playing for Tottenham Juniors and Wood Green. With the war, Dorling found himself one of the few available full-backs on the club's books and made his first team debut on 30th September 1939 in a friendly against Chelsea. He went on to play twelve Football League South games early that season. After that first season he did not play for Spurs again, although he did appear as a guest for Aldershot and Leeds United. Although still on Spurs' books after the war, he was never seriously in consideration for a place in the team and was given a free transfer in April 1947. He moved to Southern League Gillingham, where he played for four years, helping them embark on their Football League career. Dorling was the uncle of Tony Marchi.

Appearances:
Others: 14 apps.
Total: **14 apps. 0 gls.**

DOW, William

Role: Outside-left 1906-07
5ft.7ins, 11st.7lbs.
Born: Edinburgh, 15th November 1884

CAREER: Vale of Grange/Leith Athletic Jan 1904/Bury May 1905/**SPURS** May 1906/released Apr 1907/Cowdenbeath Sep 1908.

Debut v West Ham United (SL) (h) 1.9.1906 (scored once)

A 22-year old signing, William Dow was the fourth player that manager John Cameron recruited to try and fill the outside-left position which had proved so troublesome after John Kirwan's move to Chelsea in the summer of 1905. Dow followed William Murray, Chris Carrick and Alf Whyman, but was to prove no more successful than any of them-even though he scored in his first game. Described at the time as "a very sturdily built young fellow", he played in nine of the season's first ten Southern League matches and the first five Western League fixtures, but then disappeared into the reserves before being released in April 1907.

Appearances:
Southern: 9 apps. 3 gls.
Others: 6 apps.
Total: **15 apps. 3 gls.**

DOWERS, Arthur John

Role: Outside-right 1939-40
5ft.10ins.
Born: Walthamstow, London, 8th October 1923
Died: Sarasota, Florida, USA, 9th August 2007

CAREER: Markhouse Road Senior Boys School/Walthamstow Schools/Essex Schools/London Schools/England Schools/**Tottenham Juniors** Aug 1939/Northfleet United/(guest for Dartford during World War Two)/Luton Town cs. 1946/West Ham United Jul 1947/Margate Jan-Jun 1948/Guildford City 1948/Ramsgate Athletic Jul 1949-Aug 1949.

Debut v Southend United (FLS) (h) 23.12.1939 (match abandoned)

Johnny Dowers had joined Tottenham Juniors for the start of the 1939-40 season, but his career was immediately put on hold by the outbreak of war. He settled down to work as office boy for Spurs' chief scout Ben Ives, but was called on to make up the numbers in two Football League South fixtures that season. His first game was in the December in a match that had to be abandoned after 60 minutes due to fog and he played again a week later. In both matches he occupied the outside-right berth. With little opportunity for youth football, he guested for Dartford, but joined Luton Town when normal football resumed in 1946. He had only one year with Luton then moved on to West Ham United, but failed to make the League side at Upton Park before moving into non-League football. Dowers' uncle was Charlie Hannaford, a war-time guest for Spurs who went on to play for Charlton Athletic, Clapton Orient and Manchester United.

Appearances:
Others: 2* apps.
Total: **2 apps. 0 gls.**
* Includes 1 abandoned match.

DOWNER, Frederick

Role: Outside-right 1943-44

CAREER: Millwall/(guest for **SPURS** during World War Two).

Debut v Millwall (Fr) (a) 10.4.1944

Fred Downer was one of Millwall's junior players who had made several appearances in their colours during the war. He made his one appearance for Spurs as a guest in a friendly at Millwall when Spurs had to borrow three of the home club's juniors to make up a full eleven.

Appearances:
Others: 1 app.
Total: **1 app. 0 gls.**

DOWNIE, Edwin

Role: Half-back 1897-98
5ft.10ins. 12st.8lbs.

CAREER: Heart of Midlothian Sep 1894/**SPURS** Dec 1897/Chesterfield Town Jun 1899/Stockport County cs. 1900.

Debut v Wolverton (SL) (h) 22.1.1898
(Kettering (Fr) (h) 11.12.1897)

Ed Downie joined Spurs shortly after the announcement by full-back Ly Burrows of his decision to move to Sheffield, and it was expected Downie would take his place. However, he only played two matches in that role before reverting to a more accustomed half-back position where he turned out in the majority of first team games until the end of the season. Downie spent most of the following season in the reserves and at the end was released. He moved to Chesterfield, where he played with former Spurs' team-mate Bob Tannahill for a year, before transferring to Stockport County.

Appearances:
Southern: 11 apps.
Others: 26 apps.
Total: 37 apps. 0 gls.

DOWSETT, Gilbert James

Role: Outside-left 1951-55
5ft.8ins. 10st.9lbs.
Born: Widford, Essex, 3rd July 1931

CAREER: Sudbury Town/**SPURS** May 1952/Southend United May 1955/Southampton Jul 1956/Bournemouth and Boscombe Athletic Jun 1957/Crystal Palace Nov 1962/Weymouth Jun 1965/Bournemouth & Boscombe Athletic commercial manager Jun 1968-Mar 1983.

Debut v Aston Villa (FL) (a) 21.8.1954 (scored once)
(Crittalls Athletic (sub) (Fr) (h) 11.5.1952)

Dickie Dowsett made his first appearance for Spurs in a friendly within days of joining the club, but then had to wait more than two years for his only League game in Spurs' colours. He played in the first match of the 1954-55 season and scored in a 4-2 win at Villa Park, but never made the starting line-up again and joined Southend United at the end of the season. Evidently he liked the sea air, for he then moved on to Southampton and Bournemouth. A centre-forward for just over five years at Dean Court, he was more than useful in the air and a determined runner. Dowsett had cost a mere £100, yet scored 79 goals in 169 League games for the Cherries before returning to London with Crystal Palace for £3,500. In June 1965 he moved back to the coast with Weymouth and helped them win the Southern League Championship in his first season. He later returned to Bournemouth to work on the administrative side before becoming production manager of a toy firm in the town.

Appearances:
League: 1 app. 1 gl.
Others: (1) app.
Total: 1 (1) apps. 1 gl.

DOYLE, J

Role: Full-back 1915-16

CAREER: Dublin Bohemians/(guest for **SPURS** during World War One).

Debut v Fulham (LFC) (a) 19.2.1916

Doyle made his one appearance for Spurs as a trialist in a London Football Combination fixture in February 1916, but did not make any further appearances for the club.

Appearances:
Others: 1 app.
Total: 1 app. 0 gls.

DOZZELL, Jason Irvin Winans

Role: Midfield 1993-97
6ft.2ins. 13st.12lbs.
Born: Ipswich, Suffolk, 9th December 1967

CAREER: Newpark Rangers/Needham Phoenix/Langham Lions/Ipswich Town app. Jul 1984, pro. Dec 1984/**SPURS** Jul 1993/(Birmingham City trial Jul 1997)/free transfer Sep 1997/Ipswich Town training Sep 1997/Gillingham training Oct 1997/Northampton Town Dec 1997/Colchester United Oct 1998/retired Sep 2001/Canvey Island trial Jul 2002, perm Aug 2002/Grays Athletic trial Oct 2002, perm Oct 2002/Ipswich Wanderers player-manager Jun 2003-May 2006/Leiston manager Oct 2006-Nov 2007/Ipswich Town academy coach.

Debut v Newcastle United (PL) (a) 14.8.1993
(Brentford (Fr) (a) 6.8.1993)

At the age of 16 years and 57 days, Jason Dozzell was still an Associated Schoolboy when he became (and still is) the youngest goal-scorer in the top flight of English football with his goal for Ipswich Town against Coventry City in February 1984. It was the start of career that should have reached the heights but, sadly, fell far short. Dozzell was a striker when he first broke into the Ipswich team, but it was soon realised that he was most effective playing in midfield. Neat and tidy in his control with excellent passing skills, he had the ability to cover the ground rapidly with a long, loping stride. That allowed him to make runs from deep positions into the box, where his height and eye for goal were always a threat. An England Under-21 international, he made over 350 senior appearances for his home town club and looked set to remain with Ipswich for the rest of his career, but when refused a new contract Spurs moved to sign him as Ossie Ardiles set out to make his mark as Spurs' manager. Unable to agree a fee with Ipswich, an independent tribunal directed that Spurs should pay £1.75 million with another £150,000 after 60 appearances. It seemed a reasonable investment for a 26-year old with his best years still to come as Dozzell settled well in his first year. Sadly, things did not continue that way as injuries, loss of form and, more importantly, loss of confidence left Dozzell struggling. After four years, with his undoubted talent sadly unfulfilled, he was given a free transfer. Initially he returned to Ipswich, but he quickly moved on to Northampton Town and Colchester United where his coolness and obvious class often shone through in the hustle and bustle of lower level football. A toe injury finally saw Dozzell retire from top class football, but he continued to play and manage at non-League level before joining Ipswich Town's academy. Just over 32 years after Dozzell had made his goal-scoring debut for Ipswich, he was in the crowd to watch his son, Andre, repeat the feat. Andre was 16.

Appearances:
League: 68 (16) apps. 13 gls.
FA Cup: 5* (1) apps. 1 gl.
FL Cup: 8 (2) apps.
Others: 14 (6) apps. 5 gls.
Total: 95 (25) apps. 19 gls.
* Includes 1 abandoned match.

DRABBLE, Frank

Role: Goalkeeper 1909-10
5ft.11ins, 12st.0lbs.
Born: Southport, Lancashire, 8th July 1888
Died: Staines, Middlesex, 29th July 1964

CAREER: Bloxwich Wesleyans/Southport YMCA/Lancashire/**SPURS** trial Jul 1909, pro. Oct 1909/Nottingham Forest Jan 1911/Burnley Dec 1911 /Bradford Park Avenue Jun 1913/(Brentford, Fulham and Southport during World War One)/Bolton Wanderers Jul 1919/Southport Jun 1921-1922/Queens Park Rangers Mar 1924.

Debut v Preston North End (FL) (a) 23.10.1909 (match abandoned)

Frank Drabble had been playing for Southport YMCA in the Lancashire Amateur League when he arrived at White Hart Lane for a trial. Spurs were clearly impressed, for he was almost immediately signed professional and given a chance in the League side. His first appearance was at Preston North End on 23rd October 1909, but the match was abandoned after 50 minutes due to rain. He played in the next League game and in a London Professional Football Charity Fund match with Woolwich Arsenal, but then had to return the 'keeper's jersey to Frank Boreham. With the arrival later that term of both John Joyce and Tommy Lunn, Drabble was relegated to fourth choice keeper and at the end of the season allowed to move to Nottingham Forest. He quickly moved on to Burnley and then Bradford Park Avenue. During the First World War Drabble joined his home town club, Southport, and remained with them for their Football League debut. He finished his career with a brief spell at Queens' Park Rangers and later returned to his profession of a schoolmaster. He also worked as a bookmaker and finished life as an estate agent.

Appearances:
League: 2* apps.
Others: 2 apps.
Total: 4 apps. 0 gls.
* Includes 1 abandoned match.

DRAPER

Role: Left-back 1918-19

Debut v Clapton Orient (Fr) (a) 26.4.1919

Draper made his only appearance for Spurs in a friendly match when he was one of several players given a trial, who were not to progress any further with the club.

Appearances:
Others: 1 app.
Total: 1 apps. 0 gls.

DRYBURGH, William

Role: Outside-right 1902-03
Born: Lochgelly, Cowdenbeath, 22nd May 1876
Died: Kelty, Fife, 5th April 1951

CAREER: Dunfermline Juniors/Cowdenbeath Aug 1895/Sheffield Wednesday Aug 1897/Millwall Athletic Jul 1899/Sheffield Wednesday May 1901/Cowdenbeath Aug 1902/**SPURS** Dec 1902/released May 1903/Lochgelly United 1903-1905.

Debut v Portsmouth (SL) (h) 25.12.1902 (scored once)

Right from the start of the 1902-03 season Spurs were desperately seeking a successor for departed outside-right Tom Smith. The only player on the books capable of filling Smith's shoes was Alan Haig-Brown, but he was an amateur and not available on a regular basis. William Dryburgh had started with Cowdenbeath, spent two years with both Sheffield Wednesday and Millwall Athletic and another year with Wednesday before returning to Scotland. Clearly an experienced player-although not in the same class as Smith-it was hoped he might at least be able to provide  a similar sort of service. He made a goal-scoring debut on Christmas Day 1902 and played most of the remaining matches that season, but was released at its conclusion and returned home to play for Lochgelly United.

Appearances:
Southern: 16 apps. 2 gls.
FA Cup: 4 apps. 1 gl.
Others: 11 apps.
Total: 31 apps. 3 gls.

DRYSDALE, R T

Role: Half-back 1890-91

CAREER: Old St Stephens/(guest for **SPURS** Jan 1891).

Debut v Millwall Athletic (LSC) (a) 31.1.1891

Drysdale's only known appearance in Spurs first team was in January 1891 when he played in a Second Round London Senior Cup tie with Millwall Athletic that Spurs lost 1-5. He was one of several members of the Old St Stephens club who made odd appearances for Spurs.

Appearances:
Others: 1 app.
Total: 1 app. 0 gls.

DUFFUS, John Murison

Role: Centre-forward 1923-24
5ft.8ins. 11st.6lbs.
Born: Aberdeen, 10th May 1901
Died: Stockport, Cheshire, 18th September 1975

CAREER: Aberdeen Richmond/Dumbarton Jun 1919/(Bo'ness loan Nov 1919)/Dundee 1919/Scunthorpe & Lindsey United 1920/Llanelly Jun 1921 /Caerau/Clapton Orient Oct 1922/**SPURS** May 1923/Norwich City May

1924/Stockport County Jul 1927/Hyde United Aug 1928/Hurst Jul 1929/Congleton Town Nov 1929.

Debut v Norwich City (Fr) (a) 25.10.1923

Jack Duffus joined Spurs on a free transfer having accumulated plenty of experience in England as well as his native Scotland. Originally a centre-forward, he never got a chance at Spurs due to the scoring form of regular number nine Alex Lindsay, and played in only two senior matches, in one of which Spurs fielded barely more than reserve teams. Duffus played in one friendly with his only competitive match being a London FA Charity Cup replay with Crystal Palace. Released in May 1924, he joined Norwich City where he moved into the half-back line and played for Norwich for three years, before signing for Stockport County. He settled in Stockport where he ran a market gardening/nursery business. At Clapton Duffus played one game alongside his brother, Bob, who also played for Aberdeen, Dundee, Dumbarton, Scunthorpe United, Millwall and Accrington Stanley and was player-manager of Bangor City.

Appearances:
Others: 2 apps.
Total: 2 apps. 0 gls.

DUKES, Harold Parkinson

Role: Goalkeeper 1944-45
5ft.10ins. 11st.8lbs.
Born: Portsmouth, Hampshire, 31st March 1912
Died: Cambridge, Cambridgeshire, 13th August 1988

CAREER: Sleaford 1930/Martlesham 1931/Melton 1932/Orwell Works 1933/Ipswich Town am. Jan 1934/Norwich City pro. Aug 1934/(guest for Aldershot, Bedford Town, Brentford, Fulham, Queens Park Rangers and **SPURS** during World War Two)/Guildford City Jul 1947/Newmarket Town player-manager 1949–Aug 1950.

Debut v Reading (FLS) (a) 9.9.1944

Harry Dukes was on the books of Norwich City when he played as a guest for Spurs during the Second World War. After moving to Suffolk with his family, he played as a youth for several local clubs, before starting his senior career with the still amateur Ipswich Town, who he helped win the Southern Amateur League. Upon losing his job as a car salesman Dukes accepted the offer of professional terms from Norwich City and played regularly until the outbreak of the Second World War. During the war he guested for several League clubs, although most of his football was played with Bedford Town, until his return to Norwich in August 1945. His first appearance for Spurs was in September 1944 at Reading in a Football League South fixture. Spurs arrived for that match with only four men and Dukes, who had been delayed in meeting up with the Spurs party, had to run all the way from the railway station to the ground to get there in time for the kick-off. His next appearance was in February 1945 in a League South Cup tie having conceded six goals the previous week when he guested for Aldershot in the same competition at White Hart Lane. After the war he played just one season for Norwich before joining Guildford. Later in life Dukes was a publican and shopkeeper.

Appearances:
Others: 3 apps.
Total: 3 apps. 0 gls.

DULIN, Michael Charles

Role: Winger 1954-58
5ft.5ins. 10st.10lbs.
Born: Stepney, London, 25th October 1935

CAREER: Hitchin Grammar School/Arlesey Town/All England Grammar Schools/Welwyn Garden City/**SPURS** am. 1952, pro. Nov 1952/retired cs. 1958/Wingate manager 1967/Barking manager/Leyton-Wingate manager Jan 1976/Ilford manager Jan 1977/Wingate & Finchley manager, director of football, life vice-president Jan 2000.

Debut v Burnley (FL) (a) 17.12.1955
(Lille Olympique (Fr) (a) 14.8.1954)

A short but stickily-built winger who never stopped working, Micky Dulin appeared for Hertfordshire Youth and made his way up through the junior ranks at White Hart Lane after signing as an amateur whilst playing for Welwyn Garden City. His League debut was more than a year after his first team debut and, although he had played only a handful of games, he was just beginning to find his feet in First Division football when he was injured at Birmingham City in September 1957. Despite a long struggle to overcome

the problem, he was forced to concede defeat at the end of the 1957-58 season when he formally retired. He later took up the manager's post at Wingate, and despite spells with Barking and Ilford returned to Wingate in the mid-1980s. All told has given them over 30 years' service in various capacities.

Appearances:
League: 10 apps. 2 gls.
FA Cup: 1 app.
Others: 14 apps. 6 gls.
Total: 25 apps. 8 gls.

DUMITRESCU, Ilie

Role: Forward 1994-96
5ft.9ins. 11st.3lbs.
Born: Bucharest, Rumania, 6th January 1969

CAREER: Steaua Bucharest (Rumania) 1986/(Olt Scornicești (Rumania) loan Jul 1987)/**SPURS** Jul 1994/(Sevilla loan Dec 1994)/West Ham United

Mar 1996/Ciudad América (Mexico) Jan 1997/Deportivo Atalante (Mexico) Aug 1997/ Steaua Bucharest (Rumania) Aug 1998/retired Feb 1999/ Oțelul Galați (Rumania) coach Dec 2000/FC Brașov (Rumania) coach Jul-Aug 2001/Alki Larnaca (Cyprus) coach Sep 2001-Apr 2002/Petrolul Ploiești (Rumania) coach May 2002/Rumania Under-21 manager Aug-Oct 2002/FCM Bacău (Rumania) manager Oct 2002/Apollon Limassol (Cyprus) Jun 2003/AEK Athens (Greece) manager Feb-Jun 2004/Akratitos (Greece) coach Jun 2005/Kallithea (Greece) coach Oct 2005-Feb 2006/PAOK (Greece) coach Feb-Oct 2006 /Panthrakikos (Greece) Technical director May 2009/Steaua Bucharest (Rumania) coach Aug-Sep 2010.

Debut v Sheffield Wednesday (PL) (a) 20.8.1994

In July 1994 Spurs paid £2.6 million to sign Ilie Dumitrescu after he had produced one thrilling performance after another for Rumania in the World Cup. A wide midfielder, he had been with his home town club, Steaua Bucharest from the age of eight, at one time a full-back but soon recognised as an attacking force. Loaned to Olt Scornicești, favoured team of Rumanian president, Nicolae Ceaușescu, Dumitrescu developed rapidly and on his return to Steaua established himself as an integral part of an exciting team that did the Cup and League "double" in 1989, won the Cup in 1992 and the League in 1993 and 1994. Having made his international debut in April 1989, Dumitrescu was a crucial part of the national team by the time the World Cup began, with 35 appearances and twelve goals to his credit. His pace, directness, willingness to take on opponents and desire to shoot from any distance appealed to Ossie Ardiles' desire for all-out attacking football, and he arrived at White Hart Lane to become one of the short-lived "Famous Five" attacking force with Darren Anderton, Nicky Barmby, Teddy Sheringham and Jürgen Klinsmann. While the quintet produced some exhilarating football, the price was too many defeats and Ardiles lost his job. Of the players, Dumitrescu was the one to suffer most, immediately discarded by Gerry Francis and by the end of the year loaned out to Sevilla. Although he had a couple of brief opportunities in 1995-96, Dumitrescu was too unpredictable for Francis and made available for transfer. A deal was done with West Ham United in January 1996, but because he had played so rarely for Spurs, Dumitrescu had problems with his work permit and it was two months before the move could go through. He fared little better at Upton Park and within a year was playing in Mexico. He soon returned to Steaua, but in February 1999 announced persistent injury problems meant he had to bring to an end a sadly unfulfilled career. He later worked as a player's agent and coached in Rumania and Greece without any great success.

Appearances:
League: 16 (2) apps. 4 gls.
FL Cup: 2 apps. 1 gl.
Others: 6 (2) apps. 1 gl.
Total: 24 (4) apps. 6 gls.

DUNCAN, Andrew

Role: Inside-forward 1934-43
5ft.6ins. 10st.5lbs.
Born: Renton, Dumbartonshire, 25th January 1911
Died: Southall, Middlesex, 10th October 1983

CAREER: Welfare Juniors/Renton Thistle/Dumbarton May 1930/Renton Thistle/Hull City May 1930/**SPURS** Mar 1935/(Brentford, Chelmsford City and Crystal Palace during World War Two)/Chelmsford City May 1946/retired May 1948/**SPURS** ground-staff, scout.

Debut v Manchester City (FL) (h) 16.3.1935

A constructive inside-forward who used his considerable strength to advantage and also had the knack of scoring regularly, Andy Duncan, was signed for £6,000 by Spurs in March 1935 having netted 16 goals for Hull that season. Hull had received five years' great service from Duncan who helped them win the Third Division (North) in 1933. His Spurs' debut came immediately after signing, but he was unable to do anything to prevent the club finishing the season bottom of the table. Rather susceptible to injury, Duncan played fairly regularly over the next four seasons, but with the arrival of Ronnie Dix in the summer of 1939, his days at White Hart Lane seemed numbered. However, the intervention of war allowed him to turn out frequently until 29th August 1942 when, in a quite extraordinary incident midway through a poor opening game of the season against Crystal Palace, Duncan said he was not going to tolerate any more of the crowd's barracking and simply walked off the pitch! Although he remained on the books, he never wore a Spurs shirt again, and spent most of the next four years as a guest with Chelmsford City, to whom he was transferred after the war.

Appearances:
League: 93 apps. 22 gls.
FA Cup: 10 apps. 4 gls
Others: 81 apps. 22 gls.
Total: 184 apps. 48 gls.

DUNCAN, John Pearson

Role: Striker 1974-79
5ft.11in. 11st.4lbs.
Born: Dundee, 22nd February 1949

CAREER: Clepington Road School/Morgan Academy/Butterburn Youth Club/Dundee Schools/Dundee Apr 1966/(Broughty Thistle)/ **SPURS** Oct 1974/Derby County Sep 1978/Scunthorpe United player-manager Jun 1981-Feb 1983/Hartlepool United manager Apr 1983/ Chesterfield manager Jun 1983/Ipswich Town manager Jun 1987-Apr 1990/**SPURS** scout/Chesterfield manager Feb 1993-Apr 2000/ Loughborough University FC manager Aug 2007-May 2011.

Debut v Luton Town (FL) (a) 26.10.1974

Terry Neill's first signing as Spurs' manager, John Duncan was a Scotland schoolboys' trialist who had watched Alan Gilzean from the Dundee terraces and turned professional on leaving school. "Farmed out" as a junior to Broughty Athletic, Duncan was soon in the Dundee team and showing an eye for goal that twice saw him selected as a non-playing substitute for the full Scotland side, before a Scottish League appearance against the Football League in March 1973 when he scored both goals in a 2-2 draw. An immediate success following his £150,000 move, Duncan's twelve goals in his first season made him top scorer and effectively kept Spurs in the First Division. Whilst not the greatest of footballers when

away from goal, Duncan was simply lethal inside the penalty box, where his uncanny positional sixth-sense, swivel-turn and speed of reaction with both foot and head made him a deadly and regular goal-scorer. His notable average of a goal every other game whilst with Spurs is testament enough to the elegant Scot's prowess as a top-drawer finisher. Duncan led the scoring chart again the following season, but a serious back injury saw him miss most of the 1976 77 season when his goals may have saved Spurs from the ignominy of relegation. He was back in 1977 78, leading scorer as Spurs returned to Division One at the first attempt. His last match came in September 1978 when Spurs suffered a 0-7 drubbing at Liverpool. Later that month he moved to Derby County for £150,000. Recurring back injury problems restricted him to only 37 appearances for Derby. He moved to Scunthorpe, quickly taking over as manager. Harshly sacked to make way for Allan Clarke, Duncan joined Hartlepool, but after only two months in charge moved to Chesterfield, who he led to the Fourth Division championship in 1985. He then joined Ipswich Town, but despite the team's reputation for bright, adventurous football, became the first Ipswich manager to be dismissed when they failed to make the 1990 promotion play-offs. Duncan then went into school-teaching whilst keeping in touch with football as a Spurs' scout. He returned to management with Chesterfield, earning great credit as he led them to the semi-final, practically the final, of the FA Cup in 1997.

Appearances:
League: 101 (2) apps. 53 gls.
FA Cup: 7 apps. 2 gls.
FL Cup: 10 app. 7 gls.
Others: 21 (4) apps. 13 gls.
Total: 139 (6) apps. 75 gls.

DUNCAN, Adam Scott Mathieson

Role: Outside-right 1918-19
5ft.9ins. 11st.10lbs.
Born: *Dumbarton, Dunbartonshire, 2nd November 1888*
Died: *Helensburgh, Dunbartonshire, 3rd October 1976*

CAREER: Dumbarton Academy/Dumbarton Oakvale/Dumbarton Corinthians/Clydebank Juniors/Shettleston Juniors/Dumbarton Nov 1905/Newcastle United Mar 1908/Rangers May 1913/(guest for Celtic, Manchester United, Partick Thistle and SPURS during World War One)/Dumbarton Jul 1919/Cowdenbeath cs. 1920/retired 1922/Hamilton Academical secretary-manager Jul 1923/Cowdenbeath secretary-manager May 1924/Hamilton Academical secretary-manager May 1924/Cowdenbeath secretary-manager Jul 1925/Manchester United manager Jun 1932/Ipswich Town manager Sep 1937, secretary Aug 1955-May 1958.

Debut v West Ham United (LFC) (h) 16.11.1918

Scott Duncan was coming to the end of a fine playing career when he made his one guest appearance for Spurs while serving in the Royal Field Artillery. He had made his reputation as a close dribbling winger with Newcastle, helping them to the Football League title in 1909 and playing in a Scottish international trial in 1911, although never really establishing himself as a first team regular. He returned to Scotland with Rangers and it was only after the war that he wound down his playing career with Dumbarton and Cowdenbeath. He then moved into management with Hamilton Academical and Cowdenbeath, strangely signing to manage Cowdenbeath in May 1924, not quitting Hamilton and then deciding to remain with Hamilton. In June 1932, he joined Manchester United. With United for five years, he did not have a great deal of success, although he did take them to the Second Division championship in 1936, but resigned only three months into the next season to take over Ipswich Town. Duncan was manager at Portman Road for 18 years, taking them into the Football League and to the Third Division (South) title in 1954. With Alf Ramsey arriving in August 1955 to assume the

managerial duties, Duncan moved up to be secretary and only retired in May 1958 when almost 70 years old. Ipswich played Norwich City in a testimonial for him.

Appearances:
Others: 1 app.
Total: 1 app. 0 gls.

DUNMORE, David Gerald Ivor

Role: Centre-forward 1953-60
6ft.0ins. 13st.5lbs.
Born: *Whitehaven, Yorkshire, 18th February 1934*

CAREER: York Schools/North Riding Schools/Cliftonville Minors/York City am. 1950-51, part-time May 1952/SPURS part-time pro. Feb 1954, pro. Jan 1957/West Ham United Mar 1960/Leyton Orient Mar 1961/York City Jun 1965/Worcester City May 1967/Bridlington Trinity/Scarborough by 1968.

Debut v Arsenal (FL) (a) 27.2.1954

Looking to rebuild as the "Push and Run" team aged, Arthur Rowe was quickly on the trail of Dave Dunmore, who attracted scouts from several larger clubs to Bootham Crescent almost immediately after he had broken into York's League team. A tally of 25 goals in 48 League games for the Third Division (North) club, marked Dunmore as a player of considerable potential and he cost a sizeable £10,500 fee, but with his early career at White Hart Lane restricted by National Service, he never really blossomed. Unable to displace Len Duquemin, he then became reserve to Bobby Smith, but still proved a handy player who could be relied upon to give of his best. Following his transfer to West Ham as part of the £20,000 deal that saw John Smith move to Spurs, he showed his value by hitting 16 goals in 36

League games for the Hammers. Dunmore spent only twelve months with West Ham. He then joined Leyton Orient and helped them win promotion to the First Division in 1962. Dunmore finished his senior career back with York, before moving into non-League football.

Appearances:
League: 75 apps. 23 gls.
FA Cup: 6 apps. 3 gls.
Others: 13* (3) apps. 8 gls.
Total: 94 (3) apps. 34 gl.
*Includes 1 abandoned match

DUNN, Richard

Role: Inside-forward 1944-45
Born: Easington, Northumberland, 23rd December 1919
Died: January 1986

CAREER: Ferryhill Athletic/West Ham United Feb 1938/(guest for Hartlepools United, Preston North End, **SPURS** and York City during World War Two)/Hartlepools United Aug 1949/Consett/Wingate Welfare.

Debut v Reading (FLS) (a) 9.9.1944

A West Ham United player, Dickie Dunn made his one appearance for Spurs at Reading in September 1944 when Spurs arrived for the match with only four men. Fortunately, Dunn was at the game as a spectator and able to turn out at the last minute. He had joined the Hammers in 1938, but the Second World War meant he never established himself as a first choice player. He stayed with West Ham until moving to Hartlepools United where he finished his career. He then joined the prison service as a warder at Durham jail.

Appearances:
Others: 1 app.
Total: 1 app. 0 gls.

DUQUEMIN, Leonard Stanley

Role: Centre-forward 1945-57
5ft.11ins. 11st.11lbs.
Born: Cobo, Guernsey, 17th July 1924
Died: Buckhurst Hill, Essex, 20th April 2003

CAREER: Guernsey Schools/Guernsey Rangers (Guernsey)/Vauxbelet (Guernsey)/**SPURS** trial Dec 1945, am. Jan 1946, pro. Sep 1946/(guest for Chelmsford City and Colchester United during World War Two)/Bedford Town Nov 1958/Hastings United May 1960/Romford Jul 1961/retired May 1962.

Debut v Sheffield Wednesday (FL) (h) 30.8.1947 (scored once)
(Fulham (FLS) (a) 9.3.1946)

One of the few Channel Islanders to make a career in the Football League, Len Duquemin was playing for the Vauxbelet club when recommended to Spurs by a supporter on the island. He arrived for a trial at the end of 1945, was rapidly signed as an amateur and stayed for 13 years, leading the attack during those immensely successful seasons soon after the war. His first appearance was in a Football League South fixture in March 1946, but as the club had no reserve team at the time, Len played most of his football that season for Arthur Rowe's Chelmsford City. He made a goal-scoring League debut in August 1947 and was immediately secure as first choice centre-forward. A stoical, conscientious character, the "Duke" was a chunky, workmanlike player who was not as skilful as some of his day, but mobile and competitive. He was a splendid leader of the line, strong in the air, and always willing to sweat it out in support of others in the team. Duquemin also had a good shot in his armoury and hit many crucial goals-including the one that sealed the 1951 League title -, but it was his insatiable appetite for work and hard-running off the ball that allowed his clever positional movements to create as many goals as he scored and made him perfect for the "Push and Run" style that bought Spurs the

Second Division title in 1950 and the League Championship the following season. The arrival of Dave Dunmore in February 1954 put Duquemin's place in jeopardy but, typically, he fought back and also saw off the challenge of Alfie Stokes, before having to concede the number nine shirt to Bobby Smith. Duquemin moved on to Bedford Town (top-scoring as they won the Southern League in 1959) and also played for Hastings United and Romford before retiring from the game. He then ran a newsagent's business in Northumberland Park and was landlord of the Haunch of Venison in Cheshunt until his retirement. During the German occupation of the Channel Islands in the Second World War, Duquemin worked as a gardener in a monastery, He learned fluent French as the Catholic monk's command of English was so limited.

Appearances:
League: 275* apps. 114 gls.
FA Cup: 33 apps. 20 gls.
Others: 66 apps. 53 gls.
Total: 374 apps. 187 gls.
*Includes 1 abandoned match.

DURIE, Gordon Scott

Role: Striker 1991-93
6ft.0ins. 12st.0lbs.
Born: Paisley, Renfrewshire, 6th December 1965

CAREER: Hill O'Beath Hawthorn/East Fife Dec 1981/Hibernian Oct 1984/Chelsea Apr 1986/**SPURS** Aug 1991/Rangers Nov 1993/Heart of Midlothian Sep 2000/East Fife asst. manager Nov 2010, caretaker manager and permanent Mar-Nov 2012/Rangers Reserve and Under-20s coach Jul 2013, first team coach Dec 2014-Jul 2015.

Debut v Southampton (FL) (a) 17.8.1991 (scored once)

When Spurs moved to sign Gordon Durie in August 1991 it was something of a surprise. The club's financial problems were well known, and to many the £2,000,000 fee seemed beyond its resources. However, the money was somehow found by the club's new owners, Alan Sugar and Terry Venables, and it showed their determination to build upon the previous season's FA Cup success. Durie had first impressed in his time with Hibernian and, at Chelsea, soon settled to English football, forming a potent goal-scoring partnership with Kerry Dixon. Durie won four Scottish Under-21 caps, before a full international debut as a substitute against Bulgaria in November 1987. An opportunist striker, pacy, strong

running and always keen to take on defenders, he collected twelve full caps before his move to White Hart Lane. He made a goal-scoring debut in the opening match of the season and looked just the player Spurs needed to share the goal-scoring burden with Gary Lineker, but then Durie hit a drought and failed to find the net for three months as Spurs struggled. His form was not helped either by some speculation that he might return to Scotland. Durie won his first cap as a Spurs' player against Switzerland in September 1991, and continued to figure in Scotland's future international planning, even though he was in and out of the Spurs' team. A boyhood fan of Rangers, Durie eventually got his wish with a transfer to them in November 1993. Settled back in his native Scotland, Durie helped keep Rangers at the pinnacle of the Scottish game picking up six championships, three Scottish Cups and one Scottish League Cup, before finishing his career with a season at Heart of Midlothian. Having been out of the game for some years, Durie became assistant manager of East Fife in November 2010, shortly after his son, Scott, had joined the Fifers from Rangers. In November 2012 illness caused Durie to stand down from the manager's post he had occupied since March that year. On recovering he joined the coaching staff at Rangers until his services were dispensed with when Mark Warburton took over as manager.

Appearances:
League: 58 apps. 11 gls.
FA Cup: 2 apps.
FL Cup: 10 apps. 3 gls.
Euro: 8 apps. 3 gls.
Others: 8 (4) apps. 2 gls.
Total: 86 (4) apps. 19 gls.

DURSTON

Role: Half-back 1943-44

Debut v Millwall (Fr) (a) 10.4.1944.

A junior on Millwall's books, Durston played his one game for Spurs in a friendly against his own club when he and two other Millwall juniors helped make up a full team for Spurs.

Appearances:
Others: 1 app.
Total: 1 app. 0 gls.

DYSON, Terence Kent

Role: Winger 1954-65
5ft.3ins. 10st.5lbs.
Born: Malton, Yorkshire, 29th November 1934

CAREER: Scarborough/**SPURS** am. Dec 1954, pro. Apr 1955/Fulham Jun 1965/Colchester United Aug 1968/Guildford City Jul 1970/Kings Lynn 1971/Wealdstone player-coach Feb 1972, player-asst. manager 1974/Dagenham manager 1979/Boreham Wood coach 1983/Kingsbury Town manager Aug 1985-Feb 1988/Ruislip coach Dec 1988/Wingate manager/Dagenham asst. manager/FA Premier Academy League (academy observer) late 1999.

Debut v Sheffield United (FL) (h) 19.3.1955

At 5ft 3ins it is no surprise that Terry Dyson was the son of a jockey-the well-known "Ginger" Dyson. He signed for Spurs whilst doing his National Service and joined the ranks of the professionals on his discharge from the army, by which time he had already made his debut. An out-and-out winger, his early years with Spurs were spent as understudy to George Robb and Terry Medwin. This limited Dyson's senior appearances and his best chance of a first team place on Robb's retirement appeared to disappear when Cliff Jones arrived early in 1958. Several clubs were keen to give Dyson regular League football, but Bill Nicholson refused to let him go. Dyson was richly rewarded, being almost ever-present in the famous "Double" winning team of 1960-61, when he headed the crucial second goal of the FA Cup Final against Leicester City. A fast, lively, and gritty little competitor, tenacious Terry was also likely to pop up at any time with a shot on goal. Dyson loved every minute of his football and Spurs' fans in return loved his trickery and his whole-hearted endeavour as well as his enthusiasm and zest for the game. After the "Double" triumph he was back to battling it out with Medwin and Jones for a place, and lost out to Medwin in the 1962 FA Cup Final. However, his greatest match was still to come. In the 1963 European Cup-Winners' Cup Final it was Dyson's exciting thrusts down the wing and two magnificent goals that helped destroy Atletico Madrid 5-1 to make Spurs Britain's first winners of a European trophy. Medwin's enforced retirement saw Dyson a regular once again, until he eventually moved on, his loyalty recognised with a cut-price £5,000 transfer to Fulham. With age creeping up, he only stayed three years at Craven Cottage, before going to Colchester United. Dyson then moved into non-League football, helping Guildford City win the Southern League in 1971 and Wealdstone do likewise three years later. Dyson later worked as games instructor at Hampstead School and managed around the non-League circuit before opening his own sports shop.

Appearances:
League: 184 apps. 41 gls.
FA Cup: 16 apps. 6 gls.
Euro: 9 apps. 8 gls.
Others: 30* (5) apps. 13 gls.
Total: 239 (5) apps. 68 gls.
*Includes 1 abandoned match

E

EADON, John Polloc

Role: Goalkeeper 1914-19
5ft.10ins. 11st.9lbs.
Born: Glasgow, 3rd September 1889
Died: Ballieston, Glasgow, 14th January 1961

CAREER: Maryhill/**SPURS** Sep 1913/Albion Rovers Sep 1915/Dykehead Oct 1915/Ayr United Aug 1918/Dumbarton Sep 1918/St Johnstone/ (Morton loan Sep 1920).

Debut v Middlesbrough (FL) (a) 13.2.1915
(Fulham (Fr) (h) 6.2.1915)

Although John Eadon was signed in September 1913 and was with Spurs for three years, he made only six first team appearances, all in the 1914-15 season when the club were badly hit by the national call to arms and finished bottom of the First Division. Despite conceding an embarrassing seven goals on his League debut, Eadon retained his place for the next four matches, but during those let in a further twelve and gave way to Bill Jacques. Not retained for the following season, he returned to Scotland with Albion Rovers, but did play for Spurs again, turning out against Millwall in a London Football Combination fixture in April 1919.

Appearances:
League: 5 apps.
Others: 2 apps.
Total: 7 apps. 0 gls.

EAMES, Walter

Role: Centre-forward 1906-07
5ft.9ins. 11st.0lbs.
Born: Watford, Hertfordshire, 21st December 1883
Died: Leavesden, Hertfordshire, 11th March 1941

CAREER: Crescent Ramblers/Melrose/Watford am., pro. Feb 1903/ **SPURS** May 1906/Watford Apr 1907/New Brompton Sep 1908.

Debut v West Ham United (SL) (h) 1.9.1906

Wally Eames spent several years with Watford prior to joining Spurs, but stayed for only one season at White Hart Lane. He started the campaign

in the first team, but lost his place immediately Vivian Woodward was available. After that he only appeared when Woodward was absent and on his release in April 1907 returned to Watford. Eames' stay in Hertfordshire was much shorter this time, for in September 1908 he joined New Brompton, who were shortly to change their name to Gillingham, where he spent two years.

Appearances:
Southern: 7 apps. 2 gls.
Others: 4 apps.
Total: 11 apps. 2 gls.

EASTHAM, Stanley

Role: Half-back 1942-43
Born: Bolton, Lancashire, 26th November 1913

CAREER: Kingstonian/Liverpool May 1938/(guest for Brentford, Leicester City and **SPURS** during World War Two)/Exeter City Mar 1946 /Stockport County Jun 1946/Brisbane Corinthian (Australia) Jul 1949/ Perth City (Australia) 1950/Western (New Zealand) player-coach 1952-1956.

Debut v Luton Town (FLS) (a) 14.11.1942

An England amateur international in his early days with Kingstonian, Eastham represented Great Britain at the 1936 Olympics and was on Liverpool's books when he played his one game for Spurs. Although he played a few wartime matches for Liverpool and guested for other club's such as Brentford and Leicester City, he never appeared in Liverpool's League team. Late in the war he moved to Exeter City, but soon returned north signing for Stockport County where he finished his UK career before emigrating to Australia.

Appearances:
Others: 1 app.
Total: 1 app. 0 gls.

ECCLES, James W

Role: Inside-forward 1894-96

CAREER: Queen's Park 1888-90/**SPURS** cs. 1894/London Caledonians/ West Norwood.

Debut v West Herts (FAC) (h) 13.10.1894
(Uxbridge (Fr) (a) 15.9.1894)

Well known with Queen's Park (and in some reports described as a

"Scottish international") Eccles joined Spurs at the start of the 1894 95 season having moved down to London looking for work. In the early part of the season he was the regular inside-right, helping the club reach the Fourth Qualifying Round of the FA Cup and the Second Round of the Amateur Cup in what was only Spurs' second venture into the competition. He appears to have specialised in playing Cup matches, for he turned out in most of the Cup games, but few of the friendlies that made up the bulk of Spurs' fixtures at that time. This may be explained by the fact that he also turned out for London Caledonians, the major club in London for exiled Scots. In the following season he played five early matches, but disappeared from the team after December 1895, perhaps opposed to the idea of playing for a professional club. However, he continued to play for London Caledonians for the next two seasons, although in 1897-98 he appeared for West Norwood.

Appearances:
FA Cup: 6 apps. 3 gls.
Others: 22 apps. 5 gls.
Total: 28 apps. 8 gls.

EDINBURGH, Justin Charles

Role: Full-back 1990-2000
5ft.10ins. 11st.8lbs.
Born: Brentwood, Essex, 18th December 1969

CAREER: Maldon Saints/Vange United/Southend United YTS cs. 1986, pro. cs. 1988/**SPURS** loan Jan 1990, perm Jul 1990/Portsmouth loan and perm Mar 2000/retired Jun 2002/**SPURS** Academy coach Aug 2002/Billericay Town manager May 2003/Fisher Athletic manager Jan 2006/Grays Athletic asst. manager Dec 2006, manager Jan 2007-Feb 2008/Woking asst. manager Apr-May 2008/Nottingham Forest scout Jun 2008/Rushden & Diamonds asst. manager Oct 2008, caretaker manager Feb 2009, manager Apr 2009/Newport County manager Oct 2011/Gillingham manager Feb 2015/Northampton Town manager Jan 2017.

Debut v Hartlepool United (FLC) (h) 26.9.1990
(Shelbourne (sub) (Fr) (a) 1.8.1990)

A quick thinking full-back, always eager to get forward and join the attack, Justin Edinburgh so impressed Spurs' scouts with his performances for Southend United that in January 1990 he joined the White Hart Lane staff on three months' loan. At the end of that period he returned to Southend and helped the Shrimpers finish their successful Fourth Division promotion campaign, before signing for Spurs on a permanent basis for £150,000. By then he had totalled only 37 League appearances and was regarded as long term cover for the more experienced Pat Van den Hauwe. However, Edinburgh got his first team chance sooner than expected. Having played in all the pre-season friendlies when Van den Hauwe was out injured, he started the League campaign in the reserves, but was then called up to make his competitive debut in the Rumbelows League Cup match with Hartlepool United in September 1990 when Guðni Bergsson was on international duty. With Terry Fenwick suffering two serious injuries, Van den Hauwe switched to the right. By the end of the season Edinburgh had not only laid claim to the left-back slot, but also given such a highly polished performance in the 1991 FA Cup Final victory over Nottingham Forest, that it was hard to believe that only twelve months earlier, he had been playing in the Fourth Division. Never really sure of his place, Edinburgh continued to vie with the likes of Fenwick, Van den Hauwe, Sol Campbell and Clive Wilson for the left-back slot, until the arrival of Mauricio Taricco left Edinburgh on the fringes. After more than 300 games he was allowed to move to Portsmouth. When injury curtailed his career, he moved into management, initially at non-League level, but soon in the Football League.

Appearances:
League: 190 (23) apps. 1 gl.
FA Cup: 27 (1) apps.
FL Cup: 25 (4) apps.
Euro: 4 (2) apps.
Others: 56 (19) apps.
Total: 302 (49) apps. 1 gls.

EDMAN, Erik Kenneth

Role: Full-back 2004-06
5ft.10ins. 12st.4lbs.
Born: Huskvarna, Sweden, 11th November 1978

CAREER: Habo IF (Sweden)/Helsingborgs IF (Sweden) 1994/Torino (Italy) Jul 1999/(Karlsruhe (Germany) loan Jan 2000)/AIK (Sweden) Jul 2000/Heerenveen (Holland) Jul 2001/**SPURS** Jul 2004/Stade Rennais (France) Aug 2005/Wigan Athletic Jan 2008/Helsingborgs IF (Sweden) Feb 2010, coach Jan 2012-Oct 2015.

Debut v Liverpool (BPL) (h) 14.8.2004
(Feyenoord (sub) (Fr) (Seville) 3.8.2004)

Another of the flood of signings that followed the arrival of Frank Arnesen and Jacques Santini, Erik Edman was an experienced defender, a regular for Sweden and much travelled. Having started with the youth set up at Habo IF, he had quickly been spotted by Helsingborgs and soon found himself a first team regular. A transfer to Italy with Torino seemed likely to propel him to the heights, but he failed to settle to the Italian way and quickly joined Karlsruhe, where he made few appearances before returning to Sweden with AIK of Stockholm. After one season he was on the move again, joining Heerenveen in Holland, where he rediscovered the form that had made him such a highly-rated talent. When the Dutch club hit financial problems Edman, who had performed well for Sweden at Euro 2004, was one of their most saleable assets and Arnesen knew he had a bargain when Heerenveen let it be known he could be signed for little more than £1.7 million. It was a transfer that was to cause trouble between Edman and Heerenveen who were to pay 10% of any transfer fee they received for him to AIK. Edman had agreed to take a low wage on the basis he would receive 20% of any fee. Heerenveen received €2.4 million from Spurs, but, having agreed to pay €700,000 to agents they instructed to find a buyer for Edman, told Edman the fee was only €1.7 million. They also claimed he agreed to waive his 20% so the deal would go through. Edman had to take Heerenveen to a Dutch FA tribunal before receiving his cut of the full fee. He later realised he had been incorrect; nothing had been due to him. He promptly admitted his mistake and repaid the amount involved. In his one full season with Spurs, Edman did little wrong. He proved a consistent performer, solid in defence but, perhaps a little reluctant to get forward at times. Still, it was a surprise when Spurs decided to let him leave after little more than a year, having lined up Lee Young-Pyo as his replacement. France and Stade Rennais was Edman's next stop, his three years there the longest he stayed at one club. A cruciate ligament injury early in his time with Wigan, all but brought his career to an end. Struggling to recover, his final game for Wigan was in their 1-9 hammering at White Hart Lane in November 2009. He eventually returned to Helsingborgs, adding another Swedish title in 2011 to the one he had helped them win in 1999. When he stopped playing, Edman worked on Helsingborgs' coaching staff, taking charge of their academy.

Appearances:
League: 31 apps. 1 gl.
FA Cup: 2 (1) apps.
Others: 6 (2) apps.
Total: 39 (3) apps. 1 gl.

EDRICH, William John

Role: Winger 1935-37
5ft.10ins. 10st.10lbs.
Born: Lingwood, Norfolk, 26th March 1916
Died: Chesham, Buckinghamshire, 23rd April 1986

CAREER: Bracondale School/Norfolk/Norwich City am. Aug 1932/SPURS am. Oct 1934, (Northfleet United 1934), pro. Aug 1935/Chelmsford City Aug 1939/(guest for Bournemouth and Boscombe Athletic and Lincoln City during World War Two)/released May 1947.

Debut v Blackpool (FL) (h) 30.11.1935

Far better known as an outstanding cricketer, Bill Edrich moved to London from his native Norfolk specifically so he would qualify to play cricket for Middlesex. Having been an amateur on Norwich City's books and played for Norfolk, Spurs were quick to secure his services and he was sent along to the Northfleet nursery club. Edrich showed such considerable aptitude that within a year he had signed professional and made his League debut. An outside-left with considerable pace and an accurate cross, he finished the season with nine appearances and, as he began to carve out a first team niche the following season, looked set for a highly successful football career. Sadly, cricket was Edrich's first love and when he won the chance to go on tour in 1937, Spurs agreed to release him from his contract on the

understanding he would return at the end of the trip. As it was, he decided not to pursue a football future and concentrated, very successfully, on cricket. When he did decide to play some football again, in August 1939, it was with Southern League, Chelmsford City, although during war-time, when he was a squadron leader and won a DFC, he also made one appearance for both Bournemouth and Lincoln. The high regard in which Spurs held his footballing talents is evidenced by their retention of his League registration until 1947, after which they knew he would not return. That glorious summer Edrich and his brilliant Middlesex batting partner Denis Compton (Arsenal & England) were record-breaking idols who drew vast crowds everywhere they played. Edrich hit a quite remarkable 3,539 runs that season, and in a first class career between 1934 and 1958 stroked 39,965 runs with 86 centuries. He was also a fine bowler and superb slip fielder, who continued to play minor counties cricket for Norfolk until 1971.

Appearances:
League: 20 apps. 4 gls.
Total: 20 apps. 4 gls.

EDWARDS, Albert

Role: Outside-left 1896-97
5ft.7ins. 11st. 0lbs.
Died: During World War One

CAREER: Southborne/Trowbridge Town/Swindon Town 1895/**SPURS** trial Apr 1897/Trowbridge Town/Swindon Town 1900-02/Queens Park Rangers 1902-1905/Swindon Town 1905-06

Debut v Nottingham Forest (Fr) (h) 16.4.1897

At the end of the 1896-97 season Spurs were looking for new recruits. Edwards was one of the players Spurs took the opportunity to give a trial to. He played in three friendly matches in April 1897, but although regarded as one of the better forwards tried was not offered terms. He did not return to Swindon immediately, but later gave then good service from 1900 to 1903.

Appearances:
Others: 3 apps.
Total: 3 apps. 0 gls.

EDWARDS, Harold C

Role: Forward 1893-95

CAREER: Old St Stephens 1891-96/(guest for **SPURS**).

Debut v Old Harrovians (AmC) (h) 20.10.1894
(Crouch End (Fr) (a) 21.4.1894 (scored once))

Captain of Old St Stephens and a Middlesex representative player, Edwards made two appearances for Spurs. The first was in the last match of the 1893-94 season, a friendly at local rivals Crouch End, when he played centre-forward. The other was in October 1894 in a First Qualifying Round Amateur Cup tie with Old Harrovians. He scored once from the inside-right position in Spurs 7-0 victory. As Old St Stephens developed into the

Shepherds Bush club, Edwards served on their committee from 1899 to 1914.

Appearances:
Others: 2 apps. 1 gl.
Total: 2 apps. 1 gl.

EDWARDS, Marcus

Role: Midfielder 2016-
5ft. 4ins. 9st.9lbs.
Born: London, 3rd December 1998

CAREER: Winchmore Hill School/**SPURS** Academy Scholar Jul 2015, pro. Aug 2016.

Debut v Gillingham (sub) (FLC) 21.9.2016
(v Juventus (sub) (Fr) (Melbourne) 26.7.2016)

A diminutive, attacking midfielder, Marcus Edwards has long been regarded as a jewel in the crown of the Spurs Academy. With terrific ball control and dribbling ability, his low centre of gravity helps him keep the ball close in while turning in the tightest of circles to seek out space or beat a defender. A taker of chances as much as a creator, he has represented England at all youth levels after first beginning to train with Spurs as a nine-year old. The object of envious glances from several clubs, both at home and abroad, Edwards was given an early chance in the first team in the International Champions Cup matches of July 2016, impressing all with his confidence, ability on the ball and eye for the killer pass. Signing his first professional on the return from Australia, as long as he does not allow his head to be turned, Edwards is at the perfect club to learn the game and develop into a real star.

Appearances:
FL Cup: (1)
Others: 2 (3) apps. 1 gl.
Total: 2 (4) apps. 1 gl.

EDWARDS, Matthew David

Role: Midfield 1990-92
Born: Hammersmith, London, 15th June 1971

CAREER: Saltdean Tigers/Elmbridge Schools/**SPURS** trainee Jul 1987, pro. cs. 1989/(Reading loan March 1991)/Brighton and Hove Albion cs. 1992/Kettering Jul 1994/Walton and Hersham loan early 1995-96, perm. Dec 1995/ Enfield Feb 1996/ Carshalton Dec 1997/ Boreham Wood Dec 1997/ Croydon/Ashstead.

Debut v West Ham United (Fr) (a) 12.11.1990

Although principally still a youth team player, Matt Edwards made his first team debut at West Ham United in November 1990 in a testimonial for "Hammers" manager, Billy Bonds. In March 1991, he was loaned to Reading until the end of the season and on his return was a member of the touring party to Japan where he scored his first goal at senior level. He never got another look in at first team level and when given a free transfer at the end of 1991-92 joined Brighton and Hove Albion. Edwards did not fare too well with the struggling "Seagulls" and moved into non-League football. No sooner had he signed for Kettering though, than he was injured and out for the whole of the 1994-95 season. He began to rediscover his best form while with Walton and Horsham and moved on to Enfield, but was eventually forced to retire due to a bad knee injury.

Appearances:
Others: 2 (6) apps. 1 gl.
Total: 2 (6) apps. 1 gl.

EDWARDS, Reginald Charles

Role: Winger 1941-44
5ft.6ins. 10st. 0lbs.
Born: Newton-Le-Willows, Cheshire, 24th July 1919
Died: Newton-Le Williams, Cheshire 28th March 2002

CAREER: Earlestown White Star/Alloa Athletic/(guest for Queens Park Rangers, Luton Town, **SPURS**, Swansea Town and Watford during World War Two)/Luton Town am. Aug 1945, pro. Nov 1945/Accrington Stanley Aug 1946.

Debut v Brentford (LWL) (h) 25.4.1942

Another of the guest players from the Second World War, Reg Edwards was a railway electrician serving in the RAF when he played for Spurs. He had previously played for Alloa Athletic and was to go on to make war-time appearances for Swansea Town, Queens Park Rangers, Watford and Luton Town before signing professional for the "Hatters". Primarily a winger, he made the odd appearance for Spurs during the middle war years occupying any position that needed filling. Edwards was transferred to Accrington Stanley in August 1946 and played for the former Football League club for almost three years, before returning to the electrical trade.

Appearances:
Others: 8 apps. 2 gls.
Total: 8 apps. 2 gls.

EDWARDS

Role: Half-back 1891-92

Debut v St Albans (Fr) (a) 18.4.1892

Edwards is only known to have made one appearances for Spurs, a friendly at St Albans in April 1892.

Appearances:
Others: 1 app.
Total: 1 app. 0 gls.

EGGETT, John Henry

Role: Goalkeeper 1904-07
5ft.9ins. 12st.0lbs.
Born: Wisbech, Norfolk, 19th April 1874
Died: Doncaster, Yorkshire, July qtr. 1943

CAREER: Wisbech/Doncaster Rovers cs. 1894/Woolwich Arsenal cs. 1903/West Ham United Jan 1904/**SPURS** May 1904/Croydon Common Apr 1907.

Debut v Portsmouth (WL) (a) 22.10.1904

Having been a regular with Doncaster Rovers, helping them win the Midland League in 1897 and 1899, Jack Eggett contributed to their rise to Football League status in 1901. They spent only two years in the League, but in that time Eggett proved himself their star performer, and when they returned to the Midland League he was quickly snapped up by Woolwich Arsenal. He spent half a season in south London, but failed to make a League appearance before joining West Ham. Signed by Spurs, he had to wait until October 1904 before making his debut, but from then on was virtually immovable. Having been a regular with Doncaster Rovers, helping them win the Midland League in 1897 and 1899, Jack Eggett contributed to their rise to Football League status in 1901. They spent only two years in the League, but in that time Eggett proved himself their star performer, and when they returned to the Midland League he was quickly snapped up by Woolwich Arsenal. He spent half a season in south London, but failed to make a League appearance before joining West Ham. Signed by Spurs, he had to wait until October 1904 before making his debut, but from then on was virtually immovable, playing in all further matches that season, all the Southern League matches of 1905-06 and missing only the occasional game in the secondary Western League competition. Eggett started his last season with Spurs in similar fashion, but then suffered an injury that allowed the newly signed Matt Reilly to take over the 'keeper's position. Eggett was unable to get back and was released in April 1907. He immediately joined the newly professionalised Croydon Common, where he played for one season.

Appearances:
Southern: 66 apps.
FA Cup: 8 apps.
Others: 44* apps.
Total: **118 apps. 0 gls.**
*Includes 1 abandoned match.

EL HAMDAOUI, Mounir

Role: Forward 2005-06
6ft.0ins. 13st.5lbs.
Born: Rotterdam, Holland 14th April 1984

CAREER: SC Excelsior (Holland) 2001/Blackburn Rovers trial Jul 2004/Feyenoord (Holland) training Sep 2004/**SPURS** Jan 2005/(Derby County loan Sep 2005 and Jan 2006)/Willem II (Holland) Jun 2006/AZ Alkmaar (Holland) Aug 2007/Ajax (Holland) Jul 2010/(Jong Ajax (Holland) Jul 2011)/Fiorentina (Italy) Jul 2012/(Malaga (Spain) loan Aug 2013)/AZ Alkmaar (Holland) Oct 2015/Umm Salal (Qatar) Jan 2016/Al-Taawon (Saudi Arabia) Aug 2016

Debut v Boca Juniors (sub) (Peace Cup) (Suwon, Korea) 16.7.2005

Another of the budding young talents spotted by Frank Arnesen, Mounir El Hamdaoui was one of the most promising youngsters with the Rotterdam club, SC Excelsior, something of an Academy for Feyenoord who had an arrangement that allowed them to sign the cream of Excelsior's talent. This accounts for his regular appearances at Feyenoord training sessions. Principally a central striker with Excelsior, El Hamdaoui could also perform out on the left, showing a surprising degree of skill for such a well-built player. Although a Dutch Under-21 international, his family originated from Morocco and as he held two passports El Hamdaoui eventually decided his future lay with his parent's country and, although he had not made his full international debut by the time of his move to Spurs, he had been called up to a couple of squads. With Spurs, El Hamdaoui was pulled back as an attacking midfielder and it was in that role that he played most of his games during two loan spells with Derby County. He featured in the 2005 Peace Cup and made a couple of appearances in pre-season

friendlies that summer, but was never in contention for a first team spot at White Hart Lane. In August 2006 he was allowed to return to Holland with Willem II. Although he started well, a torn cruciate ligament destroyed his first season back home, and he was surprisingly transferred to AZ Alkmaar when he had recovered. Three years at Alkmaar saw El Hamdaoui fulfil his promise and in July 2010 Ajax manager Martin Jol, who had worked with El Hamdaoui at Spurs, secured his transfer. A poor start to the season saw Jol depart in December 2010. El Hamdaoui soon fell out with Jol's replacement, Frank De Boer and so bad was the breakdown in relations that El Hamdaoui was exiled to Ajax's reserve outfit, Jong Ajax, until a move to Fiorentina was arranged. Principally used as a substitute by the Italian club, El Hamdaoui was not happy and went on loan to Malaga to secure some playing time. Back with Fiorentina after a year in Spain, El Hamdaoui was given no opportunity to impress and let his contract run down. He then returned to AZ Alkmaar for a short time before continuing his career in the Middle East.

Appearances:
Others: (4) apps.
Total: **(4) apps. 0 gls.**

ELKES, Albert John

Role: Inside-forward or centre-half 1923-29
6ft.0ins. 12st.6lbs.
Born: Snedshill, Salop, 31st December 1894
Died: Rayleigh, Essex, 22nd January 1972

CAREER: Wellington Town 1911/Wellington St Georges/Stalybridge Celtic pro. 1914/Shifnal Town/Birmingham Jan 1918/Southampton Mar 1922/**SPURS** May 1923/Middlesbrough Aug 1929/Watford Aug 1933/Stafford Rangers Aug 1934/Oakengates Town 1935/retired May 1937/Ford Motor Works coach May 1937.

Debut v Middlesbrough (FL) (h) 8.9.1923

Jack Elkes started his football career with two local amateur clubs before moving into the professional arena. He had four years at Birmingham, but it was not until he joined Southampton that he began to attract much attention. He scored two goals on his Saints' debut, but a broken collarbone in his next game, meant he was forced to miss the rest of the season. He recovered to hold down a regular place the following season and so impressed were Spurs that they moved to secure his transfer for £1,000. For a tall man, he was a deceptively clever, dribbling

inside-forward and at that time was considered one of best in the country. Very unlucky not to win international honours in his time at Spurs, he played in four international trial games and represented the Football League on three occasions. He was unable to make the breakthrough into the England team, although he was once named as first reserve. A member of the FA touring party to Australia in 1925, he also played for the Professionals against the Amateurs in the FA Charity Shield the same year. Best known as a forward, he was equally at home at centre-half, being strong and tall enough to handle the best centre-forwards, and yet had the ball control and passing ability to spark attacks from deep defensive positions. In April 1929, Elkes was not retained and moved to Middlesbrough where he played over 100 games in four years before joining Watford. He eventually moved into non-League circles. When he retired in 1937, he turned to coaching and in 1937-38 looked after Ford Motor Works FC at Dagenham.

Appearances:
League: 190 apps. 50 gls.
FA Cup: 10 apps. 1 gl.
Others: 12 apps. 6 gls.
Total: 212 apps. 57 gls.

ELKIN, Bertie Henry West

Role: Full-back 1909-11
5ft.11ins. 13st.0lbs.

Born: Neasden, London 14th January 1886
Died: Cape Town, South Africa, 3rd June 1962

CAREER: Fulham 1906-07/Leyton 1907/Stockport County cs. 1908/**SPURS** Dec 1909/released May 1911.

Debut v Bolton Wanderers (FL) (h) 11.1219.09

Bert Elkin had been on the books of Fulham and Luton Town before Spurs secured his transfer from Stockport County. He went straight into the first team and while he played only ten senior games before being dropped, he started the following season as first choice right-back. However, he was unable to maintain his form and by January 1911 found himself in the reserves. A tall, strong tackler with a mighty clearance, Elkin was not retained at the end of the season and emigrated to South Africa in September 1911. In 1924 he won the South African Open golf championship.

Appearances:
League: 26 apps.
FA Cup: 2 apps.
Others: 6 apps.
Total: 34 apps. 0 gls.

ELLIOTT, Arthur

Role: Forward 1894-95
Born: Nottingham, 1870

CAREER: Notts Rangers/Gainsborough Trinity/Accrington 1891/Woolwich Arsenal cs. 1892/**SPURS** Sep 1894/Nottingham Forest Oct 1894.

Debut v Third Battalion Grenadier Guards (Fr) (h) 6.10.1894

Having made his name with Gainsborough Trinity and Accrington, Elliott spent two years with Woolwich Arsenal, an inside-forward with a good goal-scoring record, but was released at the end of the 1893-94 season. Along with his former Woolwich Arsenal captain, Bill Julian, he accepted the chance to play for Spurs, subject to being re-instated as an amateur. That was granted in September 1894 and Elliott made his first, and last, Spurs' appearance at outside-left in a friendly with the Third Battalion of the Grenadier Guards. He did not play for Spurs again, as that same month he decided to return to Nottingham and joined Forest.

Appearances:
Others: 1 app.
Total: 1 app. 0 gls.

ELLIOTT, James E

Role: Centre-forward and half-back 1911-1920
5ft.11ins. 12st.10lbs.
Born: Peterborough 1891
Died: Turkey, 1939

CAREER: South Weald/Peterborough City/**SPURS** Oct 1911/Brentford May 1920-1924/Valencia (Spain) manager Aug 1927-1929/coach in the Balkans/coach in Switzerland/AIK (Sweden) coach 1932-1934/Guatemala City (Guatemala) coach 1935/Fenerbahce (Turkey) coach 1935-1938.

Debut v Sunderland (FL) (h) 20.1.1912

Signed as a 20-year old centre-forward from Peterborough, Jimmy Elliott made just 13 Football League appearances for Spurs in nine years with the club, but after moving to half-back became a regular during the First World War. He made his League debut within a month of signing, but was unable to retain a place and had to be content to understudy Jimmy Cantrell. In the 1913-14 season he switched to half-back and made one appearance as stand-in for Bob Steel but, like so many, had an uncertain future in first class football when war broke out. However, he was readily available during the war years and played regularly at half-back, full-back or centre-forward, whichever need arose. After the war, he made just one more League appearance before moving to spend four years at Brentford. He then travelled throughout the world as a coach and manager, including preparing Guatemala City for the 1935 Central American Olympic games. In Turkey, he was responsible for the coaching of ten teams run by the Fenerbahce club, including the first team, who won the Turkish Cup in three of his four seasons with them.

Appearances:
League: 13 apps. 4 gls.
Others: 141* apps. 11 gls.
Total: 154 apps. 15 gls.
* Includes 1 abandoned match.

ELLIS, H

Role: Winger 1891-94

CAREER: Fairfield/Edmonton Albion/**SPURS** Jan 1892/Broadwater by Feb 1894/Edmonton All Saints cs. 1894/Asplin Rovers cs. 1895.

Debut v Westminster Criterion (Fr) (h) 23.1.1892

Another of the early Spurs' players that it has proved impossible to find much information on, Ellis was playing for Edmonton Albion at the time of his first appearance for Spurs. He joined Spurs for the 1892-93 season and appears to have been quite a regular for the next two seasons, but then he and his inside-forward partner, J Brigden, joined Edmonton All Saints and ceased to play for Spurs.

Appearances:
Others: 24 apps.
Total: 24 apps. 0 gls.

EMBERY, Benjamin James

Role: Full-back 1965-66
Born: Barking, London, 10th October 1944

CAREER: Essex Schools/London Schools/**SPURS** app. May 1960, pro. Jun 1962/Exeter City Jun 1966/Barnet Jul 1968-May 1975/Tilbury player-manager/Epping/Gravesend 1975-1977/Dartford 1977/Ilford/Grays Athletic manager/Canvey Island manager 1983-1990/Great Wakering Rovers manager 1990-1994/Maldon Town manager 1994–Apr 2000/Braintree Town manager Apr 2000-Oct 2002/Concord Rangers manager Jun 2003-May 2004/Benfleet manager Jul 2006.

Debut v Sarpsborg (Fr) (a) 15.5.1966

Another of the many promising young players who joined Spurs in the 1960s, but never made the grade at White Hart Lane, Ben Embery made his one appearance in the first team in an end of season friendly against the Norwegian club Sarpsborg. The following month he moved to Exeter City. He spent two years with the Grecians before returning to London to play for Barnet. Converted to centre-half, he helped them win the Southern League Cup and reach the final of the FA Trophy in 1972. After seven years with the future League club, Embery moved to Tilbury. He was manager there for three months, then returned to playing with various non-League clubs, before starting his full managerial career at Canvey Island. He led Canvey to the Essex Senior League, took Great Wakering Rovers from the Essex Intermediate to the Essex Senior League, then steered Maldon Town from the Essex Senior to the Jewson League and Braintree into the Ryman League. Such successes earnt him a reputation as of one the finest managers in the Essex non-League game. Embery ended his career at Barnet in goal. With regular 'keeper, Jack McClelland, injured, the club had no back-up so Embery filled the breach. Embery's twin brother, William John, was also on Spurs' books as an amateur.

Appearances:
Others: 1 app.
Total: 1 app. 0 gls.

ENGLAND, Harold Michael M.B.E.

Role: Centre-half 1966-75
6ft.2ins 13st.3lbs.
Born: *Greenfield, North Wales, 2nd December 1941*

CAREER: Ysgol Dinas Basing/Holywell Schools/Flint Schools/Blackburn Rovers app. 1957, pro. Apr 1959/**SPURS** Aug 1966/retired Mar 1975/Seattle Sounders (USA) May 1975/Cardiff City Aug 1975/Seattle Sounders (USA) May 1976/Wales manager May 1980-Feb 1988.

Debut v Leeds United (FL) (h) 20.8.1966

When he first joined Blackburn Rovers, Mike England was a 16-year old inside-forward who had played in the same Ysgol Dinas Basing school team as his future international team-mate Ron Davies. He played for Rovers at outside-right, half-back and centre-forward before settling in central defence, where he was soon acknowledged as the best young centre-half in the country. He made his debut for Wales against Northern Ireland in April 1962 and by the time of his £95,000 transfer to Spurs in 1966 after Rovers' relegation from the top division, had won 20 full caps to go with eleven at Under-23 level. The fee was a British record for a defender, but England was excellent value and a worthy replacement for Maurice Norman. Lean, strong, quick and brave he was Spurs' defensive kingpin for the next nine years and hardly missed a game except through injury. Not without skill, he was also sometimes pushed up-field into an emergency centre-forward role. In his first season, England helped the club lift the FA Cup, giving a superb performance in the final when he dominated Chelsea centre-forward Tony Hateley. Although he missed the 1971 League Cup Final with an ankle injury, he helped Spurs win the 1972 UEFA Cup and the 1973 League Cup. He also appeared and scored in the 1974 UEFA Cup Final. Few forwards were able to get the better of the big hard "stopper" and, together with Pat Jennings, he provided a solid core to the defence lacking since the early Sixties. England did the same for Wales; captaining his country and winning a further 24 caps whilst with Spurs. In March 1975, aged 33, troubled by ankle problems and with Spurs struggling against relegation, he suddenly announced his retirement, but re-emerged the following August to play for one season with Cardiff City, having spent the summer with Seattle Sounders. He helped Cardiff to promotion from the Third Division and then spent four further American summers playing for Seattle, appearing for Team America in the 1976 Bi-Centennial Tournament with England, Brazil and Italy. He returned to the UK to take the Welsh manager's job. With his straight-talking, honest guidance, the Welsh were desperately unlucky not to qualify for the final stages of the major tournaments, in his seven-and-a-half seasons in charge. In 1984 he was awarded the MBE for his services to Welsh soccer. When he gave up football he took to running a retirement home in Wales.

Appearances:
League: 300 apps. 14 gls.
FA Cup: 32 apps. 2 gls.
FL Cup: 30 apps.
Euro: 35 apps. 3 gls.
Others: 37 apps. 1 gl.
Total: 434 apps. 20 gls.

ERENTZ, Henry Bernt

Role: Full-back 1898-04
5ft.10ins. 12st 2lbs.
Born: Dundee, 17th September 1874
Died: Dundee, 19th July 1947

CAREER: Dundee Aug 1895/Oldham County Sep 1896/Newton Heath May 1897/**SPURS** May 1898/released May 1904/Swindon Town Dec 1904/Corinthians trainer.

Debut v Bedminster (SL) (h) 10.9.1898

A Scot of Danish extraction, Harry Erentz made his reputation with his local club, Dundee, and spent a year with Oldham County, fore-runners of, but a different club to, Oldham Athletic, before joining Newton Heath. After only a year in Manchester, he made the move to Spurs and immediately became a great favourite. An imposing figure, strong and reliable, he was described as possessing "a cast-iron forehead" and nicknamed "Tiger" for the ferocity of his tackling. A totally committed and consistent performer, Erentz helped Spurs win the Southern League title in 1899-00 and played all matches in the following season's successful FA Cup run. It was only in 1903-04, when troubled by injury, that his standards began to slip and, with a fine understudy emerging in John Watson, Spurs decided to release him. Doubts about Erentz's fitness prevented him obtaining a new club until December, when he joined Swindon Town, but in March 1905, after just 16 appearances, he broke a leg and was forced to retire. He had a spell as trainer to the Corinthians, later returning to Dundee where he became a pub landlord. At Newton Heath in 1897-98 Erentz partnered his brother, Fred, at full-back. Fred made over 300 appearances for Newton Heath in a ten year career with the future Manchester United.

Appearances:
Southern: 134 apps.
FA Cup: 21 apps.
Others: 149 (1) apps. 2 gls.
Total: 304 (1) apps. 2 gls.

ERIKSEN, Christian Dannemann

Role: Midfielder 2013-
6ft.1ins. 11st.11lbs.
Born: Middelfart, Denmark, 14th February 1992

CAREER: Middelfart G&BK (Denmark) 1995/OB (Denmark) 2005/Chelsea trials 2006 and 2007/Barcelona (Spain) trial Apr 2008/Real Madrid (Spain) trial/Manchester United trial/AC Milan (Italy) trial/Ajax (Holland) Oct 2008/**SPURS** Aug 2013.

Debut v Norwich City (PL) (h) 14.9.2013

From his very youngest days, Christian Eriksen was identified as a major talent in the making. In his early teens Europe's biggest clubs were keen have a close look at him and he took the opportunity to look at them. When it came to making a decision he chose to join Ajax, a club with a fantastic reputation for taking talented young players and developing them into exceptional players. He raced through the youth ranks, picking up international honours along the way, to make his Eredvisie debut in January 2010. Given his chance by former Spurs manager, Martin Jol, once in the team Eriksen was there to stay, quickly establishing himself as the principal play-maker. He won his first full cap against Austria in March 2010, was voted Danish "Talent of the Year" for 2010 and collected the Dutch equivalent in 2011 having helped Ajax, including Toby Alderweireld and Jan Vertonghen, win the 2010-11 Eredivisie. Ajax retained the title for the next two years with Eriksen always at the centre of their attacking play. In August 2013 Eriksen was persuaded to join Spurs as they set out to rebuild following the sale of Gareth Bale. Fitting easily into the team, he was played out wide and in the centre of midfield. In both positions his creative talents shone out, but the advanced central position always looked the one where he could have a major impact on the game. With the arrival of Mauricio Pochettino, Eriksen found himself in just that position, his neat, incisive passing cutting open defences and creating chances for Harry Kane and the midfield runners. Whether cutting through a defence with the ball at his feet, playing short passes on the edge of the box till an opening can be found or spraying the ball out wide to the overlapping full-backs, Eriksen is always in Spurs best attacking moves. He scores his fair share of goals, many of them with lovely curling free-kicks. If he has one shortcoming, it is that all too often he pulls out of tackles, but Eriksen is an artist, not a workhorse. Thirty appearances for Denmark as a Spurs player have taken his total caps near the seventy mark.

Appearances:
League: 93 (5) apps. 23 gls.
FA Cup: 5 (2) apps. 1 gl.
FL Cup: 6 apps. 2 gls.
Euro: 14 (6) apps. 4 gls.
Others: 7 (2) apps. 1 gl.
Total: 125 (15) apps. 31 gls.

ETHERINGTON, Matthew

Role: Winger 1999-2004
5ft.9ins. 10st 12lbs.
Born: Truro. Cornwall, 14th August 1981

CAREER: Cornwall/Camborne Lions/Deacons School/Peterborough United trainee Jul 1997, pro. Aug 1998/Manchester United training Jul 1999/SPURS Jan 2000/(Bradford City loan Oct 2001)/West Ham United Aug 2003/Stoke City Jan 2009-Jun 2014/Millwall trial Oct 2014/retired Dec 2014.

Debut v Liverpool (sub) (PL) (a) 9.4.2000

Something of an old-fashioned left winger, Matt Etherington made his League debut as a 15-year old for Peterborough United in May 1997, and was soon the centre of attention from the country's biggest clubs. Alongside his young "Posh" team-mate, Simon Davies, Etherington spent a week on trial with Manchester United in July 1999, but while impressed with the talented duo, United manager, Alex Ferguson, decided not to seek their transfer. As Etherington settled as a regular for Peterborough, David Pleat was tasked with rebuilding Spurs junior set-up after it had been sadly neglected during Gerry Francis' tenure as manager. Etherington was one of the players with great potential Pleat was prepared to invest in, and in January 2000 Etherington and Davies joined Spurs for a combined fee of £1.3 million. The two of them progressed through Spurs' reserves into the first team, but Etherington, who won three England Under-21 caps, never really made a place his own. Fast and tricky, there were times when he could dazzle his way down the wing, but he lacked strength and was too often knocked out of games. In August 2003 Spurs were keen to secure Fredi Kanouté from West Ham United, but the Upton Park club would only do business if Etherington was allowed to join them in part-exchange. In over five years and nearly 200 appearances, Etherington proved himself a solid, reliable performer for the "Hammers", working up and down the flank and occasionally producing some scintillating performances. His departure for Stoke City, had more to do with his gambling problems, than for football reasons. At Stoke, Etherington continued to prove an almost indispensable performer for the best part of five years. On leaving Stoke he trained with Millwall and had an offer to sign for them, but he had been carrying an injury for some time. He rejected the offer and retired.

Appearances:
League: 20 (25) apps. 1 gl.
FA Cup: 1 (1) apps. 1 gl.
FL Cup: 3 (1) apps.
Others: 10 (13) apps. 2 gl.
Total: 34 (40) apps. 4 gls.

EVANS, Albert

Role: Centre-forward 1927-29
5ft.7ins. 9st.12lbs.
Born: Camberwell, London, 17th January 1901
Died: Enfield, Middlesex, 26th January 1969

CAREER: Army/Woking/SPURS trial Mar 1927, pro. May 1927 /(Northfleet United)/Grantham Sep 1929.

Debut v Birmingham (FL) (h) 27.8.1927

Signed from Woking after impressing while on trial, Albert Evans was sent along to the Northfleet nursery club, but within three months was called up to make a surprise debut. First choice centre-forward, Jimmy Blair, was injured in pre-season training and Evans was thrown-in at the deep end against Birmingham in the opening League match of the season. Evans played only three League games before returning to Northfleet, but moved on to the permanent White Hart Lane staff at the end of the season. Only three further first team appearances followed before his release in April 1929. He then joined Grantham.

Appearances:
League: 5 apps
Others: 2 apps.
Total: 7 apps. 0 gls.

EVANS, James Llewellyn

Role: Half-back 1943-44
5ft.8ins. 11st.0lbs.
Born: Merthyr Tydfil, Mid-Glamorgan, Wales, 18th February 1911
Died: Margate, Kent, August 1993

CAREER: Shobbon Instructional Centre/ Presteigne/Merthyr Town Feb 1930/Hereford United/Arsenal am. Mar 1935, pro. Sep 1936/(Margate loan Aug 1935)/Fulham May 1937/(Guest for SPURS during World War Two)/Margate 1946, player-caretaker-manager May-Jun 1948/Snowdon Colliery Welfare cs. 1949/Margate cs. 1952-1956.

Debut v Millwall (FLSC) (h) 11.3.1944

Jimmy Evans was a right-half with Fulham who made his only appearance for Spurs as a wartime guest in a Football League South Cup-tie with Millwall in March 1944. A Welsh Schools trialist, Evans was unemployed on leaving school and sent along to one of the government run Instructional Centres to be toughened up. Spotted by Presteigne playing for the Centre, he got a job down the pits and played as an amateur in the Merthyr League. In February 1930 he joined Merthyr Town, for whom he played two Football League matches in 1929-30. He then moved to Midland League Hereford United and it was there that he was noticed by Arsenal. They took him on and "farmed" him out to their nursery club at Margate before moving him up to the Highbury staff. Unable to make the first team, he was given a free transfer at the end of his one season at Highbury and signed for Fulham. He played there until returning to Margate after the Second World War. Save for one year at Snowdon Colliery Welfare, he spent ten years with Margate and settled in the town on his retirement.

Appearances:
Others: 1 app.
Total: 1 app. 0 gls.

EVANS, Norman

Role: Half-back 1939-40
Born: Waunlwyd, Ebbw Vale, Monmouthshire, Wales

CAREER: Cwm Villa/**SPURS** cs. 1936/Northfleet United/**SPURS** pro cs. 1939.

Debut v Norwich City (FLS) (h) 27.5.1940

Another of the young Welsh players that Spurs put through their nursery club at Northfleet, Evans joined Spurs from Cwm Villa, the same club that produced Ron Burgess. A promising youngster, he played in the Welsh amateur international trial of January 1939 and performed so well that he was then selected to play in the amateur international against England at the end of that month. He moved up to the professional staff at White Hart Lane in the summer of 1939, but was very unfortunate to make only one first team appearance for Spurs. That came against Norwich City in the last match of the 1939-40 season. Shortly after that game he was found to be suffering from rheumatic fever and forced to give up the game.

Appearances:
Others: 1 app.
Total: 1 app. 0 gls.

EVANS, Raymond Leslie

Role: Full-back 1968-75
5ft.10ins. 12st.8lbs.
Born: Edmonton, London, 20th September 1949

CAREER: Edmonton Schools/Middlesex Schools/**SPURS** app. Jul 1965, pro. May 1967/Millwall Jan 1975/Fulham Mar 1977/(St Louis Stars (USA) loan May 1977)/(California Surf (USA) loan May 1978)/Stoke City Aug 1979/Seattle Sounders (USA) Apr 1982/Tacoma Stars (USA)/Columbia Basin College (USA) asst. coach, head coach Jan 2001-Dec 2001/Soccer House, Pasco (USA) director of soccer operations.

Debut v Arsenal (FL) (a) 24.3.1969

An Edmonton schoolboy who worked his way through the ranks, England Youth cap Ray Evans was an athletic, positive full-back with an excellent long range shot, but his real forte was the superb way in which he could attack on the overlap at speed and clip in wickedly swinging crosses. Most unfortunate not to win any major honours at Spurs, he always seemed to lose out to the more experienced Joe Kinnear when the big games came round. Dropped for the semi-final clashes with AC Milan in the 1971-72 UEFA Cup which Spurs went on to win, he also missed the 1973 League Cup Final despite playing in most of the previous rounds. When he did keep his place for a major final, Spurs lost out to Feyenoord in the 1974 UEFA Cup. Eventually it seemed Evans had won his battle for the right-back spot, but then Bill Nicholson retired and his successor Terry Neill turned to Kinnear to add his extra experience to the battle

against relegation. There seemed no place for Evans at Spurs, and when Millwall offered him the chance of first team football he accepted a £35,000 move. He spent two years at The Den, moved on to Fulham and had his first summer spell in America in 1977 when he played for St Louis Stars. He appeared with California Surf the following summer, joined Stoke City and finished his British career with the Potteries club, although he played for Seattle Sounders in 1982 and 1983. He finished his playing career in the American Indoor Soccer League with Tacoma Stars and then turned to coaching youngsters in the Seattle area.

Appearances:
League: 133* (4) apps. 2 gls.
FA Cup: 7 apps.
FL Cup: 13 apps.
Euro: 22 (3) apps. 2 gls.
Others: 20 (2) apps. 1 gl.
Total: 195 (9) apps. 5 gls.
*Includes 1 abandoned match.

EVANS, R L

Role: Half-back 1943-44.

CAREER: Millwall/(guest for **SPURS** during World War Two).

Debut v Millwall (Fr) (a) 10.4.1944.

A Millwall junior, Evans' only appearance for Spurs was in a friendly match against his own club. With most available senior players turning out in competitive matches for other clubs, Millwall had to lend Spurs three of their juniors in order for Spurs to put a full team in the field.

Appearances:
Others: 1 app.
Total: 1 app. 0 gls.

EVANS, Thomas

Role: Half-back 1929-37
5ft.8ins. 12st.0lbs.
Born: Ton Pentre, Glamorgan, 28th November 1907
Died: Enfield, Middlesex, March 1993

CAREER: Ton Pentre/**SPURS** trial Apr 1927, am. May 1927, pro. May 1931/Leytonstone/Haywards Sports/Northfleet United/Haywards Sports/West Bromwich Albion Jun. 1937.

Debut v Southampton (FL) (a) 26.12.1929
(Crystal Palace (LPFCF) (h) 4.11.1929)

A ceaseless worker, Tom Evans joined Spurs junior staff after playing for his local club, Ton Pentre. Sent to the nursery at Northfleet, he did not sign professional until the summer of 1931, but had already made his Football League debut by then, having been called up on Boxing Day 1929 as Spurs suffered some desperate injury problems. Evans stayed in the team for the next match, but was not called upon again until April 1930. Once professional, he joined the scramble for midfield places in the first team of the 1930s and it was only in 1933-34, when the club finished third in the First Division, and 1934-35, when by stark contrast it finished bottom, that he had an extended run in the side. Not

re-engaged in April 1937, he joined West Bromwich Albion where he finished his career without making their first team.

Appearances:
League: 94 apps. 4 gls.
FA Cup: 7 apps.
Others: 7 apps. 1 gl.
Total: 108 apps. 5 gls.

EVANS, William

Role: Winger 1930-37
5ft.6ins. 12st.11lbs.
Born: *Waunlwyd, Ebbw Vale, Monmouthshire, 7th November 1912*
Died: *Ponders End, Enfield, Middlesex, 22nd July 1976*

CAREER: Victoria Mixed School/Ebbw Vale Schools/Tottenham Juniors/**SPURS** am. May 1929/Barnet/Hayward Sports/Cardiff City am. Jul 1930/ **SPURS** May 1931/Fulham player-coach May 1937/retired May 1938.

Debut v Swansea Town (FL) (h) 7.11.1931 (scored twice)
(Arsenal (LFACC) (Stamford Bridge) 4.5.1931)

Spurs invited 16-year old Willie Evans up to London to join the ground-staff and play for Tottenham Juniors after he had gone down the coal pits believing no club had recognised his talent as an inside-forward with Ebbw Vale Schools. Switched to outside-right, his progress was rapid and after a few games for Barnet he was sent to Hayward Sports of Enfield, another club Spurs used for nurturing promising junior players. With Haywards, he represented the Spartan League, Middlesex and the London FA and played for the Southern Counties against the Northern Counties in what was, in effect, a trial for the England amateur team. Evans performed so well he was primed he would be selected for the next England amateur international team, but then pointed out he was Welsh-and proud of it. Shortly after Haywards Sports folded, but Evans had no cause for concern. Spurs asked him to sign professional and, whilst several other clubs wanted his signature, he accepted immediately, making his first team debut in the Final of the London FA Charity Cup. Within months Evans was a first team regular, having celebrated his 19th birthday by scoring twice on his Football League debut against Swansea Town. Incredibly fast with a sledgehammer shot, Evans was a regular scorer in the Spurs team of the mid 30's and created many goals for his equally swift fellow forwards, George Hunt, Taffy O'Callaghan and Willie Hall. Their collective pace earned the side their "Greyhounds" nickname. Evans international career began with a first appearance against Northern Ireland in December 1932. Sadly, with six caps to his name, Evans suffered a serious knee injury in 1936 at Aston Villa on his 24th birthday. A cartilage operation followed, but when Spurs discovered a second operation was necessary they decided not to retain his services and in May 1937 he was released. Fulham decided Evans was worth the gamble and signed him on. He underwent the second operation needed, but it was not a success and he was forced to retire in May 1938, only 25-years old, without a single game for Fulham. He took up coaching duties at Craven Cottage and in later years reported on youth football for the Daily Mirror.

Appearances:
League: 178 apps. 78 gls.
FA Cup: 17 apps. 8 gls.
Others: 8 apps. 10 gls.
Total: 203 apps. 96 gls.

F

FAIRCLOUGH, Courtney Huw

Role: Central defender 1987-89
5ft.11ins 11st.2lbs.
Born: *Nottingham, 12th April 1964*

CAREER: Nottingham Forest app. Jun 1980, pro. Oct 1981/**SPURS** Jun 1987/Leeds United loan Mar 1989, perm. Apr 1989/Bolton Wanderers Jul 1995/Wigan Athletic training Jul 1998/Notts County Jul 1998/York City loan Mar 1999, perm. Jun 1999, released Feb 2001/retired May 2001/Nottingham Forest Academy coach Jul 2001, asst. first team coach Jul 2009-Jun 2011/Charlton Athletic Professional Development Phase Coach Jul 2012.

Debut v Coventry City (FL) (a) 15.8.1987
(Exeter City (Fr) (a) 23.7.1987)

Chris Fairclough worked his way through Nottingham Forest's junior ranks to make his debut in a Football League (Milk) Cup-tie in December 1981, although it was not until September 1982 that his League debut came against Liverpool at Anfield. He proved a really outstanding prospect, soon replaced former Spurs' star Willie Young in the centre of defence, and by the time his City Ground contract expired in the summer of 1987 had over 100 League appearances and five England Under-21 caps to his name. With Brian Clough

slow to offer a new contract, Spurs' manager David Pleat was quick to move and Fairclough arrived at White Hart Lane with a £385,000 fee set by the transfer tribunal. Quiet and undemonstrative, but tidy, reliable and effective he was the only ever-present in the traumatic 1987-88 season that saw Terry Venables take over as manager from Pleat. Fairclough added two more Under-21 caps to his collection and played for the England "B" team against Malta in October 1987. A good strong athlete, Fairclough was injured at Blackburn in November 1988 and when fit, unable to recover his first team place from young Guy Butters. He did force his way in, but only at full-back, and when Spurs accepted an offer from Leeds United he moved on to become a crucial part of Howard Wilkinson's ambitious rebuilding plans at Elland Road. In order to beat the transfer deadline, he initially went on loan with the move being made permanent the following month. In 1989-90 he played regularly as Leeds won the Second Division title and collected a cherished medal as one of the consistent cornerstones of their League Championship team in 1991-92. In the summer of 1995 he joined Bolton

Wanderers and although he could do nothing to prevent them from being relegated after just one season in the Premier League, he played his part in helping them back up at the first attempt. Released by Bolton in the summer of 1998 he had a short spell training with Wigan before returning to his home town with Notts County. He finished his career with York City, injury forcing an early retirement and then went into coaching.

Appearances:
League: 60 apps. 5 gls.
FA Cup: 3 apps.
FL Cup: 7 apps.
Others: 24 (3) apps. 1 gl.
Total: 94 (3) apps. 6 gls.

FALCO, Mark Peter

Role: Central striker 1977-87
6ft.0ins. 12st.0lbs.
Born: Hackney, London, 22nd October 1960

CAREER: Hackney Schools/London Schools/Inner London Schools/Middlesex Schools/**SPURS** app. Jul 1977, pro. Jul 1978/(Chelsea loan Nov 1982)/Watford Oct 1986/Rangers Jul 1987/Queens Park Rangers loan Dec 1987, perm. Jan 1988/Millwall Aug 1991/retired Jun 1992/Worthing Nov 1992/Enfield Dec 1992/Cornard United Jan 1994, asst. manager, manager/Worthing Aug 1994/Hitchin Town Feb 1996/Worthing asst. manager Mar 1996, manager May-Oct 1996/**SPURS** Academy coach.

Debut v Bolton Wanderers (FL) (a) 8.5.1979 (scored once)
(Truro City (sub) (Fr) (a) 3.5.1978) (scored once)

A more than useful goal-scorer blessed with all the physical attributes required by central strikers in the modern game, Mark Falco also had the skill and ability to bring team mates into the game, a factor all too easily ignored when strikers are judged by goals alone. Despite making the perfect start to his senior career with a League debut goal, Falco found a permanent breakthrough difficult and the task was certainly not made any easier by the arrival of big money signings Steve Archibald and Garth Crooks. But patience had its reward. He eventually surfaced as first choice, winning a UEFA Cup medal in 1983-84. Sadly perhaps, Falco's almost traditional centre-forward's style did not fit David Pleat's plans and he was sold for £350,000 to Watford. He only stayed briefly at Vicarage Road before joining the growing band of expensive English buys at Graeme Souness' Rangers. Falco did not though stop long in Scotland either, returning to London with Queens Park Rangers after less than six months. He later moved to Millwall where injury cut short his senior playing career. He then moved into non-League circles, signing for Gerry Armstrong's Worthing, but only a month later joined Enfield to play under another former team-mate, Graham Roberts. His next stop, along with Gary Brooke, was Cornard United, before returning to Worthing to take over from Gerry Armstrong as manager.

Appearances:
League: 162 (12) apps. 68 gls.
FA Cup: 15 apps. 5 gls.
FL Cup: 19 (3) apps. 3 gls.
Euro: 21 (4) apps. 13 gls.
Others: 76 (23) apps. 62 gls.
Total: 293 (42) apps. 151 gls.

FALQUE, Iago Silva

Role: Forward 2011-15
5ft.8ins. 11st.11lbs.
Born: Vigo, Spain, 4th January 1990

CAREER: Real Madrid (Spain) 2000/Barcelona (Spain) 2001/Juventus (Italy) Aug 2008/(AS Bari (Italy) loan Aug 2009)/(Villarreal (Spain) loan Jul 2010)/**SPURS** loan Aug 2011, perm. Jan 2012/(Southampton loan Jan 2012)/(Almeira (Spain) loan Jan 2013)/(Rayo Vallecano (Spain) loan Aug 2013)/Genoa (Italy) Aug 2014/Roma (Italy) loan and perm. Jul 2015/(Torino (Italy) loan Jul 2016).

Debut v PAOK (EL) (a) 15.9.2011

A chunky, wide midfield player, Iago Falque was an example of Spurs scouring Europe looking for reasonably-price, promising youngsters who might develop into real stars. As a 10-year old he had a year at Real Madrid's schoolboy facility, but it was at Barcelona's La Masia academy that his talent was developed, international honours at youth level coming as he progressed through the ranks. Promoted to the Barcelona B squad, Falque made only one appearance, but he was already being monitored by Juventus as the "Old Lady" of Italian football continued her return to the top after the Calciopoli scandal had seen her relegated and stripped of two league titles. Falque did not make much of an impression with Juve, failing to make one senior appearance. He was loaned to Bari to garner some top level experience of Italian football, but did not get beyond Bari's youth team. Only when he returned to Spain on loan with Villarreal's second string did Falque begin to play regularly. Villarreal decided not to exercise an option to acquire Falque permanently and he arrived at Spurs on trial in August 2011. During his trial he appeared in seven Europa League matches and obviously did enough to persuade Spurs to invest €1 million in signing him, though he was immediately loaned to Southampton. Given a chance in pre-season games, Falque never really looked good enough to challenge the likes of Aaron Lennon and Andros Townsend. He performed well enough on loan in helping Almeira to promotion from the Segunda division of Spanish football, to earn another loan to Rayo Vallecano with the prospect of a permanent move. He played regularly for Rayo but at the end of the season, the option was not exercised. Instead, Falque moved to Genoa where he began to realise his earlier potential. He not only played regularly, but scored a fair few goals. He certainly did enough to impress Roma. In July 2015 they signed him in a rather strange deal. A season long loan costing €1 million would become a permanent deal with another €7 million payable as soon as Falque played a competitive game for his new club, as happened in the first match of the season. While Falque has not established himself yet, he looks to have a good career in him.

Appearances:
League: (1) app.
FA Cup: (1) app.
FL Cup: 2 apps.
Euro: 2 (5) apps.
Others: 1 (4) apps. 2 gls.
Total: 5 (11) apps. 2 gls.

FARLEY, Henry Brian

Role: Centre-half 1949-54
5ft.11ins. 11st.9lbs.
Born: Ross-on-Wye, Herefordshire, 1st January 1927
Died: Brentwood, Essex, 4th December 1962

CAREER: Chelmsford City 1945/**SPURS** Jul 1949/Sittingbourne Aug 1955/Chelmsford City cs. 1962 player-coach.

Debut v Middlesbrough (FL) (a) 18.8.1951
(Chelmsford City (Fr) (a) 24.4.1950)

Brian Farley followed his former Chelmsford City manager, Arthur Rowe, to Spurs, and although on the playing staff for six years, made only one senior competitive appearance. His first team debut was in a friendly at his old club in April 1950 and he played two more friendlies before his only Football League game- the opening match of the 1951-52 season. Regular centre-half Harry Clarke was injured and Farley was given the job of filling-in. He had a miserable time, scoring an own goal to give Middlesbrough a point and then getting injured. Derek King replaced Farley, but after two games he joined the injury list. Arthur Rowe was forced to revert to playing Bill Nicholson in the centre of defence until Clarke returned. Released in the summer of 1955, Farley moved to Sittingbourne and remained there until the 1962-63 season when he returned to Chelmsford as player-coach. He died prematurely in December 1962 from a haemorrhage sustained whilst playing football.

Appearances:
League: 1 app.
Others: 6 apps.
Total: 7 apps. 0 gls.

FAZIO, Federico Julián

Role: Central Defender 2014-17
6ft.3ins. 14st.6lbs.
Born: Buenos Aires, Argentina, 17th March 1987

CAREER: Ferro Carril Oeste (Argentina) 2005/Sevilla (Spain) Jan 2007/**SPURS** Aug 2014/(Sevilla (Spain) loan Feb 2016)/Roma (Italy) loan Aug 2016, perm. July 2017.

Debut v Partizan Belgrade (EL) (a) 18.9.2014

Sevilla spotted Federico Fazio's talent while he was a youngster playing in the Argentine National B division with Ferro Carril Oeste of Buenos Aires. An Argentine Under-20 international, he arrived in Spain as a raw talent with potential. He spent his first season with Sevilla's B side, Sevilla Atlético, helping them win the promotion to the second division. In 2008 he was a member of the Argentine squad that won Olympic Gold in Beijing. Over the next seven years he developed as an impressive central defender, his height and confidence on the ball his most obvious attributes. He was not an automatic first choice, injuries often holding him back, but he was a regular in the first team squad, appearing in roughly half of Sevilla's games as they challenged at the top of La Liga and impressed in Europe.

With Michael Dawson coming to the end of his Tottenham career, Fazio was signed to compete with Vlad Chiriches, Younes Kaboul and Jan Vertonghen. The move had an immediate effect on Fazio's international career. He played against Croatia at Upton Park in October 2014, his first international outing for more than three years. He played frequently in his first season, though he never looked really comfortable, sometimes ungainly, lacking in concentration and prone to make mistakes. In the summer of 2015 Spurs signed Toby Alderweireld and Kevin Wimmer to compete for the central defensive position alongside Vertonghen. Fazio was well down the pecking order, rarely even making the substitutes bench. With it clear he had no future at Spurs, Fazio was allowed to return to Sevilla on loan. That was followed by a year on loan to Roma before a permanent to the Italian capital. Fazio was sent off on his Premier League debut for Spurs at Manchester City in October 2014. On his first appearance back with Sevilla at Celta Vigo, he suffered the same fate.

Appearances:
League: 20 apps.
FA Cup: 2 apps.
FL Cup: 4 apps.
Euro: 6 apps.
Others: 1 (1) apps.
Total: 33 (1) apps. 0 gls.

FEEBERY, John Horace

Role: Left-back 1916-17
Born: Hucknall, Nottinghamshire, 10th May 1888
Died: Nottingham, 1960

CAREER: Hucknall/Aston Villa am. 1906/Bulwell White Star/Bolton Wanderers am. cs. 1908, pro. Sep 1909/(guest for Notts County and **SPURS** during World War One)/Exeter City May 1920/Brighton and Hove Albion Aug 1921/Mid-Rhondda cs. 1924.

Debut v West Ham United (Fr) (a) 5.5.1917

Signed as a 20-year old in 1908, Jack Feebery was a loyal servant to Bolton Wanderers, making almost 200 appearances in 12 years on their books. Originally a defensive half-back, his best position was left-back and it was in that position that he made his only appearance for Spurs. Spurs arrived for a friendly at West Ham two men short. Feebery and Jack Casey were asked to make up the numbers. Most of Feebery's football during the First World War was played back in his native Nottingham. He returned to Bolton for one season after the war. He then had a year with Exeter City and three with Brighton and Hove Albion, before finishing his career with Mid-Rhondda. Feebery had two footballing brothers, Albert, who played for Coventry City and Crystal Palace, and Harold, who played for Derby County, Bolton Wanderers and Mansfield Town.

Appearances:
Others: 1 app.
Total: 1 app. 0 gls.

FELTON, William

Role: Full-back 1931-34
5ft.9ins. 12st.13lbs.
Born: Heworth, Gateshead, 1st August 1900
Died: Manchester, 22nd April 1977

CAREER: Pelaw Albion/Pandon Temperance/Pelaw Albion/Wardley Colliery Welfare 1914/Jarrow 1917/Grimsby Town pro. Jan 1921/Sheffield Wednesday Jan 1923/Manchester City Mar 1929/SPURS Mar 1932/Altrincham Jul 1934, player-coach 1938.

Debut v Swansea Town (FL) (a) 19.3.1932

Bill Felton gradually worked his way up the football ladder in his native North East before turning professional with Grimsby Town. He then moved to Sheffield Wednesday, won an England cap against France in May 1925 and helped Wednesday win the Second Division Championship in 1926, before joining Manchester City. Transferred to Spurs three years later, Felton quickly made his debut, and was the regular right-back for the next season. Captain of the promotion winning team of 1933, he lost his place to young Fred Channell midway through 1933-34, and so highly did Spurs rate Channell, that at the end of that season Felton was released and joined Altrincham. Felton's brothers were professional players, Ted with Carlisle United and Gateshead, Bob with Port Vale and Crystal Palace.

Appearances:
League: 73 apps. 1 gl.
FA Cup: 2 apps.
Others: 3 apps.
Total: 78 apps. 1 gl.

FENN, Neale Michael Charles

Role: Forward 1996-99
5ft.10ins. 12st.7lbs.
Born: Edmonton, London, 18th January 1977

CAREER: Wilbury Way Junior School/Aylward School/Enfield Rangers/Enfield Schools/Middlesex Schools/Republic of Ireland Schools/SPURS trainee Jul 1993, pro. Jul 1995/(Leyton Orient loan Jan 1998)/(Norwich City loan Mar 1998)/(Swindon Town loan Nov 1998)/(Lincoln City loan Dec 1998)/RBC Roosendahl (Holland) trial Jul 2000/Peterborough United Apr 2001/released May 2003/Dagenham and Redbridge trial Jul 2003/Stevenage Borough trial Aug 2003/Waterford United Aug 2003/Cork City Dec 2003/Bohemians Dec 2006/Dundalk Jan-Jul 2010/Shamrock Rovers Aug 2010/Swords Celtic 2011/North Dublin Schoolboys League academy coach/Path2Pro Academy director.

Debut v Manchester United (FA Cup) (a) 5.1.1997

A local lad who was under Spurs' wing from an early age, Neale Fenn was a highly talented young striker whose abilities deserved far greater success than he achieved. Qualifying for the Republic of Ireland through his grandmother, Fenn was capped at all Youth levels before making his first team debut. That came in January 1997 when he was thrown into the team for an FA Cup tie at Old Trafford. Injuries had so devastated Spurs that his partner was another rookie, Rory Allen. Fenn was a striker who relied on positional sense, skill and subtlety to carve out opportunities. In some respects, he was similar to Teddy Sheringham, if lacking the height and strength of the England international. It was unfortunate for Fenn that Sheringham was at the peak of his powers just as Fenn needed to be making an impression. While capped at Under-21 and "B" level, both Gerry Francis and George Graham were reluctant to give young talent much of a chance so Fenn had to rely on being loaned out to several clubs to gain experience. Even when Sheringham departed, Spurs laid out big money to sign Serhiy Rebrov to play the role Fenn was best suited to. With Les Ferdinand and Steffen Iversen also in front of him, Fenn was released and joined Peterborough United. In two years at London Road he proved his value. Released in the summer of 2003, Fenn eventually went to Ireland, enjoying success with several clubs before retiring and becoming a coach.

Appearances:
League: (8) apps.
FA Cup: 1 apps.
FL Cup: 1 apps. 1 gl.
Others: 6 (3) apps. 3 gls.
Total: 8 (11) apps. 4 gls.

FENN, F

Role: Goalkeeper 1894-95

CAREER: Millwall/SPURS trial Oct 1894.

Debut v Crouch End (Fr) (a) 27.10.1894

A trialist with previous experience playing for Millwall, Fenn made his only appearance for Spurs in a friendly with Crouch End in October 1894 when he played in goal as Spurs drew 2-2 with the local club.

Appearances:
Others: 1 app.
Total: 1 app. 0 gls.

FENWICK, Terence William

Role: Defender 1987-93
5ft.10ins. 11st.12lbs.
Born: Camden, County Durham, 17th November 1959

CAREER: Durham Schools/Crystal Palace app., pro. Dec 1976/Queens Park Rangers Dec 1980/SPURS Dec 1988/(Leicester City loan Oct 1990)/Swindon Town trial Aug 1993, perm. Sep 1993/released Aug 1994/

Portsmouth manager Feb 1995-Jan 1998/Crystal Palace first team coach Jul 1998-Jan 1999/Southall Director of Football Jun 2000/CL Financial San Juan Jabloteh (Trinidad & Tobago) Technical Director Feb 2001/Northampton Town manager Jan-Feb 2003/Ashford Town Director of Football Aug 2004, manager Oct 2004-Jan 2005/CL Financial San Juan Jabloteh (Trinidad & Tobago) coach May 2005, technical director/Queens Park (Trinidad & Tobago) Technical Director Aug 2011/Central FC (Trinidad & Tobago) manager Jan 2013/CS Visé (Belgium) manager May 2014-Mar 2015/Central FC (Trinidad & Tobago) manager Mar-Jun 2015.

Debut v Watford (FL) (h) 1.1.1989

Terry Fenwick was born in the North-East, but it was Crystal Palace who saw his potential. After winning England Youth honours Terry Venables signed him to his first professional contract. He made his League debut against Spurs at White Hart Lane in December 1977 and was soon regarded as a defender with an exciting future, winning three England Under-21 caps and helping Palace to the Second Division title in 1979. Capable of playing in any of the defensive positions or in midfield, he followed Venables to Queens Park Rangers where he won a further eight Under-21 caps and played against Spurs in the 1982 FA Cup Final. Indeed, it was his headed goal that forced a replay before Spurs were able to retain the trophy. A member of Rangers' Second Division championship team of 1983, Fenwick played for them in the 1986 Milk Cup Final defeat by Oxford United. By the time Venables signed him for Spurs, Fenwick had a total of 19 full England caps to his credit, having won the first against Wales in May 1984. Within weeks of his joining Spurs he won his 20th cap, going on as a substitute against Israel in Tel Aviv in February 1988. Signed principally as a central defender, Fenwick's versatility saw him play at full-back, in central defence, in midfield and in a continental style sweeper's role, where his ability to read the game and comfort on the ball was used to good effect. The sweeper system did not, however, always suit the style of other players around him. Just when Fenwick seemed to have found his best position for Spurs at right-back, he broke his leg in a Littlewoods Cup match at Manchester United in October 1989. Part of his recovery programme was a loan to Leicester City, but he returned to White Hart Lane and was soon back in the first team picture. Just a month later he broke an ankle in the pre-match warm up for an FA Cup tie at Portsmouth. This injury put Fenwick out of the game again until the end of the season and deprived him of the chance to play in the 1991 FA Cup Final. Not offered a new contract in the summer of 1993, Fenwick was automatically entitled to a free transfer and, after a brief trial, joined Swindon. He was unable to prevent them being relegated after just one season in the Carling FA Premiership. Released by Swindon, he took on the manager's role at Portsmouth where he was soon joined by his mentor Venables. Fenwick was dismissed following Venables' departure from Fratton Park, but the pair were soon re-united when Venables took over as manager of Crystal Palace and appointed Fenwick first team coach. That lasted for only six months, Fenwick again losing his job when Venables left as Palace plunged into financial crisis. After helping Southall as director of football, Fenwick joined CL Financial San Juan Jabloteh of Trinidad & Tobago leading them to their first League title in 2002. He surprisingly quit Jabloteh to take on the manager's job at Northampton, but last only seven weeks with five defeats and two draws in his seven games in charge. Another short but unsuccessful spell in charge of a non-League club, Ashford Town, followed before Fenwick returned to his old job in Trinidad. Apart from a brief spell managing in Belgium, he continued to work in Trinidad.

Appearances:
League: 90 (3) apps. 8 gls.
FA Cup: 7 apps.
FL Cup: 14 apps. 2 gls.
Euro: 4 apps.
Others: 32 (4) apps. 5 gls.
Total: 147 (7) apps. 15 gls.

FERDINAND, Leslie MBE

Role: Central striker 1997-2003
5ft.11ins. 13st.5lbs.
Born: Paddington, London, 18th December 1966

CAREER: Barandon Eagles/Harrow Club/Christopher Wren School/Jaguars/Viking Sports/Southall/Hayes/Akna/Queens Park Rangers Apr 1987/(Brentford loan Mar 1988)/Beşiktaş (Turkey) loan Jun 1988)/Newcastle United Jun 1995/**SPURS** Jul 1997/West Ham United Jan 2003/Leicester City Jul 2003/Bolton Wanderers Jul 2004/Reading Jan 2005/Watford Sep 2005/**SPURS** coach Nov 2008-Jun 2014/Queens Park Rangers head of football operations Oct 2014, joint caretaker manager Feb 2015, Director of Football Feb 2015.

Debut v Manchester United (BPL) (h) 10.8.1997
Fiorentina (Fr) (h) 2.8.1997

There was always something about Les Ferdinand that dictated he would one play for Spurs. Perhaps it was the fact he had been a Spurs' supporter since boyhood. Unfortunately, when he did fulfil his dream of pulling on the white shirt, the best years of his career were in the past. Playing for, first Southall, then Hayes, Ferdinand appeared to have escaped the scouting network of London's professional clubs, but eventually Queens Park Rangers troubled themselves to take a look at a player who lived on their doorstep. They liked what they saw enough to pay £30,000 for his signature, £15,000 up-front, the balance in instalments once certain numbers of games had been played. When doubts about Ferdinand's attitude surfaced, he was persuaded to spend a season on loan with Beşiktaş. Winning the Turkish Cup and helping Beşiktaş finish runners-up in the League, it was a move that paid dividends. Toughened up by the fanatical atmosphere of Istanbul, he returned a determined, more focussed player. It took a couple of years, but by 1993 he was vying with Alan Shearer to be the country's most potent striker. Strong, powerful, muscular and pacy, Ferdinand had every attribute needed of a striker in the 1990s. He was excellent in the air, never afraid to take an opponent on and possessed a fearsome shot. He won his first England cap in February 1993 and would have gone on to win far more than the 17 he garnered were it not for the presence of Shearer. With a record of more than a goal every two games for Rangers, the bigger clubs were often linked with Ferdinand and it was no surprise when a £6 million offer from Newcastle United persuaded Rangers to cash in. Ferdinand spent two years on Tyneside, the second paired with Shearer, as the exciting team crafted by Kevin Keegan almost secured the

Premier League title. At 31 Ferdinand appeared to be nearing the end of his career when Gerry Francis, who had managed Ferdinand at Loftus Road, offered £3.5 for Ferdinand's services. It was a typical piece of business by Francis, who was always keen to surround himself with players he knew well. It is easy to consider Ferdinand's power was on the wane by the time he joined Spurs, certainly he did not do as well as hoped for. However, he had been fortunate to suffer few injuries in his career until then, but seemed to sustain one after another at White Hart Lane. Even then, there were times when flashes of vintage Ferdinand showed just what might have been. After five-and-a-half years, Ferdinand was allowed to move to West Ham United on a short term deal as they fought against relegation. Unable to save them from the drop and well into the veteran stage, Ferdinand still had enough admirers to finish his career with short spells at Leicester City, Bolton Wanderers, Reading and Watford, though he never made a senior appearance for the Hertfordshire club. After retiring, Ferdinand worked in television, combining that with a role on Spurs coaching staff until persuaded to join the administrative staff back at Loftus Road. Awarded the MBE in the Queen's Birthday Honours List of 2005, Ferdinand had the honour of captaining England in May 1998 when he took over the job from Sol Campbell.

Appearances:
League: 97 (21) apps. 33 gls.
FA Cup: 15 (1) apps. 1 gl.
FL Cup: 11 (4) apps. 5 gls.
Others: 14 (7) apps. 9 gls.
Total: 137 (33) apps. 48 gls.

FERGUSON, Steven

Role: Striker 2001-02
5ft.10ins. 11st.2lbs.
Born: Dunfermline, Fife, 1st April 1982

CAREER: Dunfermline High School/Britannia (Chesterfield)/Dunfermline Colts Under-15s/Dunfermline Athletic Under-16s/Musselburgh Windsor/East Fife part-time pro. Jul 2000/**SPURS** Dec 2000/(Motherwell loan Aug 2002)/contract cancelled May 2003/oking Aug 2003/AFC Wimbledon loan Jan 2007, perm. Feb 2007/Billericay Town Jun 2008/Tonbridge Angels Mar 2009/Bromley Jan 2010/Harlow Town Sep 2010/Thurrock Sep 2011/Tooting & Mitcham United Dec 2011/Harrow Borough Mar 2012/Basildon United 2012-13.

Debut v Stevenage Borough (Fr) (a) 3.7.2001 (scored twice)

When Steve Ferguson burst on the football scene in Scotland with six goals in eleven appearances for Third Division East Fife, Spurs were quick to move for him. He signed in December 2000, but apart from two outings in pre-season friendlies was never given a chance in the senior side. A penalty box predator, sharp and nippy, Ferguson was slightly built. That probably accounts for his lack of opportunities. After a season on loan at Motherwell, Ferguson was released and moved into non-League football, most notably with Woking.

Appearances:
Others: 2 apps. 2 gls.
Total: 2 apps. 2 gls.

FERRIER, Henry

Role: Full-back 1945-46
5ft.11ins. 12st.7lbs.
Born: Ratho, Midlothian, 20th May 1920
Died: Earls Colne, Essex, 16th October 2002

CAREER: Ratho Park Rangers/Ratho Amateurs/Barnsley am., pro. 1937/(guest for Arsenal Brentford, Chelsea, Clapton Orient, Crystal Palace, Fulham, Kings Park, Middlesbrough, Millwall, Portsmouth, Queens Park Rangers, **SPURS** and Watford during World War Two)/Portsmouth Mar 1946/Gloucester City player-manager Aug 1954/Chelmsford City manager Mar 1959-Apr 1963 and Sep 1966-Jan 1969.

Debut v Coventry City (FLS) (h) 26.1.1946

Introduced to Spurs by goalkeeper Archie Hughes, with whom he was serving in the forces, Harry Ferrier was on Barnsley's books when he played his one game for Spurs in a Football League South match in January 1946. Two months after that match he was transferred from Barnsley to Portsmouth. Serving with the Royal Artillery, he was at a cinema in Greenwich when a message was flashed onto the screen asking him to contact Barnsley. When he did his transfer was arranged and he ended up signing for Portsmouth in a telephone box. He went on to make over 250 senior appearances in an eight year career at Fratton Park.

Appearances:
Others: 1 app.
Total: 1 app. 0 gls.

FERRIS

Role: Full-back 1918-19

Debut v Clapton Orient (Fr) (a) 26.4.1919

Ferris was one of several trialists who played their only match for Spurs in a friendly with Clapton Orient in April 1919. He played at left-back, but was not considered good enough to be taken on.

Appearances:
Others: 1 app.
Total: 1 app. 0 gls.

FINCH, John A

Role: Winger 1941-42
5ft.5ins, 10st 10lbs
Born: West Ham, London, 3rd February 1910
Died: Worthing, Sussex, 15th November 1993

CAREER: Gainsborough Road School/St Margarets/Walthamstow Avenue/Lowestoft Town/Walthamstow Avenue/Aston Villa trial/Fulham am. Oct 1930, pro. Nov 1930/(guest for Brentford, Crystal Palace and **SPURS** during World War Two)/Sittingbourne player-manager 1943-1946/Colchester United Aug 1946/Nigeria coach 1949/Valur (Iceland) coach Apr 1950-1952.

Debut v Fulham (LWL) (h) 2.5.1942

Jack Finch started playing football as a schoolboy with a local junior club before joining the well-known amateurs at Walthamstow Avenue, where he played for one season. Work as a coach driver took him to Lowestoft, and he played with the local club for two years, before returning to London and Walthamstow. His reputation in non-League football well established, he attracted the attention of several League clubs and, after an unsuccessful trial with Aston Villa, joined Fulham. Perfectly able to operate in any of the forward positions, he was primarily regarded as a winger, equally at home on either flank, and created many goals for team-mates by his fast orthodox style of wing play. He served Fulham with distinction throughout the 1930s and continued to turn out for them during the Second World War. He made his one appearance for Spurs against his own club in May 1942 in a London War League fixture. He joined Colchester United at the end of the war and later became a coach.

Appearances:
Others: 1 app.
Total: **1 app. 0 gls.**

FINCH, P

Role: Inside-forward 1900-01

CAREER: Waverley/**SPURS** Mar 1901.

Debut v Bristol City (WL) (a) 27.3.1901

A local player with the Waverley club, Finch played his only game for Spurs in a Western League fixture with Bristol City in March 1901. Spurs fielded a reserve team due to an FA Cup replay with Reading which was fixed for the following day. He played at inside-right in a match that Spurs lost 1-4, but compensation came the following day as Reading were beaten 3-0 on the way to Spurs' first FA Cup victory.

Appearances:
Others: 1 app.
Total: **1 app. 0 gls.**

FINCHAM, Edward J

Role: Half-back 1893-94

CAREER: Matlock Swifts by 1892/**SPURS** trial Mar 1894/Noel Park/Leyton by 1897.

Debut v 2nd Battalion Scots Guards (Fr) (h) 23.3.1894

"Tiddler" Fincham played in four friendly matches for Spurs in March and April 1894 during a month's trial from Matlock Swifts. He scored once, but was not seen in Spurs' colours after that. This probably had something to do with the fact Spurs had two excellent half-backs in Stanley Briggs and Jack Shepherd assisting them regularly, and the following season signed the former Woolwich Arsenal captain Bill Julian. With three such fine players, Fincham would have found it very difficult to make the first team. However, he went on to make a good career for himself in amateur football playing initially for Noel Park and then for Leyton and representing Essex.

Appearances:
Others: 4 apps. 1 gl.
Total: **4 apps. 1 gl.**

FINDLAY, Andrew

Role: Inside-forward 1920-21
5ft.8ins. 11st.9lbs.
Born: *Newburn-On-Tyne, Northumberland, 6th November 1896*
Died: *1969*

CAREER: Newburn-On-Tyne/**SPURS** Oct 1919/Wigan Borough cs. 1922 –1924/Dundee May 1925

Debut v Arsenal (LPFCF) (h) 25.10.1920

22-year old Andy Findlay joined Spurs from his home town club along with Matt Forster, but he was not to enjoy the same success with Spurs as his former team-mate. Findlay's only first team appearance was against Arsenal in a London Professional Football Charity Fund match in October 1920. While he remained with the club until being given a free transfer in May 1922, he never got another chance in the senior eleven. He joined Wigan Borough where he played for two years before moving on to Dundee.

Appearances:
Others: 1 app.
Total: **1 app. 0 gls.**

FINLAY, Donald Osborne

Role: Winger 1942-43
Born: *Christchurch, Hampshire, 27th May 1905*
Died: *Great Missenden, Buckinghamshire, 19th April 1970*

CAREER: RAF/Casuals 1934/Corinthians/(Guest for **SPURS** during World War Two)/Corinthian Casuals to Mar 1961

Debut v Crystal Palace (FLS) (h) 29.8.1942

Group Captain Donald Finlay DFC played three Football League South matches for Spurs during the 1942-43 season. A typical amateur, fast and quick-passing, he played on the right wing in all three games, exhibiting a totally unorthodox style of play alien to professional football of that time. However, his fame was not on the football field, but on the athletics track where he won eight AAAs hurdles titles and represented Great Britain in both the Berlin and London Olympics. He won bronze in the first and silver in the second. He also captained the men's team in the 1948 Olympics, where he had the honour of taking the Olympic oath on behalf of all competitors. In addition, he was Empires Games champion in 1934 and European champion in 1938.

Findlay played for Corinthian Casuals until 1961, but was sadly paralysed from the waist downwards in a 1966 car accident. In the Church of St George at RAF Halton there is a stained glass window dedicated to Findlay. During the Battle of Britain he shot down four Luftwaffe intruders before being shot down himself over Canterbury. He parachuted to safety with German shrapnel in his head.

Appearances:
Others: 3 apps.
Total: 3 apps. 0 gls.

FISHER, John Thomas

Role: Inside-forward 1883-84
Born: Pancras, London, March qtr. 1867

Debut v Brownlow Rovers (Fr) (h) 6.10.1883

One of the schoolboys who joined Spurs shortly after their formation, the only match Fisher is known to have played in was a friendly with Brownlow Rovers in October 1883. He may well have played in other matches that season, but as no records of the club's early games exist, this is not certain.

Appearances:
Others: 1 app.
Total: 1 app. 0 gls.

FITCHIE, Thomas Tindal

Role: Inside-forward 1901-02
5ft.9ins. 11st.12lbs.
Born: Edinburgh, Midlothian, 11th December 1881
Died: Streatham, London, 17th October 1947

CAREER: Hazelrigge School, Clapham/South London Schools 1893-97/Wingfield House 1894/West Norwood 1898/Woolwich Arsenal Nov 1901/(guest for SPURS Apr 1902)/Fulham 1904/London Caledonians/Pilgrims Sep 1905/Queen's Park Oct 1906/Norwich City Nov 1906/Brighton and Hove Albion Oct 1907/Woolwich Arsenal Sep 1908/Glossop North End cs. 1909/Fulham Oct 1912/London Caledonians Jan 1914-1915.

Debut v Luton Town (SL) (h) 12.04.1902
(Sheffield United (Fr) (h) 1.4.1902 (scored once))

Born in Scotland, Tom Fitchie came to the attention of the footballing public when he made his first appearance for South London Schoolboys at Northumberland Park on 20th February 1897. He was the star of the Boys match against their Tottenham counterparts. Instead of seeking to make a career in professional football, Fitchie went into business. He played as an amateur for the well-respected West Norwood, who were credited on the occasions he was selected to represent London. He made just two appearances for Spurs in April 1902, but as an amateur he was free to appear for any club and also played for Woolwich Arsenal earlier that season. For the next four years he played regularly for West Norwood and London Caledonians and also turned out frequently for Arsenal. During this time Fitchie won three Scottish caps, the first against Wales in March 1905, and it was the "Gunners" who were listed as being his club. A member of the Pilgrims team that toured the USA in 1905, he would probably have played more often for Arsenal were it not for various business commitments. These saw him move to Scotland in autumn 1906 where he became associated with their premier amateur club, Queen's Park. He made a single appearance for Norwich City in November 1906 and won a further Scottish cap before his return to London and Arsenal. Fitchie spent one season back in the capital before joining Glossop North End and played with the former Football League club for three seasons. He finished his involvement with senior football at Fulham. Fitchie also played for the English Wanderers, like the Pilgrims a touring side founded to promote the game abroad.

Appearances:
Southern: 1 app.
Others: 1 app. 1 gl.
Total: 2 apps. 1 gl.

FITZGERALD, Alfred Malcolm

Role: Half-back 1941-42
5ft.9ins. 11st 0lbs
Born: Conisborough, Yorkshire, 25th January 1911
Died: Brighton, Sussex, 1981

CAREER: Denaby United/Reading trial Jul 1934, pro. Aug 1934/Queens Park Rangers Nov 1936/(guest for Aldershot, Chelsea, SPURS, Watford and West Ham United during World War Two)/Aldershot Nov 1945/Tonbridge Jun 1948.

Debut v Fulham (LWL) (h) 2.5.1942

Having previously played for Denaby United and Reading, Alf Fitzgerald was with Queens Park Rangers when he made his one appearance for Spurs as a war-time guest. He played in the last match of the London War League against Fulham on 2nd May 1942 and helped Spurs to a 7-1 victory. Towards the end of the war he joined Aldershot where he played for two seasons until joining Tonbridge.

Appearances:
Others: 1 app.
Total: 1 app. 0 gls.

FLACK, Douglas W

Role: Goalkeeper 1941-42
Born: Staines, Middlesex, 24th October 1920

CAREER: Spring Grove Grammar School/Fulham ground-staff 1935, am. Oct 1936, pro. Dec 1938/(guest for Brentford, Brighton and Hove Albion, Clapton Orient, Portsmouth, Reading, SPURS and West Ham United during World War Two)/Walsall Aug 1953/Corinthian Casuals coach cs. 1954-1964/Tooting and Mitcham manager 1964-1970/retired 1970.

Debut v Chelsea (LWL) (a) 7.9.1940

Doug Flack was recommended to Fulham by one of his school teachers, Bernard Joy. He worked his way through their junior ranks, to make his debut during the Second World War when most of his football was played as a guest for other clubs in the London area. Flack only established himself as Fulham's first choice keeper in the 1948-49 season when he played in the majority of matches as Fulham won the Second Division, but then fell into the reserves, where he remained until moving to Walsall. He finished his career with one season in the Midlands and was then made coach of Corinthian Casuals, leading them to the FA Amateur Cup Final in his first season in charge. In 1964 he joined Tooting and Mitcham as manager retiring in 1970. His five Football League South appearances for Spurs were made in September and October 1940

Appearances:
Others: 5 apps.
Total: 5 apps. 0 gls.

FLACK, William Leonard Wallace

Role: Half-back 1943-44
5ft.8ins. 11st.6lbs
Born: Cambridge, 1st June 1916
Died: Bury St Edmunds, Suffolk, 29th March 1995

CAREER: Higher Grade Central School/Cambridgeshire Schools/ England Schools/Cambridge Town by Dec 1931/West Ham United am. Sep 1930/Arsenal am Jul 1931/Norwich City am. May 1933, pro. Jul 1933/ (guest for Arsenal, Fulham, Lincoln City, Southport, **SPURS** and Walsall during World War Two)/Bury Town player-coach, committee member, Vice-President.

Debut v Aldershot (FLS) (a) 22.1.1944

An England amateur international who had turned professional with Norwich City, Len Flack played two matches for Spurs as a guest in the Football League South in 1943-44 whilst serving in the RAF. He remained with Norwich for the first season of normal football after the cessation of hostilities and later joined Bury Town as player/coach.

Appearances:
Others: 2 apps.
Total: 2 apps. 0 gls.

FLAVELL, Robert Wilson

Role: Centre-forward 1944-45
Born: Annathill, Lanarkshire, 1st September 1921
Died: Airdrie, 17th March 2005

CAREER: Kirkintilloch Rob Roy Jul 1937/Airdrie Jan 1938/(guest for Arsenal, Brentford, Crystal Palace and **SPURS** during World War Two)/ Heart of Midlothian Dec 1947/Millonarios (Colombia) cs. 1950/Dundee Sep 1951/Kilmarnock Dec 1954/St Mirren Jul 1956, coach 1958/Ayr United manager Oct 1961/St Mirren manager Nov 1961/Ayr United manager Oct 1963-Dec 1964/Albion Rovers manager Mar 1965-Sep 1966/Cliftonhill director/Albion Rovers manager Nov 1969-May 1972, general manager Jul 1972, director/Berwick Rangers scout.

Debut v Charlton Athletic (FLS) (h) 30.9.1944

An aggressive and dangerous centre-forward with Airdrie, Bobby Flavell guested regularly for Spurs during the 1944-45 season. Having started with Kirkintilloch Rob Roy he joined Airdrie and was only 18 by the time war broke out. He gained valuable experience against seasoned professionals during the war and played for Scotland against England in February 1944 in a war-time international. He remained with Airdrie after the war, winning two Scottish caps in May 1947 against Belgium and Luxembourg after playing twice for the Scottish League. Transferred to Heart of Midlothian, Flavell was one of several leading British players lured to Colombia by the promise of untold riches and played for the Millonarios club of Bogota. Like most of the players who tried their luck in South America, he did not enjoy the experience even though Millonarios won the title of a Columbian League not recognised by UEFA. Flavell returned to Hearts in December 1950 as the Columbians returned to UEFA, but had to serve a six month's ban imposed by the Scottish FA. Having walked out on Hearts, Flavell clearly had no future at Tynecastle, so joined Dundee with whom he appeared in the 1952 Scottish Cup Final and won his only domestic honours as a member of their teams that won the Scottish League Cup in 1952 and 1953. After Dundee he played for Kilmarnock and St Mirren, where he finished playing and moved onto the coaching staff. In October 1961 he was appointed manager of Ayr United, but the job only lasted 17 days for the next month he took up the same role with St Mirren. Two years later he went back to Ayr and this time stayed with them for over a year. He later managed Albion Rovers over two terms, and also served them as a director.

Appearances:
Others: 15 apps. 2 gls.
Total: 15 apps. 2 gls.

FLEMING, John

Role: Centre-forward 1913-15
5ft.8ins. 11st.8lbs.
Born: Slamannan, Stirlingshire, 1890
Died: Richmond Camp, Yorkshire, 21st March 1916

CAREER: Musselburgh Union/St Bernards Nov 1909/Newcastle United Apr 1911/**SPURS** Apr 1913/Armadale Thistle May 1915/Rangers Nov 1915.

Debut v Burnley (FL) (a) 18.10.1913
(Red Star Amical (Fr) (Paris) 4.5.1913 (scored three))

John Fleming spent two years with Newcastle United, scoring four goals on his debut in a tour match against Köln. He made his League debut at White Hart Lane in November 1912, but by the end of the campaign was back in the more familiar surroundings of the reserves, where he had spent most of his time. He made his first appearance for Spurs within a month of signing, as with Newcastle

in a tour match. The game was against Red Star Amical of Paris, but Fleming only managed to score a hat-trick! His senior debut for Spurs was not until October 1913, when he played at outside-right in the absence of injured Fanny Walden. All Fleming's other appearances that season were at inside-right. The following season he was tried at right-half in the absence of Finlay Weir. He made three appearances before Weir returned and then reverted to inside-right, but he was not a success. He slipped back to the reserves and was only called upon again when injuries dictated. At the end of the 1914-15 season he returned to Scotland to play for Armadale Thistle. Fleming died in Yorkshire having returned to England after being injured whilst serving in Belgium. Fleming's brother, Bill, joined Spurs in August 1914. A centre-half, he made only one appearance during the 1917-18 season.

Appearances:
League: 19 apps. 3 gls.
Others: 11 apps. 5 gls.
Total: 30 apps. 8 gls.

FLEMING, William

Role: Centre-half 1917-18
Born: Musselburgh, Midlothian

CAREER: Bathgate/SPURS trial, pro. Aug 1914.

Debut v Millwall (LFC) (a) 25.12.1917

Bill Fleming was the brother of Jim Fleming and joined Spurs after impressing in the club's pre-season trial matches. He made no further impression though, making his only first team appearance against Millwall on Christmas Day 1917 in a London Football Combination fixture which Spurs won 6-0.

Appearances:
Others: 1 app.
Total: 1 app. 0 gls.

FLEMING, William Thomas

Role: Centre-forward 1896-97
Born: Renton, Glasgow 11th December 1871
Died: Glasgow, 17th September 1934

CAREER: Partick Thistle 1890-92/Darlington/Sheffield United 1893-94/Abercorn Jun 1895/Bury Jan 1896/SPURS Nov 1896.

Debut v Millwall Athletic (SL) (h) 28.11.1896 (scored once)
(Luton Town (Fr) (a) 16.11.1896)

Signed from Bury, Billy Fleming had a very short career with Spurs which appears to have had nothing to do with his performances on the pitch. He scored three goals in five games in the month he signed, but the following month was suspended by Spurs for reasons which it has not been possible to establish. However, he must have committed some serious crime for he left the club immediately; his departure apparently met with few regrets by fans, officials and press alike.

Appearances:
Southern: 2 apps. 1 gl.
Others: 3 apps. 2 gls.
Total: 5 apps. 3 gls.

FLETCHER, Henry George

Role: Centre-forward 1945-46
Born: Hackney, London, 7th July 1927
Died: Cuffley, Hertfordshire, 5th May 2011

CAREER: Hackney Wick/Tottenham Juniors/SPURS.

Debut v Aston Villa (FLS) (a) 2.2.1946

An 18-year old former Hackney Wick player who had played under Spurs' wing with Tottenham Juniors, Harry Fletcher was playing in the reserves when he was called up for his one first team appearance at Aston Villa in a Football League South game in February 1946.

Appearances:
Others: 1 app.
Total: 1 app. 0 gls.

FLINT, Kenneth

Role: Outside-left 1947-48
5ft.6ins. 10st.8lbs.
Born: Selston, Nottinghamshire, 12th November 1923
Died: Barnet, Hertfordshire, 21st May 2010

CAREER: Bagthorpe School/Notts Schools/Notts County am./Leicester City am./Bedford Town/(guest for Leicester City and Notts County during World War Two)/SPURS Jun 1947/Aldershot Jun 1950/Leyton Orient Jun 1958/Bath City Oct 1958/Sittingbourne.

Debut v Millwall (FL) (a) 26.3.1948

An outside-left of speed and potential, Ken Flint played only five League matches in his three years at White Hart Lane scoring once, all in his first season. He remained a reserve at the club until released in May 1950. The following month he signed for Aldershot where he gave marvellous service over the next eight years. He played well over 300 senior games for them and represented the Third Division (North) against the Third Division (South) in October 1956. After Aldershot, he returned to London for one year with Leyton Orient and then moved to Bath City and Sittingbourne.

Appearances:
League: 5 apps. 1 gl.
Total: 5 apps. 1 gl.

FLOWERS, J

Role: Goalkeeper 1895-96

CAREER: Royal Ordnance/SPURS trial Apr 1896.

Debut v Gravesend (Fr) (a) 22.4.1896

Another of the many players who made their only appearance as a trialist, Flowers was with Royal Ordnance when he played in a friendly with Gravesend in April 1896.

Appearances:
Others: 1 app.
Total: 1 app. 0 gls.

FORD, Frederick George Luther

Role: Centre-half 1945-46
Born: Dartford, Kent, 10th February 1916
Died: Oxford, 16th October 1981

CAREER: Erith and Belvedere/Arsenal am./Charlton Athletic am. Feb 1936, pro. Mar 1936/(guest for Brighton and Hove Albion, Fulham, Millwall and **SPURS** during World War Two/Millwall Nov 1945/Carlisle United player-coach Aug 1947/Bristol Rovers coach May 1955/Bristol City manager Jun 1960/Swindon Town coach Sep 1967/Bristol Rovers manager Apr 1968/Swindon Town manager Aug 1969-May 1971/Torquay United coach/asst. manager Nov 1971-Jan 1992/Oxford United coach and scout.

Debut v West Bromwich Albion (FLS) (h) 29.9.1945

Fred Ford was associated as an amateur with Arsenal before joining Charlton Athletic, and it was as a guest from Charlton that he made three Football League South appearances for Spurs in 1945-46. A strong, dominant centre-half, most of his Charlton career was spent in the reserves, before moving to Millwall and then on to the coaching side of the game at Carlisle United. He finished his playing career at Brunton Park and then moved to Bristol where he coached Bristol Rovers until taking his first managerial job. That was with Bristol City, who he led to promotion to the Second Division in 1966. Dismissed in September 1967, he coached Swindon Town, returned to Bristol Rovers as manager in April 1968 and then took over as manager at Swindon. He left in May 1971 and then worked with Torquay United and Oxford United.

Appearances:
Others: 3 apps.
Total: 3 apps. 0 gls.

FOREMAN, George Alexander

Role: Centre-forward 1944-47
Born: Walthamstow, London, 1st March 1914
Died: Waltham Forest, Essex, 19th June 1969

CAREER: Walthamstow Schools/Leyton/Walthamstow Avenue/West Ham United am. Mar 1938, pro. 1939/(guest for Clapton Orient, Crystal Palace and **SPURS** during World War Two)/**SPURS** Feb 1946/released Apr 1949, "A" team coach/Harris Lebus (renamed Finuby) coach Aug 1949-Nov 1956 at least.

Debut v Birmingham City (FL) (h) 31.8.1946 (scored once)
(Luton Town (FLS) (a) 21.10.1944 (scored once))

With eight goals in five games, it is no surprise that Spurs were impressed with George Foreman when he guested for them in 1944-45. In fact, they were so impressed that when the time came to start rebuilding for the challenges of post-war football, his was the first transfer secured. An amateur with Leyton and Walthamstow Avenue, he played in the amateur international against Ireland in February 1939 before signing professional for West Ham United. With instinctive reactions and an eye for goal, he helped West Ham win the Football League War Cup in 1940 and was their top scorer throughout the war years. He scored on his first appearance for Spurs in a 9-1 Football League South defeat of Luton Town in October 1944, and celebrated his permanent transfer with both goals in a 2-0 win over Plymouth Argyle on 23rd March 1946. Starting the initial post-war season as first choice centre-forward, he was replaced midway through by Charlie Rundle and moved to inside-forward. Len Duquemin then emerged as Spurs' long-term number nine and although Foreman was not to make the first team again, he remained on the staff until being released in April 1949.

Appearances:
League: 36 apps. 14 gls.
FA Cup: 2 apps.
Others: 18 apps. 25 gls.
Total: 56 apps. 39 gls.

FORMAN, Thomas

Role: Winger 1910-12
5ft.8ins. 12st.7lbs.
Born: Basford, Nottinghamshire, 26th October 1879

CAREER: Nottingham Forest Aug 1900/Manchester City Apr 1902/Sutton Town/Barnsley Jun 1907/**SPURS** Feb 1911/Sutton Junction Jun 1912.

Debut v Middlesbrough (FL) (h) 13.2.1911 (scored once)

Having made only three senior appearances in his two years with Nottingham Forest, and none with Manchester City, Tom Forman spent the bulk of his early career with Sutton Town of the Notts & Derbyshire League, He returned to the Football League with Barnsley in the summer of 1907 and was soon recognised as one of the fastest wingers in the Second Division. He played regularly for Barnsley, including both games of the 1910 FA Cup Final, and joined Spurs within a year of Newcastle's success in the Old Trafford replay. Foreman scored on his Spurs' debut, but was badly injured in the next game and forced to miss the rest of the season. Although he played the first six matches of the following campaign, he was never able to recover the form he showed with Barnsley. At the end of the season he was allowed to join Sutton Junction, where he played until the outbreak of the Great War. His brothers Frank and Fred both played for Aston-Upon-Trent, Beeston Town, Derby County and Nottingham Forest.

Appearances:
League: 8 apps. 1 gl.
Others: 1 app.
Total: 9 apps. 1 gl.

FORSTER, Matthew

Role: Full-back 1920-30
5ft.10ins. 11st.10lbs.
Born: Newburn-on-Tyne, Northumberland, 24th August 1900
Died: St Albans, Hertfordshire, 18th October 1976

CAREER: Northumberland Schools/Scotswood/Newburn/**SPURS** Oct 1919/Reading Jul 1930/Charlton Athletic Oct 1933/(Goldsmiths College and London University coach)/Bexleyheath and Welling Nov 1935/Fulham scout 1938.

Debut v West Bromwich Albion (FL) (h) 26.2.1921

Spurs noticed Matt Forster's talent early on, for he was only 19-years old when signed from Northern Alliance League club Newburn. He did not make his debut until February 1921, when he stood in for Tommy Clay and spent his first three seasons as reserve to the 1921 Cup Final full-backs Clay and Bob McDonald. Midway through the 1922-23 season Forster replaced McDonald and for the next six seasons appeared regularly in one of the full-back positions. During this period, he developed as a solid, reliable defender and was not far from international recognition, playing for the Football League against the Army in October 1926 and the Rest against England in an international trial in February 1927. However, the late 1920s were not good years for Spurs and this may well have prevented Forster from earning the honours his consistent displays merited. With the arrival of Bert Lyons imminent, Forster was not retained in April 1930 and joined Reading, moving on to Charlton Athletic three years later. An elder statesman in Charlton's reserves, he coached Goldsmith's College and London University FC before leaving to join Bexleyheath and Welling. He later served Fulham as a scout and then worked in the fur trade. At the time of his death he was employed by electronics firm Marconi in St Albans.

Appearances:
League: 236 apps.
FA Cup: 8 apps.
Others: 28 apps.
Total: 272 apps. 0 gls.

FORTNAM, Walter H

Role: Inside-forward 1892-93
Born: Battersea, London, 1870

CAREER: Robin Hood/guest for **SPURS** 1893/Robin Hood/City Ramblers/Waverley by Sep 1898.

Debut v London Welsh (Fr) (h) 18.2.1893. (scored once)

A player with the local Robin Hood club, Fortnam made three appearances in Spurs' first team as a "guest" in the 1892-93 season. The following season he continued to help Spurs out when needed, although all his further known games were with the reserves. He mainly played for Robin Hood and City Ramblers, with whom Robin Hood merged in September 1895.

Appearances:
Others: 3 apps. 2 gls.
Total: 3 apps. 2 gls.

FORTNUM, W

Role: Inside-forward 1900-01

CAREER: Waverley/Novocastrians/**SPURS** 1900.

Debut v Portsmouth (SL) (a) 24.4.1901

A local youngster with the Novocastrians club who had previously played for another local junior club, Waverley, Fortnum was associated with Spurs for just the 1900-01 season. He made two Southern League appearances as Spurs were forced to play eight matches in eleven days and fielded reserve teams in both games. His first appearance was just three days before the FA Cup Final replay with Sheffield United and the second, a 5-0 win over Gravesend United, on the same day as the first eleven were at Burnden Park winning the FA Cup.

Appearances:
Southern: 2 apps. 1 gl.
Total: 2 apps. 1 gl.

FOX, C

Role: Forward 1891-92

Debut v Clapton (Fr) (h) 24.10.1891

Fox is only known to have made three appearances for Spurs early in the 1891-92 season. Two weeks after his known debut, he played against the Coldstream Guards in a London Charity Cup tie, and three weeks later in a friendly against Old St Stephens when Spurs only managed to field ten men.

Appearances:
Others: 3 apps.
Total: 3 apps. 0 gls.

FOX, Ruel Adrian

Role: Winger 1995-2000
5ft.6ins. 10st.0lbs.
Born: Ipswich, Suffolk, 14th January 1968

CAREER: Whitton United 1980/Ipswich Town trial/Norwich City app. Aug 1984, pro. Jan 1986/Newcastle United Feb 1994/**SPURS** Oct 1995/West Bromwich Albion loan then perm Aug 2000/released May 2002/Southend United training Sep 2002/Stanway Rovers Sep 2002/Whitton United Feb 2004, manager 2004-May 2005/Montserrat coach Oct 2004/Suffolk College coach Nov 2008/Whitton United chairman.

Debut v Nottingham Forest (PL) (h) 14.10.1995

An elusive and at times mesmerising little winger, Ruel Fox was one of the outstanding members of the Norwich City team that took the unfashionable club to unknown heights in the late 1980s and early 1990s. His performances earnt him a big money move to Newcastle United as Kevin Keegan built an exciting, title-challenging team. Fox collected two England B caps in 1995 and looked set to make the move up to the full squad, but when Newcastle signed David Ginola, Fox found himself on the side-lines. Far too talented to be an understudy, Spurs moved quickly to sign Fox, expecting him to provide service from wide for the two central strikers, Teddy Sheringham and Chris Armstrong. At times Fox performed the job admirably, beating his opposing full-back with a

burst of pace or a piece of trickery, and laying on chances for the big men. Although not the best of finishers, he was also adept at cutting in from the wing and having a crack at goal himself. Unfortunately, he was not the most consistent of players. While he could lift the team, and crowd, with a flash of brilliance, all too often he would disappoint, lose possession or run down a blind alley. He was far too unpredictable for a manager who demanded players he could depend upon, even if they were incapable of breaking down a defence. Soon after George Graham's appointment as Spurs' manager, Fox found himself not simply out of the team, but out of the first team squad. He was allowed to move to West Bromwich Albion, where he played for a couple of years before announcing that he would be quitting the game at the end of his contract. In fact, he continued playing, making a few appearances for his home town Whitton United and playing at international level! With family roots in Montserrat, he was asked to help in identifying players who might be qualified to play for the Caribbean island. From there he quickly moved on to coaching the island's team and made two appearances for them.

Appearances:
League: 95 (11) apps. 13 gls.
FA Cup: 12* (1) apps. 1 gl.
FL Cup: 7* (3) apps. 1 gl.
Euro: 1 app.
Others: 22 (9) apps. 4 gls.
Total: **137 (24) apps. 19 gls.**
* Includes 1 abandoned match

FRAZER

Role: Half-back 1918-19

Debut v Crystal Palace (LFC) (a) 5.4.1919

Apart from the fact Frazer played his one match for Spurs as a trialist right-half, it has not been possible to unearth any information on this player.

Appearances:
Others: 1 app.
Total: **1 app. 0 gls.**

FREDERICKS, George Henry

Role: Inside-forward 1902-03
Born: 1876

CAREER: Chelmsford City/**SPURS** Apr 1902/released May 1903/Chelmsford City by Feb 1908

Debut v West Ham United (SL) (a) 14.2.1903

George Fredericks was an amateur who played with Vivian Woodward at Chelmsford, and it was on Woodward's recommendation that Spurs signed him to Southern League forms in April 1902. He played only two first team matches the following season, one in the Southern League and one in the Western League, before being released.

Appearances:
Southern: 1 app.
Others: 1 app. 1 gl.
Total: **2 apps. 1 gl.**

FREDERICKS, Ryan Marlowe Brown

Role: Full-back 2011-14
6ft.0ins. 11st.9lbs.
Born: Potters Bar, Hertfordshire, 10th October 1992

CAREER: SPURS Academy Scholar Jul 2009, pro. Jul 2010/(Brentford loan Aug 2012)/(Millwall loan Jan 2014)/(Middlesbrough loan Aug 2014)/Bristol City Aug 2014/Fulham Aug 2014.

Debut v Heart of Midlothian (EL) (h) 25.8.2011

An exciting young winger with bags of pace, Ryan Fredericks was impressive with his bursts down the right wing as he moved through the Academy and into the Development Squad. He made his debut in a Europa League match against Hearts and looked to have the makings of a decent player. With wingers rapidly disappearing from the game Fredericks dropped deeper, playing nominally as a full-back, but effectively a wing-back. He gained experience and a bit of toughness playing for Millwall and Middlesbrough in the Football League and looked to be at the point where he would make the grade or not, when he was suddenly transferred to Bristol City. He had an exceptionally short career in the West Country, signing for Fulham within days of the first move. In a miserable season for Fulham as it flirted with relegation, Fredericks was one of the few bright spots.

Appearances:
Euro: 2 (2) apps.
Others: (4) apps.
Total: **2 (6) apps. 0 gls.**

FREEBOROUGH, James

Role: Half-back 1904-06
6ft.0ins. 12st.7lbs.
Born: Stockport, Cheshire, 13th February 1879
Died: Stockport, Cheshire, January qtr. 1961

CAREER: Stockport County cs. 1902/**SPURS** May 1904/Leeds City Apr 1906/Bradford Park Avenue Jul 1908/Rochdale cs. 1909-cs. 1911/Denton/(guest for Stockport County during World War One).

Debut v Plymouth Argyle (WL) (h) 21.11.1904

When Stockport County failed to secure re-election to the Football League in 1904, Spurs were quick to secure the signature of utility defender James Freeborough. He went on to make 15 first team appearances in his two seasons at White Hart Lane, scoring one goal. Never little more than a reserve, only two of his games were played in the Southern League, the majority of them coming in the secondary Western League competition. Freeborough left Spurs at the end of the 1905-06 season to join Leeds City, where he played for two years before moving on to Bradford Park Avenue and Rochdale.

Appearances:
Southern: 2 apps.
Others: 13 apps. 1 gl.
Total: **15 apps. 1 gl.**

FREEMAN, Ernest

Role: Forward 1918-19
Born: Northampton, 5th June 1886
Died: Northampton, 7th December 1945

CAREER: Northampton Town cs. 1906/(guest for **SPURS** during World War One).

Debut v Clapton Orient (LFC) (a) 23.11.1918

A stalwart forward with his home town club, Northampton Town, where he spent the whole of his senior career, Ernie Freeman made two appearances for Spurs in the London Football Combination in 1918-19. He played at centre-forward in the first, but reverted to his more accustomed outside-right position for the second, seven days later. Prior to the war Freeman had represented the Southern League in inter-League matches against the Football League and the Scottish League. After the war, he continued to turn out for Northampton until retiring in 1921.

Appearances:
Others: 2 apps.
Total: 2 apps. 2 gls.

FRENCH, William G

Role: Goalkeeper 1918-22
5ft.10ins. 12st.7lbs.
Born: Gillingham, Kent

CAREER: Gillingham/Sheppey United 1918-19/**SPURS** Apr 1919/Clapton Orient May 1922.

Debut v Crystal Palace (Fr) (a) 26.4.1919

22-year old Bill French, holder of the Military Medal, captained the football team of the 5th Battalion, Rifle Brigade during the First World War. Wounded in March 1918, he was discharged from the Army and played for Sheppey United before joining Spurs. French was on Spurs' books for four years, playing only the same number of matches in that time. He first played in a friendly at Crystal Palace in April 1919, a day when Spurs fielded two "first teams" in matches designed to give several potential recruits a run-out. French apparently did enough to impress, for he was then signed on, but he was always very much third or fourth choice 'keeper. Apart from playing a couple of games in the London FA Charity Cup, he was never seriously considered for a first team place. In May 1922 French was given a free transfer and joined Clapton Orient, where he remained for one year before again being released on a "free".

Appearances:
Others: 4 apps.
Total: 4 apps. 0 gls.

FREUND, Steffen

Role: Midfielder 1998-2003
5ft.11ins. 12st.8lbs.
Born: Brandenburg, East Germany 19th January 1970

CAREER: Motor Süd Brandenburg (East Germany)/Stahl Brandenburg (East Germany) 1988/FC Schalke 04 (Germany) 1991/Borussia Dortmund (Germany) Jul 1993/**SPURS** Dec 1998/1FC Kaiserslautern (Germany) Jul 2003/(Leicester City loan Jan 2004)/ESV Lok Estal junior coach Feb 2007/Germany Under-20 asst. coach Sep 2007/(Nigeria asst. coach Dec 2007)/Germany Under-16 coach Jul 2009, Under-17 coach/**SPURS** asst. head coach Jul 2012, international technical co-ordinator Aug 2014.

Debut v Sheffield Wednesday (FL) (a) 9.1.1999

It did not take a genius to recognise that Spurs' weakness in the early part of the 1998-99 season lay not in its attacking prowess, but in its defensive capabilities. George Graham's first task on arriving as manager was to strengthen the defence and he did that by signing Steffen Freund. Freund was one of Europe's premier defensive midfielders, a workaholic content to patrol the midfield in front of his back four, break up attacks and lay the ball off for his more gifted colleagues to take his team forward. It was an unglamorous task, but one Freund had excelled at from his early days in East Germany. A member of Borussia Dortmund's Bundesliga winning teams of 1995 and 1996, he took his talents onto the international stage, winning 21 full caps and anchoring the midfield as Germany won the European Championship in 1996, Freund sadly missing the final due to injury. At White Hart Lane his impact was immediate as he helped Spurs overcome Wimbledon in two ugly Worthington cup semi-final ties. In the final, Freund's stubborn refusal to yield the midfield after Justin Edinburgh had been sent off was crucial in Spurs

overcoming Leicester City, with Allan Nielsen's last gasp winner. There was nothing elegant about Freund. He was a hustler, snapping at opponents, launching into tackles. When he got possession he looked uncomfortable, but he knew his limitations and quickly got rid of the ball. Not the type of player that would normally endear himself to Spurs' supporters, his limitations and his own recognition of them, together with his incredible work ethic and ability to relate to the crowd, made him immensely popular and a cult figure. Even Glenn Hoddle appreciated Freund's value, frequently finding a place for him in the team. Indeed, had Hoddle not allowed Freund to move to Kaiserslautern in the summer of 2003, his qualities might have been enough to save Hoddle's job. Freund spent only a few months back in Germany before ending his career with a brief spell on loan to Leicester City. His playing days over, Freund took to coaching and was soon working at international level with Germany's youth teams. He even helped former international manager, Bertie Vogts, prepare Nigeria for the 2008 African Cup of Nations. Freund returned to Spurs as assistant to Andre Villas-

Boas in July 2012, but was marginalised on the arrival of Mauricio Pochettino. Freund's son, Niklas, was a goalkeeper on Spurs' books as a youth. He went on to play for Chelmsford City and Harlow Town.

Appearances:
League: 92 (10) apps.
FA Cup: 11 apps.
FL Cup: 14 apps.
Euro: 4 apps.
Others: 15 (5) apps. 1 gl.
Total: 136 (15) apps. 1 gl.

FRICKER, Frank G

Role: Winger 1914-15
Born: Pentonville, London, 1891 or south Haggerston, London 1895

CAREER: Tottenham Thursday/**SPURS** am. Jan 1912/Tufnell Park.

Debut v Arsenal (LFC) (a) 4.9.1915

A good class cricketer with Stamford Hill, Frank Fricker played for the local amateur club Tottenham Thursday but, despite the fact they used to play on Spurs' White Hart Lane ground, it was only when he was playing in a trial for the London amateur team at Stamford Bridge in January 1912 that Spurs spotted his potential. Immediately signed to amateur forms, he played only one first team game, that coming at Highbury in the opening match of the London Football Combination in September 1915. After the war, Fricker played regularly for the local amateurs Tufnell Park, helping them reach the FA Amateur Cup Final in 1920 when they lost to Dulwich Hamlet.

Appearances:
Others: 1 app.
Total: 1 app. 0 gls.

FRIEDEL Bradley Howard

Role: Goalkeeper 2011-15
6ft.1ins. 14st.4lbs.
Born: *Lakewood, Ohio, USA, 18th May 1971*

CAREER: Bay High School (USA)/University of California Bruins (USA) 1989/US Soccer Federation (USA) 1992/Nottingham Forest trial Dec 1992, signed Dec 1992 but refused work permit/Celtic trial/(Newcastle United signed May 1994)/St Patricks Athletic (Ireland) training/Brøndby (Denmark) Jan 1995/Sunderland Jul 1995/Viborg (Denmark) training Aug 1995/Galatasaray (Turkey) Sep 1995/Columbus Crew (USA) Jul 1996 /Liverpool Dec 1997/Blackburn Rovers Nov 2000/Aston Villa Jul 2008/ **SPURS** Jun 2011/retired May 2015/USA Under-19 coach Jan 2016.

Debut v Manchester United (PL) (a) 22.8.2011
(v Orlando Pirates (Fr) (a) 19.7.2011)

Goalkeepers are known for the longevity of their careers, but for any footballer to still be playing at the highest level in their 44th year is quite remarkable, a word that sums up Brad Friedel. An all-round sportsman in his schooldays, Friedel played tennis and basketball and as a forward in football before taking to goalkeeping. An outstanding performer at University, he finished his studies early to try and make a career in the English game. Nottingham Forest wanted to sign him, but while Friedel

had been first choice for the Americans at the 1992 Olympics, he had only one full international appearance to his credit, so was unable to get a work permit. He returned to the States, but did not sign for any of the American clubs desperate to secure his services, just playing for the national team as it built up to the 1994 World Cup finals. Newcastle United were the next English club who wanted to take Friedel on. They even signed him to a contract, but again a work permit was refused. With Tony Meola the established number one for the States, Friedel had not played a game in the World Cup finals. He did not have the same problem in Denmark and joined Brøndby where he stayed for several months without playing a senior game. After the 1995 US Cup and Copa America, Friedel, who was just about winning the battle with Kasey Keller to be the States regular 'keeper, joined Galatasaray after Sunderland had become the third English club unable to secure a work permit for him. He had one season in Turkey and followed that with eighteen months at Columbus Crew, the only American team he played for in his career. In December 1997 Friedel was at last granted a British work permit after Liverpool had taken an initial refusal to appeal. After so much had gone into Friedel getting a chance in the English game, it was disappointing that in three years at Anfield, he played barely 30 games, but David James and Sandor Westerveld were ahead of him and they were experienced, quality 'keepers. Friedel's career seemed at the crossroads when Liverpool allowed him to move on a free transfer to Blackburn Rovers, linking up with his manager from Galatasaray. He helped Blackburn secure promotion in his first season and beat Spurs in the 2001-02 Worthington Cup, when he was "Man of the Match". In eight years with Blackburn Friedel established himself as one of the most consistent and reliable 'keepers in the country, a regular for his country and hardly ever missing a Rovers' game. He continued in much the same way when he moved to Aston Villa. After three years with Villa, Friedel was 40 and his contract was up. Heurelho Gomes had found life tough at Tottenham and Carlo Cudicini never looked much more than a back-up, but it was still a surprise when Friedel was signed. It was not expected that he would be first choice, but he was. He played every league game in his first season at White Hart Lane, the seventh successive season he had been ever-present. In ten seasons of Premier League football, he missed only four games. It was only with the arrival of Hugo Lloris that Friedel was forced to take a back seat. Even then, he remained with Spurs for another three years, ever ready if needed. When Lloris was preferred to Friedel in October 2011 it brought to an end a run of 310 successive Premier League games. Friedel is the oldest player to have appeared for Aston Villa and Spurs in top-flight football. He made 82 full appearances for the USA.

Appearances:
League: 50 apps.
FA Cup: 2 apps.
FL Cup: 2 apps.
Euro: 12 apps.
Others: 12 (5) apps.
Total: 78 (5) apps. 0 gls.

FRYERS, Ezekiel David

Role: Defender 2012-15
6ft. 12st.8lbs.
Born: *Manchester, Lancashire, 9th September 1992*

CAREER: Manchester United Academy Scholar Jul 2009, pro. Jul 2011/ **SPURS** trial Aug 2012/Standard Liege (Belgium) Aug 2012/**SPURS** Jan 2013/Crystal Palace Sep 2014/(Rotherham United loan Jan 2015)/(Ipswich Town loan Mar 2015).

Debut v Dinamo Tbilisi (sub) (EL) (h) 29.8.2013
(v Swindon Town (sub) (Fr) (a) 16.7.2013)

Zeki Fryers was an up-and-coming defender who had made a few appearances for Manchester United. While he was rated a good prospect, he decided his future lay away from Old Trafford and refused the offer of a new contract when his existing one expired. When news leaked out that Spurs were interested in signing him, Sir Alex Ferguson let it be known how highly he rated Fryers, how he had big plans for him and that a player of Fryers' potential was worth a good £4 or 5 million. Whether that was true or just bluster to try and up the price, Spurs took Fryers on trial. While they tried to reach a deal with United, Fryers accompanied Spurs Development Squad to Portugal for pre-season preparations. Having played in one friendly game, Spurs decided they could not meet United's demands. Fryers immediately signed for Standard Liege. He played in seven matches for the Belgians but when the manager was dismissed and he was left out of the first team squad, he made his displeasure clear and announced he was homesick. Spurs moved in and signed him in the January transfer window. The fee was reputed to be in the region of £1 million, far below what United had been demanding of Spurs. It also gave Standard a good, quick profit, for the development compensation that they had paid United was far below what Spurs would have had to pay if the fee had been set by a tribunal. The whole process was not appreciated by Ferguson who was quick to voice his concerns. If United made any complaint at Spurs' actions, they did not go anywhere. Fryers started in the Development Squad at White Hart Lane and was given a few outings in the first team early in the 2013-14 season. Full-back seemed to be his position, but with Kyle Walker, Danny Rose and Kyle Naughton already established, Fryer was going to have a tough job usurping any of them. When Ben Davies was signed, the prospects of a breakthrough diminished and Fryers was allowed to join Crystal Palace.

Appearances:
League: 3 (4) apps.
FL Cup: 1 (1) apps.
Euro: 6 (1) apps.
Others: 4 (7) apps.
Total: 14 (13) apps. 0 gls.

FULLWOOD, James

Role: Full-back 1934-38
5ft.11ins. 11st.3lbs
Born: Ilkeston, Derbyshire, 17th February 1911
Died: Wokingham, Berkshire, March qtr. 1981

CAREER: Frickley Colliery Jun 1929/Hatfield Main Welfare Nov 1929/Thorne Colliery/**SPURS** trial Oct 1934, pro. Nov 1934/Reading Aug 1938/ (guest for Brentford, Chelsea and Clapton Orient during World War Two).

Debut v Blackburn Rovers (FL) (a) 1.1.1935

Spotted by Spurs playing for Thorne Colliery and invited down to White Hart Lane for a trial, Jim Fullwood impressed in the reserves. After playing against the Corinthians for the Dewar Shield, he signed professional and stayed at White Hart Lane for four years, proving himself valuable as cover, but never quite good enough to make a first team place his own. His whole Spurs' career was spent as understudy to Bill Whatley and indeed, all his appearances came as stand-in for the Welsh international, the first on New Year's Day 1935. Fullwood was transferred to Reading in August 1938 and served the Royals throughout the war years, at the end of which he retired.

Appearances:
League: 34 apps. 1 gl.
FA Cup: 1 app.
Others: 3 apps.
Total: 38 apps. 1 gl.

FÜLÖP, Márton

Role: Goalkeeper 2004-07
6ft.6ins. 15st.2lbs
Born: Budapest, Hungary, 3rd May 1983
Died: Budapest, Hungary, 12th November 2015

CAREER: MTK Budapest (Hungary) 1995/(BKV Előre SC (Hungary) loan 2002-03)/(Bodajk FC Siófok (Hungary) loan) 2003-04/**SPURS** Jun 2004/Chesterfield loan Mar 2005)/(Coventry City loan Oct 2005)/ Sunderland loan Nov 2006, perm. Jan 2007/(Leicester City loan Aug 2007) /(Stoke City loan Feb 2008)/(Manchester City loan Apr 2010)/Ipswich Town Aug 2010/West Bromwich Albion Aug 2011/Asteras Tripolis (Greece) Jul 2012

Debut v Trollhättan (Fr) (a) 17.7.2004

Márton Fülöp started his career as a 12-year old with his home town club MTK Budapest, a club his father, Ferenc, served as player and technical director. After loan spells with two lower division Hungarian clubs, he was selected for the Hungarian Under-21 team where he caught Spurs' attention. Although Fülöp had not played a single game for his parent club or in the Hungarian top flight, Spurs had seen enough to secure his transfer. Arriving at the same time as Paul Robinson, Fülöp was expected to compete with the experienced Kasey Keller to provide cover for Robinson. It was an uneven contest and Fülöp was soon embarking on more of the

loan moves that were to be his lot for most of his career. Having made his first appearance at full international level in May 2005, Fülöp continued to collect Under-21 honours while on a season's loan to Coventry City. A further full appearance followed his return to Spurs, but by now it was obvious he was not going to displace Robinson. Keller had departed, but Radek Černý had arrived as back-up for Robinson. Fülöp made it clear he wanted a permanent move and eventually got his way, signing for Sunderland, with Ben Alnwick joining Spurs as part of the deal. Despite helping Sunderland win the Football League title in his first season, Sunderland signed Scotland's Craig Gordon as the next got underway. Fülöp went out on loan again, proving his value when called back to Sunderland because of injury to Gordon, but never making the number one position his own. He at last got a full season as first choice under his belt following a transfer to Ipswich Town, but after just a year moved to West Bromwich Albion as cover for Ben Foster. A year on and he was off to Greece to play for Asteras Tripolis, but his career there was brought to a halt in the summer of 2013 when he was found to have a cancerous growth in his arm that required removal. It appeared the surgery had done its job, but the disease re-appeared and led Fülöp's premature death in November 2015. Fülöp's father played at centre-forward for the German team in the film, Escape to Victory, the match at the centre of the story being played at MTK's Hungária körúti stadium. When the stadium was rebuilt as the Hidegkuti Nándor stadium, the southern goal was named after Fülöp to provide a permanent memorial.

Appearances:
Others: 4 (3) apps.
Total: 4 (3) apps. 0 gls.

FURR, William Stanley

Role: Winger 1918-19
Born: Hitchin, Hertfordshire, 22nd July 1891
Died: Biggleswade, Bedfordshire, 1975

CAREER: Hitchin Town/Everton trial Dec 1911/Brentford Jan 1912/Leicester Fosse Jul 1912/Luton Town trial Aug 1913/Lincoln City Sep 1913/(guest for **SPURS** during World War One)/Luton Town trial and pro. cs. 1919.

Debut v Arsenal (Fr) (a) 24.5.1919

A winger happy to operate on either flank, Billy Furr started his career in his home town with Hitchin Town. After a trial, Everton were prepared to pay him between 30 and 35 shillings (£1.50 and £1.75) a week to play for them, but he found the offer unacceptable. He quickly found Brentford interested in him and played one match for them in 1911-12 before signing for Leicester Fosse. Furr spent only one season at Filbert Street before being released, and after an unsuccessful trial with Luton Town joined Lincoln City. He made two appearances for Spurs, the first a friendly at Arsenal and the second in May 1919 in the National War Fund match with Fulham. He had another trial with Luton after the war and this time was taken on. His brother, Harry, was a professional goalkeeper with Croydon Common, Brentford and Leicester Fosse, another brother, George, played for Watford and Manchester City and a fourth brother, Vic, also played for Watford. His nephew, Romilly Melville Vaughan Furr played for Hitchin Town and was on Spurs' amateur books in November 1931. His sister Amelia married Billy Grimes and another sister, Miriam, married George Payne.

Appearances:
Others: 2 apps.
Total: 2 apps. 0 gls.

G

GAIN, Peter Thomas

Role: Midfielder 1998-99
5ft.9ins. 11st.7lbs
Born: Hammersmith, London, 2nd November 1976

CAREER: St James School/West London Schools/Inner London Schools Republic of Ireland Schools/**SPURS** assoc. schl. Apr 1991, trainee Jul 1993, pro. Jul 1995/Lincoln City loan Dec 1998, perm. May 1999/Peterborough United Sep 2005/Dagenham & Redbridge Jan 2008-May 2012

Debut v Birmingham City (sub) (Fr) (a) 22.7.1998

Starting as a schoolboy, Peter Gain was associated with Spurs for seven years, making his one appearance as a substitute in a pre-season friendly at Birmingham City. A busy midfielder, Gain qualified for the Republic of Ireland through his parents and played for the country winning honours at youth, Under-21 and B level. A consistent reserve performer, Gain was allowed to join Lincoln City on loan in December 1998. Although he made few appearances, he evidently impressed, for at the end of the season the move was made permanent. Gain went on to give Lincoln six years' terrific service, making over 200 appearances and proving a model of consistency. Approaching the veteran stage, he went on to play for nearly three years at Peterborough and finished his career with four more at Dagenham & Redbridge.

Appearances:
Others: (1) app.
Total: (1) app. 0 gls.

GAIR

Role: Inside-forward 1896-97

Debut v London Caledonians (Fr) (a) 26.4.1897

A young trialist from the Midlands, Gair's only appearance for Spurs was in April 1897 when he played at inside-left to fellow trialist Hobson in a friendly with London Caledonians. The match only lasted 45 minutes as it was abandoned when one of the opposition broke a leg.

Appearances:
Others: 1 app.
Total: 1 app. 0 gls.

GALBRAITH, David James

Role: Midfield 2003-04
5ft.9ins. 10st. 0lbs.
Born: Luton, Bedfordshire, 20th December 1983

CAREER: Putteridge High School/St Joseph's/Crawley Green Sports and Social Club/**SPURS** scholar Jul 2000, pro. Jul 2003, released Dec 2003/Northampton Town trial Mar 2004, perm. Aug 2004/Boston United loan Nov 2005, perm. Jan 2006/Kettering Town Jan 2008-Mar 2009/Kings Lynn Jun-Jul 2009/St Albans City Sep-Oct 2009, Dec 2010/Bedford Sep 2011/Arlesey Town Mar 2012

Debut v Wycombe Wanderers (sub) (Fr) (a) 19.7.2003

David Galbraith attended Ron Henry's Soccer School before being invited to train at White Hart Lane. From there he progressed to the professional ranks and made his first and only appearances in the first team during the 2003-04 pre-season friendlies. That was as far as Galbraith was to get at Spurs as he was released within six months. He accepted the offer of a short-term deal at Northampton Town where Colin Calderwood, who knew Galbraith from his days as reserve team coach at Spurs, was manager and did enough to earn a longer contract. From there Galbraith moved to Boston United where he had the best years of his career, holding down a regular place when fit. Unfortunately, there were too many occasions when he was not fit, one injury after another holding him back. At his best a nippy, little winger with pace and a bit of trickery, he fared little better after leaving Boston, spending more time on the injured list than the pitch.

Appearances:
Others: 1 (3) apps.
Total: 1 (3) apps. 0 gls.

GALLACHER, Joseph Patrick

Role: Winger 1904-05
6ft.0ins. 12st.4lbs.
Born: Glasgow, 17 March 1881
Died: Tottenham, London, 11 April 1951

CAREER: Duntocher Hibs 1899-1901/Rockvale 1901-02/**SPURS** Apr 1904/Luton Town cs. 1905/Partick Thistle 1906-07/Workington/Barrow/Ton Pentre.

Debut v Brentford (WL) (a) 3.4.1905
(Cambridge University (Fr) (h) 28.11.1904)

One of Scotland's most promising young juniors, Pat Gallacher played for his junior club in all positions, but preferred the right wing role. At 6ft tall he brought a big reputation with him, but totally failed to live up to it. Apart from two friendly matches, he made only one senior appearance for the club, in a Western League fixture against Brentford towards the end of the season. Released shortly after that game, he joined Luton Town along with another Spurs man, Alf Warner, but in the two seasons he was on their books still failed to reproduce the form he had shown in Scotland. He returned to Scotland, then moved around Workington, Barrow and Ton Pentre. He served in the 17th Footballers Battalion of the Middlesex Regiment during the First World War and then took up a career as a groundsman, working at the St Ignatius College Sports Ground in Tottenham, the West Ham Stadium used by Thames FC in their short career and Enfield Cable Works. Gallacher passed away at his home in Trulock Road, Tottenham, within sight of White Hart Lane.

Appearances:
Others: 3 apps.
Total: 3 apps. 0 gls.

GALLAS, William Éric

Role: Defender 2010-13
6ft.0ins. 12st.13lbs.
Born: Asnières-sur-Seine, France, 17th August 1977

CAREER: Villeneuve-la-Garenne (France) 1987/RCF Paris (France) 1992-INF Clarefontaine (France) 1992/Caen (France) 1995/Olympique de Marseille (France) 1997/Chelsea Jul 2001/Arsenal Aug 2006/**SPURS** Aug 2010/released Jun 2013/Perth Glory (Australia) Oct 2013/retired Oct 2014.

Debut v West Bromwich Albion (PL) (a) 11.9.2010

Harry Redknapp was a manager who was never afraid to make a difficult signing if he thought it would improve his team. So it was with William Gallas. Not only was the 33-year old approaching the end of his career, but he had played for both Chelsea and Arsenal and proved a controversial figure on and off the pitch. Gallas was taken into the Clarefontaine Academy as a youngster and joined Caen when he graduated. In his first season, he helped Caen secure promotion from the French second division. A rapidly developing talent, Olympique de Marseille were quick to take him on and in four years established himself as the defensive lynchpin, collecting 11 Under-21 caps, but not forcing his way into the full international team. That was rectified a little more than a year after joining Chelsea with his full debut coming against Slovenia in October 2002. Alongside John Terry, Gallas formed the central defensive barrier for Chelsea as they won the Premier League and Carling Cup in 2005 and retained the Premier League title the following year. Athletic and gangly, Gallas was all arms and legs, smothering his opponent like a rash, marking as tight as anyone ever could. He had plenty of pace that gave him had great powers of recovery and meant he was not out of place playing at full-back when circumstances demanded. A regular for France, Gallas complained at his wages when he returned from the 2006 World Cup in Germany. Approaching the last year of his contract and refusing to sign a new one, Chelsea allowed him to move to Arsenal when Arsène Wenger demanded the Frenchman as part of the deal to let Ashley Cole move to Stamford Bridge. In four years at Highbury Gallas enhanced his reputation as a top class defender, though not without some unprofessional incidents. He positioned himself in the opposition half when Birmingham City were awarded a late penalty at St Andrews in February 2008, confronted the home crowd at the end of the game and then sat on the pitch and refused to budge until Wenger talked him round. Hardly the conduct expected of the club captain. As Gallas' Arsenal contract was drawing to its May 2010 end, he again complained at what he was being paid. Arsenal considered his demands excessive and would not meet them. It was then Redknapp moved to sign Gallas for Spurs on a one-year contract. He performed well enough to earn a two-year extension. While Gallas had slowed down, his vast experience could not be denied and while there were times when he could be caught out of place and unable to recover, his reading of the game could rarely be faulted. Despite frequent injuries, he gave Spurs three years' good service. Following his release, he had a year in Australia as the marquee signing of Perth Glory. Gallas did not become one of Spurs' French internationals, playing his 84th and last game for his country in June 2010

Appearances:
League: 57 (4) apps. 1 gl.
FA Cup: 2* (1) apps.
Euro: 14 apps.
Others: 11 (2) apps.
Total: 84 (7) apps. 1 gl.
* Includes 1 abandoned match

GALLOWAY, Septimus Randolph

Role: Centre-forward 1928-29
Born: Sunderland, 22nd December 1896
Died: Mapperley, Nottinghamshire, 10th April 1964

CAREER: Sunderland Tramways 1921/Derby County Oct 1922/Nottingham Forest Nov 1924/Luton Town Jun 1927/Coventry City Dec 1927/**SPURS** trial Jul 1928, pro. Aug 1928/Grantham Town Sep 1929/Real Sporting de Gijón (Spain) trainer 1929-31/Valencia (Spain) manager 1931-33/Racing Santander (Spain) trainer 1933-35/Royal Ordnance Nottingham 1937-38/Costa Rica trainer 1946/Peñarol (Uruguay) trainer by 1948/Young Fellows (Switzerland) trainer 1949-50/Sporting Lisbon (Portugal) trainer 1950-53/Vitória de Guimarães (Portugal) coach 1954-55/Gillingham coach.

Debut v Southampton (FL) (a) 1.9.28 (scored once)

A schoolboy full-back, it was while serving in the Yorkshire Regiment that Randolph Galloway was converted to the centre-forward's role. Tremendously experienced, he arrived at White Hart Lane in July 1928 having been released by Coventry City at the end of the previous season. His football career had started just after the First World War with Sunderland Tramways and he played for Derby County, Nottingham Forest and Luton Town before his six months at Coventry. He was unable to find a new club after leaving Coventry, but Spurs decided to give him a month's trial, and he impressed enough to be signed as cover for former England international Tom Roberts who had just arrived from Preston North End. Roberts was a great disappointment and after just two games was out of the team with Galloway stepping in. He scored in his first two matches, but after only one more game was injured. Troubled by injuries for the remainder of the season, he did not get another chance. In April 1929 Galloway was released and in the absence of interest from any other League clubs joined Grantham Town. From Grantham he set out on a coaching and managerial career that saw him travel the world, his greatest successes coming with Sporting Lisbon, who he led to three successive Portuguese titles from 1951 to 1953.

Appearances:
League: 3 apps. 2 gls.
Total: 3 apps. 2 gls.

GALVIN, Anthony

Role: Wide midfield 1978-88
5ft.9ins. 11st.5lbs.
Born: Huddersfield, Yorkshire, 12th July 1956

CAREER: Yorkshire Schools/England Schools/Hull University/Goole Town/**SPURS** Jan 1978/Sheffield Wednesday Aug 1987/Swindon Town Jul 1989, asst. manager Feb 1991, caretaker manager Mar 1991/Newcastle United asst. manager Mar 1991-Feb 1992/(Gateshead Nov 1991)/Worthing Nov 1992/Royston Town manager Aug 1994 to cs. 1997/Buntingford Town asst. manager by Feb 2006/Royston Town asst. manager Nov 2007/Potton United coach Jul 2009.

Debut v Manchester City (FL) (h) 3.2.1979
(Saudi Arabian XI (Fr) (sub) (Jeddah) 9.10.1978)

Tony Galvin had shelved ideas of a professional football career to take a Bachelor of Arts degree in Russian Studies at Hull University and, when work permitted, play for the University team. After obtaining his degree he went to Teacher Training College. While there he played for Northern Premier League Goole Town, where he was spotted by Spurs. Signed in January 1978 for what proved a bargain £30,000 fee, he did not become a full time professional until that summer, preferring to complete his Teacher Training course. He made his League debut in February 1979, but it was not until early 1981, when he was called up for the FA Cup third round replay with Queens Park Rangers, that the chance arose to establish himself. From there on it was only injuries, of which he suffered quite a few, that kept him out of the team, and his deep-lying brand of wing play was crucial to Spurs' successes in the early 1980's. With his non-stop running from deep positions, ability to beat a man and produce accurate crosses, Galvin's workmanlike style was the perfect foil to the more artistic talents of Glenn Hoddle and Ossie Ardiles. A member of the FA Cup winning teams of 1981 and 1982, he also collected a League (Milk) Cup runners-up tankard in 1982 and was outstanding in the 1984 UEFA Cup winning side. Galvin qualified to play for the Republic of Ireland through his grandfather, and won his first cap against Holland in September 1982. In total he collected 20 caps for the Republic as a Spurs player, and after his £130,000 transfer to Sheffield Wednesday picked up a further nine. Again suffering more than his fair share of injuries, Galvin spent two difficult seasons at Hillsborough before moving to Swindon Town, the first purchase by his former team-mate, Ardiles, who had just taken over as manager. Winning a final international cap, he helped Swindon reach the First Division via the promotion play-offs in his first season-although they were subsequently relegated without taking their place in the elite due to financial irregularities. Promoted to assistant manager, he only held the post for a matter of weeks. When Ardiles decided to join Newcastle United, Galvin took over as the Robin's caretaker manager, but with the appointment of Glenn Hoddle to the manager's role, Galvin immediately left to renew his partnership with Ardiles. In November 1991 he signed on with Gateshead, although only to play midweek matches when his duties with Newcastle would permit. Unfortunately, it was all short-lived. In February 1992 he and Ardiles were summarily dismissed from St James Park following a re-shuffle in the Newcastle boardroom. Galvin later combined teaching with coaching at non-league level. His brother, Chris, played in midfield for Leeds United, Hull City and Stockport County during the 1970's.

Appearances:
League: 194 (7) apps. 20 gls.
FA Cup: 23 (1) apps. 2 gls.
FL Cup: 20 (3) apps. 3 gls.
Euro: 25 apps. 6 gls.
Others: 88 (14) apps. 16 gls.
Total: 350 (25) apps. 47 gls.

GAMBLE, S

Role: Centre-half 1892-93

CAREER: Foxes/**SPURS** guest Mar 1893, perm Apr 1893/Robin Hood/Foxes cs. 1894.

Debut v Old St Stephens (SA) (h) 25.3.1893

At the time of his first known appearance for Spurs, Gamble, was playing for the local club, Foxes. He had impressed Spurs with his performance for Tottenham against Edmonton the previous week, but was not due to play for Spurs. He only turned out as regular half-back Stanley Briggs failed to arrive for the game. After his second appearance the following month, Gamble switched allegiance to Spurs. He was not to play another first team game, spending the next season either in Spurs reserves or turning out for Robin Hood. At the end of the 1893-94 season he returned to Foxes and continued to perform well in local junior football, representing Tottenham again in March 1895.

Appearances:
Others: 2 apps.
Total: 2 apps. 0 gls.

GARBUTT, Henry Penty

Role: Centre-forward 1929-30
5ft.10ins. 10st.10lbs.
Born: Pontefract, Yorkshire, 12th November 1907
Died: Knottingley, Yorkshire 6th February 1986

CAREER: Castleford Town Mar pro. 1927/**SPURS** Mar 1927/Northfleet United Aug 1927/**SPURS** Sep 1927/Clapton Orient Jun 1930/Accrington Stanley Nov 1931/free transfer cs. 1932.

Debut v British Army XI (Fr) (Malta) 16.5.1929 (scored once)

Harry Garbutt had built himself quite a reputation as a goal-scoring centre-forward with Castleford Town, but had few chances to enhance that reputation at White Hart Lane. He was to make a total of only four appearances, and three of those were on Spurs' tour to Malta in May 1929. He scored four goals in three games on that tour, but back home his only first team outing was against Crystal Palace in November 1929 in the London Professional Football Charity Fund match. He played in a strong Spurs' eleven and scored a hat-trick in a 5-1 victory. Despite the fact Spurs were doing poorly in the League and Garbutt was scoring well for the reserve and "A" teams, he never got a chance in the League side and was released at the end of the season. He signed for Clapton Orient and after one season in east London moved to Accrington Stanley. He played there for just one season, before being released on a free transfer despite having scored seven goals in only twelve League games.

Appearances:
Others: 4 apps. 7 gls.
Total: 4 apps. 7 gls.

GARDINER

Role: Goalkeeper 1896-97

Debut v Northfleet (Fr) (h) 29.12.1896

Gardiner made five appearances for Spurs in friendly matches in the 1896-97 season. Although he continued to be associated with Spurs for the next two seasons, all his other games were with the reserves.

Appearances:
Others: 5 apps.
Total: 5 apps. 0 gls.

GARDNER, Anthony Derek

Role: Central Defender 1999-2008
6ft.5ins. 14st.0lbs.
Born: Stafford, Staffordshire, 19th September 1980

CAREER: Falcons/Rising Brook School/Staffordshire Schools/Stafford Falcons/Port Vale YTS May 1997, pro. Jul 1998/**SPURS** Jan 2000/(Everton loan Jan 2008)/Hull City loan Jul 2008, perm Aug 2008/Crystal Palace loan Aug 2010, perm Aug 2011/Sheffield Wednesday Jul 2012-May 2014/Port Vale training Nov 2014.

Debut v Derby County (sub) (PL) (a) 3.3.2001
(Portsmouth (sub) (Fr) (a) 9.5.2000)

Another of the young talents signed from a lower division club with the intention of being groomed for greater things, Anthony Gardner was only 19 when Spurs laid out £1million to sign him from Port Vale. Physically he seemed to possess everything needed of a central defensive pivot. Not surprisingly for someone of 6ft 5in, he was strong in the air, but his long legs not only gave him height. They carried him across the ground with deceptive speed and would snake out to pinch the ball or block a pass when least expected. Sadly, niggling little injuries continually interrupted his development. They were rarely serious, but one seemed to follow another, leaving him on the side-lines for long periods. When he did cast off his injury woes in 2003-04, he proved himself a commanding performer, with such confidence, composure and sheer class that he was called into the full England squad. Collecting his one England cap as a substitute against Sweden in March 2004, adding the honour to the Under-21 cap he had won two years earlier, was to be the high point of Gardner's career. The niggling injuries returned and

Gardner was never again to sustain a run in the Spurs' team. Eventually transferred to Hull City, injuries continued to afflict him and it was not until he moved to Crystal Palace, initially on loan, that he once again played regularly. Approaching the veteran stage, his experience proved invaluable in helping Palace recover from administration and lay the foundations for a return to the Premier League. By the time that was achieved, Gardner had moved on to Sheffield Wednesday, where he finished his career after two years,

Appearances:
League: 94 (20) apps. 2 gls.
FA Cup: 11 (3) apps.
FL Cup: 13 apps. 1 gl.
Euro: 3 apps.
Others: 20 (9) apps. 1 gl.
Total: 141 (32) apps. 4 gls.

GARLAND, Peter John

Role: Midfielder 1989-91
5ft.10ins. 12st.4lbs.
Born: Croydon, Surrey, 20th January 1971

CAREER: London Schools/Surrey Schools/Croydon/SPURS trainee Jul 1987, pro. cs. 1989/Newcastle United Mar 1992/Charlton Athletic loan and perm. Dec 1992/(Wycombe Wanderers loan Mar 1995)/Orient trial May 1996, perm. Jul 1996/Crawley Town cs. 1997/Dulwich Hamlet during 1997-98/Croydon Dec 2000/Whyteleafe Aug 2002-Feb 2004/Dulwich Hamlet Jul 2004/Erith Town Aug 2004/Greenwich Borough Dec 2004, player-coach Dec 2005, player-caretaker manager cs. 2006, manager till Nov 2006.

Debut v Norwich City (sub) (FL) (a) 10.4.1991
(Caen (sub) (Fr) (Cherbourg) 31.10.1989)

An England Under-17 international, Peter Garland was a tenacious midfield player with a powerful long range shot, who never really had a chance to make the grade at White Hart Lane. His only League appearance for Spurs was as a substitute at Norwich City in April 1991 just before the FA Cup Final. On transfer deadline day 1992 Garland was transferred to Newcastle United for £60,000. One of Kevin Keegan's earliest signings as Newcastle manager, he had as little opportunity to shine at St James' Park as he had at White Hart Lane, and made only two substitute appearances in the League. He fared better at Charlton making over fifty appearances in four years before moving to Leyton Orient. Released by Orient he joined Crawley Town where his father, Dave, was coach and when his father took over as manager of Dulwich Hamlet, Garland followed him to the south London club. He continued in non-League football until trying his hand with a short, but unsuccessful spell, as manager of Greenwich Borough. His brother, Mark, had been a trainee at Crystal Palace and later played non-League football in London and Kent.

Appearances:
League: (1) app.
Others: 1 (6) apps.
Total: 1 (7) apps. 0 gls.

GARWOOD, Leonard Frank

Role: Half-back 1945-51
5ft.8ins. 10st.3lbs.
Born: Ranikwet, India, 28th July 1923
Died: Biggleswade, Bedfordshire, 16th July 1979

CAREER: Eton Bray/Cambridge Town/Hitchin Town/SPURS am. 1944, pro. May 1946/(guest for Hitchin Town and Cambridge City during World War Two)/Bedford Town Aug 1952.

Debut v Luton Town (FL) (a) 23.10.1948
(Coventry City (FLS) (a) 4.5.1946)

Born in India where his father was serving with the forces, Len Garwood signed for Spurs as an amateur having been noticed playing for Eton Bray, the team run by printers Waterlow and Son Limited, at Dunstable. During the war he played for Hitchin Town and Cambridge City and made his first appearance for Spurs in the club's last Football League South fixture in May 1946. Garwood signed professional following that match, but, unfortunately, he was a left-half, and in the years after the war Ron Burgess was immoveable from that position. In his six years at White Hart Lane, Garwood played only two League games, the first when Burgess was on international duty and the second when Burgess was injured. Transfer-listed in May 1952 Garwood joined Bedford Town the following August and was a member of the Bedford team that took Arsenal to an FA Cup replay in 1956.

Appearances:
League: 2 apps.
Others: 4 apps.
Total: 6 apps. 0 gls.

GASCOIGNE, Paul John

Role: Midfielder 1988-91
5ft.10ins. 11st.7lbs.
Born: Gateshead, Tyne and Wear, 27th May 1967

CAREER: Redheugh Boys Club/Dunston Juniors/Gateshead Schools/Durham Schools/Newcastle United app. Jun 1983, pro. May 1985/SPURS Jul 1988/Lazio (Italy) Jul 1991-transfer completed Jun 1992/Rangers May 1995/Middlesbrough Mar 1998/Everton Jul 2000/Burnley Mar 2002-May 2002/DC United (USA) trial Jul 2002/Morpeth Town training Oct 2002/DC United (USA) Dec 2002 trial/Liaoning Bodao (China) trial Jan 2003/Gansu Tianma (China) player-asst. coach Jan 2003/Wolverhampton Wanderers training Oct 2003/Boston United player-coach Jul-Sep 2004/Algarve United (Portugal) manager Jun-Jul 2005/Kettering Town manager Oct-Dec 2005/Newcastle United part-time Academy coach Oct 2009.

Debut v Newcastle United (FL) (a) 3.9.1988
(Vederslöv-Dänningelanda (Fr) (a) 26.7.1988)

When manager Terry Venables paid a British record fee of £2,000,000 to sign Paul Gascoigne in July 1988, many people in the game thought it an enormous gamble investing so much money in a sometimes over-

exuberant 21-year old who had yet to fulfil his undoubted potential. The so-called gamble was to prove an inspired decision by Venables, who always believed he could harness the Geordie's maverick spirit without crushing his impudent footballing gifts. He was proved right as Gascoigne rapidly developed into one of the most exciting talents in European football. An Associate Schoolboy with Newcastle, he progressed through the ranks to make his League debut a month before turning professional. His rise from then on was meteoric. In June 1987 he made his debut for England Under-21's against Morocco, and when he arrived at White Hart Lane he had 13 Under-21 caps to his name although he had yet to make a senior breakthrough. Voted "Young Player of the Year" by the Professional Footballers' Association in 1988, he won his first full England cap playing as a substitute against Denmark just days after his senior debut for Spurs. A richly talented midfield player, Gascoigne combined direct and often unorthodox dribbling skills, with an ability to cut defences wide open with a lovely sweeping pass or incisive through ball. Cunning with his free-kicks and a cool finisher in front of goal, "Gazza" quickly proved himself not only one of the brightest stars in British football, but also a genuine "character". A player who clearly revelled in playing the game, his desire to entertain helped put a smile on the face of football fans throughout the country. Forever demanding the ball and desperate to be involved, his carefree and well-publicised slap-stick humorous antics both on and off the field may well have held back his international development on the grounds of immaturity, but some outstanding performances in the build-up to the 1990 World Cup finals meant Bobby Robson simply could not afford to leave him out of the team. The undoubted star of England's march to the semi-finals, Gascoigne displayed not only the expected special skills and talent, but an unexpected sense of discipline and responsibility that proved he had truly come of age. His televised, anguished tears when he realised a booking in the semi-final would rule him out of the final should England get through, endeared him to the nation, who in turn voted him the BBC Sports Personality of 1990. Gascoigne suffered a serious stomach muscle injury early in 1991, but returned to almost single-handedly steer Spurs through to the 1991 FA Cup Final. Unfortunately, one of the greatest days of his life was ruined when he was badly hurt after only ten minutes of the Final, following an inexplicably rash challenge on Nottingham Forest's Gary Charles. Gascoigne had to be stretchered off with a serious knee injury. The career-threatening damage to his cruciate ligament put in jeopardy a proposed world record £8.5 million move to the Italian club Lazio, but after medical opinion had indicated he should make a full recovery, it was agreed he should join the Italian club in May 1992 subject to proving his fitness by that time. The long-running transfer saga was eventually completed for a reduced fee of £5.5 million after Gascoigne passed a series of strenuous medical examinations and fitness tests. In total he won 20 full and 2 "B" caps whilst with Spurs. Although he did not win any honours with Lazio, his three years in Italy were almost as eventful as his time with Spurs. In May 1995 he moved to Rangers, helping them win the Scottish League and Cup double in 1996. Spells with Middlesbrough, Everton and Burnley followed, but injuries and the controversial life he led off the pitch all took their toll. He never gave up hope of resurrecting his career and finished his playing days with a spell in Chinese football before turning his short-lived attentions to management. A short time as coach to Boston United was followed by an ever shorter, 39-day, and, as usual, controversial spell as manager of Kettering Town. Unable to cope with life out of football and the public eye, Gascoigne turned to drink, with the personal problems that followed, all too readily seized upon by the press. It was a sad way for a great talent to go, but no matter what, Gascoigne will always have a special place in the hearts of those fortunate enough to have seen him hold centre stage at White Hart Lane.

Appearances:
League: 91 (1) apps. 19 gls.
FA Cup: 6 apps. 6 gls.
FL Cup: 13 (1) apps. 8 gls.
Others: 29 (3) apps. 13 gls.
Total: 139 (5) apps. 46 gls.

GAUSDEN, C G

Role: Winger 1905-06

CAREER: Richmond Association/**SPURS** trial Oct 1905.

Debut v West Ham United (WL) (a) 6.11.1905

A winger with the London junior club Richmond Association, Gausden was given a trial in October/November 1905, playing in one first eleven game, a Western League fixture against West Ham United. Gausden's play in his second match, a reserve friendly against Cambridge University, was described as being "erratic" and he was not given another chance.

Appearances:
Others: 1 app.
Total: 1 app. 0 gls.

GAVIN, John Thomas

Role: Winger 1954-56
5ft.7ins. 11st.0lbs.
Born: Limerick, Eire, 20th April 1928
Died: Cambridge, 20th September 2007

CAREER: Jamesborough United/Limerick City 1947/Norwich City Aug 1948/**SPURS** Oct 1954/Norwich City Nov 1955/Watford Jul 1958/Crystal Palace May 1959/Cambridge City Jul 1961/Newmarket player-coach Aug 1962/Fulbourn Nov 1967.

Debut v Newcastle United (FL) (a) 16.10.1954

A diminutive winger with a good goal-scoring record, Johnny Gavin had played over 200 League games for Norwich City and won four caps for the Republic of Ireland, the first against Finland in September 1949, by the time he joined Spurs. He quickly settled in at White Hart Lane, and with his speed, strength and good positional sense, became a great crowd favourite, adding two further caps to his total against Holland and West Germany in May 1955. The following season he played the first three League games, but with only one point gained was replaced by Sonny Walters. Spurs suffered defeat in eleven of the first 14 matches that season, and when manager Jimmy Anderson sought to sign the Norwich defender Maurice Norman to bolster the leaky defence, the Canaries would only do

business if Gavin's return was part of the deal. Spurs' need was desperate, so Anderson agreed. Gavin proceeded to make another 100 plus appearances for Norwich, won another cap for his country and represented the Third Division (South) against the Third Division (North) before joining Watford. He finished his senior career at Crystal Palace, then joined Cambridge City and was later player-coach of Newmarket. Later in life he was publican for several years and also a painter and decorator.

Appearances:
League: 32 apps. 15 gls.
FA Cup: 2 apps. 1 gl.
Others: 9 apps. 3 gls.
Total: 43 apps. 19 gls.

GEE

Role: Full-back 1918-19

CAREER: SPURS trial Oct 1918.

Debut v Millwall (LFC) (a) 26.10.1918

Gee made his only appearance as a trialist in a London Football Combination fixture with Millwall in October 1918. Playing at full-back, the experiment was described as "hardly successful".

Appearances:
Others: 1 app.
Total: 1 app. 0 gls.

GEMMELL, George

Role: Centre-forward 1913-14
Born: Kings Lynn, Norfolk, 1889
Died: Langham, Rutland, 25th January 1965

CAREER: Queen's College, Cambridge/Kings Lynn/Lynn Town/Watford am. Nov 1911/Ilford by Nov 1912/**SPURS** am. Oct 1913/Watford Aug 1914.

Debut v Leicester Fosse (FAC) (h) 15.1.1914

An England amateur international centre-forward, having played against Wales and France in 1912-13, George Gemmell signed for Spurs early in the 1913-14 season whilst playing for Ilford. He had previously played a few games in the Southern League for Watford. He scored four goals in as many reserve matches for Spurs, but his first team debut still came as something of a surprise. On 10th January 1914 Spurs drew an absolute thriller of an FA Cup first round tie at Leicester Fosse 5-5. Regular centre-forward Jimmy Cantrell was injured in the match and unable to take his place for the replay five days later. Gemmell was called up and played his part as Spurs won 2-0 for the right to meet Manchester City in the next round. That was to be his only appearance in Spurs' first team. Gemmell also played for Norfolk and Hertfordshire and was a cricketer with Norfolk and in Rhodesia where he lived for 13 years.

Appearances:
FA Cup: 1 app.
Total: 1 app. 0 gls.

GEORGE, John Spencer

Role: Half-back 1904-06
5ft.11ins. 12st.6lbs.
Born: Irchester, Northamptonshire, 4th February 1884
Died: Wellingborough, Northamptonshire, 29th October 1931

CAREER: Rushden Town Jul 1902/Kettering cs. 1903/**SPURS** Apr 1904/Leeds City Apr 1906/Croydon Common cs. 1907/Hastings and St Leonards United cs. 1908.

Debut v Fulham (WL) (a) 14.11.1904
(Brighton and Hove Albion (Fr) (h) 12.9.1904)

Although signed from Kettering in April 1904, John George had to wait until November that year for his competitive debut in a Western League fixture with Fulham. Retained for the following season, he never progressed past the level of a reserve and in April 1906 moved to Leeds City. With the Yorkshire club, he occupied a half-back position, until being replaced in the last match of the season by his former Spurs' reserve team-mate, John Freeborough. George remained with Leeds the following season, but then returned to London to play for Croydon Common. After one season with the newly-professionalised club, he moved to Hastings and St Leonards United in the 1908 close season.

Appearances:
Southern: 4 apps. 1 gl.
Others: 7 apps.
Total: 11 apps. 1 gl.

GHALY, Hossam El-Sayed

Role: Midfield 2006-07
5ft.11ins. 12st.7lbs.
Born: Kafr El-Sheikh, Egypt 15th December 1981

CAREER: Biala (Egypt) 1996/Al Ahly (Egypt) 1997/Feyenoord (Holland) trial Jul 2003, perm Aug 2003/**SPURS** Jan 2006/(Al Ahly training Nov 2007)/(Derby County loan Jan 2008)/Al Nasr (Saudi Arabia) Jan 2009/Al Ahly (Egypt) Jul 2010/Lierse SK (Belgium) Jul 2013/Al Ahly (Egypt) Jun 2014.

Debut v Manchester United (PL) (a) 9.9.2006
(OGC Nice (Fr) (Evian) 14.7.2006)

Hossam Ghaly was a talented midfielder who would have enjoyed a far more successful career than he did, were it not for a suspect temperament that was always likely to explode. It certainly all but finished him with Spurs. Having come to prominence as a boy prodigy with Al Ahly and been voted Egypt's "Best Youth Player", Feyenoord jumped ahead of several interested European clubs in to sign him after a brief trial. He was advised of the merits of joining the Dutch giants by his international team-mate, Mido, who had previously played for Ajax. While clearly very talented, Ghaly was inconsistent, too often disappearing from games and unable to hold down a regular place. When given the chance of a run in the team, he too often spurned it with his maverick attitude, preferring to play his

own game rather than follow his coach's instructions. It was frustration with Ghaly's attitude that led to Feyenoord accepting Spurs' offer of £2.5 million. Made to bide his time, it was eight months before he was given his chance in the first team. Initially, he impressed and looked to have the makings of a fine midfield general, but he soon showed the bad side of his game, self-indulgent, lazy and too quick to blame others for his shortcomings. The final straw came in late May 2007. Sent on as an early substitute against Blackburn at White Hart Lane, he took exception to being substituted himself after a totally ineffective half-hour performance. As he trudged off he ripped off his shirt and threw it at Martin Jol. Such action was never going to be forgiven, certainly not by the fans. An early exit from Spurs was on the cards when a permanent transfer to Birmingham City was arranged in July 2007. Subject only to him securing a work permit, the deal fell through when Ghaly took exception to being expected to undertake extra training to improve his fitness. Initially exiled to the reserves, Ghaly was allowed to return to Egypt and train with Al Ahly in preparation for the 2008 Africa Cup of Nations, but missed the competition when Derby County offered him the chance to rebuild his career by taking him on loan. Ghaly did well enough at Pride Park, but any chance of him rebuilding his career at Spurs ended in January 2009. Recalled to the first team squad by Harry Redknapp, Ghaly was preparing to go on as a substitute against Wigan Athletic in the FA Cup, when the crowd made its feeling so clear with a chorus of booing that Redknapp recalled Ghaly to the bench. By the end of the month, Ghaly had been transferred to Al Nasr of Saudi Arabia. He returned to Ah Ahly in July 2010 and enjoyed the three best years of his career with them. He helped them lift the Egyptian League title in 2011 (adding that to the three he had helped them secure in 1998, 1999 and 2000) and the CAF Champions League in 2012 (adding that to the victory in 2001). On the international stage, Ghaly made 55 appearances for his country, eight of them as a Spurs player, and helped Egypt win the Africa Cup of Nations in 2010.

Appearances:
League: 17 (4) apps. 1 gl.
FA Cup: 2 (2) apps. 1 gl.
FL Cup: 2 (1) apps.
Euro: 3 (3) apps. 1 gl.
Others: 4 (3) apps.
Total: 28 (13) apps. 3 gls.

GIBBINS, Edward

Role: Centre-half 1943-53
5ft.10ins. 12st.0lbs.
Born: Shoreditch, London, 24th March 1926
Born: Kingston St. Mary, Devon, 7th August 2011

CAREER: Dalston Schools/Tottenham Juniors/Finchley/SPURS am. Apr 1944/(Chelmsford City loan 1947-48)/SPURS pro. Aug 1948, coach cs. 1954/Jervis Bay Old Boys/Edmonton manager-coach Jan 1957/Tufnell Park, Edmonton coach Jul 1957, manager Jun 1961-1963/Hounslow Town manager Oct 1963-1964/Fulham Youth manager 1965-66/Hayes manager cs. 1966-Jan 1970.

Debut v Tranmere Rovers (FAC) (h) 12.1.1953
(Millwall (Fr) (a) 10.4.1944)

Eddie Gibbins joined Tottenham Juniors on leaving school and was then loaned out to Finchley. He made his debut in Spurs' first team as an 18-year old in April 1944 when they fielded such a young and inexperienced side in a friendly at Millwall, that Spurs had to be brought up to full strength by the inclusion of three Millwall juniors. Gibbins' competitive debut was later that month in a Football League South game against Clapton Orient, but he then had to wait no less than nine years for his next senior appearance! Signing amateur on his demob in 1946 he played for Chelmsford in the 1947-48 season, before joining the professional ranks at White Hart Lane in August 1948. He played only one League game for Spurs, on 7th March 1953 against Blackpool, but had already played three FA Cup matches that season in place of the injured Harry Clarke. Gibbins remained on Spurs' playing staff until the end of the 1953-54 season when he moved onto the coaching side. His son, Roger, was on Spurs' books as a youth but never made the first team, although he did go on to play for Oxford United, Norwich City, New England Teamen, Cambridge United, Cardiff City, Swansea City, Newport County and Torquay United.

Appearances:
League: 1 app.
FA Cup: 3 apps.
Others: 5 apps.
Total: 9 apps. 0 gls.

GIBBONS, Albert Henry

Role: Centre-forward 1937-38 and 1940-46
5ft.9ins. 11st.5lbs.
Born: Fulham, London, 10th April 1914
Died: Johannesburg, South Africa, 4th July 1986

CAREER: Uxbridge/Kingstonians/Hayes 1937/SPURS am. Mar 1937/Brentford am. Jul 1938/SPURS pro. Aug 1939/(guest for Bradford Park Avenue, Brentford, Chelsea, Fulham and Reading during Second World War)/Bradford Park Avenue am. Dec 1945, pro. May 1946/Brentford Aug 1947, caretaker player-manager Feb 1949, manager-secretary May 1949-Aug 1952/Royal Daring (Belgium) coach 1952-1954/Hapoel Petah Tikva (Israel) coach 1956/Israel National coach 1956/Hapoel Petah Tikva (Israel) coach 1958/coach in Sydney, Australia 1959-1961/Hapoel Jerusalem (Israel) coach 1961-1963/Rangers (South Africa) coach 1963-1965/Transvaal (South Africa) coach 1963-1965/Kenya manager 1966/coached in South African townships in 1970s.

Debut v Sheffield Wednesday (FL) (a) 16.9.1937 (scored once)

A phenomenal scoring rate made Jack Gibbons arguably the outstanding amateur footballer of the 1940's. Good on the ground and strong in the air, he made goal-scoring seem simple. An RAF aircraftsman, he started his career with Uxbridge and Kingstonians, before playing for Hayes and first signed amateur forms for Spurs during the 1936-37 season. Playing inside-forward to John Morrison, he made a goal-scoring debut at Sheffield Wednesday in September 1937, scored 18 goals in 33 senior games that season and collected the first of seven England amateur caps in January 1938. Having just missed promotion, Spurs were expecting

great things from Gibbons in 1938-39, but were extremely disappointed when he announced he had decided to turn out for Brentford instead. An amateur throughout his playing career, he made only 12 First Division appearances for the "Bees" and in August 1939 re-signed for Spurs. He appeared regularly for Spurs throughout the war years, was a constant member of the Football Association and Royal Air Force representative sides and played for England in the war-time international against Wales in October 1942. Spurs were hopeful he would stay with them after the war, but were again disappointed when Gibbons decided in December 1945 that he would be moving up North to work. He signed for Bradford PA and was top-scorer in his one year in Yorkshire, before returning to London and Brentford. He took over as their manager-secretary in May 1949 and held the position until his resignation in the summer of 1952. Thereafter, he travelled the world coaching. Coach to the first Israeli touring team to the USA in April and May 1956, he also prepared the South African teams that played Spurs in the summer of 1963. Gibbons worked as sports consultant for Coca-Cola in Nairobi, Kenya until ill health forced retirement and a return to South Africa. Even then, he was still to be found coaching in the townships.

Appearances:
League: 27 apps. 13 gls.
FA Cup: 6 apps. 5 gls.
Others: 115 apps. 91 gls.
Total: 148 apps. 109 gls.

GIBSON, Terence Bradley

Role: Striker 1978-84
5ft.5ins. 10st.0lbs.
Born: Walthamstow, London, 23rd December 1962

CAREER: Waltham Forest Schools/London Schools/Essex Schools/England Schools/**SPURS** app. Apr 1979, pro. Jan 1980/(GAIS (Sweden) loan summer 1981)/Coventry City Aug 1983/Manchester United Jan 1986/Wimbledon Aug 1987/(Swindon Town loan Mar 1992)/Charlton Athletic trial Aug 1993/Peterborough United trial Dec 1993/Watford trial Dec 1993/Barnet Feb 1994, player-youth team coach Apr 1994, caretaker-manager Oct 1996, first team coach Oct 1996/Wycombe Wanderers assistant manager Feb 1999/Northern Ireland coach Feb 2004, asst. manager/Bolton Wanderers scout Oct 2004/Manchester City scout Sep 2005/Fulham asst. manager Apr-Dec 2007.

Debut v Stoke City (FL) (h) 29.12.1979
(Gillingham (sub) (Fr) (a) 11.5.1979)

Winning England Youth honours on the way, little Terry Gibson developed through the ranks at Spurs to make his League debut against Stoke City in December 1979 whilst still an apprentice. Signing professional the next month he retained his place for two epic FA Cup ties with Manchester United before returning to the reserves and spent the summer of 1981 on loan to the Swedish club GAIS. A dynamic little forward, he proved to be an absolute handful for any defender, was unafraid to get stuck in when necessary and generally gave the opposition rear-guard little peace. Gibson was at his most effective in the penalty box, where his keen reflexes and speed of thought were best demonstrated. Despite this, he was unable to maintain a regular place at Spurs and was allowed to move to Coventry City for a £100,000 fee. After 43 goals in 97 League appearances for Coventry, he was transferred to Manchester United with former Spurs colleague Alan Brazil moving in the opposite direction. Gibson never really had an opportunity to prove himself at Old Trafford, and after a miserable 18 months returned to London. He signed for Wimbledon, where he rediscovered the goal-scoring instincts he had shown at Highfield Road. He helped the Dons establish themselves in the First Division and played his part in their shock FA Cup Final victory over Liverpool in 1988. Hindered by injuries, he joined former Spurs colleague Glenn Hoddle at Swindon Town in March 1992 with a view to possibly securing a permanent move. This did not materialise and after trials with Charlton Athletic, Peterborough United and Watford he joined Barnet, where he combined playing with duties coaching the youth team. Following Ray Clemence's departure to join the England set-up, Gibson was appointed first team coach and expected to have control of team affairs. However, he resigned without taking charge for even one game when Alan Mullery was appointed Director of Football. Out of football for a while, Gibson later worked as assistant manager to former Wimbledon team-mate Lawrie Sanchez, at Wycombe Wanderers, Northern Ireland and Fulham.

Appearances:
League: 16 (2) apps. 4 gls.
FA Cup: 5 apps. 1 gl.
FL Cup: 1 app. 1 gl.
Euro: (2) apps. 1 gl.
Others: 7 (10) apps. 9 gls.
Total: 29 (14) apps. 16 gls.

GILBERG, Harold

Role: Forward 1941-50
5ft.8ins. 10st.10lbs.
Born: Tottenham, London, 26th June 1923
Died: Torquay, Devon, 16th September 1994

CAREER: Tottenham Schools/Middlesex Schools/Tottenham Juniors/**SPURS** groundstaff Jun 1937, am. May 1939/Walthamstow Avenue Aug 1940/Northfleet United/**SPURS** pro. Sep 1944/(guest for Charlton Athletic, Chelmsford City and Southend United during World War Two)/Queens Park Rangers Aug 1951/Brighton and Hove Albion Dec 1952/retired 1955.

Debut v Newcastle United (FL) (a) 18.1.1947
(Watford (LWL) (a) 13.12.1941)

Harry Gilberg, whose father played for Tunbridge Wells Rangers, was taken on the Spurs ground-staff as a 14-year old schoolboy. He then played for the Tottenham Juniors, and after signing amateur forms Spurs arranged for him to play for Walthamstow Avenue and Northfleet. He was called back for his first team debut in December 1941 in a London War League match against Watford. Signed professional in September 1944, most of Gilberg's football during the war was spent as a guest with Southend United and Charlton Athletic. After the war, he continued on the professional staff, but played only two League and one FA Cup match and, after a series of injuries side-lined him for most of the 1950-51 season, decided he had no future at White Hart Lane. His transfer request was granted and he moved to Queens Park Rangers. He later played for Brighton until another bad injury forced him to retire.

Appearances:
League: 2 apps.
FA Cup: 1 app.
Others: 22 apps. 9 gls.
Total: 25 apps. 9 gls.

GILBERTO, Da Silva Melo

Role: Full-back 2007-09
5ft.11ins, 12st. 4lbs.
Born: Rio de Janeiro, Brazil, 25th April 1976

CAREER: América FC (Brazil) pro. 1993/Flamengo (Brazil) 1996/ Cruzeiro (Brazil) 1998/Internazionale (Italy) 1999/Vasco da Gama (Brazil) 1999/Grêmio (Brazil) 2002/São Caetano (Brazil) Jan 2004/Hertha Berlin (Germany) Jul 2004/**SPURS** Jan 2008/Cruzeiro (Brazil) Jul 2009-Sep 2011/ Vitória (Brazil) Sep 2011/Comercial (Brazil) Jan 2012/America-MG (Brazil) Apr-Dec 2012/Araxá EC (Brazil) player/youth coach Feb 2014.

Debut v PSV Eindhoven (UEFA) (h) 6.3.2008

Any Brazilian playing for a top flight European football club is expected to have real quality. Sadly, Gilberto exposed that as a myth. Signed from Hertha Berlin in January 2008, the 31-year old was the first Brazilian to play for Spurs at senior competitive level. He made ten such appearances, but in none of them did he do anything to justify his £2 million transfer fee. Starting with the América club in his home town of Rio de Janeiro, Gilberto did well enough for Internazionale to secure his services, but after just two games in a year in Italy he returned to Brazil. Over the next couple of years, he developed well enough to play for Brazil, establish himself as back-up to the great Roberto Carlos and earn another crack in Europe with Hertha Berlin. In nearly four years in Germany, Gilberto proved a competent, if not spectacular, left-back who was also able to perform in midfield. With Gareth Bale and Assou-Ekotto injured, Spurs needed competition for Lee Young-Pyo, but the fee was a large one for a player who would be a free agent at the end of the season, and proved even larger as Gilberto was soon injured. He did not make his debut until March 2008 and when he did, had a nightmare. Having gifted PSV Eindhoven an early goal, his performance just went from bad to worse and he was taken off at half-time. Gilberto remained at White Hart Lane for 18 months, but never did anything to justify his signing. In July 2009 his contract was cancelled after he had arranged to join Cruzeiro. He played for three more years before retiring. In total Gilberto made 35 appearances for Brazil, five of them during his Spurs' career. Gilberto's brother, Nélio, was a midfielder with several Brazilian clubs and played in Hungary. Another brother, Nildeson, was a striker who played in Brazil, El Salvador, Costa Rica and Mexico and represented El Salvador after taking out citizenship of that country.

Appearances:
League: 4 (3) apps. 1 gl.
Euro: 3 apps.
Others: 3 (1) apps.
Total: 10 (4) apps. 1 gl.

GILDERSON, E

Role: Inside-forward 1892-94

CAREER: High Cross Institute/Robin Hood/guest for **SPURS**/Robin Hood/Ilford cs. 1894.

Debut v Windsor and Eton (SA) (a) 4.3.1893 (scored once)

When Gilderson made his first recorded appearance for Spurs, he was playing for the local clubs, High Cross Institute and Robin Hood. His only other known appearance was in a friendly the following season. Although he did not make a career with Spurs, after playing again for Robin Hood in 1893-94, he found himself in trouble the following season when he signed forms for both IRMAC and Broadwater. He was refused permission to sign for either, so spent that and the following season in the Southern League with Ilford.

Appearances:
Others: 2 apps. 1 gl.
Total: 2 apps. 1 gl.

GILHOOLEY, Patrick

Role: Forward 1901-04
5ft.7ins. 11st.7lbs.
Born: Draffan, Lanarkshire, 6th July 1876
Died: Cleland, Lanarkshire, 20th February 1907

CAREER: Vale of Avon Juveniles/Larkhall Thistle/Cambuslang Hibernian/Celtic Oct 1896/Sheffield United Sep 1900/**SPURS** Sep 1901/ Brighton and Hove Albion Apr 1904/retired 1905.

Debut v Reading (WL) (h) 9.9.1901

Principally a winger, but also quite at home at inside-forward, Patrick Gilhooley started with Larkhall Thistle before joining Celtic where he rose to the level of playing for the Scottish League against the Football League in April 1898. Towards the end of 1900 he joined Sheffield United, but at the start of the following season was transferred to Spurs. While he played several matches at the beginning of the season, he was not in the same class as regular outside-right, Tom Smith, or inside-right, John Cameron. He stayed at Spurs for three years, but had to be content with a place in the reserves for the majority of that time. When released in April 1904 Gilhooley signed for Brighton where he spent just one season before retiring and returning to Scotland. He died less than two years later, after a lengthy illness.

Appearances:
Southern: 17 apps. 2 gls.
FA Cup: 3 apps.
Others: 38 apps. 5 gls.
Total: 58 apps. 7 gls.

GILLINGWATER, David

Role: Inside-forward 1965-66
Born: *Tottenham, London, 3rd February 1945*

CAREER: Tottenham Schools/London Schools/Middlesex Schools/Chelsea am./**SPURS** May 1962/released cs. 1966/Kettering/Ashford Town 1967.

Debut v Sarpsborg (Fr) (a) 15.5.1966

David Gillingwater was a local youngster almost poached from Spurs' doorstep. He signed as an amateur for Chelsea, and helped them win the FA Youth Cup in 1960-61, but when they failed to offer him professional terms, Spurs stepped in to sign him in May 1962. A regular goal-scorer for the reserves, the only first team match he played was in May 1966 when several reserves played in a friendly against the Norwegian club Sarpsborg. Gillingwater was released at the end of the season and moved into non-League soccer, combining football with a trade as a plumber and central heating engineer.

Appearances:
Others: 1 app.
Total: 1 app. 0 gls.

GILMORE, J

Role: Inside-forward 1895-96

Debut v Vampires (FAC) (h) 16.11.1895

Gilmore's four appearances for Spurs were all made within the space of a month in November/December 1895. The first was in an FA Cup Second Qualifying Round replay with Vampires, which had been ordered because the pitch had been wrongly marked out for the first match. He played in two friendly matches and the next round of the Cup, but then disappeared from the Spurs scene.

Appearances:
FA Cup: 2 apps.
Others: 2 apps.
Total: 4 apps. 0 gls.

GILZEAN, Alan John

Role: Forward 1964-75
6ft.0ins. 12st.4lbs.
Born: *Coupar Angus, Perthshire, 23rd October 1938*

CAREER: Coupar Angus Juvenilles/Dundee Violet/Dundee am. Jan 1956, pro. Aug 1957/(guest for Aldershot)/**SPURS** Dec 1964/Highland Park (South Africa) Jun 1974/Stevenage Athletic manager May-Aug 1975.

Debut v Everton (FL) (h) 19.12.1964

Alan Gilzean made an impressive debut at White Hart Lane when he scored twice for a Scotland XI against Spurs in a memorial match for John White in November 1964. A month later, he was a Spurs player and went on to give the club almost ten years' brilliant service. His career began in his home town with Coupar Angus Juvenilles, before he joined Dundee. While doing National Service in Aldershot he played for the local club, although never in a League game. Returning to Scotland Gilzean scored over 100 League goals and was a key figure in the Dundee teams that won the Scottish League title in 1961-62, reached the semi-final of the European Champions Cup the following season and the 1964 Final of the Scottish Cup. He won three Under-23 caps, played three times for the Scottish League and won five full Scottish caps, the first in November 1963 against Norway, before his £72,500 move to Spurs. An out-and-out centre-forward with Dundee, Gilzean had Jimmy Greaves alongside him at White Hart Lane and had to adapt his style accordingly to suit Spurs' principal goal-scorer, but from the first game they struck up a productive rapport. A member of the 1967 FA Cup winning team his place appeared under threat with the signing of Martin Chivers in January 1968, but Gilzean showed his adaptability once again and it was Greaves who eventually left Spurs. Instead of helping create numerous chances for the small, quicksilver Greaves, Gilzean now turned to supplying the ammunition for the big, bustling Chivers. Between them they led the forward line as Spurs won the Football League Cup in 1971 and 1973 and the UEFA Cup in 1972. Deceptively strong and wickedly cunning, Gilzean always seemed able to find space and dangerous positions, but his great forte was his exceptional heading ability. Not merely powerful, "Gilly's" touch was deft and delicate, and the abiding memory for Spurs fans of the day was how he seemed able to pass or flick the ball as well with his balding head, as many players could with their feet. He won a further 17 caps at Spurs before finishing his career on the 1974 tour to Mauritius, although he did return to White Hart Lane in November 1974 to play, and score, in his Testimonial match against Red Star Belgrade. After Spurs Gilzean went to South Africa, but only stayed three months and between May and August 1975, when they folded, was manager of Stevenage Athletic. He later worked as manager of a transport company in Enfield. His son, Ian, was a Scottish Youth international striker on Spurs' books, but did not manage to make his League breakthrough. Injuries and two knee operations disrupted his development, and, following his release in the summer 1992 he joined his father's other former club Dundee, later playing for Northampton Town, Ayr United and in Ireland. Another son, Kevin, had a brief spell with Cheshunt.

Appearances:
League: 335 (8) apps. 93 gls.
FA Cup: 40 apps. 21 gls.
FL Cup: 27 (1) apps. 6 gls.
Euro: 27 (1) apps. 13 gls.
Others: 62 (5) apps. 40 gls.
Total: 491 (15) apps. 173 gls.

GILZEAN, Ian Roger

Role: Striker 1988-92
Born: Enfield, Middlesex, 10th December 1969

CAREER: Enfield Schools/Middlesex Schools/London Youth/**SPURS** trainee Jul 1986, pro. cs. 1988/Dundee Jul 1992/(Doncaster Rovers loan Feb 1993)/Northampton Town cs. 1993/Ayr United Jul 1994/Sligo Rovers cs. 1995/Cheltenham Town trial Jul 1997/Drogheda United trial Sep 1997/St Patricks Athletic Oct 1997/Glentoran Oct 1999/Shelbourne Jul 2000/St Patricks Athletic Sep 2000/Sligo Rovers Dec 2000/Elgin City Jun 2001/Montrose Jul 2002/retired Oct 2003/Montrose coach Apr 2003, asst. manager Nov 2003, caretaker manager Nov 2005-Dec 2005/Lochee Harp jt. manager/Tayport jt. manager Mar 2007-Jun 2008/Arbroath youth development coach Apr 2009/Carnoustie Panmure manager Jun 2009-Mar 2013.

Debut v Bordeaux (sub) (Fr) (h) 4.3.1989

Like his father, Alan, Ian Gilzean was a central striker, but unlike his father he did not arrive at Spurs as a big-money signing. He joined the club from school and worked his way through the junior ranks, playing for Scotland Under-18s on the way. His only first team appearances were in March 1989 and Apr 1992 when he played as a substitute in friendlies with Bordeaux and Cardiff, but his career was hampered by a series of injuries. When released in the summer of 1992, he joined another of his father's old clubs, Dundee. He then moved around rapidly to Northampton Town and Ayr United before settling to football in Ireland, achieving most success with Glentoran. After five years in Ireland, he returned to finish his playing career in Scotland, before coaching at Junior level.

Appearances:
Others: (2) apps.
Total: (2) apps. 0 gls.

GINOLA, David Desire Marc

Role: Winger 1997-2000
6ft.1ins. 11st.10lbs.
Born: Gassin, France, 25th January 1967

CAREER: OGC Nice (France) 1983/Toulon (France) 1984/Matra Racing (France) 1988/Brest Amorique (France) 1990/Paris Saint-Germain (France) 1991/Newcastle United Jul 1995/**SPURS** Jul 1997/Aston Villa Jul 2000/Everton Feb-May 2002.

Debut v Manchester United (PL) (h) 10.8.1997
(Fredrikstad (Fr) (a) 18.7.1997)

David Ginola first came to the attention of English football fans in March and April 1994 when he played for Paris St Germain against Arsenal in the European Cup-Winners' Cup semi-final. It led to stories he would sign for Arsenal, but there was never any chance of that. Ginola was far too much a flair player for a club managed by George Graham, who still believed defence was all that mattered. Instead, Ginola joined Newcastle United, where Kevin Keegan gave him the freedom to flourish in a team that came so close to winning the League, before another manager who believed in the ethos of hard work, Kenny Dalglish, decided flair had to be sacrificed for functionality. It was rather a surprise when Gerry Francis laid out £2.5 million to sign Ginola for Spurs in July 1997. Francis had quickly dismantled Ossie Ardiles' team of attacking talents, and adopted the pragmatic approach of building a team to do a job. Results had improved, but the football being played was far from exciting. Spurs' fans have always demanded a hero, a star on whom they could pin their hopes. From his very first game it was clear Ginola was to be that man. With the Gallic good looks and physique many a movie star would envy and the graceful poise of a dancer, he added a sense of style and panache even before he got on the ball. Ginola was regarded as a winger when he joined Spurs, a man who would beat his man and provide the crosses for Les Ferdinand, who joined at the same time and also from Newcastle, to feed off. He did that, but he also showed there was a lot more to his game, often playing as a second striker or dropping back to a midfield position where time on the ball was at a premium. Most of his games for Spurs were played out on the wing and it is testament to his ability that even in that position he was invariably the most influential player on the pitch. When in possession, Ginola would glide over the surface, the ball under control, but temptingly close to his marker, inviting the lunging tackle that would miss the ball by inches as Ginola nicked it away, before speeding off. His exquisite ball control and perfect balance enabled him to take the ball close in on an opponent before a sudden drag back or quick flick took him past his man. Ginola arrived with the reputation of being a typical continental. When

things were going his way he would be demanding the ball, trying all his tricks and dominating matches. When things went against him or he just did not fancy it, he would disappear, complain at every decision that did not go his way and blame anyone but himself if anything went wrong. Early in his first season though, with Spurs struggling, Francis gone and Christian Gross installed in his place, Ginola seemed to realise that if relegation was to be avoided, he would have to buckle down and contribute fully. He showed a side of his game not seen too often in the past, working back, encouraging his team-mates, even making tackles! The returning Jürgen Klinsmann may have got much of the credit, but in truth it was the performances of Ginola that did most to keep Spurs up. With the arrival of George Graham as manager there was a risk Ginola would be side-lined, but the arch disciple of defensive football seemed to realise that leaving out the fan's favourite would definitely alienate the 50% of Spurs' supporters who were prepared to give Graham a chance to prove he could change his ways. Ginola rose to the challenge, and despite Graham's continual criticism of his work rate and penchant for substituting him, played his part in helping Spurs lift the Worthington Cup in 1999. His outstanding performances were recognised with both the PFA and FWA Player of the Year awards. They were added to the French Player of Year and Players' Player of Year awards he collected in 1994, a year after helping Paris St Germain win the French Cup, they were to collect again in 1995. Ginola was never a consistent scorer, but when he did score they were not simple goals. Just like the man himself, his goals were something special. He could find the back of the net with perfectly placed shots after cutting in from the wing, as he did against Liverpool in March 1998. He could hammer home a vicious first-time volley, as he did against Leeds United in the FA Cup in February 1999, or he could finish with a simple push past the keeper after a mazy dribble past four men, as he did in the FA Cup at Barnsley in March 1999. Every goal a stunner and every one of them just one more reason to remember one of the most thrilling players to don a Spurs' shirt.

Appearances:
League: 100 apps. 13 gls.
FA Cup: 11 apps. 5 gls.
FL Cup: 13 apps. 4 gls.
Euro: 2 (1) apps.
Others: 23 (2) apps. 2 gls.
Total: **149 (3) apps. 24 gls.**

DOS SANTOS RAMIREZ, Giovani Alex

Role: Forward 2008-12
5ft.8ins. 11st.5lbs.
Born: Monterrey, Nuevo León, Mexico, 11th May 1989

CAREER: Sao Paolo (Mexico)/Barcelona (Spain) 2002/SPURS Jul 2008/(Ipswich Town loan Mar 2009)/(Galatasaray loan Jan 2010)/(Racing Santander (Spain) loan Jan 2011)/RCD Mallorca (Spain) Aug 2012/Villarreal (Spain) Jul 2013/LA Galaxy (USA) Jul 2015.

Debut v Middlesbrough (PL) (a) 16.8.2008
(Hercules (Fr) (a) 24.7.2008)

The son of Gerardo dos Santos, better known as Zizinho, a Brazilian who spent practically his whole career playing in Mexico, principally for America and Leon, Giovani and his younger brother, Jonathan, were spotted by Barcelona playing for their local Monterrey junior club, Sao Paolo, in a youth tournament in France. Though Giovani was only eleven, and his brother a year younger, they were quickly taken under the wing of the Spanish giants, with the Dos Santos family moving to Spain. Giovani worked his way through the junior ranks at La Masia and by the age of 19 was a regular member of the first team squad and a full Mexican international. An attacking midfielder, he had to compete with the likes of Lionel Messi and as the Argentine was well on the way to becoming a world superstar, Barca were prepared to let Giovani leave when Spurs made an approach in the summer of 2008. It still cost Spurs £4.7 million to secure his signature, with the fee to rise to nearer £8 million if Giovani did as well as expected. From his first days at Spurs it was obvious Giovani was a player of tremendous talent and even greater potential, but Spurs had a miserable start to his first season. There was no time for Giovani to settle. Strength and experience were needed to turn Spurs' season around, particularly after Juande Ramos was dismissed, and they were not qualities Giovani possessed. He went to Ipswich Town on loan, where four goals in eight appearances proved his value, but back at White Hart Lane he was just unable to prove himself. Each season started with hopes high he could make the breakthrough, but with Aaron Lennon and Niko Kranjčar preferred, come the turn of the year he was out on loan again. With the ball at his feet Giovani was always a threat, prepared to take men on, alive in the box and with a powerful shot from range. He was not a player to work back, and too often ran up blind alleys, perhaps trying too hard to make an impression. He needed to be surrounded by players who knew and trusted him, as was the case with his national team. He frequently showed his true class at that level, notably in the 2012 London Olympics when he helped Mexico win the gold medal, though injury forced him to sit out the final. Not the type of player Andre Villas-Boas appreciated and with his contract into its last year, Giovani moved to Mallorca and then Villarreal. With those clubs he began to play regularly, before trying his luck in the USA with LA Galaxy. A third dos Santos brother, Éder, played for Socio Águila, Club America's reserve outfit.

Appearances:
League: 2 (15) apps.
FA Cup: 1 (1) apps. 1 gl.
FL Cup: 4 (1) apps.
Euro: 8 (1) apps. 2 gls.
Others: 6 (2) apps. 2 gls.
Total: **21 (20) apps. 5 gls.**

GIPPS, Thomas Savill

Role: Half-back 1907-10
5ft.7ins. 11st.0lbs.
Born: Walthamstow, London, January quarter 1888
Died: Walthamstow, London, 7th January 1956

CAREER: Walthamstow Imperial/SPURS trial Sep 1907, pro. Oct 1907/Barrow cs. 1911/Manchester United May 1912/free transfer May 1920.

Debut v Crystal Palace (WL) (h) 2.12.1907

Tommy Gipps performed well on his outings with the reserve team during a trial period and was signed to the professional staff. He made a first team debut two months later in a Western League fixture, but although he remained with Spurs for almost four years, his only other appearances were in Charity Cup competitions two years later. A regular for the reserves, Gipps was released at the end of the 1910-11 season and joined Barrow where he played exceptionally well and after just one season was transferred to Manchester United. In the three seasons before the First World War he made 23 appearances, but appeared regularly in the first season of war-time competition. Called up to do his duty he did return to Old Trafford after the War, but was released on a free transfer in May 1920. Gipps' brother, R, also played for Walthamstow Imperial.

Appearances:
Others: 3 apps.
Total: **3 apps. 0 gls.**

GLEN, Alexander

Role: Inside or Centre-forward 1904-06
6ft.1ins. 12st.0lbs.
Born: Kilsyth, Stirlingshire, 11th December 1879

CAREER: Fitzhugh Rovers/Glasgow Parkhead/Clyde/Grimsby Town Jul 1902/Notts County May 1903/SPURS May 1904/Southampton May 1906/Portsmouth May 1907/Brentford Jul 1908.

Debut v Fulham (SL) (h) 3.9.1904

Alex Glen had studied medicine at Glasgow Royal Infirmary in his native Scotland, before enlisting and serving in the Boer War as a surgical

dresser. On his discharge, he took up football and played for the Glasgow junior club Parkhead and then Scottish Second Division Clyde before moving down to England with Grimsby Town and Notts County. Although he made his Spurs debut in the first game of the season, he became an intermittent fixture in the team as Spurs went through a rather nondescript period between the remarkable FA Cup success of 1901 and the entry into the Football League in 1908. A neat and elegant dribbler of the ball for a tall man, he could also swerve and weave past defenders to good effect. However, in May 1906 Spurs decided not to retain his services and Glen joined Southampton where he was instantly made vice-captain. He was doing well with Southampton until March 1907 when he was suspended indefinitely for a breach of club discipline; being drunk. Released at the end of the season, he then spent a year with each of Portsmouth and Brentford. Glen later resumed his medical career and qualified as a doctor.

Appearances:
Southern: 32 apps. 12 gls.
FA Cup: 8 apps. 1 gl.
Others: 29* apps. 12 gls.
Total: 69 apps. 25 gls.
* Includes 1 abandoned match.

GLEN, P

Role: Centre-forward 1915-16
Born: Motherwell

CAREER: Gillingham cs. 1912 /(guest for **SPURS** during World War One).

Debut v Brentford (LFC) (h) 11.9.1915. (scored once)

A Gillingham player for three seasons before the outbreak of war, Glen played his only game for Spurs in September 1915 when he scored Spurs' goal in a London Football Combination fixture with Brentford.

Appearances:
Others: 1 app. 1gl.
Total: 1 app. 1 gls

GLIDDON, George

Role: Full-back 1912
5ft.10ins. 12st.6lbs.

CAREER: Tottenham Thursday/**SPURS** am. Jan 1912/Merthyr Town May 1914.

Debut v Hull City (Fr) (Brussels) 12.5.1912

George Gliddon was a Tottenham Thursday player signed to amateur forms by Spurs in January 1912, after impressing in a trial for the London amateur team at Stamford Bridge that month. Only three first team appearances have been traced for him, all from May 1912 during Spurs' European tour. The first was in a match against Hull City for the Becker Cup played in Brussels. Full details of five of the other matches played on that tour are unknown, and he may have played in one or more of them. Whatever, he never made the first team at White Hart Lane again before his departure to Merthyr Town in May 1914.

Appearances:
Others: 3 apps.
Total: 3 apps. 0 gls.

GODDARD, G Harold

Role: Outside-left 1888-89
Born: Swaffham, Suffolk

CAREER: Bakewell/Derbyshire/**SPURS** 1888.

Debut v Windsor Phoenix (Fr) (h) 2.3.1889

Harry Goddard's only traced appearance for Spurs was in March 1889 when he played outside-left in a friendly match with Windsor Phoenix during his first season with the club. An extremely fast winger, work took him from his native Suffolk to Bakewell, Derbyshire and whilst there he played for the local club and also represented Derbyshire. Although he is not known to have played any more senior matches for Spurs, he did continue to be associated with the club, spending more than 30 years working in the programme department.

Appearances:
Others: 1 app.
Total: 1 app. 0 gls.

GOLDSMITH, George

Role: Full-back 1934-35
5ft.11ins. 11st.6lbs.
Born: Loftus, Yorkshire, 11th March 1905
Died: Barnsley, September 1974

CAREER: Denaby Main/Bishop Auckland/Loftus Albion/Hull City Dec 1928/**SPURS** Jun 1934/Bolton Wanderers Mar 1935/retired 1936.

Debut v Derby County (FL) (a) 29.9.1934

George Goldsmith established himself as a fast and sure tackling right-back with Hull and, like Andy Duncan, was a member of their Division Three (North) winning team of 1933. He joined Spurs in June 1934, but made only one Football League appearance for them, against Derby County in September 1934 at left-back, before leaving to join Bolton Wanderers where he played for two years.

Appearances:
League: 1 app.
Total: 1 app. 0 gls.

GOLDTHORPE, Ernest Holroyd

Role: Inside-forward 1917-19
5ft.9ins. 11st.0lbs.
Born: Middleton, Leeds, Yorkshire, 8th June 1898
Died: Leeds, Yorkshire, 5th November 1929

CAREER: Yorkshire Schools/(guest for Bradford City and **SPURS** during World War One)/Bradford City Jun 1919/Leeds United Jun 1920/Bradford City Mar 1922/Manchester United Nov 1922/Rotherham County Oct-Nov 1925.

Debut v West Ham United (LFC) (h) 16.3.1918

Ernie Goldthorpe was a Lieutenant Corporal serving with the Scots Guards, whose only football experience had been playing for a junior club near his native Leeds. He was introduced to Spurs by Archibald Jack, an occasional guest player who served in the same regiment, and made his first appearance in March 1918 in a London Football Combination match against West Ham United when he played at left-back. Thereafter, he moved to inside-right and had scored five goals in seven appearances by the end of the season. He played again the following season at either inside or centre-forward. After the war Goldthorpe signed for Bradford City and spent twelve months there before moving to Leeds United. Less than two years later he returned to Bradford City, but eight months later was on the move again joining Manchester United where he played for nearly three years until a transfer to Rotherham County. His career at Millmoor was very short, just two games, before a leg injury flared up and his contract was cancelled by mutual consent. A member of the renowned Goldthorpe Northern Union rugby family, he collapsed and died at the age of 31 in 1929 on his way home. The inquest found he had died from heart failure having been suffering from double pneumonia for 24 hours, with severe exhaustion from playing badminton a secondary factor.

Appearances:
Others: 17 apps. 9 gls.
Total: 17 apps. 9 gls.

GOMES, Heurelho da Silva

Role: Goalkeeper 2008-14
6ft.3ins. 13st.10lbs.
Born: João Pinheiro, Brazil, 15th February 1981

CAREER: Democrata de Sete Lagoas (Brazil)/CRB Alagoas (Brazil) 1998/Guarani (Brazil)/Cruzeiro (Brazil) 2000/PSV Eindhoven (Holland) Jul 2004/**SPURS** Jul 2008/(TSG Hoffenheim (Germany) loan Jan 2013)/Watford Jun 2014.

Debut v Middlesbrough (PL) (a) 16.8.2008
(Hercules (Fr) (a) 24.7.2008)

If Heurelho Gomes was not on Spurs' radar before March 2008, he certainly was after starring for PSV Eindhoven in the second leg of the round of 16 UEFA Cup tie against Spurs that month. If ever a goalkeeper won a match that was such an occasion. With Paul Robinson struggling to rediscover the form he had shown in his early days at White Hart Lane, his performance propelled Gomes to the top of the list of possible replacements. Gomes had been with PSV for four years and established himself as one of the top 'keepers in Europe, helping PSV dominate Dutch football. In each of his four seasons in Holland he won the Eredivisie title, to add to the Campeonato Brasileiro he had won in his last season with Cruzeiro. Spurs laid out £7 million to secure Gomes' transfer but a series of early blunders cast doubt over the wisdom of such an outlay. It took time and the appointment of Tony Parks as goalkeeping coach, but gradually Gomes began to show the form that had made his reputation. He had been tremendously popular with the PSV fans and perhaps too keen to impress his new supporters. He proved a terrific shot-stopper, but too often that ability had to be called upon because of poor positional sense or a failure to dominate the penalty area. There were times when Gomes looked the part, but overall he was too inconsistent to be relied upon. In the summer of 2011 Brad Friedel was signed. It was expected he would provide cover for Gomes, but in no time the 40-year old had taken over the 'keeper's position. Gomes was rarely able to challenge for the role and with the signing of Hugo Lloris as the long-term number one, his days were clearly numbered. A spell on loan with Hoffenheim was brought to a premature end due to injury, leaving Gomes a forgotten man while his contract ran down. It was a terrible waste of talent. When his contract did expire he signed for Watford. As he helped them win promotion to the Premier League and then secure their spot in the top flight, so he began to rebuild his reputation. Gomes made two full appearances for Brazil during his time with Spurs.

Appearances:
League: 95 apps.
FA Cup: 10 apps.
FL Cup: 9 apps.
Euro: 21 apps.
Others: 15 (3) apps.
Total: 150 (3) apps. 0 gls.

GOODALL, Donald

Role: Inside-forward 1894-95

CAREER: Old St Stephens 1892-94/**SPURS** cs. 1894/Clapton cs. 1895/Ilford.

Debut v West Herts (FAC) (h) 13.10.1894 (scored twice)
(Uxbridge (Fr) (a) 15.9.1894)

In the last decade of the 19th Century it was quite common practise for members of other local clubs to turn out occasionally for Spurs. One such club was Old St Stephens-one of Spurs greatest rivals. Yet it is surprising how many of their players assisted Spurs for odd games, although few of their members actually joined Spurs. Goodall was one of the exceptions, joining Spurs for the 1894-95 season. He was a regular in the early part of the season. In the summer of 1896 he switched allegiance to the famous amateurs Clapton, and his only further

appearance for Spurs was in a friendly with that club. In the 1895-96 season he also played the odd game for Ilford, another amateur outfit.

Appearances:
FA Cup: 4 apps. 4 gls.
Others: 18 apps. 14 gls.
Total: 22 apps. 18 gls.

THE SPURS ALPHABET

GOODMAN, Albert

Role: Forward 1940-45

CAREER: Islington Corinthians/Leytonstone/Clapton Orient/Nottingham Forest/(guest for **SPURS** during World War Two).

Debut v Charlton Athletic (FLS) (a) 19.10.1940

An experienced amateur, Albert Goodman played two matches for Spurs as a guest during the Second World War. The first was at Charlton Athletic in a Football League South fixture in October 1940 when he played inside-left, and the second against Arsenal in the same competition almost four years later, when he played outside-left. By the time of that last game Goodman was 36 and had retired from playing. Les Stevens had been selected for the game, but failed to arrive on time and Goodman stood in as a last minute replacement. He performed remarkably well considering he had not trained for some time and helped Spurs to a 4-0 victory.

Appearances:
Others: 2 apps.
Total: 2 apps. 0 gls.

GOODMAN, Albert Abraham

Role: Full-back 1919-20
5ft.8ins. 11st.10lbs.
Born: Dalston, London, 3rd September 1890
Died: Ilford, Essex, 7th December 1959

CAREER: London Fields/Tottenham Thursday/Tufnell Park 1911/SPURS am. 1913/Page Green Old Boys/Maidstone United 1913/Reading/Croydon Common cs. 1914/(guest for Clapton Orient during World War One)/Maidstone United Mar 1919/Gnome Athletic 1919/SPURS trial Sep 1919, pro. Oct 1919/Margate cs. 1920/Northfleet United/Charlton Athletic Jan 1921/Gillingham Jun 1925/Clapton Orient Mar 1926/Guildford City Nov 1927/Tooting Town coach.

Debut v Lincoln City (FL) (h) 27.9.1919
(Millwall (LFACC) (h) 22.9.1919)

Bert Goodman first played as an amateur in north London before moving to Maidstone United where he really began to develop. Shortly before the First World War he joined Croydon Common, and continued to play for them until their demise in March 1917 when he chose to assist Clapton Orient. Immediately after the war he joined Orient, and it was from there that Spurs secured his transfer, although he had played a few games for Maidstone late the previous season. In his first three games he appeared in his recognised full-back position, but his next three appearances, in which he scored his only goal, came at centre-forward. He then reverted to full-back in place of the injured Tommy Clay and deputised until Clay was fit to return in January 1920. After that, his only game was the following month when he stood in for injured Bob Brown. At the end of the season Goodman was released and moved back to the Kent coast with Margate. He only stayed a short while before joining Charlton Athletic where, fondly known as "Kosher", he became one of the most consistent performers during their early seasons of Football League membership. His best years were spent in south London, although he later played for Gillingham and Clapton Orient again, before finishing his playing career at Guildford City. He then took to the coaching side of the game with Tooting Town. In January 1935 Goodman was imprisoned for a year after being the getaway driver in a raid on a tailor's shop in Ilford.

Appearances:
League: 16 apps. 1 gl.
FA Cup: 1 app.
Others: 3 apps.
Total: 20 apps. 1 gl.

GOODMAN, H

Role: Full-back 1896-97.

Debut v Luton Town (Fr) (a) 16.11.1896.

A sergeant in the 3rd Battalion of the Grenadier Guards, Goodman played his one match for Spurs as a guest in a friendly with Luton Town in November 1896. Also in Spurs' team for that game was his fellow Guardsman, Milarvie.

Appearances:
Others: 1 app.
Total: 1 app. 0 gls.

GORMAN, John

Role: Full-back 1976-79
5ft.7ins. 11st.10lbs.
Born: Winchburgh, nr Edinburgh, 16th August 1949

CAREER: Uphall Saints 1963-1965/Edina Hearts/Celtic prov. Oct 1964, full pro. Dec 1967/Carlisle United Sep 1970/SPURS Nov 1976/Tampa Bay Rowdies (USA) Mar 1979-1982/Phoenix Inferno (USA) 1982-1985/Gillingham youth team coach 1985, asst. manager Dec 1987, youth team manager Nov 1988/Leyton Orient trainer Dec 1988/Swindon Town asst. manager Apr 1991, manager Jun 1993-Nov 1994/Bristol City asst. manager Dec 1994/England asst. coach. Jul 1996-Feb 1999/Wycombe Wanderers coach Feb 1988/Ipswich Town asst. manager Mar-Jun 1999/West Bromwich Albion asst. manager Jul 1999, caretaker manager Jul 1999, asst. manager Jul 1999/Reading asst. manager Sep 1999/Southampton asst. manager Jan 2000/SPURS asst. manager Apr 2001-Sept 2003/Wycombe Wanderers caretaker-manager Oct 2003, asst. manager Oct-Nov 2003/Charlton Athletic scout/Gillingham coach Oct 2004, caretaker-manager Nov 2004/Wycombe Wanderers manager Nov 2004-May 2006/Northampton Town manager Jun-Dec 2006/Southampton chief scout Jun 2007, coach Jul 2007, joint caretaker-manager Jan-Jun 2008/Ipswich Town asst. manager Dec 2008-Apr 2009/Queens Park Rangers asst. manager Jun-Dec 2009/MK Dons asst. manager May 2010-May 2012/retired May 2012

Debut v Bristol City (FL) (h) 13.11.1976

John Gorman was first associated with Celtic as a 13-year old when they spotted him playing for Uphall Saints. A trialist for the Scottish Schools side, he joined Edina Hearts where he played alongside Alfie Conn and succeeded the future Spurs' star as captain. At 17, he signed professional for Celtic, but was unable to make his mark with the Glasgow giants and moved on to Carlisle United. At Brunton Park he developed into one of the best full-backs in the Second Division, a strong over-lapping defender with a distinctive hunched shoulders style of running. With Spurs struggling at the wrong end of the table he was signed for £60,000 in November 1976, but could do little to help the vain fight against relegation as he was badly injured after only four months and unable to play again until August 1978. Unfortunately, his career at White Hart

Lane was all too short, as serious injuries side-lined him for long spells, despite brave attempts to overcome them. He moved to Tampa Bay Rowdies in the North American Soccer League, and after four years returned to Britain and took up the post of youth team coach at Gillingham, even playing a couple of games in the League Cup, before joining Leyton Orient as trainer. In March 1991 he moved to Swindon Town as assistant to their new manager, Glenn Hoddle, and took over the hot seat when Hoddle moved to Chelsea. Unable to keep Swindon in the Premiership, he was dismissed in November 1994. He soon found a place back in the game with Bristol City, but in July 1996 was recruited by Hoddle to his England coaching staff. He lost his position when Hoddle was dismissed, assisted George Burley at Ipswich for a short time and then joined West Bromwich Albion. Initially assistant to Dennis Smith, he almost immediately took over as caretaker manager on Smith's dismissal, reverting to assistant with Albion's appointment of Brian Little. Preferring to work in the South, Gorman joined Reading, but as soon as Hoddle took over at Southampton, Gorman joined him. He followed Hoddle to White Hart Lane, but when they were both dismissed decided to go his own way. He has had a variety of coaching and managerial jobs, finding most success with Wycombe Wanderers. He looked like leading the Buckinghamshire club to new levels, but in late 2005 Gorman's wife developed cancer. With the full blessing of Wycombe Gorman supported her in what was eventually a lost battle. He returned to Wycombe but, naturally, found it hard to get over his wife's death, though not helped when Wycombe cruelly decided to dispense with his services. A coach of his quality was never going to be unemployed for long, and he held several more coaching and managerial positions before deciding to retire. Gorman made only one appearance for Celtic, against Hamilton Academical in the Scottish League Cup in September 1968. A certain Kenny Dalglish made his debut in the same game.

Appearances:
League: 30 apps.
FA Cup: 2 apps.
Others: 5 (5) apps.
Total: 37 (5) apps. 0 gls.

GORMAN, W

Role: Full-back 1893-94

CAREER: 1st Batt. Scots Guards/(guest for **SPURS** Apr 1894)/Luton Town cs. 1894.

Debut v Old St Stephens (Fr) (h) 7.4.1894

A member of the 1st Battalion Scots Guards, Kempsie Gorman helped Spurs out at right-back when the last surviving player from the days of Spurs' formation, Jack Jull, was unavailable. Gorman, who played regularly for Middlesex during his career, played in three friendly matches in April 1894. For the following season he signed for Luton Town.

Appearances:
Others: 3 apps.
Total: 3 apps. 0 gls.

GORMLEY, Edward Joseph

Role: Midfield 1989-90
5ft.10ins. 11st.0lbs.
Born: Dublin, Eire, 23rd October 1968

CAREER: Cabinteely Community School/St Joseph's Boys Club/Bray Wanderers 1987/Liverpool trial/**SPURS** Nov 1987/ (Chesterfield loan Nov 1988)/(Motherwell loan Feb 1989)/(Barnet loan Mar 1989)/(Shrewsbury Town loan Sep 1989)/Doncaster Rovers Jun 1990/Drogheda United loan Jul 1993, perm. Aug 1993/St Patricks Athletic Dec 1993/Bray Wanderers Jul 2000/(Ballymena United loan Jan 2003)/Pearse Rovers/Bray Wanderers coach, manager Sep 2006-Aug 2010/Cabinteely director of coaching, manager Jan 2015.

Debut v Caen (sub) (Fr) (Cherbourg) 31.10.1989

Eddie Gormley was playing as a semi-professional for League of Ireland side Bray Wanderers when persuaded to sign for Spurs in November 1987. He had made his debut for Bray as a 16-year old and was a promising young player who Liverpool were keen to sign. Unfortunately, the promise was not to develop with Spurs, although he was not helped by persistent injury problems and the stiff competition for places that meant he could not even be sure of one in the reserves. To gain experience he was loaned to Chesterfield and made four League appearance before returning. He then went on loan to Motherwell but, typical of the luck he seemed to have, was injured before he could make a senior appearance for the Scottish club. He recovered in time to spend the end of the season on loan to Barnet and then made three appearances for the Republic of Ireland at Under-21 level at the annual end-of-season Toulon competition. At the start of the next season Gormley was off on loan again, this time with Shrewsbury Town, and on his return made his first team debut, playing as substitute in a friendly against Caen. He remained at White Hart Lane for the rest of the season and made one further substitute appearance, against a Northern Ireland XI in the Danny Blanchflower Benefit match. At the end of the season though, Gormley was given a free transfer and signed for Doncaster Rovers. After three years with Doncaster he returned to Ireland, helping St Patricks Athletic lift the title in 1996, 1998 and 1999 and then going into management.

Appearances:
Others: 2 apps.
Total: 2 apps. 0 gls.

GOSNELL, Albert Arthur

Role: Outside-left 1910-11
5ft.11ins. 12st.3lbs.
Born: Colchester, Essex, 10th February 1880
Died: Norwich, Norfolk, 6th January 1972

CAREER: The Albion cs. 1898/Colchester Town/Essex/New Brompton Jul 1901/Chatham cs. 1902/Newcastle United May 1904/**SPURS** Jul 1910/Darlington cs. 1911/Port Vale cs. 1912/Newcastle United coach 1919/Norwich City manager Jan 1921-Feb 1926/Colchester Town coach.

Debut v Middlesbrough (FL) (a) 1.10.1910
(Clapton Orient (LFACC) (h) 19.9.1910)

Bert Gosnell started his career with a local junior club, The Albion, before progressing through Colchester Town, Essex County, New Brompton and Chatham to join Newcastle United, where he enjoyed the most successful years of his career. Outside-left in the famous Newcastle teams that won the Football League in 1905 and 1907, but lost the FA Cup Finals of 1905 and 1906, he also made one appearance for England, playing against Ireland in February 1906. A rather big man for a winger, he was an orthodox yet extremely effective team-man who linked play along the left flank for several years at St James Park. Although he began the 1909-10 season well, his form fell away and at the end of the season he was released by the Magpies and signed for Spurs, essentially to provide cover for Bert Middlemiss. Gosnell played only nine first team matches in his year at White Hart Lane, and at the end of the season was considered surplus to requirements and released. In summer 1911 he joined Darlington, but lasted less than a year before finishing his playing days with Port Vale. He then worked as a coach with Newcastle, spent five years as Norwich City manager and coached Colchester Town before moving into the licensed trade.

Appearances:
League: 5 apps.
FA Cup: 2 apps.
Others: 2 apps.
Total: 9 apps. 0 gls.

GOUGH, Charles Richard

Role: Central defender 1986-88
6ft.0ins. 11st.12lbs.
Born: Stockholm, Sweden, 5th April 1962

CAREER: Southern Transvaal/South Africa Schools/Wits University (South Africa) pro. 1979/Charlton Athletic 1978/Rangers trial/Dundee United app. 1979, pro. Mar 1980/**SPURS** Aug 1986/Rangers Oct 1987/Kansas City Wizard (USA) May 1997/Rangers Oct 1997/San Jose Clash (USA) May 1998/(Nottingham Forest loan Mar 1999)/Everton May 1999/Livingston manager Nov 2004-May 2005/Rangers global ambassador Sep 2015.

Debut v Aston Villa (FL) (a) 23.8.1986
(PSV Eindhoven (Fr) (Barcelona) 19.8.1986)

A Scotsman, born in his mother's home city of Stockholm, Sweden, brought up in South Africa and playing for an English club-that was Richard Gough. His father, Charlie, was a former wing-half with Charlton Athletic who settled in South Africa after finishing his playing career over there with Highlands Park. Young Gough spent seven months at Charlton as a 16-year old, but returned to Johannesburg because of homesickness. However, the following year he decided to have another go at making a career in professional football and joined Dundee United. He succeeded in spectacular fashion. His Scottish League debut came in April 1981 against Celtic and he quickly established himself as an outstanding defender, equally at home at full-back or in central defence. He won five Scottish Under-21 caps and made his bow for the full Scotland team against Switzerland in March 1983. He also helped Dundee United win the 1983 Scottish League title and reach the Finals of both the Scottish Cup and Scottish League Cup in 1985. By the time of his £700,000 move to Spurs he was a Scotland regular with 26 caps to his credit, the star of Scotland's disappointing World Cup campaign and Scottish PFA Player of the Year for 1986. Swiftly made Spurs' captain by manager David Pleat, he missed only two games in his first season and led the team to the 1987 FA Cup Final. A tall, commanding player, his calm assurance instilled great confidence in those around him and, as with many quality footballers, he was not easily ruffled. He always seemed to have ample time to play his way out of trouble. Having added eight further caps to his total, and played for the Football League against the Rest of the World in the League's Centenary match in August 1987, Gough looked to have a long and illustrious future ahead of him at White Hart Lane. Most unfortunately for Spurs, his family was unable to settle in London, and in October 1987 Spurs reluctantly allowed him to move to Rangers (who had been keen to sign him when he left Dundee United) for £1,500,000. Alongside former Spurs team-mate Graham Roberts, he helped Rangers win the Skol Cup in his first season at Ibrox Park and went on to add to his list of honours with the Scottish League title in nine successive years from 1988, further Skol Cups in 1989, 1990 and 1993 and the Scottish Cup in 1992 and 1993. Continuing to display the form that made him one of the most accomplished defenders in the British game, he was also voted Player of the Year by the Scottish Football Writers' Association in 1989. A member of the Scotland's 1990 World Cup squad in Italy-although injury restricted him to only one game-he added more than 20 caps to his collection with Rangers, before leaving to start a new career in America with Kansas City Wizard, but after barely five months was recalled to Ibrox as an injury hit Rangers strove unsuccessfully for that elusive ten-in-a-row. Gough returned to the Major Soccer League with San Jose Clash, but was recruited by Ron Atkinson in a desperate bid to save Nottingham Forest from relegation from the Premiership. He then spent two years with Everton, showing that even though near 40 he remained good enough for top flight football. When the time came to quit playing Gough returned to America where his family had made their home, but was tempted back to Scotland as the manager of struggling Livingston. He soon fell out with the club's owner, staying for just long enough to see Livi safe from the threat of relegation.

Appearances:
League: 49 apps. 2 gls.
FA Cup: 6 apps.
FL Cup: 10 apps.
Others: 10 (1) apps.
Total: 75 (1) apps. 2 gls.

GOWER, Mark

Role: Midfield 1998-2000
5ft.11ins. 11st.12lbs.
Born: Edmonton, London, 5th October 1978

CAREER: Havering Schools/Essex Schools/England Schools/FA National School of Excellence/**SPURS** trainee Jul 1995, pro. Mar 1997/Motherwell loan Mar 1999)/Wigan Athletic trial Nov 2000/Barnet Jan 2001/Southend United Jun 2003/Swansea City Jun 2008/Charlton Athletic loan Mar 2013, perm Jun 2013-May 2014/Ebbsfleet United Feb-May 2015.

Debut v Brentford (sub) (FLC) (a) 15.9.1998
(Birmingham City (sub) (Fr) (a) 26.7.1998)

A schoolboy star of whom much was expected, Mark Gower was a neat, well-balanced midfielder who joined Spurs after graduating from the FA School of Excellence. Apart from substitute appearances in a couple of Worthington Cup-ties shortly before George Graham's appointment, and some run-outs in pre-season games, he was not given an opportunity to make a mark at Spurs. After a loan spell with Motherwell and an unsuccessful trial with Wigan Athletic, Gower moved to Barnet. He was unable to prevent them falling out of the Football League, but in the next two years at Underhill proved himself a more than competent performer, certainly too good for non-League football. During his time at Barnet he represented England at semi-pro level, adding to his schoolboy honours. Transferred to Southend United, Gower established himself as an almost ever-present as the Essex club climbed from Division 3 to the Championship, fell back to League 1 and only failed to return to the Championship after defeat in the promotion play-offs. A regular goal-scorer, always happy to advance from midfield and get in a shot, Southend were keen to retain Gower's services when his contract expired, but he decided to accept an offer from Swansea City. An elder statesman at a club going places, his experience and remarkable consistency played a major role in taking the Welsh club into the Premier League and then making a marked impression in its first season. Reaching the veteran stage, Gower moved to Charlton Athletic on loan before making the move permanent, and finished his playing days with Ebbsfleet.

Appearances:
FL Cup: (2) apps.
Others: 2 (5) apps.
Total: **2 (7) apps. 0 gls.**

GRAY, Andrew Arthur

Role: Midfield 1991-94
5ft.11ins. 13st.3lbs.
Born: Lambeth, London 22nd February 1964

CAREER: Lambeth Schools/Corinthian Casuals Oct 1982/Dulwich Hamlet Jun 1984/Crystal Palace Nov 1984/Aston Villa Nov 1987/Queens Park Rangers Feb 1989/Crystal Palace Aug 1989/**SPURS** loan Feb 1992, perm. May 1992/(Swindon Town loan Dec 1992)/(Molenbeek (Belgium) trial Sep 1993)/(Udinese (Italy) trial Sep 1993)/Atlético Marbella (Spain) trial Jul 1994, perm. Aug 1994/Falkirk Jan 1996/Bury Aug 1997/Millwall Jan 1998/Sierra Leone consultant.

Debut v Leeds United (FL) (h) 7.3.1992

Although Andy Gray made a late entry into the professional game, he showed it was possible to bridge the gap between non-League football and the international arena. A hard-working, muscular midfielder, he was picked-up by Crystal Palace from Dulwich Hamlet and was soon playing in the Eagles' first team. After joining Aston Villa he won two England Under-21 caps and helped the Midlands side regain their First Division place, before returning to London with Queens Park Rangers. However, he did not settle in west London and was soon back with Palace where his talents were more suited to their aggressive, long-ball game. His qualities received international recognition with a debut for the full England team against Poland in November 1991. With Spurs slipping worryingly close to relegation trouble and Gray out of favour at Selhurst Park, he arrived on loan in February 1992 with a permanent transfer being completed at the end of the season, as part of Spurs' major team rebuilding. The fee was £700,000 plus a further £100,000 if Spurs were still in the Premier League two years later. Never really suited to the Spurs' style, Gray was unable to find a regular place in the team and it was soon clear he would not be part of the club's long-term plans. Allowed to find himself a new club, he went on trial to Molenbeek of Belgium and Udinese of Italy before being given a free transfer in the summer of 1994. He spent 18 months with Atletico Marbella before joining Falkirk, later playing for Bury and Millwall.

Appearances:
League: 23 (10) apps. 3 gls.
Others: 8 (7) apps. 3 gls.
Total: **31 (17) apps. 6 gls.**

GRAY, James A

Role: Half-back 1907-08
5ft.8ins. 11st.10lbs.
Born: Bristol, 1878
Died: 1937

CAREER: Cambuslang/Clyde Nov 1899//Royal Albert/Bristol Rovers 1902/Aston Villa Aug 1904/Rangers cs. 1905/**SPURS** May 1907/Leyton cs. 1908.

Debut v Bristol Rovers (WL) (a) 18.9.1907

James Gray was a talented young player whose career at Spurs was very short for reasons totally unconnected with his performances on the pitch. Having started out with Bristol Rovers, he joined Aston Villa, but made only seven first team appearances early in the 1904-05 season. Released at the end of that season, he moved to Rangers and was a regular choice for them until his release in April 1907. He made his Spurs' debut at Bristol Rovers in a Western League fixture in September 1907 and by the following February had displaced Jabez Darnell as first choice left-half. However, that month he was suspended, along with Bob Walker, for what was described as "a breach of club discipline". A further breach whilst suspended led to an indefinite ban and Gray made no further appearances for the club. He was released at the end of the season, when he joined Leyton.

Appearances:
Southern: 15 apps.
FA Cup: 1 app.
Others: 7 apps.
Total: **23 apps. 0 gls.**

GRAY, Philip

Role: Striker 1986-92
5ft.10ins. 11st.8lbs.
Born: Belfast, Northern Ireland, 2nd October 1968

CAREER: Belfast Schools/Northern Ireland Schools/Ballyclare Comrades/**SPURS** app. Apr 1985, pro. Aug 1986/(Barnsley loan Jan 1990)/(Fulham loan Dec 1990)/Luton Town Aug 1991/Sunderland Jul 1993/Nancy-Lorraine (France) Aug 1996/Fortuna Sittard (Holland) Dec 1996/Luton Town Sep 1997/Burnley Jul 2000/Oxford United Nov 2000/(Boston United loan Oct 2001)/Released May 2002/Aldershot trial Jul 2002/Chelmsford City Jul 2002/(Stevenage Borough loan Jan 2003)/Maidenhead United player-asst. manager May 2003-Dec 2004/Stotfold Feb 2005

Debut v Everton (FL) (a) 11.5.1987

A strong running striker, Phil Gray played for Northern Ireland at youth level as he worked his way up to the professional ranks at White Hart Lane. He made his League debut in the virtual reserve team that fulfilled a fixture at Everton five days before the 1987 FA Cup Final, but after that first game struggled to make an impact, mainly due to numerous injury problems that sidelined him for lengthy spells. Loaned to Barnsley, he made three League appearances and added three more games to his total while on loan to Fulham. Towards the end of the 1990-91 season he seemed to be back in real contention for a place in the League side but, when John Hendry edged ahead in the pecking order as a possible first team regular of the future, Gray found himself out of favour. In August 1991 he was allowed to move to Luton Town for £275,000 and within a month of arriving at Kenilworth Road had been elevated to Northern Ireland's full international squad. After that, however, he suffered further injury problems which restricted his appearances for the Hatters who were relegated in 1992. Moving on to Sunderland for £750,000 he proved a goal scorer of the top order. With the Bosman ruling and Gray out of contract he moved to Nancy of France, and soon moved on to Fortuna Sittard of Holland. He returned to Luton, where he resumed finding the net with regularity. As he reached his thirties he dropped down the divisions, ending his playing days in non-League circles.

Appearances:
League: 4 (5) apps.
FA Cup: (1) app.
Others: 1 (22) apps. 2 gls.
Total: 5 (28) apps. 2 gls.

GREAVES, James Peter

Role: Inside-forward 1961-79
5ft.8ins. 10st.8lbs.
Born: East Ham, London, 20th February 1940

CAREER: Lakeside Manor Boys Club/Dagenham Schools/London Schools/Essex Schools/Chelsea am. Apr 1955, pro. May 1957/AC Milan Jun 1961/**SPURS** Dec 1961/West Ham United Mar 1970/Barnet May 1971/Brentwood Dec 1975/Chelmsford City Sep 1976/Woodford Town 1979/Witham Town temp. asst. manager Jan 2011.

Debut v Blackpool (FL) (h) 16.12.1961 (scored three)

The greatest goal-scorer in Spurs' history, and arguably the greatest ever in British football, Jimmy Greaves was a goal-poaching phenomenon right from his early school days. All London's clubs were soon on his trail. As a Spurs supporter it was expected he would join the White Hart Lane staff, but during the 1954-55 season manager Arthur Rowe fell ill and before Jimmy Anderson had settled in as his successor Greaves had been persuaded to join other east London talent including Les Allen and Terry Venables, on the junior staff at Chelsea. Greaves made an immediate impact at Stamford Bridge, playing for Middlesex Youth and scoring 114 goals for the Juniors before signing professional in May 1957. An England Youth international still only 17-years old, Greaves made his League debut in the opening match of the following season. It came on 24th August 1957 against Spurs at White Hart Lane and he scored, as he did on all his debut days, in a 1-1 draw. It was the first of 357 goals in the Football League, all of them in the First Division. After only six League games, he made his debut for the England Under-23's, scoring twice against Bulgaria at Stamford Bridge. He stayed with Chelsea until June 1961 when the lure of the Italian lira took him to AC Milan. He had actually signed a contract with Milan some months earlier, but it was all subject to the Italians lifting an embargo on foreign players. By the time of his departure Greaves had already scored 124 League goals, three in the FA Cup and two in the Football League Cup. His 41 in 1960-61 still stands as Chelsea's League record. He had played for England Under-23's on eleven occasions scoring eleven goals, for the Football League four times scoring once, for Young England

against England twice scoring once, and for the full England team 15 times scoring a remarkable 16 goals. His full England debut, and first goal, had come in Peru on 17th May 1959. His goal-scoring debut for Milan was on 7th June 1961 in a friendly against Botafoga and he soon showed his natural scoring talent, even in the tough, defensive Italian League. Nine goals in 14 matches was a great return. but Greaves, a naturally effervescent Cockney character, could not stomach the rigid and often petty disciplines the Italians imposed on their players. He soon made clear his desire to return to England. In December 1961 he got his wish, signing for Spurs for £99,999 (Bill Nicholson did not want to make him the first £100,000 footballer) and responded in spectacular fashion by scoring a hat-trick on his debut. Spurs had just won the coveted "Double" and many reckoned them the best club side in Europe, but Greaves made them even better. Quick and cunning, he was quite simply a completely natural scorer, doing all his best work in the penalty area. With immaculate ball control, a positional sense second to none, perfect balance and unnerving anticipation, he was able to fool defenders and goalkeepers with a little feint here and a little jig there. But his strongest points were his incredible coolness when a chance arose and the way he always passed the ball into the back of the net, rarely blasting it. A member of Spurs' FA Cup winning teams of 1962 (when he scored the first goal) and 1967 he also scored twice in the European Cup-Winners' Cup success of 1963 and formed superb goal-scoring partnerships with Les Allen, Bobby Smith and Alan Gilzean. His 37 League goals in 1962-63 still stands as a record for Spurs, as do his totals of 220 League and 32 FA Cup goals. When he topped the First Division scoring chart in 1964-65 he became the first player to do so in three consecutive seasons and holds the record of top scoring in the top flight on six occasions. In his time with

Spurs Greaves won one England Under-23 cap (two goals), 42 full caps (28 goals), played six times for the Football League (four goals), once for England against the Football League (one goal), three times for England against Young England (one goal), and for UEFA against Scandinavia. Unfortunately, hepatitis caused him to miss out on England's greatest success. He played in the early stages of the 1966 World Cup Finals, but had not completely recovered from the debilitating disease and Geoff Hurst replaced him for the later stages. In March 1970 Greaves left Spurs to join West Ham as a £54,000 part of the £200,000 Martin Peters transfer. He scored twice on his debut for the Hammers, but after 13 goals in 38 games retired at the end of the 1970-71 season when still only 31 years old. Jimmy Greaves will always hold a special place in the hearts of Spurs' fans, as was well shown in October 1972 when a crowd of 45,799 turned out to pay tribute in his Testimonial match against Feyenoord. The first player in modern Spurs' history to be honoured in such a way, he responded in the only way he knew; scoring inside three minutes. Later he played in non-League football and also returned to guest in other testimonial matches, but Greaves fell victim to a creeping illness far worse than hepatitis-serious alcoholism-a harrowing condition he graphically described and confronted in his classic book "This One's On Me". Happily, he overcame that problem and built a successful career as a witty and respected television sports personality. Greaves' son, Danny, was a young striker on Spurs' books in 1978-79. He did not make the grade with Spurs, but went on to play for Southend United and Cambridge United, coached at Southend and managed at non-League level.

Appearances:
League: 322* apps. 220 gls.
FA Cup: 36 apps. 32 gls.
FL Cup: 8 apps. 5 gls.
Euro: 14 apps. 9 gls.
Others: 40 apps. 40 gls.
Total: **420 apps. 306 gls.**
* Includes 1 abandoned match.

GREENFIELD, George William

Role: Inside-forward 1931-35
5ft.10ins. 12st.11lbs.
Born: *Hackney, London, 4th August 1908*
Died: *1981*

CAREER: Lea Bridge Gasworks/**SPURS** Nov 1930/retired Feb 1935.

Debut v Wolverhampton Wanderers (FL) (a) 29.8.1931

Although George Greenfield made a total of only twelve appearances in his first season, he was regarded as a rare talent and one of the finest inside-forwards to play for Spurs for many years. After a few outings early in the 1931-32 season he replaced Taffy O'Callaghan towards the end of the season. He played the first three matches of the following campaign, missed the next five, but when recalled Spurs set out on a run of eleven unbeaten games which included nine victories and provided the foundation for their successful promotion campaign. Unfortunately, just as he was being hailed as the best schemer in the country and virtually certain of international honours, Greenfield suffered a broken leg in the penultimate game of that sequence. He missed the rest of the season and the whole of the following campaign. Although he managed to return for half a dozen games in 1934-35, he was never able to overcome the injury. After a long, hard struggle, he retired in February 1935 to become a member of the groundstaff.

Appearances:
League: 31 apps. 11 gls.
Others: 2 apps. 2 gls.
Total: **33 apps. 13 gls.**

GRENFELL, Stephen John

Role: Midfield 1985-86
Born: *Enfield, Middlesex, 27th October 1966*

CAREER: Enfield Schools/Middlesex Schools/London Schools/Ajax/**SPURS** app. Apr 1983, pro. Aug 1984/Colchester United loan Oct 1986, perm Dec 1986/Bromley cs. 1989/Dagenham United/Aylesbury cs. 1992/Purfleet 1994-95/**SPURS** coaching staff 1996, Community Officer Jul 1998/London Lions coach by Aug 2008/Takeley asst. manager Jan-Apr 2014

Debut v Maidstone United (sub) (Fr) (a) 14.10.1985

Steve Grenfell signed for Spurs after being spotted playing for his local Sunday club, Ajax. He made just one first team appearance, as a substitute in a testimonial match at Maidstone in October 1985. In October 1986 he joined Colchester United on loan, making the move permanent two months later. He remained with the Essex club until the end of the 1988-89 season when he was given a free transfer. He joined Bromley and later played for Dagenham, Aylesbury and Purfleet. Working as a PE instructor at Albany School Enfield, Grenfell also ran his own coaching school and coached at Spurs Centre of Excellence for two years before becoming the club's Community Officer.

Appearances:
Others: (1) app.
Total: **(1) app. 0 gls.**

GRICE, Frank

Role: Half-back 1935-39
5ft.10ins. 12st.7lbs.
Born: *Derby, 13th November 1908*
Died: *Dundee, 29th April 1988*

CAREER: King's Own Scottish Borderers/Aldershot Command/Army/Linby Colliery/Linfield Mar 1930/Notts County am. Jun 1931, pro. Aug 1931/**SPURS** Mar 1936/released cs. 1939/Glentoran Oct 1939/Dundalk 1940/Distillery 1943/Glentoran secretary Jul 1946, manager May 1948, secretary-manager 1953-Dec 1954/Chelmsford City manager Jan 1955-Feb 1959.

Debut v Swansea Town (FL) (a) 21.3.1936

Frank Grice bought himself out of the army in order to make a career in football. He soon showed he had made the right decision, winning the

Irish Cup with Linfield in 1930 and 1931. Signed by Spurs after five years with Notts County, he was the sort of strong defensive wing-half urgently needed at the time to strengthen a Spurs defence that conceded goals too easily. He performed the task admirably for a season-and-a-half, but with Vic Buckingham rapidly maturing soon melted into the reserves. Retained by the club until the outbreak of the Second World War Grice played for Glentoran during the war, helping them win the Co. Antrim Shield in 1940 and 1941, and Dundalk, who collected the Eire Cup, League of Ireland Shield and Inter-City Cup during his time there. He also appeared for the Irish League against the League of Ireland in March 1940. Grice was later manager of Glentoran, helping them pick up 11 trophies including the Irish Cup and the League title twice and was the man who sold Danny Blanchflower to Barnsley. He returned to England and spent four years as manager of Chelmsford City.

Appearances:
League: 47 apps. 1 gl.
FA Cup: 8 apps.
Total: 55 apps. 1 gl.

GRIFFITH, H

Role: Full-back 1889-90.

Debut v Royal Arsenal (Fr) (a) 21.9.1889.

The only match Griffith is known to have played for Spurs was in September 1889 when Spurs lost a friendly 1-10 to Royal Arsenal.

Appearances:
Others: 1 app.
Total: 1 app. 0 gls.

GRIFFITHS, Frederick John

Role: Goalkeeper 1901-02
6ft.2ins. 15st.0lbs.
Born: Presteigne, Radnorshire, 13th September 1873
Died: Passchendaele, France, 30th October 1917 (killed in action)

CAREER: South Shore 1894/Clitheroe Jan 1896/South Shore 1897/Blackpool Dec 1899/Stalybridge Rovers 1900/Millwall May 1900/**SPURS** Apr 1901/(Preston North End loan Mar 1902)/West Ham United Sep 1902/New Brompton Jul 1904/Middlesbrough 1906/Moore's Athletic/Shirebrook coach.

Debut v Reading (WL) (h) 9.9.1901

The son of a Presteigne coal merchant, Fred Griffiths started his career in junior football in his native Wales, but it was whilst playing for South Shore and Blackpool (who amalgamated in December 1899) that he really established his name, representing his country against Scotland in February 1900 and England the following month. A fearless goalkeeper with an imposing frame and presence, Griffiths was signed as reserve to George Clawley, but received an extended run in the team during the middle of the season when Clawley was injured. When Clawley recovered, it was back to the reserves for Griffiths, but in March 1902 Spurs allowed him to join Preston North End on loan as their regular 'keeper was injured. At the end of the season Griffiths returned to London to play for West Ham United, where he stayed for two years before effectively finishing his football career with a two-year spell at New Brompton. Griffiths later worked as a coalminer in Shirebrook, where he coached the local Central Alliance team. He died in France during the Great War whilst serving with the Sherwood Foresters.

Appearances:
Southern: 9 apps.
FA Cup: 3 apps.
Others: 11 apps.
Total: 23 apps. 0 gls.

GRIFFITHS, J

Role: Outside-right 1945-46

CAREER: SPURS am./Arsenal am./(guest for Fulham, Queens Park Rangers, **SPURS** and Watford during World War Two).

Debut v Chelsea (Fr) (h) 2.3.1946

A pre-war amateur on the books of both Spurs and Arsenal without making a League appearance for either club, 27-year old Griffiths made his one appearance for Spurs in a friendly with Chelsea in March 1946. Spurs had been due to meet Charlton Athletic that day, but they were playing in the first leg of the sixth round of the FA Cup against Brentford who had knocked Spurs out in the third round. Griffiths played outside-right as Spurs won 4-2.

Appearances:
Others: 1 app.
Total: 1 app. 0 gls.

GRIFFITHS, W

Role: Inside-forward 1893-94.

CAREER: Shaftesbury Rovers/(guest for **SPURS** Sep 1893).

Debut v Romford (Fr) (h) 23.9.1893.

A player with the local club, Shaftesbury Rovers, Griffiths only recorded first team appearance was in a friendly with Romford in September 1893.

Appearances:
Others: 1 apps.
Total: 1 apps. 0 gls.

GRIMES, William John

Role: Outside-right 1916-17
Born: Hitchin, Hertfordshire, 27th March 1886
Died: Arlesey, Bedfordshire, 6th January 1936

CAREER: St John's/Hitchin Town by 1904/Hertfordshire/Watford May 1906/Glossop North End May 1907/Bradford City Dec 1908/Derby County Mar 1910/(guest for **SPURS** during World War One)/Watford Apr 1917/Luton Town Jul 1919-cs. 1920.

Debut v Watford (LFC) (a) 7.10.1916

Billy Grimes spent the most successful years of his career with Derby County, helping them win the Second Division title in 1911 12 and again in 1914-15. He turned out for Derby in 1915-16, their only season of War-time football, and joined Spurs early the following season. Grimes scored once in three appearances before moving back to Watford where he remained until July 1919. At that time he signed for Luton Town where he finished his career after one season. His wife, Amelia, was one of Billy Furr's sisters. Another, Miriam, married former Spurs player George Payne.

Appearances:
Others: 3 apps. 1 gl.
Total: 3 apps. 1 gl.

GRIMSDELL, Arthur

Role: Half-back 1911-29
5ft.10ins. 12st.2lbs.
Born: Watford, Hertfordshire, 23rd March 1894
Died: Watford, Hertfordshire, 12th March 1963

CAREER: Watford Field School/Watford St Stephens Apr 1909/Watford Schools/England Schools/Watford am. Cs. 1909/St Albans City 1910-11/Watford pro. Nov 1911/**SPURS** Apr 1912/(guest for Watford during World War One)/Clapton Orient player-secretary-manager Aug 1929-Apr 1930/Orient director/Watford director 1945-Aug 1951.

Debut v Bolton Wanderers (FL) (h) 20.4.1912

As a schoolboy star Arthur Grimsdell was a centre-forward, but when he joined Watford they converted him to the centre-half role. He appeared regularly for Watford in that position, developing the heading ability that was to serve him well in later years. A good class cricketer with Hertfordshire, he was still only 18 when transferred to Spurs and played his first few games at centre-half. But when Peter McWilliam was appointed manager in December 1912, he soon realised that Grimsdell's excellent ball control and accurate passing made him ideally suited to a more adventurous wing-half role. He was immediately installed at left-half, a position he was to grace for the rest of his career, and by the age of 19 was already close to England honours, playing in the international trial match in November 1913. One of the first to enlist, Grimsdell was lost to Spurs for most of the war years, but when he returned in 1919, he had developed from a youth into a powerfully built man with a fierce determination to succeed. He was quickly back to his best, played in the international trial of April 1919 and for England in the Victory internationals against Scotland in April and May of that year. In the first League season after the war, he captained Spurs to the Second Division title, contributing 14 goals with his powerful long range shooting, as Spurs walked back into the First Division from which they had been cruelly demoted. Recognised as quite simply the best equipped all-round left-half in the country, he played in the two international trials of February 1920 before collecting his first official cap against Wales the following month. He followed that by playing for the Football League against the Scottish League. Grimsdell's most obvious attributes were his non-stop running and an aggressive never-say-die attitude, but this tended to obscure a fine tactical brain and great skill in possession, which allowed him to embark on incisive attacking forays in support of his forwards, and led to many chances being created. Captain of the 1921 FA Cup winning side, he was immovable from the team except when injured or adding a further five caps to his total, captaining his country three times. October 1925 saw Spurs on top of the First Division, but on the last day of the month Grimsdell broke his leg at Leicester City. He did not return until the end of April 1927 and it is a measure of his influence that without his leadership and inspiration Spurs struggled and tumbled down the table. He played most of the matches in the 1928-29 season, but was not the force he had been before the injury and in April 1929 Spurs decided to release a man who, without doubt, was one of the greatest players to have served the club, and possibly the most complete wing-half in the history of the game. He joined Clapton Orient as player/secretary/manager, but only held the post for a year before moving into schoolboy coaching. He was later a director of both Orient and Watford and ran a sports outfitters business in Watford. Grimsdell's brother, Ernie, played for St Albans City, Watford, Queens Park Rangers, Chatham, Guildford City and Dartford and was an England amateur international.

Appearances:
League: 324 apps. 26 gls.
FA Cup: 36 apps. 1 gl.
Others: 60 apps. 11 gls.
Total: 420 apps. 38 gls.

GROVES, Victor George

Role: Forward 1952-54
5ft.9ins. 12st.3lbs.
Born: Stepney, London, 5th November 1932

CAREER: Leytonstone Schools/Essex Schools/England Schools/Leytonstone/**SPURS** am. Jun 1952/Walthamstow Avenue/Leyton Orient am. May 1954, pro. Oct 1954/Arsenal Nov 1955/Canterbury City Sep 1964.

Debut v Liverpool (FL) (h) 15.9.1952 (scored twice)

England Youth and amateur international Vic Groves, signed amateur forms for Spurs in June 1952. He scored twice on his League debut against Liverpool in September that year from the outside-left position. He played only two more games that season and one the following season when he scored the only goal of the game against Charlton Athletic whilst wearing the number nine shirt. Groves continued to play with Leytonstone and then joined Walthamstow Avenue, but when eventually persuaded to turn professional it was with Leyton Orient. 24 goals in 42 League games and one appearance for England "B" marked him as a player worthy of a bigger stage. He was transferred to Arsenal, where he made over 200 senior appearances in a variety of forward positions and collected one England Under-23 cap. After nine years at Arsenal, he joined Canterbury City. Groves won two amateur caps whilst with Leytonstone and a similar number with Walthamstow Avenue.

Appearances:
League: 4 apps. 3 gls.
Total: 4 apps. 3 gls.

GRUBB, Alan Johnstone

Role: Outside-right 1952-53
5ft.8ins. 9st.11lbs.
Born: Leven, Scotland, 5th November 1928

CAREER: Largo Villa/Leslie Harps/East Fife Nov 1950/Gloucester City Sep 1951/**SPURS** Mar 1952/Walsall Aug 1953/Worcester City Jul 1954.

Debut v West Bromwich Albion (FL) (h) 23.8.1952

Having previously played for East Fife, Alan Grubb was signed in March 1952 from Gloucester City, who were managed by former Spurs centre-forward Doug Hunt. Grubb appeared in the first two matches of 1952-53, but did not make the first eleven again. Transfer-listed in May 1953 he moved to Walsall three months later, but played only 15 more League games in his one season at Fellows Park before moving back to non-League football with Worcester City.

Appearances:
League: 2 apps.
Total: 2 apps. 0 gls.

GUÐJOHNSEN, Eiður Smári

Role: Striker 2009-10
6ft.1ins. 12st. 4lbs
Born: Reykjavik, Iceland, 15th September 1978

CAREER: Valur (Iceland) 1994/PSV Eindhoven (Holland) Dec 1994/KR (Iceland) Jun 1998/Bolton Wanderers Aug 1998/Chelsea Jul 2000/Barcelona (Spain) Jun 2006/Monaco (France) Aug 2009/(**SPURS** loan Jan 2010)/Stoke City Aug 2010/(Fulham loan Jan 2011)/AEK Athens (Greece) Jul 2011/Seattle Sounders (USA) trial Sep 2012/Cercle Brugge (Belgium) Oct 2012/Club Brugge (Belgium) Jan 2013/Bolton Wanderers training Nov 2014, perm Dec 2014/Shijiazhuang Ever Bright (China) Jul 2015/Molde (Norway) Feb-Aug 2016/Pune City (India) Aug 2016.

Debut v Wolverhampton Wanderers (BPL) (a) 11.2.2010

As the proposed loan move of Robbie Keane to Celtic in January 2010 would leave Spurs with only Jermaine Defoe, Peter Crouch and a sadly misfiring Roman Pavlyuchenko as front-line strikers, a replacement had to be found. Eiður Guðjohnsen had proved himself a class act with Bolton Wanderers, Chelsea and Barcelona. He had not reached the heights with Monaco, but injuries had done nothing to assist and his services were only required short term. Guðjohnsen had been a star performer as a youngster in Iceland and quickly attracted the attention of PSV Eindhoven but, hampered by injury, his three-and-a-half years in Holland were not a success. He returned home and no sooner had he begun to play again than Bolton decided he was worth taking a risk on. It proved a wise decision as Guðjohnsen soon established himself as a more than competent First Division performer. When Bolton failed

to secure promotion for a second year, Chelsea paid out £4 million to take Guðjohnsen to Stamford Bridge. Powerful and versatile, he proved a shrewd purchase, scoring regularly and creating openings for others. Whether playing as an out-and-out central striker, a second striker, on the wing or even as a pure midfielder, Guðjohnsen was consistent, influential and scored some exceptional goals. He maintained a starting place even when Roman Abramovich and his mega signings arrived, helping Chelsea win the Premier League in 2004-05 and 2005-06 and the League Cup in 2005. When Chelsea did decide to dispense with Guðjohnsen's services, he did not take a step down, but joined Barcelona. He continued to perform at the highest level, helping Barca win La Liga and the Champions League Final in 2008-09, though he remained on the bench as Manchester United were beaten in Rome. By the time he arrived at White Hart Lane, Guðjohnsen's career was on a downward slope, though there were still flashes of his class. After Spurs, he had brief, but unsuccessful, spells with Stoke City, Fulham and AEK Athens before finding some success in Belgium. In November 2014, Guðjohnsen was without a club and began training back at Bolton. He so impressed manager Neil Lennon, that he was offered a contract. He linked up with Emile Heskay to provide one of the oldest forward lines in the English game. After Bolton, Guðjohnsen played in China and Norway. He signed for Indian Super League outfit, Poune City, but was injured in pre-season training and nver turned out for them. Guðjohnsen made 77 appearances for Iceland scoring 24 goals. He made his debut against Estonia in April 1996 when he replaced his father, Arnór, the man whose penalty Tony Parks had saved to win Spurs the UEFA Cup in 1984. The Guðjohnsens did not manage to play in the same international team. After that first appearance, Eiður suffered an ankle injury and by the time he was fit to resume playing, his father had retired.

Appearances:
League: 3 (7) apps. 1 gl.
FA Cup: 1 (2) apps. 1 gl.
Total: 4 (9) apps. 2 gls.

GUNTER, Christopher Ross

Role: Full-back 2007-10
5ft.11ins. 12st.4lbs.
Born: Newport, Gwent, 21st July 1989

CAREER: Durham Colts/Albion Rovers (Newport)/Cardiff City Scholar Jul 2005, pro. Oct 2006/**SPURS** Jan 2008/Nottingham Forest loan Mar 2009, perm Jul 2009/Reading Jul 2012.

Debut v Reading (FAC) (a) 15.1.2008

With barely thirty senior appearances for Cardiff City to his credit, Chris Gunter was another example of Spurs signing promising British youngsters hoping they would develop into stars. A talented, attack minded right-back, Gunter had been with Cardiff from the age of eight, working his way through their youth structure to make his senior bow in August 2006, when just turned 17. By the end of his debut season he had collected his first full Welsh cap, adding to those he had gained at Youth and Under-21 levels. Gunter made his Spurs' debut shortly after his arrival at White Hart Lane and did not look out of his depth. He was keen to get forward and comfortable when defending. Alan Hutton was signed at the same time as Gunter and another experienced right-back was added to the squad with the arrival of Vedran Ćorluka at the start of the 2008-09 season. With such competition, and Harry Redknapp preferring established defenders, Gunter was allowed to join Nottingham Forest on loan in March 2009. Wales' first choice at right-back, he was surprisingly transferred to Forest four months later. Gunter wasted no time establishing himself at Forest while also becoming an automatic choice for his country. First choice for Forest, it was clear Gunter was too good for Championship football. After three years he joined Reading, but was unable to prevent the new-promoted club from immediately returning to the Championship.

Appearances:
League: 3 (2) apps.
FA Cup: 2 (1) apps.
FL Cup: 1 app.
Euro: 6 (1) apps.
Others: 3 (4) apps.
Total: 15 (8) apps. 0 gls.

GURR, Harold D

Role: Inside-forward 1942-45

CAREER: Erith and Belvedere 1939/(guest for **SPURS** during World War Two).

Debut v Reading (FLS) (h) 23.1.1943

A young amateur with the Erith and Belvedere club, Harry Gurr made his one competitive appearance for Spurs as a guest in the Football League South fixture with Reading in January 1943. His services were not called upon again until April 1945 when he played in a friendly against Crystal Palace.

Appearances:
Others: 2 apps.
Total: 2 apps. 0 gls.

GUTHRIE, Peter John

Role: Goalkeeper 1988-89
Born: Newcastle, 10th October 1961

CAREER: Newcastle Schools/Forest Hall Legion/Whickham/Middlesbrough/Blyth Spartans Oct 1986/Weymouth May 1987/**SPURS** Jan 1988/(Swansea City loan Feb 1988)/(Charlton Athletic loan Dec 1988)/Barnet Aug 1989/AFC Bournemouth Aug 1990/Tsing Tao (Hong Kong) Jul 1991/Gateshead/Whitley Bay 1993-94/Hong Kong Rangers (Hong Kong) by May 1995/Happy Valley (Hong Kong) by 2000/Bedlington Terriers by Mar 2001/Blucher Social Club by Apr 2005/Heatington Stannington by Jan 2006.

Debut v Vederslov/Danningelanda (sub) (Fr) (a) 26.7.1988

Centre-forward with Newcastle Schools, Peter Guthrie began keeping goal in local football and after helping Whickham reach the semi-final of the FA Vase joined Middlesbrough. He was released without making the first team and signed for Blyth Spartans, before making the move to GM Vauxhall Conference Weymouth. It was with Weymouth that Spurs noticed his talent and negotiations for his transfer were opened by David Pleat. Pleat left White Hart Lane, but Terry Venables completed the deal and when Guthrie moved to Spurs in January 1988 he was not only Venables' first signing but, at £100,000, the first player from Non-League football to be transferred for a six figure fee. Sadly things did not work out for Guthrie at White Hart Lane. Within a month of signing, he was loaned to Swansea City and played for them till the end of the season. He played in a few friendly and tour games for Spurs, but was never really in contention for a place in the League team. In August 1989 he was transferred to Barnet, but by the end of the year had lost his place. He was to receive a further chance to make a name in League football when he joined Bournemouth, but failed to take it and went to Hong Kong to play for the Tsing Tao club. He settled well to football in the former British colony and played there for a total of eleven seasons with Tsing Tao, Hong Kong Rangers and Happy Valley. He was widely regarded as the best goalkeeper in the Hong Kong league, and often called upon in representative games. He eventually returned to the UK in 2001 and joined Bedlington Terriers. After 18 months he announced his retirement, but for some years continued to turn out for the Terriers in emergencies, also playing for fun with Sunday League teams when well into his forties. To earn a living Guthrie worked as a coach driver, even driving the Blyth Spartans coach to away games.

Appearances:
Others: 1 (4) apps.
Total: 1 (4) apps. 0 gls.

H

HADDOW, David

Role: Goalkeeper 1899-01
5ft.8ins. 12st.4lbs.
Born: *Dalserf, Lanarkshire, 12th June 1869*

CAREER: Coatbridge junior football/Albion Rovers 1888/Derby County Aug 1890/Albion Rovers Jan 1891/(guest for Royal Albert May 1891)/Rangers Jul 1891/Motherwell Jun 1895/Burnley Dec 1895/New Brighton Tower Aug 1898/**SPURS** Nov 1899/Albion Rovers Jul 1901.

Debut v Bristol City (SDC) (a) 15.11.1899
(Ilkeston (Fr) (h) 11.11.1899)

In two years with Albion Rovers, David Haddow impressed enough for Derby County to offer him a chance in the Football League, but he did not settle in England and returned to his old club after only five months. Still only 22, he was clearly very talented and in the 1891 close season joined Glasgow Rangers. Very small for a goalkeeper, he made up for his lack of inches with great agility and judgment and was good enough to play for Scotland against England and for the Scottish League against the Football League in April 1894, on the way to helping Rangers win the Scottish Cup. In 1895 he moved to Motherwell and in December of that year decided to have another try in the Football League, joining Burnley. After playing in Burnley's Second Division Championship team of 1897-98 he moved to the ambitious New Brighton Tower, but only played for them for one season as he was unable to agree terms. In late October 1899 Spurs' regular 'keeper George Clawley broke a leg and Haddow was secured as a ready-made replacement. He turned out in many games that season as Spurs won the Southern League title, but the following season saw Clawley back to his best, and at its conclusion Haddow was released. He returned to Albion Rovers. In January 1903 the "Tottenham & Edmonton Weekly Herald" quoted an interview Haddow had given the Salvation Army's "War Cry" magazine, in which he confessed to being a "professional drunkard". The "Herald" claimed he had been teetotal in his time at Spurs.

Appearances:
Southern: 26 apps.
FA Cup: 1 app.
Others: 31 apps.
Total: **58 apps. 0 gls.**

HAIG-BROWN, Alan Roderick

Role: Winger 1901-03
Born: *Charterhouse School, Surrey, 6th September 1877*
Died: *Bapaume, France, 25th March 1918 (killed in action)*

CAREER: Charterhouse 1895/Cambridge University/Old Carthusians by Mar 1901/Corinthians/Godalming by Nov 1900/Sussex/**SPURS** am. Oct 1901/Clapton Orient/Brighton and Hove Albion 1903-1906/Worthing/Shoreham/Clapton Orient Feb 1906/Shoreham

Debut v West Ham United (SL) (h) 15.2.1902
(Army Association (Fr) (h) 2.12.1901)

Born at Charterhouse, where his father was headmaster, Alan Haig-Brown was, not surprisingly, a pupil of the school and first played football there. On going to Pembroke College, Cambridge he turned out for the Old Carthusians, won his Cambridge "blue" and was playing for the Corinthians when he signed Southern League forms for Spurs in October 1901. A winger able to hit over excellent, accurate crosses whilst on the run, he was a player Spurs would dearly love to have had as a permanent member of the professional staff, particularly after the departure of Tom Smith. However, football was little more than a pleasurable hobby for Haig-Brown, while building a career teaching at Lancing College, and his services were rarely available. Only associated with the club for two seasons, he later played for Clapton Orient. He made odd appearances for Brighton and Hove Albion in 1903-04 and 1905-06, but most of his football was played with Worthing and Shoreham in the West Sussex Senior League. Serving with the Middlesex Regiment and awarded the Distinguished Service Order, Haig-Brown reached the rank of lieutenant-colonel, before falling at the second Battle of the Somme.

Appearances:
Southern: 4 apps.
Others: 3 apps.
Total: **7 apps. 0 gls.**

HALL, Alex Richmond

Role: Half-back 1897-99
5ft.10ins. 12st.4lbs.
Born: *Kirkcaldy, Fife, 1865*
Died: *Dunfermline, Fife, 1938*

CAREER: Dundee Our Boys/East End/Dundee Wanderers/Raith Rovers/Sheffield Wednesday May 1891/Raith Rovers Aug 1893/Heart of Midlothian Apr 1894/Dundee May 1896/**SPURS** cs. 1897/retired May 1899/Aberdour.

Debut v Sheppey United (SL) (a) 4.9.1897
(Glossop North End (Fr) (h) 2.9.1897)

The experienced Sandy Hall, who had helped Heart of Midlothian win the Scottish League in 1895, was the regular half-back in Spurs' second season in the Southern League, 1897-98, missing only one match in that competition and playing every match in the United League and FA Cup. With the arrival of James McNaught, he was unable to command a first team place the following season, but did himself few favours by getting suspended by the club in January 1899 for "neglect of training rules". He remained with Spurs until his release in May 1899 when he retired. Hall made one of his appearances for Spurs in goal. He occupied that position in a Thames and Medway League fixture against Thames Ironworks on 3rd September 1898 when regular 'keeper Joe Cullen was suddenly unavailable.

Appearances:
Southern: 24 apps.
FA Cup: 2 apps. 1 gl.
Others: 46 apps.
Total: 72 apps. 1 gl.

HALL, Albert Edwards Benjamin

Role: Forward 1935-47
5ft.5ins. 10st.7lbs.
Born: Cadoxton, Barry, North Wales, 3rd September 1918
Died: Shrewsbury, Shropshire, 3rd February 1998

CAREER: Wales Schools/Tottenham Juniors/**SPURS** am. May 1934, pro. Oct 1935/(guest for Chelmsford City, Luton Town, Norwich City, Millwall, Port Vale and Watford during World War Two)/Plymouth Argyle Jun 1947/Chelmsford City May 1948.

Debut v Norwich City (FL) (a) 18.4.1936

Welsh Schoolboy international Albert Hall worked his way through the Tottenham Juniors to professional status. Capable of playing in any of the forward positions. he made his debut in April 1936, but it was several years before he earned a sustained run in the team. He played in most of the matches in the 1938-39 season, but the arrival of Ronnie Dix in the summer of 1939 left Hall in the reserves when the Second World War began. He guested for Norwich City during the first war-time season, but was captured by the Japanese in Singapore in February 1942 whilst serving as a gunner with the Royal Artillery. He was not released until September 1944, when he was rescued from a Japanese transport ship sunk in the Pacific. After recovering from the experience, he returned to Spurs and played regularly in the last two seasons of war-time football, but when the normal League programme resumed found himself back in the reserves. Transfer-listed in April 1947, he moved to Plymouth Argyle three months later, linking-up with his former Spurs manager Jack Tresadern. He only remained at Home Park until the end of the season, when he dropped into non-League football.

Appearances:
League: 40 apps. 10 gls.
FA Cup: 4 apps. 1 gl.
Others: 37* apps. 11# gls.
Total: 81 apps. 22 gls.
* Includes 1 abandoned match
. #Includes 2 in an abandoned match.

HALL, Almeric George

Role: Inside-forward 1934-36
5ft.8ins. 10st.7lbs.
Born: Hove, Sussex, 12th November 1912
Died: Margate, Kent, 7th November 1994

CAREER: Brighton Schools/England Schools/Southwick/Brighton and Hove Albion am. Oct 1930, pro. Feb 1931/**SPURS** trial Sep 1934, pro. Oct 1934/Southend United May 1937/Bradford City Jun 1939/(guest for Reading during World War Two)/West Ham United Dec 1945/Margate player-manager Jun 1950-May 1953, manager May 1953-Jun 1970/Luton Town scout/Chelsea scout.

Debut v Grimsby Town (FL) (h) 26.12.1934 (scored twice)

A hat-trick for the reserves against the Corinthians in a match for the Dewar Shield, clearly shows why Almer Hall was signed to the professional staff at the end of his month's trial in October 1934. He scored twice on his League debut later in the season, but that was Spurs' last League win before a dismal run of 16 games without victory that saw Hall dropped and Spurs relegated at the end of the season. He played only four games the next season, but remained at White Hart Lane until April 1937 when he was not on the retained list and moved to Southend United. He signed for Bradford City just before the outbreak of the Second World War and finished his League career with West Ham United. In 1949 Hall moved to Margate, where he later became manager, serving the Kent League club for a total of 34 years before retiring. Made a life member of Margate, he led them to promotion in 1962 and 1967 and to the Southern League Cup final, winning it in 1968.

Appearances:
League: 16 apps. 3 gls.
FA Cup: 5 apps.
Others: 2 apps. 2 gls.
Total: 23 apps. 5 gls.

HALL, Berthold Alan Couldwell

Role: Centre-forward 1933-34
5ft.10ins. 12st.0lbs
Born: Deepcar, Yorkshire, 29th March 1908
Died: Saxilby, Lincolnshire, 2nd February 1983

CAREER: Victoria Hall Juniors/Sheffield Park Labour Club 1924/Doncaster Rovers Aug 1926/Middlesbrough Mar 1928/Bradford City Jun 1930/Lincoln City May 1931/**SPURS** Jun 1933/Blackpool Mar 1934/Gainsborough Trinity Jul 1935/(Guest for Lincoln City and Manchester City during World War Two).

Debut v Huddersfield Town (FL) (a) 26.12.1933

Having started with Doncaster Rovers, Alan Hall joined Middlesbrough, but as understudy to George Camsell made only seven League appearances in their colours before moving to Bradford City. Twelve months and only eleven League games later, he was on the move again, signing for Lincoln City. At last given a chance of regular action, he scored 65 goals in 72 appearances during his two years there, and this

THE SPURS ALPHABET

prompted Spurs to sign him. While a prolific scorer for the reserves, he was unable to break into the first team due to the presence and peak form of George Hunt. Hall made only two League appearances and by the end of the season had moved to Blackpool. At the end of the 1934-35 season Blackpool placed Hall on the transfer list seeking a fee of £1,000. It was more than any League club was prepared to pay, but Blackpool refused to reduce the asking price. Hall was left to sign for non-League Gainsborough Trinity where he finished his career.

Appearances:
League: 2 apps.
Total: 2 apps. 0 gls.

HALL, Frederick Wilkinson

Role: Centre-half 1944-46
5ft.11ins. 13st.2lbs.
Born: Chester-Le-Street, County Durham, 18th November 1917
Died: 8th January 1969

CAREER: Ouston Juniors/Blackburn Rovers am., pro. Nov 1935/(guest for Arsenal, Norwich City and **SPURS** during World War Two)/Sunderland Aug 1946/Barrow Sep 1955/Ransome & Marles Aug 1956.

Debut v Chelsea (FLS) (h) 14.10.1944

A full-back with Blackburn Rovers prior to the War, it was whilst playing as a guest for Spurs that Fred Hall was converted to the centre-half position. A tall commanding figure, he appeared regularly for Spurs in the last two seasons of war-time football and proved a valuable asset in those difficult times. First reserve for England's Victory international against France in May 1945, after the war he joined Sunderland and came close to the international recognition he would probably have achieved had he not lost his best years to the war. He made over 200 senior appearances for Sunderland before moving to Barrow, where he finished his senior career with just one season.

Appearances:
Others: 23 apps.
Total: 23 apps. 0 gls.

HALL, George William

Role: Inside-forward 1932-44
5ft.7ins. 10st.7lbs.
Born: Newark, Nottinghamshire, 12th March 1912
Died: Newark, Nottinghamshire, 22nd May 1967

CAREER: Lovers Lane School/Nottinghamshire Schools/Ransome & Miles/Notts County Nov 1930/**SPURS** Dec 1932/(guest for Reading and West Ham United during World War Two)/retired Feb 1944/Clapton Orient coach Aug 1945, manager Sep-Nov 1945/Chingford Town manager Aug 1949.

Debut v Notts County (FL) (a) 24.12.1932

When George Greenfield broke his leg in December 1932 Spurs lost one of the outstanding talents of the era, an inside-forward destined to win international recognition. Yet the replacement they signed was rated every bit as exciting a prospect, and so it proved. Willie Hall was playing for works team Ransome and Miles when Notts County first spotted his talent. At the end of his first season County were promoted from the Third Division (South) as champions. Hall made his Spurs' debut against his old club, and at the end of the season tasted further success as Spurs were promoted to the First Division. Within a year of joining Spurs, Hall had made his England debut, playing against France in December 1933. Strangely, it was four years before he won another cap, although in the intervening period he had suffered badly from injuries and Spurs' relegation to the Second Division. A clever dribbler with a controlled, slide-rule pass, his performance for the Football League against the Irish League in October 1937 led to an England recall against Northern Ireland later that month. He played eight more

games for England, including a memorable match against Northern Ireland at Old Trafford in November 1938 when his five goals included possibly the fastest ever international hat-trick. In addition to his full caps he played three times for the Football League. Hall appeared regularly for Spurs in the early war years, dropping into the half-back line, and even played at full-back. He continued to win various representative honours and played in three war-time internationals against Wales. Sadly, a serious leg disease forced him to retire in February 1944 and subsequently the lower parts of both legs were amputated. He was appointed Clapton Orient coach and quickly promoted to manager, but found his disabilities too much of a problem and resigned after two months. He later had spells as manager of Chelmsford City and Chingford Town, and for many years was licensee of a pub in east London. In February 1959 Hall was the subject of TV's "This is Your Life". When Hall made his first England appearance, Spurs had to pay Notts County £500. County had been so confident he would win international recognition they insisted on a clause to that effect being part of the transfer deal. In 1967 the Newark Football Alliance introduced the Willie Hall Memorial Trophy.

Appearances:
League: 205 apps. 27 gls.
FA Cup: 20 apps. 2 gls.
Others: 151 apps. 16 gls
Total: 376 apps. 45 gls.

HALL, John

Role: Goalkeeper 1936-46
5ft.11ins. 11st.12lbs.
Born: Prestwich, Lancashire, 23rd October 1912
Died: Manchester, August 2000

CAREER: Failsworth/Newton Heath Locomotives/Manchester United Sep 1932/**SPURS** Jun 1936/(guest for Blackburn Rovers, Bolton Wanderers, Hartlepools United, Nottingham Forest, Oldham Athletic, Rochdale and Stockport County during World War Two)/Stalybridge May 1946/Runcorn 1946/Stalybridge Celtic.

Debut v West Ham United (FL) (a) 26.8.1936

In the 1935-36 season only Manchester United stopped Spurs scoring in both their League meetings and much of that was down to the outstanding performances of United's goalkeeper, Jack Hall. At the end of the campaign United were promoted, but Spurs still persuaded Hall to move to White Hart Lane. Having played as a youth with local junior clubs, Hall spent four years with Manchester United, gradually building a reputation as an outstanding 'keeper for whom a big future was predicted. He made his Spurs' debut in the first game of the season and was virtually an ever-present. However, at the outset of the following season, his form dipped significantly. He was replaced by Percy Hooper, who performed so well that Hall was unable to get back. Unavailable to Spurs throughout the war years he returned to White Hart Lane in 1945, but by then Archie Hughes had also been signed, while Ted Ditchburn had emerged as the likely long-term 'keeper. Hall was not retained and moved to Stalybridge, later playing for Runcorn.

Appearances:
League: 53 apps.
FA Cup: 5 apps.
Others: 9 apps.
Total: **67 apps. 0 gls.**

HALLE, W

Role: Inside-left 1917-18

Debut v West Ham United (LFC) (a) 19.1.1918

Halle's only appearance for Spurs was in January 1918 when he played in a London Football Combination match with West Ham United.

Appearances:
Others: 1 app.
Total: **1 app. 0 gls.**

HAMPTON, Colin McKenzie Kenneth

Role: Goalkeeper 1921-22
5ft.11ins. 11st. 4lbs
Born: Brechin, Angus, 1st September 1888
Died: Brechin, Angus, January 1968

CAREER: Brechin Arnot by 1903/Montrose Waverley by Sep 1905/Brechin Hearts by Mar 1906/Brechin Rovers 1906/Brechin City trial Mar 1907, perm Dec 1907/Motherwell Aug 1909/Chelsea Apr 1914/(guest for **SPURS** May 1922)/Brechin City Aug 1924/Crystal Palace Dec 1925-May 1926.

Debut v Chelsea (Fr) (Camberley) 13.5.1922

Colin Hampton was Chelsea's reserve goalkeeper when he made his one appearance for Spurs. It was in May 1922 when Spurs met Chelsea in a friendly match at Camberley to raise funds for the Cadet Unit of the Royal Military College at Sandhurst. Spurs arrived for the match with only regular keeper Herbert Blake and when he suffered a leg injury just prior to kick-off, Chelsea allowed Hampton to turn out for Spurs. Captured by the Turks in 1918 Hampton was released when the armistice was declared and awarded the Military Medal. In his Motherwell days he was a member of the Scottish League team that played the Irish League in November 1912. In his one appearance for Spurs, Hampton helped Spurs to a 1-1 draw.

Appearances:
Others: 1 app.
Total: **1 app. 0 gls.**

HANCOCK, Kenneth Paul

Role: Goalkeeper 1969-71
6ft.1ins. 13st.8lbs.
Born: Stoke-on-Trent, Staffordshire, 25th November 1937

CAREER: Stoke-On-Trent Schools/Stoke City am./Port Vale am. Nov 1958, pro. Dec 1958/Ipswich Town Dec 1964/**SPURS** Mar 1969/Bury Jul 1971/Stafford Rangers cs. 1973/Northwich Victoria/Port Vale coach Jul 1975/Leek Town manager 1978-79.

Debut v Sunderland (FL) (a) 17.1.1970
(Aston Villa (Fr) (Atlanta) 17.5.1969)

Ken Hancock was signed from Ipswich Town for £7,000 to provide experienced cover for Pat Jennings. That alone explains why he made only four senior appearances. Hancock had five years as an amateur with Stoke City, but when they failed to offer him professional terms, he joined Port Vale and in his first year helped them win the Fourth Division title. He spent six years with Vale and with over 250 appearances to his credit was almost ever-present. A reliable, clean-handling and competent 'keeper, he eventually left to join Ipswich Town and was a member of their 1967-68 Second Division championship team. His first appearance for Spurs was in Atlanta during a North American tour two months after signing, but he did not play a League match until January 1970. With Barry Daines developing from the juniors to understudy Jennings, Hancock was allowed to move to Bury, later playing at non-League level before a brief spell as a coach and manager. Hancock's elder brother, Ray, was also a goalkeeper with Port Vale and Northwich Victoria.

Appearances:
League: 3 apps.
FL Cup: 1 app.
Others: 4 apps.
Total: **8 apps. 0 gls.**

HANDLEY, Charles Harold James

Role: Forward 1921-29
5ft.7ins. 10st.9lbs.
Born: Edmonton, London, 12th March 1899
Died: Edmonton, London, 21st January 1957

CAREER: Edmonton Juniors/**SPURS** trial Mar 1921, pro. Apr 1921/Swansea Town Apr 1929/Sittingbourne Nov 1930/Sheppey United Feb 1931/Thames Oct 1931/Sittingbourne 1932/Norwich City Sep 1932/Young Boys Berne (Switzerland) coach Nov 1932-Aug 1934/coach in Switzerland.

Debut v Everton (FL) (a) 15.3.1922
(Corinthians (Fr) (h) 6.10.1921)

Charlie "Tich" Handley learnt his football while serving in the Army during the First World War, and on his return played for Edmonton Juniors before joining Spurs. A hard working player, perfectly capable at inside-forward or on the wing, he was never able to settle in one position throughout his career at Spurs, having to compete with the likes of Jimmy Dimmock, Jack Elkes, Jimmy Seed and Frank Osborne. However, he was a valuable player to have in reserve and rendered Spurs many useful performances before being released in April 1929. After Spurs he spent a season with Swansea Town before they released him although they retained his League registration. Unable to find another League club, he signed for Sittingbourne and also appeared for Sheppey United and Thames before a brief stint at Norwich City. Eventually he went to Switzerland to help his old team-mate Bert Smith as a coach at Young Boys Berne and remained there for nearly two years, returning home in August 1934. He was unable to find a coaching position in the UK and returned to Switzerland.

Appearances:
League: 120 apps. 26 gls.
FA Cup: 11 apps. 9 gls.
Others: 24 apps. 14 gls.
Total: 155 apps. 49 gls.

HANNAFORD, Charles William

Role: Outside-left 1916-17
5ft.7ins. 11st. 0lbs.
Born: Finsbury Park, London, 19th November 1896
Died: Aylesbury, Buckinghamshire, July quarter 1970

CAREER: Belmont Road School (Tottenham)/Tottenham Schools/London Schools/England Schools/Page Green Old Boys/**SPURS** am./Tufnell Park 1912/(guest for **SPURS** during World War One)/Maidstone United cs. 1920/Millwall Mar 1921/Charlton Athletic Jul 1923/Clapton Orient Mar 1924/Manchester United Dec 1925/released Jun 1927/Clapton Orient Feb 1929/retired cs. 1929.

Debut v Brentford (LFC) (a) 25.12.1916 (scored once)

Associated with Spurs as an amateur prior to the outbreak of war whilst playing for Page Green Old Boys, Charlie Hannaford was a 5ft 7ins, 11st outside-left whose talent was clearly overlooked by Spurs. An amateur with Tufnell Park, he made his one appearance on Christmas Day 1916 in a London Football Combination match. He played at inside-right and scored one of Spurs' goals in a 5-1 defeat of Brentford. In 1920 he helped Tufnell Park reach the FA Amateur Cup Final before joining Maidstone United. He then played for Millwall and Charlton Athletic but enjoyed the best spell of his career at Clapton Orient. A member of the FA party that toured Australia in 1925, he played for the Professionals against the Amateurs in the FA Charity Shield in October 1925 and two months later was transferred to Manchester United. He remained with United for a year and a half, making a dozen senior appearances. He re-joined Clapton Orient in February 1929, but retired at the end of that season.

Appearances:
Others: 1 app. 1gl.
Total: 1 apps. 1 gl.

HARBIDGE, Charles William

Role: Half-back 1918-19
Born: Tipton, Staffordshire, 15th July 1891
Died: Ash, Surrey, 10th October 1980

CAREER: Civil Service Strollers/Corinthians/Reading Aeronautic School /Reading am. cs. 1918 (guest for **SPURS** during World War One)/ Charlton Athletic Aug 1921/Civil Service.

Debut v Chelsea (LFC) (h) 25.1.1919

A former player with Edinburgh's Civil Service Strollers, Charlie Harbidge made two London Football Combination appearances for Spurs in the 1918-19 season. He spent the first two seasons of post-war football with Reading although he was also a member of the Corinthians. During this time he rose to amateur international status winning four caps for England and representing Great Britain against Norway in the 1920 Olympic Games. In August 1921 he signed for Charlton Athletic but played only six League games in his one season on their books.

Appearances:
Others: 2 apps.
Total: 2 apps. 0 gls.

HARES, Wilfred

Role: Inside-forward 1942-43

CAREER: Tredegar/Newport County 1938/(guest for **SPURS** during World War Two).

Debut v Queens Park Rangers (FLS) (a) 5.9.1942

A guest player from Newport County, Wilf Hares made his one appearance for Spurs against Queens Park Rangers on 5th September 1942 at inside-left in a Football League South fixture.

Appearances:
Others: 1 app.
Total: 1 app. 0 gls.

HARGREAVES, Ellis

Role: Winger 1897-98

CAREER: Burnley/**SPURS** Sep 1897/Darwen cs. 1898.

Debut v Luton Town (UL) (a) 11.10.1897
(Third Battalion Grenadier Guards (Fr) (h) 7.10.1897)

Another player about whom little is known, Ellis Hargreaves was a winger signed from Burnley, where he had played only one game in five years, in September 1897. He played two matches in Spurs' first team the following month, one friendly and one United League fixture, but was released at the end of the season. He joined Darwen where he played for a year.

Appearances:
League: 1 app.
Others: 1 app.
Total: 2 apps. 0 gls.

HARGREAVES, Henry Harold

Role: Inside-forward 1923-26
5ft.9ins. 11st.10lbs.
Born: Higham, Lancashire, 3rd February 1899
Died: Nelson, Lancashire, 18th September 1975

CAREER: Great Harwood/East Lancashire Regiment/Nelson Aug 1921/Wolverhampton Wanderers Nov 1921/Pontypridd Jun 1923/**SPURS** Jan 1924/Burnley Mar 1926/Rotherham United May 1928/Rossendale United Oct-Dec 1930/Barnoldswick Town Mar 1931-Apr 1932.

Debut v West Ham United (FL) (a) 9.2.1924

An experienced inside-forward, Hargreaves was released by Wolverhampton Wanderers having scored only eight goals in 55 senior outings. He joined Welsh League outfit Pontypridd and immediately began to score regularly. When Spurs signed him, he had already scored 49 goals in the season. The mid-1920s were a barren period for Spurs with the club struggling to establish itself in the First Division and many players signed were not really up to the required standard. Primarily an inside-left, Hargreaves had to play second fiddle to Jack Elkes and was only able to occupy his preferred position on the rare occasions Elkes was either injured or playing at centre-half. This meant many of Hargreave's appearances came at centre-forward, a position he was not really suited to. He had few opportunities before leaving to play for two years at Burnley. When he finally ceased playing, Hargreaves opened a fish and chip shop near the Turf Moor ground.

Appearances:
League: 34 apps. 7 gls.
Others: 4 apps. 4 gls.
Total: **38 apps. 11 gls.**

HARKINS, H

Role: Outside-left 1891-92

Debut v Forest Swifts (Fr) (h) 12.12.1891

Harkin's only known appearance in Spurs' colours was in a friendly with Forest Swifts in December 1891. He played at outside-left in a match where Spurs fielded only ten players, and that had to be abandoned after only 60 minutes due to bad light with the score 1-1.

Appearances:
Others: 1 app.
Total: **1 app. 0 gls.**

HARMER, Thomas Charles

Role: Inside-forward 1949-60
5ft.6ins. 8st.9lbs.
Born: Hackney, London, 2nd February 1928
Died: Edmonton, London, 25th December 2007

CAREER: Hackney Schools/Tottenham Juniors/**SPURS** am. Aug 1945/(Finchley)/**SPURS** pro. Aug 1948/Watford Oct 1960/Chelsea Sep 1962, coach cs. 1965/retired Jun 1967/Hastings United Aug 1967–cs. 1968/Wingate manager.

Debut v Bolton Wanderers (FL) (h) 8.9.1951
(Hibernians (Fr) (h) 1.5.1950)

Little Tommy Harmer was affectionately nicknamed the "Charmer", and there can be few more apt descriptions, for he was a player simply adored by the crowds. Such a lightweight by build that various ideas were tried in his early days to encourage him to gain weight, he was certainly a heavyweight when it came to sheer entertainment. Source of a seemingly endless repertoire of ball juggling tricks and with a supreme confidence on the ball, opposing defences never quite knew how to handle his wizardry, for despite his slight frame he was neither easily shackled, nor shaken out of the game by heavy challenges. At his best at inside-forward, where he could see a lot of the ball, he played for the Tottenham Juniors, was signed as an amateur and then "farmed out" to Finchley. He would have been signed as a professional much earlier than August 1948 had it not been for concerns over how so small and apparently frail a player would cope in the hurly-burly of League football. However, Harmer's individualistic skills did not really suit the "Push and Run" style that had bought Spurs so much success in the early 1950's. It undoubtedly held him back, and although he won an England "B" cap against Holland in March 1952, it took some time for Harmer to convince the management he was worth a regular place in the team. It was only after Eddie Bailey's departure in January 1956 that Harmer was able to take over the main creative role in the team and for the next four years he was virtually ever-present. Sadly though, Harmer did not really fit in with Bill Nicholson's plans for 1960-61, and with the first team doing so well, Harmer was allowed to move to Watford in October 1960. He finished his career as a coach with Chelsea where he played only eight League games, but will always be remembered as the man whose goal secured promotion in 1963. When his football career was over he worked as a messenger for an Israeli bank in London's West End. In November 2013, at the end of a trial involving Watford, High Court Judge Mackie QC recorded his gratitude and admiration for Harmer. He recalled one particular game when he had witnessed Harmer weave his magic.

Appearances:
League: 205 apps. 47 gls.
FA Cup: 17 apps. 4 gls.
Others: 51 (2) apps. 18 gls.
Total: **273 (2) apps. 69 gls.**

HARPER, Edward Cashfield

Role: Centre-forward 1928-32
5ft.11ins. 11st.10lbs.
Born: Sheerness, Kent, 22nd August 1902
Died: Blackburn, Lancashire, 22nd July 1959

CAREER: Whitstable Town/Sheppey United/Blackburn Rovers May 1923/Sheffield Wednesday Nov 1927/**SPURS** Mar 1929/Preston North End Dec 1931/Blackburn Rovers Nov 1933, coach May 1935-May 1948.

Debut v Clapton Orient (FL) (a) 16.3.1929 (scored once)

A prolific marksman throughout his career, Ted Harper started with Whitstable and Sheppey before joining Blackburn Rovers. 43 goals in a season won him an England cap against Scotland in April 1926. He moved to Sheffield Wednesday, and it was from the Yorkshire club that Spurs secured his transfer for a stiff £5,500 fee at a time when Tottenham were renowned as refusing to pay high prices for players. In the 1930s Spurs signed rather too many who were not up scratch, but Harper was an exception as he showed from his opening game, netting the first of 83 goals in only 78 senior matches. His record could have been much better, but his reputation preceded him and he always came in for some rough handling from opponents, which in turn meant frequent absences through injury. In 1930-31 he set a Spurs record of 36 goals in the League and they came in only 30 matches. Had he not been injured at Swansea in March 1931 and forced to miss six of the last eight games, he might well have set a record that even Jimmy Greaves could not have surpassed. More importantly, Spurs would probably have won promotion instead of finishing third to Everton and West Bromwich Albion. Harper's injury did at least give Spurs the chance to try George Hunt in the team, and he did so well Harper was eventually unable to recover his place. He was allowed to move to Preston North End in a £5,000 joint transfer with Dick Rowley, and soon showed he was as sharp as ever, netting 43 goals in 1932-33 to leave him holding the enviable record of having scored most goals in a season for three different clubs. He wound down his career by returning to Blackburn Rovers and when he gave up playing in May 1935 joined Rovers' coaching staff. Leaving Ewood Park in May 1948, he was employed by English Electric until his death.

Appearances:
League: 63 apps. 62 gls.
FA Cup: 4 apps. 1 gl.
Others: 11 apps. 20 gls.
Total: **78 apps. 83 gls.**

HARRIS, H

Role: Inside-forward 1943-44

CAREER: Distillery/(guest for Arsenal and **SPURS** during World War Two).

Debut v Portsmouth (FLSC) (a) 18.3.1944

An inside-forward with the Belfast club Distillery, Harris made three appearances for Spurs in the 1943-44 season whilst serving with the Irish Guards, two in the Football League South Cup and one in the Football League South. Harris also guested for Arsenal, playing against Spurs in May 1945.

Appearances:
Others: 3 apps.
Total: 3 apps. 0 gls.

HARRIS, William

Role: Full-back 1909-10
5ft.10ins. 12st.7lbs.
Born: Govanhill, Glasgow, 25th September 1890

CAREER: Benburb/Rutherglen Glencairn/**SPURS** May 1909/released cs. 1910/Bo'ness United/Airdrieonians Mar 1913/(Albion Rovers loan Aug 1918)

Debut v Newcastle United (FL) (a) 6.11.1909
(Croydon Common (LFACC) (h) 11.10.1909)

Signed in the 1909 close season, Bill Harris was a 19-year old who had previously played for Benburb and the Rutherglen club of Glasgow. A left-back, he made his first team bow in the London FA Charity Cup in October 1909 as Spurs struggled to make a mark in their first season in Division One. He played regularly from then until December 1909 when he was replaced by the more experienced Bert Elkin. Harris was perhaps too young and inexperienced for the rigours of League football and although he remained at White Hart Lane until his release at the end of the season, he did not make the first team again. He returned to Scotland and played for Bo'ness, Airdrie and Albion Rovers.

Appearances:
League: 7 apps.
Others: 5 apps.
Total: **12 apps. 0 gls.**

HARRISON, Shayon

Role: Striker 2016-
6ft. 0ins.10st. 8lbs.
Born: Hornsey, London, 13th July 1997

CAREER: SPURS Academy Scholar Jul 2013, pro. Jul 2015/(Yeovil Town loan Jan 2017).

Debut v Juventus (sub) (Fr) (Melbourne) 26.7.2016

Another of the Academy graduates to be given a chance in the first team during the International Champions Cup visit to Australia, Shayon Harrison is a central striker who has shown throughout his time with Spurs that he knows where the goal is and how to put the ball in it. Although not big or powerful, Harrison has terrific strength, holds the ball up well and will not be bullied by bigger, more physical opponents. He is beautifully balanced while running with the ball, shields it well and is adept at bringing team-mates into play. He has a long way to go yet, but with the perfect role model in Harry Kane and a coach who believes in giving youngsters their chance, there is no reason why he should not establish himself at White Hart Lane.

Appearances:
Others: (2) apps. 1 gl.
Total: (2) apps. 1 gl.

HARSTON, William Robert

Born: Edmonton, London, December qtr. 1867
Died: Tottenham, London, 30th August 1953

CAREER: SPURS/Tottenham College/Broadwater cs. 1892.

Debut v Brownlow Rovers (Fr) (h) 6.10.1883

Billy Harston is not credited as being one of the founder members of Spurs, but he was certainly with the club by its second season, being Vice-Captain of the first eleven. He played at inside-forward to Bobby Buckle. For ten years they formed Spurs' regular left-wing pairing and, along with Jack Jull, were the longest serving players with Spurs from the early days. Considering they were only schoolboys when they played, Harston and Buckle began a long tradition of famous left-wing combinations at Spurs that was carried on by such as Copeland and Kirwan, Steel and Middlemiss, in the 1900s, Bliss and Dimmock in the 20s, Hall and Evans in the 30s, Bennett and Medley in the 40s and 50s and Greaves and Jones in the 60s. As many match details from Spurs' early days were unrecorded it is certain Harston played in far more games than are detailed here, although in the late 1880s he also played for Tottenham College whilst studying there. Harston ceased to play for Spurs in about 1892, just as the club was beginning to be recognised as a force in London football, and then played for one of the local junior clubs, Broadwater. He had probably the longest association with the club of anyone in history, still working for Spurs until his death at the age of 86 in August 1953, his last job being as press box steward.

Appearances:
Others: 40 apps. 13 gls.
Total: 40 apps. 13 gls.

HART, W

Role: Goalkeeper 1892-93.

CAREER: Robin Hood/SPURS 1892/Robin Hood/City Ramblers/Cheshunt/Ilford/SPURS 1896/Novocastrians player, secretary 1899.

Debut v London Welsh (Fr) (h) 18.2.1893.

Another of the local players who served the club when it was still an amateur outfit, Hart played for the Robin Hood club. He helped Spurs out in the 1892-93 season, making five known appearances. He was associated with Spurs for more than just the one season as he frequently turned out for the reserves in later years although most of his football was played with Robin Hood and City Ramblers who merged in September 1895. In 1895-96 he played a few games for Cheshunt and Southern League Ilford. The following season he signed Southern League forms for Spurs, although that was just as cover for regular 'keeper Charlie Ambler and most of his time was spent between City Ramblers' posts. In fact, it was in that season that he first played regularly for Novocastrians. He finished his playing days with the Novos, and when they were over, acted as secretary of that club for several years. He represented Middlesex against Kent in October 1896.

Appearances:
Others: 5 apps.
Total: 5 apps. 0 gls.

HARTLEY, Frank

Role: Inside-forward 1922-23 and 1927-31
5ft.9ins. 11st.8lbs.
Born: Shipton-under-Wychwood, Oxfordshire, 7th February 1896
Died: Shipton-under-Wychwood, Oxfordshire, 20th October 1965

CAREER: Burford Grammar School/Oxford City/SPURS am. Nov 1922/Corinthians/SPURS pro. Feb 1928/released cs. 1932/Hoxton Manor/Eton Manor secretary.

Debut v Birmingham (FL) (a) 14.4.1923

An amateur international with Oxford City, Frank Hartley was first associated with Spurs in November 1922 when he signed amateur forms. He made a Football League debut in April 1923 and the following month won a full England cap against France. Curiously, at the end of the season he decided not to continue playing at senior level due to the high risk of injury and joined the famous amateur club Corinthians. However, in February 1928 with seven amateur caps to his name, he was finally persuaded by Spurs to sign professional and thereby became one of the very few Corinthian players to join the professional ranks. Unfortunately, his move to full-time status was not a success. He played only six more League games for Spurs and was released at the end of the 1931-32 season when he became secretary of Eton Manor, the Hackney Wick Boys Club that was to help in the development of several Spurs players and is now based in Waltham Abbey. Hartley was a fine all round sportsman, representing Oxfordshire and the Minor Counties at cricket, and having a trial for England at hockey.

Appearances:
League: 7 apps. 1 gl.
Others: 6 apps. 4 gls.
Total: 13 apps. 5 gls.

HARTLEY, James Milburn

Role: Forward 1897-99
5ft.6ins. 11st.4lbs.
Born: Dumbarton, 29th October 1876

CAREER: Dumbarton 1894/Sunderland Oct 1895/Burnley Nov 1896/(Lincoln City loan Mar 1897)/SPURS May 1897/Lincoln City May 1899/Rangers May 1903/(Port Glasgow Athletic loan Sep 1904)/Brentford cs. 1905/New Brompton May 1906-1908/Port Glasgow Athletic Sep 1909.

Debut v Gravesend United (SL) (h) 9.10.1897 (scored twice)
(Glossop North End (Fr) (h) 2.9.1897) (scored once)

Jimmy Hartley had gained considerable experience of the professional game with Dumbarton, Sunderland, Burnley and Lincoln City when he arrived at Spurs in the summer of 1897, although he had failed to make much impression this side of the border. Released by Burnley at the end of the previous season, he had spent the end of it on loan to Lincoln City, helping them win the Lincolnshire Cup. He scored both Spurs' goals on his competitive debut at outside-right and kept the position for the remainder of the season, eventually ousting Bob Tannahill. With the arrival of Tom Smith in the summer of 1898, Hartley lost that spot and had to be content with a reserve role until the following summer when, along with Joe Cullen, he moved to Lincoln. He played there for two years, had one season at each of Rangers, Port Glasgow Athletic and Brentford then two years at New Brompton. Hartley's brother, Abraham, played for Dumbarton, Everton, Liverpool, Southampton, Woolwich Arsenal and Burnley, appearing for Everton in the 1897 FA Cup final.

Appearances:
Southern: 18 apps. 9 gls.
FA Cup: 3 apps. 1 gl.
Others: 43 apps. 25 gls.
Total: 64 apps. 35 gls.

HATFIELD, Thomas

Role: Goalkeeper 1896-97
Born: Woolwich, London, 1874

CAREER: Woolwich Arsenal am. Jan 1895, pro. Apr 1895/**SPURS** Sep 1896/released Apr 1897/Royal Engineers.

Debut v Wolverton (SL) (h) 1.4.1897
(First Battalion Coldstream Guards (Fr) (h) 1.10.1896)

Tom Hatfield joined Spurs after playing for Woolwich Arsenal, where he had played two League games the previous season. He was signed to provide reasonably experienced cover for first choice goalkeeper Charlie Ambler, and as such Hatfield played only ten first team games for Spurs, most of them friendlies. Hatfield did not make his Southern League debut until April 1897 but was released the same month. He later played for the Royal Engineers.

Appearances:
Southern: 1 app.
Others: 10 apps.
Total: 11 apps. 0 gls.

HATFIELD

Role: Goalkeeper 1918-19

CAREER: Guest for Fulham and **SPURS** during World War One.

Debut v Fulham (NWF) (h) 10.5.1919

A Canadian soldier, Hatfield made his one appearance for Spurs in the National War Fund match with Fulham in May 1919 when he played in a very "scratch" eleven. He had previously played a couple of games for Fulham including the match at Tottenham in November 1918 when Spurs only managed a 1-0 win.

Appearances:
Others: 1 app.
Total: 1 app. 0 gls.

HAWKINS, William

Role: Winger 1916-19

CAREER: Grantham/Page Green Old Boys/(guest for **SPURS** during World War One)/**SPURS** trial Oct 1919.

Debut v Crystal Palace (LFC) (h) 24.2.1917 (scored once)

A former Grantham player, Billy Hawkins was playing for the local Page Green Old Boys when Spurs gave him a trial in February 1917 in a London Football Combination match with Crystal Palace. He performed extremely well, showing confidence and the ability to hit over good centres and capped a fine display with a goal. From then on he appeared regularly until the conclusion of the war, principally a winger, but filling any role when necessary. He proved a useful player to have around during the war, but when things began to return to normal he was unable to progress further, being rejected by Spurs after a trial.

Appearances:
Others: 68 apps. 9 gls.
Total: 68 apps. 9 gls.

HAWLEY, Alfred

Role: Forward 1900-01

CAREER: **SPURS**/Southampton Sep 1901/Southern United by Oct 1904.

Debut v Bristol City (WL) (h) 27.3.1901
(Millwall Athletic (Fr) (h) 15.10.1900 (scored once))

The son of Jim Hawley, a Spurs director from November 1898 till his death in May 1907, Alf Hawley was an amateur winger or inside-forward. He appeared in the reserves for several years and all his appearances bar the first one were in matches when Spurs fielded reserve elevens whilst the normal first team was rested. He made his debut in a Benefit match for Tom Smith and Jim McNaught against Millwall Athletic in October 1900, scoring in a 2-1 win, and made five more appearances late in the season when the first team were rested in preparation for FA Cup ties. In September 1901 he went to Winchester Training College and agreed to play for Southampton, although he did not make their Southern League eleven. Indeed, on his visits back to Tottenham a game was usually found for him with the reserves. On 12th January 1901 Hawley walked off the pitch during a reserve game with Chesham Generals, unable to take any more of the continual abuse directed at him by the Spurs' crowd. He decided to sever his connections with Spurs there and then, but re-joined the club shortly after having been persuaded to reconsider his position. However, his return was short-lived. He later played with the short-lived Southern United.

Appearances:
Southern: 3 apps. 2 gls.
Others: 3 apps. 1 gl.
Total: 6 apps. 3 gls.

HAY, William

Role: Full-back 1894-97
6ft.2ins. 13st.7lbs.
Born: Maryhill, Glasgow, 1871

CAREER: Glasgow Academy (rugby)/Maryhill/Partick Thistle 1888/Rangers cs. 1889-1893/Queen's Park/London Caledonians/Clapton/**SPURS** Mar 1895/Rangers 1896.

Debut v Stoke (FAC) (a) 1.2.1896
(Old Westminsters (LSC) (a) 2.3.1895)

William Hay was one of the leading amateur full-backs at the end of the last century and enjoyed a reputation that spread from his native Glasgow down to his adopted London, where he played for London Caledonians, a top class amateur team of expatriate Scots. A rugby player at Glasgow Academy, he began his football career with Maryhill and played for Partick Thistle before beginning a long association with Rangers. He was also a member of the Queen's Park club but once in London joined up with the "Calies", although he continued to turn out for Rangers when he visited Glasgow. A regular for London and Middlesex, his loyalties always lay with Rangers and the Calies and whilst much in demand with London's senior clubs he was rarely able to accept many of the numerous offers that came his way. However, he did manage to fit in the odd game for Clapton and Spurs. His one major appearance for Spurs was against Stoke on 1st February 1896 in the First Round of the FA Cup, the first time Spurs had progressed beyond the qualifying rounds. When business demanded his return to Glasgow, Hay quickly took to playing for Rangers, though he did turn out for Spurs again on one of his trips back to London.

Appearances:
FA Cup: 1 app.
Others: 3 apps.
Total: **4 apps. 0 gls.**

HAYES, John Franklin

Role: Goalkeeper 1952.
Born: Northern Ireland, 25th March 1913
Died: 3rd September 1974

CAREER: Saskatoon Sons of England (Canada) 1929/Thistle (Canada) 1932/**SPURS** guest May 1952.

Debut v Saskatchewan FA (sub) (Fr) (Saskatoon) 28.5.1952.

A veteran goalkeeper, who had emigrated to Canada in 1929, John Hayes made his only appearance for Spurs when he replaced Ted Ditchburn for the second half of Spurs' match against the Saskatchewan FA in Saskatoon during the club's North American tour. By prior arrangement, Ditchburn played for the Canadian team in the second half. Spurs won the match 18-1 with Sid McClellan scoring nine goals, both records for Spurs. Hayes was one of the most experienced and competent players in Saskatoon, primarily a 'keeper, but often pressed into service in an outfield position. He had played at junior level for Saskatoon Sons, before graduating to Thistle, He played for several other local clubs before giving up playing in 1959. He then coached several minor clubs as well as refereeing. Hayes was inducted into the Saskatchewan Sports Hall of Fame in 1974.

Appearances:
Others: (1) app.
Total: **(1) app. 0 gls.**

HAYHURST, Stanley Michael

Role: Goalkeeper 1948-49
5ft.11ins. 10st.12lbs.
Born: Leyland, Lancashire, 13th May 1925
Died: Leyland, Lancashire, 8th November 1998

CAREER: Leyland Senior School/Leyland Motors 1939/Blackburn Rovers Jan 1943/**SPURS** Oct 1948/Barrow Jun 1950/Grimsby Town Jan 1951/Weymouth Jul 1953/Leyland Motors/Chorley RTM manager 1968-1970.

Debut v Cornwall County XI (Fr) (Penzance) 9.5.1949

When Spurs allowed Archie Hughes to join Blackburn Rovers in October 1948 they needed to ensure cover for Ted Ditchburn. The only other 'keeper on the books was Stan Markham, a young, inexperienced player whose first team experience had been limited to one friendly outing the previous month. They therefore made the transfer of Stan Hayhurst part of the deal. Hayhurst had been with Blackburn since the War, and though still in his early twenties had made almost 30 League appearances for them. He was to stay at White Hart Lane for almost two years, but made only one first team appearance. That was in an end of season friendly at Penzance against a Cornwall County XI. Hayhurst was one of the first Spurs' goalkeepers to suffer from Ditchburn's incredible consistency and freedom from injury. Hayhurst joined Barrow in the summer of 1950, quickly moving on to Grimsby Town. He enjoyed the best days of his career at Weymouth and later returned to Leyland.

Appearances:
Others: 1 app.
Total: **1 app. 0 gls.**

HAZARD, Michael

Role: Midfield 1979-86 and 1993-95
5ft.7ins. 10st.5lbs.
Born: Sunderland, 5th February 1960

CAREER: St Cuthbert's School/St Aidan's Catholic School/Sunderland Schools/Durham Schools/**SPURS** app. Jul 1976, pro. Feb 1978/Chelsea Sep 1985/Portsmouth Jan 1990/Swindon Town Sep 1990/**SPURS** Nov 1993/Hitchin Town Nov 1995, joint coach Feb 1996/**SPURS** Academy coach/Crystal Palace Academy coach Nov 2004/Dunton Green Jul 2009/Sevenoaks Town youth coach/director of football May 2010-Mar 2014/Chigwell Athletic adviser Jul 2011/Hoddesdon Town coach Apr 2014/Hadley manager Jun 2014.

Debut v Everton (FL) (h) 19.4.1980
(Crystal Palace (Fr) (a) 15.4.1980)

An exceptionally talented midfield play-maker with superb passing ability, delicate ball control, and a knack of scoring crucial goals, Micky Hazard was perhaps unfortunate to be with Spurs at the same time as Glenn Hoddle. Although he had the potential to emulate the England international, he was too often in Hoddle's shadow. When Hoddle was absent, Hazard would come into his own and show the ability to

dominate a game, but when they played together Hazard was less effective and seemed to defer to his senior partner. A member of the team that lost to Liverpool in the 1982 League (Milk) Cup Final, he collected an FA Cup winner's medal that season, playing in both matches, and appeared in both legs of the UEFA Cup Final victory over Anderlecht in 1983-84. A little suspect on stamina, he left Spurs for £310,000 in search of regular first team football. At Chelsea, he continued to show the potential he exhibited at White Hart Lane but, due to injuries and disputes with the management, was not to find the stage he needed to showcase his considerable talents. He moved on to Portsmouth and then linked up with his former Spurs' team-mate Ossie Ardiles at Swindon Town. Under Ardiles and then his successor, who somewhat ironically, turned out to be his other old midfield partner, Glenn Hoddle, Swindon's play revolved around Hazard's silken skills. With Hoddle departing for Chelsea having taken Swindon into the Premiership, Hazard was joined by another of the midfield playmakers developed by Spurs, John Moncur, but with Swindon struggling to make an impact in the top-flight Hazard was discarded. His talents were not wasted though, as Ardiles moved quickly to take Hazard back to White Hart Lane, one of very few players to leave and return. Although Hazard still showed at times the sort of skills that were in desperately short supply, injuries got the better of him. At the end of the 1994-95 season he was released and moved into the non-League scene, later taking on coaching roles that allowed him to pass on the talents so crucial to football.

Appearances:
League: 88 (31) apps. 15 gls.
FA Cup: 9 (3) apps. 2 gls.
FL Cup: 12 (4) apps. 5 gls.
Euro: 22 (1) apps. 3 gls.
Others: 41 (17) apps. 11 gls.
Total: 172 (56) apps. 36 gls.

HEDLEY, Foster

Role: Outside-left 1933-35
5ft.6ins. 10st.8lbs.

Born: Monkseaton, Northumberland, 6th January 1908
Died: Wembley, London, 22nd December 1983

CAREER: St Andrews FC/South Shields/Corinthians (Newcastle)/Jarrow/Hull City May 1928/Nelson May 1929/Manchester City Mar 1930/Chester Jul 1931/**SPURS** Sep 1933/Millwall Jun 1937/Swindon Town Apr 1939/(guest for Millwall and Reading during World War Two)/retired Sep 1946.

Debut v Sheffield Wednesday (FL) (h) 28.4.1934

Well-travelled Foster Hedley was signed from Chester, where he had spent the most successful spell of his career, scoring 29 goals in 88 League games and helping Chester win the Welsh Cup in 1933. Starting out in his native North-East, he had appeared for Hull City, Nelson and Manchester City before joining Chester. Hedley did not make his Spurs' debut until the last League match of the 1933-34 season, and played only seven further matches despite being on the staff until his release in May 1937. He joined Millwall where he played for two years, and then turned out for Swindon Town until his retirement in September 1946.

Appearances:
League: 4 apps. 1 gl.
FA Cup: 1 app. 0 gls.
Others: 3 apps. 1 gl.
Total: 8 apps. 2 gls.

HEFFERNAN, Thomas Patrick

Role: Defender 1977-78
Born: Dún Laoghaire, Eire, 30th April 1955

CAREER: St Joseph's Boys Club/Dún Laoghaire Celtic/**SPURS** trial Sep 1977, pro. Oct 1977/AFC Bournemouth May 1979/Sheffield United Aug 1983/AFC Bournemouth Jun 1985/Swanage Town and Herston Jul 1988/Bournemouth FC/Downton/Sturminster Marshall/Hamworthy Engineering/Parley Sports.

Debut v Arsenal (sub) (Fr) (a) 22.11.1977 (scored once)

Born in the Sallynoggin district of Dún Laoghaire, Tom Heffernan was recommended to Spurs whilst playing for Dún Laoghaire Celtic. After a trial, he signed professional, giving up his job as an orderly at a rehabilitation centre to do so. His only appearance in the first team was in November 1977 when he substituted in a testimonial match at Arsenal, and promptly scored. He was unable to make the breakthrough at Spurs and moved to Bournemouth where he held down a regular position in the centre of defence for four years. He was transferred to Sheffield United where he played for two years, returning to AFC Bournemouth after being given a free transfer. He remained at Dean Court until the end of the 1987-88 season when he was again given a "free" and moved into non-League football.

Appearances:
Others: (1) app. 1 gl.
Total: (1) app. 1 gl.

HEGGARTY, Archibald E

Role: Outside-left 1913-14
5ft.11ins. 12st.4lbs.
Born: Larne, 1884
Died: Belfast, 1951

CAREER: Distillery 1909/Belfast Celtic Aug 1910/Distillery Apr 1911/Stoke City Aug 1912/**SPURS** Jul 1913/Distillery Aug 1914/Belfast United Aug 1915/Belfast Celtic manager cs. 1929-cs. 1932

Debut v Woolwich Arsenal (LFACC) (Stamford Bridge) 10.11.1913

Archie Heggarty had shuttled between Distillery and Belfast Celtic in his native Ireland before trying his luck in the Football League. Whilst with Belfast Celtic he had represented the Irish League against the Football League and Scottish League in October 1910. He joined Stoke City and made 22 senior appearances before moving to Spurs. Heggarty did not fare so well at White Hart Lane, making just one first team appearance. That was against Woolwich Arsenal in the semi-final of the London FA Charity Cup in November 1913. At the end of that season he was released and returned home to play for Distillery.

Appearances:
Others: 1 app.
Total: **1 app. 0 gls.**

HELLIWELL, Sydney

Role: Centre-half 1927-29
6ft.1ins. 12st.12lbs.
Born: Sheffield, Yorkshire, 30th January 1904
Died: Sheffield, Yorkshire, November 1939

CAREER: Wycliffe/Sheffield Wednesday am. Aug 1923, pro. Nov 1923/Reading May 1926/**SPURS** May 1927/Walsall Jun 1929/Hednesford Town Jul 1932/Halifax Town Mar 1934/Goole Town 1934.

Debut v Manchester United (FL) (a) 24.9.1927

Sid Helliwell joined Spurs from Reading in the summer of 1927, another example of the more cheaply acquired players signed around that time who were not really of sufficient quality for a club like Spurs. He had previously been with Sheffield Wednesday without making the senior side and, in his one season at Elm Park had played just five Second Division games-although he did score twice in them. Helliwell was never able to establish a place at White Hart Lane and was released in April 1929. He joined Walsall, where he played regularly for three years, later serving Hednesford Town of the Birmingham & District League. He returned to the Football League with Halifax Town but made only a single appearance for the Shaymen before finishing his career with Goole Town.

Appearances:
League: 8 apps.
FA Cup: 1 app.
Others: 4 apps. 1 gl.
Total: **13 apps. 1 gl.**

HENDON, Ian Michael

Role: Defender 1989-94
6ft.0ins. 12st.10lbs.
Born: Hornchurch, Essex, 5th December 1971

CAREER: Havering Schools/Essex Schools/London Schools/England Schools/**SPURS** trainee Jul 1988, pro. Dec 1989/(Portsmouth loan Jan 1992)/(Leyton Orient loan Mar 1992)/(Barnsley loan Mar 1993)/Leyton Orient Aug 1993/(Birmingham City loan Mar 1995)/Sunderland trial/Notts County Feb 1997/Northampton Town Mar 1999/Sheffield Wednesday Oct 2000/(Barnet loan Dec 2002)/Peterborough United non-contract Jan 2003/Barnet May 2003, jt. temp. manager Mar 2004, player-coach Mar 2004, asst. manager May 2007, caretaker manager Dec 2008, perm. manager Apr 2009-Apr 2010/Dover Athletic manager May 2010/Gillingham asst. manager Jun 2010/West Ham United Development coach Jul 2011, first team coach Dec 2012/Leyton Orient manager May 2015-Jan 2016.

Debut v Aston Villa (sub) (FL) (a) 16.3.1991
(Bohemians (sub) (Fr) (a) 29.7.1989)

Ian Hendon was one of the most promising of an excellent crop of young players developing through the ranks at White Hart Lane in the early 1990s. He joined Spurs as a trainee in the summer of 1988 and signed professional in December 1989, having already played as a substitute in first team friendlies. Captain of England Youth he did not settle to one position, being equally at home at full-back, in the centre of defence and even in midfield where his solid tackling and sound distribution could be put to their best use. Having made his League debut as a substitute at Aston Villa in March 1991 Hendon was loaned to Portsmouth, Leyton Orient and Barnsley in order to gain League experience. Unfortunately, he did not develop as hoped and rarely looking likely to break into the first team. He was eventually allowed to move to Leyton Orient and went on to play nearly 500 senior games for several lower league clubs He finished his playing career with Barnet, where he took his first steps into management. In his first season in charge, things started well and promotion looked a realistic prospect, but when performances fell off, Barnet ended up in a relegation battle and Hendon was shown the door. He quickly found a new position at Dover Athletic, only to leave after less than three weeks when his former Barnet team-mate and predecessor at Dover, Andy Hessenthaler, offered him the assistant manager's job at Gillingham. After coaching at West Ham, Hendon returned to management with Leyton Orient, appointing Hessenthaler as his assistant.

Appearances:
League: (4) apps.
FL Cup: 1 app.
Euro: (2) apps.
Others: 7 (16) apps.
Total: **8 (22) apps. 0 gls.**

HENDRY, John Michael

Role: Striker 1990-95
5ft.11ins. 10st.6lbs.
Born: Glasgow, 6th January 1970

CAREER: Paisley Schools/Hillingdon Youth Club/Dundee Jul 1988/ (Forfar Athletic loan Feb 1990)/**SPURS** Jul 1990/(Charlton Athletic loan Feb 1992)/(Swansea City loan Oct 1994)/Notts County trial/Motherwell Jul 1995/Stirling Albion trial Aug 1998/Keith/Pollock 1999.

Debut v Norwich City (FL) (a) 10.4.1991 (scored once)

Spotted by Dundee playing for Hillingdon Youth Club in the Scottish Amateur League, John Hendry signed professional for Dundee in July 1988 and made his first appearance as substitute in the derby match against Dundee United two months later. After only one more substitute appearance in his first season, he was unable to make their first team again, but when loaned to Forfar Athletic for the last three months of the 1989-90 season scored six goals in eleven games as Forfar narrowly avoided relegation. Spurs were quick to move for him, and he arrived at White Hart Lane for a £50,000 fee in July 1990. Not helped by injuries, he took a while to settle and it was not until April 1991 that he made his League debut, scoring at Norwich City when Spurs fielded a weakened team prior to the FA Cup semi-final with Arsenal. A player with a pleasing, easy style who carefully conserved his energy for use in the penalty box, he looked to have those important striker's abilities to find space in the most crowded of areas and get his shot on target. Loaned to Charlton in February 1992, he could have proved an absolute bargain, but probably because he was not the largest of strikers he was rarely given an opportunity, even when Spurs were in desperate need of his undoubted goal-scoring abilities. In July 1995 he returned to Scotland with Motherwell in a £200,000 deal, but persistent injury problems did nothing to help his cause. Forced to quit the game because of a thigh injury, Hendry was out of the game for a year before joining Pollock where he played for four years, usually in midfield.

Appearances:
League: 5 (12) apps. 5 gls.
FA Cup: (1) app.
FL Cup: (2) app.
Others: 11 (6) apps. 5 gls.
Total: 16 (21) apps. 10 gls.

HENLEY, Leslie Donald

Role: Inside-forward 1940-45
Born: Lambeth, London, 26th September 1922.
Died: 1st May 1996

CAREER: South London Schools/England Schools/Nunhead/Margate 1938/Arsenal am. May 1939, pro. 1941/(guest for Brentford, Brighton and Hove Albion, Crystal Palace, Fulham, Northampton Town, Queens Park Rangers, Reading, **SPURS** and West Ham United during World War Two)/Reading Dec 1946/Bohemians coach, manager 1953/Wimbledon manager Jul 1955-Apr 1971.

Debut v Arsenal (FLS) (h) 12.10.1940

Les Henley was an amateur on the books of Arsenal at the time of his two appearances for Spurs as a war-time guest. The first was in a Football League South match against Arsenal in October 1940 which had to be abandoned just after half-time due to an air raid warning, and the second against Aldershot in the same competition in March 1945, when he scored one of Spurs' goals. He did not appear for Arsenal in the Football League, before being transferred to Reading where he made almost 200 senior appearances over a six-year period. He then coached and managed the Irish club, Bohemians until returning to London in July 1955 as manager of Wimbledon, a position he held until April 1971. During that time Henley led Wimbledon to four Isthmian League titles, the FA Amateur Cup and into the professional ranks.

Appearances:
Others: 2 apps. 1 gl.
Total: 2 apps. 1 gl.

HENRY, Ronald Patrick

Role: Full-back 1954-67
5ft.11ins. 11st.13lbs.
Born: Shoreditch, London, 17th August 1934
Died: Harpenden, Hertfordshire, 27th December 2014

CAREER: Manland Secondary Modern School/Harpenden Schools/ Hertfordshire Schools/Luton Town am./St Albans City/Harpenden Town/Redbourn/**SPURS** am. Nov 1954, pro. Jan 1955/retired May 1969, **SPURS** coach.

Debut v Huddersfield Town (FL) (a) 12.4.1955
(FC Servette (Fr) (h) 30.3.1955)

Although born in London, Ron Henry settled in Redbourn, Hertfordshire after being evacuated there during the war. An amateur on Luton Town's books for a while, after a trial with Wolverhampton Wanderers was postponed, he settled to playing for Harpenden Town and Redbourn. Signed to Spurs' amateur ranks in November 1954, he joined the professional staff in January 1955. Henry made his League debut at centre-half three months later, but for the next three seasons was unable to make any headway in gaining a regular first team place. In February 1958, he did replace Mel Hopkins after the Welshman was injured on international duty, but when Hopkins was fit to resume, Henry returned to the reserves. When Hopkins broke his nose-again playing for Wales-in November 1959, Henry stepped in once more, but this time did not surrender the left-back position. He missed only one of the next 188 games during which he collected a League Championship medal in 1961, FA Cup winners' medals in 1961 and 1962 and a European Cup-Winners' Cup winners medal in 1963. A solidly built man, he was a strong determined tackler who was quick to recover, had intelligent positional sense and distributed the ball easily and without fuss. Henry and his full-back partner, Peter Baker, were both locally born and neither cost a big fee, but their contribution as unsung

stalwarts of the "Double" winning side was just as important to Spurs' success as that of anyone else in the team. Henry's consistency for Spurs was rewarded by an England cap against France in February 1963. It was Alf Ramsey's first game as manager and England were hammered 5-1, but he would surely have won more honours had it not been for the presence of Ray Wilson. Henry was a truly loyal servant to Spurs. Troubled by a cartilage injury, he finally dropped down to the reserves with the arrival of Cyril Knowles in the summer of 1965. His final season was spent playing for the "A" team, passing on his wealth of experience to the more junior members of the playing staff. He moved into coaching the Spurs juniors following his retirement from playing, combining that with his business as a Hertfordshire nurseryman. When he eventually gave up the nursery, he returned to Spurs coaching the youngsters at the School of Excellence. Henry played for the same Royal Artillery team during his National Service as Terry Dyson, only he played at outside-left and Dyson at right-back. Henry's son, Steve, was on Spurs' schoolboy books for a while without making an impression. His grandson, Ronnie, did somewhat better, playing in some first team friendlies before going on to give great service to Stevenage and Luton Town.

Appearances:
League: 247 apps. 1 gl.
FA Cup: 23 apps.
Euro: 17 apps.
Others: 51 (4) apps. 1 gl.
Total: 338 (4) apps. 2 gls.

HENRY, Ronnie Stephen

Role: Defender 2002-04
5ft. 11ins. 11st. 10lbs.
Born: *Hemel Hempstead, Hertfordshire, 2nd January 1984*

CAREER: Hemel Lions/Hemel Hempstead School/Hemel Hempstead Schools/Dacorum District Schools/Herts County Schools/**SPURS** trainee Jul 2000, pro. cs. 2002/(Southend United loan Mar 2003)/Luton Town trial/Yeovil Town trial/Rushden & Diamonds trial/Fisher Athletic Feb 2004/Dagenham & Redbridge trial Jul 2004/Dublin City Aug 2004/Stevenage Borough Jan 2005/Luton Town Jun 2012/Stevenage Jun 2014

Debut v Stevenage Borough (sub) (Fr) (a) 21.7.2002

The grandson of Spurs' legend, Ron Henry, Ronnie Henry may not have done as well as his grandfather, but he built himself a solid career in the lower levels of football, tasting success at Wembley just as many times as the "Double" winning full-back. Signed to trainee terms as soon as he was old enough, Henry progressed to the reserve team, but was unable to make a senior breakthrough, playing just a handful of pre-season friendly games at first team level. With the decision being taken in November 2003 to release Henry at the end of the season, Spurs allowed him to have trials with several smaller clubs, but no offers for his services were forthcoming. It was not until August 2004 that he was able to arrange a short term contract with Dublin City, but even that ended early when the Irish club found itself in financial difficulties. On his return to England, Henry signed for Stevenage Borough on a six-month contract and ended up staying for seven years. During that time he became the first player to lift a competitive trophy at Wembley when Stevenage won the FA Trophy in 2007, a feat it repeated in 2009. He helped Stevenage win a place in the Football League and promotion to League One at the first attempt. On a personal level he played for and captained the England C side. After well over 300 appearances for Stevenage, Henry surprising dropped back into the Conference when he joined Luton Town. At the end of his second year there, Luton were promoted back to the Football League as Conference champions. Henry then returned to Stevenage.

Appearances:
Others: 4 (3) apps. 1 gl.
Total: 4 (3) apps. 1 gl.

HENTY, Ronald

Role: Full-back 1950-51
Born: *Rainham, Essex*

CAREER: SPURS pro. 1946/Chelmsford City Jul 1953-cs. 1955.

Debut v Lovells Athletic (Fr) (h) 18.9.1950

Recommended to Spurs whilst serving in the Royal Navy during the Second World War, Ronnie Henty rapidly progressed to reserve level, but was to make only one appearance in the first team. That was in September 1950 in a friendly against Lovell's Athletic. Never really challenging for a place in the senior XI, he remained with Spurs until the summer of 1953 when he was released and joined Chelmsford City.

Appearances:
Others: 1 app.
Total: 1 app. 0 gls.

HEPBURN, A E

Role: Inside-forward 1891-94

CAREER: Hermitage/Tottenham College/Robin Hood/**SPURS**.

Debut v St Albans (Fr) (a) 6.2.1892

One of two brothers who played for Hermitage, Tottenham College and Robin Hood, Hepburn's first known appearance for Spurs was in a friendly with St Albans in February 1892. He appears not to have played the next season, but then came back to make five appearances in the 1893-94 season. During that season he also assisted the reserves, whilst principally playing for Robin Hood.

Appearances:
Others: 9 apps. 5 gls.
Total: 9 apps. 5 gls.

HEROD, Edwin Redvers Baden

Role: Full-back 1928-31
5ft.10ins. 10st.8lbs.
Born: *Ilford, Essex, 16th May 1900*
Died: *Redbridge, Essex, 9th May 1973*

CAREER: Barking Town/Ilford/Great Eastern Railway Works/Charlton Athletic pro. Sep 1921/Brentford Jun 1928/**SPURS** Feb 1929/Chester Jul 1931/Swindon Town Jul 1933/Clapton Orient Jul 1935/retired cs. 1937.

Debut v Grimsby Town (FL) (a) 2.3.1929

Edwin Herod started out as an amateur with Barking and Ilford, turning professional when he joined Charlton Athletic. By the time of his move to Spurs he had considerable experience. He finished his first season at White Hart Lane as first choice left-back, but early the following term switched to the right and alternated between the two positions throughout the season. He missed only one game, but with the arrival of Bert Lyons in May 1930 and Bert Hodgkinson in August 1930 found himself out of the team. Released at the end of the 1930-31 season, he moved to Chester and helped them win the Welsh Cup in 1933 before signing for Swindon Town. He finished his career with two years at Clapton Orient.

Appearances:
League: 57 apps.
FA Cup: 2 apps.
Others: 10 apps.
Total: 69 apps. 0 gls.

HEWITSON, Robert

Role: Goalkeeper 1908-09
5ft.10ins. 12st.6lbs.
Born: Blyth, Northumberland, 1st June 1880
Died: Northumberland, 1957

CAREER: Amble Athletic 1894-95/Amble 1896/Radcliffe 1897/Amble 1898-99/Morpeth Harriers Nov 1900/Barnsley May 1903/Crystal Palace May 1905/Oldham Athletic Aug 1907/**SPURS** Jun 1908/Croydon Common Apr 1909/Doncaster Rovers cs. 1910.

Debut v Wolverhampton Wanderers (FL) (h) 1.9.1908

When Bob Hewitson made his debut in Spurs' first Football League match he achieved a remarkable double, for he had also been the last line of defence when Oldham Athletic made their bow in the Football League a year earlier. A solid if not spectacular 'keeper, he retained his position with Oldham until March 1908 and the same thing happened to him at Spurs. He played in the first 37 senior matches of the season, but at the end of March 1909 lost his place to Fred Boreham. He left at the end of the season to join Croydon Common, playing there for just one term. Quite a character, Hewitson was suspended by the Football League in February 1908 for allegedly throwing a lump of mud at the referee. In Oldham Athletic's FA Cup tie with Kidderminster in January 1907 a penalty was awarded against Oldham. The referee placed the ball for the kick to be taken but when he turned round Hewitson had disappeared. He was in the crowd, taking bets on whether he would save the penalty or not. He saved it!!

Appearances:
League: 30 apps.
FA Cup: 4 apps.
Others: 3 apps.
Total: 37 apps. 0 gls.

HEWITT, Charles William

Role: Inside-forward 1906-07
5ft.6ins. 11st.4lbs.
Born: Greatham, nr Hartlepool, County Durham, 10th April 1884
Died: Darlington, County Durham, 31st December 1966

CAREER: Greatham Schools/West Hartlepool Schools/Billingham Schools/Christ Church/West Hartlepool trial Apr 1903, perm. Apr 1903/Middlesbrough Feb 1905/**SPURS** May 1906/Liverpool May 1907/West Bromwich Albion Apr 1908/Spennymoor United May 1910/Crystal Palace Oct 1910/Verein für Rasenspiele (Mannheim, Germany) coach cs. 1912/Italy coach cs. 1913/(guest for Huddersfield Town during World War One)/retired 1917/Hartlepools United May 1921/Caerphilly manager/Mold manager till Nov 1924/Wrexham manager Nov 1924-Dec 1926/Flint Town manager 1927-May 1928/Connahs Quay & Shotton manager May 1928-May 1930/Chester manager May 1930–Apr 1936/Millwall manager Apr 1936-Apr 1940/Leyton Orient manager Jan 1946-Apr 1948/Millwall manager Aug 1948-Jan 1956.

Debut v West Ham United (SL) (h) 1.9.1906

Within weeks of signing for Spurs, and without having played a single game, Charlie Hewitt wanted to leave. After signing from Middlesbrough he heard Liverpool had offered Middlesbrough £400 for his transfer and was keen to move to Anfield. Spurs were simply not prepared to release him, and the FA decided he had to honour his one-year contract. Hewitt accepted the decision, made his debut in the opening fixture of the season against West Ham United and played regularly throughout the year.

However, it was always clear that when the season was over he would leave, and when Spurs made no effort to persuade him otherwise, he immediately signed for Liverpool. He only spent one season on Merseyside and then played for West Bromwich Albion, Spennymoor United and Crystal Palace. He retired in 1917 but returned to football four years later when he played six games for Hartlepools United during their first season in the Football League. Hewitt then took to management, initially with the ill-fated Caerphilly club. He moved around Welsh clubs, building a reputation as a manager who signed the players, but left them to get on with job he had signed them to do. He took Chester into the Football League in 1931 and established them in the Third Division (North) before moving on to Millwall. In his first season in south London he took the Third Division (South) club to the FA Cup semi-final, and the following season into the Second Division as champions. In July 1940 Hewitt was suspended for six months by the FA after a joint FA/Football League commission had looked into the affairs of Millwall amid allegations of illegal payments. Out of football for the rest of the war,

Hewitt returned to management with Leyton Orient. After two years he went back to Millwall, but in nearly eight years was unable to repeat the success of his earlier time in charge. He was awarded the Humane Society's medal for saving nine lives from drowning in the bay at Hartlepool.

Appearances:
Southern: 30 apps. 11 gls.
FA Cup: 5 apps.
Others: 12 apps. 3 gls.
Total: 47 apps. 14 gls.

HICKLING, William

Role: Left-back 1905-06
5ft.10ins. 11st.7lbs.
Born: Basford, 1883

CAREER: Basford/Ashby/Somercotes United May 1902/Derby County Apr 1903/SPURS May 1905/Middlesbrough Apr 1906/Mansfield Mechanics cs. 1908/Ilkeston United cs. 1909.

Debut v West Ham United (WL) (h) 26.3.1906

Originally with Somercotes United, a Derbyshire mining district club, William Hickling made nine Football League appearances for Derby County in the 1903-04 season, but was unable to get into the team the following season. Signed by Spurs in May 1905, he was to make only one appearance in a Western League fixture, before his release in April 1906. He joined Middlesbrough, but was unable to establish himself with the Teesside club either. He returned to his Midlands' roots playing for Mansfield Mechanics and Ilkeston.

Appearances:
Others: 1 app.
Total: 1 app. 0 gls.

HICKSON J

Role: Inside-forward 1898-99

CAREER: Liverpool South End/SPURS May 1898/released cs. 1899.

Debut v Sheppey United (TML) (h) 16.1.1899

An inexperienced junior inside-forward from Merseyside, Hickson spent one season with Spurs at the end of the 19th century making a total of four appearances. Only three of them were in competitive matches and they were in the Thames and Medway League, the minor of the three leagues Spurs competed in.

Appearances:
Others: 4 apps. 1 gl.
Total: 4 apps. 1 gl.

HILL, Daniel Ronald Louis

Role: Midfield 1992-98
5ft.9ins. 12st.5lbs.
Born: Enfield, Middlesex, 1st October 1974

CAREER: Idsall School/Albany School/Enfield Schools/Middlesex Schools/FA National School of Excellence/SPURS trainee Aug 1991, pro. Sep 1992/(Birmingham City loan Nov 1995)/(Watford loan Feb 1996)/Crewe Alexandra trial Jul 1997/(Cardiff City loan Feb 1998)/Oxford United Jul 1998/Cardiff City Nov 1998/Dagenham & Redbridge trial Jul 2001, perm Aug 2001/Hornchurch Oct 2004/Heybridge Swifts Aug 2005/Leyton Aug 2006/Billericay Town Oct 2006/Concord Rangers-Harlow Town Aug 2007-Mar 2008/Welling United U-18 manager-coach Sep 2007–Oct 2012/East Grinstead Town caretaker reserve manager Aug–Dec 2011/Leyton Orient Youth scout 2011–Sep 2012/Millwall sport science internee Jan–May 2013/Phoenix Sports therapist-coach Jun 2012–Jun 2013/Football Opposition Analyst Aug 2011–Jul 2013/Wigan Athletic 1st team opposition scout Aug 2013–Jul 2014/Chatham Town Under 18-21s asst. manager-coach Jun 2013-May 2015/Stoke City 1st team opposition scout Jul 2014/Thamesmead Town U-18 coach Aug 2015.

Debut v Chelsea (sub) (PL) (a) 20.3.1993

With Spurs from the age of ten, Danny Hill was a creative little midfield player who looked to have the skill to make a career in the top flight. Sadly, his undoubted talent sadly failed to blossom when it mattered. Given a chance in the first team shortly after turning professional, Hill was a neat, midfield general, always looking for the killer pass, and frequently capable of producing it. Perhaps a little lightweight and not the best at working back, when not out on loan he flitted around the fringes of the first team for five years, good enough to play for England at Under-21 level, but rarely given an outing at Spurs. Eventually, he left his boyhood club and moved to Oxford United, but within a few months their financial problems forced him to join Cardiff City. Hill struggled to make an impression with the Welsh club despite playing more than sixty matches, before being given a free transfer and moving into Essex non-League football.

Appearances:
League: 4 (6) apps.
FL Cup: (2) apps.
Others: 11 (13) apps. 1 gl.
Total: 15 (21) apps. 1 gl.

HILL, W

Role: Half-back 1917-18

CAREER: Wellingborough Town/Cuckfield/Brighton and Hove Albion trial Feb 1902, perm Mar 1902/Cuckfield/(guest for SPURS and Crystal Palace during World War One).

Debut v Clapton Orient (LFC) (h) 1.4.1918

Hill was a former Spurs' programme seller who had turned professional with Brighton and Hove Albion, making four appearances for them at the end of the 1901-02 season. He made two appearances for Spurs in the

London Football Combination competition of 1917-18, the first at right-half and the second at outside-right.

Appearances:
Others: 2 apps.
Total: 2 apps. 0 gls.

HILLIER, Ian Michael

Role: Defender
6ft.1ins. 11st.12lbs.
Born: Neath, 26th December 1979

CAREER: Cimla Youth/Afan Nedd Schools/West Glamorgan Schools/Wales Schools/Wales Youth/SPURS assoc. schl. Dec 1994 (Cardiff City May 1996), trainee Jul 1996, pro. Jul 1998/Luton Town trial Aug 2001, perm Oct 2001/(Chester City loan Dec 2004)/Bristol Rovers trial Apr 2005/Oxford United trial May 2005/Grimsby Town trial Jul 2005/Newport County Jul 2005/Neath Apr 2009/Carmarthen Town Jun 2012/Afan Lido Sep 2013/Goytre United Jan 2014/Briton Ferry Llansawel Oct 2014, coach Jun 2016

Debut v Bishops Stortford (sub) (Fr) (a) 3.9.1999

While Ian Hillier's early career with Spurs has some similarities to that of Ron Burgess, it did not develop in the same way as the legendary half-back. Originally a winger, Spurs decided to release the young Welshman in May 1998 following completion of his training contract. On calling in at White Hart Lane to tie up his departure, he was asked to fill in at full-back in a youth team match. He did so well he was signed to a full professional contract. A strong-tackling, adventurous defender, comfortable at full-back or in the centre of defence, he was also capable of playing in midfield. Hillier spent just over three years in the paid ranks of Spurs, collecting five Welsh Under-21 caps, but was unable to make the step up to the first team. He made just three substitute appearances in friendly games before being released to join Luton Town, managed by former Spurs' full-back, Joe Kinnear. Hillier started well in Bedfordshire, but failed to maintain his early promise. With no future at Kenilworth Road, he was allowed to look for a new club and eventually joined Newport County. He played regularly there, captaining the club until breaking his leg in three places in August 2008 while working as a tree surgeon's assistant. Newport promptly sacked Hillier, but offered him a new deal before an appeal hearing at the Welsh FA took place. However, he was not to play for Newport again. He joined his home town club, Neath, and remained with them until the club was liquidated. After that he continued to play in Welsh non-League circles.

Appearances:
Others: (3) apps.
Total: (3) apps. 0 gls.

HILLS, John Raymond

Role: Full-back 1954-60
5ft.9ins. 11st.4lbs.
Born: Gravesend, Kent, 24th February 1934

CAREER: Dashwood Athletic/Gravesend and Northfleet 1948-1952/SPURS am. Mar 1950, pro. Aug 1953/Bristol Rovers Jul 1961/Margate cs. 1962.

Debut v Blackpool (FL) (a) 14.12.1957
(Queens Park Rangers (Fr) (a) 11.10.1954)

John Hills signed amateur forms for Spurs whilst playing for Gravesend and Northfleet. Three years later he signed professional, but it was to be another four years before he made his League debut. Initially his first team opportunities were limited by the presence of Alf Ramsey, but he was unable to take advantage of Ramsey's departure in May 1955. That was mainly due to an injury sustained whilst on National Service which kept him out of action for the whole of the 1955-56 season. By the time he was fit to play again, Peter Baker had claimed the right-back spot. When Hills did step up for his debut in December 1957, he did so well that he retained the position on merit and finished the season as a member of the FA squad on its tour to Ghana. A classy full-back with plenty of composure, his development did not continue the following season though and he quickly lost his place to the more consistent Baker. Unable to recover the position, he spent the rest of his Spurs' career as Baker's understudy, though he also played one game at right-half in place of Danny Blanchflower. With no hope of dislodging Baker, Hills finally left to sign for Bristol Rovers in July 1961. A year later he moved on to Margate, after suffering a recurrence of cruciate ligament damage. Hills later became a PE teacher, working in Brussels, Paris and Sri Lanka.

Appearances:
League: 29 apps.
FA Cup: 3 apps.
Others: 9 apps.
Total: 41 apps. 0 gls.

HINTON, William Frederick Weston

Role: Goalkeeper 1924-26
5ft.9ins. 12st.7lbs.
Born: Swindon, Wiltshire, 25th December 1895
Died: Poole, Dorset, 8th March 1976

CAREER: Sanford Street School/Swindon Boys/Swindon Town am. Sep 1914/Bolton Wanderers May 1920/SPURS Jun 1924/ Swindon Town Sep 1928.

Debut v Bolton Wanderers (FL) (h) 30.8.1924

Fred Hinton started his career with his local club before joining Bolton Wanderers, where he played only 36 senior games in four years before making the move to White Hart Lane. His Spurs' debut came against his old club at the start of the following season. From then on he was ever-present, before illness struck early in the 1925-26 campaign. He struggled through only 18 games, competing with Jimmy Smith, Bill Kaine and Jock Britton. Although he was retained at the season's end, he did not play another senior game. Given a free transfer in April 1927, he returned to Swindon Town. Later in life he ran a timber and box making business.

Appearances:
League: 57 apps.
FA Cup: 7 apps.
Others: 6 apps.
Total: 70 apps. 0 gls.

HIRSCHFELD, Lars Justin

Role: Goalkeeper 2002-04
6ft.4ins. 13st.8lbs.
Born: *Edmonton, Alberta, Canada, 17th October 1978*

CAREER: Lafayette and Maranga Soccer Club (LMSC Spurs) (USA)/Edmonton Drillers (Canada) Oct 1996/Energie Cottbus (Germany) trial Apr 1998, perm. Jul 1998-May 2000/Barnsley trial Aug 2000/Calgary Storm (USA) 2001/(Vancouver Whitecaps loan Aug 2001)/Heart of Midlothian trial Dec 2001/Motherwell trial Dec 2001/Portsmouth trial Feb 2002/Wolverhampton Wanderers trial Feb 2002/**SPURS** trial Mar 2002, loan Mar 2002, trial Jul 2002, perm. Aug 2002/(Luton Town loan Feb 2003)/Plymouth Argyle trial Dec 2003/(Gillingham loan Feb 2004)/released May 2004/Dundee United trial Jul 2004, perm. Aug 2004/Leicester City Jan 2005/Tromsø (Norway) Jul 2005/Rosenborg (Norway) Nov 2005/CFR Cluj (Rumania) Jan 2008/Energie Cottbus (Germany) Jun 2009/Vålerenga (Norway) Jan 2010/KFUM (Norway) Jan 2016.

Debut v Stevenage Borough (sub) (Fr) (a) 21.7.2002

Lars Hirschfeld began his professional football career playing indoor football with Edmonton Drillers, before moving to his parents' homeland of Germany. Signed on by Energie Cottbus, he played for them for two years, but played only one senior game in their colours. During that time, though, he won four Under-23 caps and collected his first at senior level when he played against Bermuda in January 2000. Returning to Canada, he played with Calgary Storm and Vancouver Whitecaps, catching the eye of clubs in England and Scotland, but not doing enough on trials to earn a contract. Hirschfeld first had a trial with Spurs in March 2002 and was immediately taken on loan for the rest of the season. He made the bench for several Premier League games, but was not called upon to play. Invited back for pre-season so Spurs could have another good look at him, Hirschfeld played in five pre-season games before being signed on. That was as good as it got for Hirschfeld. He made one more outing in a pre-season game and was released after just two years. After Spurs he moved around Europe, spending most of his time, and enjoying limited success, in Norway. In total he made 48 full appearances for Canada, eight of them as a Spurs' player.

Appearances:
Others: 3 (3) apps.
Total: 3 (3) apps. 0 gls.

HITCHINS, Arthur William

Role: Centre-half 1937-42
5ft.11ins. 11st.3lbs.
Born: *Devonport, Devon, 1st December 1913*
Died: *Barnet, Hertfordshire, 10th October 1975*

CAREER: Lea Bridge Gasworks/Walthamstow Avenue/**SPURS** pro. Jan 1935/(Northfleet United Aug 1935)/**SPURS** Sep 1936/(guest for Crystal Palace and Watford during World War Two)/retired 1942.

Debut v Plymouth Argyle (FL) (h) 23.10.1937

An Essex County player and captain of Lea Bridge Gasworks, Arthur Hitchins was a full-back when he signed professional for Spurs in January 1935. After spending the rest of that season in the reserves he was sent along to the Northfleet nursery for a year, returning to White Hart Lane as a half-back. He made a League debut at centre-half in October 1937 and gradually became established before taking over from Albert Page. By the end of the 1938-39 season he was being tipped as a future England international, but his career was totally destroyed by the war. Almost ever-present in the first three seasons of war-time football, a shoulder injury sustained in January 1942 and a subsequent illness brought his career to a premature end.

Appearances:
League: 37 apps. 1 gl.
FA Cup: 7 apps.
Others: 112* apps.
Total: 156 apps. 1 gl.
* Includes 1 abandoned match.

HOAD, Sidney James

Role: Outside-left 1916-17
Born: *Blackpool, Lancashire, 27th December 1890*
Died: *Whitefield, Manchester, 1st January 1973*

CAREER: St Annes/Blackpool am. pro. ???/Manchester City May 1911/(guest for **SPURS** during World War One)/Rochdale Sep 1920/Nelson 1921/retired 1927/Hurst Oct 1927.

Debut v Clapton Orient (LFC) (a) 6.1.1917

Sid Hoad made his Football League debut as an amateur with Blackpool, and won two England amateur caps in his two years there before joining Manchester City, where he played until the end of the First World War. Engaged in the London area on transport work for the Army, he made four appearances for Spurs in the London Football Combination in January 1917. After the war he spent a further season with Manchester City before joining Rochdale. He finished his career at Nelson and Hurst, retiring in 1927.

Appearances:
Others: 4 apps.
Total: **4 apps. 0 gls.**

HOBDAY, Alfred

Role: Right-back 1913-14
5ft.10ins. 12st.8lbs.
Born: Blackhill, Consett, County Durham, 12th December 1886.
Died: Ypres, Belgium, 16th June 1915 (Killed in action)

CAREER: West Stanley/Allandale Park/Consett Swifts/**SPURS** trial, pro. Apr 1913/North Shields Athletic cs. 1914.

Debut v Woolwich Arsenal (LFACC) (Stamford Bridge) 10.11.1913

An amateur with Consett Swifts, Alf Hobday signed professional for Spurs after a short trial period. His only first team appearance was in November 1913 when he played in the London FA Charity Cup semi-final with Woolwich Arsenal at Stamford Bridge. Released at the end of the 1913-14 season he joined North Shields but made few appearances for them. Hobday had served in the Army for six years, from 1906 to 1912, before the First World War and when that great conflict erupted was among the first reservists to be called up. Serving with the Northumberland Fusiliers he won the Legion of Honour and was nominated for the Victoria Cross for rescuing a wounded officer before being killed in action in June 1915.

Appearances:
Others: 1 app.
Total: **1 app. 0 gls.**

HOBSON

Role: Outside-left 1896-97

CAREER: Coldstream Guards/guest for **SPURS** Jan 1897.

Debut v Loughborough (UL) (a) 24.4.1897 (scored once)
(Chatham (Fr) (h) 28.1.1897)

A soldier with the Coldstream Guards, Hobson made three appearances for Spurs, only one of which was in a competitive game. Apart from the friendly against Chatham and the last United League fixture of the season against Loughborough he also played in a friendly with the London Caledonians on 30th January 1897 which was abandoned after 45 minutes because one of the Calies players broke a leg.

Appearances:
Others: 3 apps. 1 gl.
Total: **3 apps. 1 gl.**

HODDLE, Glenn

Role: Midfielder 1975-87
6ft.1ins. 11st.6lbs.
Born: Hayes, Middlesex, 27th October 1957

CAREER: Spinney Dynamoes/Harlow Schools/Essex Schools/**SPURS** app. Apr 1974, pro. Apr 1975/Monaco (France) Jul 1987-Dec 1990/Chelsea non-contract Jan 1991/Swindon Town player-manager Mar 1991/Chelsea player-manager Jun 1993/England head coach May 1996-Feb 1999/Southampton manager Jan 2000/**SPURS** manager Apr 2001-Sep 2003/Wolverhampton Wanderers manager Dec 2004-Jul 2006/Queens Park Rangers first team coach Aug 2014-Feb 2015.

Debut v Norwich City (sub) (FL) (h) 30.8.1975

One of the great names in Spurs' modern day history, Glenn Hoddle had trained at the club with many other hopeful youngsters, but it was a recommendation by former centre-forward Martin Chivers, who spotted him in a local junior cup final where he had gone along to present the trophies, that sealed Hoddle's link with Tottenham. Overcoming a bad knee injury in his early teens, Glenn rapidly worked his way through the schoolboy and apprentice levels to sign professional. Having collected England Youth caps he made his League debut as a substitute in August 1975, but had to wait until February 1976 for his full League bow. He announced his arrival by beating England goalkeeper Peter Shilton with a splendid long range goal against Stoke City. Under new manager Keith Burkinshaw, Hoddle quickly established himself as Spurs' principal midfield playmaker and although the club were relegated at the end of 1976-77, the one season spent in the Second Division probably gave Hoddle the necessary time to fully hone his talents before unleashing them on the First Division. Winning his first Under-21 cap against Wales in December 1976 he gathered seven more at that level and played twice for the England "B" team before marking his arrival on the full international scene with a debut goal against Bulgaria in November 1979. Winner of the PFA Young Player of the Year award in 1980 Hoddle was perhaps the most naturally gifted player of his generation and became the fulcrum of the Spurs' team for eleven years, delighting football fans with his unchallenged skills. He had extraordinary vision, coupled with an ability to hit telling passes up to 50 yards with inch perfect precision. In addition he had superb close control, perfect balance, an ability to curl cunning free kicks onto the target that even the South Americans would admire, plus a powerful and accurate long range shot. The only criticisms ever levelled at Hoddle were that he was not capable of chasing around the pitch for 90 minutes and that he neglected defensive duties. But Hoddle was an artist, not an artisan, a player who could conjure a goal out of nothing or turn a game with a flash of brilliance that others could only dream of. A member of the Spurs teams that won the FA Cup in 1981 (when his free-kick sparked the equaliser) and 1982 (when he scored in both games), he also appeared in the League (Milk) Cup Final in 1982 and the FA Cup Final in 1987, missing only the 1984 UEFA Cup victory due to

injury. He won a total of twelve Under-21 caps, two for England "B" and 44 full caps with Spurs, a wholly inadequate total, restricted by England's dreary preoccupation with hard-work when the national team of the 1980's should have been built around his unique skills. After thirteen years, Hoddle took his continental skills abroad in a £750,000 move to Monaco and the French League, where his talents were, perhaps, more fully appreciated. Winning nine more England caps, he helped Monaco to the French title in 1987-88 and was voted the best foreign player in the League. Sadly, he was then troubled by a serious knee injury that all but ended his career. In December 1990, he bought up his contract and returned to England to try and recover full fitness, signing for Chelsea on a non-contract basis. Without playing a senior game he left in March 1991 and took the first steps on a managerial career joining Swindon Town as player-manager replacement for Ossie Ardiles. Operating from the sweeper role, he inspired Swindon to promotion, but left before they made their debut in the top flight to take over at Chelsea. In three years he turned the sleeping giant of west London football into a potentially lethal force and took them to the FA Cup final in his first season in charge. Building a Chelsea side in his own image, he left the job incomplete, but in the good hands of Ruud Gullit in May 1996 when he took over from Terry Venables as England coach. Hoddle led England to the 1998 World Cup Finals, but then suffered the same fate as many of his predecessors as England manager-the so-called popular press. Turning against him as if they just wanted to show their power, Hoddle was put under continual pressure and eventually stood down in February 1999. Southampton gave Hoddle the opportunity to rebuild his career, appointing him manager on a short-term contract as Dave Jones fought child abuse charges. The pressure on Jones had seen Southampton struggling, but Hoddle led them clear of the relegation places. So well was Hoddle doing that when the charges against Jones were thrown out, the Saints paid up his contract and gave Hoddle the job on a permanent basis. When the Joe Louis regime took over Spurs and dismissed George Graham, Hoddle was the only man wanted to replace him. Despite the ill-feeling it generated on the south coast, there we no way Hoddle could turn the opportunity down. His first match in charge was an FA Cup semi-final against Arsenal. The game was lost, but Hoddle's influence was soon apparent as Spurs began to play again with the style the club has always been famous for. While the quality of football improved, results did not. The Worthington Cup Final in 2002 was lost to Blackburn Rovers, while mid-table remained the best Spurs could achieve in the League. When the 2003-04 season started with just four points from six games, the board gave in to pressure and Hoddle was shown the door. After a couple of years in which his Wolverhampton Wanderers' team was unable to mount a serious promotion challenge, Hoddle again found himself out of work when he resigned. He turned his attention to setting up the Glenn Hoddle Academy in Spain, giving players rejected by English clubs another chance to make a career in football. While he had numerous offers to return to management, Hoddle turned them all done, although he did have a brief spell on the coaching staff of Queens Park Rangers.

Appearances:
League: 370 (7) apps. 88 gls.
FA Cup: 47 (1) apps. 11 gls.
FL Cup: 44 apps. 10 gls.
Euro: 17 (4) apps. 1 gl.
Others: 88 (12) apps. 22 gls.
Total: 566 (24) apps. 132 gls.

HODGE, Stephen Brian

Role: Midfield 1986-88
5ft.8ins. 9st.11lbs.
Born: Nottingham, 25th October 1962

CAREER: Nottingham Schools/Nottinghamshire Schools/Nottingham Forest app. May 1978, pro. Oct 1980/Aston Villa Aug 1985/**SPURS** Dec 1986/Nottingham Forest Aug 1988/Leeds United Jul 1991/Sporting Lisbon (Portugal) trial May 1994/(Derby County loan Aug 1994)/Queens Park Rangers Oct 1994/Watford Dec 1995 on monthly contract/Walsall trial Jan 1996/Coventry City training Feb 1996/Notts County trial Jul 1996 /Norwich City trial Sep 1996/Bristol City trial Oct 1996/Hong Kong/Leyton Orient trial Aug 1997, non-contract Aug 1997/Coventry City trial Aug 1997/Hong Kong/Notts County Academy coach/Nottingham Forest Academy coach/Gresley Rovers training Jul 2002/Blackstone United Feb 2003/Chesterfield coach 2005, reserve team manager by Oct 2006/Nottingham Forest Academy coach/Notts County coach Apr 2013, Development Squad manager Jul 2013, caretaker manager Oct 2013, Development Squad manager Nov 2013-cs. 2014/Wolverhampton Wanderers coach Jul 2014-Feb 2015.

Debut v West Ham United (FL) (h) 26.12.1986 (scored once)

Steve Hodge worked his way through the junior ranks at Nottingham Forest to make his League debut in the final match of the 1981-82 season. A busy, left-sided midfield player always likely to pop up in useful goal-scoring positions, he made an England Under-21 debut against Greece in March 1983 and had a total of five caps to his credit at that level before moving to Aston Villa in August 1985. He won two further Under-21 caps at Villa Park together with eleven full England caps, the first against the USSR in March 1986. A regular member of the World Cup team in 1986, Hodge was establishing himself as an England fixture, but with Villa struggling at the wrong end of the First Division table he took the chance of a £650,000 move to Spurs. He marked his Boxing Day debut with a goal against West Ham and was an automatic choice for the FA Cup Final against Coventry City. Despite winning another four full caps for England, Hodge, along with the rest of the team, struggled to find his true form during the traumatic start to the 1987-88 season that saw the departure of manager David Pleat and, after a lengthy gap, the arrival of Terry Venables. First impressions were not too good as Hodge got sent off in Venables' opening match in charge and by the end of the season he made it clear he was unhappy, saying he was unable to settle in London. He returned to home-town Nottingham Forest in August 1988 for £575,000 and soon rediscovered the electric form he had shown earlier in his career, helping Forest win the 1989 finals of both the Littlewoods and Simod Cups. Back to his best, he helped the Reds retain the Littlewoods Cup in 1990 and returned to the England team in the summer as a member of the World Cup squad in Italy, but then suffered a series of troublesome minor injuries that restricted his appearances. He appeared as a substitute for Forest against Spurs in the 1991 FA Cup Final, but it was clear his place was under threat from rising young star Roy Keane and a £900,000 summer move took him to Leeds United. He continued to be hampered by injury problems, but still scored a few vital goals and made enough appearances to earn a Championship medal as Leeds lifted the League title in 1992. Released by Leeds, he had a short spell with Queens' Park Rangers and then moved around the lower reaches of League football and in Hong Kong before taking up coaching. At both Nottingham Forest and Notts County one of the charges under his wing was his son, Elliot.

Appearances:
League: 44 (1) apps. 7 gls.
FA Cup: 7 apps. 2 gls.
FL Cup: 2 apps.
Others: 12 (5) apps. 3 gls.
Total: 65 (6) apps. 12 gls.

HODGES, Lee Leslie

Role: Forward 1991-94
5ft.9ins. 11st.6lbs.
Born: Epping, Essex, 4th September 1973

CAREER: Cheshunt Youth/England Youth/**SPURS** assoc. sch. Feb 1988, trainee Jul 1990, pro. Feb 1992/(Plymouth Argyle loan Feb 1993)/(Wycombe Wanderers loan Dec 1993)/Barnet May 1994/Reading Jul 1997-May 2001/Northampton Town trial Jul 2001/Luton Town trial Jul 2001/Plymouth Argyle trial and perm Aug 2001/Torquay United Jun 2008/Truro City loan Oct 2009, caretaker manager Mar 2010, manager May 2010-May 2013/St Austell Jun 2013/Torquay United asst. manager Jan 2014-Jun 2015/Plymouth Argyle development coach Jan 2016/Truro City manager Jun 2016.

Debut v Wimbledon (sub) (PL) (h) 1.5.1993
(Hull City XI (sub) (Fr) (a) 8.5.1992)

With a pretty good scoring record at youth and reserve level, Lee Hodges always looked like making a career in football. It was just a question of at what level? At Spurs he had Teddy Sheringham, Gordon Durie and the rapidly developing Nick Barmby ahead of him and the likes of Steve Robinson and Paul Mahorn coming through from the youth ranks. It was stiff competition and led to Hodges making only four substitute appearances in the Premier League before being released. He moved to Barnet where his former Spurs' coach Ray Clemence was general manager. In four years he established himself as a more than competent goal-scorer before spending a similar time at Reading where he dropped back into midfield. It was Plymouth Argyle who got the best of Hodges. In seven years he made over 200 appearances, a consistent and reliable performer, creating chances for others, but still with the eye for goal he had first shown at Spurs. In his time with Plymouth they won the Third and Second Division titles. After a year with Torquay, Hodges joined Truro City, initially as a player, but later combining the manager's job. He led them to the Southern League Premier Division title in 2011 but was surprising released in May 2013 when Truro said they could not afford to retain his services. After serving St Austell and Torquay United, Hodges returned to Plymouth to work on coaching players coming through the ranks.

Appearances:
League: (4) apps.
Others: 2 (9) apps.
Total: 2 (13) apps. 0 gls.

HODGKINSON, Herbert

Role: Left-back 1930-32
5ft.8ins. 10st.10lbs.
Born: Penistone, Derbyshire, 26th December 1903
Died: Dudley, Worcestershire, 1st April 1974

CAREER: Penistone Juniors/Barnsley Nov 1923/**SPURS** Aug 1930/Colwyn Bay United Aug 1932/Crewe Alexandra Aug 1933.

Debut v Reading (FL) (h) 30.8.1930

Signed from his first club Barnsley in August 1930, Bert Hodgkinson was a good, strong left-back who immediately went into the team, making his Spurs' debut in the season's opening game. He missed only three matches-all due to injury-in that first season as the club finished third in the Second Division, but lost his place to Cecil Poynton during the 1931-32 campaign as the team failed to match its bright form of the previous year. Although the forwards continued to score freely, the defence leaked goals and Hodgkinson was the one to carry the can. In April 1932 he was placed on the not retained list and in August that year moved to Colwyn Bay.

Appearances:
League: 56 apps.
FA Cup: 2 apps.
Others: 5 apps.
Total: 63 apps. 0 gls.

HOFFMAN (HOLT), Ernest Henry

Role: Goalkeeper 1917-18
Born: Hebburn, Northumberland, 16th July 1892
Died: South Shields, County Durham, 20th January 1959

CAREER: Hebburn Argyle/South Shields am. cs. 1914/(guest for **SPURS** during World War One)/South Shields am. cs. 1919, pro. May 1920/Derby County Apr 1923/Ashington Aug 1923/Darlington Aug 1924/Wood Skinners Oct 1925/Jarrow Sep 1926/York City Aug 1929/Blyth Spartans secretary-manager May 1933-May 1937/Birmingham City north-east scout/South Shields manager/Jarrow manager.

Debut v Fulham (LFC) (a) 1.12.1917

An amateur goalkeeper who won two international caps for England at amateur level while with Hebburn Argyle, Ernie Hoffman was on the books of South Shields when he made his one appearance for Spurs against Fulham in December 1917 in a London Football Combination fixture. Regular keeper Bill Jacques was unable to turn out because his mother was seriously ill and Hoffman was drafted in as a last-minute replacement. Very inexperienced, he was described as being the difference between the teams as Spurs lost 3-4. After the First World War he continued to turn out for South Shields until signing for Derby County. Hoffman played only one League game for Derby, then had twelve months with Ashington before going on to play and manage some of the north east's senior non-League clubs. He won the North Eastern League championship with Blyth Spartans (1935-36) and South Shields (1938-39).

Appearances:
Others: 1 app.
Total: 1 app. 0 gls.

HOFFMAN

Role: Outside-left 1918-19

CAREER: Brentford/(guest for **SPURS** during World War One).

Debut v Brentford (LFC) (a) 9.11.1918

One of Brentford's junior players, Hoffman made his one appearance for Spurs in the London Football Combination in November 1918 when he played against his own club at Griffin Park, as Spurs arrived with only nine men. Spurs lost the match 1-7 which, along with the defeat at Queens Park Rangers the same season, ranks as their heaviest defeat of the War years.

Appearances:
Others: 1 app.
Total: 1 app. 0 gls.

HOLDER, Philip

Role: Midfield 1971-76
5ft.4ins. 10st.6lbs.
Born: Kilburn, London, 19th January 1952

CAREER: Brent Schools/Middlesex Schools/London Schools/**SPURS** app. Apr 1967, pro. Feb 1969/Crystal Palace loan Feb 1975, perm Mar 1975 /Memphis Rogues (USA) summer 1978/AFC Bournemouth Mar 1979/ Crystal Palace coach/Brentford asst. manager, caretaker-manager Aug 1990, manager Oct 1990-May 1993/Watford asst. manager May 1993-Jul 1993/Southend United asst. manager Aug 1993-May 1994/Reading youth team coach Jan 1995, asst. manager till Jul 1996/Shimizu S-Pulse (Japan) asst. manager May 1999.

Debut v Keflavik (UEFA) (sub) (h) 28.9.1971 (scored once)

Phil Holder joined Spurs at the same time as Steve Perryman, with whom he had played in schoolboy representative soccer. He then had to compete with the future Spurs' captain and was not to have anything like the same amount of success. Holder won an England Youth cap and made his Spurs' debut as substitute in a UEFA Cup tie with Keflavik with his League debut, again as a substitute, coming at Liverpool in December 1971. A tiny but tough, competitive midfielder, he had precious few opportunities to play in a senior team which could boast midfield players of the calibre of Perryman, Martin Peters, John Pratt and Ralph Coates. Similar in all-action style to Perryman in that he gave everything and was always busily involved in the game, he was transferred to Crystal Palace and after a short spell there and a summer spent playing for Memphis Rogues finished his League career with Bournemouth. Once his playing days were over he moved onto the coaching side of the game and was Steve Perryman's assistant at Brentford until Perryman's surprise resignation in August 1990. At that time Holder was appointed caretaker-manager, but took on the role permanently two months later and led Brentford to the Third Division title in 1992. Dismissed by Brentford in May 1993, he succeeded Peter Taylor as assistant manager to Steve Perryman at Watford that same month, but was sacked two months later following Perryman's appointment as assistant manager at Spurs. Holder then worked as assistant manager to Peter Taylor at Southend United and with Reading and back with Perryman at Shimizu S-Pulse. Holder's brother, Jim, was on Spurs' books in 1968-69.

Appearances:
League: 9 (4) apps. 1 gl.
Euro: (6) apps. 1 gl.
Others: 3 (5) apps.
Total: 12 (15) apps. 2 gls.

HOLLEY, Thomas

Role: Centre-forward 1942-43
6ft 2ins, 13st.0lbs.
Born: Wolverhampton, Staffordshire, 15th November 1913
Died: September 1992

CAREER: North Eastern junior football/Wolverhampton Wanderers/ Sunderland trial/Barnsley cs. 1933/Leeds United Jul 1936/(guest for Aldershot, Fulham, Huddersfield Town, **SPURS** and York City during World War Two).

Debut v Clapton Orient (Fr) (h) 1.5.1943 (scored twice)

The son of former Sunderland, Wolverhampton Wanderers and England centre-forward, George, Tom Holley had been a regular war-time guest for Fulham when he made his one guest appearance for Spurs. That was in May 1943 when he played centre-forward in a friendly against Clapton Orient and scored twice. Described as well-built and dashing, he had joined Barnsley, where his father was trainer, from North Eastern junior football having failed to make the grade as an inside-forward with Sunderland. Barnsley soon realised that his best position was in the half-back line and it was as such that he was transferred to Leeds United. After the war, he spent two seasons of normal League football with Leeds playing at centre-half. On leaving football he made a career in journalism with the Sunday People and Yorkshire Evening Post before retiring to Spain.

Appearances:
Others: 1 app. 2 gls.
Total: 1 app. 2 gls.

HOLLIS, Roy Walter

Role: Centre-forward 1952-53
6ft.1ins. 11st.6lbs.
Born: Great Yarmouth, Norfolk, 24th December 1925
Died: Great Yarmouth, Norfolk, 12th November 1998

CAREER: Yarmouth Town am. Aug 1946/Norwich City am. May 1947, pro. Feb 1948/ **SPURS** Dec 1952/ Southend United Feb 1954/ Chelmsford City Jul 1960/ Yarmouth Town Oct 1961/ Lowestoft Town Dec 1962-Mar 1963.

Debut v Tranmere Rovers (FAC) (h) 12.1.1953 (scored twice)

Roy Hollis scored 52 goals in 96 League games as Norwich

fought to get out of the Third Division (South) and, with 20 of them in only 27 games during the 1951-52 season, Arthur Rowe was persuaded to sign him for Spurs. He netted twice on his debut as Spurs thrashed Tranmere Rovers in an FA Cup replay, but made only three League appearances, all in that first season. Although a prolific goal-scorer in the reserves, he was unable to displace Len Duquemin and was allowed to move back to the Third Division (South) with Southend United. In five years with Southend he scored scoring 122 goals in 240 League games and represented the Third Division (South) against the Northern section twice, before winding down his career with Chelmsford City, Yarmouth Town and Lowestoft Town. Later in life he worked as a Turf Accountant and betting shop manager.

Appearances:
League: 3 apps. 1 gl.
FA Cup: 1 app. 2 gls.
Total: 4 apps. 3 gls.

HOLLOWBREAD, John Frederick

Role: Goalkeeper 1956-64
5ft.11ins. 11st.4lbs.
Born: Ponders End, Enfield, Middlesex, 2nd January 1934
Died: Torrevieja, Spain, 7th December 2007

CAREER: Chase Side Junior School/Tottenham Technical College/ Enfield Schools/Tottenham Schools/Middlesex Schools/England Schools/ England Youth/Enfield/**SPURS** am. Jun 1950, pro. Jan 1952/ Southampton May 1964/Mullard Sports/Netley Sports trainer.

Debut v Blackburn Rovers (FL) (a) 30.8.1958
(Heart of Midlothian (Fr) (h) 12.11.1956)

First attracting attention playing for Enfield, John Hollowbread patiently spent more than six years at Spurs as third choice 'keeper facing the almost impossible task of trying to displace Ted Ditchburn and Ron Reynolds. A Middlesex Youth player, he made his League debut in August 1958 when both Ditchburn and Reynolds were injured. While it was not a happy start, Spurs losing 0-5 to Blackburn, he kept his place for the rest of the season as Spurs fought to stave off relegation. Tall and well-built, but very acrobatic and agile for a big man, he used his height to good advantage and was well appreciated by the crowd. However, he managed only one season as first choice, for in the summer of 1959 Scottish international Bill Brown was signed and Hollowbread returned to the reserves. Several clubs had been impressed by his performances for Spurs and were keen to sign him, but manager Bill Nicholson rated him highly enough to refuse to let Hollowbread leave. Due to Brown's consistency Hollowbread made few further appearances in the first team, but he had enough of a run in the 1963-64 season to rekindle interest from other clubs. When Spurs announced they were now prepared to release him for £3,000 several clubs were eager. He instantly chose Southampton, where he succeeded former Spurs' colleague Reynolds. After only 36 games for the Saints Hollowbread suffered a knee injury so serious he was forced to retire from the professional arena, although he was still able to play local football in the Southampton area, where he settled and later ran a pub in Romsey. John's father, Fred, also played for Enfield and was on the books of Northfleet United in the 1930s.

Appearances:
League: 67 apps.
FA Cup: 6 apps.
Others: 9 apps.
Total: 82 apps. 0 gls.

HOLMES, James Paul

Role: Defender 1976-81
5ft.11ins. 11st.0lbs.
Born: Dublin, Eire, 11th November 1953

CAREER: Strand Street Christian Brothers School/ Emmet Road Technical School/ Dublin Schools/Eire Schools/St John Bosco Boys Club/ Coventry City app. Aug 1969, pro. Nov 1970/**SPURS** Mar 1977/Vancouver Whitecaps (Canada) Feb 1981/Leicester City non-contract Oct 1982/ Brentford non-contract Feb 1983/Torquay United non-contract Mar-Nov 1983/ Peterborough United player-asst. manager Nov 1983/ Nuneaton Borough player-manager Dec 1985/Leicester United cs. 1987/ Hitchin Town manager 1987-88/Bedworth United manager Oct 1988/ Nuneaton Borough cs. 1989/retired cs. 1990.

Debut v West Bromwich Albion (FL) (h) 12.3.1977

An Eire Youth international, Jimmy Holmes made his League debut for Coventry City in January 1972-but he had already won his first full cap for his country. He was called on as a substitute against Austria in May 1971, becoming the youngest ever international for the Republic. At Coventry he gradually replaced the experienced Chris Cattlin and built a reputation as a genuinely classy, football-playing full-back, solid in defence, cool and confident in possession. In March 1977, with 17 caps to his credit and Spurs sliding towards the Second Division, he was signed for £100,000 in a desperate attempt to shore up a leaky defence that had just been deprived of the services of John Gorman by injury. Injured himself after only eight games, Holmes was unable to prevent Spurs being relegated, but in the next two seasons proved himself an elegant defender of outstanding ability, who could not only play at full-back, but also in the centre of defence. Collecting his twelfth cap as a Spurs player against Bulgaria in Sofia in May 1979, Holmes suffered a broken leg. The injury was serious, but it was not helped by the sub-standard treatment he received from the Bulgarian medical services. It was another eleven months before Holmes was able to play again, and by that time young Chris Hughton had become established as Spurs' left-back of the future. Unable to get back in the team Holmes, was allowed to move to Vancouver Whitecaps of the North American Soccer League. After almost two years there, during which time he won his final cap, he returned to England and played on a non-contract basis for Leicester City, Brentford and Torquay United. He then joined Peterborough United as player-assistant manager before moving to Nuneaton Borough as player-manager. Holmes later had spells as manager of Hitchin Town and Bedworth United before making a new career for himself as a member of the West Midlands police force.

Appearances:
League: 81 apps. 2 gls.
FA Cup: 9 apps.
FL Cup: 2 apps.
Others: 25 (4) apps. 2 gls.
Total: 117 (4) apps. 4 gls.

HOLTBY, Lewis Harry

Role: Midfielder 2012-
5ft.9ins. 12st.2lbs.
Born: Erkelenz, Germany, 18th September 1990

CAREER: Sparta Gerderath (Germany) 1994/Borussia Mönchengladbach (Germany) 2001/Alemannia Aachen (Germany) youth 2004, pro. Sep 2008/Schalke 04 (Germany) Jul 2009/(Vfl Bochum (Germany) loan Jan 2010)/(1FSV Mainz 05 (Germany) loan Jul 2010)/SPURS Jan 2013/(Fulham loan Jan 2014)/Hamburger SV (Germany) loan Sep 2014, perm Jul 2015.

Debut v Norwich City (PL) (a) (sub) 30.1.2013

Born in Germany to a British serviceman, Lewis Holtby was a busy little midfielder reckoned a certainty for the top when signed by Spurs. Rejected by Borussia Mönchengladbach as too small, Holtby had to drop into the German second Division with Alemannia Aachen to get his career underway, but after breaking into the team as a 17-year old and winning selection for the German Under-18s and 19s, it was not long before the top division clubs were watching him. Schalke 04 signed Holtby and while her spent most of his first two years with them out on loan, he continued to progress at international level. At last getting a regular place with Schalke, Holtby began to attract attention from further afield. A regular with the German Under-21s, he collected three caps at full level. Spurs had been monitoring Holtby for a while and in January 2013 it was announced that he would be moving to White Hart Lane once his contract with Schalke had expired at the end of the season. By the end of the month, Spurs had decided to lay out €1.75 million to sign him immediately. A non-stop worker, Holtby favoured a role just off the central striker, but Christian Eriksen was preferred in that position. It meant that Holtby was forced to play out of position, a fact that did nothing to help him impress and make a position his own. Within a year of his arrival, Holtby was out on loan with Fulham. Despite his former Schalke manager, Felix Magath, being appointed manager, Holtby had little effect on Fulham's unsuccessful relegation battle. Back with Spurs, Mauricio Pochettino clearly felt he had more than enough midfielders. Holtby returned to Germany with Hamburger, initially on loan, with the move made permanent in July 2015 after Holtby had helped his new club in a successful relegation battle.

Appearances:
League: 10 (15) apps. 1 gl.
FL Cup: 1 (1) apps.
Euro: 8 (7) apps. 2 gls.
Others: 5 (2) apps. 2 gls.
Total: 24 (25) apps. 5 gls.

HOOPER, Percy George William

Role: Goalkeeper 1934-45
6ft.1ins. 13st.2lbs.
Born: Westminster, London, 17th December 1914
Died: Kings Lynn, Norfolk, 3rd July 1997

CAREER: Cheddington Athletic/Tufnell Park/Islington Corinthians/SPURS am. Oct 1933/Northfleet United 1933/SPURS pro. Jan 1935/(guest for Arsenal, Bath City, Brighton and Hove Albion, Crystal Palace, Gillingham and West Ham United during World War Two)/Swansea Town Mar 1947/Chingford Town Aug 1948/Kings Lynn 1949/Downham Town manager-coach 1955/Kings Lynn coach, caretaker manager 1965, till 1974.

Debut v Blackburn Rovers (FL) (h) 19.4.1935

Having previously played for the Edmonton club Cheddington Athletic, Percy Hooper was reserve goalkeeper with Islington Corinthians when Spurs' reserve 'keeper Alan Taylor was injured. Hooper, who had been associated with the club as an amateur, was asked to stand in. He so impressed that he was taken onto the staff, sent along to the Northfleet nursery, and then signed professional. He made his League debut near the end of the 1934-35 season, but his real chance came early the following term when Taylor was injured and Hooper played half the League games. The signing of Jack Hall saw Hooper edged out of the team, but he eventually replaced the more experienced Hall and by the outbreak of the Second World War was recognised as first choice 'keeper. Initially his military service allowed him to turn out for Spurs, but his appearances diminished as the war went on. His absence allowed Ted Ditchburn to step in as Spurs' future number one and the end of the war saw Hooper third choice to Ditchburn and Archie Hughes. Early in 1947 he decided he had no future at White Hart Lane, was placed on the transfer list at his own request and moved to Swansea Town. He only stayed one season before joining Southern League Chingford, and when they folded moved to Kings Lynn in the Eastern Counties League where he finished his playing career. He later became their trainer and coached in East Anglia. After retiring he worked for the Eastern Electricity Board.

Appearances:
League: 100 apps.
FA Cup: 11 apps.
Others: 132* apps.
Total: 243 apps. 0 gls.
*Includes 1 abandoned match.

HOPKIN, Frederick

Role: Outside-left 1915-16
5ft.8ins. 11st.6lbs.
Born: Dewsbury, Yorkshire, 23rd September 1895
Died: Darlington, County Durham, 5th March 1970

CAREER: Darlington/(guest for SPURS and Manchester United during World War One)/Manchester United Feb 1919/Liverpool May 1921/Darlington Aug 1931-cs. 1932/Redcar Borough trainer 1933-34/Leeds United asst. trainer late 1930s.

Debut v Arsenal (LFC) (h) 8.4.1916

On the books of Darlington before the First World War, Fred Hopkin made four appearances for Spurs during the 1915-16 season. He played most of his war-time football with Manchester United and in the close season of 1919 was formally transferred to the Old Trafford club. United

found themselves in trouble with the League over Hopkin's transfer, being fined £350 for paying him more than the maximum permitted wage and promising him a cut of the transfer fee. In 1921 he was transferred to Liverpool where he made over 300 senior appearances and helped them win the League title in 1922 and 1923. He also played in an international trial match in February 1923 before returning for a final playing season with Darlington. Hopkin then had a season as trainer with Redcar Borough and in the late 1930s was on the coaching staff of Leeds United.

Appearances:
Others: 4 apps. 1 gl.
Total: **4 apps. 1 gl.**

HOPKINS, A

Role: Forward 1891-92

CAREER: SPURS by Apr 1892.

Debut v St Albans (Fr) (a) 18.4.1892

Nothing is known about this player whose only known appearance was in April 1892.

Appearances:
Others: 1 app.
Total: **1 app. 0 gls.**

HOPKINS, Melvyn

Role: Full-back 1952-64
5ft.11ins. 10st.6lbs.
Born: *Ystraad Rhondda, Wales, 7th November 1934*
Died: *Worthing, Sussex, 18th October 2010*

CAREER: Ystraad Boys Club/Tottenham Juniors/**SPURS** trial Feb 1951, am. May 1951, pro. May 1952/Brighton and Hove Albion Oct 1964/Canterbury City Jul 1967/Ballymena 1967-68/Bradford Park Avenue Jan 1969/Wimbledon//Derby County scout/Lancing.

Debut v Derby County (FL) (a) 11.10.1952

Mel Hopkins was spotted by both Spurs and Manchester United playing for the Ystraad Boys Club in Glamorgan and offered the chance to join the ground-staff of either club. He picked Spurs and rapidly developed, making his League debut within six months of signing professional. It was another two years before he was able to replace Arthur Willis and Charlie Withers as first choice left-back, but by the mid-1950s Hopkins was recognised as one of the best full-backs in the country. Fast, tenacious, strong in the tackle, keen on joining in the attack but always able to recover quickly when necessary, Hopkins was most unlucky to miss out on club honours during his many years at Spurs. He made his international debut for Wales in April 1956 and immediately became an automatic choice for his country, playing throughout the 1958 World Cup in Sweden when the Welsh were the surprise team of the tournament. Although Ron Henry had been challenging Hopkins' place for some time, the long-legged defender was able to hold him off until he broke his nose playing for Wales in November 1959. Just as the famous

"Double" team was taking shape, Henry took Hopkins' place and, despite remaining at White Hart Lane another five years, Hopkins was ousted and never able to get back in the team on a permanent basis. A reserve for Spurs, he was still a first choice for Wales, and in total won 34 full caps plus one at Under-23 level. In October 1964 he moved to Brighton and helped them collect the Fourth Division title, later playing for Canterbury City, Ballymena and Bradford Park Avenue. Mel also played a few games for Lancing and eventually became a sports instructor for the Brighton Education Authority and then Sports Officer of the Horsham Sports Centre.

Appearances:
League: 219 apps. 0 gls.
FA Cup: 20 apps. 0 gls.
Euro: 1 apps. 0 gls.
Others: 31 apps. 1 gl.
Total: **271 apps. 1 gls.**

HOUGHTON, Scott-Aaron

Role: Midfield 1990-93
5ft.5ins. 11st.6lbs.
Born: *Arlesey, Hitchin, Hertfordshire, 22nd October 1971*

CAREER: North Herts Schools/England Schools/FA-GM School of Excellence/**SPURS** trainee Aug 1988, pro. May 1990/England Youth/(Ipswich Town loan Mar 1991)/(Cambridge United loan Sep 1992)/(Gillingham loan Dec 1992)/(Charlton Athletic loan Feb 1993)/Luton Town Jul 1993/Walsall trial Jul 1994, loan Aug 1994, perm Sep 1994/Peterborough Jul 1996/Southend United loan Nov 1998, perm Dec 1998/Leyton Orient Oct 2000, released Jan 2002/Halifax Town Feb 2002/Peterborough United training Mar 2002/Stevenage Borough Mar 2002/Cambridge City Oct 2002/Arlesey Town Nov 2002/Wootton Blue Cross Feb 2003/Blackstone Jul 2003/St Neots Town player-asst. manager Sep 2004/Arlesey Town player-asst. manager Nov 2004/St Neots Town manager Jan-Sep 2007/Deeping Sports Jan 2008, then Aug 2010.

Debut v Manchester United (sub) (FL) (h) 28.9.1991
(West Ham United (Fr) (a) 12.11.1990) (scored once)

One of a crop of talented young midfielders on Spurs' books at the start of the 1990's, Scottie Houghton joined Spurs after graduating from the FA/GM School of Excellence. An England Youth cap he helped Spurs win the 1990 FA Youth Cup and made his first team debut in a testimonial at West Ham United in November 1990. To gain League experience

Houghton was loaned to Ipswich Town in March 1991 and early the following season began to make his mark as a regular member of the first team squad. At his best playing wide in midfield where he could run at an opponent, Houghton had a lethal long-range shot and an ability to swing over a variety of crosses capable of unsettling the best organised defences. His development did not continue at Spurs and in August 1993 he moved to Luton Town. He proved himself a more than competent performer lower down the League ladder with Walsall, Peterborough United and Southend. His League career over, Houghton joined the Cambridgeshire Constabulary, but continued to be involved in local football until September 2007 when he decided football had to take third place to his family and police career.

Appearances:
League: (10) apps. 2 gls.
FL Cup: (2) apps.
Euro: (2) apps.
Others: 1 (4) apps. 1 gl.
Total: 1 (18) apps. 3 gls.

HOUSTON, Robert

Role: Centre-forward 1902-03
5ft.11ins. 12st.0lbs.
Born: Leven, Fife, 9th January 1877
Died: Edmonton, 29th November 1954

CAREER: Leven Thistle/St Bernards Nov 1897/Heart of Midlothian Nov 1900/**SPURS** May 1902/released cs. 1903/East Fife/**SPURS** ground-staff 1924.

Debut v Queens Park Rangers (SL) (h) 6.9.1902

A fast-rushing style of centre or inside-forward, Bob Houston built a big reputation for himself in his native Scotland, helping Heart of Midlothian win the Scottish Cup in 1901. Joining Spurs, he started as the regular centre-forward but as soon as Vivian J Woodward was available found himself in the reserves. Houston spent the rest of the season competing with John Barlow for the role of Woodward's understudy. He was released at the end of the season, but returned to White Hart Lane in 1924 as a member of the ground-staff, assisting his father-in-law and Spurs' groundsman, John Over. He retained the position, with his wife, Alice, running the Spurs' laundry, until the Second World War. Houston's son Billy played a few games for the Spurs "A" team in the 1920s, but the bulk of his football was played at Northfleet.

Appearances:
Southern: 9 apps. 3 gls.
Others: 17 apps. 8 gls.
Total: 26 apps. 11 gls.

HOWE, Leslie Francis

Role: Utility 1930-46
5ft.10ins. 10st.8lbs.
Born: Bengeo, Hertfordshire, 5th March 1912
Died: Tottenham, London 23rd February 1999

CAREER: Lancastrian School/Tottenham Schools/London Schools/England Schools/Tottenham Argyle/Tottenham Juniors/Enfield 1928-29/**SPURS** am. Oct 1928/Northfleet United 1929/**SPURS** pro. Aug 1930/Northfleet United Aug 1931/**SPURS** May 1932/(guest for Bath City, Chelmsford City, Crewe Alexandra, Fulham, Hull City, Middlesbrough, Millwall, Nottingham Forest, Reading, Rotherham United and Swansea Town during World War Two)/**SPURS** coach, "A" team manager/Edmonton Borough trainer-coach Jun 1947/Enfield manager 1948-49.

Debut v Southampton (FL) (a) 26.12.1930
(Chelsea (LFACC) (a) 27.10.1930)

Les Howe was a valuable and extremely versatile player throughout his 16 years' service with Spurs. A local lad taken into the Tottenham Juniors on leaving school, he was then placed with Enfield before being sent to the nursery club at Northfleet. He joined the professional ranks in the summer of 1930 and made his League debut on Boxing Day 1930, when an injury crisis saw him called up to play in the right-half spot at Southampton. Although he was drafted in twice more that season, he did not get an extended run in the League team until October 1932 and then played most of his matches at outside-right. A fine all round footballer, Howe is probably best remembered as a right-half, but in his long spell with Spurs he actually played in every position, even taking over in goal in an emergency. In an age of specialisation, Howe was the proverbial "Jack of all trades, yet master of none". He was a regular in the early war years until an injury in September 1945 led to serious complications. He gained some experience as coach and manager of the "A" team and when given a free transfer in April 1947 he decided to retire from first class football to take up the role of trainer and coach with the newly-formed Edmonton Borough club. After a year with Edmonton, he spent a season managing Enfield. Having completed an apprenticeship in plumbing in case a career in football never materialised, Howe continued the trade in later life.

Appearances:
League: 165 apps. 26 gls.
FA Cup: 17 apps. 2 gls.
Others: 103* apps. 19 gls.
Total: 285 apps. 47 gls.
* Includes 1 abandoned match.

HOWELLS, David Glyn

Role: Midfield 1985-98
5ft.11ins. 11st.10lbs.
Born: Guildford, Surrey, 15th December 1967

CAREER: Guildford Schools/Surrey Schools/Hartley Wintney/**SPURS** YTS Jul 1984, pro. Jan 1985/Southampton Jul 1998/(Bristol City loan Mar 1999)/retired Aug 2000/Hartley Wintney Mar 2001/Aldershot trial Jul 2002/Havant & Waterlooville Aug 2003/AFC Guildford (Guildford United/City) player-coach-asst. manager by Jul 2004, director of football by Jun 2006/Havant & Waterlooville Feb 2005/Westfield coach Jun 2007/Crown and Anchor Nomads by Aug 2007/Guildford Athletic by Oct 2007/Charterhouse School Jul 2014.

Debut v Sheffield Wednesday (FL) (a) 22.2.1986 (scored once)

Originally a central striker, good in the air and calm in the penalty box, David Howells made the perfect start to his senior career, scoring the winning goal on his debut at Hillsborough. He was capped as a forward at England Youth and Under-19 level, but new manager Terry Venables quickly recognised that there was more to Howells that just an ability to get into the danger areas and score goals. He identified that Howells had the vision, control and passing ability to make much more of an impact in midfield, where his late runs into the penalty box and goal-scorers' instincts could be better harnessed to Spurs' needs. A good reader of the game, always conscious of the action going on around him, he developed into the perfect foil for Paul Gascoigne, operating just in front of the defence and covering for his more unpredictable colleague. As a home-produced player Howells contribution to the team is often overlooked as the spotlight falls on more obvious stars, but his first class technical skills and willingness to work for the team were acknowledged in November 1990 with selection for the Football League against the Irish League. Promoted to the England "B" squad in January 1991 he was unfortunately forced to withdraw from the team to play Wales because of injury. That injury problem threatened to rule him out of the 1991 FA Cup run, but he returned just in time to play in the memorable semi-final defeat of Arsenal, where his role wide on the left shackled the probing runs of Lee Dixon and deprived Arsenal of one of their most potent attacking options. In the final, he more than played his part, particularly after the early departure of Gascoigne through injury. Playing just in front of the back line Howells proved himself a crucial if underrated member of the first team and were it not for a series of niggling injuries at the wrong times could have developed as well on the international stage. Having established himself as one of the first names on the team sheet, Howells found himself marginalised when Ossie Ardiles was appointed manager. Committed to all-out attack, Howells' regard for the defensive side of the game was not what Ardiles wanted. It was an unfortunate decision by Ardiles. Howells was the perfect man to provide the solid base that would have allowed Ardiles' stellar attackers to flourish and may well have turned Ardiles' dream into reality. After 14 years of great service Howells was not offered a new contract in the summer of 1998 and joined Southampton, but he had difficulty making an impact as the Hampshire club continued their almost compulsory battle with relegation, and in March 1999 he joined Bristol City on loan. Continual injury problems forced Howells to retire from the top flight game in August 2000, but he was not lost to football. Initially running a soccer school in Spain, he was injured in a trial game for Aldershot, but soon returned at non-League level. Howells' brother, Gareth, was a goalkeeper on Spurs' books at one time. He failed to make the grade and went on to play for Torquay United and in non-League football.

Appearances:
League:	238 (39) apps. 22 gls.
FA Cup:	17 (4) apps. 1 gl.
FL Cup:	26 (5) apps. 4 gls.
Euro:	6 apps.
Others:	62 (26) apps. 13 gls.
Total:	**349 (74) apps. 40 gls.**

HOWSHALL, Thomas

Role: Half-back 1945-46

CAREER: Clapton Orient/(guest for Chester, Grimsby Town, Plymouth Argyle, Queens Park Rangers, Reading, Southport, Stoke City, **SPURS** and Watford during World War Two)/Plymouth Argyle Apr 1946/ Worcester City Jul 1947.

Debut v Coventry City (FLS) (h) 26.1.1946

A Clapton Orient player who appeared as a war-time guest, Tom Howshall made his one appearance for Spurs in a Football League South fixture with Coventry City in January 1946. Although it was at one time rumoured that he was going to be transferred to Spurs as part of an exchange deal, when he left Orient in April 1946 it was to join Plymouth Argyle.

Appearances:
Others:	1 app.
Total:	**1 app. 0 gls.**

HOY, Roger Ernest

Role: Centre-half 1965-68
5ft.10ins. 12st.4lbs.
Born: *Poplar, London, 6th December 1946*

CAREER: East London Schools/**SPURS** am. 1964, pro. May 1964/Crystal Palace Sep 1968/Luton Town Jun 1970/Cardiff City Aug 1971/Bath City Jan 1974/Dagenham/Palm Beach (Australia).

Debut v Sunderland (FL) (a) 26.3.1966

Roger Hoy originally joined Spurs as a full-back, but was converted to centre-half before signing professional. He made his League debut as replacement for Laurie Brown in March 1966. While Brown left Spurs the following September that was not because Hoy had taken his place, but as a result of Spurs signing Mike England. Hoy spent the next two years as England's deputy, playing only a few games when England was injured. He was never in the same class as the big Welshman, and when Bill Nicholson signed the promising Peter Collins from Southern League Chelmsford City it was clear Hoy was surplus to requirements. He was transferred to Crystal Palace, moved on to Luton Town and finished his career in this country with Cardiff City. Cardiff paid £25,000 for his signature, but his time there was plagued by injuries and eventually Cardiff terminated his contract on medical grounds. Hoy was not prepared to accept their actions, joined Bath City and subsequently successfully sued Cardiff for breach of contract. After serving Bath and Dagenham, Hoy emigrated to Australia

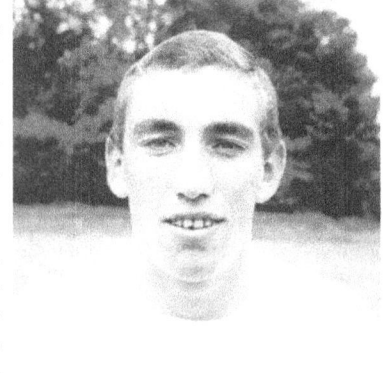

where he played for the Palm Beach club before becoming the Reverend Roger Hoy, a man of the cloth.

Appearances:
League: 10 apps.
Euro: 2 apps.
Others: 3 apps.
Total: **15 apps. 0 gls.**

HUBBLE, John Charlton

Role: Inside-forward 1902-03
Born: Wateringbury, Kent, 10th February 1881
Died: St Leonards-On-Sea, Sussex, 26th February 1965

CAREER: Maidstone/guest for **SPURS** Apr 1903.

Debut v Queens Park (Fr) (h) 6.4.1903

An amateur from Maidstone, Jack Hubble's only appearance was on 6th April 1903 when he played at inside-left in a friendly against Queen's Park. Details of his football career are unknown, but it is known that he had a lengthy and impressive career in cricket. A wicketkeeper, in 25 years he played 360 first class matches and scored over ten thousand runs.

Appearances:
Others: 1 app.
Total: **1 app. 0 gls.**

HUDDLESTONE, Thomas Andrew

Role: Midfielder 2005-14
6ft.3ins. 14st.12lbs.
Born: Nottingham, 28th December 1986

CAREER: Nottingham Forest schoolboy/Derby County Academy Scholar Jul 2003, pro. Feb 2004/**SPURS** Jul 2005/(Wolverhampton Wanderers loan Oct 2005)/Hull City Aug 2013.

Debut v Fulham (sub) (PL) (a) 31.1.2006
(Boca Juniors (sub) (Fr) (Suwon) 16.7.2005)

Rejected by Nottingham Forest as a schoolboy, Tom Huddlestone proved how wrong his home town club had been by rushing through the youth ranks of their bitter rivals, Derby County. Capped by England at all youth levels, he made his debut for Derby as a 16-year old and immediately established himself a First Division regular, the outstanding performer as Derby went from a bottom of the table club to the promotion play-offs. Spurs did a deal to take him to White Hart Lane in January 2005, though Huddlestone remained at Pride Park until the summer. By then he had added Under-21 caps to his honours. Michael Carrick was the main creative force in midfield for Spurs and at the peak of his powers when Huddlestone arrived, so to keep his career on an upward path, Huddlestone was loaned to Wolverhampton Wanderers. There, he came under the influence of England's finest midfielder, Glenn Hoddle. Over the next few years and with Carrick departing, Huddlestone developed as a quality midfield general. Big and powerful, his most obvious strengths were his long-range passing and ferocious shooting, bringing obvious comparisons to Hoddle. Huddlestone was rather more defensive minded than Hoddle and was frequently called upon to play as a central defender, comparisons then being drawn with Franz Beckenbauer. Huddlestone was a substitute in the 2008 Worthington Cup final, involved in the incident that led to the equalising penalty. Harry Redknapp, in particular, appreciated Huddlestone's talents and in 2009-10 installed him as first choice in midfield. That quickly led to him winning the first of four full England caps to add to the thirty at Under-21 level he had collected since joining Spurs. Having seemingly established himself at White Hart Lane, Huddlestone was then struck by injury, one after another decimating his career for three years and seemingly having a lasting effect. He had never been the  quickest of players, but appeared to have lost a little of his speed and become reluctant to go in for some physical challenges. Never sure of a starting place under Andre Villas Boas, the wholesale arrival of midfield players in the summer of 2013 saw Huddlestone surplus to requirements. He was allowed to join Hull City.

Appearances:
League: 104 (40) apps. 8 gls.
FA Cup: 11 (3) apps.
FL Cup: 11 (6) apps. 5 gls.
Euro: 26 (8) apps. 2 gls.
Others: 32 (17) apps.
Total: **184 (74) apps. 15 gls.**

HUDSON, E G

Role: Inside-forward 1900-01

CAREER: Rochdale Rovers/Novocastrians/**SPURS**/St Louis.

Debut v Luton Town (SL) (h) 25.4.1901

Hudson's only appearance was in a Southern League fixture with Luton Town in April 1901 when he played in a reserve team fulfilling a first eleven fixture two days before the FA Cup Final replay victory over Sheffield United. A player with the Novocastrians club, he had appeared in a junior trial at the start of the season, but was only called upon to help out the reserves on rare occasions. By October 1903 Hudson was turning out for St Louis, one of the junior clubs in Tottenham.

Appearances:
Southern: 1 app.
Total: **1 app. 0 gls.**

HUDSON, W

Role: Outside-right 1887-88

CAREER: St Lukes by Nov 1883/**SPURS**

Debut v Bowes Park (Fr) (a) 14.1.1888

Another of those players from the 1880s about whom it has proved impossible to unearth much information, Hudson was a reserve player for several years whose only known appearance in the first team was in a friendly with Bowes Park in January 1888.

Appearances:
Others: 1 app.
Total: **1 app. 0 gls.**

HUDSON

Role: Half-back 1888-89

Debut v St Albans (Fr) (a) 29.9.1888

One more of those players from late Victorian times who remain a mystery, Hudson is only known to have played in one friendly early in the 1888-89 season.

> **Appearances:**
> Others: 1 app.
> **Total: 1 app. 0 gls.**

HUDSON

Role: Centre-forward 1898-99

CAREER: Edmonton Thursday/**SPURS** Dec 1898.

Debut v Grays United (TML) (h) 6.2.1899

Another of those local players given a trial, but who progressed no further with Spurs, Hudson made his only appearance in a Thames and Medway League fixture with Grays United in February 1899 when he played in a forward role.

> **Appearances:**
> Others: 1 app.
> **Total: 1 app. 0 gls.**

HUGHES, Edward

Role: Half-back 1899-08
5ft.8ins. 11st.4lbs.
Born: Ruabon, Clwyd, Wales 1876
Died: Tottenham, London, 6th June 1936

CAREER: Formby Aug 1894/Everton Jul 1896/**SPURS** Jul 1899/Clyde cs. 1908.

Debut v Brighton United (SL) (h) 7.10.1899
(Richmond (Fr) (a) 13.9.1899)

Ted Hughes played only eight League games during three years with Everton, yet was good enough to win two caps for Wales, the first against Ireland in March 1899, when he played alongside his future Spurs' captain John L Jones. Either Everton had an abundance of first class half-backs or they were simply unable to recognise a great talent, for after joining Spurs, Hughes became one of the most important and influential figures in the club's rise to League status. His first appearance for Spurs was in the Southern League against Brighton United on 7th October 1899 and his second against Cowes on 16th December 1899, but both those matches were later expunged from the records; in Brighton's case because they resigned from the League in February 1900 and in Cowes' case because they resigned immediately after Spurs' 6-1 victory. Principally a half-back, but a more than competent full-back when necessary, Hughes slowly began to establish himself in the team. His real breakthrough came when skipper James McNaught was injured in a first round FA Cup match with Preston North End in February 1901. Hughes switched to McNaught's central half-back position for the replay and played so well McNaught was never able to regain his place, and it was Hughes who collected a Cup-winner's medal. A brave, tireless worker, Hughes was always anxious to push upfield and help out the forwards. He possessed a terrific shot when the opportunity arose. A masterful header of the ball too, his performances during the FA Cup run earned him a recall to the Wales team, with his first international as a Spurs' player against Scotland in March 1901. He would have won more than the twelve caps he collected as a Spurs player were it not for a row Spurs had with the Welsh FA. Selected for the match against England at Portsmouth in March 1903, the Welsh refused to insure Hughes against injury as Spurs requested so he was withdrawn from the squad. Hughes remained with Spurs until the summer of 1908 when he was released and signed for Clyde. However, he spent barely one month with the Scottish club before returning south to run a public house in Enfield Highway. He stayed there until the end of the First World War, when he emigrated to the USA, settling in Springfield, Massachusetts. Hughes later returned to the Tottenham area and passed away at the local Prince of Wales Hospital.

> **Appearances:**
> Southern: 151 apps. 9 gls.
> FA Cup: 31* apps. 2 gls.
> Others: 130 (1) apps. 9 gls.
> **Total: 312 (1) apps. 20 gls.**
> * Includes 1 abandoned match.

HUGHES, Mark Anthony

Role: Midfield 2003-05
5ft.10ins. 12st.3lbs.
Born: Dungannon, Northern Ireland, 16th September 1983

CAREER: Donaghmore Youth/Dungannon United/Dungannon Swifts/**SPURS** Scholar Jul 2000, pro. Jul 2001/(Northampton Town loan Aug 2004)/Oldham Athletic loan Nov 2004, perm. Feb 2005/Thurrock Jul 2006/(Chesterfield loan Nov 2006)/Stevenage Borough Jan 2007/Chester City trial Jul 2007, perm. Aug 2007/Barnet Feb 2009/Gillingham training Jul 2012/Eastleigh Aug 2012/Chelmsford City Jul 2013/Eastbourne Borough Jul 2016.

Debut v Oxford United (Fr) (a) 20.7.2003

Northern Ireland youngster Mark Hughes, was a tenacious little midfielder who made a few senior appearances for Spurs in friendly matches after working his way through the youth ranks, but had to move on to progress his career. From Spurs, Hughes, who won one Under-23 and eleven Under-21 caps for the province while on Spurs' books, went to Oldham Athletic. Initially on loan with the move quickly made permanent, he performed admirably and regularly for two seasons. Having picked up two full caps on Northern Ireland's summer tour to the USA in 2006, it was a surprise when he was released by Oldham and even more of one that he moved to a non-League club in Thurrock. He soon returned to the League with Chester, but had his best time at Barnet, rising to be captain and scoring the goal that kept them in the League in 2012.

> **Appearances:**
> Others: 5 (4) apps.
> **Total: 5 (4) apps. 0 gls.**

HUGHES, Matthew R

Role: Half-back 1895-96

CAREER: London Welsh/(guest for **SPURS** Feb 1896).

Debut v Royal Ordnance (Fr) (a) 14.2.1896

A regular with London Welsh, who at that time were as well known for their prowess with the round ball as with the oval, Matt Hughes made his one appearance for Spurs as a guest in a friendly with Royal Ordnance in February 1896. He stood in for Spurs' captain Stanley Briggs who had decided to play for Clapton that day.

Appearances:
Others: 1 app.
Total: 1 app. 0 gls.

HUGHES, William Arthur

Role: Goalkeeper 1944-48
6ft.2ins. 12st.13lbs.
Born: *Colwyn Bay, 2nd February 1919*
Died: *11th March 1992*

CAREER: Colwyn Bay United/Larne/Newry Town 1936/Huddersfield Town May 1939/(guest for Arsenal, Darlington, Queens Park Rangers, **SPURS** and West Ham United during World War Two)/**SPURS** Oct 1945 /Blackburn Rovers Oct 1948/Nelson 1950/Rochdale Sep 1950/Crystal Palace Feb 1951/retired Jun 1952.

Debut v Brentford (FAC) (h) 5.1.1946
(Coventry City (Fr) (a) 19.8.1944)

First appearing for Spurs as a war-time guest, Archie Hughes was one of only two guest players who went on to join the permanent staff. A regular from his first game in August 1944, he turned out for several other clubs, but it was at Spurs that his reputation grew. Such was his success that, as football began to return to normality, he was permanently transferred from Huddersfield and played most of the games in the transitional 1945-46 season. However, the return of Ted Ditchburn saw Hughes relegated to the reserves and he became the first of several 'keepers to experience the frustrations of being Ditchburn's understudy. Ditchburn's remarkable consistency and freedom from injury meant Hughes played just two Football League games for Spurs. Clearly far too good for continuous reserve football, he was allowed to move to Blackburn Rovers. Back on the League stage he was able once more to display his considerable talents, being rewarded with five caps for Wales, the first in November 1948 against England. He finally lost his place at Blackburn to John Patterson and joined Nelson. Hughes then wound down a career that would surely have flourished further had it not been so seriously curtailed by the Second World War, with Rochdale and Crystal Palace. He turned down an offer to re-join Colwyn Bay in the summer of 1952, preferring a clean break from football. Hughes later worked as an engineer for the Hotpoint Company and then ran a gentleman's clothing shop in Colwyn Bay until his retirement.

Appearances:
League: 2 apps.
FA Cup: 2 apps.
Others: 55 apps.
Total: 59 apps. 0 gls.

HUGHTON, Christopher William Gerard

Role: Full-back 1978-90
5ft.7ins. 10st.10lbs.
Born: *Forest Gate, London, 11th December 1958*

CAREER: St Anthony's Catholic School/Newnham Schools/Strone United/**SPURS** part-time pro. May 1977, pro. Jun 1979/West Ham United loan Nov 1990, perm Dec 1990/Brentford Mar 1992/retired Apr 1993/ **SPURS** Under-21 coach Jun 1993, reserve team manager Jun 1994, asst. manager Nov 1997, reserve team manager Jul 1994, first team coach Apr 2001, first asst. to head coach Nov 2004-Oct 2007/(Republic of Ireland asst. manager Feb 2003-Oct 2005)/Newcastle United asst. manager Feb 2008, caretaker manager Sep 2008, coach Sep 2008, caretaker manager Feb 2009, manager Oct 2009-Dec 2010/Birmingham City manager Jun 2011/ Norwich City manager Jun 2012-Apr 2014/Brighton & Hove Albion manager Dec 2014.

Debut v Manchester United (FLC) (h) 29.8.1979
(IFK Gothenburg (Fr) (a) 26.9.1978)

Chris Hughton played for Spurs as a part-time professional for two years, preferring to complete his apprenticeship as a lift engineer before signing full-time. The move soon paid dividends with his debut against Manchester United coming only two months later. A first international cap soon followed. Qualifying on his mother's side, he made his first appearance for the Republic of Ireland against the United States in October 1979. A winger in his youth days, Hughton was converted into a fast, overlapping full-back, ever keen to attack and get in a shot on goal. Wiry, well-balanced and quick on the turn, he was perfectly capable of playing in either full-back berth, but eventually settled on the left and was a member of the teams that won the FA Cup in 1981 and 1982, reached the League (Milk) Cup Final in 1982 and won the UEFA Cup in 1984. When Mitchell Thomas followed David Pleat from Luton in May 1986 Hughton appeared to have lost out, and with Danny Thomas and Gary Stevens also in competition for the full-back positions, his appearances were limited, although he was not helped by a series of injuries which particularly affected his ability to launch attacking forays. He was, though, too valuable for Spurs to release and, even when not in the team, his mere presence meant those in possession could never afford to become complacent. He continued to give his best whenever called upon, and when Danny Thomas was cruelly injured in March 1987 Hughton had only Stevens to compete with for the right-back spot in the 1987 FA Cup Final team, and got the nod. Whilst unable to secure a regular place in Spurs' line-up, he continued to represent the Republic and was a member of their highly successful team in the 1988 European Championships and the squad for the 1990 World Cup. His great service to Tottenham was rewarded with a free transfer in June 1990. Although several clubs were interested in acquiring his services, no permanent move was immediately forthcoming. In

November 1990, having raised his number of international caps to 50 the previous month, he was loaned to West Ham to cover for long term injury victim Julian Dicks and made the move permanent the following month. Hughton helped West Ham win promotion from the Second Division in 1990-91 and collected two more caps, but with the return of Dicks moved to Brentford where his vast experience helped them lift the Third Division title in 1992. A knee injury forced his retirement, but he returned to Spurs to join the coaching staff under Ossie Ardiles, rising to the position of assistant manager to Christian Gross. The dismissal of Gross and the arrival of George Graham might have been expected to herald Hughton's departure from White Hart Lane, but even when Stewart Houston arrived to take the assistant manager's post, Graham realised Hughton's commitment to Spurs could not be lost, and he remained on the coaching staff at first team level. Assistant to Martin Jol, Hughton was dismissed along with Jol in October 2007. In February 2008 he was appointed to Kevin Keegan's coaching staff at Newcastle, embarking on remarkable near three years with the Geordie club. Caretaker manager when Keegan left, coach under Joe Kinnear, caretaker and joint caretaker when Kinnear was taken ill and coach under Alan Shearer, Hughton was back as caretaker manager when the 2009-10 season got under way. With the relegated club up for sale, he did such a remarkable job as the season got underway that in October 2009 he was given the manager's job on a permanent basis. He finished the season by leading Newcastle back to the Premier League. Despite Newcastle lying in mid-table he was unbelievably sacked in December 2010 as new owner, Mike Ashley, brought in his own people. Hughton was soon back in a managerial seat, taking over at Birmingham City and leading them to the Championship promotion play-off before moving on to Norwich City. Unable to steer Norwich from the relegation zone, Hughton was sacked, but within six months was back as a manager, taking over at Brighton and leading them into the Premier League. Hughton's elder brother, Henry, was also a professional footballer, playing as a defender with Orient, Crystal Palace and Brentford, while his eldest son, Leon, was on Spurs' books as an associated schoolboy in 1992-93. His youngest son, Cian, joined the professional staff at Spurs in 2007, but did not make the grade.

Appearances:
League: 293 (4) apps. 12 gls.
FA Cup: 34 (2) apps. 1 gl.
FL Cup: 33 (2) apps. 2 gls.
Euro: 29 (1) apps. 4 gls.
Others: 96 (5) apps. 3 gls.
Total: 485 (14) apps. 22 gls.

HUGHTON, Cian James

Role: Full-back 2007-09
5ft.8ins. 10st.9lbs.
Born: Enfield, Middlesex, 25th January 1989

CAREER: SPURS Scholar Jul 2005, pro. Jul 2007/released May 2009/Charlton Athletic trial May 2009/Lincoln City trial and perm Jul 2009-May 2011/Vancouver Whitecaps (Canada) trial Jun 2011/Bristol Rovers trial Aug 2011/Milton Keynes Dons trial Aug 2011/Dundalk trial Aug 2011/Aberdeen trial Aug 2011/Birmingham City training Aug 2011/Malmö (Sweden) trial Feb 2012/Birmingham City Feb-Jul 2012/Norwich City scout.

Debut v Stevenage Borough (sub) (Fr) (a) 7.7.2008

A full-back like his father, Chris, Cian Hughton made his one appearance for Spurs at first team level as a substitute in a pre-season friendly at Stevenage Borough in July 2008. Released at the end of his contract, Hughton joined Lincoln City and played regularly for two years until released following City's relegation from the Football League. During his time with Lincoln he won two caps Under-21 caps for the Republic of Ireland to add to those he had collected at Under-18 and Under-19 level. Unable to secure a contract with another club, he trained with his father's Birmingham City and was eventually given a short term contract, but did not play for Birmingham before it expired.

Appearances:
Others: (1) app.
Total: (1) app. 0 gls.

HUMBER, C

Role: Centre-forward 1889-90

CAREER: Robin Hood/SPURS Jan 1890

Debut v Old St Stephens (MSC) (a) 18.1.1890 (scored twice)

A member of the Robin Hood club, Humber appears to have assisted Spurs for only one season. He is recorded as having played in three matches in 1889-90 although many other games were played that season for which the team line-ups have not been traced. His first known appearance was in January 1890 when he scored twice against Old St Stephens in the Middlesex Senior Cup and his two other appearances were two months later in friendly matches.

Appearances:
Others: 3 apps. 2 gls.
Total: 3 apps. 2 gls.

HUMPHREYS, Percy

Role: Centre or inside-forward 1909-12
5ft.8ins. 12st.6lbs.
Born: Cambridge, 3rd December 1880
Died: Stepney, London, 13th April 1959

CAREER: Cambridge St Marys/Cambridgeshire/Queens Park Rangers May 1900/Notts County May 1901/Leicester Fosse Jun 1907/Chelsea Feb 1908/SPURS Dec 1909/Leicester Fosse Oct 1911/Hartlepools United player-manager May 1912/FC Basel (Switzerland) player-coach 1913/Norwich City Nov 1914/Alessandria (Italy) manager 1920/FC Basel (Switzerland) coach 1922-23.

Debut v Bolton Wanderers (FL) (h) 11.12.1909

Percy Humphreys established himself as an exciting young marksman with Queens Park Rangers, finishing his one season with them as top scorer and clearly far too good a player for a club that could only finish eighth in the Southern League. He joined Notts County where he developed into a regular goal-scorer playing for the Football League against the Scottish League in March 1903 and for England against Scotland in April 1903, partnering Spurs' Vivian J Woodward.

After six years in Nottingham he found himself out of favour and moved to promotion chasing Midlands neighbours Leicester Fosse where he was leading scorer with 19 goals in 26 games at the time of his £350 transfer to Chelsea. By December 1909 he had lost his place at Stamford Bridge to Woodward, who had been persuaded out of retirement. He moved to Spurs the same month. Tottenham were struggling during their first season in Division One and desperately needed Humphreys' impressive goal-scoring talents. They proved absolutely crucial, not only for Spurs, but also for Chelsea. In the final match of the season Spurs faced Chelsea at White Hart Lane; if Bristol City won their last game, the losers would be relegated. Bristol did win and it was Humphreys' goal that gave Spurs a 2-1 victory and sent Chelsea down. From then on though, Humphreys was in and out of the first team until returning to Leicester, where he was unable to spark a modest side. He moved to Hartlepools United as player-manager in the 1913 close season and later went to coach for three years in Switzerland, returning in November 1914 to join Norwich City when the war broke out. Humphreys committed suicide in 1959 when he jumped from the roof of a building.

Appearances:
League: 45 apps. 23 gls.
FA Cup: 5 apps. 5 gls.
Others: 4 apps.
Total: 54 apps. 28 gls.

HUNT, Douglas Albert

Role: Centre-forward 1934-37 and 1939-43
5ft.10ins. 11st.8lbs.
Born: Shipton Bellinger, nr Andover, 19th May 1914
Died: Yeovil, Somerset 1989

CAREER: Winchester City/Southampton am. Jan 1932/**SPURS** am. 1932/Northfleet United 1932/**SPURS** pro. Mar 1934/Barnsley Mar 1937/Sheffield Wednesday Mar 1938/(guest for Aldershot, Brentford, Fulham, **SPURS** and West Ham United during World War Two)/Clapton Orient player-coach Apr 1946, asst. manager Aug 1947/Gloucester City player-coach Jun 1948, player-manager Nov 1948-Sep 1951/Tonbridge manager Jan 1954/Yeovil Town trainer-coach-physio 1958-1986.

Debut v Grimsby Town (FL) (a) 25.12.1934

Doug Hunt followed Ted Drake as leader of Winchester City's attack before being spotted by Spurs and nurtured at their Northfleet nursery. He moved up to the professional staff at White Hart Lane and made his League debut on Christmas Day 1934, replacing his namesake George. However, he had few chances in the first team due to the irrepressible goal-scoring form of George Hunt and Johnny Morrison and was little more than a first reserve behind the pair of them. With scant prospects of a regular first team place, he was transferred to Barnsley and then moved on to Sheffield Wednesday, but returned to help out Spurs as a guest during the Second World War. Indeed, he guested for several clubs during the War and was a member of the Brentford team that won the London War Cup in 1942. After the War he was transferred to Leyton Orient where he finished his playing career and moved into management later serving Gloucester

City, Yeovil and Tonbridge. Hunt led Tonbridge to the Southern League Cup Final in both 1955 and 1957. In April 1936 with Arthur Rowe injured, Hunt was called up to play at centre-half against Leicester City. He performed quite well against City centre-forward Fred Sharman in a 1-1 draw. The following week he was back in his usual centre-forward role with the reserves. To his surprise, marking him was Sharman who had been dropped from Leicester's first team and switched to centre-half in their reserves. Hunt had the better of the game scoring both Spurs' goals!

Appearances:
League: 17 apps. 6 gls.
FA Cup: 2 apps.
Others: 5 apps. 7 gls.
Total: 24 apps. 13 gls.

HUNT, George Samuel

Role: Centre-forward 1930-37
5ft.8ins. 10st.13lbs.
Born: Barnsley, Yorkshire, 22nd February 1910
Died: Bolton, Lancashire, 19th September 1996

CAREER: Regent Street Congregationals/Barnsley (trial)/Sheffield United (trial)/Burslem Port Vale (trial)/Chesterfield Sep 1929/**SPURS** Jun 1930/Arsenal Oct 1937/Bolton Wanderers Mar 1938/(guest for Liverpool, Luton Town and Rochdale during World War Two)/Sheffield Wednesday Nov 1946/retired May 1948/Bolton Wanderers coach May 1948/retired Sep 1968.

Debut v Stoke City (FL) (a) 20.9.1930

Known as the "Chesterfield Tough", George Hunt had the chance to follow his grandfather of the same name onto the books of his home town club, Barnsley, but turned their offer down as he did not think the terms offered good enough. Sheffield United and Burslem Port Vale both had the chance to sign him, but rejected him after trials. All three clubs must have cringed every time Hunt scored as he went on to net 151 goals in only 205 senior matches. It was Chesterfield who realised Hunt had the raw talent worth investing in. Once signed, he quickly began to score and was soon attracting the attention of bigger clubs. Arsenal manager Herbert Chapman was keen, but decided to let Hunt develop a little more

before seeking to take him to Highbury. Chapman's decision let in Spurs and Hunt, probably the best capture of Percy Smith's reign as manager, was signed in June 1930. He made a League debut for Spurs in September, but did not make the League team again until March 1931 when he was given the unenviable task of replacing the injured goal-scorer supreme, Ted Harper, in the crucial final weeks of the season. He did a remarkable job, netting five goals in eight games, but was unable to completely compensate for Harper's absence as Spurs went six games without a win. The result was that they just missed out on promotion to West Bromwich Albion, who finished three points ahead. However, Hunt had shown enough. Smith persevered with him and his loyalty was rewarded as the skilful centre-forward began to score with amazing regularity. He led the team to promotion in 1933, picking up three England caps on the way, the first against Italy in March that year. A muscular, tenacious, never-say-die player with tremendous speed off the mark and an unquenchable thirst for goals, Hunt always worked diligently throughout the ninety minutes, and his exciting solo dashes at the centre of opposing defences thrilled the Spurs crowds. Such ability meant he was the recipient of some punishing tackles and injuries in 1934-35 limited his effectiveness as the club was relegated, while the following season he found his position under challenge from Johnny Morrison. Perhaps not quite as quick as he had been, Hunt was still regarded as an extremely valuable asset and the announcement of his move to Arsenal, where he was to replace Ted Drake, was met with enormous surprise. He only stayed at Arsenal for six months, scoring three goals in 18 appearances as they took the League title, before joining Bolton Wanderers. A regular for Bolton during the war he helped them win the League North Cup in 1945. Hunt later finished his playing career at Sheffield Wednesday and then returned to Bolton where he spent twenty years on the coaching staff before running the car-wash department of a Bolton garage.

Appearances:
League: 185 apps. 125 gls.
FA Cup: 13 apps. 13 gls.
Others: 7 apps. 10 gls.
Total: 205 apps. 148 gls.

HUNT, Kenneth Reginald Gunnery

Role: Half-back 1916-17
6ft. 12st. 8lbs.
Born: Oxford, 24th February 1884
Died: Heathfield, Sussex, 28th April 1949

CAREER: Wolverhampton Boys Grammar School/Trent College 1902/Queens College, Oxford 1904/Oxford University/Corinthians/Oxford City/Wolverhampton Wanderers 1907/Leyton/Crystal Palace May 1913/(guest for **SPURS** during World War One)/Eccleshall Comrades and Stafford Rangers 1918-19 and 1920-21/Southern Amateur League president chairman 1928-1939/Pegasus president May 1948.

Debut v Portsmouth (LFC) (h) 16.12.1916 (Abandoned after 35 minutes-fog)

The Reverend Kenneth Hunt was one of the most famous amateur internationals prior to the First World War, an England regular and member of the Great Britain team that won the Olympic Gold medal in 1908. He first came to prominence with Trent College, Oxford University and the Corinthians before making his Football League debut for Wolverhampton Wanderers in March 1907. Little more than twelve months later, he scored one of their goals in the 1908 FA Cup Final with Newcastle United. He continued to assist Wolves until the 1912-13 season. As he took up a scholastic appointment in Highgate, moving south in August 1908, he was not always available to play for Wolves and accordingly turned out regularly in the Southern League for Leyton. Indeed, it was Leyton who were credited as being his club when he made two appearances for the full England team against Wales and Scotland in March and April 1911. He continued to play for Leyton until their relegation from the Southern League First Division at the end of the 1912-13 season when he switched to Crystal Palace, although he also turned out for Oxford City and played for them in the 1913 FA Amateur Cup Final. Still with Crystal Palace after the First World War, his only appearance for Spurs was in December 1916 in a London Football Combination match against Portsmouth, an appearance that lasted a total of 35 minutes. Twenty minutes were played before fog caused play to be suspended for another 20 minutes. Fifteen minutes were then played before the referee abandoned the game. Hunt's appearance for Spurs led to Crystal Palace complaining to the Football Association that Spurs should not have played Hunt without their consent. Although he had not played for Crystal Palace for two years, he was still registered with them. Spurs' explanation that they were not aware of this was accepted. As an amateur Hunt was free to play for any club he wished and this has meant there is little consistency in the clubs credited with his services when he won representative honours. Hunt continued playing after the War and at 36 was still good enough to help the GB team at the 1920 Olympic Games in Antwerp.

Appearances:
Others: 1* app.
Total: 1 app. 0 gls.
* Includes 1 abandoned match.

HUNTER, Alexander Campbell

Role: Goalkeeper 1920-22
5ft.8ins. 11st.10lbs.
Born: Renfrew, Scotland, 27th September 1895

CAREER: Renfrew Juniors/Queen's Park Aug 1918/**SPURS** pro. May 1920/Wigan Borough May 1922/transfer listed Dec 1923/Armadale Aug 1924/Fall River (USA)/New Bedford Whalers (USA).

Debut v West Bromwich Albion (FL) (h) 26.2.1921

Alex Hunter was signed as a professional having made his name with the leading Scottish amateur club Queen's Park. A daring 'keeper, perhaps rather too adventurous in leaving his line, he still proved a sound enough piece of business for a player who did not cost a fee. Signed as reserve to regular choice Bill Jacques, Hunter was called in for a League debut in February 1921 when Jacques was injured. He performed so impressively that even when Jacques was fit, Hunter retained his place. He also proved a player for the big occasion, conceding only one goal in three important ties as he picked up an FA Cup winners' medal just two months later. Such a dramatic rise to fame was,  however, followed by an almost equally swift fall, for after only twelve games of the following season, Jacques won his place back. At the end of the season, several clubs were keen to sign Hunter. He chose to join Wigan Borough where he started as first choice. Transfer listed in December 1923, he was released at the end of the season and returned to Scotland before emigrating to the USA.

Appearances:
League: 23 apps.
FA Cup: 3 apps.
Others: 8 apps.
Total: 34 apps. 0 gls.

HUNTER, Peter J

Role: Centre-forward 1894-97

CAREER: London Caledonians/**SPURS** cs. 1894/London Caledonians cs. 1896/London Welsh.

Debut v West Herts (FAC) (h) 13.10.1894 (scored once)
(Uxbridge (Fr) (a) 15.9.1894)

An incredibly prolific goal-scorer, Peter Hunter first played for Spurs in September 1894. He was already a familiar figure in London football, playing for London Caledonians and representing London and Middlesex. His debut, in what would today be regarded as a senior competition, came in the club's first FA Cup tie when he claimed the honour of scoring Spurs' opening goal of the competition. He was almost ever-present during the two most important seasons in Spurs' short history, 1894-96, first helping them become a club popular enough to take the plunge into professionalism, and then helping prove the wisdom of that decision. Ironically, such commitment to the cause probably helped end his Spurs' career, for there was no place for him when Willie Newbigging was signed in the summer of 1896. Hunter returned to London Caledonians, although he also played for London Welsh, and his three further appearances for Spurs in 1896-97 were simply to help out when Newbigging's absence left the club in difficulty.

Appearances:
FA Cup: 11 apps. 6 gls.
Others: 64 apps. 45 gls.
Total: 75 apps. 51 gls.

HURRY, J

Role: Outside-left 1891-95

Debut v St Albans (Fr) (a) 6.2.1892

Hurry played most of his matches for Spurs in the reserve side and is known to have made only two first team appearances. His first recorded senior appearance was in a friendly match with St Albans in February 1892 and he played again the following week. Hurry later went on to serve on the committee that ran Spurs, an office he held until the club became a limited company in 1898.

Appearances:
Others: 2 apps.
Total: 2 apps. 0 gls.

HUTCHINSON, George Henry

Role: Outside-right 1953-54
5ft.7ins. 10st.8lbs.
Born: Allerton Bywater, nr Castleford, Yorkshire, 31st October 1929
Died: Sheffield, South Yorkshire, 30th July 1996

CAREER: Huddersfield Town am. May 1945, pro. Jan 1947/Sheffield United Mar 1948/**SPURS** Jun 1953/Guildford City Jul 1954/Leeds United Aug 1955/Halifax Town Jul 1956/Bradford City Jul 1958/Skegness Town/Worksop Town.

Debut v Manchester United (FL) (h) 26.9.1953

George Hutchinson was signed from Sheffield United as experienced cover for first choice outside-right Sonny Walters. He started his career with Huddersfield Town, but played only one senior game before moving to Bramall Lane where he fared little better, making just over 50 appearances in five years. A fast, nimble winger he managed only five League outings for Spurs as replacement for Walters, was released in May 1954 and joined Guildford. Hutchinson spent one season in Surrey and another with Leeds United before finishing his senior career at Bradford City. He later played for Skegness Town and Worksop Town.

Appearances:
League: 5 apps. 1 gl.
Others: 2 apps. 1 gl.
Total: 7 apps. 2 gls.

HUTTTON, Alan

Role: Full-back 2007-12
6ft.1ins. 13st.2lbs.
Born: Penilee, Glasgow, 30th November 1984

CAREER: Troon Thistle/Rangers pro. 2001/**SPURS** Jan 2008/(Sunderland loan Jan 2010)/Aston Villa Aug 2011/(Nottingham Forest loan Nov 2012)/(RCD Mallorca (Spain) loan Jan 2013)/(Bolton Wanderers loan Feb 2014).

Debut v Manchester United (PL) (h) 2.2.2008

A £9 million purchase from Rangers, Alan Hutton had established himself as the best left-back in Scotland, a regular for Rangers with six full international caps to his credit. Pacy and attack-minded, Hutton was at his best going forward, but he could be strong and combative when defence was needed. In only his third appearance for Spurs he picked up the second medal of his senior career, a Worthington Cup winners medal, to add to the Scottish Premier League champions medal he had collected in 2004-05. That was to be very much the high point of his Spurs' career. While he played in most of the matches following the Wembley success, by the end of the season he was on the injury list. That was where he spent much of his time, one persistent injury after another all but ruining his career. Loaned to Sunderland, he played regularly, but once back at White Hart Lane, injury struck again. Only for a spell in the 2010-11 season did he

regain full fitness, but by then Gareth Bale and Benoit Assou-Ekotto were dominating the left flank and Hutton had to be content playing on the right. With Kyle Walker establishing himself as the long-term right-back, Hutton was surplus to requirements and allowed to join Aston Villa, renewing acquaintance with one of his former Rangers' managers, Alex McLeish. Hutton had added another fourteen full internationals to his total while a Spurs player. He did reasonably well in his first season at Villa but at the start of the following campaign new manager, Paul Lambert, made it clear Hutton had no future at Villa Park. The only football he played for the next two years was while on loan to RCD Mallorca and Bolton Wanderers and for Scotland. Hutton forced himself back into Villa's plans as the famous old club began to struggle when owner, Randy Lerner, began to tighten the purse strings. When Lambert departed, Hutton was the only quality full-back left and he held down a regular position, one of the few players to perform to anywhere near the standard expected as Villa eventually plunged out of the Premier League.

Appearances:
League: 39 (12) apps. 2 gls.
FA Cup: 3 apps.
FL Cup: 6 apps.
Euro: 6 apps.
Others: 11 (3) apps.
Total: 65 (15) apps. 2 gls.

HYDE, Leonard Joseph

Role: Winger 1899-02
5ft.8ins. 11st.8lbs.
Born: Birmingham, 6th May 1876
Died: Winson Green, Birmingham, 30th December 1932

CAREER: Summersfield Eclipse 1889/Harborne 1894/Kidderminster Harriers 1896/Grimsby Town trial Apr 1897, pro Jun 1897/Bristol St Georges Jan 1898/Wellingborough May 1898/**SPURS** May 1899/ Wellingborough Apr 1902/Brighton and Hove Albion Jul 1903/Doncaster Rovers Sep 1904-May 1905.

Debut v Reading (SDC) (a) 9.10.1899
(Clapton (Fr) (a) 27.9.1899 (scored twice))

Leon Hyde began his football career as a 13-year old with the local club, Summersfield Eclipse, joined Harborne in the Birmingham Junior League and then moved to Kidderminster Harriers. Towards the end of his first season with Kidderminster he was offered a trial by Grimsby Town and signed in the 1897 close season. Released in January 1898, Hyde spent the rest of that season with Bristol St Georges, then played for Wellingborough. It was as a result of his performances there that Spurs signed him. A winger who could play on either flank, he was required as cover for the first choice pair, Tom Smith and John Kirwan, but their consistency and freedom from injury meant Hyde made few appearances in his three years at the club. He returned to Wellingborough in April 1902 and had one more year there, later playing for Brighton and Doncaster Rovers.

Appearances:
Southern: 18 apps. 5 gls.
Others: 30 apps. 4 gls.
Total: 48 apps. 9 gls.

IFIL, Philip Nathan

Role: Full-back 2004-08
5ft.10ins. 12st.5lbs.
Born: Park Royal, London, 18th November 1986

CAREER: Springfield/ **SPURS** Academy Scholar Jul 2003, pro. Nov 2004/ (Millwall loan Sep 2005 and Jan 2006)/(Southampton loan Sep 2007)/Colchester United Jan 2008/(Milton Keynes Dons trial Jul 2009)/Crystal Palace trial Aug 2010/ Watford trial Aug 2010/ Dagenham & Redbridge Sep 2010-May 2011/Kettering Town trial and perm Jul 2011 /Wrexham trial Jan 2013/ Evergreen Sep 2014.

Debut v Liverpool (PL) (h) 14.8.2004
(Falkenbergs (sub) (Fr) (a) 14.7.2004)

In much the same way as it was obvious from their time as youth team players that Sol Campbell and Ledley King were destined for the very top, so it was that Phil Ifil stood out as a youngster that had everything needed for a top career in front of him. Called up to the first team as a 17-year old, Ifil had skill, pace and, for a player of such tender years, not a little confidence. An England player at all levels from Under-16 through to Under-20, perhaps his initial performances raised expectations too high. He failed to progress as expected and after that first season was to play only one more competitive game before being allowed to join Colchester United. Sadly, it was all downhill for Ifil from there. After short spells with Dagenham & Redbridge and Kettering Town, Ifil was unable to get a new club. Eventually, he had to content himself with playing for fun, joining Evergreen of the Watford Sunday League. Ifil's brother, Jerel, was a defender who played for Watford, Swindon Town and Aberdeen amongst others.

Appearances:
League: 3 apps.
FL Cup: 1 (1) apps.
Others: 5 (9) apps.
Total: 9 (10) apps. 0 gls.

ILEY, James

Role: Half-back 1957-59
5ft.11ins. 10st.13lbs.
Born: Kirkby, Yorkshire, 15th December 1935

CAREER: East Yorkshire Schools/Yorkshire Schools/Moorthorpe St Joseph's Boys Club/Yorkshire Boys Clubs/National Association of Boys

Clubs/Pontefract/Sheffield United junior Mar 1951, pro. Jun 1953/**SPURS** Aug 1957/Nottingham Forest Jul 1959/Newcastle United Sep 1962/Peterborough United player-manager Jan 1969-Sep 1972/Cambridge United scout Oct 1972-Mar 73/Barnsley manager Apr 1973-Apr 1978/Blackburn Rovers manager Apr 1978-Oct 1978/Bury manager Jul 1980-Feb 1984/Exeter City manager Jun 1984-Apr 1985/Charlton Athletic coach/Luton Town scout.

Debut v Newcastle United (FL) (a) 31.8.1957

When he first joined Sheffield United, Jim Iley combined playing part-time with a job at Frickley Colliery, before signing as a full professional in June 1953. During his four years at Bramall Lane he played over 100 senior games for the Blades and gained his first senior representative honour for the Football League against the Irish League in April 1956. Signed for £16,000 to replace Tony Marchi who had departed to Italy, Iley at first found it difficult to settle with Spurs, but matters were hardly helped by the fact he continued to live in Sheffield and trained with his former club. After only twelve appearances he was languishing in the reserves. Towards the end of his first season he recovered some form, got back in the first team and collected an England Under-23 cap against Wales in April 1958. A skilful ball player whose game was highlighted by some precision passing, he started the 1958-59 season as first choice left-half and played for the Football League against the Scottish League in October 1958. However, the arrival of Dave Mackay in March 1959 signalled Iley's departure and in July Spurs recouped their outlay when he moved to Nottingham Forest for £16,000. He spent just over three years with Forest before joining Newcastle. It was there that he enjoyed the best years of his career; a solid regular for over six years. In January 1969, he took on the player-manager's position at Peterborough and went on to manage Barnsley, Blackburn Rovers, Bury and Exeter City before working on the coaching staff at Charlton.

Appearances:
League: 53 apps. 1 gl.
FA Cup: 4 apps.
Others: 9 apps.
Total: 66 apps. 1 gl.

ILLINGWORTH, John William

Role: Full-back 1929-35
5ft.8ins. 10st.3lbs.
Born: Castleford, Yorkshire, 3rd September 1904
Died: Weymouth, Dorset, 4th September 1964

CAREER: Castleford Town am., pro Aug 1926/**SPURS** Mar 1927/Northfleet United Mar 1927/**SPURS** May 1929/Northfleet United/**SPURS** Nov 1932/Swansea Town May 1935/Barry Town May 1936.

Debut v Charlton Athletic (FL) (a) 14.12.1929
(Sliema Wanderers (sub) (Fr) (a) 11.5.1929)

John Illingworth joined Spurs' Northfleet nursery from Castleford Town and spent two years down in Kent before signing professional for Spurs. He immediately accompanied the first team on a six-match tour of Malta where he made his debut as a substitute. His League bow followed in December 1929 and he retained his place for the next ten matches before returning to the reserves. Released at the end of 1930-31 he was not on the club's books in 1931-32, but was back in the reserves the following season. However, he was to make only one further senior appearance, in April 1935, before being released. He then joined Swansea Town, where he spent one season followed by a similar spell with Barry Town.

Appearances:
League: 10 apps.
FA Cup: 2 apps.
Others: 7 (1) apps.
Total: 19 (1) apps. 0 gls.

INNES, A

Role: Inside-forward 1918-19

Debut v Arsenal (Fr) (a) 24.5.1919

Innes made his only appearance for Spurs when a weak Spurs' team containing several juniors, reserves and trialists drew 0-0 in a friendly at Arsenal.

Appearances:
Others: 1 app.
Total: 1 app. gls.

IRELAND, Jeffrey John Charles

Role: Outside-right 1957-59
5ft.8ins.
Born: Paddington, London, 1st December 1935
Died: Elham, Kent, 25th December 2010

CAREER: St Pancras Schools/Finchley/**SPURS** am. Oct 1957, pro. Nov 1957/Shrewsbury Town Jun 1959/Folkestone Town Aug 1960/Gravesend & Northfleet Jun 1968-1970/New Romney manager.

Debut v Nottingham Forest (FL) (a) 15.2.1958
(Vfb Stuttgart (Fr) (h) 11.11.1957)

As an amateur with Finchley, Jeff Ireland represented the London FA before joining Spurs. He spent most of his time at White Hart Lane as a reserve and played only three League games. His debut was in February 1958, but he did not play again until October 1958, appearing in the two games either side of Spurs 10-4 victory over Everton on the day Bill Nicholson was appointed Spurs' manager. He left at the end of the season and joined Shrewsbury where he played for one season before moving into non-League circles. He helped Folkestone to the Southern League First Division title in 1963-64.

Appearances:
League: 3 apps.
Others: 2 (1) apps.
Total: 5 apps. 1 gl.

IVERSEN, Steffen

Role: Striker 1996-2003
6ft.1ins. 11st.10lbs.
Born: Oslo, Norway, 10th November 1976

CAREER: SK Nationalkameratene (Norway) Feb 1984/Astor (Norway) 1989/Norway Youth/Rosenborg (Norway) pro. 1993/**SPURS** Dec 1996/Wolverhampton Wanderers Jul 2003/Vålerenga (Norway) Jul 2004/Portsmouth training Jan 2006/Rosenborg (Norway) Feb 2006/Crystal Palace Jan 2011-Jan 2012/Rosenborg (Norway) Feb-Nov 2012/retired Dec 2012/SK Herd (Norway) Sep 2013/Haugar (Norway) player-coach Dec 2015.

Debut v Coventry City (BPL) (a) 7.12.1996

Following in the footsteps of a father rated as one of his country's finest ever goal-scorers, was never going to be easy for Steffen Iversen, but were it not for a catalogue of injury problems, he would surely have gone on to be rated as highly as his father. For 17 years Odd Iversen was an outstanding striker for Rosenborg, Racing Mechelen, Vålerenga and Norway, setting numerous records. It was while he was playing for Vålerenga in Oslo that his son arrived, but by the time the youngster started to show his footballing abilities, the family had returned to Trondheim. Thus it was that after playing for a couple of junior clubs, Steffen Iversen joined Rosenborg. He was an immediate success, helping them win the Tippeligaen in 1995 and 1996 and attracting scouts from all over Europe. A regular for Norway's Under-21s, from the minute he signed for Spurs in a £2.6 million deal his potential was obvious as he settled in alongside Teddy Sheringham, until injury brought his first season to an early end. With the departure of Sheringham and the arrival of Les Ferdinand, Spurs replaced one master of centre-forward play with another. Iversen could not have had better tutors, but injuries continually disrupted his education, not only hampering him physically, but also damaging his confidence. They meant he did not make his first senior appearance for Norway until October 1998 when he played against Albania. After another injury absence he returned to help Spurs win the Worthington Cup in 1999, but it was only in 1999-2000 that he really hit peak form. Leading the line in Ferdinand's injury-induced absence, Iversen showed all the attributes then demanded of a central striker. Well-built with strength and power, he was good in the air, pacy and adept at holding up the ball. He did not, perhaps, score as many goals as he should have, but that was in part due to his unselfishness. One of his great strengths was his stamina. It saw him working as hard at the end of a game as the start, as evidenced by his lung-bursting thrust down the wing to set up Allan Nielsen's winning goal in the 1999 Worthington Cup final. Just when Iversen should have been approaching his peak years he was to spend most of his time on the treatment table. Rarely was he able to play and on the odd occasions he did, he was clearly not right, reluctant to challenge, lacking pace and confidence, often clearly not fit. After three years of struggle and with Spurs deciding that he was not going to get back to his best, Iversen was released and signed for Wolverhampton Wanderers. After an unsuccessful season at Molineux Iversen returned to Norway with Vålerenga and helped them win the Tippeligaen in 2005 before moving back to Rosenborg. With his experience and a return to some of the form that had first attracted Spurs to him, Iversen led Rosenborg to further Tippeligaen titles in 2006, 2009 and 2010 before having a final twelve month stint in England with Crystal Palace. He then returned to Rosenborg for a third time, retiring in November 2012. Iversen scored 21 goals in 79 full internationals for Norway, 39 of the appearances and eight of the goals as a Spurs' player.

Appearances:
League: 112 (31) apps. 36 gls.
FA Cup: 10 (5) apps. 4 gls.
FL Cup: 11 (4) apps. 6 gls.
Euro: 4 apps. 1 gl.
Others: 21 (11) apps. 26 gls.
Total: 158 (51) apps. 73 gls.

J

JACK, Archibald

Role: Forward 1917-19
Born: Grangemouth, Stirlingshire, 1882

CAREER: Forth Rangers/Falkirk Aug 1913/Armadale Aug 1915/Leith Athletic Oct 1915/(guest for **Spurs** during World War One)/South Shields 1919.

Debut v Brentford (LFC) (h) 2.3.1918

A player with Falkirk prior to the First World War, Archibald Jack was serving with the Royal Field Artillery when he appeared for Spurs in the London Football Combination. He made his first appearance in March 1918 and finished the season with four goals in six games. Two of those goals were against Clapton Orient on 1st April 1918 after which he was arrested for going "Absent Without Leave". His Commanding Officer usually let him off duties so he could play football, but all leave had been cancelled over that weekend, a fact Jack well knew. Spurs however did not, and when he turned up they were just grateful he was there. At least his arrest was delayed until the match was over. The following season, having presumably served his time in the "Glasshouse", Jack turned out for Spurs on 14 occasions netting three goals.

Appearances:
Others: 20 apps. 7 gls.
Total: **20 apps. 7 gls.**

JACKSON, Harold

Role: Forward 1942-43
Born: Blackburn, Lancashire, 30th December 1918
Died: 1984

CAREER: Darwen/Burnley/(guest for Accrington Stanley, Halifax Town, Notts County, Southend United, **SPURS** and Watford during World War Two)/Manchester City Jun 1946/Preston North End Dec 1947/Blackburn Rovers Dec 1948/Chester City Jul 1949/Hyde United/Ashton United/Nelson.

Debut v Portsmouth (FLS) (a) 24.10.1942

A guest player from Burnley, Harry Jackson made two appearances for Spurs in the Football League South during the 1942-43 season, the first at centre-forward and the second at inside-left. After the war he joined Manchester City, but made only nine senior appearances before moving to Preston North End. He later played for Blackburn Rovers and Chester City.

Appearances:
Others: 2 apps.
Total: **2 apps. 0 gls.**

JACKSON, Herbert E

Role: Half-back 1893-94
Born: Grantham, 1870.
Died: Southfields, London, Jul 1906

CAREER: Old Sherbrookians/Fulham Sep 1893/(guest for **SPURS** Mar 1894)/retired 1896, Fulham Secretary 1903.

Debut v 2nd Batt. Scots Guards (Fr) (h) 23.3.1894

One of the pioneers of Fulham, Jackson's only appearance for Spurs was in March 1894 when he played in a friendly with the 2nd Battalion of the Scots Guards. On retiring from playing in 1896 Jackson worked on Fulham's administrative staff eventually taking on the role of club secretary. He committed suicide at Southfields railway station in July 1906 having been diagnosed as having brain cancer. Fulham played a Rest of the Southern League XI in September of that year to raise money funds for his wife and family.

Appearances:
Others: 1 app.
Total: **1 app. 0 gls.**

JACKSON, John

Role: Goalkeeper 1944-45
5ft.9ins. 10st 7lbs
Born: Glasgow, 29th November 1906
Died: Nova Scotia, Canada, 12th June 1965

CAREER: Kirkintilloch Rob Roy/Partick Thistle Jun 1926/Chelsea Jun 1933/Guildford City/(guest for Aldershot, Brentford, Portsmouth, Queens Park Rangers and **SPURS** during World War Two)/retired.

Debut v Charlton Athletic (FLS) (h) 30.9.1944

Former Scottish international Jakey Jackson, was nearing the end of his career when he made two guest appearances for Spurs in the Football League South competition of 1944-45. He had first come to prominence with Partick Thistle, where he went seven seasons without missing a game, before a move to Chelsea. Although short for a 'keeper at only 5ft 9ins, he was regarded as a brilliant custodian, making up for his lack of inches with masterly anticipation and positioning. In his time with Partick Thistle he played for the Scottish League four times and won four Scottish caps, the first against Austria in May 1931 when five goals were put past him. After his move to London, he added another four to his total. By the time of his appearances for Spurs he had lost the position of first choice 'keeper at Stamford Bridge to England international Vic Woodley, but was a regular guest for other clubs, and helped Brentford win the London War Cup in 1942, He retired before peace returned and later emigrated to Nova Scotia, Canada, where he became a professional golfer. He returned to Britain in 1950 to compete in the British Open.

Appearances:
Others: 2 apps.
Total: 2 apps. 0 gls.

JACKSON, John Alec

Role: Defender/Midfielder 2003-06
6ft.1ins. 12st 11lbs
Born: Camden, London, 15th August 1982

CAREER: Westward Boys/London Oratory School/South East England Schools/**SPURS** assoc. schl. 1996, Scholar Jul 1998, pro. Mar 2000/(Swindon Town loan Sep 2002)/(Colchester United loan Mar 2003)/(Coventry City loan/trial Nov 2003)/(Watford loan Dec 2004)/(Derby County loan Sep 2005)/Colchester United Jun 2006/Notts County Aug 2009/Charlton Athletic loan Feb 2010, perm Jul 2010.

Debut v Portsmouth (BPL) (a) 26.12.2003
Stevenage Borough (sub) (Fr) (a) 13.7.2001

Another of the schoolboys stars of whom much was expected, Johnnie Jackson was a left-sided midfielder or full-back who possessed a sweet passing ability and a good long-range shot. Particularly adept at taking free-kicks, he managed to find space in the tightest of situations, always looking calm and in control. Moving through the junior ranks, he was given some experience in a few friendly games before making his senior debut in December 2003. He did well as the season moved to a conclusion and looked likely to make the grade, but injuries and competition from more experienced campaigners like Mauricio Taricco and Christian Ziege pushed Jackson back into the shadows. After a few loan spells he was released and moved to Colchester United. Despite the more frenetic nature of football lower down the League ladder, Jackson settled well in a Colchester side that tried to play quality football and even harboured dreams of making the top flight at one time. When Jackson was injured, Colchester suffered and slid back to Division One. Jackson was released, joined Notts County but struggled to impress in a poor County outfit. Allowed to move to Charlton Athletic, he soon got his career back on track, dominating the midfield and contributing a remarkable number of goals as Charlton won the First Division title and secured their place in the Championship. Appointed captain, he was unable to prevent the financially troubled club returning to League One.

Appearances:
League: 12 (8) apps. 1 gl.
FA Cup: 1 (2) apps.
FL Cup: 1 app.
Others: 15 (9) apps. 1 gl.
Total: 29 (19) apps. 2 gls.

JACQUES, William

Role: Goalkeeper 1914-23
5ft.10ins. 12st.7lbs.
Born: Erith, Kent, 8th December 1888
Died: Dartford, Kent, 6th June 1925

CAREER: Northumberland Oddfellows/Northfleet 1908//Coventry City Aug 1911/**SPURS** May 1914/retired 1923.

Debut v Everton (FL) (h) 2.9.1914

Before joining Spurs, Bill Jacques had played in a fine Gravesend team that included future England international Charles Buchan, and spent three years with Coventry City, building a reputation as a brave, consistent 'keeper with a promising future. He made his debut in the first match of the last pre-war season and was main choice throughout a disrupted campaign which saw Spurs, decimated by service calls, finish bottom of the First Division. Jacques played regularly throughout the war years and when normal League football resumed in 1919, was ever-present in the team that practically waltzed away with the Second Division title. An unlucky injury against West Bromwich Albion in February 1921 caused him to miss out on an FA Cup winners' medal that year as his place was taken by Alex Hunter, but by October 1921 he had recovered his first team place. The arrival of Herbert Blake in February 1922 put Jacques spot under jeopardy, but sadly it was illness, not Blake, that cost Jacques his place. The first symptoms became apparent in late 1922 and forced retirement early the following year. He died two years later aged only 36. The definitive spelling of Bill's surname has never been established. It also appears as Jaques.

Appearances:
League: 123 apps.
FA Cup: 15 apps.
Others: 124 apps.
Total: 262 apps. 0 gls.

JANES, William Henry

Role: Outside-right 1896-97
Born: St Pancras, London, April qtr. 1879

CAREER: Barnet Alston/Barnet/**SPURS** trial Apr 1897/Watford am. Jan 1899/Thames Ironworks pro. May 1899/Fulham Dec 1899/Grays United Oct 1900/Queens Park Rangers Sep 1902/Clapton Orient am. 1906.

Debut v London Caledonians (Fr) (h) 26.4.1897

Another player who made only one appearance for Spurs, Janes was a 17-year old with Barnet who impressed as they won the North Middlesex League and Alliance. As a trialist he played his only game in April 1897. It was a friendly with London Caledonians abandoned after 45 minutes when one of Spurs' opponents broke a leg. Janes went on to play for several London clubs, though he never became a regular at any of them.

Appearances:
Others: 1 app.
Total: **1 apps. 0 gls.**

JANSSEN, Vincent

Role: Striker 2016-
5ft.11ins. 12st.6lbs.
Born: Heesch, Holland, 15th June 1994

CAREER: SV Top (Holland) 2000/FC Oss (Holland) 2002/NEC Nijmegen (Holland) 2006/Feyenoord (Holland) 2009/Almere City (Holland) Jun 2013/AZ Alkmaar (Holland) Jun 2015/**SPURS** Jul 2016.

Debut v Everton (sub) (PL) (a) 13.8.2016
(Juventus Fr (Melbourne) 26.7.2016)

Throughout the 2015-16 season Harry Kane was Spurs sole senior out-and-out striker. After more than two years of non-stop football at the highest level for club and country, the effort was beginning to take its toll. Kane needed support, a colleague who could not only take over for a while, but who could also push Kane to higher levels. Vincent Janssen is the man identified to do that job. Having worked his way through the Dutch youth structure, playing for his country along the way, before failing to make the grade at Feyenoord, Janssen dropped down to the Second Division with Almere City. With increasing confidence engendered by being given a regular starting place, Janssen scored regularly, made his debut at Under-21 level in November 2014 and after two years returned to the Eredivisie with AZ Alkmaar. Less than a year later, on 25 March 2016, he won his first full cap as a substitute against France, making his first start four days later against England at Wembley and scoring from a penalty. With 31 goals in 49 games for AZ, Janssen was attracting attention from Europe's biggest clubs. Spurs were continually linked with him and eventually invested £17 million in his talents. Similar to Kane in that he possesses strength, power and a willingness to work hard for the team, Janssen is never afraid to take a shot at goal. He should certainly prove a regular scorer and is as likely to develop as a partner to Kane, rather than simply as cover.

Appearances:
League: 7 (20) apps. 2 gls.
FA Cup: 1 (2) apps. 2 gls.
FL Cup: 2 apps. 2 gls.
Euro: 2 (4) apps.
Others: 3 (1) apps. 2 gls.
Total: **15 (27) apps. 8gls..**

JANSSON, Oscar

Role: Goalkeeper 2008-10
6ft.0ins. 12st.12lbs.
Born: Örebro, Sweden, 23rd December 1990

CAREER: Karslunds IF (Sweden)/**SPURS** Academy, pro. Jan 2008/ (Exeter City loan Sep 2009)/(Northampton Town loan Aug 2010)/ (Bradford City loan Aug 2011)/Shamrock Rovers (Ireland) loan Feb 2012, perm Jul 2012/Örebro SK Dec 2012.

Debut v Leyton Orient (Fr) (A) 30.7.2008

Oscar Jansson was a novice 15-year old 'keeper playing for the Karslunds club in his home town of Orebro when he caught the attention of Spurs and several other clubs. He opted to join the Spurs Academy, signed professional and worked his way to the reserve side. Unable to make the breakthrough except in a few friendly matches, he spent much of his career out on loan garnering experience, but never enough to make him a serious challenger for the number one spot at White Hart Lane. A Swedish Under-21 international, Jansson impressed Shamrock Rovers enough on a three month loan that they wanted to sign him permanently. To enable that to happen Spurs agreed to release Jansson. He played regularly for a year in Dublin, but the season was not a success for the Irish club. When they re-signed two of their former 'keepers, it was obvious Jansson would see little senior action. He secured his release and returned home, signing for Örebro SK. In January 2014 he made his first full international appearance, going on as a substitute in a Kings Cup match against Iceland in Thailand.

Appearances:
Others: 1 (2) apps.
Total: **1 (2) apps. 0 gls.**

JEFFREY, George

Role: Inside-forward 1937-38
5ft.7ins. 10st.5lbs.
Born: Motherwell, Lanarkshire, 15th August 1916
Died: 1979

CAREER: Wishaw Boys Brigade/Wishaw Juniors/**SPURS** Nov 1936/ Motherwell May 1939/Dumbarton Jan 1941/(Guest for Aberdeen and Wishaw Juniors during World War Two)/Hamilton Academical Aug 1945/ Dundee United Aug 1945/ Stirling Albion Dec 1946/ Montrose cs. 1947/Stranraer.

Debut v Plymouth Argyle (FL) (h) 23.10.1937 (scored once)

George Jeffrey joined Spurs in November 1936, made his one League appearance almost a year later, scoring in a 3-2 win over Plymouth, and then disappeared back into the reserves. Made available for transfer in April 1939 he returned home to play for Motherwell and later moved on to Dumbarton where he played for a year in war-time competition. Jeffrey's career suffered due to his army service when he served with the Gordon Highlanders. He was wounded while fighting in Crete, captured and spent time as a prisoner of war.

Appearances:
Others: 1 app. 1 gl.
Total: 1 app. 1 gl.

JENAS, Jermaine Anthony

Role: Midfielder 2005-13
5ft.11ins. 11st.2lbs.
Born: Nottingham, 18th February 1983

CAREER: Clifton All Whites/Nottingham Forest Academy scholar Jul 1999, pro. Feb 2000/Newcastle United Feb 2002/**SPURS** Aug 2005/(Aston Villa loan Aug-Dec 2011)/(Nottingham Forest loan Sep 2012)/Queens Park Rangers Jan 2013-May 2014/retired Jan 2016.

Debut v Liverpool (PL) (h) 10.9.2005

Having played for England from Under-16 to Under-20 level, it was no surprise Jermaine Jenas made an immediate impression when given his chance in Nottingham Forest's senior team. Clearly immensely gifted, Jenas was a true-box-to-box player, working back to break up attacks, thrusting forward to support his strikers and often get ahead of them. After just a year of first team football Newcastle United invested £5 million in his talents, making him one of the most expensive teenage transfers. They were rewarded with several outstanding performances, enough to win Jenas the PFA's Young Player of the Year award for 2003 and see him make his full England debut after winning nine caps at Under-21 level. Such early success was never likely to be sustained, but when his form dipped he found it difficult to turn things around. Although still being selected for England, Jenas found the criticism, particularly from the Geordie fans, difficult to handle. When Spurs made an offer, he was glad to swap what he termed "the goldfish bowl" of Newcastle for the anonymity of London. He rediscovered his best form at White Hart Lane, initially working alongside Michael Carrick and then taking on added responsibility when Carrick departed. Working the full length and width of the pitch, Jenas had fantastic stamina, pace, an eye for the through ball and could be relied upon for his fair share of goals. He also had an appreciation of what his team-mates needed, an asset readily acknowledged by his colleagues if not always recognised by observers. For four years Jenas was a regular for Spurs, not an outstanding player, but a member of the team whose value was often only appreciated when he was absent. A member of the 2008 Worthington Cup-winning team, he won two caps at "B" level and eight at full level as a Spurs' player, but when injury afflicted him in 2009-10, and with Luka Modrić approaching his best, Jenas slipped down the pecking order. Loaned to Aston Villa and Nottingham Forest, when Harry Redknapp was desperate for experienced hands to try and save Queens Park Rangers from relegation, Jenas was one of the men he called upon. Though it proved futile, Jenas established himself as a regular in the engine room until a serious cruciate ligament injury put on him the side-lines and eventually led to his retirement.

Appearances:
League: 133 (21) apps. 21 gls.
FA Cup: 8 (1) apps. 2 gls.
FL Cup: 13 apps. 2 gls.
Euro: 21 (4) apps. 1 gl.
Others: 28 (6) apps.
Total: 203 (32) apps. 26 gls.

JENKINS, David John

Role: Forward 1968-70
5ft.9ins. 10st.12lbs.
Born: Bristol, 2nd September 1946

CAREER: Wick Road School/Bristol Schools/Arsenal app. Jul 1962, pro. Oct 1963/**SPURS** Oct 1968/Brentford Jul 1972/Hereford United Mar 1973/(Newport County loan Mar 1974)/Shrewsbury Town Aug 1974/Dorchester Town Nov 1974/Durban City (South Africa) 1975/Workington Oct 1975/Guisborough Town/Taunton Town asst. manager/Bridlington Town admin.

Debut v Liverpool (FL) (h) 19.10.1968

David Jenkins trained with Bristol City as a schoolboy, but it was with Arsenal that he began his football career. He overcame the setback of a broken leg in a pre-season practice match at the start of 1965-66 and made his League debut in November 1967. Although he only played a few games in the first team that season he was a member of the Arsenal side beaten by Leeds United in the 1968 League Cup Final. Jenkins joined Spurs in a £55,000 swap deal that saw Jimmy Robertson move to Highbury but, in honesty, was nowhere near an adequate replacement for one of Spurs' FA Cup winning heroes of 1967. A forward whose best position was probably as a winger, Jenkins was simply not a success at White Hart Lane and, although he stayed until July 1972, the vast bulk of his Spurs career was spent in the reserves. He eventually joined Brentford and spent further years in the lower divisions with Hereford, Newport County on loan and at Shrewsbury. He was unable to make an impact with any of these clubs and after a short spell with Dorchester moved to South Africa, before returning to finish his League career with Workington. On 9th March 1974 Jenkins played for Newport when they lost at Peterborough. It was an outing that cost Newport £200 and one League point because his loan transfer from Hereford was not registered until three days later.

Appearances:
League: 12* (3) apps. 2 gls.
FA Cup: 2 (1) apps.
Others: 1 app.
Total: 15 (4) apps. 2 gls.
*Includes 1 abandoned match.

JENKINS W

Role: Outside-left 1907-08

Debut v Clapton Orient (Fr) (a) 30.4.1908

A trialist from Clacton, Jenkins' made his only appearance in an end of season friendly at Clapton Orient in April 1908.

Appearances:
Others: 1 app.
Total: 1 app. 0 gls.

JENNINGS, Alfred W

Role: Centre-forward 1923-24
Born: London, 1904

CAREER: Barnet/Hertfordshire/Granville (Australia)/**SPURS** Sep 1922/Poole Town Jul 1925/Oldham Athletic Jun 1926/Poole Town cs. 1927.

Debut v Clapton Orient (LFACC) (a) 5.11.1923

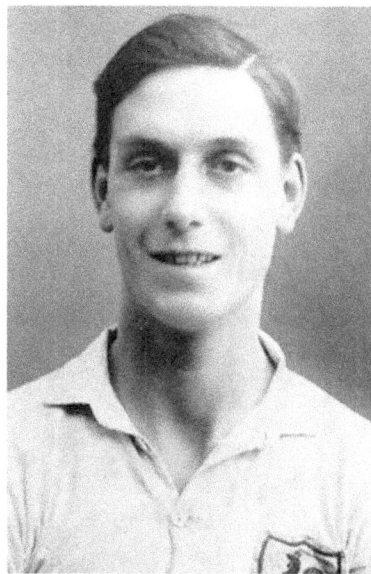

Alf Jennings started his career with Barnet, winning representative honours for Hertfordshire before emigrating to Australia, where he played for the Granville club who finished the 1922 season as runners-up in the New South Wales championship. He played for New South Wales against Queensland and was soon regarded as the country's number one player. In early 1922 he announced he was returning to the UK and by July had accepted Spurs offer of professional terms. A very skilful player who relied on skill far more than brawn and was at his best with the ball at his feet, he arrived at Spurs in a fanfare of trumpets, but totally failed to live up to expectations. His only appearance in the first team was in November 1923 against Clapton Orient in the London FA Charity Cup and although he spent two seasons at White Hart Lane he was never really in contention for a first team place. Quite simply, he was considered far too lightweight and delicate a footballer for Football League action. In April 1925 he was placed on the transfer list and moved to Poole Town. Jennings had another try with a League club making two League appearances for Oldham Athletic in his one season with them, but he was simply not up to the demands of top level football and returned to Poole.

Appearances:
Others: 1 app.
Total: **1 app. 0 gls.**

JENNINGS, Patrick Anthony M.B.E.

Role: Goalkeeper 1964-77 and 1983-86
6ft.0ins. 12st.6lbs.
Born: Newry, County Down, 12th June 1945

CAREER: Newry United/Newry Town/Watford May 1963/**SPURS** Jun 1964/Arsenal Aug 1977/**SPURS** Aug 1985/(Everton loan Mar 1986)/retired Jun 1986/**SPURS** goalkeeping coach Jul 1993, goalkeeping consultant Jul 1998/Northern Ireland goalkeeping coach Feb 1998-Nov 1999/Oxford United part-time goalkeeping coach Feb 2001.

Debut v Sheffield United (FL) 22.8.1964
(Feyenoord (Fr) (a) 8.8.1964)

The argument as to whether Pat Jennings or Ted Ditchburn was the best goalkeeper Spurs have ever had, could rage forever and will probably never be settled. What is indisputable is that at his peak, Jennings was the best 'keeper in the world and a strong candidate for the best of all time. He had every attribute a top goalkeeper needs and more. Apart from height, strength, a massive pair of hands, great positional sense and the ability to pull off reaction saves that looked impossible, he possessed an unflappable temperament, coolness under pressure and the ability to inspire great confidence among his defenders. But perhaps his greatness quality was the sheer consistency that kept him at the peak of his profession for over twenty years. Having played Gaelic football for North Down Schools, he turned to football with Newry Town's junior club, Newry United. He spent a season with the juniors and just six months with Newry Town before becoming a £6,000 signing by Watford manager, Ron Burgess, who spotted him playing for Northern Ireland in a youth tournament at Bognor Regis. Pitched straight into Watford's senior team, he progressed rapidly, played for the Northern Ireland Under-23's against Wales in February 1964 and by the end of the season had won two full international caps, the first against Wales in April 1964. Despite Jennings having made only 48 League appearances, Spurs boss Bill Nicholson paid £27,000 to take him to White Hart Lane. It was one of the best purchases Nicholson ever made. Although Jennings had a little difficulty settling in at first, by the start of the 1966-67 season he was the undisputed first choice. A member of the Spurs' teams that won the FA Cup in 1967, the League Cup in 1971 and 1973 and the UEFA Cup in 1972, and the team that lost in the Final of the UEFA Cup in 1974, Jennings went on to set a record number of appearances for Spurs, a figure bettered only by Steve Perryman. The Football Writers' Association Player of the Year in 1972-73 and the Professional Footballers' Association Player of the Year in 1975-76, Jennings was awarded the MBE for his services to the game in the 1976 Queen's Birthday Honours list. His achievements were also honoured by Spurs, with a testimonial against Arsenal in November 1976. Rarely injured during the bulk of his Spurs career, he did finally succumb to a bad ankle injury during the difficult 1976-77 season. Significantly, during his enforced absence Spurs were relegated, but worse, manager Keith Burkinshaw decided Barry Daines was a better long term prospect than the 32-year old Jennings. It was the most serious error of judgment Burkinshaw ever made, more especially as the popular Jennings was also allowed to leave for a token £45,000 fee to join his former Spurs manager and international team-mate and manager Terry Neill, then in charge of rivals Arsenal. By the time of his departure he had represented his country 66 times as a Spurs' player and had also appeared for the UK against Wales, All Ireland against Brazil and in The Three against The Six game to celebrate the enlargement of the Common Market. In eight years at Highbury Jennings proceeded to alter modern thinking about the peak years and longevity of goalkeepers by maintaining the same superb standards of performance and consistency he had shown at White Hart Lane, He made over 300 senior appearances for Arsenal, winning another FA Cup winners' medal in 1979, runners-up medals in 1978 and 1980, a European Cup-Winners' Cup runners-up medal-also in 1980-as well as collecting another 42 caps for his country. A true gentleman, he was most upset when discarded by Spurs, but showed he bore Burkinshaw no grudge by returning to don a Spurs' shirt as a guest in Burkinshaw's Testimonial match against an England XI in May 1984. Midway through the 1984-85 season he lost his Arsenal place to John Lukic and although granted a second testimonial in May 1985-this time against Spurs-was on the verge of retiring, but for the fact he was needed by Northern Ireland for their World Cup campaign. He returned to Spurs, primarily to keep fit, but also as cover for Ray Clemence, and played in the odd friendly and one match in the Screen Sport Super Cup. He also had a spell on loan to Everton who were involved in the 1986 FA Cup Final but, with Neville Southall injured, needed cover in case anything happened to their only experienced 'keeper, Bobby Mimms. Jennings' services were not called upon and by the time the 1986 World Cup began he was back with

Spurs. Including the World Cup Finals, Jennings won a further nine caps in his second spell at Spurs, giving him a total of 119, a world record. The conclusion of the World Cup saw Jennings formally retire but, he was still not quite finished with football for he captained the Rest of the World against the Americas in a FIFA/UNICAF charity match in July 1986. With clubs realising the increasing specialisation of goalkeepers Jennings was taken on the White Hart Lane coaching staff in July 1993, providing a mentor no budding young 'keeper could better. Featured on TV's "This is Your Life" in November 1983, Ireland's Personality of the Year in 1984 and International Personality of the Year in 1985 and 1986, his son, also Pat, had a brief spell as a goalkeeper on the books of Wimbledon, Chesham, Enfield and Kingstonians and represented Northern Ireland at Under-21 level. In August 1967 Jennings performed that coveted and extremely rare feat for a 'keeper when he scored a goal with a long downfield punt in the 2-2 draw against Manchester United at Old Trafford in the FA Charity Shield.

Appearances:
League: 473* apps.
FA Cup: 43 apps.
FL Cup: 39 apps.
Euro: 36 apps.
Others: 82 (3) apps. 1 gl.
Total: 673 (3) apps. 1 gl.
*Includes 1 abandoned match.

JENNINGS, Samuel

Role: Inside-forward 1918-19
5ft.11ins. 12st.0lbs.
Born: Cinderhill, Nottingham, 26th December 1898
Died: Battle, Sussex, 21st August 1944

CAREER: Highbury Vale Methodists/Basford United/Coldstream Guards/(guest for Notts County and **SPURS** during World War One)/Norwich City May 1919/Middlesbrough Apr 1920/Reading Jun 1921/West Ham United Jun 1924/Brighton and Hove Albion Mar 1925/Nottingham Forest May 1928/Port Vale May 1929/Stockport County Sep 1931/Burnley Jan 1932/Wisbech Town player, secretary-coach/Olympique de Marseilles (France) coach May 1932/Scarborough Town Sep 1934/Wisbech Town secretary-coach/coach in Switzerland 1935/Middlesbrough coach/Glentoran coach Jun 1936/Rochdale manager Oct 1937-Sep 1938.

Debut v Brentford (LFC) (h) 14.9.1918

A youngster serving in the Coldstream Guards, Jennings had very limited experience of football when he made his only appearance for Spurs in a London Football Combination match in September 1918. After the First World War though, he went on to have a lengthy career in the game proving himself a prolific scorer. He started his senior career with Norwich City and after one season was a target for bigger clubs. He moved to Middlesbrough, but had few opportunities to show what he could do due to the presence of England international George Elliott. Reading got the best out of him, but again a bigger club, this time West Ham United, gave him few chances and he dropped down to play for Brighton and Hove Albion. Brighton, Nottingham Forest and Port Vale got good service from, before he turned to coaching and management. At Norwich he played alongside his older brother, Bill, who also served Notts County, Merthyr Town, Luton Town and Northampton. His nephew Henry, Bill's son, played for Northampton Town, Ipswich Town and Rochdale.

Appearances:
Others: 1 app.
Total: 1 app. 0 gls.

JINKS, James Thomas

Role: Centre-forward 1945-46
5ft.8in. 11st.2lbs.
Born: Camberwell, London, 19th August 1916
Died: Eltham, London, 23rd November 1981

CAREER: Downham Common/Millwall am. Aug 1938, pro. Nov 1938/(guest for **SPURS**, West Bromwich Albion, West Ham United and Wolverhampton Wanderers during World War Two)/Fulham Aug 1948/Luton Town Mar 1950/Aldershot Sep 1951/Ashford Town Aug 1952.

Debut v Aston Villa (FLS) (h) 20.2.1946 (scored twice)

A war-time guest from Millwall, where he had made only one League appearance before the outbreak of War, Jimmy Jinks scored twice for Spurs on his only appearance against Aston Villa in a Football League South fixture in February 1946. A regular scorer for Millwall, he was a member of their 1945 Football League South Cup final team. By the time of his transfer to Fulham in 1948, he was well past his best and finished his career with brief spells at Luton Town and Aldershot.

Appearances:
Others: 1 app. 2 gls.
Total: 1 app. 2 gls.

JOEL

Role: Inside-forward 1891-92

Debut v Queens Park Rangers (Fr) (h) 9.1.1892

Joel's only appearance was in January 1892 when he played inside-left in a friendly against Queens Park Rangers.

Appearances:
Others: 1 app.
Total: 1 app. 0 gls.

JOHNSON, A

Role: Half-back 1895-96

CAREER: Lewisham St Marys/**SPURS** trial Mar 1896.

Debut v Royal Ordnance (Fr) (a) 9.3.1896

As a trialist from Lewisham St Mary, the only appearance Johnson made for Spurs first team was in a friendly with Royal Ordnance in March 1896. He played at half-back, a position he occupied in a few games later that season for the reserves, but was not taken on.

Appearances:
Others: 1 app.
Total: 1 app. 0 gls.

JOHNSON, Neil Joseph

Role: Winger 1965-71
5ft.9ins. 10st.11lbs.
Born: Grimsby, Humberside, 3rd December 1946

CAREER: Grimsby Schools/Lincolnshire Schools/Notre Dame Boys Club/**SPURS** app. May 1963, pro. Jun 1964/(Charlton Athletic loan Feb 1971)/Torquay United Jul-Oct 1971/Dover.

Debut v Sunderland (FL) (h) 6.10.1965
(Walton & Hersham (sub) (Fr) (a) 22.9.1965)

A scampering little winger who could fall back to help out in midfield and generally liked to be involved throughout the game, Neil Johnson made his League debut against Sunderland in October 1965. He played in the next nine matches, but was competing for a place with several decent home-produced players, such as Keith Weller and Derek Possee, and unable to retain his position. It was not until towards the end of the 1968-69 season that he appeared to have established himself, but the emergence of Jimmy Pearce early the following season saw Johnson slip back into the reserves. Unable to command a permanent position he spent a month on loan to Charlton, before moving to Torquay United, but his contract was cancelled after only a few weeks as he refused to move to Devon. He subsequently joined Dover.

Appearances:
League: 28* (7) apps. 5 gls.
FA Cup: 4 apps. 1 gl.
Others: 4 (10) apps.
Total: **36 (17) apps. 6 gls.**
*Includes 1 abandoned match.

JOHNSTON, Richard William

Role: Midfielder 1987-89
Born: Portadown, Northern Ireland, 15th October 1969

CAREER: Northern Ireland Schools/Lisburn Youth Club/**SPURS** trainee Jul 1986, pro. Jul 1987/(Dunfermline Athletic loan Apr 1990)/Linfield Aug 1990/Tandragee Rovers cs. 1998/Armagh City Aug 2002/Richhill by Apr 2005.

Debut v Brentford (sub) (Fr) (a) 5.12.1987

A midfield player who represented Northern Ireland at Under-17, Under-19, Under-21 and Under-23 level, Ritchie Johnson made just two senior appearances for Spurs, both as a substitute in friendly matches. Never in the running for a place in the League team he was loaned to Dunfermline Athletic in April 1990. When given a free transfer at the end of the season he returned to Northern Ireland with Linfield for whom he scored the goal that won the Smirnoff League title in 1992-93. He later played for Armagh City and Richhill.

Appearances:
Others: (2) apps.
Total: **(2) apps. 0 gls.**

JOLIFFE

Role: Centre-forward 1941-42

Debut v Queens Park Rangers (LWL) (a) 3.1.1942

Having scored 50 goals for the Honourable Artillery Company already that season, Joliffe was invited to appear for Spurs as a guest in a London War League match with Queens Park Rangers in January 1942. He was unable to add to his season's total as Spurs lost 0-1.

Appearances:
Others: 1 app.
Total: **1 app. 0 gls.**

JONES, Arthur Ernest

Role: Forward 1900-01
Born: St Pancras, London, January qtr. 1878
Died: Edmonton, London, October qtr. 1939

CAREER: Shrewsbury Town/Market Drayton 1896/**SPURS** May 1900/Doncaster Rovers cs. 1901-cs. 1902/St Louis by October 1903.

Debut v Chatham (SL) (h) 15.9.1900

Arthur Jones joined Spurs in the summer of 1900 and while a forward like his namesakes John L and John "Bristol", he was not to have so long or successful a career with Spurs as either of them. He made his debut in September 1900 in a Southern League fixture with Chatham which was to be expunged from the records due to Chatham's withdrawal from the League three months later. Most of his appearances came at outside-right in place of Tom Smith, but he never seriously challenged Smith for the shirt and was always regarded very much as a reserve. Indeed, the majority of his first team outings were late in the season when the reserves fulfilled first team fixtures to ensure senior players were fit for important matches in the 1901 FA Cup success. At the end of the season Jones was released and signed for Doncaster, where he played for a season. In October 1903 he was reported as playing for one of the Tottenham area junior clubs, St Louis.

Appearances:
Southern: 8 apps. 1 gl.
Others: 17 apps. 7 gls.
Total: **25 apps. 8 gls.**

JONES, Charles

Role: Centre-half 1934-36
5ft.11ins. 12st.0lbs.
Born: Penmaer, Monmouthshire, 20th November 1911
Died: Norfolk, 4th June 1985

CAREER: Ebbw Vale/Northfleet United Sep 1932/**SPURS** May 1934/Southend United May 1937/(guest for Colchester United during World War Two).

Debut v Leeds United (FL) (h) 22.12.1934

Charlie Jones is another player from the inter-war period who developed through the Northfleet nursery onto the White Hart Lane staff. He made eight League outings in his first season at Spurs, but, with the centre-half position the property of Arthur Rowe, Jones was one of several players who tried in vain to displace the man who was later to bring so much success to the club as manager. Jones was more fortunate than some for he did at least make a few appearances when Rowe was absent, but the task was not eased by a cartilage operation in the summer of 1936. In April 1937 he was given a free transfer and moved to Southend United where he played until the outbreak of war. Serving with a trawler fleet he was reported missing in October 1940, but was rescued and survived. He later emigrated to Canada.

Appearances:
League: 18 apps.
Others: 1 app.
Total: 19 apps. 0 gls.

JONES, Christopher Harry

Role: Striker 1974-82
5ft.11ins. 10st.7lbs.
Born: Jersey, Channel Islands, 18th April 1956

CAREER: Jersey Schools/Jersey-Guernsey Schools/**SPURS** app. May 1971, pro. May 1973/Manchester City Sep 1982/Crystal Palace Nov 1982/Charlton Athletic Sep 1983/Orient Sep 1984/St Albans City cs. 1987/St Peters (Jersey) manager.

Debut v Ipswich Town (FL) (h) 17.8.1974
(Heart of Midlothian (Fr) (a) 3.8.1974)

The arrival of Chris Jones on the first team scene at White Hart Lane revived memories of the only other Channel Islander to play for Spurs, Len Duquemin, but unfortunately Jones was not to enjoy the same success as his predecessor. His debut came at the start of the 1974-75 season in place of that great Spurs favourite Martin Chivers, but, after the club suffered three successive defeats, Jones was consigned to the reserves. He returned towards the end of a season of continual struggle and then, alongside Chivers, certainly played his part in the successful late battle to avoid relegation. Lean and lank-haired, Jones was a very skilful, but rather unlucky player, who never really got a grip on a first team place, always battling Chivers, John Duncan, Gerry Armstrong, Colin Lee and Ian Moores for one of the two central striking roles. He did though win an England Under-21 cap in May 1978 when he appeared as a substitute against Yugoslavia. The arrival of Steve Archibald and Garth Crooks in the summer of 1980 provided even stiffer competition for Jones, but his cause was not helped by injuries which left him side-lined for lengthy periods. In September 1982, with Mark Falco developing into the main threat to the Archibald and Crooks partnership, Jones was transferred to Manchester City for £110,000. After only three League games in two months he returned to London with Crystal Palace. He had little more success at Selhurst Park, joining Charlton in September 1983 and Orient twelve months later. Not retained by Orient in May 1987 he went into non-League football with St Albans City before returning home to Jersey to manage the St. Peters club.

Appearances:
League: 149 (15) apps. 37 gls.
FA Cup: 10 (2) apps. 4 gls.
FL Cup: 7 (1) apps. 1 gl.
Euro: (1) app.
Others: 52 (10) apps. 25 gls.
Total: 218 (29) apps. 67 gls.

JONES, Clifford William

Role: Winger 1957-78
5ft.7ins. 10st.7lbs.
Born: Swansea, Glamorgan, 7th February 1935

CAREER: Swansea Schools/Wales Schools/Swansea Town part-time pro. May 1952/**SPURS** Feb 1958/Fulham Oct 1968/Kings Lynn Jul 1970/Bedford Town Jan 1971/Wealdstone Jul 1971/Cambridge City Nov 1971, player-coach 1973/Wingate player-coach.

Debut v Arsenal (FL) (a) 22.2.1958

Spurs had to pay a £35,000 fee-a record for a winger-to secure the transfer of Cliff Jones from Swansea Town in February 1958, but every penny of that fee was recovered during ten years of the most outstanding service. With Swansea he played in the same team as his brother, Bryn, won his first full cap against Austria in May 1954 when just turned 19, and became one of the most exciting players in the game. By the time of his transfer to Spurs he had 16 full caps to his credit, yet it was only after moving to Tottenham that he began to train on a full time basis! A member of the Welsh side that did so well in the 1958 World Cup in Sweden, he broke his leg during pre-season training later that summer, but he returned to become an indispensable member of the team, capable of playing on either wing or even at inside-forward. Fast and direct, Jones possessed an elusive body swerve that left defenders tackling thin air and, for a slender-framed player of only 5ft 7ins, a prodigious leap. There were few more exciting sights than Jones leaving his marker for dead with an incredible burst of speed down the wing, arrowing in to meet a cross from the opposite flank, or soaring high above defenders to power a spectacular header at goal. But perhaps his greatest asset was his extraordinary bravery. Courageous to the point of madness, he was never afraid to throw himself-sometimes head first-at the flying feet of defenders if there was half a chance of getting to the ball or scoring a goal. Not surprisingly, he frequently paid the penalty with some nasty injuries. A key member of the team that won the "Double" in 1961, the FA Cup in 1962 and the European Cup-Winners' Cup in 1963, Jones picked up a third FA Cup winners' medal in 1967 as the first non-playing substitute. Throughout his career with Spurs he continued to represent his country, picking up 41 caps at full level and one at Under-23 level. He also represented the Football League on three occasions, quite a feat for a non-English player. In October 1968 his great service to Spurs was recognised with a cut-price £5,000 transfer to Fulham where he won his final two caps before winding down his career in non-League circles. Unfortunately, a butcher's shop in Tottenham High Road that he set up whilst still a player did not prove a success and for a spell Jones returned briefly to the sheet metal working trade he learned as a 16-year old in Swansea dry-dock. He then worked at a Sports Centre before becoming games instructor at Highbury Grove School. Jones returned to play at White Hart Lane in May 1978, guesting for Spurs in John Pratt's testimonial match against Arsenal when he still showed some of the wonderful skills that mark him out as one of Spurs greatest ever players. Jones was the fourth member of his family to make his name in professional football following his father Ivor, who played for Swansea Town, West Bromwich Albion and Wales, his uncle Bryn, who played for Wolverhampton Wanderers, Norwich City, Arsenal and Wales and his brother Bryn, who played for Swansea Town, Newport County, Bournemouth and Boscombe Athletic, Northampton Town and Watford. His grandson, Matt Wells, was an Academy Scholar with Spurs in 2005.

Appearances:
League: 314 (4) apps. 135 gls.
FA Cup: 35 (4) apps. 16 gls.
FL Cup: 2 apps. 1 gl.
Euro: 19 apps. 7 gls.
Others: 38 (2) apps. 15 gls.
Total: 408 (10) apps. 174 gls.

JONES, Eric Norman

Role: Outside-left 1942-44
Born: Stirchley, Birmingham, 5th February 1915
Died: Louth, Lincolnshire, 2nd October 1985

CAREER: Bournville & Selly Park Schools/Shirley/Kidderminster Harriers 1931/Wolverhampton Wanderers Oct 1936/Portsmouth Nov 1937/Stoke City Sep 1938/West Bromwich Albion May 1939/(guest for Aldershot, Arsenal, Brentford, Cardiff City, Chelsea, Crystal Palace, Exeter City, Fulham, Leeds United, Luton Town, Northampton Town, Nottingham Forest, Portsmouth, Queens Park Rangers, Southend United, **SPURS** and Watford during World War Two)/Brentford Nov 1945/Crewe Alexandra Jul 1946/Kidderminster Harriers Jul 1948/BSC Young Boys (Switzerland) coach 1949-50/Beerschot AC (Belgium) coach 1953-1955/Egypt national coach 1955-56/Bromsgrove Rovers manager 1959-1960/De Graafschap (Holland) coach 1960-1962/Port Vale coach Jun-Oct 1962/Coach in Belgian Congo, Denmark, Finland, Nigeria, Turkey, West Indies.

Debut v Charlton Athletic (FLS) (h) 11.9.1943
(Charlton Athletic (Fr) (h) 24.4.1943 (scored once))

A West Bromwich Albion player, Eric Jones is another of those players who made his only appearances for Spurs as a war-time guest. A very popular guest player he first appeared for Spurs in an end of season friendly in April 1943, but the following season played quite regularly in the Football League South. Having started out with Kidderminster Harriers, Jones rapidly moved around from Wolverhampton Wanderers to Portsmouth and Stoke City, with few outings, before signing for West Bromwich Albion, just in time for the outbreak of war. In the build up to the resumption of normal football after the war, he was transferred to Brentford, but after only seven months moved to Crewe Alexandra where he finished his League career. He then travelled the world, working as a coach.

Appearances:
Others: 17 apps. 8 gls.
Total: 17 apps. 8 gls.

JONES, Gordon

Role: Half-back 1912-13
5ft.10ins. 11st.8lbs.
Born: Birkenhead, Lancashire, 1st February 1889

CAREER: Bebington St Andrews/Melrose Sep 1905/Birkenhead Aug 1907/Bolton Wanderers Sep 1909/**SPURS** May 1912/Chester cs. 1913/South Liverpool Sep 1914/Hurst Feb 1915/Tranmere Rovers Jan 1916/Gresford/Chester cs. 1919/Crichtons Athletic/Wrexham Aug 1921/Connahs Quay Sep 1922/Hurst Feb 1924/Flint Town Dec 1924.

Debut v Sheffield Wednesday (FL) (h) 7.9.1912

Towards the end of the 1909-10 season Gordon Jones was the regular inside-right for Bolton Wanderers scoring six goals in 18 games, but he made only five more appearances in the next two seasons, the last of them at centre-half. Released by Bolton, he joined Spurs and stayed for only one undistinguished season. He made most of his eleven appearances for Spurs in the half-back line, though he also played at inside-left and centre-forward. Spurs won only one of those matches, against Bromley in the London FA Charity Cup. Jones spent most of the season as a reserve until released in May 1913. He joined Chester but quickly moved to South Liverpool, and continued his wanderings after the Great War.

Appearances:
League: 8* apps.
Others: 3 apps.
Total: 11 apps. 0 gls.
*Includes 1 abandoned match

JONES, Jimmy

Role: Half-back 1899-1900
Born: Birkenhead, Lancashire, 1st February 1889

CAREER: Waverley/**SPURS** am. Sep 1899, pro. Oct 1899/Watford Apr 1904.

Debut v Southampton (SDC) (a) 30.4.1900

Joining Spurs from the local junior outfit, Waverley, Jimmy "Spider" Jones, was associated with Spurs for one year, making only one appearance in the first team. Not connected with Spurs again, he resurfaced four years later signing for Watford. He played there for one season, a regular in their half-back line.

Appearances:
Others: 1 app.
Total: **1 app. 0 gls.**

JONES, John Leonard

Role: Inside-forward 1897-07
5ft.10ins. 12st.8lbs.
Born: Rhuddlan, nr Rhyl, Denbighshire, 1866
Died: Sunderland, County Durham, 24th November 1931

CAREER: Rhuddlan 1882/Bootle 1888/Stockton 1891/Grimsby Town May 1893/Sheffield United May 1894/SPURS May 1897/Watford May 1904/Worcester City May 1905.

Debut v Sheppey United (SL) (a) 4.9.1897
(Glossop North End (Fr) (h) 2.9.1897)

John L Jones began his illustrious career with his local club Rhuddlan and played for Bootle and Stockton before moving up to the Football League with Grimsby Town. It was at Sheffield United that he really came to the fore, making his Welsh international debut against Ireland in March 1895 and establishing himself as Wales' first choice left-half. When Spurs secured his signature, it was hailed as a considerable coup, for the club had played only one season of Southern League football, and Jones was a current international with nine caps to his credit. He spent most of his first season at centre-half, although in those days centre-halves were not quite the defensive players expected in the modern game. A heavily-built man, Jones was rather short on pace, but more than compensated for this with highly intelligent passing and skilful positional play. He formed the base of a superb triangle with David Copeland and John Kirwan. This influential trio were responsible in no small measure for Spurs winning the Southern League in 1899-1900 and the FA Cup for the first time in 1901 when, although player/manager John Cameron was also in the team, Jones was the captain who collected the trophy. A fine cricketer, he coached both football and cricket at Rugby School when his duties with Spurs allowed. A great captain and servant of the club, he remained an inspirational figure until leaving to join Watford only two months after winning his twelfth Welsh cap as a Spurs player. He only spent a season at Watford and then finished his senior career at Worcester City. Jones did appear once more in Spurs' colours, returning in April 1907 to play for Spurs' 1901 FA Cup winning squad in a Benefit match for trainer Sam Mountford. When his senior football days were over Jones continued to be associated with sport, initially playing in exhibition matches on a synthetic surface at Olympia. He then concentrated on coaching cricket, working in Leinster and South Africa and took up the position of coach/groundsman to Whitburn Cricket Club of the Durham Senior League in March 1923. In later life, while employed as a pattern maker, he fell down a stairway at work and sustained fatal head injuries. When he played for Wales against Ireland on 19th February 1898 Jones became the first Spurs player to win international honours.

Appearances:
Southern: 135* apps. 7 gls.
FA Cup: 31 apps. 1 gl.
Others: 171 apps. 8 gls.
Total: **337 apps. 16gls.**
*Includes 1 abandoned match.

JONES, John Thomas

Role: Inside-forward 1902-04
5ft.8ins. 11st.4lbs.
Born: West Bromwich, West Midlands, 18th October 1874
Died: Edmonton, London, 13th September 1904

CAREER: Gunns Lane School/Tantany Rovers/Shaftesbury White Rose/Sandwell Albion/Dudley/Halesowen/Small Heath Dec 1894/Eastville Rovers Aug 1898/SPURS Jul 1902.

Debut v Queens Park Rangers (SL) (h) 6.9.1902

Signed from Bristol Rovers, in the summer of 1902, John Jones was nicknamed "Bristol" to distinguish him from his more illustrious namesake and Spurs captain, John L. Originally with Small Heath, he had joined Bristol Rovers when they were still known as Eastville Rovers and 50 goals for the West country club in 1901-02 earned him the reported reputation of "The deadliest forward in the South". An inside-forward who could also play on the wing, he went straight into the first team and was settling in well until an injury in November 1902 put him out for the rest of the season. In the short time available he had impressed manager John Cameron enough to be retained for the following season when he became the regular inside-right. A consistent scorer and highly valued member of the team he did not, contrary to popular belief, join Watford in the 1904 close season. That was reserve inside-forward Jimmy Jones. Whilst in demand with several clubs "Bristol" Jones did in fact re-sign for Spurs and reported for training in September that year. He had the symptoms of what was thought to be flu, but in fact it was typhoid and he died two months later aged only 29. Tottenham marked his untimely death with a memorial benefit match in December 1904 against a team selected by George Robey to raise funds for his dependants.

Appearances:
Southern: 32 apps. 19 gls.
FA Cup: 5 apps. 2 gls.
Others: 28* apps. 15 gls.
Total: **65 apps. 36 gls.**
*Includes 1 abandoned match

JONES, Leonard

Role: Half-back 1942-43
Born: Barnsley, Yorkshire, 9th June 1913
Died: April 1998

CAREER: Wombwell/Huddersfield Town am./Barnsley Aug 1933/Chelmsford City cs. 1938/Plymouth Argyle cs. 1939/(guest for Chelmsford City, Fulham, Southend United and SPURS during World War Two)/Southend United Aug 1949/Colchester United Jul 1950/Ipswich Town Jul 1953.

Debut v Arsenal (Fr) (h) 8.5.1943

Originally a wing-half with Barnsley and Chelmsford City, Len Jones was still on the books of Plymouth Argyle when he made his one appearance for Spurs in a friendly against Arsenal in May 1943. After the war he switched to outside-right and served Plymouth in that position for two years before moving to Southend United and a year later moved on to Colchester United for their debut season in the Football League. He broke his leg during his second season in Essex and never really recovered. In July 1953, over 40-years old, he signed for Ipswich Town, although he did not make their first team as they won the Third Division (South).

Appearances:
Others: 1 app.
Total: 1 app. 0 gls.

JONES R

Role: Inside-forward 1894-95

Debut v Sheffield & District League XI (Fr) (h) 25.12.1894 (scored once)

Jones played in two friendly matches for Spurs in December 1894 scoring once in each game.

Appearances:
Others: 2 apps. 2 gls.
Total: 2 apps. 2 gls.

JONES, Richard Lewis

Role: Inside-forward 1893-94
Born: Chirk, 1867

CAREER: Swindon St Marks/Swindon Town/London Welsh/(guest for **SPURS** Dec 1893)/Queens Park Rangers/London Caledonians/Clapton/Swindon Town/Trowbridge cs. 1897/Bridge Street Victoria cs. 1898/Swindon Town.

Debut v Southampton St Marys (Fr) (a) 26.12.1893

At the time of his only appearance for Spurs, Dick Jones was reported as being a member of the London Welsh club and a Middlesex representative player. In fact his playing association with London Welsh was very short and he was primarily renowned for his success with various clubs in Swindon. During his brief association with London Welsh, he also turned out for Queens Park Rangers, London Caledonians and Clapton. His one appearance for Spurs was on Boxing Day 1893 when he played at inside-left as a late replacement for Taylor in a friendly with Southampton St Marys, regular opponents for Spurs over the Christmas period. Apart from playing for Middlesex, Jones, who played in one of Wales' unofficial internationals against the touring Canadians in October 1891, also made 17 appearances for Wiltshire.

Appearances:
Others: 1 app.
Total: 1 app. 0 gls.

JONES, William Ernest Arthur

Role: Winger 1946-49
5ft.9ins. 10st.13lbs.
Born: Cwmbwrla, Swansea, 12th November 1920
Died: November 2002

CAREER: Cwmbwrla Juniors/Swansea Schools/Swansea Town am. Aug 1937/Bolton Wanderers pro. Aug 1938/(Bury and Chester City during World War Two)/Swansea Town 1941, pro. Oct 1943/**SPURS** Jun 1947/Southampton May 1949/Bristol City Nov 1951, player-coach/Rhyl Town Apr 1954, manager Aug 1954-Aug 1955/Poole Town Jan 1956/Southampton coach Jan 1956-58/Horwich RMI chairman.

Debut v Barnsley (FL) (h) 7.6.1947

Ernie "Alphabet" Jones started his career as an amateur with Swansea Town, but turned professional with Bolton, although he failed to make their League team. He returned to Swansea during the War and quickly built a big reputation as a fast attacking winger. He won his first cap against Scotland in October 1946 and collected a second before moving to Spurs in June 1947. Jones only spent two full seasons at White Hart Lane, winning two more Welsh caps, before finding his place taken by Les Medley. In May 1949 he moved to Southampton as part of the deal that brought Alf Ramsey to Spurs. He served the Saints for over two years before a transfer to Bristol City where he finished his League career. He retired from senior football at the end of the 1953-54 season and played for Rhyl Town where he even helped design and erect the floodlights. He played one game for Poole Town before spending two years coaching the juniors at Southampton. Jones then moved back to Bolton where he worked as an engineer for Hawker Siddeley. A member of the Association of Inventors and Innovators, he kept active in retirement designing water leisure products.

Appearances:
League: 56* apps. 14 gls.
FA Cup: 2 apps.
Others: 7 apps. 2 gls.
Total: 65 apps. 16 gls.
*Includes 1 abandoned match.

JONES, William M

Role: Half-back 1906-07
5ft.8ins. 12st.4lbs.
Born: Brighton, Sussex, 6th March 1876
Died: Bristol, Gloucestershire, 25th September 1959

CAREER: Heaton Rovers/Willington Athletic/Loughborough Town cs. 1895/Bristol City May 1897/**SPURS** May 1906/Swindon Town May 1907/retired cs. 1908.

Debut v Plymouth Argyle (WL) (h) 3.9.1906

Billy Jones was signed from Bristol City as cover for Spurs' regular half-back line of Ted Hughes, Tom Morris and Walter Bull. Originally a forward with Heaton Rovers, Willington Athletic and Loughborough Town, he had spent nine years with Bristol City, dropped into the half-back role, but rising to international level with an appearance for England against Ireland in March 1901. He lost his place with Bristol in January 1906 as they moved towards the Second Division title, and, when they decided not to retain his services at the end of the season, Spurs were quick to move for a solid, dependable 30-year old who, whilst not quite the player he had been, was clearly likely to be a short term asset. He filled the reserve half-back role for one season, scoring twice in a total of 14 first team appearances. He left Spurs in May 1907 to join Swindon, but spent only a season with the Wiltshire club before retiring from the game.

Appearances:
Southern: 8 apps.
Others: 3 apps. 2 gls.
Total: **11 apps. 2 gls.**

JORDAN, John William

Role: Inside-forward 1947-48
5ft.8ins. 11st.0lbs.
Born: Romford, Essex, 8th November 1921
Died: Cambridge, 9th January 2016

CAREER: Bromley/Grays Athletic/West Ham United am. 1946/**SPURS** am. Jul 1947, pro. Aug 1947/Juventus (Italy) Aug 1948/Birmingham City Mar 1949/Sheffield Wednesday Sep 1950/Tonbridge Jul 1951/Bedford Town Jul 1953-1954.

Debut v Sheffield Wednesday (FL) (h) 30.8.1947 (scored twice)

Johnny Jordan was one of the country's most promising amateurs in the immediate post-war years. Playing with Bromley and Grays Athletic, he was also on West Ham's books. Named as reserve for the England amateur team in 1946-47, he announced his intention, a month after signing amateur forms for Spurs, to move from Grays to Sutton United. This prompted Spurs, who had been impressed by his performances in trial games, to offer him a professional contract and he went straight into the first team. An impressive inside-forward with a superb first touch and lovely vision, he scored ten goals in 27 senior appearances during his one season at White Hart Lane. He should have stayed much longer, but in August 1948 Spurs accepted an excellent transfer offer from Juventus of Italy. Like many players who followed, Jordan did not enjoy his time in Italy and returned to England only seven months later when he signed for Birmingham City. He then had a year with Sheffield Wednesday before finishing with League football and joining Tonbridge. Jordan's cousin, Clarrie, was a centre-forward with Doncaster Rovers and Sheffield Wednesday in the late 1940's and early 1950's.

Appearances:
League: 24 apps. 10 gls.
FA Cup: 3 apps.
Others: 1 app.
Total: **28 apps. 10 gls.**

JOSEPH, Leon

Role: Winger 1946-47
Born: Stepney, London, 26th February 1920
Died: Barnet, Hertfordshire, June 1983

CAREER: Oxford St. Georges School/London Schools/West Ham United am. 1935/Leytonstone 1936-1956/**SPURS** am. Feb 1947/Wingate.

Debut v Burnley (FL) (a) 18.2.1947

The absence of Les Stevens early in 1947 caused Spurs unexpected and serious problems. Harry Gilberg and Charlie Whitchurch were tried in his outside-left position without success and so Spurs turned to Leytonstone's England amateur international Leon Joseph to fill the gap. As it was, he was only required for one game as Stevens was then able to return. Joseph was an England amateur international who collected twelve caps in total. He was offered the chance to turn professional by Spurs, but he ran his own men's outfitters' business in Leytonstone and knew the money was much better there than he could hope to earn as a footballer.

Appearances:
League: 1 app.
Total: **1 app. 0 gls.**

JOSLIN, Philip James

Role: Goalkeeper 1945-46
Born: Kingsteignton, Devon, 1st September 1916
Died: 1981

CAREER: Kingsteighton Athletic/Plymouth Argyle 1936/Torquay United 1936/(guest for Aldershot, Arsenal, Crystal Palace, Exeter City, Fulham, Reading, Southend United, **SPURS** and York City during World War Two)/Cardiff City May 1948-1951.

Debut v West Ham United (FLS) (a) 8.9.1945

Torquay United's goalkeeper Phil Joslin, made four appearances for Spurs in the Football League South as a guest during September 1945. A guest for several other clubs during those times he returned to Torquay upon the resumption of normal football and remained there for another two years. After his transfer to Cardiff City he played over 100 League games for the Welsh club before a broken leg in pre-season 1951 led to his retirement.

Appearances:
Others: 4 apps.
Total: **4 apps. 0 gls.**

JOYCE, John William

Role: Goalkeeper 1909-16
6ft. 15st.10lbs.
Born: Burton-on-Trent, Staffordshire, 26th June 1877
Died: Greenwich, London, June 1956

CAREER: Burton Pioneers 1895/Woodville 1896/Overseal Town 1897/Southampton May 1898/Millwall May 1900/Burton United Aug 1901/Blackburn Rovers May 1902/Millwall cs. 1903/**SPURS** Nov 1909/Millwall

1916/(Gillingham loan Nov 1919)/Reading/retired 1919/Northfleet United 1920/Millwall asst. trainer, ground-staff, temp. manager.

Debut v Sheffield United (FL) (h) 27.11.1909

John "Tiny" Joyce spent six years with Spurs, but is best remembered for his many years' service as Millwall's custodian. His football career began in hometown Burton-On-Trent, with Burton Junior League club Overseal Town and he had two years with Southampton before joining Millwall for the first time. After two years in Docklands, he spent a season with Blackburn, but returned to Millwall where he became first choice for the next six years, until losing his place in October 1909. Spurs were finding life hard during their opening season in the First Division, and Joyce was just the type of experienced 'keeper needed to provide a solid last line of defence. His transfer was secured and he duly replaced Fred Boreham. A big, strapping, but still agile man, he kept his place until the end of the season, but the arrival of Tom Lunn meant that for the next two years he had to be content with a reserve role. He enjoyed a lengthy run in the first team in 1912-13, but then had to see off the challenge of Arthur King. Having continually bounced back, the arrival of Bill Jacques eventually finished Joyce's career with Spurs although it was not until early in 1916 that he returned to Millwall. He continued with them until his retirement in 1919 when he was made assistant trainer, although in November 1919 he was transferred to Gillingham on "loan" to help out the Southern League club who were suffering a severe injury crisis. Back at Millwall he helped with work on the construction of the ground and even briefly held the managerial reins when Bob Hunter was ill in the early 1930s. He remained assistant trainer with Millwall until 1938 when he moved onto the ground-staff. Renowned for his huge punted kicks upfield, Joyce remains the only goalkeeper to score for Spurs in a Football League game, netting against Bolton Wanderers on 10th April 1914; he also scored a penalty for Spurs, in a tour match against Bayern Munich in May 1914. In a match for the reserves against Peterborough in 1911 Joyce was reported as having punched the ball 76ft 2ins. To that can be added a dead ball kick of 94yds 2ft before the ball touched the ground measured in a competition with Chelsea inside-forward "Pom Pom" Whiting in 1906. Joyce's brother, Tom, was a goalkeeper with Burton Swifts at the turn of the 19th century.

Appearances:
Southern: 73 apps. 1 gl.
FA Cup: 8 apps.
Others: 33 apps. 1 gl.
Total: 114 apps. 2 gls.

JOYCE, William

Role: Centre-forward 1897-99
5ft.5ins. 11st.2lbs.
Born: 1877

CAREER: Greenock Morton/Bolton Wanderers Mar 1894/**SPURS** May 1897/Thames Ironworks cs. 1899/Portsmouth May 1900/Burton United cs. 1901/Morton Oct 1903/Motherwell Oct 1904.

Debut v Sheppey United (SL) (a) 4.9.1897 (scored once)
(Glossop North End (Fr) (h) 2.9.1897 (scored once))

Bill Joyce was a centre forward whose single-minded objective was to bury the ball in the net-and he certainly did it to great effect for Spurs. While he may have been a footballer with few fancy frills, his scoring record bears ample testimony to his ability to do a specific job. He scored on his debut and continued to find the net regularly in his two peak years with Spurs, hitting 93 goals in only 119 appearances including 4 hat-tricks, three fours and one five goal haul. Despite this outstanding record, the only representative honour he won during his time with the club was in November 1898 when he played for the United League against the Thames and Medway League at Northumberland Park, and, predictably, scored twice. Joyce had started his career with Greenock Morton, then joined Bolton Wanderers where a broken leg in 1896 put him out of the game for the best part of a year. In the summer of 1899 Spurs signed David Copeland and Joyce moved on to Thames Ironworks. In a struggling team he did not find goals so easy to come by and after one year left to join Portsmouth as replacement for Sandy Brown who had joined Spurs. Only a year later he moved to Burton United where he played for two seasons, before returning home to Scotland.

Appearances:
League: 40 apps. 34 gls.
FA Cup: 12 apps. 7 gls.
Others: 66 apps. 52 gls.
Total: 118 apps. 93 gls.

JULIAN, John William

Role: Half-back 1894-96
5ft.9ins. 11st.3lbs.
Born: *Boston, Lincolnshire, 10th July 1867*
Died: *Enfield, Middlesex, 14th March 1957*

CAREER: Boston Excelsior/Boston Town/Royal Arsenal cs. 1888/Luton Town player-coach cs. 1893/**SPURS** Sep 1894/British Ladies FC coach 1894/Woolwich Polytechnic Sep 1895/Dartford cs. 1896/Shepherds Bush 1898-99/MVV Maastricht (Holland) coach/VVV Venlo (Holland) coach/ PSV Eindhoven (Holland) coach/HFC Haarlem (Holland) coach/HBS Den Haag (Holland) coach/Feyenoord (Holland) coach May 1921-1922/ Helder (Holland) coach.

Debut v West Herts (FAC) (h) 13.10.1894
(London Caledonians (Fr) 29.9.1894)

One of the leading lights in London football during the final years of the 19th century, Bill Julian started out with Boston Excelsior, but it was his performance for Boston Town against Royal Arsenal in April 1888 which really set him on the road to footballing fame. He played so well that Arsenal immediately arranged a job for him at the Royal Arsenal armaments factory, simply so he could play for them. He soon became a regular, appeared for London and Middlesex and, as Arsenal skipper, had the honour of captaining the first professional football team in the South. After five years with Arsenal he moved to Luton Town as player-coach, but twelve months later he was back in the capital. Spurs were still an amateur club at the time and if Julian was to play for them he needed be reinstated as an amateur. That status was secured in September 1894. Julian immediately went into the team and was first choice for the rest of the season. However, he only played four matches the following season

having decided to turn out for Woolwich Polytechnic, and then joined Dartford. He later went abroad to Holland where he played at full-back for six years, before embarking on a lengthy career in the country coaching both football and cricket. In 1927 he led the Helder club on a tour of England. Julian had first secured some coaching experience when with Spurs. In 1894 attempts were made to popularise women's football and Julian trained the British Ladies FC in preparation for a countrywide tour. Julian's son, also JW, played for Spurs "A" team in 1909.

Appearances:
FA Cup: 5 apps.
Others: 28 apps. 4 gls.
Total: 33 apps. 4 gls.

JULL, H

Role: Half-back 1891-92

Debut v Luton Town (Fr) (a) 26.3.1892

Apart from the fact that he was related to Jack and Tommy Jull, no other information is known about this player whose sole appearance was in a friendly with Luton Town in March 1892.

Appearances:
Others: 1 app.
Total: 1 app. 0 gls.

JULL, John Charles

Role: Full-back 1883-97
Born: Edmonton, London, June qtr. 1867
Died: 22nd December 1920

Debut v West Herts (FAC) (h) 13.10.1894
(Brownlow Rovers (Fr) (h) 6.10.1883)

Jack Jull will always be remembered not only as one of the founders of Spurs, but also one of the finest players associated with the club in those late Victorian days. A little older than many of the other schoolboys who formed Spurs, he was normally a full-back but, typical of his dedication to the cause, was always prepared to turn out in any position required. His first known appearance was in a friendly with Brownlow Rovers in October 1883 which was the first Spurs match to be reported in the local newspapers. Strangely, he was mentioned in the match report, but was not included in the team line-up. The first Spurs' player to win a representative honour when he played for Middlesex against Surrey at Guildford on 18th February 1891, Jull was described by no less a figure than the outstanding amateur Stanley Briggs as "one of the finest captains and most fearless" and certainly Spurs seemed a much stronger outfit when he played. After the first couple of seasons of Spurs' existence Jull was not always available, being away at boarding school, but he was always there when Spurs were involved in a major match. He played in the clubs' first ever cup-tie, against St Albans in the London Senior Cup on 17th October 1885, first ever "League" game, against Polytechnic on 24th September 1892, first Amateur Cup game, against Vampires on 11th November 1893 and first FA Cup game, against West Herts on 13th October 1894. He continued to play for Spurs right up until April 1897 when he made two appearances in the United League. Apart from turning out for Middlesex he also represented Tottenham and London and served as a member of the Spurs' committee for several years, always remaining at the forefront of the club's development and a true guiding light. His splendid service to Spurs was recognised in 1895 when he was made the club President. After Spurs Jull played a few games for Old Tottonians in 1898-99 and when his playing days were over he was a referee in the Southern League for a time.

Appearances:
FA Cup: 8 apps.
Others: 153 apps. 24 gls.
Total: 161 apps. 24 gls.

JULL, Thomas Edward

Role: Forward 1894-97
Born: Tottenham, London, 22nd December 1875.
Died: 1963

CAREER: Asplin Rovers by Nov 1893/**SPURS**/Avondale/Cheshunt cs. 1897.

Debut v Loughborough (UL) (a) 24.4.1897

The younger brother of Jack, Tommy Jull did not reach the same heights as his brother, but was still regarded as a very useful footballer in the north London area. He appears to have first played for Spurs in 1893 when he assisted the reserves, but did not make his debut in the first team until April 1895. Indeed, Jull played most of his football for the reserves and only got into the first team on rare occasions. He played for Avondale at the end of the 1895-96 season and almost certainly turned out for some of the other local clubs. His only competitive appearance for Spurs came in April 1897 when he played at full-back in the last United League match of the season against Loughborough. His selection was apparently intended as a "trial", but in view of Jull's long association with the club that would only have been appropriate if Spurs were thinking of taking him on as a professional. Although he reportedly "did well" in the match, he was not engaged and went to play for Cheshunt, where he had probably the most memorable day of his career in February 1899, as a member of the Cheshunt team that, surprisingly, knocked the Casuals out of the Amateur Cup.

Appearances:
Others: 3 apps.
Total: 3 apps. 0 gls.

K

KABOUL, Younès

Role: Central Defender 2007-08 and 2009-15
6ft. 3ins. 11st.11lbs.
Born: Saint-Julien-en-Genevois, France, 4th January 1986

CAREER: Bellegarde (France) 1991/Concordia (France) 1993/Plastics Vallee (France) Jul 1999/AJ Auxerre (France) 2000/SPURS Jul 2007/Portsmouth Aug 2008/SPURS Jan 2010/Sunderland Jul 2015/Watford Aug 2016.

Debut v Sunderland (PL) (a) 11.8.2007
(St Patricks Athletic (Fr) (a) 12.7.2007)

France's Under-21 captain and a French Cup winner with Auxerre in 2005, Younès Kaboul was rated one of the best young defenders in Europe when Spurs signed him for £8 million in the summer of 2007. He was expected to be given time to make the transition to Premier League football, but as Spurs started the 2007-08 season with one central defender after another hit by injury, Kaboul found himself thrust into the firing line. Strong, well-built and powerful, his potential was obvious, but so was his inexperience. As Spurs struggled, so Kaboul's confidence suffered, every error highlighted and punished, his place constantly in jeopardy. The signing of Jonathan Woodgate should have allowed Kaboul time to re-start his Spurs' career, but it just marked the beginning of the end. While he made a late substitute appearance in the Worthington Cup final in 2008, there were to be no further opportunities and he was transferred to Portsmouth. Under the guidance of Harry Redknapp, Kaboul's confidence was quickly restored as he re-built his career and showed just what a good player he could be when those around had faith in him. When Redknapp joined Spurs, Kaboul was one of the first signings he made, taking him back to White Hart Lane in January 2010. Kaboul soon displayed every indication of realising the potential he had shown first time around. Now showing consistency and reliability, he was calmer under pressure, relaxed on the ball and more adventurous in possession. By the summer of 2011 he was on the international stage, making his full international debut for France against Ukraine and adding to the ten Under-21 caps he had collected in his first spell in north London. Just when he looked to have established himself as a regular first choice, Redknapp departed. Needing to impress his successor, Andre Villas-Boas, Kaboul was injured in the first League game of the season and out for the rest of the campaign. Throughout Villas-Boas' time with Spurs, doubts over Kaboul's fitness were ever-present. Only when Tim Sherwood was put in temporary control did Kaboul begin to look the part again. His future seemed assured when Mauricio Pochettino made Kaboul club captain, but Kaboul then reverted to his unsure, error-prone old self. Competing with the equally unreliable Federico Fazio and Vlad Chiriches, Kaboul played a few games, but when Pochettino eventually decided he preferred to pair the novice Eric Dier with Jan Vertonghen, Kaboul's days were numbered. He was allowed to move to Sunderland and soon moved on to Watford.

Appearances:
League: 101 (8) apps. 6 gls.
FA Cup: 6 apps.
FL Cup: 5 (1) apps.
Euro: 16 (2) apps. 2 gls.
Others: 17 (6) apps. 1 gl.
Total: 145 (17) apps. 9 gls.

KAINE, William Edward John Charles

Role: Goalkeeper 1925-26
6ft. 12st.10lbs.
Born: East Ham, London, 27th June 1900
Died: Chippenham, 3rd November 1968.

CAREER: Stirling Athletic/West Ham United May 1923/SPURS May 1925/Luton Town Jul 1926/Bradford City Mar 1928.

Debut v Bury (FL) (a) 10.10.1925

Having started with the Stirling Athletic club of Dagenham, Bill Kaine joined Spurs from West Ham United to provide both back-up and a challenge to Fred Hinton for the goalkeeper's position. He was one of four 'keepers used by Spurs in the 1925-26 campaign, the others being Hinton, Jimmy Smith and Jock Brittan, but none of them were able to satisfactorily fill what became a problem position throughout the season. Kaine made just twelve appearances before being discarded and on his release moved to Luton Town, later joining Bradford City.

Appearances:
League: 11 apps.
FA Cup: 1 app.
Total: 12 apps. 0 gls.

KAMANAN, Yannick Etienne Stanislas

Role: Forward 2001-02
6ft. 11st.8lbs.
Born: Saint-Pol-sur-Mer, France, 5th October 1981.

CAREER: Élancourt (France)/Le Mans Union Club 72 (France) Jul 1998 /SPURS trial and perm Jul 1999/Bristol Rovers trial Jan 2002/Racing Club Strasbourg (France) trial Jan 2002, perm Jun 2002/(Dijon (France) loan Jul 2003)/Grimsby Town trial Jul 2004/(Ajaccio (France) loan Jul 2004)/KV Oostende (Belgium) Jul 2005/FC Schaffhausen (Switzerland) Jul 2006/Maccabi Herzliya (Israel) Jan 2007/Maccabi Tel Aviv (Israel)

Jul 2007/Sivasspor (Turkey) Jan 2009/Mersin İdmanyurdu (Turkey) Jul 2011/Gabala (Azerbaijan) Jan 2012-Apr 2014/Ermis Aradippou (Cyprus) Aug 2014/AS Aulnoye (France) Aug 2015/ES Viry Chantillon (France) Jul 2016.

Debut v Stevenage Borough (sub) (Fr) (a) 13.7.2001

A pacy young striker signed as a youth, Yannick Kamanan appeared as a substitute in three pre-season friendlies in 2001, scoring three goals. With strikers of the calibre of Les Ferdinand, Steffen Iversen, Serhiy Rebrov and Teddy Sheringham ahead of him, Kamanan was not given another chance. When Spurs decided to release him in January 2002, he initially returned to France before setting out on a career that took him around the less exalted leagues of Europe.

Appearances:
Others: (3) apps. 3 gls.
Total: **(3) apps. 3 gls.**

KANE, Harry Edward

Role: Striker 2011-
6ft.1in. 12st.2lbs.
Born: Walthamstow, London, 28th July 1993.

CAREER: Ridgeway Rovers/Arsenal Academy/Ridgeway Rovers/Watford Academy/**SPURS** Academy Scholar Jul 2009, pro. Jul 2010/(Leyton Orient loan Jan 2011)/(Millwall loan Jan 2012)/(Norwich City loan Aug 2012)/(Leicester City loan Feb 2013).

Debut v Heart of Midlothian (EL) (h) 25.8.2011

From his earliest days at the Spurs Academy, Harry Kane exhibited the skills and attitude that have made him one of football's most potent strikers. Powerfully built and with an insatiable thirst for work matched only by his desire to score, he showed he could play as part of an attacking duo, or on his own, when his ability to hold up the ball and bring his attacking midfielders into play came to the fore. Still young enough to be playing youth team football, Kane went on loan to Leyton Orient where he scored 5 goals in 18 games in the rough, tough world of Division One football. Back at Spurs he had just turned 18 when he made his senior debut in a Europa League match against Hearts. He won a penalty, had the confidence to step up and take the kick himself, but saw his shot saved. A lesser character would have let the disappointment get the better of him, but not Kane. If anything, the failure to score just spurred him on. With the likes of Emmanuel Adebayor, Jermaine Defoe and Roberto Soldado the senior strikers at

White Hart Lane, Kane went out on loan to secure game time at senior level. He performed more than well at Millwall and Leicester City while injury restricted his opportunities at Norwich City. With Soldado proving a disappointment, Kane was given a starting role in the Premier League team in April 2014, netting three goals in as many games to show that given the opportunity, he could score the goals Soldado and Adebayor were failing to provide. The 2014-15 season proved the turning point. Given his chance by Mauricio Pochettino, Kane grabbed it with both hands, leading the line and scoring regularly. With less than a full season of top flight football under his belt, Kane made his England debut against Lithuania in March 2015, scoring within 80 seconds of being introduced as a substitute. At both club and international level, he has continued to flourish. Strong and powerful, he has a natural instinct for scoring, always prepared to have a crack at goal, and never afraid to miss. While not looking the fastest of players, he is deceptively quick and particularly adept at getting his body between ball and opponent. Whether bursting through the centre with the ball at his feet, cutting in from the wing, or racing forward to get on the end of a pass, his all round game continues to improve rapidly. All the time, the tremendous work ethic that had first propelled him forward remains at the forefront of his game, endearing him to team-mates and supporters. Spurs have had a long line of world class English central strikers, from Vivian Woodward, through George Hunt and Bobby Smith, to Martin Chivers and Teddy Sheringham. After barely three full seasons at the top level, Harry Kane must be added to that list.

Appearances:
League: 101 (12) apps. 78 gls.
FA Cup: 5 (4) apps. 5 gls.
FL Cup: 7 (2) apps. 4 gls.
Euro: 18 (16) apps. 12 gls.
Others: 10 (9) apps. 10 gls.
Total: **141 (43) apps. 109 gls.**

KANOUTÉ, Frédéric Oumar

Role: Striker 2003-06
6ft.3ins. 13st.8lbs.
Born: Sainte-Foy-lès-Lyon, France, 2nd September 1977

CAREER: Olympique Lyonnais (France) app, pro. Jun 1997/West Ham United loan Mar 2000, perm. May 2000/**SPURS** Aug 2003/Sevilla (Spain) Aug 2005/Beijing Guoan (China) Jun 2012/retired Nov 2013.

Debut v Leeds United (sub) (PL) (h) 23.8.2000

A striker of immense talent, Fredi Kanouté was also an immensely frustrating performer. Having made his name with his local club, Olympique Lyonnais, Kanouté initially joined West Ham United on loan, another of the many foreign players Harry Redknapp identified as having the potential to make their mark in the English game. After his loan spell, Kanouté signed on a permanent basis and soon proved what a shrewd judge Redknapp could be. Scoring regularly, he helped West Ham maintain a place in the top half of the League, but when injured West Ham suffered. With relegation in 2003, Kanouté made it clear he wanted

away and got his wish when Spurs added him to a powerful looking attack of Hélder Postiga, Bobby Zamora and Robbie Keane. He impressed immediately with seven goals in his first nine games, which was fortunate as both Postiga and Zamora disappointed. As expected for someone of 6ft 3ins, Kanouté was strong in the air, but not simply with his heading ability. He had a particular penchant for climbing high and taking the ball down on his chest before making for goal or laying the ball off. Intelligent, pacy and always ready to have a shot at goal, Kanouté had great vision and was also adept at holding the ball up and bringing others into play. He looked set for a great debut season in a Spurs shirt, but then decided he wanted to play in the Africa Cup of Nations that was due to start in January 2004. Although he had played for France at youth level, that did not disqualify him from playing for his father's country, Mali. The thought of losing Kanouté for more than a month was not appreciated at White Hart Lane, but Kanouté was determined to go and Spurs could not stop him. Kanouté was away for four weeks, joint top-scorer as Mali reached the semi-finals of the competition. He failed to score for Spurs again following his return. Kanouté stayed with Spurs for another year, without ever looking anything like the player his early outings had promised. There were times when he looked a world-beater. There were other times, too many of them, when he seemed lazy, uninterested, just going through the motions. While Jermaine Defoe and Robbie Keane could be relied upon to give maximum effort even if they were not having any luck, Kanouté was unpredictable. It was no surprise when Spurs cut their losses and accepted an offer from Sevilla. Kanouté spent seven years in Spain, scoring regularly and leading the line as Sevilla mounted a serious challenge to the established powerhouses of Spanish football. African Player of the Year in 2007, he helped Sevilla lift the UEFA Cup in 2006 and 2007. Kanouté had been remarkably free from injury during his career but as he began to age, so the years of continuous play began to take their toll. With Alvaro Negredo coming through to lead Sevilla's attack, Kanouté was released and moved to China, retiring after a year.

Appearances:
League: 41 (19) apps. 14 gls.
FA Cup: 6 apps. 3 gls.
FL Cup: 5 (2) apps. 4 gls.
Others: 5 (3) apps. 7 gls.
Total: 57 (24) apps. 28 gls.

KEANE, Robert David

Role: Striker 2002-2008 and 2008-12
5ft.9ins. 11st.10lbs.
Born: Dublin, Republic of Ireland, 8th July 1980.

CAREER: Fettercairn United/Crumlin United/Wolverhampton Wanderers YTS Jun 1996, pro Jul 1997/Coventry City Aug 1999/Internazionale (Italy) Jul 2000/Leeds United loan Dec 2000, perm. May 2001/**SPURS** Sep 2002/Liverpool Jul 2008/**SPURS** Feb 2009/(Celtic loan Jan 2010)/(West Ham United loan Jan 2011)/Los Angeles Galaxy (USA) Aug 2011-Nov 2016/(Aston Villa loan Jan 2012)/Al Ahli (Dubai) training Jan 2017.

Debut v West Ham United (PL) (h) 15.9.2002

Some players will readily admit that, for them, playing football is just a job. For others, the pleasure they get from doing what any supporter would give everything for is obvious. Robbie Keane was one of the latter breed of footballers. For him playing was always a pleasure, a pleasure to be shared with the supporters. Spotted by Wolverhampton Wanderers as a schoolboy in Dublin, Keane had barely turned professional before he made his League debut for Wolves, scoring twice against Norwich City. He quickly established himself as a regular, scoring regularly, the star of the Football League. Premier League clubs were soon monitoring Keane, but there were concerns as to whether such a young talent could make the step up, particularly with Wolves demanding £6 million for his signature. While the big clubs dithered, Coventry City took the plunge. In one season with them Keane proved such a success that Internazionale more than doubled Coventry's outlay to take him to Italy. Within weeks Marcello Lippi, the manager who had wanted Keane to become the future of Inter, had been sacked. His successor, Marco Tardelli, was not prepared to risk his job on a comparative unknown barely out of his teens. Keane joined Leeds United on loan in December 2000, the transfer made permanent at the end of the season. He performed more than adequately in his early days at Elland Road, but as Leeds financial problems became known and big names left to keep the club afloat, so Keane suffered the first dip in his career. Leeds' shortage of money allowed Glenn Hoddle to take Keane to White Hart Lane for what proved to be a bargain £7 million. For six years Keane flourished in the lilywhite shirt, an effervescent will-o-the-wisp, continually probing for weaknesses and, if not threatening to score himself, creating opportunities for others. Keane was not an out-and-out striker, frequently dropping back into midfield to collect the ball and utilise his dribbling skills to attack from deep. He often ran up blind alleys, and there were certainly times when he held on to the ball too long, but such shortcomings were more than compensated for by his enthusiasm and never-ending hard work. Whether playing alongside Teddy Sheringham, Fredi Kanouté, Mido, Darren Bent or Dimitar Berbatov, Keane could always be relied upon to give of his best. Having won the battle with Jermain Defoe to partner Berbatov,

Keane's game reached a whole new level with the goals flowing at a greater rate than ever before in 2007-08. Such was his success that Liverpool, desperate to keep up with Manchester United, offered nearly £20 million for Keane's transfer. It was an offer Spurs did not invite and not one they were interested in, but with Keane proclaiming his boyhood support for Liverpool, they eventually had to accept the offer. Any dreams Keane may have had of starring in front of the Kop never looked remotely like coming true. He spent a miserable few months on Merseyside before new Spurs' manager, Harry Redknapp, persuaded him to return to Tottenham. Keane was one of three former Spurs' players to return to the club during the transfer window, Jermain Defoe and Pascal Chimbonda the others. Short though Keane's time at Anfield had been, it had taken something from his game. As hard-working as ever, he was never able to rediscover the form that had made him such a star at Spurs and while his popularity rarely waned, he rarely held down a regular place. After loan spells with Celtic and West Ham United, Keane was sold to Los Angeles Galaxy in August 2012. The move was perfect for Keane. A personable chap, married to a former Miss Ireland contestant, he was everything the Americans love. While the MLS is not as good or tough as the Premier League, the quality is still there and Keane has put himself right at its peak. Keane holds the record of appearances and goals for the Republic of Ireland, scoring, as at 1 April 2016, 67 goals in 141 games, 36 of the goals coming in his 66 outings while a Spurs' player. There is no reason why more may not be added.

Appearances:
League: 189 (49) apps. 91 gls.
FA Cup: 16 (5) apps. 12 gls.
FL Cup: 16 (7) apps. 10 gls.
Euro: 15 (9) apps. 8 gls.
Others: 35 (13) apps. 26 gls.
Total: 271 (83) apps. 147 gls.

THE SPURS ALPHABET

KEELEY, Andrew James

Role: Defender 1975-77
5ft.10ins. 11st.4lbs.
Born: Basildon, Essex, 16th September 1956

CAREER: Basildon Schools/**SPURS** app. Sep 1972, pro. Jan 1974/Sheffield United Dec 1977/Scunthorpe United Jul 1981/Bowers United by 1993-94.

Debut v Birmingham City (FL) (h) 20.10.1976
(Brighton and Hove Albion (sub) (Fr) (a) 23.3.1976)

An England Youth player, Andy Keeley is one of the many youngsters who, perhaps inevitably at a big club like Spurs, work their way through the junior ranks, make a few appearances in the first team and are then released to move on to a club lower down the League ladder and prove their worth. Keeley was maybe more unfortunate in that he was with Spurs as the club sank on a downward spiral and was only able to make the first team in 1976-77, the year relegation became a reality for the first time since 1935. He had six League outings that season and looked a player who, given time, might develop into a useful defender, but in Spurs' position the one thing they just could not afford was the luxury of an inexperienced player learning his trade. He only remained with Spurs until December 1977 when he joined Sheffield United but, unable to establish himself at Bramall Lane, eventually moved on to Scunthorpe United. His brother, Glenn, was a central defender with Ipswich Town, Newcastle United, Blackburn Rovers and Oldham Athletic.

Appearances:
League: 5 (1) apps.
Others: (3) apps.
Total: 5 (4) apps. 0 gls.

KEITH

Role: Centre-half 1896-97

Debut v Northfleet (Fr) (h) 29.12.1896

Keith's only appearance for Spurs was in December 1896 when he played in a friendly against Northfleet, standing in for regular half-back Bill Almond.

Appearances:
Others: 1 app.
Total: 1 app. 0 gls.

KELLER, Kasey C

Role: Goalkeeper 2001-05
6ft.2ins. 13st.2lbs.
Born: Olympia, Washington, USA, 27th November 1969

CAREER: Portland Pirates (USA)/University of Portland (USA)/Portland Timbers (USA)/Millwall Feb 1992/Leicester City Aug 1996/Rayo Vallecano (Spain) Jul 1999/**SPURS** Aug 2001/(Southampton loan Nov 2004)/Borussia Mönchengladbach (Germany) Jan 2005/Fulham Aug 2007/Seattle Sounders (USA) Aug 2008-Oct 2011/retired Oct 2011/USA Under-20 goalkeeping coach Apr 2012, USA goalkeeping coach Jul 2013.

Debut v Torquay United (FLC) (h) 13.9.2001

With the departure of Ian Walker, Spurs needed experienced cover for first choice 'keeper, Neil Sullivan, and Kasey Keller was regarded as the perfect man for the job. As it transpired, he soon became more than a back-up. Keller had first played in England for Millwall, joining them after coming to prominence in the United States with the University of Portland, Portland Timbers and the US national team. First capped in February 1990, Keller was a member of American's squad for the 1990 World Cup finals, though he did not play a game in Italy. Making his Lions' debut in the last match of the 1991-92 campaign, Keller soon established himself as first choice and one of the outstanding 'keepers in the First Division. He was unable to save Millwall from being relegated in 1996, but, far too good for Third Division football, after captaining the American

Under-23s at the Olympic Games, joined Leicester City for close to £1 million. A member of Leicester's Coca-Cola League Cup winning team of 1997, Keller also played in the Worthington Cup final of 1999 when Leicester were beaten by Alan Nielsen's late winner for Spurs. Keller next played for Rayo Vallecano, spending two years with Madrid's third club before arriving at White Hart Lane. Keller had few chances to impress at Spurs until late in the 2001-02 season. He then replaced Sullivan for the last few games of the season and was ever-present for the next two years proving a solid, reliable, if not spectacular last line of defence. With the arrival of Paul Robinson, Keller lost his place. Approaching the veteran stage and needing regular games if he was to play for the USA in the 2005 CONCACAF Gold Cup and World Cup qualifiers, Keller moved to Borussia Monchengladbach in January 2005. He enjoyed eighteen months in Germany and a year with Fulham before returning to the US and Seattle Sounders. Keller retired just short of his 42nd birthday to take on a commentator's role for the Sounders while also doing some coaching of the national teams. Keller was voted US Soccer Athlete of the Year in 1997, 1999 and 2005. Of his 101 appearances for the USA, 25 of them were in his time with Spurs.

Appearances:
League: 85 apps.
FA Cup: 4 apps.
FL Cup: 10 apps.
Others: 13 apps.
Total: 112 apps. 0 gls.

KELLY, Gavin

Role: Goalkeeper 2001-02
6ft.0ins. 13st.7lbs.
Born: Hammersmith, London, 3rd June 1981

CAREER: Court Park Colts/West Middlesex Colts/Hillingdon Borough Schools/Middlesex Schools/Republic of Ireland Schools/**SPURS** trainee Jul 1997, pro. Jul 1999/(Chelmsford City loan Dec 1999)/(Kingstonian loan Dec 2000)/(Southend United trial Mar 2002)/(Cambridge United trial Apr 2002)/(Colchester United trial Jul 2002)/(Kettering Town loan Oct 2002)/(Rushden & Diamonds trial Jan 2003)/(Mansfield Town trial Feb 2003)/released Jun 2003/Leyton Orient trial Sep 2003/Kettering Town Sep 2003/Welling United Oct 2003/Cambridge United Mar 2004/Leatherhead 2005-06.

Debut v Stevenage Borough (sub) (Fr) (a) 13.7.2001

Gavin Kelly had picked up a bit of experience on loan to non-League Chelmsford City and Kingstonian before making three appearances for Spurs in pre-season friendlies in 2001. With Neil Sullivan and Kasey Keller competing for the first team role, Kelly was never in serious consideration for the place himself. Spurs announced he was available for transfer in December 2002 but it was some time before he fixed up a position at Kettering Town.

Appearances:
Others: 2 (1) apps.
Total: 2 (1) apps. 0 gls.

KELLY, Stephen Michael David

Role: Full-back 2002-06
6ft. 12st.4lbs.
Born: Dublin, Republic of Ireland, 6th September 1983

CAREER: St Kevin's School/Belvedere/SPURS scholar Jul 2000, pro. Sep 2000/(Southend United loan Jan 2003)/(Queens Park Rangers loan Mar 2003)/(Watford loan Sep 2003)/Birmingham City Jun 2006/(Stoke City loan Feb 2009)/Fulham Jun 2009/Reading Jan 2013-Jul 2015/Rotherham United trial and perm. Nov 2015.

Debut v Charlton Athletic (PL) (h) 28.12.2003
(DC United (sub) (Fr) (h) 17.10.2002)

Republic of Ireland youth international Stephen Kelly, joined Spurs on leaving school in Dublin, following in the footsteps of his fellow right-back, Steve Carr. There the similarity ended. Kelly was not as pacy and did not possess the same scoring threat as Carr. He was just as keen to get forward, but a little less adventurous, more cautious and conscious that his first duty was to defend. In doing that he was equally as effective and being somewhat taller than Carr could double up as a central defender when needed. After gaining experience with loan spells at Southend United and Queens Park Rangers, Kelly was given his first team opportunity towards the end of the 2003-04 season. With Carr departing for Newcastle United before the new season began, Kelly might have expected to be given the chance to make the right-back position his own. However, the arrival of Jacques Santini and Frank Arnesen and the signings of the vastly experienced Noureddine Naybet and Noe Pamarot left Kelly as back-up. While a regular for the Republic at Under-21 level, he was given few opportunities to impress and when Paul Stalteri was signed the writing was on the wall. Having made his first full international appearance, Kelly moved to Birmingham City in June 2006. First choice for two years, when he found himself out of the team, he made his displeasure known. Loaned to Stoke City, the arrival of Steve Carr at Birmingham allowed Kelly to move to Fulham and from there to Reading and Rotherham. Although never certain of a place, Kelly collected a total of 37 full caps for the Republic.

Appearances:
League: 29 (8) apps. 2 gls.
FA Cup: 6 apps.
FL Cup: 1 app.
Others: 10 (5) apps.
Total: 46 (13) apps. 2 gls.

KEMPES (Chiodi), Mario Alberto

Role: Striker 1984-85
6ft.0ins. 12st.4lbs.
Born: Belville, Cordoba, Argentina, 15th July 1954

CAREER: Atlético Talleres (Argentina)/Instituto AC Córdoba (Argentina) Mar 1972/Rosario Central (Argentina) Jan 1974/Valencia (Spain) Aug 1976/River Plate (Argentina) Mar 1981/Valencia (Spain) Jul 1982/SPURS trial Jul 1984/Hercules (Spain) Jul 1984/1FK Vienna (Austria) Apr 1986/VSE St. Pölten (Austria) Jul 1987-1990/Kremser (Austria) Jul 1990-1992/Valencia (Spain) asst. manager 1993/Arturo Fernández Vial (Chile) Aug 1995/Pelita Jaya (Indonesia) player-manager Mar-Oct 1996/Lushnjë (Albania) coach Dec 1996-Jan 1997/Mineros de Guayana (Venezuela) manager Oct 1998-Apr 1999/The Strongest (Bolivia) manager Jun 1999/Santa Bárbara (Bolivia) manager Sep 2000/Blooming Santa Cruz (Bolivia) manager Oct 2000-Feb 2001/Independiente Petrolero (Bolivia) manager Mar-Apr 2001/Casarano (Italy) coach Dec 2001-Jan 2002/San Fernando (Spain) coach Jan-May 2002/Panama manager Dec 2005 (effective Aug 2006).

Debut v Stjørdals-Blink (Fr) (a) 27.7.1984 (scored three)

One of the most exciting players of the late 70s/early 80s Mario Kempes sprang to world prominence with his performances for Argentina in the 1978 World Cup Finals where, aided by the astute promptings from midfield of Ossie Ardiles he formed a formidable attacking partnership with Leopoldo Luque. He scored six goals in the competition including two against Holland in the final as the host nation won the Cup. As a ten-year old, Kempes played for his home town team of Atlético Talleres, but was rejected by Boca Juniors so he began his senior career at Instituto Córdoba before moving to Rosario Central. An exceptional goal-scorer he made his debut at international level against Bolivia in 1973 and with 14 goals in his first 23 internationals soon had Europe's leading clubs on his trail. In 1976 he joined Valencia and quickly proved himself in the Spanish League, finishing his first two seasons as top scorer. Shortly after that move the Argentine FA banned transfers abroad and national manager César Luis Menotti declared he would only use home-based players for the forthcoming World Cup. Fortunately, not only for Kempes but for football in general, Argentina failed to perform and Kempes was one of the first stars recalled. Returning to Spain after the World Cup finals, he helped Valencia win the Spanish Cup in 1979 and defeat Arsenal on penalties in the 1980 European Cup-Winners Cup Final. In 1981 he returned to Argentina. He signed for River Plate in a £1 million deal and played for Argentina in the 1982 World Cup Finals. When the competition was over he re-joined Valencia as River Plate where unable to keep up the transfer payments. Kempes remained in Spain until his release at the end of the 1983-84 season. He made five appearances for Spurs on trial at the start of the following season, scoring a hat-trick against Stjørdals-Blink in his first match on the club's pre-season tour to Sweden and Norway. He failed to score in the other matches and although Spurs were very interested in signing him, they were unable to agree terms and he went to play in Austria. He later had a brief spell in Chile before embarking on a coaching career that took him throughout the world before he turned his talents to TV presentation. In October 2010 the Estadio Córdoba was renamed Estadio Mario Alberto Kempes in tribute to the city's most famous football son.

Appearances:
Others: 5 apps. 3 gls.
Total: 5 apps. 3 gls.

KENDALL, Mark

Role: Goalkeeper 1975-81
6ft. 12st.4lbs.
Born: Tredegar, Gwent, 30th September 1958
Died: Blackwood, Gwent, 1st May 2008

CAREER: Tredegar Schools/Gwent Schools/Wales Schools/**SPURS** app. Mar 1975, pro. Jul 1976/(Chesterfield loan Nov 1979)/Newport County loan Sep 1980, perm Nov 1980/Wolverhampton Wanderers loan Dec 1986, perm Jan 1987/Swansea City Jul 1990/(Burnley loan Dec 1991)/Newport AFC Aug 1992/Ebbw Vale/Cwmbran Town Sep 2002/Welsh Police coach.

Debut v Norwich City (FL) (a) 4.11.1978
(North Herts XI (sub) (Fr) (Stevenage) 21.4.1976)

A Welsh Youth international, Mark Kendall made his only appearance for his country at Under-21 level when he played against Scotland in February 1978, nine months before his Football League debut. That did not come until November when he was called up to replace Barry Daines. Promising, but not really ready for First Division football, it looked as if it was back to the reserves for Kendall the following month when Spurs signed Milija Aleksic, but the new arrival was injured in only his second game and Kendall was immediately recalled. Despite keen competition from Daines and Aleksic he retained the position for most of the remaining games of the 1978-79 season but, unable to maintain his form the following term, went back to the reserves. After a spell on loan to Chesterfield, he joined Newport County, initially on loan, and went on to give the now defunct club excellent service, playing more than 270 senior games over the next six years. With Newport's financial situation growing ever worse he moved to Wolverhampton Wanderers where he at last had some deserved success, being almost ever-present as the famous old club won the Fourth and Third Division titles in successive seasons and picked up the 1988 Sherpa Van Trophy along the way. Released in the summer of 1990, Mark joined Swansea City and although he spent most of the season in the reserves he did help them lift the Welsh Cup. He left Swansea in the summer of 1992 to join the police force but was still able to play for Newport AFC, Ebbw Vale and Cwmbran Town. Kendall's son Lee, the Welsh Schoolboys' captain, signed for Crystal Palace in January 1998, later playing for Cardiff City and Shrewsbury.

Appearances:
League: 29 apps.
FA Cup: 6 apps.
FL Cup: 1 app.
Others: 9 (18) apps.
Total: 45 (18) apps. 0 gls.

KENNEDY, James John

Role: Half-back 1908-12
6ft.0ins. 11st.12lbs.
Born: Dundee, Angus, 8th May 1883
Died: Glasgow, Lanarkshire, 20th July 1947

CAREER: Celtic Dec 1903/Brighton and Hove Albion May 1905/Leeds City Jun 1906/Stockport County Aug 1909/**SPURS** Mar 1910/Swindon Town Apr 1912/Norwich City Jul 1913/Watford Dec 1913/(Guest for Airdrieonians, Brentford and Motherwell during World War One)/Gillingham Dec 1919, trainer May 1920-1922/Partick Thistle trainer till Jul 1947.

Debut v Sunderland (FL) (h) 25.3.1910

Jimmy Kennedy joined Spurs from Stockport County along with Ernest Newman in March 1910, having previously played for Celtic, Brighton and Leeds City. He made his Spurs League debut later that month, standing in for Danny Steel at centre-half, but on 10th April had the misfortune to break his shoulder blade playing for the reserves. Although with Spurs for another two years, he never rose above reserve status at White Hart Lane and moved to Southern League Swindon Town in April 1912. After a season in Wiltshire, Kennedy joined Watford and helped them win the Southern League title in the last full pre-war season. Kennedy's playing career was effectively brought to a close by the First World War, but he did appear for Gillingham and was later their trainer. He returned to Scotland after Gillingham and was still working as Partick Thistle's trainer when he passed away.

Appearances:
League: 13 apps. 1 gl.
Others: 4 apps.
Total: 17 apps. 1 gls.

KERRY

Role: Full-back 1898-99

CAREER: SPURS trial and pro. Aug 1898.

Debut v Grays United (TML) (h) 6.2.1898

Arthur Kerry was a 19-year old full-back from Leigh-On-Sea signed in August 1898 after impressing in a series of trial matches held by Spurs for junior players. One of 40 potential recruits, Kerry was the only one who did enough to be signed on. He appeared regularly in the reserves, but made only one senior appearances, at half-back in a Thames and Medway League fixture.

Appearances:
Others: 1 app.
Total: 1 app. 0 gls.

KERRY, Arthur Henry Gould

Role: Winger 1909-10
Born: *Headington, Oxford, 21st July 1889*
Died: *1967*

CAREER: City of Oxford High School for Boys/St Johns College, Oxford/Oxford University/Oxford City/Corinthians/**SPURS** Mar 1910.

Debut v Chelsea (FL) (h) 30.4.1910

Arthur Kerry was one of the country's leading amateurs, an England amateur international, former Oxford blue and player with Oxford City, when he signed League forms for Spurs in March 1910. It was feared that regular outside-left Bert Middlemiss would be absent through injury and Kerry was considered the perfect stand-in. As it was, Middlemiss was passed fit, but he was injured for the last match of the season against Chelsea on 30th April 1910, a match Spurs had to win to be sure of avoiding relegation. Kerry stood in and helped Spurs clinch a 2-1 victory that kept them in Division One, but saw Chelsea go down.

Appearances:
League: 1 app.
Total: 1 app. 0 gls.

KERSLAKE, David

Role: Full back or midfield 1993-97
5ft.9ins. 12st.11lbs.
Born: *Stepney, London, 19th June 1966*

CAREER: St Mary's and St Michael's Catholic School/East London Schools/Senrab/England Schools/Queens Park Rangers app. Jun 1982, pro. Jun 1983/England Youth/Swindon Town Nov 1989/Leeds United Mar 1993/**SPURS** Sep 1993/(Swindon Town loan Nov 1996)/Charlton Athletic trial Aug 1997/Ipswich Town Aug 1997/(Wycombe Wanderers loan Dec 1997)/Swindon Town Mar 1998/released May 1999/Cambridge United trial Jul 1999/Canvey Island Nov 1999/**SPURS** academy coach, asst. Community Officer & Academy coach Apr 2002/Northampton Town reserve team manager Jan 2004/Nottingham Forest first team coach May 2006-Dec 2008/Watford first team coach Jul 2009/Cardiff City asst. manager Jun 2011, caretaker manager Dec 2013-Jan 2014/Wigan Athletic first team coach Nov 2014-Apr 2015/Gillingham asst. manager Jul 2015.

Debut v Everton (PL) (h) 3.10.1993

Although David Kerslake trained at Spurs as a 13-year old, it was Queens Park Rangers that decided to invest in his potential and gave him a professional contract. A neat, concise, midfielder at Rangers, he never really established himself, often looking full of potential, but frequently failing to impose himself. His calmness and simple style appealed to Ossie Ardiles who signed him for Swindon Town. Ardiles installed Kerslake at left-back where his keenness to attack and accurate passing were used to best effect as Ardiles built a team that looked to attack from all positions. Almost ever-present, Kerslake served Swindon well until moving to Leeds United in March 1993. His stay at Elland Road was brief,

Ardiles securing his transfer to Spurs five months later when Dean Austin's leg was broken. Kerslake competed with Austin for a regular starting position when Austin recovered, winning the battle in the early part of the 1994-95 season when Ardiles all-out attacking policy was at its most exciting. When miserable results saw Ardiles dismissed and Gerry Francis replace him, Kerslake was one of the first to suffer. Left out of the team, he rarely featured in the senior squad for the near two years before being released to join Ipswich Town. When his playing days were over, Kerslake took to coaching at the Spurs Academy before following Colin Calderwood to Northampton Town and Nottingham Forest. He then linked up with Malky Mackay at Watford, Cardiff City and Wigan Athletic and Justin Edinburgh at Gillingham. Kerslake's brother, Micky, was on the books of Fulham and Brighton & Hove Albin without making an impact in the game.

Appearances:
League: 34 (3) apps.
FA Cup: 1 (1) apps.
FL Cup: 5 apps.
Others: 15 (5) apps. 2 gls.
Total: 55 (9) apps. 2 gls.

KHUMALO, Bongani Sandile

Role: Central Defender 2011-15
6ft. 2ins. 13st. 3lbs.
Born: *Manzini, Swaziland, 6th January 1987*

CAREER: Arcadia Sheppards (South Africa)/Montreux Sports (South Africa)/University of Pretoria (South Africa) 2005/Supersport United (South Africa) 2007/**SPURS** trial Sep 2010, perm. Jan 2011/(Preston North End loan Mar 2011)/(Reading loan Jul 2011)/(PAOK (Greece) loan Jul 2011)/(Ipswich Town trial Jul 2013)/(Doncaster Rovers trial and loan Jul 2013)/(Colchester United loan Mar 2015)/Supersport United (South Africa) training Jul 2015, perm. Aug 2015/Bidvest Wits (South Africa) Jan 2016.

Debut v Kaizer Chiefs (Fr) (a) (sub) 16.7.2011

Bongani Khumalo is a fine example of Spurs scouring the world looking for rough diamonds who could be polished into the finished article. Although born in Swaziland, Khumalo's family had moved to South Africa in search of work. After playing as a youth at the University of Pretoria, Khumalo joined Supersport United, also in Pretoria. He made his debut for Bafana Bafana in March 2008, only the third player born outside

South Africa to represent the country. The outstanding player at the club, after a trial at Spurs the previous month, in October 2010 it was announced Khumalo would join Spurs in January 2011. No sooner had he arrived than he was out on loan to Preston, the first loan of what became the norm during his time with Spurs. The only first team appearances Khumalo made for Spurs were in July 2011 when the club visited South Africa for the Vodacom Challenge. A big, strong centre half he was never in contention for a regular place at Spurs. His most successful spell was when on loan to Doncaster Rovers, the level at which he was best suited. When his contract was up, he returned to South Africa, eventually re-signing for Supersport. During his time with Spurs Khumalo continued to represent South Africa, collecting 22 of his total 42 caps.

Appearances:
Others: 2 (1) apps.
Total: 2 (1) apps. 0 gls.

KIERNAN, Thomas

Role: Inside-forward 1941-42
5ft.8ins. 10st.10lbs.
Born: Coatbridge, Lanarkshire, 20th October 1918
Died: Coatbridge, Lanarkshire, 26th June 1991

CAREER: Viewpark Celtic 1935/Clydebank Juniors Apr 1936/Albion Rovers Jan 1938/(guest for Aldershot, Brentford, Chelsea, Fulham, Southampton and **SPURS** during World War Two)/Celtic Jul 1945/Stoke City Sep 1947/Luton Town Nov 1948/Gillingham 1950/St Mirren Dec 1950/Barry Town Aug 1951/Albion Rovers Sep 1952/Alloa Athletic Aug 1954/Barry Town 1955/Albion Rovers coach Oct 1958.

Debut v Charlton Athletic (LWC) (h) 11.4.1942

Tom Kiernan had been on the books of Albion Rovers before the outbreak of the Second World War and had been assisting Fulham as a guest, when he made his two appearances for Spurs in the London War Cup in April 1942. He played in both matches against Charlton Athletic in the group competition which preceded the knockout rounds although with little effect as Spurs lost the home match 0-3 and the away match 0-4. After the war Kiernan signed for Celtic and played for the Scottish League against the Football League in March 1947. He then joined Stoke City and later played for Luton Town and Gillingham before returning home to Scotland. When he left Barry Town in the summer of 1952 it was said he was emigrating to the USA, but that never transpired and he returned to Albion Rovers instead.

Appearances:
Others: 2 apps.
Total: 2 apps. 0 gls.

KING, A H

Role: Centre-forward 1893-94

Debut v London Hospital (Fr) (h) 8.2.1894

Another of those players from the late 19th century about whom nothing is known, King made his only appearance for Spurs in a friendly match against the London Hospital in February 1894.

Appearances:
Others: 1 app.
Total: 1 app. 0 gls.

KING, Arthur

Role: Goalkeeper 1913-14
6ft. 12st.4lbs.
Born: Kentore, nr Aberdeen, 6th August 1887

CAREER: Artillery/East End/Aberdeen May 1908/ **SPURS** May 1913/Belfast Celtic Jul 1914/Dunfermline Athletic 1920/Dumbarton Dec 1921-1924.

Debut v Sheffield United (FL) (a) 1.9.1913

Arthur King joined Spurs from Aberdeen where he had spent five years, the first two as a reserve, after starting his career with local junior clubs Artillery and East End. He played in 19 of the first 22 League games in his first season, but after conceding five goals at Leicester Fosse in the 1st round of the FA Cup in January 1914 was dropped. The following month he was placed on the transfer list at his own request but, with no clubs showing any interest, walked out on Spurs in March 1914. He returned to Scotland where he kicked his heels until his contract ran out. In July that year he signed for Belfast Celtic and played there until the suspension of football due to the First World War. After the War, King re-surfaced in Scotland, playing for Dunfermline and Dumbarton. .

Appearances:
League: 19 apps.
FA Cup: 1 app.
Others: 5 apps.
Total: 25 apps. 0 gls.

KING, Derek Albert

Role: Centre-half 1951-55
5ft.11ins. 11st.11lbs.
Born: Hackney, London, 15th August 1929
Died: Huntingdon, Cambridgeshire, 16th June 2003

CAREER: Glynn Road School/Alexander Palace/Albion/Tottenham Juniors/**SPURS** am. 1945, pro. Aug 1950/Swansea Town Aug 1956/Romford Aug 1959.

Debut v Fulham (FL) (h) 20.8.1951

A resolute defender, Derek King played two matches for Spurs at the start of the 1951 52 season after Brian Farley had been injured in his first game as stand-in for the injured Harry Clarke. He performed well enough in his first game, but fifteen minutes from the end of the second the injury jinx that had struck Spurs saw King leave the field with the same problem afflicting Clarke and Farley; a wrenched knee. Clarke was the first to recover, so it was back to the reserves for King. His further opportunities were limited by the consistency of Clarke and some minor injury problems. It was only towards the end of the 1952 53 season that he ever looked likely to take over Clarke's role as the defensive pivot.

Although he served Spurs for six years King's appearances were nearly always restricted to those occasions when Clarke was injured. In August 1956, he moved to Swansea Town where injuries continued to trouble him. He spent just one season at the club, before becoming one of several former Spurs' players to turn out for Romford. King was the nephew of former Spurs full-back, Eddie King.

Appearances:
League: 19 apps.
Others: 7 apps.
Total: **26 apps. 0 gls.**

KING, Edgar Frederick

Role: Full-back 1934-35
5ft.9ins. 11st.10lbs.
Born: Hackney, London, 25th February 1914

CAREER: Tottenham Juniors/Tufnell Park/Northfleet United 1932/ SPURS pro. Nov 1933.

Debut v Aston Villa (FL) (h) 22.9.1934

On leaving school Eddie King joined Tottenham Juniors and worked his way through the Tottenham system with Tufnell Park and Northfleet, before moving onto the White Hart Lane staff in November 1933. Regarded as a highly promising full-back, he suffered a severe leg injury from which he never recovered on his League debut at Aston Villa in September 1934. It forced him into a cruelly premature retirement in the summer of 1936. King was the uncle of future Spurs centre-half, Derek King.

Appearances:
League: 1 app.
Total: **1 app. 0 gls.**

KING, Ledley Brenton

Role: Defender 1998-2012
6ft.2ins. 14st.5lbs.
Born: Bow, London 12th October 1980

CAREER: Blessed John Roche School/Senrab/Hackney Schools/Tower Hamlets Schools/London Schools/England Schools/SPURS trainee Jul 1997, pro. Jul 1998/retired Jul 2012.

Debut v Liverpool (sub) (PL) (a) 1.5.1999

One of the finest central defenders of modern times, Ledley King was marked down as a star of the future right from his earliest days as a schoolboy training at White Hart Lane two evenings a week. An England

international at Under-16 and Under-18 level, he made his senior debut as a second half substitute at Liverpool as Spurs sought to defend a 2-0 lead with ten men after Mauricio Taricco had been the victim of one of those refereeing decisions that only ever seemed to go the home team's way. Playing in an unaccustomed left-back role and with Liverpool awarded a more than dubious penalty within minutes of the second half kicking off, Anfield was a cauldron, but King immediately exhibited the calmness that was to be his trademark. Under George Graham, King was brought on slowly, frequently called on to play in a defensive midfield role. It was a job he was well able to do, but the centre of defence was always where his career lay. Sol Campbell's decision to walk out on Spurs in 2001 was a big blow. It could have been a massive one, but Spurs had a ready-made replacement in King. He took over Campbell's role and, if anything, Spurs became a better team for it. King was the perfect defender. Tall, strong, he had fantastic pace and the most perfect timing, whether nipping in front of a forward to pinch the ball or sliding in with a last ditch tackle. At his best King was imperious, totally in command, calmness personified, a master craftsman making his job look easy. He collected his first full cap in March 2002 when he played against Italy. He went on to collect another 20 to add to one at "B" level and twelve at Under-21 level. There can be no doubt that his name would have been the first on England's team-sheet for years were it not for injury problems that afflicted him for much of his career. As it was, a variety of injuries restricted King's appearances, not just for England, but also for Spurs. One after another had him in the treatment room and unable to train properly. It got to the stage where King suffered so badly from knee injuries that he had his own training regime, designed to keep him on top of his game without making his injuries any worse. It got to the stage where he barely trained at all. Fortunately, he was naturally fit and able to maintain the highest level of performance with the minimum of preparation. Captain of the 2008 Worthington Cup-winning team, King was eventually forced to concede defeat to his injuries and retired in July 2012 to become a club ambassador.

Appearances:
League: 265 (3) apps. 10 gls.
FA Cup: 20 (1) apps. 3 gls.
FL Cup: 20 apps. 1 gl.
Euro: 14 apps.
Others: 26 (5) apps.
Total: **345 (9) apps. 14 gls.**

KINGAN

Role: Half-back 1893-94

Debut v Romford (Fr) (h) 23.9.1893

Another trialist, Kingan played his only match for Spurs in September 1893 in a friendly against Romford. He was clearly unimpressive, being described as "a novice to the Hotspur and from his form a novice to football"

Appearances:
Others: 1 app.
Total: **1 app. 0 gls.**

KINNEAR (REDDY), Joseph Patrick

Role: Full-back 1965-80
5ft.9ins. 11st.4lbs.
Born: Dublin, Eire, 27th December 1947

CAREER: Watford Schools/Hertfordshire Schools/St Albans City/**SPURS** am. Aug 1963, pro. Feb 1965/Brighton and Hove Albion Aug 1975/Dunstable Town Aug 1978/Woodford Town player-coach/Nepal trial manager 1985/Sharjah (UAE) 1985 coach/Al Shabab (Dubai) coach/Nepal manager Oct 1987/coach in Malaysia/Doncaster Rovers asst. manager Dec 1987, manager Mar-Jun 1989/Wimbledon reserve team coach Sep 1989, asst. manager June 1990, coach Oct 1991, manager Jan 1992–Jun 1999/Oxford United Director of Football Oct 2000-Jan 2001/Luton Town manager Feb 2001-May 2003/Nottingham Forest manager Feb-Dec 2004/Newcastle United manager Sep 2008-May 2009, Director of Football Jun 2013-Feb 2014.

Debut v West Ham United (FL) (h) 8.4.1966

Joe Kinnear moved to London with his family when only seven. Having captained Watford and Hertfordshire Schoolboys, he joined St Albans City, where he was noticed by Spurs. He made his League debut in April 1966, but his big breakthrough came in February 1967. Just three days after Kinnear had won his first full cap for the Republic of Ireland against Turkey, regular full-back Phil Beal suffered the broken arm that was to put him out of action for the rest of the season. Kinnear was the natural replacement and finished the season with an FA Cup winners' medal. Despite being the youngest player on the pitch, and one of only two Spurs' players who had not cost a large fee, he gave a thoroughly impressive Wembley performance in the final against Chelsea. Kinnear settled into the team so well that when Beal returned it was in central defence and not in his old position. A compact, quick and hard tackling defender, who enjoyed getting forward to support the forwards in an era when wingers were falling out of fashion, Kinnear formed an excellent full-back partnership with Cyril Knowles until January 1969 when a broken leg put Kinnear out of the game for the best part of a year. When fit to resume, he found his position taken by first Tony Want and then Ray Evans, but he regained his place and, although frequently left out in favour of Evans, played in the League Cup winning teams of 1971 and 1973 and the successful 1972 UEFA Cup side. Eventually the younger Evans gained the upper hand and, although Kinnear was recalled to add his valuable experience to the battle against relegation in 1974-75, in the summer of 1975 he was transferred to Brighton. He only played on the South Coast for a year before retiring from top-flight football, adding one more cap to the 24 he had won with Spurs. Spurs played a testimonial for Kinnear at the Goldstone Ground in March 1976, and although he returned to Spurs to play in Terry Naylor's testimonial against Crystal Palace in April 1980, at first he left football completely. He later tried the management side with a three week trial as manager of Nepal before assisting Dave Mackay coaching in the Near East and as assistant manager at Doncaster Rovers. He took over as Rovers' manager on Mackay's departure, but after only three months was dismissed to make way for Billy Bremner. Kinnear returned to London coaching with Wimbledon. He was upgraded to assistant manager and then took over the reins on the dismissal of Peter Withe. It was largely due to Kinnear's efforts that the Dons changed from an aggressive "hit and hope" outfit to a more responsible football team. In March 1999 Kinnear suffered a heart attack that caused him to stand down as Wimbledon manager at the end of the season, but football was a drug he could not give up. He returned to the game, managing Luton Town, Nottingham Forest and Newcastle United until further health concerns arose in February 2009 that caused him to stand down from the St James' Park job. Over four years later he was back at Newcastle as Director of Football, but it was a difficult time and after continual pressure from the fans, he was forced to resign.

Appearances:

League:	190* (7) apps. 2 gls.
FA Cup:	24 apps.
FL Cup:	20 apps.
Euro:	18 apps.
Others:	40 (3) apps. 4 gls.
Total:	**292 (10) apps. 6 gls.**

*Includes 1 abandoned match.

KIRWAN, John Francis

Role: Outside-left 1899-07
5ft.7ins. 10st.8lbs.
Born: Dunlavin, County Wicklow, Ireland, 12th December 1872
Died: Hendon, Middlesex, 9th January 1959

CAREER: Southport Central/Everton Feb 1898/**SPURS** May 1899/Chelsea May 1905/Clyde May 1908/Leyton Jun 1909/Ajax (Holland) trainer Sep 1910–1914/Dublin Bohemians coach Jul 1914/Southport Vulcan coach Aug 1918/Livorno (Italy) coach Sep 1923.

Debut v Millwall Athletic (SL) (a) 2.9.1899 (scored twice)

John Kirwan had won an All-Ireland medal at Gaelic Football, before deciding to cross the sea in the summer of 1897 and try his hand at professional football with Southport Central in the Lancashire League. He impressed immediately, with Football League clubs taking an interest and Everton and Blackburn Rovers bidding for his services. A major argument developed between the two of them as to who was entitled to his services. His decision to opt for Everton, resulted in a fine being levied on the Merseyside outfit. He was officially transferred to them in February 1898 and appeared regularly in their Football League team throughout the 1898-99 season. However, he was not happy in Liverpool and when John Cameron, who had played with Kirwan for a couple of months before his move to Spurs, got to learn of this he was quick to offer Kirwan the chance of joining him in London. Kirwan was just as quick to accept it. Again his impact was immediate. Initially playing outside Cameron but soon partnered by David Copeland, he proved a devastating little winger, incredibly popular with the Spurs' crowd and instantly taken to their hearts. With pace and trickery, he used to run at his full-back and torment the life out of him with his feints and little tricks. His opponent would never know what Kirwan was going to do next. He would make the same move two or three times but just

as his marker thought he knew what was coming, Kirwan would pull another trick out of the bag and leave his man on the seat of his pants. Nimble of foot, he had the ability to head in one direction before stopping dead in his tracks and going off in another and when past his man covering defenders could never be sure what he was going to do. He was unorthodox in that he did not finish a run down the wing with a hopeful punt into the centre like so many of his contemporaries. He would take a second to consider his options and if a pass to his centre-forward was not on, cut the ball back to the edge of the box for Copeland or Cameron to burst onto. Kirwan needed his trickery for he was not the biggest of men and when defenders did get to him he took some really hard challenges, but when clattered to the ground he just picked himself up and got on with the game, confident that skill would tell. One of the stars of the team that won the Southern League in 1900, Kirwan was responsible for many of the goals scored by Tom Pratt but chipped in with quite a few of his own, netting a total of twenty as Spurs not only won their first major title, but finished second in the Southern District Combination. It was no surprise when he collected his first Irish cap against Wales in February 1900. Having really made his mark in Southern football, Kirwan's talents were then seen on the national stage as Spurs went on to win the FA Cup the following season. Ever-present throughout the run to the final, Kirwan was at his absolute best in the Villa Park semi-final. Sandy Brown took the plaudits with all four Spurs' goals, but it was the first two, both set up by Kirwan, that were to prove so decisive. While Spurs were unable to repeat their earlier triumphs over the next few years, Kirwan continued to dazzle, spectators prepared to pay their money just to see him perform. All the time his partnership with Copeland continued to develop. It was almost as if they had a telepathic understanding, seeming to know what each was going to do as if they had played together all their lives. Kirwan took his total of Irish caps as a Spurs' player to twelve and it is just unfortunate Copeland was a Scot. Together on the international stage they would certainly have flourished. Almost regarded as indispensable, it was a considerable surprise to all at White Hart Lane when, in 1905, Kirwan and Copeland were enticed away, becoming the first major signings of west London's newly-formed club, Chelsea. As Everton were a Football League club and Spurs in the Southern League, Spurs had avoided paying a transfer fee when Kirwan was signed. Throughout his time at White Hart Lane, Everton had continued to offer Kirwan a new contract each close season. It meant they retained his Football League registration, so when Chelsea signed him Everton were entitled to a transfer fee and demanded £150. Chelsea's offer of £30 was rejected, but just before the dispute was to go to the Football League for a decision, a deal was done at £100. Kirwan, in particular, proved highly instrumental in helping Chelsea finish third in their first season in the Football League and secure promotion in their second. He later played for Clyde and Leyton before embarking on a coaching career that took him to Holland and Italy, but he always retained one souvenir of his time with Spurs. At the final whistle of the 1901 FA Cup final replay, he was first to grab the ball and kept it until his death.

Appearances:
Southern: 157* apps. 41 gls.
FA Cup: 24 apps. 2 gls.
Others: 159 (1) apps. 55 gls.
Total: 340 (1) apps. 98 gls.
*Includes 1 abandoned match

KLINSMANN, Jürgen

Role: Striker 1994-95, 1997-98 & 2002-03
6ft.2ins. 12st.13lbs.
Born: Goppingen, West Germany, 30th July 1964

CAREER: TB Gingen (West Germany) 1972/SV Geislingen (West Germany) 1974/Stuttgart Kickers (West Germany) 1978/Vfb Stuttgart (West Germany) cs. 1984/Inter Milan (Italy) May 1989/AS Monaco (France) Jul 1992/**SPURS** Jul 1994/Bayern Munich (Germany) Jul 1995/Sampdoria (Italy) May 1997/**SPURS** Dec 1997/retired Jan 1999/Orange County Blue Stars (USA)/Los Angeles Galaxy (USA) technical adviser/Germany head coach Jul 2004-Jul 2006/Bayern Munich head coach Jul 2008-Apr 2009/Toronto FC (Canada) consultant Nov 2010/USA head coach Jul 2011-Nov 2016.

Debut v Sheffield Wednesday (PL) (a) 20.8.1994 (scored once)
(Watford) (Fr) (a) 6.8.1994)

Spurs are a club named after a knight, Harry Hotspur, son of the Duke of Northumberland, famously slain at the Battle of Shrewsbury in 1403. Like most clubs they have at one time or another needed a saviour, a knight in shining armour. Twice Jürgen Klinsmann proved to be that man. In the summer of 1994 Spurs were in a desperate situation, financial irregularities under the Venables' regime seeing them banned from the FA Cup and given a twelve point deduction even before the League season began. Gloom and despondency hung heavy over White Hart Lane. It was all the more astonishing, therefore, that Spurs' Chairman, Alan Sugar, was somehow able to persuade Klinsmann to join Spurs. Perhaps it was the opulent surroundings of Sugar's yacht moored in Monaco harbour where the deal was done, perhaps it was the money or perhaps, as Klinsmann himself suggested, it was the challenge of playing for a famous, but beleaguered club. Whatever the reason, his signing was hailed a coup as big as that of Ossie Ardiles and Ricky Villa 16 years earlier. A World Cup winner in 1990 Klinsmann, a true superstar of the European game, had already played in his native Germany, in Italy and in France and was keen to sample football in the Premiership, but there was one fear. He had a reputation as a "diver", a man who would fall over at the slightest touch, particularly if there was a chance of winning a penalty. It was a fear Klinsmann turned into an attribute. At his first press conference he asked the assembled hacks for directions to the nearest diving school, immediately winning over the public with his charm and sense of humour. On the pitch, Klinsmann started in the perfect way, with a cracking header against Sheffield Wednesday followed by an exaggerated celebratory dive to the touchline, before being stretchered off after a sickening clash of heads. It was the first of several scintillating performances from Ardiles' "Famous Five" of Klinsmann, Teddy Sheringham, Nick Barmby, Darren Anderton and Ilie Dumitrescu, but not all ended so well. The football was brilliant, but the results were not, and Ardiles was dismissed. His "devil may care" football gave way to Gerry Francis' more pragmatic "results first, performance second" style, but the change had little effect on Klinsmann. A natural goal-scorer, he continued to find the back of the net regularly, forming a devastating partnership with Teddy Sheringham. Klinsmann was all-action, forever on the move, wandering wherever there was space, just waiting for the moment to burst into action. Although thirty he still possessed that vital burst of pace, that little edge and all-important killer instinct. Equally proficient with either foot or head, he could finish with simple knock-ins from a few yards, searing volleys from twenty or delicate chips past even the best positioned 'keeper. His most outstanding attribute, though, was his attitude. For a man some critics had labelled a mercenary, he worked tirelessly from start to finish, harassing defenders, pressurising goalkeepers, encouraging those around him. And he did it all with a smile, clearly enjoying every minute and relishing a fantastic rapport with the fans. With the points' deduction and FA Cup ban replaced by a fine, Klinsmann almost made it a fairy tale first season, but hopes of a Wembley visit were dashed by Everton in the FA Cup semi-final. Worse was to follow when Klinsmann, voted Player of the Year by the FWA to add to the awards he had collected as German Player of the Year in 1988 and 1994, announced he was returning to Germany to join Bayern Munich. Sugar was not happy with the announcement. Klinsmann explained that he wanted to win the Bundesliga before retiring. While Spurs struggled to find a replacement, Klinsmann helped Bayern lift the 1996 UEFA Cup, captained Germany to the 1996 European Championship and, in 1997, won the Bundesliga title he so yearned for. He then joined Sampdoria, but late in 1997 found himself out of the team and was concerned for his international place with the 1998 World Cup on the horizon. He had already announced he would be retiring after the competition. Spurs were having a bad time, again finding goals hard to come by and not safe from relegation. In December 1997 Klinsmann returned to White Hart Lane. He was not the power he had been, but his return gave the whole club a lift. Showing flashes of his old brilliance, he helped Spurs pull clear of the relegation zone, scoring six goals in his last three games. Four of them came in his last but one outing against Wimbledon at Selhurst Park, when he gave a master class in finishing. Each goal was different, each was clinical and each was joyously celebrated as if it was the first he had ever scored. After the 1998 World Cup Klinsmann had plenty of offers for his services, but early in 1999 decided to call it a day for his playing career, although he actually continued to play. It was not until August 2003 that it was revealed that for five years Klinsmann had been playing under the name of Jay Goppingen, for an amateur outfit, Orange County Blue Stars, in California where he had settled. With little coaching experience, it was a surprise when Klinsmann was announced as Germany's new head coach in July 2004, charged with rebuilding German football from the top. He did a remarkable job, leading an exciting and offensive German team to third place in the 2006 World Cup and rekindling pride in the national team. Although the DFB wanted Klinsmann to continue, he refused all offers when his contract expired after the World Cup finals. He was out of the game for another two years, then returned to Bayern Munich, but left within a year when he fell out with the board. In July 2011 he was appointed head coach to the USA. Klinsmann scored 47 goals in 108 appearances for Germany, ten of the goals and 17 of the appearances, as a Spurs' player.

Appearances:
League: 56 apps. 29 gls.
FA Cup: 9 apps. 5 gls.
FL Cup: 3 apps. 4 gls.
Others: 4 apps. 3 gls.
Total: 72 apps. 41 gls.

KNIGHT, John George

Role: Centre-half 1928-29
5ft.9ins. 11st.9lbs.
Born: Edmonton, London, 18th August 1902
Died: Bury St Edmunds, Suffolk, 20th January 1990

CAREER: Crayland Road School/Latymer Secondary School/London University/Casuals/Corinthians 1923/**SPURS** am. Aug 1927/released Aug 1930.

Debut v Bradford Park Avenue (FL) (h) 23.2.1929

An England amateur international half-back who had played for Casuals and the Corinthians, John Knight signed amateur forms for Spurs in August 1927, but it was not until February 1929 that he made his one Football League appearance. In the interim he had continued to play for, and captain Casuals, collect England international caps and play for the Amateurs against the Professionals in the full international trial in January 1928. He did not make the Spurs' first team again and in August 1930 was removed from the list of retained players. Knight was a Master at Haberdasher's Aske's School.

Appearances:
League: 1 app.
Total: 1 app. 0 gls.

KNIGHTON, Thomas

Role: Centre-forward 1915-16

CAREER: Glossop am. Sep 1914/(guest for Grimsby Town, Manchester United, **SPURS** and Watford during World War One)/Lincoln City am. Sep-Oct 1919.

Debut v Crystal Palace (LFC) (a) 11.12.1915

A member of the Officers Training Corp who had played for Glossop before the outbreak of war, Knighton made four appearances for Spurs in the London Football Combination during the 1915-16 season, scoring twice. After the war he joined Lincoln City on amateur forms, but was not up to standard and made only two appearances before his release. The first of those appearances was against Spurs.

Appearances:
Others: 4 apps. 2 gls.
Total: 4 apps. 2 gls.

KNOTT, Victor J

Role: Inside-forward 1923-26
Born: Edmonton, London

CAREER: Cheshunt/**SPURS** Oct 1923/Fulham May 1926/Northfleet United Nov 1927.

Debut v Crystal Palace (LFACC) (h) 29.10.1923

A local lad who played for several of the area's junior clubs, Vic Knott signed professional for Spurs in October 1923 and made his first team debut that month, scoring in a London FA Charity Cup tie with Crystal Palace. Normally an inside-forward, he stayed at White Hart Lane for three seasons playing regularly in the reserves, but never able to

force his way into the first team. Released at the end of the 1925-26 season, he joined Fulham, never managed to make the senior XI at Craven Cottage and moved on to Northfleet United.

Appearances:
Others: 2 apps.
Total: 2 apps. 0 gls.

KNOWLES, Cyril Barry

Role: Full-back 1964-77
6ft.0ins. 13st.13lbs.
Born: Fitzwilliam, Yorkshire, 13th July 1944
Died: Middlesbrough, Cleveland, 31st August 1991

CAREER: South Emshall Schools/Manchester United/Hemsworth/Blackpool trial/Monckton Colliery Welfare/Middlesbrough pro. Oct 1962/**SPURS** May 1964/retired May 1976/Hertford Town manager cs. 1976/**SPURS** Yorkshire scout/Doncaster Rovers coach 1977/Middlesbrough coach 1981, asst. manager Feb 1982/Darlington manager May 1983-Mar 1987/Torquay United manager Jun 1987-Oct 1989/Hartlepool United manager Dec 1989-Jun 1991.

Debut v Sheffield United (FL) (h) 22.8.1964
(Feyenoord (Fr) (a) 8.8.1964)

Born in the same mining village as cricketer Geoff Boycott, Cyril Knowles was an outside-left as a schoolboy and had a year on the junior staff of Manchester United before he was rejected. He continued with his local club, Hemsworth, but a trial with Blackpool and a brief spell with Wolves' nursery club Monkton Colliery both met with further rejections. However, Middlesbrough shrewdly recognised that whilst he might not be good enough to make the grade as a pure winger, he had considerable promise as a full-back, and they took him on their amateur staff. Certainly Spurs would never regret that Middlesbrough spotted qualities overlooked by others, for Knowles was to become one of the best left-backs ever to serve the club. He made his League debut in April 1963 and almost immediately caught the eye of Bill Nicholson who was looking to replace the ageing Peter Baker, Ron Henry and Mel Hopkins. When he joined Spurs, Knowles had made only 39 senior appearances, but the club still had to fork out £45,000 for his signature. Occupying the right-back position in his first season at White Hart Lane, he won his first England Under-23 cap against Wales in November 1964 and at the end of the season played for Young England against England in the annual eve of FA Cup Final match. He then moved across to left-back and for the next ten years was only absent from the team due to injury. A strong, lithe defender, skilful and stylish, always cool and confident on the ball, he put his experience as a winger to good use, developing the overlapping style of full-back flank play that became so important in an era when wingers were out of favour. Always quick to recover, he rarely missed an opportunity to get forward and support the front runners, and his ability to fire in accurate crosses from a variety of angles created many goals for the likes of Martin Chivers, Alan Gilzean and Martin Peters. A member of the teams that won the FA Cup in 1967, the League Cup in 1971 and 1973 and the UEFA Cup in 1972, he won a total of six Under-23 caps, played for the Football League against the Scottish League in March 1968, represented England against Young England in both 1968 and 1969, but won only four full caps, the first against the USSR in December 1967. That was no reflection on his ability, but testimony to the brilliance of Leeds United's Terry Cooper who kept Knowles out of the England team. A national cult figure due to the success of the pop record "Nice One Cyril", the title of which became a national catchphrase, Knowles was always enormously popular with the Spurs' fans, not only because of his football ability but also for his ever cheery outlook. It was with great sadness that news of his retirement was announced in the summer of 1976. The root of the problem was a serious knee injury suffered in December 1973 and, although he recovered to help save the club from relegation in 1975 with two goals in the final vital match with Leeds, the injury flared up again the following season and he was advised to quit. Granted a testimonial against Arsenal in October 1975, he also played in a benefit for his long-time team-mate Pat Jennings in November 1976. After his retirement, Knowles had a short spell as Hertford Town manager and then returned to Yorkshire acting as Spurs scout. He worked as a coach with Doncaster Rovers and Middlesbrough until being appointed assistant manager at Ayresome Park, and then took on the manager's job at Darlington. He led the Quakers to promotion from Division Four in 1985, but left in March 1987 when they were relegated. The following season he joined Torquay United, taking them to the Sherpa Van Trophy final in 1989, but resigning in October of the same year. Clearly a man able to eke out success on even the most limited of resources, he was appointed manager of Hartlepool United and they were in the running for promotion when he faced the shattering diagnosis in February 1991 that he was suffering from a serious brain illness. He died just six months later, but will never be forgotten by all those who had the great privilege of watching him play for Spurs. Cyril's brother, Peter, was an outstanding inside-forward with Wolverhampton Wanderers and an England Under-23 international who gave up his career as he felt football conflicted with his religious convictions as a Jehovah's Witness. He played just once after retiring, turning out as a substitute in Cyril's testimonial against Arsenal.

Appearances:
League: 401* (1) apps. 15 gls.
FA Cup: 42 apps. 1 gl.
FL Cup: 32 (1) apps.
Euro: 30 apps. 1 gl.
Others: 62 apps. 3 gls.
Total: 567 (2) apps. 20 gls.
*Includes 1 abandoned match

KNOWLES, Joseph

Role: Full-back 1897-98
5ft.6ins. 11st.6lbs.
Born: Monkwearmouth, Wearside, 22nd May 1872

CAREER: Monkwearmouth 1892/Sunderland Nov 1895/**SPURS** May 1897/South Shields cs. 1898/Queens Park Rangers Aug 1899.

Debut v Sheppey United (SL) (a) 4.9.1897
(Glossop North End (Fr) (h) 2.9.1897)

Joe Knowles spent two years with Sunderland, but had played only one Football League game when he arrived at Spurs along with several other new recruits for the 1897-98 season. He was a regular throughout, but with Spurs signing Bob Cain and Harry Erentz twelve months later, was released. He moved on to South Shields. After a year back in the North East he returned to London, joining Queens Park Rangers in preparation for their first season in the Southern League. At Rangers, he linked up with Jock Campbell, the QPR trainer who had been Spurs' trainer when Knowles was there.

Appearances:
Southern: 19 apps.
FA Cup: 1 app.
Others: 30 (1) apps.
Total: 50 (1) apps.

KNOWLES, Peter

Role: Inside-forward 1975-76
Born: Fitzwilliam, Yorkshire, 30th September 1945

CAREER: Wath Wanderers/Wolverhampton Wanderers 1961, pro Oct 1962/retired Sep 1969.

Debut v Arsenal (sub) (Fr) (h) 22.10.1975

Peter Knowles was an inside-forward with beautiful, silky skills who had a very big future in the game in front of him, but gave it all up as he found the demands of professional football incompatible with his beliefs as a Jehovah's Witness. He joined Wolverhampton Wanderers from their nursery club of Wath Wanderers and worked his way through the apprentice ranks to make his League debut in October 1963. An England Youth cap, he helped Wolves return to the First Division in 1967 and collected four England Under-23 caps. In 1969 he played for Wolves under the pseudonym of Kansas City Spurs in the North American Soccer League international cup tournament. He made over 170 League appearances for Wolves before announcing his retirement early in the 1969-70 season. Wolves retained his registration for a further twelve years but there was never any chance of him returning to the game. His one appearance in a Spurs' shirt was when he played for a short while as substitute in brother Cyril's testimonial match against Arsenal in October 1975.

Appearances:
Others: (1) app.
Total: (1) app. 0 gls.

KONCHESKY, Paul Martyn

Role: Full-back 2003-04
5ft.10ins. 10 st.5lbs.
Born: Barking, Essex, 15th May 1981

CAREER: Great Danes Youth/Senrab/West Ham United Academy/Charlton Athletic YTS Aug 1997, pro May 1998/(**SPURS** loan Sep 2003)/West Ham United Jul 2005/Fulham Jul 2007/Liverpool Aug 2010/(Nottingham Forest loan Jan 2011)/Leicester City Jul 2011/ (Queens Park Rangers loan Aug 2015)/released Jun 2016/ Gillingham Jul 2016/ Billericay Town Feb 2017..

Debut v Chelsea (sub) (PL) (a) 13.9.2003

An East End boy who once had a season ticket at West Ham United and was an Academy player there, Paul Konchesky made his mark at Charlton Athletic, a tough, uncompromising full-back of whom much was expected. Charlton's youngest debutant when he first appeared in a League game for them in August 1997, he played for England at all youth levels as his career progressed rapidly. Recognised as a potential regular full international left-back, Konchesky collected his first cap against Australia in February 2003. He was appointed captain of the England Under-21s and harboured ambitions of playing in Euro 2004, but when Chris Powell, his ageing rival for the left-back slot, was offered a new contract by Charlton, Konchesky demanded a move. With no takers, he joined Spurs on loan, initially for a month, but eventually staying for three months. During that time, he made a dozen appearances for Spurs

and collected two more Under-23 caps. Konchesky returned to Charlton, did not make England's Euro 2004 squad, but took his total number of appearances over the 150 mark before being transferred to West Ham. He picked up a second full England cap, played in the 2006 FA Cup final and turned out regularly for two years before joining Fulham. With the Cottagers, Konchesky established himself as a Premier League regular and helped Fulham reach the Europa League final in 2010. His manager that season was Roy Hodgson and when he took over at Liverpool, Konchesky was one of the first players he wanted to sign. Unfortunately for Konchesky, Hodgson's reign at Anfield was not a success. When Kenny Dalglish replaced Hodgson, Konchesky was one of the first to find himself dropped. Within weeks, he was shipped out on loan to Nottingham Forest, a permanent transfer to Leicester City soon following.

Appearances:
League: 10 (2) apps.
FL Cup: 2 (1) apps.
Total: 12 (3) apps. 0 gls.

KORSTEN, Willem

Role: Midfielder 1999-2002
6ft.3ins. 12st.13lbs.
Born: Boxtel, Holland, 21st January 1975

CAREER: Gwen (Holland)/NEC Nijmegen (Holland) Jul 1992/Vitesse Arnhem Jul 1993/(Leeds United loan Jan-Mar 1999)/**SPURS** May 1999/retired Oct 2001/NEC Nijmegen (Holland) Academy coach Apr 2002/ SC Velp '58 (Holland) 2002/Achilles '29 (Holland) May 2011, asst. trainer Jun 2011-Mar 2012/NEC Nijmegen (Holland) asst. coach Apr 2012.

Debut v Sheffield Wednesday (sub) (PL) (h) 22.1.2000
(Queens Park Rangers (sub) (Fr) (a) 28.7.1999)

A classy, wide left attacking midfielder, Willem Korsten's career seemed about to take off when he joined Leeds United on loan from Vitesse Arnhem for the latter part of the 1998-99 season. Leeds, under George Graham's management, had been monitoring Korsten for some time, but it was only after Graham had left for Spurs that they managed to secure his temporary transfer. In three months in Yorkshire Korsten's simple but effective style so impressed that a permanent transfer seemed a formality. That was until Graham stepped in and persuaded Korsten to join Spurs in a £1.5 million deal.

Unfortunately, no sooner had Korsten arrived than injury struck. In more than two years Korsten was rarely available, struck down by one injury after another. On the rare occasions he was able to play, he showed flashes of his talent, but he was never able to put together any sort of a run in the team. In October 2001 Korsten conceded defeat to persistent hip problems and retired. He returned to Holland and began coaching with his first club NEC Nijmegen. Korsten tried to resume playing again. His first attempt at SC Velp failed after five games, but he had a little more success with Achilles '29. In just over a month playing for them, he helped them win the KNVB Amateur Cup, scoring the only goal of the game in the final.

Appearances:
League: 12 (11) apps. 3 gls.
FA Cup: (3) apps.
FL Cup: 1 app.
Others: (3) apps.
Total: 13 (17) apps. 3 gls.

KRANJČAR, Niko

Role: Midfielder 2009-12
6ft. 13st.3lbs.
Born: Zagreb, Yugoslavia 13th August 1984

CAREER: Rapid Vienna (Austria)/Dinamo Zagreb (Croatia)/Hadjuk Split (Croatia) Jan 2005/Portsmouth Aug 2006/**SPURS** Sep 2009/Dynamo Kiev (Ukraine) Jun 2012-Jan 2016/(Queens Park Rangers loans Sep 2013 and Sep 2014)/New York Cosmos (USA) training Feb 2016, perm. Mar 2016/Rangers Jun 2016.

Debut v Manchester United (sub) (PL) (h) 12.9.2009

Almost as soon as he was able to kick a ball, Niko Kranjčar began training with Rapid Vienna, where his father, Zlatko, one of Dinamo Zagreb's finest footballers, was playing. On the family's return to Croatia, Kranjčar junior joined Dinamo Zagreb's youth set-up. He made his senior debut when 16 and was still only 19 when he helped Dinamo win the Croatian League and Cup "Double" in 2003, retaining the League trophy in 2004. Already being lauded as one of Croatia's midfielders, the Croatian manager, Kranjčar's father, selected his son for his full international debut in August 2004, adding to his appearances at youth and Under-21 level. Kranjčar seemed set for a lengthy career with Dinamo, but then fell out with the club and was surprisingly allowed to move to Dinamo's great rival, Hadjuk Split, immediately helping them win the Prva HNL Ožujsko in 2005. Dinamo presumably knew that in Luka Modrić they had the perfect replacement for Kranjčar. The 2006 World Cup brought Kranjčar to the international stage and he was hailed as one of the stars of the tournament. Quickly signed by Harry Redknapp for Portsmouth, he made his Premier League debut at White Hart Lane and soon established himself as an attacking midfielder of true quality and class. He was a member of the Portsmouth team that won the FA Cup in 2008, but soon realised Portsmouth's financial problems meant it was not a club that could match his ambitions. When he made it clear he would see out his contract and leave, Redknapp moved in to bring Kranjčar to Tottenham. A technically gifted player, Kranjčar was at his most effective operating out wide, gliding over the surface, cutting inside and slipping passes through to the forwards. He worked hard, covering back, had a cracking shot and was expert in dead ball situations. Unfortunately for Kranjčar, they were similar qualities to Gareth Bale. While Kranjčar played a fair number of games, many of them were as a substitute and with niggling injuries holding him back, he was never truly able to impose himself with Spurs. Released after three years, he joined Dynamo Kiev, started well, but then suffered a couple of injuries that saw him side-lined. When fit he was unable to secure a place in the team so joined Queens Park Rangers on two season long loans, again linking-up with Redknapp. On his release by Dinamo Kiev, Kranjčar took his talents to America and the re-born New York Cosmos. Between 2004 and 2013 Kranjčar made 81 appearances for Croatia, 22 of them in his time with Spurs.

Appearances:
League: 30 (19) apps. 9 gls.
FA Cup: 8 (4) apps. 2 gls.
FL Cup: (1) app.
Euro: 3 (6) apps.
Others: 5 (5) apps.
Total: 46 (35) apps. 11 gls.

KYLE, Peter

Role: Centre-forward 1905-06
5ft.9ins. 11st.4lbs.
Born: Rutherglen, September 1880
Died: Glasgow, 19th January 1957

CAREER: Glasgow & District Schools/Glasgow Parkhead Jun 1896/Partick Thistle/Clyde Oct 1898/Liverpool May 1899/Leicester Fosse May 1900/Wellingborough cs. 1901/West Ham United Sep 1901/Kettering Dec 1901/Aberdeen Sep 1902/Cowdenbeath Jan 1903/Heart of Midlothian Aug 1903/Leicester Fosse Oct 1903/Port Glasgow Athletic Apr 1904/Royal Albert Nov 1904/Heart of Midlothian/Larkhall Thistle Apr 1905/Royal Albert May 1905/**SPURS** May 1905/Woolwich Arsenal Apr 1906/Aston Villa Mar 1908/Sheffield United Oct 1908/Royal Albert Aug 1909/Watford Nov 1909/Royal Albert cs. 1910.

Debut v Reading (SL) (a) 2.9.1905 (scored once)

A more than colourful character, following the career of Peter Kyle is exceptionally difficult, partly due to the lack of any regulated transfer system between English and Scottish clubs, but also because he seems to have suffered from a lack of discipline that saw him move quickly from one club to another, often without any obvious reason. A bustling centre-forward with a good eye for goal, he had little difficulty making the transition from Scottish Junior football to the English professional game, and does not seem to have got himself into any trouble while playing for Liverpool or Leicester. However, he then moved quickly from Wellingborough, West Ham United, Kettering and Aberdeen before spending 18 months with Cowdenbeath. Port Glasgow Athletic and Royal Albert provided only temporary homes, a trial with Heart of Midlothian did not prove any better and only a month after signing for Larkhall Thistle, Kyle was on his way to Spurs. He scored in each of his first four competitive matches for Spurs and led the attack well in the absence of first choice

Vivian J Woodward, moving comfortably to the inside-left spot when Woodward was available. He was clearly a valuable member of the team and appeared to have a lengthy career with Spurs in front of him but, together with Chris Carrick, was guilty of a breach of the club's training rules between Western League fixtures at Bristol Rovers and Plymouth Argyle in March 1906. Both players were suspended as a result and neither played for Spurs' first team again. The following month Kyle was transferred to Woolwich Arsenal where he scored 22 goals in 60 senior games and played in the Scottish international trial match of March 1907. His last appearance for Arsenal was against Aston Villa in February 1908, and the following month he moved to Villa Park. By October 1908 he had joined Sheffield United but ran into further disciplinary trouble with the management for failing to train properly and began the next season back home in Scotland with Royal Albert. He returned to the Southern League with Watford in November 1909, but within three months was dismissed for what was described as "disgraceful conduct" and returned home again to Scotland.

Appearances:
Southern: 25 apps. 8 gls.
FA Cup: 4 apps. 3 gls.
Others: 13 apps. 8 gls.
Total: 42 apps. 19 gls

LACY, John

Role: Centre-half 1978-83
6ft.3ins. 12st.4lbs.
Born: Liverpool, 14th August 1951

CAREER: Merseyside Schools/Lancashire Schools/Marine/London University/British Universities/Kingstonians/Fulham am. cs. 1970, pro. Jun 1971/**SPURS** Jul 1978/Crystal Palace Jul 1983/Stenungsunds (Sweden) Nov 1984/Barnet 1985/St Albans City Oct 1986, player-manager Jul 1987-1988/Wivenhoe cs. 1988, asst. manager 1990/Cornard United 1993-94.

Debut v Nottingham Forest (FL) (a) 19.8.1978
(Aberdeen (Fr) (a) 5.8.1978)

Born in the Everton district of Liverpool, John Lacy played for Liverpool Marine, but essentially gave up thoughts of a professional football career to pursue a Bachelor of Science Degree at the London School of Economics. Whilst studying he played for London University, who were coached by former Fulham and England full-back George Cohen, and after Lacy had gained his degree in Economics, Cohen persuaded him to join the amateur staff at Fulham. He made his League debut in November 1972 and developed rapidly, no doubt helped by the vast experience of former England stars Alan Mullery and Bobby Moore. He played for Fulham in the 1975 FA Cup Final against West Ham. Attracting the attention of the bigger clubs, Lacy was signed by Spurs for a £200,000 fee in the shadow of the  tickertape arrival of Ricky Villa and Ossie Ardiles, and the presence of the two Argentines allowed Lacy to settle in almost unnoticed. A tall, somewhat gangling centre-half, he was not the most constructive of footballers, but his job was to defend. He did that well enough in what was a difficult period for a Spurs' team newly back in the top flight, but still short of enough class players to make a real impact. A regular for most of that first season, his place came under increasing threat with the emergence of Paul Miller, and much of the following campaign was spent in the reserves. Having apparently recovered a starting place in 1980-81, the growing multitude of talent now available to Spurs crowded him out shortly after the FA Cup run began, and he was never able to break through again. He stayed with Spurs until July 1983 when he moved to Crystal Palace, but his contract there was cancelled so he could play in Norway. On his return from Scandinavia he spent a year with

Barnet and three more at St Albans City before moving down the non-League ladder.

Appearances:
League: 99 (5) apps. 2 gls.
FA Cup: 12 apps.
FL Cup: 11 apps. 1 gl.
Euro: 4 (1) apps.
Others: 37 (5) apps. 2 gls.
Total: **163 (11) apps. 5 gls.**

LAMELA, Érik Manuel

Role: Forward 2013-
5ft.11ins. 12st.4lbs.
Born: Florida, Buenos Aires, Argentina, 4th March 1992

CAREER: River Plate (Argentina)/Roma (Italy) Aug 2011/**SPURS** Aug 2013.

Debut v Arsenal (PL) (a) (sub) 1.9.2013

At £30 million, Érik Lamela was, and remains, the most expensive signing Spurs have ever made. After four years it still remains to be seen whether his signing will be regarded as a good piece of business or a mistake. A child prodigy at home in Argentina, it is claimed that even before he was ten-years old, Barcelona had offered his family £100,000 a year plus a house and jobs to take him to Spain, in much the way Lionel Messi's family had been encouraged to move to Europe. If the stories are true, the offer was rejected for Lamela remained at River Plate where he had begun to play at the age of seven. He made his debut for River Plate when aged 17, but was not an immediate success. It was two years before he began to establish himself as a first team regular, and no sooner had he done that and made his full international debut against Paraguay, then he was off to Roma in a €14 million deal. In two years he proved a tricky, elusive winger who not only created chances but proved adept at converting them himself. Franco Baldini had been General Director at Roma. When he joined Spurs in July 2013 as Director of Football he was clearly instrumental in Lamela signing for Spurs. Lamela's career at White Hart Lane did not start too well. For two years he did little to live up to the reputation that had accompanied him. He seemed, lightweight, indecisive, too easily prepared to give up. With countryman, Mauricio Pochettino, settling on a high pressure game that demanded 90 plus minute's effort from every player, Lamela might have been expected to be on his way. However, he buckled down and wholeheartedly adopted the Pochettino ideology. Pressing from the front as the first line of defence, working back to help his full-back, the expected dainty player with skill but little else, was replaced by a strong, determined worker. He still has his faults, over anxious sometimes, liable to make a rash challenge and collect a card, but if he continues to show the willingness to give his all, that £30 million may prove money well spent.

Appearances:
League: 62 (23) apps. 8 gls.
FA Cup: 3 apps.
FL Cup: 4 (4) apps. 2 gls.
Euro: 19 (6) apps. 9 gls.
Others: 8 (4) apps. 5 gls.
Total: **96 (37) apps. 24 gls.**

LANCASTER, Cameron Paul

Role: Striker 2011-12
5ft.11ins. 13st.3lbs.
Born: Camden, London, 5tth November 1992

CAREER: Oakhill Tigers/**SPURS** Academy Scholar Jul 2009, pro. Jul 2011/(Dagenham & Redbridge loan Mar 2011)/released Jun 2014/Crewe Alexandra trial Jul 2014/Stevenage trial and perm. Aug 2014/St Albans City Dec 2014/Louisville City (USA) trial and perm. Mar 2015.

Debut v Wigan Athletic (PL) (h) (sub) 31.1.2012

The appearance of Cameron Lancaster's name on the team-sheet for Spurs Premier League meeting with Wigan Athletic in January 2012 was a considerable surprise. Although he had made a few appearances, and scored a few goals, for the Development Squad, there had been little suggestion of him being ready for Premiership football. At the time he was not even a full professional, still being on Scholarship forms and with his experience limited to four games on loan to Dagenham & Redbridge. He was called upon as a 78th minute substitute, having no time in which to impress. That was the full extent of his senior career with Spurs. Seriously hampered by injuries, he remained with the club until being released in the summer of 2014. After playing for Stevenage and St Albans, Lancaster was taken on by Louisville City after impressing in a trial. The day after making his first appearance, Lancaster was injured in training and side-lined for the rest of the season.

Appearances:
League: (1) app.
Total: **(1) app. 0 gls.**

LANDON, Christopher Stephen

Role: Defender 1992-93
5ft.7ins. 9st.7lbs.
Born: Epsom, Surrey, 20th October 1974

CAREER: Epsom and Ewell High School/London Schools/Surrey Schools/**SPURS** trainee cs. 1991, pro. Jul 1993/free transfer Feb 1994.

Debut v Watford (sub) (Fr) (a) 8.8.1992

18-year old full-back Chris Landon was still only a trainee when called up to play for the first team in a couple of pre-season friendly games in August 1992. Signed professional almost a year later, he was given a free transfer in February 1994, but was unable to secure another club and disappeared from the game.

Appearances:
Others: 1 (1) apps.
Total: **1 (1) apps. 0 gls.**

LANE (LOHN), William Henry Charles

Role: Centre-forward 1924-27
5ft.10ins. 11st.2lbs.
Born: Tottenham, London, 23rd October 1904
Died: Chelmsford, Essex, 10th November 1985

CAREER: London City Mission/Gnome Athletic/Park Avondale/Tottenham/Charlton Athletic trial/**SPURS** am. 1920/Summerstown Nov 1923/Barnet Jan 1924/Northfleet United 1924/**SPURS** pro. May 1924/Leicester City Nov 1926/Reading May 1928/Brentford May 1929/Watford May 1932/Bristol City Jan 1936/Clapton Orient Jul 1937/Gravesend cs. 1938, manager/Brentford asst. manager 1938/(guest for Brighton and Hove Albion, Clapton Orient, Reading and Watford during World War Two)/Guildford City manager Jun 1947/Brighton and Hove Albion asst. manager Apr 1950, caretaker-manager Mar 1951, manager cs. 1951-May 1961/Gravesend and Northfleet manager Dec 1961-cs. 1963/Arsenal scout 1963/Queens Park Rangers scout Jan 1968/Arsenal scout/Brighton and Hove Albion scout Sep 1978.

Debut v Notts County (FL) (a) 6.9.1924

A local lad who played for three of the area's junior clubs and was then placed by Spurs at Barnet, Bill Lane was born under the name of Lohn. He was one of the first graduates from the nursery club at Northfleet, when he joined the White Hart Lane staff in the summer of 1924. He made his League debut in the third game of the season, but spent most of his career with Spurs as a reserve, only being regarded as a first team regular in the last three months of 1924-25. When Spurs signed Frank Osborne, Lane moved to Leicester City for £2,250, but was again a frustrated understudy, this time to the prolific Arthur Chandler. From Leicester he spent the rest of his career moving rapidly from one club to another. Although he did not stay long with any of his many clubs for long, they all got good value from a player who had the priceless ability to score goals, albeit in the lower reaches of the League. At Brentford he netted 84 goals in just 114 games. Another 72 goals followed at Watford. When his playing career was over Lane went into management with Brentford, Guildford City and Brighton. After twice finishing second in the Third Division (South), he eventually led Brighton into the Second Division as champions in 1957-58, the last year in which the division was divided into North and South sections. He remained with Brighton until May 1961 when he retired, complaining the game was "too commercialised". He was not out of the game for long, returning as manager of Gravesend and Northfleet and leading them on their FA Cup run of 1963 which only ended in a fourth round replay defeat by Sunderland. The highlight of his career probably came on 20th December 1933 when he scored a hat-trick in only three minutes for Watford against Clapton Orient. His brother, R, played for Barnet and helped Spurs reserves in 1926-27.

Appearances:
League: 25 apps. 7 gls.
FA Cup: 4 apps. 2 gls.
Others: 7 apps. 3 gls.
Total: 36 apps. 12 gls.

LANHAM, Charles Hamilton

Role: Inside-forward 1895-97
Born: Stanley, 20th December 1877
Died: 8th October 1953

CAREER: SPURS trial Jan 1896, pro. Aug 1896, am. Aug 1897/Millwall Athletic Dec 1897/Southall/West Hampstead/Old St Stephens (Shepherds Bush) 1898-1903/Brighton and Hove Albion Aug 1902/Brentford cs. 1903.

Debut v Stoke (FAC) (a) 1.2.1896
(Reading (Fr) (h) 4.1.1896 (scored once))

A good friend of Spurs winger Ernie Payne, who recommended him, Charlie Lanham was given a trial in a friendly against Reading in January 1896. A lively 18-year old, he promptly scored and became a regular for the rest of the season. Although he performed well in his first season and was persuaded to sign professional for Spurs' entry into the Southern League, he found himself out of favour the following season when the inside-right position he so favoured was taken by Jimmy Milliken. Lanham remained with Spurs until the end of that season when, along with practically the whole playing staff, he was released. Re-instated as an amateur in August 1897, he re-signed for Spurs but was unable to get back in the first team. Other clubs were keen to acquire his services and in December 1897 it was reported Spurs had complained to the United League of an illegal approach to Lanham by Millwall Athletic. As it was, Spurs released Lanham anyway, and he duly joined Millwall, but was unable to establish a place and moved on to Southall, West Hampstead and Shepherds Bush. He later played the odd game for Brighton and Hove Albion and Brentford.

Appearances:
Southern: 2 apps.
FA Cup: 1 app.
Others: 34 apps. 18 gls.
Total: 37 apps. 18 gls.

LATHAM, Fredrick

Role: Goalkeeper 1896-97
Born: Crewe, Cheshire, 1876

CAREER: Crewe Alexandra/Stoke May 1896/**SPURS** trial Apr 1897/Crewe Alexandra.

Debut v Kettering Town (UL) (h) 17.4.1897
(Nottingham Forest (Fr) (h) 16.4.1897)

Fred Latham played just three matches for Spurs in April 1897 whilst on trial. At the time he was on the books of Stoke but had made only five League appearances before slipping out of favour. His first game was a friendly with Nottingham Forest, and he also played in a United League fixture with Kettering Town the following day when he seemed well regarded and was admired "for the neat way he cleared danger". However, he was not taken on by Spurs and returned to the Potteries. In his final trial appearance Latham appeared under the pseudonym of "Stokeley".

Appearances:
Others: 3 apps.
Total: 3 apps. 0 gls.

LATYMER, T

Role: Half-back 1888-89

CAREER: SPURS/Old St Stephens.

Debut v Windsor Phoenix (Fr) (h) 2.3.1889

Latymer's only known appearance for Spurs was in March 1889 when he played in a friendly against Windsor Phoenix. It is more than likely that he played in other matches that season but details of the line-ups, indeed even many of the matches played, have proved impossible to trace. He appears to have been associated with Spurs for just the one season and later played for Old St Stephens.

Appearances:
Others: 1 app.
Total: 1 app. 0 gls.

LAUREL, John Albert

Role: Centre-half 1957-58
Born: Dartford, Kent, 11th June 1935

CAREER: Gravesend & Northfleet 1951-52/**SPURS** am. Nov 1951, pro. Jul 1952/ Ipswich Town Jun 1959/ Kings Lynn.

Debut v Rotterdam Select XI (Fr) (a) 27.3.1958

Although a Middlesex and England Youth international, John Laurel was never able to replace the established centre-halves such as Harry Clarke, John Ryden and Maurice Norman and never played a League game for Spurs. His only first team appearance was in March 1958 when he played against a Rotterdam Select XI in Rotterdam in a friendly match. In June 1959, he joined Ipswich Town who were under the management of Alf Ramsey, but had no greater success there, playing only four games in his three years with the club.

Appearances:
Others: 1 app.
Total: 1 app. 0 gls.

LAWRENCE, Walter Henry

Role: Centre-half or inside-forward 1917-18
Born: London

CAREER: Summerstown/Crystal Palace am. Nov 1906/Woolwich Arsenal am. May 1909, pro. May 1909/Crystal Palace cs. 1910//Northfleet United cs. 1912/Merthyr Town cs. 1913/(guest for Crystal Palace, Queens Park Rangers and **SPURS** during World War One)/Northfleet United 1919/Ramsgate cs. 1920/Dartford.

Debut v Clapton Orient (LFC) (h) 20.10.1917

In two spells, Billy Lawrence spent seven years associated with Crystal Palace as an amateur, making about 30 senior appearances and collecting an England amateur cap against Wales in February 1909. After a year with Northfleet, he moved to Merthyr Town and was still on the books of the Southern League club when the First World War broke out. Back in London for war service, he made five appearances for Spurs in the London Football Combination in 1917-18 scoring once. His first appearance was against Clapton Orient in October 1917 on their Homerton ground in what was a home match for Spurs, played at Homerton because White Hart Lane was being used for the manufacture of gas marks. He returned to Northfleet after the War, had a year there and at Ramsgate before finishing his career at Dartford.

Appearances:
Others: 5 apps. 1 gl.
Total: 5 apps. 1 gl.

LAYBOURNE, John Sylvester

Role: Centre-forward 1952-53
Born: Durham, County Durham, 26th May 1927

CAREER: Emmanuel College, Cambridge/Cambridge University/ Pegasus/**SPURS** am. Jun 1953/Corinthian Casuals.

Debut v West Ham United (Fr) (a) 16.4.1953

The goal-scoring centre-forward of the Universities team Pegasus that beat Harwich & Parkeston 6-0 to win the 1953 Amateur Cup, Jack Laybourne was recommended to Spurs by the Pegasus coach, Vic Buckingham. He made his one appearance as a trialist in a friendly at West Ham United in April 1953, the first match to be played at Upton Park under floodlights, five days after helping Pegasus lift the Amateur Cup. Although he signed amateur forms for Spurs that June he did not play any further games for the club at any level. He did however go on to play for Corinthian Casuals, win four England amateur caps, play in the 1956 Amateur Cup final and lead the line for Great Britain in the 1956 Olympic Games.

Appearances:
Others: 1 app.
Total: 1 app. 0 gls.

LAYCOCK

Role: Inside-forward 1894-95

Debut v Liverpool Casuals (Fr) (h) 12.4.95 (scored once)

Laycock made his only appearance for Spurs in April 1895 when he scored once in a friendly with Liverpool Casuals.

Appearances:
Others: 1 app. 1 gl.
Total: 1 app. 1 gl.

LEACH, George

Role: Centre or inside-forward 1905-06
6ft.0ins. 13st.4lbs.
Born: Malta, 18th July 1881
Died: Rawtenstall, Lancashire, 10th July 1945

CAREER: Eastbourne by 1899/Hailsham/Eastbourne Old Town/Brighton and Hove Albion Aug 1904/ **SPURS** Apr 1905/Tunbridge Wells Rangers Apr 1907/ Brighton and Hove Albion Mar-May 1909.

Debut v Fulham (WL) (h) 16.10.1905

A useful County cricketer who played 225 matches for

Surrey between 1903 and 1914, and was a regular member of the Hailsham Cricket Club, George Leach had played a few games for Brighton and Hove Albion before joining Spurs. In his first season, he appeared in seven competitive matches, but, although he remained with Spurs for the following season, all his only other outings were in friendly matches. Released in April 1907 he joined Tunbridge Wells Rangers and later played a few more games for Brighton.

Appearances:
Southern: 2 apps. 2 gls.
Others: 5 apps. 1 gl.
Total: 7 apps. 3 gls.

LEACH-LEWIS, Allan Francis

Role: Centre-half 1903-05
Born: Margate, Kent, 11th March 1883
Died: Thanet, 7th July 1963

CAREER: Margate by 1901-02/Cambridge University/**SPURS** am. Mar 1904/Casuals/Corinthians.

Debut v Luton Town (SL) (h) 2.4.1904

Allan Leach-Lewis was a student at Pembroke College, Cambridge when he signed amateur forms for Spurs in March 1904. Centre-half in the Cambridge University team he played one Southern League match for Spurs the following month. A player for the Casuals and Corinthians, he continued to be associated with Spurs the following season, but made only one further first team appearance in a friendly.

Appearances:
Southern: 1 app.
Others: 1 app.
Total: 2 apps. 0 gls.

LEAMAN, Stuart

Role: Goalkeeper or half-back 1883-90
Died: Rose Park, Adelaide, Australia, September 1902

Debut v Brownlow Rovers (Fr) (h) 6.10.1883

Stuart Leaman, a pupil at St Johns Middle Class School, has come to be regarded as Spurs' first goalkeeper as he occupied that position in the first

Spurs' match for which a team line-up has been traced. That was in October 1883 in a friendly against Brownlow Rovers that Spurs won 9-0. One of the founder members of the club, he probably played most of his football for the reserve side of which he was captain. His only other known appearance in the first team was in October 1889 when he played at half-back in a friendly against Vulcan. Until 1896 he was a member of the committee that ran Spurs, although he was associated with other local clubs, notably Avondale. In 1896-97 he was one of the club's joint auditors. He was still in the Tottenham area in the late 1890's; an organ teacher and concert performer. His association with Spurs did not end until he emigrated to Australia early in the 20th Century.

Appearances:
Others: 2 apps.
Total: 2 apps. 0 gls.

LEE, Charles

Role: Defender 2006-07
5ft.11ins. 11st.7lbs.
Born: Whitechapel, London, 5tth January 1987

CAREER: SPURS Academy 2003, pro. Jul 2005/(Millwall loan Nov 2006)/Peterborough United May 2007/Gillingham loan Nov 2010, perm Jul 2011/Stevenage Jul 2014.

Debut v Girondins de Bordeaux (sub) (Fr) 13.7.2006

With Spurs from eight years old, Charlie Lee was a hard-working midfielder or defender who worked his way through the ranks onto the professional staff. He made a couple of substitute appearances on the pre-season tour of France in July 2006, but apart from making the substitutes bench for a few games never seriously got close to the League team. Lee joined Peterborough United in the summer of 2007. He went on to play more than 150 games for the "Posh" and more than 100 for Gillingham before moving on to Stevenage.

Appearances:
Others: (2) apps.
Total: (2) apps. 0 gls.

LEE, Colin

Role: Striker 1977-80
6ft.0ins. 11st.9lbs.
Born: Torquay, Devon, 12th June 1956

CAREER: Torbay Schools/Buckfastleigh Rangers/Bristol City app. Aug 1971, pro. Jul 1974/(Hereford United loan Nov 1974)/Torquay United loan Jan 1977, perm Feb 1977/**SPURS** Oct 1977/Chelsea Jan 1980/Brentford player-Youth Development Officer Jul 1987/Watford Youth team manager Jul 1989, manager Mar-Nov 1990/Reading Youth Development Officer Jul 1991, asst. manager by May 1993/Leicester City asst. manager Dec 1994/Wolverhampton Wanderers asst. manager Dec 1995, caretaker manager Nov 1998, perm. Nov 1998-Jan 2001/Leeds United scout Jan 2001/Torquay United technical consultant Feb 2001, manager Mar-Apr 2001/Leeds United scout Jul 2001/Wigan Athletic coach Dec 2001/Walsall manager Jan 2002-Apr 2004/Millwall coach Jul 2005, manager Jul 2005, director of football Dec 2005-Jan 2006/Torquay United asst. manager Jan 2007, caretaker manager Feb 2007, director of football Feb-May 2007, Chief Executive May 2007-May 2011/Notts County asst. manager Feb 2012-Feb 2013/Buckfastleigh Rangers president.

Debut v Bristol Rovers (FL) (h) 22.10.1977 (scored four)

Colin Lee joined Bristol City as a central striker, but opportunities in that position were so limited at Ashton Gate, that he switched to full-back. It was in that role that he was loaned out to Hereford and Torquay before a permanent transfer to the Devon club. At Plainmoor he reverted to striker and caught the eye of Spurs' manager Keith Burkinshaw. Regarded as one for the future, Spurs invested £60,000 in his potential, but due to injuries Lee was immediately thrown into the first team. He grabbed the headlines in quite remarkable fashion, with four debut goals as Bristol Rovers were crushed 9-0. Not surprisingly, Lee was unable to

maintain such a fairy-tale start and although he played regularly during the season's successful promotion campaign, he was unable to hold down a regular first team place up front in 1978-79. He responded by showing considerable versatility, dropping back to centre-half or even full-back, but while this made him a useful squad member, he was perhaps not really good enough in any one position for First Division football. Even so, Chelsea still laid out £200,000 to sign him and he spent seven years with the west London club, both as a striker and defender. Indeed, it was as a full-back that he won a Second Division Championship medal in 1984, while his Full Members' Cup medal in 1986 came as a two-goal centre-forward! In July 1987, Lee joined former Spurs team-mate Steve Perryman at Brentford as player/Youth Development Officer and then moved to Watford to take charge of their Youth team. Following the dismissal of Steve Harrison in March 1990, he took over as caretaker-manager and was handed the job permanently at the end of that season. However, he was unable to rebuild the Hornets and in November 1990, with the club seven points adrift at the foot of Division Two, was dismissed and replaced by Perryman. In July 1991 Lee joined Reading as Youth Development Officer where he first linked up with Mark McGhee whom he followed as assistant manager to Leicester City and Wolverhampton Wanderers. Lee took over the manager's job at Molineux following McGhee's dismissal and later went on to manage Walsall, Millwall and Torquay, rising to be Chief Executive at Plainmoor.

Appearances:
League: 57 (5) apps. 18 gls.
FA Cup: 6 (1) apps. 3 gls.
FL Cup: 2 apps.
Others: 20 (3) apps. 9 gls.
Total: 85 (9) apps. 30 gls.

LEE, David John Francis

Role: Midfielder 1999-2000
5ft.10ins. 12st.7lbs.
Born: Basildon, Essex, 28th March 1980

CAREER: Corringham Boys/SPURS assoc. schl. 1994, trainee Jul 1996, pro. Jul 1998/(Luton Town loan Sep 1999)/Norwich City trial Jan 2000/Luton Town trial Feb 2000/Norwich City trial Feb 2000/Gillingham Mar 2000/Southend United Aug 2000/Hull City May 2001/Brighton and Hove Albion Jan 2002/(Bristol Rovers loan Oct 2002)/(Yeovil Town trial Feb 2003)/(Cambridge United trial Apr 2003)/(Thurrock United loan Oct 2003)/Oldham Athletic training Oct 2004, perm Oct-Nov 2004/Thurrock Dec 2004/Kidderminster Harriers trial Jan 2005/Stevenage Borough Feb 2005/Aldershot Town Feb 2005/Harlow Town Feb 2007/Braintree Town Mar 2007/AFC Hornchurch Aug 2007/Harlow Town Oct 2007/Canvey Island Jul 2008/retired May 2009.

Debut v Bishops Stortford (sub) (Fr) (a) 3.9.1999

David Lee was a talented young midfielder who made his only first team appearance as a substitute in a friendly at Bishop Stortford in September 1999 to officially open Stortford's new Woodside Park ground. With many players away on international duty, several youngsters were given an outing. Lee was made available for transfer early the following year and went on to play for numerous clubs lower down the football ladder. While at Aldershot in August 2005 he suffered a serious injury, dislocating his ankle, breaking his ankle socket and cracking his tibia and fibular. He was lucky to play again, but, not surprisingly, was never quite the player he was before the injury.

Appearances:
Others: (1) app.
Total: (1) app. 0 gls.

LEE, J

Role: Outside-left 1907-08

CAREER: Chelmsford/SPURS trial Oct 1907/Brighton and Hove Albion.

Debut v Reading (WL) (h) 14.10.1907

An amateur with Chelmsford, Lee made his only appearance for Spurs on trial in October 1907 against Reading. He did not impress enough to sign for Spurs but later played for Brighton and Hove Albion.

Appearances:
Others: 1 app.
Total: 1 app. 0 gls.

LEE, Terence William George

Role: Goalkeeper 1973-75
5ft.11ins. 11st.10lbs.
Born: Stepney, London, 20th September 1952
Died: Torbay, Devon, 22nd June 1996

CAREER: North Island (New Zealand)/Havering Schools/Mid Essex Schools/SPURS app. Apr 1968, pro. May 1970/(Cardiff City loan Aug 1974)/(Gillingham loan Feb 1975)/Torquay United Jul 1975/Newport County trial Nov 1978, perm. Dec 1978-Mar 1979/Minehead Apr 1979.

Debut v Newcastle United (FL) (a) 11.5.1974

Terry Lee emigrated to New Zealand in 1964 and before returning to the U.K. represented North Island against South Island in an international trial as an inside-forward. On his return, he took up goalkeeping and caught the eye of Spurs' scouts. Signed as an apprentice in April 1968 and professional in May 1970 his only full first team appearance was in May 1974 when he kept a clean sheet in the last League match of the season at Newcastle United. The following season he made one substitute appearance in a friendly and, after spells on loan to Cardiff and Gillingham, was transferred to Torquay. He went on to make over 100 appearances for the West Country club before his release and then spent a year with Newport County. In April 1979 he moved on to Minehead. Lee died of a heart attack while playing cricket.

Appearances:
League: 1 app.
Others: (1) app.
Total: 1 (1) apps. 0 gls.

LEE, Young-Pyo

Role: Full-back 2005-2007
5ft.8ins. 10st.13lbs.
Born: Hongchun, South Korea, 23rd April 1977

CAREER: Konkuk University (South Korea) am./Anyang LG Cheetahs (South Korea) pro. 2000/PSV Eindhoven (Holland) loan Jan 2003, perm. Jul 2003/**SPURS** Aug 2005/Borussia Dortmund (Germany) Aug 2008/Al-Hilal (Saudi Arabia) Jul 2009/Vancouver Whitecaps (Canada) Dec 2011/ retired Oct 2013.

Debut v Liverpool (PL) (h) 10.4.2005

If ever there was a perfect example of how football truly is the global game, then Lee Young-Pyo is that example. In a distinguished career, Lee has taken his talents to all corners of the globe, a success wherever he has been. Initially playing for Konkuk University while studying for a degree in Governmental Issues and Politics, he made his first appearance for South Korea in June 1999 and played all three games for the Under-23s

as they represented South Korea in the 2000 Sydney Olympics. Following the Olympic Games, he signed professional for Anyang Cheetahs and helped them win the K-League in his first year there. A regular for his country, Lee was one of the outstanding performers as South Korea reached the semi-finals of the 2002 World Cup. His national manager then was Gus Hiddink and when he returned to Holland, Lee was one of the first players he secured for PSV Eindhoven. Initially signed on loan, Lee played in

practically all PSV's remaining games as they collected the Eredivisie title. An attack minded full-back who could also play in midfield, Lee was at his best on the left, but when needed would switch to the right. Having helped PSV win another Eredivisie title in 2005, Lee became a target for some of Europe's bigger clubs and when a move to Roma fell through, Martin Jol was quick to bring him to White Hart Lane. In his first season, Lee proved a fine acquisition, sharp, quick to tackle, defensively competent, but at his best using his terrific pace to get forward. His lack of height and less than effective crossing were, perhaps, his obvious weaknesses and when Benoît Assou-Ekotto and Pascal Chimbonda were signed he found himself out of the team. For two years he competed with Assou-Ekotto for the left-back slot, but eventually conceded defeat and moved to Borussia Dortmund. A year later he moved on to Al-Hilal in Saudi Arabia, helping them win the Saudi Professional League in both his years there. The final stop on Lee's world tour was Vancouver for another two year stay. When Lee retired from international football in January 2011 he had an amazing 127 appearances for his country to his credit, 16 of them in his days with Spurs.

Appearances:
League: 68 (2) apps.
FA Cup: 7 apps.
FL Cup: 6 apps.
Euro: 10 apps.
Others: 2 apps.
Total: 93 (2) apps. 0 gls.

LEECH, William

Role: Half-back 1898-99
5ft.7ins. 10st.7lbs.
Born: Newcastle-under-Lyme, Staffordshire, 15th July 1875
Died: Leicester, 24th November 1934

CAREER: Newcastle White Star/Newcastle Swifts/**SPURS** cs. 1898/ Burslem Port Vale Jun 1899/Stoke May 1900/Plymouth Argyle Jul 1903/ Leicester Fosse Jul 1906, coach 1912-1915.

Debut v Chatham (TML) (a) 2.1.1899

Previously with Newcastle White Star and Newcastle Swifts in his native Staffordshire, Billy Leech joined Spurs as a defensive half-back. Basically a reserve, he spent just one year at Tottenham, with most of his 13 appearances coming towards the end of the season. On his release he returned to Staffordshire, established himself with Burslem Port Vale and quickly moved on to Stoke where he held down the centre-half position until his leg was broken in February 1902. Unable to recover his position, in the summer of

1903 he joined the newly professionalised Plymouth Argyle where he played for three years until moving on to Leicester Fosse. An almost ever-present in his first two seasons, which saw Leicester promoted to the First Division in 1908, he then led the reserves before taking up a position on the coaching staff until the First World War.

Appearances:
Southern: 4 apps. 2 gls.
Others: 9 apps. 4 gls.
Total: 13 apps. 6 gls.

LEESE, F J

Role: Half-back or full-back 1891-92

CAREER: Tottenham Park/**SPURS** 1891-92/Old St Marks 1892.

Debut v Uxbridge (Fr) (h) 2.1.1892

Another of the players from Spurs' early days about whom information has proved impossible to find, Leese played for Spurs in two friendly matches in January 1892. The brother of H Leese, in the first, he played in the half-back line and in the second at full-back. As details of all Spurs' matches that season are not known he may well have made further appearances. The following season he played for Old St Marks and in the early 1900s was a referee in the Southern and Western Leagues. He has been noted playing for Tottenham Park in December 1882.

Appearances:
Others: 3 apps.
Total: 3 apps. 0 gls.

LEESE, H

Role: Outside-left 1891-92

CAREER: Tottenham Park/**SPURS** 1891-92.

Debut v Hampstead (Fr) (h) 26.9.1891

Like his brother, FJ, it has proved impossible to discover any information on this player's career. His first known appearance was in a friendly with Hampstead in September 1891 and he appears to have been the regular outside-left for most of the season. He also played for Tottenham Park in December 1882.

Appearances:
Others: 12 apps. 4 gls.
Total: 12 apps. 4 gls.

"LEIGH, A K"

Role: Outside-right 1900-01

Debut v Queens Park Rangers (WL) (h) 15.4.1901

"A local amateur with a good reputation", Leigh made his one appearance for Spurs in a Western League fixture in April 1901. With the FA Cup success causing a fixture backlog, Spurs were expected to play 15 matches that month and, along with several local players and reserves, Leigh's services were called upon. It is quite possible AK Leigh is not the player's real name. There was a player of that name with Shepherds Bush, a west London club that eventually merged with Queens Park Rangers, but the use of inverted commas in match reports would indicate the name was a pseudonym-perhaps for a player with the London Caledonians, who were known as the "Calies".

Appearances:
Others: 1 app.
Total: 1 app. 0 gls.

LENNON, Aaron Justin

Role: Wide Midfield 2005-2015
5ft.6ins. 10st.1lbs.
Born: Leeds, South Yorkshire, 16th April 1987

CAREER: Leeds United Academy Scholar Jul 2003, pro. Apr 2004/**SPURS** Jul 2005/Everton loan Feb 2015, perm. Sep 2015.

Debut v Chelsea (sub) (BPL) (h) 27.8.2005
(Sundowns (sub) (Fr) (Suwon) 18.7.2005)

In an age when size and power count for so much in professional football, Aaron Lennon continues to add proof to the old adage that if you're good enough, you're big enough. Barely into his teens, Lennon was identified as a potential wing star, his pace and trickery outstanding as he worked his way through the ranks at Leeds United to make his Premier League debut as a substitute at White Hart Lane in August 2003. At 16 years and 129 days, he was the youngest player in Premier League history. In a Leeds side plummeting downwards because of financial problems, Lennon was the precious home grown star that provided a spark of hope for the future, but when Spurs made a cheeky offer of £1 million for his signature, even that was too much for Leeds to refuse. Lennon was another of the young, talented English players Spurs identified and earmarked for careful development. He was not expected to seriously challenge for a regular first team spot for a year or two, but from his first outing it was clear he was already good enough. Within a few weeks of signing Lennon collected his first England Under-21 cap, adding to the international honours he had won at all junior levels. At the end of his first season as a Spurs player he was selected for the World Cup squad, only making his full international debut in the run up to the tournament. His incredible pace, both the initial speed off the mark and the sustained burst over a distance, was always his most obvious attribute, but while he lost none of that in the ten years he played at White Hart Lane, Lennon proved there is much more to his game than just pace. He has trickery, an ability to beat a man and is never afraid to cut inside. He has learnt that football is a team game and that he has a part to play in helping defend as well as going forward. Sometimes his crossing has been lacking, and he is not always the most composed in front of goal, but the positives vastly outweigh the negatives. His style has often meant that even slight injuries side-lined him for longer than anyone would like. The absences cost him more full caps than the 21 he collected. Given a bit of luck, Lennon should have been a more than influential performer for Spurs for years. Sadly, the style of football Mauricio Pochettino wanted to play meant there was no place for wingers. Attacking from out wide became the job of the full-backs. Lennon was rarely given a chance by Pochettino and it was no surprise when he was allowed to move to Everton.

Appearances:
League: 220 (46) apps. 26 gls.
FA Cup: 14 (5) apps. 1 gl.
FL Cup: 16 (5) apps. 1 gl.
Euro: 46 (12) apps. 2 gls.
Others: 28 (18) apps. 5 gls.
Total: 324 (86) apps. 35 gls.

LEONHARDSEN, Øyvind

Role: Midfield 1999-2002
5ft.10ins. 11st.7lbs.
Born: Kristiansund, Norway, 17th August 1970

CAREER: Clausenengen (Norway) Aug 1987/Molde (Norway) Jun 1989/Rosenberg (Norway) Aug 1992/**SPURS** trial Oct 1993/Wimbledon Nov 1994/Liverpool Jun 1997/**SPURS** August 1999/Schalke 04 (Germany) trial Aug 2002/Aston Villa Aug 2002/Portsmouth trial Jan 2004/Lyn Oslo (Norway) Mar 2004/Strømsgodset IF (Norway) Dec 2005/retired Dec 2007/Lyn Oslo youth development coach Mar 2009/Haslum IL (Norway) coach/Norwegian Football Academy coach Aug 2009.

Debut v West Ham United (sub) (PL) (a) 7.8.1999

Having won the award as Norway's best midfielder in 1991, Øyvind Leonhardsen was on the way to winning it a second time when invited to Spurs for a trial in November 1993. A busy little midfielder, he impressed, but not enough for Spurs to secure his transfer. Little more than a year later, and having been voted Player of the Year by his fellow Norwegian players for 1994, he joined Wimbledon. Joe Kinnear was the Wimbledon manager then and trying to move the club away from the crudity of its "Crazy Gang" style. Leonhardsen fitted in well with Kinnear's plans, a busy, scurrying midfielder, technically strong and always likely to score. His form attracted the attention of Liverpool and he quickly moved to Anfield, linking up with fellow Norwegian internationals Stig Inge Bjørnebye and Bjørn Tore Kvarme. For a year Leonhardsen was a regular for the Merseysiders, but when Gerard Houllier took charge his plans for a more cultured style saw Leonhardsen marginalised. His non-stop work ethic and willingness to give everything for the team was exactly what George Graham demanded and his transfer to White Hart Lane was secured for a fee of £2.75 million. Somewhat similar to his experience at Liverpool, for 18 months, Leonhardsen was a regular performer, hard-working, professional and at times outstanding. He was not a Glenn Hoddle style of player, though, and when the Spurs' legend replaced Graham, Leonhardsen was out in the cold. He was eventually transferred to Aston Villa where he played for 18 months before returning to Norway, moving into coaching when his playing days were over. While Leonhardsen was rarely an automatic choice for Spurs, he was for his country. Out of 86 appearances for Norway, 18 were in his time at White Hart Lane.

Appearances:
League: 46 (8) apps. 7 gls.
FA Cup: 3 (3) apps. 1 gl.
FL Cup: 6 (2) apps. 2 gls.
Euro: 4 apps. 1 gl.
Others: 8 (10) apps. 1 gl.
Total: 67 (23) apps. 12 gls.

LESLIE, Thomas Scott

Role: Half-back 1908-11
5ft.10ins. 11st.8lbs.
Born: Tollcross, Glasgow, 26th February 1885
Died: Hackney, London, Apr qtr. 1948

CAREER: Vale of Clyde/ **SPURS** May 1908/Leyton Aug 1911/Gillingham Sep 1912/(Guest for Clyde during World War One)/Caerphilly cs. 1920/Barry Town cs. 1921.

Debut v Blackpool (FL) (a) 10.10.1908

Tom Leslie was signed as cover for regular left-half Jabez Darnell and when he made his League debut against Blackpool in October 1908 it was in place of the absent Darnell. Leslie stayed three years with Spurs, but was never to rise above the role of reserve, his best run coming in February and March 1910 when he played at full-back in the absence of Bert Elkin. Released at the end of the 1910-11 season, he moved to Leyton and after just one season joined Gillingham. He rendered the "Gills" many years valuable service before finishing his career with a year at both Caerphilly and Barry Town.

Appearances:
League: 10 apps.
FA Cup: 2 apps.
Others: 4 apps.
Total: 16 apps. 0 gls.

LESNIAK, Filip

Role: Midfielder 2013-17
5ft.8ins. 10st.11lbs.
Born: Košice, Slovakia, 14th May 1996

CAREER: MFK Košice (Slovakia)/**SPURS** Academy Scholar Jul 2012, pro. Jul 2014/(Slovan Liberec (Czech Republic) loan Jul 2016/released June 2017.

Debut v Leicester City (sub) (PL) (a) 18.5.2017
(Ledley King XI (Fr) (h) (sub) 12.5.2014)

Filip Lesniak proves that in the ever-expanding search for talented youngsters, modern football knows no boundaries. Lesniak was training with his home town second division club, MFK Košice, in Slovakia when noticed by Spurs. Taken on to the Academy, he was signed professional by Spurs at the first opportunity. A defensive midfielder, neat and tidy in possession, always backing up his colleagues and looking for the ball, his first senior appearance was in Ledley King's Testimonial match in May 2014. Although selected for his country at Under-21 level, he was unable to make a breakthrough into Spurs' senior squad. Sent on loan to Slovan Liberec, he was given few opportunities before returning to Spurs after six months. It was back to the Development Squad until a surprise call-up to the Premier League team for an end of season visit to Leicester and a late debut as a substitute. That was as good as it got for Lesniak at Spurs. Less than a month later, he was released.

Appearances:
League   (1) app.
Others: 1 (1) apps.
Total: 1 (2) apps. 0 gls.

LEVENE, David Jack

Role: Half-back 1932-35
5ft.9ins. 12st.6lbs
Born: Bethnal Green, London, 25th February 1908
Died: Southend, Essex, October qtr. 1970

CAREER: Hugonians/Northfleet United Mar 1931/**SPURS** am. Jan 1931, pro. May 1932/Crystal Palace Dec 1935/Northern France cs. 1937/Clapton Orient trial and perm. Aug 1938/(Guest for Chesterfield during World War Two).

Debut v Manchester United (FL) (h) 10.9.1932

David Levene served his apprenticeship at the Northfleet nursery before moving up to Spurs in the summer of 1932. He soon made his League debut in a 6-1 thrashing of Manchester United, but as a half-back he found few openings in the first team due to the form of Tom Meads and Arthur Rowe. He spent two and a half years at White Hart Lane, but, with only ten appearances to show for it, it was no surprise when the prospect of regular first team football led him to join Crystal Palace. He only stayed one season in south London, played for a year in northern France, and then returned to London. After a trial with Clapton Orient he was taken on and finished his career there during the Second World War.

Appearances:
League: 8 apps.
FA Cup: 2 apps.
Total: 10 apps. 0 gls.

LEVY, Ernest William

Role: Inside-forward 1899-00
Born: Atcham, Shropshire, Apr qtr. 1877

CAREER: Aston Villa/Park Mills Oct 1897/Chesham Jan 1900/**SPURS** Jan 1900/Fulham Jul 1900-Jun 1901/Erith Oct 1901/Southern United Oct 1905.

Debut v Gravesend United (Fr) (a) 21.2.1900

Levy, who was reputed to have played for Aston Villa's reserves, joined Spurs from Chesham in January 1900, and made his only first team appearance in a friendly at Gravesend United the following month. He was released at the end of the season and spent the following season with Fulham, later playing for Erith and Southern United.

Appearances:
Others: 1 app.
Total: 1 app. 0 gls.

LEWORTHY, David John

Role: Striker 1984-86
5ft.9ins. 12st.0lbs.
Born: Portsmouth, Hampshire, 22nd October 1962

CAREER: Portsmouth Schools/Portsmouth app. Apr 1979, pro. Sep 1980, contract cancelled Apr 1982/Fareham Town Jul 1982/**SPURS** Aug 1984/Oxford United Dec 1985/(Shrewsbury Town loan Oct 1987)/Reading Jul 1989/(Colchester United loan Mar 1991)/Farnborough Town Feb 1992/Dover Athletic Jul 1993, player-joint caretaker manager Jan 1995/Rushden and Diamonds Jan 1997/Kingstonians Jul 1997/Havant and Waterlooville player-coach Jun 2000, youth team manager Oct 2002, reserve team manager Jul 2003, manager Jan-Nov 2004/San Pedro (Spain) coach/Kingstonians player-coach Nov 2006/Croydon Athletic first team coach Jun-Oct 2007/Carshalton Athletic asst. manager/Banstead Athletic manager Dec 2007-Oct 2008/Croydon manager Nov 2008-Jan 2009.

Debut v Arsenal (FL) (h) 15.4.1985
(Guernsey FA XI (Fr) (a) 8.4.1985)

When he was only eight months old David Leworthy's family emigrated to Australia. They returned to the U.K. eight years later. On leaving school Leworthy signed for Portsmouth and worked his way up to professional level, but made only one League appearance, as a substitute, in October 1981. His contract was cancelled by mutual consent in April 1982 and three months later he joined Fareham Town, becoming a regular scorer for the Hampshire club. Spurs moved to sign the chunky forward for £5,000 in August 1984, no doubt hoping he might emulate Tony Galvin and Graham Roberts who had been plucked from non-League obscurity and developed into international players. Leworthy made his League debut for Spurs against Arsenal in April 1985 and looked to be developing satisfactorily when Oxford United offered a substantial £250,000 for his transfer. With forwards Mark Falco, Clive Allen, Chris Waddle and John Chiedozie on the books, Spurs decided it was too good to refuse. Unfortunately, life did not work out too well for Leworthy at Oxford, the pressure of being a big money buy at a small club perhaps too much for him. He failed to justify the fee and, after being loaned out to Shrewsbury, was given a free transfer at the end of the 1988-89 season. He joined Reading, but again things did not work out for him and he returned to non-League football in March 1991 on loan to Colchester United as they sought, in vain, a return to the Fourth Division. When Reading gave him a free transfer, he signed for Farnborough Town and began to re-discover his goal-scoring form, playing for England at semi-professional level. Top scorer in the GM Vauxhall Conference, he was transferred to Dover for £50,000, a record between non-League clubs and then moved on to Rushden & Diamonds and Kingstonians. His last game for the "Kings", as a substitute in the 2000 FA Vase final, was shortly followed by a move to Havant and Waterlooville where he moved into coaching and management. Leworthy's son, Craig, failed to make the grade with Peterborough United but joined his father at Havant.

Appearances:
League: 8 (3) apps. 3 gls.
FL Cup: (1) app. 1 gl.
Others: 8 (9) apps. 11 gls.
Total: 16 (13) apps. 15 gls.

LIGHTFOOT, Edward John

Role: Half-back 1911-18
5ft.9ins. 11st.0lbs.
Born: Litherland, Lancashire, 13th November 1889
Died: France, 20th July 1918 (Killed in action)

CAREER: Harrowby/Southport Central 1910/**SPURS** May 1911/Southport Central Aug 1915.

Debut v Middlesbrough (FL) (a) 14.10.1911

Ed Lightfoot was signed from Lancashire Combination club Southport Central to provide cover for the regular half-backs Dan Steel, Charlie Rance and Jabez Darnell. He made his League debut in October 1911 and eventually replaced Darnell at left-half until losing the position to the emerging Arthur Grimsdell in December 1912. Only called upon in 1913-14 in an emergency, he remained a useful reserve and rendered the club valuable service in the 1914-15 season when Spurs were badly hit by players joining the forces. Eventually called up himself, Ed played in just two war-time matches before being killed in action in France during July 1918.

Appearances:
League: 62* apps. 2 gls.
FA Cup: 5 apps.
Others: 19 apps.
Total: 86 apps. 0 gls.
*Includes 1 abandoned match.

LINDSAY, Alexander Findlay

Role: Half-back or forward 1917-30
5ft.6ins. 11st.0lbs.
Born: Dundee, 8th November 1896
Died: Dundee, 9th December 1971

CAREER: Dundee Violet/Raith Rovers Oct 1916/(guest for **SPURS** during World War One)/**SPURS** Aug 1919/Thames Aug 1930/Dundee Jul 1931.

Debut v Coventry City (FL) (a) 30.8.1919
(Arsenal (LFC) (h) 22.9.1917)

Alex Lindsay made several guest appearances for Spurs during the latter years of the First World War and when the time came to rebuild in readiness for the resumption of League football, his transfer from Raith Rovers was quickly secured. Originally a centre or inside-forward he had few first team opportunities in the early 1920s when Spurs were blessed with talented players like Jimmy Cantrell and Jimmy Banks, but Lindsay gradually proved himself a more than competent performer in any of the forward positions. He won selection for the Anglo-Scots against the Home Scots in a Scottish international trial match in March 1923, and by the end of the season had replaced Cantrell as first choice centre-forward. A willing, industrious player who chased the remotest of scoring opportunities, Lindsay never shirked a challenge either and this accounted for many of the injuries which dogged him throughout his career. With Frank Osborne shifting from the wing to centre-forward in October 1925, Lindsay lost his place in the forward line. He switched to left-half where his buzzing, non-stop style of play was used to try and compensate for the absence of broken leg victim, Arthur Grimsdell. With Grimsdell's return in September 1927 Lindsay was left out, but continued to prove himself a valuable member of the first team squad for the next three years, filling in whenever needed at half-back or in the forward line. In April 1930 he was released and moved to Thames. When they gave him a free transfer he returned to Scotland with Dundee, where he made just two appearances

Appearances:
League: 211 apps. 42 gls.
FA Cup: 15 apps. 8 gls.
Others: 53 apps. 18 gls.
Total: 279 apps. 68 gls.

LINDSAY, D

Role: Goalkeeper 1917-19
Born: Sint Jorisweg, Holland, 14th December 1890

CAREER: Dordrechtsche (Holland)/Sparta (Holland)/**SPURS** trial and pro. Aug 1914.

Debut v Fulham (LFC) (a) 23.3.1918

Lindsay played regularly for Spurs from March till December 1918. In many newspaper reports of the time his name appeared in inverted commas and it is believed Lindsay was a pseudonym used by Geert van Driel, a Dutchman working at the JAP factory in Edmonton who had previously played for Dordrechtsche FC and Sparta in Holland. Van Driel helped Sparta win the Dutch League in 1911-12 and 1912-13 before arriving at Tottenham for a trial in August 1914. Taken on, as a professional after playing for the reserves under the name of "Smith", he was reprimanded for breach of training rules in October 1914, but remained with the club. He played in all but one of the last eight matches of the 1917-18 season and in 15 of the first 16 matches the following season. His place was then taken by Bill McIver and Bill Jacques and Lindsay made only one more appearance; in February 1919.

Appearances:
Others: 24 apps.
Total: 24 apps. 0 gls.

LINDSAY, James

Role: Inside-forward 1895-96
Born: 1874

CAREER: Scottish football/Anchor/Millwall Athletic cs. 1892/Old Castle Swifts Nov 1894/Ilford Oct 1895/Thames Ironworks Oct 1895/South West Ham/**SPURS** Dec 1895/Ilford.

Debut v Casuals (Fr) (h) 21.12.7895

When centre-forward Jimmy Lindsay was released by Millwall at the end of the 1893-94 season he accepted the offer of playing for Spurs. However, he had been a professional at Millwall and as Spurs were still an amateur club he needed to be re-instated as an amateur before Spurs could utilise his experience. Unfortunately, his application for re-instatement was turned down in October 1894, so he was not able to play for Spurs that season and instead joined Old Castle Swifts. When a further application was granted in October 1895, Lindsay joined Ilford but did not turn out for them immediately. A boilermaker at the Thames Ironworks he turned out for the newly-founded Ironworks team for a couple of months, then played for South West Ham, although he continued to help out the Ironworks team. He made four appearances for Spurs in friendly matches in the space of just eight days at the end of December 1895. Thereafter he played a few games for the reserves, but did not make the first team again. He later made a few appearances for Ilford in 1896-97.

Appearances:
Others: 4 apps.
Total: 4 apps. 0 gls.

LINEKER, Gary Winston O.B.E.

Role: Striker 1989-92
5ft.11ins. 12st.2lbs.
Born: Leicester, 30th November 1960

CAREER: Leicester City app. Jul 1977, pro. Dec 1978/Everton Jun 1985/Barcelona (Spain) Jul 1986/**SPURS** Jun 1989/Grampus Eight (Japan) Nov 1991.

Debut v Luton Town (FL) (h) 19.8.1989
(Bohemians (Fr) (a) 23.7.1989)

One of England's leading goal-scorers and outstanding talents of his generation, Gary Lineker was signed by Spurs from Barcelona for £1.2 million, renewing his partnership with Terry Venables who had first signed him for the Spanish giants. A career that took him around the world started with his home town club, Leicester City. He made his League debut in January 1979 and once City found his best position Lineker's predatory instincts surfaced, it was soon clear that if allowed to display his growing talents at the highest level, he would have a superb career ahead of him. A member of Leicester's team that won the Second Division Championship in 1980 and promotion again in 1983, his great asset in his early days was his blistering pace. He top-scored for four successive seasons at Leicester, many of the goals down to his speed off the mark. But Leicester were a team who spent too much time at the wrong end of the table and, although he made an England debut in May 1984 as a substitute against Scotland, it was only towards the end of the following season that Lineker began to get a regular chance at international level. With 103 League and Cup goals for Leicester, a move was inevitable, and in June 1985 he was transferred to Everton for £800,000. In his one season on Merseyside he showed exactly what he was capable of with top class players around him. He scored 40 goals-many unexpectedly with his head-as Everton finished runners-up to Liverpool in both the League and FA Cup, and hit the "Toffees" goal in the FA Cup Final. Lineker's career and value escalated dramatically as he then went to the Mexico World Cup Finals with England, became a national hero with a hat-trick against Poland, and finished as the competition's "Golden Boot" top scorer. If Europe's leading clubs had not been checking him out already, his electrifying performances on the world stage immediately had them queuing up for a signature. On his return from Mexico he moved to Barcelona in a £2.75 million deal. The Football Writers' Association and Professional Footballers' Association Player of the Year for 1986, he helped Barcelona lift the Spanish Cup in 1988 and the European Cup-Winners' Cup in 1989, but could not help the Catalan club prise the coveted Spanish League title away from great rivals Real Madrid. An attack of hepatitis left Lineker drained and below par for the 1988 European Championships. When fit to resume, he found that he did not fit in with the plans of Barcelona's new coach, Johann Cruyff. Played as a winger, quite clearly not his best position, Lineker typically did not complain about the situation but merely got on with the job. The way he conducted himself greatly enhanced his already considerable reputation as a model professional. The move to White Hart Lane allowed Lineker to return to his preferred central striking role and it was soon clear that his time in the tough Spanish game had done nothing to dull the sharpness of his quick-witted skills. Indeed, he looked a more complete, all-round player than when he left England. His first appearance for England as a Spurs player was against Sweden on 6th September 1989 and he was ultimately desperately unlucky not to surpass Bobby Charlton's record of 49 England goals. Going into the 1992 European Championship Finals having already announced his decision to retire from the international stage at the tournament's end, he was unable to net the one goal necessary to equal Charlton's record. Top scorer for Spurs in all three of his seasons at the club, a member of the 1991 FA Cup winning side and captain of England it was announced in November 1991 that Lineker would be leaving Spurs. At the end of the season he was to join the Japanese club, Grampus Eight of Nagoya, in time for the start of the first professional League in Japan during March 1993. With the Japanese paying £900,000 to sign Lineker, Spurs all but recovered what they had paid out to sign him. Never booked during his whole career, his services to football were rewarded in the 1992 New Year's Honours List with the O.B.E. A long-standing toe injury hampered his career in Japan and after two years he returned home to a career with BBC radio and television.

Appearances:
League: 105 apps. 67 gls.
FA Cup: 9 apps. 3 gls.
FL Cup: 16 apps. 8 gls.
Euro: 8 apps. 2 gls.
Others: 24 (3) apps. 10 gls.
Total: 163 (3) apps. 90 gls.

LITTLEFORD, A

Role: Full-back 1889-90

Debut v Iona (Fr) (h) 12.10.1889

Littleford only played for Spurs in the 1889-90 season and details of all matches played that season are not known. His first known match was a friendly against Iona on 12th October 1888, but he appeared in most of the matches that a team has been traced for.

Appearances:
Others: 5 apps.
Total: 5 apps. 0 gls.

LIVERMORE, Jake Cyril Leonard

Role: Midfielder
5ft.10ins. 12st.8lbs.
Born: Enfield, Middlesex, 14th November 1989

CAREER: SPURS Academy Scholar Jul 2006, pro. Nov 2006/(Milton Keynes Dons loan Feb 2008)/(Crewe Alexandra loan Jul 2008)/(Derby County loan Aug 2009)/(Peterborough United loan Jan 2010)/(Ipswich Town loan Sep 2010)/(Leeds United loan Mar 2011)/Hull City loan Aug 2013, perm Jun 2014/West Bromwich Albion Jan 2017.

Debut v Stoke City (sub) (BPL) (a) 20.3.2010
(Stevenage Borough (sub) (Fr) (a) 7.7.2007)

An industrious, bustling midfielder, Jake Livermore is a perfect example of the gifted home-produced talent side-lined by the arrival of established foreign players, that has been able to take advantage of the loan system in an effort to prove he is good enough for Spurs. A local lad, he joined Spurs academy and quickly worked his way up to first appear in the senior team in a 2007 pre-season friendly. To gain experience he began a series of loan moves, gradually moving up the football ladder. In 2011, Harry Redknapp installed Livermore as a member of the first team squad. Providing cover for, if not an immediate challenge to, Sandro and Scott Parker, Livermore grew in confidence as he got more games. Strong and determined, he prowled the midfield, breaking up opponents' attacks and providing a platform for Spurs to go forward. Just when it seemed Livermore was about to establish himself at Spurs, Redknapp was sacked. Among the first signings his replacement, Andre Villas-Boas, made were Mousa Dembélé and Gylfi Sigurdsson, expensive signings and serious competition. Even though Livermore collected a full cap against Italy in August 2012, he was given few chances by Villas-Boas. With Lewis Holtby, Étienne Capoue, Paulinho, Nacer Chadli and Christian Eriksen added to the available midfield players, it was clear Livermore would have even less opportunities. When Tom Huddlestone moved to Hull City on a permanent transfer, Livermore was allowed to go with him. The initial move was on a year's loan. That was made permanent immediately after the 2014 FA Cup Final, Livermore having played a full part in helping unfancied Hull reach the final. Livermore was unable to help in Hull's final battle to avoid relegation at the end of the 2014-15 season, having failed a drugs test. It was later revealed he had taken cocaine following the death of his new born child. Fortunately, both the FA and Hull showed the compassionate side of football and he received no further punishment than the initial short-term suspension that had been imposed.

Appearances:
League: 11 (25) apps.
FA Cup: 4 (1) apps.
FL Cup: 3 apps.
Euro: 9 (5) apps. 1 gl.
Others: 10 (13) apps. 2 gls.
Total: 37 (44) apps. 3 gls.

LLORIS, Hugo

Role: Goalkeeper 2012-
6ft.2ins. 12st.11lbs.
Born: Nice (France), 26th December 1986

CAREER: CEDAC Cimiez (France) Sep 1993/OGC Nice (France) Jul 1997/Olympique Lyonnais (France) Jul 2008/SPURS Aug 2012.

Debut v Lazio (EL) (h) 20.9.2012

Hugo Lloris caught the attention of his local club, OGC Nice, while a ten-year old playing at a local cultural centre, Centre de Diffusion et d'Action Culturelle. A promising tennis player, he decided to concentrate on football and worked his way through the youth and B ranks to establish himself as Nice's first choice 'keeper. He had been called up for several French full international squads without making a start by the time he transferred to Olympique Lyonnais, reportedly with Spurs interested in signing him. Lloris collected his first full cap playing against Uruguay in November 2008 and soon established himself as his country's number one. Practically ever-present for his club in over four years, it took a £20 million deal for Spurs to secure Lloris' services. With Heurelho Gomes totally out of favour and both Carlo Cudicini and Brad Friedel well into the veteran stage, fresh blood was urgently needed. Initially Lloris alternated with Friedel, but it was soon clear the Frenchman more than merited the starting berth. Once he was installed as first choice, his confidence soared and apart from the odd game when he has been rested, Lloris has played every game of consequence. Lloris is consistent, unflappable, reliable and rarely makes mistakes. As demanded of modern goalkeepers, he is quite comfortable with the ball at his feet, always there to take the ball from back pass and start the play from deep. There are no histrionics with Lloris, no grandstanding. He gets on with the job and does it as simply as possible. Commanding in the box, strong in the air and with terrific reflex, he is better than most in one-on-one situations. His country's automatic first choice, he was installed as national captain in February 2012 and led France throughout Euro 2016.

Appearances:
League: 170 apps.
FA Cup: 2 apps.
FL Cup: 3 apps.
Euro: 37 apps.
Others: 8 (4) apps.
Total: 220 (4) apps. 0 gls.

LLOYD, William Harold

Role: Inside-forward 1915-19
Born: Tottenham, London

CAREER: Tufnell Park/SPURS am. 1908/Clapton 1914/(guest for SPURS during World War One)/Tufnell Park.

Debut v West Ham United (LFC) (h) 27.11.1915

A local amateur player, Lloyd first became associated with Spurs during the 1908-09 season. He was playing for Tufnell Park and signed amateur forms, turning out for the reserves at centre-forward. However, his services were not called upon very often until the First World War began by which time he had joined Clapton. In the 1914-15 season he played for the reserve side that was decimated by the demands of the first team after so many senior players had joined the services. When the War-time London Football Combination began Lloyd's skills were needed by the first team and by the end of the 1915-16 season he was a regular. A fine inside-forward with Clapton, he started in that position with Spurs, but was quite comfortable in any role demanded of him. It was his versatility that made him such a valuable member of Spurs' squad in the 1916-17 season. He played in any position the club needed him, winger, centre-forward, half-back, full-back. He was so successful that it was expected Spurs would sign him as a professional when the war was over, but service demands then made him unavailable and he was not to be offered terms. He continued to turn out for Tufnell Park and played for them in the 1920 FA Amateur Cup Final when they lost to Dulwich Hamlet.

Appearances:
Others: 40 apps. 7 gls.
Total: 40 apps. 7 gls.
*Includes 1 abandoned match.

LOGAN, John Theodore

Role: Inside-forward 1895-96
Born: Glasgow, 1871

CAREER: Linthouse/SPURS Jan 1896/Parkhead/Partick Thistle Jun 1896/Newton Heath Oct 1896/Musselburgh.

Debut v Reading (Fr) (h) 4.1.1896

Possibly Spurs' first professional player, Logan was signed in January 1896 as a result of trainer John Campbell making a visit to Scotland to implement the previous month's decision to employ professionals.

Basically, an inside forward, although he also appeared as a winger, he scored 14 goals in 19 appearances in friendly matches that season. At the end of the season he was not retained and joined Partick Thistle. He only remained in Scotland until December 1896 when he was transferred to Newton Heath. While the transfer fee of £40 was a reasonable sum in those days, he never appeared in Newton Heath's first team.

Appearances:
Others: 20 apps. 12 gls.
Total: 20 apps. 12 gls.

LOMAS, William

Role: Half-back 1883-87
Born: Edmonton, London, 13 July 1868

CAREER: SPURS/Park by Jan 1887.

Debut v Brownlow Rovers (Fr) (h) 6.10.1883.

Another of those players from the dim and distant past about whom it has proved impossible to unearth much information, Lomas is known to have played only three matches for Spurs. The first was a friendly against Brownlow Rovers in October 1883, the first reported match played by the club, when he played at half-back. He played in a friendly against Grange Park in January 1885 in an outfield position and his only other known appearance was in October 1886 when he played in goal as Spurs lost 0-6 to Upton Park in a London Association Cup-tie. In that season he also played for Spurs' great local rivals, Park FC, along with his brothers H and P.

Appearances:
Others: 3 apps.
Total: 3 apps. 0 gls.

LOMAX, John Charles

Role: Inside-forward 1892-93

CAREER: Luton/SPURS cs. 1892.

Debut v Paddington (Fr) (h) 14.9.1892

Lomax joined Spurs for the start of the 1892-93 season from Luton, but made only two known appearances in the first team. Both of these were in friendly matches, the first against Paddington in the first match of the season and the second against Royal Arsenal Athletic on 1st October 1892. By January of 1893 he was playing in the reserve side.

Appearances:
Others: 2 apps.
Total: 2 apps. 0 gls.

LÓPEZ (SABATA), Pau

Role: Goalkeeper 2016-
6ft.2ins. 12st. 2lbs,
Born: Girona, Catalonia, Spain, 13th December 1994

CAREER: Girona (Spain)/RCD Espanyol (Spain) 2006, pro. Jun 2014/SPURS loan Aug 2016.

Debut v Kitchee (sub) (Fr) (a) 26.5.2017.

A relatively inexperienced young 'keeper, Pau López was well-known to Mauricio Pochettino and his goalkeeping coach, Toni Jimenez, from their time with Barcelona's second club. First associated with Espanyol as a twelve-year old, López progressed through the ranks and by the age of twenty was holding down a regular starting position. Although he was clearly talented had played for Span at Under-21 level and been called into the full squad, Lopez was not the experienced stopper Espanyol's new manager, Quique Sánchez Flores, wanted and the signing of Roberto in June 2016 relegated López to the bench. This allowed Spurs to make their move for a player who had reportedly been on the radar for some time. He signed in August 2016, initially on a season's loan, but with an option for the move to be made permanent. Although yet to play for Spain at full international level, López does already have one full international appearance to his credit.

While Catalonia is not affiliated to Fifa or Uefa, it does have a long-established "national" football team and in December 2015 López played for it against Basque Country.

Appearances:
Others: (1) app.
Total: (1) app. 0 gl.

LORIMER, Hugh Harper

Role: Winger 1919-22
5ft.7ins. 10st.10lbs.
Born: Paisley, Renfrewshire, 11th November 1896
Died: Leavesdale, Pittsburgh, Pennsylvania, USA, 1920s

CAREER: St Mirren Juniors/SPURS Aug 1919/Dundee Nov 1921/Dalbeattie Star/Carlisle United Nov 1922/Boston Wonder Workers (USA) 1924-26/J&P Coats (Rhode Island) (renamed Pawtucket Rangers) (USA) 1926-27.

Debut v South Shields (FL) (h) 13.9.1919

Hugh Lorimer was a talented winger expected to provide both cover and stiff competition to Fanny Walden. He made his League debut in September 1919 as a replacement for Walden and played in the next six matches, but returned to the reserves when Walden was again available. Lorimer failed to live up to expectations and although he did a useful enough job as Walden's reserve, never mounted a serious challenge to the England winger. He stayed with Spurs until November 1921 when he was transferred to Dundee where he played for one season. After short spells with

Dalbeattie Star and Carlisle, Lorimer emigrated to the USA. He helped the Boston Soccer Club's Wonder Workers win the American Professional Championship in 1925, before playing for J&P Coats.

Appearances:
League: 5 apps.
Others: 8 apps.
Total: 13 apps. 0 gls.

LOVIS, Francis Bedford

Role: Outside-right 1883-94
Born: Shoreditch, London, December qtr. 1866

CAREER: SPURS/Tottenham College/High Cross Institute/Tottenham Thursday.

Debut v Brownlow Rovers (Fr) (h) 6.10.1883

A pupil at Lancasterian Boys School, although Frank Lovis is not credited as being one of Spurs' founder members, he was certainly playing for the club by its second season of existence. His first known appearance was in a friendly with Brownlow Rovers on 6th October 1883 and he appears to have played regularly for the next few seasons. In most games he played on the right wing. He was associated with the club for at least ten years and also played for Tottenham College, High Cross Institute and Tottenham Thursday.

Appearances:
Others: 28 apps. 5 gls.
Total: 28 apps. 5 gls.

LOVIS, Herbert

Role: Outside-left 1892-93
Born: Tottenham, London.

CAREER: Tottenham College/SPURS/High Cross Institute by Feb 1894/Tottenham Thursday 1895-96/Asplin Rovers 1895-96.

Debut v Slough (SA) (a) 21.1.1893 (scored once)

Brother of Frank, Herbert Lovis, is only known to have played one game for Spurs. That was a Southern Alliance fixture with Slough in January 1893 when he scored one of Spurs' goals in a 3-3 draw. He also studied at Tottenham College and played for the College football team and in 1895-96 played for Tottenham Thursday and Asplin Rovers.

Appearances:
Others: 1 app. 1 gl.
Total: 1 app. 1 gl.

LOVIS, John S

Role: Half-back 1892-93
Born: Islington, London

CAREER: Tottenham College/SPURS.

Debut v Slough (SA) (a) 21.1.1893

As with his brother, Herbert, this player's only known appearance for Spurs was in the Southern Alliance match at Slough on 21st January 1893. Again a player for Tottenham College. although he does not appear to have had a very long association with Spurs he certainly had a lengthy involvement with first class football. He was a referee in the Southern and Western Leagues in the early years of the 20th century.

Appearances:
Others: 1 app.
Total: 1 app. 0 gls.

LOVIS, Percy

Role: Half-back or outside-left 1892-93
Born: Tottenham, London.

CAREER: Invicta 1888-89/Tottenham College/SPURS 1892-93/High Cross Institute by Feb 1894/Broadwater and Tottenham Thursday 1895-96.

Debut v Casuals (LSC) (h) 28.1.1893

Yet another member of the Lovis family who played for Spurs, Percy Lovis is known to have made two appearances in the 1892-93 season. The first was in January 1893 as Spurs lost 0-1 to the Casuals in the fifth round of the London Senior Cup and the second four days later in a Southern Alliance match with Slough. Like his brothers a player for Tottenham College, in the first match he played at outside-left and in the second at half-back. He is also known to have played for several other local clubs

Appearances:
Others: 2 apps.
Total: 2 apps. 0 gls.

LOVIS, S

Role: Outside-left 1892-93

CAREER: Tottenham College/SPURS/Broadwater 1893-94.

Debut v Slough (SA) (a) 23.1.1893

The final member of the Lovis family, this player is only known to have played two matches for Spurs in the Southern Alliance competition of 1892-93. He also played for Tottenham College and in the 1893-94 season with Broadwater, but was still helping out Spurs reserves in early 1895.

Appearances:
Others: 2 apps.
Total: 2 apps. 0 gls.

LOW, Anthony Roy

Role: Half-back 1964-67
5ft.8ins.
Born: Watford, Hertfordshire, 8th July 1944

CAREER: England Schools/SPURS am. Aug 1958, pro. Jul 1961/Watford Feb 1967-cs. 1969/Bedford Town Aug 1970.

Debut v Sheffield Wednesday (FL) (h) 5.12.1964

Principally regarded as a wing-half, Roy Low played for Spurs during that difficult period when a great team is breaking up and a new one is struggling to take shape. Supporter's memories are still fresh and newcomers almost inevitably suffer a period of unfavourable comparison, particularly when not a "big money buy". Low made his debut in December 1964 and had six outings that season, two at half-back and four in the forward line. Although he stayed another two years, he only made two substitute appearances before moving to Watford. He does at least have a permanent place in Spurs' history, being the first substitute used by the club in a League match. That came

on 11th September 1965 when he replaced the injured Derek Possee against Arsenal at White Hart Lane.

Appearances:
League: 6 (2) apps. 1 gl.
Others: 3 (1) apps. 1 gl.
Total: 9 (3) apps. 2 gls.

LOWDELL, Arthur Edward

Role: Half-back 1927-30
5ft.6ins. 10st.8lbs.
Born: Edmonton, London, 7th November 1897
Died: Canvey Island, Essex, 29th July 1979

CAREER: London Schools/Ton Pentre 1918/Sheffield Wednesday Jan 1922/**SPURS** Aug 1927/released May 1931/retired Feb 1932.

Debut v Birmingham (FL) (h) 27.8.1927

Although born on Spurs' doorstep, "Darkie" Lowdell travelled almost the length and breadth of the country before arriving on the White Hart Lane staff. He joined the forces at the age of sixteen and, having served throughout the First World War, signed for the Welsh club Ton Pentre on his discharge. He quickly built a big reputation in Wales and began to attract the attention of several League clubs, including Spurs. However, when Spurs sent their scout specifically to watch Lowdell in a match against Mid-Rhondda, his attention was distracted by Mid-Rhondda's inside-forward, Jimmy Seed, and it was Seed who was signed in February 1920. Lowdell did not remain outside the Football League for long though as Sheffield Wednesday moved in to snap him up. He developed well in Sheffield, moved from his original inside-forward slot to half-back, played over 100 games for Wednesday and was close to international honours, playing in an international trial match in January 1927. A strong, mature, defender, when Wednesday sought to secure Seed's transfer, Spurs insisted Lowdell move to White Hart Lane as part of the deal. Although Spurs were relegated at the end of his first season, Lowdell was Spurs' regular right-half for two years until suffering a thigh injury in November 1930. He never fully recovered, but remained with the club until being released in April 1931. Unable to find a new club, he formally retired in February 1932.

Appearances:
League: 86 apps.
FA Cup: 4 apps.
Others: 9 apps.
Total: 99 apps. 0 gls.

LOWE, Horace Harold

Role: Half-back 1914-27
5ft.9ins. 10st.7lbs.
Born: Northwich, Lancashire, 10th August 1886
Died: Camden Town, London, 15th July 1966

CAREER: Northwich Victoria/Brighton and Hove Albion trial Aug 1913, perm Sep 1913/**SPURS** Apr 1914/Fulham May 1927/Beckenham Jan 1930/Real Sociedad (Spain) 1930-35 coach/Club Esportiu Espanyol (Spain) coach till Dec 1935/Islington Corinthians player-coach cs. 1937/**SPURS** reserve team coach 1938/Bournemouth and Boscombe Athletic manager Aug 1947–Feb 1950/Yeovil Town manager Jul 1951-May 1953.

Debut v Middlesbrough (FL) (a) 13.2.1915
(Crystal Palace (LFACC) (a) 19.10.1914)

Originally a forward, Harry Lowe was signed from Brighton where he had spent most of his one season on the coast in the reserves. He made his debut in a bizarre 5-7 defeat at Middlesbrough in February 1915. He kept his place for the next match, but then did not make the League team again until after the war. By that stage he had moved into the half-back line and whilst never really a first choice, he did have several lengthy runs at centre-half and was retained until May 1927. When released he joined Fulham, but spent only one season at Craven Cottage before bringing his playing days to an end. He then turned to coaching and worked in San Sebastian for Real Sociedad for four years. Espanyol were his next club, but he resigned in December 1935, leaving Spain just before the outbreak of the Spanish Civil War. Lowe returned to Spurs in 1938 as reserve team coach, having led Islington Corinthians on a world tour the previous season. From 1947 to 1950 he managed Bournemouth and Boscombe Athletic and later had two years as manager of Yeovil Town.

Appearances:
League: 65 apps.
FA Cup: 7 apps.
Others: 13 apps.
Total: 85 apps. 0 gls.

LUDFORD, George Albert

Role: Forward or half-back 1936-50
5ft.7ins. 10st.12lbs.
Born: Barnet, Hertfordshire, 22nd March 1915
Died: Enfield, Middlesex, 2nd January 2001

CAREER: **SPURS** ground-staff May 1931/Tottenham Juniors 1931-33/Enfield Aug-Dec 1933/Northfleet United Jan 1934/**SPURS** am. May 1933, pro. May 1936/(guest for Chelsea, Clapton Orient, Fulham, Millwall, Queens Park Rangers, Reading, Southend United, Watford and West Ham United during World War Two)/**SPURS** coach 1954/Enfield manager Apr 1957-Jun 1965, stadium manager.

Debut v West Ham United (FL) (a) 29.8.1936

George Ludford began a 24-year association with Spurs when he joined the ground-staff on leaving school. After playing with Tottenham Juniors for two years he was sent along to Enfield, but quickly moved on to the Northfleet nursery, where he scored 101 goals from centre-forward in the 1935-36 season. Such goal-scoring prowess resulted in a move to the professional ranks at White Hart Lane, and he made his League debut against West Ham in August 1936. Whilst always a prolific scorer for the reserves, Ludford had few first team opportunities before the Second World War due to the equally impressive scoring form of regular centre-forward Johnny Morrison. It was only during the war that he really had his chance, but even then it was rarely in his favoured centre-forward role due to the presence of the great amateur Jack Gibbons. Frequently filling in on either wing, he still managed to score regularly and, when unable to turn out for Spurs, was in great demand to guest for other clubs. Indeed, he played for Millwall against Chelsea in

the 1945 Football League South Cup Final. A loyal club man in every sense of the description, he was happy to play for Spurs in whatever position they wanted and in an emergency was even moved to half-back. By the end of the war he had settled comfortably into that role and, as right-half, had his best season in the first team, missing only one game in 1946-47. With Bill Nicholson's move to right-half in 1947, Ludford lost his place, but continued to serve the club well, even playing a few games at left-back in 1949. However, most of his football was played with the reserve and junior teams where he passed on the benefit of his experience until he finished playing in 1954 and moved onto the coaching staff. Ludford finally left Spurs in 1957 to take up the manager's job at Enfield, and was later their stadium manager.

Appearances:
League: 77 apps. 8 gls.
FA Cup: 6 apps. 1 gl.
Others: 192 apps. 83 gls.
Total: 275 apps. 92 gls.

LUNN, Thomas Henry

Role: Goalkeeper 1909-13
5ft.9ins. 12st.10lbs.
Born: Bishop Auckland, County Durham, 9th July 1883
Died: Edmonton, London, 29th March 1960

CAREER: Hednesford Swifts/Brownhills Albion/Wolverhampton Wanderers Aug 1904/**SPURS** Apr 1910/Stockport Jun 1913.

Debut v Bolton Wanderers (FL) (a) 23.4.1910

A member of Wolves' FA Cup winning team of 1908, Tommy Lunn joined Spurs in April 1910 as they struggled desperately to avoid relegation after just one season in the First Division. He made his debut in the penultimate game as Spurs won 2-0 at Bolton, but the club still went into the last match of the season against Chelsea needing victory to ensure they stayed up and Chelsea went down instead. Although Percy Humphreys was widely acclaimed as Spurs' saviour for scoring the winning goal, Lunn turned in a superb performance, and were it not for some of his magnificent saves, the match would have been lost before Humphreys' winner. The regular custodian for the next two seasons, Lunn played for the Football League against the Southern League at White Hart Lane in November 1910 and it was only in December 1912 that his place was taken by John "Tiny" Joyce. Although re-instated for two games early in 1913, Lunn then took out a publican's license which was frowned upon by the Spurs' hierarchy and in breach of his contract. Suspended as a consequence, he did not play another game for Spurs before his contract expired in June 1913. He signed for Stockport County, but played just two games before a serious leg injury forced him to retire. Lunn appeared in the first Football League game played at White Hart Lane-playing for Wolverhampton Wanderers on 1st September 1908.

Appearances:
League: 89* apps.
FA Cup: 5 apps.
Others: 13 apps.
Total: 107 apps. 0 gls.
*Includes 3 abandoned matches.

LUONGO, Massimo Corey

Role: Midfielder 2011-12
5ft.10ins. 11st.11lbs.
Born: Sydney, Australia, 25th September 1992

CAREER: Waverley College (Australia)/Sydney Olympic (Australia)/APIA Leichhardt Tigers (Australia)/Rushden & Diamonds Jan 2011/**SPURS** Nov 2009/Rushden & Diamonds Jan 2011/**SPURS** pro. Jan 2011/(Ipswich Town loan Jul 2012)/Swindon Town loans Mar 2013 and Jul 2013, perm. Aug 2013/Queens Park Rangers May 2015.

Debut v Stoke City (FLC) (a) (sub) 21.9.2011

An energetic midfield dynamo, Massimo Luongo joined Spurs youth team in November 2009. Playing regularly for the youth and development teams he signed professional a little over a year later, from Rushden & Diamonds who he had strangely signed for the same day. An impressive performer, playing deep and bursting forward with pace and aggression, his only senior appearance came in September 2011 when he went on as a substitute in a Carling Cup match at Stoke City. It was a short outing and not one Luongo will want to remember. Called on to replace Sandro after 70 minutes, a young Spurs team did well to hang on for a 0-0 draw. After extra-time the tie went to penalties. Luongo's effort was saved and Spurs went out of the competition. From that point Luongo's career has been all uphill. After gaining experience on loan to Ipswich Town and Swindon Town, he joined Swindon again in July 2013 for what was intended to be a season-long loan. A month later a £400,000 fee made the move permanent. Nailing down a regular position, he thrived just in front of the back four, providing defensive cover before opponents got at the Swindon defence and the driving force of attacks. He collected his first cap for Australia against Ecuador in March 2015 and was the star of the show as Swindon battled for promotion in 2015. After an unsuccessful play-off he returned to Australia to play in the Asia Cup, helped his country win the tournament and returned to England as the competition's Most Valuable Player. A £2.5 million transfer to Queens Park Rangers followed, allowing Luongo to link up with Chris Ramsey, his youth team coach at Spurs.

Appearances:
Others: (1) app.
Total: (1) app. 0 gls.

LYLE, Archibald

Role: Inside-forward 1909-10
5ft.8ins. 11st.0lbs.
Born: 10th February 1886

CAREER: Falkirk trial Oct 1907/Blackburn Rovers trial Dec 1907/Elmbank 1907-08/Raith Rovers trial 1908/Third Lanark trial/Glasgow Perthshire trial/Maryhill FC/Dundee trial Jan 1909/**SPURS** Aug 1909/released May 1910/South Side ASC 1911/Queen's Park trial 1912/Queen's Park Strollers 1912.

Debut v Sheffield Wednesday (FL) (h) 25.9.1909

A journeyman inside-forward who had plied his trade around Scottish clubs for some time, Alex Lyle was signed from the Glasgow club Maryhill FC. He made one ill-fated appearance during his year at Spurs. That was in September 1909 in a match with Sheffield Wednesday when he suffered a serious injury. At the end of the season Spurs felt he would not recover sufficiently to justify being retained. He was released and returned to Scotland.

Appearances:
League: 1 app.
Total: 1 app. 0 gls.

LYMAN, Colin Charles

Role: Winger 1937-46
5ft.8ins. 10st.6lbs.
Born: Northampton, 9th March 1914
Died: Cambridge, 9th May 1986

CAREER: East End Rangers/Semilong United/Northampton Town/Rushden Town/West Bromwich Albion trial/Northampton Town/Southend United am. Jul 1933/Northampton Town am. Mar 1934, pro. Nov 1934/**SPURS** Oct 1937/(guest for Aldershot, Chesterfield, Coventry City, Derby County, Leicester City, Northampton Town, Nottingham Forest, Notts County and Port Vale during World War Two)/Port Vale May 1946/ Nottingham Forest Oct 1946//Ransome & Marles player-manager Jun 1947/Notts County Aug 1947/Nuneaton Borough player-coach Jun 1948, manager 1950-Jan 1951/Long Eaton Town player-manager Jan 1951/British Timken.

Debut v Manchester United (FL) (h) 9.10.1937

Colin Lyman joined Rushden Town of the East Midlands League straight from school, had a trial for West Bromwich Albion who rejected him as being "too frail", and played one match for Southend. However, he impressed Northampton Town enough with his performances for Rushden to sign amateur forms and then be taken on as a professional. Lyman soon established himself with the "Cobblers" as an out-and-out winger who hit over accurate crosses and packed a powerful shot himself. Spurs secured his transfer in October 1937 and he went straight into the first team, playing regularly in the last two full seasons before the Second World War. During the war, service demands meant he was rarely able to play for Spurs, but he guested for several other clubs and played in representative matches for the Royal Air Force and Football Association. When he was demobbed, it was apparent his peak years had been lost, and in May 1946 he was allowed to move to Port Vale. He was only with the Potteries club for five months before moving on to Nottingham Forest and eight months later joined Ransome & Marles as player-manager. He only had two months in that role before signing for Notts County. Lyman spent just the one season with County before returning to playing and managing with Nuneaton Borough and Long Eaton Town.

Appearances:
League: 47 apps. 10 gls.
FA Cup: 8 apps. 1 gl.
Others: 32 apps. 9 gls.
Total: 87 apps. 20 gls.

LYONS, Albert Thomas

Role: Full-back 1930-32
Born: Hednesford, West Midlands, 5th March 1902
Died: Great Yarmouth, Norfolk, 10th May 1981

CAREER: Hednesford/Army/Port Vale 1924/Walsall 1925/Clapton Orient am. Jun 1926, pro. Sep 1926/**SPURS** May 1930/Colwyn Bay Aug 1932.

Debut v Reading (FL) (h) 30.8.1930

Although he never played a senior game for them, Bert Lyons had been on the books of Hednesford, a club with close family ties. His father, Tommy, who played for Aston Villa in the 1903 FA Cup final, had joined the club before the First World War and played during the War years. As his career came to an end his son, Jim, took over until he was transferred to Derby County, later playing for Wrexham. Another brother, Alfred, had been on Villa's books before the Great War. It was while serving in the Army that Bert Lyons came to be noticed by League clubs. After playing for Port Vale and Walsall, Spurs signed him from Clapton Orient. A strong tackling, safe full-back, he made his Spurs debut against Reading in the first match of the 1930-31 season and brought some much needed stability to a suspect defence. However, at the end of his first season, Spurs signed Jack Moran and Lyons found he had lost his place. While he soon won it back again, Spurs signed Bill Felton in March 1932 and, with it clear Felton was considered first choice, Lyons was released in April 1932. He moved to Colwyn Bay in the August.

Appearances:
League: 54 apps. 3 gls.
FA Cup: 3 apps.
Others: 6 apps. 1 gl.
Total: 63 apps. 4 gls.

Mc

McALLISTER, Donald

Role: Defender 1974-81
5ft.10ins. 11st.2lbs.
Born: *Radcliffe, Lancashire, 26th May 1953*

CAREER: Prestwich, Radcliffe and Whitefield Schools/Lancashire Schools/Coventry City trial/Bolton Wanderers app. 1968, pro. Jun 1970/ **SPURS** Feb 1975/Washington Diplomats (USA) summer 1977/Charlton Athletic Aug 1981/Tampa Bay Rowdies (USA) summer 1984/Charlton Athletic trial Sep 1984/Vitória Setúbal (Portugal) 1984/Rochdale trial/ Luton Town trial/Rochdale non-contract Nov 1984/Tampa Bay Rowdies (USA)/Barnet manager Dec 1985-Jul 1986.

Debut v Coventry City (FL) (a) 15.2.1975

Rejected by Coventry City as a youngster, Don McAllister had better luck with his local club Bolton Wanderers and after serving his apprenticeship, signed professional in June 1970. Although relegated in his first season, he helped Bolton win the Third Division title in 1972-73 and in over 150 senior games earned a reputation as one of the best central defenders in the Second Division. With Spurs fighting against the very real threat of relegation midway through the 1974-75 season, manager Terry Neill felt the determined and uncompromising McAllister could strengthen the defence and his £80,000 transfer to Spurs was secured. After five defeats in six games, Neill reverted to the more experienced players and McAllister found himself replaced by long-serving Phil Beal for the final crucial games. However, Beal left in the summer and McAllister was re-instated at the centre of defence at the start of 1975-76, only to lose his place again in September with the arrival of Willie Young. With Cyril Knowles battling in vain to overcome an old knee injury, the following month saw McAllister tried at left-back, and he kept the position until injured in November 1976. After spending the summer of 1977 in America playing for Washington Diplomats, he returned to take over in central defence following Keith Osgood's departure. A strong, versatile, no frills defender McAllister performed his job competently enough to help Spurs climb out of the Second Division at the first attempt in 1977-78 and re-establish themselves as a First Division force. Following a further injury in 1980-81 McAllister left Spurs in August to join Charlton Athletic, where he spent two years before returning to America to play for Tampa Bay Rowdies. He returned to England, but after an unsuccessful trial at Charlton and a very short stay in Portugal with Vitória Setúbal, finished his League career with three games as a non-contract player for Rochdale. The circumstances of McAllister's departure from Spurs were a little unusual. With his contract up at the end of the season, Spurs said they had written to him with a new offer. McAllister claimed not to have received any letter from the club and was therefore entitled to a free transfer and able to sign for Charlton. Spurs appealed to the Football League, but the appeal was turned down.

Appearances:
League: 168 (4) apps. 9 gls.
FA Cup: 16 (1) apps.
FL Cup: 13 apps. 1 gl.
Others: 55 (3) apps. 3 gls.
Total: 252 (8) apps. 13 gls.

McCABE, Michael John

Role: Forward 1981-82
Born: *Waterford, Eire, 21st August 1964*

CAREER: Eire Schools/Johnville/**SPURS** app. Jun 1980, pro. Sep 1982/SK Vard (Norway) Apr 1984/Tromsø IL (Norway) Apr 1988/Viking (Norway) Oct 1990, coach, asst. manager/Hana IL (Norway) by Apr 2001/ Vidar (Norway) coach 2002/Hundvåg (Norway) coach Apr 2003/Hana IL (Norway) coach 2004/SAFK Fagernes (Norway) coach by Oct 2004/Hana IL (Norway) coach 2005/Hana IL (Norway) coach Nov 2006/Sandved IL (Norway) coach Dec 2008-Sep 2009/Hundvåg (Norway) coach Nov 2012-Jul 2013.

Debut v Luton Town (sub) (Fr) (a) 12.10.1981

Apart from football, Mike McCabe was a schoolboy star at Gaelic football and hurling, representing Waterford County at both sports, but it was when playing for his local Johnville club that Spurs recognised his potential. After playing for the Eire Youth team, he signed professional forms having already made his one first team appearance. That was as a substitute at Luton Town in a testimonial match for Paul Price. His career with Spurs was sadly disrupted by injury and in April 1984 he moved to the Norwegian club Vard. He made a good career for himself in Norway, playing for Tromsø and Viking, where he became assistant manager. He settled in Norway working as a coach for several lower level clubs.

Appearances:
Others: (1) app.
Total: (1) app. 0 gls.

McCALMONT

Role: Centre-forward 1918-19

CAREER: Linfield/(guest for **SPURS** during World War One).

Debut v Arsenal (LFC) (h) 7.12.1918 (scored once)

A Linfield player, McCalmont made his only appearances for Spurs in December 1918. The first was in a home London Football Combination match against Arsenal played at Highbury, when he scored the only goal of the game. He played again four days later when Spurs sent a team to Reading to play a friendly against an RAF team.

Appearances:
Others: 2 apps.
Total: 2 apps. 0 gls.

McCARTHY, Albert Charles

Role: Goalkeeper 1940-41
Born: *Edmonton, London, 2nd April 1919*

CAREER: Edmonton Schools/Tottenham Juniors/**SPURS** am. May 1937

Debut v Queens Park Rangers (FLS) (h) 7.12.1940

Little more than a schoolboy, metal worker Albert McCarthy made his one appearance for Spurs in a Football League South fixture with Queens Park Rangers in December 1940. He was quite a well-known goalkeeper in north London having been the hero of Edmonton Schools' performance in the English Schools Shield Final against Sunderland Schools in 1933.

Appearances:
Others: 1 app.
Total: 1 app. 0 gls.

McCLELLAN, Sydney Benjamin

Role: Forward 1950-56
5ft.8ins. 10st.7lbs.
Born: *Bromley-by-Bow, London, 11th June 1925*
Died: *Dagenham, Essex, 16th December 2000*

CAREER: Chelmsford City cs. 1946/**SPURS** Aug 1949/Portsmouth Nov 1956/Leyton Orient Jul 1958/Romford Jul 1959-Jul 1960/Dagenham coach 1963-1969 and 1971-72.

Debut v Sunderland (FL) (h) 23.9.1950

Sid McClellan first made his mark at White Hart Lane in January 1948 when he scored a hat-trick for Chelmsford in a friendly against Spurs reserves. A prolific scorer for the Southern League club, he followed his Chelmsford manager Arthur Rowe to White Hart Lane in August 1949, but it was more than a year before he made his Spurs League debut. With Len Duquemin the established centre-forward leading a line that shared around the goals, his services were simply not needed. A deadly finisher with a remarkable burst of speed, McClellan stayed with Spurs for seven years, but was never regarded as a first team regular. A more than competent replacement for any of the forward positions, his speed off the mark was frequently put to good use in one of the wing positions, and he scored in a healthy percentage of his appearances. Unlucky not to do better with Spurs, he was transferred to Portsmouth for £8,500 when his speed began to wane. He finished his senior career with a year at Leyton Orient, then had a year with Romford and was coach to the Dagenham team that reached the FA Amateur Cup final in 1970. McClellan has the distinction of scoring more goals for Spurs in a single match than any other player. He scored nine in an 18-1 defeat of the Saskatchewan FA in May 1952 during Spurs' tour of North America.

Appearances:
League: 68 apps. 29 gls.
FA Cup: 2 apps 3 gls.
Others: 23 (4) apps. 30 gls.
Total: 93 (4) apps. 62 gls.

McCLENEGHAN, Harry

Role: Goalkeeper 1913-14

CAREER: Belfast Distillery/Norwich City trial/**SPURS** Feb 1914/released May 1914.

Debut v Chelsea (Fr) (h) 21.2.1914

Harry McCleneghan joined Spurs after impressing for Norwich City reserves in a South Eastern League fixture against Spurs at White Hart Lane while on trial with Norwich. His signing bought the number of goalkeepers on Spurs' books to five, a high number in those days as all were in contention for the first team place. McCleneghan in fact played only one first team game, a friendly with Chelsea on 21st February 1914 when he conceded seven goals. With John Joyce, Arthur King, John Eadon and John Tate all senior to him, he only managed to make two appearances for the reserves, having to be content with playing for the more junior teams. He was released at the end of the season.

Appearances:
Others: 1 app.
Total: 1 app. 0 gls.

McCONNACHIE, John

Role: Winger 1903-04
5ft.11ins. 12st.4lbs.
Born: *Alexandria, Dumbartonshire, 25th October 1884*

CAREER:
Maryhill/Celtic/Rangers/**SPURS** Jun 1903/Southampton cs. 1904/**SPURS** trial Sep 1905/Leyton Oct 1905/Southampton May 1906.

Debut v Brentford (SL) (a) 14.9.1903

Signed as a 19-year old from Rangers in the face of stiff competition from Celtic, Vale of Leven and Third Lanark, John McConnachie was a "boy wonder" who, having been saddled with an inflated reputation, unfortunately failed to live up to it. Starting with Glasgow's Maryhill FC he had played a few matches for both Celtic and Rangers before his move to Spurs. A typically tricky, flying Scottish winger he made his debut for Spurs in a Southern League match early in the season but played only ten senior matches before his release and move to Southampton. He fared little better with the "Saints" and was released after one season on the South Coast. He turned up again at Spurs for an unsuccessful trial before signing for Leyton where he played for a year before going back to Southampton.

Appearances:
Southern: 6 apps.
Others: 4* apps.
Total: 10 apps. 0 gls.
*Includes 1 abandoned match

McCONNON, Patrick

Role: Forward 1909
5ft.7ins. 11st.4lbs.

CAREER: South Bank/South Bank St Peters/Grangetown/**SPURS** May 1909/ released May 1910.

Debut v Uruguay League Select XI (Fr) (Montevideo) 10.6.1909

Signed from the Northern League team Grangetown as a 21-year-old, Patrick McConnon's first two appearances for Spurs senior team were in South America during the club's 1909 tour to Argentina and Uruguay. The first was against a Uruguay League Select XI in Montevideo and the second against the club side Argentinos in Palermo. He scored once in each game. McConnon spent the following season in the reserve side, with just one first team appearance in an early season friendly at Reading. He was not retained at the end of that season.

Appearances:
Others: 3 apps. 2 gls.
Total: **3 apps. 2 gls.**

McCORMICK, James

Role: Outside-left 1932-46
5ft.7ins. 11st.0lbs.
Born: Rotherham, Yorkshire, 26th April 1912
Died: Marbella, Spain, 3rd January 1968

CAREER: South Grove School/Yorkshire Schools/ Rotherham YMCA/ Rotherham United am. Sep 1930, pro. Apr 1931/ Chesterfield Aug 1932/ **SPURS** Mar 1933/(guest for Birmingham, Chelmsford City, Chester, Crewe Alexandra, Derby County, Fulham, Leicester City, Lincoln City, Liverpool, Rochdale, Southend United, Tranmere Rovers, Walsall and West Bromwich Albion during World War Two)/ Fulham Nov 1945/Lincoln City Aug 1947/Crystal Palace Feb 1949/Sliema Wanderers (Malta) player-coach Jun 1949/Turkish FA coach May 1950/Wycombe Wanderers coach 1951-52/Lincoln City coach/Sheffield United coach 1952-53/Walton & Hersham coach, manager/York City manager May 1953-Sep 1954/ Marlow Town manager Aug 1955.

Debut v Port Vale (FL) (a) 18.3.1933

Jimmy "Boy" McCormick was signed from Chesterfield in March 1933 following injuries to Les Howe and Taffy O'Callaghan that threatened Spurs' push for promotion. He had attracted the attention of Rotherham while playing for the local YMCA, but it was Chesterfield who offered professional terms. His speedy, orthodox wing play had already alerted Spurs to his potential prior to the injury crisis. He made his debut immediately, helped Spurs through a difficult final push for promotion and then missed only two games as the club finished third in the First Division in 1933-34. Although Spurs slumped and were relegated the following season, McCormick's crafty work on the wing continued as one of the most positive attractions of Spurs' play until injury early in 1937-38 virtually finished his White Hart Lane career. Rarely available for Spurs during the war, although he guested for many other clubs, he eventually moved on to Fulham. Continual injury problems restricted his appearances for the "Cottagers" to only nine, before he joined Lincoln City. Combining a part-time career with a men's outfitters business in Haringey, he helped Lincoln win the Third Division (North) in 1948. He also had three months with Crystal Palace before ending his playing career. McCormick then turned to coaching abroad, firstly with the Maltese club, Sliema Wanderers and then the Turkish National team. It was with Walton and Hersham that he first moved into management. In May 1953, he took on the manager's job at York City, but resigned in September 1954 after a dispute with the board over team selection. McCormick then worked in the licensing trade and at the time of his death, in a road accident in Spain, ran a pub in Lemsford, Hertfordshire. His father, John, was a forward with Rotherham Town in the 1890s.

Appearances:
League: 137 apps. 26 gls.
FA Cup: 13 apps. 2 gls.
Others: 20 apps. 2 gls.
Total: **170 apps. 30 gls.**

McCRACKEN

Role: Half-back 1918-19

Debut v Haydn Price's XI (Fr) (St Albans) 31.8.1918

An amateur trialist, McCracken made his only appearance for Spurs in a pre-season friendly at St Albans against Corporal H Price's XI in August 1918, Spurs fielded several trialists in a charity match. He suffered with cramp early in the game and had no real chance to impress.

Appearances:
Others: 1 app.
Total: **1 app. 0 gls.**

McCUDDEN, Joseph Francis

Role: Outside-right 1923-24
5ft.9ins. 11st.8lbs.
Born: Edmonton, London, 17th January 1899
Died: Beckenham, Kent, 14th October 1976

CAREER: Park Avondale/Gnome Athletic/Clapton Orient am. Dec 1920/ Edmonton Mar 1921/**SPURS** pro. Mar 1922/Norwich City May 1924/ Clapton Orient Aug 1926/Grays Thurrock United Oct 1926/Whitbreads Aug 1927.

Debut v West Ham United (Fr) (a) 23.2.1924

A local lad and regular with the Edmonton club, Frank McCudden was first associated with Spurs during the 1921-22 season when he played for the junior sides. Signed as a professional, he played regularly for the reserves for the next two seasons, but made only one first team appearance. That was in a friendly at West Ham United in February 1924. Released at the end of the season, he had one season with each of Norwich City and Clapton Orient, before moving to Grays Thurrock.

Appearances:
Others: 1 app.
Total: **1 app. 0 gls.**

McCURDY, William

Role: Full-back 1904-05
5ft.10ins. 12st.0lbs.
Born: Bridgton, 4th September 1876

CAREER: Vale of Clyde/Luton Town Jun 1900/Nottingham Forest Feb 1901/New Brompton May 1902/**SPURS** May 1904/New Brompton Jul 1905/Luton Town Aug 1906/retired May 1910.

Debut v Queens Park Rangers (WL) (h) 19.9.1904

Scottish full-back Bill McCurdy was much in demand when he decided to leave his first club, Vale of Clyde, with both Partick Thistle and Clyde keen to sign him on. He decided instead to move to England, and played for Luton Town, Nottingham Forest and New Brompton, a first team regular for all of them. Signed by Spurs as cover for John Watson, he spent the whole of his only season at White Hart Lane in a stand-by role, and was usually only able to make the first team when injuries dictated. Released at the end of the season, he returned to New Brompton and then went back to Luton where he played until retiring.

Appearances:
Southern: 12 apps.
Others: 17* apps.
Total: 29 apps. 0 gls.
*Includes 1 abandoned match.

McDERMOTT, John

Role: Inside-forward 1896-97
Born: Burnley, Lancashire, 1876

CAREER: Rossendale May 1895/Sheffield United Dec 1895/**SPURS** trial Sep 1896

Debut v Rossendale (Fr) (h) 3.9.1896

A 21-year old previously associated with Sheffield United, McDermott made two appearances for Spurs in friendly matches at the start of the 1896-97 season whilst on a month's trial. He could not have impressed too much as he was not subsequently taken on.

Appearances:
Others: 2 apps.
Total: 2 apps. 0 gls.

McDIARMID, Frederick

Role: Half-back 1906-07
5ft.8ins. 11st.7lbs.
Born: Dundee, 1880

CAREER: Partick Thistle Sep 1897/Dundee May 1899/**SPURS** May 1906/Northampton Town Apr 1907/Distillery cs. 1911.

Debut v West Ham United (SL) (h) 1.9.1906

Originally a winger but later converted to half-back, Fred McDiarmid spent seven years with Dundee and played for the Scottish League against the Irish League in February 1902. A solid performer whose strengths lay in the defensive side of his game, he joined Spurs with a view to replacing the ageing Ted Hughes. Although he played in the first few games of the season it was soon clear the Scot was not in the same class as Hughes. He spent most of the season in the reserves, making a total of only twelve senior appearances, before moving on to Northampton Town, where he commanded a regular first team place for four years. He then joined Distillery.

Appearances:
Southern: 7 apps.
Others: 5 apps.
Total: 12 apps. 0 gls.

MacDONALD, A

Role: Inside-forward 1893-94

Debut v Chesham (W&DCC) (h) 27.1.1894

MacDonald's only appearance for Spurs was in January 1894 when he played in a Wolverton and District Charity Cup match against Chesham.

Appearances:
Others: 1 app.
Total: 1 app. 0 gls.

McDONALD, David Hugh

Role: Full-back 1991-93
5ft.11ins. 11st.7lbs.
Born: Dublin, Republic of Ireland, 2nd January 1971

CAREER: Galtee Celtic/Republic of Ireland Schools/Home Farm/**SPURS** trainee May 1987, pro. Jul 1988/Republic of Ireland Youth/(Gillingham loan Aug 1990)/(Bradford City loan Aug 1992)/(Reading loan Mar 1993)/Peterborough United Aug 1993/Barnet Mar 1994/Cambridge United trial Feb 1998/St Albans trial Jul 1998/Welling United Aug 1998/Bishops Stortford Jan 1999/Barnet training Jul 1999/Canvey Island Aug 1999/Enfield Dec 1999/Boreham Wood Dec 1999/Enfield Jul 2000/Boreham Wood Jul 2001/Hendon/Billericay Town Jun 2002/Potters Bar Town Jan 2003/Boreham Wood Mar 2003/Enfield, player-manager Apr 2004-Jun 2005/Boreham Wood asst. manager Jul-Aug 2008.

Debut v Liverpool (BPL) (a) 9.5.1993
(Cardiff City (Fr) (a) 5.5.1992)

Young Irish full-back Dave McDonald was a surprise call-up to the first team for the visit to Anfield in May 1993. With injuries taking their toll, Dean Austin, Guðni Bergsson and Terry Fenwick were all unavailable, while Stuart Nethercott's lack of pace had been exposed in the two previous games. McDonald had been spotted by Spurs while playing for the famous Dublin club, Home Farm. An Irish schoolboy international at all levels, he had moved up to Under-21 and "B" level and gained League experience on loan to Gillingham, Bradford City and Reading. McDonald did not perform badly against Liverpool and was in no way to blame for the 2-6 defeat as Spurs' season drew to a poor close. McDonald maintained his place for the last game of the season, a 3-1 success at Highbury, but by the start of the next campaign had been transferred to Peterborough United. He enjoyed the best spell of his career at Barnet and later stepped down to non-League level, playing, coaching and managing for several southern clubs.

Appearances:
League: 2 apps.
Others: 2 (1) apps.
Total: 4 (1) apps. 0 gls.

McDONALD, Daniel Roy

Role: Centre-half 1920-21
6ft.0ins. 13st.0lbs.
Born: *East Wemyss, Fife, 12th September 1894*

CAREER: Wemyss Athletic/Dundee May 1913/**SPURS** May 1920/Bradford Park Avenue Jun 1921.

Debut v Watford (Fr) (a) 22.9.1920

An experienced performer who had spent seven years with Dundee, Roy McDonald arrived at White Hart Lane in the summer of 1920 to provide cover for centre-half, Charlie Rance. As it was, Charlie Walters, signed just a few weeks earlier and not expected to provide competition to Rance, proved remarkably quick at making the step up from amateur football. McDonald was never given a chance to make his mark and after just one appearance in a friendly at Watford was released to join Bradford PA.

Appearances:
Others: 1 app.
Total: 1 app. 0 gls.

MacDONALD, Robert James

Role: Full-back 1919-26
5ft.10ins. 11st.7lbs.
Born: *Inverness, 25th February 1895*
Died: *Glasgow, 1st April 1971*

CAREER: Inverness Caledonians/**SPURS** Aug 1919/Heart of Midlothian trial Sep 1927/Clapton Orient Oct 1927.

Debut v Birmingham (FL) (a) 1.5.1920
(Millwall (LFACC) (h) 22.9.1919)

Bob MacDonald was playing as an amateur with Inverness Caledonians when Spurs persuaded him to try his luck in the professional game. A typically strong, hard-tackling Scottish full-back, he made a first team debut against Millwall in a London FA Charity Cup tie in September 1919, but had to wait until the last match of the 1919-20 season before making his League bow. A right-back with Inverness, his chances of establishing himself in that position with Spurs were always going to be limited by the consistent brilliance of Tommy Clay, but MacDonald

performed so well as Clay's deputy in two matches early the following season, that when Clay returned, MacDonald was tried at left-back. Not only was the experiment a success, but he ousted Bob Brown, finished the season with an FA Cup Winner's medal and retained his place in the team until Matt Forster was signed in February 1923. Appearances after that were limited, in part due to several bad injuries, but he remained at White Hart Lane until released in April 1927. He had an unsuccessful trial with Hearts so joined Clapton Orient where he played for two years.

Appearances:
League: 109 apps.
FA Cup: 16 app.
Others: 24 apps.
Total: 149 apps. 0 gls.

McELHANEY, Ralph

Role: Outside-left 1896-97
Born: *1876*
Died: *Romford, Essex, 5th December 1930*

CAREER: Dreghorn Juniors/Third Lanark 1894/Celtic Apr 1895/Clyde Aug 1895/Partick Thistle Dec 1895/**SPURS** cs. 1896/Swindon Town cs. 1897/Beith Sep 1898/East Stirling Jun 1899/Dunipace Sep 1899/Brentford Jan 1900/Grays United Jan 1903/Southall 1904.

Debut v Sheppey United (SL) (a) 5.9.1896

Ralph McElhaney was almost ever-present during Spurs first Southern League season of 1896-97, when his dashing wing play was responsible for many of the goals plundered by top scorer Bob Clements. McElhaney made his debut in the club's first Southern League match at Sheppey United, went on to score 18 goals in a total of 53 senior appearances and would surely have been retained for the following season had it not been for some undisclosed "act of insubordination" in April 1897. That resulted in him being suspended  along with James Devlin, Frank Wilson and Jimmy Milliken. McElhaney was released at the end of the season without having played a further game for Spurs. He joined Swindon Town and moved quickly around, only Brentford getting more than a year's service from him.

Appearances:
Southern: 19 apps. 6 gls.
FA Cup: 3 apps. 1 gl.
Others: 31* apps. 11 gls
Total: 53 apps. 18 gls.
*Includes 1 abandoned match.

McELHENEY, J

Role: Inside-forward 1894-95

Debut v Liverpool Casuals (Fr) (h) 12.4.1895 (scored twice)

McElheney was a member of the 3rd Battalion of the Grenadier Guards who played four friendly matches for Spurs in April 1895, scoring three goals.

Appearances:
Others: 4 apps. 3 gls.
Total: 4 apps. 3 gls.

McENEFF, Aaron

Role: Midfielder 2013-14
5ft.10ins. 11st.9lbs.
Born: Cornshell Fields, Derry, Northern Ireland 9th July 1995

CAREER: Don Bosco's Boys Club/Maiden City Academy/Institute FC/ **SPURS** Academy Scholar Jul 2012, pro. Jul 2014/(Sheffield Wednesday trial Apr 2015)/(Nottingham Forest trial Apr 2015)/ released Jun 2015/Derry City training and perm. Jul 2015.

Debut v Ledley King XI (Fr) (h) (sub) 12.5.2014

One of the youngsters who made their senior debut as a substitute in Ledley King's testimonial in May 2014, Aaron McEneff was a Northern Ireland youth international who had been in the Spurs Academy for nearly two years. He signed professional shortly after his one game but was to go no further with Spurs. A bit lightweight for the hustle and bustle of midfield, injury early in the 2014-15 season did nothing to help his cause. With the decision to release him made before the season was over, he had trials at Sheffield Wednesday and Nottingham Forest without an offer. He returned home to Derry, signing for Derry City.

Appearances:
Others: (1) app.
Total: (1) app. 0 gls.

McEVOY, Kenneth

Role: Wide Midfielder 2013-14
5ft.9ins. 11st.1lbs.
Born: Waterford, Republic of Ireland, 4th September 1994

CAREER: **SPURS** Academy Scholar Jul 2011, pro. Jul 2013/ (Peterborough United loan Jul 2014)/(Colchester United loan Jan 2015) /(Stevenage loan Sep 2015)/York City loan Nov 2015, perm. Jan-May 2016/South Normanton Athletic Sep 2016.

Debut v Ledley King XI (Fr) (h) 12.5.2014

Kenny McEvoy was unfortunate to be a winger at White Hart Lane at the same time as Gareth Bale. Regular comparisons with the Welsh wizard were not simply inappropriate, but they put unnecessary pressure on a young man trying to make his way in the game. McEvoy played out wide, but there the similarity ended. He had pace over a short distance, but he did not have the power of Bale. When he got away from his man, he did so with skill and trickery, not power. Once he got away, he looked to set up chances for his strikers with crosses, not cut in for a strike on goal. Often on the fringe of selection, the Northern Ireland youth international's only senior game was in Ledley King's testimonial. Playing at first team level while out on loan, McEvoy believed he was worth an opportunity at Spurs and annoyed when it did not come. When he began agitating to leave, he was allowed to move to York City, but after less than a year was released and joined South Normanton Athletic.

Appearances:
Others: 1 app.
Total: 1 app. 0 gls.

McEWAN, Francis Fowler

Role: Inside-forward 1939-40
Born: Airdrie
Died: September 1944 (Killed in action)

CAREER: Whitburn/Airdrieonians Nov 1935/**SPURS** Nov 1938/(Guest for Hamilton Academical during World War Two).

Debut v Crystal Palace (FLS) (h) 9.12.1939

Joining Spurs from Scottish Second Division side Airdrieonians, Frank McEwan was regarded as "one for the future". His only first team appearances for the club were all in December 1939 when he played three matches in the Football League South competition. War service prevented him playing for Spurs again and in September 1944 he was killed in action.

Appearances:
Others: 3* apps.
Total: 3 apps. 0 gls.
*Includes 1 abandoned match

McEWEN, David

Role: Striker 1999-2001
6ft. 11st.0lbs.
Born: Westminster, London 2nd November 1977

CAREER: Crouch End Vampires 1997/Crawley Town Aug 1998/ Brentford trial Jul 1999/Dulwich Hamlet Aug 1999/**SPURS** part-time pro.

Jan 2000, pro. March 2000/Queens Park Rangers Jul-Oct 2001/Aldershot trial Jul 2002/Crawley Town/Hertford Town Mar 2003.

Debut v Derby County (sub) (PL) 29.4.2000

Making the leap from non-League to Premier League football is the stuff dreams are made of. For Dave McEwen it was a dream that came true. McEwen was banging in the goals for Dulwich Hamlet in the Isthmian League when he was spotted by Director of Football, David Pleat. As he was studying at the University of London, McEwen initially signed as a part-time professional, not taking the plunge into the professional game totally until he had completed his Business Studies course. A tall, bustling style of striker, he was called up for senior action in April 2000 as cover for Steffen Iversen and Chris Armstrong, making his debut as a substitute for the Norwegian. He made three further substitute appearances in January 2001, but that was as far as McEwen's career at Spurs went. Released in the summer of 2001, he moved to Queens Park Rangers, but fared no better in west London than he had in north London and returned to the non-League game.

Appearances:
League: (4) apps.
Others: (1) apps.
Total: (5) apps. 0 gls.

MacFARLANE, Dugald

Role: Centre-forward 1908-10
5ft.8ins. 11st.0lbs.
Born: Barrow-in-Furness, Cumbria, 24th August 1880
Died: Barrow-in-Furness, Cumbria, 22nd April 1965

CAREER: Barrow/Burnley cs. 1903/**SPURS** Jun 1908/Barrow cs. 1910.

Debut v Wolverhampton Wanderers (FL) (h) 1.9.1908

Originally a centre-forward, Doug McFarlane was signed from Burnley where he had played for five years, latterly either on the wing or at centre-half. With Spurs, he reverted to his original role and made his debut in the club's first Football League game against Wolves. He scored twice in the 16 League games he played that season, but most matches were as deputy for first choice Vivian J Woodward, and McFarlane spent much of his time in the reserves. The following year he stepped into the half-back line and made only five further League appearances before moving to Barrow.

Appearances:
League: 21 apps. 2 gls.
Others: 7 apps. 2 gls.
Total: 28 apps. 4 gls.

McFARLANE

Role: Outside-right 1941-42

CAREER: St Bernards/(guest for **SPURS** during World War Two).

Debut v Watford (LWC) (a) 6.4.1942

A former St Bernards full-back serving in the Royal Air Force, McFarlane was introduced to Spurs by Vic Buckingham. He played his only game at outside-right in a London War Cup match against Watford in April 1942.

Appearances:
Others: 1 app.
Total: **1 app. 0 gls.**

McGAHEY, Charles Percy

Role: Full-back 1893-99
6ft.1ins. 13st.8lbs
Born: Hornsey, London, 12th February 1871
Died: Whipps Cross, Leytonstone, London, 10th January 1935

CAREER: Wanstead Flats/Forest Gate Alliance/Ilford Park/Clapton/Ilford/City Ramblers/(guest for Millwall Athletic, Sheffield United, **SPURS**, Vampires and Woolwich Arsenal)/Richmond Association/Corinthians/Clapton/Northampton Town manager 1903-04.

Debut v London Hospital (Fr) (h) 8.2.1894

One of the stars of London amateur football at the end of the 19th century, Charlie McGahey was a fine all-round sportsman, representing Essex at cricket and London and Middlesex at football. He was, perhaps, best known in football circles as a City Ramblers' player, turning out and captaining them for several years, while very much in demand with all London's emerging clubs. He started his career with Wanstead Flats, before moving up the football ladder with Forest Gate Alliance, Ilford Park, Clapton, Ilford and then City Ramblers. Although he could have had his pick of the London clubs, his first loyalty always lay with the Ramblers, though he did turn out for other clubs such as Millwall, Sheffield United, Vampires and Woolwich Arsenal on occasions. It was as a guest that he made his first appearance for Spurs,

playing in a friendly against London Hospital on 8th February 1894 in a very inexperienced Spurs team. In 1895-96 he played quite often for Spurs, although all but one of his appearances were in friendly games as he apparently refused to take part in serious competitive football. On medical advice he spent quite a bit of time in Australia in the late 1890s and this may have had something to do with his rejection of the Spurs' captaincy at the start of the 1897-98 season. In fact, he was to make only one further appearance in Spurs' colours after that. He preferred to continue with City Ramblers, the Corinthians and Clapton until the 1902-03 season. He then decided to concentrate on cricket with Essex, although he did spend the 1903-04 season as manager of Northampton Town.

Appearances:
Others: 18 (1) apps.
Total: **18 (1) apps. 0 gls.**

McGEE, Luke Paul

Role: Goalkeeper 2014-17
6ft.4ins. 12st.7lbs.
Born: Edgware, Middlesex, 2nd September 1995

CAREER: SPURS Academy Scholar Jul 2012, pro. Jul 2014/(Harlow Town work experience Feb 2014)/(Peterborough United loan Aug 2016)/Portsmouth Jul 2017.

Debut v Chicago Fire (Fr) (a) (sub) 26.7.2014

Luke McGee was a highly thought of young 'keeper, who was unable to make his mark at White Hart Lane. He made a few appearances in pre-season matches, but the Academy graduate spent most of his time as back-up to the regular 'keepers, Hugo Lloris and Michel Vorm. Unable to displace either, a year's loan to Peterborough United was followed by a permanent transfer to Portsmouth.

Appearances:
Others: 1 (3) apps.
Total: 1 (3) apps. 0 gls.

McGLASHAN, G

Role: Right-half 1916-17

Debut v West Ham United (LFC) (h) 28.9.1916

McGlashan's only appearance in Spurs' colours was in September 1916 when he played in a London Football Combination fixture with West Ham United.

Appearances:
Others: 1 app.
Total: 1 app. 0 gls.

McGRATH, Roland Christopher

Role: Forward 1973-77
5ft.9ins. 11st.0lbs.
Born: Belfast, 29th November 1954

CAREER: Belfast Schools/Northern Ireland Schools/**SPURS** app. Jul 1970, pro. Jan 1972/(Millwall loan Feb 1976)/Manchester United Oct 1976/Tulsa Roughnecks (USA) Feb 1981-Sep 1982/South China (Hong Kong).

Debut v Arsenal (FL) (h) 13.10.1973

Chris McGrath was a promising young striker who proved particularly effective in European matches. He scored several important goals during the 1973-74 UEFA Cup and appeared in both legs of the final with Feyenoord. Although he had to be content with a runners-up medal as Spurs lost the first major final in their history, consolation came in the form of international honours with his first appearance for Northern Ireland in May 1974 against Scotland. Unfortunately, the talent he displayed that first season did not develop as expected and under Terry Neill, who as manager of Northern Ireland gave McGrath his international chance, he was rarely able to get a first team game. He was not helped by a general uncertainty as to his most effective position, sometimes playing on the wing, sometimes as a central striker and even in a more withdrawn midfield role. With six international caps to his credit and after a loan spell with Millwall, McGrath was transferred to Manchester United for £35,000, leaving the feeling that he simply under achieved. Although at Old Trafford for five years, McGrath played only twelve full League games for the Reds, and in fact, made more appearances at international level, 16, than for his club! He spent the summers of 1981 and 1982 in America with Tulsa Roughnecks and when released by United joined the South China club of Hong Kong.

Appearances:
League: 30 (8) apps. 5 gls.
FL Cup: 1 app.
Euro: 7 (1) apps. 5 gls.
Others: 8 (7) apps.
Total: **46 (16) apps. 10 gls.**

McGREGOR, T

Role: Centre-forward 1915-16

Debut v Norwich City (Fr) (a) 24.4.1916 (scored once)

A private serving in the 4th Battalion of the Cameron Highlanders, McGregor played his one match for Spurs in a friendly at Norwich City in April 1916. Operating at centre-forward, he scored Spurs' goal in a 1-1 draw converting "a smart centre from the left" by Ramsay, another soldier who had been called into the Spurs' team as they were two men short.

Appearances:
Others: 1 app. 1 gl.
Total: **1 app. 1 gl.**

McINROY, David

Role: Inside-forward 1895-96

CAREER: Our Boys/Dundee May 1893/Millwall Athletic cs. 1895/(guest for **SPURS** Feb 1896)/Dundee Apr 1896/(Dundee Wanderers loan Apr 1896).

Debut v Luton Town (Fr) (a) 10.2.1896

Millwall Athletic's Davie McInroy made his only appearance for Spurs in February 1896 when he played in a friendly against Luton Town. McInroy had started with the Our Boys club of Dundee that merged with East End to form Dundee in May 1893. He started his one season with Millwall as first choice at inside-forward, but lost his place with the arrival of Tom

Malloch from another Dundee club, Dundee Harps. McInroy returned to Scotland and later turned out again for Dundee.

Appearances:
Others: 1 app.
Total: 1 app. 0 gls.

McIVER, William

Role: Goalkeeper 1918-19
Born: *Whittle-le-Woods, Lancashire, 1877*
Died: *Darwen, Lancashire, 4th April 1934*

CAREER: Whittle-le-Woods/Darwen 1898/Blackburn Rovers Jul 1901/Brentford Jun 1908/Hartlepools United Oct 1909/Stockport County Jun 1911/Darwen 1913/(guest for Blackburn Rovers and **SPURS** during World War One)/Nelson/Blackburn Trinity.

Debut v Millwall (LFC) (h) 21.12.1918

Willie McIver played three games for Spurs in the London Football Combination over the Christmas 1918 period. The first was on 21st December in a home match with Millwall played at Clapton Orient's Homerton ground and the other two against Queens Park Rangers on Christmas and Boxing Day. A well-experienced 'keeper, he had spent over seven years at Blackburn playing more than 100 games before a season with Brentford. He spent the 1909-10 season with Hartlepools United, two years with Stockport County and immediately before World War One was playing for Darwen. After the war he turned out for Nelson and Blackburn Trinity.

Appearances:
Others: 3 apps.
Total: 3 apps. 0 gls.

McKAY, Kenneth

Role: Inside-forward 1898-99
5ft.6ins. 10st.11lbs
Born: *Larkhall, Lanarkshire, 1877*

CAREER: Albion Rovers/Hamilton Acadaemical/Sheffield United Jan 1897/**SPURS** May 1898/Thames Ironworks May 1899/Wishaw Thistle Sep 1900/Fulham Jan 1901-Jun 1902/Royal Albert Oct 1902.

Debut v Thames Ironworks (TML) (h) 3.9.1898 (scored once) (Gainsborough Trinity (Fr) (h) 1.9.1898 (scored three))

In his one full season at Bramall Lane, 1897-98, Kenny McKay had proved an important member of Sheffield United's League Championship team and it was a considerable surprise when he was persuaded to join Spurs. A hard-working player with an eye for goal, he played throughout the season, providing valuable support to Bill Joyce and creating many goals for the centre-forward. Having performed so well, the decision to release him at the end of one season was rather mystifying, but the flow of goals had dried up after Christmas and manager John Cameron believed he had secured the signature of a more lethal scorer in Tom Pratt. McKay moved on to Thames Ironworks where he spent one season before joining Fulham. He played for two years at Craven Cottage, helping Fulham win the Second Division of the Southern League in 1901-02. The only representative honour he won in his time with Spurs was in November 1898, when he scored twice for the United League against the Thames and Medway League at Northumberland Park. McKay scored on his first appearances for Spurs in a friendly, the United League, Thames and Medway League and FA Cup. It was only in the Southern League that he failed to mark his first outing in the competition with a goal.

Appearances:
Southern: 18 apps. 5 gls.
FA Cup: 9 apps. 1 gl.
Others: 26 apps. 19 gls.
Total: 53 apps. 25 gls.

McKENNA, Kieran Thomas

Role: Midfielder 2004-06
5ft.10ins. 11st.5lbs
Born: *Kilburn, London, 14th May 1986*

CAREER: Enniskillen Town/Ballinamallard Youth/**SPURS** scholar Jul 2002, pro. Aug 2003/retired Mar 2009/**SPURS** Academy coach/Leicester City Academy coach Aug 2009/Nottingham Forest Academy coach/Loughborough University second team coach/Vancouver Whitecaps (Canada) guest asst. coach Jun 2010/St Thomas Aquinas College, New York (USA) coach/Loughborough University coach Sep 2010, first team coach Mar 2011, player Jan 2012/St Thomas Aquinas College, New York (USA) coach/**SPURS** Under-18 coach/Manchester United Academy (Under-18) coach Aug 2016

Debut v Stevenage Borough (sub) (Fr) (a) 20.7.2004

A talented young midfielder born in London but brought up in Northern Ireland, Kieran McKenna looked to have the talent to build a good career in football. Hard-working and blessed with good passing skills, although he had only made a few substitute appearances for the first team, he was recognised as good enough to play for Northern Ireland Under-21s, winning six caps at that level. Just when McKenna seemed set for a breakthrough with Spurs he was side-lined by a hip injury. Despite two years of treatment, the injury proved too much and at only 23 McKenna was forced to retire. Initially helping out with coaching at the Spurs Academy, he set out to quickly gather experience at home and in North America. Impressing in a full-time role with Spurs, he was tempted way by Manchester United.

Appearances:
Others: (6) apps. 1gl.
Total: (6) apps. 1 gl.

McKENZIE, Lewis H

Role: Half-back 1894-96

CAREER: Minerva/Caledonian Athletic/London Caledonians/guest for SPURS Dec 1894/SPURS Sep 1895/London Caledonians Oct 1895.

Debut v Luton Town (FAC) (a) 12.10.1895
(Sheffield & District League XI (Fr) (h) 25.12.1894)

Originally with the London club Minerva, McKenzie had progressed to playing for Caledonian Athletic and the London Caledonians when he made his first appearances for Spurs as a guest over the Christmas holiday period of 1894. He did not play again that season, but was a regular in the first few games of the following campaign, including the first FA Cup tie of the season at Luton. However, it seems fair to assume that he was of those against professionalism, for once the club had taken the decision to pay players, McKenzie reverted to playing for London Caledonians. He made only one further appearance for Spurs, on Christmas Day 1895, when the "Calies" were without a game.

Appearances:
FA Cup: 1 app.
Others: 9 apps.
Total: 10 apps. 0 gls.

McKIE, Marcel

Role: Defender 2004-05
5ft.11ins. 11st.9lbs
Born: Edmonton, London, 22nd September 1984

CAREER: SPURS scholar Jul 2001, pro. Sep 2001/Wycombe Wanderers trial Apr 2006/West Ham United trial Apr 2006/Crewe Alexandra trial Jun 2006/Dagenham & Redbridge trial Aug 2006/Kettering Town Sep 2006-March 2007/Lewes Mar 2007/Fabril (Spain) trial Jul 2007/St Albans City Aug 2007/Potters Bar Town Sep 2008/Enfield Town Dec 2008/Grays Athletic Jun 2009/Butlins Bognor Regis by 2010

Debut v Falkenburgs (Fr) (a) 13.7.2004

Another of the talented youngsters developed by Spurs of whom much was expected, but who failed to quite make the grade, Marcel McKie was a cultured left-back given a chance in pre-season friendlies when Frank Arnesen and Jacques Santini were taking stock of the talent at their disposal. Though he played regularly for the youth and reserve sides, that was as far as McKie progressed at Spurs. On being released he had trials with several League clubs, but eventually had to settle for playing at non-League level.

Appearances:
Others: 2 (4) apps.
Total: 2 (4) apps. 0 gls.

MacLACHLAN, Charles Fellowes

Role: Inside-forward 1893-94
Born: Hackney, London 1875
Died: Roche, Cornwall, 28th September 1951

CAREER: SPURS Dec 1893/West Herts am. 1894/Crouch End Vampires by Dec 1896.

Debut v Erith (Fr) (h) 16.12.1893

Charlie MacLachlan made his first appearance for Spurs in a friendly with Erith in December 1893. Although he did not play again for another six weeks, he was then a regular in the team until the end of the season. He usually played at inside-left, but also turned out on the left wing when Ernie Payne was not available. MacLachlan's association with Spurs came to an end when the season was over and he played for West Herts, the forerunners of Watford, for the next two seasons. In December 1896 he was to be found playing for Crouch End Vampires.

Appearances:
Others: 15 apps. 2 gls.
Total: 15 apps. 2 gls.

McMAHON, Gerard Joseph

Role: Forward 1992-97
5ft.11ins. 11st.8lbs.
Born: Belfast, 29th December 1973

CAREER: Lurgan United/Glenavon assoc. schl, Jul 1988/SPURS Jul 1992/(Barnet loan Oct 1994)/Stuttgart (Germany) trial Sep 1996/Udinese (Italy) trial Sep 1996/Stoke City Sep 1996/St. Johnstone Feb 1998-May 2000/Notts County trial Jul 2000/Macclesfield trial Aug 2000/Glenavon Aug 2000, asst. manager, caretaker manager Jan 2009, reserve team manager/Loughgall asst. manager Oct 2012/Dromara Village player/manager Jan 2014.

Debut v Coventry City (PL) (h) 9.5.1995

Ged McMahon was drawing scouts from English clubs to Glenavon's Mourneview Park as soon as he began to turn out regularly for the Lurgan club. That was not surprising though, as he was only 14-years old. A tricky little winger, there were several clubs keen on securing his services and it took £100,000 to persuade Glenavon to let him join Spurs. The deal was done in July 1992, but McMahon stayed with Glenavon until the end of the season, helping them win the Irish Cup, before moving to London. At first, McMahon seemed a disappointment. He made a few appearances in friendly games, but while he played for Northern Ireland at Under-21 and "B" level, it was not until the last two games of the 1994-95 season that he was brought into the League XI. That breakthrough was followed by his full international debut against Canada in May 1995. For the 1995-96 season McMahon regularly found himself in the senior squad, but with competition from Ruel Fox and Ronnie Rosenthal, it was never easy for McMahon. With Northern Ireland manager, Bryan Hamilton, making it clear McMahon needed regular first team action if his international ambitions were to be satisfied, McMahon decided to move as his

contract ran out. After trials in Germany and Italy, he decided to join Stoke City. He did not go cheaply. The transfer fee was set by the Premier League at an initial £250,000 with another £25,000 payable after each of 10, 20, 30 and 40 appearances. His continuing potential was recognised with Stoke also liable to pay 25% of any profit they were to make on him being transferred. McMahon settled immediately at Stoke, playing regularly and looking sure to fulfil his potential, but when Stoke struggled and Brian Little was appointed manager, the new man made it clear there would be no place for an out-and-out winger. Clearly unwanted, McMahon moved to St Johnstone, a club that was on an upward curve. For two years they challenged Celtic and Rangers, even qualifying for European football. When released by St Johnstone, McMahon returned home to Ireland and Glenavon, initially as a player. He then moved on to the coaching and management side.

Appearances:
League: 9 (7) apps.
FA Cup: (1) apps.
FL Cup: 3 apps.
Others: 7 (7) apps. 1 gl.
Total: 19 (15) apps. 1 gl.

McMULLAN, Francis

Role: Inside-forward 1905-06
5ft.10ins. 11st.4lbs.
Born: Castlewellan, Ireland, 1882

CAREER: Old Xaverians/Liverpool/**SPURS** May 1905/released Apr 1906.

Debut v Brentford (WL) (a) 26.2.1906

Little is known about McMullan who made his only appearance for Spurs in a first team competition in February 1906 when the club fielded a reserve side for a Western League fixture with Brentford, two days before the first team were due to play Birmingham in a Third Round FA Cup replay. For the rest of the season he had to be content with a place in the reserves and was released in April 1906.

Appearances:
Others: 1 app.
Total: 1 app. 0 gls.

McNAB, Neil

Role: Midfielder 1973-79
5ft.7ins. 10st.10lbs.
Born: Greenock, Renfrewshire, 4th June 1957

CAREER: Greenock Schools/Scotland Schools/Morton 1972/**SPURS** am. Feb 1974, pro. Jun 1974/Bolton Wanderers Nov 1978/Brighton and Hove Albion Feb 1980/(Leeds United loan Dec 1982)/(Portsmouth loan Mar 1983)/Manchester City Jul 1983/Tranmere Rovers Jan 1990/(Huddersfield Town loan Jan 1992)/Hibernians (Malta) Jun 1993/Derry City Jul 1993/Ayr United Jul 1993/Darlington Sep 1993/Witton Albion Jan 1994/Manchester City youth team manager Jun 1994-May 1998/Portsmouth reserve team coach May 1998-Apr 2000, Oct 2000/Exeter City head coach Oct 2002-Feb 2003/Weymouth asst. manager Jun 2003/Tucker Youth Soccer Association-Triumph Soccer Club (USA) coach Oct 2003/Cobb Futbol Club (USA) Director of Coaching/Chiefs Futbol Club (USA) coach 2008,

Debut v Chelsea (sub) (FL) (h) 3.4.1974

Neil McNab joined Spurs in February 1974 for £40,000-a hefty fee for a raw 16-year old. McNab had played for Morton in the Scottish First Division when only 15 and was trumpeted by the press as "the new John White". On signing he had to revert to amateur status, but that lasted only four months during which time he made his League debut. A hard working, gritty midfield player, neat and concise with great skill on the ball and an ability to hit superb long passes, it took McNab until 1977-78 to establish a place in the first team, but he was ever-present in the Second Division promotion campaign and won a Scottish Under-21 cap against Wales in February 1978 to add to his schoolboy and youth honours. With the arrival of World Cup stars Ossie Ardiles and Ricardo Villa from Argentina in the summer of 1978, McNab lost his place. A midfield of Ardiles, Hoddle, McNab and Villa meant that there was nobody in that crucial area capable of winning the ball, although it would certainly have provided one of the most talented and creative midfields in the English game! McNab made his last senior appearance for Spurs in a miserable 0-7 defeat at Anfield in September 1978. He was transferred to Bolton for £250,000 two months later. He then moved around with Brighton, Leeds United (loan) and Portsmouth (loan) before a permanent move to Manchester City. The Maine Road fans probably saw McNab's best performances, as he developed into a mature player thriving on the responsibility of being the most experienced man in an exciting young team. He proved invaluable in helping City win promotion to the First Division in 1989, and was voted "Player of the Year", but struggled to retain his place the following season. Sold to Tranmere Rovers, he promptly helped them win promotion and then consolidate their position in the Second Division, giving them three years' great service. Released by Tranmere, McNab moved around from club to club quickly before joining the coaching staff at Maine Road. He then spent several years on the coaching and management side in England before moving to the United States where he has continued to help develop young players. At the time of his debut McNab was the youngest player to appear for Spurs in the Football League. That record has since been overtaken by Ally Dick. McNab's sons, Neil junior and Joe, played for Portsmouth and several American clubs before coaching alongside their father in the States.

Appearances:
League: 63 (9) apps. 3 gls.
FA Cup: 2 apps.
FL Cup: 5 (1) apps.
Others: 26 (8) apps. 3 gls.
Total: 96 (18) apps. 6 gls.

McNAIR, William D

Role: Centre-forward 1907-08
5ft.10ins. 11st.7lbs.
Born: Renfrew, Renfrewshire, 29th April 1885

CAREER: Forth Rangers/Celtic Jan 1905/(Hamilton Acadaemical loan

Dec 1905)/(East Stirling loan Aug 1906)/Falkirk/**SPURS** May 1907 Aberdeen May 1908/Reading 1909/Alloa May 1909/Reading Feb 1910.

Debut v Queens Park Rangers (SL) (a) 2.9.1907 (scored once)

Formerly with Celtic, East Stirling and Falkirk, Willie McNair was signed specifically to provide cover for Vivian J Woodward, and it was in that capacity that he made the majority of his appearances for Spurs early in the 1907-08 season, when Woodward was unavailable. McNair did reasonably well, scoring six goals in his first ten games, and when Woodward was able to play, McNair was tried at inside-forward. Sadly, without the same success. He dropped into the reserves, but still turned out frequently for the first team in the principally midweek Western League competition that several senior players were unable to trouble with. During the middle of the season he played a few games on what was proving to be a troublesome right wing, but was not really cut out for that role. By March 1908 his place as Woodward's understudy had been taken by Max Seeburg. On being released at the end of the season, McNair returned to Scotland where he played for a year with Aberdeen and later turned out for Reading and Alloa.

Appearances:
Southern: 15 apps. 5 gls.
FA Cup: 1 app.
Others: 11 apps. 2 gls.
Total: 27 apps. 7 gls.

McNALLY, John Brendan

Role: Full-back 1954-55
Born: Drimnagh, Dublin, 22nd January 1935
Died: Luton, Bedfordshire, 6th July 2011

CAREER: Shelbourne/**SPURS** trial Nov 1954/Luton Town trial Apr 1956, perm May 1956/Cambridge City Jun 1963/Dunstable Town/Chesham United manager 1970/Dunstable Town manager 1977-1983.

Debut v Accrington Stanley (Fr) (a) 29.11.1954

Brendan McNally played his one match for Spurs as a trialist bought over from the Shelbourne club by its manager and former Arsenal star, David Jack. McNally had little opportunity to impress with the match being abandoned after 52 minutes due to torrential rain. Although subsequently watched by Spurs in a few games for Shelbourne, they decided not to sign him. However, he did go on to make his mark in the Football League with Luton Town. He was immediately signed by Luton after a trial in April 1956, made 134 League appearances in six years, played in the 1959 FA Cup Final and won three full caps for the Republic of Ireland plus one at "B" level.

Appearances:
Others: 1* app.
Total: 1 app. 0 gls.
*Includes 1 abandoned match

McNAUGHT, James Rankin

Role: Half-back 1898-07
5ft.6ins. 9st.10lbs.
Born: Dumbarton, 8th June 1870
Died: West Ham, London, March 1919

CAREER: Nethlan Park/Dumbarton 1890/Linfield/Newton Heath Feb 1893/**SPURS** May 1898/Maidstone Apr 1907/retired 1909/Asplin Rovers vice-president.

Debut v Thames Ironworks (TML) (h) 3.9.1898
(Gainsborough Trinity (Fr) (h) 1.9.1898)

James McNaught began his career as an inside-forward with Dumbarton, helping them win the Scottish League title in both 1891 and 1892 and reach the Scottish Cup final in the first of those years. After a short spell in Ireland with Linfield, he joined Newton Heath and made his name as a ball-playing centre-half who could also operate at inside-forward, although he personally preferred the half-back position. With Spurs, he proved a hard uncompromising centre-half who was never afraid to venture upfield and assist the forwards, but whose great strength lay in his defensive play. Close to Scottish international honours, he played for the Anglo-Scots against the Home Scots in the international trial in March 1899, having earlier that month played for an England XI (!) against a Scotland XI in a match to raise money for the Player's Union. In an age when players only signed one year contracts and were all too frequently released at the end of them, he gave Spurs nine years' great service, originally as a first team regular, but later in the reserves, with whom he also worked on the coaching side. A member of the team that won the Southern League title in 1900, he was unfortunate to miss out on the FA Cup success of 1901, collecting an injury in the First round match against Preston North End and unable to recover his place. Released in April 1907 he, along with Tom Purdie, joined his former team-mate Bob Stormont (who had experienced a similar fate in the 1901 Cup run) at Maidstone, where he remained until his retirement. McNaught retained his association with the Tottenham area for many years, being a vice-president of Asplin Rovers, one of the area's junior clubs.

Appearances:
Southern: 105 apps.
FA Cup: 13 apps. 1 gl.
Others: 133 apps. 8 gls.
Total: 251 apps. 9 gls.

McQUEEN, Alexander Luke

Role: Defender 2013-14
5ft.11ins. 11st.7lbs.
Born: Rush Green, Essex, 24th March 1995

CAREER: SPURS Academy Scholar Jul 2011, pro. Jul 2014/ (Nottingham Forest trial Apr 2015)/released Jun 2015/Carlisle United trial and perm. Jul 2015-May 2016, trial Sep 2016, perm. Dec 2016.

Debut v Ledley King XI (Fr) (h) (sub) 12.5.2014

An athletic and stylish performer, Alex McQueen was a defender at Spurs Academy when he played as a substitute in Ledley King's testimonial. Able to play anywhere across the back line or in midfield he signed professional terms, but a year later the decision was taken that he would not make it in the top flight. Released, he was snapped up by Carlisle United on a one-year deal. They were keen to retain his services but McQueen looked elsewhere. When he was unable to secure an offer elsewhere, he returned to Carlisle on trial, until signing a short-term contract.

Appearances:
Others: (1) app.
Total: (1) app. 0 gls.

McTAVISH, John Kay

Role: Outside-right 1910-12
5ft.7ins. 11st.2lbs.
Born: *Govan, Glasgow, 7th June 1885*
Died: *Falkirk, Stirlingshire, 4th April 1944*

CAREER: Ibrox Roselea/Fairfield/Petershill/Falkirk Jun 1905/Oldham Athletic Jun 1910/**SPURS** Dec 1910/Newcastle United Apr 1912/Partick Thistle May 1913/York City May 1914/Goole Town Feb 1915/(guest for Heart of Midlothian and Falkirk during World War One)/Bo'ness/East Fife cs. 1920/(Falkirk loan Sep 1920)/(Dumbarton loan Oct 1920)/East Stirling Aug 1921/Dumbarton/retired 1924.

Debut v Newcastle United (FL) (a) 21.1.1911

John McTavish met with more success at Falkirk than his brother, Bob, representing the Scottish League against the Football League twice and winning an international cap for Scotland against Ireland in March 1910. At Oldham for only six months, he vied with George Woodger, who was also later to join Spurs, for the inside-right position, but had to concede defeat to the England international. With Spurs, he made his League debut in January 1911 and after playing two games at inside-left in place of his brother, moved to outside-right. He started the following season in that role and was soon hailed as one of the best right wingers in the country, but by the middle of the season his form had

strangely fallen away and he was out of the team. In February 1912, he demanded a transfer, but it was not until the end of April that he moved to Newcastle United for £650, where he played in the last League match of the season. He stayed with Newcastle until May 1913 and then played for Partick Thistle, York City, Goole Town, East Fife, Dumbarton and East Stirling before retiring in 1924.

Appearances:
League: 40* apps. 3 gls.
FA Cup: 2 apps.
Others: 3 apps.
Total: 45 apps. 3 gls.
*Includes 2 abandoned matches.

McTAVISH, Robert

Role: Inside-forward 1910-12
5ft.9ins. 12st.0lbs.
Born: *26th October 1888*
Died: *1972*

CAREER: Ibrox Roselea/Avondale/Rangers trial/Petershill 1906/Falkirk Apr 1907/**SPURS** Jun 1910/Brentford Feb 1912/Third Lanark Jul 1913/ (Guest for Raith Rovers during World War One).

Debut v Preston North End (FL) (h) 8.10.1910
(Clapton Orient (LFACC) (h) 19.9.1910)

When Bob McTavish arrived from Falkirk, where he had played alongside his brother John, he was expected to provide cover for inside-forward Bobby Steel, but his League debut came at centre-forward as Spurs searched desperately to find an adequate replacement for the injured Percy Humphries. McTavish was not up to the task and returned to the reserves. The remainder of his senior appearances came in place of Steel. In total, he managed just 15 appearances for the club and although retained for the following

season, he left in February 1912 to sign for Brentford. He played in west London until the summer of 1913 when he moved to Third Lanark. Curiously, although John and Bob McTavish were together at Tottenham for 14 months, they only played together for Spurs in one League match-against Blackburn Rovers on 22nd April 1911. McTavish's son, John, played for Manchester City during the 1950s.

Appearances:
League: 10 apps. 3 gls.
FA Cup: 1 app.
Others: 4 apps. 1 gl.
Total: 15 apps. 4 gls.

McVEIGH, Paul Francis

Role: Forward 1996-98
5ft.6ins. 11st.0lbs.
Born: *Belfast, 6th December 1977*

CAREER: St John Baptist Primary School/St Mary's School/Belfast Schools/Lisburn Youth/**SPURS** trainee Jul 1994, pro. Jul 1996/Cambridge United trial Feb 2000/Norwich City trial and perm. Mar 2000/(Burnley loan Mar 2007)/Pisa (Italy) training Jul 2007/Plymouth Argyle trial Jul

2007/Luton Town Aug 2007/San Jose Earthquakes (USA) trial May 2009/Norwich City trial and perm Jul 2009-May 2010.

Debut v Aston Villa (PL) (a) 19.4.1997

At 5ft 6ins tall, Paul McVeigh had an obvious disadvantage in an age when strikers were increasingly expected to be six foot plus, but the lack of inches did not hold him back and, if anything, just reinforced what a good footballer he was. McVeigh was in his first year as a professional when he was called up for his Spurs' debut against Aston Villa in April 1997 as the season was drawing to a close. Playing alongside Teddy Sheringham, he buzzed around the Villa defence, a nippy, ever-active bundle of energy, keeping the defenders on their toes. He made two more appearances, netting his only League goal for Spurs in the last of them. He played in the pre-season friendlies of the following July, but was not to appear in the first team again. A regular for Northern Ireland at Under-21 level, he collected his first full cap before Spurs decided to allow him to leave. McVeigh moved to Norwich City, giving them great service, initially as a striker and later in midfield. He made over 200 appearances in seven years and won another 19 full caps before spending 18 months with Luton Town. On being released by Luton McVeigh had a trial with San Jose Earthquakes, but when no offer of a contract was forthcoming he returned to England. While looking for a new club he trained with Norwich and impressed them so much that they offered him a year's contract.

Appearances:
League: 2 (1) apps. 1 gl.
Others: 2 (4) apps. 1 gl.
Total: 4 (5) apps. 2 gls.

McVEY, J

Role: Forward 1916-17

CAREER: Shelbourne/(guest for **SPURS** during World War One).

Debut v Chelsea (LFC) (a) 2.9.1916

With Shelbourne prior to the outbreak of the First World War, McVey made two appearances for Spurs in the London Football Combination in 1916-17, the first at Chelsea on 2nd September and the other four weeks later at Millwall.

Appearances:
Others: 2 apps.
Total: 2 apps. 0 gls.

MABBUTT, Gary Vincent M.B.E.

Role: Midfield or defender 1982-1999
5ft.9ins. 12st.9lbs.
Born: Bristol, 23rd August 1961

CAREER: Bristol Parkway/Bristol Schools/Avon Schools/Bristol Rovers app. Aug 1977, pro. Jan 1979/**SPURS** Jul 1982/released Jun 1998/retired Jan 1999.

Debut v Luton Town (FL) (h) 28.8.1982 (scored once)
(Lausanne (Fr) (a) 6.8.1982)

England Youth international Gary Mabbutt made his League debut for Bristol Rovers in December 1978 and rapidly built a reputation as a highly versatile player, occupying every outfield position in his four years at Eastville. He won a first England Under-21 cap against Poland in March 1982 and had three such caps to his credit by the time of his £120,000 move to Spurs. Although expected to start the season in the reserves, a crop of early injuries forced a first senior appearance against Liverpool in the FA Charity Shield at Wembley and from that opening game, it was apparent Spurs had secured a player destined for the very top. Initially played in midfield, his stamina, hunger for the ball, non-stop running and strong tackling allied to quick and accurate passing were all most encouraging signs. Skilful athletic and always composed Gary settled so well into the upper echelons of football that, after just one more Under-21 cap, he won full international honours against West Germany in October 1982, not in midfield but at right-back. He retained a place in the England team as a midfield player but his admirable ability to play anywhere had drawbacks for Gary was never able to truly command one particular role and always tended to be viewed as a "bits-and-pieces" player who would do a good job wherever he was asked to perform. A member of the Spurs team that won the UEFA Cup in 1984, injury caused him to miss much of the 1984-85 season but, when fit, he was invariably in the first team squad, if not the team. When David Pleat arrived as manager in May 1986 he identified that Mabbutt's ability to out-jump taller players, strength in the tackle, speed of recovery and organisational abilities would best serve the team in central defence and he teamed him with Richard Gough in a defensive duo that was not only solid and reliable but could also play constructive football out of defence. Gary appeared in that position in the 1987 FA Cup Final when he scored Spurs' second goal but then had the

appalling misfortune to deflect in the decisive goal that won a dramatic match for Coventry City. Appointed captain on the departure of Gough, Mabbutt received some real consolation for the 1987 FA Cup Final disappointment when, as the highlight of his career, he led the club to its record eighth FA Cup win in 1991. Although at one time he appeared out of favour with the England management, his tremendous consistency and reliability saw him recalled to the England team early in 1991-92 for the final qualifying games of the European Championship when England's hopes of going through were badly threatened by injuries. Typically, Gary did not let his country down. Even the misfortune of suffering a broken leg in the first match of the 1996-97 season was overcome. Although many pundits thought his career might be over and he was out of the team for a year he returned to show he was still as good a player as ever although it almost certainly prevented him overtaking Steve Perryman's record of League appearances for Spurs. Released in June 1998 Mabbutt had several offers but refused to consider them while still suffering from a knee injury. In January 1999 he announced the injury would not recover and retired. Apart from his footballing talents, Mabbutt proved an inspiration to many, for he is a diabetic. He has never let the condition hold him back and has shown other sufferers what can be achieved if the determination and desire is strong enough. He was rewarded for his services to football with the M.B.E. in the 1994 New Year's Honours List. Gary is part of a useful footballing family; his father, Roy, was a forward with Bristol Rovers and Newport County and his brother Kevin a striker with Bristol City and Crystal Palace. He was the subject of TV's "This Is Your Life".

Appearances:
League: 458 (19) apps. 27 gls.
FA Cup: 46* (2) apps. 5 gls.
FL Cup: 60 (2) apps. 2 gls.
Euro: 22 (3) apps. 4 gls.
Others: 143 (23) apps. 15 gls.
Total: 729 (49) apps. 53 gls.
*Includes 1 abandoned match.

MABIZELA, Mbulelo

Role: Defender 2003-05
5ft.11ins. 13st.1lbs.
Born: Maritzburg, South Africa, 16th September 1980

CAREER: Edendale Stars (South Africa)/Sundowns Junior Soccer Academy (South Africa)/Ashdown Young Buccaneers (South Africa)/Maritzburg City (South Africa)/Orlando Pirates (South Africa) 2001/**SPURS** trial Jul 2003, perm. Aug 2003/released Oct 2004/Fulham trial Nov 2004/Vålerenga (Norway) Mar 2005/Mamelodi Sundowns (South Africa) Aug 2006/Platinum Stars (South Africa) Jan 2009-May 2011/Ajax Cape Town (South Africa) training Aug 2011/Bidvest Wits (South Africa) Aug 2011/Chippa United (South Africa) Jan 2013/Mpumalanga Black Aces (South Africa) training and perm Oct 2013-Dec 2014/Amazulu (South Africa) trial and perm Jan 2015-Jun 2015/Royal Eagles (South Africa) Oct 2015-Mar 2016.

Debut v Leicester City (sub) (PL) (a) 19.10.2003 (scored once)
(Sporting Portugal (Fr) (h) 10.8.2003)

Spurs returned from their pre-season trip to South Africa in July 2003 with one player more than went out with them. South African Player of the Year, Mabizela Mbulelo, so impressed Director of Football David Pleat playing for Orlando Pirates against Spurs, that he arranged for the Bafana Bafana captain to join Spurs on trial. It was a short-lived arrangement, as Mabizela's transfer was secured immediately a work permit was obtained. A powerful central defender, reputedly nicknamed "Old John" because he showed a footballing maturity well beyond his years, Mabizela had made his first international appearance in November 2001 and was soon captaining his country. Primarily viewed as a central defender, he could play all across the back line or operate in central midfield where his calmness and simple ball-playing skills were not out of place. Having played in a pre-season friendly, Mabizela made his League debut at Leicester in October 2003, replacing Gus Poyet and scoring with a fantastic volley. Sadly, that was to be the high point of Mabizela's Spurs' career. Lacking in self-discipline, he was unable to adapt to life as a highly paid professional sportsman in a foreign country. Stripped of the South African captaincy, his personal problems eventually led to him being released by Spurs. Vålerenga of Oslo gave him a second chance to make an international career for himself but he rarely made their starting eleven. He returned to South Africa, but no sooner had he signed for Mamelodi Sundowns than he was suspended from football for six months after a drugs' test found traces of marijuana. Having signed for Platinum Stars, Mabizela was lucky to be acquitted of driving while under the influence of alcohol on a technicality. Despite his problems, there were clubs prepared to take him on and there were times when he repaid them with fine performances. Demands were even made for his international recall, but the manager decided he could not trust a player who had, and continued, to let himself down all too often. Mabizela's father, Dumisana, was a striker with Amazulu, Benfica (of Mpumalanga) and Swift Swallows, while his brother, S'bongiseni, played for Maritzburg City.

Appearances:
League: 1 (6) apps. 1 gl.
FL Cup: 1 (1) apps.
Others: 4 (2) apps.
Total: 6 (9) apps. 1 gl.

MACKAY, David Craig

Role: Half-back 1958-68
5ft.8ins. 11st.6lbs.
Born: Edinburgh, Midlothian, 14th November 1934
Died: Nottingham, 2nd March 2015

CAREER: Balgreen Primary School/Carrickvale Secondary School/Edinburgh Schools/Scotland Schools/Gorgie Boys Brigade/Slateford Athletic/Newtongrange Star/Hutcheson Vale/Heart of Midlothian Am. Nov 1951, part-time pro. Apr 1952/**SPURS** Mar 1959/Derby County Jul 1968/Swindon Town player-manager May 1971, manager Nov 1971/Nottingham Forest manager Nov 1972/Derby County manager Oct 1973-Nov 1976/Walsall manager Mar 1977-May 1978/Al Arabi Sporting Club (Kuwait) manager Aug 1978/Al Shabab (Dubai) manager 1986/Doncaster Rovers manager Dec 1987-Mar 1989/Birmingham City manager Apr 1989-Jan 1991/Zamalek (Egypt) manager Oct 1991/Qatar Under-17 coach.

Debut v Manchester City (FL) (h) 21.3.1959

David Mackay was signed for £30,000 from Hearts, reportedly as an alternative after Bill Nicholson had failed in an attempt to capture Mel Charles. The failure to secure the transfer of the great Welsh international may have been a blessing in disguise, for the craggy-faced, barrel-chested Mackay soon became a folk hero at White Hart Lane and, with hindsight, must be considered one of Spurs greatest ever players. A half-back from his school days, he joined Hearts as a part-time professional in April 1952, made his League debut in 1953-54 and, after signing as a full-time professional on completing his National Service, helped Hearts win the

Scottish League Cup in 1955 and the Scottish Cup the following year. Success with Hearts soon brought representative honours and after playing for Scotland Under-23's against England and the Scottish League against the Football League in March 1957, Mackay made his full international debut against Spain in May 1957. Although he won two more Under-23 caps and helped Hearts win the Scottish League the following season, it was not until June 1958, after he had been voted Scotland's Player of the Year, that he won his next full cap playing against France in Scotland's last match of the 1958 World Cup in Sweden. Two more full caps plus a 1959 Scottish League Cup Winners' medal had been added to the Mackay trophy collection before his move to Spurs. It took Mackay no time at all to settle in. He may have lacked great pace, but his dynamic, never-say-die spirit and hand-clapping infectious enthusiasm for the game dovetailed perfectly with the more cultured play of his half-back partner, Danny Blanchflower. Strong and brave with enormous stamina, it was the shuddering power of Mackay's tackling, the drive and commitment in every crunching challenge that immediately caught the eye. But this tended to obscure his deft footballing skills and calm, accurate passing under pressure, which, coupled with a knack of scoring vital goals, knitted perfectly into Spurs style of play. A Scotland regular and a crucial member of Spurs' famous 1961 "Double" side and the 1962 FA Cup winning team, injury forced Mackay to miss the European Cup-Winners' Cup Final of 1963. The latter competition was not kind to him, for in December 1963 his leg was broken at Old Trafford in only the second match of Spurs' bid to retain the trophy. He was out of action for the rest of the season, but even worse was to follow. The next September, after just one first team friendly and three reserve outings, the same leg was broken again and there were widespread concerns as to whether he would play again. However, the fierce determination Mackay showed on the pitch now came through off it. By August 1965 he was back in League action, tackling as hard as ever and, if it were possible, perhaps even more inspirational. Taking over as skipper, he led Spurs to victory in the 1967 FA Cup Final against Chelsea. A year later, as a reward for his sterling service, he was allowed to move to Derby County for a nominal £5,000 fee. In total he won 18 full caps, played twice for a Scotland XI against the Scottish League and represented the Football League twice in his time with Spurs. At Derby he moved to a central defensive role and led the Rams to the Second Division title in 1968-69, a feat that helped earn him the Football Writers' Association Player of the Year award for 1969 along with Tony Book. After helping Derby establish themselves in the First Division, Mackay moved to Swindon Town as player-manager, had eleven months as manager of Nottingham Forest and, when his former Derby boss Brian Clough left the Baseball Ground, Mackay replaced him. He inherited a terrible situation at Derby, with the players up in arms over Clough's controversial departure, continual boardroom disputes and stories of efforts to engineer Clough's return. Again Mackay showed the courage that had made him such an exceptional player. He rode out the storm and steered Derby to the League Championship in 1974-75. He left Derby in November 1976 and after the first unsuccessful spell of his career at Walsall, took up the post as manager of the Al Arabi Sporting Club of Kuwait. He spent nine successful years coaching in the Near East with Al Arabi and the Alba Shabab club of Dubai, before returning to the Football League as Doncaster Rovers' manager, but soon left after a dispute over the sale of young players. Mackay then took on the role of general manager at Birmingham City but, unable to get the Blues out of the Third Division, resigned in January 1991 and went back to coaching in the Middle East. Mackay was the first player to appear for both the Scottish League against the Football League and the Football League against the Scottish League, when he played for the Football League against the Scots in March 1960.

Appearances:
League: 268 apps. 42 gls.
FA Cup: 33 apps. 4 gls.
Euro: 17 apps. 5 gls.
Others: 44 (2) apps. 12 gls,
Total: 362 (2) apps. 63 gls.

MADDEN, John

Role: Centre-forward 1897-98
Born: Dumbarton, 11th June 1865
Died: Prague, Czechoslovakia, 17th April 1948

CAREER: Dumbarton Albion 1884/Dumbarton Hibernian cs. 1885/Dumbarton Nov 1886/Gainsborough Trinity cs. 1887/Grimsby Town 1887/Dumbarton by Mar 1888/Celtic Aug 1889/Sheffield Wednesday Aug 1892/Celtic Aug 1892/Dundee Sep 1897/**SPURS** Dec 1897/Slavia Prague (Czechoslovakia) player-coach cs. 1898, coach Feb 1905-Jun 1930.

Debut v Rushden (UL) (h) 8.1.1898

John Madden was a member of Dumbarton's 1887 Scottish Cup Final side but it was at Celtic that his footballing talent really blossomed and he developed into one of the most important players in their early history. A centre-forward who could also operate at outside-right, he was a continual danger in front of goal with neat and clever touches and an eager eye for the half-chance. With Celtic he appeared in the first match of the 1892 Scottish Cup Final but was unable to play as they won the replay, and had to settle for loser's medals in 1893 and 1894. However, he partly made up for those disappointments by helping Celtic take the Scottish League title in 1893, 1894 and 1896. He won two Scottish caps, scoring four goals against Wales in March 1893 and another against the Welsh in March 1895. He also made four appearances for the Scottish League. Spurs

secured his transfer from Dundee in December 1897 but by then he was past his best and only stayed until the end of the season. When released he joined the Slavia club of Prague as player/coach and spent the rest of his life in Prague winning the Czech League title in 1925, 1929 and 1930 and the Czech Cup in 1908 and 1912. A legend in Czechoslovakia, even in his seventies and unable to walk he used to take training whilst sitting in a wheelchair on the touchline. In the summer of 1892 Madden was reported to have joined Sheffield Wednesday. He only played in one practise match. Immediately after the game he was "persuaded" to return to Celtic by a Roman Catholic priest!

Appearances:
Southern: 2 apps.
Others: 6 apps.
Total: 8 apps. 0 gls.

MADDISON, George

Role: Goalkeeper 1922-24
6ft. 13st.6lbs.
Born: Birtley, County Durham, 14th August 1902
Died: Hull, 18th May 1959

CAREER: Birtley Colliery/**SPURS** trial and perm Nov 1922/Hull City Jun 1924/retired 1938.

Debut v Bolton Wanderers (FL) (a) 11.4.1923

Geordie Maddison was signed from Birtley Colliery FC of the Northern Alliance in November 1922, having originally joined Spurs that month on trial. During his trial period Spurs' reserve 'keeper Bill Jacques was taken ill and Maddison was taken on to provide cover for first choice 'keeper Herbert Blake. He was not called upon for first team duty until April 1923 when he made his League debut at Bolton, but he played for the remainder of the season and by the next was first choice. With the signing of Bill Hinton in May 1924, Maddison was released and moved to Hull City where he became one of the League's most consistent and reliable 'keepers. In view of the problems experienced with the goalkeeping position over the next few years at White Hart Lane, it was perhaps a hasty decision Spurs had cause to regret more than once. Maddison was a member of Hull's Third Division (North) winning team of 1933 and spent 14 years with the Humberside club, only retiring in 1938 after a serious injury. Maddison's son, also named George, was a goalkeeper with Aldershot and York City in the late 1940s and early 1950s.

Appearances:
League: 40 apps.
FA Cup: 1 app.
Others: 7 apps.
Total: 48 apps. 0 gls.

MAGHOMA, Jacques Ilonda

Role: Midfielder 2007-08
5ft.9ins. 12st.4lbs.
Born: Lubumbashi, Congo, 23rd October 1987

CAREER: SPURS scholar Jul 2004, pro. Jul 2005/Leeds United trial Sep 2008/Hereford United trial Jul 2009/Burton Albion trial and perm. Jul 2009/Sheffield Wednesday Jun 2013/Birmingham City Jun 2015.

Debut v Stevenage Borough (sub) (Fr) (a) 7.7.2007

An attacking midfielder of power and promise, Jacques Maghoma progressed from the youth teams to become a regular at reserve level, but apart from three substitute appearances in pre-season friendlies was unable to progress any further with Spurs. Not helped by persistent injuries, he was released in May 2009 and eventually joined League newcomers, Burton Albion. In four years, he became a regular and helped Burton establish themselves in the League. Attracting attention from more established and higher level clubs, Maghoma left Burton when his contract expired in July 2013 and joined Sheffield Wednesday. He proved a crucial part of Wednesday's midfield until surprisingly released after two years, when Birmingham City were quick to take him on. Whilst with Burton, Maghoma took his talents to the international stage. After one game for DR Congo at B level in May 2010, he made his full debut against Saudi Arabia the same month. It was to be another five years before he represented his country again, but now appears to have established himself in the national squad. His brother, Christian, is a promising central defender working his way through Spurs' youth structure with another brother, Paris, also at the Academy.

Appearances:
Others: (3) apps.
Total: (3) apps. 0 gls.

MAHER, Kevin Andrew

Role: Midfield 1997-1998
6ft. 12st.11lbs.
Born: Ilford, Essex, 17th October 1976

CAREER: Cannon Palmer School/Redbridge United Boys Club/Redbridge Schools/Essex Schools/Republic of Ireland Schools/**SPURS** trainee Jul 1993, pro. Jul 1995/Southend United Jan 1998/Oldham Athletic Jul 2008/Gillingham Jun 2009/Yeovil Town trial Jul 2011/Dagenham & Redbridge Aug 2011/Bray Wanderers Aug 2013/Whitehawk Dec 2013-Mar 2014/Southend United coach Apr 2014/Chelmsford City head coach Jun 2014, temp. manager Jan 2016/Southend United asst. Academy Professional Development Stage Coach Oct 2015.

Debut v Faaberg (sub) (Fr) (a) 17.7.1997

Ilford born Kevin Maher was a tidy midfield player never afraid to make a tackle and with a fair amount of skill. A Republic of Ireland Under-21 and "B" cap, he played in all four matches of Spurs' pre-season tour to Norway in 1997 but made just one more substitute appearance before being released on a free transfer to join Southend United. Over ten years he made more than 400 appearances for the Essex club, a consistent, reliable, permanent fixture in the centre of midfield. Reaching the veteran stage, Maher was released in May 2008 but he still had enough to offer for Oldham Athletic, Gillingham and Dagenham and Redbridge to make good use of his services before he set out on a coaching career.

Appearances:
Others: 2 (3) apps.
Total: 2 (3) apps. 0 gls.

MAHORN, Paul Gladstone

Role: Striker 1992-1996
5ft.10ins. 13st.4lbs.
Born: Whipps Cross, 13th August 1973

CAREER: SPURS trainee Mar 1990, pro. Jan 1992/(Port Vale loan Aug 1993)/(Fulham loan Sep 1993)/(Burnley loan Mar 1996)/(Brentford loan Mar 1997)/released Mar 1998/Port Vale trial Mar 1998/Stevenage Borough trial Aug 1998/Cambridge United trial and perm. Nov 1998/(Bishops Stortford loan Nov 1998)/Cambridge City May 1999/Enfield trial Aug 1999/Boreham Wood trial Aug 1999.

Debut v Swindon Town (PL) (a) 22.1.1994
(Lazio (sub) (Fr) (a) 23.9.1992)

Well-built, strong, muscular and with a sharp burst of pace, Paul Mahorn had all that was needed to be a quality central striker but he lacked one crucial attribute, good luck. First given an opportunity in January 1994 having gathered some experience of League action on loan to Port Vale and Fulham, he was clearly highly thought of, for despite several lengthy injury absences there was rarely any suggestion of him being discarded. Mahorn played in three successive games in September 1997 in the absence of Les Ferdinand, but had little luck in front of goal and appeared sadly lacking in confidence. Released in March 1998, he was unable to find another League club and slipped into non-League circles where he played for a short time before leaving the game.

Appearances:
League: 3 apps.
FA Cup: (1) app.
FL Cup: (1) apps. 1 gl.
Others: 10 (7) apps.
Total: 13 (9) apps. 1 gl.

MAIR, Robert

Role: Half-back 1896-97
Born: Glasgow, 14th April 1875
Died: Gartcosh, Lanarkshire, 8th April 1939

CAREER: Glenboig/**SPURS** Nov 1896/released cs. 1897.

Debut v Reading (SL) (a) 5.12.1896
(Blackpool (Fr) (h) 21.11.1896)

An inexperienced Scottish junior who had played for the Glenboig club, Robert Mair was signed by Spurs in November 1896. He spent most of the season as virtual first choice reserve for any of the half-back positions, making 19 first team appearances before his release at the end of the season.

Appearances:
League: 2 apps.
Others: 17* apps.
Total: 19 apps. 0 gls.
*Includes 1 abandoned match.

MALBRANQUE, Steed

Role: Midfield 2006-08
5ft.8ins. 12st.0lbs.
Born: Mouscron, Belgium 6th January 1980

CAREER: US Oyonnax (France) 1991/Montpelier (France) 1994/Olympique Lyonnais (France) 1997/Fulham Aug 2001/**SPURS** Aug 2006/Sunderland Jul 2008/AS Saint-Étienne (France) Aug-Sep 2011/Olympique Lyonnais (France) trial and perm. Aug 2012/SM Caen (France) Jun 2016.

Debut v Port Vale (FLC) (h) 8.11.2006

A wide midfield schemer, Steed Malbranque had spent five years at Fulham giving a continual string of impressive performances before moving to Spurs. Born in Belgium but raised in France, he had first shown his range of talents at Olympique Lyonnais, establishing himself as a regular by the age of 21 and representing France at Under-21 level. Fulham reportedly paid £5 million to take him to Craven Cottage. Although that was twice the amount Spurs supposedly paid for his transfer five years later, Fulham still got fantastic value for their money. Malbranque proved one of the most influential players as they consolidated their place in the Premier League, his unique brand of wing play attractive as well as effective. Spurs had the pace of Aaron Lennon to call upon, but Martin Jol recognised the need for someone with Malbranque's talents on the opposite flank. At his best breaking forward down the wing and cutting inside, Malbranque was injured when Spurs signed him. It was to be three months before he was fit to make his debut but once in the team Malbranque was rarely left out. Not only combining pace with trickery, but adding a tireless work ethic that saw him tracking back as much as thrusting forward, he was one of the club's most consistent and reliable performers, a highly regarded member of the 2008 Worthington Cup-winning side. With Juande Ramos, looking to rebuild the squad he inherited from Jol, Malbranque, along with Teemu Tainio and Pascal Chimbonda, moved to Sunderland after only two years at White Hart Lane.

Every bit as reliable and effective on Wearside as he had been in London, Malbranque had three years with Sunderland before returning to France. Initially signing for St Etienne, his contract was terminated by mutual consent after only three weeks amid unfounded rumours of his retirement. Out of the game for twelve months, he then returned to his first club, Olympique Lyonnais.

Appearances:
League: 53 (9) apps. 6 gls.
FA Cup: 7 (2) apps. 1 gl.
FL Cup: 9 apps. 2 gls.
Euro: 13 (3) apps. 3 gls.
Others: 6 (1) apps.
Total: 88 (15) apps. 12 gls.

MALCOLM, Michael Dwaynee

Role: Striker 2004-05
5ft.8ins. 12st.0lbs.
Born: Harrow, Middlesex, 13th October 1985

CAREER: Bellmont United/Brent Schools/Middlesex Schools/Wycombe Wanderers/**SPURS** Schoolboy Mar 2000, Scholar Jul 2002, pro. Oct 2002/released May 2005/Stockport County trial Jul 2005, perm. Aug 2005, released May 2007/Dagenham & Redbridge trial Jul 2007/Kettering Town Aug 2007/Rushden & Diamonds Sep 2007/Thurrock Dec 2007/Weymouth Jan 2008/(Luton Town trial Jul 2008)/Crawley Town loan Nov

2008, perm May 2009/(Hayes & Yeading United loan Aug 2010)/ Farnborough Dec 2010/Lewes Jul 2011/Bromley Feb 2012/ Whitehawk Jan 2013/Maidenhead United Jun 2013/Wealdstone Jan-Oct 2014/St Albans City Jan 2015/Hayes & Yeading United Aug 2015/ Cambridge City Aug 2015/Staines Town Dec 2015/Cray Wanderers Feb 2016/ Chalfont St Peters Jul 2016/Barton Rovers Nov 2016..

Debut v Falkenburgs (sub) (Fr) (a) 13.7.2004

Spurs signing of Michael Malcolm as a schoolboy in March 2000 was a controversial deal, for the 15-year old had not even played for Wycombe Wanderers' youth team. The deal had a potential value to Wycombe of £1 million, £10,000 on his signing to be followed by stage payments depending on the player's progress. As it was, no further payments were ever made. Malcolm's only senior appearances for Spurs came in the 2004 pre-season when Frank Arnesen and Jacques Santini took every opportunity to have a look at the players on Spurs' books. Released at the end of that season, Malcolm earnt himself a deal with Stockport County and while not a prolific scorer was a target for Werder Bremen in January 2007. Unfortunately for Malcolm, nothing came of the German's interest and six months later he was released by Stockport. Since then Malcolm has moved around non-League circles.

Appearances:
Others: 1 (3) apps.
Total: **1 (3) apps. 0 gls.**

MANLEY, Thomas Ronald

Role: Half-back 1943-44
6ft.1ins. 12st.5lbs.
Born: Northwich, Cheshire, 7th December 1912
Died: Brentwood, Essex, 4th July 1988

CAREER: Brunner Monds/Norley United/Northwich Victoria Apr 1930/ Manchester United am. Sep 1930, pro. May 1931/Brentford Jul 1939/ (guest for Blackpool, Chester, Fulham, Manchester United, Norwich City, Nottingham Forest and **SPURS** during World War Two)/Northwich Victoria manager Mar-Oct 1954.

Debut v Aldershot (FLS) (a) 22.1.1944

Tommy Manley started his football career as a half-back with Brunner Monds, moved to outside-right with Northwich Victoria and played for Manchester United at inside-forward before reverting back to the half-back line. A member of United's promotion winning team of 1937-38 he was tipped as a possible England player of the future at the time of his transfer to Brentford but any hopes of an international career were shattered by the outbreak of war. He made one guest appearance for Spurs during the War in January 1944 when he played right-half in a Football League South match at Aldershot. After the war he spent four years with Brentford before retiring to run a public house back in Cheshire but later had a short spell as manager of Northwich Victoria.

Appearances:
Others: 1 app.
Total: 1 app. 0 gls.

MANNING, Gordon S

Role: Goalkeeper 1907-08

5ft.11ins. 11st.0lbs.
Born: Prescot, Lancashire, 17th May 1895
Died: St Helens, Lancashire, 23rd December 1963

CAREER: Aston Town/Preston North End/**SPURS** May 1907/released cs. 1908.

Debut v New Brompton (SL) (h) 21.9.1907
(Ostend (Fr) (a) 26.5.1907)

Gordon Manning was manager Fred Kirkham's first signing for Spurs when he joined the club from Preston North End where he had spent his time as third choice 'keeper. Originally expected to provide cover for Jack Whitbourne, he made his first team debut on an end of season trip to Belgium. The team that played Fulham on 20th May 1907 is still not known, but he certainly played against Ostend six days later. He replaced Whitbourne for his first senior match in September 1907 and remained first choice 'keeper for the whole of the season, at the end of which he was released.

Appearances:
Southern: 33 apps.
FA Cup: 1 app.
Others: 15 apps.
Total: 49 apps. 0 gls.

MANNION, Wilfred John

Role: Inside-forward 1941-42
5ft.5ins. 11st.0lbs.
Born: South Bank, North Yorkshire, 16th May 1918
Died: Redcar, Cleveland 14th April 2000

CAREER: South Bank St Peters/Middlesbrough am. Sep 1936, pro. Jan 1937/(guest for Bournemouth and Boscombe Athletic and **SPURS** during World War Two)/retired Jun 1954/Hull City Dec 1954/Poole Town Sep 1955-Mar 1956/Cambridge United Aug 1956/Kings Lynn May 1958/ Haverhill Rovers Oct 1958-cs. 1959/Earlestown player-manager Oct 1960-Oct 1962.

Debut v Crystal Palace (LWL) (a) 31.1.1942

Wilf Mannion is regarded as one of England's greatest post-war inside-forwards, a strongly built, constructive, beautifully balanced player with immaculate close control, a dangerous burst of speed and good goal-

scoring record. After shining in Schoolboy football, he played for South Bank St Peters and then joined Middlesbrough making his League debut in January 1937. Within 18 months he was a regular in the Middlesbrough team and tipped for England recognition but then the Second World War intervened and, like so many of his contemporaries, his career was put on hold. He continued to play during the war, made four appearances for England in war-time internationals and represented the Football League against the Scottish League. After the war Mannion was at his peak, winning 26 full and two "B" caps", representing the Football League on seven occasions and playing for Great Britain against the Rest of Europe at Hampden Park in May 1947 when he gave probably the best display of his career. At the end of the 1947-48 season he was in dispute with Middlesbrough and refused to re-sign. He even took a job outside football but in those days Freedom of Contract was a thing of the future and after missing much of the season he was forced to give in and re-sign. He stayed with Middlesbrough until the end of the 1953-54 season when, with 99 goals in 351 League appearances he retired. However, he was tempted back to football by Hull City and spent half a season with them scoring the one goal he needed to complete his century. He then moved into non-League football with Poole Town, Cambridge United, Kings Lynn, Haverhill Rovers and Earlestown.

Appearances:
Others: 4 apps.
Total: 4 apps. 0 gls.

MANUEL, William Albert James

Role: Full-back 1987-88
Born: Hackney, London, 28th June 1969

CAREER: Hackney Schools/East London Schools/Inner London Schools/London Schools/**SPURS** YTS Aug 1985, pro. Jul 1987/Gillingham Feb 1989/Brentford Jun 1991/Peterborough United Sep 1994/Stevenage Borough Oct 1994/Cambridge United October 1994/Peterborough United Mar 1995/Gillingham Jan 1996/Barnet Jul 1997/Folkestone Invicta player-coach Jul 1999/Horsham Dec 2000/Grays Athletic Jan 2001/Tonbridge Angels cs. 2001/Bromley Mar 2002/Windsor and Eton Sep 2002/Bromley Nov 2002/Waltham Forest Jun 2003/Metrogas 2004/Stansfield Aug 2005.

Debut v Crystal Palace (sub) (Fr) (a) 26.4.1988

Billy Manuel never got past the reserve ranks at Spurs and his only first team outings were as a substitute in friendly matches. He did that twice, against Crystal Palace on 26th April and Barnet on 6th May 1988. Stuck in the reserves with little prospect of making a breakthrough he was transferred to Gillingham where he linked up with Keith Blunt, his former Spurs' youth team coach who was Keith Burkinshaw's assistant manager. Proving himself a more than competent performer with Gillingham he was transferred to Brentford where he played for three years before a free transfer saw him move to Cambridge United. On a week to week contract with Cambridge he was sacked in January 1995 having been sent off three times in five matches. He later played for Peterborough, Gillingham again and Barnet before moving into the non-League game and was still playing well past his mid-thirties.

Appearances:
Others: (2) apps.
Total: (2) apps. 0 gls.

MAPLEY, Percy Joseph

Role: Full-back 1903-05
5ft.10ins. 11st.9lbs.
Born: Poplar, London, 24th November 1882
Died: Poplar, London 1907

CAREER: West Ham United/**SPURS** Feb 1904/released May 1905.

Debut v Queens Park Rangers (LL) (a) 15.2.1904

Percy Mapley joined Spurs from West Ham where he had enjoyed a first season of senior football, but did not make much impression at White Hart Lane. He made his debut in a London League match at Queens Park Rangers soon after signing and finished the season with ten appearances to his credit. Retained for the following term he spent most of it in the reserves although he was not helped by breaking a small bone in his foot during February 1905. At the end of the season he was not retained.

Appearances:
Southern: 5 apps.
Others: 5 apps.
Total: 10 apps. 0 gls.

MARADONA, Diego Armando

Role: Midfield 1985-86.
5ft.5ins. 12st.4lbs
Born: Lanus, Argentina, 30th October 1960.

CAREER: Los Cebolittos (Argentina)/Argentinos Juniors (Argentina)/Boca Juniors (Argentina) loan Feb 1981-May 1982/Barcelona (Spain) Jun 1982/Napoli (Italy) Jun 1984/Sevilla (Spain) Sep 1992/Newell Old Boys (Argentina) Sep 1993-Feb 1994/Boca Juniors asst. coach Oct 1994/Sporting Mudiya de Corrientes (Argentina) trainer Oct-Dec 1994/Racing Club (Argentina) coach Dec 1994-Mar 1995/Boca Juniors Jul 1995/retired Oct 1997/Almagro (Argentina) coach Nov 2000/Boca Juniors Sports vice-president Aug 2005-Aug 2006/Argentina coach Oct 2008-Jul 2010/Al Wasl (Dubai) manager May 2011-Jul 2012/Deportivo Riestra (Argentina) spiritual coach Aug 2013.

Debut v Inter Milan (Fr) (h) 1.5.1986.

The greatest footballer in the world throughout the 1980s Diego Maradona was a true child star. He started playing football with a local neighbourhood team called Los Cebolittos (the Little Onions) and so determined were Argentinos Juniors to secure Maradona that they adopted the little team as one of their junior clubs. A member of their League side at the age of 15 he made his full international debut for Argentina against Hungary when only 16-years old, the youngest player to appear for his country. At 18 he led Argentina to success in the World Youth Cup and, already being hailed as the new superstar of world soccer, was transferred to Boca Juniors for £1 million. A surprise omission from Argentina's 1978 World Cup winning squad he was voted South American Footballer of the Year in 1979 and 1980 and at last got the chance to display his talents on the world stage in the 1982 World Cup in Spain. By the time the competition started he had joined Barcelona for a world record fee of £4.8 million but he had a disappointing competition. He failed to live up to expectations and allowed his frustrations to get the better of him in the second round match against Brazil when he was sent off as Brazil comfortably beat the defending champions 3-1. In his first season with Barcelona he helped them win the Spanish League, League Cup and Super Cup but he was never really at home in Spain and in June 1984 moved to Napoli for another world record fee of £6.9 million. He made his one appearance for Spurs on 1st May 1986 playing as a guest in Ossie Ardiles' Benefit match against Inter Milan. At the end of the following month he captained Argentina to World Cup success over West Germany proving himself a worthy successor to Pele and Cruyff as "The Greatest Footballer in the World". The following season he led Napoli to the Italian League and Cup "Double" and followed that with the UEFA Cup in 1989 and the Italian League title in 1990. Such was the importance of Maradona to Napoli that he continually had to play when far from fit and shot full of pain-killers. This did not help him retain the high standards expected of him and no doubt contributed to his poor performances in the 1990 World Cup when, although he helped a poor Argentinian team reach the Final, he was clearly well below his best. It may also have been an influential factor in his decision to retire from international football after the World Cup with 79 caps and 31 goals to his credit. Being recognised as the greatest player in the World may have its benefits but it must also have its drawbacks particularly in the "pressure cooker" atmosphere of Italian football. Those pressures seemed to get to Maradona in the 1990-91 season and must have had something to do with his bizarre conduct which first saw him walk out on Napoli and then suspended in April 1991 for 15 months after a routine drug test had revealed traces of cocaine in his blood. With the suspension he returned to Argentina announcing that he had retired from football but then joined Sevilla. A miserable year full of controversy saw him sacked by the Spanish club and he again went back to Argentina signing for Newells Old Boys although at first Sevilla refused to give him international clearance. Things did not improve and in February 1994 he was again sacked. His career seemed well and truly over but he was not finished yet and returned to assist Argentina in the 1994 World Cup Finals in the USA. Failing a drug test during the competition, Maradona was suspended from playing for 15 months in August 1994 and took to coaching but rarely staying long with any club. Continually courting controversy and a pale shadow of his former self he made yet another comeback with Boca Juniors in August 1995. Frankly it would be better for him to quit the game for good and leave his fans with the memories of what a truly wonderful footballer he had been but he played on until announcing his retirement from the game in October 1997. Maradona's younger brother, Hugo, played for Argentinos Juniors, Napoli, Ascoli, Rayo Vallecano and Rapid Vienna among others and another younger brother, Raul "Lalo" for Boca Juniors, Granada of Spain, Toronto Italia of Canada and Toronto Shooting Stars in the National Professional Soccer League-a six a side indoor game.

Appearances:
Others: 1 app.
Total: 1 app. 0 gls.

MARCHI, Anthony Vittorio

Role: Half-back 1949-57 and 1959-65
6ft.0ins. 11st.4lbs.
Born: Edmonton, North London, 21st January 1933

CAREER: Raynham Road School/Edmonton Schools/Enfield Schools/London Schools/Middlesex Schools/England Schools/Tottenham Juniors/**SPURS** am. Jul 1948, pro. Jun 1950/Juventus (Italy) Jul 1957/(Lanerossi (Italy) loan Aug 1957)/Torino (Italy) cs. 1958/**SPURS** Jun 1959/(Cambridge University coach)/Cambridge City player-manager Jun 1965-Mar 1967/Northampton Town manager Sep 1967-May 1968.

Debut v Grimsby Town (FL) (h) 22.4.1950

Tony Marchi was a schoolboy prodigy who appeared in Spurs' reserve team when only 15 and then, as an England Youth international, made his League debut as a 17-year old in April 1950. A tall, constructive wing-half he gradually developed and by the end of the 1954-55 season had taken over the left-half position vacated by the departure of the great Ron Burgess. A reliable ever-present for the next two seasons, Tony was appointed captain and, with an England "B" cap against Scotland in February 1957 to his credit, his future at Tottenham looked rosy. At this stage however, Italian outfit Juventus made a £42,000 offer, much too good for either the club, or Marchi, to turn down and Spurs reluctantly agreed to let him leave. He never played for "The Old Lady" of Italian football though. As they already had their one permitted foreigner he was loaned to Lanerossi. Within weeks of moving to his father's home country he was being tipped for Italian international honours but, his lone appearance for England "B" disqualified him from playing for Italy. After a season with Lanerossi and another with Torino he was ready to return home. Arsenal were very keen to sign him but, when he had left for Italy, Spurs had been shrewd enough to ensure the contract gave them first option on any transfer outside the Italian League and had no hesitation in paying £20,000 to bring him back. With Dave Mackay having taken Marchi's old left-half berth and playing so well alongside Danny Blanchflower, Marchi was unable to get back in the team and had to settle for an almost permanent back-up role for any of the half-back positions. Good enough to walk into most other First Division teams, he may not have received the public acclaim accorded to the first team regulars during the "Double" era, but his contribution to Spurs' successes in the early 1960s was always acknowledged within the club. The only major honour he won in his time with Spurs came when he stood in for the injured Mackay in the 1963 European Cup-Winners' Cup Final against Atlético  Madrid in Rotterdam and gave such a first-class performance that it was followed by an appearance for England against Young England. In June 1965, he left Spurs for the player/manager's job with Cambridge City and then had a year as boss of Northampton Town. He later owned a wallpaper business and was engaged in the building trade in Malden, Essex. The goal Marchi scored for Spurs' reserves at Southampton on 1st October 1951 gave him the distinction of being the first player to score a competitive goal under floodlights in England. He was the nephew of George Dorling.

Appearances:
League: 232 apps. 7 gls.
FA Cup: 16 apps.
Euro: 12 apps.
Others: 57* apps. 3 gls.
Total: 317 apps. 10 gls.
* Includes 1 abandoned match

MARJORAM, Arthur E

Role: Full-back 1895-97
Born: Brighton, Sussex, 1877
Died: August 1911

CAREER: Aston Villa am./Swanscombe/SPURS trial Nov 1895, perm Dec 1895/Gravesend United cs. 1896/(Northfleet loan 1896-97)/Swanscombe/Thames Ironworks Sep 1898.

Debut v Luton Town (Fr) (a) 7.11.1895

Marjoram made his first appearance under the pseudonym "Bach" for at the time he was with the Swanscombe club and they would have been upset to learn that Spurs were giving one of their best players a trial. He performed well in the game and Spurs offered him the chance to play in the FA Cup replay with Vampires fixed for 16th November but he was unable to turn out. He continued with Swanscombe for a month and then signed on for Spurs but played only two further friendlies that season. The following season he made only one appearance in a friendly having by that time joined Gravesend United although he also played on "loan" for Northfleet during the season. A Kent County player and at one time an amateur on Aston Villa's books he returned to playing for Swanscombe and later played for Thames Ironworks. Some records give his name as Marjeram.

Appearances:
Others: 4 apps.
Total: 4 apps. 0 gls.

MARKHAM, Ernest Sowerby

Role: Full-back 1892-99
Born: Edmonton, north London, September qtr. 1880

CAREER: Robin Hood/Ilford Sep 1893/Shaftesbury Rovers/Tottenham Thursday/Ilford/Gravesend United Mar 1896/SPURS Mar 1897/Ilford cs. 1897/(guest for SPURS)/Tottenham Thursday.

Debut v Kettering Town (UL) (a) 15.3.1897 (match abandoned) (Windsor & Eton (SA) (h) 4.3.1893)

"Bunks" Markham was a local lad who played for the Robin Hood club and Shaftesbury Rovers before spending the best part of his career with Ilford. He first appeared for Spurs in March 1893 and continued to assist Rovers the following season although he also made a few appearances for Tottenham Thursday and began his association with Ilford. Principally a full-back, he began the 1896-97 season at Ilford and played for Gravesend United before transferring to Spurs. Released at the end of the season he was reinstated as an amateur in August 1897 so he could again play for Ilford, but still made several "guest" appearances for Spurs in the 1898-99 season when he also once again played for Tottenham Thursday. He later emigrated to South Africa and was still playing in 1905. He was a member of a well-known local family of footballers who all played for Spurs. His brothers, Dick and Wall, played with him for Robin Hood, Shaftesbury Rovers and Ilford, where Wall was captain for several years. Of the three, Dick was probably the best, representing Essex County and also playing for Southend Athletic before finishing his playing days with Novocastrians. All three of the brothers made their first known appearance for Spurs in the Southern Alliance fixture with Windsor and Eton on 4th March 1893.

Appearances:
Southern: 3 apps.
Others: 16* apps.
Total: 19 apps. 0 gls.
*Includes 1 abandoned match

MARKHAM, Frederick

Role: Full-back or half-back 1892-97
Died: Southend, Essex, February 1902

CAREER: Robin Hood/Novocastrians/Ilford/SPURS/Shaftesbury Rovers/Gravesend United Mar 1896/Ilford Aug 1897/Southend Athletic/Novocastrians.

Debut v Windsor & Eton (SA) (h) 4.3.1893

A local lad whose family was well known in north London football Dick Markham made his first known appearance for Spurs in March 1893 in a Southern Alliance fixture against Windsor and Eton when his brothers "Bunks" and Wall also played their first known game for Spurs. At the time he and his brothers were associated with the Robin Hood club although Dick also played for Ilford. For the following season the Markham brothers switched their local allegiance to Shaftesbury Rovers but Dick continued to turn out for Ilford doing much to enhance his reputation. He played regularly in the Southern League in 1894-95 and 1895-96 and was probably the best of the brothers going on to play for Essex County. He assisted Spurs when needed but all his appearances bar the first were in friendly matches. In August 1896 he signed for Gravesend United and appeared for them in the Southern League although he still continued to assist Ilford on several occasions. He spent one year with Gravesend and in August 1897 was re-instated as an amateur so that he could continue to assist Ilford where his brother Wall had been appointed captain. He finished his senior career with Southend Athletic and then returned to local football with the Novocastrians. In early February Markham caught a chill that turned to acute peritonitis and despite an operation he died in Southend Hospital

Appearances:
Others: 12 apps.
Total: 12 apps. 0 gls.

MARKHAM, Stanley Henry

Role: Goalkeeper 1948-49
6ft. 2ins, 12st.0lbs.
Born: Lambeth, London, 12th January 1926
Died: Tooting, London, 5th August 2003

CAREER: Bermondsey Schools/South London Schools/**SPURS** Sep 1947/retired cs. 1951/Wisbech Town/Canterbury City 1953/Crawley Town May 1956, scout and Minors XI manager, secretary Dec 1967, manager-secretary Jan 1970, secretary during 1972-73-1997, vice-president

Debut v Chelmsford City (Fr) (a) 20.9.1948

21-year old Stan Markham joined Spurs having attracted their attention playing for the Grenadier Guards when doing his National Service. With the Guards he had started as an inside or centre-forward but had then taken over the goalkeeping position. In his four years with Spurs he made his only first team appearance in a memorial match for former Spurs and Chelmsford winger Fred Sargent only playing then because Ted Ditchburn was appearing for the Football League against the Irish League at Anfield. With Ditchburn the undisputed number one Markham never got a chance at first team level before sustaining a serious injury in April 1951 which necessitated an operation the following month. The operation was not a success and he retired to join the ground-staff. He later attempted a comeback in non-League football with Wisbech and Canterbury, finally joining Crawley Town where he gave them 37 years' service in various roles and became known as "Mr Crawley Town".

Appearances:
Others: 1 app.
Total: **1 app. 0 gls.**

MARKHAM, Wilfred

Role: Half-back 1892-97
Born: Edmonton, London, September 1877

CAREER: Robin Hood/Shaftesbury Rovers/City Ramblers/Ilford/SPURS.

Debut v Windsor & Eton (SA) (h) 4.3.1893

Like his brothers, Dick and "Bunks", Wall Markham made his first recorded appearance for Spurs in a Southern Alliance fixture with Windsor and Eton on 4th March 1893. Unlike his brothers however he was to play only one further game for Spurs, a friendly against Blackburn Rovers on 20th April 1897. He had started out with Robin Hood and Shaftesbury Rovers but also played for City Ramblers before making his mark as a member of the Ilford club. He played for Ilford for several years, rising to the level of club captain, but was always an amateur and never joined the professional ranks.

Appearances:
Others: 2 apps.
Total: **2 apps. 0 gls.**

MARNEY, Dean Edward

Role: Midfield 2002-06
5ft.9ins. 11st.2lbs.
Born: Barking, Essex, 31st January 1984

CAREER: Northwick Boys Club/Correston Royals/Island Boys Club/Cornelius Vermuyden School/South Essex Schools/**SPURS** scholar Jul 2000, pro. Jul 2002/(Swindon Town loan Dec 2002)/(Queens Park Rangers loan trial Jan 2004)/(Gillingham loan Nov 2004)/(Norwich City loan Aug 2005)/Hull City Jul 2006/Burnley May 2010.

Debut v Birmingham City (sub) (PL) (a) 16.8.2003
(AFC Bournemouth (sub) (Fr) (a) 25.7.2002)

Like so many youngsters attracted to Spurs, Dean Marney made the breakthrough to play a few first team games but had to move on in order to progress his career. A strong-running, hard-tackling midfielder with more skill than he was often given credit for, Marney joined Spurs as a nine-year old, worked his way up to professional level and gathered some League experience on loan to Swindon Town before his first taste of Premier League action in August 2003. After further loans to Queens Park Rangers and Gillingham, he returned to make an unforgettable impact in his first League game at White Hart Lane, scoring twice against Everton in a 5-2 win. That was to be the high point of Marney's Spurs' career. A loan to Norwich City ended early when he suffered a serious Achilles tendon injury and with Spurs investing in some experience midfield performers such as Teemu Tainio, Didier Zokora and Edgar Davids, Marney was allowed to move to Hull City. He performed well, helping his new club win promotion to the Premier League and remaining in the top flight for a year. Injury restricted his appearances as Hull suffered "second season syndrome" and relegation in 2009-10. Burnley were quick to secure his services and he has proved invaluable in the engine room of a team battling to return to the peak of English football.

Appearances:
League: 4 (4) apps. 2 gls.
FA Cup: (3) apps.
Others: 10 (13) apps.
Total: **14 (20) apps. 2 gls.**

MARPOLE, D W

Role: Full-back or centre-forward 1889-90

Debut v Vulcan (Fr) (h) 5.10.1889

Another player from the early days Marpole is only known to have played in two matches for Spurs. The first in October 1889 in a friendly against Vulcan when he played at right-back and the other on 2nd November 1889 in a London Senior Cup tie against Old St Marks when he played centre-forward.

Appearances:
Others: 2 apps.
Total: **2 apps. 0 gls.**

MARSHALL, Alan

Role: Full-back 1979

Debut v Bermuda Select XI (Fr) (a) 6.6.1979

Alan Marshall was another of the Bermudian players who guested for Spurs in the friendly against a Bermuda Select XI on 6th June 1979 at the end of Spurs' summer tour. He appeared as a second half substitute for Peter Day, the Spurs' secretary, who was called upon to play at left-back due to the number of Spurs' players who were injured or had returned home early.

Appearances:
Others: (1) app.
Total: (1) app. 0 gls.

MARSHALL, Ernest

Role: Half-back 1942-43
5ft.11ins. 11st.7lbs.
Born: Dinnington, Yorkshire, 23rd May 1918
Died: Pwllheli, Gwynedd, 1983

CAREER: Dinnington Athletic/Huddersfield Town trial 1934/Sheffield United May 1935/Cardiff City May 1939/(guest for Aldershot, Luton Town, Mansfield Town, Reading, Southend United and **SPURS** during World War Two)/Yeovil Town/Bath City Feb 1948/Trowbridge Town Dec 1951/Bath City secretary 1956-Jan 1967

Debut v Portsmouth (FLS) (a) 24.10.1942

Ernie Marshall was a Cardiff City inside-forward who had joined the Welshmen just before the outbreak of War from Sheffield United. He made his one appearance for Spurs in the Football League South game at Portsmouth in October 1942 playing at left-half. After the war he made just one League appearance for Cardiff before being released.

Appearances:
Others: 1 app.
Total: 1 app. 0 gls.

MARSHALL, William Henry

Role: Inside-forward 1931-32
5ft.8ins. 10st.8lbs.
Born: Hucknall, Nottinghamshire, 16th February 1905
Died: Hucknall, Nottinghamshire, 9th March 1959

CAREER: Hucknall Primitives 1921/Bromley's Athletic/Bromley United/Nottingham Forest Feb 1924/Southport Aug 1926/Wolverhampton Wanderers Mar 1928/Port Vale Mar 1930/**SPURS** Mar 1932/Kidderminster Harriers Jul 1933/Brierley Hill Alliance Aug 1934/Rochdale Aug 1935/Linfield Jun 1938.

Debut v Stoke City (FL) (h) 25.3.1932

Harry Marshall was a fairly experienced player signed from Port Vale towards the end of the 1931-32 season who had enjoyed his best days with Southport and Wolves. He made just one appearance in the Spurs' first team shortly after signing, replacing Walter Bellamy for the match with Stoke City. He failed to make the first team again and in May 1933 was released and joined Kidderminster Harriers. He retired in 1940 and worked as a miner in Linby Colliery and died while working down the pit. His brother, Bob, played for Sunderland and Manchester City and managed Chesterfield.

Appearances:
Others: 1 app.
Total: 1 app. 0 gls.

MARTIN, John Rowland

Role: Inside-forward 1942-45
5ft.10ins. 11st.4lbs.
Born: Hamstead, Birmingham, 5th August 1914

CAREER: Rugeley Grammar School/St Mark & St Johns College 1931/Combined London Colleges 1932/Cannock St Lukes/Hednesford Town Oct 1934/Aston Villa pro. Jan 1935/(guest for Aldershot, Birmingham, Nottingham Forest, Portsmouth, Queens Park Rangers, **SPURS**, Wellington Town and Wrexham during World War Two)/retired 1948/Hednesford Town manager cs. 1950-May 1952.

Debut v Charlton Athletic (FLS) (h) 12.9.1942 (scored once)

Born in the Hamstead district of Birmingham, John Martin played College football whilst studying in London for a career as a schoolmaster. On his return to the Midlands he was following his profession at West Hill School, Hednesford and playing for Cannock St Lukes and then part-time for Hednesford Town when he attracted the attention of Aston Villa. They persuaded him to sign professional although he still continued his teaching career. An inside-forward with an eye for goal he took time to settle to the professional game and it was only in the last season of pre-war football that he established himself as a Villa regular. The outbreak of war though put a promising career on hold. He played throughout the war not only for Villa and as a guest for other clubs but also for Football Association, Football League and All British XIs. He also represented England in war-time internationals against Wales in November 1939 and Scotland in May 1940. Stationed in London on National Service he played regularly for Spurs during the 1942-43 and 1943-44 seasons helping Spurs win the Football League South in the second. After the war he continued with Aston Villa until his retirement in 1948 when he returned to full time teaching, played hockey for Cannock and later spent two years as manager of Hednesford Town.

Appearances:
Others: 45 apps. 15 gls.
Total: 45 apps. 15 gls.

MASON, Billy

Role: Centre-forward 1884-90
Born: Elmham, Norfolk

CAREER: Star/**SPURS** cs. 1885.

Debut v Woodgrange (Fr) (h) 18.10.1884 (scored once)

In Spurs' earliest days they played their games on the open spaces of Tottenham Marshes and one of the clubs that occupied another of the pitches there was Star FC which had previously been known as Coleraine Park Amateurs. When Star folded at the end of the 1884-85 season several of their players joined Spurs and Billy Mason was one of the most long In Spurs' earliest days they played their games on the open spaces of Tottenham Marshes and one of the clubs that occupied another of the

pitches there was Star FC which had previously been known as Coleraine Park Amateurs. When Star folded at the end of the 1884-85 season several of their players joined Spurs and Billy Mason was one of the most long-lasting and successful. He had played for Spurs when Star were still going; it was quite normal for the local clubs to lend each other players, and his first known appearance was in October 1884 when he scored as Spurs lost 4-5 to Woodgrange. He played for Spurs for over five years and also served the club off the field as a member of the club committee and as secretary. He remained associated with Spurs in one capacity or another right up until 1898 when the limited company was formed.

Appearances:
Others: 24 apps. 11 gls
Total: 24 apps. 11 gls.

MASON, Ryan Glen

Role: Midfielder 2008-
5ft.10ins. 9st.6lbs.
Born: Enfield, Middlesex, 13th June 1991

CAREER: SPURS Academy Scholar Jul 2007, pro. Aug 2008/(Yeovil Town loan Jul 2009)/(Doncaster Rovers loan Aug 2010, Jan 2011, Jul-Nov 2011)/(Millwall loan Dec 2011)/(Lorient (France) loan Jan 2013)/(Swindon Town loan Jul 2013)/Hull City Aug 2016.

Debut v NEC Nijmegen (sub) (UEFA) (a) 27.11.2008

As a youth team player, Ryan Mason was viewed as a bright, goal-scoring midfielder who had the potential to go all the way. While he was given a few outings in Europa and League Cup games and did not look out of his depth, most of his experience was gained on loan to lower Division clubs. In the summer of 2013, just when Mason might have been expected to really push for a senior breakthrough, the arrival of established international midfielders pushed him right down the pecking order. Joining Swindon on a season long deal, it looked as though he would have to make a permanent move away from White Hart Lane if he was to make a career in top-fight football. Although injuries meant he did not play regularly for the Robins, he returned to Spurs a stronger, more determined character. Mauricio Pochettino recognised that Mason was not only a neat, hard-working, box-to-box midfielder, with natural ability, but he only wanted to play for Spurs. Eventually given his chance in the Premier League in September 2014, Mason immediately established himself, the likes of Paulinho and Mousa Dembélé finding Mason not just challenging them, but taking their place. Mason flourished in the knowledge his manager had faith in him. Not the biggest of players, his strength and an them, but taking their place. Mason flourished in the knowledge his manager had faith in him. Not the biggest of players, his strength and an aggressive edge to his game came to the fore and in March 2015 made his full international debut for England, playing against Italy. While injuries restricted Mason's appearances, Eric Dier and Mousa Dembélé made the central midfield positions their own. With the likes of Harry Winks and Will Miller pushing for promotion to the senior squad, Mason accepted the chance of a regular starting place at Hull City, the player first associated with Spurs as an 8-year old, joining the former Spurs' colony at the KC Stadium.

Appearances:
League: 37 (16) apps. 2 gls.
FA Cup: (1) app.
FL Cup: 4 (1) apps. 1 gl.
Euro: 6 (5) apps. 1 gl.
Others: 8 (5) apps.
Total: 55 (28) apps. 4 gls.

MASON, Thomas Lot

Role: Inside-forward 1911-12
Born: Portsmouth, 23rd November 1886
Died: Edmonton, north London, 22nd March 1954

CAREER: Tufnell Park/Tottenham Thursday/Barnet Alston/**SPURS** Dec 1911/Southend United Mar 1913/Sittingbourne cs. 1913.

Debut v Middlesbrough (FL) (h) 17.2.1912
(Clapton Orient (Fr) (h) 3.2.1912)

Tom Mason joined Spurs during the 1911-12 season, made seven League appearances and scored one goal before spending the following season in the reserves. Not seriously considered as a first team performer he was allowed to move to Southern League Southend United in March 1913, where he played until the end of the season, then joined Sittingbourne.

Appearances:
League: 7 apps. 1 gl.
Others: 1 app.
Total: 8 apps. 1 gl.

MASSEY, Frederick James

Role: Half-back 1907-09
5ft.11ins. 10st.4lbs.
Born: East Ham, London, 2nd November 1883
Died: Watford, Hertfordshire, 26th January 1953

CAREER: Leyton/**SPURS** cs. 1907/West Ham United cs. 1909.

Debut v Reading (WL) (h) 14.10.1907

Fred Massey had two years with Leyton before his move to Spurs in the summer of 1907. He spent a similar length of time with Spurs, but made only five senior appearances, just one of which came in a major competition of the time. He played three matches in the secondary Western League during his first season, but was unable to make the team for the senior Southern League matches. Retained for Spurs' first season in the Football League he stood in for Billy Minter against Gainsborough Trinity on 27th March 1909, but when the season was over was allowed to move to West Ham where he played for three years.

Appearances:
League: 1 app.
Others: 4 apps.
Total: **5 apps. 0 gls.**

MAYOR, J

Role: Inside-forward 1894-95

CAREER: Old St Stephens/(guest for **SPURS** Apr 1895).

Debut v London Caledonians (Fr) (h) 25.4.1895

Another player with Old St Stephens, Mayor's only appearance in Spurs' colours was in April 1895 when he played in a friendly against London Caledonians which lasted only seventy minutes.

Appearances:
Others: 1 app.
Total: **1 app. 0 gls.**

MAZZON, Giorgio

Role: Midfield or defender 1979-83
5ft.10ins. 11st.9lbs.
Born: Waltham Cross, Herts, 4th September 1960

CAREER: Lea Valley Schools/Cheshunt/Waltham New Town/**SPURS** pro. Apr 1979/Aldershot Aug 1983.

Debut v Birmingham City (sub) (FL) (h) 10.1.1981
(Oxford United (Fr) (a) 4.8.1979)

A career in professional football seemed to have passed George Mazzon by when the Hertfordshire Youth player took a job working for a builder's merchants. However, in his spare time he played for Waltham New Town and it was there Spurs noticed him. A defender or defensive midfield player, he made his League debut as a substitute against Birmingham City in January 1981, but whilst often on the fringe of the first team he never had the opportunity to play regularly. He consequently moved to Aldershot where he played consistently, over 200 games, until being given a free transfer at the end of the 1988-89 season.

Appearances:
League: 3 (1) apps.
FA Cup: 1 app.
FL Cup: (2) apps.
Others: 3 (9) apps. 1 gl.
Total: **7 (12) apps. 1 gl.**

MEADE, Thomas George

Role: Centre or inside-forward 1897-99
5ft.11ins. 12st.8lbs.
Born: Plumstead, London, 14th May 1877

CAREER: Strand/Woolwich Arsenal am. Nov 1893, pro. Oct 1894/**SPURS** May 1897/released cs. 1899/Fulham Dec 1900-cs. 1905.

Debut v Sheppey United (SL) (a) 4.9.1897
(Glossop North End (Fr) (h) 2.9.1897)

A regular goal-scorer in his three-and-a-half-years with Woolwich Arsenal, Tom Meade went straight into the first team on joining Spurs, but then had to be left out after what were described as "exorbitant demands on the part of Woolwich Arsenal". This curious hitch allowed Bill Joyce to establish himself as principle goal-scorer, and although Meade stopped with Spurs for two seasons, he was always regarded as a reserve. He left at the end of the 1898-99 season and later joined Fulham where he played for four years. Given a regular chance in their attack he showed great prowess as a goal-scorer and was particularly instrumental in helping Fulham win the Second Division of the Southern League in both 1902 and 1903. Unfortunately, they failed to make the First Division each time, being beaten in the "Test Match" play-off games.

Appearances:
Southern: 15 apps. 5 gls.
FA Cup: 2 apps. 3 gls.
Others: 15 apps. 8 gls.
Total: **32 apps. 16 gls.**

MEADOWS, Horace

Role: Centre-forward 1951-52

CAREER: SPURS am. May 1952/Hayes 1952-53/Hendon 1954-56.

Debut v Ipswich Town (Fr) (a) 5.5.1952 (scored once)

A centre-forward from the Watford area, Horace Meadows signed amateur forms for Spurs in May 1952 and immediately made his only first team appearance. That was against Ipswich Town in a match played at Portman Road for the Ipswich Hospital Charity Cup, when he scored once. That was his only involvement with Spurs for he did not even play for the youth or junior teams the following season. He re-surfaced at Hendon but made only three appearances in two seasons there.

Appearances:
Others: 1 app. 1 gl.
Total: **1 app. 1 gl.**

MEADS, Thomas

Role: Half-back 1929-35
5ft.9ins. 12st.6lbs.
Born: Grassmoor, Derbyshire, 2nd November 1900
Died: Chesterfield, Derbyshire, 30th January 1983

CAREER: Grassmoor Ivanhoe/Clay Cross Town/Matlock Town/Stockport County Nov 1923/Huddersfield Town Mar 1927/Reading Oct

1928/**SPURS** May 1929/Notts County Jun 1935/Frickley Colliery player-coach Sep 1936/Dinnington Athletic 1937/Frickley Colliery player-coach Sep 1937/Scarborough player-coach May 1939/Chesterfield reserve team coach circa 1945/Middlesex AFA coach.

Debut v Bradford Park Avenue (FL) (a) 31.8.1929

Tom Meads played as an amateur for Clay Cross and Matlock Town before turning professional with Stockport County. He joined League champions Huddersfield late in the 1926-27 season, played regularly until the end, but was unable to help them retain the title for a fourth successive year. They finished second, as they did the following season. Suddenly out of favour, he moved to Reading and it was from the Berkshire club that Spurs secured his transfer. He made his debut in the first match of the new season and proved a combative and regular left-half for the next five campaigns, helping Spurs climb out of the Second Division in 1932-33. He lost his place to Wally Alsford in December 1934 as Spurs slid back towards relegation, was not retained at the end of the season and joined Notts County. Meads brother, Jack, played for Chesterfield, Scarborough and Middlesbrough and another brother, James played for Mansfield Town.

Appearances:
League: 184 apps. 6 gls.
FA Cup: 5 apps.
Others: 7 apps.
Total: 196 apps. 6 gls.

MEARNS, Frederick Charles

Role: Goalkeeper 1903-04
5ft.10ins. 12st.8lbs.
Born: Sunderland, 31st March 1879
Died: Sunderland, 22nd January 1931

CAREER: Selbourne/Whitburn/Sunderland Jan 1901/Kettering May 1902/**SPURS** Mar 1903/Bradford City May 1904/Southern United Apr 1905/Grays United cs. 1905/Southern United Dec 1905/Barrow Mar 1906/Bury Apr 1908/Stockton cs. 1908/Hartlepools United 1908/Barnsley May 1909/Leicester Fosse Jan 1911/Newcastle City cs. 1913/West Stanley Jan 1914/Sunderland West End Oct 1919/Durham City trainer Aug 1923.

Debut v Queens Park Rangers (WL) (a) 5.10.1903
(New Brompton (Fr) (a) 23.9.1903)

Fred Mearns started playing football with local clubs Selbourne and Whitburn, before joining his home town club, Sunderland. Understudy to long-serving Scottish international Teddy Doig, he made only two League appearances for the Wearsiders, and after little more than a year joined Southern League Kettering. Given the opportunity of regular first team football, he proved a most reliable 'keeper and in under one season with Kettering was reported to have saved no less than 19 penalty kicks! In March 1903 Spurs secured his transfer to provide cover for Charlie Williams after George Clawley had made it clear he would be returning to Southampton at the end of the season. Such was Mearns' blossoming reputation, Spurs knew that if they waited until the season was over, other clubs would be competing for his services. In his one season at White Hart Lane the bulky Mearns never let Spurs down, but was unable to displace Williams, and in May 1904 was released. He then moved swiftly from one club to another, with his only major honour coming in 1910 playing for Barnsley in both FA Cup Final games. His travels continued until the First World War. After the War he was trainer to Durham City for a while before returning to his trade as a joiner. He died in a building site accident.

Appearances:
Southern: 5 apps.
Others: 10 apps.
Total: 15 apps. 0 gls.

MEATES, William Percival

Role: Goalkeeper 1899-00
Born: Bournemouth, Hampshire, 1871

CAREER: Eastbourne/Small Heath Aug 1895/Warmley cs. 1897/Richmond Association/**SPURS** trial Oct 1899/Nottingham Forest trial/Olympic by Nov 1900 still there by April 1901/Shepherds Bush cs. 1903.

Debut v Southampton (Fr) (h) 28.10.1899

Bill Meates made his one appearance for Spurs in October 1899 in a friendly with Southampton. Spurs' number one 'keeper George Clawley was injured only days earlier and Meates was given the opportunity to prove that he could stand in till Clawley recovered. He had started his career with Eastbourne and then signed for Small Heath where he played a dozen Football League games. After one season he was nothing more than a reserve for the Midlands club. When released he joined Warmley, but by the time of his one game for Spurs was assisting Richmond. Unfortunately, he failed to take his chance. Although Spurs won the game 4-3, it was clear Meates was not good enough. Spurs arranged for the well-known amateur Wilfred Waller to play in the next game while they signed David Haddow as Clawley's long term replacement. Although Meates later had a trial with Nottingham Forest he failed to make a career in top class football.

Appearances:
Others: 1 app.
Total: 1 app. 0 gls.

MEDLEY, Leslie Dennis

Role: Outside-left 1938-53
5ft.7ins. 11st.11lbs.
Born: Edmonton, London, 3rd September 1920
Died: London, Ontario, Canada, 22nd February 2001

CAREER: Latymer School/Edmonton Schools/London Schools/Middlesex Schools/England Schools/Tottenham Juniors/**SPURS** am. cs. 1935/Northfleet United 1937/Harwich & Parkeston 1938-39/**SPURS** pro. Feb 1939/(guest for Aldershot, Clapton Orient, Millwall and West Ham United during World War Two)/Toronto Greenbacks (Canada)/Ulster United (Canada)/**SPURS** Jan 1948/retired May 1953/Wanderers (South Africa)/Randfontein (South Africa) player-coach 1958-61.

Debut v Brentford (FAC) (h) 5.1.1946
(Arsenal (Fr) (Colchester) 17.4.1939)

A local schoolboy star, Les Medley played for Tottenham Juniors and Northfleet before joining the professional staff at White Hart Lane. The outbreak of World War Two gave him an earlier opportunity in the first

outbreak of World War Two gave him an earlier opportunity in the first team than might otherwise have been the case, and he played regularly in the first season of war-time football. Service in the Royal Air Force then took him to Canada where he spent much of the war and also met his wife. Returning to Spurs for the latter war years, he established his place in the first team, but his wife became homesick, and in November 1946 he emigrated to Canada. Medley played for Toronto Greenbacks and Ulster United, but it was now Medley's turn to yearn for the "Old Country" and in January 1948 he returned to both England and Spurs. He took time to re-adjust to English football and it was not until April 1949 that he was able to re-establish himself in the team. When he did, he made the left wing position his own, becoming one of the most important players in the fluent "Push and Run" team that won the Second and First Division titles in successive seasons in 1950 and 1951. A stockily-built, fast and direct winger, with a natural body swerve, he worked perfectly with Eddie Baily and Ron Burgess as an orthodox winger able to cross the ball with both feet, and the trio developed a triangular understanding on the left flank to rival that of Grimsdell, Bliss and Dimmock in the 1920s. However, it was more the unorthodox nature of his play that made Medley stand out, for he adopted a wandering "free-role" on the pitch and was always liable to pop up in the most unexpected positions. It was this unpredictable aspect of his play that helped him amass so many goals, especially from Alf Ramsey's flighted free-kicks, top scoring with 18 in the promotion side of 1950. On the First Division stage, his talent was soon noticed by the international selectors and he made his England debut against Wales in November 1950. It was the first of six full caps, four of which came with Eddie Bailey as his inside-forward partner, and Medley was never on the losing side. He also played for the Football League against the Scottish League in October 1951 and collected his last major representative honour when he played for the Rest of the United Kingdom against Wales in December that year. An automatic choice for Spurs for four seasons, he retired at the end of 1952-53 to return to Canada, although from 1958 to 1961 he was player/coach of the South African club Randfontein FC.

Appearances:
League: 150 apps. 45 gls.
FA Cup: 14 apps. 1 gl.
Others: 89 apps. 28 gls.
Total: 253 apps. 74 gls.

MEDWIN, Terence Cameron

Role: Winger 1956-63
5ft.9ins. 11st.8lbs.
Born: Swansea, Glamorganshire, 25th September 1932

CAREER: St Helens School/Oxford Street School/Swansea Schools/Wales Schools/Swansea Town am. 1946, pro. Nov 1949/**SPURS** Apr 1956/retired May 1964/Enfield manager 1964-65/Cheshunt manager 1965-67/Cardiff City coach 1967-69/Fulham coach 1969-70, scout 1970-73/Norwich City reserve team coach/Swansea City assistant manager 1978-82, scout 1982-83/Mumbles Rangers life vice-president 1959.

Debut v Preston North End (FL) (a) 19.8.1956 (scored twice)

Terry Medwin proved himself a very versatile forward with Swansea Town, occupying all the front-line positions. When transferred to Spurs on the last day of the 1955-56 season for £25,000, he was Swansea's leading scorer with 16 goals from the centre-forward berth. Although he did play in that role for Spurs, he will always be best remembered at White Hart Lane as a fast, dangerous winger with immense power in both feet and the ability to whip in telling crosses with either foot. He won his first cap for Wales against Northern Ireland in April 1953 and had three in total when he joined Spurs-but had not played for his country for three years. His First Division form soon earned a recall, and he made the first of his 27 international appearances as a Spurs' player against Scotland in October 1956. A Tottenham regular for four years, he was unfortunate to lose his place to Terry Dyson in the fabulous 1960-61 "Double" season, but, with 15 outings, still played an important role as deputy for either Dyson or Cliff Jones. Some consolation for missing the club's greatest triumph came in 1962 when he was a member of the team that retained the FA Cup, but only twelve months later he suffered a broken leg playing for Spurs against a NSAFL Invitation XI on a tour to South Africa. After a long fight to regain full fitness he eventually had to admit defeat. He retired to take up the manager's post at Athenian League Enfield. He later continued to work in football as a coach and scout until ill-health forced his premature retirement in 1983. Medwin spent his childhood at Swansea prison where his father, on Southampton's books in the 1920s, worked as a prison warder. Medwin's grandson, Josh, played for Barry Town.

Appearances:
League: 197 apps. 65 gls.
FA Cup: 13 apps. 7 gls.
Europe: 5 apps.
Others: 32 apps. 18 gls.
Total: 247 apps. 90 gls.

MEEK, Joseph

Role: Inside-forward 1935-39
5ft.5ins. 11st.1lbs.
Born: Hazelrigg, Northumberland, 31st May 1910
Died: Hazelrigg, Northumberland, 17th September 1976

CAREER: Bussadon/Newcastle Co-operative/Seaton Delavel cs. 1926/Bedlington United Jul 1927Liverpool trial Mar 1928/Stockton/Middlesbrough am. Jan 1931/Gateshead am. Feb 1931, pro. Feb 1931/Bradford Park Avenue Oct 1934/**SPURS** Mar 1936/Swansea Town Feb 1939/(Burnley, Grimsby Town, Lincoln City, Liverpool, Middlesbrough, Newcastle United, Nottingham Forest, Rochdale and Southport during World War Two).

Debut v Swansea Town (FL) (a) 31.3.1936

An outside-left at school, Joe Meek switched to the right wing after sustaining a foot injury whilst working down the pits, and played for Newcastle Co-operative and Seaton Delavel. Rejected by Liverpool as being "too small", he played as an amateur with Middlesbrough and Gateshead before being taken on the professional staff at Redheugh Park, where he moved to inside-right. He then joined Bradford Park Avenue

and it was from there Spurs secured his transfer, prompted by his FA Cup performances against them in February 1936. A regular goalscorer, he did not score on his debut, but in the next match bagged a hat-trick as Spurs beat Southampton 8-0. Although he played for the rest of the season and the majority of the next, the decision to move Willie Hall to inside-right relegated Meek to the reserves, from which he was unable to escape. He was transferred to Swansea Town and retired from playing at the end of the war.

Appearances:
League: 45 apps. 15 gls.
FA Cup: 6 apps. 1 gl.
Total: 51 apps. 16 gls.

MEGGS, James W

Role: Inside-forward 1892-94

CAREER: Erith/Royal Ordnance/City Ramblers/Royal Arsenal Sep 1889-1891/City Ramblers/**SPURS** Apr 1893/Royal Ordnance Factories Oct 1893/Bromley/Royal Artillery by Oct 1895/Northfleet by May 1896.

Debut v City Ramblers (Fr) (h) 1.4.1893

Jimmy Meggs was principally associated with City Ramblers when he made his appearances for Spurs, having previously played for Royal Arsenal. His first known appearance for Spurs was in April 1893 in a friendly with City Ramblers and his only other known outing that season was later that month in a Wolverton and District Charity Cup. The following season he played in only two friendly matches, scoring once, before his association with Spurs ended. In November 1898 he was reported to have gone to Ceylon.

Appearances:
Others: 4 apps. 1 gl.
Total: 4 apps. 1 gl.

MELIA, James

Role: Full-back 1898-01
5ft.11ins. 12st.4lbs.
Born: Darlington, County Durham, 2nd April 1874
Died: Darlington, County Durham, February 1905

CAREER: Darlington St Augustine's/Darlington Town/Stockton/Sheffield Wednesday Jul 1895/**SPURS** May 1898/Preston North End Jul 1901.

Debut v Luton Town (UL) (h) 5.9.1898
(Gainsborough Trinity (Fr) (h) 1.9.1898)

After two years as a Sheffield Wednesday reserve, Jimmy Melia joined Spurs as cover for Harry Erentz. He stayed for three years providing the big Scot with stiff opposition, frequently winning a first team spot on merit. Selected for the Southern League against the Southern Amateurs in a War Fund match in February 1900, Melia left Spurs in July 1901 and signed for Preston North End. He had few first team opportunities there. He fell ill and died in February 1905.

Appearances:
Southern: 38* apps. 1 gl.
FA Cup: 3 apps.
Others: 49 apps. 2 gls
Total: 90 apps. 3 gls.
*Includes 1 abandoned match.

MENDES, Pedro Miguel Da Silva

Role: Midfield 2004-06
5ft.10ins. 12st.4lbs.
Born: Guimarães, Portugal, 26th February 1979

CAREER: Desportivo das Aves (Portugal)/FC Felgueiras (Portugal) Jul 1998/Vitória Guimarães (Portugal) Jul 1999/FC Porto (Portugal) Jul 2003/**SPURS** Jul 2004/Portsmouth Jan 2006/Rangers Aug 2008/Sporting (Portugal) Jan 2010/Vitória Guimarães (Portugal) Jul 2011/retired May 2012.

Debut v Liverpool (PL) (h) 14.8.2004
(Trollhättan (sub) (Fr) (a) 17.7.2004)

Signed from Porto as part of the deal that saw Hélder Postiga return to his former club after a miserable season at White Hart Lane, Pedro Mendes was to fare only a little better than his former team-mate, though he was to write his name in Spurs' history in a way that will never be forgotten. A hard-working midfielder, who would be breaking up an attack on the edge of his own box one minute and probing for a weakness at the other end a minute later, Mendes made his name with his home town Vitória Guimarães. With two appearances for Portugal to his credit, he moved to Porto, a vital cog in the José Mourinho coached club that won the Primeira Liga and Champions League in 2004. Frank Arnesen and Jacques Santini recognised Mendes had the potential to be Spurs' midfield workhorse and made him one of the first of the flood of signings that followed their arrival. He started his first season at Spurs as a regular, but after injury found it difficult to recover his place and in January 2006 joined relegation threatened Portsmouth, along with Sean Davis and Noé Pamarot. Mendes proved a pivotal member of the Pompey team that avoided the dreaded drop and went on to win the FA Cup in May 2008. Only three months later he signed for Rangers, helping them win the Scottish League and Cup in 2009 before returning to Portugal with Sporting. After little more than a year, his contract with Sporting

was cancelled. He returned to Vitória Guimarães where he played for a final year before retiring after injury had caused him to miss a large part of the season. Mendes' name was written into Spurs' history in January 2005. Drawing 0-0 with Manchester United at Old Trafford and with the game in added time, Mendes tried an audacious shot from his own half. The ball should have been easily held by United 'keeper, Roy Carroll, but he fumbled it into the net before pushing it back into play. A goal was not awarded as referee Mark Clattenburg and his assistant were the only people in the ground who could not see that the ball was clearly two or three yards over the line.

Appearances:
League: 25 (5) apps. 1 gl.
FA Cup: 2 apps.
FL Cup: 2 (2) apps.
Others: 9 (6) apps.
Total: 38 (13) apps. 1 gl.

MESSER, Alfred Thomas

Role: Centre-half 1930-32
6ft. 12st.10lbs.
Born: Deptford, London, 8th March 1900
Died: Reading, Berkshire, 27th July 1947

CAREER: Mansfield Colliery/Sutton Town/Mansfield Town 1922/Nottingham Forest 1922/Reading Jun 1923/**SPURS** Jul 1930/Bournemouth and Boscombe Athletic player-coach May 1934/Thorneycroft Athletic coach Aug 1937/Oxford City coach.

Debut v Reading (FL) (h) 30.8.1930

Alf Messer had moved around the South and Midlands trying to make a name for himself with little success until joining Reading. A brave, strong defender who was at his best with his back to the wall, he spent seven years at Elm Park and helped Reading gain promotion from the Third Division (South) in 1926. Making his Spurs' debut in a 7-1 victory over his former club, Messer was almost ever-present in his first season as Spurs finished third in Division Two, but lost his place to the up-and-coming talent of Arthur Rowe early the following season. Unable to re-establish a place and dogged by persistent injury worries, he was not retained. In April 1934, he joined Bournemouth and Boscombe Athletic as player/coach. His playing career ending after just ten games due to injury.

Appearances:
League: 50 apps. 2 gls.
FA Cup: 2 apps.
Others: 4 apps.
Total: 56 apps. 2 gls.

METGOD, Johannes Anthonius Bernardus

Role: Midfield 1987-88
6ft.3ins. 12st.6lbs.
Born: Amsterdam, Holland, 27th February 1958

CAREER: DWS Amsterdam (Holland)/Haarlem (Holland)/AZ 67 Alkmaar (Holland) 1976/Real Madrid (Spain) Jul 1982/Nottingham Forest Aug 1984/**SPURS** Jul 1987/Feyenoord (Holland) May 1988, youth team coach Feb 1994, asst. first team coach, first team coach 2001/Portsmouth first team coach Nov 2008-Feb 2009/Derby County first team coach May 2009-Oct 2013/Colorado Rapids (USA) coach/consultant Jan 2014, perm coach Feb-Sep 2014/ADO Den Haag (Holland) technical manager Jun 2015.

Debut v Coventry City (sub) (FL) (a) 15.8.1987
(Exeter City (Fr) (a) 23.7.1987 (scored once))

Johnny Metgod started his career with DWS Amsterdam and Haarlem, but it was after joining AZ 67 Alkmaar that he really came to prominence. Helping AZ win the Dutch League and Cup "Double" in 1981, reach the UEFA Cup Final the same year, and retain the Cup in 1982 he collected 19 full caps. Best known as a tall, elegant midfield player, he then moved to Real Madrid where he built a reputation as one of Europe's top sweepers, famed for his powerful long-range shooting, particularly from free kicks. In his first season in Spain he helped Real to the final of the European Cup-Winners' Cup and collected two more caps. He then had three good years with Nottingham Forest, usually playing in midfield, where his quick and accurate passing skills where put to their best advantage in a team renowned for playing flowing football to feet. Joining Spurs for £250,000 he was expected to fill the immense void left by the departure of Glenn Hoddle, but had a terrible time at White Hart Lane. After playing for the Football League against the Irish League in September 1987 he was soon hit by a series of injuries that limited him to only five full League games and two in the Littlewoods Cup. It was a great shame Spurs' fans never saw the best of Metgod, for he was a player whose skills were ideally suited to football in the very best Tottenham traditions. With Terry Venables looking to build a team for the future and Metgod by then over 30, he left Spurs to return to Holland with Feyenoord. He helped Feyenoord win the Dutch Cup in 1991 and returned to Spurs early the following year when, operating as a sweeper just in front of the defence, he dictated play from deep and gave a superb performance as the Dutch club knocked Spurs out of the European Cup-Winners' Cup. Voted Holland's Player of the Year in 1992, he led Feyenoord to the Dutch title in 1993 before retiring to take up coaching. Metgod's brother, Eddy, played in goal for Sparta Rotterdam and for Holland at Under-21 level and another brother, Mark, had a brief career with Haarlem.

Appearances:
League: 5 (7) apps.
FL Cup: 2 apps.
Others: 7 (5) apps. 2 gls.
Total: 14 (12) apps. 2 gls.

MIDDLEMISS, Herbert

Role: Outside-left 1907-20
5ft.10ins. 11st.5lbs.
Born: New Benwell, Newcastle, 19th December 1888
Died: Brixham, Devon, 28th June 1941

CAREER: Walker/Stalybridge Rovers/Stockport County Sep 1907/**SPURS** Nov 1907/(guest for Birmingham and Coventry City during World War One)/Queens Park Rangers Jun 1920.

Debut v Brentford (SL) (h) 16.11.1907

Although Bert Middlemiss joined Spurs from Stalybridge, Spurs had to pay a transfer fee to Stockport County. Until a few weeks before the move, Middlemiss had been an amateur, but then signed professional forms for Stockport, just so they would benefit from any transfer fee paid. A rapid, raiding winger, always keen to cut inside and take a shot at goal, he went straight into the team and became an almost permanent fixture until the First World War, making more League appearances for Spurs before the War than any other player. Only Vivian Woodward scored more goals as Spurs won promotion to the First Division at the end of the 1908-09 season, their first in the Football League. Middlemiss was often on the verge of international honours, playing in four England trial matches. The only representative honour he won though, was in April 1910 when he played for the Football League against the Southern League. Unavailable for most of the war, he was past his best when normal football resumed and on his release in June 1920 joined Queens Park Rangers for their first season in the Football League.

Appearances:
Southern: 25 apps. 8 gls.
League: 248* apps. 52 gls.
FA Cup: 17 apps. 3 gls.
Others: 72 apps. 27 gls.
Total: **362 apps. 90 gls.**
*Includes 3 abandoned matches

"MIDO", Ahmed Hossam Hussein Abdelhamid

Role: Striker 2004-07
6ft.2ins. 14st.8lbs.
Born: Cairo, Egypt, 23rd February 1983

CAREER: Zamalek (Egypt) pro. 1999/KAA Gent (Belgium) Jul 2000/Ajax (Holland) Jul 2001/(Celta Vigo (Spain) loan Mar 2003)/Olympique Marseille (France) Jul 2003/AS Roma (Italy) Aug 2004/**SPURS** loan Jan 2005, perm. Aug 2006/Middlesbrough Aug 2007/(Wigan Athletic loan Jan 2009)/(Zamalek (Egypt) loan Aug 2009)/(West Ham United loan Jan 2010)/(Ajax (Holland) loan Sep 2010)/Zamalek (Egypt) Jan 2011/Barnsley Jun 2012, contract cancelled Jan 2013/retired Jun 2013/Zamalek (Egypt) head coach Jan-Jul 2014, director of youth academy Aug 2014/Ismaily (Egypt) manager Jul-Dec 2015/Zamalek (Egypt) manager Jan-Feb 2016 /Lierse (Belgium) technical advisor Jul 2016/Wadi Degla (Egypt) manager Nov 2016..

Debut v Portsmouth (PL) (h) 5.2.2005 (scored twice)

Mido burst onto the Egyptian football scene as a 17-year old, scoring four goals in three games for Zamalek and helping them win the Africa Cup-Winners' Cup. That was enough to earn him a transfer to Genk of Belgium, where he impressed so much in one season that he was voted the best African player in the Belgian top flight, Belgian "Discovery of the Year" and Egyptian Young Player of the Year. Such outstanding promise was recognised by Ajax, who were quick to invest in his talents. They reaped the reward as Mido marked his first season in Holland by helping Ajax win the Eredivisie and lift the Dutch Cup and Super Cup. Another personal honour followed as he was voted African Young Player of the Year. Success was all Mido had known in his short career and it should have continued that way, but perhaps he had won too much, too soon. He fell out with Ajax manager, Ronald Koeman, frequently criticised for a lack of effort in training and during games and continually facing disciplinary sanctions. It was the start of a problem that resurfaced frequently for the rest of his career. Mido's situation at Ajax saw him loaned to Celta Vigo before a permanent transfer to Olympique Marseille, but, unhappy playing second fiddle to Didier Drogba, within months Mido was expressing his unhappiness. Before the start of the next season he completed a €6 million move to Roma, Marseille recovering only half of what they had paid Ajax. Things went no better in the Italian capital in what was a season of turmoil for Roma, and with Mido rarely playing, he agitated for a move. While Spurs had Jermaine Defoe, Robbie Keane and Fredi Kanouté to call on, none of them were the bustling type of central striker, Martin Jol wanted. Mido was, and his services were secured on an 18-month loan deal. He started well, netting twice against Portsmouth on his debut and certainly adding some power to a forward line that while full of guile and trickery, all too often looked lightweight. With the departure of Kanouté, more responsibility fell upon Mido. Big and powerful, he found it harder to score in England than he had before, but he could never be ignored and his mere presence created room for others. He did enough during his loan spell to merit a permanent move, even though it meant him competing with Dimitar Berbatov. With the Bulgarian impressing from his first game, Mido again found himself second choice and did not take kindly to the situation. Allowing a weight problem to get the better of him, when Mido fell out with Martin Jol, all signs pointed to the exit. He left White Hart Lane in August 2007 for Middlesbrough and remained on the Teesside club's books for over three years, though most of the time he was on loan to one club or another. He even had another spell at Ajax, where Jol was head coach, but when Ronald De Boer replaced Jol, Mido was quick to bring the loan to an end. After a spell back with Zamalek, Mido had one more venture into English football. After one game in six months for Barnsley his contract was cancelled, and unable to secure a new club, he retired in June 2013. It was a sad end to a playing career that had begun so well and should have achieved so much more. Within a year, Mido was surprisingly appointed manager of his old club, Zamalek, the youngest manager in Egyptian football. He led Zamalek to third place in the League and Egyptian Cup success, only to be almost immediately dismissed. He took charge of Zamalek's youth set-up for a year then became manager of Ismaily. That was another job that only lasted six months, longer than may have been the case as he was continually in dispute with the board and resigned more than once. In January 2016 he was back as Zamalek manager. After 37 days he was sacked! On the international stage, Mido scored on his debut for Egypt against the UAE in January 2001. He went on to make a total of 51 full appearances scoring 20 goals, four of the goals coming in his twelve appearances as a Spurs player. He would have

won many more caps but for frequent disputes with managers and the Egyptian FA that often saw him suspended or "not available for selection". Mido has one connection with a football club that should last longer than any ever did during his playing days-he is Honorary Life President of Old Wykehamist FC.

Appearances:
League: 35 (13) apps. 14 gls.
FA Cup: 2 (3) apps. 2 gls.
FL Cup: 2 (2) apps. 3 gls
Euro: 2 (2) apps.
Others: 5 (1) apps. 4 gls.
Total: 46 (21) apps. 23 gls.

MILARVIE

Role: Full-back 1896-97

CAREER: Third Batt. Grenadier Guards/Royal Ordnance/(guest for **SPURS** Nov 1896).

Debut v Luton Town (Fr) (a) 16.11.1896

A member of the Third Battalion of the Grenadier Guards who also played for Royal Ordnance, Milarvie made his only appearance for Spurs in a friendly with Luton Town in November 1896.

Appearances:
Others: 1 app.
Total: 1 app. 0 gls.

MILLARD

Role: Forward 1891-92

Debut v Caledonian Athletic (LSC) (h) 10.10.1891

Millard is recorded as having played three matches for Spurs in the 1891-92 season, scoring two goals. His first known appearance was in October 1891 against Caledonian Athletic in the London Senior Cup. His other games were later that season, one in a Luton Charity Cup match and one a friendly. He scored once in each of those games.

Appearances:
Others: 3 apps. 2 gls.
Total: 3 apps. 2 gls.

MILLER, Leslie Roy

Role: Outside-left 1936-39
5ft.7ins. 11st.3lbs.
Born: Barking, Essex, 30th March 1911
Died: Braintree, Essex, 1st October 1959

CAREER: England Schools/Barking/Northampton Town am. 1929/Barking/Sochaux-Montbéliard (France) 1931/**SPURS** Sep 1936/Chesterfield Jul 1939/(Mansfield Town during World War Two).

Debut v Newcastle United (FL) (a) 12.9.1936

Whilst manager of Northampton Town, Jack Tresadern signed Les Miller as an amateur. He offered Miller professional terms, but was unable to meet the player's demands so Miller returned to Barking. He was not forgotten by Tresadern, and when the French club, Sochaux, approached him seeking new players, he immediately recommended Miller to them. After playing in France for nearly five years, Miller announced a desire to return to the UK and Tresadern, now manager of Spurs, was quick to make an approach. This time Miller found Tresadern's offer satisfactory and signed to become the first player to join a Football League club who had played professionally in France. A well-built, intelligent winger who relied on genuine speed and skill to beat his marker, Miller played regularly for most of his first season at Spurs. He then vied for a position with Colin Lyman during the next two seasons before moving on to Chesterfield. The war effectively brought his career to a conclusion, although during those times he continued to turn out for Chesterfield and also assisted Mansfield Town. In the 1935-36 season Les Miller scored no less than 60 goals for Sochaux.

Appearances:
League: 56 apps. 22 gls.
FA Cup: 9 apps. 4 gls.
Total: 65 apps. 26 gls.

MILLER, Paul Richard

Role: Central defender 1978-87
6ft. 12st.2lbs.
Born: Stepney, London, 11th October 1959

CAREER: Senrab/East London Schools/London Schools/Middlesex Schools/**SPURS** assoc. schl. Jan 1975, app. Apr 1976, pro. May 1977/(Skeid Oslo (Norway) loan Mar-Oct 1978)/Charlton Athletic Feb 1987/Watford Oct 1988/AFC Bournemouth Aug 1989/(Brentford loan Nov 1989)/Swansea City Sep 1990/Wingate and Finchley youth team manager.

Debut v Arsenal (FL) (a) 10.4.1979

Paul Miller is one of several home-produced Spurs players of the late 1970s and early 1980s who benefited greatly from a spell on loan to a Scandinavian club. Miller played for Skeid Oslo of Norway in their 1978 season and six months later was ready for his League debut. He slowly established himself in the first team and helped Spurs win the FA Cup in 1981 and 1982, reach the League (Milk) Cup Final in 1982 and win the UEFA Cup in 1984. It was Miller who headed the crucial away goal in the first leg of the Final against Anderlecht. He may not have been the prettiest or most constructive of players, but Miller's raw commitment to the Spurs cause could never be faulted. However, Miller's position in the team always seemed under threat with the signings of players such as Paul Price and Gary Stevens, the development of young players such as Gary O'Reilly, Ian Culverhouse and Simon Webster and the versatility of Gary

Mabbutt and Graham Roberts. A Spurs man through and through, he saw off all the challenges until David Pleat signed Richard Gough and paired him with Mabbutt in the centre of defence. With little prospect of a return to first team action, Miller moved to Charlton for £130,000 and helped them retain their First Division status before moving on to Watford and Bournemouth. Unable to maintain a place with Bournemouth, he had a month on loan to Brentford where he linked-up with his former Spurs' captain and Bees' manager Steve Perryman. In September 1990 he was given a free transfer and joined Swansea City but in March 1991 was again given a "free". He then went to work as youth team manager of Wingate and Finchley whilst starting out on a career as a financial consultant.

Appearances:
League: 206 (2) apps. 7 gls.
FA Cup: 30 (1) apps. 1 gl.
FL Cup: 22 (1) apps.
Euro: 23 apps. 2 gls.
Others: 92 (6) apps. 6 gls.
Total: 373 (10) apps. 16 gls.

MILLER, William Finn

Role: Midfielder 2013-
5ft.5ins. 10st.1lb.
Born: *Hackney, London, 8th June 1996*

CAREER: Leyton Orient/**SPURS** Academy Scholar Jul 2012, pro. Jul 2014/(Burton Albion loan Aug 2016).

Debut v Ledley King XI (Fr) (h) (sub) 12.5.2014

Will Miller has made only one first team appearance, and that as a substitute in Ledley King's testimonial match, but he certainly has the talent to go a lot further. A schoolboy with Leyton Orient, he was taken into the Spurs Academy and after playing in the former captain's game signed professional at the first opportunity. Settling to a midfield role, he has a delicate touch and lovely vision, running with the ball and timing its release to perfection. Midfield would appear to be the best position for him although he has often featured as a striker where his calmness stands out. At 5ft 5ins though, he may be too small to meet the demands made of modern centre-forwards, but there is always that role just behind the striker and Miller certainly looked at home there while on loan to Burton Albion. He looks set to have a future in the game, but should the fates dictate otherwise, he could always fall back on other talents. Before settling on football as a career he was a child actor, appearing in films and on TV.

Appearances:
Others: 1 (3) app.
Total: 1 (3) app. 0 gls.

MILLER, W

Role: Half-back 1891-92

Debut v Minerva (MSC) (a) 5.12.1891

Another of the players from a time when Spurs matches were recorded only in the barest detail, Miller was a half-back who assisted the club in 1891-92. His first known match was in December 1891 in a Middlesex Senior Cup tie with Minerva. He is also known to have scored once in four friendly matches.

Appearances:
Others: 5 apps. 1 gl.
Total: 5 apps. 1 gl.

MILLIGAN, Alexander Aitken

Role: Full-back 1896-97
Born: *Glasgow 13th November 1876*

CAREER: First Batt. Scots Guards/(Guest for **SPURS** Apr 1897)/Bristol City Oct 1897/Third Lanark Nov 1902/Beith May 1903/Swindon Town cs. 1903-1905/Haydon St WMC.

Debut v Everton (Fr) (h) 22.4.1897

A soldier in the 1st Battalion of the Scots Guards who also played for the Brigade of Guards, Milligan's only appearances for Spurs were in April 1897 when he played in a friendly against Everton and in the Wellingborough Charity Cup final. The following season he turned out regularly for the newly-formed Bristol City and helped them out for three years until re-enlisting and serving in the Boer War. After that War he played for Third Lanark before joining Swindon Town in the summer of 1903 playing there for two years.

Appearances:
Others: 2 apps.
Total: 2 apps. 0 gls.

MILLIKEN, James

Role: Inside-forward 1896-97

CAREER: Third Lanark Aug 1893/Leicester Fosse 1894/St Mirren Aug 1895/**SPURS** May 1896/Clyde Jun 1897.

Debut v Sheppey United (SL) (a) 5.9.1896 (scored once)

Jimmy Milliken first made his mark with Third Lanark. His form there earnt him a move to Leicester City, but in a year with the Foxes, he failed to make a senior appearance, He returned to Scotland with St Mirren, where he caught Spurs' eye. He was the regular inside-right in the 1896-97 season, as the club took its first steps into senior League football as part of the Southern League. He made a goal-scoring debut in Spurs' first Southern League match at Sheppey United, and played in the majority of matches that season until April 1897. At that point he was suspended, along with Wilson, McElhaney and Devlin, for unspecified "acts of insubordination". At the end of the season he was not retained and returned to Scotland to play for Clyde.

Appearances:
Southern: 19 apps. 6 gls.
FA Cup: 3 apps.
Others: 30* apps. 7# gls
Total: 52 apps. 13 gls.
*Includes 1 abandoned match.
#Includes 1 in an abandoned match.

MILLS, J "Scottie"

Role: Centre-forward 1893-94

Debut v 1st Batt Scots Guards (Fr) (h) 4.11.1893

In view of his nickname Mills presumably hailed from North of the Border, but apart from that nothing more is known of him. In his first game for Spurs against the 1st Battalion of the Scots Guards he was said to have "shaped finely and fed wings beautifully". He was first choice in the centre-forward position until the end of December. After that he only played in one more game and that was at half-back. His only competitive goal came in Spurs' only Amateur Cup tie of the season when they beat Vampires 3-1. They went no further in the competition, being unable to meet Clapham Rovers after they had been suspended as a result of the "Payne's Boot" affair that led to the club turning professional.

Appearances:
Others: 9 apps. 2 gls
Total: 9 apps. 2 gls.

MILLS, Leigh

Role: Central defender
5ft.11ins. 12st.4lbs.
Born: Winchester, Hampshire, 8th February 1988

CAREER: Swindon Town/SPURS Scholar Jul 2004, pro. Jul 2005/(Brentford loan Jun 2008)/(Gillingham loan Aug 2008)/released Feb 2009/Winchester City Jul 2010/Eastleigh Sep 2012/Blackfield & Langley Jan 2013/Winchester City Jun 2013-Oct 2014, Jul 2015-Jun 2016.

Debut v Stevenage Borough (sub) (Fr) (a) 7.7.2007

An England Under-16 and Under-17 international, central defender Leigh Mills was viewed very much as "one for the future" when signed from Swindon Town. He had been with the Robins from the age of nine and worked his way through their youth ranks. He played for Spurs youth and reserve teams while winning caps at Under-18 and Under-19 level. His one first team appearance came in July 2007 when he went on as a substitute in a pre-season friendly with Stevenage Borough. That was as far as his Spurs' career went. Loaned to Brentford and Gillingham, he was released in February 2009 and, at first, gave up football. It was more than a year later that he signed for home-town Winchester City. Since then he has continued to play in the non-League game.

Appearances:
Others: (1) app.
Total: (1) app. 0 gls.

MILNE, S

Role: Centre-forward or half-back 1893-94

Debut v Chesham (W&DCC) (h) 27.1.1894

Another of the players from the 19th century about whom nothing is known, Milne was a centre-forward or half-back who played late in the 1893-94 season, scoring two goals in twelve appearances.

Appearances:
Others: 12 apps. 2 gls
Total: 12 apps. 2 gls.

MILNES, Frederick Houghton

Role: Full-back 1905-06
Born: Wortley, Yorkshire, 25th January 1878
Died: Leeds, Yorkshire, 1st July 1946

CAREER: Sheffield Wycliffe/Sheffield United am. May 1902/Sheffield Apr 1904/West Ham United am. Oct 1904/Pilgrims Sep 1905/SPURS am. Dec 1905/Manchester United am. Mar 1906/Leicester Fosse am. Feb 1907/St Mirren Mar 1907/Northern Nomads/Reading/Ilford cs. 1908/Norwich City Sep 1908/Pilgrims Oct 1909/Niagara Falls Rangers (USA) 1913.

Debut v Queens Park Rangers (WL) (h) 29.1.1906

An England amateur international, Fred Milnes was much sought after by all the country's senior teams, but is best known for his service to the famous Sheffield club. As an amateur he could play for any club he wanted to. This led to him appearing for several top names during his career, though he never formally signed for them. His first allegiance always lay with Sheffield, whom he helped win the Amateur Cup in 1904 when he scored one of their goals. He played a handful of Football League games for Sheffield United and late in 1904-05 played for West Ham. In September 1905 he was a member of the Pilgrims, a selection of England's best amateur footballers who went to North America on a tour that was one of the first efforts to popularise the game over there. When he returned Milnes signed Southern League forms for Spurs on the recommendation of his fellow Pilgrim, Vivian Woodward, but was to make only two appearances, both in the Western League. He toured the States with the Pilgrims again in 1909 and must have taken a liking to America. In 1912 he went to New York intending to emigrate to the States. Playing for Niagara Falls Rangers he was involved in the game's local administration until the end of 1915 when he was suspended indefinitely by the United States FA for "failure to satisfactorily account for the funds" of the Northwestern New York State FA. Further details are unknown, but Milnes returned to the UK.

Appearances:
Others: 2 apps.
Total: 2 apps. 0 gls.

MILTON, G W

Role: Inside-forward 1942-43

CAREER: Fulham/(guest for Aldershot, Brentford, Bristol City, Chelsea, Crystal Palace, Dunfermline and SPURS during World War Two).

Debut v Queens Park Rangers (Fr) (a) 17.4.1943

One of the junior players on Fulham's books, Milton's only appearance for Spurs was in April 1943 when he played in a friendly with Queens Park Rangers.

Appearances:
Others: 1 app.
Total: 1 app. 0 gls.

MILTON, Harold Aubrey

Role: Half-back 1903-05
Born: Hackney, 15th January 1882
Died: Islington, London, 14th March 1970

CAREER: University College School and Trinity Hall/Cambridge University/SPURS Mar 1904/Clapton 1904-05/New Crusaders 1905-09/Casuals/Corinthians 1909-12.

Debut v Brentford (WL) (a) 28.3.1904

Toby Milton was a Varsity player for Cambridge who helped Spurs out as an amateur for two seasons. Originally a winger, it was while at Cambridge University that he switched to half-back. As with many other players, it was his performances in the annual matches against Oxford University that drew him to the attention of football's senior clubs. A very strong, bustling style of player, Milton first signed for Spurs towards the end of the 1903-04 season. He went on to make three appearances, one in the Southern League, the other two in the Western League and enough to earn him a championship medal. Although he continued to be associated with Spurs, Milton was a solicitor and was not prepared to give up his career or his amateur status and only made two more appearances over the following two years. He initially preferred to play for Clapton, helping them to the Amateur Cup final in 1905, before throwing in his lot with New Crusaders and the Casuals. He also appeared for the Corinthians. The son of AG Milton, a famous Clapton player, he was a member of the Amateurs of the South team that played the Professionals of the South in an international trial match in January 1906 and later played for England in AFA internationals. During the First World War he won the Military Cross and the Croix de Guerre. In common with many "Oxbridge" gentlemen in the early years of the 20th century, Milton was an all-round sportsman. He played cricket for Southgate CC for many years and was good enough at the summer game to play three matches for Middlesex.

Appearances:
Southern: 1 app.
Others: 4 apps.
Total: 5 apps. 0 gls.

MIMMS, Robert Andrew

Role: Goalkeeper 1987-91
6ft.3" 13st.7lbs.
Born: York, 12th October 1963

CAREER: North Yorkshire Schools/Barnsley trial 1979/Sheffield Wednesday trial 1979/Preston North End trial 1979/Halifax Town app. Apr 1980, pro. Aug 1981/Rotherham United Nov 1981/Everton Jun 1985/ (Notts County loan Feb 1986)/(Sunderland loan Dec 1986)/(Blackburn Rovers loan Jan 1987)/(Manchester City loan Sep 1987)/**SPURS** loan Feb 1988, perm. Feb 1988/(Aberdeen loan Feb 1990)/Blackburn Rovers Dec 1990/York City trial Jul 1996/Bradford City training Jul 1996/Sheffield United trial Aug 1996/Crystal Palace non-contract Aug 1996/Preston North End Sep 1996/Rotherham United Aug 1997/York City loan Aug 1998, perm. Oct 1998, (St Johnstone trial Mar 1999) player-asst. manager May 1999/Mansfield Town Mar 2000/retired Jul 2001/Wolverhampton Wanderers goalkeeping coach Jul 2001/Blackburn Rovers goalkeeping coach Aug 2008-Dec 2012/Oldham Athletic goalkeeping coach Jul 2013/Bahrain National Team goalkeeping coach Feb 2014/West Ham United goalkeeping coach Oct 2014/Blackpool goalkeeping coach Jun 2015/Bolton Wanderers goalkeeping coach Aug 2015/Hull City goalkeeping coach Nov 2016-Jan 2017.

Debut v Manchester United (FL) (h) 23.3.1988

Bobby Mimms began his career with Halifax Town, but moved to Rotherham United without making the first team. He made his League debut in May 1982 and soon came under scrutiny from the bigger clubs, particularly after he played as a substitute for the England Under-21 side

against Israel in February 1985 and the Republic of Ireland the following month. He moved to Everton as cover for Neville Southall and, after a spell on loan to Notts County, returned to Goodison Park where his big chance came in April 1986. With Southall injured, Mimms stood-in and after gaining a further Under 21 cap, finished the season with an FA Cup runners up medal as Everton lost to rivals Liverpool. Although he began the following season in the team, the consistent Southall was always number one choice, and as soon as he was fit recovered his place. Only considered if Southall was injured Mimms, went on loan to Sunderland, Blackburn Rovers and Manchester City before Terry Venables decided the goalkeeping position at Spurs desperately needed strengthening and signed Mimms for £375,000. For his first Spurs appearance against Manchester United he was officially on loan, as technically that was the only way to gain official clearance in time for him to make his debut. Competent, but not really good enough to imbue defensive confidence, Mimms, along with the whole team, had a poor start to the 1988-89 season and although he started to show improved form after the signing of Erik Thorstvedt, he eventually lost his place to the Norwegian international. Mimms played a few games during 1989-90 when Thorstvedt was injured, before going out on loan to Aberdeen, but was forced to be content with a reserve position until his £250,000 transfer to Blackburn Rovers. In his second season he helped them win promotion back to the top flight via a Wembley play-off final. With England 'keeper Tim Flowers' arrival as Kenny Dalglish really began to spend Jack Walker's millions, Mimms found himself relegated to reserve and at the end of 1995-96 he was given a free transfer. He joined Crystal Palace as a non-contract player to provide cover while Chris Day, Palace's former Spurs' reserve, was on England Under-21 duty and then moved to Preston where he played for a year before returning to Rotherham. When he retired from playing Mimms took to coaching, being one of the first specialist goalkeeping coaches.

Appearances:
League: 37 apps.
FA Cup: 2 apps.
FL Cup: 5 apps.
Others: 20 (5) apps.
Total: 64 (5) apps. 0 gls.

MINTER, William James

Role: Inside-forward 1907-26
5ft.10ins. 11st.7lbs.
Born: Woolwich, London, 16th April 1888
Died: Tottenham, London, 21st May 1940

CAREER: Norwich City am. Nov 1905/Woolwich Arsenal am. Feb 1906/ Reading Jun 1906/**SPURS** Mar 1908, trainer Jun 1920, manager Feb 1927, asst. secretary Nov 1929.

Debut v Millwall (SL) (h) 7.3.1908 (scored once)

Billy Minter played two friendlies as an amateur for Norwich City before a brief but unsuccessful spell back in his birthplace with Woolwich Arsenal. He then moved to Reading and it was from the Berkshire club,

where he had been top scorer for two seasons, that Spurs secured his transfer. A well-built inside-forward who could be relied upon for his fair share of goals each season, Minter scored the first of over 100 senior goals for the club on his debut against Millwall. After helping Spurs win promotion from the Second Division in 1909 he was top scorer for the next three seasons, his goals playing a major part in helping Spurs maintain a place in the First Division. Absent for most of the First World War due to military service, he helped lift Spurs back into the First Division in 1919-20 although he was replaced by exciting young talent Jimmy Banks midway through the season. At the end of the campaign he announced his retirement from playing and took up the post of club trainer, although he still turned out in a couple of friendlies when injuries necessitated. He filled the role of trainer until Peter McWilliam resigned as manager and Minter was asked to replace him. In charge for almost three years, Spurs were relegated in his first full season. He took the failure to get the club back into the First Division so personally it made him ill, and in November 1929 he resigned. Spurs had put no pressure at all on Minter to quit, for his absolute dedication to the club was well appreciated and is best shown by the fact he was not allowed to leave. Instead, he was made assistant secretary, a position he occupied until his death.

Appearances:
Southern: 9 apps. 4 gls,
League: 248* apps. 95 gls.
FA Cup: 19 apps. 6 gls.
Others: 68 apps. 51 gls.
Total: 344 apps. 156 gls.
*Includes 4 abandoned matches.

MINTON, Jeffrey Simon Thompson

Role: Midfield 1991-93
5ft.5ins. 11st.7lbs.
Born: Hackney, London, 28th December 1973

CAREER: Hackney Schools/ Tower Hamlets Schools/ **SPURS** trainee Jul 1990, pro. Feb 1992/Brighton and Hove Albion Jul 1994/Port Vale Jun 1999/Rotherham United Mar 2001/Leyton Orient Jul 2001-May 2002/AFC Bournemouth trial Jul 2002/Rushden & Diamonds trial Jul 2002/ Southend United Jul trial 2002/Grays Athletic Aug 2002 /Canvey Island Aug 2002/ Chelmsford City Jul 2006/ Welling United Jul-Aug 2009/ Ware Nov 2012.

Debut v Everton (FL) (h) 25.4.1992 (scored once)

England Youth international Jeff Minton began the 1991-92 season as a youth team player and finished it playing in front of full houses at White Hart Lane and Old Trafford. First associated with Spurs as a schoolboy, he made his senior debut within a couple of months of turning professional. He was to get no further opportunities and was allowed to join Brighton on a free transfer. A strong-running midfielder with an eye for goal, Minton gave Brighton great service for five years before dropping down the divisions and eventually playing in non-League circles.

Appearances:
League: 2 apps. 1 gl.
FL Cup: (1) app.
Others: 1 (1) apps.
Total: 3 (2) apps. 1 gl.

MODRIĆ, Luka

Role: Midfield 2008-12
5ft.7ins. 10st.5lbs.
Born: Zadar, Yugoslavia, 9th September 1985

CAREER: NK Zadar (Croatia)/Dinamo Zagreb (Croatia) 2001/(HŠK Zrinjski Mostar (Bosnia & Herzegovina) loan 2003/ (Inter Zaprešić (Croatia) loan Jul 2004)/**SPURS** Jul 2008/Real Madrid (Spain) Aug 2012.

Debut v Middlesbrough (PL) (a) 16.8.2008
(Norwich City (Fr) (a) 28.7.2008)

At only 5ft 7ins and less than twelve and a half stone, Luka Modrić may have appeared ill-equipped to be a midfielder in some of the toughest leagues in the world, but his talents have marked him out as one of the finest performers in those leagues. Brought up during the Balkans Conflict of the early 1990s, Modrić was an outstanding youngster taken under Dinamo Zagreb's wing as a 16-year old. Loaned to Zrinjski Mostar for a year, he returned as the Bosnian and Herzegovinian League Player of the Year, quite an achievement for an 18-year old. He then went on loan to Inter Zaprešić, helping them finish runners-up in the Croatian League and qualify for the UEFA Cup while being voted Croatia's Football Hope of the Year. Back with Dinamo, he quickly established himself as the midfield maestro, a creative force and regular scorer as Dinamo won the Croatian League in 2006, 2007 and 2008 and the Croatian Cup in the last two of those campaigns. Spurs were monitoring Modrić for some time before committing £16.5 million to secure his transfer. It equalled the record fee Spurs had paid out to sign a player, but if there were ever concerns it was a risk, they disappeared from the minute Modrić first donned a Spurs' shirt. Neat and tidy in possession, with the ability to keep the ball under the severest pressure, Modrić immediately established himself as Spurs' midfield general, the perfect play-maker. With the ability to sweep the ball out wide with inch perfect precision, he could play just in front of the defence, controlling play from deep and orchestrating swift attacks, but he was at his most effective operating just behind the strikers, where he could play short, incisive passes, quick one-twos and pick out the killer pass. Rarely absent save when injured, Modrić became a vital component of a team that played some fine attacking football, taking Spurs into the Champions League for the first time.

His skill, commitment and work ethic made him a firm favourite with the supporters so it was a terrible let down when he allowed his head to be turned by interest from Chelsea. Spurs refused to allow him to join their London rivals, but the die was set. When Real Madrid made an approach, it was simply a case of getting the best deal possible. £33 million was double what Spurs had paid for Modrić, but still a bargain. Modrić did not find it easy in Spain and after a few months was even voted La Liga's worst signing of the year but, he has class and class will always succeed. Slowly he proved his value, and when Carlo Ancelotti replaced Jose Mourinho, Modrić's name became one of the first on the team-sheet. It has remained so ever since. Croatian Footballer of the Year in 2007, 2008 and 2011, Modrić played for his country at Under-17, Under-19 and Under-21 level before making his first senior appearance in March 2006. He scored four goals in 28 appearances for his country as a Spurs' player.

Appearances:
League: 123 (4) apps. 13 gls.
FA Cup: 14* (1) apps. 1 gl.
FL Cup: 3 (1) apps.
Euro: 12 (3) apps. 3 gls.
Others: 12 (8) apps. 2 gls.
Total: 164 (17) apps. 19 gls.
* Includes 1 abandoned match

MOFFATT, Joseph

Role: Forward 1900-01
6ft. 12st.0lbs
Born: Bo'ness, Linlithgowshire, 26th July 1875

CAREER: Bo'ness/Abercorn Jul 1896/Bo'ness Dec 1896/Wishaw Thistle Feb 1897/Aberdeen/Bo'ness Nov 1897/Paisley St Mirren/Chatham 1898/Gravesend United/Walsall Aug 1899/**SPURS** May 1900/St Mirren Sep 1901/Manchester City May 1903/Kilmarnock May 1905/Watford Aug 1908/Aberdeen May 1909-May 1910.

Debut v Kettering Town (SL) (h) 1.12.1900
(Notts County (Fr) (h) 8.10.1900)

Joe Moffatt gained plenty of experience in his native Scotland before moving to England with Southern League Chatham and Gravesend United and Midland League Walsall. He signed for Spurs in the summer of 1900 and stayed for just a year at White Hart Lane, operating as a reserve forward, and playing just nine competitive games. The majority of his outings came late in the season when, because of the FA Cup run, Spurs had a backlog of fixtures and frequently fielded a reserve team in order to keep the first team fresh for the Cup battles. Tall and good in the air, but less impressive with the ball at his feet, he was released at the end of the season and signed for St Mirren. In May 1903 he joined Manchester City where he played for three years, initially as a forward but then in the half-back line. He later played for Kilmarnock and Watford before finishing his career with a season at Aberdeen. At Manchester City Moffatt played in the reserves with his brother Bobby. After seven years as a regular at half-back, Bobby became City's reserve coach, but when he left to take up a coaching post with Kilmarnock, Joe followed him.

Appearances:
Southern: 6 apps. 3 gls.
Others: 8 apps.
Total: 14 apps. 3 gls.

MOGFORD, Reginald William James

Role: Inside-forward 1943-45
Born: Newport, Gwent, 12th June 1919
Died: Warndon, Worcestershire, 28th September 1992

CAREER: Newport County am. Nov 1937, pro. 1939/(guest for Aberaman, Crystal Palace, Huddersfield Town, Luton Town, Reading and **SPURS** during World War Two)/Worcester City Jul 1948/Kidderminster Harriers Jul 1952/Bromsgrove Rovers Jul 1953.

Debut v Reading (FLS) (h) 5.2.1944

Reg Mogford spent all his senior professional career with his home town club, save for the war years when he guested for several clubs. It was as a guest that he made his appearances for Spurs in the inside-forward positions, although he was perhaps more highly regarded as an outside-left. After the war he remained with Newport until the 1948 close season when he joined Worcester City and later played for Kidderminster Harriers. Mogford's son, Bryan, also played for Worcester.

Appearances:
Others: 8 apps. 1 gl.
Total: 8 apps. 1 gl.

MOLES, Walter John

Role: Half-back or goalkeeper 1900-03
Born: Tottenham, London, 1878
Died: Hertford, Hertfordshire, 1954

CAREER: Castle United/Waverley/**SPURS** trial Aug 1900, pro. Oct 1900/Bristol City Jul-Nov 1901/**SPURS** Dec 1901.

Debut v Bristol City (WL) (a) 27.3.1901
(Luton Town (Fr) (a) 12.11.1900)

Originally with the local clubs Castle United and Waverley, Walter "Tiny" Moles was first noticed in August 1900 when he took part in one of the regular pre-season trial matches that Spurs organised for local junior players. A most unusually versatile player who was equally competent at half-back or in goal, he signed professional forms two months later. His first team debut was in November 1900, but he had to wait until March 1901 for an initial appearance in a first team competition. Even this was devalued, as the reserves fulfilled a Western League fixture at Bristol City because an FA Cup replay with Reading was fixed for the next day. All his appearances in first team competitions that season were made in similar circumstances, usually at half-back, although in one game he played outside-right. Released at the end of the season he joined Bristol City where he made six Football League appearances in 1901-02-all of them in goal. Released by the Bristol club in November 1901, he returned to help out Spurs' reserves, although towards the end of the season he made two appearances in the first team, both of them this time between the posts. He continued to assist the reserves for some years, but still played two further first team matches, both at half-back. Moles' brother, John, was also on Spurs' books at one time. Originally with Asplin Rovers and Edmonton Melrose, after Spurs he joined Leyton and had two years with Birmingham before returning to Leyton. He was later manager of the Brimsdown club. Another brother, Allan, better known as Mike, also turned out for Asplin Rovers.

Appearances:
Southern: 3 apps.
Others: 6 apps.
Total: 9 apps. 0 gls.

MONCUR, John Frederick

Role: Midfield 1985-92
5ft.9ins. 11st.3lbs.
Born: Mile End, London, 22nd September 1966

CAREER: Harlow Schools/South West Essex Schools/Essex Schools/London Schools/**SPURS** app. Apr 1983, pro. Aug 1984/(Doncaster Rovers loan Sep 1986)/(Cambridge United loan Mar 1987)/(Portsmouth loan Mar 1989)/(Brentford loan Oct 1989)/(Ipswich Town loan Oct 1991)/(Nottingham Forest loan Feb 1992)/Swindon Town Mar 1992/West Ham United Jun 1994/released May 2003/retired Sep 2003/Grays Athletic chairman Jun 2009-May 2011.

Debut v Everton (FL) (a) 11.5.1987
(Maidstone United (Fr) (a) 14.10.1985)

John Moncur trained with Arsenal, Orient and West Ham before joining Spurs, no doubt influenced by his father who was the club's Youth Development Officer. A midfield player of some style and flair who was seen at his best when given room to play, Moncur made his League debut at Everton in May 1987 when Spurs fielded a virtual reserve side five days before the FA Cup Final against Coventry City-a transgression for which the League imposed a stiff fine. In fact, Moncur already had some League experience, for in September 1986 he played four League games on loan to Doncaster Rovers (an experience that ended sadly when he broke his leg) and had also played on loan for Cambridge United. Similar in style to players of the calibre of Paul Gascoigne and Vinny Samways, Moncur was always on the fringe of the first team, never quite able to make the breakthrough to claim a permanent place. He spent much of his time on loan to other clubs before his £75,000 transfer to Swindon Town on deadline day 1992. He developed well in Wiltshire, learning from his Spurs' predecessors Glenn Hoddle and Micky Hazard and helped Swindon into the Premier League in 1993. His performances were unable to keep Swindon up, but he was clearly far too good a player for the First Division and in June 1994 moved to West Ham in a £1 million deal, preferring to return to his roots rather than join Hoddle's Chelsea. West Ham got nine years' service from Moncur, proving a hard-working, combative character. Moncur's sons, George and Freddy have both played professionally. George with West Ham, Colchester United and Barnsley, Freddy with Leyton Orient.

Appearances:
League: 10 (11) apps. 1 gl.
FL Cup: 1 (2) apps.
Others: 10 (20) apps. 1 gl.
Total: 21 (33) apps. 2 gls.

MONK, Cuthbert Valentine

Role: Goalkeeper 1891-96
Born: Hackney, March qtr. 1871

CAREER: Tottenham College by Oct 1886/**SPURS** 1891/Old Tottonians.

Debut v West Herts (FAC) (h) 13.10.1894
(Hampstead (LSC) (a) 31.10.1891)

Basically a goalkeeper, although he also played several games at half-back, former Tottenham College full-back Cuthbert Monk played regularly for Spurs in the early 1890s, although he was still around and helping out even after the club had become a professional outfit. His first known appearance was in October 1891 in a London Senior Cup tie with Hampstead when he played at half-back. In the next round, against City Ramblers less than a month later, he played in goal and he was Spurs' regular custodian until November 1894 when Charlie Ambler was signed. Goalkeeper in Spurs' first FA Cup and Amateur Cup ties, the arrival of Ambler consigned Monk to the reserves. Rarely called upon again for first team action he sometimes turned out for Old Tottonians. Monk's brother, Steve, was later associated with Spurs. A full-back who played for Old Tottonians he was with Spurs from 1897 to 1899, but his only first team appearances were in two friendly matches in February and April 1898.

Appearances:
FA Cup: 2 apps.
Others: 68 apps.
Total: 70 apps. 0 gls.

MONK, Stephen M

Role: Full-back 1897-98

CAREER: Old Tottonians/**SPURS** 1897.

Debut v Chesham (Fr) (h) 28.2.1898

Steve Monk was the brother of former Spurs' goalkeeper, Cuthbert, and made two first team appearances in the 1897-98 season. After playing for most of the season in the reserves or with Old Tottonians, he made his first team debut in a friendly against Chesham in February 1898. His only other first team appearance was in the last match of the season, a friendly with Bolton Wanderers. Described as a "bustling" player he performed well in that game and continued to be associated with Spurs the following season. He did not get past reserve level again and continued to play for Old Tottonians.

Appearances:
Others: 2 apps.
Total: 2 apps. 0 gls.

MONTGOMERY, Gerald

Role: Centre-half 1901-02
5ft.7ins. 12st.0lbs.
Born: Liverpool

CAREER: Old Xaverians/Preston North End 1900/**SPURS** May 1901/Preston North End 1902/retired cs. 1902.

Debut v Woolwich Arsenal (LL) (a) 16.9.1901

Signed from Preston North End as a 20-year old in the summer of 1901, Montgomery played only one competitive match for Spurs, against Woolwich Arsenal in the London League in September 1901. Three friendly appearances and a couple of months later, he sustained a serious injury which put him out of the game for the rest of the season. He returned to Preston North End, but the injury was too serious for him to continue playing. He retired from football to pursue a business career.

Appearances:
Others: 4 apps.
Total: 4 apps. 0 gls.

MONTGOMERY, John

Role: Full-back 1895-98
5ft.8ins. 13st.0lbs.
Born: Chryston, Lanarkshire, 18th June 1876
Died: Edmonton, London, 6th April 1940

CAREER: SPURS Jan 1896/Notts County May 1898 to May 1911/Glossop North End/Preston North End trainer.

Debut v Stoke (FAC) (a) 1.2.1896
(Reading (Fr) (h) 4.1.1896)

When Jock Montgomery signed professional forms for Spurs in January 1896, he may well have become the first professional player at the club. The decision to adopt the paid game was made only the previous month, and having been sent to Scotland with instructions to find new recruits, trainer John Campbell returned with Montgomery and John Logan. Which of them actually signed first is unknown. Montgomery was pitched straight into the team and went on to give the club first class service at left-back for two-and-a-half-years before moving to Notts County. He had played for the Southern League against London in February 1897, but his play rapidly developed in the Football League and by March 1899 he was in line for international recognition, playing for the Anglo-Scots against the Home Scots in an international trial match. Although he never did win a cap for his country he spent 13 years as first choice left-back at Meadow Lane before finishing his career with Glossop North End in 1914-15. He then took on the trainer's role with Preston North End. Montgomery's brother, goalkeeper Archie, was also a professional footballer, notably with Rangers, Bury and Manchester United. In the early 1920s Montgomery's son was given a trial in Spurs reserves.

Appearances:
Southern: 36 apps.
FA Cup: 5 apps.
Others: 89* apps. 1 gl.
Total: 130 apps. 1 gl.
*Includes 1 abandoned match.

MOODIE, John

Role: Goalkeeper 1944-45
Born: Inverkeithing, Fife
Died: 1st January 1994 (aged 76)

CAREER: Lochore Welfare/Heart of Midlothian Feb 1937/Raith Rovers Aug 1939/(Guest for Aberdeen. Airdrieonians, Dundee United, East Fife, Reading and SPURS during World War Two)/Cowdenbeath May 1948/Dunfermline Jun 1951.

Debut v Queens Park Rangers (FLSC) (h) 3.2.1945

On the books of Airdrie, Jock Moodie who represented Scottish Command, the Army in Scotland and the Combined Services during the War, made his one appearance for Spurs as a guest against Queens Park Rangers in a Football League South Cup tie in February 1945.

Appearances:
Others: 1 app.
Total: 1 app. 0 gls.

MOODY, R

Role: Full-back 1892-94

CAREER: Dreadnought/London Caledonians/Clapton/SPURS Sep 1892.

Debut v Polytechnic (SA) (h) 24.9.1892
(Paddington (Fr) (h) 17.9.1892)

A well-known player in London with Dreadnought, London Caledonians and Clapton, Moody played regularly for Spurs for two seasons.

Appearances:
Others: 26 apps.
Total: 26 apps. 0 gls.

MOORES, Ian Richard

Role: Striker 1976-79
6ft.2ins. 13st.8lbs.
Born: Newcastle-Under-Lyme, Staffordshire, 5th October 1954
Died: Stoke, Staffordshire, 12th January 1998

CAREER: Edward Orme Secondary School/Staffordshire Schools/Stoke City app., pro. Jun 1972/SPURS Aug 1976/(Western Suburbs, Sydney (Australia) loan summer 1977)/Orient Oct 1978/Bolton Wanderers Jul 1982/(Barnsley loan Feb 1983)/APOEL (Cyprus) Jul 1983/Port Vale trial 1988/Newcastle Town/Tamworth Feb 1989/Landskrona BoIs (Sweden)/Port Vale trial.

Debut v Middlesbrough (FLC) (a) 31.8.1976 (scored once)

Ian Moores made his League debut for Stoke in April 1974 and by January 1975 had won his first England Under-23 cap playing against Wales. A gangling, sometimes rather awkward looking centre-forward, he had scored 14 goals in 50 League games for Stoke and collected one more Under-23 cap by the time Keith Burkinshaw moved to sign him for £75,000 in August 1976 in an effort to solve Spurs' chronic lack of goals. At first the move appeared to pay off, with Moores scoring in his first two games, but the goals then dried up and he only managed one more in a season that finished with Spurs relegated to Division Two.

In the summer of 1977 Moores was allowed to play for the Western Suburbs club of Sydney and when he returned he found it increasingly hard to get in the team. The high point of his Spurs career came in October 1977 when he scored a hat-trick against Bristol Rovers in a 9-0 victory alongside four goal debutant Colin Lee. Moores remained with Spurs until October 1978 when for £55,000 he moved to Orient, He spent four years at Brisbane Road before joining Bolton Wanderers. He had just a year with Bolton and later went to play in Cyprus where he helped APOEL win the League in 1986. On his return to the UK Moores played in non-League circles and then had a spell in Sweden. He was only 43 when he died of cancer.

Appearances:
League: 25 (4) apps. 6 gls.
FL Cup: 3 apps. 2 gls.
Others: 11 (7) apps. 9 gls.
Total: 39 (11) apps. 17 gls.

MORAH, Olisah H

Role: Striker 1991-92
5ft.11ins. 13st.5lbs.
Born: Islington, London, 3rd September 1972

CAREER: Harlow Schools/West Essex Schools/FA/GM School of Excellence/**SPURS** trainee Jul 1989, pro. May 1991/(Hereford United loan Nov 1991)/Swindon Town loan Nov 1992, perm Dec 1992/Sutton United May 1993/Cambridge United Aug 1994-May 1996 (Torquay United loan Mar 1995)/Braintree Town/Welling United Aug 1996-97/**SPURS** Academy coach/Crystal Palace Academy coach/Potters Bar Town youth coach/Wycombe Wanderers Centre of Excellence manager 2009/Dagenham & Redbridge Academy coach 2012, Lead Foundation coach.

Debut v Spurs 1981-82 (sub) (Fr) (h) 10.11.1991

England schoolboy and youth international, Ollie Morah was a well-built central striker who attended the FA/GM School of Excellence before joining Spurs. A member of the FA Youth Cup-winning team of 1990, he progressed to reserve level, but his only first team appearance was as a substitute when a weak first eleven met an Ex-Spurs team in a memorial match for Cyril Knowles in November 1991. Later that month he went out on loan to Hereford United. A year later a similar arrangement saw him join Swindon Town with the move made permanent. Morah failed to make the breakthrough in Wiltshire, but after joining Sutton United did enough to earn another crack at the League game with Cambridge United. Unfortunately injuries restricted his appearances and he moved back into non-League circles. When he finished playing Morah went into coaching, obtaining his UEFA A license and running his own soccer school.

Appearances:
Others: (1) app.
Total: **(1) app. 0 gls.**

MORAN, John

Role: Full-back 1931-32
5ft.11ins. 12st.0lbs.
Born: Wigan, Lancashire, 9th February 1906
Died: Newton-le-Willows, Lancashire, 12th October 1959

CAREER: Earlestown/Wigan Juniors/Wigan Borough am. Oct 1924, pro Apr 1925/**SPURS** May 1931/ Watford Sep 1932/Mansfield Town Mar 1936-May 1937.

Debut v Preston North End (FL) (h) 31.8.1931

Signed from Wigan Borough, Jack Moran was thrust into first team action much sooner than expected, replacing the injured Cecil Poynton for the second match of the 1931-32 season. After eight games though, it was clear he was really not up to the standard required and Bert Lyons was drafted in instead. Moran made only four more appearances that season and left in the summer of 1932 to join Watford. He proved a remarkably consistent performer there for four years before spending a year with Mansfield Town

Appearances:
League: 12 apps.
Total: **12 apps. 0 gls.**

MORAN, Paul

Role: Forward 1986-94
5ft.10ins. 11st.0lbs.
Born: Enfield, Middlesex, 22nd May 1968

CAREER: SPURS YTS Jul 1984, pro. Jul 1985/(Portsmouth loan Jan 1989)/(Leicester City loan Nov 1989)/(Newcastle United loan Feb 1991)/(Southend United loan Mar 1991)/(Cambridge United loan Sep 1992)/Peterborough Jul 1994/Enfield loan then perm 1995/East Thurrock United player-coach Feb 1996/Enfield by Aug 1996/Borehamwood) by Feb 1998/Enfield by Oct 1998/Whitewebs/Kingsbury Town 1999/Hertford Town 1999/Hendon 2000/Hertford Town Feb 2000/Potters Bar Town by May 2002, player-coach/East Thurrock United/Boreham Wood/Kingsbury Town/Potters Bar Town.

Debut v Everton (FL) (a) 11.5.1987
(Hamburg SV (Fr) (h) 4.11.1986)

Like several others in the team, Paul Moran made his League debut at Everton in May 1987 when Spurs fielded a reserve side, five days before the FA Cup Final with Coventry City. A slightly built striker with a great burst of speed who could play on the wing or through the centre, his best run in the first team followed the arrival of Terry Venables as manager in December 1987, when many of the youngsters on the staff were given an opportunity to impress. Despite a number of useful spells out on loan, Moran did not fulfil his true potential, though he did suffer persistent injury problems which held back his development just when he should be have been establishing himself. Always on the fringe of the first team Moran was given a free transfer in May 1994 and joined Peterborough United, but made only seven appearances in 18 months. Loaned to Enfield he made the move permanent, and operating in midfield at last managed to steer clear of injury and play regularly.

Appearances:
League: 14 (22) apps. 2 gls.
FA Cup: 3 (1) apps.
FL Cup: 1 (6) apps.
Euro: (1) app.
Others: 10 (25) apps. 3 gls.
Total: **28 (55) apps. 5 gls.**

MORDIN, W B

Role: Half-back 1893-94
Born: 12th November 1871

CAREER: City Ramblers/**SPURS** Feb 1894/Vampires/City Ramblers/Richmond Association.

Debut v London Hospital (Fr) (h) 8.2.1894

A half-back with City Ramblers, Mordin made his only appearance for Spurs as a guest in a friendly with London Hospital in February 1894. He later played for Vampires and back with City Ramblers.

Appearances:
Others: 1 app.
Total: 1 app. 0 gls.

MORGAN, Charles

Role: Half-back 1904-05
5ft.8ins. 11st.3lbs.
Born: Bootle, Lancashire, 1882

CAREER: Everton/**SPURS** May 1904/Leeds City Apr 1905/Bradford Park Avenue 1909/Halifax Town/Leeds United director Oct 1919.

Debut v Fulham (WL) (h) 2.1.1905

Having spent most of his time in the reserves at Everton, Charlie Morgan had the misfortune to break his jaw in one of Spurs pre-season trial matches in August 1904. Such an early setback meant his Tottenham career never got off the ground and he played in only one competitive fixture, a Western League match in January 1905, and one senior friendly. Released in April 1905 he moved to Leeds City where he spent four years until joining Bradford Park Avenue.

Appearances:
Others: 2 apps.
Total: 2 apps. 0 gls.

MORGAN, Roger Ernest

Role: Winger 1968-73
5ft.9ins. 11st.0lbs.
Born: Walthamstow, London, 14th November 1946

CAREER: Walthamstow Schools/Queens Park Rangers app., pro. Sep 1964/**SPURS** Feb 1969/West Ham United Community Development Officer.

Debut v Queens Park Rangers (FL) (a) 15.2.1969

Until Roger Morgan joined Spurs for £110,000 his career ran an almost parallel course to that of his identical twin, Ian. They played together for Walthamstow Schools, joined Queens Park Rangers as apprentices at the same time and signed professional for the west London club on the same day. The similarity did not end there. They were not only alike in appearance, but also in style, both being fast, tricky wingers who could cross accurately or cut in for a shot on goal. Of the two, Roger, an England youth cap, was regarded as slightly the better, but together they proved a real handful for opposing defences. Only Roger was a member of the Rangers side that surprisingly won the first Wembley League Cup Final in 1967, but they both played in the team that won the Third Division title the same season and then clinched promotion to the First Division in 1968. Quite comfortable with the step up to the First Division, Morgan was signed to provide the supply of crosses from the wing for Jimmy Greaves and Alan Gilzean which had been lacking following the release of Cliff Jones and Jimmy Robertson. The late 1960s were a rebuilding era for Spurs, but Morgan settled well, won an England Under-23 cap against Bulgaria in April 1970 and looked a likely long-term prospect only to be injured early in 1970-71. It was the first of several serious knee injuries that, sadly, forced him to retire in the summer of 1973. Morgan worked in recreation at Haringey Council before a return to football as West Ham's Community Development Officer. He played cricket for Essex Schools and was thought good enough to go professional in the summer game, but turned down the opportunity to concentrate on football.

Appearances:
League: 66 (2) apps. 8 gls.
FA Cup: 6 apps. 2 gls.
FL Cup: 3 apps. 1 gl.
Euro: 2 (1) apps. 1 gl.
Others: 12 (3) apps. 5 gls.
Total: 89 (6) apps. 17 gls.

MORRIS, James

Role: Winger 1915-17

CAREER: Millwall 1908/Reading cs. 1912/Merthyr Town cs. 1914/(guest for **SPURS** during World War One).

Debut v Arsenal (LFC) (a) 4.9.1915

A winger who had made a name for himself in London with Millwall, Jimmy Morris had spent the last season of pre-war football with Merthyr Town having also served Reading. He made his Spurs' debut in the club's first match of the London Football Combination and missed only one match that season, but was only available to assist Spurs in the early part of the following season.

Appearances:
Others: 43 apps. 4 gls.
Total: 43 apps. 4 gls.

MORRIS, Thomas

Role: Half-back 1899-13
5ft.10ins. 11st.9lbs.
Born: Grantham, Lincolnshire, 9th February 1875
Died: Uxbridge, Middlesex, 25th April 1942

CAREER: Grantham Rovers 1894/Gainsborough Trinity cs. 1897/**SPURS** May 1899, ground-staff 1912-42.

Debut v Queens Park Rangers (SL) (h) 9.9.1899
(Notts County (Fr) (h) 4.9.1899)

Tom Morris is one of the players who did so much to help establish Spurs as one of the leading lights of Southern football during the early part of the twentieth century. After three years with Grantham Rovers and two with Gainsborough Trinity, he joined Spurs in preference to several other clubs who were keen to acquire his services. A powerful, determined half-back, equally comfortable in defence or attack, he possessed boundless energy, never seemed to tire and was always involved at the centre of the action. His Southern League debut came in September 1899 and he went on to appear in more Southern League matches than any other Spurs' player. A member of the side that won the Southern League in 1899-00, he played in the first senior match at White Hart Lane, was ever-present in the FA Cup winning team of 1901 and the only member of that great team still with Spurs when the club entered the Football League. He played for the South against the North in international trial matches in March 1900 and January 1903, but failed to collect the England cap he so richly deserved, with the selectors each time preferring William Johnson of Sheffield United. After 13 years of tremendous service to Spurs and two benefits, Morris retired from playing in the summer of 1912 to take up a position on the Spurs' ground-staff. He remained working for the club until his death in April 1942.

Appearances:
Southern: 243 apps. 21 gls.
League: 63 apps. 2 gls.
FA Cup: 39* apps. 1 gl.
Others: 182 apps. 24 gls.
Total: 527 apps. 48 gls.
*Includes 1 abandoned match.

MORRISON, John Alfred

Role: Centre-forward 1932-46
5ft.9ins. 10st.8lbs.
Born: Belvedere, Kent, 26th March 1911
Died: Culcompton, Devon, 13th September 1984

CAREER: Bostal Heath/Luton Town trial/Callenders Athletic/**SPURS** am. Aug 1931/(Northfleet United Apr 1932)/**SPURS** pro. Jul 1933/(guest for Millwall during World War Two)/retired Jun 1946.

Debut v Chesterfield (FL) (a) 1.4.1933 (scored once)

Throughout the 1930s Spurs were fortunate to be served by three truly great goal-scoring centre-forwards, Ted Harper, George Hunt and finally Johnny Morrison. After a year at the Northfleet nursery, Morrison moved up to White Hart Lane and marked his debut in April 1933 with a goal, but failed to make the first team the following season as Hunt continued to lead the attack. Despite netting 36 goals in 28 appearances for the reserves, he surprisingly played only three matches in 1934-35 as, hit by injuries and personnel changes, Spurs relied on Hunt for the goals needed to keep them in the First Division. Through no fault of his own, Hunt failed to do so, and with relegation Jack Tresadern took over the manager's job from Percy Smith. Morrison's big chance came in September 1935, when he was called up to replace Hunt. He took the opportunity so well that Hunt was rarely able to get back in the team. In October 1937 Spurs were able to let the "Chesterfield Tough" join Arsenal, when there were clearly still plenty of goals to come from him. It is perhaps unfortunate that Hunt and Morrison were unable to play together, but they were similar in style, and in those days teams operated with just one central striker supplied by two wingers. Although he

appeared a little clumsy at times, Morrison had bags more skill than critics gave him credit for. There was no denying that he was an opportunist goal-scorer, quick off the mark and not afraid to venture in where tackles were heaviest. His remarkable goal-scoring record speaks for itself. Still first choice centre-forward on the outbreak of the Second World War, Spurs were deprived of his services soon after the conflict began. When he returned to the club in December 1945 he played only one game before deciding his best years had gone and announced his retirement.

Appearances:
League: 134 apps. 90 gls.
FA Cup: 21 apps. 14 gls.
Others: 34* apps. 26 gls.
Total: 189 apps. 130 gls.
*Includes 1 abandoned match.

MORTON, James Cowan

Role: Centre-forward 1908-09
5ft.11ins. 12st.6lbs.
Born: Leith, Edinburgh, 28th July 1887
Died: Edinburgh, 29th July 1926

CAREER: Newtongrange Star/Hibernian Dec 1906/Bradford City Jan 1908/Stoke Jan 1908/**SPURS** Jun 1908/Edinburgh St Bernards Oct 1909/Bathgate/Barnsley Oct 1913/Bristol City Apr 1914/Nuneaton coach.

Debut v Grimsby Town (FL) (h) 28.11.1908

Another former Stoke player signed by Spurs in the summer of 1908 after the Stoke club had been wound up and with Spurs expected to take their League place, James Morton made only four first team appearances in his one season with the club. Previously with Hibernian and Bradford City, for whom he failed to make a single League appearance, he failed to score in his four games for Spurs and was released at the end of the season.

Appearances:
League: 2 apps.
Others: 2 apps.
Total: **4 apps. 0 gls.**

MOSELEY, William A

Role: Half-back 1943-44

Debut v Queens Park Rangers (FLS) (a) 4.9.1943 (scored once)

Bill Moseley was introduced to Spurs by his army colleague and Spurs' full-back, Bill Whatley. He made three Football League South appearances and scored one goal during September 1943.

Appearances:
Others: 3 apps. 1 gl.
Total: **3 apps. 1 gl.**

MUIR, Alexander

Role: Full-back 1942-43

CAREER: Burnbank Athletic/Albion Rovers trial then perm. Aug 1941/ (guest for Brentford, Fulham and **SPURS** during World War Two).

Debut v Reading (FLS) (a) 17.10.1942

Signed by Albion Rovers during the war after impressing in a trial match, Chic Muir made his one appearance for Spurs at left-back in a 6-2 Football League South victory at Reading in October 1942. He continued with Albion Rovers after the war, captaining the club for some years, until leaving in the close season of 1953.

Appearances:
Others: 1 app.
Total: **1 app. 0 gls.**

MUIR, Matthew R

Role: Half-back 1944-45

CAREER: Rochdale/(guest for Brighton and Hove Albion, Fulham, **SPURS** and Wrexham during World War Two).

Debut v Crystal Palace (FLS) (a) 7.10.1944

On Rochdale's books, Muir made his one appearance for Spurs at right-half in a Football League South match against Crystal Palace in October 1944.

Appearances:
Others: 1 app.
Total: **1 app. 0 gls.**

MULLERY, Alan Patrick M.B.E.

Role: Midfielder 1963-72
5ft.9ins. 12st.4lbs.
Born: Notting Hill, London, 23rd November 1941

CAREER: West London Schools/London Schools/Middlesex Schools/Fulham am. Jun 1957, pro. Dec 1958/**SPURS** Mar 1964/Fulham loan Mar 1972, perm Jul 1972/Durban City (South Africa) 1975/retired May 1976/Brighton and Hove Albion manager Jul 1976-Jun 1981/Charlton Athletic manager Jul 1981/Crystal Palace manager Jun 1982-May 1984/Queens Park Rangers manager Jun-Dec 1984/Brighton and Hove Albion manager May 1986-Jan 1987/Southwick manager Aug-Nov 1987/Armed Forces (Malaysia) coach/Barnet Director of Football Oct 1996-May 1997/Crawley Town consultant Sep 2005.

Debut v Manchester United (FL) (h) 21.3.1964

Within two months of signing for Fulham as a 17-year old professional, Alan Mullery made his debut. He kept his place in the team alongside stars like Graham Leggatt, Johnny Haynes and Tosh Chamberlain and at the end of the season Fulham won promotion to the First Division. A permanent fixture in the team, he rapidly established himself as one of England's brightest up and coming half-backs, won the first of his three England Under-23 caps against Italy in November 1960 and after more than 200 senior appearances moved to Spurs for £72,500. In May 1964, he played for the Football League against the Italian League and after one more outing with the Football League won his first full cap against Holland in December that year. Whilst Mullery was doing well on the international front, his domestic career was not so happy. He had been bought to replace Danny Blanchflower and wore the former captain's prized number four shirt, but he was a totally different type of player to the legendary Irishman and it took a long time for Spurs supporters to appreciate that Mullery's strengths lay not in the artistry of his play, but in his enthusiasm, hard work and ceaseless toil. His appearances for England were restricted by the performances of Nobby Stiles and Mullery did not win his second cap until May 1967, four days after playing one of his best games for Spurs in the FA Cup Final victory over Chelsea. He then became an England regular winning 33 more caps, and many recall his goal against West Germany in the epic 1970 World Cup quarter-final in Mexico. An inspirational figure, forever urging the team on and leading by example, Mullery took over the Spurs' captaincy following the departure of Dave Mackay and led the club to victory in the 1971 League Cup Final. However, in October 1971 he suffered a serious pelvic injury which put him out of action for over six months. In an effort to recover full fitness he was loaned to Fulham, but was recalled after a month due to a lengthy injury list at Spurs. He responded by scoring a spectacular and crucial away goal against AC Milan in the second leg of the UEFA Cup semi-final and then headed the goal in the second leg of the 1972 Final against Wolves which gave Spurs the trophy. Mullery had been aggrieved at Bill Nicholson's decision to loan him to Fulham, and at the end of the season returned permanently to his former club for a £65,000 fee. In the next four years, he made almost 200 more appearances for Fulham, helped them to the FA Cup Final in 1975, was voted the Football Writers' Association Player of the Year for 1974-75 and awarded the MBE for his services to the game. When his top-flight career was over, he agreed to play for Durban City, but injury prevented him doing so. Instead, he moved into management, taking over at Brighton in July 1976 and leading them from the Third Division to the First before moving to Charlton. At times an outspoken boss, he only spent a year with the Valiants before two years in charge of both Crystal Palace and Queens Park Rangers and finished his managerial career with another short spell back at Brighton. In June 1993 Mullery was coaching the Malaysian Second Division side, Armed Forces, when he walked out on them because he had not been paid for several months by his employers,

Soccer Schools UK. Mullery should have won his first full England cap before December 1964. He was selected to go on England's 1964 summer tour of South America and expected to make his debut, but on the morning he was due to join the England squad he suffered a muscle spasm whilst shaving, and was forced to pull out of the tour! He was featured on "This Is Your Life" on 24 March 1976.

Appearances:
League: 313* apps. 25 gls.
FA Cup: 33 apps. 1 gl.
FL Cup: 18 apps.
Euro: 10 apps. 4 gls.
Others: 55 apps. 9 gls.
Total: 429 apps. 39 gls.
*Includes 1 abandoned match

MURPHY, Daniel Benjamin

Role: Midfielder 2005-07
5ft.9ins. 12st.4lbs.
Born: Chester, Cheshire, 18th March 1977

CAREER: Crewe Alexandra trainee Jul 1993, pro. Mar 1994/Liverpool Jul 1997/(Crewe Alexandra loan Feb 1999)/Charlton Athletic Aug 2004/SPURS Jan 2006/Fulham Aug 2007/Blackburn Rovers Jun 2012-Jul 2013/retired Oct 2013.

Debut v Sunderland (sub) (PL) (a) 12.2.2006

Danny Murphy was one of the most successful graduates of Dario Gradi's famous Crewe Alexandra football academy, going on to establish himself a consistent Premiership performer and England international.

Unfortunately, his time with Spurs was not to be among the most memorable periods of his career as he struggled to make any impression. Early in his career Murphy showed the wide range of passing that complemented his astute tactical acumen. Given the opportunity, he was happy to accept the responsibility of running the midfield, controlling a game as he orchestrated attacks from deep, snapping into tackles and covering back when necessary. He was adept at dead ball situations and could strike a shot sweetly and accurately from distance. After helping Crewe earn promotion to the Second Division and establish the club at that level, Murphy joined Liverpool, a little over 20-years old, but with nearly 150 senior appearances to his credit. It took Murphy time to establish himself at Anfield, but, after a loan spell back at Crewe, he slowly but surely secured a place in Liverpool's midfield, helping the Reds complete the "Cup Treble" of FA Cup, Worthington Cup and UEFA Cup in 2001 and add the Carling Cup in 2003. Having won the first of his nine England caps against Sweden in November 2001, Murphy was approaching his best when he found himself unwanted on Merseyside following the arrival of Rafa Benitez and his Spanish midfield contingent in the summer of 2004. Spurs tried to sign Murphy then, but when they would not give him the guarantee of first team football he demanded, Murphy decided to accept an offer from Charlton Athletic. Eighteen months later, Murphy was unhappy at the Valley. Even though the prospects of a regular first team spot were even less, he accepted another approach from Spurs. Competing with the likes of Didier Zokora, Jermaine Jenas, Teemu Tainio and Tom Huddlestone, Murphy had few opportunities. With so many younger players ahead of him, it was no surprise when he was allowed to move to Fulham. Back in the centre of midfield, a regular and given the responsibility that always brought the best out of him, Fulham got five years great service from Murphy. He finished his career with a year at Blackburn, his contract cancelled early so he could look for another club. When he failed to find one, he retired.

Appearances:
League: 7 (15) apps. 1 gl.
FA Cup: 1 app.
FL Cup: 3 apps.
Euro: 2 (1) apps.
Others: 5 (4) apps.
Total: 18 (20) apps. 1 gl.

MURPHY, Peter

Role: Inside-forward 1950-52
5ft.7ins. 11st.7lbs.
Born: Hartlepool, County Durham, 7th March 1922
Died: 7th April 1975

CAREER: Coventry Schools/Dunlop/Birmingham am./(Guest for Coventry City and Millwall during World War Two)/Coventry City pro. May 1946/SPURS May 1950/Birmingham City Jan 1952/Rugby Town cs. 1960/retired 1961/Coventry City coach.

Debut v Bolton Wanderers (FL) (a) 23.8.1950 (scored once)

Born in the North-East, Peter Murphy's family moved to the Midlands when he was four. He played for Coventry Schools, but was an amateur on Birmingham's books before signing professional for Coventry City. Top scorer for the Sky Blues in 1949-50, he joined Spurs for £18,500 to strengthen a squad that had just won the Second Division title. Murphy made a goal-scoring League debut in August 1950, provided stiff opposition to Les Bennett, and finished the season with a Football League Championship medal. Never able to command a regular place, but much too good for reserve team football, Spurs agreed to let Murphy join Birmingham City for £20,000 in January 1952. He scored more than 125 goals in over 250 senior appearances in the next eight years, helping City win the Second Division championship in 1955 and reach the FA Cup Final against Manchester City twelve months later. It was Murphy who was involved in the accident that left opposing goalkeeper Bert Trautmann with a broken neck. A regular until 1958, he retired from first class football in 1960 and finished his playing career with a year at Rugby Town. He later had a spell on Coventry's coaching staff before working as a representative for Davenports Brewery.

Appearances:
League: 38 apps. 14 gls.
Others: 11 apps. 6 gls.
Total: 49 apps. 20 gls.

THE SPURS ALPHABET

MURRAY, William B

Role: Winger 1904-06
5ft.6ins. 11st.7lbs.
Born: Forres, Morayshire, 1883
Died: Kilmallie, Inverness, 22nd April 1929

CAREER: Forres/Inverness/Sunderland Jun 1901/Northampton Town cs. 1903/**SPURS** May 1904/Leeds City May 1906/retired May 1907.

Debut v Brentford (SL) (h) 29.10.1904

Willie Murray made seven appearances for Sunderland at the end of the 1901-02 season as they moved towards the Football League Championship. After only one of those appearances he played for the Anglo-Scots against the Home Scots in the Scottish international trial. Having played just once the following season, he moved to Northampton Town where he played regularly and attracted Spurs' attention. Signed as cover for John Kirwan, Murray spent the whole of his first season at White Hart Lane deputising only when Kirwan was absent, but with the departure of Kirwan for Chelsea in 1905, Murray got his chance. He started the 1905-06 season as first choice outside-left, but lost out to Chris Carrick and, with the developing Alf Whyman coming through, the decision was taken to release Murray in April 1906. He moved to Leeds City where he joined former Spurs men James Freeborough and John George and played for one season.

Appearances:
Southern: 20 apps.
FA Cup: 1 app.
Others: 22 apps. 1 gl.
Total: 43 apps. 1 gl.

NASH, Martin

Role: Forward 1994-95
5ft.11ins. 12st.3lbs.
Born: Regina, Saskatchewan, Canada 27th December 1975

CAREER: Vancouver 86ers (Canada) 1994-96/**SPURS** trial Oct 1994/Stockport County Nov 1996-1998/St Johnstone trial Jul 1998/Dallas Burn (USA) trial/Edmonton Drillers (Canada) 1998-99/Vancouver 86ers (Canada) 1999/Bolton Wanderers trial Jul 1999/Chester City Oct 1999-2000/Detroit Rockers (USA)/St Johnstone trial Mar 2000/Rochester Raging Rhinos (USA) Mar 2000/Edmonton Drillers (Canada) Oct-Dec 2000/Detroit Rockers (USA) Dec 2000/Milwaukee Wave (USA) 2002/Macclesfield trial Dec 2003, non-contract Jan 2003/Montreal Impact (Canada) Apr 2003/La Furia de Monterrey (Mexico) May 2003/Dallas Sidekicks (USA) Jul 2003/Vancouver Whitecaps (Canada) Apr 2004, coach Oct 2010/retired Oct 2010/British Colombia (Canada) coach/Ottawa Fury (Canada) asst. coach Oct 2013-Oct 2016.

Debut v Reading (sub) (Fr) (a) 11.11.1994 (scored one)

Younger brother of the basketball superstar, Steve Nash, Martin Nash was one of Canada's most celebrated professional football players. Born in Regina, Saskatchewan but raised in Victoria, British Columbia, Nash first came to prominence with Vancouver 86ers, and it was while playing for them that he was invited for a trial with Spurs. It was during the trial that he made his one senior appearance, going on as a substitute in a friendly at Reading and promptly scoring. Not offered terms by Spurs, he returned to Canada and embarked on a lengthy career, playing both regular football and in the indoor game. He frequently returned to the UK, playing for Stockport County, Chester City and Macclesfield, but without ever making the breakthrough. Nash helped Rochester Rhinos win the A League in 2000 and 2001, Vancouver Whitecaps win the USL First Division title in 2006 and 2008, and made 38 appearances for Canada.

Appearances:
Others: (1) app. 1 gl.
Total: (1) app. 1 gl.

NAUGHTON, Kyle

Role: Full-back 2009-2015
5ft.11ins. 11st.14lbs.
Born: Sheffield, South Yorkshire, 11th November 1988

CAREER: Sheffield United Scholar Jul 2005, pro Jul 2007/(Gretna loan Jan 2008)/**SPURS** Jul 2009/(Middlesbrough loan Feb 2010)/(Leicester City loan Oct 2010)/(Norwich City loan Jul 2011)/Swansea City Jan 2015.

Debut v West Ham United (sub) (PL) 23.8.2009
(Barcelona (sub) (Fr) (Wembley) 24.7.2009)

Signed from Sheffield United in a joint deal with fellow full-back, Kyle Walker, Naughton was another of the young English talents Spurs invested in hoping to develop a star, rather than lay out big money for a proven name or foreign talent. With Sheffield United from his youngest school days, Naughton benefitted greatly from a spell on loan to Gretna when the Scottish club were embroiled in an ultimately unsuccessful relegation battle. He returned to Sheffield after five months on loan, a stronger, harder player and made his debut for his home town club early in the 2008-09 season. Once in the team, he was rarely left out and by the end of the season, was a target for Premier League clubs. When Naughton arrived at White Hart Lane, Vedran Ćorluka was firmly established in the right-back role. To continue his football education Naughton was loaned to first Middlesbrough and then Leicester City of the Championship. He performed more than well for both clubs, but it was when on a season long loan to Premier League Norwich City that he really started to make a big impression. Strong and firm in his defending, it was going forward where he really caught the eye. Always on the lookout for the chance to overlap, his speed and willingness to get ahead of his midfielders and ability to cut the ball back, created many opportunities. With Kyle Walker having made the right-back spot his own after Ćorluka's departure and rarely absent, Naughton had to be content as first reserve to Walker and left-back Danny Rose. It meant Naughton had few opportunities, most of them on the left, not his best position. With the signings of Eric Dier and Ben Davies, Naughton found it even harder to make the team. When Swansea offered £5 million for his transfer, it was a good deal for Spurs. It also gave Naughton the chance of regular football. All parties were happy. In Wales, Naughton has held his own, not always first choice, but certainly a valued player.

Appearances:
League: 37 (5) apps.
FA Cup: 2 (1) apps.
FL Cup: 6 apps.
Euro: 23 (1) apps.
Others: 18 (14) apps.
Total: 86 (21) apps. 0 gls.

NAYBET, Noureddine

Role: Central defender 2004-06
6ft.1ins. 11st.13lbs.
Born: Casablanca, Morocco, 10th February 1970

CAREER: Wydad AC (Morocco) 1985/Nantes (France) Jul 1993/Sporting (Portugal) Jul 1994/Deportivo de La Coruña (Spain) Jul 1996/**SPURS** Aug 2004/released May 2006/Morocco FA consultant Aug 2007.

Debut v Liverpool (PL) (h) 14.8.2004

With the wholesale changes Frank Arnesen and Jacques Santini planned when they arrived in the summer of 2004, there was a real risk of a lack of experience in the most important area of a team, central defence. To ensure that was not a problem, Noureddine Naybet was signed from Deportivo de la Coruna. The 34-year old cost £700,000, an absolute bargain for a man who had been one of the finest central defenders in Spain for eight years and still had an enormous amount to offer. Making his international debut in August 1990, Naybet helped his home town club,

Wydad, win the Moroccan Botola League title in 1990, 1991 and 1993 and the CAF Champions League in 1992 before experiencing European football. He played for a year with Nantes and two with Sporting, but it was after he had signed for Deportivo that he really came to the fore. With Naybet the rock at the centre of their defence, the unfashionable Galician club reached the peak of Spanish football, winning La Liga for the first time in 2000 and mounting a serious and consistent challenge to Real Madrid and Barcelona. In the four years before his departure, Deportivo were twice runners-up and finished third the same number of times. Given his age, it was not surprising Naybet had lost some of his pace by the time he joined Spurs, but that was more than made up for by his power, positional sense and simple knowhow. Rarely one to fluster, his mere presence had a calming effect as he organised those around him, not just telling them what to do, but often showing them how to do it. Ledley King and Michael Dawson could not have had a better mentor. Naybet did a fantastic job for twelve months, but then age did begin to take its toll. With Dawson, King and Anthony Gardner the future, Naybet was released and hung up his boots. In August 2007 the Royal Moroccan Football Federation wanted to appoint him as assistant coach but he did not have the necessary qualifications. He was appointed a consultant instead. In total Naybet made 115 international appearances, twelve of them in his time at White Hart Lane.

Appearances:
League: 29 (1) apps.
FA Cup: 2 apps.
FL Cup: 3 apps.
Total: 34 (1) apps. 0 gls.

(NAYIM) AMAR, Mohammed Ali.

Role: Midfield 1988-93
5ft.8ins. 11st.8lbs.
Born: Ceuta, Morocco, 5th November 1966

CAREER: AD Ceuta (Spain)/Barcelona Atlètic (Spain) 1985/Barcelona (Spain)/**SPURS** loan Oct 1988, perm Jun 1989/Real Zaragoza (Spain) Apr 1993/Logroñés (Spain) Jul 1997/retired Nov 1999/Serrallo CF (Spain) coach/AD Ceuta (Spain) asst. coach Jul 2004, caretaker coach Mar 2006/Atlético Ceuta (Spain) coach Jul-Sep 2006/Unión Africa Ceutí (Spain) Oct 2007/Real Zaragoza (Spain) asst. manager Dec 2009-Nov 2010.

Debut v Norwich City (FL) (h) 21.2.1989
(Monaco (sub) (Fr) (h) 17.1.1989)

Nayim was born in Spain's North African colony of Ceuta and after being noticed by Barcelona taken on the staff of their nursery side

Barcelona Atlètic. He developed rapidly, winning Spanish Youth and Under-21 honours after being given his chance in Barcelona's senior team by Terry Venables. He then suffered a serious knee ligament injury and when fit to return Venables' replacement, Johan Cruyff, made it clear Nayim was not part of his plans for the Spanish giants. Venables persuaded Nayim to join Spurs on loan for 18 months and, operating as a wide midfield man, he soon settled into the first team, showing the flair and ball skills expected of the continentals. Venables persuaded Nayim to join Spurs on loan for 18 months and, operating as a wide midfield man, he soon settled into the first team, showing the flair and ball skills expected of the continentals. He rapidly established himself as a player who could have a big future at White Hart Lane and such was his impact Venables insisted Nayim's permanent £300,000 transfer should form part of the deal that saw Gary Lineker signed from Barcelona. Although he suffered with a few injuries and did not always win the battle for a midfield place, Nayim proved his value to Spurs when he substituted for the injured Paul Gascoigne in the 1991 FA Cup Final victory over Nottingham Forest. Nayim returned to Spain with Real Zaragoza in April 1993, helped them win the Spanish Cup in 1994 and a year later endeared himself even further to Spurs fans when his last minute goal from the half-way line defeated Arsenal in the European Cup-Winners' Cup Final. He later joined Logroñés, but was released after two years having suffered with a bad knee injury. Unable to find a new club he formally retired in November 1999 and returned to his roots. After helping coach Serrallo CF to promotion to the Spanish Third Division in 2000, he took on the role of assistant coach with AD Ceuta. Two years later he moved to Atletico Ceuta as senior coach, but lasted barely two months, dismissed after five successive defeats. He continued to coach in the colony before a year as assistant manager back at Zaragoza. Unable to get another coaching post, Nayim went to Dubai in 2014 to set up a football school for the children of ex-pats. In 2006 Nayim's name was etched permanently into Aragónese history when a street in the village of Trasmoz was named "Gol de Nayim" ("Nayim's Goal").

Appearances:
League: 95 (17) apps. 11 gls.
FA Cup: 6 (3) apps. 4 gls.
FL Cup: 11 (6) apps. 3 gls.
Euro: 6 apps.
Others: 33 (6) apps. 3 gls.
Total: 151 (32) apps. 21 gls.

NAYLOR, Terence Michael Patrick

Role: Defender 1969-80
5ft.10" 11st.10lbs.
Born: Islington, London, 5th December 1948

CAREER: Vittoria Primary School/Risinghill Secondary Modern School/Islington Boys/**SPURS** am. 1966, pro. Jul 1969/Charlton Athletic Nov 1980/retired Nov 1983/Gravesend and Northfleet Aug 1984-1985/Haringey Borough/Empire Papermill/Tonbridge Angels manager Jul-Sep 1988.

Debut v West Bromwich Albion (FL) (a) 28.3.1970

Terry Naylor trained with both Arsenal and Millwall (where he scored a hat-trick in a trial match, but fell out after arriving late for an away game) before joining Spurs as an amateur. He then gave up his job as a porter at Smithfield Meat Market to turn professional. Originally a defensive midfield player, the array of talent available to Spurs in the early 1970's meant he had few opportunities in that position, and when his chances came they were as cover for the central defensive men, notably Phil Beal. As Beal's deputy he helped Spurs run to the 1973 League Cup Final, but in January sustained a fractured leg which deprived him of a place in the Final. However, with Cyril Knowles sustaining a serious knee injury in December 1973, Naylor was given a chance at left-back. He made the position his own, appearing in both legs of the 1974 UEFA Cup Final, and then, following the departure of Kinnear and Evans, switched to right-back where he served the club well until the emergence of Chris Hughton early in the 1979-80 season. A sterling, wholehearted player who was always ready to run his heart out for the club, he was happy to fill any role for Spurs. He finally moved across London on a free transfer to Charlton, where he played until a broken leg in August 1982 during a pre-season friendly against West Ham eventually forced his retirement from the first class game. He signed for Gravesend and Northfleet and then played for Haringey Borough and Empire Papermill before a three-month spell as manager of Tonbridge Angels. Naylor then ran a pub in Woolwich and kept in touch with the game as a football reporter for the Sunday Sport newspaper.

Appearances:
League: 237 (6) apps.
FA Cup: 17 (1) apps.
FL Cup: 23 (1) apps. 1 gl.
Euro: 13 (6) apps.
Others: 66 (8) apps.
Total: 356 (22) apps. 1 gl.

NEIGHBOUR, James Edward

Role: Winger 1970-77
5ft.7ins. 10st.8lbs.
Born: Chingford, Essex, 15th November 1950
Died: Woodford Green, Essex, 11th April 2009

CAREER: Waltham Forest Schools/London Schools/Essex Schools/**SPURS** app. Apr 1966, pro. Nov 1968/Norwich City Sep 1976/(Seattle Sounders (USA) May 1979)/West Ham United Sep 1979/(AFC Bournemouth loan Jan 1983)/retired cs. 1983/Enfield player-coach Oct 1988/West Ham United Youth Development Officer Oct 1990-Apr 1994/Doncaster Rovers Youth

Team Coach Sep 1994, asst. manager Sep-Dec 1994, youth team coach/ SPURS coach 1995/St Albans City manager Dec 1996-Mar 1998/Charlton Athletic head of youth recruitment Jun 1999/SPURS coach 2000, youth team coach Jul 2000-Jul 2005/West Ham United academy coach 2008.

Debut v Stoke City (sub) (FL) (h) 24.10.1970

Jimmy Neighbour was an old-fashioned type of winger, strong running and difficult to pin down, who liked to get to the line and send over tantalising crosses. He made his League debut in October 1970, but it was not until early in 1971 that he really made an impact, collecting a League Cup winners' tankard against Aston Villa after just a few first team games. Competing with Jimmy Pearce and Ralph Coates, he was in and out of the team, and it was not until Terry Neill arrived as manager that Neighbour had an extended run as an almost automatic choice in 1975 76. However, in September 1976 with Keith Burkinshaw then in charge, Spurs signed Peter Taylor, a more direct, regular goal-scoring winger, and Neighbour was immediately transferred for £75,000 to Norwich City-against whom he had made his last appearance for Spurs a few days earlier. He spent three years at Carrow Road and then joined West Ham, helping them reach the FA Cup Final in 1980, although he did not play in the Final itself. A member of their losing League Cup Final team the following season, he remained with the Hammers for four years until his retirement. He then managed a Sports Centre in Haringey and ran his own sports shop in Chingford. He also coached Enfield and helped them win the FA Trophy in 1988. In October 1990, he returned to West Ham as their Youth Development Officer, remaining there for four years until his retirement. He then managed a Sports Centre in Haringey and ran his own sports shop in Chingford. He also coached Enfield and helped them win the FA Trophy in 1988. In October 1990, he returned to West Ham as their Youth Development Officer, remaining there for four years before coaching at Doncaster Rovers. After a time as manager of St Albans, Neighbour returned to youth coaching with Charlton, Spurs and West Ham United.

Appearances:
League: 104 (15) apps. 8 gls.
FA Cup: 10 (1) apps. 1 gl.
FL Cup: 14 (3) apps. 1 gl.
Euro: 6 (3) apps. 1 gl.
Others: 24 (10) apps. 4 gls.
Total: 158 (32) apps. 15 gls.

NEILL, William John Terence

Role: Manager 1974-76
5ft.11ins. 12st.7lbs.
Born: Belfast, Northern Ireland, 8th May 1942

CAREER: Northern Ireland Schools/Bangor Jul 1958/Arsenal Dec 1959/Hull City player-manager Jul 1970/(Northern Ireland player-manager Oct 1971)/SPURS manager Sep 1974/Arsenal manager Jun 1976-Dec 1983.

Debut v Northern New South Wales (sub) (Fr) (Newcastle) 12.5.1976

Terry Neill is best remembered at Spurs for his time as manager, but he did in fact play once for the first team. That was on the club's tour to Canada, Fiji and Australasia in 1976 when he played as substitute against Northern New South Wales in Newcastle. Neill started his football career as a wing-half with Bangor before moving to Arsenal. He made his League debut in December 1960, was Arsenal captain by the age of 20 and won four Under-23 and 44 full caps for Northern Ireland before joining Hull City as player-manager. Appointed player-manager of Northern Ireland in October 1971 he played over 100 League games for Hull and won another 15 caps before retiring from playing to concentrate on management. His selection as successor to Bill Nicholson was quite a surprise for his time with Hull had always been looked upon as a managerial apprenticeship for an expected return to Arsenal. Due to his links with Spurs' great rivals Neill had a difficult time at White Hart Lane

and there were few regrets when he resigned, almost immediately taking over the manager's role at Highbury. With Arsenal until his dismissal in December 1983, he led them to three successive FA Cup Finals between 1978 and 1980, winning the Cup in 1979 and losing on the other two occasions, and to the European Cup-Winners' Cup Final in 1980 where they lost on penalties to Valencia. Following his dismissal he worked as a radio football commentator while running a sports bar in central London.

Appearances:
Others: (1) app.
Total: (1) app. 0 gls.

NELSEN, Ryan William

Role: Defender 2011-12
6ft.1ins. 12st.1lb.
Born: Christchurch, New Zealand, 18th October 1977

CAREER: Newman College (New Zealand)/Christchurch United (New Zealand) 1995-98/Canterbury/Greensboro College (USA) Jan 1997/Stanford Cardinal (USA) Jan 1999/DC United (USA) Jan 2001/Blackburn Rovers Jan 2005/SPURS Feb-May 2012/Queens Park Rangers Jun 2012/Toronto (Canada) head coach Jan 2013-Aug 2014.

Debut v Newcastle United (sub) (PL) (h) 11.2.2011

As Blackburn Rovers struggled at the wrong end of the Premier League table in 2011-12, former captain Ryan Nelsen spent nearly all his time in the treatment room with a knee injury. Club and player agreed that after seven years of great service, it was time for a parting of the ways and his contract was cancelled. As Harry Redknapp had allowed Sébastien Bassong to join Wolves on transfer deadline day, Spurs were a little short of defensive cover and signed Nelsen on a short term deal. The 34-year old was coming to the end of a great career that had encompassed playing in his native New Zealand, eight years in America, including four with DC United, playing for New Zealand's Under-23s in the 2008 Olympic games and 45 full caps, many of them as captain, in addition to his time with Blackburn. He was to make only five substitute appearances in the Premier League, though he did play in four FA Cup-ties, including the one with Bolton Wanderers abandoned when Fabrice Muamba suffered his heart attack. Released at the end of the season, Nelsen finished his career with a year at Queens Park Rangers before a short, but unsuccessful, time as head coach of Toronto. Nelsen became the only Spurs player to represent New Zealand when he played against Jamaica late in February 2012.

Appearances:
League: (5) apps.
FA Cup: 4* apps. 1 gl.
Total: 4 (5) apps. 1 gl.
* Includes 1 abandoned match

NELSON, David

Role: Inside-forward 1942-44
5ft.8ins. 11st.3lbs.
Born: Douglas Water, Lanarkshire, 3rd February 1918
Died: Greenwich, Connecticut, USA, September 1988

CAREER: Douglas Water Thistle/St Bernards am. Aug 1935, pro. Jan 1936/Arsenal May 1936/(guest for Brentford, Celtic, Chesterfield, Clapton Orient, Motherwell and **SPURS** during World War Two)/Fulham Dec 1946/Brentford Aug 1947/Queens Park Rangers Feb 1950/Crystal Palace Mar 1952/Ashford Town player-manager Mar 1953.

Debut v Millwall (FLSC) (h) 20.3.1943 (scored once)

David Nelson was an Arsenal player who made two guest appearances for Spurs in the Football League South Cup. He made his League debut for Arsenal in December 1936, but was never a regular having to compete with Alf Kirchen for the outside-right position. Whilst a winger at Highbury he played both his games for Spurs at inside-forward and after the War joined Fulham where he played at half-back. His best days were spent with Brentford where he made over a hundred League appearances before ending his senior career with spells at Queens Park Rangers and Crystal Palace. He had a brief spell as player-manager of Ashford before emigrating to America in December 1955.

Appearances:
Others: 2 apps. 1 gl.
Total: 2 apps. 1 gl.

NESBIT

Role: Inside-forward 1893-94

Debut v London Hospital (Fr) (h) 8.2.1894 (scored once)

Nesbit's one appearance for Spurs was in February 1894 when he played in a friendly match against London Hospital. Spurs fielded a team of mostly reserves and trialists in a 1-1 draw, with Nesbit scoring Spurs' goal.

Appearances:
Others: 1 app. 1 gl.
Total: 1 app. 1 gl.

NETHERCOTT, Stuart David

Role: Central defender 1991-97
6ft.1ins. 13st.12lbs.
Born: Chadwell Heath, Essex 21st March 1973

CAREER: Redbridge United/Claparcro/**SPURS** trainee Jul 1989, pro. Jul 1991/(Maidstone United loan Sep 1991)/(Barnet loan Feb 1992)/Millwall loan Jan 1998, perm. Feb 1998/Wycombe Wanderers loan Dec 2003, perm. Jun 2004/(Woking loan Aug 2005)/Heybridge Swifts trial Jul 2006, perm. Sep 2006/Wivenhoe Town Jan 2007/Welling United player-asst. manager May 2007-Jan 2008/Wivenhoe Town Jan 2008/Maldon Town player-asst. manager Jul 2008, player-caretaker manager Sep 2008, player-manager Oct 2008-Sep 2009/Ware manager Jun 2011, player Jul 2011-Jun 2012/Little Waltham/Coggleshall Town coach Jun 2013.

Debut v Chelsea (PL) (a) 20.3.1993
(Hull City XI (sub) (Fr) (a) 8.5.1992)

A big, powerful, central defender who gave no quarter and asked for none, Stuart Nethercott gained early League experience on loan to Maidstone United and Barnet, before slowly pushing for a place at Spurs. For five years he was on the fringes at Spurs, frequently called up, playing a couple of games, then finding himself back on the bench or in the reserves. He made eight appearances for the England Under-21 side. Particularly strong in the air, Nethercott was a bit of a throw-back to the robust centre-halves of the sixties, strong, aggressive, hard-tackling, no-nonsense. Finesse was not Nethercott's forte and that made it difficult for him to compete with central defenders like Gary Mabbutt, Sol Campbell and Colin Calderwood. With it unlikely he would ever become a regular at White Hart Lane, Nethercott was allowed to move to Millwall, a club where his talents were always more likely to be fully appreciated. He helped Millwall win promotion from the Second Division and gave the Lions six years first rate service, over 200 appearances to his credit, before moving down the football ladder. He finished his playing career at non-League level and went into management, though he was registered as a player again in June 2011 so he could turn out for Ware. He was sacked as Ware manager following the election of former Spurs' physio, Mike Varney, as club chairman.

Appearances:
League: 31 (23) apps.
FA Cup: 5 (3) apps. 1 gl.
Others: 16 (15) apps. 1 gl.
Total: 52 (41) apps. 2 gls.

NEWBIGGING, William Menzies

Role: Centre-forward 1896-97
Born: Larkhall, Lanarkshire, 27th December 1874
Died: Douglas, Lanarkshire, 16th October 1954

CAREER: Lanark County/**SPURS** Jun 1896/Motherwell Mar 1898/Folkestone May 1898/Fulham Mar 1900/Queens Park Rangers Aug 1900 Lanark Jan 1903.

Debut v Sheppey United (SL) (a) 5.9.1896
(Rossendale (Fr) (h) 3.9.1896 (scored twice))

Willie Newbigging was Spurs' regular centre-forward throughout the 1896-97 season as the club made its debut in the Southern League. A frequent scorer in friendlies, he did not find the net too often in competitive matches and was released at the end of the season. He later played for Motherwell, Folkestone, Fulham and Queens Park Rangers. Newbigging's younger brother, Alex, was a well-travelled goalkeeper in the early years of the last century playing for, amongst others, Aberdeen, Queens Park Rangers, Nottingham Forest, Reading, Rangers and Coventry City.

Appearances:
Southern: 10 apps. 2 gls.
FA Cup: 3 apps. 3 gls.
Others: 34* apps. 17 gls.
Total: 47 apps. 22 gls.
*Includes 1 abandoned match.

NEWBURY, B E

Role: Inside-forward 1893-94

Debut v Friars (Fr) (h) 19.12.1893

A reserve with Spurs for two or three years, Newbury's only first team appearance was in December 1893 when he played in a friendly with the club made up of members of the London Sporting Press, the Friars.

Appearances:
Others: 1 app.
Total: 1 app. 0 gls.

NEWBY, W

Role: Half-back 1893-95

CAREER: Robin Hood/**SPURS** cs. 1893/Shaftesbury Rovers/Edmonton Albion by Sep 1896/Vampires by Dec 1896/Edmonton Ramblers by Feb 1898/Edmonton White Star by Jan 1899.

Debut v Enfield (Fr) (a) 16.9.1893

A former player with Robin Hood, Newby played regularly for Spurs in the 1893-94 season although he still turned out in a few games for the Robins and also played for Shaftesbury Rovers. He made his debut for Spurs in the first game of the season as Spurs, with a number of trialists being given the opportunity to impress, lost 1-5 at Enfield. Newby was one of the few to take his chance and kept a place in the team until March 1894. He made only one first team appearance the following season, but continued to help Spurs out until the end of the century although all his further games were for the reserves. In September 1896 he was reported to be playing with Edmonton Albion, but by December that year he was turning out for Vampires. In February 1898 he was with Edmonton Ramblers and by January 1899 Edmonton White Star.

Appearances:
Others: 19 apps. 1 gl.
Total: 19 apps. 1 gl.

NEWMAN, Ernest Henry

Role: Outside-left 1909-14
5ft.7ins. 10st.4lbs.
Born: Birmingham, Warwickshire, 27th December 1887
Died: Edmonton, London, 3rd January 1945

CAREER: Erdington/Walsall cs. 1907/Stockport County cs. 1909/**SPURS** Apr 1910.

Debut v Bolton Wanderers (FL) (a) 23.4.1910

Ernie Newman was signed from Stockport County in April 1910 and made his first appearance that month in a League game against Bolton Wanderers. An inside-forward with Stockport, he played at outside-left in the absence of injured Bert Middlemiss. Although he remained with Spurs for four years, most of that time was spent in the reserves as cover for any of the forward positions. It was only in 1911-12 that he had an extended first team run in his recognised role after Billy Minter was moved to centre-forward on the failure of Alex Young.

Appearances:
League: 31* apps. 6 gls.
FA Cup: 2 apps.
Others: 1 app.
Total: 34 apps. 6 gls.
*Includes 1 abandoned match.

NEWMAN

Role: Inside-forward 1894-95

Debut v Casuals (Fr) (h) 6.4.1895

Newman's only appearance for Spurs was in a 60 minute friendly match with Casuals in April 1895. He was then replaced by J McElheney and it may well be "Newman" was a pseudonym McElheney played under.

Appearances:
Others: 1 app.
Total: 1 app. 0 gls.

NICHOLLS, Joseph Henry

Role: Goalkeeper 1926-36
6ft.4ins. 13st.9lbs.
Born: Carlton, Nottinghamshire, 8th March 1905
Died: Nottingham, Nottinghamshire, 20th June 1973

CAREER: Notts County trial/Darlaston/Grenadier Guards 1922/**SPURS** trial Aug 1926, am. Sep 1926, pro. May 1927/(Northfleet United 1926)/Bristol Rovers May 1936/retired 1939.

Debut v Liverpool (FL) (a) 30.4.1927

A giant of a man, Joe Nicholls first caught Spurs' attention when, serving in the Grenadier Guards, he gave a wonderful display in the Army Services Bulldog Challenge Cup Final. When Spurs heard he had decided to leave the Army they invited him to sign and, although several other clubs were keen to secure his signature, he accepted Spurs' offer. Sent to the Northfleet nursery, he made his League debut in April 1927, but had to serve a lengthy apprenticeship as understudy to Cyril Spiers before taking over at the start of the 1932-33 season. Spurs were promoted that year and the following season Nicholls was ever-present as they finished third in Division One. His reliability was recognised when he played for the Rest against England in the international trial in March 1934, but that was the closest he got to international honours. Incredibly popular with the crowd, he was remarkably agile for such a big man, but it was his strength in the air and ability to withstand the heaviest of challenges from opposing forwards that caught the eye. His form suffered at the start of 1935-36 and he lost his place to Alan Taylor as Spurs fought vainly against relegation. With the developing talent of Percy Hooper in reserve, Spurs gave Nicholls a free transfer in May 1936 and he joined Bristol Rovers. Not surprisingly for such a large and powerful man Nicholls was boxing champion of his Army battalion.

Appearances:
League: 124 apps.
FA Cup: 5 apps.
Others: 10 apps.
Total: 139 apps. 0 gls.

NICHOLSON, William Edward O.B.E.

Role: Half-back 1938-55
5ft.9ins. 11st.7lbs.
Born: Scarborough, Yorkshire, 26th January 1919
Died: Potters Bar, Hertfordshire, 23rd October 2004

CAREER: Scarborough Working Men's Club/Scarborough Young Liberals/**SPURS** trial Mar 1936/(Northfleet United)/**SPURS** pro., Aug 1938/(guest for Darlington, Fulham, Hartlepools United, Manchester United, Middlesbrough, Newcastle United and Sunderland during World War Two)/**SPURS** coach Dec 1955, first team coach Jul 1955, manager Oct 1958-Sep 1974/West Ham United scout Oct 1974-Jul 1976/ **SPURS** consultant Jul 1976, president May 1991.

Debut v Blackburn Rovers (FL) (a) 22.10.1938

Bill Nicholson may not be remembered as the best player in Spurs' illustrious history, but there can be no doubt he is the greatest and most influential servant the club has ever had. He gave up a job as a laundry boy in his home town for a trial at White Hart Lane in March 1936, joined the ground-staff, and was groomed for two years at the Northfleet nursery before signing as a professional. Originally a left-back, he made his League debut in October 1938 standing in for Bill Whatley who was on international duty with Wales, and by the start of the following season was first choice. On the outbreak of war Nicholson was called up for service in the Durham Light Infantry and rarely able to play for Spurs. Returning after the war, he initially turned out at centre-half, but for the start of the 1947-48 season moved to the right-half position he was to make his own. A solid, dependable player, robust and hard tackling, Nicholson was a ball-winning terrier rather than an artist. He possessed excellent simple qualities of distribution and frequently ferreted out the ball before laying it off to the more creative players in the team such as Sonny Walters and Eddie Bailey. A member of the famous "Push and Run" side that won the Second Division title in 1950 and the Football League Championship the following year, Nicholson collected his first representative honour in January 1950 playing for England "B" against Switzerland. It was not however, the start of a long international career, for whilst he appeared for the Football League, won two more England "B" caps and was a member of England's 1950 World Cup squad, he was to win only one full England cap. That came against Portugal at Goodison Park in May 1951 when, remarkably, he scored with his first kick of the match. Selected for the game against Austria in November 1951, he was forced to withdraw through injury and thereafter was unable to wrest the right-half position from the legendary Billy Wright. Whilst still playing, Nicholson passed his FA badge and coached Wingate and the Cambridge University team, so it was no surprise when he moved onto the White Hart Lane coaching staff following his retirement from playing. Appointed first team coach when Jimmy Anderson took over the manager's role from Arthur Rowe, Nicholson also helped Walter Winterbottom with the England Under-23 side and was an obvious appointment as Spurs' next manager. His first match in charge provided an extraordinary foretaste of the glorious era to come as Spurs thrashed Everton 10-4. As manager, Nicholson led Spurs to their greatest triumphs, the "Double" in 1961, FA Cup in 1962 and 1967, European Cup-Winners' Cup in 1963, League Cup in 1971 and 1973 and UEFA Cup in 1972. They also reached the UEFA Cup Final in 1974. A man of the "old school", renowned for his honesty and integrity, Nicholson built three fine sides during his lengthy spell in charge. He was a perfectionist and a hard taskmaster, often slow to praise even when his players had done well, but all his teams played in the traditional "Tottenham style", with great players allowed to parade their skills, and the emphasis always on attack, and above all, entertainment. However, as time wore on Nicholson became increasingly disillusioned by the attitudes and demands of some modern players, as well as the negative tactical direction the game he loved so much seemed to be taking at the time. In the wake of Spurs' poor start he resigned in September 1974 and despite pleas to remain from directors, players and supporters alike, Nicholson's mind was made up and he left the club he had served so admirably. Some sharp criticism followed that not enough was done to find him another role at White Hart Lane, but ultimately he was not away for long. He helped out West Ham during their European campaign of 1975-76 before returning to Spurs in July 1976-the very first request made by new manager Keith Burkinshaw. Appointed to the role of Consultant, he occupied that position until May 1991 when his truly great service to Spurs was recognised by his appointment as club President. His respect and immense standing within the game was also recognised earlier when he was awarded the OBE in 1975, a testimonial game at Spurs in August 1983, and the Professional Footballers' Association Merit Award in 1984. Nicholson retired in July 1997 but was still to be seen at White Hart Lane, a living legend in the Legends Executive Suite until shortly before his passing.

Appearances:
League: 318* apps. 6 gls.
FA Cup: 27 apps.
Others: 49 apps. 1 gl.
Total: 394 apps. 7 gls.
*Includes 1 abandoned match.

NICHOLSON, Jake Charlie

Role: Midfielder
6ft.1ins. 11st.5lbs.
Born: Harrow, Middlesex, 19th July 1992

CAREER: West Ham United Academy/**SPURS** Academy Scholar Jul 2008, pro. Jul 2010 /(MyPa (Finland) loan Mar 2011)/released Jun 2013/ Crystal Palace trial Jul 2013/ Ipswich Town trial Sep 2013/ Greenock Morton Nov 2013/ AFC Wimbledon trial and perm Feb 2014-Jan 2015/St Albans City Feb–Mar 2015/ Swindon Town trial Jul 2015/ Hayes & Yeading United Aug-Sep 2015/Walton Casuals Oct 2015/ Kingstonian May 2016/ Walton Casuals Aug 2016..

Debut v Heart of Midlothian (sub) (UEFA) (h) 25.8.2011

Previously with West Ham United's academy, Jake Nicholson had gained some senior experience during three months on loan to MyPa of Finland. Shortly after returning to Spurs he made his one and only first team appearance as a substitute in a Europa League tie with Heart of Midlothian. The England Under-19 international then suffered a hip injury and unable to recover full fitness was released in June 2013. He played a few games with Morton before returning to London with AFC Wimbledon. He made an immediate impression, scoring on his debut and then finding himself at the centre of a disciplinary hearing. Wimbledon registered his initial one-month contract with the Football League, but failed to continue the registration, meaning Nicholson had been ineligible to play. The Dons had three points deducted and a £5,000 suspended fine. Nicholson made less than a dozen appearances for Wimbledon before moving into non-League football.

Appearances:
Europe: (1) app.
Total: (1) app. 0 gls.

NIELSEN, Allan

Role: Midfield 1996-2000
5ft.8ins. 11st.8lbs.
Born: Esbjerg, Denmark, 13th March 1971

CAREER: Sædding/Guldager (Denmark)/Esbjerg (Denmark)/Bayern Munich (Germany) Jan 1989/Sion (Switzerland) Jul 1991/OB Odense (Denmark) Oct 1991/FC Copenhagen (Denmark) Jan 1994/Brøndby (Denmark) Apr 1995/**SPURS** Aug 1996/(Wolverhampton Wanderers loan Mar 2000)/Watford Aug 2000/Herfølge BK (Denmark) player-asst. coach Jun 2003, player-coach Apr 2004, coach Jul 2004-Apr 2005/Birkerød Sports College (Denmark) coach 2008/Viborg Sports College (Denmark).

Debut v Wimbledon (PL) (a) 4.9.1996

Allan Nielsen was not one of those creative midfield geniuses blessed with style and flair. He was a grafter, a non-stop worker with a never satisfied determination to be continually involved in the game. Whether it was making tackles, breaking up play, tracking back or bursting forward, Nielsen was always at the heart of the action, providing the support and platform without which players with finesse could not hope to flourish. Something of a boy prodigy in his native Denmark, Nielsen was whisked off to Germany as a 17-year old, but in two years with Bayern Munich made just one six-minute first team appearance. Released by the Germans, he joined Sion but did no better there, returning home to Denmark after three months and without playing even five minutes for the Swiss outfit. Such rejections might have been enough to turn a boy off football, but Nielsen was nothing if not persistent. With Odense, he began to make his mark, helping them win the Danish Cup in 1993, before moving up to FC Copenhagen and a year later to Brøndby, then Denmark's top club. It was with Brøndby that Nielsen came to the fore. He made his international debut against Armenia in August 1995, scoring within 45 seconds of his introduction as a substitute. He followed that by helping Brøndby lift the Superliga title in 1996, then played in Denmark's three Euro 96 games and was voted his country's Player of the Year. Reportedly on Spurs' radar prior to Euro 96, Nielsen was just the type of midfield hustler Gerry Francis liked. While the deal to sign him was completed in August 1996, Francis willingly waited until Brøndby's Champions League qualifier had been completed for Nielsen to arrive at White Hart Lane. Doing a lot of the hard work that often gets overlooked, Nielsen had three years as a near regular at Spurs, though sometimes the one to be omitted when more creative talents were called for. The highlight of his Spurs' career was without doubt the 1999 Worthington Cup final when he scored the only goal of the game, a goal that typified Nielsen's attitude. With only seconds remaining, Steffen Iversen broke from his own half. Nielsen had worked overtime to help compensate for the dismissal of Justin Edinburgh, but from somewhere he found the energy to burst into the Leicester box and head home Iversen's deflected cross. After that, the arrival of Øyvind Leonhardsen and Tim Sherwood saw Nielsen's career with Spurs on a downward slope. Following a loan spell with Wolverhampton Wanderers, Nielsen was transferred to Watford where he remained for three years until financial constraints dictated his release. He returned to Denmark, played for and coached Herfølge but was unable to save them from relegation and resigned. He has since coached at youth level. Nielsen played 30 games for Denmark during his time with Spurs.

Appearances:
League: 78 (18) apps. 12 gls.
FA Cup: 5 (2) apps. 3 gls
FL Cup: 10 (1) apps. 3 gls
Euro: 1 app.
Others: 8 apps. 2 gls.
Total: 102 (21) apps. 20 gls.

NILSEN, Roger

Role: Defender 1998-99
5ft.11ins. 12st.6lbs.
Born: Tromsø, Norway, 8th August 1969

CAREER: Kvaløysletta (Norway)/Tromsø (Norway) 1987-88/Viking (Norway) 1989-1993/(1.FC Köln (Germany) loan 1993)/Sheffield United Nov 1993/**SPURS** March 1999/released May 1999/Casino Graz (Austria) Jul 1999/Molde (Norway) Dec 1999/Heart of Midlothian trial Jan 2001/Bryne (Norway) loan Apr 2002, perm. Oct 2002/Stavanger (Norway) Dec 2003, manager Nov 2005/Viking (Norway) asst. manager Dec 2006-Dec 2010/Norwegian College of Elite Sports (Norway) teacher/IF Fløya (women's) (Norway) manager Jun 2014-Sep 2016/Viking (Norway) women's development officer Dec 2016.

Debut v Newcastle United (PL) (a) 5.4.1999

Roger Nilsen was signed from Sheffield United in March 1999 purely to provide short term central defensive cover. With Ramon Vega and John Scales on the injured list and an FA Cup semi-final upcoming, Sol Campbell and Luke Young were the only available centre-halves, with Young still a novice. Nilsen had bags of experience having played in Norway, Germany and for six years at Sheffield United. A dependable performer with 31 appearances for Norway to his credit, there was nothing particularly outstanding about Nilsen. He played the game simply and that was all Spurs were ever going to want from him. In the three months he was at White Hart Lane, Nilsen played just three matches. On his release, he played for a short time with Casino Graz in Austria before returning to Norway with Molde. After three years he joined Bryne, then signed for Stavanger where he moved into management, guiding the unfashionable club to the

Norwegian Second Division before moving into the top-flight with Viking. Nilsen's brother, Steinar, played for Tromsø, Inter-Milan and Norway.

Appearances:
League: 3 apps.
Total: 3 apps. 0 gls.

NIXON, Arthur Cooper

Role: Outside-left 1894-95
Born: 18th April 1867
Died: Ladysmith, Natal, South Africa, 16th February 1900

CAREER: Old Carthusians/Casuals/SPURS Jan 1895.

Debut v London Welsh (AmC) (Spotted Dog) 19.1.1895

An Old Carthusians player, Nixon made his only appearance for Spurs in the Amateur Cup Divisional Final 2nd replay with London Welsh in January 1895. He was also a member of the Casuals for some years and represented London.

Appearances:
Others: 1 app.
Total: 1 app. 0 gls.

N'JIE, Clinton Mua

Role: Forward 2015-
5ft.9ins. 10st.10lbs.
Born: Buea, Cameroon, 15th August 1993

CAREER: l'École de Football des Brasseries (Cameroon)/Olympique Lyonnais (France) 2011/SPURS Aug 2015/(Olympique de Marseille loan Aug 2016).

Debut v Crystal Palace (PL) (h) 20.9.2015

Another in the long line of exciting young strikers identified by French clubs in the nation's former African colonies, Clinton N'jie spent four years with Olympique Lyonnais, proving himself a player of tremendous potential. Best playing up against the last defender when his pace can be put to effect, he arrived at Spurs with six goals in eleven full international appearances for Cameroon. At Lyonnais N'jie had not been required to play as a loan striker and really does not have the physical attributes for that sort of role., at least not how it has developed in the English game. Whether it was intended when he was signed that he would play alongside Harry Kane did not become clear before N'jie was injured. It resulted in him missing most of his first season as Kane continued the incredible scoring form that showed Spurs at their best when he played as a lone striker. With the arrival of Vincent Janssen, a striker more in the Kane mould, opportunities for N'jie look limited. As the 2016 transfer window closed he was allowed to join Marseille on loan for the season, a permanent transfer viewed as probable.

Appearances:
League: (8) apps.
FL Cup: (1) apps.
Euro: 2 (3) apps.
Total: 2 (12) apps. 0 gls.

NKOUDOU (MBIDA), Georges-Kévin

Role: Winger 2016-
5ft.8ins. 10st. 10lbs.
Born: Versaille, France, 13th February 1995

CAREER: Petits Anges (France) Aug 2006/EST Solitaire Paris (France) Oct 2007/Paris Saint-Germain (France) Jul 2008/AC Boulogne Billancourt (France) Jul 2010/Nantes (France) Jul 2011/Olympique Marseille (France) Jun 2015/SPURS Aug 2016.

Debut v Gillingham (sub) (FL Cup) (h) 21.9.2017

Georges-Kévin Nkoudou showed enough talent as a schoolboy to be taken into the Paris Saint-Germain Academy. When they decided he would not make the grade, he did not give up hopes of making a career in the professional game but returned to youth football until Nantes gave him another chance. A winger with pace who chips in with his fair share of goals, Nkoudou made his senior debut in August 2013 and while many of his appearances were from the bench, did enough for Olympique Marseille to invest £1 million in his talents. In his one season with Marseille he proved a revelation, with ten goals in 41 appearances enough to persuade Spurs to lay out £11 million for his signature. Having played for France at youth level and with six Under-21 appearances to his name, Nkoudou now has the chance to move on to the next level.

Appearances:
League: (8) apps.
FA Cup: 1 (2) apps.
FL Cup: 1 (1) apps.
Euro: (4) apps.
Others: 1 app.
Total: 3 (15) app. 0 gls.

NOBLE, David Simpson

Role: Outside-left 1941-42
Born: Queensferry, West Lothian

CAREER: Blackhall Athletic/St Bernards Jun 1934/Clyde Sep 1936/(guest for SPURS during World War Two).

Debut v Queens Park Rangers (LWL) (h) 27.9.1941

A guest player from Clyde, Noble was serving in the Royal Air Force when he made six appearances for Spurs in the London War League during the 1941-42 season scoring three goals.

Appearances:
Others: 6 app. 3 gls.
Total: 6 app. 3 gls.

NORMAN, Maurice

Role: Defender 1955-66
6ft.1ins. 12st.2lbs.
Born: Mulbarton, Norfolk, 8th May 1934

CAREER: Norfolk Schools/Wymondham Juniors/Mulbarton FC/

Norwich City am. 1951, pro. Sep 1952/**SPURS** Nov 1955/retired May 1967.

Debut v Cardiff City (FL) (h) 5.11.1955

A centre-half with Norwich City, Maurice Norman made his League debut in February 1955. He had played only 35 League games when Spurs moved to sign him for £28,000, with winger Johnny Gavin returning to Norwich as part of the deal. Brought in to replace Alf Ramsey, he immediately settled into the right-back role and won his first England Under-23 cap against Scotland in February 1956. An injury in September 1956 forced him to miss six months of the season, and when he returned it was at left-back, for Peter Baker had taken over the number two shirt. Towards the end of that season Norman moved to centre-half in place of John Ryden and collected two more Under-23 caps, but it was not until a third of the way through the next season that he moved permanently into the pivotal position. A member of England's squad for the 1958 World Cup, he proved almost immovable at Spurs until his retirement, and developed into one of the finest centre-halves in the game. Tall and confident, Norman had a superb, strong physique which helped make him such an awesome and uncompromising tackler. His height meant he was useful enough in the air, but those earlier experiences at full-back had developed not only a fine sense of positional play, but also excellent distributional skills that helped start attacks from deep in defence. After missing only one game in the "Double" season of 1960-61 and helping Spurs retain the FA Cup in 1962, he at last won his first England cap, playing against Peru in May 1962 in the last warm up game before the World Cup. England's regular centre-half from then on, he picked up a winner's medal in the European Cup-Winners' Cup in 1963, won 22 more full caps, played for England in representative matches against the Football League and Young England and appeared for the Football League. Primarily a defensive player, although he was an early exponent of the tactic of moving up for a corner kick, Norman's contribution to Spurs' great successes in the early 1960s was maybe a little overshadowed by the brilliance

of the players around him, but his solid defensive efficiency, huge heart and ability to cover for the forward sorties of Blanchflower and Mackay, were of crucial importance to the team. Having reverted to full-back with the arrival of Laurie Brown and the semi-retirement of Ron Henry, Norman's career sadly suffered an abrupt end when he broke a leg in a friendly against a Hungarian Select XI in November 1965. Despite a long battle to recover, he never played again, retiring in the summer of 1967. Norman then ran a knitwear and wool shop in Frinton-on-Sea before becoming a self-employed gardener.

Appearances:
League: 357 apps. 16 gls.
FA Cup: 37 apps. 2 gls.
Euro: 17 apps. 1 gl.
Others: 43 apps.
Total: 454 apps. 19 gls.

NUTTALL, Thomas Albert Bradshaw

Role: Centre-forward 1917-18
5ft.8ins. 10st.8lbs.
Born: Bolton, Lancashire, January 1889
Died: Wandsworth, London, October 1963

CAREER: Heywood United/Manchester United May 1910/Everton May 1913/(guest for **SPURS**, St Mirren and Stockport County during World War One)/St Mirren Aug 1919/Northwich Victoria Jan 1920/Southend United Jul 1920/Leyland cs. 1922/Northwich Victoria May 1922/Breightmet United Oct 1926/Manchester North End Aug 1927.

Debut v Brentford (LFC) (a) 15.9.1917 (scored once)

An Everton player who regularly guested for St Mirren, Tommy Nuttall played 18 matches for Spurs in the 1917-18 London Football Combination scoring 10 goals. A centre or inside-forward he had previously played for Manchester United, scoring four goals in 16 appearances over three years. He scored on his first appearance for Spurs in September 1917 and played centre-forward in all his matches. After the War, he signed for St Mirren, but returned to the north-west with Northwich Victoria within a year. He then joined Southend United, where he played for two years before signing for Leyland, though he had put pen to paper before going back to Northwich Victoria. His father, Jack, was assistant trainer at Manchester United before the First War and his brother, Harry, a half-back, played for Bolton Wanderers, won three England caps in 1928-29 and was coach to Nelson.

Appearances:
Others: 18 apps. 10 gls.
Total: 18 apps. 10 gls.

O

OAKES, John

Role: Centre-half 1944-45
5ft.10ins. 12st.0lbs.
Born: Northwich, Cheshire, 13th September 1905
Died: Perth, Australia 20th March 1992

CAREER: Cargo Fleet Works and Cochrane/Chilton Colliery May 1928/Nottingham Forest Aug 1928/Newark 1930/Clapton Orient trial Sep 1930/Crook Town Oct 1930/Southend United May 1931/Crook Town Jul 1932/Spennymoor United Feb 1933/(Middlesbrough Police)/Aldershot Aug 1934/Charlton Athletic Mar 1936/(guest for Brentford, Clapton Orient, Crystal Palace, Millwall, Stoke City, **SPURS** and West Ham United during World War Two)/Plymouth Argyle Jul 1947/Snowdon Colliery Welfare player-manager Jul 1949-Feb 1953/Gravesend and Northfleet coach Jul 1953/coach in Sweden/coach in USA/coach in Australia.

Debut v Reading (FLS) (a) 9.9.1944

Charlton Athletic's centre-half, John Oakes made his one appearance for Spurs as a guest against Reading in September 1944, being called upon to play as Spurs arrived for the game with only four players. Originally an inside-forward, he had made several attempts to break into League football without success and close to his thirties when he switched to centre-forward and made the breakthrough. He was Aldershot's top-scorer when Charlton secured his services as they sought, successfully, to ensure promotion to the First Division. Over thirty by the time he made his top-flight debut, Oakes was soon moved back to centre-half, a decision that certainly extended his career. An England War-time international against Wales in November 1939, he was a member of the Charlton teams that reached the Football League South Cup finals in 1942-43 and 1943-44, winning on the second occasion, and also played for Charlton when they lost to Derby in the 1946 FA Cup Final. In July 1947, almost 42 years of age, he moved to Plymouth Argyle and played for them for one season before retiring. He then went into coaching. Later in life he moved to America and then on to Australia.

Appearances:
Others: 1 app.
Total: 1 app. 0 gls.

OATES

Role: Half-back 1896-97

Debut v Vampires (Fr) (h) 26.12.1896

Oates made his only appearance for Spurs on Boxing Day 1896 when he played in a friendly match with Vampires. A local reporter stated that "Oates performed creditably notwithstanding that it is some years since he won his international cap for Wales". As there does not appear to be a player of this name who played for Wales, it may be his name was wrongly given and that it should have been John Mates, a half-back with Chirk, born in Chirk on 28th February 1870. Mates had won his first cap against Ireland in February 1891 although he had to wait until March 1897 before winning two more. The Spurs' match was played in the morning with some of the Spurs' players also turning out in another friendly in the afternoon against the Third Battalion of the Grenadier Guards.

Appearances:
Others: 1 app.
Total: 1 app. 0 gls.

OBIKA, Jonathan Chiedozie

Role: Striker 2008-
6ft.0ins. 13st.0lbs.
Born: Enfield, Middlesex, 12th September 1990

CAREER: Bishops Stopford's School/**SPURS** academy scholar Jul 2007, pro. Jan 2009/(Yeovil Town loan Mar 2009 and Aug 2009)/(Millwall loan Feb 2010)/(Crystal Palace loan Aug 2010)/(Peterborough United loan Jan 2011)/(Swindon Town loan Feb 2011)/(Yeovil Town loan Mar 2011 and Aug 2011)/(Charlton Athletic loan Feb 2013)/(Brighton & Hove Albion loan Jan 2014)/(Charlton Athletic loan Mar 2014)/Swindon Town Sep 2014.

Debut v NEC Nijmegen (sub) (UEFA) (a) 27.11.2008

A big, strong, bustling type of central striker, Jon Obika was on the fringes of the first team squad at White Hart Lane for some time, without ever making the breakthrough. A prolific scorer at youth level as he worked his way through the Spurs Academy, Obika was originally a powerful, pacy, forward who played out wide, but proved at his most effective when drifting into the centre. An England Under-20 international, he was allowed out on loan to clubs lower down the football ladder to gain experience. His build and willingness to battle it out with the toughest of central defenders saw Obika play as the focal point of the attack, a role that certainly toughened him up. He was continually loaned out during his time with Spurs, impressing all the clubs he played for, but not doing enough to earn a real chance in Spurs' first team. He made just one starting appearance. That was in the second leg of a UEFA cup-tie against Shakhtar Donetsk, when Spurs were two goals down after the first leg and had little real chance of progressing further. After more than 100 League appearances while on loan, Obika moved to Swindon Town. In two years there he has proved a competent enough performer at League One level.

Appearances:
FA Cup: (1) app.
FL Cup: (1) apps.
Euro: 1 (1) apps.
Others: 4 (3) apps. 2 gls.
Total: 5 (6) apps. 2 gls.

O'CALLAGHAN, Eugene

Role: Inside-forward 1926-35 and 1940-44
5ft.8ins. 11st.10lbs.
Born: Ebbw Vale, 6th October 1906
Died: Fulham, London, 4th July 1956

CAREER: Victoria Mixed School/Ebbw Vale Schools/Wales Schools/Victoria United/Ebbw Vale Corinthians/**SPURS** am. Sep 1924, ground-staff 1925/(Barnet 1925)/(Northfleet United May 1925)/**SPURS** pro. Aug 1926/Leicester City Mar 1935/Fulham Oct 1937/(guest for Aldershot, Brentford, Reading and **SPURS** during World War Two)/Fulham coach.

Debut v Everton (FL) (a) 15.1.1927

Taffy O'Callaghan was working in the pits and playing for Ebbw Vales' junior club, Victoria United, and Ebbw Vale reserves, when invited to join the Spurs' ground-staff in 1925. "Farmed out" to Barnet and then Northfleet, he was destined to become one of the few real bright spots at White Hart Lane in the late 1920's and early 1930's when, in general, the club struggled. He made such an immediate impact following his debut in January 1927 that by August Spurs had allowed Jimmy Seed to move on to Sheffield Wednesday, leaving O'Callaghan as the mainspring of the forward line. Although light in build, he was a true ninety-minute player. He could dispense pin-point passes, and showed great flair and dash when in possession. Adored by the crowd, he was good with both feet, packed a powerful shot, and, for an inside-forward primarily recognised for his creative talents, scored plenty of goals. O'Callaghan made his first appearance for Wales against Northern Ireland in May 1929, and went on to win eleven full caps in his time with Spurs. Having helped steer the club back to the First Division in 1932-33, he was surprisingly transferred to Leicester City in March 1935 just when Spurs were struggling to avoid relegation. He helped Leicester win the Second Division title in his first full season, and, in October 1937 moved to Fulham, making his debut in their colours against Spurs the same month. However, his association with Spurs was not over, for he returned to guest frequently during the Second World War. O'Callaghan stayed with Fulham until his retirement during the 1945-46 season and was then appointed assistant trainer, remaining on the Craven Cottage coaching staff until his death.

Appearances:
League: 252 apps. 92 gls.
FA Cup: 11 apps. 6 gls.
Others: 50 apps. 23 gls.
Total: 313 apps. 121 gls.

O'DONNELL, Francis Joseph

Role: Centre-forward 1943-45
6ft.0ins. 11st.10lbs.
Born: Buckhaven, Fife, 31st August 1911
Died: Macclesfield, Cheshire, 4th September 1952

CAREER: Wellesley Juniors Aug 1930/Celtic Sep 1930/Preston North End May 1935/Blackpool Nov 1937/Aston Villa Nov 1938/(guest for Blackpool, Brentford, Brighton and Hove Albion, Fulham, Heart of Midlothian, Liverpool, Notts County, Preston North End, **SPURS**, Wolverhampton Wanderers and York City during World War Two)/Nottingham Forest Jan 1946/Raith Rovers 1946-47/Buxton player-manager Dec 1948-May 1952.

Debut v Queens Park Rangers (FLS) (a) 4.9.1943

Frank O'Donnell started his professional career with Celtic and then joined Preston North End together with his brother Hugh, an outside-left, who had played with him at Wellesley Juniors and Celtic and would go on to play alongside with him at Blackpool. A prolific scorer, Frank O'Donnell made his debut for Scotland against England in April 1937 and won three more caps in his time with Preston. Scorer of Preston's goal in the 1937 FA Cup Final when they lost to Sunderland, he won his last two caps while with Blackpool and then joined Aston Villa. It was as a guest from Villa that he played for Spurs during the war, scoring eight goals in thirteen matches and showing the form that had made him such a popular player before the conflict. One of the most travelled of war-time guest players he finished his career in the first season of normal football after the war playing for Nottingham Forest. From 1948 to 1952 he was player-manager of the Derbyshire club, Buxton.

Appearances:
Others: 13 apps. 8 gls.
Total: 13 apps. 8 gls.

O'DONNELL

Role: Inside-forward 1904-05
Born: Liverpool, Lancashire

CAREER: Belfast Distillery/**SPURS** trial Apr 1905.

Debut v Sheffield United (Fr) (h) 25.4.1905

A former Belfast Distillery player, O'Donnell played his one game for Spurs in a friendly against Sheffield United in April 1905. He played by way of a trial but whilst described as "having a pretty good style" had few opportunities to impress in a 0-0 draw.

Appearances:
Others: 1 app.
Total: 1 app. 0 gls.

O'DONNELL, James

Role: Inside-forward 1920-21
5ft 10ins, 10st.8lbs.
Born: Edinburgh, about 1899

CAREER: Edinburgh junior clubs/**SPURS** Sep 1920

Debut v Watford (Fr) (a) 22.9.1920

An inexperienced young junior who signed his first professional contract when he joined Spurs from an Edinburgh junior club, James O'Donnell made his one first team appearance within a couple of weeks of his signing. That was in a benefit match at Watford for the dependents of Tom Coulson, Watford's old trainer. Although he played a few reserve games, O'Donnell's career progressed no further with Spurs and he was released at the end of the season.

Appearances:
Others: 1 app.
Total: 1 app. 0 gls.

O'DONOGHUE, Paul

Role: Defender 2002-05
6ft 1ins, 13st.10lbs.
Born: *Lewisham, south London, 14th December 1983*

CAREER: Blackheath District Schools/Inner London Schools/Villacourt Rovers/Welling United/**SPURS** scholar Jul 2000, pro. Oct 2001/(Hornchurch loan Dec 2004)/Heybridge Swifts loan Apr 2005, perm. Jul 2005/Beckenham Town.

Debut v Colchester United (sub) (Fr) (a) 23.7.2002

A powerful centre-half who joined Spurs after impressing in London schools football, Paul O'Donoghue worked his way through the youth and reserve ranks at White Hart Lane, but made only a few appearances in senior friendly matches before being released. He joined Heybridge where he had earlier played on loan linking up with former Spurs' full-back and Heybridge manager, Brian Statham. O'Donoghue did not stay long at Heybridge and soon disappeared from the football scene. In July 2007, he was reported to have given up football, planning to join his parents in Kerry and hoping to go to technical college and play Gaelic football. That was a sport he had excelled in as a schoolboy, representing London at Under-20 level. He went on to play for Tralee Institute of Technology, John Mitchels, Austin Stacks and Round Towers.

Appearances:
Others: 3 (3) apps.
Total: 3 (3) apps. 0 gls.

ODUWA, Kelede Nathan

Role: Forward 2013-
6ft.2ins. 12st.9lbs.
Born: *Bloomsbury, London, 5th March 1996*

CAREER: **SPURS** Academy Scholar Jul 2012, pro. Jul 2013/(Luton Town loan Feb 2015)/(Rangers loan Aug 2015)/(Colchester United loan Feb 2016)/(Peterborough United loan Aug 2016)/Olimpija Ljubljana. (Slovenia) Feb 2017.

Debut v Ledley King XI (Fr) (h) (sub) 12.5.2014 (scored once)

Another of the Academy players whose only appearance to date was as a substitute in Ledley King's testimonial match, Nathan Oduwa is a precocious talent who has the ability to go to the very top, if he can harness his talents in the right direction. An old-fashioned type of winger, Oduwa impressed as he worked his way through the youth system, playing for England at all age groups up to Under-20. Very tall, pacy, direct and with an incredible array of tricks, he was given a little taste of League football on loan to Luton, before signing a season-long loan deal with Rangers. He had an immediate effect with the

Glasgow club, thrilling fans with his guile and experience, while irritating opponents who considered some of his actions disrespectful. With Rangers looking for permanent recruits to play in Oduwa's position, his loan was cut short and he returned to Spurs, to be quickly loaned to Colchester. In May 2016 he was invited to play for the Nigerian Under-23s in the Rio Olympics. He accepted the offer, making his first appearance for his parents' home country in June 2016 in a pre-Games warm-up against South Korea. Reportedly upset at failing to make a first team breakthrough at Spurs, Oduwa rarely made the starting line-up during a six-month loan at Peterborough United before a surprise transfer to top-flight Slovenian outfit Olimpija.

Appearances:
Others: (1) app.
Total: (1) app. 1 gls.

OGILVIE, Connor Stuart

Role: Defender 2013-
6ft. 12st.10lbs.
Born: *Harlow, Essex, 14th February 1996*

CAREER: **SPURS** Academy Scholar Jul 2012, pro. Jul 2014/Stevenage loan Aug 2015 and Jan 2017)/(Gillingham loan Jul 2017).

Debut v Ledley King XI (Fr) (h) (sub) 12.5.2014

Spotted early and taken into the Spurs Academy, Connor Ogilvie is one of those quiet but consistent performers who do their job well and with the minimum of fuss. A defender, comfortable at full-back or in the centre of defence, Ogilvie made his debut in the senior team as a substitute in Ledley King's testimonial. Confident with the ball at his feet, he is no slouch in the air and happy to push forward when his defensive duties allow. He joined Stevenage for a month's loan in August 2015 and was so impressive that he ended up staying for the whole season, playing regularly. He returned a few months later on another loan and for 2017-18 made on loan to Portsmouth.

Appearances:
Others: (1) app.
Total: (1) app. 0 gls.

O'HAGAN, Charles

Role: Inside-forward 1904-06
5ft.9ins. 10st.7lbs.
Born: *Buncara, County Derry, 28th July 1881*

Died: New York, USA, 1st July 1931

CAREER: St Columb's Court/Derry Celtic/Old Xaverians/Everton Mar 1903/**SPURS** May 1904/Middlesbrough Jul 1906/Aberdeen Dec 1906/Greenock Morton Sep 1910/Third Lanark May 1912/Norwich City manager Jul 1920-Jan 1921/Sevilla (Spain) coach Aug 1923/FC Berlin (Germany) coach Jul 1924.

Debut v Millwall (WL) (a) 3.10.1904
(Brighton and Hove Albion (Fr) (h) 12.9.1904) (scored twice)

Charlie O'Hagan started with Derry Celtic before moving to Liverpool and playing for Old Xaverians, one of the city's premier amateur clubs of the time. He was spotted by Everton, but was in their reserves when signed by Spurs. A neat, dainty ball player, most of his Spurs appearances were as stand-in for David Copeland, but when he did play, he fitted in well with fellow Irishman, John Kirwan. Although by no means a regular for Spurs, O'Hagan played five matches for Ireland in his time at White Hart Lane, the first against Scotland in March 1905. In all of them he partnered Kirwan. Released in May 1906, he joined Middlesbrough but only stayed on Teesside a few months before moving on to Aberdeen where he won a further six caps, the first Aberdeen player to win international honours. After four years with Aberdeen, he finished his career with Greenock Morton and Third Lanark. Having put in three years' war-time service with the Highland Light Infantry in France, O'Hagan was appointed manager of Norwich City for their debut season in the Football League, but resigned within six months. He later coached in Spain and Germany.

Appearances:
Southern: 21 apps. 6 gls.
FA Cup: 3 apps. 1 gl.
Others: 25* apps. 13# gls.
Total: 49 apps. 20 gls.
*Includes 1 abandoned match.
Includes 1 in an abandoned match.

O'HARA, Jamie Darryl

Role: Midfield 2004-10
5ft.10ins. 12st.2lbs.
Born: Farnborough, Kent, 25th September 1986

CAREER: Higham Park School/Dartford District Schools/Sutton Dynamo/Arsenal schoolboy/**SPURS** scholar Jul 2003, pro. Sep 2004/(Chesterfield loan Jan 2006)/(Millwall loan Aug 2007)/(Portsmouth loan Aug 2009-Dec 2009 and Jan-May 2010)/Wolverhampton Wanderers loan Jan 2011, perm Jun 2011-Aug 2014/(Blackpool trial Nov 2013)/Blackpool Nov 2014/Fulham Jul 2015/San Jose Earthquakes (USA) trial Aug 2016/Gillingham Aug-Oct 2016/Billericay Town Mar 2017..

Debut v Portsmouth (sub) (PL) (a) 15.12.2007
(Falkenbergs (sub) (Fr) (h) 13.7.2004)

Having trained with the club since a schoolboy, Jamie O'Hara was expected to accept a scholarship with Arsenal as soon as he was old enough to sign. Arsenal were certainly keen to take him on and made an offer, but O'Hara felt that young English players were given few opportunities to make the grade at Highbury. He rejected Arsenal's offer and instead signed for Spurs, the club he had supported as a boy. He was given an early opportunity to show what he could do, making his Spurs' debut in a pre-season friendly before he had even signed his first professional contract, but O'Hara was a young man in a hurry. While on the fringes of the first team, he wanted to sample senior football on a regular basis. A loan with Chesterfield was arranged and O'Hara did well in his three months with the Derbyshire club. Back at Spurs, he was a reserve team regular in 2006-07 as Martin Jol's team made a concerted effort to secure Champions League qualification, but when he found himself outside the first team squad the following season, again agitated for a loan move. He went to Millwall, returning when Juande Ramos replaced Jol as head coach. Ramos gave O'Hara his chance and there were times when he looked to have made the breakthrough he wanted. A creative midfielder, industrious and forever demanding the ball, he was at his best going forward when his ability to beat players or thread a pass through a defence came to the fore. Never afraid to accept responsibility, every set-piece would see O'Hara stepping forward. Going forward when things were going well, O'Hara was to the fore, but when things were going badly, when he was needed to defend, to put his foot in, make tackles, do the less glamorous work, he seemed to disappear. With the arrival of Wilson Palacios, O'Hara found himself out of favour. He played as a substitute in the 2009 Worthington Cup final, typically the first to step forward for the fateful penalty shoot-out. His shot was saved. Only used as a substitute as the 2009-10 season got underway, O'Hara joined Portsmouth on loan until January 2010 with an option to stay for the whole season. A regular for the south coast club, he returned to Spurs in January 2010 when a transfer embargo was imposed due to Portsmouth's financial problems. The embargo was lifted just in time for O'Hara to return and just as the FA Cup got underway. O'Hara was one of the most influential figures as Portsmouth progressed to the FA Cup final, though he had to miss the semi-final meeting with Spurs. Although O'Hara played in the cup final, he was suffering a serious injury having fractured his back. Major surgery was required and for several months O'Hara was on the side-lines. When able to resume playing, another loan was arranged, this time with Wolverhampton Wanderers. O'Hara played a central role in helping Wolves avoid relegation from the Premier League and was rewarded with a permanent transfer. Life soon turned sour at Molineux with successive relegations seeing Wolves drop down to League One. As they struggled so they could not afford to hold on to players of O'Hara's quality and his contract was terminated by mutual consent. He accepted a short term deal with Blackpool, then returned to London with Fulham. After a year he me moved on to Gillingham, but soon departed when a long-term injury meant he would be side-lined for some time. When fit to resume he signed for Isthmian League Premier Division, Billericay Town.

Appearances:
League: 15 (19) apps. 2 gls.
FA Cup: 2 (1) apps.
FL Cup: 6 (3) apps. 3 gls.
Euro: 5 (5) apps. 2 gls.
Others: 12 (15) apps. 2 gls.
Total: 40 (43) apps. 9 gls.

OLIVER, John

Role: Half-back 1894-95
Born: Birmingham

CAREER: Star/Westminster Criterion by Jan 1892/Old St Stephens/SPURS cs. 1894, president Jul 1894, director Mar-Nov 1898/Leeds City director Apr 1905.

Debut v West Liverpool (Fr) (h) 26.12.1894

Jack Oliver played for several London clubs after moving down from Birmingham, but it was as an administrator that he best served football. He was a player and President of Westminster Criterion and continued to play when they merged with Old St Stephens in 1892, also being President of the combined club. He held the same position with the Southern Alliance which he founded. An ambitious and successful businessman, owner of the Athletic World, he realised that the old boys club had only limited potential and switched his interest to Spurs. He was elected president in the summer of 1894, replacing John Ripsher, who had been almost a fairy godfather to the club from shortly after its formation. Oliver was to become one of the guiding lights in Spurs' development as one of the most promising clubs in London. A wealthy man with a burning ambition to establish a top level football club in London capable of challenging the dominant clubs from the north, he also owned a carpet factory and was able to tempt good quality players to Spurs by the offer of jobs. His influence was clearly important and Spurs' fortunes certainly improved under his guidance. He paid for the erection of the first stand at Northumberland Park, was responsible for the club entering the FA Cup for the first time and chairman and one of the prime movers behind the meeting that decided to adopt professionalism. He was also one of the original directors on the club becoming a limited company in 1898, although he resigned from the board shortly thereafter and ceased to have any further involvement with Spurs. His departure was due to the failure of his business ventures. He fell upon hard times, but his help for the club was not forgotten and Spurs played a match for his benefit against CW Brown's XI in January 1901. His two appearances for Spurs, both over the Christmas period of 1894, were apparently something of a surprise and by all accounts his apparel caused a good deal of hilarity amongst the spectators.

Appearances:
Others: 2 (1) apps.
Total: 2 (1) apps. 0 gls.

OLIVER, William

Role: Outside-left 1913-14
5ft.8ins. 12st.1lbs.
Born: Walthamstow, London, September 1892

CAREER: SPURS am. 1908/Walthamstow Grange/SPURS pro. Nov 1913.

Debut v Aston Villa (FL) (a) 13.12.1913

As a young amateur William Oliver was first associated with Spurs in the 1908-09 season when he played in the reserves. Not expected to make the grade he was released, but developed well in amateur football and so joined Spurs' professional staff from Walthamstow Grange in November 1913 in preference to several other clubs who were keen to sign him. He made only two League appearances the following month, and although retained for the 1914-15 season, did not to make the first team again.

Appearances:
League: 2 apps.
Total: 2 apps. 0 gls.

ONOMAH, Joshua

Role: Midfielder 2014-
6ft. 11st.7lbs.
Born: Enfield, Middlesex, 27th April 1997

CAREER: Southbury Primary School/Kingsmead Secondary School/Omonia Youth/SPURS Academy Scholar Jul 2013, pro. Apr 2014.

Debut v Burnley (FAC) (h) (sub) 14.1.2015

A local product taken into the Spurs' Academy as a nine-year old, Josh Onomah is one of possibly the most exciting crop of home-grown talent the Academy system has produced. An attacking midfielder with pace, dribbling skills and plenty of trickery, Onomah was marked down as one to watch from his earliest days, representing England at all Schoolboys levels as he progressed through the ranks at Spurs. He has been gradually introduced to top level football by Mauricio Pochettino and gives all the signs of being destined for the top. Strong and powerful, Onomah is at his most effective going forward, a neat passer of the ball, always looking for a gap to burst into. While his shooting may have

room for improvement, he certainly knows where the target is and is not afraid to have a pop at goal. A member of England's Under-20 World Cup-winning squad of 2017, the very nature of top flight football may demand that Onomah curb his natural instinct to wander into positions where feels he can do most danger and accept his defensive responsibilities. Those are skills that can be taught, not so the natural talent he clearly possesses.

Appearances:
League: (13) apps.
FA Cup: 3 (5) app.
FL Cup: 2 apps. 1 gl.
Euro: 2 (7) apps.
Others: 2 (5) apps.
Total: 9 (30) apps. 1 gl.

O'REILLY, Gary Miles

Role: Defender 1979-84
5ft.11ins. 12st.0lbs.
Born: Isleworth, Middlesex, 21st March 1961

CAREER: Harlow Schools/Essex Schools/England Schools/Arsenal schoolboy/Grays Athletic/SPURS app. Jun 1977, pro. Sep 1979/Brighton and Hove Albion Aug 1984/Crystal Palace Jan 1987/(Birmingham City loan Mar 1991)/Brighton and Hove Albion July 1991/Bognor Regis Town 1993.

Debut v Southampton (sub) (FL) (h) 26.12.1980
(AFC Bournemouth (Fr) (a) 5.5.1980)

Although Gary O'Reilly played for England Schools, he qualified for the Republic of Ireland through his parents and accepted the chance to play for Eire at Youth level. Happy in any of the defensive positions, but perhaps best in the centre, he was competent enough, but always struggled to break through at Spurs and was only a regular choice at the end of the 1982-83 season when John Lacy was absent. Unable to progress past the stage of simply being a handy member of the first team squad, he moved to Brighton and Hove Albion for £35,000 and with regular football proved himself a capable Second Division defender, before returning to London with Crystal Palace. He helped Palace win promotion to the First Division in 1989 and scored the first goal in the 1990 FA Cup Final with Manchester United which Palace lost after a replay. With Palace doing well the following season, O'Reilly found himself unable to get in the team and had a brief spell on loan to Birmingham City before returning to Brighton on a free transfer. Injury forced his retirement in 1993, although he later played for Bognor Regis before carving out a career in TV. O'Reilly was the National Schools Javelin Champion in 1978.

Appearances:
League: 39 (6) apps.
FA Cup: 2 apps.
FL Cup: 4 apps.
Euro: 2 (2) apps.
Others: 14 (4) apps. 1 gl.
Total: 61 (12) apps. 1 gl.

OSBORNE, Frank Raymond

Role: Forward 1923-31
5ft.10ins. 10st.7lbs.
Born: Wynberg, South Africa, 14th October 1896.
Died: Epsom, Surrey, 8th March 1988

CAREER: Gymnasium School (South Africa)/Netley 1911/Bromley am. 1919/Fulham pro. Nov 1921/**SPURS** Jan 1924/Southampton Jun 1931/retired May 1933/Fulham director Mar 1935, manager Sep 1948-Jun 1949, general manager Jun 1949-Oct 1953, manager Oct 1953-Jan 1956, general manager Jan 1956-Oct 1964/retired Oct 1964.

Debut v Newcastle United (FL) (h) 19.1.1924

Frank Osborne was born in South Africa where his father was a colonel in the Royal Army Medical Corps. The family returned to England in 1911 and Osborne immediately joined Netley. He signed for the well-known amateur club Bromley in 1919 and within two years was playing the professional game. Osborne made 70 League and FA Cup appearances for Fulham and won two England caps whilst at Craven Cottage, showing his versatility by operating at centre-forward against Ireland in October 1922 and on the right wing against France in May 1923. Slightly built, he could ably fill any of the forward positions, atoning for his apparent lack of physique with accurate passing and a shrewd positional sense. Spurs paid £1,500 to sign an artistic, skilful player. Osborne's versatility proved exceptionally valuable, but despite his fine scoring record at centre-forward, he did not fill that role often enough

and this probably prevented him collecting more honours than the two more caps he collected as a Spurs player. Both were won against Belgium, in December 1924 and May 1926, the first on the left wing and the second, when he scored a hat-trick, at centre-forward. With age catching up, he left Spurs to join Southampton for £450 and stayed for two years before retiring from playing. Appointed a director at Fulham in 1935 he stepped down from the board to take over as team manager in September 1948 and in his first season led Fulham to the Second Division title. He took them back up to the First Division in 1959 and served the club for 16 years as team manager, general manager and secretary-manager before retiring. Osborne's brother, Reginald, was an England amateur international who made two appearances for the full England team in his Leicester City days. Another brother, Harold, played for Chelmsford City and made one League appearance for Norwich City as an amateur in September 1924.

Appearances:
League: 210 apps. 78 gls.
FA Cup: 9 apps. 4 gls.
Others: 10 apps. 5 gls.
Total: 229 apps. 87 gls.

OSGOOD, Keith

Role: Central defender 1973-78
6ft.0ins. 11st.2lbs.
Born: Isleworth, Middlesex, 8th May 1955

CAREER: Hounslow Schools/London Schools/England Schools/Hounslow Town/**SPURS** app. Jun 1971, pro. Jun 1972/Coventry City Jan 1978/Derby County Oct 1979/Orient Dec 1981/HJK Helsinki (Finland) May 1984/Cambridge United Nov 1984/Burton Albion Feb 1986/Stapenhill Mar 1986/Örgryte (Sweden) May 1987/Leicester United.

Debut v Newcastle United (sub) (FL) (a) 11.5.1974

An England Youth international, Keith Osgood made his debut in the last League match of 1973-74, but after a couple of League outings at the start of the next season went back into the reserves. However, by the middle of March 1975, Spurs had a desperate fight on their hands to avoid relegation and he was recalled for the last eight games, with the drop only averted in the final match. A stylish defender with a really thunderous long range shot, Osgood impressed so much in those difficult times that he immediately became one of the regular centre backs and did not miss a game for the

next two seasons. Equally at home as the defensive kingpin or tidying up alongside the centre-half, he seemed set for a fine future, yet when his form faltered in December 1977 and he was dropped, he reacted by instantly demanding a transfer. The request was granted by manager Keith Burkinshaw and Osgood moved to Coventry City for £125,000. Unfortunately, things did not work out well for him away from White Hart Lane. Unable to rediscover his earlier form he stayed at Coventry for less than two years before joining Derby County, and although he appeared at times to be getting back to near his best then moved on again to Orient. He played for Helsinki FC and Cambridge United and when his contract with Cambridge was cancelled in January 1986 joined Burton Albion. Just a month later he left the Derbyshire club for Stapenhill, but retired within a couple of months, the consequence of a back injury.

Appearances:
League: 112 (1) apps. 13 gls.
FA Cup: 3 apps.
FL Cup: 11 apps. 1 gl.
Others: 32 (3) apps. 6 gls.
Total: 158 (4) apps. 20 gls.

O'SHEA, Timothy James Peter

Role: Defender or midfield 1986-88
5ft.11ins. 11st.4lbs.
Born: Westminster, London, 12th November 1966

CAREER: West London Schools/London Schools/SPURS YTS Sep 1983, pro. Aug 1984/(Newport County loan Oct 1986)/Leyton Orient Jul 1988/Gillingham loan then perm Feb 1989/Yeovil Mar 1992 /Eastern (Hong Kong) Mar 1992 /Instant Dict (Hong Kong) 1995/Farnborough Town Jul 1999/Welling United loan Dec 2002, perm Feb 2003, coach & Community Officer Jul 2004/Millwall academy coach/Grays Athletic coach Feb 2008, manager Sep-Oct 2008/Croydon Athletic manager Dec 2008-Sep 2010/Lewes manager Oct 2010-May 2011.

Debut v Sheffield Wednesday (sub) (FL) (a) 7.4.1987

As a schoolboy Tim O'Shea trained with Wimbledon and Fulham, and he was on Associated Schoolboy forms with Arsenal before joining Spurs. An England Schools trialist, he played for London and the Republic of Ireland at Youth level. Playing in the defensive midfield role, he made ten League outings on loan to Newport County between October and December 1986 before making his League debut for Spurs. He played only one full League game for Spurs, and made just two other appearances as a substitute, before moving to Leyton Orient in the summer of 1988. O'Shea moved from Brisbane Road in February 1989, when he joined Gillingham, initially on loan, linking up with former Spurs manager Keith Burkinshaw and former Spurs Youth team manager Keith Blunt. He gave Gillingham three years' service, joined Yeovil but quickly moved on to Hong Kong. He spent seven years in Hong Kong, one of English football's most successful exports to the former colony. He returned to England to play, coach and manage at non-League level, even forming part of a consortium that tried to buy Farnborough FC in November 2011.

Appearances:
League: 1 (2) apps.
Others: 1 (1) apps.
Total: 2 (3) apps. 0 gls.

OTTEWELL, Sydney

Role: Inside-forward 1939-40
5ft.7ins. 10st.12lbs.
Born: Horsley, Derbyshire, 23rd October 1919
Died: Eastbrook, Nottinghamshire, 31st January 2012

CAREER: Derbyshire Schools/Holbrook Colliery Welfare/Chesterfield Nov 1936/(guest for Birmingham, Blackburn Rovers, Blackpool, Bradford City, Chester, Fulham and SPURS during World War Two)/Birmingham City Jun 1947/Luton Town Nov 1947/Nottingham Forest Jul 1948/Mansfield Town Jan 1950/Scunthorpe United Mar 1952/Whitstable Town Jul 1953/Spalding United player-manager cs. 1954/Heanor Town Nov 1956/Bourne Town manager by 1959/Lockheed Lemington manager 1960-Jan 1969.

Debut v Chelsea (FLS) (h) 25.5.1940

Sid Ottewell was a guest from Chesterfield who, whilst recognised as an inside-forward, made his one appearance for Spurs in a Football League South game at outside-left. He was fairly inexperienced at the time, but went on after the war to play for six years with several clubs before going into management. He proved successful on this side of the game, particularly with Bourne Town and Lockheed Lemington.

Appearances:
Others: 1 app.
Total: 1 app. 0 gls.

OWEN, Aled Watcyn

Role: Winger 1953-54
5ft.7ins. 10st.11lbs.
Born: Brynteg, Anglesey, 7th January 1934

CAREER: Anglesey Schools/Bangor City 1950/SPURS Sep 1953/Ipswich Town Jul 1958/Wrexham Jul 1963/Holyhead Town Aug 1964/Bethesda Athletic Jul 1965/Penmaenmawr Sep 1966.

Debut v Preston North End (FL) (h) 19.5.1954
(Hibernian (Fr) (a) 21.9.1953)

Although Aled Owen made his first appearance in a Spurs' shirt in a friendly with Hibernians within days of signing for the club, he had to wait until the end of the season for his one League game-and only other appearance at first team level. He spent almost five years playing for the reserve and "A" teams without seriously challenging for a place in the senior side. Transferred to Ipswich Town, he made only 30 League appearances in five years at

Portman Road, before moving on to Wrexham and non-League clubs in Wales. Owen, who was Ernie Walley's brother-in-law, ran a haulage business in Anglesey after retiring from football.

Appearances:
League: 1 app.
Others: 1 app.
Total: 2 apps. 0 gls.

OWEN, M L

Role: Full-back 1895-96

CAREER: London Welsh/(guest for **SPURS** Oct 1895).

Debut v Luton Town (FAC) (a) 12.10.1895 (scored once)

A member of the London Welsh club, who at the time were as well known for their ability with the round ball as they now are with the oval, Owen played as a guest inside-forward in Spurs' FA Cup First Qualifying Round tie with Luton Town in October 1895. He scored once as Luton were beaten 2-1. Owen did not appear again until late that season, when he turned out at full-back in three friendly games. In his days with London Welsh, Owen also represented London.

Appearances:
FA Cup: 1 app. 1 gl.
Others: 3 apps.
Total: 4 apps. 1 gl.

PAGE, Albert Edward

Role: Centre-half 1936-46
5ft.11ins. 11st.11lbs.
Born: Walthamstow, London, 18th March 1916
Died: Paddington, London, 10th January 1995

CAREER: Leyton/**SPURS** May 1935, pro. Jan 1936/(guest for Bradford City, Crystal Palace, Hamilton Academical, Lincoln City and West Ham United during World War Two)/Colchester United cs. 1947/Chingford Town.

Debut v Newcastle United (FL) (h) 9.1.1937

An amateur with Leyton, where he had represented the Athenian League, Bert Page joined Spurs in January 1936 and immediately signed professional. He had to wait another twelve months before making a League debut, but slowly won the battle with Jim Blyth as to who should replace Arthur Rowe. Having just about established himself as first choice, he only held the centre-half position until December 1938 when it was taken by Arthur Hitchins. Page made a few appearances for Spurs during the war, but when he  returned to the club full time found that all that awaited him was a place in the reserves. In September 1946 he was placed on the transfer list at his own request, but it was not until the summer of 1947 that he moved to Colchester United on a free transfer. He later played for Chingford.

Appearances:
League: 56 apps.
FA Cup: 1 app.
Others: 31 apps.
Total: 88 apps. 0 gls.

PAGE, George

Role: Centre-forward 1905-07
5ft.8ins. 11st.0lbs.
Born: London

CAREER: Asplin Rovers at least Sep 1901-Nov 1902/Cheshunt by 1904/(guest for **SPURS** Apr 1906)/Redhill cs. 1906/**SPURS** Sep 1906/Leeds City Nov 1906/Redhill cs. 1907.

Debut v Norwich City (SL) (h) 17.4.1906

George Page was first associated with Spurs while playing for Asplin Rovers, appearing for the reserves in December 1902. A centre-forward, he moved on to Cheshunt, guesting for Spurs and making his first senior appearance in a Southern League match against Norwich City in April 1906, when he played at inside-forward. At the end of the season he switched from Cheshunt to Redhill. Always an amateur in his time associated with Spurs, he signed to play in the Southern League again in September 1906. He went on to play only one more first team game for Spurs, and that was a Western League fixture in October 1906. The following month he signed Football League forms with Leeds City. Page made four League appearances for Leeds, in his one season with Leeds before returning to Redhill.

Appearances:
Southern: 1 app.
Others: 1 app.
Total: 2 apps. 0 gls.

PAGE, R J

Role: Outside-right 1915-16

Debut v Brentford (LFC) (h) 11.9.1915

A local amateur half-back who had appeared in the reserve team for several years, Page made three appearances for Spurs in the 1915-16 London Football Combination competition. In all of them he played outside-right.

Appearances:
Others: 3 apps.
Total: 3 apps. 0 gls.

PALACIOS SUAZO, Wilson Roberto

Role: Midfielder 2008-12
5ft.10ins. 11st.11lbs.
Born: La Ceiba, Honduras, 29th July 1984

CAREER: CD Victoria (Honduras)/CD Olimpia (Honduras) 2002/Red Star Belgrade (Serbia) trial Jul 2007/Monaco (France) trial Aug 2007/Arsenal trial Aug 2007/Birmingham City trial Aug 2007, loan Aug 2007/Wigan Athletic Jan 2008/SPURS Jan 2009/Stoke City Aug 2011-Jun 2015/Philadelphia Union (USA) trial Jun 2015/Bolton Wanderers trial Jul 2015/Hull City trial Jul 2015/Miami FC (USA) Dec 2015-Nov 2016.

Debut v Bolton Wanderers (PL) (a) 30.1.2009

When the 2008-09 season reached the half-way stage, Spurs were in a sorry position. The worst ever start to a Premier League campaign had seen Juande Ramos dismissed. While things had improved under Harry Redknapp, Spurs were still struggling at the wrong end of the table. One of the most obvious weaknesses was in midfield. Spurs had no-one capable of breaking up attacks before they got at Spurs' back line. Palacios was signed to remedy that problem, and for eighteen months performed the job superbly. One of five brothers who played for Victoria and Olimpia in their native Honduras, Palacios was given a chance in England by Steve Bruce at Birmingham City, after trials with several other European clubs had failed to produce an offer. Birmingham took him on loan, but when Bruce moved to Wigan he made Palacios his first permanent signing. Given a regular place, he proved a revelation for Wigan, who made a substantial profit when Redknapp signed him for Spurs after just twelve months in the north-west. Palacios made an immediate impact at White Hart Lane, prowling the midfield, launching himself into tackles, harrying opponents. He did not stop working from first whistle to last, never gave anything less than all he had. Palacios' performances were in no small measure responsible for the improvement in Spurs' fortunes that followed his arrival and continued into the next season. While his effort could never be criticised, Palacios did have his limitations, principally a lack of creativity. He was not comfortable in possession, lacked ball control and did not have great vision, shortcomings that were exposed during Spurs 2010-11 Champions League sortie, but Palacios was signed as a ball-winner, and at that he excelled. Once Redknapp had arrested Spurs slide and was able to concentrate on taking the team forward, Palacios found himself on the fringes and moved to Stoke City. After four years' service to the Potteries club, Palacios was released. He again hawked his services around, before joining Miami. For much of his early career in England, Palacios laboured under the burden of his youngest brother's life being under threat. In October 2007 14-year old Edwin, was kidnapped. Although a £125,000 ransom was paid within a month, the youngster was not released and it was not until May 2009 that his body was found. Palacios made his international debut in April 2003 and made 21 appearances for his country as a Spurs player.

Appearances:
League: 56 (9) apps. 1 gl.
FA Cup: 7 (1) apps.
FL Cup: 4 apps.
Euro: 5 (4) apps.
Others: 7 (3) apps. 1 gl.
Total: 79 (17) apps. 2 gls.

PALMER

Role: Centre-forward 1892-93

Debut v City Ramblers (Fr) (h) 1.4.1893 (scored once)

Palmer's only known appearance for Spurs was in April 1893 when he scored the only goal in a friendly victory over City Ramblers.

Appearances:
Others: 1 app. 1 gl.
Total: 1 app. 1 gl.

PALMER

Role: Half-back 1942-43

Debut v Queens Park Rangers (Fr) (a) 17.4.1943

A former Spurs junior on the books of Queens Park Rangers, Palmer made his one appearance for Spurs as a guest against his own club in a friendly in April 1943.

Appearances:
Others: 1 app.
Total: 1 app. 0 gls.

PAMAROT, Louis Noé

Role: Defender 2004-06
5ft.11ins. 13st.7lbs.
Born: Fontenay-sous-Bois, France, 14th April 1979

CAREER: Fontenay-sous-Bois (France)/Paris FC (France) 1995/Martigues (France) 1997/OGC Nice (France) Jul 1999/(Portsmouth loan Sep 1999)/SPURS Aug 2004/Portsmouth Jan 2006/OGC Nice (France) training Jul 2009/Nantes (France) trial Jul 2009/Hercules (Spain) Aug 2009/Granada CF (Spain) Jul 2011-Jun 2012/Hercules (Spain) Jan 2013/CD Torrevieja (Spain) training Jan 2015/Jove Español San Vicente (Spain) Jul 2015.

Debut v West Bromwich Albion (PL) (a) 25.8.2004

A strapping defender, muscular and powerful, Noé Pamarot was another of the Arnesen/Santini signings of summer 2004 following the arrival of the new Director of Football and Head Coach. Pamarot had been with OGC Nice for five years. Apart from a brief spell on loan to Portsmouth, he had been a regular and consistent performer all across the back line and had been called up to the French international squad on several occasions without ever making an international appearance. He settled in well at Spurs, an imposing figure usually playing at right-back, but filling in at the centre of defence when needed. Quick and physical, he rarely advanced too far forward save for set pieces, when he would be a handful for opposing defenders. Pamarot appeared set to stay at Spurs for some time when he sustained a serious ligament injury in April 2005. Although he recovered, Paul Stalteri had taken his place and Pamarot was allowed to move to Portsmouth in a joint deal with Sean Davis and Pedro Mendes. He stayed far longer with Pompey than on his first visit, a regular until his contract ran out. He would have stayed longer, but Portsmouth's financial problems meant he was just one of many players that had to leave the club. He returned to France but was unavailable to find a new club until signing for Hercules of Alicante. He has remained in Spain ever since.

Appearances:
League: 23 (2) apps. 1 gl.
FA Cup: 2 apps. 1 gl.
FL Cup: 3 apps.
Total: 28 (2) apps. 2 gls.

PANGBOURNE, Thomas

Role: Inside-forward 1900-01
5ft.9ins. 11st.10lbs.
Born: Bordesley, Birmingham, 5th January 1870
Died: Lozells, Birmingham, 19th February 1926

CAREER: Warwick County/Southfield/Walsall Town Swifts cs. 1891/Southfield Oct 1892/Worcester Rovers/West Bromwich Albion Jun 1895/Ashton North End Oct 1895/Bury Oct 1896/Grimsby Town Aug 1898/Ashton North End Nov 1898/New Brompton Jun 1899/**SPURS** Apr 1900/Reading Jan 1901/Watford May 1901/Worcester City May 1902.

Debut v Millwall Athletic (SL) (a) 1.9.1900

Only 26-years old, but well-travelled, Tom Pangbourne had been a very popular player at New Brompton, and his signing for Spurs in April 1900 caused much ill feeling. At the end of that month and in the last Southern League match of the season, Spurs needed a win at the Kent club to secure the title. Pangbourne, who unknown to New Brompton had already agreed to move to White Hart Lane, did not turn out for the home club as Spurs won 2-1. When New Brompton learned how Pangbourne had already committed himself to Spurs, the recriminations began. Initially New Brompton publicly accused the match officials of being biased in Spurs' favour. The officials' complaint to the Southern League at this allegation was referred to the Football Association, with New Brompton accusing Spurs of certain "unacceptable practises". Not surprisingly, all the allegations were found to be unwarranted, but they did leave a cloud. Pangbourne had been a regular in his one season with New Brompton, but was to play only two Southern League games for Spurs. He appeared in the first match of the season, but lost his place immediately John L Jones became available. After only seven more appearances he moved to Reading, stayed there a few months and then had a year at Watford before finishing his career with Worcester City.

Appearances:
Southern: 2 apps.
Others: 6 apps. 1 gl.
Total: 8 apps. 1 gl.

PARKER, Henry Clifford

Role: Winger 1943-44
5ft.6ins. 10st. 0lbs.
Born: Denaby, Yorkshire, 6th September 1913
Died: Binstead, Isle of Wight, January 1983

CAREER: Mexborough Schools/Yorkshire Schools/Denaby United/Mexborough/Doncaster Rovers 1930/Portsmouth Dec 1933/(guest for Folland Aircraft and **SPURS** during World War Two)/Denaby United/Portsmouth scout, asst. trainer May 1954-Jul 1957.

Debut v Aldershot (FLSC) (h) 25.3.1944

Scorer of two goals in Portsmouth's FA Cup final winning team of 1939, Cliff Parker was a midget of a left-winger who made his one guest appearance for Spurs against Aldershot in a Football League South Cup game in March 1944. One of Portsmouth's star performers either side of the War, he was available to turn out regularly during the conflict and a member of the team that reached the London War Cup final in 1942. A real handful for any defender, Parker was a real tough nut who never let his lack of inches prevent him taking on the toughest of defenders, and not always with the ball. Parker remained a first choice as football resumed after the hostilities, only dropping down to the reserves as he approached his forties. With over 350 appearances for Portsmouth to his credit he eventually moved on to the coaching staff.

Appearances:
Others: 1 app.
Total: 1 app. 0 gls.

PARKER, G A

Role: Forward 1888-90

Debut v Windsor Phoenix (Fr) (h) 2.3.1889

Parker only played two known matches for Spurs, both friendlies. The first was against Windsor Phoenix in March 1889 when he played centre-forward and the second against Royal Arsenal in September 1889 when he scored Spurs' only goal from the outside-right position as they lost 1-10.

Appearances:
Others: 2 apps.
Total: 2 app. 1 gl.

PARKER, Scott Matthew

Role: Midfielder 2011-13
5ft.9ins. 12st. 2lbs.
Born: Lambeth, London, 13tth October 1980

CAREER: Haberdashers' Aske's Hatcham College/FA National School of Excellence/Charlton Athletic trainee Jul 1997, pro. Oct 1997/(Norwich City loan Oct 2000)/Chelsea Jan 2004/Newcastle United Jun 2005/West Ham United Jun 2007/**SPURS** Aug 2011/Fulham Aug 2013/**SPURS** Under-18s coach Jun 2017.

Debut v Wolverhampton Wanderers (PL) (a) 10.9.2011

Scott Parker will forever be remembered as the 13-year old schoolboy playing keepie-uppie in the McDonald's advert during the 1994 World Cup. Few could have imagined he would go from there to become a Premier League star and England international, although someone at White Hart Lane spotted his potential early on. Spurs tried to sign him as schoolboy when he was at the FA School of Excellence. Parker refused the offer and was soon rewarded for his loyalty. After leaving Lilleshall he had a few games for Charlton's reserves before being thrown into the first team in August 1997, before a professional contract had even been put before him for his signature. Progressing as an England youth and Under-21 international, Parker did not immediately establish himself at Charlton. It took him a while and a loan spell at Norwich City as Charlton won promotion to the Premier League, were relegated and promoted. As Charlton established themselves in the Premier League so Parker made a starting place his own. A holding midfielder, Parker proved an industrious player, working across the full width of the pitch, making tackles and interceptions, then pushing his team forward. The outstanding young English midfield player, Parker was tempted to Chelsea as the Abramovich millions began to roll in. Although he finished his first season at Stamford Bridge as the PFA Young Player of the Year, the move was not a success. He hardly played a game, not even the ten necessary for a medal, as Chelsea won the Premier League in 2004-05. Parker departed Chelsea for Newcastle United and got his career back on track with two years at St James Park, followed by four at the Boleyn Ground. Having played in south, west and east London, Parker completed all four points of the compass when he joined Spurs from West Ham. At 31 he was not the player he had been, but he brought a calmness to the midfield that only came with experience. He still strode through the middle of the park, still worked tirelessly, still won the ball and supported his colleagues. The move reinvigorated his England career, just in time for the 2012 Euros, when he played in all England's games. He won twelve of his 18 England caps as a Spurs player. Confident in his own ability, Parker was never afraid to hold on to the ball. All too often though, he simply turned in circles, looking for a simple pass and being dispossessed. With the signing of Moussa Dembélé, Parker found his opportunities limited. At a point in his career when he needed to be playing, he moved to Fulham.

Appearances:
League: 43 (7) apps.
FA Cup: 8* apps.
Euro: 6 apps.
Others: 3 (2) apps.
Total: 60 (9) apps. 0 gls.
* Includes 1 abandoned match

PARKS, Anthony

Role: Goalkeeper 1979-88
5ft.11ins. 10st.8lbs.
Born: Hackney, London, 28th January 1963

CAREER: Hackney Schools/Inner London Schools/**SPURS** app. Apr 1979, pro. Sep 1980/(Oxford United loan Oct 1986)/(Gillingham loan Sep 1987)/Brentford Jul 1988/(Queens Park Rangers loan Aug 1990)/Fulham loan Feb 1991, perm. Mar 1991/Southend United trial Jul 1991/West Ham United trial Aug 1991, perm. Sep 1991/Stoke City trial Sep 1992/Falkirk trial and perm. Oct 1992/Blackpool Sep 1996/Barnet training Jul 1997/Burnley Sep 1997/(Doncaster Rovers loan Feb 1998)/(Barrow loan Sep 1998)/Scarborough Feb 1999/Halifax Town player-coach Jun 1999, joint caretaker-manager Sep 2000/Crewe Alexandra goalkeeping coach Jul 2002/FA goalkeeping coach Oct 2002/**SPURS** goalkeeping coach Nov 2008-May 2014/Norwich City goalkeeping coach Jul 2014/Aston Villa goalkeeping coach Feb 2015–Jun 2016.

Debut v West Ham United (FL) (a) 10.5.1982
(AFC Bournemouth (sub) (Fr) (a) 5.5.1980)

Tony Parks had trained with Queens Park Rangers as a schoolboy before deciding to join Spurs. A competent goalkeeper who was perhaps slightly handicapped by his lack of inches, he carved a permanent niche for himself in Spurs' history in the second leg of the 1984 UEFA Cup Final against Anderlecht. When the Final finished 2-2 on aggregate and extra-time had failed to produce a winner, the outcome of the trophy went to penalties. Parks saved Anderlecht's first attempt, but when Danny Thomas stepped up for what would be the clincher, his spot kick was saved. With Spurs 4-3 ahead, the destiny of the cup rested on the 21-year-old deputy goalkeeper. He

responded with a marvellous, clawing save to his right from the Icelandic international Arnór Guðjohnsen to win the trophy for Spurs and spark wild celebrations. Parks was only playing as stand-in for the injured Ray Clemence, a situation that prevailed for all his career at Spurs, and meant he had few first team opportunities. When Clemence suffered the injury that led to his retirement in October 1987, Parks had the perfect opportunity to stake his claim as permanent replacement. He failed to impress new manager Terry Venables, who signed Bobby Mimms from Everton. Parks moved to Brentford, where his former Spurs captain Steve Perryman was manager for £60,000, and was one of the heroes of the Brentford team that reached the sixth round of the FA Cup in 1989 before losing to Liverpool. Out of favour within a year, he had a brief spell with Fulham, then joined West Ham. Although always second choice to

Ludek Miklosko, he did not disappoint whenever called on. Despite this he was released again and moved to Falkirk where he played for four years, helping them win the Scottish First Division title. A proposed move to Lillestrøm fell through in July 1996 so Parks signed for Blackpool. He finished his playing career moving around the lower reaches of the Football League and the senior level of non-League football before moving onto coaching. Firmly established alongside Ray Clemence as the FA's goalkeeping coach, Parks returned to Spurs charged with improving the performances of Heurelho Gomes. It was a task he performed so well that he remained with Spurs for another seven years, only leaving when the entire senior coaching staff was sacked along with acting manager, Tim Sherwood.

Appearances:
League: 37 apps.
FA Cup: 5 apps.
FL Cup: 1 app.
Euro: 5 (1) apps.
Others: 24 (16) apps.
Total: 72 (17) apps. 0 gls.

PARRETT, Dean Gary

Role: Midfielder
5ft.9ins. 12st.4lbs.
Born: Hampstead, London, 16th November 1991

CAREER: Queens Park Rangers Academy/**SPURS** Academy Jan 2007, Scholar Jul 2008, pro. Nov 2008/(Aldershot Town loan Sep 2009)/(Plymouth Argyle loan Aug 2010)/(Charlton Athletic loan Mar 2011)/(Yeovil Town loan Jan 2012)/(Swindon Town loan Mar 2013)/Crystal Palace trial Apr 2013/released May 2013/Notts County trial Jun 2013/Plymouth Argyle trial Aug 2013/Derby County trial Aug 2013/Shrewsbury Town trial Sep 2013/Stevenage Oct 2013/AFC Wimbledon Jul 2016.

Debut v Shakhtar Donetsk (UEFA Cup) (a) 19.2.2009

Dean Parrett was a 15-year old schoolboy when a deal was done for him to sign for Spurs in a deal that might have netted Queens Park Rangers, who had first taken him under their wing, £2million. Signed as a professional at the first opportunity, the England Under-16 and Under-17 star played in the youth and reserve teams at Spurs, but his only first team opportunities came in UEFA Cup/Europa League matches when the opportunity was taken to give some of the promising youngsters a chance on the big stage. Parrett was a neat, creative player, better going forward than doing the dirty work. Sent out on loan to gain experience and strengthen him up, he continued to progress through the England youth teams, playing at Under-19 and Under-20 level. Looking unlikely to make a first team breakthrough and with several promising youngsters coming through the Academy, the decision to release him was made towards the end of the 2012-13 season. After trials with several clubs, Parrett signed for Stevenage.

Appearances:
Euro: 1 (3) apps.
Others: 1 (1) apps.
Total: 2 (4) apps. 0 gls.

PARSONS, Horace

Role: Half-back 1918-19

CAREER: Aston Villa/(guest for Brentford and **SPURS** during World War One).

Debut v Brentford (LFC) (h) 4.1.1919

A former Aston Villa reserve, Parsons made his one Spurs' appearance in January 1919 when he played against Brentford in a London Football Combination match at Clapton Orient's Homerton ground.

Appearances:
Others: 1 app.
Total: 1 app. 0 gls.

PASS, James Ernest

Role: Inside-forward 1907-08
5ft.8ins. 10st.5lbs.
Born: Juffulpore, India, 6th November 1883
Died: Stockport, Lancashire, 2nd November 1956

CAREER: Edgley White Star/Stockport County May 1903/**SPURS** May 1907/New Brompton Mar 1908.

Debut v Queens Park Rangers (SL) (a) 2.9.1907 (scored once)

Signed by Stockport County after scoring against them for the Stockport League in April 1903, Jimmy Pass had three years as a regular before joining Spurs. He spent less than a season at White Hart Lane, competing with Bob Walker for the inside-right position. He began the season in that role, but gave way to Walker before winning the place back in February 1908. Both of them ultimately lost out with the signing of Billy Minter in March 1908. Although Pass played a couple of games at outside-right, by the end of the month he had departed for New Brompton. He was soon joined at the Kent club by Bob Walker.

Appearances:
Southern: 18 apps. 5 gls.
FA Cup: 1 app.
Others: 12 apps. 6 gls.
Total: 31 apps. 11 gls.

PATON, Thomas Gracie

Role: Forward 1940-41
5ft.10ins, 11st.4lbs
Born: Saltcoats, Ayrshire, 22nd February 1918
Died: Folkestone, Kent, 14th December 1991

CAREER: Ardeer Thistle am. Jul 1936/Wolverhampton Wanderers pro. Jun 1937/Portsmouth Aug 1937/Swansea Town Oct 1938/Bournemouth and Boscombe Athletic Feb 1939/(guest for Crystal Palace, Leeds United, Lincoln City, Manchester City and **SPURS** during World War Two)/Watford Jan 1948/Folkestone Town Aug 1952/Sheffield Wednesday scout by Sep 1959.

Debut v Portsmouth (FLS) (h) 26.10.1940

Tom Paton was on the books of Bournemouth and Boscombe Athletic when he played four matches for Spurs in the Football League South competition as a war-time guest. His first appearance was in October 1940 and he made his three other appearances the following month, prior to being shot down and captured whilst serving with Bomber Command. A member of Bournemouth's 1946 3rd Division (South) Cup winning team, he spent the best part of two post-war seasons with Bournemouth before moving to Watford where he played for five years. His brother, Andy, was a Scottish international and captain of Motherwell when they played in the 1951 Scottish Cup final. Father, Tom, played for Derby County and Sheffield United.

Appearances:
Others: 4 apps.
Total: 4 apps. 0 gls.

PATTINSON

Role: Full-back 1918-19

Debut v Fulham (LFC) (h) 22.2.1919

A local lad, Pattinson played his only match for Spurs as a late trialist against Fulham in February 1919 in a London Football Combination match played at Clapton Orient's Homerton ground.

Appearances:
Others: 1 app.
Total: 1 app. 0 gls.

PATTISON, John R Maurice

Role: Outside-left 1942-43
Born: Eastwood, Glasgow, 19th December 1918

CAREER: Motherwell Apr 1936/Queens Park Rangers May 1937/(guest for Aldershot and **SPURS** during Second World War)/Leyton Orient Feb 1950/Dover Athletic May 1951/Queensland Club (Australia) coach during 1955-56.

Debut v Reading (FLS) (a) 17.10.1942 (scored once)

John Pattison was an outside-left with Queens Park Rangers who was serving in the Army and stationed near Reading. Spurs took the opportunity to give him a run-out in October 1942 when they were playing at Reading in a Football League South fixture. He scored once in a 6-2 win and went on to make thirteen appearances for Spurs that season.

Appearances:
Others: 13 apps. 3 gls.
Total: 13 apps. 3 gls.

PAULINHO, Jose Paulo Bezerra Maciel Junior

Role: Midfielder 2013-15
6ft. 13st.3lbs.
Born: Lorne, Brazil, 25th July 1988

CAREER: Pão de Açúcar (Brazil) 2004/(Juventus (Brazil) loan 2006)/(FC Vilnius (Lithuania) loan Jan 2007)/(ŁKS Łódź (Poland) loan Aug 2007)/(Bragantino (Brazil) loan Jun 2009)/Coimbra Sports Apr 2010/Corinthians (Brazil) loan May 2010, perm Oct 2012/**SPURS** Jul 2013/Guangzhou Evergrande (China) Jun 2015.

Debut v Crystal Palace (PL) (a) 18.8.2013

(v RCD Espanyol (Fr) (h) 10.8.2103)

For so many young Brazilians, football provides the only hope of escaping a life of poverty, and perhaps worse. Even then, they would have little prospect of the hope being realised without the help of big business and wealthy individuals who have a social conscience. It was to provide sports opportunities for youngsters that the Pão de Açúcar (Sugar Loaf) Sports Club was formed in the shadow of Rio de Janeiro's most famous landmark. Originally an athletics club, it was only in 2003 that a football section was formed, with Paulinho one of the first members to graduate to the professional game. Pão de Açúcar formed an arrangement with Juventus that allowed the Sao Paulo club to take promising talent into its youth set up. Paulinho spent a year at Juventus without making the first team. However, his potential had not gone unnoticed and he moved to Europe, first with Vilnius of Lithuania and then LKS Lodz in Poland. The

youngster did not enjoy his time so far away from home. By the time he returned to Pão de Açúcar the club had turned professional and was playing in the third tier of Sao Paulo football. Paulinho's first season back home saw the club rise to the second division, but Paulinho did not play for them at the higher level as he joined Bragantino. A year later, through the Coimbra Sports agency, he moved to Corinthians, initially on loan so that if the signing did not work out, the club would not lose too much money. Paulinho settled quickly, made his debut for Brazil against Argentina in September 2011 and as European clubs began to cast envious glances, the move was made permanent. The anchor in the heart of midfield, Paulinho helped Corinthians to the Brazilian League title in 2011, the Copa Libertadores and Club World Cup in 2012. Spurs had, reportedly, been on his trail for some time. He was signed in July 2013 for £17 million, one of many arrivals following the sale of Gareth Bale. Paulinho had a big reputation, anyone a regular for Brazil had to be a top quality player, and much was expected of him. He was a disappointment. He certainly put in the effort, a box-to-box, central midfielder, happy to put as much effort into his defensive duties as those going forward. For some reason, it just never worked for him. He often looked slow, ponderous, simply out of his depth. He was soon relegated to the substitute's bench, only starting games in the cup competitions that were of secondary importance. He collected 15 of his 32 Brazilian caps as a Spurs player, his final appearance coming in the 2014 World Cup semi-final when Germany thrashed the home nation 7-1. When the Chinese club, Guangzhou Evergrande, managed by Paulinho's former international manger, Luiz Felipe Scolari, made a near £10 million offer, Spurs readily accepted, just grateful to recover a large chunk of their original outlay. In his first season in China, Paulinho helped his club win the Chinese Super League and AFC Champions League.

Appearances:
League: 31 (14) apps. 6 gls.
FA Cup: 3 apps. 1 gl.
FL Cup: 3 (3) apps. 1 gl.
Euro: 10 (3) apps. 2 gls.
Others: 1 app.
Total: 48 (20) apps. 10 gls.

PAVLYUCHENKO, Roman Anatolyevich

Role: Striker 2008-12
6ft.2ins. 13st.4lbs.
Born: Mostovski, Krasnodar Krai, Russia, 15th December 1981

CAREER: Victory Sports School/Dinamo Stavropol (Russia) 1997/Rotor Volgograd (Russia) 1999/Spartak Moscow (Russia) Oct 2002/SPURS Aug 2008/Lokomotiv Moscow (Russia) Jan 2012/Kuban Krasnodar (Russia) Jul 2015/Ural Yekaterinburg Jun 2016.

Debut v Aston Villa (PL) (h) 15.9.2008

Roman Pavlyuchenko first came to the attention of British football fans in October 2007 when he scored both Russia's goals in a 2-1 defeat of England that seriously jeopardised England's hopes of qualifying for the Euro 2008 finals. Pavlyuchenko was already an established top flight striker in the Russian Premier League with a record of almost a goal every other game for Spartak Moscow, but was a comparative novice at international level having scored only two goals in eleven full appearances after playing at Under-21 and Olympic level. He had started out with Dinamo Stavropol, first playing as a 16-year old, but when Dinamo were relegated from the Russian First Division he moved to Rotor Volgograd. In three years Pavlyuchenko was not the most prolific of strikers, but he was one of the few bright spots for a Rotor club in serious decline that was eventually forced to cash in on his talents. With Russia qualifying for Euro 2008, Pavlyuchenko had the perfect stage to display his talents and did just that with three goals as Russia progressed to the semi-finals before going out to eventual champions, Spain. His performances were enough to make him a man in demand and Spurs had to pay out nearly £14 million to sign him. Strong and muscular, Pavlyuchenko was perfectly built for a modern central striker. He was competent in the air, quick if not devastatingly so, could hold the ball up and packed a powerful shot. Unfortunately, his career at White Hart Lane did not have the best of starts. The team Juande Ramos had fashioned struggled so badly, that after eight League games the Spaniard was sacked. Pavlyuchenko's career with Spurs never really took off. For three years he was in and out of the team, never sure of a place, never building the confidence that was essential to him. Competing with Darren Bent, Jermaine Defoe, Robbie Keane and Peter Crouch, there were times when he showed just what he was capable of, but at others, he seemed out of his depth. When Emmanuel Adebayor joined at the start of the 2011-12 season, the writing was on the wall for Pavlyuchenko. A bit-part player, he knew his place in the Russian team for the 2012 Euros was at risk and when Lokomotiv Moscow made an offer for his services, he was quick to accept. The move did not have the effect he wanted-he played only one match in the competition. Pavlyuchenko retired from international football in July 2013 with 51 appearances to his credit, 22 of them as a Spurs player.

Appearances:
League: 45 (33) apps. 19 gls.
FA Cup: 6 (5) apps. 8 gls.
FL Cup: 9 (1) apps. 7 gls
Euro: 10 (4) apps. 6 gls.
Others: 6 (9) apps. 5 gls.
Total: 76 (52) apps. 45 gls.

PAYNE, Ernest George

Role: Outside-left 1893-99
5ft.9ins. 11st.6lbs.
Born: Fulham, London, 1876

CAREER: Old Sherbrookians/Fulham/SPURS Oct 1893/retired 1898/Bush Hill Rovers Mar 1898.

Debut v West Herts (FAC) (h) 13.10.1894
(Polytechnic (Fr) (h) 10.2.1894) (scored four)

The man regarded as being the catalyst behind Spurs' decision to turn professional, Ernie Payne was on Fulham's books throughout the 1892-93 season, but was only selected for their first team twice. A good, direct, speedy winger who was always likely to score goals, he deserved regular football and when Spurs invited him to play in a reserve match on 21st October 1893 he accepted the invitation with relish. When he went to Fulham to collect his kit he found it had all disappeared and arrived at Northumberland Park totally bereft of any equipment. Whilst shirt and shorts were not a problem, no suitable boots could be found, so Spurs loaned Payne ten shillings to buy a pair. When Fulham heard of this they complained to the London FA that Spurs were guilty of "poaching" and "professionalism", both cardinal sins in the eyes of the London amateurs. Spurs were acquitted of the poaching charge, but were found guilty of misconduct in offering Payne an "inducement" to play for them. As a penalty the Northumberland Park ground was closed for two weeks and Payne suspended for one. The blinkered attitude of the London FA and the high-handed manner in which Spurs were treated led directly to the decision to adopt professionalism two years later. Payne was one of those who took up the offer of paid football and continued to appear regularly until forced to retire due to a knee injury. In his time with Spurs he played on many occasions for London and Middlesex.

Appearances:
Southern: 20 apps. 5 gls.
FA Cup: 14 apps. 6 gls.
Others: 103 apps. 53 gls.
Total: 137 apps. 64 gls.

PAYNE, George Clark

Role: Inside-forward 1906-08
5ft.9ins. 10st.6lbs.
Born: Hitchin, Hertfordshire, 17th February 1887
Died: Clacton-on-Sea, Essex, 21st August 1932

CAREER: Page Green Old Boys/Hitchin Union Jack 1902/Hitchin Town 1904/Barnet Alston 1905/**SPURS** trial and perm. Nov 1906/Crystal Palace May 1909/Sunderland Apr 1911/Leyton Jan 1912/Woolwich Arsenal Jul 1912.

Debut v Portsmouth (WL) (h) 26.11.1906

George Payne first came to prominence with one of Spurs' local junior clubs, Page Green Old Boys, but it was his performances for Barnet Alston that alerted Spurs' attention. A Hertfordshire County player, he was given a trial in a friendly with Oxford University in November 1906, scored and performed with such promise that immediately after the game he was signed as a professional. He made his competitive debut in the Western League a week later, but his career at White Hart Lane never got off the ground as he was badly affected by injuries which limited his availability. He made eleven first team appearances in his first full season, but was unable to make the team the following year when Spurs made their debut in the Football League. Released at the end of 1908-09 he moved to Crystal Palace, was their top scorer in 1909-10 with 25 goals in 34 Southern League matches, and at the end of the following season moved on to Sunderland. He played only a couple of League games for the Wearsiders before returning to London midway through the season with Leyton. He tried his luck in the Football League again in 1912-13, making three appearances for Woolwich Arsenal. In September 1918 he was seriously wounded on active service and unable to play again after the war. Payne died in 1932 when a family holiday on the Essex coast turned to disaster. Returning to his bungalow on an outboard motor-boat, the vessel capsized. Payne helped save his five fellow passengers, including his son, but died himself. Payne married one of Billy Furr's sisters. Another of Furr's sisters married Billy Grimes.

Appearances:
Southern: 6 apps. 3 gls.
Others: 6 apps. 4 gls.
Total: 12 apps. 7 gls.

PAYNE

Role: 1888-89

Debut v Plaistow (Fr) (a) 15.12.1888 (scored once)

Payne' only known appearance for Spurs was in December 1888 when he scored one of Spurs' goals in a 2-1 friendly defeat of Plaistow in a 40-minute match.

Appearances:
Others: 1 app. 1 gl.
Total: 1 app. 1 gl.

PAYNE, H

Role: Inside-forward 1894-95

Debut v West Liverpool (Fr) (h) 26.12.1894 (scored once)

Younger brother of Ernie Payne, junior made his one appearance for Spurs on Boxing Day 1894 when he lined up alongside his brother and scored once in a 3-0 friendly victory over West Liverpool.

Appearances:
Others: 1 app. 1 gl.
Total: 1 app. 1 gl.

PEAKE, William Edward

Role: Inside-forward 1917-19
5ft.11ins. 11st.7lbs.
Born: Prestwich, Manchester, 1888
Died: Manchester, 12th March 1960

CAREER: Battersea Scholastic Training College/Northern Nomads/Eccles Borough/Sheffield United Jan 1910/Bury Jul 1912/(guest for **SPURS** during World War One)/Newcross cs. 1922/Macclesfield/Manchester North End 1922-24

Debut v Chelsea (LFC) (h) 29.12.1917 (scored once)

A former schoolmaster, Billy Peake was on the books of Bury when the First World War started. A goal-scoring inside-forward, he marked his Spurs' debut against Chelsea in December 1917 with a goal and appeared regularly in the final London Football Combination games of the season. In total he scored seven goals in 15 matches that season, but was not available so often the following season when he scored once in four games. After the war he continued to play regularly for three years at Bury before dropping out of senior football.

Appearances:
Others: 19 apps. 8 gls.
Total: 19 apps. 8 gls.

PEARCE, James John

Role: Forward 1968-75
5ft.10ins. 11st.6lbs.
Born: Tottenham, London, 27th November 1947

CAREER: Tottenham Schools/England Schools/**SPURS** app. May 1963, pro. May 1965/retired 1974/Walthamstow Avenue.

Debut v Arsenal (FL) (h) 10.8.1968
(Anorthosis (Fr) (a) 19.5.1968)

Jimmy Pearce was a local player first associated with Spurs whilst at school, who worked his way through the junior ranks into the senior side. A forward able to play as a central striker, winger or in midfield, he made his first team debut during Spurs' summer tour of Greece and Cyprus in 1968 and his League debut at the start of the following season. A very skilful player, at his best as an orthodox winger, he never managed to completely establish himself as a first team regular. Although he, perhaps, suffered from the syndrome of being a home-grown player at a time when Spurs were expected to field an all-star attack, he was never quite consistent enough to merit a regular spot. Most exciting on his day and capable of scoring some spectacular goals, he never settled to any

one position and spent a lot of his time as a versatile substitute. Indeed, it was his goal when brought off the bench in the second leg of the League Cup semi-final against Bristol City in December 1971 that finally saw off the gallant Third Division side and sent Spurs to their first League Cup Final. He sat out that Final as a substitute, but at least had the consolation of playing in the team that won the trophy in 1973. Shortly after that he was diagnosed as suffering from a rare bone complaint and in 1974, still only 26, was forced to retire from playing, although he did make a subsequent abortive attempt at a comeback with Walthamstow Avenue. He later went into business running a ladies-wear shop in Essex.

Appearances:
League: 109* (33) apps. 21 gls.
FA Cup: 4 (6) apps. 3 gls.
FL Cup: 21 (6) apps. 7 gls.
Euro: 8 (7) apps. 4 gls.
Others: 18 (7) apps. 8 gls.
Total: 160 (59) apps. 43 gls.
* Includes 1 abandoned match.

PEARSON, John

Role: Full-back 1913-23
5ft.10ins. 12st.7lbs.
Born: Arbroath, Angus, 22nd January 1892
Died: Arbroath, Angus, 13th April 1937

CAREER: Arbroath/**SPURS** Feb 1913/(Partick Thistle during World War One)/Luton Town Jun 1923/Arbroath Jun 1924.

Debut v Bradford City (FL) (a) 12.9.1914
(Chelsea (Fr) (h) 21.2.1914)

Along with centre-forward Alex Milne, John Pearson joined Spurs from Arbroath in February 1913. He had to wait a year for his first team debut and then another seven months for a League bow, but he fared much better than Milne, who left Spurs for Stoke City without even making the first eleven. With so many Spurs players joining the forces, Pearson played regularly towards the end of 1914-15, taking the place of fellow Scot Tom Collins. Unavailable during the war due to his own military service, he returned to start the 1919-20 season as first choice left-back and qualified for a Second Division Championship medal by playing in exactly half the League games before losing his place to Bob Brown. From then on he was limited to the odd game as reserve for Brown, before leaving to join Luton Town. After a year in Bedfordshire, he returned to Arbroath.

Appearances:
League: 47 apps.
FA Cup: 3 apps.
Others: 7 apps.
Total: 57 apps. 0 gls.

PEARSON, Thomas Usher

Role: Outside-left 1941-42
5ft.8ins. 10st.2lbs.
Born: Edinburgh, 6th March 1913
Died: Edinburgh, 1st March 1999

CAREER: Murrayfield Athletic/Heart of Midlothian trial 1933/Newcastle United Mar 1933/(guest for Birmingham, Blackburn Rovers, Blackpool, Bolton Wanderers, Heart of Midlothian, Liverpool, **SPURS**, Stoke City and Walsall during World War Two)/Aberdeen Feb 1948/retired 1953/Aberdeen youth team coach 1959, manager Nov 1959-Feb 1965/Newcastle United scout Jun 1967.

Debut v Reading (LWL) (h) 10.1.1942

Tommy Pearson was a top-class winger who made two appearances for Spurs in the London War League as a guest in January 1942. Discovered by Newcastle playing for the Edinburgh amateur club Murrayfield Athletic, Pearson has quite a record in representative football. In December 1939, with England's first choice outside-left, Eric Brook, injured in a car accident on the way to the game, he appeared for England against Scotland in a War-time international at St James' Park and in October 1941 he played for the Football League against the Scottish League. After the war, he won his first full caps for Scotland against England in April 1947 and Belgium the following month and, having been transferred to Aberdeen, played for the Scottish League against the League of Ireland. During the war years he was a popular guest player, almost guaranteed a match wherever he wanted, and helped Blackpool in the 1944 Football League North Cup Final. Following his retirement, he became a journalist with the "Scottish Daily Mail", but returned to football in 1959, initially as Aberdeen's youth team coach and then as manager. He held the post of manager until February 1965 when he resigned after Aberdeen had been knocked out of the Scottish Cup by Second Division East Fife. Pearson later worked for Newcastle as their Scottish scout while opening a jewellery business in Edinburgh. Pearson's father, also Tommy, played for Heart of Midlothian and his brother, Harry, played for Arsenal.

Appearances:
Others: 2 apps.
Total: 2 apps. 0 gls.

PERRIN, Percival Albert

Role: Goalkeeper 1893-94
6ft.1ins.
Born: Hackney, London, 26th May 1876
Died: Hickling, Norfolk, 20th November 1945

Debut v Friars (Fr) (h) 19.12.1893

A well-known Essex County cricketer, Percy Perrin, together with his brother Fred, frequently appeared in one of Spurs' junior teams, playing in any position he could simply for the fun of it, and to keep fit for his summer activities. Most often a full-back with the reserves, he made only one first team appearance. That came in December 1893 when he played in goal in a friendly against the Friars, a football club formed by members of the London sporting press. Perrin's summer activity was playing cricket, a sport he was particularly good at. He holds the record of the highest score in an innings for Essex, scoring 343 not out against Derbyshire at Chesterfield in 1904. Later in life he was a Test selector and, in 1939, Chairman of Selectors. At Essex, Perrin frequently partnered another old Spurs player, Charlie McGahey. Together they were known as "The Essex Twins".

Appearances:
Others: 1 app.
Total: 1 app. 0 gls.

PERRY, Christopher John

Role: Central Defender 1999-2004
5ft.8ins. 10st.12lbs.
Born: Carshalton, Surrey, 26th April 1973

CAREER: Wimbledon trainee Jul 1989, pro. Jul 1991/**SPURS** Jul 1999/Charlton Athletic loan Sep 2003, perm. Nov 2003/West Bromwich Albion Jun 2006/ Luton Town Jul 2007/Southampton loan Mar 2008, perm Jun 2008-May 2010/Dagenham & Redbridge coach Aug 2011.

Debut v West Ham United (PL) (a) 7.8.1999
(Elfsborg (Fr) (a) 15.7.1999

After ten years with Wimbledon, Chris Perry had developed into exactly the type of central defender George Graham liked. Solid, consistent and dependable, he had pace, could tackle, read the game and, for a player less than six feet tall, was good in the air. Particularly effective as a man-marker, he lacked creative skills, but that was of little importance. He was a destroyer, pure and simple. For three years Perry did the job demanded of him and did it well. Initially playing alongside Sol Campbell, Perry's position came under threat with the signings of Dean Richards and Goran Bunjevčević. Not the type of ball-playing defender Glenn Hoddle favoured, but with both new signings suffering injury setbacks, Perry's reliability proved invaluable. While distribution was never his strongest point and he rarely failed to take command the way a player of his experience could be expected to, his simple, no-nonsense approach, and the unfussy way he went about the job could never be faulted. It was only when a back injury side-lined Perry and youngsters like Ledley King and Anthony Gardner began to fulfil their potential, that Perry found himself surplus to requirements. He joined Charlton Athletic, initially on loan in a deal that saw Paul Konchesky arrive at White Hart Lane on the same basis, but soon moved to the Valley on a permanent basis. Approaching the veteran stage, Perry gave Charlton three years great service, helping the club maintain the Premier League status it only lost after he had been allowed to join West Bromwich Albion. From the West Midlands Perry went to Luton Town and Southampton, providing experience and a guiding hand to young, developing teams.

Appearances:
League: 111 (9) apps. 3 gls.
FA Cup: 9 apps.
FL Cup: 13 apps.
Euro: 4 apps. 1 gl.
Others: 28 (12) apps.
Total: 165 (21) apps. 4 gls.

PERRY, H

Role: Forward 1889-91

Debut v Swindon Town (Fr) (a) 1.3.1890

Another of the late 19th century Spurs' players about whom nothing is known, Perry is recorded as having played in only two Spurs' first team games. A forward, he scored once against Swindon Town in a friendly played in March 1889 with his other appearance against Millwall Athletic in a London Senior Cup tie in January 1891.

Appearances:
Others: 2 apps. 1 gl.
Total: 2 apps. 1 gl.

PERRYMAN, Stephen John M.B.E.

Role: Midfielder or defender 1969-90
5ft.8ins. 10st.10lbs.
Born: Ealing, London, 21st December 1951

CAREER: Ealing Schools/Middlesex Schools/London Schools/England Schools/**SPURS** app. Jul 1967, pro. Jan 1969/Oxford United player-coach Mar 1986/Brentford player-asst. manager Nov 1986, player-manager Feb 1987, manager May 1989-Aug 1990/Middlesbrough scout Aug 1990/Watford manager Nov 1990/**SPURS** asst. manager Jul 1993, caretaker manager Oct -Nov 1994/IK Start (Norway) manager Jun 1995/Shimizu S-Pulse (Japan) asst. manager Jan 1996, manager May 1999/Exeter City technical consultant Jan 2001/Kashiwa Reysol manager (Japan) Jun 2001-Aug 2002/Exeter City consultant May 2003, director of football Aug 2003, temporary manager Oct 2004.

Debut v Sunderland (FL) (h) 27.9.1969
(West Ham United (Fr) (Baltimore) 15.5.1969)

Steve Perryman is without doubt the most consistent and loyal player Spurs have ever had. He holds the record of having appeared in more matches for Spurs than anyone else, not only in the Football League but also in the FA Cup, the League Cup (in its various guises), European competitions and first team matches of any description. An England Youth cap, his first team debut came in May 1969 in a Toronto Cup match during Spurs' visit to North America. His League debut followed six months later. A first-teamer when he played in the 1970 Youth Cup winning side, Steve was originally a bustling midfielder of limitless energy. When he first got in the team, his job was to win the ball and make it available for more experienced players like Alan Mullery, Alan Gilzean and Martin Peters, but Perryman was not simply a fine ball-winner, he was also a very talented creator in his own right. Once in the side, his effervescence and incredible consistency made him a permanent fixture, and during the next 17 years he was only ever absent through rare injuries. A member of the team that won the League Cup in 1971 and

1973 and the UEFA Cup in 1972 he won the first of 17 England Under-23 caps against East Germany in June 1972. After playing in the 1974 UEFA Cup Final, the departure of Martin Peters in March 1975 saw Perryman take over as Spurs' captain and, whilst the club were relegated at the end of 1976-77, he led them back to Division One at the first attempt. By then he was playing as a central defender, sweeping alongside Keith Osgood. Whilst never the tallest or fastest of players, his shrewd positional sense and quite outstanding ability to read the game allowed him to operate in that position with considerable ease. Back in the First Division, he switched to right-back and in that role enjoyed some of the highlights of his career, captaining Spurs to the FA Cup victories of 1981 and 1982 and the 1982 League (Milk) Cup Final. In June 1982 Perryman, voted the Football Writers' Association's Player of the Year, won his only full cap when he played as a substitute against Iceland in what was effectively an England "B" team. He should have won more caps, and there can be little doubt he would have done, had he not earlier sacrificed his own development as a quality midfielder for the benefit of Spurs. In the UEFA Cup Final of 1984 he played in the first leg, but was forced to sit out the second due to suspension. He still received a medal though, for Ossie Ardiles insisted Perryman should have his; a clear sign of the respect and esteem in which Perryman was held by his team-mates. A truly great professional and loyal club man, nobody has won more medals as a Spurs player. Perryman was awarded a testimonial in 1979 and the MBE in the Queen's 1986 Birthday Honours List. He finally left Spurs in March 1986 to join Oxford United for £50,000. Two months later was back in a Spurs shirt playing as a guest in a friendly at Brentford. He later moved to Brentford as player-assistant manager, was promoted to manager and led Brentford to the sixth round of the FA Cup and Third Division play-offs in 1989. Building a useful team to get Brentford out of the Third Division, he surprisingly resigned in August 1990. Three months later he took over as manager at Watford. In July 1993 Perryman resigned his post at Watford, and the following day accepted the job of working as assistant manager to Ossie Ardiles back at Spurs. On Ardiles' dismissal, Perryman took charge of the team for one game as caretaker, but then found himself sacked as well. He had a short spell as a manager in Norway, a country where he has always been extremely popular, before being released from his contract so he could re-join his great friend Ardiles in Japan. In 1999 he succeeded Ardiles as manager and led Shimizu S Pulse to the title in the second stage of the J League. Unfortunately, they lost in the play-off for the overall title on penalties. Perryman was, however, voted the J League Manager of the Year. In June 2000 he led Shimizu to success in the Asian Cup-Winners' Cup. Returning to the UK, Perryman took up a consultancy role with Exeter City, a position he returned to after another spell in Japan. Settled in Devon, he was appointed Director of Football, a position he continues to occupy.

Appearances:

League:	654* (2) apps.	31 gls.
FA Cup:	69 apps.	2 gls.
FL Cup:	66 apps.	3 gls.
Euro:	63 (1) apps.	3 gls.
Others:	162 (5) apps.	12 gls
Total:	**1014 (8) apps.**	**51 gls.**

*Includes 1 abandoned match

PETERS, Martin Stanford M.B.E.

Role: Midfielder 1969-75
5ft.11ins. 11st.10lbs.
Born: Plaistow, London, 8th November 1943

CAREER: Fanshawe Primary School/Dagenham Schools/London Schools/Essex Schools/England Schools/West Ham United app. May 1959, pro. Nov 1960/**SPURS** Mar 1970/Norwich City Mar 1975/(Frankston City (Australia) guest May-Jun 1979)/Sheffield United player-coach Aug 1980, player-manager Jan-Jun 1981/retired Jun 1981/Gorleston Town 1981-82/**SPURS** non-executive director Aug 1998-Sep 2002.

Debut v Coventry City (FL) (h) 21.3.1970 (scored once)

For fifteen years Martin Peters had to live with the description of "ten years ahead of his time" given to him by England manager Sir Alf Ramsey. It was a tag he was never allowed to forget, but it was, perhaps, an astute evaluation of a classy player who could have appeared at the highest level in any era. An east London boy, he joined West Ham straight from school. Having collected his England Youth cap, he made his League debut in April 1962 and by November of that year was playing for the England Under-23 team against Belgium. A member of West Ham's European Cup-Winners' Cup winning team of 1965 and League Cup final team of 1966, he collected five Under-23 caps and played for the Football League against the League of Ireland in October 1963, before winning his first full cap against Yugoslavia in May 1966, just in time for the World Cup. With his West

Ham colleagues Bobby Moore and Geoff Hurst he helped England lift the World Cup, scoring one of the goals that defeated West Germany in the Final at Wembley. He had started with West Ham as a wing-half, but developed into an elegant goal-scoring midfield player with first class technical skills and a high work rate. By the time he moved to Spurs, for a record £200,000 with Jimmy Greaves going to Upton Park in part-exchange, Peters had played over 300 League games for West Ham, collected 33 full caps and made three appearances for the Football League. Still only 26, but very experienced, he possessed an exceptional tactical vision that helped him to almost intuitively spot potentially fruitful situations early enough to make the incisive blind side runs that brought him many goals. Indeed, the late run into the area became recognised as Peters' trademark. He won his first representative honour as a Spurs' player as a substitute for the Football League against the Scottish League in March 1970 and his first cap with Spurs against Wales the following month. In total he won 34 caps whilst at Tottenham and made two appearances for the Football League. A member of the teams that won the League Cup in 1971 and 1973 and the UEFA Cup in 1972, he also played in the UEFA Cup Final of 1974. Made captain following the departure of Alan Mullery, Peters gave Spurs five years' great service before an all rather too premature £60,000 move to Norwich City. The modest fee proved a bargain as Peters made more than 200 further League outings for the Canaries. His great contribution to the game was recognised with the award of an MBE in 1978. That was followed by a move to Sheffield United as player/coach, where he took his total Football League appearances past the 700 mark. He retired on his dismissal as United's player-manager, and, like so many before him, found he was unable to translate his success on the field into management. He subsequently returned to the playing side of the game with Gorleston Town. Peters later worked for a fruit machine firm, before linking up with his former Hammers and England team mate Geoff Hurst at a motor repair insurance company. In August 1998 he was invited on to the Spurs' board, taking on the role of supporter liaison. He held the position for four years. In 1967 Peters played for West Ham under the name of Baltimore Bays in the North American Soccer League's International Cup.

Appearances:
League: 189 apps. 46 gls.
FA Cup: 16 apps. 5 gls.
FL Cup: 23 apps. 12 gls.
Euro: 32 apps. 13 gls
Others: 27 apps. 11 gls.
Total: 287 apps. 87 gls.

PHYPERS, Ernest

Role: Half-back 1934-37
5ft.9ins. 11st.10lbs.
Born: Walthamstow, London, 13th September 1910
Died: Chingford, Essex, 28th October 1960

CAREER: Westminster Schools/Haywards Sports/Walthamstow Avenue/Aston Villa am. Sep 1932/**SPURS** am. Aug 1933/(Northfleet United 1933)/**SPURS** pro. Jun 1934/Doncaster Rovers Jun 1939/(guest for Clapton Orient, Raith Rovers, Southend United and West Ham United during World War Two).

Debut v Arsenal (FL) (h) 6.3.1935

Ernie Phypers had signed for Aston Villa as an amateur in 1932, but the registration was cancelled four months later with no professional terms offered. Phypers continued in the amateur game with Walthamstow Avenue until joining Spurs. After a short spell at the Northfleet nursery, he signed professional and made his League debut in March 1935. It was a sobering introduction. He had to mark Cliff Bastin as Arsenal won 6-0 at White Hart Lane and helped push Spurs towards relegation. Phypers' only significant run in the first team came between September 1935 and March 1936, before he slipped back into the reserves, where he spent most of his Spurs career. He was made available for transfer in April 1939, and two months later moved to Doncaster Rovers where he played for a couple of years in war-time competition before calling it a day.

Appearances:
League: 30 apps.
FA Cup: 3 apps.
Others: 2 apps.
Total: 35 apps. 0 gls.

PICKETT, Arthur Edward

Role: Inside-forward or winger 1906-08
5ft.4ins. 10st.0lbs.
Born: Bristol, 1882

CAREER: Workington/**SPURS** May 1906/New Brompton Jun 1908–cs. 1911.

Debut v Plymouth Argyle (WL) (a) 3.9.1906

Arthur Pickett was signed in May 1906 having impressed while playing for Workington in the Lancashire Combination. Although he made his debut early the next season, in his two years at Spurs he only managed to hold down a regular place in the Southern League team towards the end of each. Reliable but nothing special, he was released in May 1908 and joined New Brompton, where he played for three years.

Appearances:
Southern: 28 apps. 6 gls.
Others: 6 apps. 1 gl.
Total: 34 apps. 7 gls.

PIENAAR, Steven Jerome

Role: Midfielder 2010-12
5ft.8ins. 11st.13lbs.
Born: Westbury, Johannesburg, South Africa, 17th March 1982

CAREER: South African FA School of Excellence 2000/Ajax Cape Town (South Africa)/Ajax (Holland) Jan 2001/Borussia Dortmund (Germany) Jul 2006/Everton loan Jul 2007, perm. Apr 2008/**SPURS** Jan 2011/Everton loan Jan 2012, perm. Jul 2012/released Jun 2016/Sunderland trial and perm. Aug 2016.

Debut v Newcastle United (PL) (a) 22.1.2011

The signing of Steven Pienaar from Everton was the culmination of a long-held Spurs' ambition, made all the sweeter by his rejection of an offer from Chelsea. Pienaar had built a well-earned reputation with Everton of being a dynamic, hard-working wide midfielder, who could suddenly spark into life and change the course of a game. A product of the South African FA's School of Excellence based in his home-town of Johannesburg, he developed his talent at Ajax Cape Town for two years before joining the parent club in Amsterdam. The step up in class proved no obstacle to Pienaar and within a couple of years he was a first team regular. With team-mates including Mido and Rafael Van der Vaart, he helped Ajax win the Eredivisie and the KNVB Cup in 2002 and the Eredvisie again in 2004. In January 2006 he became another of the long list of stars Ajax were able to sell because of the conveyor belt of talent coming through their Academy. Pienaar signed for Borussia Dortmund in what was to prove a bad move. Dortmund were on a

downward spiral, and while they recovered to finish his first season in Germany well enough, the following season was a disaster from the start. While Pienaar's class was obvious, a relegation battle, three different coaches and a dressing room that never really accepted him, made Pienaar's life a misery. When the chance of a season-long loan to Everton arose, he grabbed it. Back in an environment where he was appreciated, he flourished and the move was made permanent as soon as the loan was over. An outstanding worker, willing to track back and cover his full-back partner, Pienaar had the pace and vision to burst into open spaces and provided a creativity from out wide that was priceless. With Gareth Bale still predominantly viewed as a full-back, Pienaar was needed to provide an experienced hand to bring out the best in Bale. Sadly, Pienaar never got his career at White Hart Lane underway. An early injury was just the first of many that saw him side-lined for long spells, and even when he was fit, Bale was so outstanding that Pienaar's presence would just have inhibited Spurs' star performer. After only a handful of appearances, Pienaar returned to Everton, initially on loan, but then permanently. For two years Pienaar was back at this best, but when injuries flared up again, he was rarely in contention. At the end of 2015-16 he was released. Over a ten-year period between May 2002 and October 2012 Pienaar made 71 appearances for South Africa, six of them as a Spurs' player.

Appearances:
League: 5 (5) apps.
FA Cup: 2 (1) apps.
Euro: 5 apps. 1 gl.
Others: 3 apps.
Total: **15 (6) apps. 1 gl.**

PIERCY, John William

Role: Midfielder 1999-2002
5ft.9ins. 11st.13lbs.
Born: Forest Gate, London, 18th September 1979

CAREER: Old Town Boys/South East Sussex Schools/Sussex County Schools/SPURS assoc. schl. Oct 1993, trainee Jul 1996, pro. Jul 1998, released Aug 2002/Brighton and Hove Albion Sep 2002/retired Nov 2004/Eastbourne Town Feb 2006-Nov 2007, coach Dec 2007-May 2009/Worthing Nov 2009.

Debut v Crewe Alexandria (FLC) (h) 13.10.1999 (Bishops Stortford (sub) (Fr) (a) 3.9.1999)

John Piercy was an east London lad, who moved to Maidstone with his family at an early age. He first made his name in Sussex schools football and made five appearances for England schools. Joining Spurs as a schoolboy, he worked his way up to the professional ranks and was given a few outings early in the 1999-2000 season when injuries left Spurs short of attacking options. Continuing his education in the reserves, Piercy gained experience in several positions, up front, all across the midfield, even as a wing-back. His best position was as an attacking midfielder, the type of role that would see him supporting a lone striker in the modern game. He made a few substitute appearances late in the 2000-01 season as Glenn Hoddle took the opportunity to look at the staff he had inherited from George Graham, but after that Piercy was not in first team contention again. Released in August 2002, the following month he joined Brighton and Hove Albion. He was to make only 30 appearances for the Seagulls, forced to retire after two years due to colitis. He later played for a short while with Eastbourne Town and Worthing.

Appearances:
League: 1 (7) apps.
FL Cup: 1 app.
Others: 4 (5) apps. 2 gls.
Total: **6 (12) apps. 2 gls.**

PILBROW, W

Role: Unknown 1890-91

CAREER: Douglas by Jan 1886

Debut v Unity (Fr) (a) 6.12.1890

Pilbrow's only known appearance for Spurs was in December 1890, when he scored once as a nine-man Spurs team drew 1-1 with Unity in a friendly match.

Appearances:
Others: 1 app. 1 gl.
Total: **1 app. 1 gl.**

PILCH, Robert George

Role: Half-back 1903-05
Born: Holt, Norfolk, 12th October 1877
Died: Norwich, Norfolk, 1st November 1957

CAREER: Melton Constable/Caleys 3rd XI/Norwich Church of England Young Men's Society/SPURS am. Nov 1903/Norwich City Oct 1911/Everton 1912/Norwich City director 1923-53, vice-chairman 1930-47.

Debut v Brentford (LL) (a) 16.11.1903

Originally a centre-forward, Robert Pilch developed into one of the best half-backs in Norfolk, playing for the Church of England Young Men's Society and Norfolk County. He signed amateur forms for Spurs in November 1903 and played in two London League fixtures that month, but apart from one Western League outing the following season that was the full extent of his brief association with the club. Quite capable of playing in a higher grade, he preferred to spend his time with the Young Men's team, playing in any position demanded; centre-forward, half-back, full-back, even goalkeeper. In total he gave the Society over 25 years' service, also working as committeeman, secretary, chairman and president. In 1911-12 he played a couple of games for Norwich City in the Southern League and played for Everton against Norwich when Everton turned up for a charity match a man short. Due to referee the game, he instead stood in for the England international winger Jack Sharp! Pilch was later a director and vice-chairman of Norwich. In his youth Pilch also appeared regularly as a fast bowler for the Norfolk County cricket team.

Appearances:
Others: 3 apps.
Total: **3 apps. 0 gls.**

PIPER, Gilbert Harold

Role: Half-back 1939-41
5ft.10ins. 11st.2lbs.
Born: Northfleet, Kent, 21st June 1921
Died: Gravesend, Kent, Jul 1987

CAREER: Northfleet United/(guest for Gillingham and **SPURS** during World War Two)/Gillingham Mar 1946/Dartford Jul 1951/Gravesend & Northfleet 1954-55

Debut v Crystal Palace (FLS) (a) 28.2.1940

A junior playing for Spurs' nursery club at Northfleet on the outbreak of hostilities, Piper made four appearances during the early years of the Second World War. He also guested for Gillingham and signed for them after the war. He continued to play for them until their first season of League football in 1950-51, making over 120 appearances before moving on to Dartford.

Appearances:
Others: 4 apps.
Total: 4 apps. 0 gls.

PIPER, Ronald David

Role: Inside-forward 1962-63
5ft.8ins.
Born: Crestwell, Derbyshire, 16th March 1943

CAREER: Arsenal am./**SPURS** am. Aug 1960, pro. Sep 1960/Guildford City May 1965/Wimbledon Dec 1966.

Debut v Blackburn Rovers (FL) (a) 20.5.1963

Ron Piper had been on Arsenal's books as an amateur before joining Spurs in the same capacity. Upgraded to professional status after a month, it was almost three full seasons later that he made his one and only appearance in the first team in the final Football League game of 1962-63 at Blackburn Rovers. Although he spent the next two years as a regular in the reserve and "A" teams, he never made the senior eleven again and when released in the summer of 1965 went into non-League football.

Appearances:
League: 1 app.
Total: 1 app. 0 gls.

PITT, Stephen William

Role: Winger 1965-66
5ft.7ins.
Born: Willesden, London, 1st August 1948

CAREER: Willesden Schools/London Schools/Middlesex Schools/Corinthian Casuals/**SPURS** app. Aug 1963, pro. Aug 1965/Colchester United Jun 1969/Stevenage Borough.

Debut v Blackpool (FL) (h) 27.8.1965
(Maccabi (Fr) (a) 24.6.1965)

Steve Pitt was a goal-scoring winger with the reserve and "A" teams, who made his first team debut as a 16-year-old. That was in a match against the Maccabi club of Tel Aviv for the John White Cup during Spurs' summer trip to Israel in 1965. Like several young home produced players of the 1960's, he was unable to establish himself and made only one senior appearance before returning to the reserves. His single League outing was early in the 1965-66 season when Jimmy Robertson was absent, but the rest of his Spurs' career was spent on the fringes before a move to Colchester United.

Appearances:
League: 1 app.
Others: 1 app.
Total: 2 apps. 0 gls.

PLETIKOSA, Stipe

Role: Goalkeeper 2010-11
6ft.4ins. 13st, 6lbs
Born: Split, Croatia, 6th January 1979

CAREER: Hadjuk Split (Croatia)/Shakhtar Donetsk (Ukraine) 2003/(Hadjuk Split loan 2005)/Spartak Moscow (Russia) Jan 2007/(**SPURS** loan Aug 2010)/Celtic trial Jul 2011/FC Rostov (Russia) Aug 2011/Deportivo de la Coruña (Spain) Dec 2015/retired May 2016.

Debut v Arsenal (FLC) (h) 21.9.2010

A vastly experienced goalkeeper, Stipe Pletikosa joined Spurs on loan to compete with Carlo Cudicini as cover for Heurelho Gomes. The move held the promise of a permanent transfer to join his compatriots, Vedran Ćorluka, Niko Kranjčar and Luka Modrić, if Pletikosa impressed. Having started with home-town Hadjuk Split, Pletikosa was first choice 'keeper by the time he turned 20. He represented his country at all levels from Under-15 to Under-21 and in February 1999 made his full international debut. Helping Hadjuk win the Croatian Cup in 2000 and 2002 and the Croatian League in 2001, he

picked up the individual award as Player of the Year in 2002. A move to Shakhtar Donetsk followed, but it did not work out for Pletikosa in the Ukraine. After two years he was loaned back to Hadjuk. He rebuilt his reputation, but when he returned to Donetsk was still unable to establish himself as first choice. It was only after he was transferred to Spartak Moscow that Pletikosa got back to his best. Almost ever-present for two years, it was reported that Harry Redknapp was keen on bringing him to Spurs in 2009, but a serious knee injury days before he was due to fly to London put him out of action for almost a full year. When he did make it to London, it did not turn out as he had hoped. In his year on loan, Pletikosa made just one senior appearance, an inauspicious Carling Cup defeat to Arsenal at White Hart Lane. For most of the time he lost out to Cudicini in the contest to occupy the substitute's bench. With his loan to Spurs up, Pletikosa returned to Moscow to negotiate the termination of his contract. After an unsuccessful trial with Celtic, he joined Rostov. While with Spurs, Pletikosa made two appearances for Croatia to add to the 80 he had previously made. He later took his total international appearances past the century mark.

Appearances:
FL Cup: 1 app.
Total: **1 app. 0 gls.**

POLSTON, Andrew Alfred

Role: Defender 1988-92
5ft.10ins. 11st.3lbs.
Born: *Bethnal Green, London, 26th July 1970*

CAREER: Waltham Forest Schools/Walthamstow Avenue Colts/Essex Schools/London Schools/**SPURS** trainee Jul 1986, pro. Aug 1988/(Cambridge United loan Oct 1989)/(Gillingham loan Nov 1991)/Brighton & Hove Albion trial Jul 1992/Reading trial Sep 1992/Fulham trial Oct 1992/Hendon Oct 1992/St Albans City Jun 1994/ Braintree Town Sep 1999/ Boreham Wood Jul 2000/Bishops Stortford Jul 2001/Ford United Nov 2001/Billericay Town player-asst. manager May 2003-May 2004/Aveley coach.

Debut v Crystal Palace (sub) (FL) (h) 3.3.1990
(Home Farm (Fr) (a) 18.10.1988)

Andy Polston followed his elder brother John through Waltham Forest, Essex and London Schoolboys, onto the trainee and professional staff at White Hart Lane and then into the Football League team. A defender, like his brother, he made three League appearances whilst on loan to Cambridge United in October 1989, and on his return to White Hart Lane only had to wait a few months before making his League debut for Spurs. When he went on as a substitute against Crystal Palace in March 1990 and joined John, they became the first brothers to play together in the League for Spurs since Bobby and Danny Steel in April 1912. Unfortunately, injuries then restricted Polston's further opportunities, and with Spurs' decision to rebuild, he was released in May 1992. After unsuccessful trials with League clubs, he joined non-League Hendon and went on to make a good career in non-League circles.

Appearances:
League: (1) app.
Others: 4 (9) apps.
Total: **4 (10) apps. 0 gls.**

POLSTON, John David

Role: Defender 1985-90
5ft.10ins. 11st.0lbs.
Born: *Walthamstow, London, 10th June 1968*

CAREER: Waltham Forest Schools/Essex Schools/London Schools/**SPURS** app. Jun 1984, pro. Jul 1985/Norwich City Jul 1990/Reading May 1998/retired Apr 2001/Grays Athletic asst. manager Sep 2002.

Debut v Coventry City (FL) (h) 15.11.1986
(West Ham United (sub) (Fr) (a) 12.5.1986)

England Youth cap John Polston made his League debut in November 1986, but was forced to miss most of the following season due to a serious back injury. He recovered in time to accompany the England Under-19 team on its tour to Brazil in the summer of 1988 and slowly worked his way back into Spurs' first team squad. A calm, versatile young defender, quite happy carrying the ball forward and a good judge of when to make a tackle, he was probably at his best in the centre of the back line. It was only early in 1989 that he managed a significant run in the first team, but just when it seemed Polston was set to challenge for a regular place, he was somewhat surprisingly allowed to move to Norwich City for £300,000. Linking-up with other former Spurs reserves, Mark Bowen, Ian Crook and Ian Culverhouse, he took some time to settle in Norfolk, even going on "strike" at one stage, but when the Canaries switched to a sweeper system midway through the 1991-92 season, he found himself a regular. In eight years Polston made more than 250 appearances for the Canaries before injury saw him lose his place. He moved to Reading, but never really recovered full fitness and played few games in his three years in Berkshire. After retiring, Polston worked as a personal trainer and sports therapist, although he did have a brief spell as assistant manager to his former Sours' reserve team-mate, Mark Stimson, at Grays Athletic. As a schoolboy Polston not only played for Waltham Forest Schools at football, but also at cricket and basketball.

Appearances:
League: 17 (7) apps. 1 gl.
FA Cup: 3 (1) apps.
Others: 9 (7) apps.
Total: **29 (15) apps. 1 gl.**

POPESCU, Gheorghe

Role: Defender 1994-95
6ft.2ins. 13st.1lb.
Born: *Calafat, Rumania, 6th December 1967*

CAREER: Calafat (Rumania)/Universitatea Craiova (Rumania) Jul 1985/(Steaua Bucharest (Rumania) loan Jan 1988)/PSV Eindhoven (Holland) Jul 1990/**SPURS** Sep 1994/Barcelona (Spain) Jul 1995/Galatasaray (Turkey) Jul 1997/US Lecce (Italy) Aug 2001/Dinamo Bucharest (Rumania) Aug-Nov 2002/Hanover 96 (Germany) Feb 2003/retired May 2003.

Debut v Watford (FLC) (a) 21.9.1994

Throughout the 1990s Gică Popescu was one of the finest midfielders in European football, a marvellously gifted creator with flair and style. Sadly, his short time with Spurs was probably the most disappointing of an otherwise outstanding career. Popescu started his senior career with Universitatea Craiova and by the age of 20 was the focal point of their team. In January 1988 he was surprisingly loaned to Steaua Bucharest, a move that may have had something to do with the fact the Steaua president was Valentin Ceausescu, son of the Rumanian dictator Nicolae Ceauşescu. Popescu provided the final impetus to Steaua's ultimately successful push for the Rumanian League and Cup "Double" and helped them reach the semi-final of the European Cup. Returning to Craiova, he made his first international appearance in September 1988 and was an established international by the time he was allowed to leave Rumania for PSV Eindhoven. His reputation was enhanced in Holland as helped PSV win the Eredivisie in 1991 and 1992. Popescu played in the back line for Rumania during the 1994 World Cup finals in the USA, his elegance, reading of the game and composure outstanding. Ossie Ardiles decided Popescu was the man he wanted to complete his team of attacking talents, the man to not only provide the solid midfield base that would allow, Darren Anderton, Nick Barmby, Ilie Dumitrescu, Jürgen Klinsmann and Teddy Sheringham to flourish, but also add a different dimension with his ability to provide inch-perfect long passes. Popescu's signing was not completed until the season was well underway, with disappointing results already threatening Ardiles' position. Installed

in front of a back four that had full-backs who were expected to attack more than defend, Popescu found it hard. Unaccustomed to the high intensity football typical of the English game, he was uncomfortable when put under pressure. When he had time and space, when things were going his way, his class stood out, but when hustled and harried, he would struggle, sometimes panic. With Ardiles' dismissal and the arrival of the pragmatic Gerry Francis, David Howells was reinstated as the midfield anchor. This allowed Popescu to concentrate on his offensive obligations and he was seen at his best, but he was clearly unhappy with the pace of English football. It was no surprise when he was allowed to join Barcelona. In the less frenzied football of La Liga, Popescu soon re-discovered his best form, helping Barca win the Copa del Rey and Cup-Winners' Cup in 1996-97. At 30 years of age, Popescu was released and joined Galatasaray. If that was expected to provide a winding down of his career, little could be further from the truth. In four years he helped Galatasaray lift the Süper Lig three times, the Turkish Cup twice and the UEFA Cup. He wound down his career with a year at Lecce and then joined Dinamo Bucharest, Steaua's great city rivals. His contract was cancelled after Popescu reacted to abuse hurled at him by fans after a particularly embarrassing defeat and a few months later he ended his playing days with a short spell at Hanover 96. Popescu, who made 115 international appearances, six as a Spurs player, was Rumanian Player of the Year a remarkable six times. On retiring Popescu ran a soccer school in Craiova and worked as players' agent. In March 2014, just as he was about to stand as a candidate for President of the Rumanian Football Federation, Popescu was imprisoned for three years having been convicted of money laundering and tax evasion.

Appearances:
League: 23 apps. 3 gls.
FA Cup: 3 apps.
FL Cup: 2 apps.
Total: 28 apps. 3 gls.

POSSEE, Derek James

Role: Winger 1963-66
5ft.5ins. 10st.0lbs.
Born: Southwark, London, 14th February 1946

CAREER: Redhill and Reigate Schools/Surrey Schools/**SPURS** app. Jul 1961, pro. Mar 1963/Millwall Aug 1967/Crystal Palace Jan 1973/Orient Jul 1974/Vancouver Whitecaps (Canada) May 1977/Dartford Sep 1978/Canada Soccer asst. coach by 1990, head coach by Oct 2001/British Columbia Soccer Association Provincial head coach 2003-Nov 2004/Surrey United (Canada), coach Sep 2005, asst. technical director Mar 2006/PASS soccer school coach (Canada) 2008.

Debut v Aston Villa (FL) (h) 25.1.1964 (scored once)

A speedy, dancing little winger, Derek Possee was one of several useful players who worked their way up through the junior ranks at Spurs, failed to make it at White Hart Lane, but went on to prove a more than competent performer elsewhere. A regular goal-scorer for the reserves, Possee netted on his League debut in January 1964, but was simply unable to oust either of the regular senior wingers, Jimmy Robertson or Cliff Jones. Possee moved to Millwall for £25,000 and spent his best years at the Den as a central striker, forming an effective partnership with Keith Weller, a former team-mate in Spurs' reserves, Millwall converted from a winger to a talented midfield player. Possee then played for Crystal Palace and Orient and when his League career came to an end spent the summers of 1977, 1978 and 1979 playing for Vancouver Whitecaps in the North American Soccer League. He later settled in Canada and worked as a coach.

Appearances:
League: 19 apps. 4 gls.
Others: 13 (3) apps.
Total: 32 (3) apps. 4 gls.

POSTIGA, Hélder Manuel Marques

Role: Striker 2003-04
6ft. 12st.6lbs
Born: Vila do Conde, Portugal, 2nd August 1982

CAREER: Varzim SC (Portugal)/Porto (Portugal) 1998/**SPURS** Jun 2003/Porto (Portugal) Jul 2004/(Saint-Étienne (France) loan Jan 2006)/(Panathinaikos (Greece) loan Jan 2008)/Sporting Lisbon (Portugal) Jun 2008/Real Zaragoza (Spain) Aug 2011/Valencia (Spain) Aug 2013/(Lazio (Italy) loan Jan 2014)/Deportivo de la Coruña (Spain) Sep 2014/Atlético de Kolkata (India) Jul 2015/Rio Ave (Portugal) Feb 2016/Atlético de Kolkata (India) Aug 2016.

Debut v Birmingham City (FL) (a) 16.8.2003
(Stevenage Borough (sub) (Fr) (a) 16.7.2003 (scored once))

With 22 goals in 58 appearances for Porto in the Primeira Liga, Hélder Postiga was regarded as one of Europe's most up-and-coming strikers. Spurs were thought to have got a good deal by signing him for an initial £6.25 million, but sadly for both Spurs and Postiga, it turned out to be a false belief. Under the coaching of José Mourinho, Postiga helped Porto

win both the Primeira Liga and Taça de Portugal in 2002-03. He also helped them win the UEFA Cup, though suspension meant he had to miss the final. A regular for his country at Under-21 level, Postiga made his first full appearance in February 2003 and had three full appearances to his credit when he joined Spurs. Arriving at the same time as Fredi Kanouté and Bobby Zamora, Postiga was immediately taken to by Spurs fans, but from the very start nothing went right for him. His class was obvious, as was his skill, hold up play and movement. He had an inbuilt talent for finding space. What let him down was his finishing, or perhaps more accurately his finishing was let down by the absence of the luck all good goal-scorers need. With the departure of Glenn Hoddle and the return to fitness of Robbie Keane, Postiga found himself little more than fourth choice and when Jermaine Defoe was signed, Postiga's days were numbered. Barely a year after signing, he returned to Porto with Pedro Mendes moving to Spurs as part of the deal. His experience in England seriously knocked Postiga's confidence. He struggled to rediscover anything like his old form whether back with Porto, at Sporting Lisbon or out on loan. It was only when he joined Real Zaragoza that Postiga began to score again with any regularity. His goals were not enough to save Zaragoza from relegation, but they did earn him a transfer to Valencia, replacing the Spurs bound Roberto Soldado. Again things did not work out for him, a story repeated at Deportivo de la Coruña. In July 2015, Postiga became the marque signing for Atlético de Kolkata in the Indian Super League. He scored twice on his debut, left the field injured and did not play for Kolkata again that season. After a year back in Portugal he returned to Kolkata, only for another injury to hold him back, but when recovered he showed flashes of his best. Despite his lack of goals at club level, Postiga continued to represent Portugal through most of his career, running up 65 appearances and 27 goals. Six of those appearances and two of the goals came during his year with Spurs, as did three goals in five Under-21 appearances.

Appearances:
League: 9 (10) apps. 1 gl.
FA Cup: 2 apps.
FL Cup: 1 (2) apps. 1 gl.
Others: 6 (1) apps. 2 gls.
Total: **18 (13) apps. 4 gls.**

POTTER, Cecil Bertram

Role: Inside-forward 1916-19
5ft.8ins. 11st.13lbs.
Born: West Hoathley, nr Eastbourne, Sussex, 14th November 1888
Died: Sutton, Surrey, 17th October 1975

CAREER: Melton Asylum/Ipswich Town Jul 1910/Norwich City trial then, perm. Aug 1911/(guest for Hull City and SPURS during World War One)/Hull City Aug 1918/Hartlepools United player-manager-secretary May 1920/Derby County manager Jul 1922/Huddersfield Town manager Jul 1925-Jul 1926/Norwich City manager Nov 1926-Jan 1929.

Debut v Reading (LFC) (a) 23.9.1916 (scored once)

Cec Potter made his name in the years preceding the First World War with Norwich City, having previously played for the amateur Ipswich Town. Principally an inside forward, although he could occupy any of the forward positions, he helped Spurs for three years. He was one of the most regular guest players, even though most of his football was played with Hull City. After the war he had a year with Hull before joining Hartlepools United as player-manager-secretary, giving up playing shortly after taking up the post. He then took over as manager of Derby County and almost took them to promotion to the First Division in his last two seasons in charge. On each occasion they were third and missed out. They did manage to achieve their target in 1925-26. By that time Potter was with Huddersfield Town, having succeeded Herbert Chapman. He would not have felt too upset at missing out on Derby's promotion for in the same season he led Huddersfield to their third successive Football League title. He only remained in charge of Huddersfield until the start of the following season when he resigned due to "ill health". In December 1926 he took over as Norwich City manager, a position he held for three years.

Appearances:
Others: 22 apps. 9 gls.
Total: **22 apps. 9 gls.**

POWELL, Herbert Harold

Role: Outside-left 1916-17
Born: Rotherham, Yorkshire, 1887

CAREER: Treharris FC/Nottingham Forest Aug 1904/Gresley Rovers Jun 1905/Grantham Avenue Feb 1906/Chesterfield Town Aug 1906/Barnsley Feb 1907/Carlisle United May 1907/New Brompton May 1908/Coventry City cs. 1909/Birmingham Dec 1910/Rotherham Town cs. 1911/Portsmouth May 1913/Boscombe cs. 1914/(Guest for Brentford and SPURS during World War One)/Worksop Town cs. 1919/Bethlehem Steel (USA) 1920/Grantham FC Mar 1922/Retford Town cs. 1922/Sutton Town Aug 1923

Debut v Portsmouth (LFC) (a) 17.1.1917

A well-travelled footballer who played either at centre-forward or on the left wing, Herbert Powell scored 30 goals for Rotherham Town in the 1911-12 season. He did not have the same success in his two years with Portsmouth and was released in the summer of 1914 to join Boscombe FC. His one appearance for Spurs was in February 1917 as a last minute replacement against Portsmouth in the London Football Combination. At the time of the game he was Portsmouth's assistant trainer. After the War he played for several years in senior non-League circles, with a year in America with the Bethlehem Steel club, one of America's most successful clubs.

Appearances:
Others: 1 app.
Total: **1 app. 0 gls.**

POWELL, J

Role: Inside-forward 1918-19

Debut v Arsenal (Fr) (a) 24.5.1919

Powell made his only appearance for Spurs in May 1919 when he was one of several trialists in an end of season friendly at Arsenal.

Appearances:
Others: 1 app.
Total: **1 app. 0 gls.**

POYET, (Dominguez) Gustavo Augusto

Role: Midfield 2001-04
6ft.2ins. 13st.0lbs.

Born: *Montevideo, Uruguay, 15th November 1967*

CAREER: Bella Vista (Uruguay) Dec 1985/Grenoble (France) Aug 1988/River Plate (Uruguay) Aug 1989/Real Zaragoza (Spain) Aug 1990/Chelsea Jul 1997/**SPURS** Jun 2001/retired May 2004/Uruguay FA coach/Swindon Town asst. manager May 2006/Leeds United asst. manager Oct 2006/**SPURS** asst. manager Oct 2007-Oct 2008/Brighton & Hove Albion manager Nov 2009-Jun 2013/Sunderland manager Oct 2013-Mar 2015/AEK Athens (Greece) manager Oct 2015/Real Betis (Spain) manager May 2016/Shanghai Shenhua.(China) manager Nov 2016.

Debut v Aston Villa (PL) (h) 18.8.2001
(Stevenage Borough (Fr) (a) 13.7.2001)

It might have been thought that Gus Poyet's best years were well in the past when Glenn Hoddle signed the 33-year old for Spurs. Certainly, he had enjoyed a successful and rewarding career, but Hoddle knew his man and knew Poyet still had much to offer. The former Uruguayan international had come to prominence during seven years with Real Zaragoza, helping the Spanish outfit lift the Copa del Rey in 1994 and the European Cup-Winners' Cup a year later, when a certain Nayim scored from the half-way line. A muscular midfielder, forever working the full length of the pitch and a regular goal-scorer, Chelsea manager Ruud Gullit pulled off something of a coup when he persuaded Poyet to move to Stamford Bridge when his Zaragoza contract expired, thus securing him on a free transfer. In four years Poyet, one of several international stars attracted to west London by Gullit and Luca Vialli, did much to raise Chelsea's profile, eventually attracting the Russian billionaire, Roman Abramovich. In his time with Chelsea Poyet helped the club lift the European Cup-Winners' Cup in 1998 and the FA Cup in 2000 and establish itself as a regular in the upper reaches of the Premier League. Poyet arrived at White Hart Lane at the same time as Christian Ziege and the returning Teddy Sheringham as Hoddle sought to secure immediate success by investing in experienced stars. While Poyet had lost some of his pace and had to rely on the youngsters around him to do much of the hard work, he still exuded quality and retained his greatest asset, the ability to suddenly appear, unmarked, in the opposition box and finish off play with a goal. As age and injuries took their toll, Poyet's influence diminished, but two assets that could never be lessened were his passion and love for the game. He would still strut the midfield, teaching the less experienced the tricks of the game and cajoling colleagues to greater effort, no matter their seniority. When he did stop playing it was no surprise he took to coaching and managing, transferring his animated gestures and passion from the pitch to the technical area. At first Poyet worked as assistant manager to his former Chelsea team-mate Dennis Wise at Swindon Town and Leeds United. When Juande Ramos was appointed manager at Spurs, Poyet was persuaded to leave Leeds and become Ramos' assistant. His services were dispensed with when Ramos was dismissed. Poyet returned to management with Brighton, building an exciting team that got very close to promotion to the top flight. In May 2013 he led Brighton to the Championship play-offs. The day after they had lost to Crystal Palace, Poyet, along with his assistant, Mauricio Taricco and coach Charlie Oatway, was suspended by Brighton. He was subsequently dismissed of alleged gross misconduct. Legal action resulted, but was settled shortly after Poyet had been appointed manager at Sunderland. Unable to arrest Sunderland's slide, he lasted just over a year at Sunderland, managed AEK Athens for a year and has now moved into the hot seat at Real Betis. Poyet's son, Diego, is on West Ham's books, having previously played for Charlton Athletic.

Appearances:
League: 66 (16) apps. 18 gls.
FA Cup: 6 (1) apps. 3 gls.
FL Cup: 8 (1) apps. 2 gls.
Others: 11 (10) apps. 8 gls.
Total: 91 (28) apps. 31 gls.

POYNTON, Cecil

Role: Full-back 1922-33
5ft.10ins. 11st.10lbs.
Born: *Brownhills, Staffordshire, 10th August 1901*
Died: *Tottenham, London, 12th January 1983*

CAREER: Ton Pentre/**SPURS** Aug 1922, coach Aug 1933/Ramsgate Town player-manager Jul 1934/Northmet/**SPURS** asst. trainer Jan 1946, trainer Jan 1947, physio 1972/retired 1975.

Debut v Birmingham (FL) (h) 29.12.1923
(Llanelly (Fr) (a) 16.10.1922)

Signed from the Welsh League club, Ton Pentre, Cecil Poynton gave Spurs over fifty years dedicated service as player, trainer and then physiotherapist. Signed from the Welsh League club, Ton Pentre, as understudy to Spurs' half-back and captain Arthur Grimsdell, it was as a full-back that Poynton made his mark as a player. He did not make his League debut until December 1923 when he stood in for Grimsdell, and most of his appearances that season were in a similar vein. However, the final outing was at left-back. He competed with Bob MacDonald for that position for much of the next season and seemed to have won the battle until injury struck. A member of the FA touring team to Australia in 1925, he suffered an injury on the trip which never really cleared up. He was out of the first team for the whole of 1925-26, although he did represent the Professionals against the Amateurs in the FA Charity Shield match in November 1925. He regained the left-back slot the following season and continued to appear in the first team for the next six years, despite never really making the position his own. At the end of 1932-33 he was retained to coach the young players, but a year later was released and moved to Margate as player-manager. Things did not work out on the Kent coast, and he returned to playing with Northmet. After studying physiotherapy Poynton returned to Spurs as assistant trainer, and on George Hardy's retirement took over as trainer. He continued in that role until 1972 when he became physiotherapist, a position he held until his retirement in 1975.

Appearances:
League: 152 apps. 3 gls.
FA Cup: 6 apps.
Others: 21 apps.
Total: 179 apps. 3 gls.

PRACEY, Albert J

Role: Centre-half 1889-90

CAREER: Tottenham College/**SPURS** 1889/Robin Hood.

Debut v Royal Arsenal (Fr) (a) 21.9.1889

A former Tottenham College player, Pracey's only known appearance in Spurs' first team was in September 1889 when he faced Royal Arsenal in a friendly match that was lost 1-10. He later played for the local junior club Robin Hood.

Appearances:
Others: 1 app.
Total: 1 app. 0 gls.

PRATT, John Arthur

Role: Midfield 1969-86
5ft.8ins. 10st.3lbs.
Born: Hackney, London, 26th June 1948

CAREER: SPURS am., pro. Nov 1965/Portland Timbers (USA) May 1980/**SPURS** youth team coach Jan 1983, reserve team coach, asst. manager 1984-Apr 1986/Walthamstow Avenue Aug 1986/Chesham United manager/Barkingside/coach in Nigeria/Stevenage Borough coach Oct 1994/Worthing asst. manager till Oct 1996.

Debut v Arsenal (FL) (a) 24.3.1969
(Cyprus International XI (Fr) (a) 25.5.1968)

John Pratt had represented London at Youth level and been a youth team player with Brentford, when recommended to Spurs by former winger Terry Medwin. Initially a centre-half, he switched to a wing-half position and worked his way through the junior and reserve ranks to make his League debut against Arsenal in March 1969. He gradually established himself and took over the number four shirt when Alan Mullery returned to Fulham. A substitute appearance in the first leg of the 1972 UEFA Cup Final was followed by an ever-present role in the League Cup run of 1973, although he only played 20 minutes of the Final against Norwich City before injury forced him to give way to Ralph Coates. At least he played in both legs of the following season's UEFA Cup Final. A tough, all-action midfielder with a crisp shot, Pratt was never given the credit he deserved and, indeed, was often the butt of the crowd's derision, a curious reaction, considering he was always totally committed to Spurs' cause. Never one to hide, he worked ceaselessly in midfield and it was the ball-winning base he provided that allowed his more talented colleagues to show their skills. Granted a testimonial against Arsenal in May 1978, Pratt was a regular choice under Bill Nicholson, Terry Neill and Keith Burkinshaw, and remained with Spurs until May 1980 when he went to play for Portland Timbers. After three years in America he returned to White Hart Lane as youth team coach and served as reserve team coach and assistant manager until he and Peter Shreeve were dismissed in April 1986. Pratt continued in football, working in non-League circles. During his time on the Spurs coaching staff he also made a couple of appearances in friendly matches. Pratt, who was the subject of a Monty Python sketch, later went into the office cleaning business.

Appearances:
League: 307 (24) apps. 39 gls.
FA Cup: 23 (5) apps. 2 gls.
FL Cup: 27 (4) apps. 7 gls
Euro: 24 (1) apps. 1 gl.
Others: 81 (11) apps. 15 gls.
Total: 462 (45) apps. 64 gls.

PRATT, Thomas Peet

Role: Centre-forward 1899-00
5ft.9ins. 13st.0lbs.
Born: Fleetwood, Lancashire, 28th August 1873
Died: Fleetwood, Lancashire, August 1935

CAREER: Fleetwood Rangers 1892/Grimsby Town Jun 1895/Preston North End Jun 1896/(Newtown loan Apr 1898)/**SPURS** Apr 1899/Preston North End May 1900/Fleetwood Rangers May 1902/Preston North End Oct 1902/Woolwich Arsenal Aug 1903/Fulham May 1904/Blackpool Mar 1905/Fleetwood May 1906/Blackpool Feb 1907.

Debut v Millwall Athletic (SL) (a) 2.9.1899

A big, brawny, tough centre-forward, Tom Pratt first came to prominence with Grimsby Town, but it was with Preston North End that he really showed his prowess and no little skill. His signing for Spurs caused quite a stir. He spent only a year at White Hart Lane, but left his mark, scoring the goals that won Spurs their only Southern League championship and helped them finish second in the Southern District Combination. However, he could not, reportedly, settle in London and went back to his former club. After a year at Fleetwood and a third, albeit short spell, back at Preston, he returned to London playing for Woolwich Arsenal and Fulham. He finished his career back in Lancashire with two more spells at Blackpool, either side of another few months at Fleetwood. When his playing days were over, Pratt became a motor engineer.

Appearances:
League: 30* apps. 24# gls.
FA Cup: 1 app.
Others: 29 apps. 29 gls.
Total: 60 apps. 53 gls.
*Includes 1 abandoned match.
#Includes 1 in an abandoned match.

PRICE, Ioan Haydn

Role: Outside-right 1918-19
Born: Mardy, Glamorgan, February 1883
Died: Portsmouth, Hampshire, 7th March 1964

CAREER: Mardy Corinthians/Riverside/Aberdare Athletic 1902/Aston Villa Dec 1904/Burton United Apr 1907/Wrexham cs. 1908/Leeds City cs. 1909/Shrewsbury Town Jun 1910/Walsall cs. 1911, secretary-manager Jul 1912/(guest for **SPURS** during World War One)/Mid-Rhondda United cs. manager 1919/Grimsby Town manager Jul-Nov 1920/Walsall secretary Nov 1920-1921/Mid-Rhondda United secretary-manager cs. 1921.

Debut v Clapton Orient (LFC) (h) 28.9.1918 (scored twice)

A Welsh international half back or inside forward Haydn Price played for Spurs as a guest in the 1918-19 season, despite having retired from playing six years earlier. Experienced and well-travelled, he played for Mardy Corinthians and Riverside (later to become Cardiff City) before

catching the attention of Aston Villa as he helped Aberdare to the 1904 Welsh Cup Final. He stayed with Villa for three years, but failed to make their League team although he won his first cap for Wales against Scotland in March 1907 whilst in Villa's third team. He collected two more caps with Burton United and three with Wrexham whom he helped lift the Welsh Cup in 1909. After a year with Leeds City and Shrewsbury in the Birmingham and District League Price finished his playing career with one season at Walsall. He then took on the job of secretary/manager at Walsall, his first full-time job in football, for as a player he had only been a part-time professional while maintaining a career as a Birmingham schoolteacher. He was forced to vacate the post in 1915 due to the First World War. After the War he was manager of Mid-Rhondda United and it was Price who rescued the career of Jimmy Seed after the future England international had been discarded by Sunderland. Price had just one year with Mid-Rhondda before joining Grimsby Town as manager, but only held the post for four months before taking the blame for a run of bad results. He went back to Walsall as secretary and later returned to Mid-Rhondda as manager until suspended by the Welsh FA after the club failed to pay its debts.

Appearances:
Others: 9 apps. 3 gls
Total: 9 apps. 3 gls.

PRICE, John David

Role: Centre-half 1954-5.
Born: Camden, London, 31st December 1932

CAREER: Eastbourne United/**SPURS** am. Nov 1953, pro. Sep 1954/Aldershot Jan 1957/Watford Jun 1959/Dartford Jun 1960.

Debut v Finchley (Fr) (h) 15.11.1954

Jack Price was signed in September 1954, but while he stayed with Spurs until January 1957 he played only two first team matches, both of them friendlies during his first season. On leaving Spurs he joined Aldershot where he established himself as a strong defensive pivot before moving on to Watford. He spent just one season at Watford, losing his first team place half-way through the season, but at least consoled by the fact he had helped set Watford on a successful Fourth Division promotion campaign.

Appearances:
Others: 2 apps.
Total: 2 apps. 0 gls.

PRICE, Owen

Role: Striker 2004
5ft.10ins. 11st.9lbs.
Born: Tooting, London, 20th October 1986

CAREER: Ernest Bevin College/South London Schools/London Schools/England Schools/Charlton Athletic/SPURS Scholar Jul 2002, pro. Jul 2003/released May 2005/Lewes Aug 2005/GIF Sundsvall (Sweden) Dec 2005/HJK Helsinki (Finland) trial Feb 2007/Turun Palloseura (Finland) May 2007/Fabril (Spain) trial Jul 2007/Ljungskile SK (Sweden) Aug-Dec 2007/Blackwood Town by Sep 2008/Northwich Victoria Dec 2008-Feb 2009/Farnborough Apr 2010/(Hastings United loan Dec 2010)/Cobham Sep 2011/Lewes Aug 2011/Farnborough Aug 2013/Carshalton Athletic Feb 2014/Cray Wanderers/(Erith Town loan Jan 2016)/Greenwich Borough Jul 2016/Chatham Town Aug 2016.

Debut v Falkenbergs (Fr) (a) 13.7.2004

A boy prodigy, Owen Price sprang to national prominence when he scored for Ernest Bevin College against Barking Abbey in the final of the Heinz Ketchup Cup, the FA Cup for schools, at Highbury in 2000. The 13-year old found the back of the net in a world record time of 4.07 seconds. At the time he had just joined Spurs having been associated with Charlton Athletic. His move angered Charlton who had suffered similarly when Jermaine Defoe had taken his talents to West Ham United. A Football League compensation tribunal eventually ordered Spurs to pay Charlton up to £445,000, £10,000 immediately, £15,000 on Price signing as a Scholar, £20,000 on his signing professional and £100,000 on each of 10, 20, 30 and 40 senior appearances. Charlton would also get 10% of any future transfer fee. As it turned out, Spurs only had to make the first three payments. The England schools international could play all across the front line and did quite well in Spurs youth teams, but had only one taste of senior football. That came on the pre-season tour in 2004 when new manager Jacques Santini took the whole professional squad to Norway to have a look at every player. Price made a substitute appearance in the first game of the tour, but was not seen again and at the end of that season was released. He found it hard to find a new club, but eventually played in Sweden and Finland. He had a trial with Fabril, the "B" side of Deportivo La Coruna, but was not taken on and after a few months back in Sweden, settled to playing in the non-League game.

Appearances:
Others: (1) app.
Total: (1) app. 0 gls.

PRICE, Paul Terence

Role: Defender 1981-84
5ft.11ins. 12st.0lbs.
Born: St Albans, Hertfordshire, 23rd March 1954

CAREER: Welwyn Schools/Mid-Hertfordshire Schools/Welwyn Garden City/Luton Town am. Jan 1970, pro. Jul 1971/(Minnesota Kicks (USA) summers 1977 and 1978)/**SPURS** Jun 1981/Minnesota Strikers (USA) Jul 1984/Swansea City Jan 1985/Saltash United/Peterborough United Jun

1986/Chelmsford City cs. 1988/Wivenhoe 1988/St Albans City cs. 1991/Hitchin Town 1993-94, joint coach Feb 1996/Western Knights (Australia) Youth coach 2007, coach Nov 2008-Aug 2010/Sorrento (Australia) coach Jan 2011-Sep 2013.

Debut v Middlesbrough (FL) (a) 29.8.1981
(Glentoran (Fr) (a) 8.8.1981)

As a promising youngster with Luton Town, Paul Price twice broke his leg while playing for the Hatter's reserves, but he did not let the setbacks beat him and battled back to develop into a cool, classy, cultured central defender. While building a reputation as a reliable player who performed his duties with the minimum of fuss, he helped Luton gain promotion to Division One in 1973-74. Qualifying for Wales through his Merthyr Vale born father, he made his debut at full international level against England in May 1980, and by the time of his £250,000 move to Spurs had a total of eleven full caps and one at Under-21 level. Although good enough for a place in most First Division teams, Price proved unable to displace the regular central defenders, Paul Miller and Graham Roberts, and played most of his matches when the adaptable Roberts had to move into midfield or one of the other defensive positions. Price still continued to represent his country though, winning the first of 14 Welsh caps as a Spurs' player against the USSR in November 1982. He also played in the Spurs teams that won the FA Cup, but lost out in the League (Milk) Cup Final of 1982. However, that was the pinnacle of his White Hart Lane career as a combination of niggling injuries and the form of Roberts and Miller limited his first team opportunities. At the end of the 1983-84 season he was given a free transfer, went to America to play for Minnesota Strikers and on his return to the UK joined Swansea City, moving on to Saltash United and Peterborough United. He returned to non-League circles appearing for Chelmsford City, Wivenhoe and St Albans City. At Chelmsford he was taken on to combine the duties of full time commercial manager with playing, but after only a few pre-season friendlies his contract was terminated and he successfully sued the club. After taking up coaching with Hitchin Town, Price eventually took his talents to Australia, coaching Western Knights and Sorrento, where his son, David, played.

Appearances:
League: 35 (4) apps.
FA Cup: 6 apps.
FL Cup: 7 apps.
Euro: 10 apps.
Others: 13 (3) apps.
Total: **71 (7) apps. 0 gls.**

PRITCHARD, Alex David

Role: Midfielder 2013-
5ft.5ins. 9st.13lbs.
Born: Orsett, Essex, 3rd May 1993

CAREER: SPURS Academy Scholar Jul 2009, pro. Jul 2011/(Peterborough United loan Jan 2013)/(Swindon Town loan Jul 2013)/(Brentford loan Jul 2014)/(West Bromwich Albion loan Feb 2016)/Norwich City Aug 2016.

Debut v Aston Villa (PL) (h) (sub) 11.5.2014

Alex Pritchard trained at West Ham as a boy, but when it came to a Scholarship, he chose to join a Spurs Academy that was becoming increasing well-known for the quality of its training. As he progressed through the Under-18 and Under-21 teams, there was speculation that some of Europe's top clubs were looking to pinch him from Spurs. He remained loyal, signing his first professional contract in July 2011. By now the star of the Development Squad, he went out on loan to Football League clubs to gain experience. He returned from a season long loan to Swindon Town with praise from all quarters to be rewarded by caretaker manager, Tim Sherwood. He put Pritchard on the bench for the last two games of the 2013-14 season, giving him a few minute's action in the last game. Pritchard then did particularly well in another year long loan, this time at Brentford. Promoted to the first team squad for 2015-16, an ankle injury in pre-season put him out of action for the best part of six months. With the team doing well, Pritchard was loaned to West Bromwich Albion, the intention being that he should regain full fitness while experiencing Premier League action. He would have done better staying at Spurs as he spent practically the whole loan spell warming the substitute's bench. A chunky, little midfielder dynamo, Pritchard exhibits fine technical ability and a desire to push forward into the box. Quick, both in thought and action, he has a sharp eye for the opening and an expert at dead ball situations. With a little patience, he should have proved a Spurs star of the future, but in August 2016 he was made available for transfer and joined Norwich City, a club that should fully appreciate his talents.

Appearances:
League: (2) apps.
Others: (1) apps.
Total: **(3) apps. 0 gls.**

PRYDE, Robert Ireland

Role: Centre-half 1944-45
6ft., 12st. 0lbs.
Born: Methill, Fifeshire, 25th April 1913
Died: June 1998

CAREER: St Johnstone Dec 1929/(Brechin City loan Oct 1932)/Blackburn Rovers May 1933/(guest for Aldershot, Bolton Wanderers, Brighton and Hove Albion, Fulham, Liverpool, Southport, **SPURS** and West Ham United during World War Two)/Wigan Athletic player-manager Aug 1949-Jan 1952.

Debut v Arsenal (FLS) (h) 2.9.1944

A stopper style of centre-half, Bob Pryde quickly became a regular at Ewood Park after signing for Blackburn from St Johnstone. He missed only one game as Blackburn won the Second Division title in 1938-39 and helped them reach the League War Cup Final in the first war-time season. He played for the Football League against the Scottish League in October 1941. His only game for Spurs was in September 1944 as a guest in a Football League South match with Arsenal. After the war he spent another three years with Blackburn, the dominant force in a weak team, and during that time made one further appearance for the Football League. At the end of the 1948-49 season, he retired from senior football and took on the player/manager's role at Wigan Athletic, where he remained for three years.

Appearances:
Others: 1 app.
Total: 1 app. 0 gls.

PRYOR, Harry

Role: Winger 1894-96
5ft.4ins. 9st.7lbs.

CAREER: Barking Anchor/Old St Stephens 1891-93/Old Castle Swifts/ **SPURS** Apr 1895/Dartford cs. 1896/Grays United.

Debut v Luton Town (FAC) (a) 12.10.1895
(2nd Batt. Scots Guards (Fr) (h) 13.4.1895)

Only 18-years old when he played his first FA Cup-tie, Harry Pryor was a local lad who had learnt his football with Barking Anchor and previously played for Old Castle Swifts and Old St Stephens. He made his first appearance for Spurs in April 1895 when he stood in for Ernie Payne. From then until February 1896 he was the regular outside-right until dropped and replaced by Charlie Lanham as Spurs began to plan for a future as a professional club. Pryor played only a few more matches before the end of the season when he was released. He joined Dartford and later played for Grays United.

Appearances:
FA Cup: 6 apps. 4 gls.
Others: 29 apps. 6 gls.
Total: 35 apps. 10 gls.

PURDIE, Tom

Role: Forward 1886-88
Born: Edinburgh, Scotland, 1854
Died: Davidson's Mains, Edinburgh, Scotland, 27tth December 1929

CAREER: Heart of Midlothian Aug 1875-Feb 1881/**SPURS** Dec 1886/Maidstone.

Debut v Iona (Fr) (a) 4.12.1886
(scored twice)

Heart of Midlothian's first captain, Tom Purdie was a full-back who played for Hearts from August 1875 until February 1881. He is only known to have made two first team appearances for Spurs. The first recorded appearance was in a friendly with Iona in December 1886 when he scored twice, and the other against the Old Etonians in October 1888 when he scored once in a London Senior Cup match. He moved to Maidstone with Charlie Bird and later returned to Scotland. Once a Spurs' committeeman, he was serving on Hearts' committee when the Scottish Cup winners visited Spurs in September 1901 for a "Championship of the World" friendly.

Appearances:
Others: 2 apps. 3 gls.
Total: 2 apps. 3 gls.

Q

QUINN, David

Role: Inside-forward 1902-04
5ft.7ins. 10st.0lbs.
Born: Tyrone, Ireland, 1882

CAREER: Hudson's Club/Darwen 1900/**SPURS** May 1902/released cs. 1904.
Debut v West Ham United (WL) (h) 16.2.1903
(London FA (Fr) (h) 8.12.1902) (scored once)

David Quinn started his career in England with the Hudson's club of Bootle and then spent two years with Lancashire League Darwen. He helped them win the League title prior to signing for Spurs, in preference to several Football League clubs, Everton and Sheffield United included, who were keen to acquire his signature. He scored on his debut in a friendly against the London FA in December 1902, but it was not until February 1903 that he made a competitive appearance playing against West Ham in a Western League match. Never more than a reserve in his two years at White Hart Lane, he left in the summer of 1904.

Appearances:
Southern: 1 app.
Others: 9 apps. 1 gl.
Total: 10 apps. 1 gl.

R

RABY, William Joseph

Role: Inside-forward 1899-00
5ft.6ins. 10st.6lbs.
Born: Heighington, Lincolnshire, 3rd July 1873
Died: Gainsborough, Lincolnshire, 18th December 1954

CAREER: St Catherines/Lincoln City Sep 1891/Gainsborough Trinity cs. 1894/Lincoln City Apr 1897/Gainsborough Trinity May 1897/Wellingborough cs. 1898/**SPURS** May 1899/Wellingborough cs. 1900/Gainsborough Trinity 1900/Stockport County cs. 1902/Doncaster Rovers 1904.

Debut v Reading (SDC) (a) 9.10.1899
(Richmond (Fr) (a) 13.9.1899)

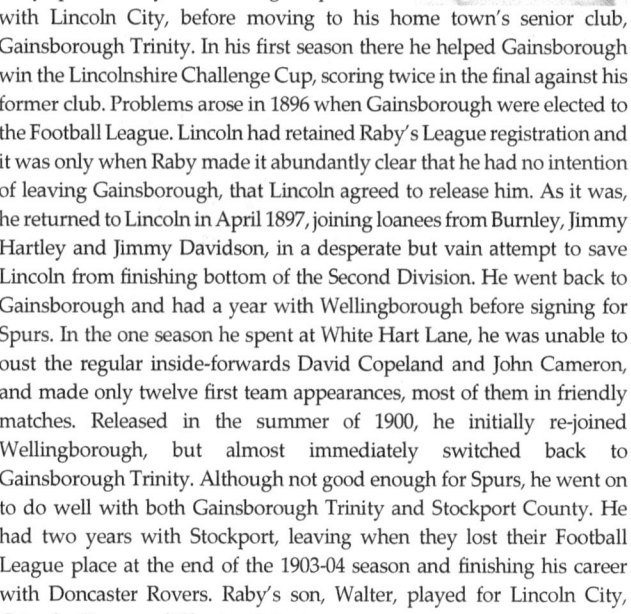

A diminutive but pacy inside-forward, Joe Raby spent three years building a reputation with Lincoln City, before moving to his home town's senior club, Gainsborough Trinity. In his first season there he helped Gainsborough win the Lincolnshire Challenge Cup, scoring twice in the final against his former club. Problems arose in 1896 when Gainsborough were elected to the Football League. Lincoln had retained Raby's League registration and it was only when Raby made it abundantly clear that he had no intention of leaving Gainsborough, that Lincoln agreed to release him. As it was, he returned to Lincoln in April 1897, joining loanees from Burnley, Jimmy Hartley and Jimmy Davidson, in a desperate but vain attempt to save Lincoln from finishing bottom of the Second Division. He went back to Gainsborough and had a year with Wellingborough before signing for Spurs. In the one season he spent at White Hart Lane, he was unable to oust the regular inside-forwards David Copeland and John Cameron, and made only twelve first team appearances, most of them in friendly matches. Released in the summer of 1900, he initially re-joined Wellingborough, but almost immediately switched back to Gainsborough Trinity. Although not good enough for Spurs, he went on to do well with both Gainsborough Trinity and Stockport County. He had two years with Stockport, leaving when they lost their Football League place at the end of the 1903-04 season and finishing his career with Doncaster Rovers. Raby's son, Walter, played for Lincoln City, Grimsby Town and Clapton Orient.

Appearances:
Southern: 2 apps.
Others: 10 apps. 8 gls.
Total: 12 apps. 8 gls.

RADOSAVLJEVIĆ, Predrag (PREKI)

Role: Inside-forward 1991-92
Born: Belgrade, Yugoslavia, 24th June 1963

CAREER: Čukarički Stankom (Serbia)/Red Star Belgrade (Yugoslavia) 1983-85/Tacoma Stars (USA) 1985-90/Estrela da Amadora (Portugal) 1987/Råslätts SK (Sweden) 1990/St Louis Storm (USA) 1990-92/**SPURS** trial

Apr 1992/Everton May 1992/San Jose Grizzlies (USA) 1992-94/Portsmouth Jun 1994/San Jose Grizzlies (USA) Jul 1995/Kansas City Wizards (USA) Feb 1996/Miami Fusion (USA) Mar 2001/Kansas City Wizards (USA) 2002/retired Oct 2005/Chivas USA (USA) asst. coach 2006, head coach Jan 2007-Nov 2009/Toronto (Canada) head coach Nov 2009-Sep 2010/Sacramento Republic (USA) head coach Jul 2013-Jul 2015/St Louis (USA) head coach Oct 2016.

Debut v Cardiff City (Fr) (a) 5.5.1992

Better known as Preki, Predrag Radosavljević, was a young midfielder making his way with Red Star Belgrade when spotted playing in an indoor tournament by the coach of Tacoma Stars, the former Arsenal full-back, Bob McNab. Persuaded to move to the USA, Preki became one of the finest exponents of the indoor game, winning numerous honours playing for the Stars, St Louis Storm and San Jose Grizzlies. For a couple of years when not wanted by Tacoma Stars he returned to the outdoor game and in April 1992 was taken on trial by Spurs. He played in an end of season testimonial match for Harry Parsons at Cardiff, but was not offered a contract. He was luckier though with a trial at Everton and spent two years on Merseyside before moving to Portsmouth. When his work permit expired Preki had to leave Pompey and returned to America. After another year playing indoor football, Preki. was allocated to Kansas City Wizards for the inaugural season of Major League Soccer. With the exception of one season at Miami Fusion, he played for ten seasons with the Wiz, the undoubted star not only of his club but the MLS. Granted American citizenship in October 1996, Preki made his first appearance for the USA team in November 1996 and went on to win 28 caps. He won the MLS Most Valuable Player award in 1997 and, at the age of 40, again in 2003. Following his retirement from playing he took to coaching and was voted MLS Coach of the Year in 2007.

Appearances:
Others: 1 app.
Total: **1 app. 0 gls.**

RAINBIRD, H A

Role: Forward 1902-03

CAREER: West Norwood/**SPURS** pro. May 1902/released cs. 1903/Southern United by Apr 1904.

Debut v West Ham United (LL) (h) 15.12.1902

(West Norwood (Fr) (a) 10.12.1902 (scored three))

An amateur with West Norwood, where he gained many representative honours for London and Surrey, Rainbird joined Spurs as a professional in May 1902. It was not until December that he made an impressive debut, scoring a hat-trick against his former colleagues in a friendly. That display not surprisingly earned him a competitive debut against West Ham five days later, but he proved unable to make the transition from amateur to professional status. He played only four first team matches in his one season with the club.

Appearances:
Others: 4 apps. 1 gl.
Total: **4 apps. 1 gl.**

RALSTON, Andrew Thomson

Role: Full-back 1915-19
Born: Trodigal, Argyllshire, 26th March 1880
Died: Ealing, Middlesex, 31st January 1950

CAREER: Thistle/London Caledonians/Aston Villa am./Watford am. cs. 1904/Civil Service/Southend United am. Dec 1911/Ilford by Oct 1914/ (guest for **SPURS** during World War One).

Debut v Clapton Orient (LFC) (a) 23.10.1915

A strong, fearless full-back, Andy Ralston assisted Spurs throughout the First World War years. He had previously spent several years playing for the famous London amateur club London Caledonians after first trying his hand at football as a youth in Glasgow with the Thistle club. He proved one of the most regular performers for Spurs at a time when it was always very difficult to get a team together. Although he also appeared as an amateur with Watford and Aston Villa, Ralston will always be associated with the Calies, playing for them for 25 years and then serving them for 20 years as club secretary. During his playing days he was one of the best full-backs in London amateur football appearing regularly for both London and Middlesex.

Appearances:
Others: 104* apps.
Total: **104 apps. 0 gls.**
*Includes 1 abandoned match.

RAMSAY, A

Role: Outside-left 1915-16

Debut v Norwich City (Fr) (a) 24.4.1916

A soldier serving with the 2/6th (Perthshire) Battalion of the Black Watch, Ramsay played his only game for Spurs in a friendly match at Norwich City in April 1916. Called upon at the last minute as Spurs only had nine men available, he set up Spurs' goal in a 1-1 draw with a smart centre from the left converted by his fellow soldier T McGregor.

Appearances:
Others: 1 app.
Total: **1 app. 0 gls.**

RAMSEY, Sir Alfred Ernest

Role: Full-back 1949-55
5ft.10ins. 11st.6lbs.
Born: Dagenham, Essex, 22nd January 1920
Died: Ipswich, Suffolk, 28th April 1999

CAREER: Beacontree Heath School/Dagenham Schools/Essex Schools/Five Elms/Portsmouth am. Jan 1940/Southampton am. Oct 1943, pro.

Aug 1944/**SPURS** May 1949/Eton Manor part-time manager Feb 1954/Ipswich Town manager Aug 1955/England manager Oct 1962-May 1974/Birmingham City director Jan 1976, caretaker- manager Sep 1977-Mar 1978.

Debut v Brentford (FL) (a) 20.8.1949

A grocer's lad from Dagenham, Alf Ramsey was spotted by Portsmouth playing for his local side, Five Elms, and signed amateur forms. He heard nothing more from them though, and with the arrival of the Second World War, it appeared professional football would miss out on his talents. However, whilst serving in Hampshire he played for his battalion at centre-half in a trial match against Southampton, and although they lost 1-10, played again the following week when Southampton's reserves were beaten 4-1. Saints were clearly impressed by his performances, for he immediately signed amateur forms and less than a year later was upgraded to professional status. Converted to right-back, he became a regular after the war and in May 1948 won his first senior representative honour when he played for England "B" against Switzerland "B". A place in the Football League team against the Irish League in September 1948 followed and in December that year he made his debut for the full England team against Switzerland. Ramsey was 29 when he joined Spurs for £21,000-a record fee for a full-back-with Ernie Jones moving to the Dell as part of the deal, but soon became recognised as one of the finest defenders in the country. The final-and by far the most expensive-component in Arthur Rowe's exciting "Push and Run" side, Ramsey played his first game for England as a Spurs' man in November 1949 against Italy at White Hart Lane and played in the next 28 internationals, captaining the side in the absence of Billy Wright. Virtually ever-present in the teams that won the Second Division and Football League titles in 1950 and 1951, Ramsey was a really stylish, unflappable defender; a careful, precision passer who combined power with polish, it was he that developed such a fine understanding with Ted Ditchburn and encouraged the goalkeeper to often throw rather than kick the ball clear as Spurs built their attacks from the back. Ramsey was a calm and accurate penalty-taker and overall, was such a clever, innovative tactician, especially from free-kick situations that he became known as "The General". Made captain of Spurs on Ron Burgess' departure, Ramsey was a consistent regular until leaving to take up the manager's position at Ipswich Town. By that time, he had a total of 32 full caps, had represented the Football League on four occasions, played for England against Young England once and for the 1950 World Cup team against the Canadian Touring Team in the 1950 FA Charity Shield. At Portman Road further great success followed as he led unfashionable Ipswich to the Third Division (South) title in 1957, the Second Division title in 1961 and then, remarkably, the Football League title in 1962. Such outstanding managerial success led to his appointment as England manager, and it was his tactical brilliance with the "Wingless Wonders" that helped England win the World Cup in 1966, an outstanding achievement for which he was knighted. He remained England manager until May 1974 when he was dismissed after the failure to qualify for that year's World Cup Finals. He later joined the board of Birmingham City and even briefly took over the managerial reins as caretaker boss between September 1977 and March 1978. Ramsey made his first senior appearance at White Hart Lane when he played for Southampton against Arsenal in December 1944.

Appearances:
League: 226 apps. 24 gls.
FA Cup: 24 apps.
Others: 33 apps. 6 gls.
Total: 283 apps. 30 gls.

RANCE, Charles Stanley

Role: Centre-half 1910-21
6ft. 12st.8lbs.
Born: Bow, London, 28th February 1889
Died: Chichester, Sussex, 29th December 1966

CAREER: West Ham Schools/London Schools/Clapton 1904/**SPURS** am., pro. Jul 1910/Derby County Mar 1921/Queens Park Rangers Sep 1922/coach in Holland/Guildford United secretary-manager May 1925-Jun 1927/Wood Green coach May 1930.

Debut v Blackburn Rovers (FL) (h) 17.12.1910
(Clapton Orient (LFACC) (h) 19.9.1910 (scored once))

An East End boy, Charlie Rance played for Clapton as a 15-year old amateur, going on to represent London and Essex County. A member of Clapton's Amateur Cup winning team of 1907, he played alongside Walter Tull in the 1909 final and scored a hat-trick as Clapton beat Eston United 6-0. Although he often played at centre-forward, Rance developed rapidly as one of the best centre-halves in the amateur game and was selected as reserve for the England amateur team on four occasions. When eventually chosen to replace RM Hawkes in the game against Denmark in May 1910, Rance missed out on the honour when the game was postponed because of King Edward VII's death. He did not get another opportunity, before accepting Spurs' offer to sign professional. A determined, intelligent centre-half who always tried to be creative with his clearances from defence, it was during the First World War years that Rance's value to Spurs was most apparent. He made more appearances in the London Football Combination than any other Tottenham player and his continued presence at the centre of defence provided the stability badly needed at a time when the availability of players was always uncertain. Sadly, the best years of his career were lost to the war, but he at least had the compensation of playing regularly in the Second Division winning team of 1919-20. The signing of Charlie Walters put Rance's place under threat and eventually he had to concede defeat. He moved to Derby County, but returned to London after eighteen months joining Queens Park Rangers. When he finished playing he was appointed manager of Guildford, but did not hold the post for long. He was later coach to Wood Green. In over a hundred Football League games for Spurs Rance scored only once, and even that has been forgotten! The goal came against Notts County in October 1912-in a game that was abandoned after 80 minutes due to fog.

Appearances:
League: 105* apps. 1# gl.
FA Cup: 7 apps. 1 gl.
Others: 151 apps. 14 gls.
Total: 263 apps. 16 gls.
*Includes 2 abandoned matches.
#Scored in abandoned match.

RANDALL, James G

Role: Forward 1883-87
Born: Dalston, London. 18th September 1864

CAREER: Radicals by 1881/**SPURS** 1883.

Debut v Latymer (Fr) (a) 15.3.1884 (score once)

Billy Randall played for at least two years with Radicals, Spurs first ever opponents. Whilst not one of Spurs' founder members, by the start of their second season in existence he was captain, although he only held that post for one season. His first known appearance for Spurs was in March 1884 when he scored in a friendly against Latymer, but he almost certainly played in many other matches that season. For the 1884-85 season he was a member of the committee that ran the club. While he continued to play after that, he took a less active part in management affairs. He played for Spurs until the 1886-87 season, but then disappeared from the scene.

Appearances:
Others: 12 apps. 6 gls.
Total: **12 apps. 6 gls**

RASIAK, Grzegorz

Role: Striker 2005-06
6ft.3ins. 13st.3lbs
Born: Stettino, Poland, 12th January 1979

CAREER: Olimpia Poznań (Poland) 1996/SKS 13 Poznań (Poland)/MSP Szamotuly (Poland)/Warta Poznań (Poland) 1996-97/GKS Bełchatów (Poland) 1998/Odra Wodzisław (Poland) 2000-01/Groclin Dyskobolia (Poland) 2001-02/Siena (Italy) Aug 2004/Derby County Sep 2004/**SPURS** loan Aug 2005, perm. Sep 2005/Southampton loan Feb 2006, perm. May 2006/(Bolton Wanderers loan Jan 2008)/(Watford loan Aug 2008)/Reading Jul 2009/AEL Limassol (Cyprus) Aug 2010-Apr 2011/Charlton Athletic trial Aug 2011/Jagiellonia Bialystok (Poland) Sep 2011/Lechia Gdańsk (Poland) Jun 2012/Warta Poznań (Poland) Jul 2013/retired Jun 2014.

Debut v Liverpool (FL) (h) 10.9.2005

Although Spurs had Mido, the sale of Fredi Kanouté to Sevilla late in the summer 2005 transfer window left the club short up front. Jermain Defoe and Robbie Keane were available, but neither of them were the big, target man style of centre-forward Martin Jol liked. Grzegorz Rasiak was. The Polish international had developed well with some of his country's lesser known clubs, proving a handful for opposing defenders and a regular goal-scorer. A goal every two games for Groclin Dyskobolia earnt Rasiak a move to Siena, but the Italian authorities refused to register the transfer as Siena already had the permitted number of foreigners on their books. Derby County stepped in and in little more than a year at the Baseball

Ground Rasiak was a success, 18 goals in 41 Championship appearances. The £2.25 million deal taking Rasiak to White Hart Lane was done so late, literally with minutes to spare before the transfer window closed, that the move was initially on a loan basis. It gave the impression of desperation. After a few games the impression had been reinforced. While he worked hard and could never be accused of giving anything less than his best, Rasiak proved a failure. Cumbersome and lacking in basic skills, he never looked a Premiership, let alone international, striker. It did not take the fans quickly turning against Rasiak for Jol to realise the signing had been a mistake. Rasiak was called upon only when there was no alternative, before moving to Southampton, initially on loan. He proved a competent enough scorer back at Championship level with Southampton, Watford and Reading. After a less than successful season with AEL Limassol, Rasiak returned to Poland, eventually re-joining and finishing his career at Warta Poznań, the club he had started his senior career with 17 years earlier.

Appearances:
League: 4 (4) apps.
FA Cup: 1 app.
Total: **5 (4) apps. 0 gls.**

REBROV, Serhiy Stanislavovych

Role: Striker 2000-03
5ft.7ins. 11st.0lbs.
Born: Gorlovka, Ukraine, 3rd June 1974

CAREER: Shakhtar Donetsk (Ukraine) 1990/Dynamo Kiev (Ukraine) Jul 1992/**SPURS** May 2000/(Fenerbahce (Turkey) loan Jan 2003)/West Ham United training Jul 2004, perm. Aug 2004/Dynamo Kiev (Ukraine) Jun 2005/Rubin Kazan (Russia) Mar 2008/retired Jul 2009/Dynamo Kiev (Ukraine) reserves coach Jul 2009, coach Dec 2012, acting head coach Apr 2014, perm. head coach May 2014/Ukraine asst. coach Sep 2012.

Debut v Ipswich Town (PL) (h) 19.8.2000
(Skellefteå AIK (Fr) (a) 19.7.2000)

When George Graham persuaded Sir Alan Sugar to lay out £11million to sign Serhiy Rebrov, he was not the only person who thought Spurs had secured one of Europe's best strikers, a man whose goals were sure to turn Spurs from mid-table also-rans to Champions League contenders. After being snapped up as an 18-year old prodigy from Shakhtar Donetsk, Rebrov had flourished at Dynamo Kiev, forming a deadly partnership at both club and international level with Andriy Shevchenko. Rebrov was the brains of the duo, the creative, nippy little player creating chances for the big, bustling, powerhouse, while at the same time, feeding off the chaos the bigger man created. He was not an out-and-out striker. He occupied the space between midfield and the main striker, the area where his deft skills could create chances but still allow him to display his clinical finishing. In many respects, he was some years ahead of his time. Shevchenko had left Dynamo a year before Rebrov and proved a stunning success with AC Milan. The expectation was that Rebrov would do just as well. Sadly, he did not. Les Ferdinand, who could be just as explosive as Shevchenko, was Spurs' principal striker and should have provided the perfect foil for Rebrov. Had

Rebrov been allowed to play in his favoured role behind the main striker, he may have done, but Rebrov was expected to play right up front alongside Ferdinand. It was not a role Rebrov was comfortable with or physically built for. He needed to have space and the play in front of him, not his back to goal while marked by a towering centre-half. He needed the ball on the floor, not flying over his head. There were times when he fell back into midfield and showed what he was capable of, but all too often those moments were submerged in exaltations to push further up. Considering the demands made of him, Rebrov did remarkably well in his first season. The arrival of Glenn Hoddle should have promised better things for Rebrov, but the truth was just the opposite. Hoddle clearly did not take to Rebrov. He gave him few real opportunities, all too often sending Rebrov on as a substitute with only minutes to play. Any confidence Rebrov possessed was destroyed. It was no way to treat a great player. For the 2002-03 season Rebrov was not even making the first team squad for games. He was allowed to join Fenerbahce on an 18-month loan and played regularly as he helped Fenerbahce win the Turkish Süper Lig in 2003-04. Rebrov did not return to Spurs. With his contract up, he faced work permit problems. When they were overcome, he joined West Ham United, but the Championship was not the place for his talents. After spending most of the season as a substitute, he returned home to Dinamo Kiev. He soon rediscovered his old form, was voted Ukrainian Premier League Player of the Season for 2005-06 as he helped Dinamo win the Ukrainian Cup and added the Ukrainian League the following season. A year with Rubin Kazan brought Rebrov's playing career to an end and he then became a coach. Rebrov scored 15 goals in 75 appearances for Ukraine, one goal and 29 appearances during his time as a Spurs' player.

Appearances:
League: 37 (22) apps. 10 gls.
FA Cup: 7 (1) apps. 3 gls.
FL Cup: 4 (4) apps. 3 gls.
Others: 15 (8) apps. 11 gls.
Total: 63 (35) apps. 27 gls.

REDDISH, John

Role: Left-back 1928-32
5ft.9ins. 11st.6lbs.
Born: Nottingham, 22nd December 1904
Died: Manchester, 18th October 1989

CAREER: Boots Athletic/**SPURS** Mar 1927/Lincoln City Aug 1933/Notts County Sep 1935/Dundee Jul 1936.

Debut v West Bromwich Albion (FL) (a) 21.4.1930

(Charlton Athletic (LFACC) (Upton Park) 26.11.1928)

Although Jack Reddish made his first appearance for Spurs in a London FA Charity Cup semi-final with Charlton Athletic at Upton Park in November 1928, he did not make a League debut until April 1930. He played in the final three matches of that season, replacing Bill Herod who had switched to the right-back slot in place of the absent Matt Forster. Reddish did not make the first team again until February 1932 and was never near to claiming a regular place. In May 1933 he was made available for transfer and joined Lincoln City in August, later moving on to Notts County and Dundee. When his playing days were over, Reddish turned to coaching. He spent most of his time in the Channel Islands, only leaving when World War Two began, but returned to the island of Guernsey after the war as games master of Elizabeth College. At one time Reddish had been on the books of Notts CC, playing one senior game for them in 1930.

Appearances:
League: 6 apps.
FA Cup: 1 app.
Others: 3 apps.
Total: 10 apps. 0 gls.

REDKNAPP, Jamie Frank

Role: Midfielder 2002-05
6ft. 13st.4lbs.
Born: Barton-On-Sea, Hampshire, 25th June 1973

CAREER: Greenfields/Bournemouth Schools/England Schools/**SPURS** Ass. Schl. 1988/AFC Bournemouth trainee Jul 1989, pro. Jun 1990/Liverpool Jan 1991/**SPURS** Apr 2002/Southampton Jan 2005/retired Jun 2005.

Debut v Everton (PL) (a) 17.8.2002
(Stevenage Borough (sub) (Fr) (a) 21.7.2002)

Jamie Redknapp was on Spurs' books as a schoolboy, but turned down the offer of a training contract to join AFC Bournemouth where his father, Harry, was manager. If it was a gamble to risk allegations of nepotism, it was not one that lasted long. Barely six months after signing professional, and with only 13 League appearances to his credit, Redknapp was snapped up by Liverpool. The fee was £350,000, a

record for a player of his age, but soon to prove an absolute bargain. Redknapp spent most of his first couple of years on Merseyside, playing for the reserves and being educated in "the Liverpool way", not that he needed much education. His natural game was perfect for Liverpool. A very talented, industrious midfielder, always demanding the ball, forever supporting his colleagues, he was at his best with the ball on the deck, working it through midfield, looking for the incisive pass or spreading play out with a long pass to the wings. He established himself as a central figure in Liverpool's midfield, chipping in with his fair share of goals, normally from long-range and often from set pieces. With Liverpool, Redknapp collected 17 full England caps to add to 18 at Under-21 and one at "A" level, but only picked up one club honour, the Coca-Cola Cup in 1995. He was made Liverpool captain in 1999, but led the team out on far fewer occasions than anyone would have liked. He had suffered a few injuries in his career, but a serious knee injury saw him play little more than a dozen games in two-and-a-half years. When his contract expired in 2002, Liverpool wanted to give him a new one, but he decided a change of scenery might herald a change in fitness. He accepted Glenn Hoddle's offer to join Spurs. At first things went well. He settled quickly, dominating midfield, showing the skills to open opposing defences. Unfortunately, the injuries problems soon resurfaced and for three years Redknapp spent as long receiving treatment as he did playing. Eventually he was released to join father Harry at Southampton in a desperate but unsuccessful attempt to save the Saints from relegation. After six months he retired to become a TV pundit and sports columnist.

Appearances:
League: 37 (11) apps. 4 gls.
FL Cup: 1 app.
Others: 15 (2) apps. 1 gl.
Total: 53 (13) apps. 5 gls.

REES, William

Role: Inside-forward 1949-50
5ft.11ins. 12st.0lbs.

Born: Blaengarw, Glamorganshire, 10th March 1924
Died: Cardiff, 25th July 1996

CAREER: Blaengarw/Caernarvon Rovers/Cardiff City Feb 1943, pro Feb 1944/SPURS Jun 1949/Leyton Orient Jun 1950/Headington United Dec 1955/Kettering Town cs. 1959.

Debut v Chesterfield (FL) (a) 27.12.1949

A coal-miner for seven years, Billy Rees was playing for Caernarvon Rovers when spotted by the Cardiff City manager and former Spurs goalkeeper Cyril Spiers. Principally an inside-forward, but capable of playing in any of the front positions, he played regularly for the Welsh club during the war and turned out for Wales against England in a war-time international in May 1945. He made over 100 League appearances for Cardiff and won three full Welsh caps, the first against Northern Ireland in March 1949, before joining Spurs for £14,000. Early on at White Hart Lane he suffered a series of minor injuries and consequently it was not until December 1949 that he made his debut. In total he made fourteen senior appearances in the 1949-50 promotion season and won one further Welsh cap-against Northern Ireland in March 1950. With Peter Murphy signed from Coventry City in June 1950, Spurs recouped their outlay as Rees was allowed to move for £14,500 to Leyton Orient. He played there for over five years, netting 66 goals in 198 appearances before moving into non-League circles with Headington United and Kettering Town. He later worked as a plant operator and then for a pharmaceutical company in Bridgend.

Appearances:
League: 11 apps. 3 gls.
FA Cup: 2 apps.
Others: 1 app.
Total: 14 apps. 3 gls.

REES

Role: Outside-right 1918-19

Debut v Clapton Orient (Fr) (a) 26.4.1919

Rees is another of those players who made their only appearance for Spurs as a trialist in April 1919. He played in the friendly that day at Clapton Orient, but was not a success and not taken on.

Appearances:
Others: 1 app.
Total: 1 app. 0 gls.

REGAN, Charles D

Role: Half-back 1895-97
Born: Romford, Essex, 22nd September 1869

CAREER: Clarendon/Woodville/Ilford 1894/Clapton/Sheffield/Glossop/SPURS Dec 1896/Gravesend United/Richmond Association/Shepherds Bush 1902-03.

Debut v Rushden (UL) (h) 4.3.1897
(Vampires (Fr) (h) 25.12.1895)

Charlie Regan was one of the many amateur players from around at the end of the 19th century who played the game purely for enjoyment, despite numerous offers to join the paid ranks. An Essex county player in his days with Woodville, he appeared regularly for Ilford in 1894-95 and 1895-96, but also assisted several other clubs. It was in the 1895-96 season that he made his first appearance for Spurs, the only game he played that year. In December 1896, at which time he was primarily associated with Clapton, he signed Southern League forms for Spurs, but did not to make any appearances for the club in that competition. He only played four further matches for Spurs, one a United League fixture and the others friendlies. He then appeared for three seasons with Gravesend United and later Richmond Association, although still associated with Clapton, who were credited as being his club when he represented London.

Appearances:
Others: 5 apps.
Total: 5 apps. 0 gls.

REID, Andrew Matthew

Role: Midfielder 2004-06
5ft.9ins. 12st.8lbs.
Born: Dublin, Republic of Ireland, 29th July 1982

CAREER: Templeogue United/Lourdes Celtic/Cherry Orchard/Nottingham Forest trainee Jul 1998, pro. Aug 1999/SPURS Jan 2005/Charlton Athletic Aug 2006/Sunderland Jan 2008/(Sheffield United loan Oct 2010)/Blackpool Jan-May 2011/Nottingham Forest Jul 2011, coach Mar 2016.

Debut v Portsmouth (PL) (h) 5.2.2005

Spurs had been chasing Andy Reid for some time when they eventually signed him and Michael Dawson from Nottingham Forest in January 2005. A creative little wide midfielder, tricky, with an eye for an opening and the ability to exploit it, Reid was rated one of the most talented midfielders playing in the Championship. He was regarded as the better prospect of the two, a Republic of Ireland international at Under-21 and full level, but it was Dawson that turned out to be by far the better signing. Right from his debut, Reid's talent was obvious, as was the difficult question of where he would be most effective. Played out wide, he had the skills to beat his man, but not the pace to get away from him. Played infield, he could pick out the killer pass, but was easily outmuscled. It was a question that was never answered as Reid struggled to adapt to football at the top level. At Forest he had been the star, the man who took charge of all the set plays. At Spurs he was one of many stars, and as the newcomer had to take second place to his seniors. A portly character, it was frequently suggested that Reid was overweight. That was always denied, but he certainly never looked trim enough for a top professional. After his first season, Reid began to suffer injury problems. Combined with serious doubts about his ability to make it at one of football's biggest clubs, the decision was made to let him leave for Charlton Athletic. He was unable to stop Charlton being relegated, but once back in the Championship began to display the form he had shown at Forest. That form earnt him another chance at the big time with Sunderland but, as with Spurs, he started well, then faded. Eventually released by Sunderland, Reid's career reached its low point with a few months on loan to Blackpool that saw him play only five games as the seaside club failed to avoid relegation. Released again, he returned to Nottingham Forest. He soon got back to playing the football that first earned him a move to Spurs, only to suffer a serious groin injury that side-lined him for two years and put his future in doubt. Reid's father, Bill, played for St Patrick's Athletic and his uncle, Victor, played for Shelbourne.

Appearances:
League: 20 (6) apps. 1 gl.
FL Cup: 1 app.
Others: 7 (2) apps.
Total: 28 (8) apps. 1 gl.

REID, James

Role: Inside-forward 1906-08
5ft.10ins. 12st.0lbs.
Born: Bells Hill, Lanarkshire, 20th February 1879

CAREER: Petershill/Hibernian Aug 1898/Burslem Port Vale Jul 1899/Thames Ironworks Jun 1900/Gainsborough Trinity Jun 1901/Worksop Town Jul 1902/Notts County Mar 1903/Watford May 1905/SPURS May 1906/Reading Mar 1908/New Brompton Aug 1908/Worksop cs. 1910.

Debut v Norwich City (SL) (h) 22.9.1906
(London Caledonians (Fr) (h) 13.9.1906 (scored three))

A well-travelled, goal-scoring inside-forward, Jimmy Reid was with Spurs for nearly two years, although it was only in the first that he had a sustained run in the senior team. Signed from Watford in May 1906, he scored a hat-trick on his first appearance and finished the season as top scorer. In the following season he was one of six players Spurs tried in the troublesome inside-left position, but none were particularly successful. The problem was only solved with the signing of Bob Steel in May 1908, two months after Reid had moved to Spurs' former Southern League rivals Reading.

Appearances:
Southern: 37 apps. 20 gls.
FA Cup: 7 apps. 2 gls.
Others: 15 apps. 10 gls.
Total: 59 apps. 32 gls.

REILLY, Mathew Michael

Role: Goalkeeper 1906-07
5ft.11ins. 12st.0lbs.
Born: Donneybrook, Ireland, 22nd March 1874
Died: Dublin, Eire, 9th December 1954

CAREER: Benburb (Dublin-Gaelic football)/Royal Artillery (Portsmouth) 1893/(Southampton St Marys loan Dec 1895)/(Freemantle loan)/Dundee cs. 1904/Notts County Jun 1905/SPURS trial and perm. Oct 1906/Shelbourne Aug 1907.

Debut v Southampton (WL) (a) 3.10.1906

Although he had played Gaelic football back home in Ireland, it was whilst performing in Army football that Matt Reilly first came to prominence. He played for the Royal Artillery, which later developed through Royal Artillery, Portsmouth to become the Portsmouth club of today. Reilly spent four years with Royal Artillery in the Southern League helping them reach the semi-final of the FA Amateur Cup in 1896, and also made two appearances in that competition for Southampton in 1895-96 as a guest player. With the demise of Royal Artillery, Portsmouth at the end of 1897-98 the Portsmouth club was founded and Reilly was their first goalkeeper. A regular for the next six years he helped them win the Southern League title in 1901-02 and played for Ireland against England in March 1900 and again in March 1902. In the summer of 1904 he moved to Dundee, but spent only one season there as a reserve before joining Notts County. At the end of 1905-06 he was released by Notts and by October that year had still not managed to fix himself up with a new club. Spurs agreed to give him a trial and he quickly made his debut against Southampton. Most impressive, he was immediately signed and stayed in the first team until March 1907 when he gave way to Jack Whitbourne. Released at the end of the season, Reilly he returned to Ireland to play for Shelbourne. Later in life he became a publican at Southsea in Hampshire. In January 1904 Reilly punched a spectator in the face after the crowd had thrown clinker at him. He was suspended for two weeks.

Appearances:
Southern: 19 apps.
FA Cup: 7 apps.
Others: 9 apps.
Total: 35 apps. 0 gls.

RENALS, James Herbert (Sir) 2nd Bt

Role: Outside-left 1891-94
Born: 5th November 1870
Died: Brighton, Sussex, 27th March 1927

CAREER: Tottenham/SPURS 1893.

Debut v St. Albans (Fr) (a) 18.4.1892

Renals, whose father was Sir Joseph Renals, Sheriff and a Lord Mayor of London, made his first appearance for Spurs in April 1892 playing at full-back, the position he occupied with the Tottenham club in 1892-93. The following season he principally played for Spurs on the left wing, but lost his place in January 1894 with the arrival of Ernie Payne. Renals was quite

a character. In November 1914, he was charged with providing a false reference so that a Marcus Barthropp, a serial fraudster, could obtain an Army commission. Renals was fined £20. The following January he appeared at the Old Bailey charged with conspiracy to defraud the public by means of a bogus money lending scheme. When acquitted the Recorder commented that Renal's involvement was down to an addiction to strong drink. His life continued on a downward spiral. When he died it was in the Brighton Poor Law Institution.

Appearances:
Others: 11 apps. 1 gl.
Total: 11 apps. 1 gl.

REVELL, Charles H

Role: Half-back 1941-42
5ft.10ins. 11st.4lbs.
Born: Belvedere, Kent, 5th June 1919
Died: Sidcup, Kent, 11th December 1999

CAREER: Picardy School/Erith Schools/Callenders Athletic/**SPURS** am. Jan 1937/Northfleet United, pro. Jul 1937/**SPURS** pro. May 1938/Charlton Athletic May 1939/(guest for Birmingham, Blackpool, Bury, Chelsea, Fulham, **SPURS** and Wrexham during World War Two)/Derby County Mar 1951/Eynesbury Rovers player-manager Jul 1952/Edgware Town manager Jul 1955-cs. 1957/Canterbury City player-coach Aug 1957/Erith and Belvedere manager Jun 1958/Crystal Palace coach and scout/Charlton Athletic coach and scout.

Debut v Charlton Athletic (LWL) (h) 7.3.1942 (scored once)

Charlie Revell was spotted by Spurs in the late 1930s playing for Callenders Athletic, the club that had produced Spurs' great goal-scoring centre-forward of that period, Johnny Morrison. Taken on the junior staff at White Hart Lane Revell was sent down to the Northfleet nursery club where he played as a forward. Spurs decided he would not make the grade and allowed him to join Charlton Athletic. Spurs' loss was Charlton's gain, for he served them well from the wing-half position, helping them to the Football League South Cup Final in 1943 and 1944, winning the competition on the second occasion. He continued to play for Charlton until March 1951 when he was transferred to Derby County, but only stayed at the Baseball Ground for just over a year before taking the first steps on a managerial career that encompassed Eynesbury Rovers, Edgware Town, Canterbury City and Erith and Belvedere. He later served both Crystal Palace and Charlton as a coach and scout. His only appearance for Spurs was as a guest when he played at outside-left in a Football League South match in March 1942. He scored one of Spurs' goals in a 2-0 win over his own club, Charlton.

Appearances:
Others: 1 app. 1 gl.
Total: 1 app. 1 gl.

REYNOLDS, Ronald Sidney Maurice

Role: Goalkeeper 1950-59
5ft.11ins. 11st.4lbs.
Born: Haslemere, Hampshire, 2nd June 1928
Died: Haslemere, Hampshire, 2nd June 1999

CAREER: Godalming Grammar School/Shottermill/Aldershot am. Jun 1945, pro. Dec 1945/**SPURS** Jul 1950/Southampton Mar 1960/retired 1963/Southampton scout/Crystal Palace scout.

Debut v Sunderland (FL) (h) 20.3.1954
(Chelmsford City (Fr) (a) 30.4.1951)

Ron Reynolds joined Aldershot as a 17-year old, making an unhappy debut in January 1946 when Bournemouth put seven goals past him. He went on to make over 100 League appearances for Aldershot, before joining Spurs as cover for Ted Ditchburn. Ken Flint moved in the opposite direction as part of the deal. Reynolds became the almost permanent understudy to Ditchburn. Such was the consistency of the England international that Reynolds had to wait until March 1954 before making his Spurs' League debut. A more than proficient 'keeper, good both in the air and dealing with low shots, he proved a thoroughly capable deputy for Ditchburn. Though there were times when Reynolds kept his place on merit, Ditchburn always seemed to bounce back. Considered at one time as a possible international Reynolds, who wore contact lenses, lost his position as first choice reserve to John Hollowbread in early 1958. He remained with Spurs until March 1960, when he joined Southampton on transfer deadline day for £10,000. He played there for three years, helping Saints win the Third Division in his first season, before a shoulder injury forced him to quit. He scouted briefly for Southampton and Palace before working for a London firm of investment consultants. He then ran his own insurance agency before retiring. He continued to live in Haslemere until passing away on his 71st birthday.

Appearances:
League: 86 apps.
FA Cup: 9 apps.
Others: 43* apps.
Total: 138 apps. 0 gls.
*Includes 1 abandoned match

REYNOLDS, W

Role: Forward 1894-95

CAREER: 1st Batt. Coldstream Guards/**SPURS** guest Mar 1895.

Debut v Old Westminsters (LSC) (h) 9.3.1895 (scored once)

A member of the Coldstream Guards and an Army representative player, Reynolds made just two appearances for Spurs in the 1894-95 season. The first was in March 1895 in a London Senior Cup tie when he scored once against Old Westminsters. Although his performance at centre-forward in that game was described as "very disappointing", he made a further appearance twelve days later, this time on the right wing, in a London Charity Cup tie with Old Carthusians.

Appearances:
Others: 2 apps. 1 gl.
Total: 2 apps. 1 gl.

RICHARDS, Dean Ivor

Role: Central Defender 2001-05
6ft.2ins. 13st.5lbs.
Born: Bradford, Yorkshire, 9th June 1974
Died: Leeds, South Yorkshire, 26th February 2011

CAREER: Sedgeberg Juniors/Queensbury Celtic/Bradford City trainee Jul 1990, pro. Jul 1992/Wolverhampton Wanderers loan Mar 1995, perm May 1995/Southampton Jul 1999/SPURS Sep 2001/retired Mar 2005/Bradford City youth team coach Aug 2007.

Debut v Manchester United (PL) (h) 29.9.2001 (scored one)

When Sol Campbell ran down his contract and walked out on Spurs in the summer of 2001, Glenn Hoddle was left with the difficult job of finding a replacement for the best central defender in the country. He turned to Dean Richards, a player who could be similar in style to Campbell and someone Hoddle knew well from their time together at Southampton. Richards had begun his career with his local club Bradford City, moving on to Wolverhampton Wanderers and soon impressing as they fought their way to the play-offs in an ultimately unsuccessful attempt to escape the First Division. Captain of the England Under-21 team for the Toulon tournament in 1995, Richards' career suffered a setback when he was injured in a car crash on his way home after starring for Wolves as they held Spurs to a draw in the FA Cup at White Hart Lane in January 1996. He seemed to fully recover, but a year later knee and back injuries that put him out of the game for a full year were attributed to the accident. As Richards got back to his best the country's biggest clubs were circling, so it was a surprise when Richards let his Wolves' contract run down and signed for Southampton. At the Dell, Richards continued to improve, pushing hard for full England recognition. Big, solid, muscular and superb in the air, he had all the physical attributes a central defender required, but he had more. He was consistent, dependable, a threat at set pieces and not afraid to bring the ball out of defence when the opportunity arose. For a man of his size and gait, he possessed unexpected skills. Hoddle earmarked Richards as a Spurs' player even before Campbell decided to jump ship. It was a stance that did not go down well with Southampton. They were aggrieved at Hoddle's departure and had no desire to lose their number one defender, even accusing Spurs of making an improper approach to Richards. It took an offer of £8.1 million to persuade Southampton to let Richards leave. At White Hart Lane, Richards immediately showed some of the qualities expected and often looked capable of forming a solid partnership with Anthony Gardner or Ledley King, but his performances rarely reached the heights expected. Injuries did nothing to help and he was frequently absent. In 2004 he suffered loss of balance, pain and unnatural tiredness. A brain scan indicated a brain haemorrhage was unlikely, but the problems persisted. In March 2005 he retired having been advised that to continue playing could seriously damage his health. Richards took to coaching but passed away in February 2011 after a long illness. At only 36 it was a particularly terrible loss.

Appearances:
League: 73 apps. 4 gls.
FA Cup: 5 apps.
FL Cup: 3 apps.
Others: 8 (1) apps. 2 gls.
Total: 89 (1) apps. 6 gls.

RICHARDSON, John

Role: Full-back 1925-29
5ft.10ins. 11st.10lbs.
Born: Motherwell, 4th April 1906
Died: Uddington, Lanarkshire, January 1986

CAREER: Burnbank Athletic/Hamilton Acadaemical May 1923/SPURS trial Oct 1924/Motherwell/Northfleet United/SPURS pro. May 1925/Reading Jun 1929/Bournemouth and Boscombe Athletic May 1934/Folkestone Town May 1935/SPURS scout.

Debut v Newcastle United (FL) (a) 16.4.1927
(La Chaux-de-Fonds (Fr) (a) 20.5.1925 (scored once))

Jock Richardson was brought up to White Hart Lane from the Northfleet nursery in May 1925. He made his first team debut that month on the club's Swiss tour, although in exactly which game is unclear as the line-ups for all the games have not been traced. He had to wait until April 1927 for a League debut, when he stood in for the injured Cyril Poynton. Richardson spent the next two years vying with Poynton for the left-back spot, but never made the position his own during a time when Spurs were first relegated, and then unable to make much impression on the battle for promotion. In April 1929 Spurs decided not to retain Richardson. Two months later he moved to Reading where he spent the next five years, before winding down his career with Bournemouth and Folkestone.

Appearances:
League: 38 apps.
FA Cup: 3 apps.
Others: 6 apps. 1 gl.
Total: 47 apps. 1gl.

RICKETTS, Rohan Antonio

Role: Midfield 2002-05
5ft.8ins. 11st.5lbs.
Born: Clapham, London, 22nd December 1982

CAREER: South London Select (Mottingham Youth)/South London Schools/London Schools/England Youth/Arsenal trainee Jun 1999, pro. Aug 2001/SPURS Jul 2002/(Coventry City loan Oct 2004)/Wolverhampton Wanderers loan Mar 2005, perm. May 2005/(Queens Park Rangers loan Mar 2007)/Barnsley trial and perm. Jul 2007/Toronto FC (Canada) Apr 2008-Jun 2009/Odense (Denmark) trial Jul 2009/Aberdeen trial Aug 2009/Orient trial/Diósgyőr (Hungary) Feb 2010/Dacia Chişinău (Moldova) Aug 2010/AEK Athens (Greece) trial

Jul 2010/Kickers Offenbach (Germany) trial Dec 2010/FC Ingolstadt 04 (Germany) Nov 2010/US Boulogne (France) trial Jan 2011/SV Wilhelmshaven (Germany) Jan 2011/Norwich City trial May 2011/ Southend United trial Jul 2011/Stevenage trial Jul 2011/Chesterfield trial Jul 2011/Shamrock Rovers Aug 2011-Jan 2012/Exeter City Mar-Apr 2012/Dempo SC (Goa, India) Aug 2012-Jan 2013/CD Quevedo (Ecuador) Jan-Jul 2013/Army United (Thailand) Jan 2014/PTT Rayong (Thailand) Feb-Oct 2014/Eastern Sports (Hong Kong) trial and perm Jan 2015/Abahani Limited Dhaka (Bangladesh) Mar 2016/ Leatherhead Nov–Dec 2016.

Debut v Birmingham City (PL) (a) 16.8.2003
(Stevenage Borough (Fr) (a) 21.7.2002)

Rohan Ricketts was released by Arsenal after a year in their professional ranks. Taken on by Spurs, he spent a year in the reserve side before Glenn Hoddle gave him his chance in the League team in August 2003. It was a surprise step up, but Ricketts acquitted himself well. Playing out wide, he showed plenty of talent, allied to a willingness to work. He had pace, could spot and exploit an opening and was not afraid to have a shot at goal. He enjoyed dribbling with the ball, sometimes too keen to do so, but that was something that could be forgiven. Even with the arrival of the experienced Stephane Dalmat, Ricketts continued to hold his own and it was only when Christian Ziege was fully recovered from injury that Ricketts found himself out of favour. The dismissal of Hoddle, followed by the mass influx of players under the Arnesen/Santini regime saw Ricketts pushed down the pecking order. A loan spell with Coventry City was followed by another at Wolverhampton Wanderers where Glenn Hoddle was manager. Hoddle showed his faith in Ricketts by signing him permanently and while he was in charge, Ricketts played regularly. When Hoddle left though, Ricketts was out in the cold. He had a year at Barnsley, but made little impression with the struggling Championship club. When released he moved to Canada, the start of a never ending journey that has taken him to all four corners of the world. He is the only Spurs player to have played for clubs in Moldova, India, Ecuador, Thailand and Bangladesh!

Appearances:
League: 17 (13) apps. 1 gl.
FL Cup: 4 (2) apps. 1 gl.
Others: 12 (11) apps.
Total: 33 (26) apps. 2 gls.

RILEY, Christopher

Role: Defender 2007-08
5ft.9ins 11st. 9lbs.
Born: Enfield, Middlesex, 2nd February 1988

CAREER: Enfield Grammar School/Middlesex Schools/**SPURS** Academy Jul 2004, pro./released May 2008/Bromley Jul 2009/Jerez Industrial CF (Spain)/Burton Albion trial Sep 2009/Ebbsfleet United Oct 2009/Enfield Town/Interwood/Horsham Feb 2010/Stansted Aug 2010/Chesham Aug 2010/(Burnham loan Aug 2011)/Cheshunt/ Caernarfon Town/**SPURS** Academy Sports Science Intern.

Debut v Stevenage Borough (Sub) (Fr) (a) 7.7.2007

First associated with Spurs as a nine-year old, Chris Riley progressed through the schoolboy ranks on to the professional staff. A talented defender, happy at centre-half or full-back, he could also play in midfield if necessary. Capped by England at Under-16, Under-17 and Under-19 level, a couple of bad injuries restricted his progress. He still worked his way up to reserve level and made one substitute appearance in a pre-season friendly, before it was decided he would not make the grade and was released. He joined Glenn Hoddle's Academy for young players discarded by senior clubs in Spain and returned to play at non-League level before making a career in sports science.

Appearances:
Others: (1) app.
Total: (1) app. 0 gls.

RINGROSE, Albert Arthur

Role: Full-back 1936-37
5ft.9ins. 10st.8lbs.
Born: Tottenham, London, 18th November 1916
Died: Chelsea, London, 16th January 1968

CAREER: Tottenham Juniors/**SPURS** am. cs. 1934/(Northfleet United 1934-36)/**SPURS** pro. May 1936/Notts County May 1939.

Debut v Norwich City (FL) (a) 2.1.1937

Like many of his Spurs contemporaries, Bert Ringrose played for the Tottenham Juniors and after signing as an amateur, was groomed at the Northfleet nursery. He spent two years there before signing professional forms at White Hart Lane. His League debut came against Norwich City in January 1937 when he replaced the injured Ralph Ward, and he made a total of ten League appearances that season as Ward's stand-in. Ward was a very consistent player, rarely absent through injury. Although he was always regarded as a valuable member of the club staff, Ringrose was unable to break into the team again. Even when Spurs signed England international Bert Sproston to replace Ward, Ringrose was kept on, but he was not called up when Sproston departed soon after signing. In April 1939 Ringrose was made available for transfer and quickly transferred to Notts County. Sadly, a broken leg in his first game for Notts County brought his career to an unhappily premature end.

Appearances:
League: 10 apps.
Total: 10 apps. 0 gls.

ROBB, George

Role: Outside-left 1951-59
5ft.8ins. 11st.8lbs.
Born: Finsbury Park, London, 1st June 1926
Died: Haywards Heath, West Sussex, 25th December 2011

CAREER: Holloway County Grammar School/Islington Schools/Finchley 1942/**SPURS** am. Aug 1944/Finchley/**SPURS** am. Dec 1951, pro. Jun 1953/retired May 1960.

Debut v Charlton Athletic (FL) (a) 25.12.1951 (scored once)

George Robb first signed amateur forms for Spurs in 1944. At the time he was playing for Finchley, where several of Spurs' junior players spent some time during the Second World War. Not offered professional terms by Spurs he became a schoolmaster, but continued to turn out for Finchley, winning 18 England amateur caps during his nine years with them. Reportedly offered a professional contract by the Italian club, Padua, he again signed amateur forms for Spurs in December 1951, and made his League debut against Charlton that month, scoring in a 3-1 win. With the departure of Les Medley to Canada at the end of the 1952-53 season, Robb was persuaded to sign professional. It was one of the cheapest and best signings Spurs made during that period. A strong, direct winger, genuinely two-footed, with a good turn of speed and a deadly shot, Robb liked to slice inside his opposing full-back for a crack at the target. His opportunism is evidenced by the number of goals he scored. A member of the Football League team against the Irish League in September 1953, he won just one full England cap. Unfortunately that came in the match against Hungary in November 1953 when England were taught a lesson with a crushing 3-6 defeat at the hands of the "Magical Magyars". Although he did not win more full honours, Robb did play in three "B". internationals at the end of the 1953-54 season. Still near his peak, he suffered a serious injury during 1957-58 which eventually forced him to retire in May 1960. He returned to teaching at Christ's College in Finchley and then at Ardingley, a public school in Sussex.

Appearances:
League: 182 apps. 53 gls.
FA Cup: 18 apps. 5 gls.
Others: 24 apps. 7 gls.
Total: 224 apps. 65 gls.

ROBERTS, Graham Paul

Role: Defender or midfield 1979-88
5ft.10ins. 12st.12lbs.
Born: Southampton, Hampshire, 3rd July 1959

CAREER: Southampton Schools/Hampshire Schools/Sholing/AFC Bournemouth app./Portsmouth app./Dorchester Town loan Mar 1977 then perm./Weymouth Aug 1979/**SPURS** May 1980/Rangers Dec 1986/Chelsea May 1988, player-coach Nov 1989-Feb 1990/West Bromwich Albion Nov 1990/Enfield Aug 1992, player-manager Oct 1992-May 1994/Slough Town player-manager Jul 1994/Stevenage Borough Oct 1994/Yeovil Town manager Jan 1995-Feb 1998/Wealdstone Feb 1998/Chesham United player-manager Feb 1998/Slough Town manager Oct 1998–Nov 1999/Hertford Town manager Feb 2000-Sep 2000/Boreham Wood manager Feb 2001-Apr 2001, Apr 2001-Jul 2001/Carshalton Athletic manager Dec 2001-Jun 2003/Braintree Town manager Mar 2004-Apr 2004/San Pedro (Spain) coach Jul 2004/Clyde manager Mar 2005–Aug 2006/Pakistan, consultant Sept 2010, head coach Oct 2010/Nepal manager Jan 2011-Mar 2012.

Debut v Stoke City (sub) (FL) (a) 4.10.1980
(AFC Bournemouth (Fr) (a) 5.5.1980)

Graham Roberts joined his local club Southampton as an associated schoolboy, but although he won Hampshire County Youth honours, they did not offer him apprentice terms. He played for the Hampshire League side Sholing before joining the junior staff of AFC Bournemouth. For financial reasons the Cherries disbanded their youth set-up and Roberts moved on to Portsmouth. They were set to offer him professional terms when he broke his ankle in a friendly match and the idea was shelved. Fully recovered, he joined Dorchester Town and spent two-and-a-half years in the Southern Premier League, before moving to Alliance League Weymouth. Originally a forward, Roberts was dropped back into midfield to such effect that he soon began to attract attention from bigger clubs. By the end of 1979-80 Spurs and West Bromwich Albion both wanted to buy him, but Roberts choose Tottenham, signing for £35,000, a record for a non-League player. It was a terrific bargain; within twelve months the tough shipyard fitter's mate was playing at Wembley and spitting out two broken teeth as he helped Spurs win the 1981 FA Cup after a replay. A hard-tackling, aggressive player, Roberts was never afraid to go in where it hurts and that, coupled with a passionate desire to win, made him a folk hero with the Spurs crowd. Playing either in central defence or providing strength and ball-winning qualities in midfield, he was also a member of the team that retained the FA Cup in 1982-when he was fouled in an early attacking foray during the replay for the match-winning penalty. Roberts won his first England cap in May 1983 when he appeared against Northern Ireland, and in total collected six full and one "B" cap in his time at White Hart Lane. The Roberts' fairy-tale peaked in 1984 when, still only 24, and captain in Steve Perryman's absence, he led the team to the 1984 UEFA Cup success over Anderlecht, scoring the crucial late equalising goal that took the Final into extra-time and the ensuing dramatic penalty shoot-out. With the arrival of David Pleat and the signing of the more cultured Richard Gough, it was obvious Roberts did not figure in Pleat's plans. He was transferred to Glasgow Rangers for £450,000, assuming the hard man role vacated by manager Graeme Souness. In his first season Roberts helped Rangers win the Scottish Premier Division title and in 1988 the Skol Cup. After a disagreement with Souness, he moved to Chelsea, captained them to the Second Division title in 1989, and was made player-coach. A row with Chelsea Chairman Ken Bates saw Roberts give up the coaching role in February 1990 and placed on the transfer list, but it was not until November 1990 that he left Stamford Bridge for West Bromwich Albion. When released by West Bromwich he was unable to find another League club, so joined Enfield, quickly taking on the player-manager's role. It was the start of a lengthy managerial and coaching career that was not without its controversial incidents. He lost his job with Yeovil when he sent Newcastle a telegram before their FA Cup-tie with Stevenage Borough telling them in no uncertain terms what he wanted them to do to Yeovil's rivals. He left Boreham Wood as manager in April 2001 but returned a week later only to leave permanently in July 2001. He was sacked by Clyde for alleged anti-Semitic and racist remarks on an end of season tour to Canada, then succeeded in a claim for wrongful dismissal against the club. After leaving Spurs, Roberts returned in March 1988 to guest in Danny Thomas' Benefit match against Manchester United.

Appearances:
League: 200 (9) apps. 23 gls.
FA Cup: 27 apps. 2 gls.
FL Cup: 24 (1) apps. 5 gls.
Euro: 25 (1) apps. 5 gls.
Others: 81 (6) apps. 10 gls.
Total: 357 (17) apps. 45 gls.

ROBERTS, R D

Role: Goalkeeper 1944-45

CAREER: Crossbrook Sports/Finchley/Walthamstow Avenue/Golders Green/(guest for SPURS during World War Two).

Debut v Arsenal (Fr) (h) 19.5.1945

Another of the players whose chance in senior football only came about because of the Second World War, Roberts was a local lad in his early twenties, whose previous experience had been gained playing for Crossbrook Sports, Finchley, Walthamstow Avenue and Golders Green. All were clubs with close associations with Spurs, and for whom many of Spurs' junior players had appeared over the years. He was called upon to play two friendly matches for Spurs in May 1945 because first choice keeper Archie Hughes was suffering from a nasty boil. The first was against Arsenal, when Spurs so totally outclassed their near neighbours in a 4-0 victory that he had very little to do, and the other a week later against Fulham.

Appearances:
Others: 2 apps.
Total: 2 apps. 0 gls.

ROBERTS, John William

Role: Centre-forward 1899-00
5ft.8ins. 11st.9lbs.
Born: Liverpool, Lancashire, 1880

CAREER: White Star Wanderers/SPURS Dec 1899/Stockport County Jan 1902/Grays United cs. 1902/Brighton and Hove Albion cs. 1903/Queens Park Rangers May 1905/Preston North End Jun 1906/Leicester Fosse trial Nov 1907.

Debut v Millwall Athletic (SDC) (a) 26.4.1900
(Thames Ironworks (Fr) (a) 2.4.1900)

Young Willie Roberts joined Spurs in December 1899 from Lancashire League club White Star Wanderers of Liverpool. He did not make his first team debut until April 1900, when he played in a Benefit match for the late Tom Bradshaw. He then played two matches in the Southern District Combination later that month, scoring one goal. Roberts was released at the end of the season. He later played for several clubs, usually appearing at outside-left where his dribbling skills were best utilised. His best time was at Brighton where he impressed enough in two years for QPR to sign him.

Appearances:
Others: 3 apps. 2 gls.
Total: 3 apps. 2 gls.

ROBERTS, William Thomas

Role: Centre-forward 1928-29
5ft.11ins. 12st.0lbs.
Born: Handsworth, Birmingham, 29th November 1898
Died: Preston, Lancashire, 13th October 1965

CAREER: Kentish Rovers/Boyce Engineers/Lord Street/Soho Villa/Leicester Fosse/(Southport Vulcan during World War One)/Preston North End May 1919/Burnley Oct 1924/Preston North End Jul 1926/SPURS May 1928/Dick Kerr's FC Aug 1929/Chorley Oct 1930.

Debut v Oldham Athletic (FL) (h) 25.8.1928 (scored twice)

Tom Roberts was signed for £1,000 from Preston North End where he had spent the best years of his career, winning England and Football League honours. Having played local football in his native Birmingham, he moved into the first class game with Leicester Fosse, but they allowed him to move on to Preston North End after the First World War without playing a senior game. Perhaps they had not seen the goal-scoring ability that Preston had noted when Roberts played for Southport Vulcan during the War. A strong, hard-running centre-forward he scored regularly for the Deepdale club and in October 1922 made his first appearance for the Football League, scoring once against the Irish League. His first England cap came in November 1923 against Belgium and he won a second against Wales in March 1924, scoring in both games. In October 1924 Roberts moved to Burnley where he suffered a broken pelvis. Preston soon secured his return and he won his final representative honour in October 1926 when he netted twice for the Football League against the Irish League. Roberts made his Spurs' debut in the first League game of 1928-29 and scored twice, but they were to be his only goals for the club. Although still only 29, he was past his best and, suffering from recurring injury problems, was a great disappointment at White Hart Lane. When released in April 1929 he had made only four League appearances in a Spurs shirt. He returned to Preston to play for Dick Kerr's FC and finished his career with Chorley. Roberts then settled back in Preston where he worked as a publican for 30 years.

Appearances:
Others: 4 apps. 2 gls.
Total: 4 apps. 2 gls.

ROBERTSON, Alexander

Role: Centre-forward 1896-97

CAREER: Dundee May 1896/SPURS Feb 1897

Debut v Northfleet (SL) (h) 13.2.1897
(3rd Batt Grenadier Guards (Fr) (h) 6.2.1897 (scored once))

When Alex Robertson joined Spurs from Dundee in February 1897 he was described as a "first League player with excellent credentials". He scored in each of his opening three games, but played only once more before dropping out of the picture. His only other appearance was in April 1897. He played at half-back in the final of the Wellingborough Charity Cup as Spurs were forced to field a team with several players operating outside their recognised positions due to injury and disciplinary problems.

Appearances:
Southern: 1 app. 1 gl.
Others: 4 apps. 2 gls.
Total: 5 apps. 3 gls.

ROBERTSON, James Gillen

Role: Outside-right 1963-69
5ft.9ins. 9st.7lbs.
Born: Cardonald, Glasgow, 17th December 1944

CAREER: Middlesbrough/Celtic/Cowdenbeath am./St Mirren pro. May 1962/SPURS Mar 1964/Arsenal Oct 1968/Ipswich Town Mar 1970/Stoke City Jun 1972/Seattle Sounders (USA) summer 1976 and 1977/Walsall Sep 1977/Crewe Alexandra Sep 1978.

Debut v Liverpool (FL) (a) 30.3.1964

Jimmy Robertson had been a junior with Middlesbrough and a part-timer with Celtic before joining Cowdenbeath. In their senior team when still a 16-year old amateur, he played for Scotland at Youth level and won an amateur cap against Northern Ireland before joining St Mirren. Three months after winning his first Under-23 cap against Wales, he moved to Spurs for £25,000. A fast, well balanced footballer who liked to cut inside and try a shot at goal, he was able to play on either flank but is best remembered at Spurs as a right winger supplying the ammunition for Jimmy Greaves and Alan Gilzean. After his move to Spurs, Robertson won three more Under-23 caps, but only one at full international level, against Wales in October 1964. Blessed with a good turn of pace and an accurate cross, he also varied his play by cleverly holding up the ball and creating chances with perceptive passes through the defence. A popular player, his finest performance for Spurs probably came in the 1967 FA Cup Final against Chelsea when he scored the opening goal to put Spurs on the way to their fifth FA Cup victory. With wingers drifting out of fashion, Robertson was allowed to leave in October 1968, moving to Arsenal in a £55,000 deal which saw David Jenkins travel in the opposite direction. It was not one of Bill Nicholson's better decisions as Robertson had plenty of good football left in him. He only stayed at Highbury for two years, then gave useful service to Ipswich Town and Stoke City, before winding down his career with Walsall and Crewe. He later became a director of a computer insurance company.

Appearances:
League: 153 (4) apps. 25 gls.
FA Cup: 18 apps. 3 gls.
FL Cup: 2 apps.
Euro: 4 apps. 3 gls.
Others: 31 (3) apps. 11 gls.
Total: 208 (7) apps. 42 gls.

ROBINSON, Martin John

Role: Striker 1975-78
5ft.8ins. 11st.5lbs.
Born: Chadwell St Marys, Essex, 17th July 1957

CAREER: Thurrock Schools/SPURS app. Jul 1973, pro. May 1975/Charlton Athletic Feb 1978/(Reading loan Sep 1982)/Gillingham Oct 1984/Southend United Jul 1987/Cambridge United Jun 1989/Enfield cs. 1990.

Debut v Leicester City (FL) (h) 28.2.1976
(Stade Rennais (Fr) (a) 29.9.1975)

Martin Robinson is yet another example of the excellent young players developed by Spurs who never really had a chance to show what they could do before leaving the club. A busy little striker, perhaps best suited to a wide position, Robinson had to compete with more established stars such as Alfie Conn, Peter Taylor and Ralph Coates, but when he did play looked to have many of the necessary qualities. However, opportunities at Spurs were very limited and for a cut-price £15,000 he was allowed to join Charlton. He played in south London for almost ten years, giving sterling value with over 50 goals in more than 200 League games before moving to Gillingham. He then played for Southend and after being given a free transfer joined Cambridge United where he spent just a year. After a course in hotel management set him on the path to a new career, he finished playing at Enfield.

Appearances:
League: 5 (1) apps. 2 gls.
Others: 2 (3) apps.
Total: 7 (4) apps. 2 gls.

ROBINSON, Paul William

Role: Goalkeeper 2004-08
6ft.2ins. 14st.6lbs.
Born: Beverley, East Yorkshire, 15th October 1979

CAREER: Beverley Town Boys/York City youth/Leeds United trainee Jul 1996, pro. May 1997/SPURS May 2004/Blackburn Rovers Jul 2008-May 2015/Burnley Jan 2016.

Debut v Liverpool (PL) (h) 14.8.2004
(Hull City (Fr) (a) 24.7.2004)

Few players who leave Spurs are welcomed back to White Hart Lane quite as much as Paul Robinson. The former England goalkeeper enjoyed such a fabulous rapport with the Spurs fans that even when events conspired against him and his form took a turn for the worse, the fans stood by him. Robinson first came to prominence as number two to England 'keeper Nigel Martyn at Leeds. When Martyn asked to be released from pre-season games after the 2002 World Cup, manager Terry Venables installed Robinson, already England's regular Under-21 'keeper, as his first choice. The big, well-built Robinson quickly impressed and barely missed a game over the next two years as Leeds' financial problems dragged them down. Spurs had been on his trail for some time and with Leeds' relegation they were at last able to secure their target. With his innate friendliness and first class goalkeeping skills, Robinson immediately won over the Spurs' support. Confident and commanding, he displayed terrific reflexes and proved a great shot-stopper as he established himself as the number one for not only Spurs, but also England. He seemed set for a career that would reach the heights. The turning point came in October 2006 in Zagreb during England's Euro 2008 qualifier against Croatia. A Gary Neville back-pass bobbled just as Robinson swung his boot at the ball. It went over his foot and rolled into the net. While barely a word was said about Neville committing the cardinal sin of playing the ball straight at goal instead of to the side, Robinson was crucified for the incident. The criticism that followed, particularly from the tabloids, badly affected his confidence, a crucial aspect of any player's armoury, but all the more so a goalkeeper's. With every little incident blown out of all proportion, his form was badly affected. Dropped in January 2008, Robinson returned for the Worthington Cup Final defeat of Chelsea, but by the end of the season had lost his Spurs' place to Radek Černý and his England spot to David James. With Juande Ramos signing Heurelho Gomes, Robinson was allowed to move to Blackburn Rovers. With the spotlight off him, Robinson began to rebuild his career and despite Blackburn being relegated, he proved worth every penny of the £3.5 million, they had paid Spurs for him. At times there was talk of him being recalled by England, but in August 2010, with 41 caps to his name, he announced his international retirement. Robinson had been fortunate with injuries for most of his career, but he was put out of the game for six months when treatment for a back injury led to a blood clot that could have proved far more serious. He recovered, fought his way back and at times looked set to resume as first choice, before deciding he had little future at Blackburn and moved to Burnley. Robinson scored for Spurs against Watford in March 2007 when a 95-yard free-kick sailed over Ben Foster's head. It was not the first senior goal he had scored. In September he headed a last-minute equaliser for Leeds in a Carling Cup-tie with Swindon, and followed that up with a crucial save in the resultant penalty shoot-out.

Appearances:
League: 137 apps. 1 gl.
FA Cup: 12 apps.
FL Cup: 10 apps.
Euro: 16 apps.
Others: 11 apps.
Total: **186 apps. 1 gl.**

ROBINSON, Stephen

Role: Striker 1993-95
5ft.8ins. 10st.7lbs.
Born: Lisburn, Northern Ireland, 10th December 1974

CAREER: Friends School/Lisburn Schools/Northern Ireland Schools/Linfield/**SPURS** trainee Jul 1991, pro. Jan 1993/Northern Ireland Youth/(Leyton Orient loan Aug 1994)/AFC Bournemouth Oct 1994/Preston North End May 2000/(Bristol City loan Mar 2002)/Luton Town Jun 2002-May 2008/Irish FA County Londonderry Performance coach 2008, Under-19 asst. manager/Lisburn Distillery asst. manager Jan 2012/Irish FA Under-21 manager Feb 2012, Under-17 and Under-19 manager Oct 2012, Under 17 and Under-21 manager Apr 2013/Motherwell asst. manager Feb 2015/Oldham Athletic manager Jul 2016.

Debut v Blackburn Rovers (PL) (a) 30.10.1993
(Brann (sub) (Fr) (a) 11.10.1993)

Northern Ireland schoolboy and youth international Steve Robinson was an unexpected selection for the game at Blackburn in October 1993. 18-years old, he had been a professional for less than a year and was only just beginning to establish himself in the reserves. With Teddy Sheringham out injured, Ossie Ardiles was desperate for someone to score some goals. Robinson had been doing that with the reserves, but it was still a surprise he should be chosen ahead of Gordon Durie and John Hendry. Robinson made a substitute appearance a month later and at the end of the season played for Northern Ireland at both Under-21 and "B" level. Apart from another substitute appearance in a friendly in July 1994, Robinson was not to see first team action for Spurs again. Allowed to move to Bournemouth, he proved a terrific performer for the Cherries, running up more than 250 appearances over six years, originally as a striker but later in a midfield role. Preston North End paid £375,000 to sign Robinson, but his two years at Deepdale were not a success and he moved on to Luton Town. He made another 200 plus appearances before retiring and returning to Northern Ireland. He moved into coaching, worked for the Irish FA and then took up management with Motherwell. Robinson won three more "B" caps and seven at full level after leaving Spurs.

Appearances:
League: 1 (1) apps.
Others: (3) apps. 1 gl.
Total: **1 (4) apps. 1 gl.**

ROBINSON

Role: Half-back 1917-18

Debut v Fulham (LFC) (h) 4.5.1918

Robinson made his only Spurs' appearance in May 1918 when he played in a London Football Combination fixture with Fulham, a home match for Spurs played at Upton Park.

Appearances:
Others: 1 app.
Total: **1 app. 0 gls.**

ROBSHAW, Henry William

Role: Half-back 1951-53
5ft.11ins. 11st.6lbs.
Born: Edmonton, north London, 10th May 1927

CAREER: Edmonton Schools/Tottenham Juniors/**SPURS** am. Sep 1944/(Golders Green)/(Crossbrook Sports by Jan 1945)/**SPURS** pro. Nov 1948/Reading Mar 1953/Tonbridge Jul 1954/Yeovil Town 1956–1961.

Debut v Liverpool (FL) (h) 1.12.1951

Harry Robshaw developed through the youth set up that served Spurs so well between the wars, playing for Tottenham Juniors before being farmed out to Golders Green after signing amateur forms. He had to wait until November 1948 before signing professional and then another three years before playing his only League game for Spurs against Liverpool. Ron Burgess and Bill Nicholson were Spurs first choice wing halves and with both still at their peak, Robshaw never got another chance. He eventually moved to Reading as part of the deal that saw Johnny Brooks join Spurs.

Appearances:
League: 1 app.
Others: 2 (1) apps.
Total: 3 (1) apps. 0 gls.

ROBSON, J

Role: Forward 1918-19

Debut v Haydn Price's XI (Fr) (St Albans) 31.8.1918

Robson was an amateur who played two games for Spurs as a trialist in friendly matches during the 1918-19 season. The first was right at the beginning of the season, against Corporal H Prices XI at St Albans in a charity game, and the second at the end of the season, in April, against Clapton Orient.

Appearances:
Others: 2 apps.
Total: 2 apps. 0 gls.

ROBSON, Mark Andrew

Role: Winger 1987-92
5ft.7ins. 10st.0lbs.
Born: Stratford, east London, 22nd May 1969

CAREER: Exeter City app. Aug 1985, pro. Dec 1986/**SPURS** Jul 1987/(Reading loan Mar 1988)/(Watford loan Oct 1989)/(Plymouth Argyle loan Jan 1990)/(Rosenborg (Norway) loan summer 1991)/(Exeter City loan Jan 1992)/West Ham United July 1992/Charlton Athletic Nov 1993/Notts County Jun 1997/(Wycombe Wanderers loan Oct 1998)/retired Sep 1999/Boreham Wood player-coach Nov 1999, caretaker manager Nov 1999/Charlton Athletic academy coach Jan 2000, asst. academy director and coach Aug 2000, reserve team manager Mar 2006, development coach May 2006, asst. head coach Nov 2006, first team coach Jan 2007-Jul 2008/Dagenham and Redbridge trial/Aveley Jan 2001/Tilbury by 2001-02/Erith & Belvedere Mar 2004/Chelmsford City Sep 2004/Hornchurch Nov 2004/Bishops Stortford Apr 2005/Gillingham coach Aug 2008-May 2010, asst. manager May-Jun 2010/Peterborough United coach Jun 2010/Burnham Ramblers Under-17 part-time manager/Barnet head coach Jun 2012, joint head coach Oct-Dec 2012/FA asst. coach England Under-17 Mar 2013/Norwich City coach Under-21 squad Oct 2013, asst. first team coach Jun-Nov 2014/Aston Villa first team coach Feb 2015-Oct 2015/FA coach Apr 2016.

Debut v West Ham United (sub) (FL) (a) 17.12.1988
(Länsi-Uudenmaan Dist (Fr) (a) 1.8.1987)

Although an east Londoner, it was in the west country with Exeter City that Mark Robson started his football career. He joined their professional ranks in December 1986, having scored on his Football League debut the previous month, and had made only 27 League appearances when Spurs secured his transfer for £50,000. Robson spent most of his first season at White Hart Lane in the reserves before joining Reading on loan towards the end of the campaign to help in the Royals' unsuccessful battle against relegation from the Second Division. A quick, talented winger, he played three League games for Spurs midway through 1988-89 in the absence of Paul Stewart and looked to be full of promise. Loaned to Watford and then Plymouth to gain further experience, he quickly got back into first team contention on his return from Home Park, but in March 1990 suffered a serious knee injury against Crystal Palace. It put him out for the rest of the season and it was only towards the end of 1990-91 that he was fit to play again. As part of his recovery programme he was loaned to the Norwegian club, Rosenberg, for the summer of 1991 and later to his former club Exeter City. Released in May 1992 as Spurs rebuilt, Robson joined relegated West Ham two months later and helped them to promotion in his first season, showing that his injury problems were behind him. Surprisingly allowed to move to Charlton in November 1993 for £125,000, he gave the south Londoners almost four years' good service before a free transfer to Notts County. Injury problems resurfaced at Meadow Lane and after two years Robson decided to retire from the first class game. He took to playing and coaching at non-League level and soon joined the coaching staff back at Charlton. He served Charlton in various coaching roles for more than eight years, playing for numerous non-League clubs when his Charlton duties permitted. Since leaving Charlton, Robson has coached and managed at various clubs.

Appearances:
League: 3 (5) apps.
FL Cup: 1 app.
Others: 5 (13) apps.
Total: 9 (18) apps. 0 gls.

ROCHA, Ricardo Sergio (Azevedo)

Role: Defender 2006-08
6ft. 13st.7lbs.
Born: Santo Tirso, Portugal, 3rd October 1978

CAREER: ARC Areias (Portugal)/Vitória de Guimarães (Portugal)/Famalicão (Portugal) Jul 1998/Sporting Braga (Portugal) Jul 1999/Benfica (Portugal) Jul 2002/**SPURS** Jan 2007/released May 2009/Standard Liege (Belgium) Aug 2009/Portsmouth Feb 2010/(Leeds United trial Sep 2010)/released May 2012/Ipswich Town trial Sep 2012/Portsmouth Nov 2012-May 2013.

Debut v Southend United (FAC) (h) 27.1.2007

In January 2007 Spurs central defensive options were seriously limited as both Ledley King and Calum Davenport found themselves on the injured list. If Michael Dawson or Anthony Gardner were to join their colleagues, Spurs hopes of progress in the Carling Cup, FA Cup and UEFA Cup, let alone the Premier League would be in real jeopardy. To cover the risk, Ricardo Rocha was signed from Benfica for £3.3 million. In more than

four years with Benfica, the strong, experienced defender, who first made his name with SC Braga, had developed into one of Portugal's best stoppers. Rocha had six full appearances for Portugal to his credit, a number that would have been substantially more had he not been in competition with such consistently brilliant performers as Fernando Couto, Ricardo Carvalho and Jorge Andrade. Highly rated as a man-marker, Rocha performed reasonably well when he first arrived at Spurs. There was nothing spectacular about him, but he appeared competent enough and certainly not out of his depth. Before he could fully establish himself though, injuries took their toll. Rocha made his final first team appearance in September 2007 and made few reserve team outings before being released in May 2009. He moved to Standard Liege, but did not settle in Belgium and soon returned to England, signing for Portsmouth. He helped Portsmouth reach the FA Cup final in 2010, but was not to add a winner's medal to the Portuguese Cup and League winners' medals he had won with Benfica in 2004 and 2005. Released in May 2012 but re-signed six months later, Rocha was one of the few constants as the financially-stricken club plummeted from the Premier League to League Two.

Appearances:
League: 13 (1) apps.
FA Cup: 3 apps.
FL Cup: (1) app.
Others: 5 (1) apps.
Total: 21 (3) apps. 0 gls.

ROE, Thomas William

Role: Forward 1925-27
5ft.8ins. 11st.7lbs.
Born: Evenwood, County Durham, 8th December 1900
Died: Durham West, County Durham, December 1972

CAREER: Evenwood Town/ Cockfield/Esperley Rovers/ Willington Athletic Aug 1922/Durham City am. Nov 1922/ Shildon Athletic Jul 1923/

Cockfield Nov 1923/ Northfleet United Aug 1924/ **SPURS** Jul 1925/Nottingham Forest May 1927/Luton Town Aug 1928/Walsall May 1929/ Coventry City May 1930/ Heanor Town/Nottingham City Transport Dec 1932.

Debut v Bolton Wanderers (FL) (a) 3.4.1926

Tommy Roe joined the nursery club at Northfleet as a youngster in 1924 before moving up onto the staff at White Hart Lane a year later. An inside or centre-forward, he made his League debut at the end of his first season, but in two years on the books made only seven League appearances before his release in April 1927. He joined Nottingham Forest and moved rapidly on to Luton Town, Walsall and Coventry City without particularly great success. His brother, Harry, was with Luton Town in 1926.

Appearances:
League: 7 apps. 4 gls.
Others: 2 apps. 1 gl.
Total: 9 apps. 5 gls.

ROPER

Role: Centre-forward 1918-19

Debut v Clapton Orient (Fr) (a) 26.4.1919 (scored once)

Yet another of the trialists who made their only Spurs' appearance in April 1919, Roper played in the friendly at Clapton Orient and scored Spurs' goal as a very young and inexperienced team was beaten 1-6.

Appearances:
Others: 1 app. 1 gl.
Total: 1 app. 1 gl.

ROSE, Daniel Lee

Role: Defender Forward 2009-
5ft.8ins. 12st.6lbs.
Born: Doncaster, South Yorkshire, 2nd July 1990

CAREER: Leeds United Scholar/**SPURS** Jul 2007/ (Watford loan Mar 2009)/ (Peterborough United loan Sep 2009)/(Bristol City loan Sep 2010)/ (Sunderland loan Aug 2012).

Debut v Doncaster Rovers (sub) (FLC) (a) 26.8.2009 (Exeter City (Fr) (a) 15.7.2009)

Capped by England from Under-16 through to Under-19 level, Danny Rose was one of the brightest gems to develop at the Leeds United Academy, but the club's financial collapse meant that even fledgling talent had to be capitalised on if it meant money being brought in. So it was that Leeds did not resist Spurs' overtures as Rose neared the end of his scholarship. A potential £1 million in development costs would be gratefully received. Rose was a forward with Leeds, often utilised as an out-and-out winger, but usually playing out wide on the left of midfield. He started as a midfielder with Spurs, quickly establishing himself in the reserves. Injuries curtailed his progress and as part of his recovery he was loaned out to Watford, impressing enough in his short time there to win a call-up to the England Under-21 squad and win his first caps at that level. Rose made his competitive debut for Spurs in the Carling Cup in August 2009. He followed that with a three-month loan at Peterborough United, and after his return made three appearances in the FA Cup, but it was in April 2010 that he really made his mark. On his Premier League debut, he scored with a thunderous 35-yard volley to set Spurs on the way to a 2-1 victory over Arsenal. With Gareth Bale making the left wing position his own, Rose had to show remarkable patience and a willingness to adapt. He worked hard on his defensive qualities and soon began to challenge Benoit Assou-Ekotto for the left-back position. For the 2012-13 season Rose was loaned to Sunderland. He returned an accomplished full-back, strong, hard-tackling, aggressive but still keen to go forward at every opportunity. He so impressed Andre Villas-Boas that Assou-Ekotto was loaned to QPR while Rose was installed as first choice left-back. With attack always at the forefront of his thoughts, there were times when he could be stranded upfield, his defensive duties suffering. When Mauricio Pochettino took over he recognised Rose's value as one of Spurs' most potent attacking weapons. He installed Eric Dier in the centre of midfield, with instructions to drop back and form a defensive three so Rose and Kyle Walker on the opposite flank, could provide some attacking width. It was a move that worked so well that Rose collected his first cap against Germany in March 2016, in the build-up to the Euros in France and was soon established as an England regular. Rose's brother, Mitchell, is a midfielder with Newport County, having started his career with Rotherham United.

Appearances:
League: 99 (9) apps. 8 gls
FA Cup: 10 (3) apps. 1 gl.
FL Cup: 4 (2) apps.
Euro: 14 (2) apps. 1 gl.
Others: 16 (12) apps. 1 gl.
Total: 143 (28) apps. 11 gls.

ROSE, L

Role: Full-back 1892-95

CAREER: Foxes/**SPURS** guest.

Debut v Old St Stephens (SA) (h) 25.3.1893

A regular performer for one of Spurs' local rivals, Foxes, Rose was called upon to make several appearances for Spurs as a guest player over a period of three years. Regarded as one of the area's best full-backs, his first recorded appearance was in a Southern Alliance fixture with Old St Stephens in March 1893. Regular full-back Moody failed to arrive for the game and Rose was called on at the last minute. Spurs were fortunate at the time to be able to call upon full-backs of the calibre of Jack Jull, Moody, Ly Burrows and Jack Welham, but Rose was a more than competent deputy for all of them and would have been readily accepted into Spurs' ranks had he ever decided to leave the Foxes. During his time with Foxes, Rose represented Middlesex.

Appearances:
Others: 11 apps. 1 gl.
Total: 11 apps. 1 gl.

ROSENTHAL, Ronald

Role: Forward 1993-97
5ft.11ins. 12st.13lbs.
Born: Haifa, Israel, 11th October 1963

CAREER: Maccabi Haifa (Israel) 1974/FC Bruges (Belgium) Jul 1986/Standard Liege (Belgium) Jul 1988/(Luton Town loan Mar 1990)/Liverpool loan Mar 1990, perm. May 1990/**SPURS** Jan 1994/Watford Aug 1997/retired Jul 1999/Golders Green Aug 2001.

Debut v Sheffield Wednesday (PL) (h) 5.3.1994 (scored once)

When Teddy Sheringham was injured in October 1993, Spurs immediately found themselves in trouble. Sheringham was the man new manager Ossie Ardiles had built his team around, the man whose goals were expected to lead an assault on the Premier League title. Without Sheringham the goals dried up, Spurs struggled and a relegation battle was looking increasingly more likely than a title challenge. Come January 1994, Ronny Rosenthal was the man Ardiles turned to in order to fill the goal-scoring void. Rosenthal had first made his name in his native Israel, helping Maccabi Haifa win the Israeli Liga Leumit in 1984 and 1985. Joining Club Brugge, he added the Belgian league title to his list of honours in 1988 before moving on to Standard Liege where his goal-scoring reached its peak. Luton Town took Rosenthal on loan with a view to a permanent deal and were quickly impressed, but while they dithered, Liverpool acted. Rosenthal moved to Anfield, initially on loan, but with a permanent summer transfer expected to follow. Seven goals in only eight League games as Liverpool clinched the Premier League title made that a certainty, even though the fee had reportedly rocketed. After such an incredible start it was perhaps to be expected that things would not continue in the same vein. As Liverpool failed to match the high standards they had set, so Rosenthal struggled to find a regular place. He became a bit part player, very popular, always a threat, but frequently a substitute. When he joined Spurs he was already over thirty and not expected to be anything more than a short-term signing. As it was he stayed for over three years, good value for the £250,000 Spurs paid Liverpool for his services. A non-stop worker whose joy at just playing was always obvious, Rosenthal was at his best running at an opponent, his arms and legs whirling like a windmill. While there were times when he was capable of genius, he was not the best of finishers but he could always be relied upon for effort. As with his time at Anfield, he was frequently used by Spurs as a substitute, though his best spell in the team came when he was used as a wide midfielder. After Spurs, Rosenthal spent two years with Watford, retiring when he was released and

becoming a player's agent and football consultant. Throughout his career Rosenthal was a regular for Israel, collecting sixty caps, 19 of them as a Spurs player. His brother, Lior, was also a professional player, notably with Maccabi Haifa. In July 1989 Rosenthal signed for Udinese but the move fell through. The Italians blamed a spinal cord problem, but the real reason was the anti-Semitic abuse heaped on Rosenthal and the club's board by so-called supporters.

Appearances:
League: 55 (33) apps. 4 gls.
FA Cup: 8 (2) app. 6 gls.
FL Cup: 3* apps. 1 gl.
Others: 14 (7) apps. 4 gls.
Total: 80 (42) apps. 15 gls.
*Includes 1 abandoned match

ROSS, George

Role: Goalkeeper 1895-96

CAREER: Broadwater/Crouch End Sep 1895/**SPURS** guest Nov 1895.

Debut v London Welsh (Fr) (h) 30.11.1895

George Ross was a well-known local goalkeeper playing for Crouch End at the time of his one appearance for Spurs. He had previously played for Broadwater and represented Tottenham in local district matches. His one game for Spurs was in November 1895 in a friendly with London Welsh. He stood in for Spurs' regular keeper Charlie Ambler, who was playing for Arsenal in a Football League fixture. Ross had much the better day, Spurs winning 3-2, while Ambler let in five as Arsenal were thrashed at Newton Heath. After the one game Ross continued to help Spurs out on odd occasions, although only with the reserves.

Appearances:
Others: 1 app.
Total: 1 app. 0 gls.

ROSS, James Donaldson

Role: Full-back 1920-24
5ft.8ins. 11st.7lbs.
Born: Bonnyrigg, Midlothian, 7th March 1895

CAREER: Raith Rovers/**SPURS** Apr 1920/released Apr 1925.

Debut v Manchester City (FL) (a) 14.3.1923
(Clapton Orient (LFACC) (Highbury) 11.4.1921)

Signed as a half-back from Raith Rovers, Jimmy Ross made his first team debut in a London FA Charity Cup semi-final with Clapton Orient in April 1921, but had to wait almost two more years for his first League game. That came in March 1923 when he appeared at right-back in place of the injured Tommy Clay. Clay was almost immovable in that position, and although Ross remained with Spurs until the end of the 1924-25 season, he was rarely in contention for a first team place. In April 1925 he was given a free transfer, but with few clubs showing an interest in securing his services, decided to finish with football. In July of that year he took up the post of manager at the Stadium Golf Club in north London. An Army Captain during the Great War, Ross was awarded the Military Cross.

Appearances:
League: 7 apps.
Others: 2 apps.
Total: 9 apps. 0 gls.

ROUTLEDGE, Wayne Neville Anthony

Role: Winger 2005-2008
5ft.7ins. 11st.13lbs.
Born: Sidcup, Kent, 7th January 1985

CAREER: Addiscombe Corinthians/Crystal Palace scholar Jul 2001, pro. Jul 2002/**SPURS** Jul 2005/(Portsmouth loan Jan 2006)/(Fulham loan Aug 2006)/Aston Villa Jan 2008/(Cardiff City loan Nov 2008)/Queens Park Rangers Jan 2009/Newcastle United Jan 2010/(Queens Park Rangers loan Jan 2011)/Swansea City Aug 2011.

Debut v Portsmouth (PL) (a) 13.8.2005
(Boca Juniors (Fr) (Suwon) 16.7.2005)

When Spurs signed England Under-21 international Wayne Routledge they were viewed as lucky to be securing one of the most exciting young talents in English football, a dazzling winger with pace and some remarkable dribbling skills. Spurs had been on Routledge's trail for months having reportedly offered Crystal Palace £3 million for his signature in January 2005. The offer was refused, but when Routledge declined a new contract, there was nothing Palace could do to prevent him moving. The clubs were unable to agree a fee, but shortly before a tribunal was set to determine how much Palace were to receive in development costs, a deal was done. Spurs paid an initial £1.25 million, with up to £750,000 more dependent on appearances. None of the further payments ever fell due, as Routledge made only five League appearances in a near three year Spurs' career. He started well enough, playing in all the pre-season games, but broke a bone in his foot on his first Premier League outing. Aaron Lennon, signed at the same time as Routledge, was two years junior to Routledge and viewed as a long-term signing. He seized the opportunity to make his mark and performed so well that Routledge rarely had another chance to show what he could do. After loans to Portsmouth and Fulham, Routledge joined Aston Villa with Spurs more than recovering what they had paid to sign him. Routledge fared no better at Villa Park and it was only after joining Queens Park Rangers that he began to fulfil the promise he had shown in his Palace days. Even then he did not settle, quickly moving to Newcastle United and then returning to Loftus Road on loan. It was only when he joined Swansea City that Routledge at last found the stage on which he would display his talents regularly.

Playing in a team that believed in fast-paced football with the ball kept on the ground, he was one of the most consistent performers as the Welsh club established itself in the Premier League and won the Carling Cup in 2012. Routledge had two Under-21 caps when he joined Spurs. He collected ten more before leaving for Aston Villa.

Appearances:
League: 3 (2) apps.
Others: 12 (7) apps. 1 gl.
Total: 15 (9) apps. 1 gl.

ROWE, Arthur Sydney

Role: Centre-half 1930-38
5ft.9ins. 12st.8lbs.
Born: Tottenham, north London, 1st September 1906
Died: Norbury, south London, 5th November 1993

CAREER: Tottenham Schools/London Schools/**SPURS** am. 1923/(Cheshunt)/(Northfleet United)/**SPURS** pro. May 1929/retired Apr 1939/Chelmsford City manager Jul 1945/**SPURS** manager May 1949–Jul 1955/West Bromwich Albion chief scout Aug 1957/Crystal Palace asst. manager Nov 1958, manager Apr 1960-Dec 1962, backroom staff till Feb 1971/Orient consultant Jan 1972-1978/Crystal Palace director/Millwall consultant Jun 1978.

Debut v Burnley (FL) (h) 10.10.1931
(Chelsea (LFACC) (a) 27.10.1930)

Arthur Rowe was such a Spurs man through and through, that it was almost destined he should bring so much success to White Hart Lane. He was born near Spurs' ground and worked his way through the ranks to become both player and manager of the club he loved so dearly. First associated with Spurs in 1921 whilst still a talented junior at school, he only missed out on an England Schoolboy cap due to injury. Signed as an amateur, he played for the Cheshunt and Northfleet nursery clubs before joining the professional ranks. His first team debut was in October 1930 in a London FA Charity Cup tie, and although it was almost a year before he made his League debut, once in the team, he was there to stay. In the next two seasons Rowe helped Spurs win back their place in Division One and reach third in the table in 1933-34. As a centre-half he may have been expected to adopt a defensive outlook on the game, but he was not in the traditional "stopper" mould of centre-half then so in fashion. He was more a footballing half-back, like those from the earlier years of the century, who just happened to be especially strong at marking the opposing centre-forward. Never one for the hurried clearance downfield

or a wild punt into the crowd, Rowe was always cool, steady and confident, looking to guide the ball out of defence to a colleague so that the forwards had a chance to do their job. Honoured with an international cap against France in December 1933 when the match was played at White Hart Lane, he suffered a serious injury a year later which kept him out of the side, and it was his absence, more than anything, that resulted in Spurs' relegation in 1934-35. Not until Rowe was manager would Spurs regain their place in the top flight. Although he returned for the start of the 1935-36 season he thereafter continually suffered with injuries and was rarely able to recover his prime form. Made available for transfer in April 1939 having failed to overcome a cartilage operation, he decided to retire from playing. Recommended by FA Chairman, Stanley Rous, he went on a lecture tour of Hungary. So impressed were the Hungarians that they wanted Rowe to set up a coaches training course and prepare the national team for the 1940 Olympics. Rowe was keen to accept the proposal, but the German invasion of Austria scuppered the plan. The War did at least give him the chance to try his hand at management, and he was in charge of the Army team for much of that time. On demob he was appointed boss of Chelmsford City and in his first season led them to the Southern League title. Having fashioned the Essex club into one of the best and most attractive non-League teams in the country, it was no surprise when he took over from Joe Hulme as Spurs' manager. With his famous philosophy of "Make it quick; make it simple" Rowe's impact at White Hart Lane was immediate. He steered Spurs to the Second Division title in his very first season and the League Championship for the first time in the club's history in 1950-51, with the neat style of football that will forever be known as "Push and Run". Always striving after that to re-create the remarkable chemistry of the "Push and Run" team, Rowe worked tirelessly for Spurs, but it had a detrimental effect on his health and, after a breakdown in 1954, he was forced to resign. He returned to football as chief scout at West Bromwich Albion and then joined the managerial staff of Crystal Palace, taking over the manager's role in April 1960. In his first season he led Palace out of Division Four, but again found the pressures too much and resigned in December 1962. A man with a deep affection for the game of football, Rowe continued to work with the backroom staff at Palace until February 1971 when he briefly returned to management with the ill-fated Football Hall of Fame in London. He was later a consultant with Orient and Millwall.

Appearances:
League: 182 apps.
FA Cup: 19 apps.
Others: 9 apps.
Total: 210 apps. 0 gls.

ROWLEY, John Frederick

Role: Centre-forward 1942-45
5ft.9ins. 11st.7lbs.
Born: Wolverhampton, Staffordshire, 7th October 1920
Died: Shaw, nr Oldham, Lancashire, 29th June 1998

CAREER: Dudley Old Boys/Wolverhampton Wanderers Nov 1935/(Cradley Heath loan Oct 1936)/(Bournemouth and Boscombe Athletic loan Feb 1937)/Manchester United Oct 1937/(guest for Aldershot, Distillery, Folkestone, Shrewsbury Town, **SPURS**, Walsall and Wolverhampton Wanderers during Second World War)/Plymouth Argyle player-manager Feb 1955, manager May 1957-Mar 1960/Oldham Athletic manager Jul 1960/Ajax (Holland) coach Aug 1963-Jul 1964/Wrexham general manager Jan 1966/Bradford Park Avenue general manager Apr 1967/Oldham Athletic manager Oct 1968-Dec 1969.

Debut v Reading (FLSC) (h) 3.4.1943

Jack Rowley started his senior career with Wolverhampton Wanderers, but it was when he was loaned to Cradley Heath and then Bournemouth and Boscombe Athletic that his goal-scoring talent caught the attention of the bigger clubs. He moved to Manchester United and stayed with them for 17 years scoring almost 200 goals in over 300 League appearances. A member of the Football League teams against the Scottish League in October 1941 and the League of Ireland in 1948, Rowley played for Spurs as a war-time guest, making his first appearance in April 1943. During the war he also guested for Wolverhampton Wanderers and scored twice in the second leg of the 1942 League Cup Final. It was as a result of his guesting for Distillery that he was introduced to Spurs. Les Bennett was playing for Distillery and he suggested Rowley should contact Spurs if he found himself in London and without a game. Although he did not score in his first two matches he was a regular and top scorer in 1943-44 as Spurs won the Football League South. It was his form for Spurs that led to his first England appearance playing in a war-time international against Wales in May 1944. When the war was over he returned to Manchester United, scored twice in the 1948 FA Cup Final defeat of Blackpool, helped United to

the Football League title in 1952 and won one "B" and six full England caps, the first against Switzerland in December 1948. Brother of Arthur Rowley who played for West Bromwich Albion, Fulham, Leicester City, Shrewsbury Town and England "B", Jack stayed with Manchester United until February 1955 when he started out with Plymouth Argyle on a managerial career that took in Oldham Athletic, Ajax of Amsterdam, Wrexham, Bradford Park Avenue and finished back with Oldham. His only managerial success was in 1959 when he led Plymouth back into Division Two.

Appearances:
Others: 27 apps. 26 gls.
Total: 27 apps. 26 gls.

ROWLEY, Richard William Morris

Role: Centre-forward 1929-32
6ft.1ins. 11st.12lbs.
Born: Enniskillen, County Antrim, 13th January 1904
Died: Southampton, Hampshire, 18th April 1984

CAREER: Fulwood Barracks/Preston Grammar School/Taunton College Grammar (Rugby)/Tidworth Garrison/Tidworth United/Andover Sep 1922/Swindon Town am. Nov 1924/London Casuals 1925/Southampton am. May 1926, pro. Nov 1926/**SPURS** Feb 1930/Preston North End Dec 1931/retired 1934.

Debut v Oldham Athletic (FL) (h) 15.2.1930

A Northern Ireland international with a good goal-scoring record, Dick

Rowley was signed to replace the injured Ted Harper. The son of an Army officer, he first played football with Fulwood Barracks and Preston Grammar School, but on going to Taunton Grammar School was forced to give up football in favour of rugby for two years. Once his schooldays were over, he took to football again and played for the Tidworth Garrison sports club, where his father was secretary. In 1920 he helped form Tidworth United, a team for under-18s. Moving down to Andover, he signed for the local club and helped them win the Hampshire League in 1925. An amateur on Swindon Town's books, he won selection for Wiltshire before joining Southampton, where his career took off with 52 goals in 102 League outings. By the time of his £3,750 move to Spurs he had already won four Irish caps, the first against Wales in February 1929. He went straight into the team, but as soon as Harper was fit to resume found himself confined to the reserves. Harper's understudy throughout 1930-31 he was still good enough to pick up two more Irish caps in April and September 1931, but with the arrival of the talented George Hunt found himself very much third choice. In December 1931 he and Ted Harper were transferred for a joint £5,000 fee to Preston North End, where Rowley played till his retirement.

Appearances:
League: 24 apps. 10 gls.
Others: 2 apps. 1 gl.
Total: 26 apps. 11 gls.

RUDDOCK, Neil

Role: Central defender 1985-88 & 1992-93
6ft.2ins. 12st.6lbs.
Born: Battersea, South London, 9th May 1968

CAREER: Ashford Schools/Kent Schools/Charlton Athletic/Millwall app. Jun 1984, pro. Mar 1985/SPURS Mar 1986/Millwall Jun 1988/Southampton Feb 1989/SPURS Jul 1992/Liverpool Jul 1993/(Queens Park Rangers loan Mar 1998)/West Ham United Jul 1998/Crystal Palace Jul 2000-Apr 2001/Oxford United training Jul 2001/Swindon Town player-coach Aug 2001-Dec 2002/Northam 75 Oct 2005.

Debut v Wimbledon (sub) (FAC) (a) 15.3.1987
(Rangers (Fr) (a) 6.4.1986.)

Neil Ruddock played one game in Charlton Athletic's youth team before joining Millwall, where he became an England Youth international. Transferred to Spurs for £50,000 without playing even one senior competitive match for the Lions, Ruddock made his mark as a tough, uncompromising defender with a good left foot who liked to get forward for set pieces or fire in a long range shot on goal. He had only played a few senior games for Spurs, but looked to have a big future at White Hart Lane, particularly when Richard Gough returned to Scotland in October 1987. Ruddock then suffered a series of unsettling injuries and had few chances to impress new manager Terry Venables. He played out the final games of his first spell as a Spurs' player in South America as a member of the England Under-20 touring party, before returning to newly promoted Millwall in a £300,000 deal. Unable to gain a place in a Millwall side that started its first season in Division One so well, he was on the move again by February 1989, when he joined struggling Southampton for £250,000. His rugged, combative style helped the Saints avoid the drop. Despite graduating to England Under-21 level in the summer of 1989, Ruddock too often marred some fine displays for his club with worrying lapses of discipline and a string of subsequent suspensions, but gaining in maturity, he was one of the most important performers as the Saints once again successfully fought off the spectre of relegation in 1991-92. Ruddock might have failed to catch Venables' eye while with Spurs, but the Tottenham manager had later seen enough to pay £750,000 in May 1992 to bring him back to White Hart Lane, a major defensive rock in Venables' plans to rebuild the team. However, Venables left Spurs in May 1993 following his dispute with co-owner Alan Sugar. Ruddock's initial staunch support for Venables endeared him to Spurs fans, but when he began to make what appeared to be unjustified financial demands, he not only alienated Sugar but also the fans. It was no surprise when he was allowed to move to Liverpool for £2.5 million. Ruddock's controversial off field career continued at Anfield, while on the pitch he showed himself a more than competent performer, good enough to collect one cap at both "B" and full level following Venables' appointment as England manager. Ruddock should have collected more honours, but doubts about his discipline persisted and such doubts could not be tolerated at international level. Liverpool proved to be the pinnacle of Ruddock's career. From there he dropped down the football ranks finishing his career at Swindon Town. Even then controversy surrounded events. With Swindon in financial trouble, Ruddock refused to accept specialist advise to quit playing because of persistent injuries. Swindon stopped paying him and it was only after Ruddock had taken the club to an Employment Tribunal that a deal was done to end his contract.

Appearances:
League: 45 (2) apps. 3 gls.
FA Cup: 6 (1) apps. 1 gl.
FL Cup: 4 apps.
Others: 24 (9) apps. 2 gls.
Total: 79 (12) apps. 6 gls.

RULE, Arthur George

Role: Centre-forward 1898-00
5ft.9ins. 11st.10lbs.
Born: Liskeard, Cornwall, 15th December 1873
Died: Edinburgh, 1937

CAREER: Millwall Athletic Feb 1893/New Brompton 1894/Sheppey United 1896/SPURS Mar 1899/Portsmouth Nov 1902/Ryde Jan 1905/Brighton and Hove Albion Sep 1905.

Debut v Woolwich Arsenal (UL) (a) 11.3.1899

Art Rule built a reputation as possibly the best centre-forward in Kent during his three years with Sheppey United, finishing top scorer in his last two years. An Admiralty clerk working in Whitehall, he joined Spurs despite keen interest from Millwall and Woolwich Arsenal, on the understanding he would only be available to play on Saturdays. He proved more than adequate cover for Spurs' regular centre-forwards, Tom Pratt and Bill Joyce, but was unable to turn out on

anything more than the odd occasion. In November 1899 he was promoted and posted to Chatham. The local club were immediately keen to sign him, but Spurs were not prepared to agree his release. However, they could not re-sign him for the 1900-01 season. Whilst he was always restricted by the demands of his civil service career, he later played for Portsmouth, Ryde and Brighton.

Appearances:
Southern: 7 apps. 1 gl.
Others: 5 apps. 3 gls.
Total: 12 apps. 4 gls.

RUNDLE, Charles Rodney

Role: Centre-forward 1945-50
5ft.11ins. 9st.13lbs.
Born: Par, Cornwall, 17th January 1923
Died: Bodmin, Cornwall, 28th June 1997

CAREER: St Blazey/Navy/SPURS am. Feb 1946, pro. Feb 1946/Crystal Palace Jun 1950/Tonbridge Aug 1952/Betteshanger Colliery Welfare player-manager Feb 1955/Ford of Dagenham sports secretary/Thorn EMI sports secretary.

Debut v Southampton (FL) (h) 9.9.1946 (scored once) (Chelsea (Fr) (h) 2.3.1946)

Spurs noticed Charlie Rundle playing representative football for the Navy and promptly signed him from his local club St Blazey. Primarily a centre-forward, but happy to play at inside-forward, he had an extended run in the first team at the end of 1946-47. With the introduction of Len Duquemin early the next season, Rundle found himself restricted to the reserves. There he remained, making a few rare appearances when Duquemin was unavailable, but also hampered by persistent injuries until May 1950, when Spurs decided not to retain his registration. He signed for Crystal Palace and then played for Tonbridge before becoming player-manager of Betteshanger Colliery FC. Later in life he was sports secretary to Fords of Dagenham and Thorn EMI. His brother, Sid, made over 50 League appearances in six years with Plymouth Argyle immediately after the Second World War and another brother, George, played for Spurs "A" team in 1947.

Appearances:
League: 28 apps. 12 gls.
FA Cup: 1 app.
Others: 10 apps. 3 gls.
Total: 39 apps. 15 gls.

RUSSELL, J

Role: Centre-forward 1895-96

CAREER: London Caledonians/SPURS guest.

Debut v Ilford (Fr) (h) 18.1.1896 (scored once)

Russell was playing for the London Caledonians when he made his one appearance for Spurs in January 1896. He played at centre-forward in a friendly with Ilford and scored once.

Appearances:
Others: 1 app. 1 gl.
Total: 1 app. 1 gl.

RUTHERFORD, John

Role: Half-back 1914-20
6ft. 13st.2lbs.
Born: Netherton Nr Newcastle, 1897
Died: Morpeth, Northumberland, September 1930

CAREER: Bedlington/Choppington/Ashington/SPURS Jan 1913/Luton Town Jul 1919/Brighton and Hove Albion May 1920/USA/Cardiff City Aug 1921/Bristol Rovers Sep 1922/Mold cs. 1923/York City/Gillingham Nov 1924.

Debut v Red Star Amical (Fr) (a) 1.5.1913

A half-back from Tyneside, John Rutherford signed for Spurs as a 21-year old. He was to make only three first team appearances. The first was in a friendly in France shortly after his arrival. His one truly competitive outing was in a London FA Charity Cup tie at Crystal Palace in October 1914 in what was basically a reserve team. Later that month it was reported his contract had been terminated, along with those of three other young players, for "breach of training regulations", but it would appear he was later given another chance for in April 1919 he played in a friendly at Arsenal. At the end of that season he was released and signed for Luton Town, going on to serve several clubs during his career, though rarely staying in one place for more than a year. It is not clear whether Rutherford played in America between his spells with Brighton and Cardiff. He was reputedly on his way back from a holiday in the States when Cardiff contacted him by radio in the middle of the Atlantic Ocean, offered him terms and he accepted. Rutherford played alongside his full-back brother, Jim, at Brighton.

Appearances:
Others: 3 apps.
Total: 3 apps. 1 gl.

RYDEN, John Johnston

Role: Half-back 1955-59
6ft.1ins. 12st.1lbs.
Born: Alexandria, Dumbartonshire, 18th February 1931
Died: Keston, Kent, 16th August 2013

CAREER: St Martin's/St Patrick's High School/Denhny Juveniles/Duntocher Hibernian/Alloa Athletic Jul 1950/Accrington Stanley Feb 1954/SPURS Nov 1955/Watford Jun 1961/Romford Oct 1962/Hastings United/Tunbridge Wells Rangers Aug 1965/Bexley United player-manager Jul 1966/retired 1968.

Debut v Preston North End (FL) (a) 2.4.1956 (scored once)

(Partick Thistle (Fr) (h) 14.11.1955)

John Ryden played for the Scottish junior clubs Denhny Juveniles and Duntocher Hibernians, before turning out as a part-timer with Second Division Alloa Athletic. It was only when transferred to Accrington Stanley that he played full-time. He developed into a powerful, tough tackling centre-half with Accrington and when signed by Spurs was regarded as the best in his position in the Third Division (North). Indeed, only the month before his £12,000 transfer he had played for the Third

Division (North) against the Third Division (South) in the annual fixture between those two sections of the League. Ryden had to wait until April 1956 for his First Division debut, playing when Harry Clarke was injured, and then had to fight hard to oust Clarke and establish himself as first choice. Made captain on Tony Marchi's big money move to Italy, Ryden then faced a strong challenge from Maurice Norman and moved to left-half-although still as a defensive player. The signings of first Jim Iley and then Dave Mackay pushed Ryden into the shadows. He was allowed to move on to Watford, where he played for one season before dropping into non-League football with Romford, Tunbridge Wells and Bexley United. Ryden later managed the Maidstone branch of a finance company and the Richmond office of a finance and insurance brokers. His two brothers also played football at professional level, George for Dundee and Hugh for several clubs including Chester, Stockport and Leeds. Curiously, all three of them share the middle Christian name, "Johnston".

Appearances:
League: 63 apps. 2 gls.
FA Cup: 5 apps.
Others: 21 apps. 1 gl.
Total: 89 apps. 3 gls.

S

SAGE, William

Role: Half-back 1919-26
5ft.9ins. 10st.7lbs.
Born: Edmonton, north London, 11th November 1893
Died: Enfield, Middlesex, 21st June 1968

CAREER: Houndsfield Road School/Tottenham Thursday/Corinthians/**SPURS** am. Oct 1919, pro. May 1920/Clapton Orient Aug 1927/Dartford Jul 1928/London Public Omnibus Company coach Nov 1929, manager Dec 1929.

Debut v Rotherham County (FL) (h) 20.3.1920

In an age when players tended to specialise in just one position, Billy Sage can only be described as a versatile utility player, although after leaving Spurs he eventually settled at half-back. An occasional player for the Corinthians and an England amateur international trialist, he joined Spurs shortly after leaving the Army. He stood by as reserve for all of England's amateur internationals in the 1919-20 season before signing professional, having made his League debut at right-half in March 1920. His next League outing did not come until October 1923, when he played at centre-forward, whilst the rest of his appearances that season came at centre-half. Sage then had a game at outside-right, before going on the FA tour of Australia in 1925. Unable to stake a claim as a regular with Spurs, he was given a free transfer at the end of 1926-27 and moved to Clapton Orient. He spent a season with Orient before joining Dartford, where he finished his senior playing career. In November 1929 he succeeded former Spurs' man Jimmy Banks as coach of the London Public Omnibus Company's football club in the Enfield Midweek League. Sage was known as "Sapper" from his days in Army representative football.

Appearances:
League: 13 apps.
Others: 3 apps.
Total: 16 apps. 0 gls.

SAHA, Louis Laurent

Role: Striker 2011-12
6ft. 11st.8lbs.
Born: Paris, France, 8th August 1978

CAREER: Soisy-Andilly-Margency (France)/INF Clarefontaine/Metz (France) Jul 1995/(Newcastle United loan Jan 1999)/Fulham Jun 2000/Manchester United Jan 2004/Everton Sep 2008/**SPURS** Jan 2012/Sunderland Aug 2012/Lazio (Italy) Feb 2013/retired Aug 2013.

Debut v Liverpool (sub) (PL) (h) 6.2.2012

When Everton made a late transfer window move to take a sadly disappointing Steven Pienaar back to Goodison Park on loan, Harry Redknapp took the opportunity to make the signing of Louis Saha part of the deal. The 33-year old was signed on a short term deal and certainly proved a worthwhile acquisition. A product of the famous French football academy at Clarefontaine, Saha was beginning to make a name for himself with Metz when Newcastle United took him on loan in January 1999. Although he showed promise in four months on Tyneside, Newcastle decided not to take him on permanently. He returned for another season with Metz, but when Jean Tigana moved from Monaco to take over as manager at Fulham, Saha was one of the first signings he wanted. With pace, neat close control and a willingness to work hard, Saha proved a great success, providing the goals that took Fulham into the Premiership. As he helped Fulham settle in the top flight, Saha became the object of Manchester United's attentions and eventually Fulham succumbed to a £12.4 million offer. Almost as soon as he arrived at Old Trafford, Saha was selected for the full French team, netting on his debut against Belgium in February 2004. He went on to make a total of twenty full appearances. In four-and-a-half years Saha was a regular performer for United, though injuries did not help him really establish himself as a first choice striker. He played in the 2006 Carling Cup final defeat of Wigan Athletic and helped United win the Premier League in 2007 and 2008, but missed the 2008 Champions League final. Such were the injury doubts that United allowed Saha to move to Everton where he initially played on a 'pay-as-you-play' basis. Everton got more than three years' good service out of him before his move to White Hart Lane. Saha might have thought he had done enough to earn a long term contract with Spurs, but he had only ever been a temporary signing and was not offered a new deal. Sunderland took a gamble on his talents, but after six months his contract was terminated so he could join Lazio on another short term deal. Unable to secure another senior club, Saha announced his retirement on his 35th birthday. In October 2013 it was announced that Saha was the first marquee signing for the professional football league to be launched in India by IMG-Reliance and to be run along similar lines to cricket's successful Indian Premier League, but when it came to actually making the move, Saha decided he had other things to do.

Appearances:
League: 5 (5) apps. 3 gls.
FA Cup: 2* (1) apps. 1 gl.
Total: 7 (6) apps. 4 gls.
* Includes 1 abandoned match

SAIB, Moussa

Role: Midfield 1997-99
5ft.9ins. 11st.8lbs.
Born: Théniet El Had, Algeria, 5th March 1969

CAREER: Théniet El Had (Algeria) 1981/JSM Tiaret (Algeria) 1987/JS Kabylie (Algeria) 1989/Auxerre (France) 1992/Valencia (Spain) Jul 1997/ **SPURS** Feb 1998/(Heart of Midlothian loan Sep 1999)/(El Nasr (Saudi Arabia) loan Dec 1999)/released May 2000/Auxerre (France) Oct 2000/ Monaco (France) Jul 2001/(Lorient (France) loan Jan 2002)/Dubai SC (UAE) Oct 2002/Al Ahly (Dubai, UAE) Nov 2002/JS Kabylie (Algeria) Dec 2002, coach May 2004-Apr 2005/retired Dec 2004/Olympique Noisy-le-Sec (France) player-coach Dec 2005/JS Kabylie (Algeria) coach Oct-Nov 2006, asst. coach Jul-Aug 2007, caretaker coach Aug 2007/Nadi El Watani (Saudi Arabia) coach Jun-Oct 2008/JS Kabylie (Algeria) coach Nov 2008-Jan 2009/ASO Chlef (Algeria) coach Jun-Aug 2009/JS Kabylie (Algeria) coach Jun-Sep 2011.

Debut v Bolton Wanderers (sub) (PL) (h) 1.3.1998

One of Europe's most cultured midfield creators, Moussa Saib should have enjoyed a long and successful career at Spurs. That he did not had nothing to do with his performances on the pitch, but everything to do with a manager who demanded nothing but total control. Saib had won the Algerian League and African Champions League with JS Kabylie in 1990 before joining Auxerre. Under the guidance of Guy Roux, a man known for spotting and developing talent, Saib became one of the continent's most wanted talents as he helped the unfashionable French club win the Coupe de France in 1994 and do the French "double" of Coupe de France and Lique 1 in 1996. Subject of serious interest from Arsène Wenger, Arsenal were not prepared to meet Auxerre's asking price so Saib was sold to Valencia. He only played in Spain for six months before joining Spurs. Gerry Francis had left a workmanlike squad that was never going to produce the type of football Spurs' fans demanded. Christian Gross knew a midfield general was needed and persuaded Alan Sugar to lay out £2.3 million on the Algerian captain. In his few games for Spurs, Saib showed glimpses of real quality. Tall and elegant, he floated over the ground, rapier-like long passes, mixed with more subtle, probing through balls. Injuries restricted his appearances and it was injury related problems that were to end his Spurs' career. Shortly after George Graham's arrival, the injured Saib reported for duty with Algeria so they could, as they were entitled to, check his injury situation. Graham took exception to Saib's actions and simply ostracised him. He totally froze Saib out, refusing to let him play for the reserves even. It was an appalling waste. After a loan spell with Hearts, Saib was allowed to join the Saudi Arabian club, El Nasr, on loan. He went straight into their team, one of the stars of the first FIFA World Club Championship held in Brazil. When eventually released by Spurs, Saib returned to France, helping Lorient lift the Coupe de France in 2002. Reaching the veteran stage he played in Dubai and helped JS Kabylie win the Algerian League in 2004, when, at 35 years of age, he was voted Algerian Player of the Year. Saib then began a short coaching career during which he led JS Kabylie to the Algerian title in 2008. Saib made 91 full international appearances for Algeria, nine of them during his time as a Spurs' player. His brother, Ramzy, played for JS Kabylie, Le Havre and Auxerre.

Appearances:
League: 3 (10) apps. 1 gl.
Others: 7 (1) apps. 2 gls.
Total: 10 (11) apps. 3 gls.

SAINSBURY, Robert

Role: Centre-forward 1940-42

CAREER: Wales Schools/Tottenham Juniors May 1939/(guest for Enfield during World War Two).

Debut v Chelsea (FLS) (h) 14.9.1940

Bobby Sainsbury moved up to London as a 14-year old to play in the Tottenham Juniors. A promising talent several clubs, including Arsenal and Wolverhampton Wanderers, were keen on signing him, but he was no doubt influenced by the fact his elder brother, Billy, was already with the Juniors. Called into the team in September 1940 he made his debut as emergency centre-forward in a Football League South game against Chelsea. The match lasted for two hours and fifty minutes because play had to be suspended after fifteen minutes due to an air raid warning and was not resumed until 80 minutes later. He made one other appearance, in a London War League game against Brighton and Hove Albion in October 1941.

Appearances:
Others: 2 apps.
Total: **2 apps. 0 gls.**

SAINSBURY, William H

Role: Half-back 1941-44

CAREER: Wales Schools/Tottenham Juniors/(guest for Enfield and Reading during World War Two).

Debut v Charlton Athletic (LWL) (h) 7.3.1942

A Welsh Schools international like Bobby, his younger brother, Billy Sainsbury had joined Tottenham Juniors prior to the Second World War and had made a couple of appearances in "A" team friendlies before war broke out. He was serving in the Army when he made his first appearance for the club in March 1942 in the London War League, but only played when Spurs were unable to field an experienced player. He played against Spurs on 17th October 1942; turning out for Reading when they were a man short.

Appearances:
Others: 5 apps. 1 gl.
Total: **5 apps. 1 gl.**

SAMWAYS, Vincent

Role: Midfield 1984-94
6ft.2ins. 11st.0lbs.
Born: Bethnal Green, East London, 27th October 1968

CAREER: East London Schools/London Schools/**SPURS** app. Apr 1985, pro. Nov 1985/Everton Aug 1994/(Wolverhampton Wanderers loan Dec 1995)/(Birmingham City loan Feb 1996)/Las Palmas (Spain) trial Oct 1996, perm. Dec 1996/Sevilla (Spain) Jul 2002/Cordoba (Spain) Jan 2003/Walsall loan Feb 2003, perm. Jul 2003-Feb 2004/Algeciras (Spain) Jul 2004/San Pedro (Spain) manager coach by Jul 2004/AFA Marbella Academy coach

Debut v Nottingham Forest (sub) (FL) (a) 2.5.1987
(Bristol Rovers (sub) (Fr) (a) 29.4.1985)

A creative midfield player, Vinny Samways followed in the steps of Glenn Hoddle, Mike Hazard and Ian Crook, winning England Youth caps before making his Football League debut in May 1987. The following season he suddenly found that with Hoddle gone, and Johnny Metgod plagued by continuous injury problems, he was expected to shoulder the responsible role of midfield playmaker. Although Spurs suffered a traumatic season with the departure of David Pleat, he more than justified the faith placed in his considerable ability, and looked a talented player who, given time, would establish himself as a first team regular and worthy successor to such gifted artists. However, time is a rare commodity in football and although Samways won the first of five Under-21 caps against Sweden in October 1988, he then suffered with several minor injury setbacks that curtailed his progress. In the meantime, Paul Gascoigne stepped in to claim the crown as midfield kingpin, and for much of the time Samways was left on the fringes of the

first team. He recovered a place in time for the 1991 FA Cup run, and gave one of his finest performances in the Final against Nottingham Forest after Gascoigne was badly injured in the opening 15 minutes. With Gascoigne's impending departure for Italy and his own maturity growing, Samways looked set to make the creative midfield role his own, but this did not prove to be the case. In the age of the more direct long ball game, too many midfield players were bypassed and simply left to chase, harass and close down the opposition. That was not Samways' forte. A compact, composed and skilful player, Samways tried to create chances with neat, simple passing, deft ball control and genuine guile. Sadly, something of a dying breed, he was a player in the best Tottenham traditions, but when he felt his special skills were not appreciated at Tottenham demanded a transfer. He moved to Everton, one of Mike Walker's first signings for the Merseysiders, but with Walker's departure was hardly given a chance to show his talents and became something of a forgotten man. Eventually he was given a cut-price transfer and moved to Spain with Las Palmas. His talents were appreciated there, though he was often regarded as something of a "hard-man" with his English style of tackling not appreciated by Spanish referees. Samways not only played football for East London and London Schools but also cricket.

Appearances:
League: 165 (28) apps. 11 gls.
FA Cup: 15 (1) app. 2 gls.
FL Cup: 27 (4) apps. 4 gls.
Euro: 6 (1) apps.
Others: 64 (13) apps. 12 gls.
Total: **277 (47) apps. 29 gls.**

SÁNCHEZ (DOMINGUEZ), Luis César

Role: Goalkeeper 2008-09
6ft.1ins. 13st.4lbs.
Born: Coria, Spain, 2nd September 1971

CAREER: Union Polideportiva Plasencia (Spain)/Real Valladolid (Spain) 1987/Real Madrid (Spain) Aug 1999/(Real Valladolid loan Aug 1999)/Real Zaragoza (Spain) Jun 2005/**SPURS** Aug 2008/Valencia (Spain) Jan 2009/Villarreal (Spain) Jun 2011/Valencia (Spain) asst. coach May-Sep 2016.

Debut v Liverpool (sub) (FLC) (h) 12.11.2008

After ten years as first choice number one with Rayo Vallecano, César Sánchez earned a move to Real Madrid where he was expected to provide back-up for the up-and-coming, Iker Casillas. With his vast experience it

was no surprise that he posed a real threat to the young 'keeper, even displacing him and appearing in the 2002 European Champions League defeat of Bayer Leverkusen. With Casillas the long-term future, Sanchez moved on to Real Zaragoza after six years. Well known to Juande Ramos, Spurs secured his free transfer in August 2008 with the veteran coming in as back-up to the newly-signed Heurelho Gomes. Regularly on the bench, Sanchez was to make only one appearance, replacing the injured Gomes in a Carling Cup-tie against Liverpool. With the signing of Carlo Cudicini in January 2009, Sanchez's contract was cancelled so he could join Valencia. Moving on to Villarreal, he became one of the few players to appear in the Spanish top flight at over 40, taking his total appearances in La Liga over the 400 mark. Sanchez won his only cap for Spain in August 2000, playing against Germany.

Appearances:
FL Cup: (1) app.
Total: (1) app. 0 gls.

SANDERS, Arthur William

Role: Centre-forward 1926-28
5ft.10ins. 11st.5lbs.
Born: Edmonton, London, 8th May 1901
Died: Winchmore Hill, London, 26th September 1983

CAREER: Raynham Road School/Latymer School/Edmonton Schools/(Guest for Rosario (Argentina) during World War One)/London University/Peterborough and Fletton United/Northfleet United 1924/**SPURS** am. cs. 1925, pro. May 1927/Northfleet United 1928/Clapton Orient Jun 1929/retired May 1933.

Debut v Bury (FL) (h) 19.2.1927

Captain of Latymer School and Edmonton Schoolboys, Arthur Sanders played for London University whilst training to become a teacher. First associated with Spurs after the First World War, he played for Peterborough and Fletton United and helped them win the Southern League in 1924 before going down to the Northfleet nursery in Kent for a season. He moved up to White Hart Lane in 1925, but only signed as an amateur, preferring to concentrate on a career as an Edmonton schoolmaster. He did not make his debut until February 1927. With seven goals in twelve games, he so impressed, that Spurs persuaded him to sign professional at the end of the season. Sanders continued to work as a teacher and played, and scored, regularly for the reserves, but strangely, made only one more League appearance. That was despite the fact Spurs were doing badly and indeed, were relegated at the end of 1927-28. The following season Sanders returned to Northfleet. On his release by Spurs he joined Clapton Orient where he played for four years, latterly at half-back, before retiring. He went back to teaching in Edmonton, where he became head of Raglan School. During the First World War Sanders served in the Royal Navy and when his ship docked in Argentina he played for the ship's team against the Rosario club. They were so impressed that he played a few games for them before sailing home.

Appearances:
League: 13 apps. 7 gls.
Total: 13 apps. 7 gls.

SANDRO, Ranieri Guimaraes Cordeiro

Role: Midfielder 2010-15
5ft.8ins. 13st.1lbs.
Born: Riachinho, Minas Gerhais, Brazil, 15th March 1989

CAREER: SC Internacional (Brazil) pro. 2007/**SPURS** Jul 2010/Queens Park Rangers Sep 2014/(West Bromwich Albion loan Jan 2016)/Antalyaspor (Turkey) Jan 2017.

Debut v Arsenal (FLC) (h) 21.9.2010

Brazilian footballers are all expected to possess exuberant skills and play Samba football. Many of them can, but no matter how talented they are, they cannot perform without players around them who are prepared to do the dirty work, to get stuck in, win the challenges and pass the ball to their more gifted colleagues. Sandro is one of that latter breed, a midfield workhorse. Spurs had their sights set on Sandro soon after he moved up from the Internacional academy to the professional staff. He quickly established himself in the Porto Alegre club's midfield, playing for Brazil at Under-20 level and attracting admiring glances form other European clubs. It took several attempts and a co-operation agreement between the clubs before Spurs were able to persuade Internacional to agree to sell Sandro. Even then, the deal was announced in March 2010, but would not be completed until Internacional's Copa Libertadores campaign had concluded. As they went all the way to, and won, the final, it was not until August 2010 that Sandro arrived at White Hart Lane. With his aggressive English style, determination and work ethic, Sandro soon endeared himself to the Spurs' crowd, becoming something of a cult figure. Injuries often left him side-lined and he was rarely sure of a starting place, but Spurs seemed better with him in the team, more solid, less likely to be overrun. Following Tim Sherwood's decision to promote Nabil Bentaleb, similar in style to Sandro, but somewhat more creative, from the Development squad, Sandro found himself pushed down the pecking order. He moved to Queens Park Rangers, but further injuries restricted his appearances and even put his work permit in jeopardy. With Rangers making little impression on the promotion race, Sandro was loaned to West Bromwich Albion. Sandro was a member of the Brazilian Under-23 team that won silver in the 2012 London Olympics. He won his first full cap for Brazil against Chile in September 2009, the only cap he had when he joined Spurs. By the time he left, he had added 16 more to his collection.

Appearances:
League: 60 (21) apps. 3 gls.
FA Cup: 2 (1) apps.
FL Cup: 3 apps.
Euro: 17 (2) apps.
Others: 1 (3) apps.
Total: 83 (27) apps. 3 gls.

SANDS

Role: Inside-forward 1900-01

Debut v Portsmouth (WL) (a) 17.4.1901

Another of the several local juniors who only made the first team as Spurs prepared for the 1901 FA Cup Final, Sands' one appearance came in April 1901 when he played in a Western League match at Portsmouth.

Appearances:
Others: 1 app.
Total: **1 app. 0 gls.**

SARGENT, Frederick Albert

Role: Outside-right 1934-46
5ft.8ins. 10st.8lbs.
Born: Islington, London, 7th March 1912
Died: New Barnet, Hertfordshire, 22nd August 1948

CAREER: Brecknock School/Islington Schools/Barnsbury 1932/Tufnell Park/**SPURS** am. Feb 1934/(Northfleet United 1934)/**SPURS** pro. Aug 1934/(guest for Aldershot, Burnley, Chelmsford City, Dundee United, Fulham, Hull City, Middlesbrough, Plymouth Argyle and York City during World War Two)/Chelmsford City May 1946.

Debut v Derby County (FL) (a) 29.9.1934

Having played in junior football for Barnsbury in the Islington Junior League, Fred Sargent was turning out for Tufnell Park when Spurs spotted his potential. He was sent along to Northfleet for three months to develop. Shortly after joining the White Hart Lane staff he made his League debut, but then went back to the reserves to continue his football education. Midway through the 1935-36 season he replaced John McCormick, but 1936-37 saw him once more back in the reserves. When McCormick was injured again in September 1937, Sargent took over and made the outside-right berth his own. A fine, attacking winger who loved to take on his full-back and beat him for pace, Sargent also scored his fair share of goals. Unfortunately, the Second World War badly disrupted his career. Not always available for selection, he broke his leg at Chelsea in February 1940 and in football terms generally had a poor time. With the end of the war he returned to Spurs, but his contract was cancelled by mutual consent in May 1946 and he joined former team-mate Arthur Rowe at Chelmsford City. Sadly, Sargent was to play for only two years before his untimely death. Spurs sent a full strength first eleven to Chelmsford to play a match in his memory a month later.

Appearances:
League: 96 apps. 25 gls.
FA Cup: 16 apps. 8 gls.
Others: 31 apps. 5 gls.
Total: **143 apps. 38 gls.**

SAUL, Frank Landen

Role: Forward 1959-68
5ft.10ins. 11st.12lbs.
Born: Canvey Island, Essex, 23rd August 1943

CAREER: **SPURS** am. Aug 1958, pro. Aug 1960/Southampton Jan 1968/Queens Park Rangers May 1970/ Millwall Mar 1972/Dagenham Mar 1976.

Debut v Bolton Wanderers (FL) (a) 7.9.1960
(Reading (Fr) (a) 21.10.1959)

Frank Saul was something of a "Boy Wonder", playing in the reserves when only 15 and making his League debut when just turned 17. An England Youth international, he scored three goals in six matches in the "Double" season as stand-in for Bobby Smith, but never quite lived up to his early promise. Whilst versatile and able to play on either wing as well as at centre-forward, he was just not consistent enough and failed to grasp the chance of claiming a permanent place in the team as his own following Smith's transfer in 1964. This resulted in the signing of Alan Gilzean, which simply provided Saul with even more competition up front. His best year was 1965-66 when he stood in for hepatitis victim Jimmy Greaves and finished the season playing for Young England against England in the annual eve of Cup Final match. The undoubted high point of his Spurs career came in 1966-67. He scored the winning goals in both the FA Cup semi-final against Nottingham Forest and the Final itself against Chelsea. A hard-grafting player who always gave everything in the Spurs cause, he eventually moved to Southampton as a £45,000 slice of the record £125,000 deal that saw Martin Chivers join Spurs. Two years at the Dell and two with Queens Park Rangers were followed by five at Millwall where he finished his senior career. He later ran a building and decorating concern in Billericay, Essex, and a fashion and knitwear business in London's East End.

Appearances:
League: 112 (4) apps. 37 gls.
FA Cup: 7 apps. 6 gls.
FL Cup: 1 apps.
Euro: 5 apps. 2 gls.
Others: 33 (6) apps. 15 gls.
Total: **158 (10) apps. 60 gls.**

SAUNDERS, Wilfred William

Role: Goalkeeper 1940-41
5ft.11ins. 12st.2lbs.
Born: Grimsbury, nr Banbury, Oxfordshire, 24 April 1916
Died: 1981

CAREER: Banbury and Middleton Cheney Schools/Banbury Spencer/West Bromwich Albion am. Mar 1938, pro. May 1938/(guest for Clapton Orient, Luton Town, Northampton Town, **SPURS** and Watford during World War Two)Banbury Spencer May 1946/retired 1950.

Debut v Luton Town (FLS) (a) 2.11.1940

A guest player from West Bromwich Albion introduced to Spurs by his RAF colleague Vic Buckingham, Wilf Saunders played three matches for Spurs in the Football League South during November 1940. He had joined West Bromwich Albion in 1938, but by the time War broke out had played only two League games. His best years were undoubtedly lost to the War and in the summer of 1946 he returned to Banbury Spencer.

Appearances:
Others: 3 apps
Total: 3 apps. 0 gls.

SAUNDERS

Role: Inside-forward 1917-18

CAREER: Brentford/(guest for SPURS during World War One).

Debut v Brentford (LFC) (a) 5.1.1918

A Brentford youngster, Saunders made his only appearance for Spurs in January 1918 in a London Football Combination match at Brentford when he was called into the Spurs' team to make up the numbers. He played at inside-left with his fellow Brentford junior, Bird outside him.

Appearances:
Others: 1 app.
Total: 1 app. 0 gls.

SCALES, John Robert

Role: Defender 1996-2000
6ft.2ins. 13st.6lbs.
Born: Harrogate, Yorkshire, 4th July 1966

CAREER: Rossett High School/Leeds United app. Jul 1982, pro Aug 1984/Bristol Rovers Jul 1985/Wimbledon Jul 1987/Liverpool Sep 1994/SPURS Dec 1996/Ipswich Town Jul 2000-May 2001/England Pro-Beach Soccer player-manager by Jun 2003/Brighton Electricity Nov 2003.

Debut v Sheffield Wednesday (sub) (PL) (h) 21.12.1996

Having failed to make the breakthrough at Leeds United, John Scales went to Bristol Rovers to get his football career underway. After two years, he followed manager Bobby Gould to Wimbledon, becoming a member of the "Crazy Gang" and appearing as a substitute in the 1988 FA Cup Final. In seven years with Wimbledon Scales developed into a strong, commanding central defender, cool and competent, with a fair amount of skill for a player at a club that built its name on aggression. With over 200 games for Wimbledon to his credit, Scales moved to Liverpool, where he won two England "B" and three full caps and picked up the 1995 Coca Cola Cup. With an abundance of competent central defenders, Liverpool let Scales move to White Hart Lane when Gerry Francis, who had played with Scales at Bristol Rovers, made an offer of over £2 million for his transfer. Scales was to spend nearly four years with Spurs, but rarely had any sort of a run in the team. There were times when he looked an accomplished defender who could prove a valuable acquisition, but all too often he was out injured. His Spurs' career totally ravaged by injuries, he was released and joined Ipswich Town. He made only two appearances in his year at Portman Road before succumbing to injury.

Appearances:
League: 29 (4) apps.
FA Cup: 4 app. 1 gl.
Others: 5 (3) apps.
Total: 38 (7) apps. 1 gl.

SCARTH, James William

Role: Winger 1949-52
5ft.8ins. 11st.12lbs.
Born: North Shields, County Durham, 26th August 1926
Died: Welwyn Garden City, Hertfordshire, 12th December 2000

CAREER: St Joseph's School/North Shields Schools/Percy Main/North Shields am./Percy Main/SPURS am. May 1948, trial Jul 1948, pro. Aug 1948/Gillingham Feb 1952/Gravesend & Northfleet Jul 1955/retired 1960/Brimsdown Veterans.

Debut v Brentford (FL) (h) 17.12.1949

Jimmy Scarth built a name for himself in the North East as a nippy little winger with Percy Main, representing the North East Amateurs. Invited down to Spurs for a trial, he impressed so much that he was immediately signed as a professional and within four months had made his League debut. At that time the great "Push and Run" team was at its peak with Les Medley and Sonny Walters integral parts of the team. Scarth was never able to threaten their positions, but for three seasons provided first class cover before moving to Gillingham. He played for the Kent club for five seasons as either a winger or centre-forward and wrote his name into the record books on 1st November 1952, when he scored a hat-trick against Clapton Orient in three minutes! His son, Bobby, who was deaf and dumb, joined Spurs' junior staff in the early 1970s, but did not make the grade and later had a spell at Gillingham.

Appearances:
League: 7 apps. 3 gls.
Others: 5 apps. 4 gls.
Total: 12 apps. 7 gls.

SCOTT, Joseph W

Role: Outside-left 1928-31
5ft.7ins. 10st.6lbs.
Born: Lye, Worcestershire, 6th July 1900
Died: Wollescote, Worcestershire, 11th March 1962

CAREER: Cradley Heath/Rotherham County Jun 1923/Barnsley Mar 1928/SPURS Jun 1928/Cradley Heath Jul 1931.

Debut v Wolverhampton Wanderers (FL) (h) 8.9.1928 (scored once)

Joe Scott started his senior football career with Rotherham County, a direct winger always likely to score a goal or two. In the 1927-28 season, he had netted 21 goals in 36 outings by March and was transferred to Barnsley where he only played for two months before joining Spurs.

Although he made his Spurs' debut early the following season, he was unable to displace Jimmy Dimmock. Whilst a regular scorer in the reserves, he played few first team games before moving back to Birmingham League champions Cradley Heath, once Spurs had decided to dispense with his services.

Appearances:
League: 18 apps. 4 gls.
Others: 3 apps. 2 gls.
Total: **21 apps. 6 gls.**

SCOTT, Kevin Watson

Role: Central defender 1993-97
6ft.4ins. 14st.3lbs.
Born: Easington, County Durham, 17th December 1966

CAREER: South Hetton Junior School/Hetton Comprehensive School/Easington Juniors/Eppleton Colliery Welfare/Middlesbrough trainee Jun 1983/Leicester City trial/Durham City/Sherburn 1984/Newcastle United trainee, pro. Dec 1984/**SPURS** Feb 1994/(Port Vale loan Jan 1995)/(Charlton Athletic loan Dec 1996)/Norwich City loan Jan 1997, perm Feb 1997-May 1999/(Darlington loan Jan 1999)/Guisborough Town 1999/Crook Town Sep 2001/Middlesbrough academy coach 2005

Debut v Sheffield Wednesday (FL) (h) 5.2.1994 (scored once)

Discarded by Middlesbrough after a year as a trainee, Kevin Scott was playing non-League football in his native North-east when Newcastle United offered him a second chance in the professional game. It was an offer that worked out well for both sides. Scott was a big, powerful lad who quickly progressed to the Magpies' senior eleven, captaining the club under Ossie Ardiles' management. A true battler, Scott was not the cultured style of central defender Ardiles' replacement, Kevin Keegan, craved and when Keegan began to build a title-challenging team in his image, Scott was on the outside. As Spurs struggled against the threat of relegation in his first season as manager at White Hart Lane, Ardiles recognised the value of Scott's qualities and persuaded the Spurs' hierarchy to invest in them. Although Scott had his limitations, the £850,000 fee was repaid with relegation avoided, but before Scott could consolidate his position Ardiles was replaced by Garry Francis. Out of favour under Francis, Scott was loaned out to Port Vale before being afflicted by a series of knee injuries. With first team opportunities limited, he moved to Norwich City and for a while looked as if he might get back to his old form, but persistent knee problems forced him to give up the game at top level.

Appearances:
League: 16 (2) apps. 1 gl.
FL Cup: (1) app.
Others: 4 (7) apps. 1 gl.
Total: **20 (10) apps. 2 gls.**

SCOTT, W J

Role: Full-back 1896-97

CAREER: Guildford/Brighton Athletic/**SPURS** Oct 1896.

Debut v Royal Scots Greys (Fr) (h) 8.10.1896

An amateur with Brighton Athletic back in the 1890s, Scott made three first team appearances for Spurs in friendlies during the 1896-97 season. A metal worker by trade although he may not have made a very big impact on the playing side at Spurs he did have a part in one of the most famous sights at Spurs. He was one of the makers of the cockerel that adorned the West Stand from 1909 to 1958 and now resides in the main entrance of the new Lilywhite House, while a replica has surveyed the ground from its position on the East Stand.

Appearances:
Others: 3 apps
Total: **3 apps. 0 gls.**

SEDGLEY, Stephen Philip

Role: Midfield or defender 1989-94
6ft.1ins. 13st.3lbs.
Born: Enfield, Middlesex, 26th May 1968

CAREER: Cheshunt Youth/Coventry City YTS. pro. Jun 1986/**SPURS** Jul 1989/Ipswich Town Jun 1994/Wolverhampton Wanderers Jul 1997-Dec 2000/Kingstonian coach Apr 2001, manager Oct 2001-Dec 2002/Crystal Palace Academy coach/Luton Town youth team coach Oct 2005-Jul 2007.

Debut v Luton Town (FL) (h) 19.8.1989
(Bohemians (Fr) (a) 23.7.1989)

Steve Sedgley really is a prime example of Spurs missing out on a young talent they could have secured for nothing, but subsequently had to pay a big fee to sign. A Spurs fan as a boy, he trained at the club in his schoolboy days and even appeared in the junior team. However, he was not offered a chance with Spurs and joined Coventry City, where he served his apprenticeship before signing professional. He made his League debut against Arsenal in August 1986 and soon settled in as a central defender or defensive midfielder. A substitute when Coventry beat Spurs in the 1987 FA Cup Final, he collected his first Under-21 cap for England against the Soviet Union in June 1987, and by the time of his transfer to Spurs for £750,000 had ten such caps to his credit. Signed to provide the defensive stability in midfield that would allow Paul Gascoigne and Vinny Samways to concentrate on unlocking opposing defences, he won his first international honour as a Spurs player in September 1989, playing for the Under-21s against Sweden. While he was settling well to his midfield task, the defence began to leak goals and he was switched to the centre of defence. Alongside Gary Mabbutt, he provided not only a more solid core to the team, but one that was made up of players equally happy to operate in midfield and able to play constructive football from deep in their own half, a quality perfectly illustrated in the 1991 FA Cup Final. With the arrival of Ossie Ardiles as manager, Sedgley's position was thought to be under threat when Colin Calderwood, the type of ball-playing central defender Ardiles liked, was signed, but Sedgley showed his versatility, playing in midfield or the centre of defence as necessary. Ever-present in Ardiles' first season, it was therefore something of a surprise when Sedgley was allowed to move to Ipswich Town for £1 million, later joining Wolverhampton Wanderers. A long term knee injury led to his contract being cancelled in December 2000 and he moved

into coaching at non-League level before moving on to Luton Town. Sedgley's father, Gordon, was an amateur on Spurs' books who went on to play for Wealdstone and Enfield, helping Wealdstone to the Amateur Cup Final in 1966 before going one step further with Enfield a year later.

Appearances:
League: 147 (17) apps. 9 gls.
FA Cup: 12 (1) app. 1 gl.
FL Cup: 24 (3) apps. 1 gl.
Euro: 4 (3) apps.
Others: 53 (5) apps. 3 gls.
Total: 240 (29) apps. 14 gls.

SEEBURG, Max Paul

Role: Forward 1907-09
5ft.6ins. 11st.7lbs.
Born: Leipzig, Germany, 19th September 1884
Died: Thatcham, Berkshire, 24th January 1972

CAREER: Coleraine Park by Sep 1900/Tottenham Phoenix /Park Aug 1903/Cheshunt by 1904/Chelsea 1906/**SPURS** May 1907/Leyton Oct 1908/ Burnley Jun 1910/Grimsby Town Jun 1911/Reading May 1912/retired cs. 1913/Reading Feb 1914.

Debut v Queens Park Rangers (SL) (h) 14.9.1907 (Royale Union Saint-Gilloise) (Fr) (Ostend) 19.5.1907 (scored three))

Although born in Germany, Max Seeburg was bought up in the Tottenham area and played for the local clubs Coleraine Park, Park-who had been around when Spurs were founded-and Cheshunt before joining his first senior club, Chelsea. He failed to make the League team at Stamford Bridge and moved to Spurs, making his debut during the trip to Belgium in May 1907. Principally regarded as a centre-forward, he started with Spurs at inside-left, reverting to centre-forward when Vivian Woodward was unable to play. In his first season he scored eight goals in 26 games, but although re-signed for the following season when Spurs made their debut in the Football League, he played only one game before moving back into the Southern League with Leyton. He later had a season and a half with Burnley, playing as a winger, half-back and centre-forward, and then a year with both Grimsby Town and Reading before retiring to run a public house in Reading. He re-signed for Reading in February 1914, but that was short-lived as he was interned early in the First World War because of his German origins. When released he was too old to continue playing. In January 1920 Seeburg became a naturalised British citizen. He later developed his trade as a carpenter.

Appearances:
Southern: 15 apps. 5 gls.
League: 1 app.
Others: 13 apps. 6 gls.
Total: 29 apps. 11 gls.

SEED, James Marshall

Role: Inside-forward 1919-27
5ft.10ins. 11st.9lbs.
Born: Blackhill, Co Durham, 25th March 1895
Died: Farnborough, Kent, 16th July 1966

CAREER: Whitburn/Sunderland Apr 1914/Mid-Rhondda Jul 1919/ **SPURS** Feb 1920/Sheffield Wednesday Aug 1927/Clapton Orient manager Apr 1931/Charlton Athletic manager May 1933-Sep 1956/Bristol City adviser Jan 1957, caretaker-manager Jan 1958/Millwall manager Jan 1958–Jul 1959, consultant, director Jan 1960-Jul 1966.

Debut v Wolverhampton Wanderers (FL) (a) 5.4.1920

Jimmy Seed was working down the pits and playing in his spare time for Whitburn in the Wearside League when invited for a trial with Sunderland. They had heard of the 80 plus goals he scored in the 1913-14 season. He quickly signed for Sunderland, but the outbreak of war saw him serving in the Army and he was limited to playing service football. After the war he returned to the North East, but the Roker club felt it doubtful he could fully recover from the effects of a slight gas attack suffered on active service. He was apparently on the football scrapheap at just 24, Fortunately, Hadyn Price, the former Welsh international who had played a few games for Spurs during the war, invited Seed to play for Mid-Rhondda. He soon showed the gas had left no ill effects. Still registered on Sunderland's books, he nursed hopes of eventually getting back into League football and was able to negotiate a free transfer. At about the same time Spurs' manager Peter McWilliam was watching Ton Pentre's inside-forward "Darkie" Lowdell, by chance in a match against Mid-Rhondda. It was Seed who really caught McWilliam's attention and his was the transfer Spurs quickly secured. In his seven months with the Welsh club Seed had set them on the way to winning the Second Division of the Southern League, the Welsh League and the Welsh Cup. At White Hart Lane he soon settled to become one of Spurs' most important and influential players of the 1920's. A fine, intelligent tactician and accurate passer, he struck up an immediate rapport with Fanny Walden, always looking for the telling pass to link in others or get the little winger heading for the goal-line. A crisp shot made Seed a regular scorer too, and it was he who really masterminded the FA Cup success of 1921. He was rewarded with a first England cap against Belgium in May 1921. Seed won four more in his time with Spurs, but late in 1926 suffered a bad ankle injury that gave Taffy O'Callaghan a chance in the first team. When fit again, Seed was unable to regain his place. At the start of the next season, manager Billy Minter made it clear he was looking to build a Spurs team around O'Callaghan's creativity and, astonishingly, Seed was allowed to move to Sheffield Wednesday. "Darkie" Lowdell, at last, joined Spurs in part-exchange. Alongside the departure of Pat Jennings to Arsenal, the premature sale of Seed must rank as quite the worst transfer decision ever made by Spurs. Towards the end of the season Spurs stood a comfortable seventh in the First Division with Wednesday rock bottom needing 16 points from ten games to stay up. Seed was made captain and inspired the Sheffield club to pick up 17 points, four at the expense of Spurs who slumped miserably and finished the season relegated! Under Seed's guidance Wednesday then went on to win and retain the League title in the next two seasons, while Spurs struggled to get out of the Second Division. A member of the 1929 FA touring party to South Africa, Seed retired at the end of 1930-31 and, at the invitation of Herbert Chapman, moved into management with Clapton Orient. Chapman had plans to turn Orient into Arsenal's nursery club, but the scheme was scuppered by the Football League, and Seed had to struggle through two seasons before resigning to take over at Charlton Athletic. He stayed at the Valley until September 1956, steering Charlton from the Third Division (South) to the First Division in successive seasons from 1934 to 1936 and then to the FA Cup Final in 1946 and 1947, winning the trophy on the second occasion. After leaving Charlton he advised Bristol City, and was briefly caretaker manager, before becoming boss of Millwall. He later worked as a consultant until invited to join the board. Such was his service to Charlton that when they returned to the rebuilt Valley one of the stands was named after him. His brother, Angus, played for Workington in their pre-League days and was later manager of Aldershot and Barnsley.

Appearances:
League: 230 apps. 65 gls.
FA Cup: 25 apps. 12 gls.
Others: 31 apps. 8 gls.
Total: 286 apps. 85 gls.

SEGERS, Johannes Cornelius Antonius

Role: Goalkeeper 1998-2000
5ft.11ins. 12st.10lbs.
Born: Eindhoven. Holland, 30th October 1961

CAREER: PSV Eindhoven (Holland) trainee Nov 1977, pro. Oct 1978/Nottingham Forest Aug 1984/(Stoke City loan Feb 1987)/(Sheffield United loan Nov 1987)/(Dunfermline loan Mar 1988)/Wimbledon Sep 1988/Wolverhampton Wanderers non-contract Aug 1996/Woking Feb-Mar 1997/Wolverhampton Wanderers Sep 1997/**SPURS** player-goalkeeping coach Jul 1998, goalkeeping coach May 2000-Oct 2007/PSV Eindhoven (Holland) goalkeeping coach Mar 2008/Fulham goalkeeping coach Jun 2011-Apr 2014/RKC Waalwijk (Holland) goalkeeping coach Jul 2014/FC Eindhoven (Holland) goalkeeping coach Sep 2014.

Debut v Southampton (PL) (A) 19.9.1998
(De Tubanters (sub) (Fr) (a) 5.8.1998)

After three years as a bit-part performer with his home-town club PSV Eindhoven, Hans Segers was signed by Nottingham Forest, but never really established himself as number one choice before moving on to Wimbledon. For eight years he was almost ever-present at Plough Lane as the unfashionable club, against all the odds, maintained a Premier League place. Solid, dependable and consistent, he would probably have served Wimbledon even longer were it not for being involved in matching fixing allegations. Together with former Wimbledon team-mate, John Fashanu, and former Liverpool goalkeeper, Bruce Grobbelaar, Segers was accused of conspiracy to corrupt. Pending the trial, he signed for Wolverhampton Wanderers on non-contract terms. He did not play for them but, as the trial was coming to an end, turned out for Woking. With the jury unable to reach verdicts, Segers' career remained in limbo and it was only after a second jury had acquitted him of the charges that he was able to play for Wolves. After a year with Wolves, Segers joined Spurs as goalkeeping coach and back-up to Ian Walker and Espen Baardsen. He was not expected to make any senior appearances, but with both regular 'keepers injured, he was called upon for two matches in late September 1998. He remained on the playing staff for two years, then concentrated on his coaching duties until dismissed along with Martin Jol. After a spell back with PSV, Segers linked up with Jol again at Fulham, remaining in his post even after Jol had departed. He then returned to Holland with RKC Waalwijk, quickly moving on to Eindhoven's other club, FC Eindhoven.

Appearances:
League: 1 app.
FL Cup: 1 app.
Others: 1 (1) apps.
Total: 3 (1) apps. 0 gls.

SHACKLETON, John

Role: Winger 1905-06
5ft.10ins. 11st.10lbs.
Born: Keighley, Yorkshire, 1884

CAREER: St Augustine's/Darlington/**SPURS** Apr 1905/Bury Apr 1906/Huddersfield Town Aug 1908.

Debut v Bristol Rovers (WL) (h) 25.9.1905

John Shackleton was signed from Darlington and arrived as a 22-year-old with the reputation of "being the best forward in the Northern League last season". His debut came early in 1905-06 in a Western League fixture, but he did not live up to his star billing and played only nine senior matches before being released in April 1906. He joined Bury where he played for one season, then moved to Huddersfield Town and appeared in the first few matches of their existence before dropping off the scene altogether.

Appearances:
Southern: 3 apps. 1 gl.
Others: 6 apps.
Total: 9 apps. 1 gl.

SHARP, Buchanan

Role: Inside-forward 1922-25
5ft.11ins. 12st.2lbs.
Born: Alexandria, Dumbartonshire, 2nd November 1894
Died: Bolton, Lancashire, 11th January 1956

CAREER: Clydebank Juniors/Vale of Leven 1912/Chelsea Nov 1919/**SPURS** Mar 1923/Leicester City Jan 1925/Nelson Jun 1926, player-manager Mar 1928/Southport Oct 1928.

Debut v Sunderland (FL) (a) 31.3.1923

Buchanan Sharp was a traditional, close-dribbling Scottish inside-forward. On joining Chelsea, he took some time to settle into English football, but was just doing so and starting to score goals when Spurs moved to sign him. He made his Spurs' debut immediately, but proved a great disappointment. He played only two more League matches in two years, before moving to Leicester City as cover for their Scottish international Johnny Duncan. He later played for Nelson where he hit 21 goals in his first season and had a short spell as player-manager, then finished his career at Southport

Appearances:
League: 3 apps.
Others: 2 apps. 1 gl.
Total: 5 apps. 1 gl.

SHARPE, Frederick Charles

Role: Half-back 1958-59
5ft.9ins. 11st.6lbs.

Born: Greenwich, London, 11th March 1937

CAREER: Stanley Street School/London Boys/Tottenham Juniors/**SPURS** am. Jun 1954, pro. May 1956/Norwich City Jul 1963/Reading Jul 1969-Jun 1971/Berks and Bucks Schools coach.

Debut v Nottingham Forest (FL) (h) 17.9.1958 (scored once)

In nine years with Spurs, Fred Sharpe made only two League appearances, both in the 1958-59 season. The first was as deputy for Danny Blanchflower, when Sharpe scored the only goal of the game against Nottingham Forest, and the second five months later when he stood-in for Dave Mackay. With two of the most famous half-backs in Spurs' history ahead of him and the club about to embark on the greatest period in its existence, it is not surprising Sharpe did not manage to make the first team again before moving to Norwich City. He played over 100 League matches for the Canaries and finished his senior career with two years at Reading. Fred was then offered a coaching job back at Carrow Road by Ron Saunders, but declined and for six years coached schools in High Wycombe and Bracknell and Finchampstead's Under-12s. He was later a salesman in the food business and ran a car valeting business.

Appearances:
League: 2 apps. 1 gl.
Total: 2 apps. 1 gl.

SHAW, W Burt

Role: Outside-right 1893-95

Debut v 3rd Batt. Grenadier Guards (MSC) (h) 13.1.1894

Another of the amateur players from the 1890s who played most of their games for the club at reserve level, Burt Shaw made his first team debut in January 1894 in a Middlesex Senior Cup tie. He played at centre-forward in that match and was described by a local reporter as "absolutely useless", which might go some way to explaining why all his other senior appearances were made at outside-right. He progressed no further in his football career than his few games with Spurs and later ran a hotel in Ramsgate. His brother, H J, also played for Spurs but only at reserve level.

Appearances:
Others: 6 apps. 2 gls.
Total: 6 apps. 2 gls.

SHEARING, William Kirk

Role: Outside-left 1893-94

Born: Melbourne, Australia, 1875

CAREER: Robin Hood/**SPURS** 1893/Avondale/Edmonton/Novocastrians/Broadwater/Old Tottonians/Park/Asplin Rovers Sep 1900/Tottenham Park.

Debut v 3rd Batt. Grenadier Guards (MSC) (h) 20.1.1894

A former member of the Robin Hood club, Shearing first joined Spurs for the 1893-94 season during which he also played for another local club, Avondale. His only first team appearance was in January 1894 when he played in a Middlesex Senior Cup tie with the 3rd Battalion of the Grenadier Guards. In demand with all the local junior clubs, he played for most of them over the next few years although he continued to turn out for Spurs reserves whenever his services were needed. Even though he was never seriously considered first team material, he was still turning out for Spurs in September 1903. His brother, Samuel D'urban, also played for Spurs, but not at first team level. The pair of them were partners in the Stock Exchange jobbers of Shearing Brothers.

Appearances:
Others: 1 app.
Total: 1 app. 0 gls.

SHEPHERD, W John

Role: Half-back 1891-97

CAREER: Irmac/Robin Hood/Shaftesbury Rovers 1893/**SPURS**/Millwall Athletic cs. 1894/Rochdale Rovers Apr 1895/London Welsh 1895/West Green Athletic Sep 1898/Cheshunt by Feb 1899.

Debut v West Herts (FAC) (h) 13.10.1894
(Forest Swifts (Fr) (h) 12.12.1891)

A local lad and a member of the Robin Hood club, Jack Shepherd's first recorded appearance for Spurs was in December 1891. He was one of a ten-man Spurs team that was drawing a friendly match with Forest Swifts 1-1, when the game was abandoned after an hour due to bad light. For the 1893-94 season he initially agreed to play for Shaftesbury Rovers, another local club, but by the end of September 1893 was back playing for Spurs and proving to be one of the most regular performers. The following season he decided to play for Millwall Athletic, but although selected to represent London, he did not make Millwall's senior eleven. However, he still turned out for Spurs and played in all the season's FA Cup and Amateur Cup matches. At the end of that campaign Spurs wanted to retain his services, but he was not happy that they only wanted him for the reserve eleven and he signed for Rochdale Rovers, one of the area's junior clubs. He also played a few matches for the London Welsh, but still managed to play a few matches in Spurs' colours over the next two years. In September 1898 he signed for another junior team, West Green Athletic, and also turned out for Cheshunt, a member of their team that surprisingly knocked Casuals out of the Amateur Cup in February 1899.

Appearances:
FA Cup: 8 apps.
Others: 67 (1) apps. 2 gls.
Total: 75 (1) apps. 2 gls.

SHERINGHAM, Edward Paul MBE

Role: Striker 1992-97 and 2001-03
6ft. 12st.8lbs.
Born: Highams Park, 2nd April 1966

CAREER: Selwyn Primary School/Waltham Forest Schools/Discus/Beaumont/Sir George Monoux Senior High School/Leytonstone-Ilford/Millwall app. Jun 1982, pro. Jan 1984/(Aldershot loan Feb 1985)/(Djurgårdens (Sweden) loan Apr 1985)/England Youth/Nottingham Forest Jul 1991/**SPURS** Aug 1992/Manchester United Jul 1997/**SPURS** May 2001/Portsmouth Jul 2003/West Ham United Jul 2004/Colchester United Jul 2007-May 2008/West Ham United coach May 2014/Stevenage manager May 2015-Feb 2016.

Debut v Ipswich Town (PL) (a) 30.8.1992

If ever a player epitomised the changing nature of centre-forward play, that player was Teddy Sheringham. As a boy he trained with Spurs, Leyton Orient and Crystal Palace, but it was Millwall who gave him his chance in professional football. With Tony Cascarino providing the raw power and strength, and Sheringham the finesse, they led the line as Millwall won promotion to the top flight of English football for the first time in 1988. When Millwall cashed in on Cascarino's talents and Sheringham was hit by injury, Millwall struggled and were relegated.

Back in the Second Division and free from injury, Sheringham blossomed. The talents that made him top scorer in the Football League deserved the highest stage and that came when Brian Clough signed him for Nottingham Forest. Having played in the basic, long-ball Millwall style, Sheringham flourished in the more refined, short-passing game Clough insisted on. It was the same style Terry Venables wanted Spurs to play, so it was not surprising Venables cast envious glances in Forest's direction. What was surprising was Clough accepting Spurs' £2million offer for Sheringham' transfer. In five years at White Hart Lane, Sheringham proved himself one of the finest all-round strikers in the game. Perfectly built to lead the line, he was not a powerful striker, though he possessed enough strength to mix it with the toughest of defenders. He was a player of guile and subtlety. His greatest strengths were his speed of thought and ability to bring others into the game. For a man who thrived on scoring goals, he was remarkably unselfish, always content to pass up the chance of a shot if a team-mate was better placed. Whether playing alongside Gordon Durie, Nicky Barmby, Jürgen Klinsmann, Ronnie Rosenthal, Steffen Iversen, Les Ferdinand or Chris Armstrong, Sheringham was simply superb, adapting his style of play to suit that of his partner, making sure that as a pair they were more effective than two individuals could be. He performed a similar role with England. Although given his first cap by Graham Taylor in May 1993, he was far too sophisticated a player for the Taylor style of play, but just perfect for that of Taylor's successor, Venables. Trusted to play his own game, Sheringham formed the perfect partnership with Alan Shearer. While Sheringham was idolised by the fans and loved playing for Spurs, there was one thing missing-trophies. The nearest he got to silverware with Spurs was two FA Cup semi-finals in 1993 and 1995. When Manchester United sought Sheringham's transfer it was an opportunity no player of 31 could refuse. After one season the move might have appeared a mistake as United failed to collect a single trophy. They responded by signing Dwight Yorke to partner Andy Cole, leaving Sheringham to compete with Ole Gunnar Solskjær as back-up. It was a job he performed admirably. In May 1999 he helped United beat Spurs in the last League game of the season to win the Premier League. Six days later he left the bench to score the first goal as Newcastle United were defeated in the FA Cup final. Another four days on and United were a goal down to Bayern United as the Champions League final went into added time. A United corner was not properly cleared and Sheringham bagged an equaliser. Two minutes later he headed on another corner and Solskjær was there to grab the winner. If his thirst for silverware had not been sated by winning club football's top three trophies in less than two weeks, it should have been as United retained the Premier League for the next two seasons and Sheringham was voted both the PFA Player of the Year and the FWA Footballer of the Year in 2001. It might have been thought that at 35 and with the signing of Ruud van Nistelrooy, Sheringham would have been content to accept a bit part role at Old Trafford. If such thoughts ever entered his head, they disappeared when Glenn Hoddle asked him to return to Spurs. In two years, his performances would have had you believe he was ten years younger than he was. He took his total number of appearances for Spurs over the 300 mark, with a goal almost every other game. With the wholesale managerial and structural changes that followed the dismissal of Hoddle, Sheringham was not offered a new contract. If he thought it might have been a good time to retire, Harry Redknapp did not. He persuaded Sheringham to join Portsmouth for their first season in the Premier League. After playing in nearly every game and scoring ten goals, his services were not required. Next stop was Upton Park. A season in the Championship and West Ham were back in the Premier League. He played for another two years in the top flight, only beginning to slow down in the last year as he moved into his forties. Awarded the MBE for services to football in 2007, Sheringham finished his top flight career as both the oldest outfield player and oldest goal-scorer to appear in the Premier League. Even then he had not finished, playing for a year with Colchester United before finally retiring. After playing Poker for some years Sheringham returned to West Ham as a coach to the forwards. He remained at Upton Park for a year then took his first steps in management with Stevenage. For the first time in his life, he was not a success, sacked after nine months with Stevenage struggling at the wrong end of the Second Division table. Sheringham scored nine goals in 38 appearances for England as a Spurs player.

Appearances:
League: 230 (6) apps. 97 gls.
FA Cup: 21* apps. 14 gls.
FL Cup: 20 (1) apps. 13 gls.
Others: 30 (1) apps. 20 gls.
Total: 301 (8) apps. 144 gls.
*Includes 1 abandoned match

SHERWOOD, Timothy Alan

Role: Midfield 1998-03
6ft.1ins. 11st.4lbs.
Born: St Albans, Hertfordshire, 2nd February 1969

CAREER: Hertfordshire Schools/Forest United/Watford trainee May 1985, pro. Feb 1987/Norwich City Jul 1989/Blackburn Rovers Feb 1992/**SPURS** Feb 1999/Portsmouth Jan 2003-Jun 2004/Coventry City Jul 2004-Jul 2005/**SPURS** coach Nov 2008, Technical Co-Ordinator Apr 2010, acting head coach and head coach Dec 2013-May 2014/Aston Villa manager Feb-Oct 2015/Swindon Town Director of Football Nov 2016-Jun 2017.

Debut v Coventry City (sub) (PL) (h) 6.2.1999

Although Tim Sherwood had been on Norwich City's books as a schoolboy, when the chance came to make a career in the game he turned them down; preferring to accept an offer from his local club, Watford. He made his League debut in September 1987 and while he could do little to

save Watford from relegation in his first season, he played regularly as the Hornets sought an instant return to the top flight. Happy to play anywhere as he strove to establish himself, he appeared all across midfield, at full-back and in the centre of defence. Midfield appeared his favoured position and it was to play there that, of all clubs, Norwich City laid out £175,000 for his transfer. In near three years in Norfolk, Sherwood established himself at the heart of midfield, a 90-minute player with plenty of skill, not afraid to put his foot in. At Norwich he also showed that he was not afraid to speak his mind, a trait that was not always an attribute. When Kenny Dalglish was spending Jack Walker's millions in an effort to win the Football League, he identified Sherwood as the abrasive, midfield general he needed to captain the team. Sherwood moved to Ewood Park for £375,000, a fee that proved a bargain. In his first season, he led the team that made Walker's dream come true. Blackburn got seven years' tremendous service from Sherwood, 250 appearances and 25 goals. Even at the age of 30 Sherwood was a perfect player for a George Graham team, hard, commanding, experienced and not afraid of a little physicality. Almost £4 million was a lot of money but it seemed money well spent as Sherwood settled to give some fine performances, at last playing for England and collecting three caps. Just as Sherwood was a Graham type of player, so he was not a Glenn Hoddle type. He struggled to impress Hoddle, his willingness to publicly express his dissatisfaction doing him no favours. In January 2003 he was allowed to leave. He signed for Portsmouth and helped them secure the First Division title. On Boxing Day 2003 his leg was broken in a challenge with Mauricio Taricco. It finished his career with Portsmouth. Coventry City invested in his leadership skills, but constant injuries saw him play few games and he was released after a year. Harry Redknapp recruited Sherwood to Spurs' coaching staff in November 2008. He worked with the younger players in the youth teams and Development Squad. In December 2013 he was made head coach following the dismissal of André Villas-Boas, despite not having obtained his Uefa Pro Licence. While results improved under Sherwood's guidance as he placed trust in some of the younger players and re-integrated the difficult Emmanuel Adebayor, he courted controversy with his blunt comments. Such honesty was refreshing, but not appreciated by millionaire footballers not used to being told a few home truths. It was his refusal to change his style that saw him dismissed after only five months. Perhaps harshly treated by Spurs, Sherwood was nothing if not confident in his own ability. As Aston Villa struggled at the wrong end of the Premier League, he took over from Paul Lambert, led Villa to safety and to the FA Cup final. Unfortunately, Villa, with an owner who wanted to sell and would not invest in the club, was only going one way, and that was downhill. With the 2015-16 season barely three months old Sherwood was dismissed. It was some time be3fore he returned, taking on the Director of Football's role at Swindon Town.

Appearances:
League: 81 (12) apps. 12 gls.
FA Cup: 13 apps. 1 gl.
FL Cup: 6 (3) apps. 2 gls.
Euro: 3 apps. 1 gl.
Others: 14 (8) apps. 4 gls.
Total: 117 (23) apps. 20 gls.

SHILLINGWORTH, M

Role: Half-back 1891-92

Debut v Forest Swifts (Fr) (h) 12.12.1891

Shillingworth's only recorded appearance for Spurs was in December 1891, when he played in a friendly match with Forest Swifts. That match, in which Spurs fielded only ten men, was abandoned after 60 minutes due to bad light.

Appearances:
Others: 2 apps.
Total: 2 apps. 0 gls.

SIBLEY, Albert

Role: Outside-right 1941-42
5ft.10ins.
Born: Southend, Essex, 6th October 1919
Died: Southchurch, Essex, 20th February 2008

CAREER: Barking/Southend United Aug 1937/(guest for Aldershot, Arsenal, Chelsea, Crystal Palace, Fulham, Millwall, Queens Park Rangers and **SPURS** during World War Two)/Newcastle United Feb 1947/Southend United Jul 1950/retired May 1956.

Debut v Reading (LWL) (h) 10.1.1942

A young winger on the books of Southend United, Joe, as he was known, Sibley made three appearances for Spurs as a guest in the London War League during the 1941-42 season scoring once. Having guested for Arsenal early in the war, he spent most of the 1941-42 season assisting Fulham, but in January 1942 they agreed he could turn out for Spurs. After the war he returned to Southend where he remained until moving to Newcastle United. He made 31 League appearances for the Magpies, scoring six goals, before returning to Southend. In five years he took his total number of appearances for the Essex club over the 200 mark.

Appearances:
Others: 3 apps. 1 gl.
Total: 3 apps. 1 gl.

SIGURÐSSON, Gylfi Þór

Role: Midfielder Striker 2012-14
6ft.1ins. 12st. 10lbs.
Born: Reykjavik, Iceland, 8th September 1989

CAREER: Fimleikafélag Hafnarfjarðar (Iceland) 2002/Everton trial Jul 2002/Preston North End trial/Breiðablik (Iceland) Feb 2003/Reading Academy Scholar Oct 2005, pro. Jul 2007/(Shrewsbury Town loan Oct 2008)/(Crewe Alexandra loan Feb 2009)/TSG 1899 Hoffenheim (Germany) Aug 2010/(Swansea City loan Jan 2012)/**SPURS** Jul 2010/Swansea City Jul 2014.

Debut v Newcastle United (PL) (a) 18.8.2012
(Stevenage (Fr) (a) 18.7.2012)

An Icelandic youngster offered a Scholarship by a Championship club shows just how much the recruitment of football talent has become a world-wide business at every level of the game. Gylfi Sigurðsson had been marked out as a potential star from an early age. He made his debut for Reading in August 2008, gained some experience out on loan. He had established himself as a crucial component of the Reading midfield when Hoffenheim, the club from a village of 3,300 with a millionaire owner, who had come from nowhere to the Bundesliga made an offer Reading could not refuse. He started well in Germany, scoring regularly and was a firm fan's favourite. Unexpectedly he fell out of favour and was made available for transfer. Swansea City secured his services on loan. In half a season, he gave one exceptional performance after another. Operating just behind a central striker, he linked the midfield and attack, playing clever little passes through to his striker or out to the wing. He possessed a real eye for the opening and could finish with an accurately placed shot or a fierce volley. Swansea were keen to sign him to a permanent deal and reportedly had one in place until Brendan Rogers left to take over as manager of Liverpool. Spurs moved quickly and a near £10 million deal saw Sigurðsson as André Villas-Boas' first signing. There can be no doubt that Sigurðsson was a class act. Played behind the main striker, given the freedom to roam and sure of his place, he would have been a success at Spurs. Sadly that rarely happened. He was never certain of a place in a team that changed from one game to another. He was rarely used in his best position, required to play as a deep midfielder, even out wide and all too often a substitute given little time to influence events. After two years he returned to Swansea in a deal that saw Ben Davies and Michel Vorm move to Spurs. He immediately showed how much his two years at Spurs had been wasted. Sigurðsson made 15 appearances for Iceland in his time at White Hart Lane.

Appearances:
League: 26 (32) apps. 8 gls.
FA Cup: 2 apps.
FL Cup: 4 apps. 2 gls.
Euro: 12 (7) apps. 3 gls.
Others: 11 (2) apps. 3 gls.
Total: 55 (41) apps. 16 gls.

SILVA, Edson Rolando Silva Sousa

Role: Striker 2004-05
6ft.1ins. 11st. 10lbs.
Born: Sao Vicente, Cape Verde Islands, 9th March 1983

CAREER: Batoque (Portugal) am./Estoril (Portugal) am./Benfica (Portugal) 1999/FC Baden (Switzerland) 2000/PSV Eindhoven 2001/(Solothurn (Switzerland) loan 2001-02/(FC Luzern (Switzerland) loan 2002-04/**SPURS** trial Jul 2004, perm. Aug 2004/(Den Haag (Holland) loan Jan-Apr 2005)/Zamalek (Egypt) Jul 2005/CS Maritimo (Portugal) 2006/Estrela de Amadora (Portugal) trial Mar 2006, perm. Jul 2006/UT Arad (Rumania) trial and perm. Jan 2007/Turun Palloseura (Finland) trial Mar 2009)/Ceahlaul Piatra Neamt (Romania) Feb 2010/Falcões do Norte (Cape Verde) manager.

Debut v Nottingham Forest (sub) (Fr) (a) 31.7.2004

There cannot be many, if any, Cape Verdean footballers who have played competitively at the top level for English clubs. Edson Silva was not to be one. Having failed to make the grade in Portugal he was with FC Baden

in Switzerland when spotted by Frank Arnesen and taken on at PSV Eindhoven. In three years he played just one game for the Dutch club, spending most of his time on loan in Switzerland, and making little impression. Silva followed Arnesen to Spurs in the summer of July 2004 and played in three pre-season friendlies by way of a trial. He was surprisingly signed on and scored 6 goals in 14 Reserve League games before returning to Holland on loan to Den Haag. Released after a year, Silva then hawked his talents around Europe, having a modicum of success at UT Arad, but otherwise making no impression.

Appearances:
Others: 2 (1) apps.
Total: 2 (1) apps. 0 gls.

SIMMONDS

Role: Forward 1979

Debut v Bermuda Select XI (sub) (Fr) (a) 6.6.1979

Simmonds was the fourth Bermudian player to appear as a substitute for Spurs at the end of the club's 1979 tour. He replaced Colin Lee in a friendly against a Bermudian Select XI. Spurs were forced to field goalkeeper Milija Aleksic as an outfield player, physio Mike Varney and club secretary Peter Day, due to injuries and players having already returned home.

Appearances:
Others: (1) app.
Total: (1) app. 0 gls.

SIMMONDS, H

Role: Centre-forward 1893-95

CAREER: Tottenham College/Edmonton/Woolwich Arsenal/**SPURS** guest/Edmonton All Saints/City Ramblers.

Debut v 2nd Battalion Scots Guards (Fr) (h) 23.3.1894 (scored twice)

A former player with Tottenham College, Simmonds was captain of the Edmonton club and kingpin of the Edmonton district side when he played as a guest for Spurs. He played in three friendly matches in 1893-94, scoring twice on his debut, and in two friendlies the following season, by which time he was playing for the newly-formed Edmonton All Saints.

Appearances:
Others: 5 apps. 3 gls.
Total: 5 apps. 3 gls.

SIMONS, Henry Thomas

Role: Centre-forward 1918-19
5ft.8ins. 11st.4lbs.
Born: Hackney, London, 26th November 1887
Died: Stoke Newington, London, 26th August 1956

CAREER: Pell Institute Mar 1906/Clapton Orient Mar 1906/Leyton Sep 1906/Tufnell Park 1907/Middlesex County/Sheffield United Jul 1907/Shepherds Bush cs. 1908/Luton Town 1908-09/Doncaster Rovers Nov 1909/Sheffield United Jul 1910/Halifax Town Aug 1912/Merthyr Town

Nov 1912/Brentford Aug 1913/Fulham Apr 1914/Queens Park Rangers Nov 1914/(guest for **SPURS** during World War One)/Norwich City Sep 1920/Merthyr Town/Margate Nov 1920.

Debut v Fulham (LFC) (h) 2.11.1918

Tommy Simmons gained plenty of experience as a youngster in his native London, but it was when he joined Doncaster Rovers that his career began to make strides. A regular scorer in the Midland League, he was transferred to Sheffield United, but had few opportunities to show his prowess in two years at Bramall Lane. He moved quickly from Halifax Town to Merthyr Town before joining Brentford. He did well for the Bees with 19 goals in 25 Southern League appearances. That persuaded Fulham to secure his transfer at the end of the 1913-14 season. After only three months with Fulham he was transferred to Queens Park Rangers and played regularly for them during 1914-15 and the first season of war-time football. It is not clear where, or even whether, he played in the 1919-20 season, but he joined Norwich City in September 1920, perhaps knocking a few years off his age. He made four appearances in Spurs' colours during the 1918-19 season, three in London Football Combination games and the other in a friendly.

Appearances:
Others: 4 apps. 2 gls.
Total: **4 apps. 2 gls.**

SIMPSON, Harold

Role: Half-back 1888-93

CAREER: SPURS/Avondale by Nov 1893.

Debut v Windsor Phoenix (Fr) (a) 16.1.1889

Yet another of the pioneers of Spurs' history who was associated with the club for several years, Simpson made his first known appearance in January 1889 in a friendly with Windsor Phoenix. Apart from the fact that he continued to turn out for the club for the next four years and by November 1893 was captaining Avondale, nothing more is known about him.

Appearances:
Others: 16 apps.
Total: **16 apps. 0 gls.**

SIMPSON, Robert W

Role: Half-back 1894-95

CAREER: SPURS/London Caledonians by Mar 1895.

Debut v Old Harrovians (AmC) (h) 20.10.1894 (scored once)

Nothing has been discovered about Simpson who made one appearance for Spurs in the 1894-95 season. That was in October 1894 when he scored once in a 7-0 thrashing of Old Harrovians in a 1st Qualifying Round Amateur Cup tie. By March 1895 he was playing in goal for the London Caledonians.

Appearances:
Others: 1 app. 1 gl.
Total: **1 app. 1 gl.**

SINTON, Andrew

Role: Midfield/Winger 1995-99
5ft.8ins. 11st.10lbs.
Born: *Newcastle, Tyne and Wear, 19th March 1966*

CAREER: Cramlington Juniors/South Northumberland Schools/England Schools/Cambridge United app. Jun 1982, pro. Apr 1983/Brentford Dec 1985/Queens Park Rangers Mar 1989/Sheffield Wednesday Jul 1993/**SPURS** Jan 1996/Wolverhampton Wanderers Jul 1999-May 2002/Walsall training Jul 2002/Burton Albion Aug 2002/Bromsgrove Rovers Mar 2004/Fleet Town Football Development manager/player-coach Jul 2004, manager Jun 2005/AFC Telford United manager May 2010-Jan 2013.

Debut v Liverpool (PL) (a) 3.2.1996

Andy Sinton had worked his way through all levels of football by the time he arrived at White Hart Lane. A Geordie born and bred, he started his career at Cambridge United, making his debut as a 16-year old. He spent three years with Cambridge, years that saw them plummeting down the Football League. By the time they reached the lowest tier, Sinton had moved to Brentford. He spent three years with the Bees, a hard-working, consistent wide man, deserving of a bigger stage. He got that with a transfer to Queens Park Rangers. Under the management of Gerry Francis, Sinton flourished as a typical winger of the time, shuttling up and down the wing, getting back to help his full-back defend, racing forward on the break. The role demanded endless energy and a commitment to hard work, both attributes Sinton possessed. Rangers had some good times with Sinton providing many of the crosses on which Les Ferdinand thrived. A record £2.75 million offer persuaded Rangers to let Sinton, who had ten of the twelve England caps he was to win, move to Sheffield Wednesday. He played there for two-and-a-half years in Sheffield, doing a competent job, but not setting the world alike. When he joined Spurs it was a typical piece of Gerry Francis business, signing a player he knew well and in whom he had implicit faith. For a year Sinton performed well, his wing play setting up chances for Teddy Sheringham, Chris Armstrong and Steffen Iversen. When age and injuries began to take their toll the level of his performances suffered. He was allowed to leave for Wolves in July 1999 and later played and managed at non-League level.

Appearances:
League: 66 (17) apps. 6 gls.
FA Cup: 4 (4) apps. 1 gl.
FL Cup: 6 (3) apps.
Others: 11 (6) apps. 4 gls.
Total: **87 (30) apps. 11 gls.**

SISSOKO, Moussa

Role: Midfielder 2016-
6ft.2ins. 13st. 1lb.
Born: *Le Blanc-Mesnil, France, 16th August 1989*

CAREER: Espérance Aulnay (France) 1995/AS Red Star 93 (France) Jul 1999/Espérance Aulnay (France) Oct 2001/Toulouse (France) Jul 2003, pro. Jan 2007/Newcastle United Jan 2013/**SPURS** Aug 2016.

Debut v Stoke City (sub) (PL) (a) 10.9.2016

At his best Moussa Sissoko can be a devastating box-to-box midfielder. Well-built and naturally powerful, he has the strength and stamina to suddenly bust forward with terrific pace to cut a swathe through opposing defences. Having joined the Toulouse youth set-up, Sissoko worked his way through the ranks alongside Étienne Capoue to make his senior debut in August 2007. Impressing with both his defensive and attacking abilities, Sissoko played for France at all youth levels, made 18 Under-21 appearances and his first at full level against the Faroe Islands in October 2009. He was soon attracting attention from abroad and Spurs were reputedly among a cluster of big names prepared to pay anything up to €30 million for his signature. Toulouse refused to let him leave and while Sissoko was content to let his contract run down, his career began to stagnate. Eventually he was allowed to sign for Newcastle United, the £1.5 million fee reflecting the six months left till he could move on for nothing. In an ever-changing "Toon" team, often packed with French colleagues, there were times when Sissoko could look awesome, but there were also times when he could just disappear. He was certainly never at his best in a struggling team. Perhaps it was the thought of playing Championship football following Newcastle's 2016 relegation that spurred Sissoko into showing what he could do at Euro 2016. Clearly relishing the big stage, his performances for the home nation as they reached the Final, and he took his total of full caps to 44, showed how good he could be and resulted in Spurs and Everton competing for his signature as the transfer window drew to a close. Sissoko chose Spurs. A £30 million signing, he has yet to justify the price tag.

Appearances:
League: 8 (17) apps.
FA Cup: 2 (2) apps.
FL Cup: 2 (3) apps.
Others: 1 app.
Total: **13 (22) apps. 0 gls.**

SKINNER, George Edward Henry

Role: Inside-forward 1940-47
Born: Belvedere, Kent, 26th June 1917
Died: Eastbourne, Sussex, 30th September 2002

CAREER: Picardy School/Kent Schools/Callenders Cable Works FC/**SPURS** am. May 1937/(Northfleet United Aug 1937)/**SPURS** pro. Sep 1938/(guest for Bristol Rovers, Charlton Athletic, Fulham, Hartlepools United, Middlesbrough, Swindon Town and York City during World War Two)/Gillingham May 1947/Brighton and Hove Albion Feb 1948/coach in Finland 1948/Hastings United player-coach/Kent FA chief coach/Finnish Olympic team coach/Eastbourne Town manager/Sussex FA coach/Director of coaching in Nigeria 1962/Libya coach 1965/Jordan coach 1968/Saudi Arabia coach 1969/Iran coach 1972/IBV (Iceland) coach 1976/retired 1978.

Debut v Birmingham City (FL) (h) 31.8.1946
(West Ham United (FLS) (a) 7.9.1940)

George Skinner was spotted by Spurs playing for Callenders FC-the same club that produced Johnny Morrison. Skinner was not destined to enjoy the same degree of success as Morrison, losing the best years of his career to the Second World War. After playing for Northfleet he joined the White Hart Lane staff in 1938. He made his debut in a Football League South game in September 1940, but was soon unavailable due to service demands. When he returned from military service in early 1946, he enjoyed his best run in the team, but only played in the first post-war Football League match. Transfer-listed at his own request in January 1947, he had to wait until May before joining Gillingham. He later signed for Brighton, although he never appeared in their League team, and then moved into management with Hastings United and the Finnish Olympic team. His debut only lasted for eighty minutes. The game against West Ham United had to be abandoned after that time due to an air raid warning.

Appearances:
League: 1 app.
Others: 15 apps. 3 gls.
Total: **16 apps. 3 gls.**

SKINNER, James Frederick

Role: Half-back 1919-26
5ft.8ins. 11st.0lbs.
Born: Beckenham, Kent, 11th October 1898
Died: Cranborne, Dorset, September 1984

CAREER: Manor Road School/West Ham Schools/England Schools/Beckenham/**SPURS** May 1919-Mar 1927.

Debut v Clapton Orient (FL) (h) 11.10.1919
(Crystal Palace (LFACC) (a) 6.10.1919)

Jimmy Skinner joined Spurs from the Beckenham club after the First World War as reserve for the England international half-backs Bert Smith and Arthur Grimsdell. As such, he had few first team opportunities until the 1924-25 season when he stood in for the injured Grimsdell and proved a reliable deputy, although not in the same class as the Spurs' captain. He served the club well as an ever-ready reserve until 1926-27 when he was troubled by a serious ligament injury. However, he did not help himself by failing to comply with the club's training regulations and other instructions. Twice suspended for fourteen days, when he committed the same offence for a third time in March 1927, Spurs terminated his contract. He appealed to the Football League, but failed to attend the hearing and thereby automatically lost the appeal. In later life he owned a greengrocer's business in Enfield and a building firm in Harlow, where he also ran a fruit farm.

Appearances:
League: 88 apps. 3 gls.
FA Cup: 6 apps.
Others: 17 apps.
Total: **111 apps. 3 gls.**

SKITT, Harry

Role: Half-back 1924-31
5ft.8ins. 10st.9lbs.
Born: Portobello, Staffordshire, 26th June 1901
Died: Poole, Dorset, 28th January 1976

CAREER: Darlaston/**SPURS** May 1923/(Northfleet United 1923)/Chester Jul 1931/Congleton Town cs. 1936.

Debut v Aston Villa (FL) (h) 1.11.1924
(Fulham (LFACC) (h) 27.10.1924)

A powerful, reliable half-back, Harry Skitt was spotted by manager Peter McWilliam after he went to watch one of Skitt's colleagues at Darlaston. He joined Spurs nursery club at Northfleet and moved up to White Hart Lane in May 1923. The majority of his appearances were at centre-half, but he was quite capable of playing in any of the half-back positions. For seven years he proved a solid, dependable player, but, during a particularly nondescript period in Spurs' history, never reached the heights his consistency merited. The nearest he came to any honours was in August 1929 when he was selected as reserve for the Football League team to meet the Irish League. With the developing talents of Wally Alsford coming to the fore during 1930-31, Skitt was released at the end of the season. He moved to Chester where he played for five years before retiring from top flight football to play for Congleton Town. When his playing career was over, he was a publican in Staffordshire for many years.

Appearances:
League: 212 apps.
FA Cup: 17 apps.
Others: 29 apps. 4 gls.
Total: **258 apps. 4 gls.**

SLABBER, Jamie

Role: Striker 2002-04
5ft.10ins. 12st.2lbs.
Born: Enfield, Middlesex, 31st December 1984

CAREER: Wormley Youth/Cuffley/Lea Valley District Schools/**SPURS** scholar Jul 2001, pro. Dec 2001/(AB Copenhagen (Denmark) loan Mar 2004)/(Swindon Town loan Dec 2004)/released Mar 2005/Aldershot Town Apr-May 2005/Bristol Rovers trial Jul 2005/Grays Athletic trial and perm. Jul 2005/(Oxford United loan Nov 2006)/Stevenage Borough Dec 2006-May 2007/Rushden & Diamonds trial Jul 2007/Havant & Waterlooville trial and perm. Jul 2007-Oct 2008/Grays Athletic Oct 2008 /Woking Dec 2009/Eastleigh Jul 2010/Chelmsford City Mar 2012/Sutton United May 2013/Bromley May 2014-Jun 2015/(Farnborough loan Oct 2014)/Hemel Hempstead Town Jul 2015/(Sutton United loan Mar 2016)/ Welling United May 2016/(Bishops Stortford loan Oct 2016).

Debut v Liverpool (sub) (PL) (h) 16.3.2003

Jamie Slabber had performed well as he worked his way through the junior ranks at Spurs. A crafty striker, with a good touch and neat control, in some ways similar to Teddy Sheringham, he was a surprise call-up to

the substitute's bench in March 2003. Spurs were going through one of those spells when goals were hard to come by. Thrown on when Spurs were 1-3 down, he set up a second goal for Sheringham, but was unable to swing the game Spurs' way. Slabber had few further opportunities. He played in a few friendly matches, but was never given another chance in a competitive game. When he was released by Spurs he was unable to get find another League club and ended up playing for several non-League outfits.

Appearances:
League: (1) app.
Others: 1 (3) apps.
Total: **1 (4) apps. 0 gls.**

SLADE, H C

Role: Inside-forward 1916-17

CAREER: Reading/(guest for **SPURS** during World War One).

Debut v Fulham (LFC) (a) 21.10.1916

A young player on the books of Reading prior to the First World War, Slade made his one appearance for Spurs in October 1916 in a London Football Combination match with Fulham. He had played regularly for Reading that season, but during the course of the previous week they had decided they were unable to continue. They resigned from the competition with their fixtures being taken over by Portsmouth.

Appearances:
Others: 1 app.
Total: **1 app. 0 gls.**

SLADE, Steven Anthony

Role: Striker 1994-96
5ft.11ins. 10st.7lbs.
Born: Hackney, London, 6th October 1975

CAREER: Marshalls Park School/Romford Schools/ Essex Schools/**SPURS** assoc. schl Mar 1991, trainee Jul 1992, pro. Jul 1994/Queens Park Rangers Jul 1996-May 2000/(Brentford loan Feb 1997)/Cambridge United Aug-Nov 2000/Luton Town trial Apr 2001/Hayes trial Aug 2001/Chesham United trial Sep 2001/Hemel Hempstead Town trial/ Harrow Borough trial Oct 2001/Leyton Orient trial Dec 2001/St Albans City trial Feb 2002/Billericay Town trial/Worthing by Mar 2005/Vikingur (Iceland)/Barking & East Ham trial Aug 2005/

Cambridge United training Aug 2005//Redbridge trial Sep 2005/Hayes trial Aug 2005/Rushden & Diamonds trial Aug 2005/Grimsby Town trial Sep-Oct 2005/Maidenhead United Oct 2005/Millwall trial Jan 2006/Worthing Mar 2006/Chesham United Mar 2006/Hornchurch Feb 2007/Barking Jan 2008/Ware Sep 2011/Wingate & Finchley.

Debut v Chester City (FLC) (sub) (a) 4.10.1995
(Reading (Fr) 11.11.1994)

Steve Slade really was a player who should have had a big career in top flight football. Unfortunately, the tremendous promise he showed as a youngster was never built upon and he ended up a bit part player with numerous non-League clubs. A lithe central striker, quick off the mark and a handful for any defence, Slade had done well progressing through the youth set-up and into the reserves. He well-merited the few appearances he made in the second half of the 1995-96 season and the four England Under-21 caps he won playing in the end of season Toulon tournament. Most of his Spurs' outings were as a substitute, but a start had to be made somewhere and it showed that he was definitely in manager Gerry Francis' thoughts. Teddy Sheringham and Chris Armstrong were the regular forward pairing with Ronny Rosenthal the number one back-up. A little patience and Slade should have been able to learn from that trio and provide another forward option. Regretfully Slade was not prepared to wait his chance. He refused the offer of a new contract and moved to Queens Park Rangers. The move was conditional on QPR accepting a transfer fee that would be set by a FA tribunal. A good indicator of the high opinion in which Slade was held is shown by the tribunal's decision. If QPR wanted him, they would have to pay £350,000 plus a slice of any sell-on fee. They paid it willingly. In three years at Loftus Road, Slade scored six goals in almost eighty appearances, the vast majority as a substitute. It was a major let down. From Rangers, Slade's career went downhill, unsuccessful trials interspersed with brief spells at several non-League clubs.

Appearances:
League: 1 (4) apps.
FA Cup: (2) apps.
FL Cup: (1) app.
Others: 3 (1) apps.
Total: 4 (8) apps. 0 gls.

SLARK, S G

Role: Full-back 1895-96

CAREER: High Cross Institute/Dartford/SPURS trial Jan 1896/Barnet 1896-98.

Debut v Notts County (Fr) (h) 25.1.1896

A local lad who had previously played for High Cross Institute, Slark was with Dartford when he made his only appearance for Spurs. That was in January 1896 when he played as a trialist in a friendly with Notts County. The following season Slark played for Barnet and helped them win the North Middlesex League and Alliance.

Appearances:
Others: 1 app.
Total: 1 app. 0 gls.

"SLENDER"

Role: Outside-right 1918-19

Debut v Crystal Palace (Fr) (a) 26.4.1919

The true name of this player has never been discovered. His only match for Spurs was in April 1919 when he played in a friendly at Crystal Palace. Several trialists were given the opportunity to impress in two friendly matches played that day. So bad was "Slender's" performance that not only was he substituted, but he was also given this pseudonym to protect him from further abuse.

Appearances:
Others: 1 app.
Total: 1 app. 0 gls.

SLOAN, Thomas

Role: Midfield 1978
5ft.6ins. 9st.10lbs.
Born: Ballymena, Northern Ireland, 10th July 1959

CAREER: Raglan Homers/Ballymena United/SPURS trial May 1978/Manchester United trial Jul 1978, pro. Aug 1978/Chester City Aug 1982/Linfield 1983/Coleraine 1986/Carrick Rangers 1987/Ballymena United 1989/Larne 1991/Raglan Homers.

Debut v FC Hamar (Fr) (a) 15.5.1978

A member of Northern Ireland's first Under-21 international team, Tom Sloan was on the books of Ballymena United and the Ulster Young Footballer of the Year when he joined Spurs for a trial during their 1978 end of season tour to Sweden and Norway. A small, creative midfielder, he played against FC Hamar and Kvik Halden, but at the end of the tour Spurs decided not to offer him a contract. Instead he tried his luck with Manchester United and after a short trial was signed on. While he won three full caps for his country, the first against Scotland in May 1979, he never managed to make the grade at Old Trafford. He spent most of his time in the reserves, before moving to Chester City where he played for just one season. He then returned to Ireland playing for Linfield, Coleraine, Carrick Rangers and Ballymena, and finished his senior career at Larne. He later returned to where it all began, reinstated as an amateur and playing for Raglan Homers in the Ballymena Saturday Morning League.

Appearances:
Others: 2 apps.
Total: 2 apps. 0 gls.

SMAILES, James

Role: Outside-left 1930-32
5ft.6ins. 10st.0lbs.
Born: South Moor, Yorkshire, 9th June 1907
Died: Tow Law, County Durham, May 1986

CAREER: Tow Law Town/Huddersfield Town Mar 1928/SPURS Mar 1931/Blackpool Dec 1932/Grimsby Town May 1935/Stockport County Jun 1936/Bradford City Jul 1938/(guest for Bradford Park Avenue, Hartlepools United and Huddersfield Town during World War Two)/Waterhouse Sports Club coach Jul 1946/Tow Law Town trainer-coach 1947.

Debut v Bradford City (FL) (h) 14.3.1931 (scored once)

In February 1931 Jimmy Smailes played for Huddersfield Town in a friendly against Spurs at White Hart Lane. Although at Huddersfield for

three years, he had been kept out of the team by international winger Billy Smith, but his direct style of wing-play impressed Spurs enough for them to secure his transfer the following month. He went straight into the side, scored on his debut and kept his place until the end of the season. Early the following campaign he lost out to Willie Evans and, never able to get back in, was sold to Blackpool for £2,000. He moved on fairly quickly to Grimsby and Stockport, with whom he won a Division Three (North) Championship medal in 1937, but that was scant reward for a career which had promised much in its early days yet never really matured. He finished his career with Bradford City, retiring at the end of the Second World War to take up a coaching job with Waterhouse Sports Club.

Appearances:
League: 16 apps. 3 gls.
Total: 16 apps. 3 gls.

SMITH, Adam James

Role: Full-back 2008-
5ft.9ins. 10st.6lbs.
Born: *Leytonstone, London, 29th April 1991*

CAREER: SPURS Academy scholar Jul 2007, pro. May 2008/(Wycombe Wanderers loan Aug 2009)/(Torquay United loan Nov 2009)/(AFC Bournemouth loan Sep 2010)/(Milton Keynes Dons loan Aug 2011-Jan 2012)/(Leeds United loan Jan-Feb 2012)/(Millwall loan Nov 2012)/(Derby County loan Jul-Dec 2013)/AFC Bournemouth Jan 2014.

Debut v Fulham (PL) (h) (sub) 13.5.2014
Leyton Orient (sub) (Fr) (a) 30.7.2008

When 17-year old Academy graduate Adam Smith was called upon to make a couple of substitute appearances in pre-season friendlies in July and August 2008, he looked a remarkably confident young man, a full-back who showed little fear and bombed forward at every opportunity. He continued to show the same attack-minded attitude in the youth squads, on loan to Football League clubs and as he worked his way up the international ladder. It was, perhaps, that attitude that cost Smith the chance of a career with Spurs. So keen to get forward was he, that he sometimes forgot that as a full-back, his first priority was defending. His sorties forward could leave space behind him and his position exposed. While he was quick to recover, he could not always get back in time. After several loans, Smith moved permanently to AFC Bournemouth, one of the clubs with whom he had

most impressed while on loan. Smith soon established himself as a regular with the Cherries. With traditional wingers out of fashion, Smith is a perfect example of the modern full-back, more a winger playing in defence. One of the successes of Bournemouth's Premier League campaigns, Smith has shown himself to be a footballer of true quality.

Appearances:
League: (1) app.
FL Cup: 1 app.
Others: (7) apps.
Total: 1 (8) apps. 0 gls.

SMITH, Anthony Brian

Role: Centre-half 1959-65
Born: *Lavenham, Suffolk, 5th October 1941*

CAREER: SPURS am. Aug 1957, pro. May 1959/Southern Suburbs (South Africa) Mar 1966/Addington (South Africa) 1968/Durban Spurs (South Africa) 1969/Durban United (South Africa) 1970-73/Durban City (South Africa) 1973-74/Hillary (South Africa) 1976-78/Bush Bucks (South Africa) manager 1982.

Debut v Reading (Fr) (a) 21.10.1959

Tony Smith's only appearances in the Spurs' first team were in friendlies at Reading in October 1959 and Leytonstone in December 1964. He stayed with Spurs until March 1966 when he left to play for Southern Suburbs of Johannesburg. He settled in South Africa and later played for Durban United and Addington of Durban where former Spurs full-back Peter Baker was coach.

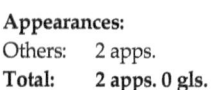

Appearances:
Others: 2 apps.
Total: 2 apps. 0 gls.

SMITH, Bertram

Role: Half-back 1916-29
5ft.7ins. 11st.4lbs.
Born: *Higham, Kent, 7th March 1892*
Died: *Biggleswade, Bedfordshire, September 1969*

CAREER: Vanbrugh Park/Crawford United/Metrogas/Huddersfield Town Apr 1913/(guest for SPURS during World War One)/SPURS Aug 1919/Northfleet United player-coach May 1930/Sheppey United coach and part-time pro. Sep 1931/Young Boys (Berne, Switzerland) player-coach Oct 1931/Harwich & Parkeston manager-coach May 1934/Stevenage Town/Hitchin Town trainer-coach 1937, groundsman.

Debut v Coventry City (FL) (a) 30.8.1919
(Arsenal (LFC) (h) 2.12.1916)

Bert Smith played for Vanbrugh Park, Crawford United and Metrogas in his native Kent, but he was overlooked by all the London clubs and had to go to Yorkshire to turn professional with Huddersfield. During the Great War he played service football, appearing for the British Army against the French Army, and one of his service colleagues was Bert Bliss. It was as a direct result of Bliss's recommendation that Smith made his first appearances for Spurs as a wartime guest. During 1918-19 he played in his recognised inside-forward role, but towards the end of the season

was given a few games at half-back. Whilst Smith was still only a reserve at Huddersfield, Spurs manager Peter McWilliam realised that he would make an excellent addition to Spurs half-back ranks, so arranged the transfer. Smith made his League debut in the first match of the 1919-20 season and went on to become a first choice for the next eight years. A member of the team that stormed away with the Second Division title in 1919-20 and followed up with the FA Cup in 1921, he played in international trial games towards the end of both the 1920 and 1921 seasons. He won his first cap against Scotland in April 1921, when he appeared alongside club colleagues Bliss, Arthur Grimsdell and Jimmy Dimmock. A non-stop, hard-grafting player, Smith was also exceptionally skilful, although this tended to be overlooked as his relentless tackling caught the eye. He won two England caps, played in four England trial games and also appeared for the Football League against the Scottish League in February 1922. The cornerstone of the team until January 1927, Smith remained as a player until May 1930 when he was released and went to Northfleet as coach. He then took up the same post with Sheppey United, but after only a month went to Switzerland where he worked as player-coach with The Young Boys club of Berne. When he returned to England he joined Harwich and Parkeston as manager-coach and also worked with Stevenage Town, before joining Hitchin Town. Initially trainer-coach he settled in Hitchin, eventually taking on the job of groundsman and remained with the club until his retirement in 1966.

Appearances:
League: 291 apps. 9 gls.
FA Cup: 28 apps. 1 gl.
Others: 52 apps. 3 gls.
Total: **371 apps. 13 gls.**

SMITH, F E

Role: Half-back 1894-95

Debut v Sheffield & District League XI (Fr) (h) 25.12.1894

Smith made his first appearance for Spurs in a friendly against a Sheffield and District League XI at Northumberland Park on Christmas Day 1894. He did not play again until late in the season when he appeared in a London Charity Cup tie with the Old Carthusians. The following season he made four more appearances.

Appearances:
Others: 6 apps.
Total: **6 apps. 0 gls.**

SMITH, George Casper

Role: Centre-half 1945-46
6ft.1ins. 12st.2lbs.
Born: Bromley-By-Bow, London, 23rd April 1915
Died: Bodmin, Cornwall, 31st October 1983

CAREER: Hackney Schools/Erith & Belvedere/Welling & Bexleyheath 1937-38/Charlton Athletic Aug 1938/(guest for Reading and **SPURS** during World War Two)/Brentford Nov 1945/Queens Park Rangers Jun 1947/Ipswich Town asst. manager-coach Apr 1949, player Dec 1949/Chelmsford City Aug 1950/Redhill Athletic manager-coach Jul 1951/Eastbourne United manager-coach 1952-55/FA coach/Sheffield United coach Sep 1955-Feb 1956/Sutton United manager-coach May 1956-May 1958/Crystal Palace manager Jul 1958-Apr 1960/Sheffield United coach Apr 1960-Apr 1961/Portsmouth manager Apr 1961-Mar 1970.

Debut v Swansea Town (FLS) (a) 20.10.1945

George Smith made four Football League South appearances for Spurs as a guest from Charlton Athletic in 1945-46. He had joined Charlton from their nursery club of Welling and Bexleyheath, but in eight years on their books made only one League appearance as his career was decimated by the War. He played regularly during the war years, was a member of their Football League South Cup-winning team of 1944 and played for England in a wartime international with Wales in May 1945. His first appearance for Spurs was against Swansea Town in October 1945 and he played in the next three games, the last two of which were against Brentford. They must have been impressed by his performances, for after the last match they secured his transfer. He later moved to Queens Park Rangers and led them to the Third Division (South) title in 1948 before starting on a coaching and managerial career with Ipswich Town. When his playing registration was transferred to Ipswich he stood down as assistant manager/coach, but played only nine League games for them before finishing his playing career with a year at Chelmsford City. He then worked for Redhill Athletic, Eastbourne United, the FA coaching staff, Sheffield United, Sutton United, Crystal Palace, Sheffield United again and Portsmouth where he succeeded former Spurs' star Freddie Cox and gave them great service until resigning in March 1970.

Appearances:
Others: 4 apps.
Total: **4 apps. 0 gls.**

SMITH, Gordon Melville

Role: Full-back 1978-82
5ft.8ins. 12st.11lbs.
Born: Partick, Glasgow, 3rd July 1954
Died: Glasgow, 5th April 2014

CAREER: Perth Schools/Rangers Boys Club/St Johnstone am. Nov 1969, pro. Jul 1971/Aston Villa Aug 1976/**SPURS** Feb 1979/Wolverhampton Wanderers Aug 1982/South Africa Jun 1984/Pittsburgh Spirit (USA) Jan 1985-1989.

Debut v Bolton Wanderers (sub) (FL) (a) 8.5.1979
(West Ham United (Fr) (h) 30.4.1979)

An industrious full-back who liked to burst through on the overlap, Gordon Smith had a disappointing and undistinguished three years with Spurs. A Scottish Youth international, he started his career with St Johnstone and collected four Scotland Under-23 caps before moving to Aston Villa. He played regularly in his first two seasons at Villa Park, helping Villa win the League Cup in 1977, albeit as a substitute, but was out of favour when Spurs moved to sign him for £150,000. His career at White Hart Lane was not helped by early injury problems, and it was not until the end of the season that he made the first team. At the time, Spurs

were trying to re-establish themselves after a year in the Second Division and the defence in particular suffered as Keith Burkinshaw sought a settled line-up. Stricken by further injuries, Smith was rarely able to make the team and in May 1982 was given a free transfer. After taking part in the "rebel" tour of South Africa in July 1982 he joined Wolves and helped them win promotion to the First Division in 1983, but did not appear very often after that. In May 1984. he went to play in South Africa and later joined the American club Pittsburgh Spirit. His father, Neil, played for the well-known minor club Kilsyth Rangers and his grandfather, Willie Salisbury, played for Partick Thistle and Liverpool in the 1920s.

Appearances:
League: 34 (4) apps. 1 gl.
FL Cup: 6 apps.
Euro: (1) app.
Others: 19 (3) apps. 1 gl.
Total: 59 (8) apps. 2 gls.

SMITH, Ian Ralph

Role: Full-back 1975-76
5ft.10ins. 10st.12lbs.
Born: Rotherham, Yorkshire, 15th February 1957

CAREER: Rotherham Schools/Yorkshire Schools/England Schools/**SPURS** app. Jul 1972, pro. Apr 1974/Rotherham United Jun 1976/Scarborough 1978/Bishops Stortford/Ipswich Town scout, Football in the Community coach 1992, Academy coach, asst. director till Apr 2004.

Debut v Norwich City (FL) (h) 30.8.1975
(Bristol Rovers (sub) (Fr) (a) 8.8.1975)

Ian Smith developed through Spurs' junior ranks and made a couple of League appearances early in 1975-76, but was never able to challenge the established right-back Terry Naylor. He was released at the end of the season and returned to his home town. Not quite up to the grade for League football, he made only three League appearances for Rotherham United before going into non-League football. Smith then spent 12 years coaching youngsters at Ipswich, rising to the position of assistant director, before departing. Sadly, Smith later took advantage of the relationship he had built up with some of the boys he had helped develop. He was convicted of stealing money from two lads who had left Ipswich. His actions were put down to gambling problems, but could not save him from having to perform 250 hours of Community Service.

Appearances:
League: 2 apps.
Others: 1 (3) apps.
Total: 3 (3) apps. 0 gls.

SMITH, James McQueen Anderson

Role: Goalkeeper 1925-27
5ft.11ins. 11st.11lbs.
Born: Leith, Edinburgh, 28th November 1901
Died: Kirkcaldy, Fife, 9th April 1964

CAREER: Rosyth Juniors/Rosyth Recreation/East Fife/**SPURS** Jun 1925/St Johnstone Nov 1928/Norwich City May 1930/Ayr United Sep 1931.

Debut v Leicester City (FL) (a) 31.10.1925
(Norwich City (Fr) (Bury St Edmunds) 22.10.1925)

Although Jimmy Smith conceded five goals at Leicester on his League debut for Spurs, he competed with Bill Kaine, John Britton and Fred Hinton for the 'keeper's jersey in 1925-26. He appeared to have won the battle at the start of the next season when, with Hinton injured and Kaine gone to Luton, he played regularly. However, the goalkeeping position was Spurs' biggest problem in the mid-1920s. In January 1927 Smith lost his place to Britton and was never able to get it back. Spurs signed Cyril Spiers and Joe Nicholls in an attempt to solve the dilemma and although Smith remained at the club until the end of 1928-29, he did not appear in the first team again. He moved to St Johnstone, and a year later signed for Norwich City, but spent only one season in East Anglia before returning to Scotland with Ayr United.

Appearances:
League: 30 apps.
FA Cup: 1 app.
Others: 4 apps.
Total: 35 apps. 0 gls.

SMITH, John

Role: Half-back or inside-forward 1959-64
5ft.7ins. 13st.0lbs.
Born: Shoreditch, London, 4th January 1939
Died: Harlesden, London, 12th February 1988

CAREER: East London Schools/London Schools/Middlesex Schools/West Ham United am. 1954, pro. Jan 1956/**SPURS** Mar 1960/Coventry City Mar 1964/Leyton Orient Oct 1965/Torquay United Oct 1966/Swindon Town Jun 1968/Walsall player-coach Jun 1971, manager Oct 1972-Mar 1973/Dundalk player-manager Jun 1973.

Debut v Everton (FL) (a) 9.4.1960

John Smith was rated a star of the future when he joined Spurs as part of a £20,000 deal that saw Dave Dunmore move West Ham United. Unfortunately, Smith never fulfilled his potential, and became an almost permanent reserve at White Hart Lane due to the form and consistency of Danny Blanchflower, Dave Mackay and John White. An England Youth cap, Smith had developed rapidly in the Upton Park academy, played for England at Under-23 level, was reserve for the full England team against Wales in October 1959 and looked to have a great career ahead of him. However, faced with three of the great players of post-war football as competitors, he was rarely in contention for a place, and after a handful of games in four years was allowed to move on to Coventry City. He also played for Leyton Orient and Torquay United before joining Swindon Town, where he enjoyed the highlight of his career, helping the Third Division side beat Arsenal to win the League Cup at Wembley in 1969. He ended his playing career in England with Walsall and was then player-manager of Dundalk. He later worked as manager of United Biscuits' Social Club in Harlesden.

Appearances:
League: 21 apps. 1 gl.
FA Cup: 2 apps.
Euro: 1 app.
Others: 3 (1) apps.
Total: 27 (1) apps. 1 gl.

SMITH, Kenneth

Role: Inside-forward 1944-45

CAREER: Bolton Wanderers/(guest for Mansfield Town and **SPURS** during World War Two).

Debut v Southampton (FLS) (a) 23.9.1944

An amateur on the books of Bolton Wanderers, with previous experience gained as a guest with Mansfield Town, Ken Smith made his one appearance for Spurs in a Football League South game against Southampton in September 1944.

Appearances:
Others: 1 app.
Total: 1 app. 0 gls.

SMITH, James Christopher Reginald

Role: Outside-right 1943-44
5ft.9ins. 11st.8lbs.
Born: Battersea, London, 20th January 1912
Died: Stevenage, Hertfordshire, 6th January 2004

CAREER: Pirton/Hitchin Town 1930/Crystal Palace trial/**SPURS** am. May 1931/Northfleet United/St Albans City Aug 1933/Millwall pro. Aug 1935/(guest for Chelsea, Dundee, Luton Town, Partick Thistle, Reading, **SPURS**, Watford and West Ham United during Second World War)/Dundee Mar 1946/Corby Town player-manager Jun 1948-1949/Dundee coach 1949/Dundee United manager Sep 1954/Western Provinces (South Africa) coach 1954-56/Falkirk manager Jan 1957-May 1959/Millwall manager Jul 1959-Jan 1961/Addington (South Africa) coach Mar 1961/Durban (South Africa) manager 1961/Bedford Town manager 1961-Sep 1963/Addington (South Africa) manager 1964/Cape Town City (South Africa) manager 1964-68/Bedford Town manager Nov 1971-Jun 1972/Stevenage Town manager.

Debut v Aldershot (FLSC) (h) 25.3.1944

Born near Millwall, Reg Smith, whose real name was Schmidt, was the son of a South African rugby international who accompanied the first Springbok tour of Britain. Smith was bought up in South Africa, and when he returned to the UK it was with Hitchin Town that he started his football career. A representative for both Hertfordshire and the Spartan League, he was spotted by Spurs, signed amateur forms and played for the nursery club at Northfleet. When Spurs decided he was not good enough to be offered a chance on the White Hart Lane staff, Smith joined Millwall. A right-winger of pace and trickery, he developed into an England international. A member of the Millwall team that won the Third Division (South) in 1938, he scored two goals on his England debut against Norway on 9th November 1938 and played again the following week against Northern Ireland when he helped Spurs' own Willie Hall score five goals. Smith continued to represent England during the early years of the Second World War. He made his one appearance for Spurs against Aldershot in March 1944 in a Football League South Cup game. In March 1946 Smith moved to Dundee, returned to England as player-manager of the newly-formed Corby Town and then went back to Dundee as trainer/coach. He moved into management with Dundee United, then spent the best part of thirty years flitting between England and South Africa.

Appearances:
Others: 1 app.
Total: 1 app. 0 gls.

SMITH, John Charles Trevor

Role: Inside-forward 1943-44
5ft.5ins. 11st.0lbs.
Born: West Stanley, County Durham, 8th September 1910
Died: Bracknell, Berkshire, 23rd October 1997

CAREER: South Moors/Annfield Plain semi-pro. 1930/Portsmouth trial Feb 1930/Charlton Athletic May 1933/Fulham Mar 1935/Crystal Palace Feb 1938/(guest for Brentford, Carlisle United, Colchester United, Fulham, Nottingham Forest, Notts County, **SPURS** and West Ham United during World War Two)/Yeovil Town cs. 1946/Colchester United/Watford Jun 1947-May 1948/Bedford Town by Apr 1949/Wingate manager Jun 1949-1972.

Debut v Chelsea (FLS) (h) 30.10.1943 (scored once)

Trevor Smith played two Football League South games for Spurs in the 1943-44 season as a guest player from Crystal Palace. Originally a winger with the junior club South Moors and a semi-professional with Annfield Plain, he joined Charlton Athletic, but it was when he was with Fulham that he was converted to the inside-forward position before moving to Crystal Palace. He played at inside-left for Spurs and scored in his first game against Chelsea. He was retained for the match against Brentford a week

later. In the close season of 1946 Smith left League football to play for Yeovil Town, moved into the half-back line and then joined Colchester United. He returned to the Football League to finish his playing career with Watford where he spent twelve months. In June 1949, he became manager of Wingate, a role he occupied for more than twenty years.

Appearances:
Others: 2 apps. 1 gl.
Total: 2 apps. 1 gl.

SMITH, Neil James

Role: Forward 1990-91
5ft.8ins. 11st.10lbs.
Born: Lambeth, London, 30th September 1971

CAREER: SPURS app. Aug 1988, pro. Jul 1990/Gillingham loan Oct 1991, perm. Nov 1991/Fulham Jul 1997/Reading Aug 1999/Gillingham training Jul 2002/Stevenage Borough Aug 2002/Woking Oct 2002, joint caretaker-manager Mar 2007/Welling United player-manager May 2007 /Bromley Jan 2008/Grays Athletic coach Feb-Oct 2008/Maidstone United Oct 2008/Croydon Athletic asst. manager Nov 2008-Sep 2010/Lewes asst. manager Sep 2010-May 2011/Bromley coach Jun 2011, asst. manager Jul 2011, interim manager Feb 2016, perm. manager Apr 2016.

Debut v West Ham United (sub) (Fr) (a) 12.11.1990

A member of Spurs FA Youth Cup winning team in 1990, Neil Smith was a forward when he first joined the club, but played in both defence and midfield for the Youth side. His one first team appearance was in November 1990 when he went on as a late substitute for Paul Walsh in a testimonial for West Ham manager Billy Bonds at Upton Park. With an abundance of midfield players at White Hart Lane, Smith was allowed to join Gillingham on loan in October 1991 with the move being made permanent the following month. He proved himself a more than competent performer in five years at Priestfield and then had two years with Fulham and three with Reading. Smith then moved into the non-League game, playing, coaching and managing.

Appearances:
Others: (1) app.
Total: (1) app. 0 gls.

SMITH, P

Role: Full-back 1918-19

CAREER: Rangers/(guest for **SPURS** during World War One).

Debut v Clapton Orient (LFC) (h) 28.9.1918

A junior on the books of Glasgow Rangers, Smith made four London Football Combination appearances for Spurs in the 1918-19 season whilst serving as an air mechanic.

Appearances:
Others: 4 apps.
Total: 4 apps. 0 gls.

SMITH, Robert Alfred

Role: Centre-forward 1955-64
5ft.10ins. 12st.11lbs.
Born: Lingdale, North Yorkshire, 22nd February 1933
Died: Enfield, Middlesex, 18th September 2010

CAREER: Lingdale Council School/Redcar Boys Club/Tudor Rose/ Redcar United May 1947/Chelsea am. Feb 1948, pro. May 1950/**SPURS** Dec 1955/Brighton and Hove Albion May 1964/Hastings United Oct 1965-Mar 1967/Leyton Orient trial Mar 1967/Banbury United Jun 1968-May 1969.

Debut v Luton Town (h) 24.12.1955

When the term "a typical old-fashioned English centre-forward" is used, Bobby Smith is the player who immediately springs to mind. The son of a Yorkshire miner, big, burly and bustling, he was not the prettiest of footballers, but as a tough, muscular, battering-ram of a centre-forward Smith's job was to score goals, and he did that with a relish that put the fear of God into opposing defenders and goalkeepers. In Chelsea's League team at the age of 17, he hit 30 goals in 86 senior games, but when Spurs moved to sign him for £16,000, was marking time in Chelsea's reserves, unable to displace Roy Bentley. Smith arrived at White Hart Lane with Spurs one place off the bottom of the First Division, scored the goals necessary to dispel the threat of relegation, and went on to play a full part in the most glorious years in the club's history. Taking over from Len Duquemin, and with little Tommy Harmer creating the openings, he scored 36 League goals in 1957-58 to equal Ted Harper's 1930-31 record and by August 1960 had overtaken George Hunt's aggregate of League goals for Spurs. He won his first England cap against Northern Ireland in October 1960 and went on to score 13 goals in 15 appearances for his country. Top scorer in the "Double" winning team, he also hit some crucial cup goals, including the first in the 1961 FA Cup Final-after netting a brace in the semi-final against Burnley-and was on target in the Final again the following season as Spurs retained the trophy. By then Smith had the magical Jimmy Greaves alongside him, and together they formed the most feared striking partnership in English-and possibly European-football. A brave, strong ox of a striker, with a fierce shoulder-charge who liked nothing more than a hard, physical battle, he also had a great deal of skill and frequently surprised spectators with the deftness of his footwork. However, there were times when manager Bill Nicholson preferred the subtler skills of Les Allen, and Smith was often left out of the team. He always came bouncing back for the bigger games though, and his very presence gave Spurs a hefty psychological advantage over Atletico Madrid in the 1963 European Cup-Winners' Cup Final. At the end of the 1963-64 season, and with Smith past 30, Nicholson decided the younger Frank Saul should partner Greaves. Smith moved to Brighton for £5,000, where 18 goals in 31 appearances helped win the Fourth Division title in his only season there. Before a new campaign started, he fell out with Brighton over comments in some newspaper articles and was sacked. He played for Hastings United until March 1967 and had a brief time at Banbury United. Smith later had a series of driving and labouring jobs, but was increasingly troubled by the effects of several old injuries that were a painful legacy of his whole-hearted style of play.

Appearances:
League: 271 apps. 176 gls
FA Cup: 32 apps. 22 gls.
Euro: 14 apps. 10 gls.
Others: 41 (1) apps. 43 gls.
Total: 358 (1) apps. 251 gls.

SMITH, Roger Anthony

Role: Outside-left 1965-66

Born: Welwyn Garden City, Hertfordshire, 3rd November 1944

CAREER: Tottenham Schools/London Schools/Middlesex Schools/SPURS app. May 1960, pro. Jun 1962/Exeter City Jun 1966/Ashford Town cs. 1969/Guildford/Banbury/Epping Town/Wimbledon academy manager/Arsenal scout/Cardiff City chief scout Aug 2008/Chelsea scout/Charlton Athletic scout.

Debut v Sarpsborg (Fr) (a) 15.5.1966

Roger Smith made only one appearance in Spurs' first team. That was in a friendly against the Norwegian club Sarpsborg in May 1966. He was given a free transfer later that month and moved to Exeter City but played there for only one season before joining Ashford Town. He later coached and finished his career scouting for several clubs.

Appearances:
Others: 1 app.
Total: 1 app. 0 gls.

SMITH, Thomas

Role: Outside-right 1898-07
5ft.7ins. 11st.2lbs.
Born: Maryport, Cumberland, 26th November 1876
Died: Carlisle, Cumbria, 26th April 1937

CAREER: Preston North End Nov 1895/SPURS May 1898/retired Jun 1902/Preston North End Mar 1904/Carlisle United/Maryport Tradesmen.

Debut v Thames Ironworks (TML) (h) 3.9.1898
(Gainsborough Trinity (Fr) (h) 1.9.1898 (scored twice))

In his four years in north London, Tom Smith was to prove one of Spurs' most influential players as the club picked up its first major honours with the Southern League title in 1899-00 and the FA Cup in 1901. He went into the first team immediately on arriving from Preston and soon settled, showing the exceptional speed that earned him a reputation as one of the fastest wingers in the game. A very tricky player, in contrast he had a very simple view of his job; it was to get to the goal line as quickly as possible and send over accurate crosses for the foraging forwards to put into the net. Smith was particularly adept at firing in high dipping crosses that gave the likes of Cameron and Copeland extra time to judge their movements, and "Sandy" Brown in particular profited from the service. Smith himself scored Spurs' second goal in the 1901 Cup Final replay but, despite a fine reputation and the fact he was coveted by many League clubs, he never won any representative honours with Spurs. The nearest he got came in March 1899 when he played for an England XI against a Scotland XI in a match to raise funds for the fledgling Players' Union. A vital cog in the team, Spurs were most surprised and upset when Smith announced his retirement at the end of 1901-02 and returned to Cumberland. In March 1904 Preston persuaded him out of retirement and he played eight games to help them take the Second Division title. He later appeared for Carlisle United in the early years of their existence and was still playing in 1909, turning out for Maryport Tradesmen in the West Cumberland League. His final appearance in a Spurs' shirt was in April 1907 when he played for the 1901 FA Cup winning side in a benefit game for former trainer, Sam Mountford. Smith was a fine all-round sportsman. In addition to football he played wing three quarter at rugby and turned out for Maryport Cricket club along with his three sons. One of them was ED Smith, who refereed the 1946 FA Cup Final. In October 1912 Smith was playing rugby for a Cumberland club, Fothergill. One of his sons was given a run-out in the reserves in the early 1920s.

Appearances:
Southern: 94* apps. 25 gls.
FA Cup: 20 apps. 2 gls.
Others: 110 apps. 27 gls.
Total: 224 apps. 54 gls.
*Includes 1 abandoned match.

SMY, James

Role: Inside-forward 1928-31
5ft.8ins. 12st.0lbs
Born: Edmonton, London, 24th November 1907
Died: Brisbane, Australia, 29th July 1997

CAREER: Eldon Road School/Edmonton Schools/London Schools/South of England Schools/Tottenham Polytechnic/Woodside/Tottenham Argyle by 1926/Lower Edmonton/Tottenham Argyle/Hampstead Town/SPURS am. 1926, pro. Jan 1929/released Jun 1932/Northfleet United Aug 1932/Sittingbourne Sep 1934.

Debut v Port Vale (FL) (h) 9.2.1929

Jimmy Smy made his name as an amateur with Hampstead Town. He represented Middlesex, the Football Association and the Athenian League and was reserve for England's amateur international with Scotland in April 1928. When he joined Spurs he left Hampstead sitting on top of the Athenian League. Smy made his debut shortly after signing, but although he stayed with Spurs until released at the end of 1931-32 he was always little more than reserve to Billy Cook. Never able to establish himself in the first class

professional game, he returned to non-League football, including a spell with Sittingbourne before emigrating to Australia.

Appearances:
League: 17 apps. 6 gls.
Others: 2 apps.
Total: 19 apps. 6 gls.

SNEE, George

Role: Forward 2002-03
5ft.10ins. 11st. 11lbs.
Born: Dublin, Republic of Ireland 26th January 1983

CAREER: Maynooth School/Dunboyne/Hartstown/Belvedere/Dublin Schools/Republic of Ireland Schools/**SPURS** trainee Jul 1999, pro. Jul 2000 /released Dec 2002/Colchester United trial Apr 2003/Leyton Orient trial/ Cambridge United trial Jul 2003/Queens Park Rangers trial/AFC Wimbledon Mar-May 2004/Crystal Palace trial Apr 2004/Crewe Alexandra trial Jul 2004/Hampton and Richmond Borough 2005-06/ Woking trial Jul 2006.

Debut v AFC Bournemouth (sub) (Fr) (a) 25.7.2002

It was not difficult for Spurs scouting network to notice George Snee, he was one of the brightest youngsters playing for Republic of Ireland schools. Taken on as a schoolboy, he joined the trainee staff and then made the step up to professional level. A regular performer in the reserves, playing wide on either flank or in central midfield, he made one substitute appearance in a pre-season friendly at Bournemouth in July 2002. Five months later he was released. After several trials, he had a brief spell with the fledgling AFC Wimbledon and continued to try and make a career outside League football.

Appearances:
Others: (1) app.
Total: (1) app. 0 gls.

SOLDADO RILLO, Roberto

Role: Striker 2013-15
5ft.11ins. 12st.4lbs.
Born: Valencia, Spain, 27th May 1985

CAREER: CF Don Bosco (Spain) 1990/Real Madrid (Spain) 1999/Real Madrid Castilla (Spain)/(Osasuna (Spain) loan Jul 2006)/Getafe (Spain) Jul 2008/Valencia (Spain) Jul 2010/**SPURS** Aug 2013/Villarreal (Spain) Aug 2015.

Debut v Crystal Palace (PL) (a) 18.8.2013
(RCD Espanyol (Fr) (h) 10.8.2013)

One of the mass influx of players who arrived following the departure of Gareth Bale, Roberto Soldado cost Spurs a then record fee of £26 million. While it was an enormous sum, Soldado was a proven goal-scorer in Spain's La Liga, at the peak of his career and expected to have no problems adapting to English football. Unfortunately, despite every effort from player, club and fans, he did not prove a success and returned to Spain after two years, regarded as a failure. Soldado had started his career with Real Madrid, working his way through the youth ranks and playing for their reserve side, Castilla. He had a few games in the first team, but with competition from the likes of Michael Owen and Ronaldo was sent out on loan to Osasuna to gain experience. He did well enough with the club from Pamplona to earn promotion from the Spanish Under-21s to the full international team. On his return to Madrid he found Ruud van Nistelrooy established as unchallenged first choice in the central striker role Soldado played. He moved to Getafe and from there to Valencia, a prolific scorer with both clubs, netting an average of roughly a goal every two games. A nippy predator who excelled at running behind defenders on to through passes, he was calm in his finishes, usually finishing with an accurate shot, rather than a simple blast. There was no obvious reason why he could not do as well for Spurs as he had in Spain. He started well enough, showing his quality with some neat touches and link-up play, if not goals, as he settled to the more physical English game. One element seemed missing though, the most crucial element for all strikers-luck. No matter what he did, the goals just would not come. As he struggled to score so he tried to change his game, dropping deep to get in the game, so not being there to finish off moves. His confidence began to visibly wane and he was soon spending most of his time on the bench. While he can always be criticised for his lack of goals, his effort can never be challenged. No matter what the situation he always gave all he had, a fact that meant Spurs' fans never turned against him. After two miserable years, Soldado returned to Spain with Villarreal. Soldado won one of his twelve full caps as a Spurs' player, making him Spurs' only Spanish international.

Appearances:
League: 29 (23) apps. 7 gls.
FA Cup: 4 apps.
FL Cup: 2 (3) apps. 2 gls.
Euro: 12 (3) apps. 7 gls.
Others: 3 (3) apps. 4 gls.
Total: 50 (32) apps. 20 gls.

SON, Heung-min

Role: Forward 2015-
6ft. 12st.2lbs.
Born: Chuncheon, Gangwon, South Korea, 8th July 1992

CAREER: FC Seoul (South Korea)/SV Hamburg (Germany) youth, pro. Jul 2010/Bayer 04 Leverkusen (Germany) Jun 2013/**SPURS** Aug 2015

Debut v Sunderland (PL) (a) 13.9.2015

Heung-Min Son was spotted by Hamburg as a 16-year old playing for FC Seoul's Under-18 team, Dongbuk High School, and enticed to Germany. He worked his way through the youth and reserve teams to make his senior debut in August 2010. Within a few months he was selected for his national team, making his debut against Syria in December 2010. A nippy attacker, usually played behind a main striker, he performed well with Hamburg, netting regularly and making himself an automatic choice. Bayer Leverkusen forked out €10 million to secure his transfer and in two years Son continued to impress, scoring roughly once every three games. Spurs paid out £22 million to bring Son to White Hart Lane, someone to take some of the

pressure off Harry Kane, though not an alternative. In Mauricio Pochettino's favoured formation of three attackers behind a central striker, Son has proved capable of occupying any of the three attacking positions, hard-working and always likely to pop up in the box to finish an opening created for him or to create one himself. While many of his appearances have come as a substitute, that is no reflection on Son's abilities, given the midfield talent available to Pochettino and the fact every player needs time to settle after moving from another country. More importantly, football has continued to develop into a squad game where players can no longer expect to play every game. Son has the mentality that puts club demands above personal gain. He has continued to represent South Korea since joining Spurs, taking his number of full appearances past the half-century mark. Son's father, Son Woong-jung played for Ilhwa Chunma and reached the national under-23 squad.

Appearances:
League: 36 (26) apps. 19 gls
FA Cup: 8 (1) apps. 7 gls.
FL Cup: (1) app.
Euro: 12 (3) apps. 4 gls
Others: 2 (1) apps. 1 gl.
Total: 58 (32) apps. 31 gls.

SOULSBY, Thomas

Role: Winger 1901-02
5ft.5ins. 11st.7lbs.
Born: Mickley Square, Northumberland, 24th October 1876.

CAREER: Mickley/Liverpool 1899/**SPURS** May 1901/released May 1902/Mickley/Lincoln City May-Nov 1905.

Debut v West Ham United (LL) (a) 16.12.1901
(Cambridge University (Fr) (h) 25.11.1901)

Tom Soulsby was signed from Liverpool where he had played for two years in the reserves. A winger, his only first team appearances for Spurs were in a friendly against Cambridge University in November 1901 and a London League match at West Ham United the next month. Released at the end of that season he returned to Mickley and later played for Lincoln, although his career there was brought to an early end by an ankle injury.

Appearances:
Others: 2 apps.
Total: 2 apps. 0 gls.

SOUNESS, Graeme James

Role: Midfield 1971-72
5ft.10ins. 12st.13lbs.
Born: Edinburgh, 6th May 1953

CAREER: Carrickvale School/Edinburgh Schools/Scotland Schools/**SPURS** app. Apr 1969, pro. May 1970/(Montreal Olympic (Canada) loan summer 1972)/Middlesbrough Jan 1973/Liverpool Jan 1978/Sampdoria (Italy) Jul 1984/Rangers player-manager Apr 1986/Liverpool manager Apr 1991-Jan 1994/Galatasaray (Turkey) manager May 1995/Southampton manager Jul 1996/Torino (Italy) manager Jun 1997, head of strategic development Oct 1997/Benfica manager Nov 1997/Blackburn Rovers manager Mar 2000/Newcastle United manager Sep 2004-Feb 2006.

Debut v Keflavik (sub) (UEFAC) (a) 14.9.1971

Throughout his career Graeme Souness exhibited a fierce desire to succeed, but it was that ambition which deprived Spurs of his services. A tough-tackling, creative midfielder, he won his Scotland Youth cap with Spurs who always knew he was destined for the very top. It was just a question of when to give him a chance, but with established midfielders of the quality of Alan Mullery, Martin Peters and Steve Perryman, the young Souness grew frustrated. Though substitute in two League games, the only first team appearance he made was as a substitute in a UEFA Cup match against Keflavik of Iceland in September 1971. After playing for Montreal Olympic in the North American Soccer League in the summer of 1972 he made clear his frustration and at one time even walked out on

the club. Reluctantly, Spurs allowed him to move to Middlesbrough for £32,000 and from there he went on to develop into one of the game's most influential performers of modern times. At the end of his first full season Middlesbrough were promoted to Division One, and Souness had won his first Scotland Under-23 cap against England in March 1974. In October 1974 he won his first full honours against East Germany and had added another Under-23 and two more full caps to his total by the time of his transfer to Liverpool. There, he blossomed into a world class player. The midfield focal point, Souness had the ability to totally dominate games, taking control and dictating the play with his strength and pin point passing. At times he strolled with almost arrogantly ease through the opposition, to then unleash a powerful long-range shot. With Liverpool, he won almost every honour the game can offer, the Football League title in 1979, 1980, 1982, 1983 and 1984, the League Cup (in its various guises) in 1981 (although he missed the replay), 1982, 1983 and 1984, the European Cup in 1978, 1981 and 1984 and 37 more Scottish caps. Having reached the pinnacle of English football, he turned his attention to Europe and moved to Sampdoria of Italy where he spent a highly successful two years picking up another 14 Scottish caps before returning to Britain as player-manager of Rangers. In his first season Rangers won the Scottish League and Scottish League Cup, in 1987-88 the League Cup, in 1988-89 the Scottish League and Skol Cup and reached the Final of the Scottish Cup, in 1989-90 the Scottish League title again and in 1990-91 the Skol Cup. Part-owner of Rangers, Souness was still striving for the only major trophy to elude Rangers, the European Cup, when he left in April 1991 to replace former Anfield team-mate Kenny Dalglish as manager of

Liverpool. In his first season he made many expensive changes and, after the shock of undergoing major heart surgery, led Liverpool to the one trophy he failed to capture as a player, the FA Cup. Sometimes controversial he left Liverpool in April 1994 and a year later went to Turkey as manager of Galatasaray. A year in the "hot seat" at Southampton followed, till Souness suddenly quit to return to Italy with Torino. He had a short and unhappy spell there before taking on the job of trying to rebuild Portugal's fallen giants, Benfica. He failed to do that, and had little success with Blackburn Rovers or Newcastle United before quitting the game to become a TV pundit. Souness attended Carrickvale School in Edinburgh, the same establishment as former Spurs' star Dave Mackay.

Appearances:
Europe: (1) app.
Total: **(1) app. 0 gls.**

SOUTHEY, Peter Charles

Role: Full-back 1979-83
5ft.7ins. 11st.0lbs.
Born: Parsons Green, London, 4th January 1962
Died: Ham, Surrey, 28th December 1983

CAREER: Wandsworth Schools/Inner London Schools/**SPURS** app. Jul 1978, pro. Oct 1978.

Debut v Brighton and Hove Albion (FL) (h) 8.9.1978
(Oxford United (Fr) (a) 4.8.1979)

A full-back of considerable potential, Peter Southey made his single League appearance for Spurs in August 1979, just two months after signing apprentice forms and a month before signing professional. Although he only played as a substitute in a few friendlies thereafter, he was continuing his development in the reserves and expected to mount a serious challenge for a first team place when he was diagnosed as suffering from leukaemia. After a long and brave fight, he passed away in December 1983.

Appearances:
League: 1 app.
Others: 2 (4) apps.
Total: **3 (4) apps. 0 gls.**

SPARROW, Henry

Role: Centre-forward 1913-15
5ft.11ins. 12st.0lbs.
Born: Faversham, Kent, 13th June 1889
Died: Lincoln, Lincolnshire, 13th June 1973

CAREER: Faversham Thursday Portsmouth Dec 1909/Sittingbourne Oct 1910/Croydon Common Oct 1911/Leicester Fosse Feb 1912/**SPURS** Jan 1914/released May 1915/Margate Town cs. 1919/Margate Juniors coach 1922.

Debut v Oldham Athletic (FL) (h) 17.1.1914 (scored twice)

The FA Cup clearly brought out the best in Harry Sparrow, for it was his performance for Leicester Fosse against Spurs in January 1914 that

persuaded Spurs to secure his transfer. Signed jointly with Tommy Clay, Sparrow was Leicester's top scorer at the time of his transfer with six goals in eleven games, and in his two years there had scored 23 goals in only 51 matches. Sparrow had built a reputation with all his previous clubs as someone who knew where the net was and reinforced that with two goals on his Spurs' debut. Spurs acquired Sparrow to provide cover for the injured Jimmy Cantrell and he did the job well in his first few months, scoring in each of his four games in his first season at White Hart Lane. He did not continue in the same vein the following season and never posed a serious threat to Cantrell. Sparrow was released at the end of the 1914-15 season. He did not get another club before the War interrupted football, but signed for Margate when hostilities ended and had a couple of productive years there before becoming a coach.

Appearances:
League: 18 apps. 7 gls.
FA Cup: 1 app.
Others: 8 apps. 7 gls.
Total: **27 apps. 14 gls.**

SPELMAN, Isaac

Role: Half-back 1937-40
5ft.9ins. 11st.2lbs.
Born: Newcastle-Upon-Tyne, 9th March 1914
Died: Newcastle-Upon-Tyne, Apr 2003

CAREER: Usworth Colliery/Leeds United Mar 1933/Southend United May 1935/**SPURS** May 1937/(Bradford City, Darlington, Fulham, Gateshead, Hartlepools United and York City during World War Two)/Hartlepools United May 1946.

Debut v Coventry City (FL) (h) 28.8.1937

Isaac Spelman was spotted by Leeds United playing for the works team of Usworth Colliery where he worked as a miner. He spent three years with Leeds and one with Southend United before joining Spurs, with Sammy Bell making the reverse journey as part of the deal. Spelman made his debut in the first League game of the 1937-38 season, but soon lost his place to Les Howe and it then took Spelman over a year to displace him. Injured in February 1939, Ron Burgess was introduced and Spelman was not to get back in, except for the early part of the 1939-40 war season. After the war Spurs were looking to start afresh and Spelman was by then 32, so he was allowed to move to

Hartlepools where he played for one season. His son, Mick, made over 100 appearances for Hartlepools in the 1970s.

Appearances:
League: 28 apps. 2 gls.
FA Cup: 4 apps.
Others: 12 apps.
Total: 44 apps. 2 gls.

SPENCER, Alfred

Role: Inside-forward 1917-18

CAREER: Clapton Orient May 1913/released cs. 1914/(guest for **SPURS** during World War One).

Debut v Clapton Orient (LFC) (a) 15.12.1917 (scored once)

Alf Spencer joined Clapton Orient on returning from military service in India, but made only one senior appearance in their colours before being released. However, he continued to appear for them during the War until wounds received on active service forced his retirement. His one appearance for Spurs was against Clapton Orient in a London Football Combination match in December 1917 when he scored once.

Appearances:
Others: 1 app. 1 gl.
Total: 1 app. 1 gl.

SPERRIN, William Thomas

Role: Inside-forward or winger 1940-44
5ft.5ins. 11st. 0lbs.
Born: Wood Green, London, 9th April 1922
Died: Sawbridgeworth, Hertfordshire, 21st June 2000

CAREER: Wood Green Schools/Middlesex Schools/Tottenham Juniors/ **SPURS** am./Finchley/(guest for Bradford City, Brighton and Hove Albion, Chelsea, Clapton Orient, Fulham and Millwall during World War Two)/Finchley/Guildford City/Brentford Sep 1949-1956/Tunbridge Wells United/Yiewsley (later Hillingdon Borough) trainer, coach, caretaker manager, asst. manager/North Greenford United manager.

Debut v Southend United (FLS) (a) 30.11.1940

Like his brother, Jimmy, Billy Sperrin was an amateur on Spurs' books playing for Finchley during the Second World War after completing his time with Tottenham Juniors. He appeared for Spurs throughout the middle war years making his first appearance as an 18-year old in November 1940 against Southend United. That was in a Football League South game played on the ground of Chelmsford City who lent Southend their facilities for the season. A wartime guest for several clubs, Sperrin was loaned by Spurs to Clapton Orient for the match against Spurs on 21st December 1940 that Spurs won 9-0. After the war he continued to play for Finchley before joining Brentford where he played for six years. He later served Yiewsley (Hillingdon Borough) for twelve years in a variety of capacities. His son, Martin, played for Luton Town, West Ham United and Barnet.

Appearances:
Others: 28 apps. 6 gls.
Total: 28 apps. 6 gls.

SPERRIN, James

Role: Winger 1940-42
Born: Wood Green, London, 10th July 1920
Died: Luton, Bedfordshire, 10th May 2000

CAREER: Tottenham Juniors/**SPURS** am./Northfleet United/**SPURS**/ Finchley loan 1939/(guest for Clapton Orient, Luton Town and Millwall during World War Two)/Finchley/St Albans City cs. 1947.

Debut v Luton Town (FLS) (a) 2.11.1940

A former Tottenham Junior, Jimmy Sperrin had played at the Northfleet nursery and in 1939-40 was loaned out by Spurs to Finchley. A tiny, flying winger he was regarded as a second Fanny Walden, but his career was ruined by the outbreak of the Second World War. He made his debut as a 20-year old against Luton Town in a Football League South fixture in November 1940 and played quite regularly, often alternating in the outside-right position with his brother, Billy. After the War, Sperrin continued with Finchley before joining St Albans City where he enjoyed his most successful years representing Middlesex, Hertfordshire, the Athenian and Isthmian Leagues and the Football Association.

Appearances:
Others: 16 apps. 4 gls.
Total: 16 apps. 4 gls.

SPIERS, Cyril Henry

Role: Goalkeeper 1927-32
6ft.2ins. 12st.13lbs.
Born: Witton, Birmingham, 4th April 1902
Died: 21st May 1967

CAREER: Aston Boys/Midlands Boys/Witton Star/Birchfield Boys Brigade/The Swifts (Perry Barr)/Brookvale United/Soho Rovers/ Handsworth Central/Halesowen/Aston Villa Dec 1920/**SPURS** trial Nov 1927, perm. Dec 1927/Wolverhampton Wanderers Sep 1933, retired May 1935, coach-asst. manager Aug 1935/Cardiff City secretary-manager Apr 1939/Norwich City manager Jun 1946/Cardiff City manager Dec 1947/ Crystal Palace manager Apr 1954-May 1958/Leicester City scout Sep 1958–Apr 1962/Exeter City manager May 1962-Feb 1963/Leicester City scout Feb 1963-May 1965.

Debut v Burnley (FL) (h) 3.12.1927

Cyril Spiers gradually worked his way through the various levels of local football to join Aston Villa. An agile and brave 'keeper, he took time to establish himself at Villa Park, but made over 100 League appearances in his seven years there and had just about consolidated his position as first choice when surprisingly released. He had been injured towards the end of 1926-27 and Villa decided he would not be fit enough to play again. However, he underwent an experimental operation during the close season and arrived at White Hart Lane for a month's trial. He played just two trial games and was then signed permanently as Jock Britton had been injured in a motorcycle accident. Consistent and reliable, Spiers went on to give Spurs four years' invaluable service and even got close to international recognition. After playing for the Football League against the Scottish League in November 1930, he played in the international trial match of March 1931 but found Harry Hibbs preferred when the selectors made a final decision. Given a free transfer in May 1933, he joined Wolves where he was eventually made assistant manager to Major Frank Buckley. In April 1939 he took on the manager's role at Cardiff City, but with the intervention of the War he remained in Cardiff concentrating his efforts in developing the Cardiff Nomads club. In June 1946 Spiers became manager of Norwich City, but within eighteen months he had returned to Cardiff. He filled the manager's role there for seven years, later serving

Crystal Palace and Exeter City as manager and Leicester City as a scout.

Appearances:
League: 158 apps.
FA Cup: 11 apps.
Others: 17 apps.
Total: **186 apps. 0 gls.**

SPIVEY, Douglas

Role: Outside-left 1954-55
Born: North Shields, North Tyneside,
Died: Monkseaton, Tyne & Wear, 14th July 2015

CAREER: SPURS 1950/released Apr 1955/ North Shields cs. 1955.

Debut v Queens Park Rangers (Fr) (a) 11.10.1954

First associated with Spurs during the 1950-51 season, Doug Spivey was a winger who made just one appearance in the first team. That was in October 1954 when he played in a friendly at Queens Park Rangers. Released at the end of that season he returned home to North Shields and signed for the local club.

Appearances:
Others: 1 app.
Total: **1 app. 0 gls.**

SPROSTON, Bert

Role: Full-back 1938-39
5ft.9ins. 12st.0lbs.
Born: Elworth, nr. Sandbach, Cheshire, 22nd June 1915
Died: Bolton, Greater Manchester, 27th January 2000

CAREER: Elworth Church of England School/Sandbach Council School/Wheelock Village/Middlewich Athletic/Sandbach Ramblers/Huddersfield Town trial/Leeds United May 1933/SPURS Jun 1938/Manchester City Nov 1938/(guest for Aldershot, Millwall, Newmarket Town and Wrexham during World War Two)/Ashton United Aug 1950/Bolton Wanderers trainer Jul 1951, coach, scout.

Debut v Southampton (FL) (a) 27.8.1938
(Arsenal (JTF) (a) 20.8.1938)

England full-back Bert Sproston had a very short career at White Hart Lane, making only nine League appearances, but winning four representative honours in his five months as a Spurs player. As a youth he played at half-back and had a trial in that position with Huddersfield Town, but was not taken on. He continued to play for Sandbach Ramblers as a right-half, but then switched to the right-back spot and replaced his brother, before coming to the attention of Leeds United. He progressed rapidly with Leeds, won his first cap against Wales in October 1936 and by the time of his transfer to Spurs for a big £9,500 fee had eight caps to his credit. Having won two more full caps and played twice for the Football League he was picked for Spurs' match at Manchester City on 5th November 1938. He played in the game, but not for Spurs. The previous day he was transferred to Manchester City for another £9,500 fee having complained he was unable to settle in London. He spent over ten years at Maine Road, helped City win the Second Division title in 1947 and collected one more England cap. He finished his playing career with twelve months at Ashton United and then joined the coaching staff at Bolton Wanderers.

Appearances:
League: 9 apps.
Others: 1 app.
Total: **10 apps. 0 gls.**

STALEY, Ronald

Role: Outside-left 1942-43
Born: 1922
Died: 5th September 2013

CAREER: Derby County/(guest for SPURS during World War Two)/Burton Town/Gresley Rovers Aug 1948-May 1950.

Debut v Queens Park Rangers (FLS) (a) 5.9.1942

A guest outside-left on the books of Derby County, Ronald Staley made his one appearance for Spurs in a Football League South game against Queens Park Rangers in September 1942. After the War he played for Burton Town and Gresley Rovers.

Appearances:
Others: 1 app.
Total: **1 app. 0 gls.**

STALTERI, Paul

Role: Full-back 2005-2008
5ft.11ins. 12st.2lbs.
Born: Etobicoke, Ontario, Canada, 18th October 1977

CAREER: Brampton Rebels (Canada)/Malton Bullets (Canada) 1990/Clemson University (USA)/Toronto Lynx (Canada) Mar 1997/ Werder Bremen (Germany) trial and perm. Nov 1997/SPURS Jul 2005/ (Fulham loan Jan 2008)/contract cancelled Dec 2008/Borussia Mönchengladbach (Germany) Jan 2009-Jun 2011/retired Mar 2013.

Debut v Portsmouth (PL) (a) 14.8.2005

A competent, unfussy defender, Paul Stalteri had played for less than a year as a professional footballer with Toronto Lynx when spotted by Werder Bremen. After a short trial he was taken on and spent two years learning the game in their reserves before making a first team breakthrough. He established himself as a solid, dependable regular, a full-back who played the game in a simple manner, and helped Bremen win the Bundesliga and Pokal in 2004. With his Bremen contract coming to an end, Stalteri was attracted to Spurs to replace the injured Noe

Pamarot. He did a great job in his first season, a consistent performer, playing an uncomplicated game that had defending as its priority. He would venture forward, often to great effect, but he rarely reached the final third of the field. After just a year as a regular, Stalteri found his place taken by a new arrival, the buccaneering Pascal Chimbonda. Stalteri saw little first team action after that, playing more games in a loan spell with Fulham than he did in his last 18 months with Spurs. With prospects of first team action and his place in the Canadian team under threat, his contract was cancelled so he could immediately return to Germany with Borussia Mönchengladbach. Stalteri won a record 84 full caps for Canada, 22 of them in his time at White Hart Lane.

Appearances:
League: 37 (5) apps. 2 gls.
FA Cup: 3 (2) apps. 1 gl.
FL Cup: 3 apps.
Euro: 4 (2) apps.
Others: 5 (2) apps.
Total: 52 (11) apps. 3 gls.

STAMBOULI, Benjamin

Role: Midfielder 2014-15
5ft.11ins. 13st.1lb.
Born: Marseille, France, 13th August 1990

CAREER: Olympique Marseille (France) Oct 1996/ L'Entente sportive Gallia Club d'Uzès (France) Sep 1997/CC Sedan Ardennes (France) Sep 2001/L'Entente sportive Gallia Club d'Uzès (France) Apr 2003/Montpellier Herault (France) Jul 2004, pro. Mar 2010/**SPURS** Sep 2014/Paris St Germain (France) Jul 2015.

Debut v Sunderland (PL) (a) (sub) 13.9.2014

Benjamin Stambouli's signing from Montpellier came as a bit of a surprise. At the time Spurs already had Nabil Bentaleb and Étienne Capoue to play in the defensive midfield role Stambouli was known to occupy. An athletic, technically sound, hard worker, the French Under-21 international had been on the radar of Europe's major clubs for some time. He helped Montpellier win Lique 1 in 2011-12 as he established himself in the centre of the Montpellier midfield and rose to captain the club. In the season before he moved to Spurs he played in all but one of his club's League games, not even being substituted in one of them. At Spurs, substitute was his usual role, practically all his senior appearances coming in the cup competitions that were becoming less important than the Premier League. Less than a year after arriving in London, Paris St Germain made an offer of £6 million for Stambouli. As it gave the player the chance to re-kindle his career and Spurs, reputedly, a 50% profit, it was an offer neither could refuse. Stambouli's father, Henri, was a goalkeeper who played two matches for Marseille, but went on to have a lengthy career as a manager and coach and his grandfather, Gérard Banide, managed several French clubs. Banide's son, Laurent, managed Monaco and numerous clubs in the Middle East.

Appearances:
League: 4 (8) apps.
FA Cup: 2 apps.
FL Cup: 5 apps.
Euro: 6 apps. 1 gl.
Others: 2 apps.
Total: 19 (8) apps. 1 gl.

STANSFIELD, Harold

Role: Forward 1904-08
5ft.7ins. 10st.7lbs.
Born: Manchester, 21st July 1878

CAREER: Berrys/Preston North End 1899/Stockport County cs. 1900/ **SPURS** May 1904/Luton Town May 1908.

Debut v Fulham (SL) (h) 3.9.1904

Harry Stansfield joined Spurs after Stockport County had failed to secure re-election to the Football League. Stansfield had spent four years with Stockport, having started his career at Preston North End. Able to occupy any of the forward positions, he played regularly throughout his first season at White Hart Lane. After that he was principally a reserve, usually called upon to fill one of the winger's roles. He stayed with Spurs for four years before moving to Luton.

Appearances:
Southern: 49 apps. 9 gls.
FA Cup: 6 apps.
Others: 38 apps. 6 gls.
Total: 93 apps. 15 gls.

STATHAM, Brian

Role: Full-back 1987-92
5ft.9ins. 11st.7lbs.
Born: Harare, Rhodesia, 21st May 1969

CAREER: Vange United/ Brentwood and Basildon Schools/London Schools/ **SPURS** app. Jul 1985, pro. Jul 1987/(Reading loan Mar 1991)/(AFC Bournemouth loan Nov 1991)/Brentford loan Jan 1992, perm. Feb 1992 /Gillingham Aug 1997/ (Woking loan Sep 1998)/ (Stevenage Borough loan Feb 1999)/Chesham United Sep 1999/Chelmsford City Oct 2001/Welling United Jun 2003- Jun 2004/East Thurrock United Jul 2004/ Erith & Belvedere Jan 2005/ Heybridge Swifts player-manager Jan 2005, manager May 2005-Aug 2008/ Billericay Town manager Apr 2009-Mar 2010.

Debut v Southampton (sub) (FL) (a) 26.12.1987
(St Albans City (Fr) (a) 10.11.1987)

Born in Zimbabwe (then Rhodesia), Brian Statham lived for a while in Saudi Arabia before settling in England with his family. A schoolboy footballer for his district, he also played cricket for Essex Schools before deciding to make a career in football. A hard tackling full-back with a strong physique who could also play in midfield, he got a first team chance early in 1988 due to the persistent injury problems that afflicted the unfortunate Gary Stevens. He grabbed the opportunity and performed so well in the First Division that by May 1988 he was in the England Under-21 team which played Switzerland, and at the end of the season appeared for the England Under-20 team on its short tour to Brazil. Although he started the next season in the team and won two further Under-21 caps, he was unable to maintain his earlier form and fell back into the reserves. Continually hampered by injuries that caused him to miss much of the 1989-90 and 1990-91 seasons, he was loaned out to Reading and Bournemouth in an effort to recover full fitness but, after a further loan period with Brentford, Spurs decided to allow him to move on. He signed permanently for Brentford, where he played his part in helping them win the Third Division in 1992. He gave Brentford five years' good service, and Gillingham another one, then played and managed in non-League circles.

Appearances:
League: 20 (4) apps.
FA Cup: (1) app.
FL Cup: 2 apps.
Others: 13 (5) apps.
Total: 35 (10) apps. 0 gls.

STEAD, Kevin

Role: Striker 1976-77
Born: West Ham, London, 2nd October 1958
Died: Dagenham, Essex, 19th January 2016

CAREER: Newham Schools/Essex Schools/England Schools/**SPURS** app. Jul 1975, pro. Apr 1976/Arsenal Jul 1977/Oxford City cs. 1980.

Debut v Swindon Town (sub) (Fr) (a) 10.8.1976

The brother of full-back, Micky, Kevin Stead made his only first team appearance as a substitute in a friendly at Swindon Town in August 1976. He followed former Spurs' manager Terry Neill to Arsenal in July 1977 and made two League appearances before being released at the end of the 1979-80 season to join Oxford City.

Appearances:
Others: (1) app.
Total: (1) app. 0 gls.

STEAD, Michael John

Role: Full-back 1975-78
5ft.8ins. 11st.7lbs.
Born: West Ham, London, 28th February 1957

CAREER: Newham Schools/**SPURS** app. Jul 1973, pro. Nov 1974/(Swansea City loan Feb 1977)/Southend United loan Sep 1978, perm. Nov 1978/Doncaster Rovers player-coach Nov 1985/Fisher Athletic cs. 1988/Stambridge/Chelmsford City Nov 1990/Braintree Town cs. 1992/Heybridge Swifts 1993-94 player-coach/Halstead Town 1993-94/Dagenham & Redbridge asst. manager Jul 1994/Fisher 93 co-manager in 1995-96/Fisher Athletic coach 1996-97, manager

Debut v Stoke City (FL) (a) 21.2.1976

Micky Stead worked his way up through the junior ranks at White Hart Lane to sign on the professional staff in November 1974. He made his League debut at Stoke City in the same game as Glenn Hoddle made his full League bow. The similarity however ends there, for while Hoddle went on to become one of the country's top stars, Stead merely progressed enough to build a good career for himself in the lower divisions. After a spell on loan to Swansea City in February 1977, Stead returned to find new signing Jimmy Holmes injured and played the last six games of the season as Spurs were relegated. With the more experienced players available, he had few chances in the first team after that and in September 1978 joined Southend United on loan, making the move permanent two months later. A competent full-back with Spurs, Micky spent over seven years with Southend making more than 300 appearances as a full-back, central defender and occasional midfielder before moving to Doncaster Rovers as player-coach. Relieved of his coaching duties when Dave Mackay took over as manager in December 1987, Stead was given a free transfer at the end of the season and went into non-League football. His brother, Kevin, was a forward on Spurs' books at the same time as Micky. Although he did not make the League team at White Hart Lane, he followed Terry Neill to Highbury and made two League appearances for Arsenal before moving on to Oxford City.

Appearances:
League: 14 (1) apps.
Others: 17 (9) apps. 3 gls.
Total: 31 (10) apps. 3 gls.

STEEL, Alexander

Role: Half-back 1909-10
5ft.7ins. 11st.8lbs.
Born: Newmilns, Ayrshire, 25th July 1886
Died: St. Albans, Hertfordshire, late January 1932

CAREER: Newmilns/Ayr United/Manchester City Feb 1906/**SPURS** trial and perm Jan 1910/Kilmarnock Aug 1911/Southend United cs. 1913/Gillingham Nov 1919.

Debut v Bradford City (FL) (h) 29.1.1910

Alex Steel's only appearance for Spurs was in a League game against Bradford City in January 1910. As his brothers, Danny and Bobby, were also in the team it was a notable event, for it is the only occasion on which Spurs have fielded three brothers in the same League game. Steel remained with Spurs until the summer of 1911 without playing another senior game and then returned to Scotland with Kilmarnock. Two years later he was back in England with Southend and then played for a year with Gillingham where he was joined by brother Bobby.

Appearances:
League: 1 app.
Total: **1 app. 0 gls.**

STEEL, Daniel

Role: Centre-half 1906-12
5ft.9ins. 10st.5lbs.
Born: Newmilns, Ayrshire, 2nd May 1884
Died: Marylebone, London, 29th April 1931

CAREER: Newmilns/Airdrie 1904/Rangers Apr 1904/**SPURS** May 1906/Third Lanark Jul 1912/(Dumbarton loan Apr 1914)/Clapton Orient Aug 1914.

Debut v West Ham United (WL) (a) 8.10.1906

Danny Steel had spent most of his time in the reserves at Rangers, and at first was just a reserve at Spurs, understudying Ted Hughes and Tom Morris, the half-backs of the 1901 FA Cup winning team. He played only 12 games in his first season at White Hart Lane and it was not until called up to replace Walter Bull early in the next that he was given the opportunity to claim a regular first team place. Steel did so well that he made the centre-half position his own, and Spurs were able to part with the experienced and highly respected Bull. Always calm and collected, Steel was a commanding individual, able to dictate the play with his strong tackling and accurate passing. For the first four years of Spurs' Football League history, he and brother Bobby formed the essential core of a team that found it very hard adjusting to life in the First Division. No representative honours came Steel's way, although he played for the Anglo-Scots against the Home Scots in the Scottish international trial matches of 1908, 1910 and 1912. At the end of 1911-12 Spurs decided that they had seen the best of Steel and the future defensive kingpin would be the promising Charlie Rance. Steel was released and moved to Third Lanark, returning to London with Clapton Orient where he finished his career.

Appearances:
Southern: 32 apps. 1 gl.
League: 131* apps. 3 gls.
FA Cup: 13 apps.
Others: 36 apps. 2 gls.
Total: **212 apps. 6 gls.**
* Includes 3 abandoned matches.

STEEL, Robert Loudoun

Role: Inside-forward and centre-half 1908-16
5ft.10ins. 11st.9lbs.
Born: Newmilns, Ayrshire, 25th June 1888
Died: Winchmore Hill, London, 28th March 1972

CAREER: Newmilns/Kilwinning Rangers/Greenock Morton 1904/Port Glasgow Athletic Oct 1906/**SPURS** May 1908/released May 1919/Gillingham Dec 1919-May 1920.

Debut v Wolverhampton Wanderers (FL) (h) 1.9.1908

The youngest of the three Steel brothers, Bobby played with Danny for Newmilns but moved on to Kilwinning and Port Glasgow before they linked up again at Spurs. Originally an inside-left, he made his debut in the club's first League game against Wolves and went on to give Spurs seven years of the most dedicated service. A real hard-worker, he was unlike many Scottish inside-forwards, in that he was not only a mazy dribbler, but also excelled at the passing game. A regular scorer, he was one of the stars of Spurs' early days in the Football League but, like Danny, never won any major representative honours although he did play for the Anglo-Scots against the Home Scots in the international trial match of March 1909. There can be no doubt that both Bobby and Danny suffered from the reluctance of the Scottish selectors to pick players who had decided to make their careers in England. Steel continued to exert his influence at inside-left until 1913-14 when he moved to the centre-half role not long vacated by Danny. With the outbreak of the First World War, Steel showed his versatility, playing in any position necessary, centre-forward, outside-left and even left-back. He was only able to appear for the first war-time season of 1915-16, but returned to White Hart Lane when the conflict was over. With his best years in the past, he was released and took up refereeing in the Southern League until persuaded to return to active participation in the game with Gillingham by his other brother, Alex. He finished playing in the summer of 1920 and returned to refereeing. After football Bobby remained keen on sport, and at one time captained the England Bowls team. Although Bobby Steel played for Port Glasgow immediately before joining Spurs he was registered as a Scottish League player with Greenock Morton and it was to them Spurs had to pay a transfer fee.

Appearances:
League: 230 apps. 41 gls.
FA Cup: 19 apps. 5 gls.
Others: 68 apps. 16 gls.
Total: **317 apps. 62 gls.**
* Includes 3 abandoned matches.

STEPHENSON, John Wallace

Role: Full-back 1900-04
5ft.9ins. 11st.12lbs.
Born: Leigh-on-Sea, Essex, 8th February 1874
Died: Much Woolton, Lincolnshire, 18 January 1908

CAREER: Liverpool am./New Brighton Tower 1897/Swindon Town cs. 1900/**SPURS** Apr 1901/retired May 1904.

Debut v Portsmouth (SL) (a) 24.4.1901

John Stephenson was signed from Swindon Town in April 1901 and went straight into the team in the absence of Sandy Tait. Previously in the reserves at Liverpool and with New Brighton

Tower, he was a full-back of considerable promise but his short career was blighted by injury. After only 25 appearances for Spurs he was forced to retire at the end of the 1903-04 season. He died of pneumonia in January 1908.

Appearances:
Southern: 1 app.
Others: 21* apps.
Total: **22 apps. 0 gls.**
*Includes 1 abandoned match.

STERLING, Kazaiah

Role: Striker 2016-
6ft.0ins. 12st.0lbs.
Born: Enfield, Middx, 9th November 1998

CAREER: Winchmore School/Leyton Orient/**SPURS** Academy Scholar Jul 2015.

Debut v Kitchee (sub) (Fr) (a) 26.5.2017 (scored once)

A talented, locally-born young striker of whom much is expected, Kazaiah Sterling started the 2016-17 with an injury that saw him side-lined just when he wanted to be making his mark. It finished with him scoring on his first team debut in a friendly against Kitchee in Hong Kong. Strong and hard-running Sterling has proved a regular scorer at all levels as he has progressed through the youth ranks. An England international at Under-17 and Under-18 level, he could be one for the future.

Appearances:
Others: (1) app. 1 gl.
Total: **(1) app. 1 gl.**

STEVEN

Role: Half-back 1902-03

Debut v Reading (SCC) (a) 14.1.1903

Steven, not to be confused with Bob Stevens, made one appearances for Spurs in the 1902-03 season. That was against Reading in January 1903 in the Southern Charity Cup when he played at centre-half in what was basically a reserve eleven.

Appearances:
Others: 1 app.
Total: **1 app. 0 gls.**

STEVENS, Gary Andrew

Role: Defender or Midfield 1983-90
6ft.0ins. 12st.0lbs.
Born: Hillingdon, Middlesex, 30th March 1962

CAREER: West Suffolk Schools/Suffolk Schools/Brighton and Hove Albion pro. Oct 1979/**SPURS** Jun 1983/Portsmouth loan Jan 1990, perm. Mar 1990/retired Feb 1992/Farnborough Town/Petersfield Town manager Jun 1993-1994/Charlton Athletic Under-21 coach Jun 1998-Jun 2001/Tunbridge Wells Director of Football Jul 2006/Gabala (Azerbaijan) asst. manager Feb 2010, manager Nov 2011-Apr 2012/Sligo Rovers (Eire) asst. manager Jan 2013-Jun 2014/Army United (Thailand) manager Aug 2014-May 2015/FC Port (Thailand) manager Jun-Jul 2015.

Debut v Ipswich Town (FL) (a) 27.8.1983
(Hertford Town (Fr) (a) 2.8.1983)

Although associated with Ipswich Town as a schoolboy, Gary Stevens had to go down to Brighton to start off his professional career. Playing at the centre of defence alongside the experienced Steve Foster, he developed rapidly, winning his first England Under-21 cap against Hungary in April 1983. The following month played for Brighton in the FA Cup Final against Manchester United. Although unfancied Brighton lost after a replay, Stevens gave a masterful performance in the first match when the Seagulls were without the suspended Foster, even managing to score one of Brighton's goals. The South Coast club were also relegated at the end of that season, but Stevens did not drop down with them, joining Spurs instead for £350,000. He found life much harder at White Hart Lane and, when Paul Miller was re-instated in one of the main defensive positions, Stevens was switched to full-back. His first representative honour as a Spurs player was in October 1983 when he played for England Under-21s against Hungary, and by the end of the season his number of Under-21 caps had increased to six. When Glenn Hoddle was injured, Stevens was tried in midfield and he played there in both legs of the 1984 UEFA Cup Final. He performed so well he retained a midfield role even when Hoddle returned, and his debut for the full England side, as a substitute against Finland in October 1984, came in a similar midfield position. Energetic and quick into the tackle, Steven's defensive experience helped him win the ball, but he also showed a flair for accurate passing and a taste for joining the attack that had not been so apparent when playing at the back. In March 1985, just as he seemed set to make a real challenge for a regular England place, Stevens suffered a serious knee injury that was to keep him out of the team for six months. Having fought his way back and collected another Under-21 and six more full caps (all but one as substitute) he picked up a further bad injury in November 1986 and from then on sustained one injury blow after another. He kept bouncing back and, if he had only been able to stay fit, his versatility would have ensured he became a valuable member of the first team squad. However, it was just not to be, and after yet another setback, Stevens was loaned to Portsmouth in a final effort to prove his fitness. He did well back on the South Coast, and after two months the transfer was made permanent. Sadly, he was still plagued by injury problems and in February 1992 was forced to give up the battle and retired. Gary did however, remain connected with football, initially working as a commentator for Capital Radio in London and taking on the manager's job at Wessex League Petersfield Town. Moving over to work for Sky TV, Stevens was a regular performer at White Hart Lane in 1996-97 as announcer. With media work always there as a back-up, Stevens took to coaching, working as far afield as Azerbaijan, Eire and Thailand. As Stevens was rejected by Ipswich Town as a schoolboy, it is somewhat ironic that he made his debut for both Brighton and Spurs against the team from Portman Road.

Appearances:
League: 140 (7) apps. 6 gls.
FA Cup: 13 (4) apps.
FL Cup: 19 (2) apps.
Euro: 15 apps. 2 gls
Others: 36 (7) apps. 4 gls
Total: **223 (20) apps. 12 gls.**

STEVENS, Leslie William George

Role: Outside-left 1941-49
5ft.7ins. 9st.8lbs.
Born: Croydon, Surrey, 15th August 1920
Died: 14th February 1991

CAREER: Acc & Tabs/Tottenham Juniors/**SPURS** am. May 1937/(Northfleet United)/**SPURS** pro. Jan 1940/(Aldershot, Arsenal, Charlton Athletic, Chelsea, Crystal Palace and Millwall during World War Two)/Bradford Park Avenue Feb 1949/Crystal Palace Aug 1950/Tonbridge Aug 1951/Snowdon Colliery Welfare/ Ashford/Cambridge United.

Debut v West Bromwich Albion (FL) (a) 7.9.1946
(Crystal Palace (FLS) (h) 28.2.1940 (scored once))

Having first joined Spurs as an amateur, Les Stevens worked his way through the ranks of Tottenham Juniors and Northfleet to sign professional in January 1940. He made his debut against Crystal Palace the next month, scoring from the inside-left position. A regular performer during the Second World War, he moved to outside-left and was first choice there during 1946-47. The following season he had to compete with Welsh international Ernie Jones, but lost out and as a consequence moved on to Bradford PA. He returned to London with Crystal Palace, but only played there for a year before moving into the non-League scene. After football Stevens ran an off-license in the New Cross district of London.

Appearances:
League: 54 apps. 5 gls.
FA Cup: 5 apps.
Others: 33 apps. 9 gls.
Total: 92 apps. 14 gls.

STEVENS, Robert Clarke

Role: Full-back 1899-03
Born: Derby, April qtr. 1875
Died: Thanet, Kent, February 1928

CAREER: Charterhouse School/London Caledonians/Cheshunt/Fulham Mar 1898/West Norwood/**SPURS** trial Aug 1899/Fulham Sep–Nov 1900/Millwall Athletic/Old Carthusians/West Norwood am. Oct 1905.

Debut v Portsmouth (WL) (a) 17.4.1901
(Middlesbrough (Fr) (a) 1.1.1900)

A well-known amateur with London Caledonians, West Norwood, Cheshunt and London, Bob Stevens first appeared in a Spurs shirt in a pre-season trial match in August 1899. Regarded as one of London's premier defenders around the turn of the century, he spent 14 years from 1898 onwards assisting Spurs, although the vast majority of his appearances came in the reserve team. The only senior competitive matches he played in were at the end of April 1901, when the first team were preparing for the FA Cup Final against Sheffield United and reserve teams were fielded. As with all traditional amateurs, he was free to play for any club he pleased and these included Fulham, Millwall and the Old Carthusians. He continued to help out Spurs' reserves until 1912, retiring from senior football once the First World War was underway. He eventually met a most unhappy end, killed in a motor car accident in February 1928 whilst travelling down to Margate for his daughter's wedding.

Appearances:
Southern: 3 apps.
Others: 5 apps.
Total: 8 apps. 0 gls.

STEWART, Kevin Linford

Role: Defender 2013-
6ft. 11st.7lbs.
Born: Enfield, Middlesex, 12th September 1990

CAREER: Enfield Grammar School/**SPURS** Academy Scholar Jul 2010, pro. Jul 2012/(Crewe Alexandra loan Mar 2013)/Liverpool Jul 2014/(Cheltenham Town loan Jan 2015)/(Burton Albion loan Mar 2015)/(Swindon Town loan Jul 2015).

Debut v Swindon Town (Fr) (a) 16.7.2013

A local lad who graduated from the Spurs Academy, Kevin Stewart played in some of the 2013-14 pre-season friendlies, but never got any closer to a senior first team outing. Released at the end of the season, the defender was offered another chance of big-time football at Liverpool. Former Spurs' Academy coach Alex Inglethorpe had left Spurs to take up a similar role at Liverpool. He remembered Stewart as a determined youngster playing at full-back or the centre of defence, but thought Stewart had better prospects as a defensive midfielder. Within a few months of arriving at Anfield, Stewart was out on loan playing in the Football League. Recalled to Liverpool when injuries began to take their toll, Jürgen Klopp gave Stewart his senior debut in an FA Cup-tie. Stewart grabbed the opportunity and performed so well that he even earned a starting position in Premier League games as the German manager got to know his new charges.

Appearances:
Others: 1 (2) apps.
Total: 1 (2) apps. 0 gls.

STEWART, Paul Andrew

Role: Striker or midfield 1988-92
6ft. 13st.4lbs.
Born: Manchester, 7th June 1964

CAREER: Blackpool app. Jun 1980, pro. Oct 1981/Manchester City Mar 1987/**SPURS** Jun 1988/Liverpool Jul 1992/(Crystal Palace loan Jan 1994)/(Wolverhampton Wanderers loan Sep 1994)/(Burnley loan Feb 1995)/Sunderland loan Aug 1995 and Mar 1996, perm. Jul 1996/Stoke City Jul 1997/retired Jun 1998/Workington Sep 1998.

Debut v Manchester United (sub) (FL) (h) 1.10.1988
(Vederslöv-Dänningelanda (Fr) (a) 26.7.1988) (scored once)

Starting off his career with Blackpool, England Youth cap Paul Stewart made his League debut in February 1982. He scored 56 goals in 201

League appearances in the next five years before a £200,000 move to Manchester City. Although he could do nothing to prevent the Light Blues from relegation at the end of 1987-88, Stewart really showed his promise the following season with 24 goals in 40 League appearances. It earnt him his first England Under-21 cap in April 1988 against France. With Clive Allen moving to France and only Paul Walsh left up front, Spurs' attack looked lightweight, so Terry Venables secured Stewart's transfer for £1.7 million, more than Spurs had ever paid out before to sign a player. A big, bustling, determined centre-forward with inexhaustible stamina, Stewart found it difficult to make an impact as Spurs struggled at the wrong end of the table, but by the end of his first season he had begun to show flashes of the form that had persuaded Venables to invest so much money, and was rewarded by selection for the end of season England "B" tour. The arrival of the prolific Gary Lineker to share the burden up front, did not provide the anticipated boost to Stewart's modest scoring rate, but although Lineker, not Stewart, was now the focal point of the Spurs attack, his immense success would not have been possible without Stewart's unselfish hard graft. It was not really until early in 1990-91 that Stewart at last began to gain the full credit he deserved, but it was one game in particular, against Luton Town in December 1990, that proved to be the turning point. Spurs had two men sent off and Stewart was forced to drop back into midfield. He showed an unexpected liking for a position where he was both continually involved, and able to find more time and space to show the full range of his skills. It was an aspect of the game never previously available to him when posted almost exclusively in the opposition's penalty area. So well did he perform that he kept a place there for the remainder of the season, which culminated in his scoring the all-important equaliser against Nottingham Forest in the FA Cup Final. By September 1991, his dynamic midfield performances had propelled him to the full England squad. He made his debut as a substitute against Germany and then continued to press for a regular spot. It had been known for some time that Stewart wanted to return North for personal reasons. Spurs resisted until July 1992 when they were unable to refuse Liverpool's £2,300,000 offer for his transfer. A Graeme Souness signing, life did not work out for Stewart on Merseyside. After loan spells with several clubs he eventually joined Sunderland and helped them secure promotion to the Premier League. When they were relegated he moved to Stoke and when they suffered the same fate, he retired. He was then persuaded to sign for non-League Workington and helped them reach the First Division of the Northern Premier League, before giving up the game for good. Stewart is one of the few players to have appeared in derby matches in Manchester, north London, Liverpool and the North East.

Appearances:
League: 126 (5) apps. 28 gls.
FA Cup: 9 apps. 2 gls.
FL Cup: 23 apps. 7 gls.
Euro: 8 apps.
Others: 43 (2) apps. 20 gls.
Total: 209 (7) apps. 57 gls.

STIMSON, Mark Nicholas

Role: Full-back 1986-89
5ft.11 ins. 11st.0lbs.
Born: Plaistow, London, 27th December 1967

CAREER: Newham Schools/Essex County/**SPURS** YTS Jul 1984, pro. Jul 1985/(Orient loan Mar 1988)/(Gillingham loan Jan 1989)/Newcastle United May 1989/Portsmouth loan Dec 1992, perm. Jul 1993/(Barnet loan Sep 1995)/Southend United Mar 1996/Queens Park Rangers trial/Leyton Orient Mar 1999/Welling United trial Jul 1999/Gillingham trial Jul 1999/Canvey Island Aug 1999/**SPURS** Academy coach Aug 2000–2005 /Grays Athletic player-coach May 2002, player-manager Sep 2002/ Stevenage Borough manager Jun-Oct 2007/Gillingham manager November 2007-May 2010/Barnet manager Jun 2010-Jan 2011/ Dagenham & Redbridge coach May 2011/Kettering Town manager Sep 2011-Jan 2012/Peterborough United coach Feb 2012/Thurrock manager May 2012.

Debut v Everton (FL) (a) 11.5.1987.

Mark Stimson is another of the clutch of Spurs' youngsters who made. He was an associate schoolboy with Queens Park Rangers, but joined Spurs under the Youth Training Scheme. An Essex and London Youth player, Stimson had few opportunities with Mitchell Thomas firmly established as first choice left-back and, after two loan spells, moved to Newcastle United for £150,000. He played regularly there until the dismissal of manager Ossie Ardiles as the Magpies struggled to return to the upper echelons of the game. A loan spell with Portsmouth turned into a permanent transfer and he served Pompey for almost three years before a similar time with Southend United. After a short spell back with Leyton Orient he moved into the non-League game while also taking the first steps on a coaching career at the Spurs Academy. While with Canvey Island, Stimson made one appearance for the England National Game XI. As coaching became his priority, he led Grays Athletic to FA Trophy success in 2005 and 2006, making it three in a row after joining Stevenage Borough. Stimson has since worked as a coach and manager at the lower League level and in the upper reaches of the non-League game.

Appearances:
League: 1 (1) apps.
Others: 6 (5) apps. 1 gl.
Total: 7 (6) apps. 1 gl.

STIRLING, J

Role: Half-back 1894-95

Debut v London Caledonians (Fr) (h) 23.3.1895

A guest from the 2nd Battalion of the Scots Guards, Sterling made five first team appearances for Spurs in friendly matches during the 1894-95 season. The first was in March 1895 against London Caledonians.

Appearances:
Others: 5 apps.
Total: 5 apps. 0 gls.

THE SPURS ALPHABET

STOKES, Alfred Edward

Role: Forward 1952-59 5ft.9ins. 11st.9lbs.
Born: Hackney, London, 3rd October 1932
Died: Worthing, Sussex, 30th March 2002

CAREER: Albion/Leyton Orient am./Clapton/**SPURS** am. Sep 1951, pro. Feb 1953/Fulham Jul 1959/Cambridge City Jul 1960/Watford Apr 1961/Nuneaton Borough Nov 1961/Ramsgate Athletic/Hastings United/Guildford City/Budapest St George (Australia) 1962.

Debut v Bolton Wanderers (FL) (a) 4.4.1953 (scored once)

Little Alfie Stokes is one of those players whose records indicate they should have experienced much more success in the game than they did. Able to play in any of the forward positions, Stokes played for Clapton until turning professional with Spurs, scored on his League debut, but only slowly made a mark at White Hart Lane. Capped at England Under-23 level against Denmark in September 1955, he was forced to compete with the likes of Dave Dunmore, Tommy Harmer and Johnny Brooks and never really succeeded in making a regular place his own. His best season was 1956-57 when, playing alongside Bobby Smith, he scored 18 goals in a 21 League outings, kept Brooks out of the team for lengthy spells, and played for England "B" against Scotland and for the Football League against the Scottish League. Ever alert and blessed with an uncanny natural knack of turning half chances into goals, Stokes did not however, fit into Bill Nicholson's thoughts and was allowed to move to Fulham for £10,000. A year at Craven Cottage and twelve months at Cambridge City were followed by a similar spell with Watford. He moved quickly through a succession of non-League clubs, and worked as a chauffeur. He moved to Australia in 1962 and later returned to the UK.

Appearances:
League: 65 apps. 40 gls.
FA Cup: 4 apps. 2 gls.
Others: 20 (2) apps. 20 gls.
Total: 89 (2) apps. 62 gls.

STORMONT, Robert

Role: Half-back or inside-forward 1897-01
5ft.7ins. 11st.10lbs.

CAREER: Johnstone Wanderers Aug 1893/Preston North End Oct 1893/Dundee May 1896/**SPURS** cs. 1897/Brentford Jul 1901/Maidstone/retired 1909.

Debut v Sheppey United (SL) (a) 4.9.1897
(Glossop North End (Fr) (h) 2.9.1897)

Bob Stormont was a rough, tough Scottish half-back or inside-forward, signed from Dundee in the summer of 1897. His aggressive style of play quickly made him a crowd favourite and, for nearly four years a Spurs' team without his imposing presence was almost unthinkable. A member of the side that won the Southern League in 1899-00, Stormont lost his place early during the 1901 FA Cup run when player-manager John Cameron decided he preferred to have John L Jones operating just behind David Copeland. With the team set fair on its way to the club's first major final, Stormont was unable to recover his place and at the end of the season moved to Brentford where he played for a year. When released by the west London club he took up refereeing, but returned to the playing side of the game with Maidstone before injury forced his retirement in early 1909.

Appearances:
Southern: 93* apps. 8 gls.
FA Cup: 14 apps. 1 gl.
Others: 125 apps. 15 gls.
Total: 232 apps. 24 gls.
*Includes 1 abandoned match.

STURGESS, L

Role: Goalkeeper 1942-43

CAREER: Reading/(guest for **SPURS** during World War Two).

Debut v Clapton Orient (Fr) (h) 1.5.1943

A goalkeeper who joined Reading during the Second World War, Sturgess made his one appearance for Spurs in a friendly against Clapton Orient in May 1943. ME Sturgess was in the same team, but they were not related, although they did live in the same road in Reading.

Appearances:
Others: 1 app.
Total: 1 app. 0 gls.

STURGESS, M E

Role: Winger 1942-43

Debut v Clapton Orient (Fr) (h) 1.5.1943

Described as crafty but on the small side Sturgess, like his namesake, made his only appearance for Spurs in a friendly with Clapton Orient in May 1943 when he scored once. It was perhaps fortunate that L Sturgess was already on the books of Reading and that the two were not related, for Spurs already had the Bennett brothers, Les and Ken, the Sainsbury brothers, Billy and Bobby, and the Sperrin Brothers, Jimmy and Billy, on the playing staff.

Appearances:
Others: 1 app.
Total: 1 app. 0 gls.

SULLIVAN, John

Role: Full-back 1894-95

CAREER: Westminster Criterion/Old St Stephens 1892-97/**SPURS** guest Oct 1894.

Debut v Old Harrovians (AmC) (h) 20.10.1894

A local man, Jack Sullivan had played for Westminster Criterion before its merger with Old St Stephens. He became a regular with Old St Stephens club, one of Spurs' regular opponents in their early days, and represented Middlesex. Sullivan made his one Spurs' appearance in an FA Amateur Cup tie with Old Harrovians in October 1894. He played several further games the following season but they were all at reserve level.

Appearances:
Others: 1 app.
Total: 1 app. 0 gls.

SULLIVAN, Neil

Role: Goalkeeper 2000-04
6ft.2ins. 15st.2lbs.
Born: Sutton, Surrey, 24th February 1970

CAREER: Wimbledon trainee Jul 1986, pro. Jul 1988/(Crystal Palace loan May 1992)/**SPURS** May 2000/Chelsea Sep 2003/Leeds United Jul 2004/Doncaster Rovers loan Nov 2006 and Feb 2007, perm Jun 2007-Jul 2013/(AFC Wimbledon loan Nov 2012)/Leeds United Academy goalkeeping coach Jul 2013, first team goalkeeping coach Jul 2014, Academy goalkeeping coach Jun 2015.

Debut v Ipswich Town (PL) (h) 19.8.2000
(Skellefteå AIK (sub) (Fr) (a) 19.7.2000)

Neil Sullivan had spent the early part of his twelve-year professional career with Wimbledon as understudy to Hans Segers before eventually replacing the Dutch international. A big, powerful, well-built 'keeper, Sullivan had proved a formidable barrier as the Wimbledon rags to riches story began to unravel, but even he was unable to prevent the club eventually being relegated. Qualifying through a grandmother, Sullivan was Scotland's first choice with 14 full caps to his name. First Division football was not going to do his international career much good. Playing for a club of Spurs' stature would. At the end of his contract, it did not take long for George Graham to persuade Sullivan to sign for Spurs. Ian Walker had been Spurs' regular 'keeper for ten years, but it was obvious Graham did not rate him. Sullivan was soon in the team and proving a good acquisition. For the best part of two years he performed well, even with the equally experienced Kasey Keller, signed as competition, but when his form took a dip and he faced criticism over his weight and attitude, he found himself out of favour. He hung around for another year before accepting the offer of a move to Chelsea where he would provide back-up to Carlo Cudicini. After a year at Chelsea, Sullivan joined Leeds United to replace Spurs-bound Paul Robinson. He was almost ever-present for two seasons, quickly racking up 100 appearances. Injury put him out of team early in 2006-07, he joined Doncaster Rovers on loan to recover match fitness and when called back to Elland Road faced further complaints about his weight. Another loan spell with Doncaster was followed by Leeds releasing him. He then joined Doncaster on a permanent basis, the start of an incredible renaissance. Ever-present in his first season, Doncaster won promotion with a play-off defeat of Leeds. He missed only one game in the next two seasons as Doncaster held on to a championship place and it was only as he entered his forties that his performances began to tail off. Even then, he was good enough to return to almost the place where it all began, playing on loan for AFC Wimbledon. He was recalled from Wimbledon to help Doncaster in their final, successful, push for a return to the Championship. At the end of the season he at last retired from playing and returned to Leeds, working on the coaching staff. As a Spurs' player, Sullivan added twelve caps to his collection.

Appearances:
League: 64 apps.
FA Cup: 9 apps.
FL Cup: 8 apps.
Others: 21 (1) apps.
Total: 102 (1) 0 gls.

SUNDERLAND, Herbert Stanway

Role: Goalkeeper 1896-97
Born: Hereford, Herefordshire, 29th August 1872
Died: Lambton, New South Wales, Australia, 6th September 1945

CAREER: Hereford Town/**SPURS** trial Sep 1896/Gravesend United trial Oct 1896, perm. Oct 1896/Millwall 1898-1900/Thames Ironworks 1899/First South Australian British FC (Australia).

Debut v London Caledonians (Fr) (h) 10.9.1896

A trialist from Hereford Town, Sunderland played in two friendly matches for Spurs in September 1896. The first was against London Caledonians and the second seven days later against Casuals. He did not do enough to impress Spurs, but the following month had a trial with Gravesend United. Although it was reported that he did not give a very good impression in his first match for the Kent club, he was signed on and played with Gravesend for the rest of the season. He later spent two years with Millwall and a year with Thames Ironworks before emigrating to Australia, where he became a member of the first South Australian British football team. Sunderland had also played cricket for Herefordshire.

Appearances:
Others: 2 apps.
Total: 2 apps. 0 gls.

SUTTON, John

Role: Striker 2002-03
6ft. 14st. 0lbs.
Born: Norwich, Norfolk, 26th December 1983

CAREER: Horsford Boys/Hellesdon High School/Norwich Middle Schools/Norwich High Schools/Norfolk Schools/**SPURS** trainee 2000/(Carlisle United loan Oct 2002)/released Dec 2002/Swindon Town Dec 2002/Southend United trial Mar 2003/Cambridge United trial Apr-Jul 2003/Leicester City trial Jul 2003/Raith Rovers Jul 2003/Millwall Jan 2004/(Dundee loan Jul 2004)/St Mirren Aug 2005/Wycombe Wanderers Jun 2007/Motherwell Aug 2008/Heart of Midlothian May 2011/(Central Coast Mariners (Australia) loan Jan 2012)/Motherwell Jun 2013/St Johnstone Jun 2015/St Mirren Jun 2016.

Debut v Gillingham (sub) (Fr) (a) 27.7.2002

Son of Mike, who played for Norwich City, Chester and Carlisle United, and brother of Chris, who played for Norwich City, Blackburn Rovers and Celtic amongst others, John Sutton was a central striker, very similar in build and style to Chris. He joined Spurs trainee ranks as a 17-year old and proved a consistent scorer as he worked his way up to reserve level. One substitute appearance in a pre-season friendly was as far as Sutton got with Spurs. After three goals in a loan spell with Carlisle United, Sutton returned to Spurs to be released so that he could sign for Swindon Town. That did not work out, but he had more success when he joined Raith Rovers, 16 goals in 24 games and Millwall secured his signature. He rarely had a look-in in south London and had one poor season with

Wycombe Wanderers, but back in Scotland, the goals have flowed regularly with all his clubs.

Appearances:
Others: (1) app.
Total: (1) app. 0 gls.

SWANN, Andrew

Role: Inside-forward 1904-05
5ft.8ins. 12st.0lbs.
Born: Dalbeattie, Kirkcudbrightshire, 1878

CAREER: Dalbeattie/Lincoln City Nov 1898/New Brompton Jul 1899/Barnsley May 1900/Woolwich Arsenal May 1901/Stockport County Dec 1901/Mexborough United cs. 1902/St Mirren May 1902/**SPURS** May 1904/Partick Thistle May 1905/Blackpool Jun 1906.

Debut v Queens Park Rangers (SL) (a) 5.11.1904
(Brighton and Hove Albion (Fr) (h) 12.9.1904)

Centre or inside-forward Andrew Swann had first come to the fore at Lincoln City as a 20-year old. He showed a lot of promise and was quickly persuaded to sign for New Brompton. He disappointed in his one season in Kent, but got his career back on track with Barnsley, and by the time he arrived at Spurs was well-travelled and experienced. Not in the same class as regular centre-forward, Vivian Woodward, Swann joined Spurs as reserve cover and it was in that role that he spent most of his one season at White Hart Lane. He did not make his senior debut until November 1904, called up after Spurs had suffered seven straight defeats and secured only one draw in their last eight games. Results definitely improved with Swann in the team, as testified by two draws and two wins in his four games, but it was soon back to the reserves for him. At the end of the season he was released and went home to Scotland. He had a year with Partick Thistle, then finished his career with three seasons at Blackpool.

Appearances:
Southern: 2 apps.
Others: 4 apps. 1 gl.
Total: 6 apps. 1 gl.

SWIFT, William Norman

Role: Centre-half 1944-45

CAREER: SPURS/Crossbrook Sports/Walthamstow Avenue.

Debut v Southampton (FLS) (a) 23.9.1944

A local-born member of Spurs' junior staff, Bill Swift was playing for Crossbrook Sports of Cheshunt and Walthamstow Avenue when he was called up to play in a Football League South game at Southampton in September 1944, his only game for the club.

Appearances:
Others: 1 app.
Total: 1 app. 0 gls.

SYKES, Dr J Louis

Role: Winger 1891-96

CAREER: United Hospital/Tottenham/**SPURS** cs. 1891/Crouch End cs. 1894.

Debut v Vampires (AmC) (h) 11.11.1893
(Uxbridge (Fr) (h) 2.1.1892)

A local medical practitioner, Louis Sykes was a well-known local footballer, a Middlesex county regular who played for United Hospitals and the Tottenham club before joining Spurs. His first known appearance was in a friendly with Uxbridge in January 1892, but he almost certainly played earlier in the season. With Spurs he continued to play for the Tottenham district and London representative teams. He proved himself a most useful and regular performer over the next two seasons, a time when Spurs started to build a name for themselves in London football. In the summer of 1894 he decided to play for Crouch End, but still returned to play a few more games for Spurs. Sykes' father, EJ, was a vice-president of Spurs during their amateur days.

Appearances:
Others: 57 apps. 13 gls.
Total: 57 apps. 13 gls.

T

TAARABT, Adel

Role: Midfielder 2006-2010
5ft.9ins. 12st.10lbs.
Born: Fes, Morocco, 24th May 1989

CAREER: RC Lens (France) 2001/**SPURS** loan Jan 2007, perm Jun 2007/Queens Park Rangers loan Mar and Jul 2009, perm Aug 2010/(Fulham loan Aug 2013)/(AC Milan (Italy) loan Jan 2014)/Benfica (Portugal) Jun 2015/(Genoa (Italy) loan Jan 2017).

Debut v West Ham United (sub) (PL) (a) 4.3.2007

Adel Taarabt is one of those footballers who so annoy coaches, managers and fans; a massive natural talent with an attitude that almost guarantees a career that will be wasted. Taarabt was plucked by Spurs from the Lens youth ranks having played in only one senior game. The signing was initially on loan as the clubs negotiated a transfer fee with a figure of £2.5 million finally being agreed. From the outset it was obvious Taarabt possessed terrific skill and ability. Running from deep in midfield, whether through the centre or out wide, he could cut a swathe through opposing defences, his pace, control and not a few tricks leaving opponents kicking out at thin air. Sadly, his shortcomings were also obvious. He regarded himself as an offensive player, give him the ball and he would play. He did not think he had to defend, tackle or make any effort to get the ball; that was for the less gifted to do. He was too easily brushed off the ball, the loss of possession a reason to complain to the referee. When things went wrong, someone else was to blame. His faults could be forgiven if he was prepared to apply himself, but he preferred to enjoy the good life. Juande Ramos was not a man to tolerate Taarabt's antics and ostracised him. He was not even given a squad number at the start of 2008-09. When Harry Redknapp arrived, he gave Taarabt another chance, but within months he was shipped out on loan to Queens Park Rangers. While injury saw an early return to Spurs, he again joined QPR for a season long loan in July 2009. He at last began to show some discipline and willingness to work and looked a cut above the Championship level he was playing in. So much did Taarabt impress himself that he talked of signing for Barcelona or Real Madrid. When he did sign again, it was not for one of Europe's super powers, but on a permanent move to QPR. With events at last going his way, Taarabt helped QPR return to the Premier League and started the top flight playing the type of football that would attract Europe's biggest clubs. However, as soon as talk of interest from bigger clubs surfaced, so Taarabt became unsettled, playing not for the team but for himself and those he believed were watching. It was surprising QPR persevered with him, but the player had value they could not afford to lose. Taarabt's career at Loftus Road took a downward turn with the arrival of Harry Redknapp, a man who was not afraid to give the type of criticism Taarabt preferred to dish out. Taarabt spent the 2013-14 season on loan to Fulham and AC Milan. He returned to play a couple of games and more criticism from Redknapp about his weight and attitude. Despite QPR struggling in vain against relegation, he rarely featured in the first team. With relegation, neither QPR nor Taarabt wanted the relationship to continue. His contract was cancelled and he signed for Benfica, soon exiled to their B team as he reverted to type. Having played for France at youth level, Taarabt opted to play for Morocco at full international level. He made 18 appearances, eight of them as a Spurs' player though only one when he was not out on loan. Even his international career was marked by controversy. When dropped after a poor performance he announced he would never play for his country again. He did, but when he was omitted from the 2013 Africa Cup of Nations squad, his international career seemed over.

Appearances:
League:	(9) apps.
FA Cup:	(2) apps.
FL Cup:	(1) app.
Euro:	(3) apps.
Others:	6 (7) apps. 1 gl.
Total:	**6 (22) apps. 1 gl.**

TAINIO, Teemu Mikael

Role: Midfielder 2005-08
5ft.9ins. 12st.4lbs.
Born: Tornio, Finland, 27th November 1979

CAREER: TP 47 (Finland) 1994/FC Haka (Finland) 1997/Manchester United trial Mar 1997/Auxerre (France) May 1997/**SPURS** Jul 2005/Sunderland Jul 2008/(Birmingham City loan Sep 2009)/Ajax (Holland) Aug 2010/New York Red Bulls (USA) Mar 2011/HJK (Finland) Jan 2013/retired Feb 2015.

Debut v Portsmouth (PL) (a) 13.8.2005
(Boca Juniors (Fr) (Suwon, Korea) 13.7.2005)

A tenacious little midfielder, capable of playing anywhere across the middle of the park, Teemu Tainio was a smart piece of business by manager Martin Jol. His contract with Auxerre up, no transfer fee was involved for an established international with 25 caps to his credit. Tainio had joined the French club as an 18-year old and given great service, helping Auxerre win the French Cup club twice. He was an industrious character, forever foraging, getting in tackles, winning the ball and then looking to get an attack underway. There were no airs and graces about Tainio, he was a real team player, more concerned with the team's performance than his own. It was the type of attitude that endeared him to fans. He gave Spurs good service over two years. He was never assured of a place, but that was no disgrace when he was competing with the likes of Michael Carrick, Edgar Davids and Jermaine Jenas. Having taken his tally of international appearances to

39, he was allowed to join Sunderland where injuries restricted his appearances. A short spell with Ajax, managed by Martin Jol, followed, before Tainio joined the ranks of aging players able to extend their careers for a couple of years in America. He concluded his playing days back home in Finland with HJK Helsinki. In January 2017, it was announced that Tainio's 15-year old son, Maximus, would be joining the Spurs Academy in Jull 2017.

Appearances:
League: 48 (13) apps. 3 gls.
FA Cup: 5 (2) apps.
FL Cup: 3 (3) apps.
Euro: 7 (2) apps.
Others: 11 (3) apps. 2 gls.
Total: 74 (23) apps. 5 gls.

TAIT, Alexander Gilchrist

Role: Full-back 1899-08
5ft.9ins. 11st.10lbs.
Born: Glenbuck, Ayrshire, 1873
Died: Croydon, Surrey, 6th April 1949

CAREER: Glenbuck Athletic/Ayr 1889/Royal Albert 1890/(Rangers loan Sep 1891)/Motherwell cs. 1892/Preston North End May 1894/**SPURS** May 1899/Leyton May 1908, then manager/Croydon Common manager Jul 1910-May 1911/Corinthians coach Sep 1922.

Debut v Millwall Athletic (SL) (a) 2.9.1899

One of 13 children, Sandy Tait worked as a boy in the pits, leading the ponies. In his free time he played for Glenbuck Athletic. After a brief spell with Ayr he had three years with Royal Albert, part of which were spent "on loan" to Rangers. Turning professional with Motherwell, he soon caught the eye, but like many of his countrymen it was only when he moved to England that he really began to build a reputation. For Tait, it reached a peak during his time with Spurs, when he developed into probably the best left-back in the country. Known as "Terrible Tait" for the ferocity of his tackling, he gave Spurs eight years' remarkable service; a member of the teams that won the Southern League in 1899-00 and the FA Cup the following year. Hard but fair, with a slick and efficient sliding tackle, he took his football very seriously but, despite his intimidating nickname, was not a dirty player. He always played the game to the rules Laws, was never booked and was generally a credit to his profession. Tait's greatest asset was his speed of thought. He always seemed to anticipate situations and opportunities far quicker than opponents. This compensated for any lack of pace, but if ever that let him down, he had enormous strength and determination to fall back on. A most consistent performer, he was a natural leader and made captain during his latter days at Spurs. The only representative honour he won in his time at Tottenham came in March 1903 when he played in a Scottish international trial match. It was precious little reward for a player who deserved far more. Tait remained a regular for Spurs until 1907-08 when Ollie Burton, very similar in style, replaced him. In May 1908 Tait was released and moved to Leyton, initially as a player but then as manager. He had one season as manager of the short-lived Croydon Common during which he also played in a few games and later took to coaching.

Appearances:
Southern: 205* apps. 3 gls.
FA Cup: 36* apps.
Others: 178^ apps. 7# gls
Total: 419 apps. 10 gls.
*Includes 1 abandoned match.
^Includes 2 abandoned matches.
#Includes 1 scored in an abandoned match.

TALESNIKOV, Jan

Role: Midfielder 1998-99
5ft.8ins.
Born: Torinsk, Russia, 11th December 1972

CAREER: Ironi Ashdod (Israel) 1990/Beitar Jerusalem (Israel) 1996/**SPURS** trial Jul 1998/Dundee United trial Jul 1999, perm. Aug 1999/Beitar Jerusalem (Israel) Jun 2000/FC Ashdod (Israel) 2003/Hapoel Jerusalem (Israel) 2005/retired May 2007/Beitar Jerusalem (Israel) youth team coach Aug 2008/Hapoel Be'er Sheva (Israel) asst. manager Jun 2009/FC Ashdod (Israel) director of football 2010-Dec 2011/Beitar Jerusalem (Israel) asst. coach Jan 2012-Jun 2013/Israel FA Girls Football Academy asst. coach Sep 2013.

Debut v Grasshoppers (sub) (a) 10.7.1998

An Israeli international with three goals in 5 appearances for his country, Jan Talesnikov joined Spurs for a month's trial in July 1998. He played as a substitute in a pre-season friendly against Grasshoppers in Zurich, a game arranged as part of the deal when Christian Gross joined Spurs as manger. It was his only outing in a Spurs' shirt. He did rather better a year later. Having impressed in a month's trial, he signed for Dundee United once work permit difficulties had been overcome. He had a year in Scotland but was unable to settle and returned to Israel. He resigned for Beitar Jerusalem, the club he had helped lift the Israeli Premier League title in 1997 and 1998 and spent the rest of his career in Israel, taking his total of international appearances to 21. While still playing, Talesnikov studied acting and graduated in screenwriting. He went on to appear in films and TV series.

Appearances:
Others: (1) app.
Total: (1) app. 0 gls.

TANNAHILL, Robert

Role: Outside-right 1897-98
5ft.6ins. 10st.10lbs.
Born: Kilmarnock, Ayrshire, 24 March (or 1st May) 1870

CAREER: Kilmarnock Aug 1889/Blackburn Rovers trial Jan 1893/Bolton Wanderers Feb 1893/**SPURS** May 1897/Millwall Athletic Oct 1898/Chesterfield Town Aug 1899/Fulham May 1901/Grays United Sep 1904/Oldham Athletic Aug 1905-May 1906.

Debut v Sheppey United (SL) (a) 4.9.1897
(Glossop North End (Fr) (h) 2.9.1897)

Another of the many Scots who played for Spurs around the turn of the century, Bob Tannahill had enjoyed four successful years with Bolton Wanderers. A winger in his early days, he moved to inside-forward late in the 1893-94 season and when Bolton were badly hit by injuries, played in the FA Cup Final against Notts County in that position. Reverting to his more accustomed outside-right role, he then helped Bolton reach the FA Cup semi-final two years later. At Spurs he played regularly in the early part of 1897-98, but then lost his place to the more free-scoring James Hartley. Having played 29 senior games he was released in the 1898 close season and joined Millwall Athletic, later playing for Chesterfield, Fulham, Grays United and Oldham Athletic.

Appearances:
Southern: 11 apps. 3 gls.
FA Cup: 2 apps.
Others: 16 apps. 6 gls.
Total: **29 apps. 9 gls.**

TARBOLTON

Role: Half-back 1893-94

CAREER: Tottenham/**SPURS** Dec 1893/City Ramblers cs. 1894.

Debut v Friars (Fr) (h) 19.12.1893

Later associated with City Ramblers, Tarbolton joined Spurs when the Tottenham club disbanded. He made his only appearance in Spurs' first team in December 1893 in a friendly with Friars, although he continued to assist Spurs' reserve side for the rest of the season.

Appearances:
Others: 1 app.
Total: **1 app. 0 gls.**

TARICCO, Mauricio Ricardo

Role: Full-back 1998-05
5ft.8ins. 11st.7lbs.
Born: Buenos Aires, Argentina, 10th March 1973

CAREER: Argentinos Juniors (Argentina) Aug 1993/Ipswich Town Sep 1994/**SPURS** Nov 1998/West Ham United Nov 2004/ASD Villasimius (Italy) by Dec 2005/Brighton and Hove Albion asst. manager Nov 2009-Jun 2013/Sunderland asst. manager Oct 2013-Mar 2015/AEK Athens (Greece) asst. manager Oct 2015/Real Betis (Spain) asst. manager May 2016/Shanghai Shenhua(China) asst. manager Nov 2016.

Debut v Wimbledon (sub) (PL) (h) 16.1.1999

A product of the Argentinos Juniors youth set-up, Mauricio Taricco had played for only one season in their first eleven when he crossed the Atlantic to join Ipswich Town. It took him a while to settle in Suffolk and establish himself. Once he had done so he developed as a cultured, solid, hard-tackling full-back, the first name on the team sheet as he ran up 200 appearances in five years. He joined Spurs shortly after George Graham's arrival as manager. Paolo Tramezzani had proved an abject failure, leaving Justin Edinburgh as the only recognised left-back. He did not immediately secure a regular starting place. His arrival seemed to spur on Edinburgh who was not going to surrender his regained position easily. The two of them were similar in many respects. Both liked to press

forward, were strong tacklers and often found themselves in trouble with officials. Taricco was, perhaps, the more cultured and his partnership with David Ginola out on the left was slightly better than Edinburgh's had been. For four years Taricco was a first choice at left-back, reliable and never complaining. It was only the arrival of Frank Arnesen, that Taricco's place came under threat. One of the numerous signings the Director of Football was responsible for was that of Erik Edman. With the Swede installed, Taricco was allowed to move on and joined West Ham United. In his first game he picked up an injury that was going to put him out of action for a good couple of months. Rather than accept wages for doing nothing he agreed to tear up his contract and retired from playing. A year later he resumed playing when he joined lower league ASD Villasimius in Sardinia. For four years he played for little more than pleasure. Taricco returned to the UK in November 2009 when Gus Poyet asked him to be his assistant manager at Brighton. He has since followed Poyet to Sunderland and AEK Athens.

Appearances:
League: 125 (5) apps. 2 gls.
FA Cup: 9 (2) apps.
FL Cup: 12 apps.
Euro: 3 apps.
Others: 28 (15) apps.
Total: **177 (22) apps. 2 gls.**

TATE, John Anthony

Role: Goalkeeper 1913-15
5ft.11ins. 11st.5lbs.
Born: Chester-le-Street, County Durham, 6th December 1892

CAREER: Chester-le-Street Osborne/West Stanley/**SPURS** Feb 1913/West Stanley Jul 1914/Shildon.

Debut v Woolwich Arsenal (FL) (h) 19.4.1913

John Tate was signed from the North Eastern League team West Stanley. He was required to provide cover for first choice 'keeper John Joyce after Spurs' other experienced custodian,

Tommy Lunn, had been suspended by the club for taking out a publican's license. Tate played in the last two games of 1912-13, but made only one more League appearance before returning to West Stanley.

Appearances:
League: 4 apps.
Others: 2 apps.
Total: **6 apps. 0 gls.**

TATTERSALL, Walter Scott

Role: Outside-right 1911-15
5ft.7ins. 11st.8lbs.
Born: Warsop, Nottinghamshire, 4th September 1888
Died: Warsop, Nottinghamshire, 28th December 1968

CAREER: Mansfield Wesleyans by Sep 1902/Warsop Athletic 1903/ Moores Athletic 1907/Shirebrook/Chesterfield Town am. Jan 1908, pro. May 1908/Mansfield Mechanics cs. 1908/Watford Jul 1910/**SPURS** Apr 1912/released May 1919/(guest for Notts County during World War One)/Shirebrook Colliery Welfare 1920/Welbeck Colliery May 1921/ Sutton Junction 1922.

Debut v Bolton Wanderers (FL) (h) 20.4.1912

Walter Tattersall was signed from Watford at the same time as Arthur Grimsdell, but did not go on to enjoy the same degree of success as the future Spurs' captain. An experienced performer, Tattersall had been a regular with Watford in his two years there, making over eighty appearances in total. He went straight into the Spurs' team on his arrival and retained the outside-right position until the signing of little Fanny Walden in April 1913. After Walden's arrival Tattersall was always second choice and was released at the end of the Great War.

Appearances:
League: 45* apps. 3 gls.
FA Cup: 3 apps. 2 gls.
Others: 16 apps. 3 gls.
Total: 64 apps. 8 gls.
*Includes 1 abandoned match

TAYLOR, Allan

Role: Goalkeeper 1929-36
6ft. 12st.0lbs.
Born: North Shields, Co Durham, 1st December 1905
Died: Whitley Bay, North Tyneside, 11th April 1981

CAREER: England Schools/ North Shields/Newcastle United cs. 1925/ South Shields May 1926/**SPURS** trial and perm Jul 1929/ Hartlepools United May 1937/retired cs. 1938.

Debut v Burnley (FL) (h) 10.10.1931
(Clapton Orient (LFACC) (a) 14.10.1929)

Allan Taylor arrived at White Hart Lane in July 1929 for a month's trial and ended up staying for eight years. Previously with North Shields, Newcastle, for whom he made only one League appearance, and South Shields he signed on to the full-time staff at the end of his trial spell. He made a first team debut in a London FA Charity Cup tie in October 1929 but, due to the consistency of Cyril Spiers, had to wait almost two more years before playing his first League game for Spurs. Once in the team, he vied with Spiers for the goalkeeper's position, but big Joe Nicholls then came to the fore and Taylor found himself third choice. Although he had extended runs in the first team in both 1934-35 and 1935-36, the emerging Percy Hooper pushed Taylor into the reserves again. In April 1937, he was not retained and moved to Hartlepools United where he played for a year until retiring.

Appearances:
League: 60 apps.
FA Cup: 10 apps.
Others: 7 apps.
Total: 77 apps. 0 gls.

TAYLOR, Peter John

Role: Winger 1976-80
5ft.7ins. 11st.7lbs.
Born: Rochford, Essex, 3rd January 1953

CAREER: South East Essex Schools/Canvey Island/Southend United app. Jan 1970, pro. Jan 1971/Crystal Palace Oct 1973/**SPURS** Sep 1976/ Orient Nov 1980/(Oldham Athletic loan Jan 1983)/Maidstone United Mar 1983 player-coach/Exeter City non-contract Oct 1983/Maidstone United player-manager to Oct 1984/Heybridge Swifts 1984/ Chelmsford City Nov 1984/Dartford player-manager Jul 1986/Enfield manager Sep 1990/Watford asst. manager Aug 1991/Harlow Town Oct 1991/Enfield player-manager 1991-92/Hendon manager May 1993/ Southend United manager Dec 1993/Chelmsford City in 1994-95/ Dover Athletic manager Nov 1995/England Under-21 manager Jul 1996-Jun 1999/Gillingham manager Jul 1999/Leicester City manager Jun 2000-Oct 2001/England part-time caretaker manager Oct 2000 and Nov 2000-Jan 2001/Peterborough United temp asst. coach Oct 2001/ Brighton and Hove Albion manager Oct 2001-May 2002/Peterborough United coach Aug 2002/Hull City manager Oct 2002/England Under-21 part-time manager Jul 2004/Crystal Palace manager Jun 2006-Oct 2007/Stevenage Borough manager Nov 2007/ Wycombe Wanderers manager May 2008-Oct 2009/ Bradford City manager Feb 2010 - Feb 2011/Bahrain national team coach Jul 2011-Oct 2012/England Under-20 manager Mar-May 2013 Gillingham interim manager Oct 2013, perm. manager Nov 2013-Dec 2014/Kerala Blasters (India) head coach May-Oct 2015/New Zealand asst. coach Nov 2016.

Debut v West Bromwich Albion (FL) (a) 2.10.1976 (scored once)

Rejected by Spurs as a youngster, Peter Taylor went on to become an England international before returning as a major £400,000 signing. At Southend, he stood out as a player of immense potential, was transferred to Crystal Palace, rose to Under-23 status and became one of the few Third Division players to appear in a full international for England. After winning four caps at Under-23 level, he made his debut for the full England team as a goal-scoring substitute against Wales in March 1976 and three further caps soon followed. A fast-raiding winger, he was one of the first more modern breed of footballer who, when necessary, could double as an extra midfielder and was quite prepared to drop back and help out in defence. He was an insatiable worker, always likely to pop up and score from any position. Although Spurs were relegated at the end of his first season, Taylor missed only one game in the following term's promotion campaign, but found himself left out to accommodate Ricky Villa. A series of injuries then took their toll and for £150,000 he was allowed to move to Orient, where he played over 50 games before joining Gola League Maidstone United. He returned briefly to League football to help out former Palace team-mate Gerry Francis as a non-contract player with Exeter City and then went back to Maidstone as player-manager. A member of the England semi-professional team on three occasions, Taylor took Maidstone to the Gola League title before moving on to play for Heybridge Swifts, Chelmsford City and Dartford where he was also made manager. Appointed boss of Spurs' non-league neighbours Enfield, he left after less than a year to join Watford as assistant manager to Steve Perryman, but still found time to sign for Harlow Town in October 1991 although he could only be available for midweek games when his duties at Watford allowed. In May 1994, he resigned from Watford intending to return to the insurance industry whilst managing Hendon on a part-time basis, but was tempted back to full-time football by the chance to manage Southend United. Given a very hard time at Roots Hall he took over as manager at Dover, but left to join Glenn Hoddle's England staff as manager of the Under-21 team. He did an excellent job helping develop England's internationals of the future and was harshly dismissed by Howard Wilkinson following Hoddle's departure from the senior job. Gillingham were quick to offer him a return to management and at the end of his first season in charge he led the Gills into the top half of English football for the first time. His success attracted Leicester City, and within weeks of joining them City were top of Premier League and Taylor was manager of England, albeit for only one game as caretaker between the departure of Kevin Keegan and the arrival of Sven-Goran Eriksson. His success at Leicester did not continue and he was dismissed in September 2001, but he was quickly appointed Brighton boss and led them to the Second Division championship. He followed that up by guiding Hull City from Division Three to the Championship in successive seasons. While doing that he was again in charge of England's Under-21s, repeating the success of his earlier tenure until new England manager, Steve McLaren, decided he wanted a full time manager in charge of the Under-21s. After spells with Crystal Palace, Stevenage Borough, Wycombe Wanderers and Bradford City, Taylor took his talents back to the international stage. He led Bahrain to success in the GCC Games and Arab Games, remarkable achievements for such a small nation with a fledgling football structure. Taylor has since been in charge of England Under-20s, Gillingham and the Indian franchise team, Kerala Blasters. After leaving Spurs, he returned twice to play as a guest in testimonials for Keith Burkinshaw and Danny Blanchflower.

Appearances:
League: 116 (7) apps. 31 gls.
FA Cup: 8 (3) apps. 2 gls.
FL Cup: 4 (2) apps.
Others: 27 (6) apps. 13 gls.
Total: 155 (18) apps. 46 gls.

TAYLOR, S G

Role: Inside-forward 1893-94

Debut v Vampires (AmC) (h) 11.11.1893 (scored once)
(1st Batt Scots Guards (Fr) (h) 4.11.1893)

Nothing is known about this player who made five appearances in November and December 1893 scoring twice, once in an Amateur Cup tie and once in a London Charity Cup tie. His other three appearances were all in friendly matches.

Appearances:
Others: 5 apps. 2 gls.
Total: 5 apps. 2 gls.

THATCHER, Benjamin David

Role: Defender 2000-03
5ft.10ins. 12st.6lbs.
Born: *Swindon, Wiltshire, 30th November 1975*

CAREER: FA School of Excellence/Millwall trainee Jun 1992, pro. Dec 1992/Wimbledon Jul 1996/**SPURS** Jul 2000/Leicester City Jul 2003/Manchester City Jun 2004/Charlton Athletic Jan 2007/Ipswich Town trial Jul 2008/Wolverhampton Wanderers trial Jul 2008/West Ham United trial Aug 2008/Ipswich Town Aug 2008-Feb 2010.

Debut v Ipswich Town (PL) (h) 19.8.2000

A graduate of the FA's Lilleshall School of Excellence, Ben Thatcher was a hard, aggressive full-back with Millwall and Wimbledon who seemed to revel in the reputation so many players seemed to believe went with playing for those clubs. At Millwall he looked a rough diamond with plenty of potential. At Wimbledon he adapted to Premiership football and at times looked to possess a fair amount of skill. He showed enough ability to make four appearances for England at under-21 level. When Wimbledon were relegated Thatcher followed Neil Sullivan to Spurs, a £5 million signing and possibly George Graham's worst signing in his time with Spurs. He played regularly while Graham was in charge, but as soon as Glenn Hoddle took over he made it clear that will he wanted competitive players in his team, he did not want the combative type Thatcher represented. He had few outings under Hoddle's management and eventually moved to Leicester City. Spurs received less than 10% of what they had paid to sign him. With Leicester's relegation he moved on to Manchester City and did alright in his first two years, never sure of a place, but more often in than out. His career really took a turn for the worse in August 2006. An outrageous elbow to the face of Portsmouth's Pedro Mendes saw the former Spurs' midfielder out cold and receiving oxygen. It was not dissimilar to an incident three weeks earlier when, in a pre-season friendly, a Shanghai Shenhua player had been left with a collapsed lung. The assault spelt the end of Thatcher's City career. The club suspended him for four games with two more suspended and fined him. The FA gave him an eight match ban with a further 15 suspended. Charlton Athletic, battling to avoid relegation from the Premier League took a chance on signing Thatcher. It did not pay off. They were still relegated. Thatcher finished his playing days with Ipswich Town, his contract terminated by manager, Roy Keane, when Thatcher refused to move closer to Ipswich. Although he had played for England at Under-21 level, Thatcher was able to play for Wales at full level due to having a Welsh grandmother. He won seven caps in 2004.

Appearances:
League: 29 (7) apps.
FA Cup: 3 apps.
FL Cup: 6 (1) apps.
Others: 11 (3) apps.
Total: 49 (11) apps. 0 gls.

THELWELL, Alton Anthony

Role: Central defender 1999-03
5ft.11ins. 12st.2lbs.
Born: *Holloway, London, 5th September 1980*

CAREER: Rokeby School/Newham Schools/Flanders Athletic/Barking Colts/**SPURS** trainee Jul 1997, pro. Jan 1999/(IFK Hässleholm loan Apr 2000)/released Jun 2003/Hull City Jun 2003/Leyton Orient loan Oct 2006, perm. Jan 2007/AFC Bournemouth trial Jul 2009/Milton Keynes Dons trial Aug 2009/Gillingham trial Aug 2009/Aldershot Town trial Sep 2009/London APSA Sep 2009/Mansfield Town trial Oct 2009/Newport County trial and perm. Oct 2009/Kettering Town Dec 2009/retired Apr 2010/Carshalton Athletic Sep 2012/Billericay Town Oct 2012.

Debut v Liverpool (PL) (h) 19.11.2000
(Bishops Stortford (Fr) (a) 3.9.1999)

George Graham was one of those managers who were rarely prepared to give youth a chance. He would rather stick to tried and experienced players, even if they were playing badly. However, there are times when circumstances force a change of attitude. So it was in November 2000. Spurs were playing poorly, pressure was building on Alan Sugar, Sol Campbell was injured, Ben Thatcher and Ramon Vega were proving totally ineffective. Graham was forced to turn to 20-year olds Ledley King and Alton Thelwell. King had played a couple of senior games, for Thelwell it was a whole new experience. Playing in a back three alongside Chris Perry and Luke Young, he gave a really accomplished performance, growing in confidence as the game progressed and looking a polished performer. He retained a place for a while, even after Campbell had recovered, before Graham reverted to his tried and trusted players. Thelwell was far from the finished article, his lack of experience sometimes showed and he did make mistakes, but there was certainly plenty to work with and even after Graham was replaced by Glenn Hoddle, Thelwell was still in the first team picture. The signings of Goran Bunjevčević and Dean Richards pushed Thelwell back into the shadows and while he remained with Spurs for another two years he was never in contention for a senior place again. On his release he joined Hull City, but a knee injury seriously restricted his appearances. Even after moving to Leyton Orient the injury continued to trouble him. He still managed about 80 appearances for the Os, before dropping into non-League football. Thelwell had made only ten competitive appearances for Spurs when he won his only England Under-21 cap, playing against Spain in February 2001.

Appearances:
League: 13 (5) apps.
FA Cup: (3) apps.
Others: 4 (2) apps.
Total: **17 (10) apps. 0 gls.**

THEODOSIOU, Andrew

Role: Central defender 1988-89
Born: Stoke Newington, London, 30th October 1970

CAREER: SPURS trainee cs. 1987/Norwich City cs. 1989/Hereford United Jul 1991/free transfer cs. 1993/Brighton and Hove Albion/Dover Athletic Jun 1995/(Chesham United loan Nov 1995)/(Crawley Town loan Feb 1996)/Billericay Town Mar 1997/Harlow Town Jul 1998/Windsor & Eton Sep 1999/Arlesey Town Aug 2000/Harlow Town/Arlesey Town Nov 2001, player-asst. coach, temp. manager Dec 2004/Hemel Hempstead Town player-coach Dec 2004/Aylesbury United coach Dec 2005-Mar 2006/Arlesey Town coach Mar 2008, asst. manager.

Debut v Charlton Athletic (sub) (Fr) (a) 4.4.1989

Andy Theodosiou spent two years with Spurs as a trainee, but was released without making the professional ranks. His only first team appearance was in April 1989 when he played as a late substitute for Brian Statham in a testimonial match for long-serving Charlton Athletic utility player Steve Gritt. On his release he joined Norwich City where he must have hoped to follow in the footsteps of former Spurs' reserves Ian Crook, Mark Bowen and Ian Culverhouse who all established themselves as First Division players. However, it was not to be and at the end of the 1990-91 season he was released. He joined Hereford United where he played for two years, making close on 100 appearances, before moving into non-League circles, playing, coaching and managing.

Appearances:
Others: (1) app.
Total: **(1) app. 0 gls.**

THOMAS, Daniel Joseph

Role: Full-back 1983-87
5ft.7ins. 10st.2lbs.
Born: Worksop, Nottinghamshire, 12th November 1961

CAREER: Worksop & Retford Schools/Nottinghamshire Schools/England Schools/Sheffield United trial/Leeds United trial/Coventry City app., pro. Dec 1978/**SPURS** Jun 1983/retired Jan 1988/West Bromwich Albion physiotherapist May 1992.

Debut v Ipswich Town (FL) (a) 27.8.1983
(Brentford (Fr) (a) 6.8.1983)

As a schoolboy, Danny Thomas had trials with Sheffield United and Leeds United before deciding to join Coventry City where he developed into a potential England regular. His League debut was against Spurs in September 1979, and he soon established himself in a talented young Coventry team, winning his first England Under-21 cap against the Republic of Ireland in March 1981. He collected four more caps at that level and played twice for the full England team on the tour to Australia in 1983 before moving to Spurs for £250,000. In his first season at White Hart Lane injuries had him in and out of the team, although he did play in both legs of the 1984 UEFA Cup

Final and won two more Under-21 caps against Italy and Spain in May 1984. At his best Thomas was an exciting full-back, able to play on both flanks. A biting, well-timed tackle helped make him an even more accomplished defender, but it was going forward he looked most thrilling. Always keen to attack, his natural talent shone through with concise, accurate passing and a good long range shot. A popular and thoroughly likeable individual, Thomas was just getting back to his very best and being tipped to gain further international honours when he suffered a terrible knee injury against Queens Park Rangers in March 1987, the victim of a particularly reckless tackle. It not only caused him to miss the 1987 FA Cup Final against his former club Coventry, but was so serious it brought his career to a premature end. In January 1988 he retired from playing and went to study for a new career in physiotherapy. By 1992 he was happily back in the game as physio at Ossie Ardiles' West Bromwich Albion, but left during the 1994-95 season to set up his own physiotherapy practise. His brother, Valmore, was on Coventry's books at the same time as Danny, but failed to make the grade at the highest level, going on to join Hereford United.

Appearances:
League: 80 (7) apps. 1 gl.
FA Cup: 4 apps.
FL Cup: 11 (2) apps.
Euro: 8 (4) apps.
Others: 48 (8) apps. 4 gls.
Total: 151 (21) apps. 5 gls.

THOMAS, Martin Richard

Role: Goalkeeper 1982-83
6ft.1ins. 13st.0lbs.
Born: Senghenydd nr Caerphilly, Glamorgan, 28th November 1959

CAREER: St Helens & Cardinal Newman Schools/Pontypridd Schools/Rhondda Schools/Bristol Rovers app. Jul 1976, pro. Sep 1977/(Cardiff City loan Jul 1982)/(**SPURS** loan Dec 1982)/(Southend United loan Feb 1983)/Newcastle United loan Mar 1983, perm. Jul 1983/(Middlesbrough loan Oct 1984)/Birmingham City Oct 1988/(Aston Villa loan Jan 1993)/(Crystal Palace loan Mar 1993)/Cheltenham Town Aug 1993/Birmingham City goalkeeping coach/Norwich City goalkeeping coach/Swindon Town goalkeeping coach/Newcastle United goalkeeping coach/FA goalkeeping coach part-time 1992, full time 1998, England Under-21 goalkeeping coach, National goalkeeping coach.

Debut v Israeli Select XI (sub) (Fr) (a) 22.12.1982

Welsh Youth and Under-21 international Martin Thomas joined Spurs in December 1982 for a two months' loan. With Tony Parks injured, cover was needed for Ray Clemence. Rated one of the best 'keepers in the lower divisions, he made his only first team appearance as a substitute against an Israeli Select XI in a friendly in Tel Aviv. Spurs were keen to sign Thomas on a permanent basis, but player and club were unable to agree terms and he returned to Bristol Rovers. He later joined Newcastle where he played for five years and collected a full Welsh cap against Finland in September 1986. He lost his place with the signing of Dave Beasant and was transferred to Birmingham City where he played for the best part of five years. He took his career total of senior appearances over the 500 mark at Cheltenham. When he finished playing he became a specialist goalkeeping coach, rising to the peak of his profession as England's national coach.

Appearances:
Others: (1) app.
Total: (1) app. 0 gls.

THOMAS, Mitchell Anthony

Role: Full-back 1986-92
6ft.2ins. 13st.0lbs.
Born: Luton, Bedfordshire, 2nd October 1964

CAREER: Limsbury Boys Club/Luton Schools/Bedfordshire Schools/Luton Town app. Sep 1981, pro. Aug 1982/**SPURS** Jul 1986/West Ham United Aug 1991/Luton Town loan Nov 1993, perm Mar 1994, player-coach Jul 1998/Burnley Jul 1999-May 2002.

Debut v Aston Villa (FL) (a) 23.8.1986
(Aldershot (sub) (Fr) (a) 4.8.1986)

Mitchell Thomas was one of the first footballers to make a career as a professional under the government sponsored Youth Opportunities Scheme. An England Youth international he made his League debut for Luton Town in February 1983 and was soon looked on as a potential full international. Thomas made his England Under-21 bow against Turkey in October 1985, and by the end of the season had won three caps at that level. When Luton manager David Pleat joined Spurs in July 1986, Thomas was his first signing and he made his Spurs' League debut in the opening match of the following season. A tall, gangling left-back, quick to the tackle and always willing

to push forward, he was a regular under Pleat, played in the 1987 FA Cup Final, won an England "B" cap against Malta in October 1987 and was promoted to the full England squad. Under Terry Venables though, he was not always able to get in the first team and midway through the 1988-89 season lost his place to long-serving Chris Hughton. The arrival of Pat Van den Hauwe the following season put Thomas' future at White Hart Lane very much in doubt, but he proved a valuable member of the squad, showing an admirable willingness to play in any role requested. At times he proved particularly effective in midfield. In August 1991 he moved to newly promoted West Ham for £500,000 as replacement for the injured Julian Dicks and when Dicks recovered played the majority of his games in midfield. He could not prevent the Hammers slipping out of the top flight in 1992 and generally had a tough time at Upton Park. He was no doubt grateful when David Pleat gave him the opportunity to return to Luton. He spent over five years back in Bedfordshire, only leaving when the club went into receivership. He signed for Burnley, playing over 100 games as a senior pro and helping the club gain promotion to the First Division. When he finished playing, Thomas acted as a player's agent.

Appearances:
League: 136 (21) apps. 6 gls.
FA Cup: 12 apps. 1 gl.
FL Cup: 28 (1) apps. 1 gl.
Others: 33 (11) apps. 2 gls.
Total: 207 (33) apps. 10 gls.

THOMAS, William S L

Role: Outside-left 1915-19
Born: Grays, Essex

CAREER: Grays United/Gillingham Jul 1914/(guest for **SPURS** during World War One)/Chatham Dec 1922/Guildford City Sep 1927.

Debut v West Ham United (LFC) (a) 18.9.1915

A guest player from Gillingham, whom he had joined from Grays United just before the outbreak of the Great War, Bill Thomas appeared on and off for Spurs during the First World War. Originally a winger, in his first season he played most of his games in his usual outside-left position, but in subsequent seasons occupied any role asked of him, winger, centre-forward and even half-back.

Appearances:
Others: 26 apps. 6 gls.
Total: 26 apps. 6 gls.

THOMPSON, Andrew

Role: Forward 1920-31
5ft.8ins. 11st.4lbs.
Born: Newcastle-Upon-Tyne, 21st January 1899
Died: Leyton, London, 1st January 1970

CAREER: Newburn/Wickham Park Villa/**SPURS** Nov 1920/Chester Jul 1931/Norwich City Nov 1931/Clapton Orient Oct 1932, coach 1933/ Ashford Town player-coach Mar 1934/Northfleet United Aug 1934, player-coach/Northfleet Amateurs coach/Chelsea coach/**SPURS** coach cs. 1938 to Aug 1960.

Debut v Sunderland (FL) (a) 26.3.1921

Originally an inside-forward, Andy Thompson played for Spurs for eleven years, but it was only when he moved to the right wing in the 1920's that he became a first team regular. A fine servant of the club, there were times when other teams were keen to acquire his services, but Spurs always resisted, knowing he was a player who, whenever called upon, would never let the club down. It was only in 1930-31, when manager Percy Smith teamed the Welsh internationals Willie Davies and Taffy O'Callaghan on the right, that Thompson became surplus to requirements. At the end of that season he was released. He went to Norwich City, spent a season in Norfolk and played for Chester and Clapton Orient before joining Spurs' nursery club at Northfleet, where he became involved on the coaching side. He then worked as a coach with Chelsea before returning to Spurs, initially in that capacity, but doing several other backroom jobs over more than twenty years.

Appearances:
League: 153 apps. 19 gls.
FA Cup: 13 apps. 2 gls.
Others: 38 apps. 12 gls.
Total: 204 apps. 33 gls.

THOMPSON, John Howard

Role: Forward 1883-84
Born: Edmonton, London, circa 1869
Died: February 1909

Debut v Albion (Fr) (a) 9.2.1884

One of the founders of Spurs, Jack Thompson is known to have played in only one first eleven match for the club. The first club secretary, he played mostly for the reserves throughout the 1880s. Elected to the club committee in 1885, he was financial secretary from 1896-98 and a director between March 1898 and July 1899. He was still a supporter when he passed away at the age of 40.

Appearances:
Others: 1 app.
Total: 1 app. 0 gls.

THORBURN

Role: Outside-right 1896-97

CAREER: Lanark Athletic/**SPURS** trial Sep 1896/Gravesend United trial Oct 1896.

Debut v Luton Town (Fr) (h) 24.9.1896

Thorburn played two friendly matches for Spurs during a period on trial in September 1896. The first was against Luton Town when he had little opportunity to impress as rain caused the match to be abandoned after 70 minutes. He had been due to make his debut a week earlier, but when the Casuals arrived at Spurs for a friendly they were a man short and Spurs let Thorburn turn out for them. He played his second game a week later, but was not taken on being described as "clever with feet but not likely to out-rival Payne". Like his fellow trialist, Sunderland, Thorburn joined Gravesend United on trial the following month. Unlike Sunderland, he had no better luck with them.

Appearances:
Others: 2 apps.
Total: 2 apps. 0 gls.

THORNLEY, J W

Role: Centre-half 1892-93

Debut v Smethwick (W&DCC) (Wolverton) 15.4.1893

Thornley's only recorded appearance for Spurs at first team level was in April 1893, when he played at Wolverton in a Wolverton & District Charity Cup semi-final with Smethwick.

Appearances:
Others: 1 app.
Total: 1 app. 0 gls.

THORSTVEDT, Erik

Role: Goalkeeper 1988-96
6ft.4ins. 14st.3lbs.
Born: Stavanger, Norway, 28th October 1962

CAREER: Vidar (Norway)/Viking Stavanger (Norway) 1974/Madla (Norway) till 1979/Viking Stavanger (Norway) 1980-81/Eik-Tønsberg (Norway) 1982-83/Viking Stavanger (Norway) by May 1984-1985/ Queens Park Rangers trial 1984/**SPURS** trial Dec 1984/Borussia Mönchengladbach (West Germany) Oct 1985/Arsenal trial 1987/1FK Gothenburg (Sweden) by Mar 1987/**SPURS** Dec 1988/Viking Stavanger (Norway) director of football 1997-98/Norway goalkeeping coach to Nov 2003.

Debut v Nottingham Forest (FL) (h) 15.1.1989

Erik Thorstvedt first began to make a name for himself in Norway when playing for Madla. He joined Viking but found several promising keepers ahead of him so dropped down to the second level of Norwegian football with Eik-Tønsberg. He performed so well in helping Eik secure promotion that he won his first cap against Kuwait in November 1982. He represented Norway at the 1984 Olympics before returning to Viking Stavanger. He was first connected to Spurs in December 1984, playing two matches in the reserves while on trial, but it was to be another four years before he was signed. By then he had developed into one of the top keepers in Europe and cost £400,000. Spurs were very interested in signing him after that initial trial, but even though he was Norway's first choice, they were unable to obtain the necessary work permit. The rules were not so tough in Germany though, and he spent two years with Borussia Mönchengladbach at the end of which he joined Arsenal on trial. They too wanted to sign him, but had no better luck than Spurs in seeking a work permit, and so he returned to Scandinavia to play for Gothenburg. With Bobby Mimms having a poor time in goal and Spurs struggling in Terry Venables' first full season in charge, Spurs tried their luck again in December 1988 and were at last able to get clearance to sign the big Norwegian who had, by that time, accumulated 51 caps for Norway. He made his Spurs' debut in a "live" televised League match against Nottingham Forest in January 1989, and whilst he made a terrible gaffe in front of the cameras to concede the winning goal, he quickly settled in and proved to be an exceptionally popular 'keeper. A member of the 1991 FA Cup winning team and first choice for his emerging national team he proved a steady last line of defence as Norway at last began to build themselves a reputation in football. His position at White Hart Lane came under threat from the talented young Ian Walker during 1991-92 and after suffering with a long-standing knee injury he had to give way to Walker. Released on a free transfer in May 1996 Thorstvedt was expected to join Wolverhampton Wanderers, but a back injury would not stand up to medical scrutiny. He was forced to retire from the game, returning to Norway as director of football at his old club, Viking Stavanger, and later going on to be a TV presenter and national goalkeeping coach. In his time with Spurs, Thorstvedt made 47 appearances for Norway.

Appearances:
League: 171 (2) apps.
FA Cup: 14 apps.
FL Cup: 25 apps.
Euro: 6 apps.
Others: 40 (5) apps.
Total: 256 (7) apps. 0 gls.

THWAITES, Arthur W

Role: Half-back 1916-18

CAREER: Alston Rangers/Tottenham Thursday/(guest for Southampton and **SPURS** during World War One)/Tufnell Park.

Debut v Arsenal (LFC) (a) 9.9.1916

A local player with the Tottenham Thursday club, Thwaites made all his appearances for Spurs during the First World War. He first played his first game as a last-minute replacement for the Derby County half-back, James Walker, when Walker was unable to appear as expected. Never a regular member of the team, Thwaites was usually called upon when Spurs were having difficulty raising a full team. After the War, he played for the local amateur side Tufnell Park.

Appearances:
Others: 12 apps. 3 gls.
Total: 12 apps. 3 gls.

TICKRIDGE, Sidney

Role: Full-back 1941-51
5ft.10ins. 11st.6lbs.
Born: Stepney, London, 10th April 1923
Died: Wingham, Kent, 6th January 1997

CAREER: Bow Central Schools/Bow Schools/East London Schools/England Schools/Tottenham Juniors/**SPURS** am., ground-staff Jun 1937/(Northfleet United Aug 1939)/(guest for Aldershot, Crystal Palace, Dartford, Fulham and Millwall during World War Two)/**SPURS** pro. Apr 1946/Chelsea Mar 1951/Brentford Jul 1955/retired Jan 1957/Millwall assistant trainer 1957-60/**SPURS** youth team trainer Aug 1960, reserve team trainer 1968, coach/retired Sep 1977.

Debut v Southampton (FL) (h) 9.9.1946
(Watford (LWL) (h) 30.8.1941)

Another of the many pre-war and war-time players who developed through the excellent youth scheme then operated by Spurs, Sid Tickridge played for Tottenham Juniors before being groomed at the Northfleet nursery. A hard, determined full-back, he played for Dartford in 1939-40 and guested for Millwall the following season, before making his Spurs debut in the first match of the London War League in August 1941. From then until the end of the season he did not miss a match, but was then called up. Serving in the Royal Navy, his further football was limited to service games and one appearance for Aldershot. It was not until his return to Spurs in 1946 that Tickridge was able to sign professional forms and,

having seen off the challenge of Arthur Willis was a regular from 1947. He eventually lost his place with the arrival of Alf Ramsey and was transferred to Chelsea, moving on to Brentford where he played for eighteen months before injury brought his career to an end. Following his retirement from playing, he took up training and assisted Millwall for three years before giving Spurs another 17 years' service.

Appearances:
League: 96* apps.
FA Cup: 6 apps.
Others: 49 apps.
Total: 151 apps. 0 gls.
*Includes 1 abandoned match.

TODA, Kazuyuki

Role: Midfielder 2002-04
5ft.10ins. 11st.9lbs.
Born: Tokyo, Japan, 30th December 1977

CAREER: Toin Gakueda High School/FC Machida (Japan)/Shimizu S-Pulse (Japan) 1995/Sunderland trial Jan 2003/(**SPURS** loan Jan 2003)/ADO Den Haag (Holland) loan and trial Jan 2004/Tokyo Verdy (Japan) Jan 2005/Sanfrecce Hiroshima (Japan) loan Jan 2006, perm Dec 2006/(JEF United (Japan) loan Jun 2008/Gyeongnam (South Korea) Mar 2009/Thespa Kusatsu (Japan) Dec 2009/Machida Zelvia (Japan) Jan 2012/Warriors (Singapore) Jan 2013/retired Dec 2013.

Debut v Manchester City (sub) (PL) (h) 18.4.2003 (Bohemians (Fr) (a) 4.3.2003)

Japanese midfield star Kazu Toda joined Spurs on a one-year loan in January 2001 with a view to a permanent transfer. He had played for eight years with Shimizu S-Pulse, some of that time under the management of Ossie Ardiles and Steve Perryman, and played for Japan in the 2002 World Cup finals. A midfield anchor man, Toda certainly put in the effort during his time at White Hart Lane, but rarely looked better than many other midfielders available to the club. He was allowed to leave before his full loan had run its course in order to have a trial with ADO Den Haag. That resulted in a one year contract and Toda played 20 games for the Dutch club before returning to Japan. He played for another eight years, mostly with Japanese clubs, though he finished his playing days in Singapore.

Appearances:
League: 2 (2) apps.
Others: 5 (1) apps.
Total: 7 (3) apps. 0 gls.

TOMKIN, Albert Harry

Role: Winger 1938-40
5ft.8ins. 10st.0lbs.
Born: Barrow-in-Furness, Lancashire, 23rd December 1915
Died: Leyland, Lancashire, 3rd September 1989

CAREER: Formby/**SPURS** am. Nov 1937/Northfleet United Nov 1937/**SPURS** pro. Dec 1937/(guest for Cardiff City, Luton Town, Southport, Sunderland and Swansea Town during World War Two).

Debut v Norwich City (FL) (a) 4.2.1939

Albert Tomkin joined Spurs after a good display for the Northern Counties against the Southern Counties in an amateur international trial. Sent to the Northfleet nursery for six months, he signed on Spurs' professional staff a month later and made a League debut in February 1939. Although he only played two matches that season, the departure of Les Miller in July 1939 left Tomkin to compete with Colin Lyman for the outside-right position. After playing in two of the three expunged League games at the start of the 1939-40 season and two more war-time matches, Tomkin left for military service and was not to appear for Spurs again.

Appearances:
League: 4 apps.
Others: 2 apps.
Total: 6 apps. 0 gls.

TOMKINS, Eric Feltham

Role: Half-back 1917-19
Born: Rushden, Northamptonshire, 18th December 1892
Died: Rushden, Northamptonshire, 20th July 1980

CAREER: Rushden Schools/England Schools/Rushden Fosse/Rushden Windmill/Northampton Town am., pro. 1911/(guest for Southampton and **SPURS** during World War One)/Rushden Town/Notts County coach.

Debut v West Ham United (LFC) (h) 24.11.1917

A former team-mate of Fanny Walden at Northampton, "Wassie" Tomkins turned out regularly for Spurs in the last two seasons of the First World War. A schoolboy star, captain of the first England Schoolboys team, he joined Southern League Northampton Town from his local junior club and quickly established himself as first choice left-half. With the outbreak of the First World War, he joined the Royal Flying Corps and after a couple of years was spending most of his time in and around London and so, on Walden's recommendation, was available to turn out for Spurs. After the War he returned to Northampton where he played until the end of the 1926-27 season. Like Walden, Tomkins was a top-class cricketer and played for Northamptonshire, playing in 13 first class matches in 1921 and 1922.

Appearances:
Others: 39 apps.
Total: 39 apps. 0 gls.

TONER, Ciarán

Role: Midfield 2001-02
6ft.1ins. 12st.2lbs.
Born: Craigavon, Northern Ireland, 30th June 1981.

CAREER: Parkside 1990/Goodyear Juniors 1993/Sunnyside Boys Club 1994/Glenavon Jul 1995/**SPURS** assoc. schl. May 1995, trainee Jul 1997, pro. Jul 1999/(Peterborough United loan Dec 2001)/(Bristol Rovers loan Mar 2002)/Leyton Orient May 2002/Lincoln City trial Jul 2004, perm. Aug 2004/(Cambridge United loan Mar 2005)/Grimsby Town Jul 2005/Rochdale Jul 2008/Luton Town trial Jul 2010/Harrogate Town Aug 2010/Guiseley Jul 2011/York City coach Oct 2012-May 2013/Gainsborough Trinity player/coach Sep 2013-Apr 2015/Dearne Valley College Football

Head Coach Aug 2013-Sep 2015/Rotherham United Youth Development Phase coach Aug 2013.

Debut v Stevenage Borough (Fr) (a) 13.7.2001

The only football played at Ciarán Toner's school in Northern Ireland was the Gaelic variety. Perhaps not the best way of training to play football with the feet, it is a physical game and certainly helped Toner toughen up. Football was always his game though and he took the chance to attend coaching sessions at St Paul's High School and play for junior clubs at the weekends. Taken on by Spurs as an associated schoolboy, Toner joined youth set-up at Glenavon before crossing the water to accept a trainee position at Spurs. An energetic midfielder with more than a little skill, he made just one senior appearance for Spurs in a pre-season friendly. Released after loan spells with Peterborough United and Bristol Rovers, Toner joined Leyton Orient. He later played around the lower reaches of the Football League and higher levels of non-League and started a coaching career with Rotherham United. Toner collected 12 Under-21 caps for Northern Ireland in his years with Spurs and made two full appearances in June 2003 when with Leyton Orient.

Appearances:
Others: 1 app.
Total: **1 app. 0 gls.**

TOULOUSE, Cyril Harvey

Role: Centre-half 1948-49
6ft.2ins. 12st.0lbs.
Born: Acton, London, 24th December 1924
Died: Pembroke, Dyfed, 22nd January 1980.

CAREER: St Cuthberts/Brentford pro. May 1946/**SPURS** Dec 1947/Guildford City Aug 1949/Headington United Mar 1950/Hastings United cs. 1954.

Debut v West Bromwich Albion (FL) (a) 11.9.1948

Spotted by Brentford playing for St Cuthberts in the Brentford Hospital Cup final of 1946 and immediately signed on, Cyril Toulouse joined Spurs as part of the deal that saw Jack Chisholm move to Griffin Park. He had made only 13 League appearances but was looked upon by Spurs as a player for the future. That did not prove to be the case, for he was to make only two appearances-in the space of three days-for Spurs in the Football League in September 1948 against West Bromwich Albion and Leeds United. He remained in the reserves until April 1949 when Spurs decided not to retain his registration. He signed for Guildford City, later playing for Headington United and Hastings United.

Appearances:
Others: 2 apps.
Total: **2 apps. 0 gls.**

TOWNLEY, James Chadwick

Role: Inside-forward 1927-28
5ft.9ins. 11st.0lbs.
Born: Blackburn, Lancashire, 2nd May 1902
Died: Thun, Switzerland, 3rd February 1983

CAREER: Hamburg Victoria (Germany) 1921/St Gallen (Switzerland) 1923/Chelsea trial 1924/**SPURS** trial Feb 1925, pro. Mar 1925/Brighton and Hove Albion Aug 1928/Clapton Orient Feb 1930/FC Berne (Switzerland) Aug 1931/St Gallen (Switzerland) manager Apr 1945-1949/FC Thun (Switzerland) manager 1949-50.

Debut v Everton (FL) (h) 1.10.1927 (scored once)

Jimmy Townley came to the UK from Switzerland, where his father worked as a coach, and arrived at White Hart Lane for a trial in February 1925 having failed to convince Chelsea of his abilities. Spurs were clearly more impressed than their south London neighbours and he was taken on the professional staff, but had the misfortune to break a leg in October 1925. It was to be two more years before Jimmy made his first team debut, standing-in for Jack Elkes, and he scored in his opening two games. Both games were lost though, and he made only one more League appearance before transferring to Brighton. He later had 18 months with Clapton Orient but when they decided not to retain his services returned to Switzerland. He played for FC Berne and later became a manager. Townley's father was William Townley, Blackburn Rover's England international of the 1880s and 1890s who scored a hat-trick in the 1890 FA Cup Final. He had two spells as manager of St Gallen in Switzerland. 1920-21 and 1923-25, and was followed into the job by Townley in April 1945.

Appearances:
League: 3 apps. 2 gls.
Others: 2 apps. 2 gls.
Total: **5 apps. 4 gls.**

TOWNSEND, Andros

Role: Wide midfield 2008-16
6ft.0ins., 12st. 0lbs.
Born: Whipps Cross, Walthamstow, London, 16th July 1991

CAREER: Rush Croft Sports College/**SPURS** Academy Scholar Jul 2007, pro. Dec 2008/(Yeovil Town loan Mar 2009)/(Leyton Orient loan Aug 2009)/(Milton Keynes Dons loan Jan 2010)/(Ipswich Town loan Aug 2010)/(Watford loan Jan 2011)/(Millwall loan Mar 2011)/(Leeds United loan Jan 2012)/(Birmingham City loan Feb 2012)(Queens Park Rangers loan Jan 2013)/Newcastle United Jan 2016/Crystal Palace Jul 2016.

Debut v Charlton Athletic (FAC) (h) 9.1.2011 (scored one)
(Hercules (sub) (Fr) (a) 24.7.2008)

A Spurs fan from his earliest days, Andros Townsend is the perfect example of the way young footballers develop in the modern game. Taken into the Spurs Academy, he progressed through the ranks to sign professional, made a few, often fleeting, first team appearances and went out on loan. Initially with lower level Football League clubs, he worked his way up the ladder to finish with a lengthy spell at a rival Premier League outfit and returned to Spurs to join the first team squad. Townsend had given Spurs supporters a taste of his quality on his competitive debut when he scored against Charlton in the FA Cup. A strong runner, he can play as an old-fashioned winger, taking his man on, beating him for pace and firing in a cross, but he is more effective carrying the ball forward and then cutting inside for a shot on goal. His shooting is not only powerful and accurate, but the way he can swerve the ball, makes the goalkeeper's job even harder. Townsend had only made a handful of appearances when he was called up to the England squad. He made his debut against Montenegro in October 2013 and brought to the team the same freedom and lack of fear he was showing at club level and celebrated with a goal. As with most players, Townsend could never be sure of a place in a starting line-up, but he was invariably involved in most games. It was only when Mauricio Pochettino settled on a formation that used over-lapping full-backs in place of wingers that Townsend, like Aaron Lennon, dropped out of favour. While Lennon accepted the situation and got on with his job, Townsend found it much harder to accept. He wanted to play, and not just play-he wanted to play for Spurs. His frustrations boiled over and led to a bust-up with a member of the training staff. Pochettino would not accept that. While Townsend was suspended and paid the financial penalty, claims that all was forgiven were not borne out with Townsend totally marginalised. Several clubs recognised that Townsend would be a terrific acquisition and sought his transfer. Eventually Townsend accepted the one that took him about as far away from White Hart Lane as possible. While he was unable to save Newcastle from relegation, he certainly gave the Toon Army hope for the future which made it all the more surprising that he was allowed to return to London with Crystal Palace..

Appearances:
League: 22 (28) apps. 3 gls.
FA Cup: 3 (2) apps. 2 gls.
FL Cup: 8 (2) apps. 2 gls.
Euro: 22 (6) apps. 4 gls,
Others: 8 (18) apps. 3 gls.
Total: 63 (56) apps. 14 gls.

TRAILOR, Cyril Henry

Role: Half-back 1941-49
5ft.10ins. 10st.7lbs.
Born: *Merthyr Tydfil, Glamorgan, 15th May 1919*
Died: *Merthyr Tydfil, Glamorgan, 28th August 1986*

CAREER: Wales Schools/Tottenham Juniors/**SPURS** am. Oct 1936/ Northfleet United Aug 1937/**SPURS** pro. 1946/Clapton Orient Aug 1949/ Bedford Town Jan 1951.

Debut v Southampton (FL) (a) 10.5.1947
(Aldershot (LWL) (h) 20.12.1941)

Cyril Trailor worked his way through Tottenham Juniors and Northfleet to make his debut in a London War League match against Aldershot in December 1941. He only signed as a professional after the war, and then had the unenviable task of understudying the great Ron Burgess. Only called into the team when Burgess was injured or on international duty, Trailor was not retained in April 1949 and joined Clapton Orient where he spent a season as a first team regular, before joining Bedford Town.

Appearances:
League: 11 apps.
FA Cup: 1 app.
Others: 6 apps.
Total: 18 apps. 0 gls.

TRAMEZZANI, Paolo

Role: Full-back 1998-99
6ft.1ins. 13st.5lbs.
Born: *Castelnovo ne' Monti, Italy, 30th July 1970.*

CAREER: Internazionale Youth (Italy) 1986-1989/(Prato (Italy) loan Oct 1989)/(Cosenza (Italy) loan 1990-91)/(Lucchese (Italy) loan 1992)/Venezia (Italy) Nov 1994/Cesena (Italy) Nov 1995/Piacenza (Italy) cs. 1996/**SPURS** Jun 1998/Pistoiese (Italy) Feb 2000/Piacenza (Italy) Jul 2001/Atalanta (Italy) Jan 2003/Empoli (Italy) Jul 2003/Pro Patria (Italy) Oct 2003/Albania national team asst. coach Jan 2012/ASD Golfodianese asst. coach Jul 2013.

Debut v Wimbledon (PL) (a) 15.8.1998
(Grasshoppers (Fr) (a) 10.7.1998)

When he signed for Spurs, Paolo Tramezzani was hailed as a star of Italian football, a full-back of quality who would strengthen Spurs' defence and bring a whole new dimension to the attacking options. It was a build-up that he came nowhere near meeting. At an age when he should have been at his peak, Tramezzani was at best a journeyman footballer. He had been with Internazionale since the age of nine, but had played few games for the Italian giants. Most of his football had been in Serie C1 and Serie B on loan to smaller clubs. Only with Piacenza had he experience playing in the top division and even then he had made barely 30 appearances in three years for a team continually fighting relegation. Tramezzani started his Spurs' career in the team, playing all the pre-season games and the first seven competitive matches, but it was quickly obvious that Tramezzani was not good enough for top level English football. He was soon out of

the team and when George Graham replaced Christian Gross, not even in the first team squad. Being generous, his failure at Spurs could be put down to injury. Being honest, he was simply not good enough. Tramezzani hung around until February 2000, when his contract was paid off. He returned to Italy where he played for another four years, rarely anything more than a squad player in his second spell with Piacenza. When he quit playing Tramezzani turned to youth coaching, combining that with the position of assistant coach to Albania.

Appearances:
League: 6 apps.
FL Cup: 1 app.
Others: 10 apps. 1 gl.
Total: **17 apps. 1 gl.**

TRAVERS, George Edward James

Role: Centre-forward 1915-17
5ft.8ins. 11st.6lbs.
Born: Newtown, Birmingham, 4th November 1888
Died: Smethwick, Birmingham, 31st August 1946.

CAREER: Birchfield Road School/Newton Abbey 1903/Bilston United 1904/Rowley United 1905/Wolverhampton Wanderers Jul 1906/Birmingham Aug 1907/Aston Villa Dec 1908/Queens Park Rangers May 1909/Leicester Fosse Aug 1910/Barnsley Jan 1911/Manchester United Jan 1914/(guest for **SPURS** during World War One)/Swindon Town Jul 1919/Millwall Jun 1920/Norwich City Oct 1920/Gillingham Jul 1921/Nuneaton Town Sep 1921/Pembroke Dock United trial Oct 1923/Cradley Heath Nov 1928/Bilston United cs. 1929/retired May 1931.

Debut v West Ham United (LFC) (a) 18.9.1915

A true football nomad, George Travers played as a 16-year old schoolboy for a year with Bilston United before travelling the length and breadth of the country, plying his trade as a consistent, if not prolific goal-scorer. He played two League games for Birmingham before crossing the city to Aston Villa where he scored a hat-trick on his League debut in their colours. He played only three more League games for Villa before moving down to London and Queens Park Rangers where he played regularly for one season. Released by Rangers, he moved quickly from Leicester Fosse to Barnsley where he experienced the high point of his career, helping the Yorkshire club win the FA Cup in 1912. Next stop was Manchester United and he played his first game for them at White Hart Lane. With the outbreak of the First World War he was one of the first to join up and played for Spurs as a guest during the early part of the war when able to get time off from his service duties. After the war he was released by United and went on to play for Swindon Town, Millwall, Norwich City, Gillingham, Nuneaton Town and Cradley Heath finishing his career back where it all began with two seasons at Bilston United. Travers' father was the old-time music hall comedian Hyram Travers, known as the "Pearly King".

Appearances:
Others: 6 apps.2 gls.
Total: **6 apps. 2 gls.**

TRIGG, Sidney A

Role: Outside-left 1942-43

CAREER: Bradford Park Avenue/(guest for Aldershot, **SPURS** and West Ham United during World War Two).

Debut v Queens Park Rangers (Fr) (a) 17.4.1943

A guest from Bradford Park Avenue, Sid Trigg made his one appearance for Spurs in a friendly against Queens Park Rangers in April 1943.

Appearances:
Others: 1 app.
Total: **1 app. 0 gls.**

TRIPPIER, Kieran John

Role: Full-back 2015-
5ft.10ins. 11st.4lbs.
Born: Bury, Lancashire, 19th July 1990

CAREER: Manchester City Academy 1999, pro. 2008/(Barnsley loans Feb 2010 & Aug 2010)/(Burnley loan Jul 2011, perm. Jan 2012/**SPURS** Jun 2015.

Debut v Bournemouth (PL) (a) (sub) 25.10.2015
(MLS All-Stars (Fr) (a) (sub) 29.7.2015)

Kieran Trippier was nine-years old when he joined the Manchester City Academy. He worked his way through the ranks, collecting England Youth honours and the 2008 FA Youth Cup on the way, into the reserve team. That was to be as far as he progressed with City. The influx of money from the club's Abu Dhabi owners and the signing of mega-stars left youngsters like Trippier on the outside. He had two loans spells with Barnsley, the first for a month, the second for a full season, quickly proving a more than competent Championship performer. Burnley was his next stop, again on a season long loan, but so impressed were they that within six months the move was made permanent. Almost ever-present for four years, Trippier was outstanding as Burnley played Premiership football in 2014-15. Pacy, strong in the tackle, quick to recover, always looking to go forward and an excellent crosser of the ball, there was little prospect of Trippier dropping back down to the Championship when Burnley were relegated. With Kyle Naughton having left for Swansea City, Kyle Walker needed someone to challenge for his position, Trippier was just the man. While Trippier initially had to play second fiddle to Walker, his mere presence brought about a noticeable immediate improvement in Walker's form. Clearly rated by the management team, Trippier finished the 2016-17 not only sharing the right-back position with Walker for Spurs, but also at international level. He made his first appearance for England against France in June 2017. If fears Walker departs for a heftier pay packet are realised, there can be few doubts Spurs have a more than adequate replacement on the books..

Appearances:
League: 11 (7) apps. 1 gl.
FA Cup: 7 apps.
FL Cup: 3 apps.
Euro: 13 apps.
Others: 3 (3) apps.
Total: **37 (10) apps. 1 gl.**

TULL, Walter Daniel John

Role: Centre-forward 1908-11
5ft.8ins. 11st.0lbs.
Born: Folkestone, Sussex, 28th April 1888
Died: Favreuil, France, 25th March 1918 (Killed in action)

CAREER: Bonner Road Orphanage/Clapton cs. 1908/**SPURS** am. Apr 1909, pro. May 1909/Northampton Town Oct 1911/(Fulham during World War Two).

Debut v Sunderland (FL) (a) 1.9.1909
(Clapton Orient (Fr) (a) 29.4.1909 (scored twice))

Born of an English mother and a West Indian father, "Darkie" Tull was probably the second black player to appear in the Football League. Orphaned at the age of nine, he first learnt football at an orphanage in Bethnal Green. He joined the famous amateur club Clapton for 1908-09 and it was his performances in helping them win the Amateur and London Senior Cups that alerted Spurs to his talents. He made his League debut at the start of the following season and played in six of the first seven League games but, whilst a skilful player, he was not considered fast enough for top class football. A transfer to Heanor Town was arranged, but called off when he joined Northampton Town as part of the transfer of Richard Brittan to Spurs. Tull moved into the half-back line where his lack of pace was not so obvious, and served Northampton until the outbreak of the First World War. Serving in the Footballers' Battalion, he has been lauded as the first black officer in the British army and was mentioned in dispatches, before being killed in action. Tull appeared as a guest for Fulham during the war. He signed to play for Rangers when he knew he would be doing his training with the Officer Training Corps in Glasgow, but was unable to be available for any matches. In July 2004 Spurs met Rangers in Glasgow in a pre-season fixture for the Walker Tull Trophy.

Appearances:
League: 10 apps. 2 gls.
Others: 8 apps. 6 gls
Total: 18 apps. 8 gls.

TUNNEY, Edward Luton

Role: Full-back 1944-45
5ft.8ins. 11st.0lbs.
Born: Wirral, Cheshire, 23rd September 1915
Died: September 2011

CAREER: Harrington Board School/Yoik House Boys' Club/Liverpool Boys' Clubs/Liverpool FA/Lancashire/Everton Aug am 1935, semi-pro. Aug 1936/Wrexham Sep 1937/(guest for Crystal Palace, Hartlepools United, Luton Town, **SPURS** and Tranmere Rovers during World War Two)/Winsford United 1952/Tranmere Rovers coach.

Debut v Aldershot (FLSC) (a) 10.3.1945

Ed Tunney was a Wrexham player who played one game for Spurs as a guest at Aldershot in a Football League South Cup tie in March 1945. Serving as a sergeant instructor in the Army, Tunney was on a course at Aldershot and when Arthur Willis was unable to play due to a head injury Tunney stood in occupying his usual left-back position. He had been on Everton's books without making the breakthrough when the chance came to play for Wrexham. It allowed him to continue with his job in the print trade. Down in Wales, he was a regular performer, occupying one of the full-back positions and rarely missing a game. He returned to Wrexham after the War and played for another five years, racking up almost 300 appearances in total.

Appearances:
Others: 1 app.
Total: 1 app. 0 gls.

TURNER, Andrew Peter

Role: Winger 1991-96
5ft.10ins. 11st.2lbs.
Born: Woolwich, London 23rd March 1975

CAREER: North Kent Schools/FA-GM School of Excellence/England Schools/**SPURS** trainee Jul 1991, pro. Mar 1992/(Wycombe Wanderers loan Aug 1994)/(Doncaster Rovers loan Oct 1994)/(Huddersfield Town loan Dec 1995)/(Southend United loan Mar 1996)/Portsmouth Sep 1996/Crystal Palace Oct 1998/Wolverhampton Wanderers Mar-Jun 1999/Rotherham United Jun 1999-May 2001/(Boston United loan Nov 2000)/(Rochdale loan Mar 2001)/Yeovil Town Jun 2001-May 2002/(Nuneaton Borough loan Jan 2002)/(Kettering Town loan Mar 2002)/Tamworth player-coach Jun 2002/Northampton Town Jan 2003/Northwich Victoria loan Mar 2003)/Moor Green Jun 2003/Sutton Coldfield Town Oct 2003/Ilkeston Town trial Feb 2004/Cinderford Town Mar 2004/Belper Town Jul 2004/Chasetown player-coach Jul 2005-Oct 2011, scholarship scheme manager Jul 2009-Aug 2013/Kidsgrove Athletic first team coach Dec 2011-May 2012/Alsager Town manager May 2012-Jan 2014/Coalville Town asst. manager Jan 2014/Romulus FC joint-manager Jan 2015, Academy head coach Jun 2015.

Debut v Southampton (PL) (a) 15.8.1992
(Hull City XI (Fr) (a) 8.5.1992)

Even though he had played in pre-season games, it was a complete surprise when Andy Turner was selected for Spurs opening game of the 1992-93 season against Southampton. The FA School of Excellence graduate was barely 17-years old and had only been a professional for a few months. Terry Venables, though, was a manager who was not afraid to give youth a chance. He had no qualms about throwing Turner into the big-time. A speedy, direct winger who would take an opponent on

for pace and head for the goal-line before firing a cross into the middle, the freshness and innocence Turner brought to the game gave Spurs an early season boost. The youngest goal-scorer in Premier League football when he scored against Everton in September 1992, Turner was unable to maintain a regular place and after one season was rarely seen at first team level again, spending much of his time out on loan. He won seven caps for the Republic of Ireland at Under-21 level before being released to join Portsmouth. Pompey probably saw the best of Turner as he played fairly regularly over two years. Since Portsmouth Turner has taken his talents around the country, becoming a coach and manager at non-League level and helping young players develop.

Appearances:
League: 8 (12) apps. 3 gls.
FA Cup: (1) app.
FL Cup: (2) apps. 1 gl.
Others: 13 (10) apps. 3 gls.
Total: 21 (25) apps. 7 gls.

TURNER, Arthur Docwra

Role: Winger 1903-04
5ft.8ins. 11st.10lbs.
Born: Farnborough, Hampshire, June 1877
Died: Hartley Witney, Hampshire, 4th April 1925.

CAREER: Aldershot North End 1892-94/South Farnborough/Camberley St Michaels/Brentford trial/Reading trial/Southampton May 1899/Derby County May 1902/Newcastle United Jan 1903/**SPURS** Jan 1904/Southampton May 1904/(Bristol City loan Feb 1905)/South Farnborough Athletic/retired Aug 1905.

Debut v Queens Park Rangers (LL) (a) 15.2.1904

Having originally played for Aldershot North End, South Farnborough and Camberley St Michaels, Arthur Turner joined Southampton and soon established himself as a regular, helping them reach the FA Cup Final in 1900 and 1902 and win the Southern League title in 1900-01. After playing for the South against the North in the international trial match in March 1900, he won his first England cap against Ireland later that month and collected a further cap against the Irish in March 1901. A speedy, attacking winger with an eye for goal and a master of the accurate centre, Turner had short spells with Derby County-alongside the legendary Steve Bloomer-and Newcastle United, from whom Spurs secured his transfer. In the two months he spent at White Hart Lane he made 13 appearances scoring six goals, four of them against Kettering on 16th April. Released at the end of the season, he returned to Southampton where he played for just one more year, including one game on "loan" to Bristol City, before retiring at the age of 28. He joined his father's business in Farnborough, although he continued to play for his local club, South Farnborough Athletic. His brother, Harry, also played for Southampton, Reading and South Farnborough.

Appearances:
Southern: 5 apps. 5 gls.
Others: 7 apps. 1 gl.
Total: 12 apps. 6 gls.

TUTTLE, David Philip

Role: Central defender 1989-93
6ft.1ins. 12st.10lbs.
Born: Reading, Berkshire, 6th February 1972

CAREER: SPURS trainee Jul 1988, pro. Feb 1990/(Peterborough United Jan 1993)/Sheffield United Aug 1993/Crystal Palace Mar 1996/(Charlton Athletic loan Mar 1999)/Barnsley Aug 1999/Millwall Mar 2000/(Wycombe Wanderers loan Feb 2002)/Retired Jan 2003/Millwall scout Feb 2003, coach, manager Dec 2005-Apr 2006/Swindon Town youth and scouting director Jun 2006, caretaker manager Oct 2006/Dorking player-advisor Jun 2007/Milton Keynes Dons chief scout Jul 2007/Blackburn Rovers chief scout Jun 2008/Bracknell Town manager Aug 2009/Henley Town manager Jul 2010-May 2012/Hartley Wintney manager Jun 2012/Newbury Oct 2012-Jan 2013.

Debut v Sheffield United (sub) (FLC) (a) 27.11.1990
(Caen (sub) (Fr) (Cherbourg) 31.10.1989)

A highly promising young player David Tuttle, who represented England at Under-17 and Under-18 level, helped Spurs win the FA Youth Cup in 1990 and it was directly because of his encouraging development that Spurs felt able to let reserve centre-half Guy Butters move to Portsmouth in September 1990. Tuttle made his competitive debut as substitute in a Rumbelows League Cup tie at Sheffield United in November 1990 and retained the place for the weekend's League match at Chelsea. Unfortunately, his inexperience was exposed by former England centre-forward Kerry Dixon and he was withdrawn at half-time, but he learnt from the lesson and returned later in the season to show what a useful player he could be. A defender pure and simple, he had a difficult job trying to get past players like Gary Mabbutt, Steve Sedgley and latterly Neil Ruddock and when Ossie Ardiles bought Colin Calderwood, Tuttle was allowed to move to Sheffield United for £350,000. A consistent, if quiet, performer, he returned to London in March 1996 following former Sheffield United manager Dave Bassett to Crystal Palace. Bassett did not remain long at Selhurst Park, but Tuttle did, helping Palace win promotion to the Premiership in 1997. After a brief spell with Barnsley, Tuttle joined Millwall, but injury forced his retirement in January 2003. Taken on the scouting and coaching staff, Tuttle was surprisingly appointed manager in December 2005 as the Lions struggled against relegation. Unable to keep them up he left before the season's conclusion and has since continued to work in football as a scout and manager.

Appearances:
League: 10 (3) apps.
FL Cup: 3 (1) apps.
Euro: 1 app. 1 gl.
Others: 8 (9) apps.
Total: 22 (13) apps. 1 gl.

TYLER, W

Role: Centre-forward 1891-94

Debut v Uxbridge (Fr) (h) 2.2.1892 (scored once)

Tyler first appeared for Spurs midway through the 1891-92 season. His first known appearance was in January 1892 when he scored in a friendly with Uxbridge and he played in the rest of the friendly matches that season. His services were not called upon the following season, but he did appear in the first team again in October 1893, as Spurs tried several players in the centre-forward position that proved a problem for the whole of the season.

Appearances:
Others: 11 apps. 5 gls.
Total: 11 apps. 5 gls.

TYRELL, William C

Role: Full-back 1883-93
Born: Edmonton, London, June qtr. 1866

Debut v Brownlow Rovers (Fr) (h) 6.10.1883

One of Spurs' earliest players, Billy Tyrell played for the club for ten years from shortly after its formation and was one of the most regular performers in those early days.

Appearances:
Others: 25 apps. 1 gl.
Total: 25 apps. 1 gl.

U

UPEX, Derek

Role: Inside-forward 1918-19
5ft.10ins. 10st.2lbs
Born: Peterborough, 26th June 1882
Died: Croydon, Surrey, 22nd May 1979

CAREER: Great Eastern Locomotive Works/Peterborough City/Croydon Common Oct 1912/(guest for Clapton Orient and **SPURS** during World War One)/Southend United Aug 1919/Charlton Athletic Aug 1920.

Debut v Crystal Palace (Fr) (a) 26.4.1919

Dick Upex started his career with Great Western Locomotive Works and Peterborough City before joining Croydon Common. He served with the Footballers' Battalion of the Middlesex Regiment during the First World War and played regularly for Clapton Orient after the demise of Croydon Common. He made his one appearance for Spurs at the end of the war in a friendly at Crystal Palace in April 1919 when Spurs included several trialists. After the war he assisted Southend United for one season and then had two years with Charlton Athletic playing three games in their first season as a Football League club.

Appearances:
Others: 1 app.
Total: 1 app. 0 gls.

UPHILL, Edward Dennis Herbert

Role: Inside-forward 1950-53
5ft.8ins. 10st.10lbs.
Born: Bath, Somerset, 11th August 1931
Died: Watford, Hertfordshire, 7th February 2007

CAREER: Odd Down/Peasedown Colliery/**SPURS** am. Mar 1948/(Finchley)/**SPURS** pro. Sep 1949/Reading Feb 1953/Coventry City guest Oct 1955, perm. Oct 1955/Mansfield Town Mar 1957/Watford Jun 1959/Crystal Palace Oct 1960/Rugby Town Apr 1963/Romford/Dartford Feb 1964/Croxley Casuals Oct 1967.

Debut v Sunderland (FL) (h) 23.9.1950

Dennis Uphill joined Spurs as a junior from Western League Peasedown Colliery and after a spell with Finchley signed professional. For almost

four years he played in the reserves and made only six League appearances, without ever posing any serious threat to Eddie Baily or Les Bennett. Transferred to Reading in part-exchange for Johnny Brooks, he went on to prove a consistent scorer in the lower divisions with Reading, Coventry City, Mansfield Town, Watford and Crystal Palace netting 145 goals in 338 League games.

Appearances:
League: 6 apps. 2 gls.
Others: 2 (1) apps. 4 gls.
Total: 8 (1) apps. 6 gls.

UPTON, Soloman

Role: Winger 1912-13
Born: Higham Ferrers, Northamptonshire, 7th February 1891
Died: Wellingborough, Northamptonshire, 29th August 1972

CAREER: Higham St Marys/Raunds Town/Sheffield United trial/Kettering Town cs. 1911/**SPURS** Dec 1911/Portsmouth May 1913/(guest for Luton Town during World War One)/Kettering Town 1919/Higham Town 1921.

Debut v Bolton Wanderers (FL) (h) 9.11.1912
(Crystal Palace (LFACC) (h) 21.10.1912)

Signed from Kettering in December 1911, Solly Upton waited almost a year for his first team debut-and then when he did play, the match was declared void! That initial appearance came in a London FA Charity Cup tie with Crystal Palace, but Spurs had not registered Jimmy Cantrell with the London FA and they ordered the game be replayed. After this "false start", Upton made his only League appearances for Spurs the following month and in between played his only other senior game in another London FA Charity Cup tie with Palace. Released in May 1913, he joined Portsmouth where he played until the outbreak of the First World War.

Appearances:
League: 2 apps.
Others: 2 apps.
Total: 4 apps. 0 gls.

VAN DEN HAUWE, Patrick William Roger

Role: Full-back 1989-93
5ft.11ins. 11st.10lbs.
Born: Dendermode, Belgium, 16th December 1960.

CAREER: Birmingham City app. Jul 1976, pro. Aug 1978/Everton Sep 1984/**SPURS** Aug 1989/Millwall Sep 1993-Jan 1995/Hellenic (South Africa) 1995/Witbank (South Africa)/Wynberg St Johns (South Africa) Mar 1997/Kapstad (South Africa) coach/Ikapa Sporting (South Africa) technical advisor.

Debut v Aston Villa (FL) (a) 9.9.1989

An uncompromising, hard-tackling defender, Pat Van den Hauwe was brought up in London, but started his football career with Birmingham City. He made his League debut two months after signing professional, but took time to establish himself at St Andrew's although his progress was not helped by being called upon to alternate between full-back and central defence in a poor team continually struggling against relegation. It was not until 1983-84 that he settled as first choice left-back, but at the end of the season Birmingham were relegated. Too good a player for Second Division football, he was transferred to Everton and with quality players around him began to blossom. By the end of his first season at Goodison, he had helped Everton win the Football League title and the European Cup-Winners' Cup, reach the FA Cup Final and won his first international cap. Although born in Belgium, where his father, Rene, had been a professional footballer, Van den Hauwe had opted out of National Service and was therefore ineligible to play for the country of his birth. Instead, he chose to play for Wales and made his debut against Spain in April 1985. Over the next four years he was a regular in the fine Everton sides which won the League again in 1987, reached the FA Cup Finals in 1986 and 1989 and also the Simod Cup Final in 1989. By the time of his £575,000 move to White Hart Lane he had taken his total number of Welsh caps to 13. At Spurs he soon settled in, adding both the bite and strength which had been missing from the defence. Although in his thirties, his vast experience and powerful physique

helped offset any lack of pace and he finally collected an FA Cup winners' medal in May 1991 when he played against Nottingham Forest. With injuries restricting his appearances and Justin Edinburgh pushing hard to become first choice left-back Van den Hauwe was released on a free transfer to join Millwall. After a couple of years, he finished playing and moved to South Africa, where he coached at several clubs.

Appearances:
League: 110 (6) apps.
FA Cup: 7 apps.
FL Cup: 16 apps.
Euro: 6 apps.
Others: 15 (1) apps.
Total: 154 (7) apps. 0 gls.

VAN DER VAART, Rafael Ferdinand

Role: Midfielder 2010-12
5ft.10ins. 12st.3lbs.
Born: Heemskerk, Holland, 11th February 1983

CAREER: De Kennemers (Holland) 1987/Ajax (Holland) Academy 1993, pro./Hamburg SV (Germany) Jun 2005/Real Madrid (Spain) Aug 2008/ **SPURS** Aug 2010/Hamburg SV (Germany) Aug 2012/Real Betis (Spain) Jun 2015/Midtjylland (Denmark) Aug 2016.

Debut v West Bromwich Albion (PL) (a) 11.9.2010

As a child Rafael van der Vaart honed his talents between the caravans on the trailer park where his family lived. At the age of 10 he began attending the Ajax Academy and shortly after he reached 17 he was playing for Ajax in the Eredivisie. A wonderfully talented midfield creator and goal-scorer, despite a serious knee injury that put him out of the game for a long spell, he became one of the most important components of an Ajax team that played an exciting brand of football as it won the Dutch League and Cup in 2002 and the League again in 2004. Like so many other Dutch

talents, van der Vaart was soon looking to take his career a stage further by playing abroad. Despite interest from some of Europe's big clubs, he decided to join Hamburg, a decision met with much surprise. A big fish in a relatively small pond, van der Vaart did well in Germany, helping Hamburg twice win the Intertoto Cup, but his talents deserved a far bigger stage. They got one in August 2008 when he signed for Real Madrid. The move to Spain meant he would play again with Wesley Sneijder, a team-mate in his Ajax days that van der Vaart was said to be unable to play with. They played together for just one year, though with van der Vaart often being used as a substitute. Before his second season in Madrid van der Vaart was told he did not figure in manager Manuel Pellegrini's plans. He was expected to leave, but remained as compatriots Sneijder, Arjen Robben and Klaas-Jan Huntelaar were shown the exit door. A year later, Spurs learnt van der Vaart was available for a bargain £8 million. Harry Redknapp was never a man to turn down the chance to manage a player of van der Vaart's stature and a deal was quickly done. Van der Vaart was just the type of top quality player Spurs needed for their first venture into the Champions League and he proved worth every penny of the transfer fee. At his best operating behind one or more central strikers, van der Vaart worked perfectly with Gareth Bale and Luka Modrić, spreading the ball out to the Welshman, seeking out space to take passes from the Croat. A sweet left foot and excellent vision that was always looking for an opening, van der Vaart was at his best given the freedom to roam, tasked Mike Varney was the club physiotherapist called upon to play for the first team in a friendly match against a Bermuda Select XI in June 1979, during a break in Spurs' return journey from Japan where the club had won the Japan Cup during its summer tour. Varney moved from Leeds to London when ten months old and after school joined the Army with the Norfolk with breaking down defences, not working back to defend his own goal. In two years he provided some magical moments, but van der Vaart was a man who needed to be sure of his place. When Luka Modrić departed, Gylfi Sigurðsson, Mousa Dembélé and Clint Dempsey arrived, van der Vaart decided it would be best for him to leave. He went back to Hamburg for another three years and then joined Real Betis. Van der Vaart's signing for Spurs was not without its problems. The deal was done as the transfer window was closing. Computer problems meant the necessary forms were not completed in time and Spurs had to get special dispensation from the Premier League for the transfer to be registered. Van der Vaart made his international debut for Holland against Andorra in October 2001. Almost guaranteed a place when fit, he made a total of 109 full appearances, 16 in his time with Spurs.

Appearances:
League: 57 (6) apps. 24 gls.
FA Cup: 6* apps. 1 gl.
FL Cup: 1 app.
Euro: 8 apps. 3 gls.
Others: 4 (2) apps. 3 gls.
Total: 76 (8) apps. 31 gls.
* Includes 1 abandoned match

VANNER, Richard Thomas

Role: Outside-right 1925-26
Born: Farnham, Hampshire, 14th November 1903
Died: Farnham, Hampshire, 15th July 1978

CAREER: Aldershot Traction Company Works FC/**SPURS** Mar 1925/Clapton Orient May 1928/Aldershot Aug 1931.

Debut v Hull City (Fr) (a) 27.3.1926

Dick Vanner joined Spurs as a 22-year old from the Aldershot Traction Company Works FC in March 1925. He made his only first team appearance in a friendly with Hull City a year later. He remained with Spurs without getting a chance in the senior side until released in May 1928, when he joined Clapton Orient. He stayed at Orient until the end of the 1930-31 season when they decided not to retain him and joined Aldershot where he played for a year.

Appearances:
Others: 1 app.
Total: 1 app. 0 gls.

VARNEY, Mike

Role: Outside-left 1979
Born: Leeds

CAREER: Kingstonians physio/Sutton United physio/Staines Town physio/**SPURS** physio cs. 1975-Jul 1986/Ware football development officer 2005-06/Hertford Town chairman to Sep 2011/Ware vice-chairman, chairman Jun 2012-Nov 2013.

Debut v Bermuda Select XI (Fr) (a) 6.6.1979

Mike Varney was the club physiotherapist called upon to play for the first team in a friendly match against a Bermuda Select XI in June 1979, during a break in Spurs' return journey from Japan where the club had won the Japan Cup during its summer tour. Varney moved from Leeds to London when ten months old and after school joined the Army with the Norfolk Regiment. He later moved to the Army Physical Training Corps as a Sergeant Instructor. Qualifying as a remedial gymnast he served at the Joint Services Rehabilitation Centre and began his involvement with football helping Kingstonians, Sutton United and Staines Town as physiotherapist. After ten years in the army Varney left and joined Spurs as first team physiotherapist in the summer of 1975. He remained with Spurs for eleven years, but left in the summer of 1986 when David Pleat's physiotherapist, John Sheridan, moved with him from Luton Town. Varney later joined Queens Park Rangers as physio, linking up with Rangers' assistant manager Peter Shreeve who he had served under at White Hart Lane.

Appearances:
Others: 1 app.
Total: 1 app. 0 gls.

VAUGHAN, W

Role: Outside-left 1903-04

CAREER: SPURS trial Nov 1903.

Debut v Millwall (LL) (h) 23.11.1903

A young Welsh trialist, Vaughan played in the London League match with Millwall in November 1903, but was not offered terms.

Appearances:
Others: 1 app.
Total: 1 app. 0 gls.

VEGA, Ramon

Role: Central defender 1996-2001
6ft.3ins. 14st.11lbs.
Born: Olten, Switzerland, 14th June 1971

CAREER: FC Trimbach (Switzerland)/FC Olten (Switzerland) 1987/FC Trimbach (Switzerland) 1989/Grasshoppers (Switzerland) 1990/Cagliari (Italy) Jun 1996/SPURS Jan 1997/Celtic loan Dec 2001/Watford Jun 2001 -May 2002/US Créteil-Lusitanos (France) Sep 2002/retired 2003.

Debut v Manchester United (PL) (h) 12.1.1997

The Swiss born son of Spanish émigrés, Ramon Vega was a striker in his early days and it was only after he had joined Grasshoppers that he began to play in the centre of defence. He was soon in the first eleven, playing regularly and providing a solid core as Grasshoppers won the Swiss Super League in 1991, 1995 and 1996 and the Swiss Cup in 1994. Vega made his first international appearance against Tunisia in March 1993 and by the time of the Euro 96 tournament had nine caps to his credit. The Swiss did not make it past the group stages, but Vega had shown himself a big, strong, capable football-playing defender who looked to have all the qualities needed to be a success in English football. However, Cagliari thought he had what was needed at the highest level of Italian football and it was they who persuaded Vega to leave Grasshoppers. Six months later Vega accepted he had made a mistake and made the move to White Hart Lane. He spent the best part of four years with Spurs. There were times when he looked the part-his former Grasshoppers' manager, Christian Gross, seemed able to get the best out of him-but at other times he looked, weak, indecisive and error-prone. Although he helped Spurs win the Worthington Cup in 1999, George Graham certainly did not trust Vega. He signed Chris Perry to play alongside Sol Campbell. Vega stayed with Spurs until December 2001 when, in the last year of his contract, he moved on loan to Celtic. He helped the giants secure the Scottish Premier League, Scottish Cup and Scottish League Cup and could have remained in Glasgow, but chose instead to sign for Watford. He played at Road for a year as Watford struggled and finished his playing career with a season at French second division outfit US Créteil-Lusitanos. When he retired Vega turned his talents to the financial world, putting to work the degree in banking and financing he had obtained while with Grasshoppers. Of the 23 games Vega played for Switzerland, eight of them were as a Spurs player, two of when playing for Celtic.

Appearances:
League: 53 (11) apps. 7 gls.
FA Cup: 8 (1) apps.
FL Cup: 9 (2) apps 1 gl.
Others: 17 (5) apps. 5 gls.
Total: 87 (19) apps. 13 gls.

VELJKOVIĆ, Miloš

Role: Defender 2013-15
5ft.11ins. 11st.7lbs.
Born: Basel, Switzerland, 26th September 1995

CAREER: FC Basel (Switzerland)/SPURS Academy Scholar Jul 2012, pro. Sep 2012/(Middlesbrough loan Oct 2014)/(Charlton Athletic loan Jan 2015)/Werder Bremen (Germany) Feb 2016.

Debut v Sunderland (PL) (h) (sub) 7.4.2014

Having been born in Switzerland to Serbian parents, Miloš Veljković began his career with FC Basel and represented his country of birth at Under-16 level. Spurs spotted his potential early, took him into the Academy and signed him to the professional staff at the first opportunity. A cultured, football playing central defender or defensive midfielder, he switched

allegiance to Serbia when the country of his parents approached and continued to work his way up the international youth structure, winning eight caps at Under-21 level while on Spurs' books. Veljković made his senior debut for Spurs as a substitute in April 2014, a similar appearance immediately following. A young man in a hurry, he went on loan to Middlesbrough and Charlton Athletic, and returned looking for a place in Spurs' first team squad. With the likes Jan Vertonghen, Toby Alderweireld and Kevin Wimmer ahead of him in the pecking order, his ambitions were not met and he made it clear he planned to leave when his contract had run its course. Before that happened he moved to Werder Bremen with Spurs banking a €400,000 fee.

Appearances:
League: (2) apps.
Euro: (1) app.
Others: 3 (2) apps.
Total: 3 (5) apps. 0 gls.

VENABLES, Terence Frederick

Role: Inside-forward 1965-69
5ft.8ins. 11st.8lbs.
Born: Dagenham, Essex, 6th January 1943

CAREER: Dagenham Schools/Essex Schools/London Schools/England Schools/Chelsea am. Jul 1958, pro. Aug 1960/**SPURS** May 1966/Queens Park Rangers Jun 1969/Crystal Palace Sep 1974/St Patricks Athletic Feb 1976/Crystal Palace coach, manager Jun 1976/Queens Park Rangers manager Oct 1980/Barcelona (Spain) manager May 1984/**SPURS** manager Dec 1988, chief executive Jul 1991-May 1993/England coach Jan 1994/Portsmouth Director of Football Aug 1996/Australia coach Nov 1996/Portsmouth owner Jan 1997-Jan 1998/Crystal Palace manager Jun 1998, part-time consultant Jan 1999/Middlesbrough first team coach Dec 2000-Jun 2001/Leeds United first team coach Jul 2002-Mar 2003/ England asst. manager Aug 2006-Nov 2007/Wembley technical advisor Mar 2012.

Debut v Blackburn Rovers (FL) (a) 9.5.1966

From schoolboy star to Chief Executive and part owner of one of England's biggest clubs, Terry Venables' rise through all levels of football was nothing short of mercurial; but his career is far from over, and as one of the most forward thinking and innovative administrators in the game, who knows what more he may achieve. An England Schools, Youth and Amateur international, Venables first showed his footballing talent as a chirpy, confident member of Tommy Docherty's young Chelsea team that won promotion to the First Division in 1963 and the League Cup in 1965. Having won four Under-23 caps, his selection for the full England team against Belgium in October 1964 made him the first player to win international honours at all levels. He also played for the Football League against the Irish League the same month, but won only one more cap, against Holland in December 1964. Transferred to Spurs in May 1966 for £80,000 he was permitted to make his debut at Blackburn Rovers that month, even though he was signed after the transfer deadline, as the result would have no effect on the final League table. He was not the most fluid or swift mover on the ball, but he had accurate passing skills-particularly over long range-and the vision to spot forward openings. In his first season with Spurs he won an FA Cup winners' medal against his old club Chelsea, but overall he had a tough time at White Hart Lane. Whilst almost ever-present for three seasons, Spurs were in a transitional stage and memories of the glorious "Double" winning side with the likes of Danny Blanchflower and John White were still far too vivid. Although he made every effort, even his extrovert, impudent Cockney personality and mischievous wit, were never enough to win over the hearts of Spurs' supporters. A victim of intolerance and unjust abuse, it was only after his £70,000 transfer to Queens Park Rangers that his true value and influence were appreciated at White Hart Lane. He spent five years at Loftus Road, then moved on to Crystal Palace, where he played only 14 matches before injury brought his first class playing days to an end. Although there were a few games for the Dublin club St Patricks Athletic, Venables then turned his talents to coaching and spent two years at Palace working under Malcolm Allison before being promoted to manager on Allison's departure. Venables took Palace from the Third to First Division and built an exciting young team tipped as the "Team of the Eighties", then left suddenly to take over at Queens Park Rangers. After steering Rangers to the FA Cup Final against Spurs in 1982, he led them to the Second Division title the following season and had established the west London club in the First Division when he accepted a lucrative offer to take over as manager of Spanish giants Barcelona. In his first season, and with former Spurs star Steve Archibald netting the goals, Barcelona won the Spanish League and in the next reached the European Cup Final, only losing to Steaua Bucharest on penalties. It was success by any measure, but arch rivals Real Madrid were now on top, winning three successive titles. After a bad start to the 1988-89 season Venables left Barcelona by mutual consent. His departure fell at just the right moment for Spurs, as David Pleat left White Hart Lane at the same time. Venables was immediately approached and in October 1988 was appointed manager, although it was not until December that he took up the position officially. Venables ambitious long-term aim was to build a Spurs team capable of challenging for the major honours, yet one which played open attacking football with the emphasis on skill and entertainment in the best Spurs traditions. His efforts appeared scuppered early in the 1990-91 season when public disclosure of the club's precarious financial situation not only meant he had no resources to go out and buy new players, it meant the club's very

existence was in doubt. However, Venables now showed his true fighting spirit and not only guided the club to a fine FA Cup success over Nottingham Forest, but also set out to put together a financial rescue package. Under tremendous pressure from all quarters and overcoming numerous obstacles, he persevered and in July 1991, with the support of not only electronics tycoon Alan Sugar, but Spurs' fans in general, he successfully took over the club. At that time, he was appointed chief executive, fulfilling a long-cherished dream that one day he could control the destiny of a major football club from the very top. The dream was shattered within two years. An acrimonious falling out with Sugar saw Venables kicked out and the start of years of bitter, sometimes vindictive litigation. With his business dealings put under microscopic public scrutiny Venables received a lot of bad, at times vitriolic, media attention. No matter what his business dealings may have been, his reputation as one of the best coaches in football could not be tarnished. Given the job of England coach (manager was one step too far for the FA), and at last able to work with the cream of English football, he did a great job leading England to the semi-finals of Euro '96. He left once the competition was over having announced before it began that he would not be seeking to have his contract renewed, as he needed time to prepare for his courtroom battles with Sugar. He could not stay out of football though, accepted the job of Director of Football at Portsmouth, combined that with the position of coach to the Australian national side and then in January 1997 took over control of Portsmouth. With all that he still managed to take Australia to the final hurdle of the qualifying rounds for the 1998 World Cup where they lost to Iran. Portsmouth's financial difficulties meant he had to relinquish control in January 1998 but he was soon back in the game as manager of Crystal Palace. That too did not last long and by early the following year, with Palace on the road to Administrative Receivership, Venables was released from day to day control although remaining as a part-time consultant. He then had two years out of the game until accepting the challenge of helping keep Middlesbrough in the top flight. The job accomplished, he had another year out of the game until called upon to rescue Leeds United. Arriving just as their financial problems were about to become public knowledge, he had little chance and was sacked with Leeds close to relegation. His last major post in football was as assistant to England manager, Steve McLaren, a post that lasted until England's failure to qualify for Euro 2008.

Appearances:
League: 114 (1) apps. 5 gls.
FA Cup: 15 (1) apps. 2 gls
FL Cup: 6 apps. 1 gl.
Euro: 4 apps. 1 gl.
Others: 28 (1) apps. 4 gls.
Total: **167 (3) apps. 13 gls.**

VERTONGHEN, Jan Bert Lieve

Role: Central Defender 2012-
6ft.2ins. 14st.2lbs.
Born: *Sint Niklaas, Belgium 24th April 1987*

CAREER: VK Tielrode (Belgium) 1993/Germinal Beerschott (Belgium) 2000/Ajax (Holland) Academy 2003, pro. 2006/(RKC Waalwijk (Holland) loan Jan 2007)/**SPURS** Jul 2012.

Debut v West Bromwich Albion (PL) (h) 25.8.2012
(Stevenage (Fr) (a) 18.7.2012)

Another young Belgian star whisked away to the Ajax Academy, it took Jan Vertonghen little time to impress the coaching staff in Amsterdam and make a first team breakthrough. The only problem was that he wanted to play in the centre of defence where Ajax already had international stars in John Heitinga and his fellow Belgian Thomas Vermaelen. It meant that in his early days Vertonghen was forced to play in midfield, a burden that has had long-lasting benefits as it taught him to be composed and confident on the ball. Since then he has never been

afraid to take the ball out of defence and embark on forward sorties. Eventually Vertonghen established himself in his favourite role, at first alongside Vermaelen, then Toby Alderweireld, in two partnerships that were also taken onto the international stage with Belgium. Having helped Ajax win and retain the Eredivisie in 2010–11 and 2011–12, Vertonghen joined Spurs in a £9 million deal and immediately settled to prove himself a very astute acquisition. Tall, commanding and elegant, he exudes confidence, normally playing football from the back, but not afraid to find row Z when necessary. On a few occasions he has been asked to play at full-back. It is not a role he likes, but one he has proved more than competent in, his strength, power and crossing ability coming to the fore. With the signing of Alderweireld, their partnership from Ajax has been re-formed and looks even stronger than before. Vertonghen won 23 Under-23 caps for Belgium and made his first appearance at full level in June 2007. He has since been a regular, though often having to play at left-back. With Vermaelen and Vincent Kompany, the Belgians have been blessed with an abundance of top quality central defenders. Vertonghen has been the most adept playing out wide.

Appearances:
League: 150 (1) apps. 4 gls.
FA Cup: 6 apps.
FL Cup: 9 (1) apps. 1 gl.
Euro: 35 (2) apps. 2 gls.
Others: 8 (8) apps.
Total: **208 (12) apps. 7 gls.**

VILLA, Julio Ricardo

Role: Midfield or forward 1978-88
6ft. 12st.5lbs.
Born: *Roque Perez, Buenos Aires, Argentina, 18th August 1952*

CAREER: Quilmes (Argentina) 1969/Club Atlético San Martín (Argentina) 1973-Sep 1975/Atlético Tucumán (Argentina) by Feb 1976/Racing Club de Avellendea (Argentina) Feb 1977/**SPURS** Jun 1978/Fort Lauderdale Strikers (USA) Jun 1983/Deportivo Cali (Colombia) 1985/Defensa y Justicia 1986-89 (Argentina)/Buenos Aires (Argentina) player-coach/CA Tigre (Argentina)/Atlético Tucumán (Argentina) technical director by Apr 1996-Sep 2000/Defensa y Justicia (Argentina) manager by Oct 2000-Mar 2001/Cañuelas (Argentina) youth co-ordinator Jan 2002/Racing Club de Avellaneda (Argentina) asst. trainer Jul 2002-May 2003/Atlético Talleres (Argentina) asst. coach Jul 2005, director of football.

Debut v Nottingham Forest (FL) (a) 19.8.1978 (scored once)
(Royal Antwerp (Fr) (a) 8.8.1978.)

Big, bearded Ricky Villa first came to world attention when he made two appearances as a substitute for Argentina in the 1978 World Cup Finals. Argentina's most expensive player when transferred from Racing Tucuman to Buenos Aires' Racing Club, he joined Spurs with his Argentine colleague Ossie Ardiles with 17 international appearances to his credit. Regarded by some as a bit of a make-weight in the sensational deal, he did not have the same outstanding success as his compatriot, but still proved worth every

penny of the £375,000 Spurs paid for him. A midfielder in Argentina, he had difficulty finding a regular role at White Hart Lane, although the many niggling injuries he suffered did not help. He was used in midfield and up front, but frequently found himself on the substitute's bench. Deceptively skilful for such a large man, Villa may not have had the lasting impact of Ardiles, but he did have a moment of glory that will never be forgotten. In the drawn 1981 centenary FA Cup Final he had a very poor game and shuffled his way to the dressing room in tears after being substituted. Manager Keith Burkinshaw stuck by him for the replay and his loyalty was rewarded in spectacular fashion. Villa netted the first goal and, after Spurs had pulled back to equalise at 2-2, he set off on a mazy run that left four Manchester City players trailing in his wake. He climaxed the run by first dummying and then slipping the ball past Joe Corrigan for the greatest individual goal seen at Wembley. Villa had scored another superb goal against Wolves in the semi-final replay, but this was extra special and few will forget his ecstatic, celebratory dash across the Wembley turf. A substitute in the 1982 League (Milk) Cup Final, he was unlucky to miss that year's FA Cup Final, but Burkinshaw decided it was better to omit Villa in view of the strong emotions surrounding the Falklands conflict. Villa remained at Spurs until June 1983 when he joined Fort Lauderdale Strikers, and later signed for Deportivo Cali of Colombia, although jaundice restricted him to few appearances. He then took up coaching back home in Argentina which he initially combined with playing in the lower reaches of Argentine football with Defensa y Justicia and Buenos Aires. After leaving he returned to play for Spurs once more guesting in Tony Galvin's testimonial match against West Ham in October 1987.

Appearances:
League: 124 (9) apps. 18 gls.
FA Cup: 21 apps. 3 gls.
FL Cup: 15 (1) apps. 3 gls.
Euro: 8 (1) apps. 1 gl.
Others: 43 (2) apps. 15 gls.
Total: 211 (13) apps. 40 gls.

VISI, Stefano

Role: Goalkeeper 1998-99
6ft.1ins. 12st.10lbs.
Born: Porto San Giorgio, Italy, 11th December 1971

CAREER: Sambenedettese (Italy) 1989-90/Santegidiese (Italy) 1990-91/Sambenedettese (Italy) 1991-94/Venezia (Italy) 1994-95/Avellino (Italy) 1995-96/Pescara (Italy) 1996-98/Birmingham City trial 1997-98/Sheffield United 1997-98 trial/Sheffield Wednesday trial Nov 1997/**SPURS** trial Jul 1998/Padua (Italy) 1998-99/Sambenedettese (Italy) 1999-2002/Tivoli (Italy) 2002-03/Grottammare (Italy) 2003-04/Tivoli (Italy) 2004-05/Giulianova (Italy) Feb 2005/Sambenedettese (Italy) Jul 2007/Ternana Jul 2008/Sporting Terni (Italy) Aug 2011/Sambenedettese (Italy) Oct 2011.

Debut v Birmingham City (Fr) (a) 28.7.1998

Stefano Visi joined Spurs for a trial in July 1998 and played in a pre-season friendly at Birmingham City. A former Italian Under-21 and Olympic international, Visi had started his career with Sambenedettese in the Italian third tier. He moved up to Serie B, a teammate of Paolo Tramezzani at Venezia, before trying his luck in England with trials at Birmingham City and the two Sheffield clubs. They did not take him on and he did no better with Spurs. He returned to Italy and continued to turn out regularly in Serie C1, particularly with Sambenedettese, signing for them five times.

Appearances:
Others: 1 app.
Total: 1 app. 0 gls.

VORM, Michel Armand

Role: Goalkeeper 2013-
6ft.1ins. 13st.1lb.
Born: IJsselstein, Holland, 20th October 1983

CAREER: JSV Nieuwegein (Holland)/FC Utrecht (Holland) 2000/(FC Den Bosch (Holland) loan Aug 2005)/Swansea City Jul 2011/**SPURS** Jul 2014.

Debut v Nottingham Forest (FLC) (h) 24.9.2014

With Brad Friedel approaching the end of his fabulous career, Spurs were in need of a competent back-up for Hugo Lloris. Michel Vorm was the man they turned to. A full Dutch international, Vorm had been with Swansea City for three years, proving himself a top-notch 'keeper good enough to be first choice for most Premier League clubs. Taken on by FC Utrecht as a youth, Vorm had to wait five years before getting a taste of Dutch League football, playing for a season on loan to Den Bosch in the Dutch second division. He returned to Utrecht to immediately make his First Division debut and for the next five years was the automatic first choice, picking up the first of 15 caps against Sweden in November 2008. With Dorus de Vries leaving Swansea for Wolves at the end of his contract, the Welsh club paid £1.5 million to sign Vorm, a more than reasonable fee that increasingly looked a bargain as Vorm helped Swansea establish its Premier League place. Vorm joined Spurs at the same time as Ben Davies moved from Swansea to Spurs and Gylfi Sigurðsson returned to the Liberty Stadium. The whole deal was valued at £10 million, all of it attributed by Spurs and Swansea to the signing of Davies. Utrecht took objection to that. The deal when Vorm moved to Swansea gave them 30% of any fee received on re-sale. Utrecht complained but the complaint was thrown out by FIFA, leaving them to take the issue to the Court of Arbitration for Sport.

Appearances:
League: 8 (2) apps.
FA Cup: 11 apps.
FL Cup: 8 apps.
Euro: 3 apps.
Others: 5 (3) apps.
Total: 35 (5) apps. 0 gls.

W

WADDLE, Christopher Roland

Role: Forward 1985-2003
6ft. 11st.5lbs.
Born: Gateshead, County Durham, 14th December 1960

CAREER: Sheffield United trial 1974/Coventry City assoc. schl. 1974/Pelaw Juniors 1975/Whitehouse Social Club 1975/Sunderland trial 1976/Mount Pleasant Social Club/HMH Printing/Pelaw Social Club 1976/Leam Lane Social Club 1977/Clarke Chapman 1977/ Tow Law Town Jul 1978/Sunderland trial Jan 1980/Newcastle United Jul 1980/**SPURS** Jul 1985/Olympique Marseille (France) Jul 1989/Sheffield Wednesday Jul 1992/Falkirk Sep 1996/Bradford City Oct 1996/Sunderland Mar 1997/Burnley player-manager Jul 1997-May 1998/Hollinsend Aug 1998/Brunsmeer 1998/Torquay United non-contract Sep 1998/Hilltop Nov 1998/Davy Sports Nov 1998/Chesterfield coach/Sheffield Wednesday coach Dec 1998, reserve team coach Jul 1999-Jun 2000/Brunsmeer Athletic (Sunday League) player-manager Dec 1998/Boston United Feb 1999/Worksop Town Jul 2000/(Parkgate loan Nov 2001)/Staveley Apr 2002/Glapwell Aug 2002/Gedling Town/South Normanton Athletic Mar 2003/Stocksbridge Park Steels Apr 2003/Staveley Miners Welfare Oct 2003/South Normanton Athletic Oct 2003/Staveley Miners Welfare Jul 2004/Teversal consultant Jan 2010/Hallam Vets Jul 2013.

Debut v Watford (FL) (h) 17.8.1985 (scored twice)
(Wycombe Wanderers (Fr) (Bisham Abbey) (18.7.1985)

Having trained with Newcastle United and been an associated schoolboy with Coventry City, Chris Waddle was not offered an apprenticeship when he left school, so played for local junior and social clubs until joining one of the North East's premier amateur outfits, Clarke Chapman. Tow Law Town noticed him, and after some impressive performances for them and an unsuccessful trial with Sunderland, he was transferred to Newcastle. Under the guidance of manager Arthur Cox, he made rapid progress at St James' Park. By October 1980 he had made his League debut and alongside Peter Beardsley helped a Kevin Keegan inspired Newcastle gain promotion in 1984. With the departure of Keegan, Waddle developed into Newcastle's star player and in October 1984 won his first England Under-21 cap against Finland. In March 1985 he made his full debut against the Republic of Ireland and, by the time of his £650,000 move to Spurs, had won eight full caps. He collected the first of 36 caps as a Spurs' player in September 1985 and soon struck up a fine understanding with Glenn Hoddle. It was a partnership and friendship that worked well off the field too, with the duo's hit record "Diamond Lights". A member of the 1987 FA Cup Final team, Waddle took over Hoddle's role as focal point of the team when the midfield maestro left for Monaco. Despite some concern at international level about a similarity to John Barnes, Waddle continued to appear regularly for England and played for the Football League against the Rest of the World in the FA Centenary match of August 1987. A tall, willowy, elusive player with pace, excellent ball control and a curious "hunched shoulders" style of running, Waddle had the priceless ability to beat an opponent in a confined space and apply a cool finish. Equally at home on the wing, as a central striker or in midfield, he had his best season in 1988-89 when given a free role and allowed to roam where he thought he could do most damage. Such was his success that French champions Olympique de Marseille made Spurs a massive £4.5 million offer for his transfer. Spurs did not want Waddle to leave, but an offer of such magnitude could not be ignored and, with the chance to set himself up for life financially, Waddle agreed to go. He became the third most expensive player in history behind Diego Maradona and Ruud Gullit. After Marseille had won the French League in his first season Waddle then helped England reach the World Cup semi-finals. With Marseille he added another 18 caps to his collection, helped them reach the European Cup Final in 1991 and retain their French League title in 1991 and 1992. He returned to England in July 1992 with another major move to Sheffield Wednesday and in 1993 was The Football Writers' Association Player of the Year. Out of favour with David Pleat, Waddle was allowed to join Bradford City in October 1996 and showed that if he had lost some of the pace he had lost none of the ability. Such was his impact at Bradford that he moved on quickly to Sunderland as they fought desperately, but ultimately unsuccessfully, to remain in the Premier League. For some time, Waddle had admitted he was attracted to the idea of being a manager and he got his chance in July 1997 with Burnley. He did not prove a success and after a season of struggle was released. A brief spell with Torquay United brought to an end his top-flight career, but Waddle has continued to coach and play at veteran level, just happy to play football. Waddle's cousin, Alan Waddle, was a much-travelled forward in the 1970's and 80's, notably with Swansea City and Liverpool.

Appearances:
League: 137 (1) apps. 33 gls.
FA Cup: 14 app. 5 gls.
FL Cup: 21 apps. 4 gls.
Others: 41 (4) apps. 11 gls.
Total: **213 (5) apps. 53 gls.**

WALDEN, Frederick Ingram

Role: Winger 1912-26
5ft.2ins. 8st.9lbs.
Born: Wellingborough, Northamptonshire, 1st March 1888
Died: Northampton, Northamptonshire, 3rd May 1949

CAREER: White Cross/All Saints/Wellingborough Redwell Stars/Wellingborough Town/Northampton Town cs. 1909/**SPURS** Apr 1913/(Leeds City during World War One)/Northampton Town May 1926/retired Aug 1927/Northampton Town coach.

Debut v Woolwich Arsenal (FL) (h) 19.4.1913

Fanny Walden was a diminutive little magician, whose intricate dribbling skills illuminated Spurs' football for a thirteen-year period either side of the First World War. He first played for three local junior clubs, but it was when he joined Northampton Town from Wellingborough Town that he came to the fore. He scored a hat-trick on his Southern League debut for Northampton from the centre-forward position. In view of his size it is surprising that he was even expected to fill that role. However, he soon displayed an amazing dribbling ability and was moved to the right wing, winning his first representative honour in September 1912 when he played for the Southern League against the Football League. He played in all the Southern League's inter-League matches that season and appeared for England against the South in an international trial in March 1913. His manager at Northampton had been Herbert Chapman, and when Chapman took over at Leeds City he wanted to take Walden with him. Northampton were in dire financial straits with the sale of Walden seemingly their only hope of survival. In a desperate attempt to keep their star, a "Save Fanny Walden Fund" was started with the aim of raising £1,000 in seven days. All sorts of schemes were tried; subscription lists, appeals to the local shoe and boot manufacturers, lemonade bottles with a hole in the neck for the insertion of coins were placed all over town. Two huge clock faces showing the progress of the appeal were erected outside the Town Hall. It was all in vain. Only £600 was raised and Northampton were left to accept Spurs' record £1,700 offer for Walden's transfer. Although he was signed after the transfer deadline, Walden was allowed to make an immediate debut against Woolwich Arsenal as the result would have no effect on promotion or relegation. His size, jinking runs down the right wing and variety of tricks made him a firm favourite of the White Hart Lane crowd. In April 1914, he won his first England cap against Scotland and played for the Football League against the Scottish League in October 1914. A regular until the First World War intervened, when Walden joined the services it allowed Chapman to see Walden in his Leeds City team, Walden playing as a guest in the 1915-16 season. After the war he was one of the stars of the Spurs' team that won the Second Division title in 1920, but was deprived of a place in the 1921 FA Cup Final by a cartilage injury. He recovered his spot early the following season and collected his second cap against Wales in March 1922. While he did not play for England again, he continued to weave his magic for Spurs until May 1926 when he returned to Northampton Town. At a mere eight and a half stone Walden had a marvellously consistent record in an age when full-backs could legitimately shoulder charge an opponent off the field, so perhaps there was some merit in the terrace joke that the tiny winger could run through an opponent's legs! He only played for one season back at Northampton, retiring to open a public house in the town, although he did later coach their "A" team youngsters. A county cricketer for Northamptonshire throughout his football career, Walden was a useful batsman (over 7,000 runs), a handy bowler (over 100 wickets) and a sharp cover fielder who played 258 matches. He later became a first class umpire, reaching Test match level umpiring in 11 test matches. Walden was given the name "Fanny" by his school pals, being named after a lady who ran a corner shop near his Wellingborough school. In 1905 he received a special award from the Prince of Wales, later King George V, for saving a boy from drowning.

Appearances:
League: 214 apps. 21 gls.
FA Cup: 22 apps. 4 gls.
Others: 87 apps. 21 gls.
Total: 323 apps. 46 gls.
* Includes 1 abandoned match.

WALFORD, Frank Scott

Role: Goalkeeper 1889-91
Born: Perry Barr, Birmingham
Died: Croydon, Surrey, 27th June 1935

CAREER: SPURS/London Caledonians/Enfield League President Oct 1902/Lincoln City/Small Heath/Aston Villa/Brighton and Hove Albion manager Mar 1905/Leeds City manager Mar 1908-Apr 1912/Nottingham Forest manager Apr 1912/Coventry City manager 1914-15.

Debut v Vulcan (Fr) (h) 5.10.1889

Although Frank Walford played a few games for Spurs it was as a manager that he had most success in football. His first known appearance for Spurs was in October 1889 in a friendly with Vulcan, but it has proved impossible to trace many of the team details from that era and he almost certainly played in most of the games in that and the following season. He then played for London Caledonians, but by 1897 was working as a journalist and had taken to refereeing in the Southern League. He was also a Football League linesman and founder of the Enfield and District League. It was several years before he took on his first managerial post with Brighton and Hove Albion. He did a good job on limited resources on the South Coast, but in April 1906 an FA Council meeting decided he had been illegally approaching players. He was suspended from any involvement in football until August of that year. The success he had achieved was noted by clubs at a higher level and he was persuaded to become manager at Leeds City, where he was again forced to operate under severe financial limitations. He left Leeds for a year at Nottingham Forest and in 1914 joined Coventry City. He had to vacate the post in 1915 due to the severe financial strains caused to the club by the demands of War.

Appearances:
Others: 8 apps.
Total: 8 apps. 0 gls.

WALFORD, Stephen James

Role: Defender 1975-76
6ft.1ins. 11st.7lbs.
Born: Islington, London, 5th January 1958

CAREER: Holloway School/Islington Schools/**SPURS** app. Apr 1974, pro. Apr 1975/Arsenal Aug 1977/Norwich City Mar 1981/West Ham United Aug 1983/(Huddersfield Town loan Oct 1987)/(Gillingham loan Dec 1988)/(West Bromwich Albion loan Mar 1989)/Lai Sun (Hong Kong) Aug 1989/Turkey 1990/Wycombe Wanderers Oct 1990/(Wealdstone loan Mar 1992)/Barnet youth team manager Nov 1993/Wycombe Wanderers youth team manager 1994, asst. manager/Norwich City youth team manager Jun 1995, caretaker manager Dec 1995/Leicester City first team coach Dec 1995, asst. manager/Celtic asst. manager Jun 2000-May 2005/Aston Villa first team coach Aug 2006-Jun 2010/Sunderland first team coach Dec 2011-Apr 2013/Republic of Ireland coach May 2014/Bolton Wanderers asst. manager Sep 2015-Apr 2016.

Debut v Liverpool (sub) (FL) (h) 13.12.1975
(Millwall (sub) (Fr) (a) 27.10.1975)

As a 17-year old, Steve Walford played two League games for Spurs, but was allowed to follow former manager Terry Neill to Highbury for £25,000 without getting a further opportunity. With hindsight, it was perhaps a poor decision, for the England Youth international went on to become a more than competent First Division defender. Substitute for

Arsenal in the 1979 FA Cup Final, he was probably most at home in central defence, though versatile enough to play at left-back or even in midfield. After making over 80 appearances for Arsenal, Walford had over 100 League outings for both Norwich City and West Ham United before being given a free transfer by West Ham. He joined the Lai Sun club of Hong Kong and after playing in Turkey returned to England with Wycombe Wanderers. Barnet gave him his first chance in coaching as youth team manager and he soon returned to Wycombe Wanderers in the same role. Re-united with Martin O'Neill, who had signed him as a player for Wycombe, Walford became part of O'Neill's coaching team following the manager from Wycombe to Norwich, Leicester, Celtic, Aston Villa, Sunderland and the Republic of Ireland. With international duty not providing a full-time role, Walford assisted Neil Lennon at Bolton in 2015-16, departing following their relegation.

Appearances:
League: 1 (1) apps.
Others: 7 (4) apps.
Total: 8 (5) apps. 0 gls.

WALKER, David

Role: Inside-forward 1944-45

CAREER: Northfleet United am./(guest for **SPURS** during World War Two).

Debut v Crystal Palace (Fr) (a) 7.4.1945

One of the amateur players at Spurs nursery club of Northfleet, Walker played his only match for Spurs in a friendly against Crystal Palace in April 1945.

Appearances:
Others: 1 app.
Total: 1 app. 0 gls.

WALKER, Ian Michael

Role: Goalkeeper 1990-2001
6ft.1ins. 11st.9lbs.
Born: *Watford, Hertfordshire, 31st October 1971*

CAREER: Colchester Athletic/FA School of Excellence/**SPURS** trainee Jul 1988, pro. Oct 1989/(Oxford United loan Sep 1990)/(Ipswich Town loan Nov 1990)/Leicester City Jul 2001/Bolton Wanderers Jul 2005-Dec 2008/Kansas City Wizards (USA) trial Jan 2010/Fort Lauderdale Select (USA) coach/Coral Springs Storm (USA) coach/Bishops Stortford manager Mar-Dec 2011/Shanghai Shenhua (China) coach Apr 2012-Nov 2013/Shanghai East Asia (China) coach Jan 2014-Nov 2016.

Debut v Norwich City (FL) (a) 10.4.1991

A highly promising young 'keeper who had been on Associated Schoolboy forms at Queens Park Rangers, Ian Walker joined Spurs' trainee staff having graduated from the FA's School of Excellence at Lilleshall. England's regular 'keeper from Under-15 through to Under-19 level, he helped the Spurs Youth team win the FA Youth Cup in 1990, but with Erik Thorstvedt, Bobby Mimms, Gareth Howells and Kevin Dearden all his senior, started the following season out on loan with Oxford United and Ipswich Town. Without making a first team appearance for Spurs he made his debut for the England Under-21 team against Wales in December 1990 and with the departures of Mimms and Howells soon found himself competing with Dearden as Thorstvedt's reserve. Late in August 1991 he was called up for his second League outing with Thorstvedt away on international duty and kept the big Norwegian out on merit until he was

taken ill. Confident and unflustered, Walker proved an excellent shot-stopper and with Thorstvedt injured in the final weeks of the season he returned to the first team. With the benefit of coaching from former England 'keeper, Ray Clemence, Walker gradually overtook Thorstvedt as first choice and collected the first of four England caps as a substitute against Hungary in May 1996. Automatic first choice for Spurs for five years, Walker was a more than reliable performer, strong in the air, an excellent shot-stopper and good organiser of his defence. A member of the team that won the Worthington Cup in 1999 and confident in his own ability, if he had one fault, it was that sometimes his phlegmatic attitude was not always appreciated by all. When things went wrong, he accepted them, rarely showed emotion and just got on with the job. Seemingly set for a long career at White Hart Lane, that all changed with George Graham's appointment as manager. One of his first signings was Neil Sullivan and Graham was never going to let a man he had bought in warm the bench. While Walker's disquiet was obvious and he sought a transfer, he remained with Spurs for a year until a £2.5 million move to Leicester. He had a difficult four years at Filbert Street, relegation followed by promotion, followed by relegation again. Released at the end of his contract, he moved to Bolton Wanderers. In three years there he rarely saw action, making no appearances in the League and only a few in cup competitions. Walker then went to the United States where he got into coaching. He had a brief spell in management back in the UK with Bishops Stortford and for the last few years has been coaching in China. On his League debut, Walker was perhaps more closely scrutinised from the Norwich bench than from Spurs'. Sitting on it was his father, Mike, the former Watford and Colchester United goalkeeper who was on the coaching staff and later manager of Norwich and Everton.

Appearances:
League: 257 (2) apps.
FA Cup: 26* apps.
FL Cup: 22 (1) apps.
Euro: 6 apps.
Others: 66 (8) apps.
Total: 377 (11) apps. 0 gls.
* Includes 1 abandoned match

WALKER, Kyle Andrew

Role: Full-back 2009-
5ft.10ins. 13st.3lbs.
Born: *Sheffield, South Yorkshire, 28th May 1990*

CAREER: High Storrs School/Sheffield United Academy Scholar Jul 2006, pro. Jul 2008/(Northampton Town loan Nov 2008)/**SPURS** Jul 2009/(Sheffield United loan Aug 2009)/(Queens Park Rangers loan Sep 2010)/(Aston Villa loan Jan 2011)/Manchester City Jul 2017.

Debut v Portsmouth (PL) (h) 27.3.2010

Associated with Sheffield United from the age of seven, Kyle Walker was snapped up by Spurs before he had played even a dozen League games. Having developed through Sheffield United's youth structure, he joined Northampton Town on loan for his first taste of senior football. When he returned to Bramall Lane he was thrown into the first team as United reached the Championship play-off final before losing out to Burnley. No sooner had the whistle blown at Wembley than Spurs were signing Walker and the man who had been United's regular right-back until Walker emerged, Kyle Naughton, in a £9 million double deal. Part of the deal was that Walker should spend the 2009-10 season on loan to United. He played practically every game until January 2010 when, with Alan Hutton loaned to Sunderland, Walker was recalled to White Hart Lane. Loans to Queens Park Rangers and Aston Villa followed, before Walker found he was first choice right-back following the departure of Hutton to Aston Villa. Once in the team Walker was rarely absent save when injured. An instinctive attacking player, perhaps a little suspect in his defensive play at times, his willingness to get forward, and incredible, sustained pace, made him one of Spurs' most potent weapons. Voted the PFA's Young Player of the Year for 2011-12, the signing of Kieran Trippier in the summer of 2015 put Walker's place came under threat, but the effect was simply to raise his game to a new level. Having made his first appearance for England at Under-21 level in March 2010 and for the full team in November 2011, injuries prevented Walker playing in Euro 2012 and the 2014 World Cup, but he was able to take his place in Euro 2016. One of England's stars of the tournament his progress continued unabated as he and Danny Rose proved the perfect combination for club and country before Manchester City's mega riches tempted him away.

Appearances:
League: 180 (3) apps. 4 gls.
FA Cup: 8* (3#) apps. 1 gl.
FL Cup: 8 (1) apps.
Euro: 27 (2) apps.
Others: 21 (7) apps.
Total: 242 (16) apps. 5 gls.
* Includes 1 abandoned match
#Includes 1 in an abandoned match

WALKER, Robert Henry

Role: Inside-forward 1906-08
5ft.9ins. 11st.3lbs.
Born: Northallerton, Yorkshire, 5th January 1884

CAREER: West Hartlepool/Heart of Midlothian/Middlesbrough Jan 1906/**SPURS** May 1906/New Brompton Mar 1908/Northampton Town cs. 1908/Millwall Sep 1910/Luton Town Mar 1911/Bristol Rovers cs. 1912.

Debut v West Ham United (SL) (h) 1.9.1906

Bob Walker spent almost two years at White Hart Lane without ever truly establishing himself. He made his debut at the start of 1906-07, but was soon out of the team and it was only towards the end of the season that he claimed a regular place. Retained for the following term, he had just about managed to clinch a place in the forward line when, in February 1908, he and James Gray were suspended for a breach of club discipline. A further transgression of rules whilst suspended led to an indefinite suspension, and the next month he moved to New Brompton, along with James Pass. Walker then moved around the Southern League clubs finishing his career during the World War One with Bristol Rovers.

Appearances:
Southern: 24 apps. 3 gls.
FA Cup: 1 app.
Others: 6 apps.
Total: 31 apps. 3 gls.

WALKER-PETERS, Kyle

Role: Full-back 2013-
5ft.8ins.9st.15lbs.
Born: Edmonton, London, 13th April 1997

CAREER: SPURS Academy Scholar Jul 2013, pro. Dec 2014/Roda JC Kerkrade (Holland) loan trial Jan 2016.

Debut v Ledley King's XI (sub) (Fr) (h) 12.5.2014

One of the most exciting talents to come through Spurs Academy in recent years, Kyle Walker-Peters is one of the modern breed of full-backs who years ago would have played as a winger. Today, they have to combine the two jobs of defending and providing options on the flank. Walker-Peters is perfectly competent to do that. A good marker and strong tackler, he does sometimes allow himself to be drawn out of position, but his speed of recovery can make up for a fault that time will probably eradicate. His forte is definitely his willingness to thrust and join the attack, his acceleration taking him past opponents. An England regular throughout the youth ranks, as yet his first team outings have been limited to friendly games. With Kyle Walker gone, he is sure to be a threat to Kieran Trippier and will not be held back for long.

Appearances:
Others: (4) apps.
Total: (4) apps. 0 gls.

WALKES, Anton

Role: Midfielder/Defender 2016-
6ft.2ins. 12st. 7lbs,
Born: Lewisham, London, 8th February 1997

CAREER: SPURS Academy Scholar Jul 2013, pro. Jul 2015/(Atlanta United (USA) loan Jan 2017).

Debut v Juventus (sub) Fr (Melbourne) 26.7.2016

The last of the Academy products to be given a chance in Australia during the International Champions Cup, Anton Walkes is one of the lesser lauded youngsters pushing for a place in the senior squad, but one who has as much potential as any of those who have been getting more publicity. A calm, controlled figure, Walkes was originally a central midfielder. When injuries left Spurs short at the back, he was called upon to cover and has proved himself a more than competent performer, both in the centre of defence and at full-back.

Appearances:
Others: 1(2) apps.
Total: 1 (2) apps. 0 gls.

WALLER, Wilfred Hugh

Role: Goalkeeper 1898-00
5ft.11ins. 12st.10lbs.
Born: South Africa, 27th July 1877

CAREER: Vampires/Corinthians/Richmond Association/Wolverton Sep 1897/guest for SPURS Jan 1899/Queen's Park/Wolverton Sep 1899/Bolton Wanderers 1899-1901/Southampton Sep 1900/Watford 1901-02/Aylesbury United Oct 1904/Camerons (South Africa).

Debut v Brighton United (SL) (a) 21.1.1899

Wilfred Waller was an amateur goalkeeper with Corinthians and Richmond Association who helped Spurs out on rare occasions. He was acknowledged as one of the best goalkeepers in amateur football, although also capable of giving a fine performance at full-back. A member of the strong FA XI that toured Germany in November 1899, his first appearance for Spurs was in a Southern League fixture with Brighton United in January 1899 when he stood-in for Joe Cullen-as he did in all his games that season. His only further appearance was in November 1899 when George Clawley was injured and Spurs were desperately seeking a long term replacement. Apart from Spurs he also assisted Queen's Park, Bolton Wanderers and Southampton during his career, but whilst he collected many minor representative caps, badges and honours he never represented England in a full international. He did however play for the FA XI in four tour matches against Germany in November 1899 and in September 1901 for an England amateur team against the visiting Germans at White Hart Lane, a match that has come to be regarded as an unofficial international. In 1906 he returned to South Africa and continued to play the game, representing South Africa against the Corinthians in 1907.

Appearances:
Southern: 4 apps.
Others: 1 app.
Total: 5 apps. 0 gls.

WALLEY, Ernest

Role: Half-back 1954-58
5ft.8ins. 10st.11lbs.
Born: Caernarvon, Gwynedd, 19th April 1933

CAREER: Caernarvon Youth Club/Caernarvon Town/SPURS am. Sep 1950, pro. May 1951/Middlesbrough May 1958/Crystal Palace May 1960/Gravesend & Northfleet cs. 1961-1963/Stevenage Athletic/Arsenal coach/Crystal Palace coach, caretaker-manager Oct 1980, joint manager Nov 1980, asst. manager Dec 1980/Barking manager Dec 1983-Jan 1985/Chelsea asst. manager Aug 1985–Mar 1986/Watford reserve team manager/Bangor City manager Aug-Oct 1992/Wales Under-21 asst. manager 1995-96.

Debut v Manchester United (FL) (h) 31.8.1955
(Lille Olympique (sub) (Fr) (a) 14.8.1954)

Ernie Walley spent seven years on Spurs' staff during the 1950's in the frustrating role of reserve wing-half. He had few opportunities to make the first team with players such as Ron Burgess, Bill Nicholson, Tony Marchi and Danny Blanchflower ahead of him and made only five League outings before moving on to Middlesbrough. He did little better on Teesside, just eight League appearances in two years. Still that was better than his next club, Crystal Palace. He failed to make a single appearance for them. He played a bit more often with Gravesend and Stevenage Athletic, but it was as a coach that Walley was best known. He had eight years with Arsenal and another 13 with Crystal Palace. He was also caretaker/manager at Palace for two months in September and October 1980 after Terry Venables had left to join Queens Park Rangers. Walley was later assistant manager to John Hollins at Chelsea and in charge of the reserve team at Watford. He was on the Watford staff at the same time as his brother, Tom, who had a long career in football, notably with Watford and Orient. Walley was manager of Bangor City for a short time when they joined the League of Wales.

Appearances:
League: 5 apps.
Others: 7 (2) apps. 1 gl.
Total: 12 (2) apps. 1 gl.

WALLIS, John Clifford M.B.E.

Role: Full-back 1940-45
Born: Finchley, Middlesex, 3rd October 1923
Died: Edmonton, London, 25th February 2003

CAREER: Mill Hill Schools/Hendon Schools/London Schools/Middlesex Schools/England Schools/SPURS am. 1936, ground-staff 1938, Tottenham Juniors cs. 1939/(guest for Brighton and Hove Albion and Enfield during World War Two)/Chelmsford City Jul 1947/Wisbech Town/SPURS coach 1948, first team trainer 1958, reserve team manager 1964, physio 1968, kit manager 1975, asst. kit manager 1987, ground maintenance staff 1992/retired May 1994.

Debut v Luton Town (FLS) (h) 23.11.1940

Johnny Wallis gave Spurs over 50 years' service most of it in backroom jobs that tend to be overlooked. He first joined Spurs as an amateur in 1936, signed on the ground-staff in 1938 and at the start of the 1939-40 season was placed with the Tottenham Juniors, but his football education was soon bought to a halt by the outbreak of war. A full-back, he was called up to make his first appearance in a Football League South match

with Luton Town in November 1940 and seemed to have a promising career in front of him. Unfortunately, he suffered serious shrapnel wounds whilst serving in Palestine during the war and at the age of 23 had to give up hopes of a professional career, though he did play in the non-League game with Chelmsford City and Wisbech. He then took coaching and medical courses and joined the Spurs' coaching staff, taking over the first team in 1958 when Bill Nicholson was appointed manager. After a spell as manager of the reserves he became club physiotherapist and held the position until 1975 when he was made kit manager. He continued to serve the club in that role for some time before moving onto the ground maintenance staff. In 1993 his great service to football, but in particular to Spurs, was recognised with the MBE in the Queen's Birthday Honours List.

Appearances:
Others: 9 apps. 1 gl.
Total: 9 apps. 1 gl.

WALSH, Paul Anthony

Role: Striker 1987-1992
5ft.8ins. 11st.2lbs.
Born: *Plumstead, south London, 1st October 1962*

CAREER: Blackheath Schools/South London Schools/London Schools/Charlton Athletic pro. Oct 1979/Luton Town Jul 1982/Liverpool May 1984/SPURS Feb 1988/(Queens Park Rangers loan Sep 1991)/Portsmouth Jun 1992/Manchester City Mar 1994/Portsmouth Sep 1995/retired Nov 1997.

Debut v Manchester United (FL) (h) 23.2.1989

From his League debut in September 1979, England Youth cap Paul Walsh showed a natural talent that marked him as a star of the future. A skilful, ball playing forward, he scored 31 goals in 100 senior appearances for Charlton and was soon attracting the attention of the game's bigger clubs, but it was Luton Town who secured his signature. He won his first England Under-21 cap against Denmark in December 1982 and had added three more at that level before making his full debut on England's tour of Australia in June 1983, playing in all three internationals. The Professional Footballers' Association's Young Player of The Year in 1984, he was clearly destined for the top, and was transferred to Liverpool where he was expected to take over from Kenny Dalglish. A member of Liverpool's 1985 European Cup Final team, he helped Liverpool win the League title the following year and reach the Littlewoods Cup Final in 1987. Walsh was perhaps too much of an individual for the Liverpool style of team play, and spent much of his time at Anfield in the reserves or on the substitute's bench. Walsh became Terry Venables' first major signing when he joined Spurs for £500,000. A tricky little striker with excellent close control who was particularly adept at spinning off his marker, he soon became a favourite of the Spurs crowd, but was unable to deliver the quantity of goals his talents promised, and his effort deserved. As a result, he again spent too much of his time on the substitute's bench, playing as such in the 1991 FA Cup final victory. In September 1991 he was suspended after an incident with reserve team manager Ray Clemence and joined Queens Park Rangers on loan with a view to a permanent transfer. That did not materialise and he returned to Spurs, where he continued to prove a valuable member of the first team squad until sold to Portsmouth as a £500,000 slice of Darren Anderton's transfer to White Hart Lane. With Portsmouth Walsh began to rediscover his old form and within two years moved back to the top flight with Manchester City. He was one of the brighter lights in a poor City team that struggled continually and returned to Portsmouth as part of the deal that saw Gerry Creaney move to Manchester. Walsh had little opportunity in his second spell in Hampshire, with injuries severely restricting his appearances and eventually forcing him out of the game. Like many ex-Spurs players, he looked to make a new career for himself as a summariser on Sky TV.

Appearances:
League: 84 (44) apps. 19 gls.
FA Cup: 4 (4) apps.
FL Cup: 9 (7) apps. 2 gls.
Euro: 1 (3) apps.
Others: 40 (12) apps. 15 gls.
Total: 138 (70) apps. 36 gls.

WALTERS, Charlie

Role: Centre-half 1919-26
5ft.11ins. 12st.6lbs.
Born: *Sandford-On-Thames, Oxfordshire, 1st April 1897*
Died: *Bath, Somerset, 13th May 1971*

CAREER: Wesleyan Higher Grade School/Oxford Schools/Thame/Oxford City/SPURS am. Dec 1919, pro. Apr 1920/Fulham Oct 1926/Mansfield Town Aug 1928-May 1929.

Debut v Stoke City (FL) (a) 10.4.1920

An amateur with Oxford City, Charlie Walters was attracting attention from quite a few leading clubs when Spurs persuaded him to sign amateur forms in December 1919. He performed well in several reserve games and by the end of the season had signed professional and made his League debut. One of the fastest players on the club's books, Walters was quickly recognised as a fine defender. He soon developed into a solid "stopper" style of centre-half, and by the middle of the following season replaced Charlie Rance. Destructive rather than constructive, Walters played exceptionally well in the 1921 FA Cup Final. His hefty clearances out of defence on a sodden pitch were particularly welcome towards the end of the game, as Wolves desperately sought an equaliser. Selected for

England against Belgium in November 1923, but forced to withdraw because of injury he did not get another chance to win an international cap. Eventually he lost his place at Spurs to Harry Skitt and moved to Fulham, finishing his career with a season at Mansfield Town. Walters was also a more than competent cricketer. He played 129 matches for Oxfordshire between 1922 and 1952, appeared for the Minor Counties and coached the game at Oxford University.

Appearances:
League: 106 apps.
FA Cup: 11 apps.
Others: 17 apps.
Total: 134 apps. 0 gls.

WALTERS, Joseph

Role: Inside-forward 1918-19
Born: Stourbridge, Worcestershire, 11th December 1886
Died: Manchester, Lancashire, 24th December 1923

CAREER: Wordsley Athletic 1900/Stourbridge Aug 1902/Aston Villa am. Jun 1905, pro. Jan 1906/Oldham Athletic Jun 1912/(Guest for **SPURS** during World War One)/Accrington Stanley Sep 1920/Southend United Sep 1920/Millwall May 1921/Rochdale Oct 1922/Manchester North End cs. 1923/Crewe Alexandra Nov 1923.

Debut v West Ham United (LFC) (h) 8.3.1919

Originally a winger, Joey Walters started out in football as a 14-year old with Wordsley Athletic and played for Stourbridge before beginning a seven-year association with Aston Villa. Converted to the inside-forward position, he was a member of Villa's team that won the League championship in 1909-10 and played in an England trial at White Hart Lane in January 1911. When he left Villa Park it was to join Oldham Athletic, where he played until the outbreak of the First World War. His one appearance for Spurs was in a London Football Combination fixture against West Ham United in March 1919. When the war was over he returned for a final year with Oldham. Past his best, he moved rapidly around with Accrington Stanley, Southend United, Millwall, Rochdale and Manchester North End. His final club was Crewe Alexandra, but he died of pneumonia a month after joining them without playing a game.

Appearances:
Others: 1 app.
Total: 1 app. 0 gls.

WALTERS, William Edward

Role: Outside-right 1943-56
5ft.8ins. 10st.3lbs.
Born: Edmonton, London, 5th September 1924
Died: Enfield, Middlesex, 25th November 1970

CAREER: Houndsfield Road School/Eldon Road School/Edmonton Schools/London Schools/**SPURS** am. 1938/Tottenham Juniors 1939/Walthamstow Avenue/Finchley/**SPURS** pro. Sep 1944/(Derry City and Millwall during World War Two)/Aldershot July 1957.

Debut v West Bromwich Albion (FL) (a) 4.1.1947
(Fulham (FLS) (h) 25.12.1943) (scored once)

Spotted by former Spurs player Billy Sage, Sonny Walters played for Tottenham Juniors before being farmed out to nursery outfits Walthamstow Avenue and Finchley. He made a goal-scoring debut in December 1943 and played regularly in the 1944-45 season, but after the war took a while to establish himself. It was only in April 1949 that he really won the battle with Freddie Cox for the outside-right slot. A fast, direct winger with a splendid burst of speed, he had a fierce shot and an instinctive opportunism that helped him finish the Second Division championship campaign of 1949-50 as top scorer. His swift and accurately pushed return passes from the wing blended perfectly with the style of Alf Ramsey and Bill Nicholson and created just as many vital goals that season as they did the following year when Spurs famous "Push and Run" side won the First Division title. Most unfortunate to play in the same international era as Stan Matthews and Tom Finney, Walters' only representative honour was an appearance for England "B" against Holland in February 1950. He gave great service to Spurs before leaving in July 1957 to join Aldershot, where he played for a further couple of years before retiring.

Appearances:
League: 211* apps. 66 gls.
FA Cup: 23 apps. 5 gls.
Others: 112 apps. 38 gls.
Total: 346 apps. 109 gls.
* Includes 1 abandoned match.

WALTON, Joseph

Role: Outside-right 1903-09
5ft.11ins. 12st.0lbs.
Born: Lunes, 8th January 1881

CAREER: Preston North End 1901/**SPURS** May 1903/Sheffield United Apr 1909/Stalybridge Celtic Jul 1911.

Debut v Woolwich Arsenal (LL) (h) 1.9.1903

Joe Walton first played for Preston North End as a 17-year old and spent five years at Deepdale, only appearing in the first team in the last two seasons before joining Spurs. A nifty, mobile winger he made his first appearance for Spurs in the first match of 1903-04, but took time to settle, and it was two years before he made the outside-right position his own. Once he did, Walton started to attract the attention of the international selectors. Although he played well in three trial matches in 1905 and 1906, he did not manage to win international recognition. In April 1909 Spurs offered Walton the maximum wage to re-sign, but he refused the offer and joined Sheffield United. He played there for two years before moving to Stalybridge Celtic for their first year as a professional club in the Lancashire Combination.

Appearances:
Southern: 105 apps. 24 gls.
League: 24 apps. 2 gls.
FA Cup: 18 apps. 4 gls.
Others: 74* apps. 23 gls.
Total: 221 apps. 53 gls.
* Includes 1 abandoned match.

WANT, Anthony George

Role: Full-back 1967-72
5ft.9ins. 11st.11lbs.
Born: Hackney, London, 13th December 1948

CAREER: Hackney Schools/**SPURS** app. Nov 1963, pro. Dec 1965/ Birmingham City Jun 1972/(Philadelphia Atoms (USA) May 1975)/ Minnesota Kicks (USA) Apr 1978/Philadelphia Fury 1979.

Debut v West Bromwich Albion (FL) (h) 1.3.1968
(FC Zurich (Fr) (a) 30.5.1967)

A competent, unspectacular full-back, Tony Want was unlucky to be with Spurs at the same time as players like Phil Beal, Joe Kinnear and Cyril Knowles. With such competition, it was always going to be hard to secure a regular first team place. An England Youth international, Want had few opportunities, and it was only in 1969-70 when he stood in for both Beal and Knowles that he had any real chance to show what he could do. He never let the team down when called upon and was clearly too good for continual reserve team football. He was allowed to move to Birmingham City for £50,000 where he played for six years, often appearing as a central defender. He finished his career in America, alongside many other former League players of his generation, playing for Minnesota Kicks for four years. When he finally returned to England, Want went into business in the Solihull area.

Appearances:
League: 46 (4) apps.
FA Cup: 3 apps.
FL Cup: 3 apps.
Others: 18 (2) apps.
Total: 70 (6) apps. 0 gls.

WANYAMA, Victor Mugubi

Role: Midfielder 2016-
6ft.2ins. 12st.0lbs.
Born: Nairobi, Kenya, 25th June 1991

CAREER: Kamukunji High School (Kenya)/JMJ Youth Academy (Kenya) 2006-08/Nairobi City Stars (Kenya) 2006/AFC Leopards (Kenya) 2006-07/Helsingborg (Sweden) 2007-08/Germinal Beerschot (Belgium) trial, perm. 2008/Celtic Jul 2011/Southampton Jul 2013/**SPURS** Jun 2016

Debut v Everton (PL) (a) 13.8.2016
(Juventus Fr (Melbourne) 26.7.2016)

Kenyan captain, Victor Wanyama was a schoolboy prodigy at home in Nairobi, making his international debut as a 15-year old in May 2007. His elevation to international status was swiftly followed by a move to the Swedish club, Helsingborg, where his brother, McDonald Mariga, was already playing. When Mariga left to join Parma, Wanyama returned to Kenya, but a year later went on trial with Germinal Beerschot in Belgium and soon signed a permanent deal. A strong, aggressive, defensive midfielder, the Belgian club resisted several approaches for Wanyama's transfer before eventually accepting Celtic's near £million offer. Relishing the tough, combative football in Scotland, Wanyama helped Celtic dominate Scottish football with the SPL title in 2011-12 and 2012-13 and the Scottish Cup in 2013. In 2012-13 he also collected the SPL Young Player of the Year award. At the end of  the season he became one of Mauricio Pochettino's first signings for Southampton, easily adapting to English football, if sometimes finding himself in trouble with referees as the game became less physical. When Pochettino joined Spurs, Wanyama was said to be the one player he wanted to follow him, but Southampton were not prepared to lose one of their most important players, as well as their head coach. It was a full year before Spurs were able to persuade Southampton to takes Spurs £11 million. During that time Wanyama had taken his total of appearances for the Saints near the one hundred mark, though with only four goals. The winner on his home debut for Spurs against Crystal Palace, gave hope that was a record he would improve upon. Wanyama's sporting family is not limited to his brother Mariga. His father, Noah Wanyama was a Kenyan international who played for AFC Leopards and two other brothers, Thomas and Sylvester, play in the Kenyan Premier League.

Appearances:
League: 35 (1) apps. 4 gls.
FA Cup: 3 apps.
FL Cup: (1) apps.
Euro: 7 apps. 1 gl.
Others: 2 (1) apps.
Total: 47 (3) apps. 5 gls.

WARD, Grant Antony

Role: Defender/Midfielder 2014-
5ft. 8ins. 11st. 5lbs
Born: Lewisham, south London, 5th December 1994

CAREER: SPURS Academy Scholar Jul 2011, pro. Jul 2013/(Chicago Fire (USA) loan Mar 2014)/(Coventry City loan Mar 2015)/(Rotherham United loan Jul 2015)/Ipswich Town Aug 2016.

Debut v Malaysia FA XI (Fr) (a) (sub) 27.5.2015

A hard-working midfielder who retains many of the qualities that initially saw him regarded as a full-back, Grant Ward's development through the Spurs Academy to become a Football League regular has been very much under the radar. Loaned to Chicago Fire as a 19-year old, it appeared he was not regarded as having what was needed to make a career in the UK, but away from home, he rapidly grew up and returned a young man with strength and confidence. After his

time in America, Ward had three months on loan at Coventry City, quickly settling and proving a firm favourite. He returned from Coventry to accompany Spurs' end-of-season trip to Malaysia and Australia, playing in both games and not looking out of place. Coventry wanted him back for a second loan, but Spurs decided Rotherham United would provide a better platform for Ward's development. In a difficult season as Rotherham struggled to maintain their Championship place, Ward played practically every game, a consistent, reliable performer. His best position appeared to be in front of the back four, providing a shield, picking up the ball and bursting forward through midfield with it. With similar style players like Eric Dier and Nabil Bentaleb already on the books, the signing of Victor Wanyam pushed Ward well down the pecking order. When Ipswich Town moved in for him the opportunity of regular first team football could not be refused. Ward made his debut for Ipswich as a second half substitute. He showed his attacking talents with a quick-fire tat-trick.

Appearances:
Others: (2) apps.
Total: (2) apps. 0 gls.

WARD, Ralph Arthur

Role: Full-back 1935-46
5ft.8ins. 11st.11lbs.
Born: Oadby, Leicestershire, 5th February 1911
Died: Oadby, Leicestershire, March 1983

CAREER: Leicester Schools/England Schools/Kettering Town/Hinckley United/Leicester City am. 1928/Bradford Park Avenue pro. Nov 1929/**SPURS** Mar 1936/(Arsenal, Bradford City, Bradford Park Avenue and Fulham during World War Two)/Crewe Alexandra Aug 1946/retired May 1949/Oadby Town Jan 1952/Crewe Alexandra manager Jun 1953-55.

Debut v West Ham United (FL) (h) 14.3.1936

Like Tommy Clay, his predecessor of the 1920's, Ralph Ward was signed by Spurs after impressing for the opposition in an FA Cup tie. Having started with Hinckley United in the Birmingham League, Ward signed amateur forms for Leicester City, but when they failed to offer professional terms, he accepted an invitation from Bradford Park Avenue. It was in February 1936 that he played against Spurs in the fifth round of the FA Cup. He gave such outstanding performances over the two matches that within a month Spurs moved to sign the solid, muscular defender who would serve them well for the next ten years. First choice for practically his whole career at White Hart Lane, his position only really came under any threat with the signing of Bert Sproston in June 1938, but Sproston only stayed at Spurs four months. On his departure Ward was recalled and continued to play throughout the Second World War years, most of the time as captain. In October 1945, Ward realised his playing career was coming to an end and took up the post of assistant golf professional at Bush Hill Golf Club. In June 1946 he asked for a transfer and when the request was granted, moved to Crewe Alexandra. He played at Crewe for three years before injury forced a retirement from senior football. He returned to the game in January 1952, when he was re-instated as an amateur so that he could play for Oadby Town in the Leicestershire Senior League. He later served Crewe as manager from 1953 to 1955 and then ran his own haulage business.

Appearances:
League: 118 apps. 10 gls
FA Cup: 17 apps. 1 gl.
Others: 244 (3) apps. 17 gls.
Total: 379 (3) apps. 28 gls.

WARD-LEAVER, J

Role: Inside-forward 1894-95

CAREER: Westminster Criterion/Old St Stephens/**SPURS** guest Apr 1895.

Debut v Southampton St Marys (Fr) (a) 15.4.1895

An Old St Stephens player, Ward-Leaver made his only appearance for Spurs in April 1895 in a friendly match with Southampton St Marys.

Appearances:
Others: 1 app.
Total: 1 app. 0 gls.

WARNER, Alfred Cragg

Role: Inside-forward 1902-05
5ft.8ins. 11st.0lbs.
Born: Hyson Green, Nottingham, April 1879

CAREER: Notts Rangers/Nottingham Olympic/St Andrews/Weal/Notts County Aug 1899/**SPURS** May 1902/Luton Town May 1905/retired May 1907/Notts County Oct 1907.

Debut v Queens Park Rangers (SL) (h) 6.9.1902

Alf Warner was one of those useful squad players often left out to give a new signing a chance, but brought back when circumstances demanded a solid dependable professional. Although in his early twenties when signed, Warner had gathered a fair degree of experience in his three years with Notts County without ever hitting the heights. At Spurs for three years, he appeared in either of the right flank positions and in his first two seasons at White Hart Lane played with reasonable regularity. However, he found himself in the reserves for most of his final season. When released he joined Luton

Town where he played for two years before announcing his retirement. In October 1907 Notts County persuaded Warner to make a comeback, but he only played a few games for them before retiring for good.

Appearances:
Southern: 47 apps. 12 gls.
FA Cup: 5* apps.
Others: 38 apps. 11 gls.
Total: 90 apps. 23 gls.
*Includes 1 abandoned match.

WATKINS, George C

Role: Goalkeeper 1914-15

CAREER: Nunhead/(guest for **SPURS** during World War One).

Debut v Chelsea (Fr) (a) 15.10.1914

A former goalkeeper with the Nunhead club, Watkins made his one appearance for Spurs in a friendly with Chelsea in October 1914.

Appearances:
Others: 1 app.
Total: 1 app. 0 gls.

WATKINS, W

Role: Goalkeeper 1915-17

CAREER: Nunhead/(guest for **SPURS** during World War One)/Clapton Orient Sep 1917.

Debut v Fulham (LFC) (a) 19.2.1916

Like his namesake, George, Watkins was an amateur with the South London club, Nunhead. He was first associated with Spurs in the 1914-15 season when he played a few games in the reserves. He did not make his first senior appearance for Spurs until February 1916 when he played in a London Football Combination fixture with Fulham. While his performance was described as "not too good", he did make two further appearances for Spurs, one in a friendly later that season and the other another London Football Combination game with Queens Park Rangers in January 1917. He joined Clapton Orient in September 1917.

Appearances:
Others: 3 apps.
Total: 3 apps. 0 gls.

WATSON, Dr Alec

Role: Winger 1883-84

Debut v Brownlow Rovers (Fr) (h) 6.10.1883

A local doctor, Alec Watson is only known to have played in four friendly matches for Spurs during the 1883-84 season. That he was associated with the club at all is rather unusual, for at the time Spurs still consisted of the schoolboys who had founded the club only twelve months earlier. In his four known matches Watson scored two goals.

Appearances:
Others: 4 apps. 2 gls.
Total: 4 apps. 2 gls.

WATSON, Claude

Role: Full-back 1906-07

CAREER: Tufnell Park/**SPURS** trial Aug 1905, am. Sep 1906/Luton Town 1910/Crystal Palace 1915.

Debut v West Ham United (WL) (a) 8.10.1906

Claude Watson played in a junior trial match organised by Spurs prior to the start of the 1905-06 season, but was not felt good enough to be offered a place on the White Hart Lane staff. However, Spurs kept an eye on his development with the Tufnell Park club and he was signed as an amateur for 1906-07. Watson turned out in one Western League match that season, playing the majority of his football with Tufnell Park or Spurs' reserves. At the time, with regular full-backs of the calibre of Ollie Burton, John Watson, John Chaplin and Sandy Tait on the books, Watson was no real threat to such experienced professionals. He continued to assist Spurs for the next five years, although his services were nearly lost in September 1908 when, after a reserve South Eastern League fixture against Crystal Palace, the south London club complained he had also signed amateur forms for them. In 1910-11 he assisted Luton Town and was still playing football during the war, appearing for Crystal Palace in 1915-16.

Appearances:
Others: 1 app.
Total: 1 app. 0 gls.

WATSON, John

Role: Full-back 1902-08
5ft.9ins. 12st.0lbs.
Born: Dundee, 1877

CAREER: Dundee Dec 1894/Dundee Wanderers Sep 1896/New Brompton Nov 1896/Dundee May 1899/Everton Mar 1900/**SPURS** May 1902/released May 1908.

Debut v Millwall Athletic (WL) (h) 15.9.1902

After experience at home in Dundee and with New Brompton, John Watson had two years as Everton's regular left-back. However, injury cost him his place at Goodison midway through the 1901-02 season and although he recovered the position, he was persuaded to make the move to Spurs at the end of the season. For the first two years at White Hart Lane Watson spent most of his time as reserve to regular full-backs Harry Erentz and Sandy Tait and it was only after Erentz's departure in the summer of 1904 that Watson emerged from his shadow. A solid hard kicking player he held the right-back spot for the next two years before losing it to fellow Scot, John Chaplin. Watson remained with Spurs until the summer of 1908 when he was released. Watson had played as a professional with Dundee so had to be re-instated as an amateur in order to play for Dundee Wanderers. Re-instatement was granted in Aug 1896, but three months later the offer came to play the paid game with New Brompton.

Appearances:
Southern: 103 apps.
FA Cup: 23* apps.
Others: 69 apps.
Total: 195 apps. 0 gls.
*Includes 1 abandoned match.

WATSON, Kevin Edward

Role: Midfield 1992-95
6ft.0ins. 12st.11lbs.
Born: Hackney, London, 3rd January 1974

CAREER: SPURS trainee Jul 1990, pro. May 1992/(Brentford loan Mar 1994)/(Bristol City loan Dec 1994)/(Barnet loan Feb 1995)/Swindon Town Jul 1996-May 1999/Rotherham United Jul 1999/Reading loan Nov 2001, perm. March 2002/Colchester United May 2004/Luton Town trial Jul 2008/Northampton Town Jul 2008/Luton Town player-coach Jul 2008-Dec 2009, coach Jan 2009-May 2010/Colchester United Academy coach Jan 2015/Maldon & Tipton manager May 2015/Stevenage asst. manager May 2015-Feb 2016/Eastleigh Aug-Dec 2016/Whitehawk asst. manager Jan 2017/Bishop's Stortford manager Mar 2017.

Debut v Brentford (FLC) (h) 22.8.1992
(West Bromwich Albion (sub) (Fr) (a) 3.8.1992)

A neat, nicely-balanced midfielder, Kevin Watson was given an opportunity in the first team early in the 1992-93 season and performed acceptably well. He showed a nice touch, got around the pitch well and was always looking creative, seeking out the opening to make a chance for his forwards. At the time Darren Anderton and Vinny Samways were the main creative forces for Spurs and with Nicky Barmby coming to the fore, it was not easy for Watson to make his mark. After several loans he was released. He joined Swindon Town and settled easily to First Division football. Three years later he moved on to Rotherham United and helped them secure successive promotions from the Third to First Division. In 2001-02 Watson led Reading from the Second to First Division and in 2005-06 Colchester United from the First Division to the Championship. When injuries deprived Colchester of his services they suffered with relegation in 2008. At Luton Town he continued to suffer from injuries and turned his attention to coaching, and was due to take up his first management job with Maldon & Tipton in May 2015. However, he never moved into the role, accepting the offer of working as assistant manager to Teddy Sheringham when his former Spurs and Colchester team-mate was appointed manager at Stevenage. He departed eight months later when Sheringham was dismissed.

Appearances:
League: 4 (1) apps.
FA Cup: (1) app.
FL Cup: 1 (1) apps. 1 gl.
Others: 2(11) apps.
Total: 7 (14) apps. 1 gl.

WEBSTER, Frederick Joseph

Role: Full-back 1911-15
5ft.9ins. 12st.0lbs.
Born: Sheffield, Yorkshire, 3rd April 1887
Died: Gainsborough, Lincolnshire, 14th September 1938

CAREER: Crown & Victoria (Sheffield)/Gainsborough Trinity Jul 1906/**SPURS** Apr 1911/Brentford Jun 1919/Gainsborough Trinity Jun 1920.

Debut v Woolwich Arsenal (FL) (h) 25.12.1911

In five years with Gainsborough Trinity, Fred Webster had developed into probably the best player on the books of the struggling Second Division club. He found life much tougher at White Hart Lane though, competing with Tom Collins, Richard Brittan and Fred Wilkes, and did not make his League debut until Christmas Day 1911 when he played in a 5-0 defeat of Woolwich Arsenal. He had to be content with a reserve place for most of his first season, but eventually replaced Richard Brittan and proved a solid and reliable performer until injured in October 1914. Joining the forces, Webster was not available throughout the years of the First World War and, when he returned to Spurs at the end of the hostilities, it was felt he was past his best. Released in the close season of 1919 he joined Brentford where he played for just one season before returning to Gainsborough.

Appearances:
League: 83* apps.
FA Cup: 4 apps.
Others: 17 apps.
Total: 104 apps. 0 gls.
*Includes 1 abandoned match.

WEBSTER, Simon Paul

Role: Central defender 1982-85
6ft.0ins. 11st.7lbs.
Born: Earl Shilton, Leicestershire, 20th January 1964

CAREER: Hatfield School/Mid-Hertfordshire Schools/Hertfordshire Schools/**SPURS** app. May 1980, pro. Dec 1981/(Barnet loan Dec 1982)/(Exeter City loan Nov 1983)/(Norwich City loan Jan 1985)/Huddersfield Town loan Feb 1985, perm. Mar 1985/Sheffield United Mar 1988/Charlton Athletic loan Aug 1990, perm. Aug 1990/West Ham United Jun 1993/(Oldham Athletic loan Mar 1995)/(Derby County loan Aug 1995)/Chertsey Town during 1996-97/St Albans City Aug 1997/Charlton Athletic Football in Community coach/West Ham United physiotherapy staff Aug 2001/Gillingham physio Mar 2004-Oct 2006/Charlton Athletic Ladies physio.

Debut v Everton (FL) (h) 3.1.1983
(Barnet (sub) (Fr) (a) 20.9.1982)

Simon Webster is another of the promising young players developed at White Hart Lane who had to move on to find football success. Loaned to Alliance League Barnet in December 1982 to gain experience, he was called back to White Hart Lane the following month due to an injury crisis and made his League debut against Everton. After one further League outing as a substitute that season he was loaned to Exeter City, but again recalled because of injury problems and made another League appearance in December

1983 before returning to Exeter for the rest of the season. With regular central defenders like Paul Miller, Gary Stevens and John Lacy ahead of him chances with Spurs were clearly limited and in March 1985 Webster moved to Huddersfield Town for a modest £15,000. Three years with Huddersfield saw Webster develop into a big, strapping defender, capable of handling the toughest of forwards. This led to him joining Sheffield United, but he had little chance to make an impression there before a double leg fracture in November 1988. It caused him to miss out on the Blades climb back to the Second Division, but he recovered to play a full part as they returned to the First Division. He was then transferred to Charlton Athletic where he rediscovered his best form as the central defensive pivot of a useful side equipped to challenge for promotion. This earnt him a £525,000 move to West Ham, but another broken leg in pre-season training put him out of the game for over a year. He did manage to play five games for the Hammers and played on loan for Oldham and Derby but never fully recovered from the injury. He was forced to retire from the first class game, although he was able to turn out for St Albans City and Chertsey Town, before building a new career as a physiotherapist.

Appearances:
League: 2 (1) apps.
Others: (2) apps.
Total: 2 (3) apps. 0 gls.

WEIR, William Findlay

Role: Half-back 1912-17
5ft.8ins. 10st.12lbs.
Born: Glasgow, 18th April 1889
Died: Brighton, Sussex. 9th July 1918

CAREER: Campvale/Waverley/Maryhill by Apr 1906/Sheffield Wednesday Feb 1909/**SPURS** May 1912.

Debut v Derby County (FL) (h) 21.9.1912

Findlay Weir had appeared regularly with Sheffield Wednesday for two and a half years before joining Spurs. Many of his games for Wednesday had been in the centre-half position, but with Danny Steel having left and Jabez Darnell nearing the end of his playing days, Spurs were in desperate need of a good, constructive and, above all, experienced half-back. Weir filled the role perfectly and missed few games in the final seasons of League football before its suspension because of the war. He joined the services to make his contribution, serving with the Tottenham Royal Engineers. Wounded in 1916, he recovered from his injuries but passed away in a Brighton hospital two years later.

Appearances:
League: 97* apps. 2 gls.
FA Cup: 5 apps.
Others: 18 apps.
Total: 120 apps. 2 gls.
*Includes 1 abandoned match.

WELCH, A

Role: Half-back 1895-96

Debut v Swindon Town (Fr) (a) 15.4.1896

Welch's two appearances in Spurs' colours were in April 1896, the first when he played in a friendly match at Swindon.

Appearances:
Others: 2 apps.
Total: 2 apps. 0 gls.

WELHAM, John W

Role: Half-back 1892-95
Born: Teignmouth, Devon

CAREER: Bedminster/**SPURS** cs. 1892/Bristol South End by Sep 1894/Clapton Oct 1894/Bristol South End by Dec 1895/Plymouth Argyle/St Albans Town 1898-99.

Debut v West Herts (FAC) (h) 13.10.1894
(Paddington (Fr) (h) 17.9.1892)

A well-built full-back with a hefty kick, Jack Welham was first associated with Spurs in 1892-93 having spent the previous season playing for Bedminster. He was virtually first choice left-back for the next three years although he also frequently appeared in the half-back line. By September 1894 he had returned to Bristol to play for South End, but made only one appearance before being persuaded to join Clapton, although he still turned out for Spurs in Cup matches that season. He then ceased to play for Spurs, but continued to play for three seasons with Clapton and certainly played a few games for Bristol South End in 1895-96 and made eleven appearances for St Albans Town between November 1898 and April 1899 in the Second Division of the Southern League. Welham's wanderings saw him play football at county level for Gloucestershire, London, Middlesex and Devon. He was a quite remarkable sportsman. He was a member of the Sterling, Ranelagh Harriers and Citizens Clubs, captain of Teignmouth Swimming Club for 22 years and represented the Amateur Swimming Association. He was stroke for Bristol Redcliffe Rowing Club and represented Middlesex, London and Devon at water polo, captaining the latter for 15 years. He played cricket for Sterling and Teignmouth, won a gold medal at Morris Tube-shooting, won the City of London 100 yards grass track sprint in 1898, and came first in the 220 yards dash at one of Spurs' athletics meetings. If that were not enough, he and his son received vellums from the Royal Humane Society for saving three ladies from drowning at Bantham in August 1918. Not to forget that in Jersey in September 1924 he saved a man from drowning.

Appearances:
FA Cup: 3 apps.
Others: 50 apps. 2 gls.
Total: 53 apps. 2 gls.

WELLER, Keith

Role: Winger 1964-67
5ft.9ins. 12st.11lbs.
Born: Islington, London, 11th June 1946
Died: Seattle, USA, 12th November 2004

CAREER: Islington Schools/Hackney Schools/Middlesex Schools/Arlington Boys Club/Islington Boys Club/**SPURS** am. Dec 1962, part-time pro. Jan 1964/Millwall Jun 1967/Chelsea May 1970/Leicester City

Sep 1971/New England Teamen (USA) loan Apr 1978, perm. Feb 1979/Fort Lauderdale Strikers (USA) Jul 1980/Enderby Town Aug 1980/Fort Lauderdale Sun (USA) player-coach 1984/South Florida Sun (USA) player-coach/Houston Dynamo (USA) player-coach 1986/Dallas Sidekicks (USA) player-coach Jul 1986-Aug 1988/San Diego Sockers (USA) player-coach/Tacoma Stars (USA) player-coach 1990-Jun 1992/Sacramento Knights (USA) coach 1994 -1997.

Debut v Wolverhampton Wanderers (FL) (h) 27.3.1965
(Leytonstone (Fr) (a) 8.12.1964)

Regarded by Spurs as a winger at a time when the role was rapidly going out of fashion, Keith Weller developed into a highly effective midfield player after leaving White Hart Lane and went on to play for England. He spent two years with Spurs as cover for the first choice wingers Jimmy Robertson and Cliff Jones, but was unable to get a regular first team slot and moved to Millwall for £18,000. Whilst at the Den he dropped back into midfield and formed a most effective partnership with his former Spurs reserve colleague Derek Possee. The excellent ball skills Weller had developed as a winger allowed him to run at opponents from deep positions, and the extra time and space created, allowed him to show off his accurate passing and ability to create chances for others. He moved to Chelsea, but although he played in their triumphant European Cup-Winners' Cup team of 1971 did not really settle at Stamford Bridge and after one season joined Leicester City for £100,000. At Leicester he really flourished and, after playing for the Football League against the Scottish League in March 1973, made his England debut against Wales in May 1974, the first of four caps. His exciting, individualist style and spectacular shooting was an integral part of Jimmy Bloomfield's attractive team and he remained at Filbert Street until the end of 1977-78. He then went to America to play for New England Teamen, where he spent two seasons, followed by a further four in Fort Lauderdale, before moving into coaching. He retired from football in 1993 and remained in the States working for a TV station, but was soon temped back to coaching. Weller's career also had its temperamental moments. At half-time in Leicester's game with Ipswich Town on 20th December 1974 he went on "strike" and refused to re-appear in protest at Leicester's refusal to grant him a transfer request.

Appearances:
League: 19 (2) apps. 1 gl.
Others: 13 (5) apps. 5 gls.
Total: 32 (7) apps. 6 gls.

WESTON, S

Role: Inside-forward 1891-93

Debut v Forest Swifts (Fr) (h) 12.12.1891

Another of those players from the early 1890s about whom little is known, Weston's first recorded appearance for Spurs was in December 1891 in a friendly with Forest Swifts. Spurs fielded only ten men in a match that was abandoned after 60 minutes because of bad light.

Appearances:
Others: 8 apps. 4 gls.
Total: 8 apps. 4 gls.

WESTWOOD, John A

Role: Centre-forward 1948-49
5ft.7ins. 10st.12lbs.
Born: Edmonton, London, 3rd December 1927

CAREER: Tottenham Juniors/Finchley/**SPURS** pro. Aug 1948/Valenciennes (France) Aug 1952/Finchley 1954/Leytonstone 1954-55/Valenciennes (France) 1955/Chelmsford City Feb 1960.

Debut v Cornwall County XI (Fr) (Penzance) 9.5.1949

John Westwood signed for Spurs as a professional after playing for the Tottenham Juniors and Finchley. He made only one appearance in the first team, in a friendly against a Cornwall County XI at Penzance in May 1949. Although he scored regularly for the reserve and "A" sides he was not able to displace Len Duquemin in the first team and was transfer-listed in May 1952. In August 1952 he took a temporary job on the ground-staff pending his move later that month to France to play for Valenciennes FC. He returned after a couple of years to play for Finchley and Leytonstone, then returned to France for a further five years.

Appearances:
Others: 1 app.
Total: 1 app. 0 gls.

WETTON, Ralph

Role: Half-back 1951-55
5ft.11ins. 10st.10lbs.
Born: Rowland Gill, County Durham, 6th June 1927

CAREER: Dartford/Cheshunt/**SPURS** am. May 1949, pro. Aug 1950/Plymouth Argyle Jun 1955/Aldershot Nov 1956/Eynesbury Rovers Jul 1958/Harlow Town manager/Cheshunt player-manager 1960-1962/Brimsdown Rovers committee.

Debut v Aston Villa (FL) (h) 20.10.1951

Originally an inside-forward, Ralph Wetton developed as a half-back in the reserves and made his League debut in October 1951 at left-half in place of Ron Burgess who was on international duty with Wales. A tall, thoughtful, creative player he provided cover for Burgess and Bill Nicholson, deputising for both in the 1953-54 season as they moved towards the end of their playing days. Looked upon as the most likely successor to

Nicholson, Wetton was unfortunately not up to the standard of two of the best wing-halves in Spurs' history, and with the arrival of Danny Blanchflower, moved on to Plymouth Argyle. He stayed in Devon for just over a season and finished his first class career at Aldershot later joining Eynesbury Rovers. Wetton's brother, Albert, was on Spurs' books at the same time as Ralph. A centre-forward, he did not make the grade with Spurs, but went on to play for Brighton and Hove Albion and Crewe Alexandra.

Appearances:
League: 45 apps.
FA Cup: 1 app.
Others: 18* apps. 3 gls.
Total: 64 apps. 3 gls.
*Includes 1 abandoned match

WHALLEY, Gareth

Role: Midfielder 1997
5ft.10ins. 11st.8lbs.
Born: Manchester, 19th December 1973

CAREER: Crewe Alexandra trainee, pro. 1992/**SPURS** trial Jul 1997/Bradford City Jul 1998/(Crewe Alexandra loan Mar 2002)/Cardiff City Jul 2002/Wigan Athletic trial Aug 2004, pro. Sep 2004/Swindon Town Jul 2005/Halifax Town trial Feb 2007/Crewe Alexandra training Jul 2007/Altrincham Aug-Dec 2007/Manchester City Academy coach, Under-18s coach Jul 2014.

Debut v Ski (sub) (Fr) (a) 15.7.1997

Another of the talented young midfielders developed by Dario Gradi at Crewe Alexandra before the modern academy structure was developed, Gareth Whalley was in dispute when he joined Spurs for a trial. He was part of the squad on a pre-season tour to Norway, playing in three of the games. Not considered better than the players Spurs already had, he returned to Crewe, settled his dispute and took his number of appearances for the club he had joined in 1992 over the 200 mark, before a £600,000 transfer to Bradford City. Providing the skill alongside all-action Stuart McCall, he helped Bradford City secure promotion to the Premier League in his first season. He enjoyed two years in the top flight with Bradford City before they were relegated, but was not to reach the same heights again. After two years at Cardiff City he linked up with his former Bradford City manager, Paul Jewell at Wigan Athletic but persistent injury concerns restricted his appearances as he moved down the leagues until becoming a coach. With his mother born in Dublin, Whalley qualified to play for the Republic of Ireland. He was called up several times without making a full appearance although he did play at "B" level.

Appearances:
Others: 1 (2) apps.
Total: 1 (2) apps. 0 gls.

WHATLEY, William John

Role: Full-back 1932-47
5ft.8ins. 11st.10lbs.
Born: Ebbw Vale, Monmouthshire, 12th October 1912
Died: Greenwich, London, December 1974

CAREER: Ebbw Vale Schools/Wales Schools/Barnet/Hayward Sports 1929/**SPURS** am. Dec 1929, pro. May 1931/Northfleet United Aug 1931/**SPURS** Mar 1932/(guest for Arsenal, Fulham, Stockport County and West Ham United during World War Two)/retired 1947, scout /Gravesend and Northfleet manager May 1954.

Debut v Nottingham Forest (FL) (h) 5.9.1932

A former baker's boy brought up to London as a 17-year old, Bill Whatley was another of the many fine players such as Willie Evans and Taffy O'Callaghan discovered by Spurs' Welsh scouting network. Under Spurs' guidance, Whatley developed through Haywards Sports and Northfleet to join the professional staff at White Hart Lane in May 1931. He made his debut more than a year later in place of the injured Cecil Poynton, and was ever-present for the rest of the season as promotion back to Division One was secured. First choice right-back until the clouds of war began to gather, he collected his first cap for Wales against England in October 1938 and retained his place for the game with Scotland the following month. It was only with the emergence of Bill Nicholson that Whatley lost his place at the start of 1939-40, but the outbreak of war saw his career extended and he played for Wales in the war-time international against England in November 1939. An ankle injury caused him to retire in 1947, but he was kept on by the club as a scout, helping to discover Harry Clarke, Mel Hopkins and Dennis Uphill. In April 1954 Bill's services were dispensed with and he joined Southern League Gravesend and Northfleet as manager. He later worked as a messenger in London's West End.

Appearances:
League: 226 apps. 2 gls.
FA Cup: 28 apps.
Others: 139* apps.
Total: 393 apps. 3 gls.
*Includes 1 abandoned match.

WHENT, John Richard

Role: Inside-forward 1943-44
Born: Darlington, County Durham, 3rd May 1920
Died: Sacramento, California, USA, 25th August 1999

CAREER: St Saviours (Canada)/(guest for Arsenal, Brighton and Hove Albion and **SPURS** during World War Two)/St Andrews FC (Canada) 1946/)/Brighton and Hove Albion Aug 1947/Luton Town Aug 1950/Kettering Town Aug 1951/Westminster Royals (Canada).

Debut v Clapton Orient (FLS) (h) 29.4.1944 (scored once)
(Millwall (Fr) (a) 10.4.1944.).

Although born in England, Jack Whent had emigrated to Canada and was serving in the Canadian Army when he made three guest appearances for Spurs during the 1943-44 season. He went back to Canada after the war and played for the St Andrews club of Vancouver as they wiped the board, winning the Anderson Cup, the Mainland Cup, the Pacific Coast League Trophy, the Nanaimo Perpetual Trophy, and the Dominion Football Association Trophy. He returned to the UK to sign professional for Brighton and played over 100 League games for them before finishing his League career with Luton Town. On returning to Canada he played for Westminster Royals, helping them to the Canadian championship in 1953.

Appearances:
Others: 3 apps. 1 gl.
Total: 3 apps. 1 gl.

WHITBOURNE, John Giles

Role: Goalkeeper 1905-08
6ft.1ins. 11st.6lbs.
Born: Farnham, Surrey, 29th December 1884
Died: Middlesbrough 1936

CAREER: South Bank/Sunderland Aug 1904/**SPURS** May 1905/Leyton Aug 1908.

Debut v Brentford (WL) (h) 13.11.1905

With the Football Association cancelling Spurs' registration of Jack Whitley, the former Stoke and Everton goalkeeper, Spurs were placed in a difficult position with no reserve 'keeper on the books. They turned to Jack Whitbourne who had spent a year with Sunderland, mostly in their reserves. He stayed three years at White Hart Lane, spending most of that time in the second eleven. For the first season he served as understudy to John Eggett, and only played for the first team in the secondary Western League fixtures but, when Eggett was injured in September 1906, his chance looked to have arrived. However, Whitbourne played only two games before Spurs signed Matt Reilly. Whitbourne was recalled in March 1907 and kept his place till the end of the season. Spurs then signed Gordon Manning and Whitbourne spent another year as second choice before being released in May 1908. He then joined Leyton where he was a regular for four years.

Appearances:
Southern: 19 apps.
Others: 13 apps.
Total: 32 apps. 0 gls.

WHITCHURCH, Charles Henry

Role: Winger 1945-47
Born: Grays, Essex, 29th October 1920
Died: Michigan, USA, July 1977

CAREER: Grays Schools/England Schools/Ford Sports/Portsmouth am./West Ham United am. Jan 1945, pro. 1945/(Charlton Athletic, Portsmouth and Southend United during World War Two)/**SPURS** Jan 1946/Southend United Jul 1947/Folkestone Town Jul 1948/Betteshanger Colliery Welfare/Margate Aug 1951-May 1952/Ford Sports.

Debut v West Bromwich Albion (FL) (a) 7.9.1946
(Luton Town (FLS) (h) 19.1.1946)

Charlie Whitchurch was a well-known athlete playing for Ford Sports of Dagenham during the Second World War when he caught the attention of West Ham United. Previously an amateur on Portsmouth's books, he joined West Ham as an amateur in January 1945 and had signed professional by the start of the 1945-46 season. Capable of playing on either flank, he used his athletic prowess to good effect and did enough in the final year of war-time competition for Spurs to secure his transfer in January 1946. He held a place in the team for the rest of that transitional season, but in the first term of normal football found Freddie Cox and Les Stevens barring his way into the first eleven. He was released in May 1947 and joined Southend United, where he spent just one season before quitting the game. Whitchurch was then employed by the Ford Motor Company at Dagenham and played for their works team until emigrating to Canada in 1951. He worked in the rocket research division of General Motors in Michigan until his death.

Appearances:
League: 8 apps. 2 gls.
Others: 19 apps. 5 gls.
Total: 27 apps. 7 gls.

WHITE, John Anderson

Role: Inside-forward 1959-64
5ft.8ins. 10st.8lbs.
Born: Musselburgh, Midlothian, 28th April 1937
Died: Crews Hill, Middlesex, 21st July 1964

CAREER: Musselburgh Junior/Bonnyrigg Rose Athletic/Alloa Athletic Aug 1956/Falkirk Aug 1958/**SPURS** Oct 1959.

Debut v Sheffield Wednesday (FL) (a) 17.10.1959 (scored once)

One of the most important elements of the "Double" winning team, John White will be remembered at Spurs as one of the greatest inside-forwards of all time. After playing in junior football, he had two years with Alloa Athletic before joining Falkirk for £3,300. Within a year of the move he was in the Scotland team, making his international debut against West Germany in May 1959. In September 1959 he played for the Scottish League against the League of Ireland with his £20,000 move to Spurs delayed to allow him to play against the Irish League the following month. With four caps to his name, White scored on his Spurs' debut and from then on was an automatic choice, taking over from the popular little Tommy Harmer. In many ways he was similar to 'The Charmer', possessing the same immaculate ball

control, the same trickery and juggling ability, the same perfectly weighted pin point passing skills, but White had a little more. Blessed with exceptional balance, he was faster and more direct. Extremely difficult to mark, he had an uncanny ability to slip, unnoticed, into goal-scoring positions, from where he could finish with a perfectly placed shot. The Spurs fans took a while to understand and accept the subtleties of his clever decoy runs and delicate style, but soon christened him "The Ghost" as White continually popped up from nowhere to receive or make, an incisive or telling pass. An invaluable ever-present cog in the 1961 "Double" winning team, he helped Spurs retain the FA Cup in 1962 and win the European Cup-Winners' Cup in 1963. His supreme talents continued to be displayed on the international stage, winning 18 full caps and one Under-23 honour in his time with Spurs. White also played for the Football League against the Irish League in October 1960 and for Scotland against the Scottish League twice. After football, golf was the passion in White's life and it was whilst sheltering from a thunderstorm on Crews Hill Golf Course at Enfield in July 1964 that his life was tragically ended when the tree he stood under was struck by lightning. It was the bitterest of blows, for White was only 27 and at the peak of his career. His brother, Tommy, was a centre-forward with Heart of Midlothian, Aberdeen, Crystal Palace, Blackpool, Bury and Crewe Alexandra. He played for Spurs as a guest in the memorial match against a Scotland XI held for White in November 1964.

Appearances:
League: 183 apps. 40 gls.
FA Cup: 19 apps. 1 gl.
Euro: 17 apps. 6 gls.
Others: 14 apps. 6 gls.
Total: 233 apps. 53 gls.

WHITE, Raymond Bernard William

Role: Half-back 1940-41
Born: Bootle, Lancashire, 13th August 1918
Died: December 1988

CAREER: Everton am./**SPURS** am. Nov 1940/(Fulham and Manchester United during World War Two)/ Bradford Park Avenue May 1946.

Debut v Brentford (FAC) (h) 5.1.1946 (Arsenal (FLS) (a) 16.11.1940)

Many players had their careers destroyed by World War Two, but Roy White was one of the rare exceptions who would probably never have made a mark in the game had it not been for those troubled times. He had played minor football in Liverpool and been with Everton as a junior, but chose to make a career in accountancy rather than football. Evacuated from Dunkirk with the British Expeditionary Force, his boat was sunk and he spent several hours in the water. Blinded for a time, he had to spend a lengthy period in hospital where he met Jock McKay, a former Blackburn Rovers and Middlesbrough forward, He recommended White to Spurs manager, Peter McWilliam. On his release from hospital, White was put on top secret work for the War Office in London and was invited along to watch Spurs play Arsenal in November 1940. Unexpectedly asked to make up the numbers, he performed so well against Cliff Bastin that Spurs immediately asked him to sign amateur forms. He did so, and played regularly throughout the war, his only absences being when away on duty or leave or playing in various representative games. He also guested for Manchester United, helping them reach the Football League (North) Cup Final in 1945. At the conclusion of war Spurs offered him professional terms. Unfortunately, he refused, choosing instead to return to Liverpool to continue his studies towards becoming a Chartered Accountant. He played his last match for Spurs in March 1946. However, he was not lost to football entirely, for Jack Gibbons, who like White had played for Spurs as an amateur during the war, persuaded White to join Bradford PA and he gave them five years sterling service before retiring.

Appearances:
FA Cup: 2 apps.
Others: 167 apps. 4 gls.
Total: 169 apps. 4 gls.

WHITE, Sidney Ernest

Role: Half-back 1923-26
5ft.11ins. 11st.7lbs.
Born: Tottenham, London, 15th February 1899
Died: Westminster, London, 6th May 1948

CAREER: Edmonton Ramblers/**SPURS** trial Mar 1921, am. Apr 1921, pro. Apr 1922/retired May 1928/ Clapton Orient coach, caretaker manager Dec 1934.

Debut v Nottingham Forest (FL) (a) 3.11.1923

Sid White learned his football whilst serving in the Army during the First World War. On his demob he joined the local junior team Edmonton Ramblers, which is where he was noticed by Spurs. He spent six years at White Hart Lane, but was never more than cover for Arthur Grimsdell and Jimmy Skinner. When released in May 1928, injury prevented him finding a new club, although he later had a spell as coach of Clapton Orient.

Appearances:
League: 20 apps.
FA Cup: 2 apps.
Others: 3 apps. 1 gl.
Total: 25 apps. 1 gl.

WHITE, Thomas

Role: Centre-forward 1964-65
Born: Musselburgh, Midlothian, 12th August 1939

CAREER: Musselburgh Juveniles/Bonnyrigg Rose/ Raith Rovers May 1958/St Mirren Oct 1962/Heart of Midlothian Nov 1963/**SPURS** guest Nov 1964/Aberdeen May 1965/Crystal Palace Jun 1966/Blackpool Mar 1968/ Bury Jun 1970/Crewe Alexandra Dec 1971/ Fleetwood/Blackpool director 1980-1992, caretaker manager Apr-Jun 1990.

Debut v Scotland XI (Fr) (h) 11.11.1964 (scored once)

Tommy White made his one appearance for Spurs in November 1964 as a guest in the Memorial match for his brother, John, against a Scotland XI. He scored once. A bustling centre-forward typical of the time, he had a good scoring record from his earliest days with Raith Rovers, scoring roughly once every two games. While he never reached the same heights as his brother, he did play for the Scottish League against Scotland in February 1964. He tried his luck in England, proving a competent performer with Crystal Palace, Blackpool, Bury and Crewe Alexandra. He settled in the Blackpool area and spent twelve years as a director of the club, serving for a short time as caretaker manager

Appearances:
Others: 1 app. 1 gl.
Total: **1 app. 1 gl.**

WHITLEY, John

Role: Goalkeeper 1905
Born: Seacombe, Cornwall, 18th April 1880
Died: London, 1953

CAREER: Seacombe Swifts/Seacombe YMCA May 1897/Liskeard YMCA 1898/Darwen Jan 1899/Aston Villa May 1900/Everton May 1902/Stoke Aug 1904/(**SPURS** Apr 1905, contract cancelled)/Leeds City Apr 1906/Lincoln City Sep 1906/Chelsea Jul 1907/retired May 19140/(guest for Fulham during World War One)/Chelsea coach-trainer 1915-May 1939.

Debut v Buda Pesth Thorna (Fr) (a) 12.5.1905

Signed in April 1905, Jack Whitley played his only recorded first team match for Spurs during a European tour in May 1905. It has not been possible to trace the details of all the Spurs teams that played seven games in Austria, Hungary and Czechoslovakia and Whitley may have played against the Vienna Athletic Club two days before his known debut. John Eggett was the only other keeper on the trip and it is quite possible he was rested for that game. An experienced keeper in his time with Darwen, Aston Villa, Everton and Stoke, Whitley had missed only two League games the previous season. In April 1905 his contract was up and Spurs appeared to have safely secured his services, but Stoke complained to the Football League that Spurs had been guilty of "poaching". The allegation was dealt with by the Football Association as Stoke were members of the Football League and Spurs the Southern League. A hearing took place after Spurs' return from the tour. The FA heard that Whitley had been offered the maximum wage by Stoke to re-sign and decided it had not heard a good enough reason to join Spurs. Stoke's complaint was upheld with the FA ordering that Whitley's registration as a Spurs' player should be cancelled. He returned to Stoke, but played only four more League games late in the season before being transferred to Leeds City. From Leeds he made the final move of his career joining Chelsea where he played until officially retiring in the summer of 1914. On his retirement Chelsea appointed him as trainer, a position he held until May 1938.

Appearances:
Others: 1 app.
Total: **1 app. 0 gls.**

WHITTINGHAM, Alfred

Role: Centre-forward 1944-45
Born: Altofts, Yorkshire, 19th June 1914

CAREER: Altofts West Riding Colliery/Bradford City Oct 1936/(guest for Bournemouth and Boscombe Athletic, Bradford Park Avenue, Chelsea, Huddersfield Town, Millwall, Norwich City, Southampton and **SPURS** during World War Two)/Huddersfield Town Feb 1947/Halifax Town Mar 1949.

Debut v Brentford (FLS) (a) 24.3.1945 (scored once)

Bradford City's Alf Whittingham made his one appearance for Spurs as a guest against Brentford in a Football League South match in March 1945. He played in that match as Spurs' regular centre-forward Jack Gibbons was not able to turn out and scored once. After the war he continued with Bradford City for almost a year and then played for Huddersfield Town and Halifax Town.

Appearances:
Others: 1 app. 1 gl.
Total: **1 app. 1 gl.**

WHITTON, William Alex

Role: Centre-forward 1921-23
Born: Aldershot, Hampshire, 1900

CAREER: Inverness Caledonians/**SPURS** Apr 1921/Chelsea Mar 1923/retired Apr 1926.

Debut v London Caledonians (LFACC) (h) 17.10.1921 (scored once)

Although a Hampshire man it was from Inverness Caledonians that Spurs signed William Whitton after the First World War. He made only two first team appearances, the first in the London FA Charity Cup in October 1921 and the second twelve months later in a friendly at Llanelly. He scored in both games, but was not given a real opportunity in the first team and was transferred to Chelsea. At first, he was unable to find his goal-scoring form, but in 1924-25 things began to look up and he netted 16 goals in 24 Football League games. However, when the goals began to dry up Whitton decided to give up football and concentrate on a business career. His contract with Chelsea was cancelled in April 1926.

Appearances:
Others: 2 apps. 2 gls.
Total: **2 apps. 2 gls.**

WHYMAN, Alfred

Role: Outside-left 1905-08
5ft.10ins. 12st.0lbs.
Born: Edmonton, London, 31st October 1884
Died: South America, 1955

CAREER: Park/Edmonton Rovers/**SPURS** Apr 1905/ New Brompton May 1908/ Queens Park Rangers May 1909/(guest for Clapton Orient during World War One)/retired 1920.

Debut v Plymouth Argyle (WL) (a) 21.3.1906

The suspension of regular left winger Chris Carrick in March 1906 for a breach of the club's training rules left Spurs with little alternative other than to call-up Alf Whyman. A 21-year old, he had been with Spurs for less than a year after signing from a local junior club. Whyman had first come to Spurs' attention when he scored twice for Edmonton Rovers on the White Hart Lane pitch in the final of the Tottenham Charity Cup in April 1905. He filled the outside-left berth for the rest of the season, but had few further chances. When Spurs signed Bert Middlemiss it was clear Whyman was no longer required. He was released and joined New Brompton, where he played for one season before moving to Queens Park Rangers. He gave Rangers great service, helping them win the Southern League title in 1911-12 and still turned out for them after the First World War making a total of over 200 appearances in their colours before retiring.

Appearances:
Southern: 18 apps. 1 gl.
Others: 16 apps. 8 gls
Total: 34 apps. 9 gls.

WILBERT, George Norman

Role: Outside-left 1939-40
5ft.9ins.
Born: Dunston, nr Newcastle-Upon-Tyne, 11th July 1924
Died: Alnwick, Northumberland, 10th September 1993

CAREER: SPURS ground-staff 1939/(guest for Gateshead and Portsmouth during World War Two)/Gateshead 1947-54.

Debut v Norwich City (FLS) (h) 27.5.1940

A member of Spurs' junior ground-staff, George Wilbert was only 15-years old when he made his one appearance for Spurs in the last Football League South game of the season against Norwich City in May 1940. That was not his first appearance in the competition though. He had played for Portsmouth against Spurs two weeks earlier when Portsmouth arrived for the game with only ten men. During the war Wilbert returned to his native North-East and played regularly for Gateshead proving to be a natural goal-scorer. He joined Gateshead permanently at the end of the war and scored 92 goals in 268 Football League games for them between 1947 and 1954. He quit football for a job with the Forestry Commission.

Appearances:
Others: 1 app.
Total: 1 app. 0 gls.

WILDING, Harry Thomas Oulton

Role: Centre-half 1928-29
6ft.1ins. 12st.12lbs.
Born: Wolverhampton, Staffordshire, 27th June 1894
Died: Earlsfield, London, 13th December 1958

CAREER: Grenadier Guards/ Chelsea Apr 1914/ (guest for Millwall during World War One)/**SPURS** Nov 1928/ Bristol Rovers Jul-Oct 1930/ Chelsea groundsman.

Debut v Clapton Orient (FL) (h) 3.11.1928

Harry Wilding joined Chelsea after impressing them whilst playing at centre-forward for the Grenadier Guards. He did not make their first team until after the First World War, during which he won the Military Medal, but once in the team played consistently for five years. Initially appearing at centre-forward, he soon dropped back to centre-half where his height and strength were put to best effect. An England international trialist in February 1923, Wilding was well past his best when signed by Spurs. After only twelve League games, he was out of the team. Surprisingly retained for the 1929-30 season, he did not make another first team appearance. Released in April 1930 he joined Bristol Rovers but did not make an appearance in their colours in the five months he was on their books before retiring.

Appearances:
Others: 12 apps. 1 gl.
Total: 12 apps. 1 gl.

WILKES, Frederick

Role: Full-back 1908-12
5ft.9 11st.7lbs.
Born: Bidford-On-Avon, Warwickshire, 26th August 1883
Died: Reading, Berkshire, 12th July 1942

CAREER: Reading am. Aug 1907, pro. Jan 1908/**SPURS** Feb 1909/Reading by Dec 1912, trainer cs. 1913-1921.

Debut v Gainsborough Trinity (FL) (h) 27.3.1909

Fred Wilkes joined Reading for the 1907-08 season after serving in the Royal Artillery. He had just established himself as first choice left-back when Spurs secured his transfer, paying a fee of £350 and guaranteeing takings of £100 for a friendly match to be played at Elm Park. Wilkes had to wait a month for a League debut, standing-in at right-back for Ernie Coquet and, by the end of the season had replaced Ollie Burton at left-back. For the next three years he competed with Burton, Coquet, Bert Elkin, Tom Collins and Tom Leslie for either of the full-back positions. With Collins establishing himself as first choice at right-back and Richard Brittan signed to play at left-back, Wilkes was allowed to return to Reading, where he became trainer.

Appearances:
League: 57 apps.
FA Cup: 3 apps.
Others: 12 apps.
Total: 72 apps. 0 gls.

WILKIE, Robert Mackintosh

Role: Winger 1956-57
5ft.10ins.
Born: Dundee, 7th October 1935

CAREER: Dundee Schools/East Craigie/Lochee Harps/Nottingham Forest am./Notts County am./**SPURS** Nov 1956/Romford Aug 1961/released Jun 1962.

Debut v Nottingham Forest (FL) (a) 29.4.1957

An amateur with both Nottingham Forest and Notts County during his National Service, Bob Wilkie signed for Spurs in November 1956. He played just one League game and made two appearances on the 1957 tour of the United States. Most of his time at White Hart Lane was spent in the Eastern Counties "A" team, and although he scored regularly at that level, he did not make the senior team again before being released.

Appearances:
League: 1 app.
Others: 1 (1) apps. 1 gl.
Total: 2 (1) apps. 1 gl.

WILKINSON, John William

Role: Full-back 1906-07
5ft.8ins. 12st.0lbs.
Born: Hucknall Torkard, Nottinghamshire, October 1882

CAREER: Hucknall White Star/Notts County am. Apr 1904, pro. May 1904/**SPURS** May 1906/released May 1907.

Debut v Luton Town (SL) (h) 25.3.1907

John Wilkinson was signed from Notts County, where he had been in the reserves for two years, on the recommendation of his former club-mate Walter Bull. He made only four appearances in his one season with Spurs, of which only two were in competitive matches, before being released.

Appearances:
Southern: 2 apps.
Total: 2 apps. 0 gls.

WILKINSON

Role: Outside-right 1894-95

Debut v Liverpool Casuals (Fr) (h) 12.4.1895 (scored once)

Wilkinson's only appearance for Spurs was in April 1895 when he scored once in a friendly match against Liverpool Casuals.

Appearances:
Others: 1 app. 1 gl.
Total: 1 app. 1 gl.

WILLIAMS, Charles Albert

Role: Goalkeeper 1902-05
5ft.11ins. 12st.3lbs.
Born: Welling, Kent, 19th November 1873
Died: Rio de Janeiro, Brazil, 1952

CAREER: Phoenix/Clarence/Erith/Royal Arsenal Nov 1891/Manchester City Jun 1894/**SPURS** May 1902/Norwich City Apr 1905/Brentford May 1906/Danish Olympic team coach Aug 1908/B93 (Denmark) coach/Olympique Lillois (France) manager Feb 1909/Le Havre (France) coach/Fluminese (Brazil) coach May 1911/Rio Grande de Sul (Brazil) trainer 1912/Botafogo (Brazil) coach 1929.

Debut v Millwall Athletic (WL) (h) 15.9.1902

Charlie Williams made more than 80 senior appearances in his three years with Arsenal, including their first Football League game, and then joined Manchester City on their formation from the remains of Ardwick FC. An unorthodox 'keeper, he helped City reach second place in the Second Division two years later, but they failed to gain promotion at the test match play-off stage then in operation. City were more successful in 1898-99 when they won the Second Division and were automatically promoted, by which time Williams had won his only senior representative honour, playing for the Football League against the Irish League in November 1897. At the end of 1901-02 City were relegated and Williams was released, joining Spurs as understudy to George Clawley. Williams had few opportunities in that first season, but when Clawley moved to Southampton in 1903 he became first choice. He maintained the role until October 1904 when he was displaced by John Eggett. At the end of the season Williams joined Norwich City, where he played for a year before finishing off his career with two years at Brentford. Williams later took to coaching and management and first worked with the Danish Olympic team leading them (one of only five entrants) to the 1908 Olympic Final where they lost to Great Britain. He later worked with the French clubs, Olympique Lillois and Le Havre and Brazilian outfit, Rio Grande de Sul. Williams settled in Rio and stayed for 40 years. On 14th April 1900, he scored for Manchester City at Sunderland when the wind caught one of his goal kicks and the opposing 'keeper fumbled the ball into the net.

Appearances:
Southern: 37 apps.
FA Cup: 5* apps.
Others: 38 apps.
Total: 80 apps. 0 gls.
*Includes 1 abandoned match.

WILLIAMS, Cyril Edward

Role: Outside-left 1941-42
Born: Bristol, 17th November 1921
Died: 21st January 1980

CAREER: Bristol Schools/Bristol City/(guest for Reading, SPURS and Swindon Town during World War Two)/West Bromwich Albion Jun 1948/Bristol City Aug 1951/Chippenham Town manager Jul 1958/Gloucester City manager Aug 1966.

Debut v Portsmouth (LWL) (a) 15.11.1941

A guest from Bristol City, Cyril Williams played three games for Spurs in the London War League in 1941-42. Although later recognised as an inside-forward all his appearances for Spurs were at outside-left. He left Bristol to join West Bromwich Albion in June 1948 and helped them to promotion from the Second Division in 1949. On returning to Bristol City he helped City win the Third Division title in 1955 and by the time he left in 1958 to take on the manager's job at Chippenham Town had taken his total of senior appearances for City to over 300. After Chippenham he was manager of Gloucester City.

Appearances:
Others: 3 apps.
Total: 3 apps. 0 gls.

WILLIAMS, F G

Role: Outside-left 1891-92

CAREER: Noel Park/(guest for SPURS Mar 1892).

Debut v Luton Town (Fr) (a) 26.3.1892

A Noel Park player, Williams made his one appearance for Spurs in a friendly with Luton Town in March 1892. He did not play for Spurs again, but continued to assist Noel Park and represented the Tottenham district side in an annual challenge match against Edmonton.

Appearances:
Others: 1 app.
Total: 1 app. 0 gls.

WILLIAMS

Role: Inside-forward 1888-89

Debut v St Albans (Fr) (a) 29.9.1888

Another of those players it has proved impossible to ascertain any information on, Williams made his one known appearance in a friendly in September 1888.

Appearances:
Others: 1 app.
Total: 1 app. 0 gls.

WILLIAMS, John Lewis James

Role: Centre-forward 1912-13
5ft.9ins. 11st.0lbs.
Born: Rhayader, Radnorshire, 15th January 1890
Died: Mold, Clwyd, 22nd October 1969

CAREER: Builth Wells/Nottingham Forest am. Mar 1912/Llandiloes/SPURS trial Aug 1912, pro. Aug 1912/released May 1913/Swansea Town Sep 1913-May 1924/Mold Town Jun 1925.

Debut v Crystal Palace (LFACC) (a) 11.11.1912

An amateur with Nottingham Forest in 1911-12 when he made four League appearances, Jack Williams arrived at White Hart Lane for a trial in August 1912. He played in a private trial match on the 8th of that month and was immediately offered and accepted professional terms. He was to play only one match in Spurs' first team, a London FA Charity Cup tie with Crystal Palace in November 1912, before being released at the end of the season. He returned to Wales with Swansea Town and impressed early on, standing by as reserve for Wales against Scotland in February 1914. After War service he returned to Swansea, moved into the half-back line and played regularly as Swansea took their first steps in the Football League. Released at the end of the 1923-24 season, it was a year before Williams signed for Mold.

Appearances:
Others: 1 app.
Total: 1 app. 0 gls.

WILLIAMS, T

Role: Left-back 1895-96

CAREER: SPURS Oct 1895.

Debut v Vampires (FAC) (a) 2.11.1895
(Ilford (Fr) (a) 19.10.1895)

Williams made three appearances in Spurs' first team during a month's trial in October-November 1895. Two of those games were friendlies with the last a second qualifying round FA Cup tie with Vampires. Spurs lost the match 2-4, but then complained the pitch had been wrongly marked out and a replay was ordered. Spurs won the replay and went on to reach the First Round proper of the competition for the first time. The left-back position was proving a problem for Spurs at the time with Jack Jull unavailable, and several players were tried out before Jock Montgomery was signed in January 1896. At the end of his trial, Williams, who usually played at right-back, was not offered terms.

Appearances:
FA Cup: 1 app.
Others: 2 apps.
Total: 3 apps. 0 gls.

WILLIAMSON, Ernest Charles

Role: Goalkeeper 1916-17
Born: Murton Colliery, County Durham, 24th May 1890
Died: Norwich, Norfolk, 30th April 1964

CAREER: Murton Red Star/Wingate Albion/Croydon Common Jun 1913/Arsenal cs. 1916/(Guest for **SPURS** during World War One)/Norwich City Jul 1923/retired May 1925.

Debut v Portsmouth (LFC) (h) 10.4.1917

"Tim" Williamson was on the books of Arsenal when he made his one appearance for Spurs in a London Football Combination game in April 1917. It was an expensive guest appearance for Spurs as they were fined five guineas for playing him in the match. Williamson had no match fixed up for that day and it was known during the week that Spurs' regular keeper Bill Jacques was unlikely to be available. Spurs told Williamson they might be able to find a place for him and he arrived at the ground ready to play. Jacques was not able to appear and Spurs were unable to find anybody else to fill his place. No Spurs' director arrived at the ground until ten minutes before kick-off, but when they went to seek Arsenal's permission for Williamson to turn out no Arsenal official could be found. They therefore decided to take the risk of fielding Williamson confident Arsenal would not object. They were wrong. Arsenal complained to the London Football Combination and Spurs were found guilty of playing a player from another club without that club's permission. Williamson had moved into the professional ranks with Croydon Common. When they suspended operations after one season of War-time football, Williamson joined Arsenal for the start of the 1916-17 season, even though he had previously agreed to play for Millwall. He developed rapidly during the war years and played for England against Wales in one of the Victory internationals of October 1919. After the war he remained with Arsenal, their regular 'keeper for three years from 1920. He collected two full international caps against Sweden in May 1923, even though he was out of favour at Highbury at the time. A month after those internationals Williamson moved to Norwich City and whilst on their books played cricket for Norfolk, not surprisingly perhaps as wicketkeeper. After two years with Norwich he retired to become a publican.

Appearances:
Others: 1 app.
Total: 1 app. 0 gls.

WILLIS, Arthur

Role: Full-back 1942-54
5ft.7ins. 11st.5lbs.
Born: Denaby Main, Northumberland, 2nd February 1920
Died: Haverfordwest, Pembrokeshire, 7th November 1987

CAREER: SPURS am. 1938/Northfleet United 1939/Finchley/**SPURS** pro. Jan 1944/(guest for Millwall during World War Two)/Swansea Town Sep 1954, player-coach Aug 1956/Haverfordwest player-manager Oct 1960.

Debut v Brentford (FAC) (h) 5.1.1946
(Charlton Athletic (Fr) (h) 24.4.1943)

Arthur Willis was working as a miner when offered the chance of a football career by Barnsley, Sunderland and Spurs. He chose to join Spurs amateur staff and went along to the Northfleet nursery, but in 1940 was strongly advised to give up the game because of duodenal ulcers. He did so, working in an aircraft factory, but still hanging around White Hart Lane. Eventually Spurs fixed him up to play with Finchley and he made his Spurs' debut during the war. His medical problems were not over though and on one occasion he was rushed to hospital in Sheffield only just in time. With the war over he signed professional and played regularly in one of the full-back positions until September 1947 when he lost his right-back place to Sid Tickridge. Again afflicted by ulcers that restricted his first team appearances he did not get back in the team until the last two matches of the 1949-50 season, playing at left-back in place of Charlie Withers. Willis took over the position regularly the next season, finishing with a League Championship medal as part of the famous "Push and Run" side, and then collected an England cap against France in October 1951. Quick, neat and studious, Willis was a good footballing full-back, but very similar to Withers. Frankly, there was little to choose between the two of them. Over the next three seasons they continually vied with each other for the first team position and played roughly half the League games each, until Willis left to follow Ron Burgess to Swansea Town. By that stage anyway, young Mel Hopkins had usurped both Willis and Withers for the place in the team. Willis played for Swansea for four years, helping them to the Welsh Cup Final in 1956, and was later on their coaching staff, before taking over as player-manager of Haverfordwest in the Welsh League. At one time Willis' brother, Annis, was on Spurs' books.

Appearances:
League: 145* apps. 1 gl.
FA Cup: 16 apps.
Others: 111 apps. 1 gl.
Total: 272 apps. 2 gls.
*Includes 1 abandoned match.

WILSON, Archibald

Role: Outside-left 1915-16
5ft.7ins. 10st.6lbs.
Born: Cambuslang, Ayrshire, 1890
Died: Somme, Belgium, 1st July 1916
(Killed in action)

CAREER: Newmilns/Nottingham Forest/**SPURS** Dec 1909/Southend United Mar 1911/Middlesbrough Jul 1914/(guest for Southend United and **SPURS** during World War One).

Debut v West Ham United (LFC) (h) 27.11.1915

Having won junior representative honours back home in Scotland, Archie Wilson spent two years in Nottingham before joining Spurs' junior staff. The club felt he was unlikely to make the grade and towards the end of the 1910-11 season he was allowed to move to Southend United. Given the opportunity of regular first team football, he developed well and was transferred to Middlesbrough where he began to establish himself as a winger of some ability. With the outbreak of war, he joined the London Scottish regiment, represented his Battalion and returned to play for Spurs as a guest in the London Football Combination. He made a total of ten appearances before returning to the front and making the supreme sacrifice.

Appearances:
Others: 10 apps.
Total: 10 apps. 0 gls.

WILSON, Charles

Role: Centre-forward 1918-23
5ft.9ins. 12st.0lbs.
Born: Atherstone, Derbyshire, 30th March 1895
Died: Atherstone, Derbyshire, 1971

CAREER: Coventry City/**SPURS** Apr 1919/Huddersfield Town Nov 1922/Stoke City Mar 1926/Stafford Rangers Jun 1931.

Debut v South Shields (FL) (a) 20.9.1919 (scored three)
(Queens Park Rangers (LFC) (h) 12.4.1919)

Charlie Wilson made his name playing services football in the First World War during which time he signed for Coventry City. He did not play for Coventry, but Spurs had seen and heard enough from service contacts to sign him in April 1919, the first signing as they prepared for the return to normal football. Although Wilson scored a hat-trick on his League debut, he spent the whole of his first full season as reserve to Jimmy Cantrell, but his seven goals in twelve games certainly helped Spurs run away with the Second Division title. With Cantrell coming to the end of his career, Wilson competed with Alex Lindsay for the next two years to establish himself as Cantrell's successor, but when Herbert Chapman's Huddersfield Town sought his transfer, Spurs decided to let him go. Top scorer as Huddersfield won the League title in 1924 and 1925, he was left out as they moved towards a third successive title and when Huddersfield announced they were prepared to release him, Stoke City were quick to move in. He could not save Stoke from relegation, but the following season, 1926-27, top scored as they won the Third Division (North). In all he was Stoke's leading scorer in four of his five full seasons with them before retiring. Wilson was one of the most prolific scorers during the inter-war period. Apart from his 27 goals in 55 League appearances for Spurs, he scored 57 in 99 for Huddersfield and 110 in 156 for Stoke. He later became a publican in Stafford. Wilson played six matches for Spurs in the 1918-19 season. In four of them he used the pseudonym "C Williams" (being described as "a colt from the Midlands"), in another the pseudonym "Forshaw" and in only one did he use his own name.

Appearances:
League: 55 apps. 27 gls.
FA Cup: 7 apps. 6 gls.
Others: 18 apps. 15 gls.
Total: 80 apps. 48 gls.

WILSON, Euclid Aklana

Role: Full back or midfield 1995-99
5ft.7ins. 11st.11lbs.
Born: Rusholme, Manchester, 13th November 1961

CAREER: Moss Side Amateurs/Manchester City non-contract Oct 1979, pro. Dec 1979/(Chester loan Sep 1982)/Chelsea Mar 1987/(Manchester City loan Mar 1987)/Queens Park Rangers Jul 1990/**SPURS** Jun 1995-May 1999/Cambridge United trial Jul 1999, perm. Aug 1999-May 2000/Wingate and Finchley player-coach Jun 2000-Dec 2002.

Debut v Liverpool (PL) (h) 26.8.1995
(Derby County (sub) (Fr) (a) 2.8.1995)

Gerry Francis was a manager who liked to have players around him he knew and trusted. After three years managing Clive Wilson at Queens Park Rangers he knew the former Manchester City and Chelsea midfielder was a dependable character who could still do a good job in Premiership football even though he was 34. As he was at college studying electrical engineering when Manchester City first approached him, Wilson did not follow the usual apprentice to professional route. Rather, he signed as a non-contract player while continuing his studies. He slowly established himself at Maine Road, an all-action midfielder, often operating out wide, with a good cross and long-range shot. As City yo-yoed between the First and Second Divisions, Wilson made a midfield place his own, before signing for Chelsea. The move was delayed as City, unsuccessfully, fought relegation. In his three years with Chelsea as they followed Manchester City with relegation then promotion, Wilson performed competently enough without ever reaching the heights his early career had promised. He moved to Queens Park Rangers in the summer of 1990 and continued to perform in midfield in his first season there. However, when Gerry Francis took over as manager he recognised that Wilson's experience, coolness under pressure and precision passing made him ideally suited to the left-back role. At White Hart Lane Wilson did a fine job for two years, usually playing at the back but often pushed into midfield. As age at last began to affect his performances he slipped down the pecking order and was released in the summer of 1999. He played for a year at Cambridge United then played and managed Wingate and Finchley. Since losing his position there, he has become a PE teacher.

Appearances:
League: 67 (3) apps. 1 gl.
FA Cup: 8* (1) apps. 1 gl.
FL Cup: 7 (1) apps.
Others: 2 (6) apps.
Total: 84 (11) apps. 2 gls.
*Includes 1 abandoned match

WILSON, Frank

Role: Centre-forward 1896-97
Born: 1875
Died: June 1898

CAREER: Bishop Auckland/Aston Villa cs. 1895/Gravesend United cs. 1896/**SPURS** Mar 1897/Blackpool May 1897.

Debut v Reading (SL) (h) 20.3.1897 (scored once)

A winger with Bishop Auckland, Frank Wilson spent only nine months with Aston Villa without breaking into the first team before moving to Spurs in March 1897. Playing at centre-forward, he quickly settled in, scoring five goals in only ten games, but within a month of signing was suspended. He, Jimmy Milliken, Ed Devlin and Rob McElhaney, were all guilty of "acts of insubordination" and paid the penalty. Wilson was released at the end of the season without playing for the first team again and joined Blackpool. He played regularly for Blackpool the following season, but during the 1898 close season he died from "maniacal exhaustion caused by football and excitement".

Appearances:
Southern: 5 apps. 3 gls.
Others: 5 apps. 2 gls.
Total: 10 apps. 5 gls.

WILSON, Joseph Alexander

Role: Inside-forward 1943-44
Born: West Wylam, Northumberland, 23rd March 1909
Died: Portslade, East Sussex, 3rd April 1984

CAREER: Spen Black & White/Winlaton Celtic/Tanfield Lea Institute/Newcastle United am. May 1933, pro. Sep 1933/Brighton and Hove Albion May 1936/(guest for Aldershot, Fulham, Reading and **SPURS** during World War Two)/Brighton and Hove Albion asst. trainer cs. 1947, trainer 1952, asst. manager, caretaker manager Feb-Apr 1963, scout.

Debut v Arsenal (FLS) (a) 22.4.1944

Joe Wilson was a guest player from Brighton and Hove Albion who played his only match for Spurs in the Football League South against Arsenal in April 1944. At the time he was serving as a Physical Training Instructor in the Army. A small but tricky inside-forward, he had moved to Brighton in the summer of 1936 from Newcastle United. He played for Brighton throughout the War and when it was over concluded his career with one further season on the Sussex coast, taking his number of appearances for the club over the 300 mark. He later joined the coaching staff and assisted at all levels, even as caretaker manager. All told, he gave Albion a total of 38 years' service.

Appearances:
Others: 1 app.
Total: 1 app. 0 gls.

WIMMER, Kevin

Role: Defender 2015-
6ft.2ins. 15st. 12lbs.
Born: Weis, Austria, 15th November 1992

CAREER: FC Edt (Austria) 1998/Fußballakademie Linz (Austria) 2000/LASK Linz (Austria) 2010/1FC Köln (Germany) Jun 2012/**SPURS** May 2015.

Debut v Qarabag (EL) (h) 17.9.2015
(MLS All-Stars (Fr) (a) (sub) 29.7.2015)

A big, powerful Austrian international with one full cap to his name, Kevin Wimmer was signed to add a bit of the muscular solidarity to a Spurs' defence that Younès Kaboul and Federico Fazio had failed to provide. Wimmer had been plucked from the second tier of Austrian football by 1FC Köln, themselves a second tier club in Germany. In his first season, he helped Köln return to the Bundesliga and then established a reputation as a solid, commanding and dependable defender. After signing for Spurs, the club acquired the services of Toby Alderweireld. He and Jan Vertonghen had played together at Ajax and for Belgium so it was no surprise they became the favoured central defensive pairing. Wimmer spent most of his first season on the bench, but when Vertonghen was injured he stepped in and did such a fine job alongside Alderweireld that Vertonghen's absence was barely noticed. A member of the Austrian squad at Euro 2016, there is nothing fancy about Wimmer. He is a defender whose only concern is to stop the opposition from scoring.

Appearances:
League: 13 (2) apps.
FA Cup: 6 apps.
FL Cup: 3 apps.
Euro: 7 apps.
Others: 2 (2) apps.
Total: 31 (4) apps. 0 gls.

WINKS, Harry

Role: Midfielder 2014-
5ft. 9ins. 11st. 8lbs
Born: Hemel Hempstead, Hertfordshire, 2nd February 1996

CAREER: SPURS Academy Scholar Jul 2012, pro. Jul 2014.

Debut v Qarabag (EL) (h) (sub) 17.9.2015
(Malaysia FA XI (Fr) (a) 27.5.2015)

Having graduated from the Spurs Academy to make his mark at White Hart Lane, Harry Winks is one of those players who should benefit immensely from the opportunity to play regularly for a season at Wembley while a new stadium rises in North London. An England international at youth levels, he had played in barely a dozen senior games before winning his first Under-21 cap. A busy, little midfielder, with an abundance of class, neat control and simple, incisive passing, Winks was very much in the style of Tom Carroll. It was his progress through the ranks and the fact he appears more physically suited to top flight football meant Spurs were able to let Carroll leave knowing a more than adequate replacement was coming through. The fierce competition for attacking midfield positions at Spurs does not make it easy for any player to establish himself, but Winks certainly has the ability, determination and attitude to hold down a regular spot.

Appearances:
League: 3 (18) apps. 1 gl.
FA Cup: 4 apps.
FL Cup: 2 apps.
Euro: 3 (6) apps.
Others: 2 (6) apps.
Total: 14 (30) apps. 0 gls.

WITHERS, Charles Francis

Role: Full-back 1947-56
5ft.7ins. 10st.12lbs.
Born: Edmonton, London, 6th September 1922
Died: Bovey Tracy, Devon, 7th June 2005

CAREER: Edmonton Schools/London Schools/Middlesex Schools/**SPURS** am. 1938/Tottenham Juniors/(Finchley)/**SPURS** pro. Oct 1947/Finchley coach Nov 1957/Boston United Jun 1958/Romford Jun 1961/Deal/Edmonton manager.

Debut v Barnsley (FL) (h) 15.3.1948

After joining Spurs' ground-staff as an amateur, England Schools trialist Charlie Withers played for the Tottenham Juniors and then went to Finchley, where he appeared until joining the services for the Second World War. On his demob in July 1947 he returned to Spurs, signed professional and made his League debut in March 1948, taking over the left-back position from Vic Buckingham midway through the following season. A powerful, resolute defender famed for his sliding tackle and speed of recovery, he played in all bar the last two matches of the 1949-50 Second Division Championship season, his calm football brain an asset to the Spurs style and tactics which put extra demands on full backs. Unfortunately, Withers lost out to Arthur Willis the following year, and consequently missed out on a "Push and Run" side League Championship medal. Thereafter he and Willis disputed the left-back position until Willis left to join Swansea Town. By then, Mel Hopkins had come through from the juniors to take the place. Withers then moved to right-back when Alf Ramsey left for Ipswich Town, but, with the arrival of Maurice Norman, found himself in the reserves. Withers remained at Spurs until the summer of 1958 when he moved to Boston United. He later played for Romford and Deal and managed Athenian League Edmonton. The only representative honour Withers collected was in March 1952 when he played for England "B" against Holland. He later worked as a messenger for the Enfield Highway branch of Barclays Bank. In over 200 appearances for Spurs Withers scored only two goals and the circumstances of those were unusual. For the FA Cup 4th round tie with Preston North End in January 1953 Spurs had an injury crisis. Withers was pressed into service as an emergency left winger and responded with both Spurs' goals in a 2-2 draw.

Appearances:
League: 153 apps.
FA Cup: 11 apps. 2 gls.
Others: 37 apps. (3) apps.
Total: 201 (3) apps. 2 gls.

WOOD F

Role: Goalkeeper 1893-94

Debut v London Hospital (Fr) (h) 8.2.1894

A corporal in the 2nd Scots Guards and a regular in representative matches for the Army, Wood played his only game for Spurs in February 1894 in a friendly against the London Hospital. He received many offers to make football a full-time career, but preferred to remain in the Army, although he did play as a guest for several clubs including Millwall.

Appearances:
Others: 1 app.
Total: 1 app. 0 gls.

WOOD, Norman Arthur

Role: Inside-forward 1908-09
Born: Tooting, London, 1890
Died: Delville Wood, France, 28th July 1916 (killed in action)

CAREER: Bromley/**SPURS** Jun 1908/Crystal Palace May 1909/Plymouth Argyle Jul 1910/Croydon Common cs. 1911/Chelsea Mar 1912/Stockport County Jun 1913/Stalybridge Celtic Mar 1915.

Debut v Queens Park Rangers (LFACC) (h) 5.10.1908

A young inside-forward spotted by Spurs playing for Bromley and the London representative team, Norman Wood spent a year at White Hart Lane making just the one first team appearance. At the end of his one season he moved to Crystal Palace, played one first team game there and double that number in a year with Plymouth. Croydon Common probably got the best out of Wood with 18 goals in 37 appearances. He certainly did well enough to earn a move to Chelsea, but he barely played a game for them. He did, at least, become a regular for Stockport County. Wood was one of the earliest to enlist in the Footballers' Battalion, and one of the first footballers to make the ultimate sacrifice.

Appearances:
Others: 1 app.
Total: 1 app. 0 gls.

WOODGATE, Jonathan

Role: Central Defender 2007-11
6ft 2ins, 12st. 8lbs.
Born: Middlesbrough, Teesside, 22nd January 1980,

CAREER: Nunthorpe Athletic/Leeds United trainee Jul 1996, pro. May 1997/Newcastle United Jan 2003/Real Madrid (Spain) Aug 2004/Middlesbrough loan Aug 2006, perm. Apr 2007/**SPURS** Jan 2008/Stoke City Jul 2011/Middlesbrough Jul 2012/retired May 2016/Leeds United scout, Middlesbrough first team coach Mar 2017.

Debut v Everton (PL) (a) 30.1.2008

There cannot be many players who have had as long and successful a top-flight career as Jonathan Woodgate, yet wonder how much more they may have achieved were it not for persistent injuries. Possibly the cream of the home-grown talent produced by Leeds United in the late 1990s/early 2000s, he was a classy central defender, powerful in the air, a good man-marker with superb positional sense and a natural athleticism. At the age of 18 he was competing with experienced professionals like Rio Ferdinand, Michael Duberry and Lucas Radebe, for a place in a team challenging at the top of the Premier League and in European competition, Leeds seemed set to remain at the peak of British football until a failure to qualify for Europe's top competition exposed a financial mess. Selling its best players was the only way Leeds could survive and Woodgate was one of the most marketable players on the books. Despite the fact niggling injuries had often held him back, Newcastle United were just one of several clubs prepared to invest heavily in his talents. £9 million secured his transfer and for most of the 2003-04 season it looked to have ensured Newcastle's entry into the Champions League.

However, injury put Woodgate out of the last few games and Newcastle only qualified for the UEFA Cup. Real Madrid had seen enough of Woodgate and even though he was on the injured list, paid out some £13 million to sign him. He had an awful two years in Madrid, injured practically all the time and making only a handful of appearances. When the Spaniards decided to cut their losses Woodgate joined the home town club he had played for as a schoolboy, Middlesbrough, on a season's loan. He appeared to have all but overcome his injury problems, playing almost every game and doing well enough to have the transfer made permanent. Juande Ramos recognised soon after replacing Martin Jol that with Ledley King suffering the persistent injury problems that were to restrict his career, Michael Dawson and Younès Kaboul were not the defensive pairing Spurs needed. Woodgate was seen as the answer and £8 million was paid to bring him to White Hart Lane. In only his fifth game for Spurs he scored the winner in the Worthington Cup final against Chelsea to collect the only trophy he has won in his career. For a season-and-a-half, Woodgate settled well in the centre of defence, rarely absent and looking a class act. Sadly, a groin injury was followed by complications and more problems. In two seasons he was hardly seen and at the end of the 2010-11 season he was released. Stoke City took a chance with him on a pay-as-you-play basis, but after a poor season when he played too often out of position at full-back, he returned to Middlesbrough. For a couple of years, he proved an inspiration, but injuries returned and in May 2016 he was released. Woodgate won eight full England caps, a mediocre return for a man who at times was the best central defender in the country.

Appearances:
League: 49 apps. 2 gls.
FA Cup: 1 app.
FL Cup: 5 apps. 1 gl.
Euro: 9 (1) apps.
Others: 3 apps.
Total: 67 (1) apps. 3 gls.

WOODGER, George

Role: Winger 1914-15
Born: Croydon, Surrey, 3rd September 1884
Died: Croydon, Surrey, 6th March 1961

CAREER: Thornton Heath Wednesday/Croydon Glenrose/Croydon Wanderers/Crystal Palace am. 1905, pro. May 1906/Oldham Athletic Oct 1910/**SPURS** May 1914.

Debut v Arsenal (WRF) (h) 22.8.1914

Nicknamed "Lady" because of the daintiness of his play, former England international George Woodger joined Spurs in May 1914, but despite the fact Spurs were decimated by the call to arms and always struggling near the bottom of the table, he never played a competitive game. As a young man he was a regular for Surrey, joined Crystal Palace on their formation and proved to be a consistent scoring winger. Within four months of his transfer to Oldham he won his first, and only, cap playing against Ireland in February 1911. Towards the end of the 1913-14 season he lost his place and at the end of the season was released to join Spurs. He made only two appearances for Spurs, against Arsenal in the War Relief Fund match in August 1914, and in a friendly in February 1915. He retired from football during the War.

Appearances:
Others: 2 apps.
Total: 2 apps. 0 gls.

WOODLEY, Victor Robert

Role: Goalkeeper 1939-40
Born: Cippenham, Berkshire, 26th February 1911
Died: Bradford on Avon, 23rd October 1978

CAREER: Cippenham/Reading am./Windsor and Eton cs. 1930/Aldershot trial/Chelsea May 1931/(guest for Brentford, Brighton and Hove Albion and **SPURS** during World War Two)/Bath City Dec 1945/ Derby County Mar 1946/ Bath City May 1947, player-manager till May 1949.

Debut v Fulham (FLS) (h) 10.4.1940

Vic Woodley was spotted by Chelsea and Aldershot playing for the Athenian League against Berks and Bucks in 1931 and offered a trial by both clubs. He chose Chelsea, made his League debut in August 1932 and was so impressive that he soon replaced Chelsea's Scottish international keeper,

Jakey Jackson. He played four times for the Football League in 1937 and 1938, won his first England cap against Scotland in April 1937, played in the last 19 internationals before the Second World War and continued to appear in the wartime and Victory internationals. His one appearance for Spurs was made in a Football League South match against Fulham in April 1940. A member of Chelsea's Football League (South) Cup Final team of 1944, when he was released he joined Bath City, but within weeks had been persuaded to return to top flight football with Derby County. A member of Derby's 1946 FA Cup winning team he stayed with Derby for the following season, but then did finish with League football. He went back to Bath City, where he later became player/manager.

Appearances:
Others: 1 app.
Total: **1 app. 0 gls.**

WOODRUFF, Charles Lewis

Role: Winger 1907-10
5ft.8ins. 11st.7lbs.
Born: Grantham, Lincolnshire, 19th January 1884
Died: Grantham, Lincolnshire, 17th July 1943

CAREER: Grantham Avenue/**SPURS** Mar 1908/Doncaster Rovers Aug 1910/Grantham cs. 1913.

Debut v Leyton (SL) (a) 28.3.1908 (scored twice)

Charlie Woodruff joined Spurs from Midland League Grantham Avenue and went straight in the team to score twice on his debut against Leyton. With Spurs' elevation to the Football League at the end of 1907-08 he was perhaps a little too inexperienced, but Spurs kept him on for two years as cover for Joe Walton and John Curtis. A fast winger with a good, accurate centre, he was neither as tricky as Walton nor as direct as Curtis, but when called upon certainly never let the team down. Released in the summer of 1910 he moved back to the Midland League with Doncaster Rovers.

Appearances:
Southern: 5 apps. 3 gls.
League: 10 apps. 1 gl.
Others: 4 apps.
Total: **19 apps. 4 gls.**

WOODS, Alan Edward

Role: Half-back 1954-55
5ft.8ins. 11st.4lbs.
Born: Dinnington, Yorkshire. 15th February 1937

CAREER: England Schools/**SPURS** am Jun 1952, pro. Feb 1954/Swansea Town Dec 1956/York City Jul 1960/retired May 1966/Boston United/Gainsborough Trinity/Bridlington.

Debut v Manchester United (FL) (h) 8.9.1954

England Youth international Alan Woods worked his way through the junior ranks at White Hart Lane to make his League debut in September 1954. He was one of two wing-halves manager Arthur Rowe used to try and replace Bill Nicholson-the other being Ralph Wetton. Woods made six League appearances that season, but neither he nor Wetton were successful, and Nicholson was recalled until the arrival in December 1954 of Danny Blanchflower. Woods remained with Spurs for another two years until joining former colleagues Ron Burgess and Arthur Willis at Swansea Town, but had little more success in Wales. It was only when he joined York City that he found a regular League place. Hard-working and consistent, he made 228 League appearances in six years until his retirement, helping York win promotion to the Third Division in 1965.

Woods remained in York when his playing days were over and became a dairyman. His son, Neil, was a forward with Doncaster Rovers, Glasgow Rangers and Ipswich Town in the early 1980's and later played for Grimsby Town.

Appearances:
League: 6 apps.
Others: (1) app.
Total: **6 (1) apps. 0 gls.**

WOODWARD, Horace John

Role: Centre-half 1941-49
5ft.10ins. 11st.11lbs.
Born: Islington, London, 16th January 1924
Died: Cricklewood, London, 3rd August 2002

CAREER: Tottenham Juniors/**SPURS** am. Mar 1939/(Finchley)/**SPURS** pro. May 1946/Queens Park Rangers Jun 1949/Tonbridge Jul 1951/Snowdon Colliery Welfare/Walsall Jul 1953/Stourbridge/Horsham player-manager/Willesden manager/Kingsbury Town manager 1966-1971/Maccabi manager.

Debut v Newport County (FL) (a) 19.9.1946
(Queens Park Rangers (LWL) (h) 27.9.1941)

Johnny Woodward joined the Tottenham Juniors straight from school, signed amateur, and played for the Juniors until the start of the 1941-42 season when he was sent to Finchley. Originally a centre-forward, he made his Spurs' debut as a 17-year old in the number nine shirt in a London War League game in September 1941. He was not called upon again during the war, although he continued to turn out for Finchley and played regularly in Services football. It was whilst serving in the Royal Navy that he was converted to centre-half and on his demob in May 1946 he signed as a professional. He made his League debut in September 1946 and with Bill Nicholson switching to right-half, was

the regular centre-half the next season. Woodward lost his first team position with the arrival of Harry Clarke, and was released in May 1949, joining Queens Park Rangers. After two years at Loftus Road he went to Southern League Tonbridge and then Snowdon Colliery before returning for a short spell in the League with Walsall. He finished his career with Stourbridge and then went into management in non-League circles. Woodward later worked as a bus driver for the British Oxygen Company.

Appearances:
League: 63 apps. 1 gl.
FA Cup: 4 apps.
Others: 9 apps. 1 gl.
Total: 76 apps. 2 gls.

WOODWARD, Vivian John

Role: Centre-forward 1900-09
5ft.11ins. 11st.0lbs.
Born: Kennington, London, 3rd June 1879
Died: Ealing, London, 31st January 1954

CAREER: Ascham College/Clacton Town Dec 1895/Colchester Town/Harwich & Parkeston/Chelmsford/**SPURS** Mar 1901, director Jun 1907-Jul 1909/retired May 1909/Chelmsford Aug 1909/Chelsea Nov 1909/retired May 1915/Clacton Town 1919-20/Chelsea director 1922-1930.

Debut v Bristol City (SL) (h) 6.4.1901

Vivian J Woodward was the epitome of everything that was good in football in the early years of the 20th century and one of the finest players of his generation. An architect by profession, he played at the highest levels but remained a true amateur throughout his career, a gentleman in every sense of the word. He started playing football while at Ascham College in Clacton and then played for Clacton and Harwich & Parkeston before joining Chelmsford City. In 1901 he first accepted the invitation to play for Spurs. Initially his appearances were limited by business commitments and his desire not to let down Chelmsford or Essex, who relied greatly on his cultured skills. It was only in 1902-03 that he began to play regularly for Spurs. By the end of the season he had made his first appearance for the full England team, scoring twice against Ireland in February 1903. He went on to score 28 goals in 23 appearances (21 of them as a Spurs player) for the full England team and also played 67 amateur internationals for England and the Great Britain, captaining the teams that won the Olympics in 1908 and 1912. A director of Spurs, he scored the club's first League goal and was top scorer in the team that won promotion to Division One at the first attempt in 1909. He would have played many more games for Spurs than he did, had he not been in such widespread demand to display his talents. For instance, in 1905 he played for "The Pilgrims" on a tour of the United States which meant he was not available for Spurs until the November. In addition to his international honours he turned out twice for the Football League and was selected for many minor representative honours. A tall, elegant, player Woodward relied on pure skill in an age when centre-forward play was invariably dominated by the big, bustling player whose main weapon was brute strength. Such crudities were not in Woodward's repertoire. He preferred to bring his team-mates into the game, but was quite prepared to dribble half the length of the field if necessary, before finishing with an accurately placed shot. "Woodward has the power of thinking with his legs" was how a contemporary described him, and he was certainly a player who relied on brains rather than brawn. Vastly respected by team-mates and opponents alike, he was often referred to as "Sir", not only by other players, but also by officials. A superb all-round sportsman; he played good class cricket with Spencer Cricket Club and competitive tennis, he surprised not only Spurs but the whole football world when, in 1909, he announced his retirement from the top level of the game in order to play again for Chelmsford. However, that was nothing compared to the shock Spurs received in November 1909 when Woodward suddenly returned again to League football-with Chelsea! He remained with Chelsea until the First World War and later served them as a director. He never won any major domestic honour in the game, although he had the opportunity to do so. When Chelsea reached the FA Cup Final in 1915, he was given leave from the Army especially so he could play. That would have meant him replacing Bob Thomson, whose goals had got Chelsea to the Final. It was no surprise that Woodward's traditional amateur spirit surfaced; he did not think that would be right and refused the chance to play. An architect for most of his life, he later became a gentleman farmer. All told, Woodward captained the full England team thirteen times during his career.

Appearances:
Southern: 104 apps. 45 gls.
League: 27 apps. 18 gls.
FA Cup: 24* apps. 5 gls.
Others: 38 apps. 28 gls.
Total: 1   93 apps. 96 gls.
*Includes 1 abandoned match.

WOOLCOTT, Roy Alfred

Role: Centre-forward 1969-70
6ft.3ins. 13st.7lbs.
Born: Leyton, London, 29th July 1946

CAREER: Eton Manor/**SPURS** am. Dec 1967, pro. Feb 1968/(Gillingham loan Feb 1972)/Chelmsford City Jul 1972-May 1974/Folkestone Aug 1975.

Debut v Ipswich Town (FL) (a) 7.12.1969

Roy Woolcott was a regular goal-scorer for the reserves, but was unfortunate to be with Spurs at the same time as Martin Chivers and Alan Gilzean. Chivers, in particular, was at his peak, and this limited Woolcott to only one Football League appearance. Five goals in 13 games while on loan to Gillingham showed Woolcott had the ability to make it in League football, but when he was allowed to leave in the summer of 1972, it was to join Chelmsford City.

Appearances:
League: 1 app.
Total: 1 app. 0 gls.

WORLEY, Leonard Francis

Role: Winger 1959-60
Born: Chalfont-St-Peters, Buckinghamshire, 29th June 1937

CAREER: Chalfont Youth Club/Chalfont St Peter/Wycombe Wanderers cs. 1954/Charlton Athletic am. Oct 1956/Wycombe Wanderers/**SPURS** am. May 1959/Chesham United/Wealdstone/Slough Town Mar-Apr 1970/Hayes Aug 1970/Chalfont.

Debut v Sheffield Wednesday (FL) (a) 17.10.1959

An England Youth and amateur international, Len Worley's trickery and crossing ability had him known as the Stanley Matthews of post-war amateur football. Having previously played one League game for Charlton Athletic, he signed amateur forms for Spurs whilst playing for Wycombe Wanderers. He gave the Buckinghamshire club tremendous service over some 15 years, helping them win the Isthmian League in 1956 and 1957 and reach the FA Amateur Cup Final in 1957. All told he made more than 500 appearances for Wycombe, quite incredible when it is remembered that he twice suffered a broken leg, in April 1957 and June 1967. His only League appearance for Spurs was against Sheffield Wednesday in October 1959 when he stood in for Terry Medwin who was on international duty for Wales against England. Worley collected 8 amateur caps, one of them when registered with Spurs, and also played for the Great Britain Olympic team. After football, Worley was involved in property development.

Appearances:
League: 1 app.
Total: 1 app. 0 gls.

WORRALL, John Edwin

Role: Full-back 1918-19
5ft 10ins, 12st.0lbs.

Born: Buxton, Derbyshire, 2nd October 1891
Died: Chesterfield, Derbyshire, 24th September 1980

CAREER: Buxton College/The Comrades (Buxton) 1908/Sheffield Wednesday Mar 1909/(guest for Chelsea and **SPURS** during World War One)/Fulham Jun 1919/Aberdare Athletic Jun 1923/Watford Jan 1925/New Brighton Jun 1925/Southport May 1927/Shirebrook Jul 1929/Gresley Rovers Aug 1930/Ripley Town May 1931/Buxton College coach/Derbyshire Schools FA coach/**SPURS** scout.

Debut v Clapton Orient (LFC) (a) 23.11.1918

Ted Worrall had been Sheffield Wednesday's regular right-back prior to the First World War and was still on their books when he played eleven games for Spurs in the London Football Combination during the 1918-19 season. After the war he was transferred to Fulham and for four years formed the full-back partnership with Alec Chaplin, who had also played for Spurs during the war. Worrall added considerably to his total League appearances while at Aberdare and New Brighton, while also playing for Watford and Southport, before winding down his career. He later turned to coaching and for a time was on Spurs' scouting staff.

Appearances:
Others: 11 apps.
Total: 11 apps. 0 gls.

WREN, George C

Role: Goalkeeper 1917-18

Debut v Fulham (LFC) (a) 27.4.1918

A young man from Wood Green, George Wren played for Spurs in a London Football Combination match against Fulham in April 1918. Although he later signed for the club he did not make any further senior appearances.

Appearances:
Others: 1 app.
Total: 1 app. 0 gls.

WRIGHT, Alexander Mason

Role: Centre-forward 1950-51
5ft.9ins. 11st.9lbs.
Born: Kirkcaldy, Fifeshire, 18th October 1925

CAREER: Bowhill Rovers/Hibernian Aug 1945/Barnsley Aug 1947/**SPURS** Sep 1950/Bradford Park Avenue Aug 1951/Falkirk Aug 1955-1959.

Debut v Chelsea (FL) (h) 3.3.1951 (scored once)

Top scorer for Barnsley in 1949-50, Alex Wright was a £12,000 buy who had less than one year with Spurs, competing with Sid McLellan to provide cover for Len Duquemin. At the time Duquemin was at his peak and Spurs were poised for their first League title. Wright scored on his debut and played the following week, but they were to be his only two senior appearances. Early the following season he was transferred to Bradford Park Avenue, where former Spurs' defender Vic Buckingham was manager, and played there for four years.

Appearances:
League: 2 apps. 1 gl.
Total: 2 apps. 1 gl.

YATES

Role: Goalkeeper 1904-05
Debut v Sheffield United (Fr) (h) 25.4.1905

A youngster from Wycombe, Yates appeared as a trialist in Spurs' friendly match against Sheffield United in April 1905. Although he did not concede a goal in a 0-0 draw his performance was described as "not very good" and he did not progress any further with Spurs.

Appearances:
Others: 1 app.
Total: 1 app. 0 gls.

YEATES. Mark Stephen Anthony

Role: Midfielder 2003-06
5ft.9ins. 13st.3lbs.
Born: Tallaght, Dublin, Eire, 11th January 1985

CAREER: Greenhill Boys/Cherry Orchard/**SPURS** Scholar Jul 2001, pro. Jul 2002/(Brighton & Hove Albion loan Nov 2003)/(Swindon Town loan Aug 2004)/Colchester United loan Sep 2005)/(Hull City loan Aug 2006)/(Leicester City loan Jan 2007)/Colchester United Jul 2007/Middlesbrough Jun 2009/Sheffield United Jan 2010/Watford Jul 2011-Jun 2013/Bradford City Jul 2013/Oldham Athletic Aug 2015/Blackpool Jan 2016/Notts County Jan 2017..

Debut v Wolverhampton Wanderers (PL) (a) 15.5.1904

Dublin born Mark Yeates is a busy little wide midfield player who, having failed to make the grade at Spurs, has moved around football, rarely staying more than a year or two at any club. A forceful talent who relies more on skill and technique than simple hard work, he was given an opportunity by Martin Jol and did alright in his one full Premier League game. However, Spurs had a glut of established and developing talent who occupied the position Yeates liked to play. He went out on loan to several clubs, never letting them down, but not setting the world alight. Released by Spurs, he has continued in the same vein. Yeates collected four caps for the Republic of Ireland at Under-21 level while with Spurs and later made one appearance for the "B" team. His father, Stephen player for Shelbourne, Shamrock Rovers, Athlone Town and Kilkenny City.

Appearances:
League: 1 (2) apps.
FA Cup: (1) app.
Others: 7 (4) apps.
Total: 8 (7) apps. 0 gls.

YEDLIN, DeAndre Roselle

Role: Full-back 2014-17
6ft.2ins. 14st.4lbs.
Born: Cheltenham, Gloucestershire, 15th January 1994

CAREER: O'Dea High School, Seattle (USA)/Washington Youth Soccer's State Olympic Development Program (USA)/Emerald City (USA)/Northwest Nationals (USA)/Crossfire Premier (USA)/Seattle Sounders (USA) Academy 2010/University of Akron (USA) Feb 2011/Seattle Sounders (USA) Jan 2013/**SPURS** Aug 2014/(Seattle Sounders (USA) loan Aug 2014)/(Sunderland loan Sep 2015)/Newcastle United Aug 2016.

Debut v Aston Villa (PL) (h) (sub) 11.4.2015

Although he has been a Spurs' player for two years, very little has been seen of Deandre Yedlin. Signed in August 2014 from Seattle Sounders, he stayed with the American club for the remainder of the 2014 season, only arriving at White Hart Lane in January 2015. After just one Premier League appearance and a few outings in friendly games, he was loaned to Sunderland for the 2015-16 season. A product of the American football education structure, Yedlin was Seattle's first Homegrown Player, that is a player signed directly from the club's Academy rather than through the Draft system. An attacking full-back, he progressed quickly, playing regularly in the MLS and making his first full international appearance against South Korea in February 2014. A member of the USA squad for the 2014 World Cup finals, Yedlin only appeared as a substitute, but his natural attacking instincts and bursts down the wing added a fresh impetus to the American's efforts. Yedlin was rated one of the best prospects of the new breed of youngsters coming though and Spurs did well to secure his services. With Kyle Walker and Kieran Trippier ahead of him in the pecking order that remains to be seen, but if Jürgen Klinsmann's view is anything to go by, Yedlin has every chance of making the grade. Since signing for Spurs he has been almost ever-present in the USA team, making more appearances for his country than he has for Spurs and Sunderland combined.

Appearances:
League: (1) app.
Others: 3 (2) apps.
Total: 3 (3) apps. 0 gls.

YORATH, Terence Charles

Role: Midfield 1979-81
5ft.11ins. 10st.12lbs.
Born: Cardiff, Glamorgan, 25th March 1950

CAREER: Gabalfa Primary School/Cathays High School/Cardiff Schools/Wales Schools/Leeds United app. 1965, pro. Apr 1967/Coventry City Aug

1976/**SPURS** Aug 1979/Vancouver Whitecaps (Canada) Feb 1981/ Bradford City asst. manager Dec 1982/Swansea City manager Oct 1986/ Wales part-time manager Jul 1988/Bradford City manager Feb 1989/ Swansea City manager Mar 1990-Mar 1991/Wales manager Mar 1991-Dec 1993/coach in Japan 1994/coach in Nigeria 1994/Cardiff City general manager Aug 1994-Mar 1995, caretaker manager Nov 1994/Lebanon coach May 1995-Aug 1997/Huddersfield Town asst. manager Oct 1997/ Bradford City asst. manager Jun 1999/Sheffield Wednesday first team coach Jun 2000, asst. manager Feb 2001, caretaker manager Oct 2001, manager Nov 2001-Oct 2002/Huddersfield Town asst. manager Jun 2003-Dec 2006/Margate director of football Jun 2008, caretaker manager Oct 2008, manager-director of football Nov 2008-Sep 2009.

Debut v Middlesbrough (FL) (h) 18.8.1979

A tenacious, shaggy-haired midfielder with a reputation for being a "hard man", it was all too easy to overlook the fact that Terry Yorath also had a fair degree of skill-essential for anyone to get into the great Leeds side of the late 1960's and early 1970's. With Leeds he won seven Welsh Under-23 and 28 full caps, his first at full level coming against Italy in November 1969 when he had made only one League appearance. Yorath took time to establish himself at Elland Road, moving up from a defensive utility role to become a hard-tackling midfield ball-winner. A substitute in Leeds 1973 FA Cup Final team, he made the starting line-ups for the 1973 European Cup-Winners' Cup and 1975 European Cup Finals, but in all three only picked up a losers' medal. He did at least collect some consolation with a League championship medal in 1974. With Coventry, Yorath enhanced his reputation as a midfield destroyer and proved a fine captain, leading by example and winning another 20 Welsh caps before joining Spurs. Signed for £275,000 to add a bit of steel to a midfield that, whilst boasting the talents of Glenn Hoddle, Ossie Ardiles and Ricky Villa, lacked a player who could win the ball, he performed the task admirably for a season. When he recovered from an injury sustained early the next term, he found his role had been taken by Graham Roberts. Having won another eight caps with Spurs, Yorath was allowed to leave and joined Vancouver Whitecaps where he won his final three caps before returning to the UK with Bradford City. Initially a player, he became assistant manager under his former Leeds team-mate Trevor Cherry and helped City win the Third Division in 1985. He officially retired as a player with Bradford City but, after joining Swansea City as manager, still turned out in one League game during an injury crisis. Appointed part-time manager of Wales, he quit Swansea to take over Bradford City but soon found himself the centre of an acrimonious legal wrangle that was only resolved when he bought out his own contract. Yorath, who had only been with Bradford for twelve months, returned to Swansea, but left again amid a further bizarre argument over whether he was sacked or resigned. Following his departure from Swansea he was made full-time manager of Wales, but was unable to lead them to the 1994 World Cup Finals in America. On his dismissal he returned to Cardiff as general manager, then left in 1994 after an abortive takeover by a consortium of which he was part. He then took on the job of coaching the Lebanon, helping to rebuild a country devastated by a long war. His talents as a coach and manager well recognised, he had further posts at Huddersfield, Bradford City and Sheffield Wednesday before winding down with Margate. An all-round sportsman at school, Yorath represented his district teams at football, cricket, rugby and baseball.

Appearances:
League: 44 (4) apps. 1 gl.
FA Cup: 7 apps.
FL Cup: 7 apps.
Others: 7 (1) apps.
Total: 65 (5) apps. 1 gl.

YOUNG, Albert Edward

Role: Full-back 1943-46
Born: Caerleon, Gwent, 11th September 1917

CAREER: Margate 1938/Arsenal Nov 1941/(guest for Chelsea, Crystal Palace, Fulham, Glentoran, **SPURS,** Swindon Town and Watford during World War Two)/Swindon Town May 1946/Chelmsford City Aug 1950-cs. 1952/Clacton Town 1952/retired 1954.

Debut v Fulham (FLS) (h) 25.12.1943

Albert Young was on Arsenal's books when he guested for Spurs in the Football League South during the Second World War. A left-back, he made his first appearance in December 1943, made one further appearance that season and one in 1945-46. Released by Arsenal after the war, he moved to Swindon Town where he played regularly for the next four years. Young was not only a talented footballer as a boy, he won a Welsh schoolboy cap at rugby.

Appearances:
Others: 3 apps.
Total: 3 apps. 0 gls.

YOUNG, Alexander Simpson

Role: Centre-forward 1911-12
5ft.9ins. 11st.8lbs.
Born: Slamannan, Stirlingshire, 23rd June 1880
Died: Portobello, Edinburgh, 17th September 1959

CAREER: St Mirren May 1899/Falkirk Apr 1901/Everton May 1901/ **SPURS** Jun 1911/Manchester City Nov 1911/South Liverpool Aug 1912/ Burslem Port Vale 1913.

Debut v Everton (FL) (a) 2.9.1911 (scored once)

Alex Young spent ten years with Everton helping them win the FA Cup in 1906-when he scored the only goal-and reach the final of the competition the next year. He also won two Scottish caps, against England in April 1905 and Wales in March 1907. An imposing, muscular centre-forward, he scored 110 League goals for Everton even though he played at inside-forward during his last two seasons at Goodison Park. He moved to Spurs in June 1911 and started well with three goals in his first two games, but failed to score in the next three and was left out of the team. Peeved, he immediately demanded a transfer and Spurs let him return north to Manchester

City. He finished the season with City and had a year with South Liverpool and Burslem Port Vale before emigrating to Australia in 1914. In December 1915, Young was charged with the wilful murder of his brother and, in June 1916 was found guilty of manslaughter. Evidence was produced from football officials in England that during his playing career Young had been subject to fits of temporary insanity. He was sentenced to three years' imprisonment, but was not released immediately on completion of his sentence. He was kept in custody on the grounds of "mental weakness" and it was sometime before he returned home to Scotland.

Appearances:
League: 5 apps. 3 gls.
Total: **5 apps. 3 gls.**

YOUNG, Christopher

Role: Centre-forward 1912-13
Born: Cleethorpes, Lincolnshire, 26th May 1886
Died: Cleethorpes, Lincolnshire, 22nd October 1956

CAREER: Grimsby Rovers/Cleethorpes Town/Grimsby Town trial 1905, am. Feb 1906/Gainsborough Trinity Aug 1911/**SPURS** Jul 1912/Burslem Port Vale May 1913/(guest for Grimsby Town during World War One)/Cleethorpes Town 1919/Charlton's 1921-Mar 1922.

Debut v Everton (FL) (h) 2.9.1912

Having finished bottom of Division Two Gainsborough Trinity were voted out of the League in 1912, and Spurs were quick to move in and sign their prize asset, Chris Young. Originally with Grimsby Rovers and Cleethorpes Town, he played five League games for Grimsby as an amateur, but spent most of his time playing for either of his earlier junior clubs. It was only in August 1911 that he joined Gainsborough with 14 goals in 27 appearances marking him as a player of some potential. He made his Spurs debut in the first match of 1912-13, but failed to score in the first four games of the season which were all lost. With Jimmy Cantrell clearly making the number nine shirt his own, Young was transferred to Burslem Port Vale at the end of the season. He proved that Spurs had not seen the best of him, scoring 78 goals for the Central League club in the two seasons before the First World War. He re-signed after the war, but injury led to him retiring without making a further appearance.

Appearances:
League: 4 apps.
Others: 2 apps.
Total: **6 apps. 0 gls.**

YOUNG, Luke Paul

Role: Defender 1998-2002
5ft.11ins. 12st.6lbs
Born: Harlow, Essex 19th July 1979

CAREER: SPURS trainee Jul 1995, pro. Jul 1997/Charlton Athletic Jul 2001/Middlesbrough Jul 2007/Aston Villa Aug 2008/Queens Park Rangers Aug 2011-May 2014.

Debut v West Ham United (PL) (a) 28.11.1998

Luke Young was a fine all-round defender, equally comfortable in either full-back position, at centre half or in the holding midfield role. He began his Spurs' career in the centre of defence and it was in that role that he played his first few games in the senior team. However, whenever there was a defensive problem Young was called upon to provide the solution. He found himself a valued member of the first team squad, but never certain of a first eleven place. His versatility was terrific for Spurs, but for Young it meant he was unable to take his career to the next level. A forceful character he made his feelings clear and was allowed to move to Charlton Athletic in a deal that saw Spurs receive £3 million up front, plus the promise of £250,000 for each of the next four seasons if Charlton retained their place in the Premier League. Spurs got their bonus payments as Young developed to become one of Charlton's most consistent performers. At Spurs he had collected ten caps for England at Under-21 level. At Charlton he moved into the full England team, his debut coming against the USA in May 2005. Despite Young's best efforts, Charlton were not a long-term Premier League club and at the end of the 2006-7 season they were relegated. Young knew demotion would do his career no good and demanded a transfer. It was granted and he joined Middlesbrough, quickly moved on to Aston Villa and then signed for Queens Park Rangers. He was a regular at Rangers until he fell out with manager, Mark Hughes. When Hughes departed injury problems saw him omitted from the League squad. He remained at Loftus Road until his contract expired when he was released. Young won all seven of his full England caps while with Charlton. His brother, Neil, was on Spurs' book as a youngster. Another all-round defender, he did not make the grade with Spurs, but went on to make nearly 500 appearances for AFC Bournemouth.

Appearances:
League: 44 (14) apps.
FA Cup: 9 (2) apps.
FL Cup: 1 (3) apps.
Euro: 2 (1) apps.
Others: 7 (7) apps.
Total: **63 (27) apps. 0 gls.**

YOUNG, William David

Role: Centre-half 1975-77
6ft.3ins. 12st.10lbs.
Born: Heriot, nr Berwick, Midlothian, 25th November 1951

CAREER: Penraitland Primary School/Tranent Secondary School/Seton Athletic/Falkirk trial/Aberdeen Jun 1969/**SPURS** Sep 1975/Arsenal Mar 1977/Nottingham Forest Dec 1981/Norwich City Aug 1983/(Brighton and Hove Albion loan Mar 1984)/Darlington non-contract Sep 1984/retired Nov 1984.

Debut v Leeds United (FL) (a) 20.9.1975

Flame-haired and well over six feet tall, Willie Young was not offered terms after an early trial with Falkirk, so continued to play for Seton Athletic whilst working as a laboratory assistant. He attracted scouts from Heart of Midlothian and Coventry City, but it was Aberdeen who moved in to sign him. An enthusiastic and determined player with a fierce will to win, he soon carved a name for himself with Aberdeen and made five appearances for Scotland at Under-23 level, the first against

Wales in January 1972. His time at Pittodrie ended in controversy as he threw his shirt at manager Jimmy Bonthrone after being substituted. Signed for Spurs by Terry Neill for £120,000, Young quickly became a cult figure at White Hart Lane but, although he had his faults-including a low temper threshold-too many people were prepared to criticise him rather than admire his plus points and the fact that, at the time, he gave a genuine lift to Spurs' 1975-76 season. An ungainly figure, he was not a pretty footballer, but he was a huge, hard-headed effective centre-half who did not mind shedding some blood in the Spurs' cause. There were few centre-forwards able to get the better of him, particularly in the air, and his height and aggression could cause havoc when he loped up into the opposition area for free-kicks and set-pieces. It was certainly a little surprising when Spurs agreed to transfer Young to Arsenal for £80,000, but Spurs were struggling, Young had been out of the team and he was keen to link up again with Neill. He spent over four years at Highbury, playing in three successive FA Cup finals between 1978 and 1980, although he only collected a winners' medal in 1979. He then had two good years with Nottingham Forest, but by the time he joined Norwich City was past his best and hampered by injury problems. He played only six League games for Norwich before finishing his League career as a non-contract player with Darlington. Young would almost certainly have made Scotland's full international team had he not been banned, along with four others, from further international recognition after misbehaving in a Copenhagen nightclub whilst on a Scotland trip abroad.

Appearances:
League: 54 apps. 3 gls.
FA Cup: 2 apps.
FL Cup: 8 apps. 1 gl.
Others: 24 apps. 3 gls.
Total: **88 apps. 7 gls.**

Z

ZAMORA, Robert Lester

Role: Striker 2003-04
6ft.1ins. 11st.11lbs.
Born: Barking, London, 16th January 1981

CAREER: Essex Junior School/Little Ilford School/Barking Abbey Secondary School/Senrab/West Ham United Academy/Bristol Rovers trainee Jul 1997, pro. Jul 1999/(Bath City loan Jan 2000)/Brighton & Hove Albion loan Feb 2000, perm. Aug 2000/**SPURS** Jul 2003/West Ham United Jan 2004/Fulham Jul 2008/Queens Park Rangers Jan 2012/ Brighton & Hove Albion Aug 2015-May 2016/retired Dec 2016.

Debut v Birmingham City (sub) (PL) (a) 16.8.2003
(Oxford United (Fr) (a) 2.7.2003 (scored two))

At the time he signed for Spurs, there was no doubt that Bobby Zamora was a prolific goal-scorer with the potential that could take him to the very top of the game. Unfortunately, the continual press stories linking him with the bigger clubs, particularly Spurs, had made him the most over-hyped of youngsters and put the type of pressure on him few players would know how to handle. Zamora was unable to live up to the hype and departed after just six months. An east London lad, Zamora began his career at Bristol Rovers having been released from West Ham's academy. It was while on loan to Bath City that he showed his goal-scoring prowess. Eleven goals in eight games had Brighton seeking his services and he spent the latter part of the 1999-2000 season on loan before a permanent transfer. In no time, Zamora was leading the line, banging in the goals and playing for England Under-21s. He top-scored as Brighton moved from the Third to First Division in successive seasons, and again as they slipped back to the Second. Spurs had been watching him for a while and laid out £1.5 million to sign him. He did alright in pre-season friendlies, three goals in three games, but when it came to the matches that matter, could do no right. While he worked hard, gave all he could in effort and maintained a positive attitude, nothing would go right for him. With Hélder Postiga also having a terrible start to his Spurs' career, Spurs struggled, the scoring burden thrust on Fredi Kanouté. When Glenn Hoddle sought to secure Jermaine Defoe from West Ham, the Irons asked for Zamora as part of the deal. It was a perfect move for all. Zamora scored on his debut. Back in the First Division, he got his career back on track. While he never got back to the free-scoring of his Brighton days, he helped West Ham secure promotion to the Premier

League and proved a competent top flight centre-forward. After five seasons at Upton Park, Zamora moved to Fulham. In a team that did not create many chances Zamora struggled, proving most effective on the European stage as Fulham surprised everyone by reaching the Europa League final. In fact, Zamora did so well that he was called up for England duty, though he might have played for Trinidad & Tobago. His father is Trinidadian and Zamora was expected to accept an invitation to play for the islands in the 2010 World Cup qualifiers. That he did not was down to injury. However, he had recovered to play for England against Hungary in August 2010, though he only won one further cap. Zamora followed three-and-a-half years at Fulham with a similar period at Queens Park Rangers, then concluded his career with a year back at Brighton, almost leading them into the Premiership.

Appearances:
League: 6 (10) apps.
FA Cup: (1) app.
FL Cup: 1 app. 1 gl.
Others: 1 (2) apps. 3 gls.
Total: 8 (13) apps. 4 gls.

ZIEGE, Christian

Role: Full/Wing-back 2001-04
6ft.1ins. 12st.13lbs
Born: Berlin, Germany, 1st February 1972

CAREER: Sudstern 08 (Germany)/TSV Rudow (Germany)/Hertha 03 Zehlendorf (Germany) 1985/Bayern Munich (Germany) Aug 1990/AC Milan (Italy) Aug 1997/Middlesbrough Jul 1999/Liverpool Aug 2000/**SPURS** Jul 2001/released May 2004/Borussia Mönchengladbach Jun 2004, retired Oct 2005, Under-17 coach, Director of Football Mar 2007-Dec 2008, interim manager Oct 2008/Arminia Bielefeld head coach and sporting director May-Nov 2010/German Under-19 coach Apr 2011, Under-18 coach Aug 2011/SpVgg Unterhaching (Germany) coach Mar 2014-Mar 2015/CD Atlético Baleares (Spain) trainer Nov 2015.

Debut v Aston Villa (PL) (h) 18.8.2001
(Wycombe Wanderers (sub) (Fr) (a) 21.7.2001)

When Glenn Hoddle persuaded Christian Ziege to put pen to paper, Spurs signed a man who was recognised as, if not the best left-wingback in the world, certainly one of the best. A tall, confident character, with a natural arrogance, he was at his best getting forward, hitting over pin-point crosses or firing in a long-range shot. Something of a free-kick specialist, he was keen to burst into the box, with his surging runs from midfield. As a boy Ziege had played in goal. It was only shortly before signing for Bayern Munich that he began to play in an outfield position. In seven years he helped Bayern lift the Bundesliga twice, in 1993–94 and 1996–97, and the UEFA Cup in 1995–96. After winning twelve German Under-21 caps, he made his full international debut in June 1993 against Brazil. He immediately established a regular position in the team and helped the Germans win Euro 96. In August 1997 he joined AC Milan and in 1998-99 added Serie A to his list of honours. While he never really settled in Italy, it was still something of a surprise when he signed for Middlesbrough. The Teesside outfit had only been in the Premier League for one season, were still building a team fit for such

exalted company and not looked upon as serious title contenders. He only stayed with Boro for a year before moving to title contenders Liverpool in controversial circumstances. Liverpool activated a buy-out clause in his contract by offering the exact £5.5 million it specified. Despite other clubs offering more, Ziege was entitled to talk to any club who matched the buy-out figure. Liverpool was the only one he was interested in. In March 2002, Liverpool were found guilty of an illegal approach to the player and fined £20,000 while Ziege was fined half that amount. By then Ziege was at White Hart Lane, having disappointed in his year on Merseyside. Liverpool won the three Cups-FA, Worthington and UEFA, but Ziege played only in the Worthington Cup final, and then only as an extra-time substitute. Playing in front of Mauricio Taricco for Spurs, he added a strength and threat from the left flank, scoring in the 2002 Worthington Cup final. He was doing well enough until injury problems. On Boxing Day 2002 he suffered what was thought to be a "dead leg", It turned out to be blood clot, with Ziege's leg swelling to twice its size. A 10 inch slit had to be made in his thigh to save the leg from amputation. He did not play again until the end of the season and was never the player he had been. Released by Spurs he joined Borussia Mönchengladbach but played few games before retiring. He then turned to coaching, initially in Germany, but latterly in Spain. Ziege collected a total of 72 German full caps, 13 as a Spurs' player.

Appearances:
League: 44 (3) apps. 7 gls.
FA Cup: 3 apps. 2 gls.
FL Cup: 5 apps. 1 gl.
Others: 10 (2) apps.
Total: 62 (5) apps. 10 gls.

ZIEGLER, Reto Pirmin

Role: Midfielder 2004-07
6ft. 13st.0lbs
Born: Nyon, Switzerland, 16th January 1986

CAREER: FC Gland (Switzerland) Sep 1993/Servette (Switzerland) Sep 1995/US Terre-Sainte (Switzerland) Aug 1997/Servette (Switzerland) Jul 1998/Lausanne-Sports (Switzerland) Aug 1999/Servette (Switzerland) Oct 1999/Grasshoppers (Switzerland) Aug 2000/**SPURS** Aug 2004/(SV Hamburg (Germany) loan Aug 2005/(Wigan Athletic loan Jan 2006)/Sampdoria (Italy) loan Jan 2007, perm. Jul 2007/Juventus (Italy) May 2011 /(Fenerbahce (Turkey) loan Sep 2011)/(Lokomotiv Moscow (Russia) loan Sep 2012)/(Fenerbahce (Turkey) loan Jan 2013)/(US Sassuolo (Italy) loan Aug 2013)/FC Sion (Switzerland) Feb 2015.

Debut v Everton (sub) (PL) (a) 2.10.2004

His ability for spotting and developing young talent was reputedly one of the main reasons Spurs went to considerable lengths to secure Frank Arnesen's appointment as Sporting Director. Reto Ziegler was one of the first youngsters he persuaded to join Spurs and probably the best of the lot. A Swiss youth international at all levels, Ziegler was in the Grasshopper's first team at 16 and was establishing himself as a regular when Spurs secured his signing. He was viewed as "one for the future", but performed so well in training and in a couple of reserve outings, that he was immediately promoted to the senior squad. Capable of playing on

the left of midfield or at full-back, Ziegler immediately impressed with his pace, directness and work rate. There were times when he could drift out of games and he was not always at this best, but it would have been unreasonable to expect otherwise from a player of his age and limited experience. Ziegler already had one Under-21 cap to his credit when he joined Spurs. He quickly added three more games and made his full international debut against France in March 2005. Things looked good for Ziegler, but suddenly, without apparent reason, he was not simply out of the first team squad, but out of the club. One loan after another culminated in a permanent move to Sampdoria. He played there for four years, but when Samp were relegated he signed for Juventus. In four years with "the Old Lady" he did not make one appearance, spending all his time out on loan. Released by Juventus, he returned to Switzerland with Sion. Ziegler's brother was a player with FC Malley.

Appearances:
League: 12 (12) apps. 1 gl.
FA Cup: 5 apps.
FL Cup: 4 apps.
Euro: 1 (1) apps.
Others: 3 (5) apps.
Total: 25 (18) apps. 1 gl.

ZOKORA, Alain Didier Maestro (Degui)

Role: Midfielder 2009
5ft.11ins. 12st.4lbs
Born: Abidjan, Ivory Coast, 14th December 1980

CAREER: Zoman FC (Ivory Coast)/ASEC Mimosas (Ivory Coast)/KRC Genk (Belgium) Jul 2000/AS Saint-Étienne (France) Jul 2004/SPURS Jul 2006/Sevilla (Spain) Jul 2009/Trabzonspor (Turkey) Jun 2011-Apr 2014/Akhisar Belediye (Turkey) May 2014-Jun 2015/Pune City (India) Jul 2015/North East United (India) Sep 2016.

Debut v Bolton Wanderers (PL) (a) 19.8.2006
(Borussia Dortmund (Fr) (a) 5.8.2006)

Although a last day defeat at West Ham in May 2006 meant Spurs failed to qualify for the Champions League, much of the success that season had been based on the hard midfield work of Edgar Davids. The "Pitbull" as he had been named by Louis van Gaal, was approaching the end of his career. A replacement with the same qualities was needed. Although they had failed to get past the group stage of the 2006 World Cup, the Ivory Coast had at its heart two players similar to Davids, Yaya Toure and Didier Zokora. Spurs could not compete with Monaco for Toure, but they were able to persuade Zokora to make the move to White Hart Lane. Zokora had been plucked from his home country by Racing Genk of Belgium. He spent four years with the Belgians, helping them win the Jupiler League in 2001–02, before moving to St Etienne. He proved a good signing for Spurs, an energetic defensive midfielder providing cover across the whole of midfield, hustling, tackling, winning the ball and laying it off. Zokora was not a creative player, he rarely got within distance of the opposition's penalty area, but his job was to stop the opposition. That was a job he performed admirably for three years. He then joined Sevilla, moving on to play in Turkey and playing in the fledgling Indian Super League. Zokora won 16 of his 125 Ivory Coast caps as a Spurs player.

Appearances:
League: 74 (13) apps.
FA Cup: 8 apps.
FL Cup: 11 (1) apps.
Euro: 26 apps.
Others: 11 (1) apps.
Total: 130 (15) apps. 0 gls.

www.ingramcontent.com/pod-product-compliance
Lightning Source LLC
Chambersburg PA
CBHW080835010526
44114CB00017B/2311